William Swan Sonnenschein

A Bibliography of Philology and Ancient Literature

Being the Sections Relating to those Subjects in The Best Books and The Reader's Guide

William Swan Sonnenschein

A Bibliography of Philology and Ancient Literature
Being the Sections Relating to those Subjects in The Best Books and The Reader's Guide

ISBN/EAN: 9783337248888

Printed in Europe, USA, Canada, Australia, Japan

Cover: Foto ©Thomas Meinert / pixelio.de

More available books at **www.hansebooks.com**

A BIBLIOGRAPHY OF

PHILOLOGY & ANCIENT LITERATURE

BEING THE SECTIONS RELATING
TO THOSE SUBJECTS IN

The Best Books and **The Reader's Guide**

BY

WILLIAM SWAN SONNENSCHEIN

London
SWAN SONNENSCHEIN & CO LIMD
PATERNOSTER SQUARE
1897

PHILOLOGY AND ANCIENT LITERATURE

WITH SPECIMENS OF THE MODERN LITERATURES OF NON-EUROPEAN LANGUAGES.

It has been deemed essential to include throughout the remainder of this CLASS *the more important modern Foreign works and editions. Where thoroughly good English books exist, covering the same ground, this has not been done quite systematically.*

XIV. The Philological Sciences and Oriental Languages Generally.

92. BIBLIOGRAPHY.

Generally —*for* Current Literature, *v. also* K § 95.

Bibliotheca Philologica [now] ed. Dr. August Blau [quarterly] *ann.* 5/- 8° *Göttingen* 47 *sqq., in prog.*
FRIEDERICI, K. [ed.] Bibliotheca Orientalis [list of new bks.; *ann.* 1876 to 1883] ea. 3/- r 8° *Leipzig* 77-83 *not cont.*
— Contin. in *Litteraturblatt f. orient. Philol.*, ed. R. KUHN, 3 vols. 45/- 4° *Leipzig*, 83-86, and thence in A. MÜLLER'S *Orient. Bibl.*, *ut infra*.
MÜLLER, A. [ed.] Orientalische Bibliographie [*quarterly*] *ann.* 6/- 8° *Berlin* 87 *sqq.*
POTT, A. F. Zur Litteratur der Sprachenkunde Europas 6/- r 8° *Leipzig* 87
SAYCE, Prf. A. H. —*in his* Introduction [*ut* K § 96] *is a short, select list of books recommended.*
ZENKER, J. Th. [ed.] Bibliotheca Orientalis, 2 vols. [useful for the earlier bks.] 22/- 8° *Leipzig* 46; 61
ZIEMER, Hermann [ed.] Jahresbericht üb. allgemeine u. vergl. Sprachwissenschaft: 1883-1888 8/- 8° *Berlin* 89

Dictionaries and Grammars.

LYONS, Rev. P. A. —*article* Dictionaries, *in* Encyclo. Brit., vol. vii. [early & mod.; v. full] 30/- 4° Black 78
TRÜBNER & Co. [bkslrs.] Catal. of Dicts. and Grammars [of all princ. langs. and dialects of world] 5/- 8° Trübner [72] 82
VATER, J. S. Literatur d. Grammatiken und Lexiken aller Sprachen der Erde, ed. B. Jülg 9/- 8° *Berlin* [15] 47

German Books.

HERRMANN, C. H. [ed.] Bibliotheca Orientalis et Linguistica [list of new books pub. in Germany 1850-68] 3/- 8° *Halle* 70

93. ORIGIN AND PHILOSOPHY OF LANGUAGE.

Generally.

CHAIGNET, A. E. La Philosophie de la Science du Langage 8° *Paris* 75
COOK, Can. F. C. The Origins of Language and Religion [5 essays] 15/- 8° Murray 84
*GEIGER, L. Der Ursprung der Sprache 6/- 8° *Stuttgart* [69] 78
" " —*in his* Entwickelungsgeschichte der Menschheit [lectures] 4/- 8° " [71] 78
GERBER, G. —*in his* Die Sprache als Kunst, 2 vols. 20/- 8° *Berlin* [71] 84; [74] 86
" " Die Sprache und das Erkennen 8/- 8° " 84
GRIMM, Jacob Ueber den Ursprung der Sprache [*also in his* Kleine Schriften, vol. i.] 1/- 8° " [51] 79
v. HUMBOLDT, W. Sprachphilosophische Werke, hrsg. H. Steinthal 18/- r 8° " [ ] 84
KEY, Prf. T. H. Language: its origin and development 14/- 8° Bell 74
Lects. on compar. grammar at Univ. Coll., Lond. Evidence drawn chfly. fr. Latin and Greek, esp. former.
KLEINPAUL, R. Sprache ohne Wörter: Idee e. allg. Wissenschaft d. Sprache 10/- 8° *Leipzig* 88
MIVART, St. George The Origin of Human Reason 10/6 8° Paul 89
MÜLLER, Prf. F. Max —*in his* The Science of Thought 21/- 8° Longman 87
Seeks the key to the sc. of thought in science of language, esp. growth of thought by comp. philology. *Vide* also his essays in K § 94; criticised by Ludwig NOIRÉ, in *Max Müller and the Philosophy of Language* [tr.] 4/- 8° Longman 79.

K §§ 94–95

NOIRÉ, Ludwig — Der Ursprung der Sprache [*v. also* Max Müller, *supra* (note)] 8/- 8° *Mayence* 77
RENAN, E. — De l'Origine du Langage 5/- 8° *Paris* [48] *n.d.* (62)
ROMANES, G. J. — Mental Evolution in Man [as part of Darwin. controversy] 14/- 8° Paul 89
*STEINTHAL, H. — Der Ursprung der Sprache 8/- 8° *Berlin* [51] 88
" " — Grammatik, Logik und Psychologie [valuable but v. controversial] *o.p.* [*w.* 20/-] 8° " 55
WEDGWOOD, Hensleigh — On the Origin of Language 3/6 f 8° Trübner 66
WHITNEY, Prf. W. D. [Am.]—*in his* Oriental and Linguistic Studies, series i. 12/- 8° " [74] 75
Conts. criticisms of Max MÜLLER'S theory of lang., BLEEK'S "Simios's theory," SCHLEICHER'S physical theory, STEINTHAL'S psychological theory.

Origin of Language fr. Evolutionist pt. of view—*v.* H § 43, *s.v.* Mental Evolution, & C § 71: Psychology.

Analogy.

WHEELER, B. I. [Am.] — Analogy and its Scope in Language [Cornell Studies]

Reduplication.

POTT, A. F. — Doppelung als eine der wichtigsten Mitteln der Sprache 6/- 8° *Detmold* 62

94. COLLECTED PHILOLOGICAL ESSAYS AND WRITINGS.

ABEL, Dr. Carl — Linguistic Essays, 9/-; Sprachwissenschaftliche Abhandlungen 10/- 8° Trübner 82; *Leipzig* 85
ASCOLI, Prf. G. J. — Studj Orientali e Linguistici, 3 pts. 14/- 8° *Milan* 54–55
" " — Studj Critici, ? *price*; Germ. tr. R. Merzdorf + B. Mangold 10/- 8° *Milan* 61 *sqq.*; *Weimar* 78
BENFEY, Prf. Theodor — Vedica und Linguistica [collected papers] 10/6 8° *Strassburg* 80
" " — Kleinere Schriften, ed. Prf. A. Bezzenberger, 2 vols. vol. i. (2 pts.) 22/- 8° *Berlin* 89 *in prog.*
BRÉAL, Michel — Mélanges de Mythologie et de Linguistique 6/6 8° *Paris* [77] 82
COLEBROOKE, H. T. — Essays: with notes Prf. E. B. Cowell, 2 vols. 28/- 8° Trübner [27–28] 73
CUST, Robert N. — Linguistic & Oriental Essays [Orient. Ser.], ser. i. 18/-, *red. to* 10/6; ser. ii. 18/- p 8° " 80; 88
DARMESTETER, J. — Essais Orientaux 8° *Paris* 83
FARRAR, Archd. F. W. — Chapters on Language 5/- c 8° Longman [65] 73
HADLEY, Prf. Jas. [Am.] — Essays: philological and critical 16/- 8° Macmillan 73
KEY, Prf. T. H. — Philological Essays [chiefly Latin and Greek] 10/6 8° Bell 68
KÖRTING, Gustav — Neuphilologische Essays 4/- 8° *Heilbronn* 87
MEYER, G. — Essays und Studien zur Sprachgeschichte und Volkskunde [chfly. Gk. & Lat.] 7/- 8° *Berlin* 85
MÜLLER, Prf. F. Max — Chips from a German Workshop, 4 vols. [*v. also* K § 96] 36/- 8° Longman [67–75] 80
i.: Essays on the science of religion; ii.: on mythol., etc.; iii.: on literature (German, etc.), biography and antiquities; iv.: on science of lang.
" " — Selected Essays on Language, Mythology and Religion, 2 vols. 16/- c 8° Longman 81
REGNAUD, P. — Essais de Linguistique Évolutionniste 8° *Paris* 85
STEINTHAL, H. — Gesammelte kleine Schriften, vol. i. 9/- 8° *Berlin* 80
WHITNEY, Prf. W. D. [Am.] — Oriental and Linguistic Studies, 2 series ea. 12/- 8° Trübner [74] 75; 74
i.: Veda, Avesta, Science of Language; ii.: East and West, Religion and Mythology, Orthography and Phonology; Hindu Astronomy.

95. MAGAZINES AND PERMANENT SERIALS.

Magazines and Serials devoted to Special Branches of Philology are classed into the Branches themselves, *infra.*

English Serials.

Philological Society: Proceedings *and* Transactions 8° Trübner 42 *sqq.*, *in prog.*
Contains annual bibliographical Reports on the Philology of various languages.

American Serials.

Journal of Philology ed. B. L. Gildersleeve [Am.], vols. i.–x.; index to same; xi. *sqq.* 8° *Baltimore* *in prog.*
Transactions of the American Philological Association, vols. i.–xix. *Cambridge, U.S.* 68–89 "

German Serials.

Einzelbeiträge zur allgemeinen u. vergl. Sprachwissenschaft, pts. i.–vi. 44/- 8° *Leipzig* 86–89 *in prog.*
i.: A. F. POTT, Allgem. Sprachwiss. u. Abel's Aegypt. Sprachstudien, 5/- '86; ii.: F. SPIEGEL, Die arische Periode, 12/- '87; iii.: Kurt BRUCHMANN, Psychol. Studien z. Sprachgesch., 9/-; iv.–vi.: C. ABEL, Wechselbeziehungen d. aegypt., indoeur. u. semit. Etymol., 3 pts., 36/- '88–'89
Neu philologische Studien, hrsg. G. Körting, pts. i.–v. 8/- 8° *Paderborn* 83–86 *in prog.*
Zeitschrift für vergleichende Sprachforschung, ed. A. Kuhn + Joh. Schmidt [bi-mthly.] *ann.* 16/- 8° *Berlin* 51 *sqq.*, "
" " Völkerpsychologie und Sprachwissenschaft, ed. M. Lazarus + H. Steinthal [qtly.] *ann.* 12/- 8° *Leipzig* 60 " "
Vols. i.–vii. ea. 9/-; x.–xvi. ea. 10/-; xvii.–xx. (1889) ea. 12/-. Vols. i.–xvi. were pub. at *Berlin.*

French Serials.

Mémoires de la Société de Linguistique de Paris, vols. i.–vi. 8° *Paris* 68–87 *in prog.*
Revue de Linguistique et de Philologie Comparée, ed. Rialle + Vinson, *etc.*, vols. i.–xxii. 8° " 67–89 "
Revue de Philologie, de Littérature et de l'Hist. Anc., ed. L. Havet + O. Riemann, *etc.*, vols. i.–xii. 8° " 77–89 "

Aryan Philology (only)—*v.* K § 119: Aryan Philology.

Classical (Greek and Latin) **Philology**—*v.* K § 173.

Oriental Philology: Generally.

Abhandlungen für die Kunde des Morgenlandes, hrsg. E. Windisch, vols. i.–x. [ed. for *DMG.*] *ea. pt. var. pr.* *Leipzig* 57 *sqq. in prog.*

Conts. valuable editions of oriental works, papers, etc.

Anecdota Oxoniensia Aryan Series, *var. prices*; Semitic Series *var. prices* s 4° Clar. Press 82 *sqq. in prog.*

A series of texts, documents and extracts, chiefly from the Bodleian and other Oxford libraries.

Giornale della Società Asiatica Italiana *ann.* 10/– 8° *Rome* 87 *sqq., in prog.*

Journal Asiatique [monthly] *ann.* 20/– 8° *Paris* 22 ,, ,,

Series i.: 12 vols., 22–27, w. 30/–; ser. ii.: 16 vols., 28–35, w. £6; ser. iii.: 14 vols., 36–43, w. £5; ser. iv.: 20 vols., 43–52, w. £7; ser. v: 20 vols., 53–62, w. £10; ser. vi.: 20 vols., 63–72, w. £10; ser. vii.: 73–84, 20 vols, w. £15; ser. viii.: vols. i.–iv., 85–88, ea. £1.

,, of the Royal Asiatic Society of Bengal, vols. i.–lviii. [compl. set to 1889, w. ab. £70] 8° *Calcutta* (Tbnr.) 32–89 *in prog.*

Eight Nos. annually, 10/–. A contin. of the *Asiatic Researches*, 21 vols. [w. £30] 4° *Calcutta*, 1788–1836, and *Gleanings in Science* (monthly; ed. J. PRINSEP), 3 vols. [w. £3 15/–] 8° *ibid.* 29–31.

,, of the Royal Asiatic Society of Gt. Brit. and Irel. *ann.*, 4 pts., ea. 5/– to 10/6 8° Trübner 34 *sqq., in prog.*

Series i.: 20 vols. 34–63, w. £10; New Series, vols. i.–xxi., 64–89, *in prog.*

,, of the American Oriental Society, vols. i.–xx. ea. 20/– 8° *New Haven* 50 *sqq., in prog.*

Literaturblatt für orientalische Philologie, ed. E. Kuhn, vols. i.–vi. [qtrly.] *ann.* 15/– 8° *Leipzig* 83–89 ,,

Vols. i.–ii. were published monthly.

Mélanges Asiatiques tirés du Bulletin de l'Acad. Imp. de St. Petersbg., vols. i.–xi. *v.p.* r 8° *St. Petersburg* 49–89 *in prog.*

Wissenschaftlicher Jahresbericht über d. Morgenländische Studien [*ann. suppl.* to *ZDMG*] 8° *Leipzig* 59 *sqq.*, ,,

Zeitschrift der Deutschen Morgenländischen Gesellschaft, [now] ed. E. Windisch, vols. i.–xl. [4 pts. = 1 vol.] ea. v. 15/– 8° ,, 46–89 ,,

Occasional Supplements and Indices are published.

,, für die Kunde des Morgenlandes, hrsg. G. Bühler and others, vols. i.–iii. [*qtrly.*] 10/– 8° *Vienna* 87 *sqq.* ,,

,, Internationale, für allgem. Sprachwiss.—*v.* K § 98.

96. COMPARATIVE PHILOLOGY (*a*): GENERAL HISTORICAL TREATISES.

Generally. —*v. also* K § 119.

BYRNE, Dr. James — General Principles of the Structure of Language, 2 vols. 31/6 8° Trübner 85

GERBER, G. — Die Sprache als Kunst, 2 vols. 20/– 8° *Berlin* [71] 84; [74] 86

HOVELACQUE, A. — The Science of Language [tr.] [popular; good] 4/– c 8° Chapman 77

v. HUMBOLDT, Wilhelm — Ueb. d. Verschiedenheit d. menschl. Sprachwiss., ed. A. F. Pott 4/6 s 8° *Berlin* [36] 83

Schasler, Max — Die Elem. d. philos. Sprachwiss. W. v. Humboldt's [adverse criticism] 4/– 8° ,, 47

Steinthal, H. — Die Sprachwiss. W. v. Humboldt's u. d. Hegel'sche Philos. [opposing Schasler] 2/– r 8° ,, 48

*MÜLLER, Fr. — Grundriss der Sprachwissenschaft, vols. i.–iii., 46/–; iv.: pt. 1 6/– 8° *Vienna* 76–87; 88

i.: (1) Einleitung, 76; (2) Wollhaarige Rassen, 77; ii.: Schlichthaar. Rassen (1) Austral., Hyperbor., Amer. 82; (2) Malay. and Mongol. 82; iii.: Lockenhaar. Rassen (1) Nuba u. Dravida, 85; (2) Mittelländische Rassen, 85–87; iv.: (1) Supplements. A monumental work.

* ,, Prf. F. Max — Lectures on the Science of Language, 2 series; ill. 16/– c 8° Longman [61; 64] 86

SERIES I.: lect. 1. Sc. of Lang. one of the Physical Sciences; 2. Growth of Lang.; 3. Empirical Stage in Sc. of Lang.; 4. Classificatory Stage in Sc. of Lang.; 5. Genealog. Classif. of Lang.; 6. Compar. Grammar; 7. Constituent Elements of Lang.; 8. Morpholog. Classif. of Lang.; 9. Theoret. Stage in Sc. of Lang.; Appendix.

SERIES II.: lect. 1. New Materials for Sc. of Lang.; 2. Language and Reason; 3. Physiolog. Alphabet; 4. Phonetic Change; 5. Grimm's Law; 6. Princ. of Etymol.; 7. Powers of Roots; 8. Metaphor; 9. Mythol. of Greeks; 10. Jupiter; 11. Myths of the Dawn; 12. Modern Mythology.

* ,, ,, — Selected Essays on Lang., Mythol., and Religion, 2 vols. 16/– c 8° Longman 81

,, ,, — Three Lects. on the Science of Lang., and its Place in General Education 2/– c 8° ,, [89] 89

Popular exposition of author's views as to origin and growth of lang., w. spec. refs. to English.

*PAUL, Prf. H. — The Principles of Philology, ed. Prf. H. A. Strong 10/6 8° Sonnenschein [88] 90

The best statement of the "New School" of Philologists.

*SAYCE, Prf. A. H. — Introduction to the Science of Language, 2 vols. 9/– p 8° Paul [80] 90

,, ,, — Principles of Comparative Philology 10/6 p 8° Trübner [74] 85

STEINTHAL, H. — Abriss d. Sprachwiss., i.: Sprache im allgemeinen [psychological] 9/– 8° *Berlin* [71] 81

WEGENER, Ph. — Untersuchungen über die Grundfragen des Sprachlebens ("New School") 5/– 8° *Halle* 85

WHITNEY, Prf. W. D. [Am.] — Language and the Study of Language [12 lectures] 10/6 c 8° Trübner [67] 84

,, ,, — The Life and Growth of Language [Internat. Scient. Series] 5/– c 8° Paul [75] 82

,, ,, — Language and its Study, ed. R. Morris 5/– c 8° Trübner [76] 81

Aryan Philology: Generally—*v.* K §§ 119–120.

Greek, Latin, Sanscrit, etc., comparatively—*v.* K §§ 167–173.

Hamitic, Semitic, and Aryan.

ABEL, Carl — Wechselbeziehungen d. ægypt., indoeurop. u. semit. Etymologie, 3 pts. 38/– 8° *Leipzig* 88–89

Seeks to prove that Egyptian and Indo-europ. roots are mainly identical, and subject to the same phonetic, conceptual, and formative changes. For his dictionary of Egyptian-Semitic-Aryan roots, v. K § 101.

DELITZSCH, Prf. Friedrich — Studien über indogermanisch-semitische Wurzelverwandtschaft 4/– 8° *Leipzig* [73] 84

RAABE, A. — Gemeinschaftliche Gramm. d. arischen u. semit. Sprachen [w. ess. on orig. of alphabet] 3/– 8° *Leipzig* 74

Classification, etc., of Languages.

ADAM, L. — Les Classifications, l'Objet, la Méthode, *etc.*, de la Linguistique 2/6 8° *Paris* 82

MÜLLER, Prf. Max — On Stratification of Languages '66; also in his Lectures, vol. i., lects. 5 and 8 [*ut supra*].

OPPERT, Prf. Gust. — On the Classification of Languages [Madras Jl. of Liter., N. S. i.] 7/6 8° Trübner 79

STEINTHAL, H. — Charakteristik d. hauptsächlichsten Typen d. Sprachbaues 6/– 8° *Berlin* [50] 60

The first edn. was pub. *sub tit. Die Classification der Sprachen dargestellt als die Entwickelung der Sprachidee.*

97. COMPARATIVE PHILOLOGY (*b*): HISTORY AND BIOGRAPHY OF THE STUDY.

History of Philology.

Early.

STEINTHAL, H. Gesch. d. Sprachwiss. bei d. Griech. u. Röm., 2 v. [w. spec. ref. to logic] 11/6 8° *Berlin* 63

Modern and Contemporary.

DENFEY, Prf. Theodor Geschichte der Sprachwissenschaft u. orient. Philologie in Deutschland 10/6 8° *Munich* 69
Since the commencement of 19th cent., w. a prelim. sketch of earlier times; and a bibliography fr. the earliest times.

BRUGMANN, Prf. Karl Zum heutigen Stand der Sprachwissenschaft 2/6 8° *Leipzig* 85
CURTIUS, Georg Zur Kritik der neuesten Sprachforschung 2/6 8° ,, 85
DELBRÜCK, B. Die neuste Sprachforschung [criticism of Curtius, *supra*] 1/- 8° ,, 85
DWIGHT, B. W. [Am.] Modern Philology: discoveries, history, influence, 2 vols. $4 4° *New York* [64] 76
de GUBERNATIS, A. Matériaux p. servir à l'Histoire d. Études Orient. en Italie 5/- 8° *Florence* 76

History of Education: Generally—*v.* D §§ 156, 157.

Biography.

Collectively.

DUGAT, G. Hist. des Orientalistes de l'Europe du 12e au 19e siècles, 2 vols. 8° *Paris* 68; 70
With a sketch of the history of Oriental study in Europe.

Greek and Latin —*v.* K § 174.

98. PHONETICS. PHYSIOLOGY OF LANGUAGE.

Books, etc., on the Phonology of Individual Languages or Groups of Langs. are classed with those Languages or Groups.

BINDSEIL, H. E. Physiol. d. Sprachlaute—*in his* Abhandlungen zur vergleich. Sprachlehre 11/- 8° *Leipzig* [38] 78
BRÜCKE, Ernst Grundzüge der Physiologie u. Systematik d. Sprachlaute 4/- 8° *Vienna* [56] 76
A very good little bk., written for philologists and teachers of the deaf-and-dumb. Gives a physiol. acc. of formation of each letter.

LEPSIUS, C. R. —*his* Standard Alphabet [*ut* K § 99] *gives the phon. alphab. wh. has found the widest acceptance.*
v. MEYER, G. H. Organs of Speech & their Applic. in Forma. of Sounds [tr.]; 47 ill. [Int. Sci. Ser.] 5/- c 8° Paul 83
MÜLLER, Prf. Max —*in his* Lect. on Science of Lang. [*ut* K § 96] ser. ii., lect. 3, *is a lucid summary.*
KUMPELT, H. B. Das natürliche System der Sprachlaute; 4 pl. in 4° 4/6 8° *Halle* 69
TECHMER, F. Phonetik, pt. i. [text and notes], pt. ii. [atlas] 18/- 8° *Leipzig* 80
THAUSSING, Moritz Das natürliche Lautsystem der menschlichen Sprache 2/6 8° ,, 63

Magazine.

Internationale Zeitschrift für allgemeine Sprachwissenschaft, ed. F. Techmer, vols. i.-vi. *ann.* 12/- r 8° *Heilbronn* 84-89 *in prog.*
Devoted to study of Phonetics in particular, and Indo-European philology in general. With good bibliographies of new books. Vols. i.-iii. and Suppl. [6/- '87] pub. at *Lpzg.*

Phonetische Studien, hrsg. Prf. W. Vietor, vol. i., 9/6; vol. ii., pt. 1 3/6 8° *Marburg* 87-88; 88 *in prog.*

Aryan —*v.* K § 120.

Musical Acoustics and Sensations of Tone—*v.* I § 125 (esp. HELMHOLTZ).

99. RELATION OF LANGUAGE TO WRITING (*a*): PALÆOGRAPHY, &c.

Books, etc., on the Palæography of Individual Langs. or Groups of Langs. are classed with those langs.

Origin and History of Writing.

ASTLE, Thomas Origin & Progress of Writing: hieroglyphic & elemen.; ill. fr. MSS., etc. 35/- 4° Chatto [1784] 76
FAULMANN, Prf. Karl Buch der Schrift: Schriften u. Alphabete aller Zeiten u. Völker 12/- 4° *Vienna* [78] 80
,, ,, Geschichte der Schrift [both this and above richly ill.] 12/- r 8° ,, 79
HALÉVY, J. Origine de l'Écriture Indienne...et l'Écriture Perse 2/6 8° *Paris* 86
HUMPHREYS, H. Noel Origin and Progress of the Art of Writing; illum. pl. and facss. *o.p.* [*pb.* 21/-] 4° Day 54
LANGLOIS, Essai sur la Calligraphie des MSS. du Moyen Age; facss. *o.p.* [*w.* 8/6] r 8° *Rouen* 41
de LACOUPERIE, Prf. Terrien The Beginning of Writing; pl. 15/-; The Ideology of Language 7/6 8° Nutt 87;
de ROSNY, Léon Les Écritures figuratives et hiéroglyphiques des différ. peuples 7/- 4° *Paris* [ ] 70
THOMPSON, E. Maunde —*article* Palæography, *in* Encyclo. Brit., vol. xviii. 30/- 4° Black 84
VAN DRIVAL, Abbé E. De l'Origine de l'Écriture; pl. 5/- 8° *Paris* [ ] 79
VOLLGRAFF, J. C. Studia Palæographica *Leyden* 70
WATTENBACH, W. Das Schriftwesen im Mittelalter 11/- r 8° *Leipzig* [71] 75
WUTTKE, H. Geschichte der Schrift und des Schriftthums, vol. i., 15/-; Atlas of 33 litho. pl. 4/- 8° *Leipzig* 72; 73

Examples, Facsimiles, etc.—*v. also* I § 110: Illuminated MSS.

Album Paléographique [Soc. de l'École des Chartes] 200 fr. 1 f° *Paris* 87
Heliographic reproductions of MSS. of 6-17 cent., chiefly of historical and of literary interest.

British Museum Catalogue of ancient MSS. in British Museum, pts. i. [Gk.] 20/-; ii. [Latin] 60/- f° Brit. Museum 81; 84
" Facsimiles of Ancient Charters in Brit. Mus., pt. i. 21/-; ii. 30/-; iii. 30/-; iv. 42/- f° " 73;76;77;78
GILBERT, J. T. [ed.] Facsimiles of Nat. MSS. of Ireland: photozinco reprods.; pt. i. *o.p.*; ii.-iii., ea. 42/-; iv. (1) 105/-, (2) 90/-. Account of same, in 4 pts., cpl. in 1 v. 10/- [earliest times to 1719] f° Ir. Rolls Ser.
Palæographical Society Facsimiles of MSS. & Inscriptions, ed. E. A. Bond + E. M. Thompson. Ser. i., 3 v.; 260 facss. ser. ii. in prog. 73-83 & seq.
A set to 1889 is worth about £14.

SICKEL, Th. [ed.] Monumenta Graphica Medii Aevi, 9 pts. [fr. Austrian colls.] ea. 50/- f° *Vienna* 59–69
SILVESTRE, M. J. V. [ed.] Universal Palæography, ed. Sir Fred. Madden, 2 v. atl f° & 2 v. r 8° *o.p.* [*w.* £30] 1 f° Bohn 49–50
A coll. of nearly 300 large facss. fr. missals and other MSS. (some illum.) fr. French, Ital., Germ. and Eng. libraries. Of all ages: European, Oriental, Gk., Lat. The work cost nearly £20,000 to produce, the expense bg. chiefly defrayed by Louis Philippe. The Small Edition, in 2 vols. f°, cont. 79 selected pl., is worth about £3.

Deciphering of Deeds —*v.* D § 36.

Alphabet.

BALLHORN, F. Grammatography: alphabets of all ages and countries 4/6 r 8° *Nuremberg.* [43] 80
BELL, A. Visible Speech [scheme f. a univ. phonet. alphab.] 67
DU BOIS-REYMOND, F. H. Kadmus: oder allgemeine Alphabetik 6/- 8° *Berlin* 62
LENORMANT, Fr. —*in his* Essai sur la Propagation de l'Alphabet Phénicien, vols. i.-ii. (1) 32/- r 8° *Paris* 72; 75
LEPSIUS, R. Standard Alphabet, f. reduc. unwritt. & for. lang. to unif. orthog. in Eur. letters 2/6 8° *Berlin* [55] 63
A recast of his *Das allgemeine linguistische Alphabet*, 1855.

TAYLOR, Can. Isaac The Alphabet: origin and development of letters, 2 vols.; ill. 36/- 8° Paul 83
Vol. i. deals with Semitic alphabets, vol. ii. with Aryan alphabets.

Cryptography.

BAILEY, J. E. —*article* Cryptography, *in* Encyclo. Brit., vol. vi. 30/- 4° Black 84

100. RELATION OF LANGUAGE TO WRITING (*b*): STENOGRAPHY (SHORTHAND).

ENGLISH.

Bibliography.

ROCKWELL, J. E. [Am.] Bibliograph. of Shorthd. Wks. in Engl. [w. many foreign entries; 122pp.]—*v. infra, s.v.* Hist. (ROCKWELL).
WESTBY-GIBSON, Dr. J. The Bibliography of Shorthand [Engl. lang. only] 5/- 8° Pitman 87

History.

ANDERSON, Thos. History of Shorthand, w. review of its present condition in Eur. & Amer. 12/6 8° W. H. Allen 82
LEVY, Matthias The History of Shorthand Writing, w. syst. used by authors 5/- 8° Trübner 62
PITMAN, Isaac History of Shorthand [repr. fr. *Phonetic Journal*] c 8° Pitman 84
REED, T. A. A Chapter in the Early History of Phonography; w. preface Isaac Pitman 1/- 8° "
*ROCKWELL, J. E. [Am.] Teaching, Practice and Literature of Shorthand [Circulars of Information, No. 2, 1884] 8° U.S. Bureau of Educ., *Washington* [84] 85
On Shorth. systems; Shorth. in Foreign Countries; Shorth. in U.S.; Bibliogr. of Shorth. (Engl. & Am. Works), w. chron. list of 483 authors.

UPHAM, W. P. [Am.] Brief History of the Art of Stenography, w. proposed New System $1.25 r 8° *Salem, Mass.* 77
WESTBY-GIBSON, Dr. J. Early Shorthand Systems 12° 83

Systems.

ALLEN, G. G. Universal Phonography, or Shorthand by the "Allen Method"
ANDERSON, Thos. [ed.] Shorthand Systems [discussion by various experts] 1/- c 8° Upcott Gill, *n.d.* (83)
ARMITAGE, M. Syllabic Writing, or Shorthand made easy [15 pp.] 6*d.* 8° Armitage, *Batley* [84] 85
BARTER, J. Self-Instructor in ABC Shorthand, 1/6; Manual of ABC Shorthand 6*d.* 12° Allman [85] 86; [85] 86
*CALLENDAR, H. L. Manual of Cursive Shorthand, 2/-; Primer of Cursive Shorthand 6*d.* c 8° Camb. Press 89; 89
CROSS, J. G. [Am.] Eclectic Shorthand Dictionary $3.50 8° *Chicago* 88
GURNEY, Joseph Textbook of the Gurney System of Shorthand. By W. B. Gurney & Sons 3/- p 8° Butterworth [1751] 84
By the present Shorthand Writers to the Houses of Parliament.

PITMAN + HOWARD, Benn J. B. [Am.] Manual of Phonography 80c. 12° *Cincinnati* [55] 85
" " Phonographic Dictionary: reptg. outlines f. 30,000 words 4/- 12° Pitman [83] 89
WATSON, John [Am.] The Phonographic Instructor: an improved method of Shorthand $2 12° *New York* 87

Abbreviated Longhand.

ANDERSON, Thos. Simplified Longhand [shorth. characters by longhand letters] 2/- c 8° W. H. Allen 82
" " Synopsis of a New System of Short Writing 1/- 8° Rankin, *Glasgow* 78
BENNETT, Eug. [Am.] Condensed Longhand, $1; Condensed Longhand as used by Press $1 12° *New York* 83; 84
DAVIES, Rev. D. S. Manual of Sonography; or Longhand-Shorthand 2/- c 8° Morgan, *Carmarthen* 87
KIMMEL, M. G. [Am.] Longhand Shorthand 75c. 12° *Valparaiso* 83
RITCHIE, Wallace Shorthand Simplified: system of abbreviated longhand 1/- 12° Russell [74] 75

K §§ 101–102

XV. Hamitic Philology, Inscriptions, etc.

101. ANCIENT EGYPTIAN AND COPTIC PHILOLOGY.

Ancient Egyptian: Hieroglyphic, Demotic, Hieratic.

Dictionaries.

ABEL, Dr. Carl — Einleitung in ein ægyptisch-semitisch-indo-europ. Wurzel-Wörterbuch, pts. i.–v. £5 s 4° *Leipzig* 85; 86

BIRCH, Dr. Samuel — Dict. of Hieroglyphics—*in* Bunsen's *Egypt* [tr.], vol. v., pp. 335–586, 5 v. 174/6 8° Longman 48–67

BRUGSCH-BEY, H. — Hieroglyphisch-Demotisches Wörterbuch, vols. i.–vi. £33 10/–, vii. £6 f° *Leipzig* 67–80; 82

" " — Dictionnaire Géograph. de l'Anc. Égypte [dict. of names on the monuments] £22 10/– f° *Leipzig* 77–80

LEVI, Dr. Simeone — Vocabolario Geroglifico Copto-Ebraico, 7 vols. ea. 30/– 4° *Turin* 87–89

PIERRET, P. — Vocabulaire Hiéroglyphique 50/– r 8° *Paris* 75

SHARPE, Samuel — Rudiments of a Vocabulary of Egyptian Hieroglyphics *o.p.* [*pb.* 10/6] 4° Moxon 61

Grammars, etc.

BIRCH, Dr. Samuel — Hieroglyphic Gram.—*in* Bunsen's *Egypt*, vol. iv., pp. 587–716; on Egypt. Gram., the Writing of Egyptians, *loc. cit.* vol. i. sects. 4 & 5, 5 vols. 174/6 8° Longman 48–67

BRUGSCH-BEY, H. — Grammaire Démotique 75/– f° *Berlin* 55

" " — Grammaire Hiéroglyphique, 24/–; Hieroglyphische Grammatik 24/– 4° *Leipzig* 72; 72

" " — Die Aegyptologie, pt. i. [elem. of Egyptian science] 10/– r 8° " 89

v. GUTSCHMID, A. — Kleine Schriften, hrsg. F. Rühl, vol. i. [Egyptol. and Gk. chronol.] 14/– 8° " 89

LORET, V. — Manuel de la Langue Égyptienne, 2 pts. [gram., texts, gloss.] 21/– 4° *Paris* 88

RENOUF, P. Le Page — Elem. Grammar of Anc. Egyptian Lang. [hieroglyph. type] 7/6 4° Bagster 75

de ROUGÉ, Visc. E. — Grammaire Égyptienne 54/– 4° *Paris* 66–75

TATTAM, H. — Compendious Grammar of Egyptian Language 9/– 8° Williams [30] 63

Chrestomathy.

BUDGE, E. A. Wallis [ed.] — An Egyptian Reading Book [Oriental Text Series] 10/6 8° Nutt 89

v. LEMM, Dr. O. [ed.] — Aegyptische Lesestücke, 1 Thl.: Schrifttafel und Lesestücke, 2 pts. [autographed] ea. 8/– 4° *Leipzig* 83

REINISCH, L. [ed.] — Aegyptische Chrestomathie, parts 1–2 11/– f° *Vienna* 73; 75

REVILLOUT, E. [ed.] — Chrestomathie Démotique, 4 pts. 84/–; Nouv. Chrest. Démot. 20/– 4° *Paris* 76–80; 78

de ROUGÉ, Visc. E. [ed.] — Chrestomathie Égyptienne, 4 pts. 72/6 s 4° " 68–76

Serial.

Zeitschrift für ägyptische Sprache u. Alterthum, vols. i.–xxvii. *ann.* 15/– r 4° *Leipzig* 63 *sqq. in prog.*
Founded by H. BRUGSCH, cont. by R. LEPSIUS, then by H. BRUGSCH + L. STERN. Index to vols. i.–xxiii. [1863–85], by Prince IBRAHIM-HILMY, *gratis*.

Coptic.

Generally.

ABEL, Dr. Carl — Koptische Untersuchungen, 2 vols. in 3 pts. 30/– 8° *Berlin* 76–77

Pott, A. F. — Allgemeine Sprachwissenschaft u. Abel's ägypt. Studien 3/– 8° *Leipzig* 86

Dictionary.

PARTHEY, G. — Vocabularium Coptico-Lat. et Lat.-Copt. [after Peyron & Tattam] *o.p.* [*w.* 30/–] r 8° *Leipzig* 44

PEYRON, Amadeus — Lexicon Copticum *o.p.* [*w.* 35/–] 4° *Turin* 35

TATTAM, H. — Lexicon Aegyptium-Latinum [Coptic] *o.p.* [*w.* 21/–] 8° *Oxford* 35

Grammar.

PEYRON, Amadeus — Grammatica Coptica 10/– 8° *Turin* 41

STERN, Ludwig — Koptische Grammatik 18/– 8° *Leipzig* 80

UHLEMANN, M. A. — Linguae Copticae Grammatica *o.p.* [*pb.* 5/–; *w.* 10/–] 8° " 53

102. ANCIENT EGYPTIAN AND COPTIC INSCRIPTIONS, LITERATURE, &c.

Bibliography.

IBRAHIM-HILMY, Prince — The Literature of Egypt and the Soudan, 2 vols. [earliest times to 1885] ea. 31/6 8° Trübner 86; 88

JOLOWICZ, Dr. H. — Bibliotheca Ægyptiaca [pubns. to 1861] 7/– 8° *Leipzig* 58–61

History of Literature.

v. GUTSCHMID, A. — Kleine Schriften, hrsg. F. Rühl, vol. i. [on Egyptol. & Gk. chronography] 14/– 8° *Leipzig* 89

Series of Translated Specimens.

Records of the Past: English trs. of Assyr. and Egypt. Monuments, ed. Dr. S. Birch, 12 vols. ea. 3/6 p 8° Bagster 75–78
Vols. ii., iv., vi., viii., x., xii. (*i.e.* the even numbers) contain Egyptian texts: odd numbers the Assyrian. New Series, ed. Prf. A. H. Sayce, vols. i.–ii. ['89; '90] ea. 4/6.

Texts and Translations: Inscriptions and Papyri—*v. also* G § 8.

Author	Title	Price	Size	Publisher	Date
BIRCH, Dr. S. [ed.]	Egyptian Texts: with transliterations and trs.	12/-	4°	Bagster	77
British Museum	Inscriptions in the Hieratic and Demotic Character	27/6	f°	British Museum	68
,, ,,	Egyptian Texts from the Earliest Period; 32 col. pl. [fr. coffin of Amamu]	42/-	f°	,,	86
,, ,,	Select Papyri in the Hieratic Character, ser. i., 3 pts., and ser. ii., pt. i.	107/-	f°	,,	41–60
	Ser. i., pt. i. [pl. 1–34] 21/- '41; ii. [pl. 35–98] 50/- '42; iii. [pl. 99–188] 56/- '44; Ser. ii. [pl. 1–19] 22/- '60				
,, ,,	Facsimile of Hieratic Papyrus of Rn. of Rameses iii.	60/-	f°	,,	76
,, ,,	Photographs of the Papyrus of Nebseni in British Museum	42/-	f°	,,	76
,, ,,	Papyrus of Ani [Book of the Dead]—*v.* note to Lepsius, *infra.*				
BRUGSCH-BEY, H. [ed.]	Recueil de Monuments Égypt., v. i.–ii.; 107 pl. (23 col.)	50/-	4°	*Leipzig*	60; 63
,, +DÜMICHEN, J.	The same, vol. iii.–iv. [Geog. Inschr. Altägypt. Denkmäler; 200 pl.]	£6	4°	,,	65; 66
,, ,,	The same, vol. v.–vi. [Geogr. Inschr., pts. 3–4; 190 pl.]	£6	4°	,,	85
,, H. [ed.]	Thesaurus Inscriptionum Aegyptiacarum, pts. i.–iv.	£10 14/-	r 4°	,,	83–84
	i.: Astronom. Inscripp., 50/- '83; ii.: Calendar Inscripp., 84/- '83; iii.: Geograph. Inscripp., 22/- '84; iv.: Mytholog. Inscripp., 50/- '84				
BUDGE, E. A. Wallis [ed.]	Martyrdom & Miracles of St. George of Cappadocia (copt. texts & trs.; Or. Txt. Ser.]	21/-	8°	Nutt	88
,, ,, [ed.]	The Sarcophagus of Queen Anxnesraneferal [text, translit. and tr.]	15/-	4°	Whiting	89
CHABAS, F. [ed.]	Mélanges Égyptologiques, 3 series; pl.		r 4°	*Paris*	62–73
,, ,, [tr.]	Voyage d'un Égyptien en Syrie, Phénicie, Palestine, etc.; 13 pl. [Fch. trss. fr. Brit. Mus.]	70/-	4°	*Paris*	66
,, ,, [ed.]	Le Papyrus Magique Harris; 10 pl. [text and Fch. tr.]	36/-	4°	*Paris*	60
DÜMICHEN, J. [ed.]	Altägyptische Kalender-Inschriften; 120 pl.	£6	f°	*Leipzig*	73
,, ,, [ed.]	Historische Inschriften Altägyptischer Denkmäler, 2 vols.; 117 pl.	£9 8/-	f°	,,	67; 73
,, ,, [ed.]	Altägyptische Tempel-Inschriften, i.: Edfu; ii.: Dendera; 160 pl.	£8	f°	,,	67
,, ,, [ed.]	Photographische Resultate der Archäolog. Expedition [of 1868]; 72 pl.	£9	f°	*Berlin*	71
EBERS, G. [ed.]	Papyrus Ebers, 2 vols.; 110 pl. [w. Hierog.-Lat. gloss.]	£10 10/-	i 4°	*Leipzig*	75
EISENLOHR, A. [ed.]	Mathemath. Handbuch d. alten Aegypter; 2 pl. and atl. of 24 pl. [= Papyr. Rhind of Brit. Mus.; w. tr.]	63/-	4°	*Leipzig*	77
GAYET, A. [ed.]	Les Monuments Coptes du Musée de Boulaq; 100 pl.	40/-	4°	*Paris*	89
HESS, J. J. [ed.]	Der demotische Roman v. Stne Ha-m-us [w. German tr., comm. & glossary]	14/-	8°	*Leipzig*	88
LEEMANS, [ed.]	Monuments Égyptiens du Musée d'Antiq. des Pays-Bas, pts. i.–xxvii.	£40	f°	*Leyden*	39–76
LEPSIUS, Dr. R. [ed.]	Denkmäler aus Aegypten u. Aethiopien; 900 pl. (some col.)	£67 10/-	f°	*Berlin*	49–60
,, ,, [ed.]	Königsbuch der alten Aegypter, 2 vols.; 73 pl.	50/-	4°	,,	58
,, ,, [ed.]	Todtenbuch der Aegypter, 79 pl. [fr. Turin papyrus]	35/-	4°	*Leipzig*	42
	A transl. of this by Dr. S. BIRCH is cont. in the 5th vol. of Bunsen's *Egypt's Place in Hist.* [tr.] 5 v. 134/6 8° Longman, '48–'67. The Brit. Mus. recension of the *Bk. of the Dead* has been reprod. in colours by Mr. Griggs. 31/6 f° '89. *Index des Mots* by J. LIEBLEIN 8° *Paris* 76.				
,, ,, [ed.]	Aelteste Texte d. Todtenbuchs; 43 pl. [fr. Brit. Mus. Sarcoph.]	48/-	f°	*Berlin*	67
MARIETTE-BEY, A. [ed.]	Listes Géographiques des Pylones de Karnak	30/-	f°	*Leipzig*	75
,, ,, [ed.]	Karnak: étude topographique et archéologique; pl.	150/-	4°	,,	75
,, ,, [ed.]	Abydos, 53 pl., 96/-; Denderah, 339 pl.; 4 vols.	ea. 64/-	f°	*Paris*	69; 70–75
,, ,, [ed.]	Monuments divers d'Égypte et de Nubie, pts. 1–24; 21 pl.	ea. 5/-	f°	,,	72–77
,, ,, [ed.]	Les Papyrus Égyptiens du Musée de Boulaq, vols. i.–iii.; 44 pl.	£15	f°	,,	72–77
,, ,, [ed.]	Le Serapeum de Memphis, 10 parts; 36 pl.	£6	f°	,,	66
MASPÉRO, G. [ed.]	Études Égyptiennes, vols. i.–ii. (pt. 1)	64/-	4°	,,	86–89
NAVILLE, E. [ed.]	Litanie du Soleil; 49 pl. [fr. tombs of Kings of Thebes]	20/-	4°	*Leipzig*	75
,, ,, [ed.]	Das Aegyptische Todtenbuch der xviii. bis xx. Dynastie; 212 pl., £12; Einleit. *sep.*	30/-	4°	*Berlin*	87; 87
,, ,, [ed.]	Textes relatifs au Mythe d'Horus; 26 pl. [fr. temple of Edfu]	40/-	f°	*Basle*	70
PIEHL, K. [ed.]	Inscriptions Hiéroglyphiques recueillés en Égypte; ser. i., 2 pts. 55/-; ser. ii., pt. i. [154 plates]	32/-	4°	*Paris*	86–88; 90
PIERRET, P., *etc.* [eds.]	Études Égyptologiques, pts. i.–xvi.		4°	,,	73–80
,, ,,	Recueil d'Inscriptions du Musée Égypt du Louvre, 2 pts.	ea. 21/-	4°	,,	73; 78
PLEYTE, W. [ed.]	Études Égyptologiques, 7 parts; 13 pl.	42/-	8°	*Leyden*	66–69
,, ,, [ed.]	Le Papyrus de Turin, 6 pts.; 150 pl.	£12	4°	,,	66–73
,, ,, [ed.]	Le Papyrus Rollin	32/-	4°	,,	68
,, ,, [ed.]	Chapitres Supplém. du Livre des Morts, 3 vols.; 27 pl. [w. Fch. tr.]	32/-	4°	,,	
REINISCH, Prf. Leo [ed.]	Die ägyptischen Denkmäler in Miramar; 43 pl. and 29 ill.	30/-	r 8°	*Vienna*	65
REVILLOUT + EISENLOHR, E.	[eds.] Corpus Papyrorum Aegypti, vol. i. [Louvre], pt. 1, 17/-; vol. ii. [Brit. Mus.], pt. 1, 15/-; pl.		4°	*Paris*	88; 88
de ROUGÉ, E. [ed.]	Rituel Funéraire des Anc. Égyptiens, pts. i.–v.	ea. 21/-	f°	,,	61–76
,, ,, [ed.]	Inscriptions hiéroglyph. copiées en Égypte pend. la Miss. Scient., 4 vols.	£3	4°	,,	77–79

103. LIBYAN PHILOLOGY.

Libyan.

Generally.

Author	Title	Price	Size	Publisher	Date
JUDAS, A. C.	Étude de la Langue Phénic. et de la Lang. Libyque; 32 pl.	27/-	4°	*Paris*	47

Dictionary.

Author	Title	Price	Size	Publisher	Date
NEWMAN, Prf. F. W.	Libyan Dictionary [reprod. in 4 modern langs.]	10/6	c 8°	Trübner	82

Berber (Tamachek).

Bibliography.

Author	Title	Price	Size	Publisher	Date
HODGSON, W. B. [Am.]	—*his* Notes on North Africa, *conts. a Berber bibliography*	$2	8°	*New York*	44

History of the Language.

RINN, Louis — Les Origines Berbères [linguistic and ethnological] 10/- 8° *Paris* 89

Dictionary.

BASSET, René — Notes de Lexicographie Berbère, pts. i.–iv. ea. 4/- 8° *Paris* [illegible]-88
BROSSELARD + JAUBERT — Dictionnaire Français-Berbère 30/- r 8° ,, 44

Grammar.

FAIDHERBE, Gen — Le Zenaga des Tribus Sénégalaises 4/- r 8° *Paris* 77
HANTEAU, A. — Grammaire de la Langue Tamachek *o.p.* [*w.* 21/-] r 8° ,, 60
NEWMAN, [Prf.] F. W. — Grammar of the Berber Language *o.p.* [*w.* 7/6] 8° Trübner *n.d.* (*c.* 40)

Inscriptions.

HALÉVY, J. — Études Berbères, vol. i.: éssai d'epigraphie Libyque [repr. fr. *Jl. Asiat.*] 12/6 8° *Paris* 75

Literature.

LOCMÂN Berbère — Berber text, w. transcription, ed. R. Basset 8/- 8° *Paris* 90
Contains also a study of the Locman legend, and four glossaries.

Kabail.

Dictionary.

BASSET, R. — Manuel de Langue Kabyle: dialecte zouaoua 7/6 8° *Paris* 87
NEWMAN, Prf. F. W. — Kabail Vocabulary supplemented by the aid of a New Science 5/- 8° Trübner 88

Grammars, etc.

BASSET, René — Manuel de la Langue Kabyle [Zouaoua dialect] 6/6 8° *Paris* 87
BELKASSEM, Ben Sedira — Cours de Langue Kabyle 7/- 8° *Algiers* 87
HANOTEAU, A. — Grammaire Kabyle 10/6 8° ,, 58
,, ,, — Essai de Grammaire Kabyle 15/- r 8° *Paris* 60

Folk-Literature —*v.* B § 34, *s.vv.* Algeria, Berber.

104. KUSHITIC PHILOLOGY.

Bilin, or Bogos.

REINISCH, Prf. Leo — Die Bilinsprache, vol. i. [texts] 10/-, vol. ii. [dictionary (in German)] 20/- 8° *Leipzig* 83; *Vienna* 87
,, ,, — Die Bilinsprache in Nord-Ost Afrika 2/6 8° *Vienna* 82

Chamir.

REINISCH, Prf. L. — Die Chamirsprache, 2 pts. [in Abyssinia] 5/- r 8° *Vienna* 84

Galla.

KRAPF, Rev. J. L. — Outlines of Elements of Galla Language *o.p.* [*w.* 12/6] 12° Trübner 40
TUTSCHEK, C. L. — Grammar of the Galla Language *o.p.* [*w.* 7/6] 8° *Munich* 45
,, ,, — Dictionary of the Galla Language, 3 pts. [Galla, English and German] 10/6 8° ,, 44–45

Kunama.

REINISCH, Prf. Leo — Die Kunama Sprache in Nordost-Afrika, pts. i.–ii. ea. 2/- 8° *Leipzig* 89; 90

Quara.

REINISCH, Prf. L. — Die Quararsprache [in Abyssinia] 6/- r 8° *Vienna* 85

Saho.

REINISCH, Prf. L. — Die Saho-Sprache, vol. i. [texts], 8/-; vol. ii. [dictionary] 24/- 8° *Vienna* 89; 90

XVI. Semitic Philology and Literature.

105. GENERAL AND COLLECTIVE WORKS.

Philology: Generally.

BARTH, J. — Die Nominalbildung in den semitischen Sprachen, vol. i. 10/- 8° *Leipzig* 89
BENLOEW, L. — La Grèce avant les Grecs [Pelasgians, Leleg., Semites, Ionians] 4/6 r 8° *Paris* 77
HERZFELD, L. — Einblicke in das Sprachliche d. semitischen Urzeit 6/- 8° *Hanover* 83
HOMMEL, Fritz — Die semitischen Völker und Sprachen, vol. i. (3 pts.) 11/- 8° *Leipzig* 81; 82; 83
,, ,, — Namen d. Säugethiere bei den südsemitischen Völkern 40/- r 8° ,, 79
A contribution to Arabic and Ethiopian lexicography, hist. of civilization, and philology.
de LAGARDE, P. — Uebersicht üb. d. im Aram., Arab. u. Hebr. übliche Bildung d. Nomina 20/- r 4° *Göttingen* 89
NÖLDEKE, Theodor — *article* Semitic Languages, *in* Encyclo. Brit., vol. xxi. [Germ. tr. of same, 1/6 8° *Leipzig* 87] 30/- 4° Black 87

RENAN, Ernest — Histoire Générale et Système Comparé des Langues Sémitiques, pt. i. 10/- 4° *Paris* [55] 63
WRIGHT, Prf. Wm. — Lectures in Comparative Semitic Grammar [posthumous] Camb. Press *in prep.*

Relation to Indogermanic Group—*v.* K § 96.

Palæography.

Alphabet.

CLARKE, J. C. C. [Am.] — Origin and Varieties of the Semitic Alphabet; 20 pl. 75c. 8° *Chicago* 87

Inscriptions.

*Corpus Inscriptionum Semit., in pts. [photo. facss., w. Fch. trs. & notes] I., 4 pts., *1 pr.*; II. i. (1) 50/- 4° *Paris* (Acad.) 81–90 *in prog.*
HALÉVY, J. — Mélanges d'Épigraphie et d'Archéologie Sémitiques 8/6 8° „ 74
Nineteen Punic, Phœnician, Egyptian, Palmyrenian, Nabatean, and Ethiopic inscriptions.
„ „ — Mission Archéologique dans le Yemen 16/- 8° „ 72
LAYARD, [Sir] A. H. [ed.] — Inscriptions in the Cuneiform Characters fr. Assyr. monum. [*v. also* G § 8] *o.p.* [*w.* 20/-] f° *London* 51
RAWLINSON + NORRIS + SMITH [eds.] — Cuneiform Inscriptions of Western Asia, 4 vols.—*v.* K § 107.
SARZEC, E. — Découvertes en Chaldée, 2 vols.; w. heliograv. pl. 50/- 4° *Paris* 87–80
de VOGUÉ, Cte. — Inscriptions Sémitiques de la Syrie Centrale; 16 pl. [w. Fch. tr.] 25/- f° „ 69
„ „ — Mélanges d'Archéologie Orientale 15/- 8° „ 69

106. ASSYRIAN, BABYLONIAN, AND ACCADIAN PHILOLOGY.

Dictionaries.

DELITZSCH, Prf. F. — Assyrisches Wörterbuch zur Keilschriftliteratur, pts. i.–iii. [to occupy ab. 10 pts] ea. 30/- 4° *Leipzig* 88–90 *in prog.*
Smith, S. A. — Why that *Assyrisches Wörterbuch* ought never to have been written 1/6 8° „ 88
NORRIS, E. — Assyrian Dictionary, pts. i.-iii. ea. 28/- 4° Williams 68–72
STRASSMAIER, Dr. J. N. — Alphab. Verzeichniss d. assyr. u. akkad. Wörter d. *Cuneif. Insc. of W. Asia*, 6 pts. [Assyr. Bibl.] 150/- r 8° *Leipzig* 82–86
„ „ — Wörterverzeichn. z. d. Babyl. Inschr. im Museum z. L'pool [repr. of pt. of above] 8/- r 8° „ 86
TALBOT, Dr. H. Fox — Contributions to a Glossary of Assyrian—*in Jl. R. A. S.* iii. and iv. 22/- 8° Trübner 68; 69

Grammars, History of the Language, etc.

BERTIN, George — Abridged Grammar of the Langs. of the Cuneif. Inscripp. [Simplif. Grams.] 5/- c 8° Trübner 88
Sumero-Akkadian, Assyro-Babylonian, Vannic, Medic, and Old Persian grammars.
DELITZSCH, Prf. F. — Assyrian Grammar, tr. A. R. S. Kennedy [w. paradigms, gloss., etc.] 15/- c 8° Williams 89
„ „ — Hebrew Language viewed in the Light of Assyrian Research [tr.] 4/- c 8° „ 83
HAUPT, Prf. Paul — Assyrische Grammatik *in prep.*
„ „ — Akkadische Sprache [a lecture] 5/- 8° *Berlin* 83
LENORMANT, Fr. — Étude sur les Syllabaires Cunéiformes 16/- 8° *Paris* 76
„ „ — La Langue Primitive de la Chaldée et les Idiomes Touraniens 21/- r 8° „ 75
„ „ — Études Accadiennes, vol. i. [gram.], 12/6; ii. (1) [texts] 17/-; iii. (1) [texts] 12/6, (2) 6/6 4° *Paris* 73–74; 74; 79; 80
Part of his *Lettres Assyriologiques*, *see* K § 107.
„ „ — Études Cunéiformes, 5 pts. [reprts. fr. var. serials] 12/6 8° *Paris* 78–80
MENANT, J. — Éléments de la Grammaire Assyrienne *o.p.* [*w.* 15/-] 8° „ 68
„ „ — Syllabaire Assyrien: système phonétique de l'écriture, 2 vols. 60/- 4° „ 69; 73
„ „ — Manuel de la Langue Assyr. [syllab., gram., readings] 15/- 8° „ 80
OPPERT, J. — Éléments de la Grammaire Assyrienne 6/- 8° „ [60] 69
„ „ — Études Sumériennes 4/6 8° „ 76
„ „ — La Peuple et la Langue des Mèdes 8/6 8° „ 79
SAYCE, Prf. A. H. — Assyrian Grammar for Comparative Purposes 7/6 12° Trübner 72
„ „ — Elementary Grammar and Reading Book of Assyrian Language 7/6 4° Bagster [75] 77
„ „ — Lectures upon the Assyrian Language and Syllabary 9/6 4° „ 77

Characters.

AMIAUD + MÉCHINEAU, A. L. — Tableau comp. d. Écritures Babyl. et. Assyr. archaiques et modernes 15/- r 8° *Paris* 87
BRÜNNOW, Dr. R. E. — Classified List of all Simple and Compound Ideographs in pub. texts, 3 v. 48/- 4° *Leyden* 88–89
MENANT, J. — Les Écritures Cunéiformes [Persian and Assyrian] *o.p.* [*w.* 12/-] 8° *Paris* [ ] 64

Chrestomathies.

BUDGE, E. A. W. [ed.] — Assyrian Texts [extracts from annals, w. notes] 7/6 8° Bagster 80
de CHOSSAT, Ed. [ed.] — Répertoire Assyrien, 21/-; Répertoire Sumérien 8/6 8° *Paris* 79; *Lyons* 82
DELITZSCH, Prf. F. [ed.] — Assyrische Lesestücke nach den Originalen 30/- f° *Leipzig* [76] 85
LYON, Prf. D. G. [ed.] — Assyrian Manual [w. sketch of Grammar (meagre)] $4 8° Amer. Hebrew Soc., *Chicago* 86
TELONI, B. [ed.] — Crestomazia Assira: con paradigmi grammaticali [Pub. Soc. As. Ital.] 8/6 8° *Florence* 87

Serials.

Beiträge zur Assyriologie u. vergl. semit. Sprachwiss., hrsg. F. Delitzsch + P. Haupt, vol. i., pt. 1 23/- r 8° *Leipzig* 89 *in prog.*
Zeitschrift für Assyriologie u. verwandte Gebiete, hrsg. C. Bezold [quarterly] *ann.* 16/- 8° „ 86 *sqq. in prog.*

107. ASSYRIAN, BABYLONIAN AND CUNEIFORM INSCRIPTIONS AND LITERATURE

History of Literature.

BEZOLD, C. — Ueberblick über die babylonisch-assyrische Literatur 12/- 8° *Leipzig* 86
BROWN, Prf. Francis [Am.] — Assyriology: its use and abuse $1 12° *New York* 88
EVANS, George — An Essay on Assyriology [w. 4° tables of inscripp.] 5/- 8° Williams 83
SAYCE, Prf. A. H. — Lectures on Babylonian Literature 4/- 8° Bagster 77
TIELE, C. P. — Die Assyriology u. ihre Ergebnisse f. d. vergl. Religionsgesch. [tr. fr. Dutch] 1/- 8° *Leipzig* 78
ZIMMERN, H. — Assyriologie [as help to study of O.T. and the classics; lect.] 8° ,, 89

History and Accounts of Discoveries and Research—*v.* A § 47.

Series of Translated Specimens.

Assyriologische Bibliothek, hrsg. F. Delitzsch + P. Haupt—*each entered separ. infra.*
Keilinschriftliche Bibliothek, vol. i., 9/-; vol. ii., 12/-; hrsg. Eberhard Schrader, vol. i., 9/-; ii., 12/- [in 4 ann. vols.; w. Germ. trss.] 8° *Berlin* 89; 90 *in prog.*
Records of the Past: Eng. tr. of Assyrian and Egyptian Monuments, ed. Dr. S. Birch ea. 3/6 p 8° Bagster 75-81
Vols. i., iii., v., vii., ix., xi., (*i.e.* the odd nos.,) contain Assyrian texts. A new series commenced in 1889. Vol. i., 4/6 [Assyrian]; vol. ii., 4/6 ['90].

Texts and Translations—*v. also* G § 10.

BEZOLD, Carl [ed.] — Achämenideninschriften [transcrip. of Babyl. text & Germ. tr.; Assyr. Bibl.] 24/- 4° *Leipzig* 82
British Museum — Cuneiform Inscriptions of W. Asia, ed. Sir H. C. Rawlinson f° British Museum 61-84
Vol. i.: *o.p.* [*pb.* 20/-] '61; ii.: 20/- '66; iii.: 20/- '70; iv.: *o.p.* 75 [*new edn. in prep.*]; v.: pl. 1-35, *o.p.* [*pb.* 10/6] '80; pl. 36-70, *o.p.* [*pb.* 10/6] '84.
STRASSMAIER, Rev. J. N. Alphabetisches Verzeichniss—*ut supra.*
British Museum — Catalogue of Cuneiform Tablets in Komunigik Collection, vol. i. 15/- 8° British Museum 89
BUDGE, Can. E. A. [tr.] — Hist. of Esarhaddon, Kg. of Assyria [son of Sennacherib; B.C. 681-668]: tr. fr. cuneif. inscripp. in Brit. Museum [Orient. Ser.] 10/6 p 8° Trübner 80
HAUPT, Paul [ed.] — Akkadische u. Sumerische Keilinscrifttexte, 4 pts. [fr. Brit. Mus.; Assyr. Bibl.] 36/- r 4° *Leipzig* 81-82
,, ,, [ed.] — Das babylonische Nimrodepos, pt. i. 20/- [fr. Brit. Mus.; Assyr. Bibl.] r 4° ,, 84
JENSEN, P. [ed.] — Kosmologie der Babylonier [cuneif. texts coll., explain., and exam.] 8° *Strassburg* 90
KOSSOWICZ, C. [ed.] — Inscriptiones Palaeo-Persicae Achaemenidarum 40/- i 8° *St. Petersburg* 72
LENORMANT, Fr. — Lettres Assyriologiques, ser. i., 2 vols., 18-; ser. ii., vol. 1, 12/6, vol. 2 (1) 16/6, vol. 3 (1-2) 19/- 4° *Paris* 71-72; 74-80
,, ,, [ed.] — Les Syllabaires Cunéiformes 16/- 8° ,, 77
,, ,, [ed.] — Choix de Textes Cunéiformes inedits, pts. 1-3 12/6 4° ,, 73-75
LYON, D. G. [ed.] — Keilinschrifttexte Sargon's [transcription, Germ. tr. & explan.; Assyr. Bibl.] 24/- r 8° *Leipzig* 83
MENANT, J. [ed. & tr.] — Annales des Rois d'Assyrie, 12/6; Babyl. et Chaldée [texts & French trss.] 12/6 r 8° *Paris* 74; 75
,, ,, — Les Achéménides et les Inscriptions de la Perse 8/6 8° ,, 73
,, ,, [ed.] — Inscriptions Assyr. de Hammourabi, roi de Babylone 8/6 8° ,, 63
OPPERT, J. [ed.] — Grande Inscription de Khorsabad, 3 vols. [w. French comm.] 25/- 8° ,, 63
,, ,, [ed. & tr.] — Les Inscriptions de Dour-Sarkayan déchiffrées 25/- f° ,, 70
,, ,, — Expéd. Scient. en Mésopotamie, 2 v. & atl. [4°] of 21 pl. [w. deciph. of inscr.] £5 i 4° ,, 56-64
,, + MENANT, J. [eds.] — Documents Juridiques de l'Assyrie et de la Chaldée 17/- 8° ,, 77
PEISER, Dr. [ed.] — Keilinschriftliche Aktenstücke; 2 pl. [21 texts fr. Berlin Museum; w. Germ. tr.] 12/- 8° *Berlin* 89
POGNON, H. [ed.] — Les Inscriptions Babyloniennes du Wadi Brissa; 14 pl. 8/6 8° *Paris* 87
RAWLINSON, Sir H. C. [ed.] — Selection from Inscriptions of Assyria; 70 pl. 12/- i f° 75
SCHEIL, P. V. [ed.] — Inscription Assyr. archaique de Samsi-Ramman iv. [824-811]; w. Fch. tr. & notes 7/- 4° *Paris* 89
SMITH, Geo. [ed. & tr.] — History of Assurbanipal: tr. fr. Cuneiform Inscriptions 28/- i 8° Williams 71
,, ,, [ed. & tr.] — Chaldean Account of Genesis: tr. fr. Cuneiform Inscriptions; ill. 16/- 8° Low [75] 80
,, ,, [ed. & tr.] — Assyrian Eponym Canon [tr., acc. of evidence, etc.] 9/- 8° Bagster 75
,, S. A. [ed.] — Miscellaneous Assyrian Texts of the British Museum: w. notes and 27 pl. 7/- 8° *Leipzig* 87
,, ,, [ed.] — Die Keilinschrifttexte Assurbanipals, pts. i. 7/-; ii. 12/-; iii. 18/- [w. transc., Germ. tr., comm. and gloss.] 8° ,, 87; 87; 89
,, ,, [tr.] — Assyrian Letters from the Royal Lib. at Nineveh: tr. and explained 6/- 8° ,, 88
STRASSMAIER, Rev. J. N. [ed.] — Babylonische Texte, pts. i.-vii. [inscripp. of Kg. Nabonidus, B.C. 555-538] c. £5 8° ,, 87-90 *in prog.*
WINCKLER, H. [ed.] — Die Keilinschrifttexte Sargons, 2 vols.; 49 pl. 48/- 4° ,, 89
ZIMMERN, H. [ed.] — Babylonische Busspsalmen [transcription, Germ. tr. & expl.; Assyr. Bibl.] 30/- r 4° ,, 85

Persian Cuneiform Inscriptions—*v.* K § 130.

108. CHALDEE (WEST OR BIBLICAL ARAMAIC) PHILOLOGY.

Primitive Language (pre-Semitic)—*v.* K § 106 (LENORMANT, *etc.*).

Dictionaries —*v. also* K § 117: Hebrew.

BUXTORF, J. — Lexicon Chaldaicum Talmudicum et Rabbinicum, ed. B. Fischer 63/- 4° *Leipzig* [1639-40] 66-74
*DAVIES, Benj. [Am.] — Student's Chaldee & Hebr. Lexicon to the O. T. [w. Hebr. & Eng. index] 21/- 8° *Andover* [ ] 83
Based on GESENIUS, FÜRST and others; ed. E. C. MITCHELL [Am.] The best student's lexicon for practical purposes.
FÜRST, Dr. Julius — Hebrew & Chaldee Lexicon to Old Test., tr. S. Davidson [conservative] 21/- r 8° Williams [67] 85
LEVY, Dr. J. — Chaldee Lexicon on the Targums, Talmud and Midraschim [tr.], 2 vols. 36/- 8° 69

Grammars.

KAUTZSCH, E.	Grammatik des Biblisch-Aramäischen	4/-	8°	*Leipzig*	84
LUZZATTO, S. D.	Grammar to Bibl. Chaldaic Language, tr. [fr. Ital.] J. S. Goldammer [Am.]	$1.50	12°	*New York*	76
PETERMANN, Dr. J. H.	Grammatica Chaldaica [w. chrest. and gloss.; Porta Ling. Orient.]	4/-	8°	*Berlin*	[6-] 72
TURPIE, Dr. D. McC.	Manual of the Chaldee Language [with chrestomathy]	7/- sq	8°	Williams	79
ZSCHOKKE, H.	Institutiones, Fundamentales Linguæ Aramaicæ	5/-	8°	*Vienna*	70

109. SYRIAC [EAST-ARAMAIC] PHILOLOGY: (*a*) CLASSICAL.

Dictionaries.

CARDAHI, P. G.	Dictionnaire Syriaque-Arabe, 2 vols.	ea. 40/-	4°	*Beyruth*	87; 89
DUVAL, R. [ed.]	Lexicon Syriacum auct. Hassano Bar Bahlule, pt. i. [in 5 pts.]	17/-	8°	*Paris*	89
*SMITH, Dn. R. Payne [ed.]	Thesaurus Syriacus, coll. Quatremère + Bernstein + Lorsbach + Jacobi + Agrell + Field, pts. i.-v. = vol. i.	£5 5/-; pts. vi.-vii. 52/6; viii. 36/-	f°	Clar. Press	68–90

Grammars, etc.

COWPER, B. H.	Syriac Grammar [tr. of Hoffmann (1827)]	9/-	8°	Williams	58
*DUVAL, R.	Traité de Grammaire Syrique	16/-	8°	*Paris*	81
MERX, A.	Grammatica Syriaca post opus Hoffmanni [1827], 2 pts.	17/6 r	8°	*Halle*	67; 70
*NESTLE, Prf. E.	Syriac Grammar, tr. A. R. S. Kennedy [Am.] [w. chrestomathy]	9/- c	8°	Williams	[81] 89
*NOELDEKE, Theodor	Kurzgefasste Syrische Grammatik	12/-	8°	*Leipzig*	80
PHILLIPS, Dr. G.	Syriac Grammar	7/6	8°	Bell	[37] 66

Chrestomathies.

BERNSTEIN + KIRSCH [eds.]	Chrestomathia Syriaca, 3/-; Lexicon to same, 5/-; in 1 vol.	7/6	8°	Williams	32; 36
MERX, A. [ed.]	Chrestomathia Targumica [Petermann's Porta Ling. Orient.]	7/6 s	8°	*Berlin*	88
NESTLE, Prf. E. [ed.]	—*in his* Grammar, *ut supra.*				
ROEDIGER, A. [ed.]	Chrestomathia Syriaca, ed. et glossario explanata	7/6	8°	*Halle*	[38] 68
WENIG, J. B. [ed.]	Chrestomathia Syriaca cum apparatu grammatico	7/6	8°	*Innsbruck*	66
ZINGERLE, P. [ed.]	Chrestom. Syriaca, c. notis philolog. et lex. Syr., 2 vols.	15/-	8°	*Rome*	71; 73

Metrology.

MARTIN, Abbé	De la Métrique des Syriens [Abhandl. f. K. d. ML.]	4/-	8°	*Leipzig*	80

Manuscripts.

Bibl. Nationale, Paris	Manuscrits Syriaques et Sabéens [by H. Zotenberg]	12/6	4°	*Paris*	74
Bodl. Lib. Oxon.	Catalogus Codicum Syriacorum Bibl. Bodleiana [by Dn. R. Payne-Smith]	21/-	4°	Clar. Press	64
British Museum	Catalogue of Syriac MSS., pt. i., 15/-; ii., 25/-; iii., 30/- [by Prf. Wm. Wright]		4°	Brit. Mus.	70; 71; 73

110. SYRIAC PHILOLOGY: (*b*) MANDAITIC [a corrupt Syriac].

History of the Dialect.

NOELDEKE, Theodor	Ueber die Mundart der Mandäer	2/6	4°	*Hanover*	62

Grammar.

NOELDEKE, Theodor	Mandäische Grammatik	15/- r	8°	*Halle*	75

Texts.

Codex Nasaraeus: Latin tr. by Norberg

At the end of Dr. A. J. H. W. BRANDT's *Die Mandäische Religion* [8/- 8° *Leipzig*, 1889: an important work] are some elaborate notes on the *Genzâ*, or *Cod. Nasar.* The preface to the bk. conts. a list of wks. on Mand. Literature, edns. and trs.

EUTING, J. [ed.]	Quolasta, Gesänge u. Lehren v. d. Taufe: text, etc.	75/-	f°	*Stuttgart*	67
PETERMANN, H. [ed.]	Thesaurus seu Liber Magnus vulgo Lib. Adamis appellatus, 2 vols.	90/-	4°	*Leipzig*	67

111. SYRIAC PHILOLOGY: (*c*) MODERN SYRIAC.

Grammars.

NOELDEKE, Theodor	Grammatik d. neusyrischen Sprache in Kurdistan	14/-	8°	*Leipzig*	68
STODDARD, Rev. D. T. [Am.]	Grammar of Modern Syriac Language	10/6	8°	*New Haven*	55

112. SYRIAC LITERATURE.

Bibliography.

NESTLE, Prf. E. Litteratura Syriaca [repr. fr. his Brevis Ling. Syr. Gram.] 2/- s 8° *Berlin* 88

History and Criticism.

CARDAHI, P. G. Liber Thesauri de Arte Poetica Syrorum 10/6 8° *Rome* 75
de LAGARDE, P. A. Analecta Syriaca, 21/-; Appendix 2/6 8° *Leipzig* 59 ; 59
MERX, A. Historia artis grammaticæ apud Syros [Abhand. Kunde ML.] 15/- r 8° ,, 89
WRIGHT, Prf. William —*article* Syriac Literature, *in* Encyclo. Brit., vol. xxii. 30/- 4° Black 87

Collections.

CURETON, Rev. W. [ed.] Ancient Syriac Documents [w. English tr.] 31/6 4° Williams 64
,, ,, Spicilegium Syriacum *o.p.* [*w.* 25/-] r 8° ,, 55
Remains of Bardesan, Melitou, Ambrose and Mara Bar Serapion, w. English trs.
LAND, J. P. N. [ed.] Anecdota Syriaca collegit, edidit, explicavit, 4 vols. 67/6 4° *Leyden* 62–75
i.: Symbolae Syr., 14/- '62; ii.: Joannis Episc. Ephes., 17/- '68; iii.: Zachariae Episc. Mityl., 18/- '70; iv.: Otia Syriaca, 18/6 '75.

Biblical Codices —*v.* A § 17.

Apocryphal Scriptures —*v.* A § 19.

Ecclesiastical Law.

de LAGARDE, P. A. [ed.] Reliquiae Juris Eccles. Antiq. Syriace 12/- r 8° *Leipzig* 57

Historians.

BAETHGEN, Fried. [ed. and tr.] Fragmente syrischer u. arab. Historiker [Abhandl. f. K. d. ML.] 7/6 8° *Leipzig* 84

Texts and Translations.

ABD-JACHOUDA ESSONBAONI Jardin de Délices, hrsg. P. G. Cardahi [verse] *Beyruth in prep.*
Addai the Apostle, Doctrine of: text and tr. Dr. G. Phillips 7/6 8° Trübner 76
ALEXANDER the Great, Hist. of: being Syriac versions of *Pseudo-Callisthenes*, ed. with tr. and notes, E. A. W. Budge 25/- 8° Camb. Press 90
APHRAATES Homilies of: ed. Prf. W. Wright, vol. i. [text] 42/- 4° Williams 69
,, ,, ,, German tr. G. Bert, w. notes 8/- 8° *Leipzig* 88
BARHEBRAEUS, Greg. Chronicon Syriacum e Codd. MSS. emend. adnot., *etc.* 36/- 4° *Paris* 90
,, ,, Œuvres Grammaticales, ed. Abbé Martin, 2 vols.; w. French notes 25/- 8° ,, 72
BEZOLD, Carl [ed.] Die Schatzhöhle, 2 pts. [w. the Arabic version and Germ. tr.] 28/- 8° *Leipzig* 86 ; 88
Book of the Bee: ed., fr. Lond., Oxon., and Munich MSS., E. A. W. Budge [w. tr.] 21/- s 4° Clar. Press 86
CLEMENTIS Romani Recognitiones Syriacae, ed. P. A. de Lagarde 20/- r 8° *Leipzig* 61
,, ,, Epistolae binae de Virginitate, ed. J. T. Beelen 14/- 8° *Louvain* 56
CURETON, Rev. W. [ed. & tr.] History of Martyrs in Palestine [w. tr.] 10/6 8° Williams 61
,, ,, [ed.] Remains of a very ancient Recension of the 4 Gospels 30/- 4° ,, 58
,, ,, [ed. & tr.] Ignatian Epistles in Syriac, Greek, Latin and English [w. tr.] 31/6 4° *Oxford* 49
EBED-JESU SOBENSIS Carmina Selecta, ed. H. Gismondi [text and Lat. tr.] 3/6 8° Trübner 88
ELIA of Sobhâ Turas Mamlâ Surjâjâ, ed. and tr. J. H. Gottheil [a treat. on Syriac gram.] 12/- 8° *Berlin* 87
EPHRAEMI Syri Carmina Nisibena, ed. Dr. W. Bickel [w. prolegom. and gloss.] 16/-; *red. to* 6/- r 8° *Leipzig* 66
,, ,, Carmina Selecta, ed. Hahn + Seiffert 4/- 8° ,, 25
,, ,, Hymni et Sermones, ed. T. J. Lamy, v. i. 17/-; ii. 30/-; iii. 12/6 [w. Lat. tr. & notes] 4° *Malines* 82; 87; 90
,, ,, Histoire de Joseph [poem in 10 bks., hitherto inedited] 8/- 8° *Paris* 87
ISAAC ANTIOCHENI Opera Omnia: Syriac text, ed. W. Bickell, pt. i. 12/-; ii. 14/- 8° *Giessen* 73; 76
JOHN OF EPHESUS Ecclesiastical History, pt. iii., ed. [in Syriac] Rev. W. Cureton 30/- 4° *Oxford* 53
JOSHUA the Stylite Chronicle of [A.D. 507]: w. tr. and notes Prf. W. Wright 10/6 8° Camb. Press 82
,, ,, ,, ["A.D. 515"]: ed. w. Fch. tr. Abbé P. Martin 9/- 8° *Leipzig* 76
Kalilag and Damnag Syriac text, ed. Bickell; w. Germ. tr., w. intro. Th. Benfey 24/- 8° ,, 76
The Fables of Bidpai (Pilpay). For Hebr. version, v. K § 118; for Persian version, v. K § 134, *s.v.* Anvari Soheili.
,, ,, Syriac text, tr. fr. the Arabic, ed. Prf. Wm. Wright 21/- 8° Trübner 84
,, ,, ,, ,, tr. w. notes Prf. I. G. N. Keith-Falconer 7/6 8° Camb. Press 85
Contains a valuable prefatory account of the literary history, various texts, etc., of the fables.

Folk-tales, Proverbs, etc.—*for some specimens*, *v.* B § 27*.

113. PHOENICIAN AND CARTHAGINIAN PHILOLOGY AND INSCRIPTIONS.

Dictionary.

LEVY, M. A. Phönizisches Wörterbuch 2/6 8° *Breslau* 64

Grammar, etc.

JUDAS, A. C. Étude de la Langue Phénic. et la Lang. Libyque; 32 pl. 27/- 4° *Paris* 47
SCHRÖDER, P. Die phönizische Sprache; 22 pl. [grammar and specimens] 14/- 8° *Halle* 69

Alphabet.

*LENORMANT, Fr. Essai sur la Propagation de l'Alphabet Phénicien, vols. i.-ii. (1) 32/- i 8° *Paris* 74; 75
de ROUGÉ, Em. Mémoire sur l'Origine Égyptienne de l'Alphabet Phénicien; 3 pl. 8/6 8° " 74

Miscellaneous Essays.

LEVY, M. A. Phönizische Studien, 4 pts. 13/- 8° *Breslau* 56–70

Inscriptions

—*v. also* K § 105: Semitic, *s.v.* Inscriptions.

British Museum Inscriptions from Carthage [researches of Nathan Davis 1856–58] 25/- f° British Museum 63
DERENBOURG, J. Notes Épigraphiques [10 notes, chiefly on Phoenician inscripp.] 3/6 8° *Paris* 77
EUTING, J. [ed.] Punische Steine; 46 f° pl. 15/- r 8° *St. Petersburg* 71
" " [ed.] Sechs Phönikische Inscriften aus Idalion; 3 pl. 4/- 4° *Strassburg* 75
GESENIUS, W. [ed.] Scripturæ Linguæque Phoeniciae Monumenta, 3 pts.; 48 pl. 50/-; *red. to* 16/- 4° *Leipzig* 37
KÄMPF, S. J. [ed.] Phöniz. Epigraphik: Grabschrift Eschumunazar's [w. Germ. tr.] 3/- 8° *Prague* 75
PRAETORIUS, F. Beiträge zur Erklärung der himjarischen Inschriften, 3 pts. 4/6 8° *Halle* 74
RENAN, Ernest La Mission de Phénicie; 70 pl. £7 f° *Paris* 74
de VOGUÉ, Cte. Mélanges d'Archéologie Orientale; pl. 20/- 8° " 69

Carthaginian.

EUTING, J. [ed.] Sammlung der carthagischen Inschriften, vol. i.; 208 pl. 60/- 4° *Strassburg* 83

114. ARABIC PHILOLOGY: CLASSICAL AND MODERN.

Dictionaries.

*BADGER, Dr. G. P. English-Arabic Lexicon [classical and modern] £4 r 4° Paul 81
BEAUSSIER, M. Dictionnaire Pratique Arabe-Française [modern Arabic] 42/- 4° *Algiers* 87
BELOT, Père J. B. Dictionnaire Français-Arabe, 2 pts. 4° *Beyrout* 90; 90
CATAFAGO, J. English and Arabic Dictionary, 2 vols. [Arab.-Eng., Eng.-Arab.] 42/- 8° Quaritch [58] 73
CHERBONNEAU, A. Dictionnaire Arabe-Française, 2 vols. [written language] 20/- 8° *Paris* 76
" " Dictionnaire Français-Arabe 10/- 8° " 72
DOZY, R. Supplément aux Dictionnaires Arabes, 8 pts. 130/- r 4° *Leyden* 77–81
FREYTAG, G. W. Lexicon Arabico-Latinum, 4 vols., 73/6; Abridged, 1 vol. 12/- 4° *Halle* 30–37; 37
GASSELIN, Edouard Dictionnaire Français-Arabe, pts. i.–xl. ea. 3/- 4° *Paris* 80–90 *in prog.*
KAZIMIRSKI de BIBERSTEIN, A. Dictionnaire Arabe-Français, 2 vols. 96/- r 8° " 46; 60
*LANE, E. W. Arabic-English Lexicon, der. fr. East. sources, ed. S. Lane-Poole; 8 v. ea. 25/- r 4° Williams 63–89
NEWMAN, Prf. F. W. Dictionary of Modern Arabic, 2 vols. 21/- c 8° Trübner 71

1. Anglo-Arabic Dictionary; 2. Anglo-Arabic Vocabulary; 3. Arabo-English Dictionary. In Roman characters.

SALMONÉ, H. A. Arabic-English Dictionary, 2 vols. 36/- p 8° " 90
STEINGASS, F. Student's Arabic-English Dictionary [tr.], 50/-; English-Arabic Dict. 28/- 8° W. H. Allen 84; 89
WAHRMUND, A. Handwörterbuch d. Neu-Arabischen-Deutschen Sprache, 2 vols. 30/- 8° *Giessen* [74;75;77] 87
" " Handwörterbuch d. Deutsch. u. Neu-Arabischen Sprache 10/- 8° " [75] 87

These "zweite Ausgaben" are merely reissues, with fresh title-pages, of the old stock of the first editions.

THOMSON-WORTABET, Prf. W. Arabic-English Dictionary 22/6 p 8° Trübner 88
ZENKER, Dr. J. H. Dictionnaire Turc-Arabe-Persan, 2 vols. £5 4° *Leipzig* 65; 70

Native Dictionaries.

As' Sihâh fi'l Logât, 2 vols. By Abu Nasr Ismail al Jauhari (d. 1007) [one of the most famous Arab. lex.] 105/- f° *Bulâq* 65
Mohit ul Mohit ["The Ocean of the Ocean"]. By Butrus-al-Butsâny, 2 vols. 168/- s f° *Beyrout* 66; 70
" Katr el Mohit ["A Drop from the Ocean"]: abridgment of above 84/- 8° " 67–70

An Arabic dictionary explained in Arabic. Contains many special and technic terms not contained in other dictionaries.

Grammars, etc.

CASPARI, C. P. Arabische Grammatik, ed. August Müller (*v. also* Wright, *infra*] 10/- 8° *Halle* [44–48] 87
GREEN, Maj. A. O. Practical Arabic Grammar, pt. i. [for use of travellers] 7/6 c 8° Clar. Press [ ] 87
HOWELL, M. S. Grammar of Classical Arabic Language, parts ii.–iii. 31/6 8° *Allahabad* 80

These two parts (in 1 vol.) contain the Verb and the Particle. Part I. is in prep.

*LANSING, J. C. [Am.] Arabic Grammar [of classical language] 8° Amer. Hebrew Soc., *Chicago* 87

The best grammar for beginners, as Wright's is for more advanced students.

LEITNER, Dr. G. W. Introduction to a Philosophical Grammar of Arabic 4/- 8° *Lahore* (Oriental Instit., *Woking*) 71
NEWMAN, Prf. F. W. Handbook of Modern Arabic 6/- 8° Trübner 66
PALMER, Prf. E. H. Grammar of Arabic Language 18/- 8° W. H. Allen 74
" " The Arabic Manual: grammar, reader, etc. 7/6 s 8° " [81] 85

Contains a condensed grammar of Classical and Modern Arabic. Readings and Exercises. Vocabulary.

" " Hindustani, Persian, and Arabic Grammar [Simplified Grammars Ser.] 5/- c 8° Trübner [82] 85
de SACY, Sylvestre Grammaire Arabe, 2 vols. [important standard work] *o.p.* [*w.* £7 7/-] 8° *Paris* [30] 31
SOCIN, Prf. A. Arabic Grammar [paradigms, liter., chrestom. and gloss.; in Engl.] 7/6 c 8° *Berlin* [85] 90
TIEN, A. Manual of Colloquial Arabic 7/6 f 8° W. H. Allen 85
WAHRMUND, A. Praktisches Handbuch d. Neu-Arabischen Sprache, 2 vols. and key 20/- 8° *Giessen* [61] 86
*WRIGHT, Prf. W. Grammar of Arabic Language, 2 vols. [orig. based on Caspari] 23/- 8° Williams [62] 74; 75

K § 115

Language Spoken in Egypt and Syria.

Author	Title	Price	Size	Publisher	Date
SABBAGH, Michail	Grammatik d. arabischen Vulgärdialecte von Syrien u. Aegypten	4/-	8°	*Stuttgart*	86
SPITTA-BEY, W.	Grammatik d. arabischen Vulgärdialects von Aegypten	25/-	r 8°	*Leipzig*	80

Proper Names.

Author	Title	Price	Size	Publisher	Date
GARCIN de TASSY	Mémoires sur les Noms Propres et les Titres Musulmans	4/6	8°	*Paris*	[ ] 78

Chrestomathies.

Author	Title	Price	Size	Publisher	Date
AMARI, M. [ed.]	Biblioteca Arabo-Sicula; w. appendix, 2 vols., ea. 20/-; appendix ii. An Italian tr. of Arabic texts contained in the pubns. of the Deutsche Morgenländische Gesellschaft.	2/-	8°	*Turin*	[57–76] 80–81; 87
ARNOLD, F. [ed.]	Chrestomathia Arabica, pt. i. [text]; pt. ii. [glossarium]	15/-	8°	*Halle*	53
BIRDWOOD, A. R. [ed.]	Arabic Reading Book	5/-	c 8°	W. H. Allen	90
DERENBOURG + SPIRO, H. J.	[eds.] Chrestomathie élém. de l'Arabe littéral [w. glossary]	5/6	s 8°	*Paris*	85
FORBES, D. [ed.]	Arabic Reading Lessons: extracts with vocabulary	15/-	r 8°	W. H. Allen	64
GIRGAS + ROSEN, W. O. W. R.	[eds.] Arabic Chrestomathy, 2 vols.	15/-	8°	*St. Petersburg*	75; 76
JACOB, Georg. [ed.]	Arabic Bible Chrestomathy: w. glossary	3/-	c 8°	Williams	89
NÖLDEKE + MÜLLER, Th. Aug.	[eds.] Chrestomathia Arabica Poetica [Porta Ling. Orient.]		8°	*Berlin*	90
de SACY, Sylvestre [ed.]	Chrestomathie Arabe, 3 vols. [w. Fch. tr. and notes] *o.p.* [*w.* £4]		8°	*Paris*	[06] 26–27
WAHRMUND, A. [ed.]	Lesebuch in Neu-Arabischen Sprache, 2 pts. [text and German tr.]	12/-	8°	*Giessen*	[ ] 80
WRIGHT, Prf. W. [ed.]	Arabic Chrestomathy, vol. i. [texts]	7/6	8°	Williams	70

Inscriptions.

Author	Title	Price	Size	Publisher	Date
AMARI, M. [ed.]	Epigrafi Arab. di Sicilia; 10 pl. [w. Italian tr.]	45/-	4°	*Naples*	75
British Museum	Inscriptions in Himyaratic Character	24/-	f°	British Museum	63
HALÉVY, J.	Études Sabéennes: examen des Inscriptions	12/6	8°	*Paris*	75
MÜLLER, D. H. [ed.]	Epigraphische Denkmäler aus Arabien; 12 pl. [reprint]	10/-	r 4°	*Leipzig*	89
THOMAS, E.	Early Sassanian Inscriptions, Seals and Coins	7/6	8°	Trübner	74

Manuscripts.

Author	Title	Price	Size	Publisher	Date
Bibl. Nationale, Paris	Catalogues des MSS. Orientaux: Arabes, pts. i.–ii. [by McGuckin de Slane] ea.	15/-	4°	*Paris*	83; 89
Berlin Roy. Lib.	Verzeichniss d. arab. Handschriften d. k. Bibl. zu Berlin, vol. i. [by W. Ahlwardt]	20/-	4°	*Berlin*	87
British Museum	Catalogue of the Arabic MSS., 3 pts.	68/-	f°	Brit. Mus.	46; 52; 71
Escurial	Les Manuscrits Arabes, decrits p. H. Derenbourg, vol. i. [École Lang. Orient. Viv.]	12/6	8°	*Paris*	85
India Office	Catalogue of the Arabic MSS. [by O. Loth]	21/-	4°	Trübner	77
Leyden Univ.	Catal. Codd. Arab. Bibl. Acad. Lugd.-Bat., vol. i. [by M. J. de Goeje + M. T. Houtsma]	8/-	8°	*Leyden*	[62–73] 88

Collected Writings.

Author	Title	Price	Size	Publisher	Date
FLEISCHER, H. L.	Kleinere Schriften, vol. i. (2 pts.), 24/-; ii., 20/-; iii., 9 pl.	20/-	8°	*Leipzig*	85; 88; 89

115. ARABIC LITERATURE.

Bibliography.

Author	Title	Price	Size	Publisher	Date
HASANEIN MOHAMMED	[ed.] Katalog der arabischen Werke der vicek. Bibl. Kairo, vol. i. [in 8 or 9 vols.]	6/-	r 8°	*Cairo*	88 *in prog.*
WÜSTENFELD, F.	Die Uebersetzungen arab. Werke in d. Latein. seit d. 11 Jahrh.	5/-	4°	*Göttingen*	77

History of Literature.

Author	Title	Price	Size	Publisher	Date
ARBUTHNOT, F. F.	Arabic Authors: a manual of Arabian History and Literature	10/-	8°	Quaritch	90
DOZY, R.	Recherches sur l'hist. et littér. de l'Espagne p. l. moyen âge, 2 vols.	17/-	8°	*Paris*	[5-] 81
HAMMER-PURGSTALL	Literaturgeschichte der Araber, 7 vols. [A.H. 656–A.D. 1258]	168/-	4°	*Vienna*	56

Grammarians.

Author	Title	Price	Size	Publisher	Date
FLÜGEL, G.	Die grammatischen Schulen der Araber, pt. i. [Basra & Kufa] [Abhand. f. K. d. ML.]	6/6	8°	*Leipzig*	62

Historians.

Author	Title	Price	Size	Publisher	Date
WÜSTENFELD, F.	Die Geschichtsschreiber der Araber u. ihre Werke	12/-	8°	*Göttingen*	82

Philosophy —*v. also* C § 2: History of Philosophy, Generally.

Author	Title	Price	Size	Publisher	Date
DIETERICI, F.	Propaedeutik der Araber, 4/6; Naturanschauung der Araber	4/-	8°	*Berlin*	65; 76
" "	Logik und Psychologie d. Araber, 7/6; Anthropologie der Araber	8/-	8°	"	68; 71
" "	Der Makrokosmos: Die Welt, 8/-; Der Mensch	8/-	8°	"	75; 76
" "	Lehre v. d. Weltseele, 8/-; Streit zwischen Mensch u. Thier	4/6	8°	"	73; 58
" "	Der Darwinismus bei den Arabern [10 cent.]	3/-	8°	"	78
DUGAT, G.	Histoire des Philosophes et de Théologiens Musulmans [A.D. 632–1258]	6/6	8°	*Paris*	78

Poets.

Author	Title	Price	Size	Publisher	Date
AHLWARDT, W.	Ueber Poesie und Poetik der Araber	4/-	4°	*Gotha*	56
BASSET, R.	La Poésie Arabe ante-islamique [Bibl. Orient. Elzévir.]	4/6	12°	*Paris*	81
NÖLDEKE, Theodor	Beiträge zur Kenntniss der Poesie d. Alten Araber	6/-	r 8°	*Hanover*	46
v. SCHACK, A. F.	Poesie u. Kunst der Araber in Spanien und Sicilien, 2 vols.	9/-	8°	*Stuttgart*	[65] 77

Biography.

Collectively.

ABU ABDALLA DAHABI Liber Classicorum Virorum, ed. F. Wüstenfeld 10/6 4° *Göttingen* 33-34
ABU ZAKARIYA YAHYA EL-NAWAWI Biographical Dictionary, ed. F. Wüstenfeld, 9 pts. 24/- 8° ,, 42-47
IBN KHALLIKAN Lives of Illustrious Men: text ed. MacGuckin de Slane, vol. i. [all pub.] 42/- 4° *Paris* 38-42
,, ,, The same, Fch. tr. MacGuckin de Slane, 4 vols. 84/- 4° ,, 42-71
Kitab al-Alghani, vols. i.-xx.; vol. xxi. ed. R. E. Brünnow, pt. i., 12/- 8° *Bulâq?; Leyden* 88

Mohammed. —*for non-native lives of Mohammed, v.* A § 13.

ABOU-'L-FÉDA Vie de Mohammed: Arabic text and Fch. tr. Desvergers 15/- 8° *Paris*
AL-WAKIDY Al Maghâzi: history of Mohammed's Campaigns, ed. A. v. Kremer. 5 pts., ea. 2/- 8° *Calcutta*
IBN HAJAR Biograp. Dictionary of Persons who knew Mohammed, vols. i.-iv., 48 pts., ea. 2/- 8° ,, *in prog.*
IBN HISCHAM ABD EL-MALIK Life of Mohammed, ed. F. Wüstenfeld: text, 21/-; commentary, etc. 7/- 8° *Göttingen* 57-60
,, ,, The same, German tr. G. Weil, 2 vols. 17/6 8° *Stuttgart* 64
Mis-chat-ul-Masabih, tr. Cpt. Matthews; w. notes by Hughes 45/- r 8° *Calcutta* [09-10] 76

These traditions constitute the second authority of Mussulman law, and are regarded as a sort of supplement to the Koran.

POOLE, S. Lane [tr.] Speeches and Table-talk of Mohammad [tr.] 4/6 18° Macmillan 82

Dictionaries —*v.* K § 114, *s.v.* Native Dictionaries.

Encyclopædias.

Athar-ul-Adhâr ["Traces of Centuries" = geog. and hist. dict.], in pts. ea. 7/6 4°
BUTRUS-AL-BUTSÂNY [Arab encyclo. of univ. knowl.], vols. i.-ix. [to occupy 15 vols.] ea. 31/6 s f° *Beyrout* 76-87 *in prog.*
Kitab-al-Fihrist [a literary encyclo.], by Abu 'l-Farraj al Warrak, ed. Rüdiger, 2 vols. 84/- i 8° *Leipzig* 71; 72

Fiction, Proverbs, etc.

Barlaam et Josaphat Extraits du Texte Grec et des Versions Arab. et Ethiop., 5/-; ed. H. Zotenberg 6/- 8° *Paris* 86
Basim le Forgeron et Harun Er-Rachid, ed. Ct. C. de Landberg, pt. i. 5/- 8° *Leyden* 88

The story of Basim the Smith in 2 Arab. versions (Egyp. and Syrian dialects) w. a French tr.

BURCKHARDT, J. L. [ed. & tr.] Arabic Proverbs, illust. Manners of Modern Egyptians 18/- 8° Quaritch [30] 75
FREYTAG, G. W. [ed.] Proverbia Arabica, 3 vols. in 4 pts. [w. Latin trs.] *o.p.* [*w.* 20/-] 8° *Bonn* 31-43
Kalilag and Damnag —*for* Syriac text, *v.* K § 112; *for* Hebrew, K § 118; *for* Persian, K § 134.
LOCMAN, Fables: text, w. French tr. and notes H. Derenbourg 2/- 12° *Berlin* 50
,, ,, text. ed. A. Cherbonneau [w. index] 1/6 12° *Paris* 88
QOLYOOBI Book of Anecdotes, ed. W. Nassau Lees 5/- 8° *Calcutta* 56
Thousand and One Nights. ("Alif Laila.") Arabic Text, ed. Sir W. H. Macnaghten, 4 vols. 60/- r 8° ,, 32-42
,, ,, Arabic Text, after Tunis MS., ed. Habicht + Fleischer, 12 vols. 96/- 12° *Breslau* 25-43
,, ,, Arabic Text, 4 vols. 63/- 4° *Cairo* A.H. 1279 [=1862]
,, ,, Arabic Text, ed. P. A. Salhani, vols. i.-ii. ea. 5/- p 8° *Beyrout* 88; 89 *in prog.*
,, ,, tr. Cpt. Sir R. F. Burton [unexpurgated], w. notes; 10 vols. and 6 suppl. vols. r 8° [*w.* £25] *pr. prin.* "*Benares*" [=*London*] 85-88
,, ,, The same, expurgated by Lady Burton, 6 vols. 63/- 8° Waterlow 87-88
,, ,, tr. John Payne, 9 vols. and 3 suppl. vols. r 8° Villon Soc. 82-84

Also *Aladdin and the Enchanted Lamp* and *Zein ul Asnam*, tr. by PAYNE, 25/- 8° Villon Society '89. This is tr. fr. ZOTENBERG'S edn. of same in *Transs. Acad. d. Inscripp.* [1890 reprinted, 6/- 8° *Paris* '88], wh. conts. an excell. account of the MSS. and literature of the *Arab. Nights*.

,, ,, tr. E. W. Lane, ed. S. Lane-Poole, 3 vols.; ill. ea. 7/6 8° Chatto [39-41] 77
,, ,, The New Arabian Nights, tr. W. F. Kirby 3/6 c 8° Sonnenschein 83

Comprising tales not included in LANE'S or GALLAND'S translations. There have been several English translations of portions (usually the same) of this work, notably those of FOSTER [1802], BEAUMONT [1810], SCOTT [1811], LAMB [1826]. Cheap editions from 1/- upwards.

,, ,, übers. Dr. G. Weil, 4 vols.; 718 ill. 14/- 4° *Stuttgart* [39-41] 89

Geography and Travels.

Collection.

Bibliotheca Geographica Arabica, ed. J. de Goeje, vols. i.-v. 75/- 8° *Leyden* 71 *sqq.*

Individual Writers.

ABULFEDA, Ismael ben-Ali [*b.* 1273] Geographie: text, ed. Reinaud + MacGuckin de Slane 45/- 8° *Paris* 40
,, ,, The same: French tr. Reinaud + Stan. Guyard, w. notes & ill. 2 v. in 3 45/- 8° ,, 48
ABU OBEID EL-BEKRI Geographical Dictionary, ed. F. Wüstenfeld. 4 vols. 37/- 4° *Göttingen* 76-77
AL-BERUNI [*b.* 973] India: its relig., liter., astron., etc.: text, ed. Prf. E. Sachau [Ind. Off. Pub.] 63/- r 4° Trübner 87
,, ,, The same, tr. w. preface Prf. E. Sachau, 2 vols. [Oriental Series] 36/- p 8° ,, 89
CAZWINI, Cosmography: text, ed. F. Wüstenfeld, 2 vols. 24/- 8° *Göttingen* 48; 56
,, The same: German tr. H. Ethé, vol. i. 11/- r 8° *Leipzig* 69
CHEMS-ED-DIN Cosmography: text, ed. A. F. Mehren 10/- 4° *St. Petersburg* 66
,, The same: French tr. 11/6 8° *Leipzig* 74
EDRISI, Description de l'Afrique et de l'Espagne. ed. R. Dozy + J. de Goeje [w. Fch. tr.] 16/- r 8° *Leyden* 66
FARIS EL SHIDIAC Description of Malta and Geography of Europe: text 16/- 8° *Tunis* 62
IBN BATOUTAH Voyages: text, w. Fch. tr. Defrémery + Sanguinetti, 4 vols. 27/6 8° *Paris* 58-59
IBN JUBAIR Travels: text, fr. Leyden MS., ed. Prf. W. Wright 12/- 8° *Leyden* 52
JACUT, Geograp. Dict., ed. F. Wüstenfeld, 6 vols. [fr. MSS. at Berl., Petersb., Paris] £9 8° *Leipzig* 66-73

K § 115

KREMER, A. [ed.] Description de l'Afrique du 6e Siècle de l'Hégire : text 6/6 8° *Vienna* 52

Lexicon Geographicum, e II. Cod. Arab., ed. Juynboll + Gaal, 6 vols. 50/- 8° *Leyden* 49–64

VAN DER LITH Livre d. Merveilles de l'Inde p. Capitaine Bozorg. ed. M. Devic ; facs. miniatures 21/- 4° *Leyden* 83–86

Grammarians.

IBN DJANAH (ABOU 'L WALID MERWAN) Opuscules et Traités Grammaticaux, ed. J. + H. Derenbourg 12/6 8° *Paris* 80

IBN HICHAM Traité de Flexion et Syntaxe Arabe, trad. A. Goguyer 10/- 8° *Leyden* 87

SIBAWAIHI, Kitab Sibouya, ed: H. Derenbourg, vols. i.–ii. (1) 25/- 8° *Paris* 81 ; 86

History.

Collections.

BAETHGEN, Fried. [ed. & tr.] Fragmente syrischer u. arab. Historiker [Abhand. f. K. d. ML.] 7/6 8° *Leipzig* 84

Fragmenta Histor. Arab., ed. J. de Goeje + P. de Jong, vols. i.–ii. 29/6 4° *Leyden* 69 ; 72

i.: Kitabo 'l-Oyun, 16/- ; ii.: Tadjaribo 'l-Omami, by Ibn Maskowaih, 13/6.

ABULFEDA, Ismael ben-Ali [*b.* 1273] Historia Ante-Islamitica, ed. H. O. Fleischer 9/- 4° *Leipzig* 31

ABD-EL-RAHMAN EL DJABARTI Chroniques du : French tr. 10/- 8° *Paris* 89

ABOUL-GHAZI BEHADOUR KHAN Hist. of Mogols and Tatars: text & Fch. tr. Bar. Desmaisons, 2 v. 10/6 8° *St. Petersburg* 71 ; 74

ABD 'OL WAHID al MARREKOSHI History of Almohades and of Spain, ed. R. Dozy 8/6 8° *Leyden* [ ] 81

ABOUL-MAHASIN Annales, ed. Juynboll + Matthes, 2 vols. [annals of Kings of Egypt] 30/- r 8° „ 55 ; 61

AL-BONDARI Hist. des Seldjoucides de l'Iraq, ed. M. T. Houtsma 5/- 8° „ 89

AL-HARIRI Les Séances de, ed. Silvestre de Sacy, revue Reinaud + Derenbourg, 2 v. 33/- 4° *Paris* 47 ; 53

„ Durrat-al-Gawwâs, ed. H. Thorbecke 18/- 8° *Leipzig* 71

„ Assemblies of, tr. w. intro. and notes T. Chenery 18/- ; *red. to* 10/- 8° Williams 67

AL-MAKKARI Analectes sur l'Hist. and Litt. des Arabes d'Espagne, ed. Dozy + Dugat + Krehl + Wright, 2 vols. 110/- 4° *Leyden* 55 ; 61

de Gayangos, P. Hist. of Moham. Dynasties of Spain, 2 v. [= tr. of pts. of Makkari] [*w.* 42/-] 4° Orient. Tr. Fd. 40 ; 43

AL-WAQIDI Futuh ul Sham, ed. W. N. Lees, 9 pts. [conq. of Syria] ea. 2/- 8° *Calcutta*

FOURNEL, H. [ed.] Les Berbers : text, vol. i. [conq. of Africa by Arabs] 25/- 4° *Paris* 75

IBN ABI ZER' Annales Regum Mauritaniae, ed. C. J. Tornberg, 2 vols. [w. Latin tr.] 42/- 4° *Upsala* 43 ; 45

IBN ADHARI History of Africa and Spain, w. French intro. R. Dozy, 2 vols. 30/- 8° *Leyden* 48 ; 51

IBN-AL-ATHIRI Chronicon, ed. C. J. Tornberg, 14 vols. 174/- r 8° *Upsala* 51–76

IBN-COTEIBA Handbook of History : text, ed. F. Wüstenfeld, 2 pts. 8/- r 8° *Göttingen* 50

IBN ED-DIN Conquest of Syria and Palestine, ed. Ct. C. de Landberg, vol. i. [text] 15/- 4° *Leyden* 88

IBN-ETTHIQTHAQA ELFACHRI History of Islam. Kingdom, ed. W. Ahlwardt 15/- 8° *Gotha* 60

IBN WADHIH Historiæ, ed. M. T. Houtsma, 2 vols. 22/6 8° *Leyden*

MOHAMED ESSEGHIR BEN ELHADJ Nozet-Elhâdj, ed. O. Houdas [hist. of saad. dyn. 1511–1670] 12/6 8° *Paris* 88

MOUDJIR-ED-DIN Histoire de Jérus. et Hebron : French tr. H. Sauvaire 12/6 8° „ 76

TABARI Chronique : French tr. by H. Zotenberg, 4 vols. 32/6 8° „ 67–74

„ Annales, ed. J. Barth + Th. Nöldeke + O. Loth + E. Prym, *etc.*, 3 ser., v. i.–xvi. 165/- 8° *Leyden* 78–90 *in prog.*

„ Geschichte der Perser u. Araber z. Zeit d. Sasaniden, übers. Th. Nöldeke 12/- r 8° „ 79

Composed in Arabic in 10 cent. It is the oldest general history in Mahomedan literature, and is of special importance for the history of the conquest of Persia by the Arabs.

Oratory.

MEHREN, A. F. [ed.] Rhetorik der Araber [selections ; Arabic texts] 14/- 8° *Copenhagen* 53

Philosophy and Religion—*v. also* Biogr. of Mohammed, *supra*, and A § 13 : Mohammedanism and Hist. of Islamism.

AL-FARABI [ALPHARABIUS] Leben und Schriften. v. M. Steinschneider 8/- 4° *St. Petersburg* 69

„ „ Philosophische Abhandlungen, hrsg. F. Dieterici [fr. Lond., Leyd., & Berl. MSS.] 5/- 8° *Leyden* 90

AVERROES Philosophie und Theologie, ed. J. Müller 12/- 4° *Munich* 59

„ Commento medio alla *Poetica* di Aristotele, ed. F. Lasinio, vols. i.–ii. 19/6 4° *Pisa* 72

Arabic text, w. notes and appendix ; Hebr. tr. by TODROS TODROSI ; Italian tr. by LASINIO, w. index.

Renan, Ernst Averroes et l'Averroisme [historical essay] 6/6 8° *Paris* 61

BOKHARI, Abn Abdallah Muhammed Jami'u s-Sahîh, 4 vols. 93/- 4° *Leyden* 62–66

The great body of canonical traditions, reverenced almost equally with the Koran by orthodox Moslems.

Ikhwanu s-Safa ["Brothers of Purity"] *o.p.* [*w.* 50/-] r 8° *Calcutta* 1263 [= 1846]

The Arabic original of the Hindustani bk. so-named by Prf. FORBES [v. K § 37]. The Ikhwanu-s-Safa were a society of thinkers and writers flourishing about end 10th cent., and this is one of their treatises.

Koran with comm. of Al-Zamakhshari, ed. W. Nassau Lees, 2 vols. 108/- r 4° *Calcutta* 56–61

„ Arabic text : crit. ed. G. Flügel 20/- 4° *Leipzig* [58] 81

„ „ „ ed. Prf. G. M. Redslob 17/- 4° *Paris* [68] 80

„ English Trans. by Geo. Sale, w. notes ; new ed. w. addns. fr. Salvary's version 8/- 8° Ward & Lk. [1734] 77

„ „ „ „ J. M. Rodwell, with notes [arranged in chronolog. order] 12/- 8° Quaritch [61] 76

„ „ „ [Qur'an] by Prf. E. H. Palmer, pts. i.–ii. [Sacr. Bks. of East ; w. val. intro.] ea. 10/6 8° Clar. Press 80 ; 82

„ „ „ Selections, tr. E. Lane, ed. S. Lane-Poole [nephew ; Orient. Ser.] 9/- p 8° Trübner [43] 79

„ Extracts tr. Sir W. Muir : with the texts 3/6 c 8° „ 80

„ French Trans. trad. M. Kasimirski 3/- s 8° *Paris* [57] 87

„ German „ übers. Friedrich Rückert, hrsg. Aug. Müller 4/- 8° *Frankfort* [ ] 88

„ „ „ „ L. Ullmann 2/- 16° *Bielefeld* [40] 82

„ Analysis by J. La Beume, *sub tit.* Le Koran analysé [fr. Kasimirski's tr. ; Bibl. Orient.] 17/- 8° *Paris* 76

„ Commentary on the Quran, by E. M. Wherry, 4 vols. [w. Sale's tr. ; Oriental Ser.] 48/- p 8° „ 82–86

„ „ „ Coran, Beidhawi's, in Latin, ed. H. O. Fleischer, 2 vols. 52/6 4° *Leipzig* 44–48

„ Concordantiae Corani Arabicae, by G. Flügel 15/- 4° „ 42

Koran Dictionary and Glossary of the Koran, by Maj. J. Penrice 21/- 4° Paul 73
,, History of Geschichte des Qorân's. By Theodor Nöldeke 6/- 8° *Göttingen* 60
,, ,, —*article* Koran, in Encyclo. Brit., vol. xvi. 30/- 4° Black 83
,, Introduction to Einleitung in den Koran. By G. Weil [the prophet, his bk., his dominion] 1/6 16° *Bielefeld* [44] 78

Poetry.

Collections.

AHLWARDT, Prf. W. [ed.] The Divans of the Six Ancient Arabic Poets: text 12/- 8° Trübner 70
Ennabiga, Antara, Tharafat, Zuhair, Alqama, Imruulqais.

Translations.

CLOUSTON, W. A. [tr.] Arabian Poetry, translated 8° *priv. prin., Glasgow* 81
GARCIN de TASSY [tr.] Allégoires, Récits, *etc.*, de l'Arabe, Persan, Hindustani et Turc 10/- 8° *Paris* [ ] 76
LYALL, C. J. [tr.] Ancient Arabic Poetry, translated; w. intro. & notes [chiefly pre-Islamic] 10/6 f 4° Williams 85

Individual Writers.

ABU-L'-WALID Moslim ibno 'l-Walid al-Ancari cogn. Cairo-'l-ghawani Poetae Diwan, ed. J. de Goeje 23/- 4° *Leyden* 75
ABU NOWAS Diwân, ed. W. Ahlwardt, 4/-; Germ. tr. A. v. Kremer 4/- 8° *Greifswald* 61; *Vienna* 55
ABU-TEMAN [*b.* 806] Hamasa, ed. G. W. Freytag, w. Latin tr. *Bonn* 28–51
,, ,, German tr. Friederich Rückert 46
BEHA ED DIN ZOHEIR Poems, ed. w. tr. Prf. E. H. Palmer, vol. i. [text]; vol. ii. [metrical tr.] ea. 10/6 c 4° Camb. Press. 76
,, Divan de, ed. Stanislas Guyard [variants; complement to above] 2/6 8° *Paris* 83
Carmina Hudsailitarum, ed. J. C. Kosegarten, vol. i. [text] 15/- 4° *Griefswald* 54
HAMASAH Arabic Poems, ed. Ahmad + Rabbani 15/- r 8° *Calcutta* 56
,, Carmina Arabica, cum Tebrisii Scholiis, ed. G. Freytag, 2 vols. 80/- 4° *Bonn* 28; 51
HATIM TAI [6 cent.] Diwân of, ed. R. Hassoun; ill. 3/6 4° Trübner
IBN-EL-ARABI Divân Ferazdak: text, ed. R. Boucher, 4 pts. [w. Fch. tr.] ea. 12/6; *red. to* 12/6 *the set* 4° *Paris* 70–75
IBN FARIDH Taijet ["Book of Love"]: text and German tr. Hammer-Purgstall 10/- 4° *Vienna* 54
,, ,, Diwân, and Commentary: text ed. Rochaid Ed-Dahdah 25/- r 8° *Paris* 55
JAMI, MULLA Salaman U Absal, ed. F. Falconer [allegor. romance] 7/6 4° Trübner 50
MO' ALLAKAT Septem Carmina Antiquissima, ed. F. A. Arnold 15/- 4° *Leipzig* 60
MUTANABBII Carmina, cum comm. Wâhidii, ed. F. Dieterici, 5 pts. 35/- 4° *Berlin* 58–61
NABIGA DHOBYANI Diwân: text, with French tr. H. Derenbourg 7/6 8° *Paris* 69
SCHEMEIL, Emin Ibrahim El Mubtaker, or First Born: text 5/- 4° *Beyrout* 70
URWA IBN ALWARD Diwân: text, German tr., and notes Th. Nöldeke 4/- 4° *Göttingen* 64

Proverbs —*v.* B § 27.

Science —*v. also* Geography, *supra.*

ABD-ER-REZZAG-ED-DJEZAIRY Kachef-er-Roumoûz: Fch. tr., w. notes [treat. on medical matters] 8/6 8° *Paris* 75
DAWUD AL HAKIM [16 cent.] Tezkiret Uli ul Albab, 4 vols. [a medical encyclo.] 70/- r 8° *Bulâq* A. H. 1288
IBN-AL-AWWAM Kitab-al-Felahah ["Book of Agriculture"], ed. Clement-Müller, vol. i. 8/6 8° *Paris* 64
MOHAMMED BEN MUSA Algebra: text, w. English tr., ed. F. Rosen 8° Oriental Trsl. Fd. 31

History of Medicine.

LECLERC, L. Histoire de la Médecine Arabe, 2 vols. 17/- 8° *Paris* 76

116. ETHIOPIC PHILOLOGY (GEEZ, AMHARIC, TIGRÉ, TIGRIÑA).

Ethiopic [Geez].

Dictionary.

DILLMANN, A. Lexicon Linguae Aethiop. cum indice latino, 3 vols. £4 4° *Leipzig* 62–65

Grammar, etc.

*DILLMANN, A. Grammatik der äthiopischen Sprache 14/- 8° *Leipzig* 57
KÖNIG, E. Neue Studien üb. Schrift, Aussprache u. Formenlehre d. Aethiopischen 12/- 8° ,, 77
PRAETORIUS, F. Grammatica Aethiopica: cum paradigmis, chrest. and gloss. 6/-; Germ. tr. 6/- s 8° *Berlin* 86; 86

Chrestomathy.

DILLMANN, A. [ed.] Christomathia Aethiopica, edita et glossario explan. 9/- 8° *Leipzig* 66

Manuscripts.

Bibliothèque Natl., Paris Catalogue des MSS. Éthiopiens [by H. Zotenberg] 12/6 4° *Paris* 77
British Museum Catalogue of the Ethiopic MSS. 10/- f° British Museum 47
,, ,, Catalogue of the Ethiopic MSS. acquired since 1847; 13 pl. [by Prf. Wm. Wright] 28/- 8° ,, 77

K § 117

Literature.

Adam's Kampf: oder das christl. Adambuch d. Morgenlandes, ed. E. Trumpp 15/- 4° *Munich* 80
Chronique de Jean, Evêque de Nikiou, ed. H. Zotenberg [w. French tr.; 7th cent.] 12/6 4° *Paris* 88
Corpus Juris Abessinorum Ethiopic and Arabic text, ed. Dr. J. Bachmann, pt. i. [Jus connubii] 16/- 4° *Berlin* 90 *in prog.*
Liber Jubilæorum ed. A. Dillmann 18/- 4° *Kiel* 59
Physiologus: Aethiop. Uebersetzung, ed. Fr. Hommel [w. German tr.] 16/- 8° *Leipzig* 77
Edited from London, Paris, and Vienna MSS., with an historical introduction.

Apocryphal Scriptures —*v.* A § 19, *s.vv.* Adam and Eve, Confl. of H. Apostles, Enoch, Hermas Pastor.

Amharic [modern Ethiopic].

Dictionaries.

d'ABBADIE, A. Dictionnaire de la Langue Amarinna 40/- 8° *Paris* 81
v. BEURMANN, M. Vocabulary of the Tigré Language: w. grammat. sketch Dr. A. Merx 3/6 8° *Halle* 68
ISENBERG, C. W. Dictionary of the Amharic Language, in 2 pts. £2 4° Trübner 41

Grammars.

ISENBERG, C. W. Grammar of the Amharic Language 21/- 8° Trübner 42
MASSAJA, G. Lectiones grammaticales . . . linguae Amharicae 20/- i 8° *Paris* 67
*PRAETORIUS, F. Die Amharische Sprache, 2 pts. ea. 15/- 4° *Halle* 78; 79

Tigré and Tigriña [modern Ethiopic].

Dictionary.

v. BEURMANN + MERX, M. A. Vocabulary of the Tigré Language 2/6 8° *Halle* 68
MUNZINGER, W. Vocabulaire de la Langue Tigré [= Append. to Dillmann's *Lex. Æth.*] 3/- 8° *Leipzig* 65

Grammars.

PRAETORIUS, F. Grammatik der Tigriña Sprache in Abessinien 13/6 4° *Halle* 72
SCHREIBER, J. Manuel de la Langue Tigraï [for missionaries] 6/- 8° *Vienna* 87

117. HEBREW AND SAMARITAN PHILOLOGY.

Generally.

DELITZSCH, Prf. Fried. The Hebrew Language viewed in the light of Assyrian research [tr.] 4/- 8° Williams 83

Dictionaries —*v. also* K § 108: Chaldee, *s.vv.* *DAVIES, FÜRST.

FÜRST, Dr. Julius Hebräisches Handwörterbuch, 2 vols., 13/6 8°; Hebr. Schulwörterbuch 3/- 16° *Leipzig*
*GESENIUS, W. Heb. & Eng. Lex. to O. T., tr. [fr. Lat. 1829-58] w. addns. E. Robinson [Am.] 36/- r 8° *Boston* [44] 80
There is also an edition by Dr. S. P. TREGELLES, which some prefer. 11th edn. of orig., ed. MÜHLAU + VOLCK + MÜLLER, 15/- r 8° *Lpzg.* '90.
LEVY, Dr. J. Neuhebraisches Wörterbuch über d. Talmud u. Midraschim, 4 vols. £7 7/- r 4° *Leipzig* 76-89

Grammars and Exercise-books.

BICKELL, Gustav Outlines of Hebrew Grammar, tr. w. notes S. I. Curtiss, jun. [syntax poor] 3/- 8° *Leipzig* 77
BOWMAN, T. A Hebrew Course [grammar, exercises, lexicon; elementary] 2 vols. 18/- 8° Clark, *Edin.* 79-82
DAVIDSON, Prf. A. B. Introductory Hebrew Grammar [w. good exercises; elementary] 7/6 8° " " [74] 84
*GESENIUS, W. Hebrew Grammar, ed. Rödiger + B. Davies, tr. E. C. Mitchell [Am.] $1.50 8° *Andover* [74] 82
*GREEN, Dr. W. H. [Am.] Grammar of the Hebrew Language, 2 pts. ea. $2 *New York* [61] 89-90
KALISCH, M. M. Hebrew Grammar: with exercises, pt. i. 12/6 [Key 5/-], ii. 12/6 8° Longman [62] 78; [63] 75
KENNEDY, Prf. J. Introduction to Biblical Hebrew [graduated instruction] 12/- 8° Williams 89
LAND, Prf. J. P. N. Principles of Heb. Grammar, tr. [fr. Dutch] R. Lane-Poole [syntax poor] 7/6 8° Trübner 76
LEATHES, Prf. Stanley Short Practical Hebrew Grammar: w. vocabulary [elementary] 7/6 c 8° Murray [68] 79
MASON, P. H. Hebrew Exercise Book; w. grammar of word-forms [conservative] 18/-; Key 4/6 8° Simpkin [73] 76; [76] 80
STRACK, Prf. H. L. Heb. Gram. [tr.; w. exx., liter. and vocab.], 4/6; Paradigms, 6*d.*; Addl. Exx. 1/6 8° Williams [86] 88; 87; 88

Samaritan.

NICHOLLS, G. F. Grammar of the Samaritan Language: with extracts and vocabulary 6/- 12° Bagster *n.d.*
PETERMANN, J. H. Brevis Linguæ Samaritanæ Grammatica 4/- 12° *Berlin* 73

Syntax.

DAVIDSON, Prf. A. B. Syntax of the Hebrew Language *in prep.*
EWALD, Heinr. Syntax of the Hebrew Language, tr. Jas. Kennedy 8/6 8° Clark, *Edin.* 79
Contains some 4,500 citations of illustrated passages from the Old Testament
MÜLLER, Prf. Aug. Outlines of Hebrew Syntax, tr. Prf. J. Robertson 6/- 8° MacLehose, *Glasg.* [83] 88

Tenses.

DRIVER, S. R. Treatise on the Use of Tenses in Hebrew 7/6 f 8° Clar. Press. [74] 81

Accentuation.

WICKES, Dr. Wm. Hebrew Accentuation of Poetical Books of Old Test. [Psalms, Prov., Job] 5/- 8° Clar. Press 81
" " Treatise on Accentuation of the 21 Prose Books of Old Testament 10/6 8° " 87

Roots.

IBN JANÂH Book of Hebrew Roots, ed. A. Neubauer 47/6 4° Clar. Press 75

Synonyms.

GIRDLESTONE, Rev. R.B. Synonyms of the O.T.: their bearing on Christian faith and practice 15/- 8° Longman 71
TEDESCHI, Moise Thesaurus Synonymorum linguæ hebraicæ 3/6 r 8° *Padua* 80

Serials.

Magazin für d. Wissenschaft d. Judenthums, hrsg. A. Berliner + D. Hoffmann [quarterly] *ann.* 12/- 8° *Berlin 73 sqq. in prog.*
Monatsschrift für Geschichte u. Wissenschaft d. Judenthums, ed. Z. Frankel, cont. H. Graetz [monthly] *ann.* 9/- 8° *Krotoschin 51 sqq. in prog.*

118. HEBREW AND SAMARITAN LITERATURE.

Bibliography.

BENJACOB, I. A. Ozar Ha-Sepharim ["Treasury of Hebrew Books"], 3 vols. [to 1863; in Hebrew] 20/- 8° *Wilna* 80
Supplement and Alphabetical List of Authors, by Dr. Steinschneider, announced to appear in 1886. ? Not pub. yet.
Bodleian Lib., Oxon. Catalogus Librorum Hebræorum [by M. Steinschneider] £5 4° *Berlin* 52–60
British Museum Catalogue of the Hebrew Books [by J. Zedner] 25/- 8° British Museum 67
FÜRST, Julius Bibliotheca Judaica, 3 vols. [in German] 42/- 8° *Leipzig* 49–64
LIPPE, Ch. D. Bibliographisches Lexikon d. gesammt. jüd. Litter.: 1880-87, 2 vols. 12/- 8° *Vienna* 81; 87

History of Literature.

DELITZSCH, F. Zur Geschichte d. jüdischen Poesie [post-Biblical and modern] *o.p.* [*w.* 4/-] 8° *Leipzig* 36
FÜRST, Julius Geschichte d. Biblischen Literatur u. Jüd.-Hellen. Schriftthums, 2 vols. 14/6 8° " 67; 70
KARPELES, G. Geschichte der jüdischen Literatur 18/6 8° *Berlin* 86
KOHN, S. Zur Sprache Literatur u. Dogmatik d. Samaritaner [Abh. f. K. d. ML.] 12/- 8° *Leipzig* 76
MEIER, E. Geschichte der poetischen National-Literatur der Hebräer 9/- 8° *Berlin* 56
NUTT, J. W. Sketch of Samaritan History, Dogma and Literature 5/- 8° Trübner 56
TAYLOR, Isaac The Spirit of Hebrew Poetry [Bk. of Psalms, etc.] 10/6 8° Bell 61

Manuscripts.

Facsimiles of Hebrew MSS. in the Bodleian Library, Oxon. 8° Clar. Press 86
HARKAVY + STRACK, A. H. L. [eds.] Catalog der Handschriften d. k. öff. Bibl., Petersburg, vols. i.–ii. 16/- r 8° *St. Petersburg* 75; 76
" A. [ed.] Neu-aufgefundene Hebräische Bibelhandschriften; 5 photo. tables 4/- 4° " 84
NEUBAUER, A. [ed.] Catalogue of Hebrew MSS. in Bodleian Lib., Oxon. 73/6 4° Camb. Press 86
Palaeographical Society —*v.* K § 99.
SCHILLER-SZINESSY, S.M. [ed.] Catalogue of Hebrew MSS. in Univ. Lib., Camb., vol. i. [Bible] 9/- 8° " 76
STEINSCHNEIDER, M. [ed.] Die Hebraischen Handschriften in München 9/- i 4° *Munich* 75
" " Catalog der Hebr. MSS. in Hambg., 6/-; Verzeichn. d. Hebr. MSS. in Berlin r 8° *Hambg.* 78; *Berlin* 78
ZOTENBERG, H. [ed.] Manuscripts Hébreux et Samaritains de la Bibl. Nat., Paris 12/6 4° *Paris* 66

Biblical Codices (edited)—*v.* A § 17.

Inscriptions.

Moabite Stone.

Facsimile: w. English tr. and commentary Dr. C. D. Ginsburg 10/6 8° Reeves & Turner 70

Accounts, etc.

COLENSO, Bp. J. C. Lectures on the Pentateuch and the Moabite Stone 12/- 8° Longman 73
KING, Rev. Jas. Moab's Patriarchal Stone: its story and teaching [quite popular] 3/6 c 8° Bickers 78
KAUTSCH + SOCIN, E. + A. Die Aechtheit d. Moabit. Altertümer; 2 pl. [advoc. authenticity] 4/- 8° *Strassburg* 76
WALSH, Bp. W. P. The Moabite Stone 1/6 c 8° *Dublin* [72] 73

in Algiers.

BLOCH, Isaac [ed.] Inscriptions Tumulaires d. anc. cimetières Israël d'Alger 4/6 8° *Paris* 88

Texts and Translations.

Kabbala —*v.* A § 12, *s.v.* Judaism.
Kalilag and Damnag Hebrew edn. of R. Joel, ed. J. Derenbourg [fr. MSS. in Roy. Lib., Paris] r 8° *Paris* 84
" " " " " " Lat. tr. by John of Capua [13 cent.], ed. J. Derenbourg " 8–
Under the titles "Directorium Humanae Vitae," and "Parabolae Antiquorum Sapientium." For Pers. version, *v.* K § 134, for Syriac, K § 1[illegible].
Midrash —*v.* A § 12.
Mishnah —*v.* A § 12.
Talmud —*v.* A § 12.
MAIMONIDES, Moses [1131–1204] Guide to the Perplexed, tr. Dr. M. Friedländer, 3 vols. 31/6 8° Trübner 85
A tr. of the *Moreh Nebuchim*, by one of the most celebrated of the Jewish rabbis, a pupil of AVERROES (the Arabian philosopher), and chief physician to the Sultan of Egypt. A Latin tr. was pub. in 3 vols., 12/- s 4° *Berlin* 75.
Münz, I. Die Religionsphilosophie des Maimonides und ihr Einfluss, pt. i. 1/6 8° *Berlin* 87

XVII. Aryan (Indo-Germanic) Philology.

119. ARYAN (a): COMPARATIVE TREATISES (a) GENERAL.

Generally

—*v. also* K § 94 (esp. WHITNEY).

BARTHOLOMAE, Dr. Chr. Studien zur indogermanischen Sprachgeschichte, pt. I. [Indogerm. *ss, etc.*] 5/- 8° *Halle* 89
" " Arische Forschungen, pt. i. 5/-; ii. 7/-; iii. 2/6 [*v.* K § 130] 8° " 82; 86; 87
DELBRÜCK, B. Introduction to the Study of Language [tr.] 5/- 8° Trübner 82
Gives a good account of the history and methods of compar. philol. of Aryan langs. of the "New School."
FICK, A. Die ehemalige Spracheinheit der Indogermanen Europas 8/6; *red. to* 5/- 8° *Göttingen* 73
PAPILLON, T. L. Compendium of Comparative Philology 6/- c 8° Clar. Press [76] 82
PEILE, J. Philology [Literature Primers; elementary] 1/- 18° Macmillan 77
PEZZI, Domenico Aryan Philol. acc. to most recent researches, tr. [fr. Ital.] by E. S. Roberts 6/- c 8° Trübner 79
*SCHLEICHER, A. Compendium of Indo-European, Sanskrit, etc., Languages [tr.], 2 vols. 13/6 8° " 74; 77
I.: Phonology, 7/6; II.: Morphology, 6/-. Somewhat antiquated, but indispensable. First edn. of original, 1861.
SCHMIDT, Johannes Die Verwandtschaftsverhältnisse der indogermanischen Sprachen 1/6 8° *Weimar* 72

Universal Philology —*v.* K § 96.

Magazines and Permanent Serials—*v. also* K § 95: Magazines.

BEZZENBERGER, Prf. A. [ed.] Beiträge zur Kunde der indogermanischen Sprachen, vols. i.-xv. ea. 10/- 8° *Göttingen* 77-88 *in prog.*
Vols. i.-x. may be had at the reduced price of £3 10/-.
OSTHOFF + BRUGMANN, H./K. [eds.] Morphologische Untersuchungen auf d. Gebiete d. indogerm. Sprachen vols. i.-iv. 27/-, v. 7/- 8° *Leipzig* 78-81
Represents the "New School." Is not to be continued. Vol. v. contains an index to the 5 vols.
Zeitschrift für vergleichende Sprachforschung, ed. A Kuhn + Joh. Schmidt, vols. i.-xxx. [bi-mthly.] *ann.* 16/- 8° *Gütersloh* 52-89 *in prog.*

Table.

ATTWELL, Prf. H. Table of the Aryan Languages, 7/6 4°; as a wall map 10/- Williams 74; 75

Aryan and Semitic: Connection between—*v.* K § 96.

Greek and Latin Comparatively—*v.* K §§ 168-173.

Aryan Peoples.

d'ARBOIS de JUBAINVILLE, H. Les Premiers Habitants de l'Europe, vol. I. 8/6 8° *Paris* [ ] 89
I.: Cave-dwellers, Iberians, Pelasgians, Etruscans, Phœnicians; II. [Aryans]: Scythians, Thracians, Illyrians, Ligurians.
v. BRADKE, P. Ueber Methode u. Ergebnisse der arischen Alterthumswissenschaft 7/6 8° *Giessen* 90
BRUNNHOFER, H. Iran und Turan: histor.-geograph. u. ethnograph. Untersuchungen 9/- 8° *Leipzig* 89
DIEFENBACH, L. Origines Europaeae: die alten Völker Europas, nebst ihren Sippen u. Nachbarn 10/- 8° *Frankfort* 61
KUHN, A. Zur ältesten Geschichte des indogermanischen Volkes 8° *Berlin* 45
LASSEN, Chr. —*in his* Indische Alterthumskunde—*v.* B § 14.
MORRIS, Charles [Am.] The Aryan Race: its origin and achievements $1.50 12° *Chicago* 88
MÜLLER, Prf. F. Max —*in his* Biographies of Words, etc. [*ut* K § 120].
PENKA, Karl Origines Ariacae [anthropological; "Aryans come fr. N. Europe"] 7/- 8° *Teschen* 83
" " Die Herkunft der Arier 5/6 8° " 86
PICTET, A. Les Origines Indo-Européennes: ou les Aryas primitifs., 3 v. [standard] 30/- 8° *Paris* [59-63] 78
RENDALL, Prc. G. H. The Cradle of the Aryans [first home in Scandinavia] 3/- 8° Macmillan 89
SCHRADER, Dr. O. Prehistoric Antiquities of the Aryan Peoples [tr.] [lang. and culture] 21/- m 8° Griffin 90
v. SPIEGEL, F. Die arische Periode und ihre Zustände 12/- 8° *Leipzig* 87
TAYLOR, Can. Isaac Origin of the Aryans; ill. [Contemporary Science Ser.] 3/6 c 8° Walter Scott 90

120. ARYAN (b): COMPARATIVE TREATISES (β) GRAMMAR.

Generally.

Bibliothek indogerman. Grammatiken, ed. F. Bücheler + B. Delbrück—*ea. ent. separ. infra.*
BOPP, Fr. Vergleichende Grammatik, 3 vols. 36/- 8° *Berlin* [33-52] 69-71
Sanscrit, Zend, Greek, Latin, Lithuanian, Gothic, German, and Slavonic. The original standard work on Comparative Forms. Later researches have corrected some erroneous details.
Arendt, Sach- und Wortregister zu Bopp's *Vergl. Grammatik* *Berlin* 63
" " Grammaire Comparée d. Langues Indo-eur., trad. Michel Bréal, 5 vols. [a good tr.] 32/6 8° *Paris* [66-74] 88-90
" " Comparative Grammar, tr. E. B. Eastwick, 3 vols. [a poor tr.] 31/6 8° Williams [45] 85

*BRUGMANN, Prf. Karl — Elements of Compar. Grammar of Indo-Germ. Langs. [tr.], v. i. [Intro. and Phonology] 18/- 8° Trübner 88
Sanst., Old Iran. (Avestic and O.-Pers.), O.-Armen., O.-Gk., Lat., Umbrian-Samnitic, O.-Irish, Gothic, O.-H. Germ., Lith. & O.-Bulgarian.

" " — Grundriss d. vergleich. Gramm. d. indogerm. Sprachen, vol. i., 14/-; vol. ii., pt. i 12/- 8° *Strassburg* 86; 88

" " — *—in his* Griechische Grammatik [*see* K § 175].

The Five School Languages.

HORNEMANN, F. — Gedanken u. Vorschläge zu e. Parallelgramm. d. 5 Schulsprachen 1/6 8° *Hanover* 88

SONNENSCHEIN, Prf. E. A. [ed.] — Parallel Grammar Series [the 5 school langs.] ea. 3/- 16° Sonnenschein [87–90] 90
English, French, German, Latin, Greek; by various contributors. Each treated on a uniform and parallel. Other Aryan languages to follow.

Chrestomathy.

SCHLEICHER, A. [ed.] — Indogermanische Chrestomathie 8/- 8° *Weimar* 69

SCHRUMPF, G. A. [ed.] — A First Aryan Reader 7/6 c 8° Nutt 90
Specs. of Indic, Eranic, Armen., Hellen., Alban., Italic, Teuton., Keltic, Baltic, Slavon., w. translit., trn., and comm.

Phonetics

—v. also K § 98: Phonetics: Generally.

ASCOLI, Prf. G. J. — Corsi di Glottologia [Sanscrit, Gk., Latin; lectures] 7/- 8° *Turin* 70

" " — The same: German tr., *sub tit.* Vorlesungen üb. d. Vergleich. Lautlehre 4/6 8° *Halle* 71

" " — Studj Critici 8° *Milan* 61

" " — The same: German tr., *sub tit.* Kritische Studien zur Sprachwissenschaft 10/6 8° *Weimar* 78

" " — Lettera Glottologica 8° *Turin* 81

CORSSEN, W. — *—in his* Aussprache der lateinischen Sprache—*v.* K § 202.

FOY, K. — *—in his* Lautsystem der griechischen Vulgärsprache 3/- 8° *Leipzig* 79

HÜBSCHMANN, H. — Das indogermanische Vocalsystem 4/6 8° *Strassburg* 85

MAHLOW, Geo. — Die langen A E O in den Europäischen Sprachen 4/- 8° *Berlin* [79] 88

RUTHERFORD, Dr. W. G. — Rex Lex: digest of princ. rel. 'tween Lat., Gk. and Ang.-Sax. Sounds 8° Macmillan *in prep.*

de SAUSSURE, F. — Système primitif des Voyelles dans les Langues Indoeurop. 10/- 8° *Leipzig* [79] 88

SCHMIDT, Johannes — Zur Geschichte des indogermanischen Vocalismus, 2 vols. 17/- 8° *Weimar* 71; 75

SCHUCHARDT, Prf. H. — Ueber die Lautgesetze [antagonistic to "new school"] 1/- 8° *Berlin* 85

*SIEVERS, Ed. — Grundzüge der Phonetik [Bibl. Indogerman. Grammatiken] 5/- 8° *Leipzig* [76] 86
A recast of his *Grundzüge der Lautphysiologie*, pub. in 1876, and forming vol. i. of the *Indogermanische Grammatiken* series.

*SWEET, Henry — Primer of Phonetics [new edn. of Hdbk. of Phon. (77)] 3/6 c 8° Clar. Press [77] 90
A very good compendium, w. a phonetic account of most modern European languages, but spec. English, Fch., Germ., Lat., Gk.

TRAUTMANN, Prf. M. — Die Sprachlaute im allgemeinen u. d. Eng., Französ. u. Deutsch. 6/- 8° *Leipzig* 84

VIETOR, Prf. W. — Elemente d. Phonetik u. Orthoepie d. Deutsch., Engl. u. Französ. 5/- 8° *Heilbronn* [84] 87

Grimm's Law. "Lautverschiebung."

DOUSE, T. Le Marchant — Grimm's Law: a study of the so-called Lautverschiebung 10/6 p 8° Trübner 76

KRÄUTER, J. F. — Zur Lautverschiebung 4/- 8° *Strassburg* 77

Verner's Law.

CONWAY, R. Seymour — Verner's Law in Italy 5/- 8° Trübner 88
An essay in the hist. of Indo-eur. sibilants. With a Dialect-Map of Italy by E. NEAWOOD.

Etymology.

Generally.

CURTIUS, Prf. Georg — *—in his* Princip. of Gk. Etymology, to Prf. A. S. Wilkins + E. B. England, 2 v. 28/- 8° Murray [75–76] 86

HEHN, Victor — Wanderings of Plants and Animals 7/6 8° Sonnenschein [85] 88
An account, chiefly etymological, of the migrations of plants and animals fr. the East to Europe. Full of research and erudite illustrations.

OSTHOFF, Hermann — Forschungen im Gebiete d. indogerm. nominalen Stammbildung, 2 pts. ea 6/- 8° *Jena* 75; 76

Dictionaries.

DIEFENBACH, L. — Lexicon Comparativum Linguarum Indogerman., 2 v. [rather antiquated] 27/- 8° *Frankfort* 46–51

*FICK, Aug. — Vergleichendes Wörterbuch der indogermanischen Sprachen, 4 vols. 45/- 8° *Göttingen* [68] 74–76
A dict. of roots and words supposed to have existed in the Indoeurop. tongue, w. corresp. words and derivatives in the various langs. The best Dictionary, but not wholly trustworthy.

POTT, A. F. — Wurzelwörterbuch der indogermanischen Sprachen, 6 vols. 150/- 8° *Detmold* [33] 67–76
A second edition of his *Etymologische Forschungen aus dem Gebiete der indogerman. Sprachen.*

ZEHETMAYR, S. — Analogisch-vergleich. Wörterbuch üb. d. Gesammtgebiet d. indogerm. Sprachen 8° *Leipzig* [73] 79
The first edn. was pub. *sub tit. Lexicon Etymolog. Latino-Sanscrit. Comparativum, Vienna* '73.

Names

—v. also K § 179: Greek Philology, *s.v.* Names, K § 228: German; K § 279: Celtic.

DELBRÜCK, B. — Die indogermanischen Verwandtschaftsnamen 8/- 8° *Leipzig* 90

KLEINPAUL, R. — Menschen u. Völkernamen: etymologische Streifzüge a. d. Gebiete d. Eigennamen 8/- 8° *Leipzig* 85

POTT, A. F. — Die Personennamen, insbesondere die Familiennamen 15/- 8° " [53] 59

Place-Names.

BLACKIE, [Miss] C. — Dictionary of Place-Names [1st edn. *sub tit. Etym. Geography*] 7/- c 8° Murray [75] 88

EDMUNDS, F. — Traces of History in the Names of Places 7/6 c 8° Longman [69] 72

*EGLI, Dr. J. — Nomina Geographica: Versuch einer allgem. geograph. Onomatologie 24/- r 8° *Leipzig* 75

" " — Etymologisch-geographisches Lexicon [part of above] 12/- r 8° " [75] 80

" " — Geschichte der geographischen Namenkunde 10/- 8° " 86

TAYLOR, Isaac — Words and Places; maps 6/- c 8° Macmillan [64] 73

K §120

Roots.

BYRNE, James — Origin of the Greek, Latin and Gothic Roots — 18/- 8° Trübner 87

Vowels.

de SAUSSURE, F. — Mémoire sur le systéme primitif d. Voyelles — 10/- 8° *Paris* [79] 88
Showing what form the Indo-european vowels take in the several languages of the family.

Words: Life, etc., of —*v. also* Whitney [*ut* K § 96].

DARMESTETER, A. — The Life of Words as Symbols of Ideas [tr.] [Intern. Scient. Ser.] — 4/6 c 8° Paul 86
Acct. of influences wh. produce chgs. of meaning, occasion rise of new and disuse of old words; illns. all drawn fr. French.

GARLAND, Dr. F. — The Fortunes of Words, 5/-; The Philosophy of Words [both popular] — 5/- c 8° Trübner 88; 88

MÜLLER, Prf. F. Max — Biographies of Words [repr. fr. *Good Words*] — 7/6 c 8° Longman 88
Contains also a full discussion of the question of the original home of the Aryans.

PALMER, Rev. W. Smythe — Leaves from a Word-hunter's Note book — 7/6 8° Trübner 76

TRENCH, Abp. R. C. — On the Study of Words, ed. Rev. A. L. Mayhew [Lects. i.–iii. ed. same 1/6 '90] — 5/- f 8° Paul [51] 88

Accidence.

Parts of Speech.

SCHÖMANN, G. F. — Die Lehre von den Redetheilen nach d. Alten dargestellt — 4/6 8° *Berlin* 62

Flexion.

BARTOLOMAE, Ch. — Beiträge zur Flexionslehre d. indogerman. Sprachen [reprint] — 5/- 8° *Gütersloh* 88

COLLITZ, H. — Flexion der Nomina im Altindischen und Griechischen — 2/- 8° *Leipzig* 85

Verb.

CURTIUS, Prf. Georg — —*in his* Das Verbum der griechischen Sprache, 2 vols. — 18/- 8° *Leipzig* [73]77; [76]80

OSTHOFF, Hermann — Das Verbum in d. Nominalcomposition [Germ., Gk., Slav., Romance] — 11/6 8° *Jena* 78

MÜLLER, H. D. — Entwickelungsgeschichte d. indogermanischen Verbalbaus — 4/- 8° *Göttingen* 90

WESTPHAL, R. — Vergleichende Grammatik d. indogerman. Sprachen, pt. i. [verb] — 20/- 8° *Jena* 73

Moods.

BENFEY, Theodor — Ueber die Entstehung des indogermanischen Optativs — 2/6 4° *Göttingen* 71

BERGAIGNE, A. — De Conjunctivi et Optativi in indoeurop. linguis — 8° *Paris* 77

JOLLY, Julius — Geschichte des Infinitivs im Indogermanischen — 6/- 8° *Munich* 73

WILHELM, E. — De Infinitivi ling. Sanscr., Bact., Pers., Graec., Osc., Umb., Lat., Goth. forma et usu — 4/- 8° *Eisenach* 73

" " — De Infinitivi vi et natura — 1/- 4° " 69

Tenses.

HOFFMANN, Otto — Das Praesens d. indogerm. Grundsprache — 4/- 8° *Göttingen* 89

*OSTHOFF, Hermann — Zur Geschichte des Perfects im Indogermanischen [spec. Gk. & Lat.] — 14/- 8° *Strassburg* 84

Verbal Nouns.

FRITSCHE, C. — De Substantia in Verbo constituta [on the participle and infinitives] — 2/- 4° *Görlitz* 65

Noun.

Case.

HOLZWEISSIG, F. — Wahrheit und Irrthum der localischen Casustheorie — 2/- 8° *Leipzig* 77

HÜBSCHMANN, H. — Zur Casuslehre — 7/- 8° *Munich* 75

STOLLE, H. A. — Ueber die Bedeutung des Accusativs — 2/6 4° *Kempten* 47

Number and Gender.

MEIER, Ernst — Bildung u. Bedeutung d. Plural in d. semit. u. indog. Sprachen — 2/6 8° *Mannheim* 46

MEYER, Wilhelm — Die Schicksale des lateinischen Neutrums im Romanischen — 4/- 8° *Halle* 83

SCHMIDT, J. — Die Pluralbildungen der indogermanischen Neutra — 12/- 8° *Weimar* 89

Degrees of Comparison.

WEIHRICH, F. — De Gradibus comparationum Sanscritæ, Græcæ, Latinæ, Gothicæ — 2/- 8° *Giessen* 69

WÖLFFLIN, E. — Lateinische und Romanische Comparation — 2/- 8° *Erlangen* 79

Pronoun.

STEINTHAL, H. — De Pronomine Relativo commentatio philologica — 2/- 8° *Berlin* 47

*WINDISCH, E. — Untersuch. üb. d. Urspr. d. Relativpronomens—*in* Curtius' *Studien* [*ut* K § 173].

Numerals.

BENLOEW, L. — Recherches sur l'Origine des Noms de Nombre Japhétiques et Sémitiques — 2/- 8° *Giessen* 61

POTT, A. F. — Die Quinäre u. Vigesimale Zählungsmethode [universal] — 5/- 8° *Brunswick* 47

" " — Sprachverschiedenheit in Europa an d. Zahlwörtern, sowie d. quin. u. viges. Zahlmethode — 2/- 8° *Halle* 68

RUMPELT, H. B. — Die deutschen Zahlwörter sprachvergleichend dargestellt [programme] — 2/- 4° *Breslau* 64

SCHMIDT, J. — Die Urheimath d. Indogermanen u. d. europ. Zahlsystem — 2/6 8° *Berlin* 90

SCHRADER, E. — Ursprung u. Bedeutung d. Zahlwörter in d. indoeur. Sprache — 2/6 4° *Stendal* 54

ZEHETMAYR, S. — Verbalbedeutung der Zahlwörter — 2/- 4° *Leipzig* 54

Particles.

MEYER, Leo — "An" im Griechischen, Lateinischen und Gothischen — 2/- 8° *Berlin* 80

Syntax.

Generally.

AUTENRIETH, G. Terminus in quem, syntaxis comparativæ particula 2/- 4° *Erlangen* 68
DELBRÜCK, B. Ablativ Localis Instrumentalis [in Sanscrit, Gk., German] 1/6 8° *Berlin* 67
* ,, + WINDISCH, E. Syntaktische Forschungen, pts. i.-v. 29/- 8° *Halle* 71; 77; 78; 79; 88
Conjunct. u. Optat. im Sansk. u. Griech., 4/6; ii.: Altind. Tempuslehre, 3/; iii.: Altind. Wortfolge, 3/-; iv.: Grundlagen d. griech. Syntax, 4/-; Altindische Synt., 15/-
JOLLY, Julius Ein Kapitel vergleich. Syntax [Conj. & Opt. in Zend., O.-Pers., Sansc., Gk.] 2/6 8° *Munich* 72
ZIEMER, H. Jung-grammatische Streifzüge im Gebiete d. Syntax 3/- 8° *Kolberg* [82] 83
,, ,, Vergleichende Syntax der indogermanischen Comparation 5/- 8° *Berlin* 84

Order of Words.

WEIL, Henri Order of Words in Anc. Langs. comp. w. Modern [chfly. Fch.], tr. Prf. C. W. Super [Am.] $1.25 8° *Boston* 88

Prosody.

GERBER, G. —*in his* Die Sprache als Kunst, 2 vols. 20/- 8° *Berlin* [71; 73] 84; 86

Metrics.

SCHMIDT, Dr. J. H. H. —*in his* Introduction to Rhythmic & Metric of Classical Languages [tr.] 10/6 8° Macmillan 78
WESTPHAL, R. —*his* Intro. *to* A. Rossbach + R. Westphal's *Theorie d. musischen Künste d. Hellenen*, 2 vols. 14/- 8° *Leipzig* [54–65] 84

121. INDIC PHILOLOGY AND LITERATURE (*a*): SANSKRIT PHILOLOGY.

Bibliography.

TRÜBNER & Co. [bkslrs.] Catalogue of Sanscrit Literature [a useful list in one alphabet] 2/6 8° Trübner 75
WEBER, Dr. Albrecht Krit.-bibl. Streifend. ind. Philol. seit 1849, 9/-; . . . seit 1869, 20/- [= *Ind. Streifen*, ii.-iii] 8° *Ber.* 69; *Lpz.* 79

Phonology and Orthography.

SACHAU, Dr. Ed. Indo-Arabische Studien zur Aussprache des Indischen 4/6 4° *Berlin* 88
WHITNEY, Prf. W. D. [Am.] —*in his* Oriental and Linguistic Studies, series ii. 12/- 8° Trübner 75

Palæography: *Inscriptions—v. also* G § 10: Antiquities of India (CUNNINGHAM, *etc.*)

Corpus Inscriptionum Indicarum, ed. A. Cunningham, vols. i. and iii. [Govt. of India] 4° Trübner 79–89
i.: Inscriptions of Asoka, 42/- '79; ii.: *not out yet;* iii.: Inscripp. of Early Gupta Kgs. and Successors, 50/- '89.
SENART, E. Notes d'Épigraphie Indienne [*repr. fr.* Journal Asiatique] 2/6 8° *Paris* 88

Serial.

Epigraphia Indica ed. Dr. James Burgess [record of Archæol. Surv.; govt. pub.] *ann.* 18/- r 4° *Simla & Calc.* 88 *sqq. in prog.*

South Indian Inscriptions—v. K § 149: Dravidian, *s.v.* Inscriptions (BURNELL, HULTSCH) *and* Coorg (RICE).

Grammars, etc.

BALLANTYNE, J. R. First Lessons in Sanscrit Grammar 3/6 p 8° Trübner [62] 82
BENFEY, Prf. Theodor Practical Grammar of the Sanscrit Language [tr.] 10/6 r 8° ,, [63] 69
BERGAIGNE, A. Manuel p. étudier la Langue Sanscrite [*v. also* K § 124 I., *s.v.* Aids to Rigveda] 8° *Paris* 84
BOPP, Fr. —*v.* K § 119: Aryan: Generally.
BÜHLER, Prf. G. Sanscrit Primer, ed. E. D. Perry [Am.] $1.50 c 8° *New York* 86
EDGREN, A. Sanscrit Grammar, ed. Dr. R. Rost [Simplified Grammars] 10/6 c 8° Trübner 85
*GEIGER, Dr. Wilhelm Elementarbuch der Sanskrit Sprache [excellent easy introduction] 6/- 8° *Munich* 88
KELLNER, H. C. Sâvitrî: prakt. Elementarbuch zur Sanskrit-sprache 5/- 8° *Leipzig* 88
MÜLLER, Prf. F. Max Sanscrit Grammar for Beginners, ed. A. A. MacDonnell 6/- c 8° Longman [6-] 86
STENZLER, A. F. Elementarbuch der Sanskrit Sprache [gram. and vocab.] 4/- 8° *Breslau* [69] 85
*WHITNEY, Prf. W. D. [Am.] Sanscrit Grammar [undoubtedly the best gram.] 12/- 8° *Leipzig* (Trübner) [79] 89
WILLIAMS, [Sir] Monier Practical Grammar of Sanscrit Lang., w. refer. to Eur. Lang. 15/- 8° Clar. Press [46] 77
,, ,, Sanscrit Manual: w. vocabulary by A. E. Gough, 7/6; Key, by Gough 4/- 18° W. H. Allen 89; 89

Etymology.

Lexicography.

ZACHARIAE, T. Beiträge zur indischen Lexicographie 3/- 8° *Berlin* 83

Roots.

WESTERGAARD, N. L. Radices Linguæ Sanskritæ [in double columns] 25/6; *red. to* 12/- r 8° *Bonn* 41
WHITNEY, Prf. W. D. [Am.] The Roots, Verb-forms and Primary Derivations of Sanscrit 7/6 8° Trübner 85

Dictionaries, etc.

BENFEY, Prf. Theodor Sanskrit-English Dictionary [tr.] 52/6 8° Longman 66
With references, etymologies, and comparisons of cognate words in Greek, Latin, Gothic, and A.-S.
*BÖHTLINGK + ROTH, O. + R. Sanskrit-Wörterbuch, 7 vols. £9 s f° *Petersburg* (*Acad.*) 55–75
* ,, O. Sanskrit Wörterbuch in kürzerer Fassung [w. additions], 7 vols. 62/6 8° ,, 79–89
BOPP, Fr. Glossarium Compar. Linguæ Sanscritæ, 2 pts. [in Lat.; largely etymolog.] 20/- 4° *Berlin* [30] 66

K § 122

BOROOAH, A. Practical English-Sanskrit Dictionary, vols. i.–iv. ea. 31/6 8° *Calcutta* 77–83
*CAPPELLER, Prf. Carl Sanskrit Wörterbuch [an excellent concise dictionary] 15/- r 8° *Strassburg* 87
Based on BÖHTLINGK'S two dictionaries. Conts. complete list of roots and primitive words. Eng. tr. in prep. by Trübner.
RÂMAKAMALA VIDYÂLANKÂRA Prakritibâda, ed. Ramesha Chandra Bandyopadhyânga; ill. [Sansc. & Bengali dict.] 8° *Calcutta* [ ] 89
WILLIAMS, [Sir] Monier English and Sanskrit Dictionary [Hon. East India Company's pubn.] 63/- 4° Trübner 51
" " Sansk.-Eng. Dict.: etym. & philolog. arrgd. w. ref. to Gk., Lat., Gr., A.-S., Eng., &c. 94/6 4° Clar. Press [72] 88
WILSON, Prf. H. H. Sanskrit-English Dictionary 31/6 4° Williams [19] 80

Accidence.

Noun.

LANMAN, Prf. C. R. [Am.] Statistical Account of Noun Inflection in the Veda $2 8° *Boston* 78
LINDNER, B. Altindische Nominalbildung 5/6 8° *Jena* 78

Gender.

FRANCKE, Dr. R. O. Die indischen Geschlechtslehren [w. excursus on double-gender] 9/- 8° *Kiel* 89

Verb.

DELBRÜCK, B. Das altindische Verbum [ill. fr. Hymns of *Rig Veda*] 6/- 8° *Halle* 74
" " Altindische Tempuslehre [= Syntakt. Forschungen, pt. ii., *v.* K § 120] 3/- 8° " 77
" " Das Conjunctiv und Optativ im Sanskrit und Griechischen [= Synt. Forsch., pt. i.] 4/6 8° *Halle* 71

Syntax.

DELBRÜCK, B. Ablativ Localis Instrumentalis [*v.* K § 120] 1/6 8° *Berlin* 67
On the origin of the various Ablative constructions.
* " " Altindische Syntax [= Syntakt. Forschungen, pt. v., *v.* K § 120] 15/- 8° *Halle* 88
SPEIJER, Dr. T. S. Sanskrit Syntax: w. intro. Dr. H. Kern [in English] 15/- r 8° *Leyden* 86

Sequence of Words.

DELBRÜCK, B. Altindische Wortfolge [ill. fr. *Catapathabrahmana* = Syntakt. Forsch. pt. iii.] 3/- 8° *Halle* 78

Metrology.

KÜHNAU, Dr. R. Die Trishtubh-Jagatî-Familie: Versuch e. rhyth. u. hist. Behandg. d. ind. Metrik 10/- 8° *Göttingen* 87
WEBER, Dr. Albrecht Ueber die Metrik der Inder [= Indische Studien, vol. viii.] 12/- 8° *Berlin* 63

Chrestomathies.

BENFEY, Prf. Theodor [ed.] Chrestomathie aus Sanskritwerken, pt. i. [text, notes]; ii. [gloss.] 27/- 8° *Leipzig* 53–54
BÖHTLINGK, O. [ed.] Sanskrit Chrestomathie 5/- 8° *St. Petersburg* [45] 77
A very representative selection. Nala [from the Mahabharata], Ramayana, Manu, Hitopadesa, Amaru-Sataka, Bhartrihari, etc.
BOURNOUF + LEUPOL, E. + L. [eds.] Selectæ e Sans. Scriptoribus paginæ [w. French trs.] 6/- 8° *Paris* 67
DELBRÜCK, B. [ed.] Vedische Chrestomathie: w. Germ. notes and glossary 3/- 8° *Halle* 74
HILLEBRANDT, A. [ed.] Vedachrestomathie 5/- 8° *Berlin* 85
Kavya-Sangraha: ed. Jibananda Vidyasagara [a Sansc. anthology of minor poems] 18/- 8° *Calcutta* 72
LANMAN, Prf. C. R. [Am.; ed.] Sanskrit Reader: w. vocab. and notes $2 c 8° *Boston* [85] 88
LASSEN, Chr. [ed.] Anthologia Sanscrita, glossario instructa, etc., ed. J. Gildemeister 5/6 8° *Bonn* [38] 68
SCHLEICHER, A. [ed.] Indogerman. Chrestomathie [to accompany his *Indogerm. Gram.*] 8/- 8° *Weimar* 69

122. INDIC (*b*): SANSCRIT LITERATURE (*a*): BIBLIOGRAPHY AND HISTORY. MSS.

Bibliography.

British Museum Catalogue of the Sanscrit and Pali Books [by Dr. Ernst Haas] 21/- 4° British Museum 76
EGGELING, Prf. J. —*in his article* Sanskrit *in* Encyclo. Brit., vol. xxi. 30/- 4° Black 86
GILDEMEISTER, J. Critical Catalogue of Sanskrit Books, printed in India and Europe 4/- 12° *Bonn* 47

Manuscripts.

Berlin Royal Lib. Verzeichniss d. Sanskrit- u. Prakrithandschriften, 2 v. [by Dr. A. Weber] 52/- r 4° *Berlin* 53–88
Cambridge: Trin. Coll. Catalogue of the Sanscrit MSS. [by Dr. S. T. Aufrecht] 7/6 8° Camb. Press 64
" Univ. Lib. Catalogue of the Buddhistic Sanscrit MSS. [by C. Bendall] 12/- 8° " 83
Ceylon Govt. Lib. Catalogue of the Sanscrit MSS. [by L. de Zoysa] 8° *Colombo* 76
India Papers on Collections of Ancient MSS. in India [by A. E. Gough] 8° *Calcutta* 78
" Fort William Coll. [late] Catalogue Raisonnée of Oriental MSS., 3 vols. [by Rev. W. Taylor] *o.p.* [*w.* 15/-] r 8° *Madras* 57–63
" Bombay Pres. Report on Search for Sanscrit MSS. in. By R. G. Bhandarkar 7/6 r 8° *Bombay* 87
" " Third Report on same. By Prof. P. Peterson [= extra No. of *Jl. Bomb. Brch. R. As. Soc.*] 8/- 8° " 87
" Office Lib. Catalogue of the Sanscrit MSS., pt. i. [Vedic MSS.] [by Dr. J. Eggeling] 10/6 4° Trübner 88
" Private Libraries of: List of Sanscrit MSS. in, vol. i., 21/-; ii., 15/- [by Dr. Gustav Oppert] r 8° *Madras* 80; 85
Maharaja of Bikaner's Lib. Catalogue of the Sanscrit MSS. [by Rajendralala Mitra] 14/- 8° *Calcutta* 80
Tanjore Palace Lib. Classified Index to the Sanscrit MSS., 3 vols. [by Dr. A. C. Burnell] ea. 10/- 4° " 79–80
Leyden Academy Catalogus Codd. Orient., vols. i.–vi. [by R. Dozy + P. de Long + M. J. de Goeje + M. T. Houtsma] 48/- 8° *Leyden* 51–77
London: British Museum —*v.* K § 4.
MITRA, Rajendralala [ed.] Notices of Sanscrit MSS., vols. i.–viii. ea. 6/- 8° " 70–86 *in prog.*
Oxford: Bodleian Lib. Catalogue of the Sanscrit MSS., pt. i., 10/-; pt. ii. 21/- 4° Clar. Press 59; 64
Vienna Imper. Lib. Katalog der orientalischen Handschriften, 3 vols. [by Dr. G. Flügel] ea. 15/- 4° *Vienna* 65–67

History of Literature.

MANNING, Mrs. Ancient and Mediæval India, 2 vols. [popular] 30/- 8° W. H. Allen 69
Contains a useful analysis of most of the chief Sanscrit works.

MÜLLER, Prf. F. Max History of Ancient Sanskrit Literature *o.p.* [*pb.* 21/-; *w.* 50/-] 8° Williams [59] 60
A history of the literature in as far as it illustrates the primitive religion of the Brahmans.

NÈVE, F. Les Époques Littéraires de l'Inde [on Sanscrit poetry] 7/6 8° *Brussels* 83
NYAYALAMKARA, N. M. Introduction to Sanskrit Literature, 2 vols. 12° *Calcutta* 80
POOR, Mrs. L. E. [Am.] Sanskrit and its Kindred Literatures [popular] 6/- c 8° Paul 80
v. SCHRÖDER, L. Indiens Literatur und Kunst in historischer Entwickelung 18/- 8° *Leipzig* 87
SMALL, Rev. G. Handbook of Sanskrit Literature 6/- c 8° Williams 66
SOUPÉ, Prf. Philibert Études sur la Littérateur Sanscrite [Littératures de l'Orient] 6/6 8° *Paris* 77
Vedas, Mahâbhârata, Râmâyana, Kalidasa, Drama, Poetry, Didactic Works.

WARD, W. View of Hist., Liter. and Relig. of Hindus; col. pl. [repr. of 3rd ed. (1811)] 40/- 8° *Madras* [11] 63
*WEBER, Dr. Albrecht History of Indian Literature [tr.] [the best introd. bk.] 10/6 8° Trübner [78] 82
" " Indische Streifen, vol. i., 8/-; vol. ii., 9/-; vol. iii. [repr. of mag. articles] 20/- 8° *Berlin* 68; 69; *Lps.* 79
WILLIAMS, [Sir] Monier Indian Epic Poetry: substance of lectures deliv. at Oxford 5/- 8° Williams 6
" —*his* Indian Wisdom [*ut* K § 123] *gives an excellent view of Sans. literature.*
WILSON, Prf. H. H. —*v.* K § 123.

Biography: Collectively.

BEALE, Thomas Oriental Biographical Dictionary, ed. H. G. Keene 42/- r 8° W.H.Allen [*Calc.*81] *in prep.*
Short articles on lives and writings of most eminent Kings and soldiers, poets and philosophers.

Treatises, etc., on Vedic Religion, etc.—*v.* A § 14: Religions of India.

123. INDIC (*γ*): SANSCRIT LITER. (*β*) COLLECTIONS OF TEXTS AND TRANSL. SELECTIONS.

Original Texts —*v. also* K § 95, *s.v.* Magazines and Serials.

BÖHTLINGK, O. [ed.] Indische Sprüche, 3 vols. [w. German trss.] 24/- 8° *St. Petersburg* [§§] 7§
MUIR, Dr. John [ed.] Original Sanskrit Texts, 5 vols. [w. trs. and notes] ea. 21/- p 8° Trübner [68] 89; 60; 68; 63; 70
i.: Mythical and Legendary Accounts of Origin of Caste, 21/-; ii.: Trans-Himalay. Origin of Hindus, 21/-; iii.: The Vedas: Opinions of their Auth. and later Ind. Writers, 16/-; iv.: Vedic and later Repres. of Indian Deities, 21/-; v.: Cosmogony, Mythology, Life and Manners of Vedic Age, 21/-.

*WEBER, Dr. Albrecht [ed.] Indische Studien, vols. i.-xvii. ea. 12/- or 15/- 8° Berlin *later* Leipzig 49–84; *in prog.*
A most important series of treatises and papers, incl. edns. and trs. of texts, by the EDITOR, R. ROTH, A. F. STENZLER, W. D. WHITNEY [Am.], R. RUST, N. L. WESTERGAARD, SPIEGEL, Th. AUFRECHT, etc. Vols. i.-iii. are *o.p.* and rare; vols. i.-viii. were pub. at *Berlin* 1849-63 at 12/- ea., vols. ix.-xii. at *Leipzig* at 15/- ea., vols. xiii. *sqq.* sold at 15/- ea. Vols. vi.-vii. cont. AUFRECHT'S edn. of the Rig Veda, vols. xi.-xii. WEBER'S edn. of the Black Yajurveda.

Translated Selections —*for* Sacred Bks. of the East, ed. Max Müller, *v.* A § 9.

ARNOLD, Sir Edwin [tr.] Indian Poetry [Oriental Series] 7/6 p 8° Trübner [81] 90
Contains *Indian Song of Songs* [*Gita Govinda*], 2 books of *Mahabharata*, and other Oriental poems.

" " " Poetical Works: tr. from Sanskrit, 6 vols. *not sold separately.* 36/- c 8° " [*v.y.*] 86
i.: The Light of Asia [anon.]; ii.: Indian Poetry [*Gita Govinda*]; iii.: Pearls of the Faith [anon.]; iv.: Indian Idylls [fr. *Mahabh.*]; v.: The Secret of Death [*Katha Upanishad*]; vi.: The Song Celestial [*Bhagavad Gita*]. For separ. edns., *v.* K § 124.

FAUCHE, Hippolyte [tr.] Une Tétrade: ou drame, hymne, roman et poème, 3 vols. 30/- 8° *Paris* 61–63
French trs. of SÛDRAKA'S Mrichchhakatika, the *Mahimna stava*, DANDIN'S *Dasakumara-charita*, MAGHA'S *Sisupala-badha*.

GRIFFITH, R. T. H. [tr.] Scenes from Ramayana, Meghaduta, etc. 6/- c 8° Trübner 70
" " Specimens of Old Indian Poetry *o.p.* [*pb.* 5/-; *w.* 4/6] f 8° Hall 52
MUIR, Dr. J. [tr.] Metrical Translations from Sanskrit Writers [Oriental Series] 14/- p 8° Trübner 79
" " [tr.] Religious and Moral Sentiments of the Hindus [metrical tr.] 2/- f 8° Williams 75
WILLIAMS, [Sir] Monier [tr.] Indian Wisdom: examples of religious doctrines *o.p.* [*pb.* and *w.* 15/-] 8° W. H. Allen [75] 76
WILSON, Prf. H. H. Works, 12 vols. in 13 £7 2*s.* 6*d.* 8° Trübner [13 *sqq.*] 62–77
i.-ii.: On Relig. of Hindus, ed. Dr. R. ROST, 21/-; iii.-v.: On Sansc. Liter., ed. ROST, 3 v., 36/-; vi.-x.: Tr. of *Vishnu Purana*, ed. F. Hall, 64/6; xi.-xii.: Specimens of Theatre of Hindus, trs., 21/-.

124. INDIC (*δ*): SANSCRIT LITERATURE (*γ*) INDIVIDUAL TEXTS AND TRANSLATIONS.

I. The Vedas.

Aids —*v. also* A § 14: Religions of India.

BENFEY, Theodor Vedica und Verwandtes, 6/-; Vedica und Linguistica 10/6 s 8° *Stuttgart* 77; 80
BERGAIGNE, Abel La Religion Védique, 3 vols. [practically a comment. on the Hymns] 8° *Paris* 78-83
" " Études sur le Lexique du Rig Veda, pt. i. 5/- 8° " 84
" + HENRY, Victor Manuel pour étudier le Sanscrite Védique 10/- 8° " 90
BURNOUF, Émile Essai sur le Véda *o.p.* [*w.* 10/-] 8° " 63
COLEBROOKE, H. T. —*in his* Essays, w. notes Prf. E. B. Cowell, 2 vols. 28/- 8° Trübner [27; 28] 73
HIRZEL, A. Gleichnisse u. Metaphern im Rigveda [comp. w. Gk. writers] 3/- 8° *Leipzig* 90
KAEGI, Prf. A. The Rig Veda: the oldest literature of the Indians, tr. R. Arrowsmith [Am.] $1.50 8° *Boston* 86

K § 124

LUDWIG, Prf. Alfred — Introduction and Commentary [in German], *to his tr. of the* ig Veda, *ut infra.*
" " — Die philosophischen und religiösen Anschauungen des Veda 2/6 8° *Prague* 75
MÜLLER, Prf. F. Max — *—ut* K § 94.
PISCHEL + GELDNER, R. K.F. — Vedische Studien, pt. i. 4/6; pt. ii. 7/- 8° *Stuttgart* 88; 89
SCHERMANN, L. — Philosoph. Hymnen d. Rig- u. Arth.-Veden verglich. m. d. älteren Upanishads 2/6 8° *Strassburg* 87
WALLIS, H. W. — The Cosmology of the Rig Veda [Hibbert Trust Essay] 5/- 8° Williams 87
WHITNEY, Prf. W. D. [Am.] — Orient. and Ling. Studies, Ser. i. [Veda, its doctrines and trs.] 12/- 8° Trübner [73] 75
Date of Vedas — *—cf.* Whitney's Oriental and Ling. Stud., pp. 21 & 73; Max Müller's Chips, v. i., pp. 11 & 114 [K § 94].
Dictionary — by H. Grassmann, *sub tit.* Wörterbuch zum Rig Veda 30/- r 8° *Leipzig* 73–75

I. RIG VEDA [Hymns].

Samhitâ.

Text.

ed. Dr. Th. Aufrecht, 2 vols. [In Roman transliteration = Weber's *Ind. Stud.*, vv. vi.–vii.] 20/- 8° *Berlin* [61] 77; [63] 77
ed. Prf. F. Max Müller: w. comm. of Sayana [14 cent.] and gloss., 6 vols. £15 4° Trübner 49–74
ed. S. Pandit: Samhita and Pada texts, w. Marathi and Eng. trs., in pts. ea. 3/6 8° *Bombay* 75 *sqq. in prog.*
Hymns — in Samhita and Pada texts, ed. Prf. F. Max Müller, 2 vols. 32/- 8° Trübner [69] 77

Reprinted from the *Editio Princeps*, *ut supra*, with the two texts on parallel pages.

" — ed. Prf. Peter Peterson: text, commentary and tr. [Bombay Sanscrit Ser.] 10/6 8° *Bombay* 88
" — ed. Dr. H. Oldenberg, vol. i. [metrical and textual prolegomena] 14/- 8° *Berlin* 88
" — ed. Râjârâm Bodas + Shivrâm Gore 16/- 8° *Bombay* 89
Selection — Zwölf Hymnen d. RV., ed. E. Windisch [w. Sayana's comm., dict. to same & append.] 5/- 8° *Leipzig* 83

Translations.

English — [*in part*] Prf. H. H. Wilson [contin. by Prf. E. B. Cowell + W. F. Webster] 6 v.: vols. i.–iv., 77/-; v., 21/-; vi. 21/- 8° Trübner [50–66] 66–88
" — tr. Max Müller, w. runng. comm., v. i. [Hymns to Maruts] [Sacr. Bks. of East] 8° Clar. Press [69] *in prep.*
" — tr. Prf. C. Delbos + Prf. K. Telang, *etc.*, ed. Nandalal Dhole 50/- r 8° *Calcutta* *in prog.*
French — traduit p. A. Langlois 17/- r 8° *Paris* [48–51] 70
German — übers. v. Prf. A. Ludwig; w. comm. and intro., 6 vols. 78/- 8° *Prague* 76–88

i.–ii.: Translation, 28/-; iii.: Introduction to the Hymns, 15/-; iv.–vi.: an elaborate commentary on the translation, 35/-.

" — übers. v. H. Grassmann, 2 vols. 30/- 8° *Leipzig* 76; 77
" — Siebenzig Lieder des Rig-Veda, übers. v. K. Geldner + A. Kaegi 3/- 8° *Tübingen* 75

Brahmanas.

Aitareya-Brâhmana — ed. w. English tr. and notes Martin Haug, 2 vols. 42/- f 8° *Bombay* 63
" " — " extracts fr. Sâyana's comm. Dr. Th. Aufrecht 11/- 8° *Bonn* 79

Conts. the earliest speculations of the Brahmins on meaning of sacrificial prayers.

Kaushitaki- [or Sankhâyana-] Brâhmana, ed. w. Germ. tr. Dr. B. Lindner, vol. i. [text] 10/- 8° *Jena* 87

Upanishads.

Aitareyâranyaka — ed. Râjendralâla Mitra, with Sâyana's comment., pts. 1–5 [Bibl. Indica] ea. 2/- 8° *Calcutta* 75–76
Aitareya-upanishad — ed. Dr. E. Röer, 3 pts. [Bibl. Indica], ea. 2/- 8° *Calcutta*, w. others—*v. infra*, *s.v.* Black Yajus.
" " — tr. Dr. E. Röer, w. others—*v. infra*, *s.v.* White Yajus.
Kaushitaki-upanishad — ed. & tr. Prf. E. B. Cowell; w. Sankarananda's comm., 2 pts. [Bibl. Indica] ea. 2/- 8° *Calcutta* 61; 62
Maitri-upanishad — ed. and tr. Prf. E. B. Cowell, w. Ramatirtha's comm. 3 pts. [Bibl. Indica] ea. 2/- 8° " 62–69
Upanishads, The — tr. Prf. F. Max Müller, pts. i.–ii. [Sacr. Bks. of E.] ea. 10/6 8° Clar. Press 79–84

Pt. i.: Khândogya-upanishad. Talavakâra-upanishad. Aitareya-âranyaka. Kaushîtaki-upanishad. Vâjasaneyi- (or Isa-) upanishad. | Pt. ii.: Katha-upanishad. Mundaka-upanishad. Taittirîyaka-upanishad. Brihadâranyaka-upanishad. Svetâsvatara-upanishad. Prasña-upanishad. Maitrâyana-upanishad.

GOUGH, A. E. — The Philosophy of the Upanishads & Anc. Ind. Metaphysics [Orient. Ser.] 9/- 8° Trübner 82

Sûtras (or Vedângas).

Shishâ-sûtra [pronunciation].

Shishâ-sûtra — ed. w. Germ. tr. Dr. A. Weber—*in his* Indische Studien, v. iv., pp. 275–371 12/- 8° *Berlin* 58

Chandah-sûtra [metre].

Chandah-sûtra — of Pingâla Achârya, ed. Visvanâtha Sâstri, 3 pts. [Bibl. Indica] ea. 2/- 8° *Calcutta*
" " — ed. w. Germ. tr. & comm. Dr. A. Weber—*in his* Indische St. viii., pp. 209 *sqq.* 12/- 8° *Berlin* 63

Nirukta-sûtras [etymology].

YÂSKA [*c.* 500 B.C.] — Nirukta sammt den Nighantavas, hrsg. u. erläutert Rudolf Roth, 3 pts. 15/- 8° *Göttingen* 52

Prâtisâkhya-sûtras [phonetics, etc.].

SAUNAKA — Prâtisâkhya, ed. w. Germ. tr. Prf. Max Müller, 4 pts. 42/- 4° *Leipzig* 56–69
" — " ed. w. French tr. Ad. Regnier, 3 vols. [repr. fr. *Jl. Asiatique*; rare; *w.* 55/-] 8° *Paris* 56–59

Kalpa-sûtras [aphorisms on sacrifices, etc.].

Srauta-sûtras [prescriptions for sacred ceremonies].

Asvalâyana-srauta-sûtra, ed. Vidyâratna, w. comment. of Nârâyana, 11 pts. [Bibl. Indica] ea. 2/- 8° *Calcutta* 64–74

Smârta-sûtras [observances prescribed by ritual].

(1) *Grihya-sûtras* [rules of domestic ceremonies].

Asvalâyana-grihya-sûtra, ed. A. F. Stenzler 8° *Leipzig* 64
" ed. Vedantavagisa, 4 pts. [Bibl. Ind.] ea. 2/- 8° *Calcutta*
Grihya-sûtras tr. Dr. H. Oldenberg, vols. i.–ii. [Sacred Books of East] ea. 12/6 8° Clar. Press 87; 89

(2) *Dharma-sûtras* [rules of daily conduct and life].

Vâsishtha-dharmasâstra ed. w. commentary of Krishnapandita 8° *Benares*
" tr. G. Bühler—*in his* Sacred Laws of the Aryas, v. ii. [Sacred Bks. of E.] 10/6 8° Clar. Press 82

Jyotisha [astronomy and seasons of ceremonies].

Jyotisha-vedanga ed. w. German tr. and comm. Dr. A. Weber 4° *Berlin* 62
" Contributions to Explanations of. By Dr. G. Thibaut 1/6 8° Trübner

Anukramanis [indices to the Hymns].

Kâtyâyana's Sarvânukramanî of Rig Veda, ed. A. A. Macdonell [Anecdota Oxon.] 16/- s 4° Clar. Press 87

II. SAMAVEDA [Songs].

Samhitâ.

Text: ed. Rev. J. Stevenson + H. Wilson 12/- r 8° W. H. Allen 43
ed. crit.: w. German tr. and Glossary, Prf. Th. Benfey, 30/-; Text only 18/- r 8° *Leipzig* 48; 48
ed. Sâmasramî, w. the Gânas & Sâyana's comm. [Bibl. Indica], 5 v. 74/-; or 37 pts. ea. 2/- 8° *Calcutta* 71–79
Translation: by Rev. J. Stevenson *o.p.* [w. 7/6] 8° Orient. Trans. Fd. 41

Brâhmanas.

Tândya-mahâ-brâhmana ed. Anandachandra Vedântavâgîsa; w. Sâyana's comm., 19 pts. [Bibl. Ind.] ea. 2/- 8° *Calcutta* 69–74
Abdhuta-brâhmana [last pt. of Sadvinsa-brâhm.] ed. w. Germ. tr. A. Weber—*in his* Zwei Vedische Texte üb. Omina u. Portente 3/- 4° *Berlin* 59

The other text is the *Abhinaddhyâya* of the *Kaushikâ-sûtra*.

Arsheya-brâhmana ed. w. comm. of Sâyana Dr. A. C. Burnell [properly a sûtra] 10/6 8° *Mangalore* 76
" Jaiminîya text, ed. Dr. A. C. Burnell 7/6 8° " 78
Devatâ-dhyâya-brâhmana, ed. Dr. A. C. Burnell, w. comm. of Sâyana [properly a sûtra] 5/- 8° " 75
Sâmavidhâna-brâhmana ed. Dr. A. C. Burnell, w. comm. of Sâyana [properly a sûtra] 12/6 p 8° Trübner 73
Samhitopanishad-brâhmana, ed. Dr. A. C. Burnell, w. comm. [properly a sûtra] 7/6 8° *Mangalore* 77
Vamsá-brâhmana ed. Dr. A. C. Burnell; w. comm. of Sâyana [properly a sûtra] 10/6 8° " 73
" ed. Dr. A. Weber—*in his* Indische Studien, vol. iv. 12/- 8° *Berlin* 55

Cf. also Prf. W. D. WHITNEY (Am.), in *Proc. Amer. Orient. Soc.*, May, [illegible] (*New Haven*). Max MÜLLER [*Academy*, 7 June, [illegible]] announces the discovery by SATYAVRATA Sâmâsrami of the *Sixth* Brâhmana, the existence of wh. at some time he first pointed out in the first. vol. of his edn. of *Rig Veda* in [illegible].

Upanishads.

Chandogya Upanishad ed. Dr. E. Röer; w. comm. of Sankara Achârya, 6 pts. [Bibl. Indica] ea. 2/- 8° *Calcutta*
" " ed. Jibananda Vidyasagara; w. comm., ed. Dr. E. Röer ea. 2/- 8° " 73
" " hrsg. O. Böhtlingk [w. German tr.] 12/- 8° *Leipzig* 89
" " tr. Râjendralâla Mitra, 2 pts. [Bibl. Indica] ea. 2/- 8° *Calcutta* 54–62
Talavakâra- or Kena-Upanishad, ed. Dr. E. Röer [Bibl. Indica; also in Müller's *Upan.*] 8° "
" " " English tr. Dr. E. Röer [Bibl. Indica] 8° "

Sûtras.

Chandas.

Nidâna-sûtra —*two chaps. of*, ed. Dr. A. Weber, *in his* Indische Studien, vol. viii. 12/- 8° *Berlin* 63

Kalpa-sûtras.

Srauta-sûtra.

LÂTYÂYANA Srauta-sûtra, ed. w. Agnisvâmin's comm., Anandachandra Vedântavâgîsa, 9 pts. [Bibl. Ind.] ea. 2/- 8° *Calcutta* 72 *sqq.*

Smarta-sûtra.

Grihya-sûtra.

Gobhiliya-grihya-sûtra ed. w. German tr. Dr. F. Knauer, pt. i. [text & intro.], 2/-; ii. [tr. & notes] 4/- 8° *Dorpat* 84; 87
" ed. Tarkâlankâra; w. comment., 12 pts. [Bibl. Indica] ea. 2/- 8° *Calcutta* 71–81

K § 124

III. YAJURVEDA [Prayers].

A. Black Yajus (Taittirîya; text of the school of Âpastamba).

Samhitâ.

Taittirîya-samhitâ ed. Mahesachandra Nayaratna; w. comm. of Madhava Acharya, pts. 1–34 ea. 2/- 8° *Calcutta* ?-87
" ed. Dr. A. Weber—*in his* Indische Studien, vols. xi.–xii. ea. 12/- 8° *Leipzig* 71; 72
Katha-samhitâ —*v.* Dr. A. Weber—*in his* Indische Studien, vol. iii. pp. 451–479 *o.p.* [rare] 8° *Berlin* 53
Mâitrayanî-samhitâ ed. L. v. Schroeder, books i.–iv. [pub. for D. M.L. Gesellsch.] 36/- 8° *Leipzig* 81–86
Ueber die Mâitrayanî-samhitâ 8° *Dorpat* 79

Brâhmanas.

Taittirîya Aranyaka ed. Râjendralâla Mitra, 11 pts. [Bibl. Indica] ea. 2/- 8° *Calcutta* 72 *sqq.*
" Brâhmana ed. Râjendralâla Mitra; w. Sâyana's comm., pts. 1–24 [Bibl. Indica] ea. 2/- 8° "

Upanishads.

Katha Upanishad tr. Sir Edwin Arnold, *sub tit.* The Secret of Death 7/6 c 8° Trübner (85) 85
Taittirîyaka Upanishad tr. Prf. Max Müller—*in his* Upanishads, vol. ii. [Sacred Bks. of East] 10/6 8° Clar. Press 84
" " ed. Dr. E. Röer—*in his* Taittirîyaka, Aitareya and Swetaswatara Upanishads, 3 pts. [Bibl. Ind.] ea. 2/- 8° *Calcutta*
" " tr. Dr. E. Röer—*v. infra, s.v.* White Yajus.

Sûtras.

Prâtisâkhya-sûtra.

Prâtisâkhya-sûtra [of Taittirîya] ed. & tr. Prf. W. D. Whitney [Am.]; w. comm. & notes [Jl. Am. Or. Soc.] $5 8° *New Haven* 71
" ed. Râjendralâla Mitra; w. comm., 3 pts. [Bibl. Indica] ea. 2/- 8° *Calcutta*

Kalpa-sûtras.

Srauta-sûtra.

Âpastambîya-srauta-sûtra, ed. Dr. Richard Garbe, pts. i.–xii. [Bibl. Indica] ea. 2/- 8° *Calcutta*

Smârta-sûtras.

(1) *Grihya-sûtras.*

Âpastambîya-grihya-sûtra ed. M. Winternitz 5/- 8° *Vienna* 87
Hiranyakesin-grihya-sûtra ed. J. Kirste, w. extr. fr. comm. of Matridatta 10/- 8° " 89

(2) *Dharma-sûtras.*

Âpastamba Dharma-sûtra ed. w. Engl. tr. and notes G. Bühler—*in his* Aphorisms of the Sacred Laws of Hindus, 2 vols. 24/- 8° *Bombay* 68; 71
" " tr. by the same [Sacred Books of East] 10/6 8° Clar. Press 79
Baudhayana Dharma-sûtra tr. G. Bühler—*in his* Sacred Laws of the Hindus—*ut supra.*
Gautama Dharma-sûtra ed. A. F. Stenzler [Auctores Sanscriti] [tr. G. Bühler, *ut supra*] 4/6 8° *London* 76
Vishnu-smriti tr. Julius Jolly, *s.v.* Institutes of Vishnu [Sacred Books of East] 10/6 8° Clar. Press 80

Dharmasâstra —*v. infra,* ¶ VIII.: Law.

B. White Yajus (Vâjasaneyi).

Samhitâ.

White Yajurveda, ed. Dr. A. Weber, 3 vols. *o.p.* [w. £9 9/-] 4° *Berlin* 49–59
i.: Vâjasaneyi-samhitâ; ii.: Satapatha-brâhmana; iii.: Srauta-sûtra of Kâtyâyana.
" " Mâdhyandina recension; w. Mahîdhara's comm., 36 pts. [Bibl. Indica] ea. 2/-sq 8° *Calcutta* 74 *sqq.*
Isa Upanishad [= 40th (last) bk. of Vâjasaneyi]—*v. infra, s.v.* Upanishads.

Brâhmanas.

Satapatha-brâhmana, tr. Prf. J. Eggeling, pts. i.–ii. [Sacred Books of the East] ea. 12/6 8° Clar. Press 82; 85
" " German tr. of pts. by Dr. A. Weber—*in his* Indische Streifen, vol. i. 8/- 8° *Berlin* 68
Conts. several legends of general interest—story of the flood, fountain of youth, punishment after death.
Brihad-Aranyaka Upanishad [= 14 bk., bk. of Satapatha-brâhmana]—*v. infra, s.v.* Upanishads.

Upanishads.

Brihad Aranyaka Upanishad, tr. and ed. Dr. E. Röer, w. comm., 14 pts. [Bibl. Indica] ea. 2/- 8° *Calcutta*
" " " tr. Prf. Max Müller—*in his* Upanishads, pt. ii. [Sacred Bks. of East] 10/6 8° Clar. Press 84
" " " in der Mâdh-jamdina Recension. hrsg. u. übers. O. Böhtlingk 5/- r 8° *St. Petersburg* 89
Isa, Kena, Katha, Prasna, Munda, Mandukya Upanishads, ed. Jibananda Vidyasagara 21/- 8° Clar. Press 73
The same (all of them), tr. Dr. E. Röer; w. comm., 3 pts. [Bibl. Indica] ea. 2/- 8° "
Includes also the *Taittirîya and Aitareya* Upanishads.
The same, tr. Prf. Max Müller—*in his* Upanishads, pt. i. [Sacred Books of East] 10/6 8° Clar. Press 79

Sûtras.

Prâtisâkhya-sûtra.

KATYÂYANA Prâtisâkhya, ed. Yugalkisora Pathaka, w. comm. of Uvata; pts. i.-vi. ea. 3/- 8° *Benares* 85-89 *in prog.*

Kalpa-sûtras.

Srauta-sûtra.

KATYÂYANA Srauta-sûtra, ed. Dr. A. Weber; w. extr. fr. comms. of Karka and Yâjnikadeva—*v. supra, s.v.* Samhitâ.

Smârta-sûtras.

(1) *Grihya-sûtra.*

PARASKARA Kâtîya-grihya-sûtra, ed. A. F. Stenzler, 8/-; Germ. tr. by same [Abh. f. Kunde d. Morgenl.] 4/6 8° *Leipsig* 76; 78

(2) *Dharma-sûtra.*

ÂPASTAMBA Dharma-sûtra [of *Vâjasaneyi*] ed. w. German tr. Dr. A. Weber—*in his* Indische Studien, vol. iv. 12/- 8° *Berlin* 58

IV. ATHARVA [OR BRAHMA]-VEDA [Incantations].

Samhitâ.

Text ed. Prf. R. Roth + Prf. W. D. Whitney [Am.], vol. i. [text only] 28/6 4° *Berlin* 55-56

Translation.

German Artharva Veda, Buch vi., Hymne 1-50, übersetzt u. erklärt C. A. Florenz 4/- 8° *Göttingen* 87

" *by* A. Ludwig—*in his* tr. of Rig Veda, *ut supra*, 2 vols. 28/- 8° *Prague* 76

" *by* Dr. A. Weber—*in his* Indische Studien, bk. i. [in vol. iv.], bk. ii. [in vol. xiii.], bk. xiv. [in vol. v.], bk. xv., by Aufrecht. [in vol. i.], ea. vol. 12/- 8° *Berlin* 58;73;61-62;49

" Hundert Lieder d. Artharva Veda, übersetzt Julius Grill [w. notes] 5/- 8° *Stuttgart* [79] 89

Aids.

ROTH, Dr. Rudolf Abhandlung über den Artharva Veda [36 pages] 1/6 4° *Tübingen* 56

" " Der Artharvaveda in Kaschmir [25 pages] 1/6 4° " 75

WHITNEY, Prf. W. D. [Am.] Index Verborum to the pub. text of Arth. Veda [= *Jl. Am. Or. Soc.*, vol. xii.] $5 i 8° *New Haven* 81

Brâhmana.

Gopatha-brâhmana, ed. Harachandra Vidyâbhushana, 2 pts. [Bibl. Indica] ea. 2/- 8° *Calcutta* 70-72

Upanishads —*Several are edit. and tr. by* Prf. W. D. Whitney [Am.] *in* Jl. Am. Or. Soc.

Artharvana Upanishads, ed. Tarkaratna, w. Narayana's comm., pts. 1-5. [Bibl. Indica] ea. 2/- 8° *Calcutta* 72 *in prog.*

Gopâla Tâpanî Upanishad, ed. Harachandra Vidyâbhushana; w. comm., pt. 1. [Bibl. Indica] 2/- 8° " 70 *in prog.*

Mahanarayana Upanishad, ed. Col. G. A. Jacob [w. Dîpikâ of Nârâyana] 2/6 8° *Bombay* 88

Prasnopanishad, tr. Dr. E. Röer [ed. Jibananda Vidyasagara, *ut supra*] 8° *Calcutta* 53

Sûtras.

Saunakîyâ Chaturâdhyâyika, ed. w. tr. and notes Prf. W. D. Whitney [Am.] [*Jl. Am. Or. Soc.*] $6.50 8° *New Haven* 62

" " ed. Prf. Bloomfield *in prep.*

Prâtisâkhya-sûtra.

Prâtisâkhya-sûtra, ed. w. English tr. Prf. W. D. Whitney [Am.]—*in Jl. A. O. S.*, vii. 333-615; Addenda x. 156-171 8° *New Haven* 62; 65

Kalpa-sûtra.

Srauta-sûtra.

Vaitâna-sûtra, ed. w. English notes Dr. Richard Garbe [Auctores Sanscriti] 5/- r 4° Trübner 78

" German tr. w. notes Dr. Richard Garbe 4/- 8° *Strassburg* 78

II. National Epics.

(1) MAHÂBHÂRATA [ascribed to VYÂSA]

Text, w. comm. of Nîlakantha, 18 bks., 5 vols. £7 7/- obl *Bombay* [63] 88

With a short alphab. index, and an elaborate index to each *Parva*.

" ed. by four Natives, w. indexes [Asiatic Soc. of Bengal] *o.p.* [w. £8 8/-] f° *Calcutta* 34-39

" Selections ed. F. Johnson *o.p.* 8° *London* 42

Translation: English by Protap Chandra Roy, w. notes [after the first pt.]; in 100 pts. *Calcutta* 83-90 *in prog.*

Pts. i.-xlv. ea. 3/-; xlvi. sqq. ea. 1/6. For translated selections, v. *infra*, V.: Lyrical Poetry, etc., *s.v.* Translated Specimens

" 2 bks. tr. Sir Edwin Arnold—*in his* Indian Poetry [Oriental Series] 7/6 p 8° Trübner [81] 90

" selns. tr. Sir Edwin Arnold—*in his* Indian Idylls 7/6 p 8° " 83

" French, par H. Fauche, vols. i.-x. [in 12 vols.; rough paraphrase] ea. 8/6 8° *Paris* 63-72

" " Onze Episodes de Mahâbhârata, trad. P. E. Foucaux 7/6 8° " 62

K § 124

BHAGAVAD-GITÂ [episode of Mahâb.]
Text ed. A. G. v. Schlegel, cura Chr. Lassen 12/- r 8° *Bonn* [23] 46
" w. comms. of Sankara, Anandagiri & Sridharaswamin & 2 Beng. comms. [*w.* 60/-] f° *Calcutta* 53
" ed. J. Garrett *o.p.* [*w.* 20/-] r 4° *Bangalore* 46
Sansc., Canar., Engl.; w. WILKINS' tr. [1785], and tr. of W. v. HUMBOLDT's notes ['25-'26]. Append. conts. SCHLEGEL'S Latin vers. & R. T. GRIFFITHS' *Ess. on B. G.*
Translation: English by Prf. K. T. Telang, w. Sanatsugatiya and Anugitâ [Sacr. Bks. of East] 10/6 8° Clar. Press 82
" " by Rev. John Davies, *sub tit.* Hindu Philosophy [Oriental Series] 8/6 p 8° Trübner [82] 89
" " by J. M. Chatterji, *sub tit.* The Lord's Day; w. comm. and notes 8/6 8° " [88] 89
" " paraphrased by [Sir] Edwin Arnold—*in his* Song Celestial 5/- c 8° " [82] 85
" German, by Dr. F. Lorinser; w. notes [incl. Sanatsugâtiya and Anugitâ] 9/- 8° *Breslau* 69
Nalopâkhyânam [episode of Mahâb.]. Nalus Eposodium, ed. F. Bopp [w. Germ. metr. tr. & notes] 12/- 4° *Berlin* [19] 68
The work that laid the foundation of Sanscrit philology in Europe.
" Story of Nala, ed. w. notes [Sir] Monier Williams, & tr. by [Dn.] H. H. Milman 15/- 8° Clar. Press [60; 35] 79
" ed. w. vocab., etc., Rev. T. Jarrett [Roman character] 10/- 8° Camb. Press 75
" German tr., by Fr. Rückert 5/- 16° *Frankfort* [28] 74
" " by H. C. Kellner [Universal-Bibl.] 3*d.* 16° *Leipzig* 87
There is an excellent analysis of the *Mahâb.* in Sir Monier WILLIAMS' *Indian Epic Poetry* [*o.p.*], afterwards repr. in his *Indian Wisdom* [*o.p.*].

(2) RÂMÂYANA [ascribed to VÂLMÎKI]
Text ed. w. Latin notes A. G. v. Schlegel, vols. i. (in 2 pts.) and ii. 31/6 8° *Bonn* 29–46
" w. commentary, pts. 1–10 [Bibl. Indica] ea. 2/6 8° *Calcutta* 70–76
" w. Ital. tr. and notes G. Gorresio, 10 vols. *o.p.* [*w.* £10] r 8° *Paris* 43–58
The Introduction (143 pp.) and Prefaces to the various vols. give full account of all then known conc. the Ramayana. Text, etc., in 5 vols. [*w.* £6 6/-], tr. in 5 vols. [*w.* £3 15/-].
Translation: English tr. R. T. H. Griffith, 5 vols. [tr. in metre of *Lady of the Lake*] *o.p.* [*w.* 147/-] 8° *Benares* (Tbnr.) 70–74
" French trad. H. Fauche, 2 vols. 6/- 12° *Paris* 64
Uttara-Kanda ed. G. Gorresio, 25/-; Italian tr. G. Gorresio 25/- r 8° " 67; 70

Aids to Mahâbhârata and Ramâyana—*v. also* K § 123, *s.v.* Translated Selections.
GRASBERGER, L. Noctes Indicae seu questt. in Nalum Mahâbhârateum 10/- 8° *Vienna* 68
PEILE, J. Notes on the Tales of Nala [for classical students] 12/- 8° Camb. Press 82
RICHARDSON, [Miss] F. [tr.] The Iliad of the East [sel. of legends of Ramâyana (tr.); popular] 7/6 8° Macmillan [70] 73
WEBER, Dr. Albrecht On the Râmâyana [tr.] [fr. *Abhandl. d.* (Berl.) *Acad. d. Wiss.*] 5/- f 8° Trübner 70
Westminster Review —*for* April, 1868, *conts. a learned article on the* Mahâbhârata 6/- 8° " 88
WHEELER, J. Talboys —*his* Hist. of India, v. i.–ii., cont. condensed stories [tr.] of the great epic 39/- 8° " 67; 69
WILLIAMS, [Sir] Monier Indian Epic Poetry [lects. on Ramâyana and Mahâb.; w. analyses] 5/- 8° Williams 63

III. Puranas and Tantras.

Agni-Purâna ed. with tr. Harachandra Vidyabhushana, 14 pts. [Bibl. Indica] ea. 2/- 8° *Calcutta* 70 *sqq.*
Bhâgavata-Purâna [the earliest philosoph. and relig. poem of India].
" " ed. with French tr. E. Burnouf + Hauvette-Besnault, 4 vols. £8 4° *Paris* 40–84
" " w. comm. in Sanscrit by Shridhar Pandit, 3 vols. 42/- obl *Bombay* 87
Kalki-Purâna pts. i.–ii. [in Bengali characters] 5/- 8° *Calcutta* 70; 73
Linga-Purâna [rel. to Siva and his achievements] 42/- f° *Bombay* 57
Mârkandeya-Purâna ed. K. M. Banerjea; w. intro., 7 pts. [Bibl. Indica] ea. 2/- 8° *Calcutta* 51 *sqq.*
Vayu-Purâna ed. Rajendralala Mitra, pts. 1–13 [Bibl. Indica] ea. 2/- 8° "
" " tr. Prf. Ramkrishna Gobal Bhandarkar [Sacred Bks. of East] 8° Clar. Press *in prep.*
Vishnu-Purâna: system of mythology, ed., w. Ratnagarbhabhatta's comm. *Bombay* 7–
" ed. Tarânâtha Tarkavâchaspati; w. comm., vols. i.–iii. [w. Bengali tr.] 47/- 8° *Calcutta* 70 *in prog.*
" English tr., w. notes and index Prf. H. H. Wilson, ed. F. Hall, 5 vols. in 6 64/6 8° Trübner [40] 64–77
Invaluable as a guide to the worships of Vishnu. Preface contains a good survey of the several Purânas. These 5 vols. = vols. vi.–x. of WILSON'S *Works*.

Aids to the Purânas.
WILSON, Prf. H. H. —*his* Essays on Sanscrit Liter. [*ut* K § 123], cont. analyses of several of the Purânas.

IV. Modern Epics.

BHÂRAVI [6 cent.] Kirâtârjuniya, ed. w. Mallinâtha's comm., 2 vols. 15/- 8° *Calcutta* 68
BHARTRIHÂRI [7 cent.] Ravâna-badha: text 8° "
A selection is in BÖHTLINGK'S *Chrestomathie*, 5/- 8° *St. Petersburg* ['45] '77 (*ut* K § 121).
HARSHA-DEVA [king; 12 cent.] Naishadhiya, w. comm. of Tarkalagisha, pts. 1–3 ea. 5/- 8° *Calcutta* [ ] 70–72
" " ed. Dr. E. Röer, w. comm., 12 pts. [Bibl. Indica] ea. 2/- 8° "
KÂLIDÂSA [6 cent.] Kumâra-sambhava, ed. w. Latin tr. A. F. Stenzler *o.p.* [*pb.* 10/-; *w.* 7/6] 4° Or. Trans. Fund 38
" " ed. w. English notes K. M. Banerjea 10/- 8° *Calcutta* 67
" " ed. Jibananda Vidyasagara [canto viii. to xvii.] 5/- 8° " [ ] 87
" " English tr. R. T. H. Griffith, *sub tit.* Birth of War God 5/- 8° Trübner [53] 79
" " French tr. H. Fauche—*in his* Oeuvres Complètes de Kâlidâsa, 2 vols. 18/- 8° *Paris* 59; 60
" Nalodaya, ed. Jibananda Vidyasagara. 4/-; ed. Jagannâtha Sukla 4/6 8° *Calcutta* 73; 70
" " ed. w. Latin tr. and comm., F. Benary *o.p.* [*pb.* 9/-; *w.* 6/-] 4° *Berlin* 30
" " ed. w. English tr. [verse] and notes W. Yates 18/- 8° *Calcutta* 44
" " English tr. [verse] Dr. Taylor
" " French, tr. H. Fauche—*ut supra.*
" Raghuvamsa, ed. w. Latin tr. A. F. Stenzler 42/- 4° Or. Trans. Fund 32
" " ed. Shânkar P. Pandit; w. comm., 3 pts. [Bomb. Sansk. Ser.] ea. 4/- 8° *Bombay* 69–76
" " ed. Kâshinâtha Pandurang Paraba, w. comm. of Mallinâthâ 3/6 8° " 86

KÂLIDÂSA [6 cent.] Raghuvamsa, ed. w. English notes K. M. Banerjea, pt. i. 4/- 8° Trübner 66

,, ,, French, tr. H. Fauche—*ut supra.*

KAVIRÂJA [10 cent.] Râghava-pândavîya, ed. Premachandra Tarkavagisa; w. comm. 18/- 8° *Calcutta* 54

MÂGHA [11 cent.] Sisupâla-badha [or Mâghakâvya]: text 8° ,,

,, ,, German tr. and notes, D. C. Schütz, pt. i. 5/- 8° *Bielefeld* 43

,, ,, French, tr. H. Fauche—*in his* Une Tétrade [v. K § 123], 3 vols. 30/- 8° *Paris* 61–63

V. Drama.

Translated Specimens.

WILSON, Prf. H. H. [tr.] Select Specimens of the Theatre of the Hindus, 2 vols. 21/- 8° Trübner [35] 71

Religious Drama.

JAYDEVA [12 cent.] Gîtagovinda, ed. w. Lat. tr. and notes C. Lassen 10/- 4° *Bonn* 36

,, ,, ed. Becharama Vasaka; w. comm. 3/- 8° *Calcutta* 72

,, ,, tr. [Sir] Edwin Arnold—*in his* Indian Song of Songs 5/- p 8° Trübner 75

Individual Writers.

BHATTA NÂRÂYANA [6–10 cent.] Venisambâra, ed. w. German intro. and notes Julius Grill 16/- 4° *Leipzig* 71

,, ,, ,, ed. Jibananda Vidyasagara; w. comm. 5/- 8° *Calcutta* [ ] 75

BHÂVABHÛTI [6 or 7 cent.] Mahâvîracharita ("History of Rama"), ed. F. H. Trithen *o.p.* [w. 5/-] r 8° *London* 48

,, ,, ed. Jibananda Vidyasagara 5/- 8° *Calcutta* 73

,, ,, English tr. J. Pickford [in prose] 5/- c 8° Trübner 71

,, Uttararâmacharita, ed. Prf. E. B. Cowell 5/- 8° *Calcutta* 62

,, ,, ed. Shrinivâs Govind Bhânap; w. English notes 4/- 8° *Bombay* 88

,, ,, ed. Jibananda Vidyasagara 3/6 8° *Calcutta* [ ] 89

,, ,, English tr. Prf. H. H. Wilson—*in his* Specimens, *ut supra.*

,, ,, ,, tr. C. H. Tawney 4/- 8° Williams 63

The above two works together form a dramatised version of the Râmâyana.

,, Mâlatî-mâdhava, ed. R. G. Bhandarkar; w. comm. 14/- 8° *Bombay* 76

,, ,, English tr. Prf. H. H. Wilson—*in his* Specimens, *ut supra.*

,, ,, French tr. G. Strehly 3/6 f 8° *Paris* 85

ANUNDORAM BOROOAH Bhavabhûti and his Place in Sanskrit Literature 5/- 8° Trübner

HARSHA-DEVA [king; 12 cent.] Nâgânanda ["Joy of Snake World"], ed. Mâdhava Chandra Ghosha 6/- r 8° *Calcutta* 64

,, ,, English tr. P. Boyd; w. preface Prf. E. B. Cowell 4/6 c 8° Trübner 72

Attributed by COWELL to the poet DHÂVAKA (12 cent.).

,, ,, French tr. A. Bergaigne 2/6 s 8° *Paris* 79

,, Priyadarsika, ed. Vishnu Daji Gadre [of doubtful authorship]

,, ,, French tr. G. Strehly [Bibl. Orient. Elzévir] 2/6 12° *Paris* 88

,, Ratnâvalî, ed. Târânâtha Tarkavâchaspati 4/- 8° *Calcutta* 66

,, ,, ed. C. Cappeller — *in* O. Böhtlingk's Sanskritische Chrestomathie 5/- 8° *St. Petersburg* [45] 77

,, ,, English tr. Prf. H. H. Wilson—*in his* Specimens, *ut supra.*

WILSON places this poem in 12 cent., and attributes it to DHÂVAKA. Attrib. by HALL to BÂNA (beg. 7 cent.).

KÂLIDÂSA [6 cent.] Œuvres complètes, trad. p. H. Fauche, 2 vols. 18/- 8° *Paris* 59; 60

,, Œuvres choisies, trad. par H. Fauche [Sakuntala, Raghuvansa, Megha-Duta] 3/6 s 8° ,, 65

,, Mâlavikâgnimitra, ed. crit., w. notes, Shankar Pandurang [Bombay Sans. Series] 6/- 8° *Bombay* [70] 89

,, ,, ed. w. German notes F. Bollensen 12/- 8° *Leipzig* 79

,, ,, English tr. C. H. Tawney

,, ,, French tr. Prf. Victor Henry: with the *Mudrârâkshasa*—*v. infra* 4/6 s 8° *Paris* 88

,, ,, ,, ,, by P. E. Foucaux [also by Fauche, *ut supra*] 2/6 s 8° *Paris* 77

,, ,, German tr. Dr. A. Weber 3/- 8° *Berlin* 56

HAAG, Fr. Zur Textkritik u. Erklärung v. Mâlavikâgnimitra, pt. i., 2/6 4° *Frauenfeld* 72

,, Sakuntalâ. (1) *Bengali version*, ed. w. French tr. A. L. Chézy [w. 21/-]; tr. only [w. 10/-] 4° *Paris* 30; 32

,, ,, ,, ,, ed. Jibananda Vidyasagara 5/- 8° *Calcutta* [79] 87

,, ,, ,, ,, ed. w. English notes Dr. Richard Pischel 12/- 8° *Kiel* 77

,, ,, ,, ,, tr. Sir W. Jones; ed. T. W. Rhys-Davids 3/6 c 8° Unwin [1790] 90

The first book ever translated from Sanskrit.

,, ,, (2) *Western* [*Devanâgarî*] *version*: Text, ed. w. Germ. notes O. Böhtlingk 10/6 r 8° *Bonn* [42] 46

The 1842 edn. contains also a German tr.; worth 16/-.

,, ,, ,, ,, ed. w. tr. & notes [Sir] Monier Williams [prose & verse] 7/6 p 8° Murray [53] 87

,, ,, ,, ,, The same: tr. only, 8/-; Illum. Edn., *o.p.* [w. 63/-] s 4° Austin, *Hertford* [53] 72: 55

PISCHEL, R. De Kalidasæ Sakuntali Recensionibus [diss. inaug.] 1/- 8° *Breslau* 70

,, Vikramorvasi, ed. crit. S. P. Pandit 6/- 8° *Calcutta* 79

,, ,, ed. [Sir] Monier Williams 5/- 8° Austin, *Hertford* 59

,, ,, ed. R. Pischel [Southern text]

,, ,, ed. w. German tr. and notes F. Bollensen 17/6 8° *St. Petersburg* 46

,, ,, English tr. Prf. H. H. Wilson *o.p.* [w. 3/6] 8° *Calcutta* 26

,, ,, ,, tr. Prf. E. B. Cowell [prose] *o.p.* [w. 10/6] 8° Austin, *Hertford* 41

,, ,, French tr. P. E. Foucaux [also by Fauche, *ut supra*] 2/6 s 8° *Paris* [61] 79

,, ,, German tr. Edm. Lobedanz 2/6 16° *Leipzig* [61] 84

,, ,, ,, tr. L. Fritze [metrical; Univ. Bibl.] 3*d.* 18° ,, 81

K § 124

KRISHNAMISRA [12 cent.] Prabodha-chandrodaya, ed. Prf. H. Brockhaus, 2 pts. 7/6 8° *Leipzig* 35 ; 45
" " ed. Jibananda Vidyasagara 8/6 12° *Calcutta* 74
" " ed. w. German tr. [by T. Goldstücker] 5/- 8° *Königsberg* 42
RÂJA-SEKHARA [bef. 10 cent.] Pracandapandava, ed. Prf. Carl Cappeller 3/6 8° *Strassburg* 85
SÛDRAKA [5 cent.] Mrichchhakatikâ ["Toy Cart"], ed. A. F. Stenzler [text, Prakrit comm. & notes] 21/- i 8° *Bonn* 47
" " English tr. Prf. H. H. Wilson—*in his* Specimens, vol. i., *ut supra.*
" " German tr. by O. Böhtlingk + L. Fritze
" " French tr. and notes P. Regnaud, 4 vols. 8/6 s 8° *Paris* 76–77
" " " H. Fauche—*in his* Une Tétrade, 3 vols. [v. K § 123] 30/- 8° " 61–63
VISÂKHADATTA [7 cent.] Mudrârâkshasa, ed. K. T. Telang [Bombay Sanscrit Series] 8° *Bombay* 84
" " French tr. Prf. Victor Henry [*w. Mâlavikâgnimitra, v. supra*] 4/6 s 8° *Paris* 88
" " German tr. Ludwig Fritze [Universal-Bibl.] 3*d.* 16° *Leipzig* 87

VI. Poetry: Lyrical, Descriptive, and Didactic.

Translated Specimens.

ARNOLD, Sir Edwin [tr.] Indian Poetry [fr. Gita Govinda, Mahâb., Hitopad., *etc.*; Or. Ser.] 7/6 p 8° Trübner [75, etc.] 90
" " [tr.] Indian Idylls [from the Mahabharata] 7/6 p 8° " [83] 89
GRIFFITH, R. T. H. [tr.] Idylls from the Sanskrit 5/- 16° Smith & Elder [66] 69
" " [tr.] Specimens of Indian Poetry 6/- c 8° Trübner 70
MUIR, Dr. John [tr.] Metrical Translations from Sanskrit Writings [Oriental Ser.] 14/- 8° " 79

Individual Writers.

BHARTRIHARI Nîtisaka & Vairâgyasataka, ed. w. notes Prf. K. T. Telang [Bombay Sansk. Ser.] 9/- 8° *Bombay* 74
" The Satakas of, tr. Rev. B. Hale Wortham [Oriental Series] 5/- p 8° Trübner 86
" Sententiæ, ed. P. v. Bohlen 13/- 4° *Berlin* 33
" The same, trad. P. Regnaud 2/6 12° *Paris* 75
KÂLIDÂSA [6 cent.] Megha-dûta ["Cloud Messenger"], w. German notes & vocab. A. F. Stenzler 4/6 8° *Breslau* 74
" " ed. w. tr. Prf. H. H. Wilson, and vocab. S. Johnson [verse tr.] 10/6 4° Trübner [14] 67
" " ed. Kâshinâth Pândurang Paraba; w. comm. of Mallinâtha 2/6 8° *Bombay* [85] 86
" " English tr. Col. H. A. Ouvry [prose] 5/- c 8° Trübner 68
" " " tr. Rev. Thos. Clark 1/- f 8° " 82
" " French tr. H. Fauche—*in his* Œuvres Complètes de Kalidasa, 2 v. 18/- 8° *Paris* 59 ; 60
" " German tr. [Prf.] F. Max Müller 1/- 12° *Königsberg* 47
" Ritu-samhâra ["Assemblage of Seasons"], ed. w. Latin notes P. v. Bohlen 4/6 8° *Leipzig* 40
" " ed. Damaru Panta; w. Commentary 2/6 8° *Calcutta* 69
" " English tr. Satyam Jayati 3/6 12° Williams 67
" " " tr. [in part] R. T. H. Griffith 5/- 8° " [53] 79
" " French tr. [in part] H. Fauche—*ut supra.*
SRI-HÂLA Saptaçatakam, ed. w. transcription & Germ. notes Dr. A. Weber [Prakrit] 32/- 8° *Leipzig* 81
Weber, Dr. A. Ueber das Saptaçatakam [Abhand. f. Kunde d. ML.] 8/- 8° " 70

Anthology.

SÂRNGADHARA [? 14 cent.] The Paddhati, ed. Prf. P. Peterson, vol. i. [Bomb. Sansc. Ser.] 12/6 8° *Bombay* 88

This first vol. comprises the text; vol. ii. is to consist of a full crit. apparatus, w. notes. This important Anthology contains quotations from upwards of [illegible] poets.

VII. Fables and Novels.

Baitâl-Pachisî ["25 Tales of a Demon"]—*for Hindustani version, v.* K § 128, *s.v.* Hindustani.
Hitopadesa ["Salutary Counsel"; summary of *Panchatantra*], ed. w. tr. F. Johnson, 25/-; Translation only 5/- 4°; Williams [47] 64; W. H. Allen [48] 80
" ed. with [interlin.] tr. Prf. Max Müller: book i. 7/6; ii.–iv. 7/6 r 8° Longman 64 ; 65
" ed. Prf. P. Peterson [Bombay Sanscr. Ser.] 4/6 8° *Bombay* 87
" ed. w. Latin notes A. G. v. Schlegel + Chr. Lassen, 2 pts. 16/6 4° *Bonn* 29 ; 31
" German tr. J. Schoenberg 2/6 8° *Vienna* 84
" French tr. E. Lancereau [Littératures Populaires] 6/6 s 8° *Paris* [55] 82
Kathâ-sarit-sâgara [By SOMADEVA (12 cent.): "Oceans of Streams of Story"] ed. w. German tr. H. Brockhaus 24/- r 8° *Leipzig* 39

The German tr. was repub. alone (2 vols. 5/- 12° *Leipzig* 43), but is now out of print, and worth about 7/6.

" Bks. vi.–xviii., ed. H. Brockhaus, 6/-; ix.–xviii. [end] 16/- 8° " 62 ; 66
" tr. C. H. Tawney, 12 pts. [Bibl. Indica] ea. 2/- r 8° *Calcutta* 80 *sqq.*
Panchatantra ["Five Books"—*v. also* K § 112, *s.v.* Kalilag], ed. G. Kosegarten, vols. i.–ii. 24/- 8° *Bonn* 48 ; 59
" ed. F. Kielhorn + G. Bühler, w. notes; book i., 3/-; ii.–iii., 2/6; iv.–v. 2/6 8° *Bombay* [68–69] 85–87
" *German tr., with valuable intro. and notes H. Benfey, 2 vols. 24/- 8° *Leipzig* 59
" " " by L. Fritze 6/- 8° " 84
" French tr. E. Lancereau 8/6 8° *Paris* 71
Suka-saptati ["70 (stories) by the Parrot"] Vier Erzählungen aus, ed. R. Schmidt [w. Germ. tr.] 2/- 8° *Kiel* 90
Vetâla-pañchavimsati ["25 (stories) of the Vetâla"] ed. Jibananda Vidyasagara 2/6 8° *Calcutta* [73] 89
" ed. H. Uhle; w. crit. comm. in German [Abh. f. d. K. d. Morgenl.] 8/- 8° *Leipzig* 81

Novels.

BANA [7 cent.] Kâdambarî, ed. Madana Mohana Sarman 8° *Calcutta* 50

" " ed. with comm. Tarkavachaspati, 2 vols. 18/- 18° " 72

" " new edition with full Commentary announced *Bombay*

DANDIN [6 cent.] Dasakumâra-charita ["Adven. of Ten Princes"], ed. Prf. H. H. Wilson *o.p.* [*w.* 16/-] 8° *London* 46

" " ed. G. Bühler, w. notes, pt. i. [Bombay Sanscrit Series] 3/- 8° *Bombay* [74] 88

" " tr. P. W. Jacob [a free tr.] 6/- 12° Trübner 73

" " tr. E. J. Rapson p 8° " 90

SUBANDHU [7 cent.] Vâsavadattâ, ed. Fitzedward Hall, w. commentary, 3 pts. ea. 2/- 8° *Calcutta* 59

VIII. Law

—*see also* D § 111.

BAUDHÂYANA Dharma Sâstra, ed. F. Hultzsch [Abhandl. f. K. d. ML.] 8/- 8° *Leipzig* 85

MANU Mânava-Dharmasâstra, ed. G. C. Haughton, w. Sir Wm. Jones' tr., ed. Percival [standard ed.] 21/- 8° *Madras* [25] 63

" " ed. w. notes Prf. J. Jolly [Oriental Series] 10/6 p 8° Trübner 87

" " tr. A. C. Burnell + E. W. Hopkins [Oriental Series] 12/- p 8° " 84

" " tr. Georg Bühler [Sacred Books of the East] 21/- 8° Clar. Press 86

NÂRADA Dharma Sâstra: Institutes, tr. Dr. Julius Jolly 10/6 s 8° Trübner 76

" and some Minor Law Books, tr. Dr. Julius Jolly [Sacred Books of East] 10/6 8° Clar. Press 90

PARÂSARA Parâsara-mâdhavîyam—chap. on Inheritance, tr. Dr. A. C. Burnell 68

" Institutes, tr. Krishnakamal Bhattacharyya [Bibl. Indica] 2/- 8° *Calcutta*

VIDYÂSÂGARA, Jîbânanda [ed.] Dharmashastrasangraha, 2 pts. [coll. of texts] " 76

Vishnu-smriti Institutes of Vishnu, ed. Dr. J. Jolly; w. comm. of Nanda Pandita, & notes, 2 pts. [Bibl. Ind.] ea. 2/- 8° "

YÂJÑA-VALKYA Dharma Sâstra, ed. with German tr. A. F. Stenzler 8/- 8° *Berlin* 49

" " ed. with English tr. and notes V. N. Mandlik, 2 vols. in 1 60/- r 8° *Bombay* 80

" " English tr. with notes Dr. E. Röer + M. A. Mantriou 18/- 8° *Calcutta* 59

Dharma-sûtras —*v. supra, s.v. Sûtras of Rig and Black Yajur Vedas.*

IX. Philosophy

—*v. also s.v.* Upanishads of each of the Vedas, *supra.*

Bibliography.

HALL, Fitzedward Contrib. towards an Index to Bibliog. of Indian Philos. Sys. [ab. 800 wks.] 12/- 8° *Calcutta* 59

General Accounts.

BALLANTYNE, J. R. Christianity Compared with Hindu Philosophy *o.p.* [*w.* 7/6] 8° Madden (Williams) 59

BANERJEA, Rev. K. M. Dialogues on the Hindu Philosophy [Nyaya, Sankhya, Vedant] 18/- 8° " " 62

COLEBROOKE, H. T. Essays on Relig. & Philos. of Hindus, ed. Sir T. E. Colebrooke [son], 3 vols. ea. 14/- 8° Trübner [07] 73

Contains the best general view of the systems, besides valuable papers on the Vedas, Hindu Philosophy, Jain sect, *etc.*

GOLDSTÜCKER, Th. —*in his* Literary Remains, *is a good brief abstract* 2 vols. 21/- 8° W. H. Allen 79

GOUGH, A. E. Philosophy of the Upanishads & Ancient Indian Metaphysics [Orient. Ser.] 9/- 8° Trübner 82

HALL, Fitzedward [tr.] Hindu Philosophy: refutation of Hindu philosophical systems 12/- 8° *Calcutta* 62

MÂDHAVA ACHÂRYA [14 cent.] Sarva-darsana-sangraha, ed. Vidyasagara, 2 pts. ea. 2/- 8° " 53–58

" " " tr. Prf. E. B. Cowell + A. E. Gough [Oriental Series] 10/6 8° Trübner [75] 82

By far the ablest general view of the philosophical systems (except the *Vedânta*) produced by a native scholar.

REGNAUD, Paul Matériaux pour servir à l'histoire de la Philosophie de l'Inde, 2 vols. 8° *Paris* 76; 78

SIMON, Dr. Richard Beiträge zur Kenntniss der vedischen Schulen 5/- 8° *Kiel* 89

Religions of India —*v.* A § 14: Religions of India.

Theosophy —*v.* A § 94: Theosophy.

Translated Selections.

MUIR, Dr. John [tr.] Religious and Moral Sentiments of the Hindus [metrical tr.] 2/- 12° Williams 75

WILLIAMS, [Sir] Monier [tr.] Indian Wisdom: examples of religious doctrines *o.p.* [*pb.* and *w.* 15/-] 8° W. H. Allen [75] 76

1. MÎMÂMSÂ Brahma Sûtras—*v. infra, s.v.* Vedânta sûtras

MÂDHAVA ÂCHÂRYA [14 cent.] Jaiminîya-Nyâya-mâlâ-vistara, ed. Th. Goldstücker + Prf. E. B. Cowell 73/6 r 4° *Bombay* 70–74

Mîmâmsâ Darsana, ed. Nyayaratna, w. comm. of Savara Svami; pts. 1–19 [Bibl. Indica] ea. 2/- 8° *Calcutta ?–87 in prog.*

2. VEDÂNTA.

Accounts.

BAIERLEIN, E. R. Lehre d. Vedânta v. Gott, d. Welt, d. Menschen u. Erlös. d. Mensch. 1/- 8° *Dresden* 89

BALLANTYNE, J. R. Lecture on the Vedânta [with text of Vedânta-sara] 10/6 8° *Allahabad* 51

*DEUSSEN, Dr. Paul Das System d. Vedânta nach d. Brahma-sûtras des Bâdarâyana u. d. Commentare d. Sankara 12/- 8° *Leipzig* 83

Texts and Translations.

FOULKES, Rev. T. [tr.] Translations from the Tamil on Vedantic Philosophy, 6 pts. 11/6 8° *Madras* 60–64

SADÂNANDA Vedânta-sara, ed. O. Frank 6/6 4° *Munich* 35

" " English tr. w. notes Col. G. A. Jacob, *sub tit. Manual of Hindu Pantheism* [Oriental Ser.] 6/- p 8° Trübner [81] 89

" " " tr. Dr. E. Röer *o.p.* [*w.* 7/6] 8° *Calcutta* 45

" " German tr. O. Böhtlingk—*in his* Sansk.-Chrestom. 5/- 8° *St. Petersburg* [45] 77

K § 124

Vedânta-sûtras	ed. E. Röer + Vidyaratna, w. Sankara's Commentary, 13 pts. [Bibl. Ind.] ea.	2/-	8°	*Calcutta*	54-63
"	English tr. K. M. Bauer, pt. i.	2/-	8°	"	70
"	" tr. Prf. G. Thibaut [Sacred Bks. of East]	12/6	8°	Clar. Press	90
"	Germ. tr. Dr. P. Deussen, *s.v. Die sûtras d. Vedanta d. Badarayana* [w. S's comm.]	18/-	8°	*Leipzig*	87
VIDYÂRANYA	Panchadashi, w. comm. of Râmkrishna	8/- r	8°	*Bombay*	88

3. SÂNKHYA.

Accounts.

BALLANTYNE, J. R.	A Lecture on Sânkhya Philosophy	7/6	8°	*Mirzapore*	54
DAVIES, Rev. J.	Hindu Philosophy [exposition of system of Kapila; Oriental Ser.]	6/- p	8°	Trübner	81
RÖER, Dr. E.	Lecture on Sânkhya Philosophy			*Calcutta*	54

Texts.

ISVARA-KRISHNA [6 cent.]	Sânkhya-kârikâ, ed. Chr. Lassen	3/-	4°	*Bonn*	32
" "	" tr. H. T. Colebrooke *o.p.* [*pb.* 10/6; *w.* 6/-]		4°	*Oxford*	37
" "	" tr. J. Davies [Orient. Ser.—*v. supra*]	6/- p	8°	Trübner	81
"	tr. Debendra Nath Goswâmi	14/-	8°	*Calcutta*	89
KAPILA	Sânkhya-pravachana, ed. Fitzedward Hall, 3 pts. [Bibl. Indica] ea.	2/-	8°	"	
"	Sânkhya-darsana, ed. Jibananda Vidyasagara; w. commentary	7/6	8°	"	72
"	" tr. J. R. Ballantyne, *sub tit.* Sânkhya Aphorisms of Kapila [Oriental Ser.]	p	8°	Trübner [*Calc.* 53-56]	86
SANKHYÂVANA	Srauta-sûtra, ed. A. Hillebrandt, pts. i.-iv. [Bibl. Indica]	2/-	8°	*Calc.*	85-87 *in prog.*
VIJÑÂNA BHIKSHU [16 cent.]	Sânkhya-sâra, ed. Fitzedward Hall [Bibl. Indica]	2/-	8°	"	

4. YOGA.

Account.

PAUL, N. C.	Treatise on the Yoga Philosophy	1/6	8°	*Bombay*	[ ] 88

Texts.

NARADA	Pancharatra, ed. K. M. Banerjea, 4 pts. [Bibl. Indica] ea.	2/-	8°	*Calcutta*	61-65
PATANJALI	Aphorisms of Yoga Philos. of, ed. w. tr. J. R. Ballantyne	9/-	8°	*Mirzapore*	52-53
"	" pts. 1-5 [Bibl. Indica.] ea.	2/-	8°	*Calcutta*	
"	" tr. Col. Olcott; w. Bhoja Raja's comm.	7/6	8°	*Bombay*	85
SANDILYA	" ed. J. R. Ballantyne, 2/-; tr. Prf. E. B. Cowell [Bibl. Indica]	2/-	8°	*Calcutta*	61; ?

5 & 6. NYÂYA AND VAISESHIKA [Logic]

Bhâshâparichbeda, tr. and	annotated Dr. E. Röer	8/-	8°	*Calcutta*	50
KANADA	Aphorisms of Vaiseshika Philosophy of, ed. J. R. Ballantyne	6/6	8°	*Mirzapore*	51
"	" " tr. A. E. Gough	14/-	8°	*Benares*	73
LANGÂKSHI BHÂSKARA	Tarkakaumudi: intro. to Vaish. & Nyâya philos., ed. Manilâl Nabhubâi Dvivedi [Bomb. San. Ser.]	3/- p	8°	*Bombay*	87
GOTAMA, Nyaya Darsana of,	ed. Jayanârâyana Tarkapanchânana, 3 pts. [Bibl. Ind.] ea.	2/-	8°	*Benares*	64-65
" "	Jebananda Vidyasagara	10/6	8°	*Calcutta*	74
RÖER, Dr. E. [ed.]	Division of Categories of Nyaya Philosophy, w. Engl. tr., 2 pts. ea.	2/-	8°	"	
Turka-Sangraha	ed. J. R. Ballantyne		8°	*Allahabad*	59
UDAYANA ACHÂVA [12 cent.]	Kusumâñjali, ed. and tr. Prf. E. B. Cowell; w. comm.	5/6	8°	*Calcutta*	64
Vaiseshika Darsana,	w. Sankara's comm., ed. Jayanârâyana Tarkapanchânana, 5 pts. [Bibl. Ind.] ea.	2/-	8°	"	60-61

X. Heretical Systems.

Lalita-vistara	ed. and [partly] tr. Râjendralâla Mitra, pts. 1-6 [Bibl. Indica] ea.	2/-	8°	*Calcutta*	81 *sqq.*
"	tr. [anon.]; pts. i.-iii. [Bibl. Indica] ea.	2/-	8°	"	
"	German tr. by S. Lefmann; w. Germ. notes, pt. i.	9/- r	8°	*Berlin*	74
"	French tr. by C. E. Foucaux [tr. of the Tibetan version]		4°	*Paris*	48
	The standard authority of the Northern Buddhists on life and doctrines of Buddha in Sanskrit verse.				
OLDENBERG, Dr. H.	Ueber d. Lalita Vistara	1/6	8°	*Berlin*	82
Maha-vastu	ed. E. Senart		8°	*Paris*	
Narada-Pañcharâtra	ed. Rev. K. M. Banerjea, 4 pts. [Bibl. Indica] ea.	2/-	8°	*Calcutta*	61-65
Saddharma-pundarika:	Lotus of the True Law, tr. H. Kern [Sacred Books of the East]	12/6	8°	Clar. Press	84
" "	French tr. E. Burnouf, *sub tit.* Lotus de la bonne Loi *o.p.* [*w.* 63/-]		4°	*Paris*	52
	One of the most importan canonical bks. of Buddhists. BURNOUF'S edn. has commentary and 21 memoirs on Buddhism.				
Vagra-kkedikâ	ed. Prf. Max Müller [anecdota Oxon., *v.* K § 151]	3/6 s	4°	Clar. Press	81

XI. Grammarians —for a list of Sansc. Gram., *etc.*, *v.* Colebrooke's Misc. Essays, ii. 38 *sqq.* [*ut* K § 94].

Criticism.

BENFEY, Prf. Theodor	—*in his* Gesch. d. Sprachwiss. [*ut* K § 97] *gives an excell. survey of Ind. grammar.*				
BURNELL, Dr. A. C.	On the Aindra School of Sanskrit Grammarians	10/6	8°	Trübner	75
PISCHEL, Dr. Richard	De Grammaticis Pracriticis	1/6	8°	*Breslau*	74
	supplementing the accounts in Chr. LASSEN'S *Institutiones Linguae Pracriticae* [3 pts., 10/- 8° *Bonn* 37				
WHITNEY, Prf. W. D. [Am.]	The Study of Sanskrit and the Hindu Grammarians—*in* Jl. Am. Or. Soc., v. pp. 279-297.				

Texts.

BHATTOJIDÎKSHITA [17 cent.]
Siddhanta-Kaumudi ed. Târânâtha Tarkabâchaspati, w. extr. fr. 3 comms., 2 vols. 42/- 8° *Calcutta* [64]70; [65]71
" ed. and partly tr. J. R. Ballantyne
" abridged by Varaarâja
BHARTRIHARI [7 cent.] Vakya-padiya; ed. w. commentaries Gangadhara Sastri Manavalli, pts. i.-ii. ea. 3/- 8° *Benares* 85-86 *in prog.*
The oldest known treatise on the philosophy of grammar and syntax.
HEMACANDRA [12 cent.] Desinamamala, ed. w. gloss. R. Pischel+G. Bühler, pt. i. [Bombay Sansc. Ser.] 10/- 8° *Calc.* 81 *in prog.*
" " ed. R. Pischel, pt. i. [text] 8/-; pt. ii. [German tr. and notes] 8/- 8° *Halle* 77; 80
Kâsikâ vritti ed. Pandit Bâla Sâstrî, 2 pts. ea. 16/- 8° *Benares* 76; 78
Kâtantra [or Kâlâpa] [7 cent.] ed. with commentary Prf. J. Eggeling, pts. 1-6 [Bibl. Indica] ea. 2/- 8° *Calcutta* 73 *in prog.*
NÂGOJÎBHATTA Paribâshendusekhara, ed. w. Engl. tr. F. Kielhorn, 4 pts. [Bomb. Sansk. Soc.] ea. 10/6 & 7/6 8° *Bombay* 68-74
i.: Text, and various readings; ii.-iv.: Translation and notes.
PÂNINI [? 3 cent.] Ashtâdhyâyî, ed. w. commentary 8° *Calcutta*
" " " ed. w. English tr. W. Goontilleke 8° *Bombay* 82 *sqq.*
" " " ed. w. German tr. and notes O. Böhtlingk 60/- r 8° *Leipzig* [39-40] 86-87
GOLDSTÜCKER, Th. Panini: his place in Sanskrit Literature *o.p.* [*pb.* 42/-; *w.* 7/6] i 8° Trübner 61
This is the celebrated work in wh. Dr. GOLDSTÜCKER assailed all contemporary Sanscritists.
PATAÑJALI Mahâ-bhâshya ["Great Comm."] ed. Prf. Th. Goldstücker, 6 vols. [photo-litho.] r 4° Ind. Off. (Trübner) 74
" " ed. Dr. F. Kielhorn, vol. i. 8/6 8°
" " ed. crit. F. Kielhorn, in pts. ea. 6/- 8° *Calcutta* 82 *in prog.*
" " ed. Dr. J. R. Ballantyne, pp. 1-808 [all pub.] *o.p.* [*w.* £3]; w. Eng. tr. [*w.* £5] f° *Mirzapore* 55
SÂNTANAVA Phit-sûtras, ed. Dr. F. Kielhorn 66
SIRADEVA Paribhâshavritti, ed. Harinâtha Dube, pts. i.-ii. [Benares Sanscrit Ser.] 8° *Benares* 86; 87 *in prog.*
Unâdi-sûtras Comment. on, by Ujjvaladatta, ed. Dr. Th. Aufrecht 10/- r 8° *Bonn* 59
Rules on the formation of irregular derivatives.
VÂMANA [? 13 cent.] Kâsikâ, ed. Bâlashâstrin 8° *Benares*
VARADARAJA Laghu Kaumudi, ed. J. R. Ballantyne, w. Engl. tr. and notes 31/6 8° " [49] 67
VARDHAMÂNA Ganaratna-Mahodadhi, ed. Prf. J. Eggeling, 2 pts. [Auctt. Sanscriti] ea. 6/- 8° Trübner 79; 81
VOPADEVA [13 cent.] Mugdhabodham Byâkaranam, ed. O. Böhtlingk 9/- 8° *St. Petersburg* 47
" " " ed. Rajani Kânta Gupta 9/- 8° *Calcutta* 88

XII. Lexicography.

AMARA-SIMHA [? 12 cent.] Amara-Kosha ["Immortal Treasury"], ed. A. Loiseleur-Deslongchamps, 2 v. 15/- 8° *Paris* 39; 45
" " ed. H. T. Colebrooke; w. English tr. and notes *o.p.* [*w.* 63/-] 8° *Serampore* [08] 25
HALÂYADHA [12 cent.] Abhidhâna-ratnamala, ed. Dr. Th. Aufrecht; w. gloss. 18/-; *red. to* 10/- 8° Williams 61
HEMACHANDRA [12 cent.] Abhidhâna-Chintâmani, ed. O. Böhtlingk+C. Rieu 14/- 8° *St. Petersburg* 47
" " " " ed. Dr. T. Aufrecht [w. Sanskrit-English glossary] 8° *London* 61
SÂSVATA Anekartha-samuchchaya ["Collection of Homonyms], ed. Th. Zachariæ

XIII. Rhetoric, etc.

DANDIN [6 cent.] Kâvyâdarsa ["Mirror of Poetry"], ed. Premachandra Tarkavâgisa, w. comm., 5 pts. [Bibl. Indica] ea. 2/- 8° *Calcutta* 63
" The same, hrsg. O. Böhtlingk [w. German tr.] 10/- r 8° *St. Petersburg* 90
DHANANJAYA [10 cent.] Dasa-rûpa ["Ten Forms" (of plays], ed. Fitzedward Hall, 3 pts. [Bibl. Ind.] ea. 2/- 8° *Calcutta* 65
JAGANNÂTHA Rasagângâdhara: treat. on poet. comp., ed. Gangadhara Sastri Manavalli, pts. i.-vi. ea. 3/- 8° *Benares* 86-89
MAMMATA [10 cent.] Kavya-prakâsa [" Lustre of Poetry"], ed. Nyâyaratna 12/- 8° *Calcutta* 66
" " w. comment. of Vâmanâchârya 14/- r 8° *Bombay* 89
VISVANÂTHA KAVIRÂJÂ [15 cent.] Sâhitya-darpana ["Mirror of Composition"] ed. Dr. Röer, w. tr. J. R. Ballantyne, pts. i.-v. [Bibl. Ind.] ea. 2/- 8° *Calcutta* 51-66
" " tr. Pramadadasa Mitra, pts. 1-4 [Bibl. Ind.] ea. 2/- 8° " -78

XIV. Astrology and Astronomy.

Accounts.

BIOT, J. B. Études sur l'Astronomie Indienne [*Journal des Savants*] 6/- 4° *Paris* 62
MÜLLER, Prf. F. Max On Ancient Hindu Astronomy and Chronology 7/6 4° *Oxford* 62
WHITNEY, Prf. W. D. [Am.] Hindu Astronomy, *in his* Oriental and Ling. Studies, ser. ii. 12/- 8° Trübner 75

Texts.

ARYABHATIYA [5 cent.] ed. Dr. H. Kern, w. Paramâdisvara's comm. 9/- 4° *Leyden* 74
BHASKARA [12 cent.] Siddhanta-Siromani, ed. Bâpû Deva Sâstrî 12/- 8° *Benares* 66
" " Engl. tr. L. Wilkinson, ed. Bâpû Deva Sâstrî, 2 pts [Bibl. Ind.] ea. 2/- 8° *Calcutta* [ ]
Surya-Siddhanta ed. Fitzedward Hall+Deva Sâstrî, 4 pts.; tr. Deva Sâstrî, 1 pt. [B. Ind.] ea. 2/- 8° " 54-59; 60
" tr. w. notes Rev. E. Burgess, ed. Prf. W. D. Whitney [Am.] 31/6 8° *New Haven* 60-61
VARÂHA-MIHIRA Brihat Samhita, ed. Dr. H. Kern, 7 pts. [Bibl. Ind.] ea. 2/- 8° *Calcutta* 64-65
" " English tr. Dr. H. Kern [Jl. Roy. As. Soc.] 18/- 8° Trübner 70-76
" " " tr. N. Chidambaram Dyer, 2 pts. (20 numbers) 15/- 8° *Madras* 7-*sqq. in prog.*
" Hora Sastra, w. Bhattotpala's commentary 8° *Bombay* 67

K § 125

XV. Mathematics.

Accounts, etc.

COLEBROOKE, H. T. —*on the* Algebra of the Hindus, *in his* Miscell. Essays, ed. Cowell, *ut* K § 94.
HANKEL, Hermann —*in his* Zur Geschichte der Mathematik im Alterth. u. Mittelalter 9/- 8° *Leipzig* 74
WOEPCKE Sur l'Introduction de l'Arithmétique Indienne en Occident 8° *Roma* 59
" Mémoire sur la Propagation des Chiffres Indiens 8° *Paris* 63

Texts.

Bhahmegupta & Bhascara: algebra w. arithmetic and mensuration, tr. H. T. Colebrooke *o.p.* [*w.* 36/-] 4° *London* 17
Sulva-sûtras, The The English tr. w. intro. Dr. G. Thibaut; 4 pl. 5/- 8° Trübner 7-

XVI. Medicine.

Accounts, etc.

LIÉTARD, G. Lettres historiques sur la Médecine chez les Indous 5/- 8° *Paris* 63
ROYLE, Dr. J. F. The Antiquity of Hindu Medicine 6/6 8° Smith & Elder
WISE, Dr. T. A. Commentary on the Hindu System of Medicine 7/6 8° Trübner 45
" " Review of History of Medicine among Asiatic Nations, vol. i. *o.p.*, vol. ii. 10/- 8° Churchill 67

Texts.

Asvavaidyaka ed. K. U. C. Gupta Kaviratna; pts. i.-v. [treat. on diseases of horse; Bibl. Indica] ea. 2/- 8° *Calcutta*
Bhava-Prakasha ed. Jibânanda Vidyasagara 36/- 8° *Calcutta* 75
CHAKRAPANI DATTA Chakradatta, ed. Jibânanda Vidyasagara 6/- 8° " 88
Charaka-samhitâ ed. Jibananda Vidyasagara 8° " 77
Karaka-sangitâ tr. into Bengali Avinash Chundra Kaviratna + Chandrakumâra 85
Mâdhava Nidâna tr. into Bengali, the same + the same 85
Sannyasimati Ayurveda-Sangraha, by Bhûvanacandra Vasaka 2/- 8° " 82
SUSRUTA-samhitâ ed. Jibananda Vidyasagara 12/6 8° " [73] 89
" ed. Avinash Chundra Kaviratna Chandrakumara, w. comm. of Dalvana 8° " 8-
" ed. Vijayaratna Sen Kaviranjana, vol. i. 8-
" tr. Udoy Chand Dutt, pts 1-2 [Bibl. Indica] ea. 2/- 8° "
VÂGBHATA Ashtânga-hridaya, ed. Vijayaratna Sen Kaviranjana [w. comm. of Arundatta] 35/- r 8° *Bombay* 88

125. INDIC (*e*): PRAKRIT PHILOLOGY AND LITERATURE.

Grammar.

COWELL, Prf. E. B. Introduction to the Ordinary Prakrit of Sanskrit Dramas 3/6 c 8° Trübner 75
With a list of common irregular Prakrit words.
LASSEN, Chr. Institutiones Linguæ Pracriticæ, 3 pts. 20/- 8° *Bonn* 36-37

Native Grammars.

COWELL, Prf. E. B. [ed.] Prakrita-Prakasa: Prakrit gram. of Vararuchi [text, var. read., notes, & tr.] 14/- 8° Trübner [54] 68
HEMACANDRA [12 cent.] —*v.* K § 124, *s.v.* Grammariana.

Chrestomathy.

JACOBI, H. [ed.] Erzählungen in Mâhârâshtrî [w. vocabulary] 6/- 8° *Leipzig* 86

Literature.

Gaina Sutras tr. H. Jacobi—*v.* A § 14.
Ravanavaha oder Setubandha, ed. w. German tr. S. Goldschmidt, pt. i. [text] 25/-; ii. [tr.] 18/- 4° *Strassburg* 80; 84
Uvasagadaso ed. A. F. R. Hoernle, pts. i.-iii. [w. Sansc. comm. and Eng. tr.; Bibl. Indica] ea. 2/- 8° *Calcutta* 86-87 *in prog.*
VAKPATI Gaüdavaho, ed. Shankar Pandurang Pandit [a histor. poem; Bomb. Sansc. Ser.] 15/- p 8° *Bombay* 88

Jain Literature.

The chief Jain Scriptures are the 11 *angas* ("members")—*v.* Hemacandra's *Abhidhanacintamani*, pp. [illegible] *sqq.*, and Wilson's *Essays*. The last *anga* is subdiv. into 5 *upangas*. Nos. [illegible] *infra* are *angas*: [illegible] has 2 comments., only one of them bg. in Sansc. No. 9 is an *upanga*. Both texts and comms. are in Jaina Prakrit. The ser. is pub. under auspices of Raya Dhanapatasimha.

1. HEMACANDRA Jaina-râmâyana [life of Rama, in 10 cantos], ed. Sri Jagannatha-sukha 10/- 8° *Calcutta* 73
2. Sripâlacarita [advents. of Kg. Sripala], ed. Pandit Krishnacandraka 5/- obl " 73
3. Sûyagadâmga-sûtra [on Jain philos. = 2nd *anga*], ed. Sha Bhimasimha Mankahkya £4 4° *Bombay* 79
4. Jnâtâdharmakathânga-sûtra [acquis. of sacr. knowl. = 6th *anga*], text by Sudharmâ 60/- obl *Calcutta* 76
5. Upâsakadasâ-sûtra [duties of Srâvakas = 7th *anga*], text by Sudharmâ 10/- obl " 76
6. Prasnavyâkarana-sûtra [on philos. and ethics = 10th *anga*], text by Sudharmâ 21/- obl " 76
7. Vipâka-sûtra [on good and evil actions = 11th *anga*], text by Sudharmâ 21/- obl " 76
8. Uttarâdhyayana [moral discipline], ed. Vijaya 60/- obl " 79
9. Uvavâî-sûtra [an *upanga* sûtra], text by Sudharmâ 18/- obl " *n.d.*

BHADRABÂHUSVÂMIN Kalpa-sûtra, ed. H. Jacobi [Abhandl. f. K. d. ML.] 10/- 8° *Leipzig* 79
" " tr. J. Stevenson 48

126. INDIC (*f*): PALI AND SINGHALESE PHILOLOGY.

Pali Dictionaries and Grammars.

Author	Title	Price	Size	Publisher	Date
*CHILDERS, R. C.	Pali-English Dictionary; w. Sanskrit equiv., references, etc.	63/- i	8°	Trübner	75
	The first Pali dictionary ever published in a European language.				
CLOUGH, B.	Compendious Pali Grammar	*o.p.* [*w.* £3]	8°	*Colombo*	24
*FRANKFURTER, Dr. O.	Pali Handbook [grammar, chrestom., glossary]	16/-	8°	Williams	83
KUHN, E. W. A.	Beiträge zur Pali Grammatik	4/-	8°	*Berlin*	75
MASON, Francis	Pali Grammar, 2 pts. [on basis of Kaccâyana]	4/-	8°	*Toungoo*	67; 68
MINAYEFF, J.	Pali Grammar [tr.] [tr. fr. Russian viâ the Fch. tr. of M.S. Guyard (1874)]	8/-	8°	*Maulmain*	82
MÜLLER, Dr. E.	Simplified Grammar of the Pali Language, ed. Dr. R. Rost [Simpl. Grams.]	7/6 c	8°	Trübner	84

Native Dictionaries and Grammars.

Author	Title	Price	Size	Publisher	Date
Abhidhanappadipika:	dict. of Pali lang., ed. Moggallâna Thero + Waskaduwe Subhuti	18/-	8°	*Colombo*	65
KACCÂYANA's Grammar:	ed. w. English notes, 3 pts.	52/6	8°	*Toungoo*	70; 71
" "	tr. and arrgd. on European Models; w. vocab.	4/-	8°	"	67
" "	ed. Rev. F. Mason [Bibl. Indica]	ea. 2/-	8°	*Calcutta*	
" "	ed. E. Senart, w. French tr. and notes	12/-	8°	*Paris*	71
" "	Introduction to. By J. de Alwis	12/-	8°	Williams	64
SUBHÛTI, Waskadawe	Nâmamâla: a work on Pali grammar	16/-	8°	*Colombo*	76

Singhalese Dictionaries and Grammars.

Author	Title	Price	Size	Publisher	Date
de ALWIS, James	Introduction to Singhalese Grammar	*o.p.* [*w.* 63/-]	8°	*Colombo*	49
" Rev. C.	Singhalese Handbook [Romanized characters]	14/-	8°	"	[ ] 80
BRIDGNELL, Rev. W.	School Dictionary: Singhalese and English	*o.p.* [*w.* £5 5/-]	24°	"	47
CARTER, Chas.	New English-Sinhalese Dictionary, pt. i. [to occupy 5 pts.]	ea. 5/- p	8°	"	89 *in prog.*
CLOUGH, Rev. B.	Dictionary of Eng.-Singh. & Singh.-Eng. Langs., 2 vols.	*o.p.* [*w.* £7 7/-]	8°	"	21-30
CHOUNAVEL, C.	Grammar of the Sinhalese Language	10/-	8°	"	85
GUNASEKARA, Abraham Mendis	Sinhalese Grammar for European Students	10/-	8°	"	89
Singhalese Made Easy	[phrase-book in Roman and Singh. characters]	7/6 s	8°	"	73

Native Grammars.

Author	Title	Price	Size	Publisher	Date
Balavataro	Text, 7/6; Romanized text, Nagari text and English tr. L. Lee		8°	"	69; ?
SIDATH SANGARAWA	Grammar of Singhalese Language, tr. J. de Alwis	42/-	8°	"	52
" "	" " " tr. D. Andris	*o.p.* [*w.* 21/-]	8°	"	57

127. INDIC (*g*): PALI AND EARLY BUDDHISTIC SANSCRIT LITERATURE.

Bibliography.

Author	Title	Price	Size	Publisher	Date
de ALWIS, J.	Catal. of Sanskrit, Pali, & Singh. Liter. Wks. of Ceylon, v. i. [in 3 vols.]	8/6	8°	Trübner	70
British Museum	Catalogue of the Sanscrit and Pali Books [by Dr. Ernst Haas]	21/-	4°	British Museum	76

Texts and Translations.

Author	Title	Price	Size	Publisher	Date
Avadâna Sataka	Le Livre des Cents Légendes: études Bouddhiques, par H. L. Feer	10/-	8°	*Paris*	81-84
*Buddhist Suttas [7]	tr. T. W. Rhys-Davids [Sacred Books of East]	10/6	8°	Clar. Press	81
Dasaratha-Jâtaka	ed. w. English tr. and notes Fausböll [Buddh. story of King Rama]	3/-	8°	*Copenhagen*	71
Dâthâvansa	Hist. of Tooth-relic of Buddha, ed. w. Engl. tr. Coomara Swamy, 10/6; tr. only	6/-	8°	Trübner	74; 74
Dhammapada	ed. V. Fausböll, with Latin tr. and comment.	12/6	8°	*Copenhagen*	55
For Chin. Vers., see G § m.					
"	tr. Prf. M. Müller and Sutta Nipata, tr. V. Fausböll [Sacr. Bks. of East]	10/6	8°	Clar. Press	81
Udanavarga [Northern Version]	tr. W. W. Rockhill [Oriental Series]	9/-	8°	Trübner	83
	The *Dhammapada* tr. was originally pub. in Max MÜLLER'S *Science of Language* (v. K § 96).				
Digha	ed. Prf. T. W. Rhys-Davids			Pali Text Soc.	*in prep.*
*Dipavamsa	ed. w. English tr. Dr. H. Oldenberg [hist. of Buddha in Ceylon]	21/-	8°	Williams	79
Divyâvadâna:	early Buddhist legends, tr. Prf. E. B. Cowell + R. A. Neil	18/-	8°	Camb. Press	86
	Tr. from Nepalese Sanscrit MSS. in Cambridge and Paris.				
Iti-vuttaka	ed. Prf. E. Windisch		8°	Pali Text Soc.	90
*Jâtaka, The	ed. V. Fausböll, w. comm., vols. i.-iv. [in 5 vols.]	ea. 28/-	8°	Trübner	75-83
* "	The same, tr. T. W. Rhys-Davids, *sub tit.* Budd. Birth Stories [Orient. Ser.]	18/- p	8°	"	80
Jatakas, Five	ed. w. English tr. V. Fausböll	6/-	8°	*Copenhagen*	61
" Ten	" " "	7/6	8°	"	72
" Nine	ed. L. H. Elwell (Am.) [in transliteration, w. vocab.]	75c.	16°	*Boston*	88
Feer, H. L.	Étude sur les Jatakas	3/6	8°	*Paris*	75
Kalpa-sûtra and Nava-tatva,	tr. Rev. J. Stevenson [2 wks. ill. Jain religion]	*o.p.* [*w.* 9/-	8°	*London*	48
Lalita Vistara	—*v.* K § 124 (X).				
Mahaparinibbanasutta of	the Sutta-Pitaka, ed. R. C. Childers	5/-	8°	Trübner	78

K § 128

Mahawanso — xxxvii. chapters from, ed. Sumangala, 2 vols. [a hist. of Ceylon] 42/- 8° *Colombo* 77
" — ed. w. Engl. tr. G. Turnour, vol. i. [first 38 chaps.] *o.p.* [*w.* 25/-] 4° " 37
" — tr. E. Upham, 3 vols. [w. other tracts illustr. of Buddhism] *o.p.* [*w.* 24/-] 8° *London* 33
Milinda Panho — ed. V. Trenckner [dial. 'tween Kg. Milinda and Nagasena] 21/- 8° Williams 80
" " — Introductory Part, ed. w. English tr. V. Trenckner [Pali Miscellany, pt. i.] 4/- 8° " 80
" " — tr. T. W. Rhys-Davids, *sub tit.* Questions of King Milinda [Sacr. Bks. of East] 10/6 8° Clar. Press 90
Peta Vatthu — ed. Prf. Minayeff — Pali Text Soc. *in prep.*
Samyutt — ed. Léon Feer, vols. i.–iii. 8° " 90
Sella Lihini Sandese — ed. w. English notes and gloss. W. C. Macready 9/- 8° *Colombo* 65
Sutta Nipata [v. Dhamm. sup.] Dial. & discourses of Gotama, tr. Coomara Swamy [w. intro. & notes] 6/- c 8° Trübner 74
Suttas Palis Sept — ed. Paul Grimblot [fr. *Digha-Nikaya*; texts & French trs.] 12/- 8° *Paris* 76
Vimana-Vatthu of the Khuddhaka Nikaya Sutta Pitaka, ed. E. R. Gooneratne 8° Pali Text Soc. 86
*Vinaya Pitakam — ed. Dr. H. Oldenberg, 5 vols. ea. 21/- 8° Williams 79–82
* " " — tr. Rhys-Davids + H. Oldenberg, 3 vols. [Sacred Books of East] ea. 10/6 8° Clar. Press 81–83
i.: Pātimokkha, Mahāvagga 1–4; ii.: ditto, 5–10, Kullavagga, 1–3; iii.: ditto, 4–12. One of the principal Buddhist Scriptures.

Serial.

Journal of the Pali Text Soc. — Pali Text Soc. (Williams) ℗ *in prog.*

Manuscripts —*v.* K § 122, *s.v.* MSS.

Buddhism —*v.* A § 14. **Chinese Buddhism** —*v.* A § 10.

128. INDIC (*h*): MODERN ARYAN LANGUAGES OF INDIA AND SPECIMENS OF THEIR LITERATURES.

Collectively.

*BEAMES, John — Comparative Grammar of Modern Aryan Languages of India, 3 vols. ea. 16/- 8° Trübner 72–79
Hindi, Panjabi, Sindhi, Gujarati, Marathi, Uriya, Bengali. i.: Sounds; ii.: Noun and Pronoun; iii.: Verb.
" " — Outlines of Indian Philology 5/- c 8° " [ ] 68
BIDDULPH, Maj. J. — Tribes of the Hindoo Koosh; pl., tables and map 15/- r 8° *Calcutta* 80
Conts. grammars and vocabularies of Bushgali, Bushkarik, Chilim, Gowro, Khowar, Narisati, Shina, Torwālik, Vidghah.
CAMPBELL, Sir J. [ed.] — Specimens of the Languages of India [Bengal, Cent. Prov., E. frontier] 31/6 f° " 74
HODGSON, B. H. — Miscellaneous Essays relating to Indian Subjects, 2 vols. 28/- 8° Trübner 80
Conts. grammars, vocabularies, etc., of Bahing Dialect, Bodo, Koech and Dhimdi, Tribes, Kiranti, Nepalese, Vāyu.
POWELL, J. W. — Intro. to Study of Indian Languages: w. phrases and sentences to be collected 4° [ ] 80

Dictionary.

WILSON, Prf. H. H. — Glossary of Judicial and Revenue, *etc.*, Terms *o.p.* [*pb.* 42/6; *w.* 25/-] 4° W. H. Allen 55
Words fr. Arabic, Pers., Hindust., Sansc., Bengali, Marathi, Telugu, Tamil, *etc.*; w. index.
YULE + BURNELL, Col. H. / Dr. H. C. — Hobson-Jobson: an Anglo-Indian glossary [colloq. words and phrases] 36/- 8° Murray 86

Literature.

GRIERSON, G. A. — The Modern Vernacular Literature of Hindustan 8° *Calcutta* 89
A very good bk.; by Hindustan is meant Rajputana and the valleys of the Jumna and Ganges as far east as river Kosi: neither the Panjaub nor Lower Bengal are included. The languages dealt with are, roughly, Marwari, Hindi, Bihari, etc. w. its various dialects and sub-dialects.

Assamese —*v. also* Bengali, *infra* (*s.v.* NICHOLL).

BRONSON, M. — Dictionary in Assamese and English 42/- 8° *Sibsagor* 67
BROWN, N. — Grammatical Notices of the Assamese Language 12/6 8° " [48] 62
CUTTER, H. D. L. — Phrases in English and Assamese 5/- 8° " 77

Angāmi-Nāgā.

MCCABE, R. B. — Outline Grammar of the Angāmi Nāgā Language [w. vocab.] 8° *Calcutta* 87

Hill Tippera.

ANDERSON, J. D. — Short List of Words of the Hill Tippera Language 8° *Shillong* 85

Kachari (Bara).

ENDLE, S. — Outline Grammar of the Kachari Language [w. sentences, vocab., etc.] 8° *Shillong* 84
SOPPITT, C. A. — Short Account of the Kachcha Naga Tribe [w. gram., vocab., etc.] 8° " 85

Lhōtā Nāgā.

WITTER, W. E. — Outline Grammar of the Lhōtā Nāgā Language [w. vocab.] 8° *Calcutta* 88

Manipuri.

PRIMROSE, A. J. — Manipuri Grammar, Vocabulary and Phrase-Book 8° *Shillong* 88

Rangkhol-Lushai.

SOPPITT, C. A. — Short Account of the Kuki-Lushai Tribes [w. gram.] 8° *Shillong* 87

Shaiyâng-Miri.

NEEDHAM, J. F. — Outline Grammar of the Shalyâng Miri Language [w. vocab.] 8° *Shillong* 86

Singpho.

MACGREGOR, C. R. — Outline Singpho Grammar [w. Singpho and Khâmpti vocab.] 8° *Shillong* 88

Bengali.

Bibliography.

British Museum — Catalogue of the Bengali Books in British Museum [by J. F. Blumhardt] 10/- 4° British Museum 86

Dictionaries.

CAREY, Rev. W. — Dictionary of Bengalee Language [in two parts; abridged] 31/6 8° *Serampore* 71
HAUGHTON, Rev. G. C. — Bengali, Sanscrit and English Dictionary; w. index *o.p.* [*w.* 30/-] 4° W. H. Allen 33
SYKES, J. — English and Bengali Dictionary for the Use of Schools, ed. G. K. Mitter 7/6 8° *Calcutta* [ ] 74

Grammars, etc.

BROWNE, J. F. — Bángáli Primer [in Roman character] 2/- c 8° Trübner 81
FORBES, D. — Grammar of Bengali, 12/6; Bengali Reader, w. trs. and vocab. 12/6 r 8° W. H. Allen 62; 62
NICHOLL, G. F. — Bengali Grammar, and Assamese Grammar, 2/-; Bengali Manual 12° W. H. Allen 85; *in prep.*
YATES, Rev. W. — Intro. to Bengali Language, ed. J. Wengler, 2 vols. [gram., reader, vocab.] 15/- 8° *Calcutta* [ ] 74
" " — Bengali Grammar, ed. J. Wengler 4/- 8° " [47] 85

Bihari.

GRIERSON, G. A. — Introduction to the Maithili Lang. of N. Bihar, 2 pts. [gram., chrest., vocab.] 12/- r 8° *Calcutta* 80–82
" " — Seven Grammars of Dialects & Subdialects of Bihari Lang., pts. i.–viii. ea. 2/6 f 4° *Calcutta* 83–88 *in prog.*
" " — Handbook to the Kayathi Characters 18/- 4° " 81

Brahui

—*v.* K § 149: Dravidian Philology.

Concani.

DA CUNHA, J. G. — The Koncani Language and Literature 5/- r 8° *Bombay* 81
MAFFEI, A. F. X. — Koncani Grammar 18/- 8° *Mangalore* 82

Gaudian.

HÖRNLE, A. F. R. — Comparative Grammar of the Gaudian Language [w. spec. ref. to E. Hindi] 18/- 8° Trübner 80

Gujarati.

BHATT, Purnanand M. — Handbook of Gujarati Grammar 6/- 12° *Bombay* 89
MINOCHEHERJI, J. D. — Pahlavi, Gujarâti and English Dictionary, 5 vols. ea. 14/- 8° " 77 *sqq.*
MOOS, A. Framjee — English-Gujarati Dictionary, pts. i.–ix. ea. 7/6 4° " 80–89 *in prog.*
EDALJI, Shapurji — Dictionary: Gujarati and English 21/- c 8° " [ ] 68
" " — Grammar of the Gujarati Language 10/6 c 8° " 67

Literature.

Parahian Tells athvâ 1001 Divasni Vârtâ: tr. into Guj. by Jijibhâi Kharshedji Kâpadyâ ["1001 days," a coll. of tales] 12/6 8° *Bombay* [ ] 88
Prabodha Kâvya Dohana: ed. Bâlâbhâi Nagindâs + Harilâl Chhotâlâl [a poetical anthology] 7/6 r 8° *Ahmedabad* 88

Gurmukhi.

Literature.

Adi Granth, The: or Holy Scriptures of the Sikhs, tr. Prf. E. Trumpp [India Office Pub.] 52/6 r 8° Trübner
SINGH, Sirdar Attar — Sakhee Book, tr. [thro' Hindi] into English 15/- 8° *Lahore* 76
A description of Gooroo Gobind Singh's Religion and Doctrines.
Sikkhan de Raj di Vikhia tr. Maj. H. Court [a history of the Sikhs] 24/- 8° " 88

Gypsy

—*v.* K § 166: Gypsy Philology.

Hindi.

Dictionaries.

BATE, J. D. — Dictionary of the Hindee Language [in Devanagari characters only] 52/6 8° *Benares* 75
MATHURAPRASADA MISRA — Trilingual Dictionary: English, Urdú, Hindí 42/- 8° " 65
THOMPSON, J. T. — Dictionary of the Hindee and English 25/- i 8° *Calcutta* [46] 70

Grammars, etc.

BROWNE, J. F. — Hindi Primer [in Roman character] 2/6 c 8° Trübner 82
ETHERINGTON, Rev. W. — Student's Grammar of the Hindi Language 12/- c 8° *Benares* [70] 73
KELLOGG, Rev. S. H. — Grammar of the Hindi Language 21/- r 8° *Allahabad* 76
PINCOTT, Fred — Hindi Manual [grammar, syntax, exx., dialogues, vocab.] 6/- 12° W. H. Allen [82] 89

Chrestomathy.

GARCIN DE TASSY [ed.] — Chrestomathie Hindie et Hindouie [w. vocabulary] *o.p.* [*w.* 10/-] 8° *Paris* 49
HALL, Fitzedward [ed.] — Hindi Reader [w. vocabulary] *o.p.* [*w.* 21/-] 4° Austin, *Hertford* 70

Literature.

Mahabharata [*v.* K § 124 II.] tr. into Hindi by Krishnachandradharmadhikarin, 3 vols. 63/- 8° *Benares*
Râmâyana [*v.* K § 124 II.] in Hindi by Tulsidâs 15/- 8° *Lucknow* [ ] 88

Hindustani [Urdu].

Bibliography.

British Museum — Catalogue of the Hindustani Books in the British Museum 12/- 4° British Museum 89
GARCIN DE TASSY — La Langue et la Littérature Hindoustanies en 1871...1878 ea. 3/6 8° *Paris* 72–79
Commenced in 1851 (= literature of 1851), but *o.p.* as far as 1872.
„ „ — Les Auteurs Hindoustanies et leurs Ouvrages 2/6 8° „ 68

Dictionaries.

BLOCHMANN, H. — English and Urdu School Dictionary [Romanized] 12° *Calcutta* [ ] 77
CRAVEN, Rev. T. — Popular Dictionary in English and Hindustani [both parts] 3/6 18° Trübner [82] 88
*FALLON, S. W. — New Hindustani-English Dictionary £5 5/- r 8° *Benares* 79
* „ „ — New English-Hindustani Dictionary, 12 pts. ea. 3/- r 8° „ 80–83
„ „ — Hindustani-English Law and Commercial Dictionary 21/- 8° „ 79
„ „ — English-Hindustani Law & Commerc. Dict., ed. Lâla Fhakir Chand Vaidya 7/6 r 8° „ [ ] 88
FORBES, Dr. Duncan — Hind.-Eng. Dict. [in Pers. char.] and Engl.-Hind. Dict. [in. Eng. char.] 42/- r 8° W. H. Allen [47] 62
„ „ — Hindustani-Eng. and Eng.-Hind. Dictionary in Roman character 36/- r 8° „ [48] 57
„ „ — Smaller Hindustani Dictionary [in English character] 12/- 16° „ 76
SHAKESPEAR, J. — Hindustani-English & English-Hindustani Dictionary *o.p.* [*pb.* 105/-; *w.* 42/-] 4° Richardson [17] 49
*PLATTS, J. T. — Hindustani Dictionary: Urdu & classical Hindi [the most useful smaller work] 63/- r 8° W. H. Allen

Grammars, Manuals, etc.

DOWSON, Prf. J. — Grammar of Urdu Language, 10/6; Hindustani Exercise Book 2/6 12° Trübner [72] 87; 72
FORBES, Dr. Duncan — Gram. of Hindust. Lang. [w. specs. & vocab.; in Orient. & Rom. charact.] 10/6 8° W. H. Allen [46] 73
„ „ + PLATTS, J. T. — Hindustani Manual [gram. and vocab.; Romanised] 3/6 18° „ [45] 89
HOLROYD, Col. W. R. M. — Tas-hil ul kalam: Hindustani made easy 6/- f 8° „ [89] 89
KEMPSON, M. — The Syntax and Idioms of Hindustani [exx., w. comm., notes & vocab.] 5/6 c 8° „ 90
PALMER, Prf. E. H. — Hindustani, Persian and Arabic Grammar Simplified [Simplified Gram.] 5/- c 8° Trübner [82] 85
PLATTS, J. T. — Grammar of the Hindustani or Urdu Language 12/- 8° W. H. Allen 74
RANKING, G. S. A. — Talim-i-Zaban-i-Urdu [guide to Hindustani] 7/6 c 8° Thacker, *Calcutta* 90
SHAKESPEAR, J. — Grammar of the Hindustani Language 14/- r 8° W. H. Allen [13] 55
„ „ — Introduction to Hindustani [grammar, vocab., dialogues] *o.p.* [*pb.* 24/-; *w.* 15/-] r 8° „ 45

Chrestomathy.

BALLANTYNE, J. R. [ed.] — Hindustani Selections [w. vocabulary] 5/- r 8° W. H. Allen 45
GARCIN DE TASSY [ed.] — Chrestomathie Hindi et Hindouie *o.p.* [*w.* 10/-] 8° *Paris* 49
SHAKESPEAR, J. [ed.] — Muntakhabat-i-Hindi, 2 v. [selns. in Hind. w. Eng. trs.] *o.p.* [*pb.* 42/-; *w.* 15/-] 4° W. H. Allen [14–16] 40–44

Literature.

General History.

GARCIN DE TASSY — Histoire de la Littérature Hindouie et Hindoustanie, 3 vols. *o.p.* [*w.* 30/-] 8° *Paris* [39–47] 71–72

Texts, etc. (Hindi and Hindustani).

Araish-i-Mahfil ["Ornament of the Assembly"], tr. Court 15/- r 8° *Allahabad* 71
Based on the *Khulâsatu-t-tawârîkh*, it conts. a good histor. and topogr. account of India.
Bagh o Bahar — ed. D. Forbes: in Pers. char. 12/6: in Eng. char., w. vocab., 5/-; Eng. tr. 8/- r 8° W. H. Allen 46; 59; 51
„ „ — tr. E. B. Eastwick: with notes 10/6 8° „
„ „ — trad. Garcin de Tassy 10/- 8° *Paris* 78
Baital Pachisi ["25 tales of a Demon"] ed. w. English tr. E. B. Eastwick 15/- 8° Austin, *Hertford* 55
„ „ — ed. D. Forbes [in Nagari character] 9/- r 8° W. H. Allen 57
„ „ — tr. J. T. Platts 8/- 8° „ 6–
„ „ — übers. Hermann Oesterley 3/- 8° *Leipzig* 73
Ikhwanu-s Safa ["Brothers of Purity"] ed. D. Forbes [in Persian character] 12/6 r 8° W. H. Allen 61
„ „ — tr. Prf. J. Dowson 7/- c 8° Trübner 69
„ „ — tr. J. T. Platts 10/6 8° W. H. Allen 69
A Hindustani tr. of an Arabic original—*v.* K § 115; Arabic Literature, *s.v.* Philosophy.
Khirad Afroz ["Illuminator of Understanding"] ed. E. B. Eastwick: w. notes 18/- i 8° Austin, *Hertford* [57] 67
Lutaifi Hindee — ed. W. C. Smyth [a jest-book] 5/- 8° Trübner 40
Prem Sagar ["Ocean of Love"] tr. E. B. Eastwick 42/- 4° „ 67
Tota Kahani ["Tales of a Parrot"] ed D. Forbes [in Persian character] 8/- r 8° „ *n.d.* (52)
„ „ „ „ — tr. Rev. G. Small 8/- 8° „

Kashmiri.

ELMSLIE, W. J. — Vocabulary of the Kashmiri Language, 2 pts. 7/6 12° Trübner 72

Khasia.

PRYSE, Rev. W. Introduction to the Khasia Language [gram., selections, vocab.] 6/- 12° *Calcutta* 55

ROBERTS, Rev. H. Anglo-Khassi Dictionary 10/6 12° ,, 75

Khyeng.

FRYER, G. E. Khyeng People of Sandoway District [grammar, notes, vocab.] 4/- 8° *Calcutta* 75

Marathi.

Dictionaries.

MOLESWORTH + CANDY, J. T. + T. G. Dictionary: Mahratti-English and English-Mahratti [both parts] ea. 42/- r 4° *Bombay* [31 ; 47] 57

PADMANJI, Baba Compendium of Molesworth's Marathi and Eng. Dictionary 14/- 8° ,, [63] 89

Grammars.

BELLAIRS + ASKHEDKAR, H. S. K. + L. G. Grammar of the Marathi Language 5/- 8° *Bombay* 68

BHIDE, Ganesh Hari Marathi English Primer 3/6 8° ,, 89

NAVALKAR, G. R. Student's Marathi Grammar 18/- 8° ,, [68] 80

PANDURANG, Dadoba Grammar of the Marathi Language 4/- 8° ,, [ ] 89

STEVENSON, Rev. J. Principles of Murathee Grammar 12/- 8° ,, [43] 68

Literature.

Bhagavat Puran [K § 124 III.] in Marathi by Ecknâth [lithographed] 15/- r 8° *Poonah* 86

Kathâsârâmrita Grantha: in Marathi by Mahipati, ed. Krishna Pitre 12/6 obl *Bombay* 88

An abstract of the Padma, Vâyu, Skanda, and some other Purânas.

Râmâyana [*v.* K § 124 II.] in Marathi by Ecknâth 78/- obl ,, 88

ECKNÂTH is one of the most popular saints and poets.

TUKARAMA Complete Poems of, ed. Vishnu Parashuram Shastri, 2 vols. ea. 31/6 r 8° ,, 73

Nepali.

TURNBULL, Rev. A. Nepali Grammar: w. English-Nepali and Nepali-English vocab. 10/6 r 8° *Darjeeling* 88

Oriya.

BROWNE, J. F. Uriyâ Primer [in Roman character] 2/6 c 8° Trübner 82

HALLAM, E. C. B. Oriya Grammar for English Students 7/6 8° *Calcutta* 74

MALTBY, T. J. Practical Handbook of Uriya or Odiya Language 10/6 8° ,, 74

MILLER + MESRA, W. + R. Oriya Dictionary: with Oriya synonyms 7/6 12° *Cuttack* 68

Peguan.

HASWELL, Rev. J. M. Grammar, Notes and Vocabulary of the Peguan Language 15/- 8° *Rangoon* 74

Punjabi.

Lodiana Mission Dictionary of the Punjabi Language 63/- 4° *Lodiana* 54

,, ,, Grammar of the Punjabi Language 7/6 8° ,, [51] 66

STARKEY + SING, Cpt. + B. English Punjabee Dictionary [w. gram., dialog., etc.] *o.p.* [*w.* 28/-] 8° *Calcutta* 49

TISDALL, Rev. W. St. Clair Simplified Gram. & Reading Bk. of Punjabi, ed. Dr. R. Rost [Simpl. Grams.] 7/6 c 8° Trübner 90

Rong.

MAINWARING, G. B. Grammar of the Rong (Lepcha) Language 15/- 4° *Calcutta* 76

Santal.

PHILLIPS, J. Introduction to Sântal Language [grammar, readings, vocab.] 7/6 12° *Calcutta* 52

SKREFSRUD, Rev. L. O. Grammar of the Sântal Language 21/- 12° *Benares* 73

Sindhi.

SHIRT + MIRZA, Rev. G. + S. F. Sindhi-English Dictionary s 4° *Kurrachee* 79

STACK, Cpt. G. Dictionary: English-Sindhi, 28/-; Sindhi-English 21/- i 8° *Bombay* 49 ; 55

,, ,, Grammar of the Sindhi Language 15/- 8° ,, 49

*TRUMPP, E. Grammar of the Sindhi Language [India Off. pub.] 15/- 8° Trübner 72

Compared with the Sanscrit, Prakrit, and cognate Indian vernaculars.

,, ,, Sindhi Reading Book [in Sansk. and Arabic chart; Ind. Off. pub.] 12/6 8° ,, 58

Somali.

HUNTER, Cpt. F. M. Grammar of the Somali Language [with vocabulary] 16/- 16° *Bombay* 80

Urdu

—*v.* Hindustani, *supra.*

Uriya

—*v.* Oriya, *supra.*

Zillah.

BROWN, C. P. Zillah Dictionary [in Roman character] 12/- 8° *Madras* 52

129. IRANIC PHILOLOGY AND LITERATURE (a): GENERAL PHILOLOGY.

Grammar.

*SPIEGEL, Fr. Vergleichende Grammatik der altiranischen Sprachen 14/- 8° *Leipzig* 82

130. IRANIC (b): ZEND (OLD BACTRIAN) AND OLD PERSIAN (a) PHILOLOGY AND INSCRIPTIONS.

Generally.

BARTHOLOMAE, Dr. Chr. Arische Forschungen, pt. i. 5/-; ii. 7/-; iii. 2/6 [language of Avesta] 8° *Halle* 82; 86; 87

*HAUG, Dr. Martin Essays on the Sacr. Language, Writings, and Religion of the Parsis, ed. Dr. E. W. West [Oriental Series] 16/- 8° Trübner [62] 78

Dictionary.

HAUG, Dr. Martin [ed.] An Old Zand-Pahlavi Glossary; w. tr. 15/- 8° *Bombay*

Grammars, etc. —*for other wks. on Zend lang.*, v. K § 131, *s.v.* Aids.

BARTHOLOMAE, Dr. Chr. Handbuch der altiranischen Dialekte [grammar, selections, glossary] 6/- 8° *Leipzig* 83

GEIGER, W. Handbuch der Awesta-Sprache [grammar, selections, glossary] 12/- 4° *Erlangen* 79

de HARLEZ, C. Manuel de la Langue de l'Avesta [gram., chrestom., gloss.] 10/- 8° *Paris* [79] 82

HAUG, Dr. Martin Outline of a Grammar of Zend Language [*extr. fr. his Essays*] *o.p.* [*w.* 21/-] 8° *Bombay* 62

HOVELACQUE, A. Grammaire de la Langue Zende 8/6 8° *Paris* [69] 78

JACKSON, A. V. W. [Am.] Sketch of Avesta Grammar and Syntax *Boston* *in prep.*

JUSTI, F. Handbuch der Zend-Sprache [dict., grammar, selections] 24/- 8° *Leipsic* 64

SPIEGEL, Fr. Grammatik der Altbaktrischen Sprache 12/- 8° ,, 67

" " Grammatik der Huzvâresch-Sprache 9/- 8° *Vienna* 56

Verb.

BARTHOLOMAE, Dr. Chr. Das altiranische Verbum in Formenlehre und Syntax dargestellt 5/- 8° *Munich* 78

Prosody.

GELDNER, K. Ueber die Metrik d. jüngeren Avesta 5/- 8° *Tübingen* 77

Old Persian Inscriptions: (*Cuneiform*).

BENFEY, Theod. Persische Keilinschriften [w. trs. and glossary] 3/6 8° *Leipzig* 47

KOSSOWICZ, C. [ed.] Inscriptiones Palaeo-Persicae Achaemenidarum; ill. 54/- 8° *St. Petersburg* 73

SPIEGEL, Fr. [ed.] Die alt-persischen Keilinschriften [w. Germ. gram., gloss., and tr.] 9/- 8° *Leipzig* [62] 81

131. IRANIC (c): ZEND LITERATURE.

Zend Avesta.

Text ed. w. gloss. and index Dr. H. Brockhaus *o.p.* [*w.* 15/-] 4° *Leipzig* 50

ed. K. F. Geldner, pts. i.-v., ea. 8/-; vi. 12/-; Eng. Edn., pts. i.-v. ea. 12/6, vi. 18/- 4° *Stuttgart* 85-89; 90

ed. w. Huzvâresch tr. Dr. F. Spiegel, vols. i.-ii., pt. i. 42/- 8° *Leipzig* 51; 58

ed. N. L. Westergaard, vol. i. [text] 28/6 4° *Copenhagen* 52-54

Gâthâs, of Zoroaster ed. w. English tr. Dr. L. H. Mills [w. Pahl., Sansc., & Pers. comms.] *in prep.*

" " Fünf. ed. Dr. Martin Haug, w. German tr. & notes, 2 pts. [songs & proverbs of Zoroaster] 12/- 8° *Leipzig* 58; 60

Selection Decem Sendavestae Excerpta, ed. w. Lat. tr. and notes C. Kossowicz 9/- 8° *Paris* 65

" Avesta Texts for Easy Reading, ed. A. V. W. Jackson [Am.] [w. notes and vocab.] *Boston* *in prep.*

English Translation tr. J. Darmesteter + Dr. L. H. Mills, 3 pts. [Sacred Books of East] i.-ii. ea. 10/6; iii. 12/6 8° Clar. Press 80; 85; 87

i.: Vendîdâd (DARMESTETER); ii.: Sîrôzahs, Yasts and Nyâyis (DARMESTETER); iii.: Yasna, Visparad, Âfrînagân, Gâhs, and miscell. fragments (MILLS).

tr. A. H. Bleeck, 3 v. in 1 [tr. viâ Spiegel's Germ. version, *ut inf.*] *o.p.* [*pb.* & *w.* 25/-] 8° Austin, *Hertford* 64

French Translation trad. C. de Harlez; pl. 17/- 8° *Paris* [ ] 81

German Translation übers. Dr. F. Spiegel, *s.v.* Die Heiligen Schriften d. Parsen, 3 v. 20/6 8° *Leipzig* 52-63

AIDS —*v. also* A § 15: Parsism.

BURNOUF, E. Études sur la Langue et sur les Textes Zends, vol. i. *o.p.* [*w.* 35/-] 8° *Paris* 40-50

DARMESTETER, Prf. J. Ormuzd et Ahriman: origines et histoire [comparative treatment] 12/- 8° ,, 77

" " Études Iraniennes, 2 vols. 35/- 8° ,, 83

" " Haurvatât et Ameretât: essai sur la myth. de l'Aveste, 4/-; Eng. tr. of same 5/- 8° ,, 75; *Bombay* 88

v. DILLON, J. E. The Home and Age of the Avesta, tr. T. A. Walsh 3/- 8° *Bombay* 88

*HAUG, Dr. Martin —*in his* Essays, *ut* K § 130.

de HARLEZ, C. De l'Exégèse et de la Correction des Textes Avestiques 6/6 8° *Leipzig* 83

HOVELACQUE, Abel L'Avesta, Zoroastre et le Mazdéisme 8/6 8° *Paris* 80

" " Le Chien dans l'Avesta: les soins qui lui sont dus 2/6 8° ,, 75

SPIEGEL, Dr. Fr. Commentar über das Avesta, 2 vols. 27/- 8° *Leipzig* 64; 66

" " Einleitung in die traditionelle Literatur der Parsen, vol. ii. 14/- 8° ,, 60

Vol. i. is a Grammar of the Huzvâresch lang.; vol. ii. a hist. of Parsee literature in rel. to those of neighbouring peoples.

WHITNEY, Prf. W. D. [Am.] On the Avesta—*in* Journal of Amer. Orient Soc. 1856.

132. IRANIC (*d*): MIDDLE PERSIAN PHILOLOGY AND LITERATURE.

Pahlavi.

Dictionaries.

HAUG, Dr. Martin [ed.] An Old Pahlavi-Pazand Glossary; w. tr., ed. Asa [15 cent.] 28/- 8° *Bombay* [67] 70
MINOCHEHERJI, J. D. Pahlavi, Gujarâti, and English Dictionary, 5 vols. ea. 14/- 8° „ *in prog.*
WEST + HAUG, Dr. E. W. / Dr. M. Glossary and Index of Pahlavi Texts of Book of Arda Viraf, Gosht-i-Fryano, Hadokht Nask, and extr. fr. Dinkard and Nirangistan 25/- 8° „ 74

Grammars, etc.

BEHRAMJEE, Pahlavi Grammar [in Gujarati] 24/- 8° *Bombay* 71
de HARLEZ, Prf. C. Manuel du Pehlevi [grammar, anthol., gloss.] 8/6 8° *Paris* 80
HAUG, Dr. Martin Essay on Pahlavi Lang. [extr. fr. his *Old Pahlavi Glos. ut sup.*] 3/6 8° *Stuttgart* 70
SUNJANA, P. D. B. Grammar of the Pehlwi Language [in Gujarati] 25/- 8° *Bombay* 71

Literature.

Arda Viraf, Book of ed. w. English tr. and intro. Drs. Martin Haug + E. W. West 26/- 8° *Munich* 72
„ „ French tr. by A. Barthélemy [Bibliothèque Elzevirienne] 4/6 12° *Paris* 87
Bundahis ed. F. Justi [transcrip., gloss. and German tr.] 42/- 4° *Leipzig* 68
Dinkard, The ed. w. trs. in Gujarati & Engl., ed. Peshotan Behramjee Sanjana, 5 vols. 70/- 8° *Bombay* 74-88 *in prog.*
Ganjeshayagan Andarze Atrepat Maraspandan Madigane Chatrang, *etc.* [orig. text] 20/- 8° *Bombay* 84
Mainyo-i-Khard, Bk. of w. old fragm. of Bundehesh: facs. of a Pahlavi MS. fr. Pers., ed. F. C. Andreas 20/- 8° *Kiel* 87
„ „ Sanskrit and Pazand texts, w. Eng. tr., ed. Dr. E. W. West 15/- r 8° *Stuttgart* 71
Pahlavi Texts* tr. Dr. E. W. West, pts. i.-iii. [Sacred Books of East] 35/6 8° Clar. Press 80; 82; 83

* i.: Bundahis, Bahman Yast, Shâyast lâ-shâyast, 10/6; ii.: Dâdistân-i Dînîk and Epp. of Mânûshîhar, 12/6; iii.: Dînâ-i Mainôg-i Khirad, Sikand-gûmânîk, Sad-dar, 10/6.

Vendidad Sade trad. en lang. Huzvaresch [Pahlavi], ed J. Thonnelier, pts. i.-ix. [16 pts. in all] ea. 17/- f° *Paris* 55-62

Parsi (Pazand).

Grammar.

SPIEGEL, Fr. Grammatik der Parsi-Sprache 7/- 8° *Leipzig* 51

Literature.

Shikand-Gûmânik Vijâr ed. w. intro. and vocab. H. D. J. Jamasp-Asânâ + Dr. E. W. West 21/- 8° *Bombay* 87

133. IRANIC (*e*): MODERN PERSIAN PHILOLOGY.

Manuscripts.

British Museum Catalogue of the Persian MSS. in Brit. Mus., v. i.-iii. [by Dr. C. Rieu] ea. 25/- 4° Brit. Mus. 79; 81; 83
Bodleian Library, Oxon. Catal. of Pers., Turk., Pushtoetc. MSS. pt. i. [Pers.] [by Drs. E. Sachau + H. Ethé] 63/- 4° Clar. Press 90

Dictionaries.

PALMER, Prf. E. H. Concise Dictionary of Persian Language [Persian-English] 10/6 r 8° Trübner [76] 83
„ „ English-Persian Dictionary 10/6 sq 16° „ 83
VULLERS, J. A. Lexicon Persico-Latinum Etymologicum, 2 vols. 84/-; Suppl. 7/- 4° *Bonn* 55-64; 67
WOLLASTON, A. N. English-Persian Dictionary 25/- 8° W. H. Allen 82
„ „ Complete English-Persian Dictionary 94/6 r 4° „ 89
ZENKER, Dr. J. H. Dictionnaire Turc-Arabe-Persian, 2 vols. £5 4° *Leipzig* 65-76

Grammars, etc.

CHODZKO, A. Grammaire de la Langue Persane [Arab. and Rom. char.] 9/- 8° *Paris* [ ] 83
CLARKE, Cpt. H. W. Persian Manual [grammar, phrases, dialogues, and vocabulary] 7/6 18° W. H. Allen 78
FORBES, Dr. D. Grammar of Persian Language [w. readings, trs., and vocab.] 12/6 r 8° „ 76
GUYARD, Stanislas Manuel de la Langue Persane Vulgaire [w. vocab. in Fch., Engl. and Pers.] 4/6 12° *Paris* 80
PALMER, Prf. E. H. Hindust., Pers., and Arabic Gram. Simplified [Simplif. Grams.] 5/- c 8° Trübner [82] 85
SALEMANN + SHUKOVSKI, C. / V. Persische Grammatik [w. parad., chrest., and gloss.; Porta Ling. Gr.] 8° *Berlin* 89
VULLERS, J. A. Grammatica Linguae Persicae comparativa 8/- 8° *Giessen* 70
„ „ The same; pt. ii. [Syntax and Prosody] 6/- 8° „ 50
WAHRMUND, A. Praktisches Handbuch der neupersischen Sprache [w. Key] 14/- 8° „ [75] 89

Prosody.

BLOCHMANN, Prf. H. The Prosody of the Persians [*v. also* Vullers, *ut sup.*] 10/6 8° *Calcutta*

Chrestomathies.

BARB, H. A. [ed.] Persische Chrestomathie, 3 pts. 12/6 8° *Vienna* 64
GRÜNERT, Dr. M. [ed.] Neupersische Chrestomathie, pt. i. [texts], pt. ii. [vocab.] *together* 16/- 8° *Prague* 87
PIZZI, J. [ed.] Chrestomathie Persane [w. brief gram. and dict.] 7/6 r 8° *Turin* 89
SCHEFER, Ch. [ed.] Chrestomathie Persane, 2 vols. [École d. Langs. Orient. Vivantes] 25/- 8° *Paris* 82
SPIEGEL, Fr. [ed.] Chrestomathia Persica Glossario explanavit 7/- 8° *Leipzig* 46
VULLERS, J. A. [ed.] Chrestomathia Schahnamiana: w. Latin notes and glossary 7/- 8° *Bonn* 33

134. IRANIC (*f*): PERSIAN LITERATURE.

History of Literature.

Author	Title	Note	Price	Size	Publisher	Date
ARBUTHNOT, F. F.	Persian Portraits	[chiefly on Pers. poets, poetry and tales]	5/-	c 8°	Quaritch	89
BACHER, W.	Memoir of the Life and Writings of Nizami [tr.]		1/6	18°	Williams	73
DARMESTETER, Prf. James	Origines de la Poésie Persane	[Bibl. Elzevirienne]	2/6	12°	*Paris*	87
Encyclopædia Britannica	—*article* Persian Literature, *in* vol. xviii.		30/-	4°	Black	84
ETHÉ, Dr. H.	Das höfische und romantische Poesie der Perser	[48 pp.]	1/-	8°	*Hamburg*	87
" "	Die mystische und didaktische Poesie der Perser	[52 pp.]	1/-	8°	"	88
LEES, W. Nassau	Biographical Sketch of the mystic philosopher and poet Jami		1/-	8°	*Calcutta*	59
OUSELEY, G.	Biographical Notes of Persian Poets			8°		46
PIZZI, Italo	L'Epopea Persiana e la vita dei tempi eroici di Persia		4/6	8°	*Florence*	88
RÜCKERT, Friedrich	Grammatik, Poetik und Rhetorik d. Perser, hrsg. w. Pertsch		21/-	8°	*Gotha*	[ ] 74

Texts and Translations.

Anvari Soheili ["Fables of Pilpay" (Bidpai)]—*for Syriac version*, *v.* K § 112; *for Hebrew*, K § 118, *s.vv.* Kalilag.

Author	Title	Note	Price	Size	Publisher	Date
" "	ed. Sir W. Ouseley		*o.p.* [*w.* 30/-]	4°	Austin, *Hertford*	51
" "	ed. H. G. Keene	[w. English tr.]	*o.p.* [*w.* 10/-]	8°	" "	35
" "	tr. E. B. Eastwick		*o.p.* [*w.* 25/-]	r 8°	" "	54
* " "	tr. A. N. Wollaston		42/-	r 8°	W. H. Allen	76
Bakhtyar Nama	tr. G. Ouseley, ed. W. A. Clouston	[Sindibad Series]	7/6	c 8°	*priv.prin.*, *Glasgow*	83
FARID-UDDIN ATTAR	Mantic Uttair, ed. Garcin de Tassy, 10/-; Frch. tr. by same		10/-	8°	*Paris*	57; 63
FERDUSI's Shah-Nameh	ed. J. A. Vullers + S. Landauer, vols. i.-iii.	[to occupy 4 vols.]	70/-	8°	*Leyden*	76-83
["Livre des Rois"]	text w. French tr. J. Mohl, vols. i.-vii. £25; f° French tr. only, 7 vols.		42/-	12°	*Paris*	38-68; 78
	tr. and abridged J. Atkinson	[prose and verse; Chandos Lib.]	2/-	p 8°	Warne [*O. T. F.* 32]	86
["Book of Kings"]	English tr. Helen Zimmern	[through French tr.]	5/-	c 8°	Unwin	[82] 86
["Heldensagen"]	German tr. A. F. v. Schack	[a free tr.]	7/6	r 8°	*Berlin*	[53] 65
["Königsbuch"]	" tr. Friedrich Rückert, hrsg. Bayer, pt. i.		8/-	8°	"	[ ] 90
HAFIZ of Shiraz						
Poems:	ed. H. Brockhaus [Turkish], w. comment of Sudi, 3 vols.		93/-	4°	*Leipzig*	54-63
Diwan:	ed. Rosenzweig-Schwanau; w. German tr. and notes, 3 vols.		56/-	r 8°	*Vienna*	58-64
Selections	from the Poems of Hafiz, tr. H. Bicknell; ill.		42/-	4°	Trübner	75
Twelve Odes of Hafiz:	tr. Rev. W. H. Lowe; w. Sudis commentary				Camb. Press	77
Century of Ghazels:	tr. S. R[obinson]	[100 odes fr. Diwan, excellently rendered]	2/-	18°	Williams	75
JAMI						
Allegorische Gedichte, ed. Rosenzweig-Schwanau, w. German trs., 2 vols.			18/-	4°	*Vienna*	40
Beharistan ["Abode of Spring"], ed. Schlechta-Wssehrd, w. German tr.			12/-	8°	"	46
"	tr.		[*w.* 21/-]	c 8°	Kama Shastra Soc.	87
" [6th bk.]	tr. C. E. Wilson, *sub tit.* Persian Wit and Humour		4/-	c 8°	Chatto	83
Tuhfat-ul-Ahrar	ed. F. Falconer	[w. German tr.]	16/-	f°	*Vienna*	24
Yusuf and Zulaikha	ed. V. v. Rosenberg		7/6	4°	Williams	48
" "	tr. R. T. H. Griffith	[verse; Oriental Ser.]	8/6	8°	Trübner	82
" "	Specimens of, tr. S. R[obinson]	[w. analyses]	1/6	18°	Williams	73
Masnavi, The	tr. J. W. Redhouse	[Bk. i. only; prose and verse; Oriental Series]	21/-	8°	Trübner	81
"	abridgment of the entire work by the Rev. E. H. Whinfield [Oriental Ser.]		7/6	8°	"	87

The *Masnavi* is one of the great authorities on the doctrine of the Sufis.

Author	Title	Note	Price	Size	Publisher	Date
MENOUTCHEHRI [11 cent.]	Text, French tr., notes and intro. A. de Biberstein Kazimirski		25/-	8°	*Paris*	87
NAWAZ KHAN	Maasir-ul-umara, ed. Abdur Rahim, vol. i., pts. 1-4	[Bibl. Indica]	ea. 2/-	8°	*Calcutta*	87 *in prog.*
OMAR KHÁYYAM [11 cent.]	ed. J. B. Nicolas: w. French tr.		12/6	8°	*Paris*	67
*Rubaiyat:	tr. Edward Fitzgerald: w. 53 ill. Elihu Vedder [Am.]		*o.p.* [*w.* 126/-]	4°	*Boston* (Quaritch)	[58] 84
"	" " 53 ill.; reduced edition		42/-	4°	" "	[58] 86
"	tr. Justin H. McCarthy	[prose; prtd. in capital letters thro'out]	15/-	16°	Nutt	89
"	übers. Friedr. Bodenstedt		5/6	s 8°	*Stuttgart*	[ ] 90
Quatrains of, ed. E. H. Whinfield; w. [verse] tr. 10/6; Tr. only			5/-	c 8°	Trübner	[81] 83
SADI of Shiraz						
Bostan:	ed. C. H. Graf, w. Persian commentary		25/-	4°	*Vienna*	58
"	German tr. by the same, 2 vols.		3/6	12°	"	50
"	English tr. by Cpt. H. W. Clarke	[prose]	30/-	8°	W. H. Allen	
"	" " Ziauddin Gulam Moheiddin Munshi, ed. R. Davies		7/6	r 12°	*Bombay*	[ ] 89
" [chap. 3]	tr. Sir Edwin Arnold, *sub tit.* With Sa'di in the Garden		7/6	c 8°	Trübner	88
Gulistan:	ed. F. Johnson	[w. vocabulary]	15/-	r 8°	Williams	63
"	ed. John Platts	["]	12/6	r 8°	W. H. Allen	71
"	ed. E. H. Whinfield, w. tr. and notes		10/6	4°	Trübner	80
"	tr. E. B. Eastwick	[prose and verse]	10/6	8°	"	[52] 80
"	tr. James Ross; w. an essay	[Camelot Series]	1/-	16°	Walter Scott	90
"	Complete Analyses of Same, by Major F. P. Anderson		40/-	r 8°	*Calcutta*	61
R[OBINSON], S.	Flowers from the Gulistan and Bostan	[tr. selections]	1/6	18°	Williams	76
SHARFUDDIN ALI YAZDI	Zafarnamah, ed. Muhammad Ilahdad, vol. i., 9 pts. and v. ii. pts. 1-3 [Bibl. Indica]		ea. 2/-	8°	*Calcutta*	?-87 *in prog.*

Sikandar Nama e Bara ["Book of Alexander"] tr. Cpt. H. W. Clarke [prose] 42/- r 8° W. H. Allen
Sindibád, Book of [The Seven Sages]
CASSEL, Paulus Mischle Sindbad, Secundus-Syntipas [w. Intro. on the bk. of the *Seven Wise Masters*] 10/- 8° *Guben* [ ] 90
CLOUSTON, W. A. [tr.] The Book of Sindibád, tr. fr. the Persian and Arabic 12/6 8° *priv. prin., Glasgow* 84
COMPARETTI, D. Researches respecting the Book of Sindibad 15/- 8° Folklore Soc. 82
COMPARETTI is based on Syriac, Hebr., Pers., and Arab. texts; an O. Span. version is added. It is the better for textual, CLOUSTON for comparative study.

Cyclopædias.

Farhang Djahangiri: Persian Dictionary of History and Literature, 2 vols. [in Persian] 12/- r 8° *Lucknow* 76
" Endjumen " " " " ["] £6 6/- f° *Lahore* 71

Translated Selections.

CLOUSTON, W. A. [tr. & ed.] Flowers from a Persian Garden 6/- 8° Nutt 90
Tr. extracts fr. SADI'S *Gulistan*, w. notes; essays on the *Tuti Námeh*, the love-story of *Majnun and Layla* [Arabic], Rabbinical legends of the Talmud, etc.
" " A Group of Eastern Stories from the Persian, Tamil and Urdu 10/6 8° *priv. prin., Glasg.* 89
The Pers. contents are *Hist. of Nasser*, *Hist. of Farrukhrus*, and other shorter stories from the *Mahbúb ul Kulúb*, and a tr. of the Urdu vers. of *The Rose of Bakáwali*, originally a Persian romance.
CHODZKO, A. [tr.] Théâtre Persan [Fch. trs. of selected dramas] 4/6 12° *Paris* 78
COSTELLO, Louis S. [tr.] Rose Garden of Persia; col. ill. fr. Pers. MSS., etc. [trs. specimen], 16/-; *red. to* 7/6 8° Bell (Slark) 87
FITZGERALD, Edward —*in his* Works [*ut* K § 89].
PALMER, Prf. E. H. [tr.] Song of the Reed, and other Pieces, translated 5/- c 8° Trübner 76
Translations from Hafiz, Omar Khayyam, and other Persian and Arabian Poets.
ROBINSON, S. [tr.] Persian Poetry for English Readers *Glasgow* 83

135. IRANIC (*g*): BALOCHI PHILOLOGY.

Grammars.

DAMES, M. L. Sketch of North Balochi Language [w. gram., vocab., and specs.] 8/- 8° *Calcutta* 81
GLADSTONE, C. E. Biluchi Handbook [grammar, vocab., and conversations] 21/- f° *Lahore* 74

Mekranee Dialect.

MARSTON, E. W. Grammar and Vocabulary of the Mekranee Dialect 7/6 8° *Bombay* 77
MOCKLER, Maj. E. Grammar of Baloochee Language as spoken in Makran 5/- f° Paul 77
PIERCE, E. Description [= Grammar & Vocabulary] of Mekranee Dialect—*in Jl. Bombay Branch R.A.S.*, No. 31 10/6 8° *Bombay* 75

136. IRANIC (*h*): PUSHTO (AFGHAN) PHILOLOGY AND LITERATURE.

Dictionaries.

BELLEW, H. W. Dictionary of Pukkhto Language [both parts] 42/- r 8° Williams 47
*RAVERTY, Cpt. [Maj.] H. G. Dictionary of Pukhto Pushto; with remarks on the language [Pukhto-Eng.] 70/- 4° " 60

Grammars, etc.

BELLEW, H. W. Grammar of the Pukkhto Language 21/- r 8° Williams 67
DORN, B. Ueber das Puschtu 21/- 4° *St. Petersburg* 45
HENRY, Prf. Victor Études Afghanes 4/6 8° *Paris* 82
RAVERTY, Cpt. [Maj.] H. G. Grammar of the Pukhto Pushto [w. selections] 17/6 4° " [55] 69
" " The Pushto Manual [grammar, exercises, dialogues, vocab.] 5/- f 8° W. H. Allen [80] 90
*TRUMPP, Dr. Ernest Grammar of the Pasto, compared with Iranian, etc. 21/- 8° Trübner 73

Chrestomathy.

DORN, B. [ed.] Chrestomathy of the Pushtoo Language [w. Afghan and English Glossary] 21/- 4° *St. Petersburg* 47

Literature.

Collections: Texts and Translations.

DARMESTETER, Prf. J. [ed. & tr.] Collection of Afghan Songs, w. French tr., notes & gloss., ser. I.-II. ea. 16/- 8° *Paris* 89; 90
RAVERTY, Cpt. [Maj.] H. G. [tr.] Selections from the Poetry of the Afghans [translations] 16/- c 8° Williams 62
" " [ed.] The Gulshan-i-Roe: prose and poetical selections 35/- 4° " 60

Individual Pieces.

Kalid-i-Afghani tr. Cpt. T. C. Plowden, w. English notes 50/- s 4° *Lahore* 75

Brahui —*v.* K § 149: Dravidian Philology, *s.v.* Brahui.

137. IRANIC (i): KURDIC PHILOLOGY.

Dictionary.

JABA, A. Dictionnaire Kurde-Français, ed. F. Justi 6/6 8° *St. Petersburg* 79

Grammar.

JUSTI, F. Kurdische Grammatik 4/- 8° *St. Petersburg* 80

Miscellaneous Works.

JABA, A. Recueil de Notices et Recits Kourdes serv. à la connaiss. de la langue 3/- 8° *St. Petersburg* 60
JUSTI, F. Les Noms des Animaux en Kurde [w. Iranic synonyms] 4/6 8° *Paris* 78

Literature

—*for some specimens of* Folk-tales & Folk-songs, *v.* B § 27*

138. IRANIC (k): OSSETIC PHILOLOGY.

Grammars, etc.

SJÖGREN, A. J. Ossetische Sprachlehre [w. Osset.-Germ. and Germ.-Osset. vocab.] 9/- 4° *St. Petersburg* 44
" " Ossetische Studien [w. spec. refer. to Indo-Europ. langs.] 3/6 s 8° " 48

Etymology and Phonology.

HÜBSCHMANN, H. Etymologie und Lautlehre der ossetischen Sprache [Samml. Indog. Wtb.] 4/- 8° *Strassburg* 87

Syntax.

v. STACKELBERG, R. Beiträge zur Syntax des Ossetischen 1/- 8° *Strassburg* 86

139. IRANIC (l): ARMENIAN PHILOLOGY.

Bibliography.

HÜBSCHMANN, H. —*v. his* Report, *in the* Transactions of the Philological Society, 1877 8° Trübner 87

Dictionaries.

ANANIAN, Rev. F. J. B. Dictionary of the Modern Armenian Language. ed. E. Hürmüz 9/- 8° *Venice* [ ] 69
AUCHER + BRAND, Rev. P. P. + J. Dictionary: English and Armenian 21/- c 8° " 68
AWKER, Rev. F. J. B. English-Armenian Dictionary [Classical Armenian-Modern Armenian] 10/6 12° " [1-] 64
BEDROSSIAN, Rev. F. M. English-Armenian Dictionary, 20/-; Armen.-Eng. Dictionary 21/- c 8° " [ ] 68; 75-79
GOILAW, A. Deutsch-Armenisches Wörterbuch, pts. i.-ii. ea. 3/- 8° *Vienna* 87 *in prog.*

Etymology.

BUGGE, Sophus Beiträge zur etymolog. Erläuterung d. armen. Sprache 1/6 8° *Christiania* 89

Grammars, etc.

de LAGARDE, P. Armenische Studien [*repr. fr.* Abh. d. Gött. Ges. d. Wiss.] 8/- 4° *Göttingen* 77
LAUER, M. Grammatik der classischen armenischen Sprache, 2/6, Fch. tr. Prf. A. Carrière 6/6 8° *Vienna* 69; *Paris* 83
PETERMANN, J. H. Brevis Linguae Armenicae gramm., liter., chrestom. [w. glossary] 4/- 12° *Berlin* [41] 72

Etymology.

HÜBSCHMANN, H. Armenische Studien, pt. i. [elem. of Armen. etymol.] [Indogerm. Gram.] 3/- 8° *Leipzig* 83

Chrestomathies

—*in* Petermann, *ut supra, is a short chrestomathy.*

LAUER, M. [ed.] Armenische Chrestomathie [Classical Armenian] 6/- 8° *Vienna* 81

Literature.

History.

NEUMANN, C. F. Geschichte der armenischen Literatur *o.p.* [w. 7/6] 8° *Leipzig* 36

Text.

JEANVI (Jean le Catholicos) Histoire d'Arménie, trad. F. Lajard 6/6 8° *Paris* 41

Lycian, Phrygian and other languages of Asia Minor—*v.* K § 184, *s.v.* Inscriptions.

XVIII. Non-Aryan and Non-Semitic Philology (European and Asiatic).

140. BASQUE PHILOLOGY.

Bibliography.

VINSON, Prf. Julien — Bibliographie Basque ; facs. [to be pub. Oct. 1890] r 8° *Chalon sur Saône, in prep.*

History of the Basque Language.

BLADÉ, J. F. — Études sur l'Origine des Basques 8/6 8° *Paris* 69
BONAPARTE, Prince L. L. — Langue Basque et Langues Finnoises 21/- 4° *London* 62
ELLIS, Dr. Robert — Sources of the Etruscan and Basque Languages 7/6 8° Trübner 86
Seeks to connect Basque with the Caucasian Languages.
GRIMM, A. — Ueber die baskische Sprache und Sprachforschung 2/- 8° *Breslau* 84
HANNEMANN, K. — Prolegomena zur baskischen Sprache 2/- 8° *Leipzig* 84
RIBARY, F. — Essai sur la Langue Basque [tr. fr. Hungarian] 4/6 8° *Paris* 77
VINSON, J. [ed.] — Documents pour Servir à l'Histoire de la Lang. Basque *o.p.* [*w.* 18/-] 8° *Bayonne* 74

Dictionaries.

CHAHO, O. — Dictionnaire Basque, Franç., Espan., Latin, pts. 1–54 [A–La] 36/- 4° *Bayonne* 67–68
van EYS, W. J. — Dictionnaire Basque-Français 20/- 8° *Paris* 73
FABRE, L. M. — Dictionnaire Français-Basque 16/- r 8° *Bayonne* 69
de LARRAMENDI, P. — Diccionario Trilingue : Castell., Bascu. y Lat., ed. Zuazua, 2 vols. [*w.* 56/-] r 4° *San Sebastian* [1745] 53
NOVIA de SALCEDO, Pedro — Diccionario etimológico del idioma vascongado, vols. i.–ii. ea. 1 y 1,25 pes. 4° *Toulouse* 87 ; 88

Grammars.

van EYS, W. J. — Outlines of Basque Grammar [Simplified Grammars] 3/6 c 8° Trübner 83
" " — Grammaire comparée des Dialectes Basques 12/6 8° *Paris* 79
" " — Essai de Grammaire de la Langue Basque 7/6 8° *Amsterdam* 67

Verb.

van EYS, W. J. — Le Verbe Auxiliare Basque 3/6 8° *Paris* 74
" " — Études sur la Formation des Verbes Auxiliares Basques 4/6 8° " 75

Dialogues.

Dialogues Basques : Guipuscoans, Biscaiens, Labourdins, Souletins [251 copies only printed] *w.* 25/- 8° *priv. pr.* (Pce. Bonaparte) 57
FABRE, H. L. — Guide de la Conversation Français-Basque 3/- 12° *Bayonne* 62

Literature

—*for* Folk-Literature, *v.* B § 38: Basque Folklore.

141. URAL-ALTAIC PHILOLOGY (*a*): GENERALLY AND LAPPONIC, FINNISH & ESTHONIAN.

Generally.

CASTREN, A. — —*in his* Ethnographische Vorlesungen über d. altaischen Völker 7/- r 8° *St. Petersburg* 57
SCHOTT, W. — Altajische Studien, 5 pts. 10/- 4° *Berlin* 60–72
" " — Ueber das altaische oder finnisch-tartarische Sprachengeschlecht 5/- 4° " 49
de ÚJFALVY, C. E. — Mélanges Altaïques [ethnographical & linguistic] 4/6 8° *Paris* 74
WINKLER, H. — Das Uralaltaische und seine Gruppen, pts. i.–ii. 4/- 8° *Berlin* 85

Lapponic.

Dictionary.

FRIIS, J. A. — Lexicon Lapponicum [w. Lat. and Dan. explans.] 20/- 4° *Christiana* 85–87

Grammar.

FRIIS, J. A. — Formenlehre d. lappischen Sprache [*repr. fr. his* Lex. Lappon., *ut sup.*] 2/- 4° *Christiana* 87

Finnish.

Ethnology, Generally.

AHLQUIST, A. — Die Culturvölker der westfinnischen Sprachen 9/- 8° *Helsingfors* 75

Dictionaries.

AHLMAN, F. — Svenskt-Finskt Lexicon 16/- 8° *Helsingfors* 72
GODENHJELM, B. F. — Saksalais-Suomalainen Sanakirja [a German-Finnish dict.] 16/- 8° " 73
LÖNNROT, Elias — Finskt-Svenskt Lexicon, 14 pts. £4 8° " 74–80
MEURMANN, A. — Dictionnaire Français-Finnois 12/- 8° " 77

K §§ 142-143

Grammars.

KELLGREN, H. Die finnische Sprache und der ural-altaische Sprachstamm 14/- 8° *Berlin* 47
KOCHSTRÖM, V. R. Grammatik der finnischen Sprache 3/- 12° *Helsingfors* 76
de UJFALVY + HERTZBERG, C.E./K. Gramm. Finnoise d'après les Principes d'Euren et de S. Budenz 5/6 8° *Paris* 76

Phonetics.

de UJFALVY, C. E. Phonétique Finnoise 4/6 8° *Paris* 75

Chrestomathy.

TENGSTRÖM, R. [ed.] Finsk Anthologie, vol. i. 4/- 8° *Helsingfors* 45

Esthonian.

Dictionaries.

KÖRBER, K. Esthnisch-Deutsches und Deutsch-Esthnisches Handwörterbuch 6/- 8° *Dorpat* 66
WIEDEMANN, F. J. Esthisch-Deutsches Wörterbuch 24/- 1 4° *St. Petersburg* 69

Grammar.

WIEDEMANN, F. J. Grammatik d. esthnischen Sprache Mittelesthlands 8/- 8° *St. Petersburg* 75

Chrestomathy.

JAKOBSON, C. R. [ed.] Kooli lugemise raamat, 2 vols. [an Esthonian reading-bk.] 6/- r 8° *Tartus* 75

Folk-Literature —*v.* B § 33: Finnish and Finnish-Tatar Folklore.

142. URAL-ALTAIC (*b*): MAGYAR (HUNGARIAN) PHILOLOGY AND LITERATURE.

Dictionaries.

BIZONFY, F. English-Hungar. Dictionary, 8/-; Hungar.-Eng. Dictionary 16/- 8° *Pesth* 78; 86
CZUCZOR + FONGARASI, G./T. A Magyar nyelv Szotara, 6 vols. [dictionary of Hung. Acad.] 60/- r 8° „ 62-74
FONGARASI, T. Wörterbuch der Deutsch. und Hungarisch Sprache, 2 vols. 17/- 8° „ 70
MÁRTOUFFY, F. Dictionnaire d. Langues Franç. et Hongr., vol. i.: Fr.-Hong. 9/- 8° „ 79
PODHORSZKY, L. Etymol. Wörterbuch d. Magyarischen Sprache [fr. Chinese roots] 10/- 8° *Paris* 77
SZARVAS + SIMONYI, [eds.] Historisches Wörterbuch der ungarischen Sprache, pt. i. 2/- 8° *Pesth* 88 *in prog.*

Grammars.

BALLAGI, M. Grammatik der ungarischen Sprache, ed. J. Jonas 5/- 8° *Pesth* [7-] 81
CSINK, Practical Grammar of the Hungarian Lang. [w. selections] 5/- 8° Williams 53
v. NEY, Franz Anleitung zur Erlernung der ungarischen Sprache [Ollendorff method] 4/- 8° *Pesth* [ ] 88
SINGER, Ignatius Grammar of Hungarian Language Simplified [Simplified Grammars] 4/6 c 8° Trübner 82
de UJFALVY, C. E. Éléments de Grammaire Magyare 5/- 8° *Paris* 76

History of Literature—*for some* Specimens of Folk-Literature, *v.* B § 31.

SCHWICKER, J. H. Geschichte der ungarischen Literatur 15/- 8° *Leipzig* 89

Serial.

Ungarische Revue hrsg. P. Hunfalvy + G. Heinrich [10 pts. yearly] *ann.* 10/- 8° *Pesth* 80 *sqq. in prog.*

143. URAL-ALTAIC (*c*): FINNISH-UGRIAN PHILOLOGY.

FINNISH-TATAR LANGUAGES OF THE VOLGA, N.-E. RUSSIA AND SIBERIA (together with SAMOYEDIC).

Comparatively.

Dictionary.

DONNER, Prf. O. Vergleichendes Wörterbuch der finnisch-ugrischen Sprachen, pts. i.-iii. ea. 5/- 8° *Helsingfors* 74;76;88

Grammar, etc.

ANDERSON, N. Studien z. Vergleichung d. indogerm. u. finn.-ugr. Sprachen 6/- 8° *Dorpat* 79
BUDENZ, J. Ueber die Verzweigung der ugrischen Sprachen 2/- 8° *Göttingen* 79
de UJFALVY, C. E. Les Langues Ougro-Finnoises, vol. i. 8/6 8° *Paris* 75
SETÄLÄ, E. N. Gesch. d. Tempus- u. Modusstammbild. d. finn.-ugr. Sprachen 3/6 8° *Helsingfors* 86
WESKE, M. Vergleichende Grammatik des finnischen Sprachstammes 2/- 8° *Leipzig* 73

Individual Languages.

Koibalic.

CASTREN, M. A. Versuch einer koibalisch. u. karagass. Sprachlehre 4/- 8° *St. Petersburg* 57
„ „ Koipabisch-deutsches Wörterverzeichniss 2/6 8° „ 86

Mordwinic.

WIEDEMANN, F. J. Grammatik der ersa-mordwinischen Sprache [w. short vocab.] 7/- s f° *St. Petersburg* 65

Ostjakic.

CASTREN, M. A. Versuch einer ostjakischen Sprachlehre 3/- 8° *St. Petersburg* [ ] 58

Polabic.

SCHLEICHER, A. Laut- und Formenlehre der polablschen Sprache 5/- r 8° *St. Petersburg* 72

Samoyedic.

CASTREN, M. A. Wörterverzeichnisse aus d. samojedischen Sprachen, ed. A. Schiefner 7/- r 8° *St. Petersburg* 55
" " Gramm. d. samojedischen Sprachen, ed. A. Schiefner 9/- r 8° " 57

Syrenic.

CASTREN, M. A. Elementa Grammatices Syrjaenae 3/- 8° *Helsingfors* 44
WIEDEMANN, F. J. Gram. d. syrjän. Sprache, 4/- ; Syrjän.-Deutsches Wörterbuch 7/- 8° *St. Petersburg* 84; 80

Tsheremiss.

CASTREN, M. A. Elementa Grammatices Tscheremissae 3/- 8° *Kuopio* 45
WIEDEMANN, F. J. Grammatik der Tscherem. Sprache 7/- 8° *Reval* 47

Thush, and Udic.

SCHIEFNER, A. Thusch-Sprache, 7/- ; Sprache der Uden 3/- 4° *St. Petersburg* 56; 63

Vêpse.

de UJFALVY, C. E. Grammaire Vêpse 8/6 8° *Paris* 75

Wotyakic.

WIEDEMANN, F. J. Grammatik der wotjakischen Sprache [*also in his* Gram. Syr., *sup.*] 6/- 8° *Reval* 51

Yeniseian.

CASTREN, M. A. Versuch einer jenissei-ostjak. u. kottischen Sprachlehre 5/- 8° *St. Petersburg* 58

144. URAL-ALTAIC (*d*): OSMANLI-TURKISH PHILOLOGY AND LITERATURE.

Dictionaries.

BARBIER DE MEYNARD, A. Dictionnaire Turc-Française, pts. i.-vii. [in 8 pts.; École Langs. Or. Viv.] ca. 8/6 8° *Paris* 81–88, *in prog.*
REDHOUSE, J. W. Turkish and English Dictionary, pts. i.-iv. ca. 9/- l 8° Quaritch [56] 84-87
YOUSSOUF, R. Dictionnaire Turc-Français, 2 vols. [in Roman and Turkish characters] 15/- 8° *Constantinople* 88
WIESENTHAL, W. Dictionnaire Français-Turc 7/6 16° " 88
ZENKER, Dr. J. H. Dictionnaire Turc-Arabe-Persan, 2 vols. £5 r 8° *Leipzig* 66; 76

Grammars.

ARNOLD, E. Simple Transliteral Grammar of Turk. Lang. [Simplif. Grams.] 2/6 p 8° Trübner 77
HOPKINS, F. L. Elementary Grammar of the Turkish Language 3/6 c 8° " 77
MACKENZIE, Cpt. C. F. Turkish Manual [gram., phrases, dialogues, vocab.] 6/- f 8° W. H. Allen 89
MÜLLER + GIES, Aug. H. Türkische Grammatik [w. parad., chrest. and gloss.: Porta Ling. Orient.] 8/- 8° *Berlin* 89
REDHOUSE, J. W. Turkish Vade Mecum [grammar. vocab., dialogues] 6/- 32° Trübner [77] 82
" " Simplified Grammar of Turkish Lang. [Simplif. Grams.] 10/6 c 8° " 84
TARRING, C. J. Practical Elementary Turkish Grammar 6/- c 8° Paul 86
WAHRMUND, A. Prakt. Handbuch d. osmanisch-türk. Sprache, 2 pts. and Key 20/- 8° *Giessen* [69] 86
WELLS, Dr. Chas. Practical Grammar of Turkish Language: spoken and written 15/- 8° Quaritch 80

Dialogues.

MALLOUF, N. New Guide to English and Turkish Conversation 2/- 12° *Paris* 80

Literature.

History of Poetry.

v. HAMMER-PURGSTALL, J. Geschichte der osmanischen Dichtkunst, 4 vols. 21/- 8° *Pesth* 36–38
REDHOUSE, J. W. History, System and Varieties of Turkish Poetry [w. selns. and trs.] 2/- 8° *Leipzig* 79

Manuscripts.

British Museum Catalogue of the Turkish Manuscripts. By Prf. Chas. Rieu [Turki and Osmanli] 17/6 8° British Museum 89

Inscriptions.

BLAU, O. [ed.] Bosnisch-Türkische Sprach-Denkmäler [Abh. f. d. K. d. Morgenl.] 10/- 8° *Leipzig* 68

Selections.

GIBB, E. J. W. [tr.] Ottoman Poems: translated [verse trs.] 21/- f 4° Trübner 82
KUNOS, Ignace [ed.] Orta-Oyonnou: théâtre pop. Turc [w. Hungar. transcript. and tr.] 4/- 8° *Pesth* 88

Individual Works —*for* Specimens of Folk-Literature, *v.* B § 31.

ABULGHASI BAHADUR CHAN Historia Mongolorum et Tatarorum, ed. with French tr. and notes Bar. Désmaisons, 2 vols. 10/6 r 8° *St. Petersburg* 71; 74

FASLI, Gül und Bülbül ["Rose and Nightingale"]: ed. w. Germ. tr. J. v. Hammer-[Purgstall] 4/6 r 4° *Pesth* 34

FETH-ALI Deux Comédies Turques, trad. A. Cillière [Bibl. Orient. Elzevir.] 4/6 12° *Paris* 88

Sajjid Batthâl, Fahrten des, übers. H. Ethé, 2 vols. 8/- 8° *Leipzig* 72

145. URAL-ALTAIC (*e*): TURKI (TATAR-TURKISH) PHILOLOGY AND LITERATURE.

Generally.

Dictionaries.

BUDAGOFF, L. Comparative Dictionary of Turkish and Tataric Dialects, 2 vols. 37/6 4° *St. Petersburg* 69; 71

RADLOFF, W. Versuch eines Wörterbuches der Türk-Dialekte, pt. i. 4/-; ii. 3/-; iii. 3/- 4° " 89-98

VAMBÉRY, Hermann Etymologisches Wörterbuch d. turko-tatar. Sprachen 8/- 8° *Leipzig* 70

Grammar, etc.

KASEM-BEG, Mirza Grammatik d. türk.-tatar. Sprache, ed. Dr. J. H. Zenker 12/- 8° *Leipzig* 48

MIKLOSICH, F. Die türk. Elemente in d. südost. and osteurop. Sprachen, & 2 Suppls., pt. i. 24/- 4° *Vienna* 84; 88; 90

RADLOFF, W. Die Sprachen d. nördl. türk. Stämme, Abtheil. I., pts. i.-vi. 45/- 8° *St. Petersburg* ?-86 *in prog.*

VAMBÉRY, Hermann Die primitive Cultur d. turko-tatar. Volkes [linguistic] 6/- 8° *Leipzig* 79

Phonetics.

RADLOFF, W. Phonetik der nördlichen Türksprachen 9/- 8° *Leipzig* 83

Turki.

SHAW, R. B. Sketch of the Turki Lang.: i. Grammar, 7/6; ii. Vocab 4/- r 8° *Calcutta* 78; 80

Texts and Translations.

Uigurische Sprachmonumente; ed. w. Germ. tr. and dict. H. Vambéry 24/- 4° *Innsbruck* 70

Cagataic.

VAMBÉRY, Hermann Cagataische Sprachstudien [gram., chrestom., Germ. dict.] 21/- 4° *Leipzig* 67

Jakutic.

BÖHTLINGK, O. Die Sprache der Jakuten [gram., texts, Germ. trs.] 21/- 4° *St. Petersburg* 51

146. URAL-ALTAIC (*f*): MONGOLIC PHILOLOGY AND LITERATURE.

East Mongolian.

Dictionary.

SCHMIDT, I. J. Mongolisch-Deutsch-Russisches Wörterbuch *o.p.* [*w.* 15/-] 4° *St. Petersburg* 35

Grammar.

SCHMIDT, I. J. Grammatik der mongolischen Sprache *o.p.* [*w.* 7/6] 4° *St. Petersburg* 31

Literature.

Ardschi-Bordschi: Selection from, ed. B. Jülg 2/6 8° *Innsbruck* 67

Busk, Miss R. H. [tr.] Sagas from the Far East [=tr. of *Ardschi-Bordschi*] 9/- p 8° Griffith 72

Jülg, B. [tr.] Mongolische Märchen [=trs. fr. *Ardschi Bordschi*] 2/6 r 8° *Innsbruck* 67

Bogda Gesser Chan's Thaten: ed. I. J. Schmidt 12/- 4° *St. Petersburg* 36

*RADLOFF, W. [tr.] Proben der Volksliteratur Süd-Siberiens, pts. i.-vi. [Germ. metrical trs.] 45/- i 8° " 66-87

Ssanang Ssetsen Chung taidschi, ed. w. Germ. tr. I. J. Schmidt [hist. of East Mongols] 16/- 4° " 29

Calmuc (West Mongolian).

ZWICK, H. A. Grammatik der west-mongolischen Sprache 9/- 4° *Donau* 52

" " Wörterbuch der west-mongolischen Sprache 15/- 4° *Freiburg* 54

Literature —*v. also* B § 32: Mongolic Folklore.

Siddhi-Kur: ed. B. Jülg [w. German tr. and dict.] 15/-; tr. alone, 2/6 r 8° *Leipzig* 66; 66

Buryatic.

CASTRÉN, M. A. Versuch einer burjätischen Sprache 5/- 8° *St. Petersburg* 57

147. URAL-ALTAIC (g): TUNGUSIC AND MANTSHOU PHILOLOGY AND LITERATURE.

Tungusic.

Grammar.

CASTREN, M. A. Grundzüge einer tungusischen Sprachlehre 3/6 8° *St. Petersburg* 56

Mantshou.

Grammars and Vocabulary.

ADAM, L. Grammaire de la Langue Mandchou 6/- 8° *Paris* 73
de HARLEZ, C. Manuel de la Langue Mandchoue [gram., chrestom., gloss.] 8/6 8° ,, 84
KAULEN, P. Linguae Mandschuricae Institutiones [w. chrest. and vocab. in Latin] 6/- 8° *Ratisbon* 56

Chrestomathy.

KAULEN, P. —*ut supra.*
KLAPROTH, J. [ed.] Chrestomathie Mandchou [with French trs.] *o.p.* [*w.* 4/-] 8° *Paris* 28
VASILEV, [ed.] Mantschjurskaa Christomatia 3/6 8° *St. Petersburg* 63

Texts —*v. also* B § 32: Mongolic, *etc.*, Folklore.

Aisin Gurun i Suduri Bithe, tr. C. de Harlez [hist. of empire of Kin] 8/- 8° *Louvain* 87
Shi-king: in Mantshou tr. w. Mant.-Germ. vocab., ed. H. C. v. Gabelentz, 2 pts. 18/- 8° *Leipzig* 64

148. CAUCASIAN PHILOLOGY.

Generally.

v. ECKERT, R. —*in his* Der Kaukasus und seine Völker; map and ill. 12/- 8° *Leipzig* 87
de MORGAN, J. Mission Scientifique au Caucase; ill. 22/6 8° *Paris* 90

Circassian.

Dictionary.

LOEWE, L. Dictionary of the Circassian Language [Eng.-Circass.-Turkish] *o.p.* [*w.* 10/-] 8° *London* 54

Georgian.

Dictionary.

TSCHOUBINOFF, D. Dictionnaire Géorgien-Russe-Français [w. brief grammar] 40/- 4° *St. Petersburg* 40

Literature.

LEIST, Arthur [tr.] Georgische Dichter [Germ. trs. fr. Georgian poets] 2/- 8° *Leipzig* 88

Kurinic.

SCHIEFNER, A. Bericht über P. v. Uslar's Kürinische Studien 7/- r 4° *St. Petersburg* 73

Ossetic —*v.* K § 138: Ossetic Philology.

149. DRAVIDIAN (SOUTH INDIAN) PHILOLOGY AND LITERATURE.

Collectively.

VINSON, J. La Science du Langage et les Études Dravidiennes [inaug. address] 1/6 8° *Paris* 81

Grammar.

*CALDWELL, R. Comparative Grammar of the Dravidian Languages 28/- 8° Trübner [56] 75
Tamil, Malayâlam, Telugu, Canarese, Tulu, Kudagee (Coorg), Tuda, Kôta, Gônd, Khônd (Ku), Mâler (Rajmahal), Orâon.

Verb.

VINSON, J. Le Verbe dans les Langues Dravidiennes 3/- 8° *Paris* 78

Dictionary.

HUNTER, [Sir] W. W. Compar. Dict. of the Non-Aryan Languages of India and High Asia 42/- 4° Trübner 68
Polyglot Vocabulary: English, German, Canarese, Tulu and Malayalim 5/- s 8° *Mangalore* 80

Palæography and Inscriptions—v. also G § 10, *s.v.* Southern Indian.

*BURNELL, Dr. A. C. Elements of South Indian Palæography; 35 pl. [inscripp. & MSS., 4-17 cent.] 52/6 4° Trübner [74] 78
HULTZSCH, Dr. [ed.] South Indian Inscriptions, vol. i [Sansc., Tamil and Grantha] Madras Archæol. Surv. 90

Serial.

Taprobanian, The: a Dravidian journal of Orient. studies in Ceylon, ed. H. Nevill *ann.* 20/- f° *Bombay* 86 *sqq.*, *in prog.*

K § 149

Andamanese.

Author	Title	Price	Size	Place	Date
PORTMAN, M. V.	Manual of the Andamanese Languages	10/6	8°	W. H. Allen	88
de ROEPSTORFF, F.	Vocabulary of Dialects spoken in Nicobar and Adaman Isles *o.p.* [*w.* 30/-]		f°	*Fort Blair*	74

Brahui.

Author	Title	Price	Size	Place	Date
BELLEW, H. W.	—*his* Indus to the Tigris, *conts. a gram. and vocab. of the Brahoe lang.*	14/-	8°	Trübner	74
BUX, Alla	Handbook of the Biroubi Language [fr. Forbes' *Manual*]	14/-	8°	*Kurrachee*	77
TRUMPP, E.	Grammatische Untersuchungen über die Sprache der Brahuis	4/-	8°	*Munich*	81

Canarese.

Author	Title	Price	Size	Place	Date
BOUTELOUP, R. A.	Grammatica Canarico-Latina ad usum scholarum	6/-	8°	*Bangalore*	[ ] 69
Dictionarium Canarense-Latinum, 2 vols.		36/-	8°	,,	55 ; 61
GARRETT, J.	English and Kanarese Dictionary	18/-	8°	,,	[65] 72
HODSON, Th.	Elementary Grammar of the Kannada	12/-	8°	,,	[59] 64
KESIRAJA	Sabdamanidarpana ["Jewel Mirror of Grammar"], ed. F. Kittel	4/-	8°	*Mangalore*	72
KITTEL, Rev. F.	Canarese Dictionary			,,	89 *in prog.*
NAGAVARMA	Canarese Prosody : w. essay on Canarese literature F. Kittel	3/6	8°	,,	75
REEVE, Rev. W.	Dictionary, Canarese and English [both parts]	63/-	8°	*Bangalore*	[ ] 58
SANDERSON, D. [ed.]	Katha Sangraha : or Canarese Selections	21/-	8°	,,	68
ZIEGLER, F.	Practical Key to the Canarese Language	6/6	8°	*Mangalore*	82

Coorg.

Author	Title	Price	Size	Place	Date
COLE, Cpt. R. A.	Elementary Grammar of the Coorg Language	15/-	8°	*Bangalore*	67

Inscriptions.

Author	Title	Price	Size	Place	Date
RICE, L. [tr.]	Coorg Inscriptions : translated [49 pp. only]	9/-	4°	*Bangalore*	86

Khond.

Author	Title	Price	Size	Place	Date
SMITH	Grammar of the Khond Language		8°	*Cuttack*	76

Malayalim.

Dictionaries.

Author	Title	Price	Size	Place	Date
BAILEY, Rev. B.	English-Malayalim Dictionary	21/-	8°	*Cottayam*	49
,, ,,	Dictionary of High and Colloquial Malayalim and English *o.p.* [*w.* 50/-]		4°	,,	46
*GUNDERT, Rev. H.	Malayalim-English Dictionary	30/-	r 8°	*Mangalore*	71–72
LASERON, E.	Dictionary of Malayalim-English and English-Malayalim Languages	15/-	8°	*Cottayam*	56
School Dictionary	Malayalim and English	12/-	8°	*Mangalore*	70

Grammars.

Author	Title	Price	Size	Place	Date
FROHNMEYER, L. J.	Progressive Grammar of the Malayalam Language		8°	*Mangalore*	89
GRUNDERT, Rev. H.	Malayalim Grammar [in Mayalalim]	3/6	8°	,,	[ ] 68
PEET, Rev. J.	Grammar of the Malayalim Language	14/-	8°	*Cottayam*	[41] 60

Chrestomathies.

Author	Title	Price	Size	Place	Date
ARBUTHNOT, A. J. [ed.]	Malayalim Selections, w. trs., anal. and vocab.	9/-	8°	*Cottayam*	64
COLLETT [ed.]	Malayalam Reader	12/6	8°	W. H. Allen	

Nicobari.

Author	Title	Price	Size	Place	Date
de ROEPSTORFF, F.	Vocab. of Dialects spoken in Nicobar and Andaman Isles *o.p.* [*w.* 30/-]		f°	*Fort Blair*	74
,,	Dictionary of Nancowry Dialect of Nicobarese Language [both parts]	7/6	r 8°	*Calcutta*	84

Tamil.

Grammars, etc.

Author	Title	Price	Size	Place	Date
BESCHIUS, C. J. [S.-J.]	Clavis Humaniorum Litt. Sublimioris Tamulici Idiomatis, ed. K. Ihlefeld	10/6	8°	*Tranquebar*	[13] 76
GRAUL, Ch.	Outline of Tamil Grammar [w. specimens and gloss. ; in English]	18/-	8°	*Leipzig*	55
LAZARUS, John	Tamil Grammar [for school use]	5/6	12°	Snow	78
POPE, Rev. G. U.	Larger Grammar of the Tamil Language [in both its dialects]	18/-	8°	*Madras*	[ ] 59
,, ,,	Tamil Handbook : w. vocabularies, readings, etc., 3 pts.	ea. 12/6	8°	W. H. Allen	[ ] 83–84
RHENIUS, Rev. C. T. E.	Grammar of the Tamil Language	12/6	8°	*Madras*	[36] 88

Dictionaries.

Author	Title	Price	Size	Place	Date
KNIGHT + SPAULDING + HUTCHINGS, Revs.	English and Tamil Dictionary	42/-	r 8°	*Madras*	[44] 88
PERCIVAL, P.	Dictionary, English and Tamil	10/-	8°	,,	[62] 70
PILLAI, V. Visvanatha	Dictionary : Tamil-English	7/6	p 8°	,,	[ ] 89
ROTTLER, J. P.	Dictionary of the Tamil and English Languages	42/-	4°	,,	34–41
WINSLOW, M.	Comprehensive Tamil and Engl. Dictionary of High and Low Tamil	73/6	4°	,,	62

Chrestomathies.

Author	Title	Price	Size	Place	Date
POPE, Rev. G. U. [ed.]	Tamil Prose Reading Book : with notes and glossary	7/6	8°	*Madras*	59
,, ,,	Tamil Poetical Anthology : with notes and vocabulary	10/6	8°	,,	59

Literature.

Bhagavad Gita [*v.* K § 124 II.] tr. into Tamil [and English] Rev. H. Bower — 6/- p 8° *Madras* 89

GRAUL, Ch. [ed.] — Bibliotheca Tamulica, 4 vols. — 50/- 8° *Leipzig* 54–65

i: Tria Opera Indorum Philos., 8/-; ii: Gram., *ut supra*; iii: *Kural of Tiruvalluver*, Germ. tr., 6/-; *The same*, trs. into Common Tamil and Latin, w. notes and glossary, 24/-.

PERCIVAL, P. [ed. & tr.] — Tamil Proverbs; with their English translations — 9/- p 8° *Madras* [43] 74

Manuscripts.

TAYLOR, Wm. [ed.] — Oriental and Histor. MSS. in Tamil Lang.: tr. w. notes, 2 vols. — 16/- 4° *Madras* 35

Telugu.

Grammars.

ARDEN, Rev. A. H. — Progressive Grammar of Telugu Language; w. examples — 14/- 8° *Madras* 73

BROWN, C. P. — Grammar of the Telugu Language — 21/- 8° ,, [40] 57

CAREY, Rev. W. — Grammar of the Telinga Language — 7/6 8° *Serampore* 74

MORRIS, Henry — Simplified Telugu Grammar [Simplified Grammars Series] c 8° Trübner *in prep.*

RICCAZ, Rev. A. — Abridgment of Telugu Grammar [for school use] 12/- 8° *Vizagapatam* 69

Dictionaries.

BROWN, C. P. — Dictionary: Telugu-English, 63/-; English-Telugu — 42/- 8° *Madras* 52; 53

,, ,, — Dictionary of Mixed Dialects and Foreign Words used in Telugu — 12/- 8° ,, 54

PERCIVAL, P. — English-Teloogoo Dictionary, 2 vols. [both parts] 10/6 8° ,, 62; 67

Chrestomathies.

ARDEN, Rev. A. H. [ed.] — Companion Telugu Reader (companion to his Grammar, *ut sup.*) 7/6 8° *Madras* 79

BROWN, C. P. [ed.] — The Telugu Reader, 3 vols. [w. trs. and anal. of words] 36/- 8° ,, 51–52

MORRIS, J. C. [ed.] — Telugu Selections (for the use of officers) 21/- 8° ,, [58] 81

Literature.

CARR, Cpt. M. W. [tr.] — Collection of Telugu Proverbs: translated — 31/6 r 8° *Madras*

Tulu.

BRIGEL, Rev. J. — Grammar of the Tulu Language — 7/6 8° *Mangalore* 72

150. JAPANESE AND COREAN PHILOLOGY.

Comparatively.

ASTON, Dr. W. G. — Compar. Study of Japan. & Korean Langs.—*in Jl. R. A. S., N. S.*, xi. 3 8/- 8° Trübner 79

Corean.

Dictionary.

Dictionnaire Coréen-français, par les missionaires de Corée — £4 4° *Yokohama* 80

OPPERT, Ernest — —*his* A Forbidden Land [Corea], *conts. a vocab., 2 pl. of alphab., etc.* 12/0 8° Low 80

Grammars, etc.

IMBAULT-HUART, C. — Manuel de la Langue Coréenne parlée — 5/- 8° *Paris* 89

Les Missionaires de Corée — Grammaire Coréenne — 37/6 r 8° *Yokohama* 81

ROSS, Rev. John — Corean Primer: lessons in Corean on ordinary subjects — 10/- 8° *Shanghai* 77

SCOTT, James — En-moun Mai Ch'aik: Corean manual and phrase-bk., w. introd. gram. 8° ,, 87

Japanese.

History of Japanese.

CHAMBERLAIN, B. H. — Language, Mythology, etc., of Japan, in the light of Aino Studies [Mems. Coll. Jap. No. 1] 10/- i 8° *Tokio* 87

Dictionaries.

HEPBURN, Dr. J. C. — Japanese and English Dictionary: w. Engl.-Japanese index — 30/- i 8° *Shanghai* [67] 86

,, ,, — Abridgment of the same, *s.v.* Japanese Pocket Dictionary [both parts] 14/- s 4° *Tokio* [73] 88

HOFFMANN, J. J. — Japanese-English Dictionary, ed. L. Serrurier, 2 vols. — 12/6 r 8° *Leyden* 81

MEDHURST, Rev. W. H. — English-Japanese and Japanese-English Vocabulary [lithographed] *o.p.* [*w.* 21/-] 8° *Batavia* 30

SATOW + MASARATA, E. + I. — English-Japanese Dictionary of Spoken Language — 12/6 i 32° Trübner [76] 79

Loan Words.

GUBBINS, J. H. — Dictionary of Chinese-Japanese Words in Japanese Language, pt. i. 7/6 8° Trübner 90 *in prog.*

Grammars.

ASTON, Dr. W. G. — Short Grammar of the Japanese Spoken Language — 12/- c 8° Trübner [ ] 89

,, ,, — Grammar of the Japanese Written Language — 28/- r 8° ,, [72] 77

CHAMBERLAIN, B. H. — Simplified Gram. of Japan. Lang. [mod. written style; Simplif. Grams.] 5/- c 8° ,, 86

,, ,, — Handbook of Colloquial Japanese — 12/6 c 8° ,, 89

HOFFMANN, J. J. — Japanese Grammar — 21/- r 8° *Leyden* [68] 76

NOACK, P. — Lehrbuch der japanischen Sprache — 15/- 8° *Leipzig* 86

TATUI BABA — Elementary Grammar of the Japanese Language — 5/- c 8° Trübner [ ] 88

K §§ 151–152

Etymology.

IMBRIE, W. Handbook of English-Japanese Etymology 6/- 8° *Tokio* [80] 89

Chrestomathies.

CHAMBERLAIN, B. H. [ed.] Japanese Reader [anecdotes, maxims, etc., romanized] 6/- c 8° Trübner 86
PFIZMAIER, A. [ed.] Chrestomathie Japonaise; ill. [with German trs.] 12/- r 8° *Paris* 47
de ROSNY, L. [ed.] Anthologie Japonaise [with French trs.], 25/-; text only 4/- 8° „ 70; 71

Dialogues.

EASTLAKE, J. W. Easy Conversations in English, German, and Japanese 4/6 8° *Tokio* [ ] 86
HOFFMANN, J. J. Shopping Dialogues in Japanese, English, and Dutch 5/- obl 8° *The Hague* 61

Aino.

DAWIDOW Wörtersammlung der Ainos
Pfizmaier, A. Kritische Durchsicht von Dawidow's Wörtersammlung der Ainos 3/6 8° *Vienna* 52
PFIZMAIER, A. Abhandlungen über die Aino-Sprache 2/6 8° „ 52
„ „ Bau der Aino-Sprache, 3/-; Vocabul. der Aino-Sprache 6/- 8° „ 51; 54

151. JAPANESE LITERATURE.

Bibliography.

HOFFMANN, J. J. Catal. Librorum Jap. a Siebold collect. 12/- 4° *Leyden* 45
PAGÈS, L. Bibliographie Japonnaise [15 cent. to present time] 5/- 4° *Paris* 59
SATOW, Em. The Jesuit Mission Press in Japan: 1591–1610; 11 pl. 15/- 4° Trübner 88

Collections.

CHAMBERLAIN, B. H. The Classical Poetry of the Japanese 7/6 p 8° Trübner 80
DICKINS, F. V. [ed. and tr.] Hyak Nin Is'shiu [seln. of Jap. odes, w. trss. and notes] 5/- 8° *Leyden* 66
MÜLLER, Prf. F. Max [ed.] Buddhist Texts from Japan, i.–iii. [ill. w. plates] 21/- s 4° Clar. Press 81; 83; 84
i.: *Vagrakkhedikâ*, the Diamond-cutter, 3/6; ii.: *Sukhâvatî-Vyûha*, 7/6; iii.: *Pragñâ-Pâramitâ-Hridaya-Sûtra*, etc.

v. SIEBOLD + HOFFMANN, P. F. + J. J. [eds.] Bibliotheca Japonica: sex selecta quaedam opera Sinico-Jap £20 f° *Leyden* 33–41

Individual Writings.

Bunyiu Nanjio [hist. of 12 Jap. Buddhist sects], translated 6/- s 8° *Tokio* 86
Chinshingura: a Japanese romance [w. col. native drawings] 10/6 r 8° W. H. Allen 80
Genji Monogatari tr. Suyematz Kenchio [classical Japanese romance] 7/6 c 8° Trübner 82
Ko-ji-ki: records of ancient matters [tr.] ed. B. H. Chamberlain; map [Trans. As. Soc. Jap., vol. x.] 17/6 8° *Yokohama* 83
Muramasa Blade, A. tr. L. Wertheimber; 5 pl. and native ill. 15/- 8° *London* 87
de ROSNY, Léon [ed. and tr.] Histoire des Dynasties divines pub. en japonnais, traduite [w. the text] 25/- 8° *Paris* 87
SERRURIER, L. [ed.] Encyclopédie Japonnaise: chapitre des quadrupèdes, 2 vols.; pl. 12/- 4° *Leyden* 75
Taketori no Okina no Monogatari, tr. F. V. Dickins; 3 col. native pl. ["Old Bamboo-Hewer's Story"; 10 cent. romance] 7/6 8° Trübner 88
TAMENAGA SHUNSUI The Loyal Ronins, tr. E. Greey + Shiuichiro Saito; ill. [histor. romance] $1.75 8° *New York* [ ] 89
Zitu-go Kyan & Dozi Kyan [instruction of truth & of youth], w. transcrip. & Fch. tr. L. de Rosny, 3 pts. 12/6 8° *Paris* 76–87

Folk-Literature —*v.* B § 37: Japanese Folklore.

152. MONOSYLLABIC LANGUAGES (a): CHINESE PHILOLOGY (a): GENERALLY.

History of Chinese Language.

DOUGLAS, Prf. R. K. Chinese Language and Literature [two Roy. Inst. lects.] 5/- c 8° Trübner 75
EDKINS, Rev. Jos. China's Place in Philology 10/6 c 8° „ 71
Seeks to prove the common origin of the languages of Europe and Asia.
„ „ Evolution of the Chinese Language [as exemplifying origin of language] 4/6 8° „ 88
WATTERS, Rev. T. Essays on the Chinese Language 8° *Shanghai* 89

Characters and Writing.

AULAIRE + GROENEVELDT, R. + W. Manual of Chinese Running Handwriting 10/6 4° *Amsterdam* 61
BALL, J. Dyer How to Write Chinese, pt. i., 10/6; How to Write the Radicals 3/6 r 8° *Hong Kong* 88; 88
CHALMERS, Dr. J. Structure of Chinese Characters, under 300 primary forms 10/6 8° Trübner 82
*EDKINS, Rev. J. Introduction to the Study of the Chinese Characters 18/- r 8° „ 76
GILES, H. A. Synoptical Studies in Chinese Character 15/- 8° *Shanghai* 74
de ROSNY, L. Dictionnaire des Signes Idéographiques de la Chine 17/- 8° *Paris* 67

Dictionaries.

CHALMERS, Dr. J. Concise Dictionary of Chinese 24/- 8° Trübner [ ] 81
EITEL, Dr. E. J. Handbook of Chinese Buddhism [= a Sanscrit-Chinese dict.] 18/- 8° " [70] 88
LOBSCHEID, Rev. W. English and Chinese Dictionary, 4 pts. £8 8/- f° *Hong Kong* 66–69
" " Chinese and English Dictionary 48/- i 8° " 71
MEDHURST, Rev. W. H. Chinese-English and Eng.-Chin. Dict., 4 vols. [acc. to Radicals] 105/- 4° *Batavia* [38] 42–57
MORRISON, Rev. Rob. Dictionary of the Chinese Language, 6 vols. £6 6/- r 4° *Macao* [15–22] 55–72
i.: Chinese-English (acc. to the Radicals) 3 vols.; ii.: Chinese-English (alphab.) 2 vols.; iii.: English-Chinese, 1 vol.
STENT, G. E. Chinese and English Pocket Dictionary 15/- 16° Trübner 74
WILLIAMS, S. Wells [Am.] Syllabic Dictionary of the Chinese Language 75/- 4° *Shanghai* (Trübner) [74] 89
Index to same, by ACHESON, 18/- r 8° *Hong Kong* 79.

Grammars, etc.

DOOLITTLE, Rev. J. Vocabulary & Handbk. of Chinese Lang., 2 vols. [romanized] 35/-, *or* ea. 21/- 8° *Shanghai* [72] 90
DOUGLAS, Prf. R. K. Chinese Manual [grammar, phrases, dialogues] 10/6 f 8° W. H. Allen 89
EDKINS, Dr. Joseph Simplified Chinese Grammar [Simplified Grammars Series] c 8° Trübner *in prep.*
FOSTER, Rev. Arnold Elementary Lessons in Chinese 2 6 8° Clar. Press 87
v. d. GABELENTZ, G. Anfangsgründe der chinesischen Grammatik, 8/-; Chines. Grammatik 38/- 8° *Leipzig* 81; 83
JULIEN, Stanislas Syntaxe nouvelle de la Langue Chinoise, 2 vols. 25/- 8° *Paris* 69; 70
LOBSCHEID, Rev. W. Chinese-English Grammar, 2 pts. ea. 7/6 8° *Hong Kong* 64; 64
MARSHMAN, J. Elements of Chinese Grammar 42/- 4° *Serampore* 44
SUMMERS, Rev. J. Handbook of Chinese Lang., 2 pts. [gram. and chrestom.] 28/- 8° Clar. Press 63

Colloquial.

EDKINS, Rev. J. Progressive Lessons in Chinese Spoken Language, 3 vols. 14/- 8° *Shanghai* [ ] 81
WADE, T. F. Progressive Course in Colloquial Chinese, 3 vols. 80/- 4° Trübner

Syntax.

Han-Wen-Tchi-Nan trad. Stanislas Julien, 2 vols. [Chinese syntax] 30/- 8° *Paris* 69; 70

Serial.

China Review: notes and queries on the far east, vols. i.–xvii. *ann.* 25/- 8° *Hong Kong* 72–89 *in prog.*

Chrestomathies —*v. also* K § 154: Chinese Literature, *s.v.* Collections.

MARTIN, Rev. W. A. P. [ed.] Analytical Reader: learning to read and write Chinese 31/6 4° *Shanghai* 63
MAYERS, W. F. [ed.] The Chinese Reader's Manual 25/6 8° " 74
de ROSNY, Léon [ed.] Textes faciles en Langue Chinois 5/- 8° *Paris* 88

Dialogues.

MEDHURST, Rev. W. H. Chinese Dialogues, Questions and Sentences 18/- 8° *Shanghai* [5+] 63

Prae-Chinese Language of China.

*de LACOUPERIE, Prf. Terrien Languages of China before the Chinese 10/6 8° Nutt 87
Finds the earlier seat of the Chinese in Western Asia, and here gives evidence that they were subject to the influence of Susiana, having moved eastwards about 23 cent. B.C. The evidence is derived chiefly fr. the remains of the early lang. in the Chinese language and literature.

153. MONOSYLLABIC (δ): CHINESE PHILOLOGY (β): DIALECTS.

Amoy.

DOUGLAS, Rev. C. Chinese-English Dictionary of Vernacular Lang. of Amoy 63/- 4° Trübner 73
MACGOWAN, Rev. J. Manual of the Amoy Colloquial 30/- 8° *Amoy* [71] 80
" " English and Chinese Dictionary of the Amoy Dialect 63/- r 4° " 83

Canton.

BALL, J. Dyer Cantonese Made Easy, 15/-; Easy Sentences in Cantonese 7/6 8° *Hong Kong* [86] 88; 87
" " How to Speak Cantonese [50 conversations in Cantonese colloquial] 15/- r 8° " 89
BRIDGMAN, Chinese Chrestomathy in the Canton Dialect *o.p.* [105/-] 4° *Macao* 41
DENNYS, Rev. N. B. Handbook of Canton Vernacular of Chinese Language 30/- r 8° *Hong Kong* 74
*EITEL, Rev. E. J. Chin. Dict. in Cantonese Dialect, 4 pts., ea. 12/6; supplement 2/6 r 8° " 77–82; 87
STEDMAN + LEE, T. L. / K. P. [Am.] Chinese and English Phrase-Book [dialogues] $1.50 8° *New York* 88
WILLIAMS, S. Wells [Am.] Easy Lessons in Chinese [esp. Canton dialect] 21/- 8° *Macao* 42
" " Tonic Dictionary of the Chinese Language [Canton dialect] *o.p.* [*w.* £4] 8° *Canton* 56

Foochow.

BALDWIN, Rev. C. C. Manual of the Foochow Dialect 18/- 8° *Foochow* 71
MACLAY + BALDWIN, R. S. / C. C. Alphabetical Dictionary of Chin. Lang. in Foochow Dialect 84/- 8° " 71

Formosa.

de LACOUPERIE, Prf. T. Formosa Notes; 3 pl. [repr. fr. *J. R. A. S.*; on MSS., races, langs.] 5/- 8° Nutt 87

K § 164

Hakka.

BALL, J. Dyer	Easy Sentences in the Hakka Dialect [w. vocab.]	5/6	8°	*Hong Kong*	81

Mandarin.

EDKINS, Rev. J.	Grammar of Chinese Colloquial Lang. : Mandarin Dialect	30/-	8°	*Shanghai*	[57] 64
GILES, Herbert A.	Dictionary of Colloquial Idioms in Mandarin Dialect	28/-	4°	Trübner	73
" "	Chinese without a Teacher [easy sentences in Mand. dial., w. vocab.]	7/6	8°	*Shanghai*	[ ] 87
PERNY, P.	Dictionnaire Français-Lat.-Chin. : Mand. Dial., 50/- ; Appendix	50/-	4°	*Paris*	69 ; 72
RUDY, C.	Chinese Mandarin Lang., vol. i. : Grammar [Ollendorf meth.]	21/-	8°	*Geneva*	74
SYDENSTRICKER, A.	Exposition of Construction and Idioms of Mandarin Dialect	6/-	c 8°	*Shanghai*	89

Ningpo.

PILLAY, P. S.	Chinese Vocabulary and Dialogues in Ningpo Dialect	52/6	r 8°	*Chusan*	56

Pekin.

STENT, G. E.	Chinese and English Vocabulary in Pekinese Dialect	40/-	8°	*Shanghai*	[ ] 77

Shanghai.

EDKINS, Rev. J.	Vocabulary of the Shanghai Dialect	21/-	8°	*Shanghai*	69
" "	Grammar of Colloquial Chinese : Shanghai Dialect	21/-	8°	"	[ ] 68
MACGOWAN, Rev. J. [ed.]	Collections of Phrases in the Shanghai Dialect	22/6	8°	"	62

Swatow.

FIELDE, A. M.	First Lessons in the Swatow Dialect	30/-	s 4°	*Swatow*	78

Pidgin-English : *Literature.*

LELAND, C. G. [Am.]	Pidgin-English Sing-Song [songs and stories in Pidgin-English]	5/-	f 8°	Trübner	[76] 88

164. MONOSYLLABIC (c): CHINESE LITERATURE.

Bibliography.

ANDREAE + GEIGER, V. J.	Bibliotheca Sinologica : Wegweiser durch sinolog. Literatur	6/-	8°	*Frankfort*	64
British Museum	Catalogue of Chinese Books in the British Museum [by R. K. Douglas]	20/-	4°	British Museum	77
CORDIER, H.	Bibliotheca Sinica, 2 vols. [L'École d. Langs. Orient. Viv.]	62/6	8°	*Paris*	78-81
V. MÖLLENDORFF, P. G. O. F.	Manual of Chinese Bibliography	30/-	8°	*Leyden*	77
WYLIE, A. [tr.]	Notes on Chinese Literature : tr. fr. Chinese, etc.	36/-	4°	Trübner	

History.

BAZIN, A.	Le Siècle de Youen : tableau histor. de la littér. Chinoise	*o.p.* [*w.* 21/-]	8°	*Paris*	50
BEAL, Prf. S.	Abstract of Four Lectures on Buddhist Literature in China			*London*	82
PFIZMAIER, A.	Die elegische Dichtung d. Chinesen [*fr.* Denksch. Wien. Akad.]	4/-	4°	*Vienna*	88
SCHOTT, W.	Entwurf einer Beschreibung der chinesischen Literatur	6/-	4°	*Berlin*	54
WYLIE, A.	Notes on Chinese Literature	*o.p.* [*w.* 25/-]	4°	*Shanghai*	67

Texts.

Collections : Texts.

de ROSNY, Léon [ed.]	Chrestomathie Religieuse de l'Extrème Orient	6/6	8°	*Paris*	87
	Selected passages from Yi King, Shoo-King, Lihi, Tao-Tchou, Hiao King. In the original texts.				
SMITH, A. H. [ed.]	The Proverbs and Common Sayings of the Chinese	30/-	r 8°	*Shanghai*	88
ZOTTOLI, A. [ed.]	Cursus Litteraturae Sinicae, 2 vols.		8°	"	79

Collections : Translations.

GILES, H. A. [tr.]	Gems of Chinese Literature : translated	7/6	8°	Quaritch	84
de ROSNY, Léon [tr.]	Textes Chinois Anciens et Modernes : traduits	10/-	8°	*Paris*	87

Individual Texts and Translations.

Confucian Texts —*for* Treatises on Confucianism, *v.* A § 10.

CHOO-FOO-TSZE	Confucian Cosmogony, tr. w. notes Rev. T. McClatchie	21/-	s 4°	Trübner	74
CHUANG TSZE	Divine Classic of Nan-Hua, ed. w. English notes F. H. Balfour	14/-	8°	"	81
Giles, H. A. [tr.]	Chuang Tzŭ : mystic, moralist and social reformer	16/-	8°	Quaritch	89
Confucian Analects :	Great Learning, Doctrine of Men, ed. w. tr., & notes J. Legge [Chinese Classics]	42/-	r 8°	"	61
CONFUCIUS,	Life and Teachings, tr. J. Legge [Chinese Classics Translated]	10/6	c 8°	"	[66] 87
DOUGLAS, Prf. R.K. [ed.]	Life of Jenghiz Khan ; tr. fr. Chinese	5/-	c 8°	Trübner	77
Dukes Yin, Hwan, Chwang,	Min, He, Wan, Seuen, and Ching, ed. w. tr. & notes J. Legge [Chin. Class.]	42/-	r 8°	"	72
" Seang, Chaou,	Ting, and Gai, ed. w. tr. and notes J. Legge [Chinese Classics]	42/-	r 8°	"	72
LAU TSZE	Speculations on Metaphys., Polity, etc., tr. J. Chalmers	4/6	f 8°	"	68
"	übersetzt, eingeleitet und commentirt von Victor von Strauss	12/-	8°	*Leipzig*	70
"	trad. Stanislas Julien, *sub tit.* Le Livre de la Voie et de la Vertu	30/-	r 8°	*Paris*	[35] 42

Li Ki [Ceremonial Usages], tr. J. Legge, 2 vols. [Sacred Books of East] ea. 12/6 8° Clar. Press 85

Mai Yu lang toú chen hoa koueï ["The Vendor of Oil"], ed. w. Fch. tr. G. Schlegel 10/- 8° *Leyden* 77

MENCIUS, Works of, ed. w. tr. and notes J. Legge [Chinese Classics] 42/- r 8° Trübner 61

" Life and Works of, tr. J. Legge [Chinese Classics Translated] 12/- c 8° " 75

Shi King, *etc.* ed. w. tr. and notes J. Legge, 2 pts. [Chinese Classics] 42/- r 8° " 71

" tr. J. Legge [Chinese Classics Translated (metrical)] 12/- c 8° " 76

Shoo King, Chow, *etc.* ed. w. tr. and notes J. Legge, 2 pts. [Chinese Classics] ea. 42/- r 8° " 65

" " and Shi King [pts. of prose; tr.] and Hsiâo King, tr. J. Legge [Sac. Bks. of East] 12/6 8° Clar. Press 79

Tripitaka Catal. of Chinese Transl. of, ed. Bunyiu Nanjio 32/6 4° " 83

Yi King tr. J. Legge [Sacred Books of East] 10/6 8° " 82

Buddhist Texts —*for* Treatises on Buddhism, *v.* A § 10.

Abhinishkramana Sutra: the romantic legend of Buddha, tr. Prf. S. Beal 12/- p 8° Trübner 75

A Sanscrit Life of Buddha, tr. into Chinese in the 6th century, and thence by BEAL into English.

Asvaghosha Bodhisattva, Fo-Sho-Hing-Tsan-King, tr. Prf. S. Beal [Sacred Books of East] 10/6 8° Clar. Press 83

A life of Buddha, translated from the Sanscrit, A.D. 420.

BEAL, Prf. Samuel [tr.] A Catena of Buddhist Scriptures [tr. fr. Chinese] 15/- 8° Trübner 71

Dhammapada Texts fr. Buddhist Canon, w. accomp. narratives, ed. Beal [Orient. Ser.] 7/6 p 8° " 78

A Chinese version of the text generally conn. w. hist. of Buddha, gathered fr. ancient canonical bks. of the Buddhists.

Fa Hian and Sung Yun, Travels of. By S. Beal [travels of Chin. Buddh. priests fr. China to India] 10/6 8° " 69

Hiuen Tsiang Si-Yu-Ki: Buddh. records of Western World [A.D. 629], ed. Beal, 2 v. [Orient. Ser.] 24/- p 8° " 84

Records of travels of Chinese Buddhist priests in India during the early centuries of the Christian era.

" " " Life of. By the Shamans Hwui & Yen-Tsung, tr. Prf. S. Beal [sup. to above] 10/- p 8° " 88

155. MONOSYLLABIC (*d*): THIBETAN PHILOLOGY AND LITERATURE.

Generally.

BASTIAN, Dr. A. Sprachvergleichliche Studien [w. spec. ref. to indo-chin. langs.] 7/6 8° *Leipzig* 70

HODGSON, B. H. Essays on the Languages, Liter. and Relig. of Nepal and Tibet 14/- r 8° Trübner 74

Dictionaries.

JAESCHKE, H. A. Tibetan-English Dictionary: w. English-Tibetan Vocabulary 30/- i 8° Trübner 81

SCHMIDT, I. J. Tibetanisch-deutsches Wörterbuch 32/- 4° *St. Petersburg* 41

" " Tibetan-Russian Dictionary 25/- 4° " 43

Grammars and Exercises.

FOUCAUX, P. E. Grammaire de la Langue Tibetane 5/- 8° *Paris* 58

JAESCHKE, H. A. Tibetan Grammar [Simplified Grammars] 5/- c 8° Trübner [65] 83

LEWIN, Maj. T. H. Manual of Tibetan: in a series of Exercises 21/- obl 4° *Calcutta* 79

SCHMIDT, I. J. Grammatik der tibetanischen Sprache 15/6 4° *St. Petersburg* 39

Texts and Translations.

Dsanglum ed. w. German tr. I. J. Schmidt, 2 vols. 20/-; suppl. by A. Schiefner 5/6 4° *St. Petersburg* 48; 52

FEER, L. [ed.] Textes tiré du Kandjuur, 11 pts. 25/- 8° *Paris* 64; 71

Lama Saskya Pandita: ed. w. French tr. P. E. Foucaux [coll. of maxims] 3/6 8° " 58

Rgya-Tcher-Rol-Pa [= Lalita Vistara, *v.* K § 124 X.]: ed. w. French tr. P. E. Foucaux 30/- 4° " 47; 48

156. MONOSYLLABIC (*e*): ANNAMITIC. COCHIN-CHINESE. SIAMESE. TONQUINESE.

Annamitic.

Dictionaries.

Dictionnaire Annamite-Français 21/- 8° *Tân-Dinh* 79

des MICHELS, A. Chu Nom an Nam [Annam. dict.-text and transcription] 6/6 8° *Paris* 78

RAVIER, M. H. Dictionarium Latino-Annamiticum completum 40/- 4° *Ninh Phu* 80

TABERD, J. L. Dictionarium Annamitico-Latinum, ed. J. S. Thewel 50/- 4° " [38] 77

Grammar.

AUBARET, G. Grammaire Annamite, avec un Vocabulaire [in Rom. and Chin. char.] 15/- r 8° *Paris* 67

Literature.

DUMOUTIER, G. [tr.] Les Chants et les Traditions pop. d. Annamites; ill. [Coll. d. Contes] 4/- 12° *Paris* 90

Kim Vân Kiêu Truyên text, French notes and tr. A. des Michels, 2 vols. [a poem] 35/- 8° " 83-85

Luc Vân Tiên Ca Diên text, transcription and French tr. A. des Michels 21/- 8° " 83

LANDES, A. [ed.] Contes et Légendes Annamites 8/- 8° *Saigon* 86

Tam Tu Kinh —*the* Chinese bk., text, Annam. transcript & French tr. A. des Michels 21/- 8° *Paris* 88

Trân Bô transcrite Phan Dú'c Hóa, w. Fch. tr. & notes A. Landes; 23 pl. [an Annam. comedy] 3/- 8° *Saigon* 87

K § 157

Cambodian.

MOUHOT, H. —*his* Travels [1858–60] in Siam, Camb. and Laos, vol. ii., pp. 207–40 *cont. a Cambod. vocab.*, 2 vols. 32/- 8° *Murray* 64

Cochin-Chinese.

Dictionary.

AYMONIER, E. Dictionnaire Khmêr-française 35/- r 8° *Saigon* 78

Dialogues.

des MICHELS, A. Dialogues Cochinchinois [in French, English and Latin] 16/- 8° *Paris* 71

Siamese.

Dictionary.

PALLEGOIX, Dictionarium Linguæ Thai [expl. in Lat., Fch. and Engl.] *o.p.* [w. £3] f° *Paris* 54

Grammar.

EWALD, L. Grammatik der Tai-Sprache 9/- 8° *Leipzig* 81

Tonquinese: *Literature.*

Les Pruniers Refleuris transcrite Phan Dú'c Hóa, trad. A. Landes 7/- 8° *Saigon* 84

157. MONOSYLLABIC (*f*): BURMESE PHILOLOGY AND LITERATURE.

History of Burmese Language.

FORCHHAMMER, Dr. E. Notes on the Languages and Dialects spoken in British Burmah 2/6 8° Trübner 87

Dictionaries.

JUDSON, A. Dictionary: Burmese-English and English Burmese ea. 25/- 8° *Rangoon* [26] 83; [52] 77
" " Burmese Pocket Dictionary, 9/- r 12°; Engl.-Burmese Dict. [abgd.] 7/6 c 8° *Rangoon* 87; [ ] 89
LANE, Charles English and Burmese Dictionary [English-Burmese only] 31/6 4° *Calcutta* 41
PHINNEY + EVELETH, F.D./F.H. Burmese Pocket Dictionary [both parts abridged from Judson's *Dict.*] 8/6 obl 8° *Rangoon* 87
WADE, J. The Anglo-Karen Dictionary, ed. Mrs. J. P. Binney 36/- 4° " [6-] 83

Grammars, etc.

DAVIDSON, Cpt. F. A. Manual of Anglicised Colloquial Burmese 3/6 f 8° W. H. Allen 89
GORDON, H. K. Handbook to Colloquial Burmese, 3/-; Companion to same 3/- 12° *Rangoon* [ ] 86; 86
JUDSON, A. Grammar of the Burmese Language 3/- 8° " [66] 89
LATTER, Th. Introduction to a Grammar of the Language of Burmah 10/6 4° *Calcutta* 45
SLACK, Cpt. Chas. Manual of Burmese; 2 maps 4/6 f 8° Trübner [88] 89
SLOAN, W. H. Practical Method with the Burmese Language 10/6 r 8° *Rangoon* [76] 87
WADE, J. Karen Vernacular Grammar 7/6 8° *Maulmain* 61

Chrestomathy.

MAINWARING, T. A. Anglo-Burmese Preceptor [stories, w. trs. and vocab.] 12/6 s 8° *Maulmain* 53

Literature.

Collections.

GRAY, J. (ed.) Ancient Provbs. & Maxims fr. Burmese Sources: the Niti-Literature [Orient. Ser.] 6/- p 8° Trübner 86

Individual Texts and Translations.

Damathat Burmese text and English tr., ed. D. Richardson [laws of Manu] 18/- r 8° *Rangoon* [ ] 76
Ka-Wee-Letkana-Deepanee-Kyan [a work on literature in Burmese] 30/- r 8° " 80
Kesasiri Jataka [a Burmese drama] 4/- 8° "
Kome-Ma-Rah-Pyah-Zat [a Burmese drama] 6/- 8° " 79
Mahachakkinda Jataka [a Burmese drama] 6/- 8° " 80
M'Mogandanobone 3 pts. [Prime minister's tales to the king on politics] ea. 7/6 8° "
Moung Pho Kyaw Sakkyathagiminthapyah-Zat [a Burmese drama] 5/- 8° " 80
Sadoodamathaya and Thauwaya Pyo, ed. Thaya [two Burmese epics] 5/- 8° " 81
SLADEN + SPARKS, E. B./T. D. [trs.] The Silver Hill, translated [a Burmese drama] 2/6 8° " 56
Thoodammasari tr. C. J. Bandow; w. notes and vocab. ["Precedents of the Princess"] 4/6 8° " 81
Tsan Mya Thinge Meng Thami Pyah-zat [a Burmese drama] 6/- 8° " 80

Burmese Buddhism—*v.* A § 14.

Shan Language.

CUSHING, Rev. J. N. Shan and English Dictionary 31/6 r 8° *Rangoon* 81
" " Grammar of the Shan Language 14/- 8° " [71] 87
" " Elementary Handbook of the Shan Language 12/6 4° " 80

XIX. Malayo-Polynesian Philology and Literature.

158. MALAIC PHILOLOGY.

Generally.

BOPP, F. — Ueb. d. Verwandtschaft d. malay.-polynes. Sprachen m. d. indo-europ. 10/- 8° *Berlin* 41

CUST, R. N. — Sketch of the Modern Langs. of East Indies [Orient. Ser.] 12/-; *red. to* 7/6 p 8° Trübner 78

Batta (SUMATRA).

van der TUUK, N. H. — Bataksch-Nederduitsch Woordenboek; 30 col. pl. 36/- 8° *Amsterdam* 61

" " — Bataksch Leesboek, 4 vols., 38/6; Tobasche Spraakkunst, pt. i. 2/6 8° " 60-62; 64

Borneo.

HARDELAND, A. — Grammatik d. Dajackschen, 9/-; Dajacksch-Deutsches Wörterbuch 32/- r 8° *Amsterdam* 58; 59

SWETTENHAM, F. A. — Comparative Vocabulary of Wild Tribes of Borneo [*Jl. R.A.S.*] 9/- 8° *Singapore* 80

Bugis, Makassar (CELEBES).

Chrestomathies Océaniennes, pt. i.: Textes Bonghis 3/6 8° *Paris*

MATTHES, B. F. — Makassaarsch-Hollandsch Woordenboek; w. atl. of col. pl. 35/- r 8° *The Hague* [59] 75

" " — Makassaarsch Spraakkunst, 7/-; Makassaarsch Chrestomathie 12/6 8° " 58; [60] 83

" " — Boegineesch-Holl. Woordenboek, 35/-; Boegineesch Spraakkunst 7/- 8° " 74; 75

Javanese.

Bibliography.

van der CHIJS, J. A. — Proeve eener Nederl-Indische Bibliographie [1659-1870] 12/- 8° *Batavia* 75

Dictionaries.

BRUCKNER, G. — Vocabulary of the Dutch, English & Javanese Langs. *o.p.* [*pb.* 16/; *w.* 18/-] 8° *Batavia* 42

FAVRE, Abbé P. — Dictionnaire Javanais-Français 15/- r 8° *Vienna* 70

JANSZ, P. — Nederlandsch-Javaansch Woordenboek 12/- 8° *Samarang* [ ] 77

" " — Javaansch-Nederlandsch Woordenboek [Roman characters] 21/- 8° 77

Grammars.

FAVRE, Abbé P. — Grammaire Javanaise: avec exercises 10/- 8° *Paris* 66

JANSZ, P. — Kleine Javaansche Spraakkunst 12/6 8° *Samarang* [ ] 80

Kawi.

v. HUMBOLDT, W. — Ueber die Kawi-Sprache, 3 vols.; 11 pl. *o.p.* [*w.* 40/-] 4° *Berlin* 36-39

An important work on compar. philol., with an intro. of 430 pp. Batta is related to Sanscrit and Pali.

Sunda.

OOSTING, H. J. — Soendasche Grammatica, 2 vols. 4/6 r 8° *The Hague* 84; 84

" " — Nederduitsch-Soend. Woordenb., 7/-; Soend.-Nederduitsch Woordenb., 3 v. 15/- r 8° " 87; 87

RIGG, Jonathan — Dictionary of the Sunda Language 42/- 4° *Batavia* 62

" " — On the Sunda Language 12/- 4° " 62

Malayan.

Dictionaries.

*FAVRE, Abbé P. — Dictionnaire Malaise-Français, 2 v. £2; Dictionnaire Français-Malais, 2 v. ea. £2 8° *Vienna* 75; 80

HAPPART, G. — Dictionary of Favorlang Dialect of Formosan Language 7/6 12° *Batavia* 40

SWETTENHAM, F. A. — Vocabulary of English and Malayan Langs., 2 vols. [both parts] ea. 10/- 8° *Singapore* 81; 87

Grammars, etc.

CRAWFURD, J. — Grammar and Dictionary of the Malay Language, 2 vols. *o.p.* [*w.* 63/-] 8° Smith & Elder 52

DENNYS, Dr. N. B. — Handbook of Malay Colloquial 21/- 8° *Singapore* 78

*FAVRE, Abbé P. — Grammaire de la Langue Malaise 12/6 8° *Vienna* 76

MAXWELL, W. E. — Manual of the Malay Language [w. sketch of Sanscr. elem. in Malay] 7/6 c 8° Trübner [82] 88

MEURSINGE, A. — Maleisch Leesboek, 3 pts. 16/- 12° *Leyden* [42-47] 79-80

159. MELANESIAN AND POLYNESIAN PHILOLOGY.

Generally.

*CODRINGTON, R. H. — The Melanesian Languages [incl. grammars and vocabularies] 18/- 8° Clar. Press 85

CUST, R. N. — Sketch of the Modern Languages of Oceania p 8° Trübner *in prep.*

*FORNANDER, A. — Acct. of Polynes. Race — vol. iii. *is a compar. vocab. of Polyns. & Indo-Eur. langs.* 9/- p 8° " [86] 90

v. d. GABELENTZ, H. C. — Die melanesischen Sprachen nach ihrem Bau, 2 pts. 16/- 4° *Leipzig* 60; 73

MACDONALD, Rev. D. [Austral.] Oceania: linguistic and anthropological; 7 ill. 6/- c 8° *Melbourne* 88

United States Exploring Expedition [1838-42] under Wilkes r 4° *Philadelphia* 48

Vol. vii: Ethnography and Philology, by H. HALE [Am.]. The Philological section contains a Polynesian and a Vitian (Fijian) grammar and vocabulary, and grammars vocabularies, etc., of dialects and languages of several other islands.

Fijian.

HALE, H. [Am.] Vitian Grammar and Vocabulary, *v. sup, s.v.* United States Explor. Exped.
HAZLEWOOD, D. * Fijian-English & English-Fijian Dictionary & Grammar, ed. Calvert *o.p.* [*w.* 25/-] 8° Wesley. Mis. Pub. [ ]72

Hawaiian.

ANDREWS, Lorrin Grammar of the Hawaiian Language 10/6 8° *Honolulu* 54
" " Vocabulary of Words in the Hawaiian Language 26/- 8° *Lahainluna* 46
" " Dictionary of Hawaiian Language: w. Eng.-Haw. Vocab. 31/6 8° *Honolulu* 65
EMERSON, English-Hawaiian Dictionary 25/- 8° *Lahainluna* 45
HITCHCOCK, H. R. [Am.] English-Hawaiian Dictionary $2 12° *San Francisco* 88

New Zealand. —*v.* K § 160.

Samoan.

Dictionary: Samoan [both pts.]; with grammar and dialect *o.p.* [*w.* 7/6] 8° *Samoa* 62
PRATT, Rev. G. Grammar and Dictionary of Samoan Language, ed. Whitmee 18/- 8° Trübner [62] 78
VIOLETTE, Père L. Dictionnaire Samoa-Franç.-Angl. et Franç.-Samoa-Anglais 17/- 8° *Paris* 79

Tahitian.

Dictionary: Tahitian and English [w. introd. remarks on the language] *o.p.* [*w.* £3] 8° *Tahiti* 51
JAUSSEN, Bp. E. Grammaire de la Langue Maori, Dialecte Tahitien 8/6 12° *St. Cloud* 60

Tongan.

Missionaires Maristes Dictionnaire Tonga-Français et Français-Tonga 17/- 8° *Paris* 90

160. AUSTRALIAN PHILOLOGY (INCL. MALAGASY, MAORI AND NEW GUINEAN).

Australian.

CURR, E. M. The Australian Race: its origin, languages, customs, etc., vols. i.–iv. 42/- c 8° & i f° Trübner 89
127 Engl. words w. their representatives in 250 native languages, printed separ. for ea. tribe. Vol. iv., f°, gives half the words in parallel columns. *Vide* E § 63
DAWSON, James Australian Aborigines 14/- 4° *Melbourne* (Macmillan) 81
On the languages and customs of several tribes in Western District of Victoria.
RIDLEY, Rev. W. Kámilarói and other Australian Languages 10/6 s 4° *Sydney* [66] 77
TEICHELMANN + SCHÜRMANN, C. G. / W. Grammar, Vocab. & Phraseol. of Aborig. Lang. of S. Australia 16/- 8° *Adelaide* 40
THRELKELD, Rev. T. E. Grammar of the Aborigines of New South Wales *o.p.*; Key *o.p.* 8° 30; 51
WILLIAMS, W. Vocabulary of the Language of Adelaide District *o.p.* [*w.* 7/6] 8° *Adelaide* 40

Malagasy (MADAGASCAR).

Dictionaries.

FREEMAN + JOHNS, J. / D. Dictionary of Malagasy Language, 2 vols. [both parts] *o.p.* [*w.* £5] 8° *Tananarivo* 35
French Cathol. Missionaries Dictionnaire Franç.-Malgache *o.p.* [*w.* £6 6/-] 8° *Ile Bourbon* 55
Vocabulaire Franç.-Malgache 14/- 8° *Tananarivo* 80
GRIFFITHS, David English and Malagasy Vocabulary, w. sentences in both languages p 8° 63
RICHARDSON, Rev. J. New Malagasy-English Dictionary: w. intro. Rev. W. E. Cousins 8° *Antananarivo* 85
SEWELL, J. S. Dictionary: English-Malagasy 12/6 8° " 75

Grammars.

GRIFFITHS, David Grammar of the Malagasy Lang. in Ankova Dialect *o.p.* [*w.* 18/-] 12° *Woodbridge* 54
KESSLER, Julius Intro. to Gram. and Liter. of Madagascar [gram., voc., phrases] 3/6 f° Hunt 70
PARKER, G. W. Concise Grammar of the Malagasy Language 5/- c 8° Trübner 83

Maori (NEW ZEALAND).

MAUNSELL, R. Grammar of the New Zealand Language *o.p.* [*w.* 42/-] 8° *Auckland* 42
WILLIAMS, W. Dictionary of New Zealand Language [w. grammar] 10/6 8° Williams [52] 71
" " First Lessons in Maori Language [w. vocabulary] 2/6 s 8° Trübner [62] 87

Literature —*for Folk-literature, v.* B § 29.

GREY, Sir George [ed.] Poetry of the New Zealanders [texts] *o.p.* [*w.* 35/-] 8° *Wellington, N.Z.* 53

New Guinean.

LAWES, Rev. W. G. Grammar and Vocabulary of the Motu Tribe 10/6 8° *Sydney* 85

XX. African Philology.

161. GENERAL AND SPECIAL TREATISES.

Generally.

Dictionaries.

BARTH, H. [ed.] Collection of Vocabs. of Central-African Languages [in Eng. and Germ.] 30/- 4° *Gotha* 62–66
KOELLE, S. W. Polyglotta Africana: comparative vocab. of 300 words in 100 langs. 21/- i f° Trübner 54
KRAPF, Rev. J. L. Vocabulary of Six East-African Languages [in 7 cols.] 12/- 4° *Tübingen* 50
LAST, J. T. Polyglotta Africana Orientalis [250 wds. and sentences in 48 langs and dial.] 3/- 8° Trübner 85
REINISCH, Leo Sprachen von Nordost-Afrika, vols. i.–iii. [Barea and Nubian] 20/- 8° *Vienna* 74–79

Grammars, etc.

BLEEK, W. H. J. Compar. Grammar of S.-African Langs. I. (i.) [phonol.], ii. (1) [noun] 36/- 8° Trübner 62; 69
*CUST, R. N. Sketch of the Modern Languages of Africa, 2 vols. 25/-; *red. to* 18/- p 8° „ 84

Folk-Literature —*v.* B § 34: African Mythology and Folklore.

Magazine.

Zeitschrift für afrikanische Sprachen, ed. C. G. Büttner (quarterly) *ann.* 12/- 8° *Berlin* 87 *in prog.*

'Afar.

COLIZZA, G. Lingua 'Afar nel Nord-est dell' Africa 8° *Vienna* 87
REINISCH, Prf. L. Die 'Afar Sprache, 3 pts. 5/- 8° „ 85–87

Akra, or Ga (GOLD COAST).

CHRISTALLER + LOCHER, J. G. / W. Dictionary: Tshi (Asante), Akra, Tshi (Chwee) 4/- 8° *Basle* 74
ZIMMERMANN, Rev. J. Grammatical Sketch of Akra or Ga Lang., 2 vols. [w. specimens] 4/- 8° *Stuttgart* 58

Amharic (ABYSSINIA)—*v.* K § 116: Ethiopic.

Asante (FANTI).

CHRISTALLER, Rev. J. G. Dictionary of the Asante and Fante [Tshi] Language 25/- 8° *Basle* 81
„ „ Grammar of the Asante and Fante [Tshi] Language 8/- 8° „ 75
RIIS, H. N. Grammatical Outline and Grammar of the Oji Language [tr.] 10/- 8° „ 54
„ „ Elemente des Akwapim Dialektes der Odschi-Sprache 8/6 8° „ 53

Bantu.

KOLBE, Rev. F. W. A Language-Study based on Bantu 6/- p 8° Trübner 88

Barea (ABYSSINIA).

REINISCH, Prf. Leo Die Barea Sprache [grammar, text, dictionary] 6/- 8° *Vienna* 74

Bari (UPPER NILE BASIN).

MITTERRUTZNER, Dr. J. C. Sprache der Bari [grammar, text, dictionary] 7/- 8° *Brixen* 67
MÜLLER, J. Sprache der Bari [grammar, selections, glossary] 2/- 8° *Vienna* 64

Benga (ISLE OF KONISKO, W. AFRICA).

MACKEY, J. L. Grammar of the Benga Language $2 12° *New York* 55

Berber (ALGERIA, TUNISIA, MOROCCO)—*v.* K § 103, *s.v.* Libyan.

Bilin, or Bogos —*v.* K § 104: Kushitic Philology.

Bishari (NUBIA).

ALMKVIST, Hermann Die Bischari-Sprache Tu-Bedawie in Nordost-Afrika, 2 vols. 35/- 4° *Upsala* 81; 86
MUNZINGER, W. Ostafrikanische Studien [w. grammar and vocab.] 11/- 8° *Schaffhausen* 64

Bornu.

KOELLE, S. W. Grammar of Bornu or Kanuri Language 10/6 8° Trübner 54
„ „ African Native Literature in Bornu Lang. [w. trss. and gloss.] 7/6 8° Williams 54
NORRIS, E. Grammar of Bornu Lang. [w. dial., trss. and vocab.] *o.p.* [15/-] 8° Trübner 53

Bunda (LOANDA, W. AFRICA).

CANNECATTIM, B. M. Observaçoes gram. sobre a lingua Bunda [in Portuguese] 20/- 8° *Lisbon* [05] 59
„ „ Diccionario da Lingua Bunda [in Portuguese] *o.p.* [*w.* 25/-] 4° „ 04
CHATELAIN, H. Grammatica do Kimbundu [in Portuguese] 8° *Genebra* 88–89
WOODWARD, W. H. Collections for a Handbook of the Boondei Language 4/- 8° Trübner 82

Chamir (ABYSSINIA)—*v.* K § 104: Kushitic Philology.

K § 101

Chigogo or Gogo [near UNYA NYAMBE].

CLARK, G. J. — Vocabulary of the Chigogo Language — 12/6 8° Trübner 77

Congo (WEST AFRICA).

BENTLEY, Rev. W. H. — Dictionary of the Kongo Language [both parts] 21/- 8° Trübner 88
" " — Grammar of the Kongo Language [w. tales, proverbs, etc.] " *in prep.*
BRUSCIOTTO, — Grammar of Congo Lang. as spoken 200 years ago 8/- 8° " 82
Translated from the Latin by Rev. H. Grattan GUINNESS.
CRAVEN + BARFIELD, H. + J. — English-Congo and Congo-English Dictionary [w. phrases] 6/- 8° " 83
GUINNESS, Rev. H. Grattan — Grammar of the Congo Language 12/6 8° " 82

Creolese —*v.* Negro-English, *infra.*

Dahomy.

COURDIOUX, Ph. E. — Dictionnaire de la Langue Fongbé, vol. i. [French-Fongbé] 4/- 8° *Paris* 79

Dinka (UPPER NILE BASIN).

BELTRAME, D. G. — Grammatica e Vocabulario della Lingua Denka [Mem. Soc. Geog. Ital., vol. iii.] 7/6 8° *Rome* 81
MITTERRUTZNER, Dr. J. C. — Die Dinka Sprache [grammar, text, dictionary] 7/- 8° *Brixen* 66

Dualla.

SAKER, A. J. — Grammatical Elements of Dualla Lang. [w. vocab.] *o.p.* [*w.* 12/-] 8° *Cameroons* (*W. Africa*) 55

Efik (WEST AFRICA).

GOLDIE, H. — Dictionary of the Efik Language [both parts] *o.p.* [*w.* 25/-] 8° *Glasgow* 74

Enguduk.

ERHARDT, J. — Vocabulary of the Enguduk Iloigob [Masai of East Africa] 3/- 8° *Ludwigsburg* 57
KRAPF, Rev. J. L. — Vocabulary of Engutuk Eloikob 2/- 8° *Tübingen* 54

Ethiopic —*v.* K § 116.

Fernandian.

CLARKE, J. — Introduction to Fernandian *o.p.* [*w.* 10/-] 8° *Berwick-on-Tweed* 48

Fulah (WEST AFRICA).

KRAUSE, G. A. — Beitrag zur Kenntniss d. Fulischen Sprache 4/- 8° *Leipzig* 84
MACBRIAR, Rev. R. M. — Grammar of Fulah Lang., [posthumously] ed. E. Norris *o.p.* [*w.* 15/-] 16° Trübner 54
REICHARDT, C. A. L. — Grammar of Fulde Language, 12/6; Vocabulary of Fulde Language 10/6 8° *Leipzig* 76; 78

Galla (EAST AFRICA)—*v.* K § 104: Kushitic Philology.

Ghat (SAHARA).

KRAUSE, G. A. [ed.] — Proben der Sprache von Ghat [w. German trns.] 4/- 8° *Leipzig* 84

Grebo (CAPE PALMAS).

PAYNE, J. [Am.] — Dictionary of the Grebo Language 15/- 8° *New York* 60
TUTSCHEK, C. — Galla Grammar, and Galla-Eng.-Germ. and Eng.-Galla-Germ. Dict. 9/- 8° *Munich* 44-45

Haussa.

LE ROUX, J. M. — Essai de Dictionnaire Français-Haoussa et Haoussa-Français 12/6 4° *Algiers* 87
SCHÖN, Rev. J. F. — Dictionary of the Haussa Language [both parts] 10/6 8° Trübner [43] 76
" " — Haussa Reading Book [w. grammar and vocab.] 2/6 8° " 77
" " — Grammar of the Haussa Language 7/6 8° " 62

Herero (SOUTH AFRICA).

BRINCKER, Rev. H. — Wörterbuch und Grammatik des Otji-Herero 25/- 8° *Leipzig* 87
HAHN, C. H. — Grundzüge einer Grammatik der Herero Sprache 8/- r 8° *Berlin* 57
KOLBE, Rev. F. W. — The Vowels: primeval laws in Herero 3/- 8° *Cape Town* 60
" " — English-Herero Dictionary, ed. Rev. H. Brincker 15/- p 8° " [ ] 88

Hottentot —*v.* Namaquha, *infra.*

Kabail —*v.* K § 103, *s.v.* Kabail.

Kafir —*v.* Zulu, *infra.*

Kanuri —*v.* Bornu, *supra.*

Kiniassa.

REBMAN, Rev. J. — Dictionary of the Kiniassa Language, ed. Dr. L. Krapf 15/- 8° *Basle* 77

Kisuaheli —*v.* Swahili, *infra.*

Libyan —*v.* K § 103: Libyan Philology.

Lunda (N. of Zambesi).

Dias de Carvalho, Maj. H. A. Methodo Pratico para fallar a lingua da Lunda [in Portuguese] 5/- 8° *Lisbon* 89

Makua.

Maples, Chauncy — Collections for a Handbook of the Makua Language 1/6 32° Trübner 79
" " — Notes on Makua Lang.—*in Trans. Philolog. Soc.* 1880–81, pt. i. 10/- 8° " 81

Malagasy —*v.* K § 160, *s.v.* Malagasy.

Mande.

Steinthal, H. — Die Mande-Neger Sprache [psycholog. and phonetically] 8/- 8° *Berlin* 67

Mozambique.

Bleek, Dr. W. H. J. — Languages of Mozambique: vocabularies 21/- obl 8° Trübner 56
Drawn from the MSS. of Dr. W. Peters and M. Beal.

Namaquha (Hottentot).

Hahn, Th. — Die Sprache der Nama [w. specimens] 3/6 8° *Leipzig* 70
Krönlein, J. G — Wortschatz der Khoi-Khoin 25/- r 8° *Berlin* 89
Olpp, J. — Nama-deutsches Wörterbuch 3/- 8° *Barmen* 88
Tindall, H. — Grammar and Vocabulary of the Namaqua-Hottentot Language 6/- 8° Longman 57

Negro-English (Creolese).

Addison, van N. [Am.]. — Contributions to Creole Grammar—in *Tr. Am. Phil. Ass.* 1869–70 5/- 8° 69–70
Schuchardt, Prf. Hugo — Kreolische Studien, pts. i–viii [repr. fr. Sitzber. Wien. Akad.] 5/- 8° *Vienna* 82–88
Thomas, J. J. — Theory and Practice of Creole Grammar 12/- 8° *Port of Spain* 69
Wullschlägel, H. R. — Deutsch-Neger-Englisches Wörterbuch 7/6 8° *Löbau* 56

Nubian.

*Lepsius, R. — Nubische Grammatik [w. texts and Nubian-German gloss.] 26/- 8° *Berlin* 80
Reinisch, Prf. Leo — Die Nubische Sprache, 2 vols. [i.: grammar and texts; ii.: dictionary] 14/- 8° *Vienna* 79

Nyamwezi.

Steere, Bp. E. — Collections for a Handbook of Nyamwezi Language 1/6 12° Trübner

Oji —*v.* Asante, *supra.*

Pongwe.

Delorme, A. — Dictionnaire Français-Pongué 8/6 12° *Paris* 77
Gachon, Rev. — — Dictionnaire Pongué Français [w. brief grammar] 8/6 12° " 81
Le Berre, Rev. — — Grammaire de la Langue Ponguée 7/- 8° " 73
Missionaries of A.B.C.F.M. — Grammar of the Mpongwe Language *o.p.* [*w.* 21/-] 8° *New York* 47

Quara (Abyssinia) —*v.* K § 104: Kushitic Philology.

Saho —*v.* K § 104: Kushitic Philology.

Sechuana (Bechuana, Sotho).

Casalis, E. — Études sur la Langue Sechuana 10/- r 8° *Paris* 41
Endemann, K. — Versuch einer Grammatik des Sotho 8/6 8° *Berlin* 76

Shambála.

Steere, Bp. E. — Collections for a Handbook of the Shambála Language 3/6 12° *Zanzibar* 67

Soso.

Raimbault, R. P. — Dictionnaire Français-Soso et Soso-Français 6/- s 8° *Paris* 85

Swahili.

Krapf, Rev. L. — Dictionary of Suahili Language [w. outline of grammar] 30/- r 8° Trübner 82
Steere, Bp. E. — Handbook of the Swahili Language 7/6 8° Bell [71] 75

Tamachek —*v.* Berber, *supra.*

Tigré, Tigrinna —*v.* K § 116.

Tshi (Fanti) —*v.* Asante, *supra.*

Vei.

Koelle, S. W. — Outline of Gram. of Vei Lang. [w. Vei-English vocab.] *o.p.* [*pb.* 16/-; *w.* 7/6] 8° Trübner 54

Wolof (Senegambia).

Boilat, Abbé — Grammaire de la Langue Woloffe 16/- r 8° *Paris* 58
Dard, J. — Dictionnaire Français-Wolof et Wolof-Français 12/- 12° *Dakar* [25] 55
Kobès, Bp. — Grammaire de la Langue Volofe 10/6 8° *S. Joseph d. Ngasobil* 69

K §§ 162-163

Yao.

HETHERWICK, Rev. A. Introductory Handbook and Vocabulary of the Yao Language 5/- c 8° S.P.C.K. 90
STEERE, Bp. E. Collections for a Handbook of the Yao Language 2/- 16° Trübner 71

Yoruba.

BOWEN, F. J. [Am.] Grammar and Dictionary of the Yoruba Language $5 4° *Washington* 58
CROWTHER, S. Vocabulary of Yoruba Lang., 8/6 ; Grammar of Yoruba Lang. 6/- 8° Seeley 52 ; 52

Zulu (Kafir and Xosa-Kafir).

COLENSO, Bp. J. W. Zulu-English Dictionary *o.p.* [w. 28/-] 8° *Pietermaritzburg* 61
" " Zulu-Kafir Reading Book pt. i., 1/- ; ii., 3/- ; iii., 5/- ; iv., 7/- 16° & 8° *Natal* *n.d.* (59)
DAVIS, Rev. W. J. English and Kaffir Dictionary : princ. Xosa-Kaffir 5/- s 8° Trübner 77
" " Dictionary of Kaffir Language ; pt. i. : Kaffir-English 8/- 8° Wesley Miss. Pub. 72
" " Kaffir Grammar 5/- 8° " " 72
DÖHNE, T. L. Zulu-Kafir Dictionary : etymologically explained 21/- r 8° *Cape Town* 57
GROUT, Rev. L. The Isizulu : grammar of Zulu language 21/- 8° *Natal* 59
ROBERTS, Rev. C. The Zulu-Kafir Language Simplified [Simplified Grammar Series] 6/- 8° Trübner 80
" " English-Zulu Dictionary : with pronunciation 8/- 8° " 80

XXI. American (Aboriginal) Philology & Literature.

162. GENERAL WORKS.

Bibliography —*v. also* E § 53.

*LUDEWIG, Dr. H. E. The Literature of American Aboriginal Languages [tr.] 10/6 8° Trübner 58
PILLING, J. C. [Am.] Bibliography of Languages of N.-American Indians 4° *Washington* 85
PLATZMANN, J. Verzeichniss amerikanischer Grammatiken, Wörterbücher, etc., etc. 4/- 8° *Leipzig* 76

Philology —*v. also* E § 53 : American Indians (Ethnology, etc.).

BRINTON, Prf. D. G. [Am.] Essays of an Americanist ; ill. $2.50 8° *Philadelphia* 90
1. Ethnologic and Archaeologic ; 2. Mythol. and Folklore ; 3. Graphic Systems and Liter. ; 4. Linguistic.
GATSCHET, A. S. [Am.] Indian Vocabularies = *appendix to* Reports on Archæol. & Ethnol. [U.S. Geog. Surv.] $10 r 4° *Washington* 79
MALLERY, G. [Am.] Introduction to Study of Sign Language among N.-A. Indians $5 4° " 80
POWELL, J. W. [Am.] Introduction to Study of Indian Languages $5 4° " [ ] 81

Folk-Literature —*v.* B § 35 : American Aboriginal Mythology and Folklore, and § 53 : American Indians.

163. NORTH AMERICAN INDIAN PHILOLOGY AND LITERATURE.

Blackfoot [a tribe of the Algonquin family].

TIMS, Rev. J. W. Grammar and Dictionary of the Blackfoot Language 6/- c 8° S.P.C.K. 89

Catawba.

CHAMBERLAIN, A. F. [Am.] Catawba-Siouan Vocabulary 8° *Toronto* 88

Chiapanek.

ADAM, L. La Langue Chiapanèque 8/- 8° *Vienna* 87

Chinook.

GIBBS, G. [Am.] Dictionary of the Chinook Jargon, or Trade Language of Oregon $2 8° *New York* 63
" " Alphabetical Vocabulary of the Chinook Language 8° " 7-

Chippeway.

BARAGA, Bp. R. A. [Am.] Grammar and Dict. of the Otchipwe Language $4 8° *Montreal* [79] 82
PETITOT, le R. P. E. Dictionnaire de la Langue Déné-Dindjie [w. grammar] £3 4° *Paris* 76

Choctaw.

BYINGTON, C. [Am.] Grammar of the Choctaw Lang., [posth.] ed. D. G. Brinton [Am.] $1.50 c 8° *Philadelphia* 70

Clallam and Lummi.

GIBBS, G. [Am.] Alphabetical Vocabularies of the Clallam and Lummi $5 8° *New York* 7-

K § 163

Cree.

HORDEN, Rev. J. [Am.] Grammar of the Cree Language as Spoken 2/- 8° Trübner 81
HOWSE, Joseph [Am.] Grammar of Cree Lang.: w. analysis of Chippeway dialect 7/6 8° ,, [44] 65
HUNTER, Archd. [Am.] Lectures on Grammatical Construction of Cree Language $3 s 4° 75
LACOMBE, le R. P. A. Dictionnaire et Grammaire de la Langue des Cris 25/- 8° *Montreal* 74

Creole —*v.* K § 161.

Dakota.

v. d. GABELENTZ, H. C. Grammatik der Dakota-Sprache 2/6 8° *Leipzig* 52
RIGGS, Rev. S. R. [Am.] Grammar and Dictionary of the Dakota Language $10 4° *Washington* 52
ROEHRIG, F. L. O. [Am.] The Language of the Dakota, or Sioux Indians 50c. 8° ,, 72
WILLIAMSON, J. P. [Am.] English-Dakota Vocabulary $2 12° *Nebraska*

Delaware.

DUPONCEAU, P. S. [Am.] Grammar of Lang. of Lenni Lenape Indians *o.p.* [*w.* 18/-] 4° *Philadelphia* 27

Etchemin.

BARRATT, J. [Am.] —*his* India of New England, *conts. vocabs. of Etchemin & Micmac langs.* 75c 8° *Connecticut* 51

Heve.

SMITH, Buckingham [Am.] Grammatical Sketch of the Heve Language $5 8° *New York* 6-

Hidatsa.

MATTHEWS, W. [Am.] Grammar and Dictionary of Language of the Hidatsa $6 i 8° *New York* 73
,, ,, Ethnology and Philology of the Hidatsa $6 8° *Washington* 77
Ethnography, Philology, Grammar, Dictionary, and English-Hidatsa Vocabulary.
,, ,, Hidatsa [Minnetakee]-English Dictionary $6 8° *New York* 75

Iroquois.

Bibliography.

PILLING, J. C. [Am.] Bibliography of the Iroquoian Languages $2 8° *Washington* 88

Kiriri.

v. d. GABELENTZ, H. C. Grammatik der Kiriri-Sprache 2/6 8° *Leipzig* 52

Lummi —*v.* Clallam, *supra.*

Micmac —*v. also* Etchemin, *supra.*

MAILLARD, Abbé Grammar of the Mikmaque Language, tr. Bellenger [Am.] $4 8° *New York* 64
Reading Book in Micmac Language [Micmac and English] $1 s 8° *Halifax, U.S.* 75

Mohawk.

BRUYAS, Rev. J. [Am.] Radical Words of Mohawk Language: w. derivations $7 8° *New York* 62

Mosquito.

COTHEAL, A. [Am.] Gram. Sketch of Lang. of Indians of Mosquito—*in Trs. Am. Eth. Soc. II.* $7 8° *New York* 48
HENDERSON, Alex. [Am.] Grammar of the Moskito Language *o.p.* [*w.* 6/6] 8° ,, 46

Mutsun.

de la CUESTA, F. A. [Am.] Grammar of the Mutsun Language of Alta California $3 r 8° *New York* 61
,, ,, Vocabulary or Phrase-Book of the Mutsun Language $2.50 r 8° ,, 62

Onondaga.

SHEA, J. G. [Am.; ed.] Onondaga and French Dictionary $5 8° *New York* 60

Pima.

SMITH, Buckingham [Am.] Grammar of the Pima or Névome $5 8° *New York* 6-

San Antonio.

SITJAR, B. [Am.] Vocabulary of the San Antonio Mission, California $4 8° *New York* 61

Selish (FLAT-HEAD).

MENGARINI, G. [Am.] Selish Grammar $5 8° *New York* 6-

Yakama.

PANDOSY, Rev. M. C. [Am.] Grammar and Dictionary of Yakama Language [tr.] $3 4° *New York* 62

164. CENTRAL AND SOUTH AMERICAN PHILOLOGY AND LITERATURE

Andes.

ADAM, Lucien — Arte de la Lengua Andé ó Campa [Bibl. Ling. Amér.] 12/6 8° *Paris* 89

Araucanian (Chilian).

CREVAUX+SAGOT+ADAM, J.;P.;L. Grams. et Vocabulaires, Roucouyenne, Arrouague, Piapoco, et autres langues des Guyanes [Bibl. Ling. Amér.] 21/- 8° *Paris* 82

FEBRES, Andres — Gram. de la Lengua Chilena, ed. F. M. Astraldi, 42/-; abgd. edition 12/6 8° *Santiago* [1765] 46:64

" " — Diccionario Chileno Hispaño, ed. the same 8/- 8° " [ ] 46

HAVESTADT, C. — Chilidúgu: sive tractatus linguæ Chilensis, ed. J. Platzmann, 2 vols.; 10 pl. 36/- 8° *Leipzig* [ ] 84

LARSEN, J. M. — Gramática Araucana 20/- 8° *Buenos Ayres* [1765] 84

de VALDIVIA, Luis — Arte, Vocabulario e Confessionario de le lengua de Chile 18/- 8° *Leipzig* 87

Arawack — *v. also* Roucouyan, etc., *supra*.

BRINTON, Prf. D. G. [Am.] Arawack Lang. of Guiana: in linguistic and ethnolog. relations 5/- 4° *Philadelphia* 71

Baures.

MAGIO, Antonio — Arte de la Lengua de los Indios Baures [Bibl. Ling. Amér.] 12/6 8° *Paris* 80

Edited by L. ADAM+Ch. LECLERC from the MS. written [illegible].

Bogota.

URICOECHEA, E. — Gramatica, Vocab. i Catec. de la lengua Chibcha [Bibl. Ling. Amér.] 17/- 8 *Paris* 71

Brazilian.

Dictionaries.

de MONTOYA, A. R. — Bocabulario y Tesoro de la Leng. Guarani, 4 vols. 48/- 4° *Leipzig* 76

Grammars, etc.

de ANCHIETA, Jos. — Arte de Gram. da Lingua do Brasil, ed. J. Platzmann 20/- 16° [74] 76

FIGUEIRA, P. Luiz — Grammatica de Lingua do Brasil, ed. J. Platzmann 5/- 16° *Leipzig* 78

de MAGALHAES, Conto — Curso da Lingua Geral, 2 vols. [Ollendorf system] 21/- 8° *Rio de Janeiro* 76

MARTIUS, C. F. P. — *in his* Beiträge zur Ethnographie u. Sprachenkunde Amerika's, 2 vols. 13/6 8° *Leipzig* 67

de MONTOYA, A. R. — Arte de la Lengua Guarani, 2 vols. [vocab., seins., etc.] 25/- s 4° *Vienna* 76-77

SYMPSON, P. L. — Grammatica de Lingua Brazilica 10/6 8° *Manaos* 77

Chrestomathies.

FERREIRA, Dr. E. F. F. — Chrestomathia de Lingua Brazilica 4/6 12° *Leipzig* 59

de MONTOYA, A. R. — *in his* Bocabulario, *ut supra*.

Caribbean.

BRETON, le P. R. — Grammaire Caraïbe, ed. L. Adam+Ch. Leclerc [Bibl. Ling. Amér.] 12/6 8 *Paris* [ ] 78

Chiquitan.

ADAM+HENRY, Lucien/Victor — Arte y Vocabul. de la Lengua Chiquita [Bibl. Ling. Amér.] 12/6 8° *Paris* 80

Jágan (Tierra del Fuego, PATAGONIA).

ADAM, Lucien — Grammaire de la Langue Jágane 2/6 8° *Paris* 85

Koggaban.

CELEDON, Rafael — Gramatica de la Lengua Koggaba [w. vocab.; Bibl. Ling. Amér.] 12/6 8° *Paris* 86

Maya (YUCATAN).

Codex Peresianus: facsimile reprod. by Léon de Rosny; 42 pl. [w. intro. and gloss. in Fch.] £6 f° *Paris* 90

Manuscript Troano — reprod. Brasseur de Bourbourg, 2 vols.; 70 col. pl. [Miss. Scient. en Méx., ii.-iii.] £6 4° *Paris* 69-70

" " — The same, without the pl., *sub tit.* Dict. Gram. et Chrest. Maya 25/- 4° *Paris* 71

PEREZ, J. P. — Diccionario de la Lengua Maya 75/- 4° *Yucatan* 77

de ROSNY, L. — Essai sur le Déchiffr. de l'écriture hiér. de l'Amér. Cent.; 19 col. pl. £4 f° *Paris* 77-82

" " — The same: with only 2 plates 12/6 8° " 76-84

" " — Vocabulaire de l'Écriture Hiératique Yucatèque [*extr. fr.* Codex Cortés.] 4/6 4° " 83

" " — Les Documents écrits de l'antiquité Américaine; 10 pl. [report] 7/6 4° " 82

" " — Interpretation des Anciens Textes Mayas [w. short grammar] 8/6 8° " 75

Maya.

STOLL, O. — Die Sprache der Ixil-Indianer [ethnolog. and philolog.] 8/- 8° *Leipzig* 87

" " — Die Maya-Sprachen der Pokom-Gruppe, pt. i. [Pokonchi Indians] 10/6 8° *Vienna* 88

Literature.

BRINTON, Prf. D. G. [Am.; ed.] Books of Chilam Balam: prophet. and histor. records of Mayas 2/6 12° *Philadelphia* 82

Mexican (Aztec, Nahuatla).

Bibliography.

BRASSEUR de BOURBOURG Bibliothèque Mexico-Guatémalienne [nearly 500 books, etc.] 10/- 8° *Paris* 71
ICAZBALCETA, J. G. Bibliografia Mexicana del siglio xvi.; 50 facss. 50/- 4° *Mexico* 86

Dictionaries.

BIONDELLI, B. Glossarium Azteco-Lat. et Lat.-Aztecum 21/- 4° *Milan* 69
de MOLINA, F. A. Vocabulario de la Lengua Mexicana, publ. J. Platzmann 50/- 4° *Leipzig* [1571] 80
del RINCON, Antonio Gramatica y Vocabulario Mexicano 17/- 4° *Mexico* [1595] 85
SIMÉON, R. Dictionnaire Mexicain-Français 8° *Paris* *in prep.*

Grammars, etc.

BUSCHMANN, J. C. Grammatik der sonorischen Sprachen, pt. i., 3/-; ii. 16/- 4° *Berlin* 64; 69
CABALLERO, D. J. Grammatica del Idioma Mexicano 21/- 8° *Mexico* 80
de OLMOS, André Arte de la lengua Nahuatl, ed. R. Siméon [written in 1547] 10/- 8° *Paris* 75
PIMENTEL, F. Cuadro Descript. y Compar. d. l. Lenguas ... d. México, 3 vols. 42/- 8° *Mexico* [ ] 75

Classification.

OROSCO Y BERRA, L. M. Geografia de las Lenguas d. México 90/- 4° *Mexico* 64
Contains [illegible] the languages of Mexico

Place-Names.

BUSCHMANN, J. C. F. Ueber die aztekischen Ortsnamen, pt. i. 6/- 4° *Berlin* 53

Literature —v. also B § 35.

BIONDELLI, B. [ed.] Evangelium, Epistolarium et Lectionarium Aztecum 50/- 4° *Milan* 58
BRINTON, Prf. D. G. [Am.; ed.] Ancient Nahuatl Poetry [27 poems w. trs. & notes; Lib. Abor. Am. Lit.] $3 12° *Philadelphia* 88
" " [Am.; ed.] Rig Veda Americanus [sacred songs of the anc. Mexicans] $2.50 8° " 90
SIMÉON, Rémi [ed.] Annales Mexicaines de Chimalpahin; w. Fch. tr. [Bibl. Ling. Amér.] 8° *Paris* 89

New Granada.

CASTILLO I OROZCO, E. Vocab. Paéz-Castellano, Catecismo, *etc.* [Bibl. Ling. Amér.; written early 18 cent.] 12/6 8° *Paris* 77
CELEDON, Rafael Gramatica, Catecismo i Vocab. Goajira [Bibl. Ling. Amér.] 17/- 8° *Paris* 78

Quichua (Peru).

Dictionary.

de ARONA, J. Dictionario de Peruanismos 40/- 8° *Buenos Ayres* 84
MIDDENDORF, E. W. Wörterbuch der Keshua-Sprache 8° *Leipzig* *in prep.*

Grammars, etc.

BRASSEUR DE BOURBOURG Gramatica de la Lengua Quiche [w. vocabulary] 21/- 8° *Paris* 62
ELLIS, R. [Am.] Peruvia Scythica: the Quichua lang. of Peru, derived fr. Central Asia 6/- 8° Trübner 75
MARKHAM, C. R. Quichua Grammar and Dictionary 31/6 c 8° " 64
MIDDENDORF, E. W. Das Runa Simi [Quichua; = "Einheim. Sprachen Perus," vol. i.] 16/- 8° *Leipzig* 90
NODAL, Dr. J. F. Elementos de la Gramática Quichua 21/- r 8°
v. TSCHUDI, J. J. Die Kechua Sprache: grammar, specimens, dictionary, 3 pts. 21/- r 8° *Vienna* 53

Literature —v. also B § 35.

Ollanta: drama in Quichua language: ed. and tr. C. R. Markham 7/6 c 8° Trübner 71
" " ed. Dr. J. F. Nodal 7/6 r 8° 74
" " ed. P. Zeggara; w. French tr. and notes [Bibl. Ling. Amér.] 21/- 8° *Paris* 78
" " Germ. tr. by J. J. v. Tschudi, w. notes 14/- i 4° *Vienna* 76
" " " by G. Flammberg [verse] 1/6 16° *Stuttgart* 77

Taensa.

HAUMONTÉ + PARISOT + ADAM, J. D. / L. L. Grammaire et Vocabulaire de la Langue Taensa [Bibl. Ling. Amér.] 12/6 8° *Paris* 82

Timuquana.

PAREJA, P. F. Arte de la Lengua Timuquana [written 1614], ed. L. Adam + J. Vinson [Bibl. Ling. Amér.] 12/6 8° *Paris* 86

XXII. Hyperborean Philology.

166. ALEUTIC AND ESQUIMAUX PHILOLOGY.

Asia.

Ainos —v. K § 150: Japanese Philology, s.v. Aino.

America.

Aleutic.

PFIZMAIER, A. Die Sprache der Aleuten and Fuchsinseln, 2 pts. 3/- 8° *Vienna* 84

K § 166

Esquimaux.

Bibliography.

PILLING, J. C. [Am.] Bibliography of the Eskimo Language [Smithsonian Instit.] 75c. f° *Washington* 87

Generally.

HENRY, Prf. Victor Equisse d'une grammaire de la langue Innok 2/- 8° *Paris* 78

KLEINSCHMIDT, S. Grammatik der grönländischen Sprache *o.p.* [w. 3/6] 8° *Berlin* 51

PETITOT, le R. P. E. Vocabulaire français-esquimaux [w. gram. notes & monogr. on the tribe] 42/-; *red. to* 21/- 4° *Paris* 76

PFIZMAIER, A. Die Abarten der grönländischen Sprache 1/6 8° *Vienna* 84

" " Darlegung grönländischer Verbalformen 1/6 8° " 85

RASMUSSEN, C. Grönlandsk Sproglaere 4/6 8° *Copenhagen* 89

RINK, Dr. H. The Eskimo Tribes—*deals largely with them in regard to languages* 4/6 8° *Copenhagen* (Williams) 88

XXIII. Unclassed Languages.

166. GYPSY PHILOLOGY.

Generally.

COLOCCI, A. Gli Zingari; ill. [a hist. of the gypsies, w. specs. of poetry] 8° *Turin* 89

Gypsy Lore Society Journal [quarterly] *ann.* 20/- 8° Constable, *Edin* 88 *sqq. in prog.*

'JOSEPH, Archduke of Hungary Czigány Nyelvtan ("the Gypsy Tongue") 8° *Pesth* 88

A copious vocabulary and grammar, comp. w. the Indian languages; w. crit. acc. of the var. wks. upon the Gypsies. French and Germ. trs. are in prep.

POTT, A. F. Die Zigeuner in Europa u. Asien, 2 vols. [gram. dict., specs.] 16/- 8° *Halle* 44; 45

Cf. also G. J. ASCOLI'S *Zigeunerisches* [Suppl. to above] 4/- 8° *ib.* 65

SIMSON, Walter —*his* History of the Gipsies, *conts.* specimens of the language $2 12° [*Lond.* 65] *New York* 78

History, etc. —*v.* F § 76: History of the Gypsies.

Literature —*v.* B § 39: Gypsy Folklore.

SMITH, Laura A. [ed.] Through Romany Song-Land [texts and trs.] 5/- f 8° Stott 89

Europe.

MIKLOSICH, Fr. Ueber die Mundarten und Wanderungen der Zigeuner Europa's, 12 pts. 40/6 4° *Vienna* 72–80

" " Beiträge zur Kenntniss der Zigeunermundarten, 4 pts. [*fr.* Sitzsb. Wien. Akad.] 2/- 4° " 74–78

Austria.

MIKLOSICH, Fr. Glossar zu d. Märchen u. Liedern d. Zigeuner d. Bukowina 5/- 8° *Vienna* 75

England.

Generally —*v. also* K § 241: English, *s.v.* Slang.

LELAND, C. G. [Am.] The English Gipsies and their Language 7/6 8° Trübner [73] 74

SMART + CROFTON, B. C. / H. T. Dialect of the English Gypsies 15/- 8° Philolog. Soc. (Tbnr.) [63] 75

Dictionary

BORROW, George Romano Lavo-Lil: wordbk. of the Romany [w. specs.; for his other bks., *v.* F § 76] 5/- s 8° Murray [74] 88

Germany and Hungary.

AVÉ-LALLEMENT, F. C. B. Das deutsche Gaunerthum, 4 vols. *o.p.* [w. 30/-] 8° *Leipzig* 58–62

MÜLLER, Friedrich Beiträge zur Kenntniss d. Rom-Sprache, 2 pts. [*fr.* Sitzb. Wien. Akad.] 2/- 8° *Vienna* 69; 72

Norway.

SUNDT, E. Beretning om Fante-eller Landstrygerfolket [w. dict. of Norweg. gypsies] 8° *Christiania* [50] 52

Roumania.

VAILLANT, J. A. Grammaire, Dialogues, et Vocabul. de la Langue des Bohémes 8° *Paris* 68

Slavonic Countries.

BÖHTLINGK, O. Ueber die Sprache d. Zigeuner in Russland; w. supplement *St. Petersburg* 52; 54

JESINA, J. Romani Cib: die Zigeuner Sprache (Germ. tr.) [gram., dict., chrestom.] 8/- 8° *Leipzig* 86

KALINA, A. La Langue des Tsiganes Slovaques 3/6 8° *Posen* 82

LISZT, F. Des Bohémiens et de leur Musique en Hongrie 12/- 8° *Leipzig* [59] 81

v. SOWA, Dr. Rudolf Die Mundart der slovakischen Zigeuner 7/- 8° *Göttingen* 87

Spain.

BORROW, George The Zincali: account of the gypsies of Spain 2/6 c 8° Murray [41] 88

HUDSON, G. Gli Zingari in Ispagna [not very good] 6/- 8° *Milan* 78

JIMENEZ, D. A. Vocabulario del Dialecto Jitano 16° *Madrid* [46] 54

MAYO y QUINDALE El Gitanismo [history, dialects, customs, *etc.*] 8° " 70

Transylvania.

v. WLISLOCKI, H. Die Sprache der transsilvanischen Zigeuner [w. dictionary] 3/- 8° *Leipzig* 83

Turkey.

PASPATI, Dr. A. G. Études sur les Tchinghianés de l'Empire Ottoman *o.p.* [*w.* 28/-] 8° *Constantinople* 70
" " Memoir of Language of Gypsies as used in Turkey [Am. tr.] 8/- 8° *Newhaven* 63
Contains an introduction, grammar, dictionary, dialogues, tales, etc.

166*. UNCLASSED ASIATIC PHILOLOGY.

Dardistan.

LEITNER, Dr. G. W. The Languages and Races of Dardistan, 3 pts.; maps and pl. [Govt. pub.] 25/- 4° *Lahore* 73-74

Hunza and Nagyr.

LEITNER, Dr. G. W. The Hunza and Nagyr Handbook, pt. i. [Govt. pub.] 42/- r 4° *Calcutta* 88
An important work, opening an entirely new field of philology. The Hunza lang., Dr. Leitner states, is one of a class in wh. nouns can be conceived of only in conn. w. a possessive pronoun, there being no abstract words of any kind. This bk. is largely ethnological.

Indian Trade Dialects, etc.

LEITNER, Dr. G. W. Linguistic Fragments discovered in 1870, '72 and '79, 4 pts. [Govt. pub.] 42/- f°. *Lahore* 80-82
Indian trade dialects, the dialects of the criminal and wandering tribes, with an account of the Shawl Alphabet and Shawl Weaving.

Prae-Chinese Languages of China—*v.* K § 152.

XXIV. Greek-and-Latin Philology: jointly.

167. BIBLIOGRAPHY, ENCYCLOPÆDIA AND INTRODUCTION.

For editions before 1700, *v.* SCHWEIGER: *Handbuch d. klass. Bibliographie*, *o.p.* 8° *Leipzig* 30; and for the Earliest Editions, *v.* PANZER: *Annales Typographici* [to A.D. 1536], 11 vols. *Nuremberg*, 1793-1803.

Bibliography, Encyclopædia and Methodology.

Bibliotheca Philologica, ed. C. H. Herrmann [German books 1852-72 in all departments] 5/6 8° *Halle* 73-74
" " [now] ed. Aug. Blau [biennial list of titles, etc., of new philol. bks.] *ann.* 5/- 8° *Göttingen* 48 *sqq. in prog.*
1848-1853, by C. J. F. RUPRECHT; 1854-79, by W. MÜLDENER; 1880-1882, by E. EHRENFEUCHTER; 1883, by G. KOBINNA; 1884, by Max HEYSE; 1885 *sqq.*, by Aug. BLAU.

Bibliotheca Philologica Classica: 1874-1889 [quarterly] *ann.* 6/- Calvary, *Berlin* 74-90 *in prog.*
Notices of classical books taken fr. the *Jahresber. üb. d. Fortschritte d. class. Alterthumswiss.*

*BOECKH, August Encyclopädie u. Methodik der philolog. Wissenschaften 12/- 8° *Leipzig* [77] 86
Posthumously ed. Ernest BRATUSCHEK, and now re-ed. Rudolf KLUSSMANN.

BOTFIELD, B. [ed.] Prefaces to First Editions of Gk. & Rom. Classics & of Scriptures *o.p.* [*pb.* 105/-; *w.* 20/-] 4° Bohn 61
BURSIAN, C. [ed.] Jahresbericht üb. d. Fortschritte d. class. Alterthumswiss. *annually* 30/- 8° *Berlin* 73 *sqq.*
Consists of reviews of classical books, magazine articles, etc. (of all countries), by eminent German specialists. As companion to it is pub. the *Bibliotheca Philologica Classica* (biennial), comprising full titles, prices, references to reviews, etc., of all new classical books, articles, etc., *annually* 6/- 8° *Berlin* 74 *sqq.*

*ENGELMANN, W. Bibliotheca Scriptorum Classicorum, ed. E. Preuss, 2 vols. 36/- 8° *Leipzig* [58] 80; [58] 82
Exhaustive lists of Editions of Texts and Monographs fr. 1700 to 1878. i: Scriptores Graeci, 20/-; ii: Scriptores Latini, 16/-.

HÜBNER, Dr. E. Grundriss zu Vorlesungen üb. d. Geschichte u. Encyclop. d. class. Philologie 4/- 8° *Berlin* 76
MAYOR, Prf. J. B. Guide to the Choice of Classical Books [good short book] 4/6 c 8° Bell [74] 85
*MÜLLER, Iwan [ed.] —*in his* Handbuch der klassischen Alterthumswissenschaft, pts. i.-x. ea. 5/6 8° *Nördlingen* 85-89 *in prog.*
A resumé of the latest results of scholarship by leading specialists, with bibliographies, etc. To occupy 10 half-volumes.

Vol. i.: Grundleg. u. Gesch. d. Philol. (v. URLICHS, etc.)—*v.* inf. [illegible]
" ii.: Griech. u. lat. Sprachwiss. (BRUGMANN, STOLZ, etc.)—*v.* K § [illegible]
" iii.: Geogr. u. polit. Gesch. (Fr. HOMMEL, LOLLING, PÖHLMANN, etc.) 10/6.
" iv.: Lehre v. d. Alterthümern (BUSOLT, BAUER, SCHILLING, etc.); Gk. 9/6; Lat. 5/6.
" v. (1): Gesch. d. antik. Naturwiss. (GÜNTHER+WINDELBAND)—*v.* K § [illegible]
" v. (2): Gr. Mythol. u. Sakralalterth. (Ad. VOIGT+P. STENGEL) 5/6.
" v. (3): Gr. Kultusalterthümer (OEHMICHEN) 6/6.
Vol. vi.: Klass. Kunstarchaeol. (FLASCH); Numismat. (WEIL).
" vii.: Griech. Literaturgesch. (v. CHRIST)—*v.* K § 187.
" viii.: Gesch. d. röm. Litteratur (M. SCHANZ)—*v.* K § 211.
" ix. (1): Bühnenwesen d. Gr. u. Röm. (OEHMICHEN)—*v.* K § [illegible]
" ix. (2): Abriss d. byzant. Litteraturgesch. (K. KRUMBACHER)—*v.* K § [illegible]
" ix. (3): Abriss d. lat. Litter. im Mittelalter (TRAUBE)—*v.* K § [illegible]
Alphabet. Index to the whole is to be publd.

Introduction.

FREUND, W. Triennium Philologicum: Grundzüge d. philol. Wissensch., 6 pts. ea. 4/- 8° *Leipzig* [74-76] 79-85
French adaptation of same by S. REINACH *s.t.*, *Manuel de Philologie Classique*, 2 v. 14/- 8° *Paris* [ ] 83-84.

GOW, Dr. James Companion to the School Classics; pl. [a good little bk.] 6/- c 8° Macmillan [88] 89
A hdbk. to the commentaries on school classics, giving in systematic form under the following heads what dicts. of class. antiq. give in dislocated articles: Textual Criticism, Gk. Govt. (espec. Athenian), Roman Govt., Theatre, Philosophy.

v. URLICHS, Dr. Grundlegung u. Geschichte d. Philologie [I. Müller's *Hdbk. Klass. Alterth.*, v. i.] 12/- r 8° *Nördlingen* 85
Includes also Hermeneutik (BLASS), Palaeogr. (BLASS), Epigraphie (HINRICHS+E. HÜBNER), Chronol. (UNGER), Metrologie (NISSEN).

168. GREEK-AND-LATIN GRAMMAR (a): GENERALLY.

BAUDRY, F. — Grammaire Comparée des Langues Classiques, 2 vols. 8° *Paris* [68] 78; 73

BAUR, Prf. Ferd. — Philological Introduction to Greek and Latin, tr. C. Kegan Paul + Stone 6/– c 8° Paul [76] 79

BRUGMANN & STOLZ, *etc.* — Griech. u. latein. Sprachwissenschaft [= Iwan Müller's *Hdb. Klass. Alterth.*, vol. ii.] 15/6 r 8° *Nördlingen* [88] 89

Gr. Gram. (BRUGMANN), Lat. Gram. (STOLZ), Gk. and Lat. Lexikogr. (AUTENRIETH + HEERDEGEN), Rhetorik (VOLKMANN), Metrik (GLEDITSCH).

FARRAR, W. H. — Comparative Grammar of Sanskrit, Greek and Latin, vol. i. 12/– 8° Longman 71

HENRY, Prf. Victor — Compar. Gram. of Gk. & Latin, tr. & ed. R. T. Elliott, w. pref. Prf. H. Nettleship 7/6 c 8° Sonnenschein 90

Affords an excellent summary of the researches of the past 10 or 15 yrs., wh. have so largely modified our notions of classical phonol. and morphology.

KING + COOKSON, $\frac{J. E.}{C.}$ — Principles of Sound and Inflexion as ill. in the Gk. and Latin Languages 18/– 8° Clar. Press 88

Based on BRUGMANN and STOLZ, *ut supra*.

" " — Introduction to the Comparative Grammar of Gk. & Lat. [abgmt. of above] 5/6 c 8° " 90

MEYER, Leo — Vergl. Grammatik. d griech. u. lat. Sprache, vol. i., 2 pts. ca. 18/– 8° *Berlin* [61] 82; [65] 84

PAPILLON, T. L. — Compendium of Comparative Philology as appl. to Gk. & Lat. Inflections 6/– c 8° Clar. Press [76] 82

Behind the times, but a convenient synopsis of the doctrine of forms.

Collected Essays —*v. also* K § 94 *and* K § 179, *s.v.* Textual Criticism.

BAUNACK, J. + Th. — Studien auf d. Gebiete d. griech. u. d. arischen Sprachen, vol. i., pt. i. 6/– 8° *Leipzig* 86

BERGK, T. — Kleine philolog. Schriften, vol. i. 10/–; ii. [Zur griech. Liter.] 12/– 8° *Halle* 84; 86

BERNAYS, J. — Gesammelte Abhandlungen, hrsg. H. Usener, 2 vols. 18/– 8° *Berlin* 85

BOECKH, August — Gesammelte kleine Schriften, hrsg. F. Ascherson, *etc.*, 7 vols. 74/– 8° *Leipzig* 58-74

CURTIUS, G. — Kleine Schriften, hrsg. E. Windisch, 2 pts.; pt. i. [speeches, lects.] 3/–; ii. [essays] 4/– 8° *Berlin* 86; 86

GITLBAUER, M. — Philologische Streifzüge 10/– 8° *Freiburg* 86

GÖTTLING, K. W. — Gesammelte Abhandlungen, *etc.*, 16/6; Opusc. Academ., ed. Kuno Fischer 6/– 8° *Halle* 51, 63; *Lps.* 69

HADLEY, Prf. J. — Essays: philological and critical 16/– 8° Macmillan 73

HAUPT, Moritz — Opuscula, 3 vols. (4 pts.) 38/– 8° *Leipzig* 75-77

HERMANN, C. F. — Gesammelte Abhandlungen und Beiträge zur class. Liter. u. Alterth. *o.p.* 8° *Göttingen* 49

KEY, Prf. T. H. — Philological Essays 10/6 8° Bell 63

KOCH, G. A. — Opuscula Philologica, ed. G. Kinkel + E. Böckel, 2 vols. 26/– 8° 81

KOECHLY, Hermann — Opuscula Philologica, 2 vols. i. Latin, 15/–; ii. German 11/– 8° *Leipzig* 81; 82

LACHMANN, Karl — Kleinere Schriften zur klassischen Philologie, hrsg. J. Vahlen 4/– 8° *Berlin* 76

LANGE, Ludwig — Kleine Schriften aus d. Gebiete d. klass. Altertumswiss., vol. i. 10/–; ii. 15/– 8° *Göttingen* 87; 87

MADVIG, J. N. — Kleine philolog. Schriften [*for his* Adversaria Crit., *v.* K § 179; Opuscula, *v.* K § 199] 14/– 8° *Lps.* 75

NIPPERDEY, C. — Opuscula 12/– 8° *Berlin* 77

RITSCHL, Friedrich — Opuscula Philologica—*v.* K § 177.

SCHOELL, Adolf — Gesammelte Aufsätze zur klassischen Literatur alter u. neuer Zeit 7/– 8° *Berlin* 84

SCHOEMANN, G. F. — Opuscula Academica, 4 vols. 30/– 8° " 56-71

TEUFFEL, W. S. — Studien u. Charakteristiken zur griech., röm. u. deut. Liter., 10/–; Suppl. 2/– 4° *Lps.* 71; *Tübingen* 79

THIRLWALL, Bp. Connop — Essays: classical and theological 15/– 8° Bentley

VISCHER, W. — Kleine Schriften, 2 vols. i. 12/–; ii. 20/– 8° *Leipzig* 77; 78

WOLF, F. A. — Kleine Schriften, hrsg. G. Bernhardy, 2 vols. 13/6 8° *Halle* 69

Palæography —*v.* K § 99; *also* K § 177, K § 201.

169. GREEK-AND-LATIN GRAMMAR (b): ACCIDENCE.

Parts of Speech.

SCHROEDER, L. — Die formelle Unterscheidung d. Redetheile im Griech. u. Lateinischen 6/– 8° *Leipzig* 74

Noun.

Case.

HARTUNG, J. A. — Ueber die Casus: ihre Bildung u. Bedeutung [in Gk. and Latin] 4/– 8° *Erlangen* 31

Declension.

MEYER, Leo — Gedrängte Vergleichung d. griech. und latein. Declination 1/6 8° *Berlin* 62

Degrees of Comparison.

FÖRSTEMANN, E. — De Comparativis et Superlativis Linguae Graecae et Latinae 1/– 8° *Nordhausen* 44

GONNET, Th. J. — Degrés de Signification en Grec et en Latin [comparative treatment] *Paris* 76

Particles.

FRITSCH, K. A. — Philolog. Studien, vol. i. (2 pts.): Vergl. Bearb. d. Gr. u. Lat. [advbs. & prep.] 4/– & 6/– 8° *Giessen* 56; 58

SCHWARZ, A. H. — De Praepositionibus Graecis et Latinis [inaug. dissert.] 1/– 8° *Königsberg* 59

Pronoun.

SCHMIDT, M. — De Pronomine Graeco et Latino [comparative; good] *o.p.* 4° *Halle* 32

Verb.

Conjugation.

BIRKENSTAMM, Th. — Die lateinische Conjugation im Vergleich mit der griechischen — 2/- 4° *Rinteln* 69

Tense and Mood.

AUTENRIETH, G. — Grundzüge d. Moduslehre im Griechischen u. Lateinischen — 6d. 8° *Zweibrücken* 75
CURTIUS, G. — Die Tempora und Modi in Griechischen u. Lateinischen [= Sprachvergl. Beitr., i.] 4/6 8° *Berlin* 46
ERNAULT, E. — Le Parfait en Grec et en Latin — 8° *Paris* 83
KOHLMANN, R. — Verhältniss d. Tempora d. lat. Verb. z. d. des griechischen — 4° *Eisleben* 8r
" " — Modi d. griech. u. d. lat. Verb. in ihrem Verhältniss [*repr. fr.* Symbolae Isleb.] 4° " 83
OSTHOFF, H. — Geschichte d. Perfects im Indogerman. [w. spec. ref. to Gk. and Lat.] 14/- 8° *Strassburg* 84
SCHRAMINEN, J. — Ueber die Bedeutung der Formen des Verbums — *Heiligenstadt* 84

170. GREEK-AND-LATIN GRAMMAR (*c*): SYNTAX.

HAVESTADT, B. — Parallelsyntax des Lateinischen und Griechischen, 2 pts. — ea. 2/- 8° *Emmerich* 63; 68
HEIDELBERG, H. — System der griechischen und lateinischen Syntax, pt. i. — 1/- 8° *Norden* 57
LUND, G. W. F. — De Parallelismo Syntaxis Graecae et Latinae — *Copenhagen* 45

Position of Words.

BOLDT, H. — De Liberiore Ling. Graec. et Lat. Collocatione — *Göttingen* 84

171. GREEK-AND-LATIN GRAMMAR (*d*): ETYMOLOGY. LEXICOGRAPHY, DICTIONARIES.

Generally.

AHRENS, F. H. L. — Beiträge zur griechischen u. lateinischen Etymologie, vol. i. — 5/- 8° *Leipzig* 79
AUTENRIETH + HEERDEGEN — Griech. u. lat. Lexikographie—*in* Iwan Müller's *Hdb. Klass. Alterth.*, vol. ii. [not v. good] 15/6 r 8° *Nördlingen* [85] 89
BYRNE, Dr. James — Origin of Greek, Latin, and Gothic Roots — 18/- 8° Trübner 87
HALSEY, C. S. [Am.] — An Etymology of Greek and Latin — $1.25 12° *Boston* 82
PEILE, J. — Introduction to Greek and Latin Etymology — 10/6 c 8° Macmillan [69] 75

Dictionary.

VANICEK, Alois — Griechisch-Lateinisch Etymologisches Wörterbuch, 2 vols. — 24/- *Leipzig* 77; 78
Indo-European roots in alphabetical order, with the Greek and Latin words derived from them.
WHARTON, E. R. — Etyma Graeca: etymological lexicon of classical Greek, 7/6; Etyma Latina 7/6 8° Rivington 82; 90

Loan Words: Greek in Latin—*v.* K § 203.

Synonyms.

SCHMIDT, J. H. H. — Handbuch der lateinischen u. griechischen Synonymik — 12/- 8° *Leipzig* 89

172. GREEK-AND-LATIN METRICS.

BENLOEW, L. — Précis d'une Théorie des Rhythmes, 2 pts. [Fch., Gk., Lat. metres] *Leipzig* 62
*CHRIST, W. — Metrik der Griechen und Römer — 12/- 8° " [74] 79
GLEDITSCH, H. — Metrik d. Griechen u. Römer—*in* Müller's *Hdb. d. class. Alterth.*, vol. ii. 15/6 r 8° *Nordlingen* [85] 89
*HAVET, I. — Cours élément. de Métrique Grecque et Lat., rédigé L. Duvau — 8° *Paris* [ ] 86
MÜLLER, Lucian — Metrik der Griechen und Römer — 1/6 p 8° *Leipzig* [80] 85
REIMANN, H. — Handbuch der griechischen und römischen Metrik [Calvary's *Bibliothek*] 12° *Berlin* *in prep.*
RÜCKERT, F. W. — —*in his* Antike und deutsche Metrik [school bk.; useful] 1/6 s 8° " [47] 74
*SCHMIDT, Dr. J. H. H. — Intro. to Rhythmic & Metric of Class. Langs., tr. Prf. J. W. White [Am.] 10/6 8° Macmillan 80
ZAMBALDI, Fr. — Metrica Graeca et Latina — *Turin* 82

173. GREEK-AND-LATIN: MAGAZINES AND PERMANENT SERIALS.

English.

Classical Review [monthly] ea. 1/6 m 8° Nutt 87 *sqq.*, *in prog.*
Hermathena: a series of papers on Liter., Science, and Philosophy (by members of Trin. Coll., Dubl.) 8° *Dublin* 73 " "
Journal of Philology, ed. W. Aldis Wright + I. Bywater + H. Jackson, vols. i.-xviii. [hf.-yearly] ea. pt. 4/6 8° Macmillan & B., *Camb.* 68–89 "

American.

American Journal of Philology, ed. B. L. Gildersleeve [Am.], vols. i.-x.; Index to same; xi. *sqq.* [qrtly.] ea. pt. 4/6 8° *Baltimore* (Macm.) *in prog.*
Harvard Studies in Classical Philology, vol. i. [organ of class. teachers of Harv. Coll.] 8° *Boston* 89 "
Studies in Classical Philology, ed. I. Flagg + W. G. Hale + B. I. Wheeler [Am.] [papers by staff and students of Cornell Univ.] 8° *Ithaca, N. Y.* (Macm.) 87–89 "

i: W. G. HALE: The "Cum" Constructions, 2 pts., sor. and 8or. '87; '89; ii: B. I. WHEELER: *Analogy and its Scope*, 8or. 87.

K § 174

Danish.

Nordisk Tidskrift for Philologi, ed. Thomsen — *Copenhagen in prog.*

Dutch.

Mnemosyne — ed. G. C. Cobet + H. W. van der Mey, series i., 9 vols., and ser. ii., vols. i.–xvii. ea. vol. of 4 pts. 9/- 8° *Leyden* 52 *sqq., in prog.*

Chiefly textual criticism, emendations, etc.

French.

Bibliothèque de l'École des Hautes Études — 8° *Paris in prog.*
Revue de Philologie — ed. O. Riemann + Chatelain — 8° ,, ,,

German.

Berliner Philologische Wochenschrift, hrsg. Chr. Belger + O. Seyffert + K. Thiemann [weekly] *ann.* 24/- r 4° *Berlin* 81 *sqq., in prog.*
,, Studien für classische Philologie u. Archæol., hrsg. F. Ascherson, vols. i.–x. [Doctor disserts. of best Berlin students] *ann. v.p.* (10/- *to* 17/-) 8° ,, 83 ,, ,,

New subscribers can obtain vols. i.–x. *for* 90/- in place of 124/-.

Göttingische Gelehrte Anzeigen, und Nachrichten, hrsg. F. Bechtel [weekly] *ann.* 27/- 8° *Göttingen in prog.*
Hermes — hrsg. G. Kaibel + C. Robert [quarterly] ea. vol. 12/- 8° *Berlin* 66 *sqq.*, ,,
Jahrbücher, Neue, für class. Philologie, hrsg. A. Fleckeisen + H. Masius [monthly] *ann.* (2 vols) 30/- 8° *Leipzig* 31 ,, ,,

The volume for 1876 contains an index for 1826–1875.

Jahresbericht üb. d. Fortschritte d. class. Alterthumswissenschaft, hrsg. C. Bursian *later* Iwan Müller *ann.* 36/- *to* 48/- 8° *Berl.* 72 ,, ,,
Philologus — ed. E. von Leutsch, vols. i.–xlvi.; by O. Crusius, New Ser., vol. i., ea. vol. 17/- 8° *Götting.* 46–88; 89 ,,

Monthly supplement to same: *Philologischer Anzeiger* [monthly] *ann.* 12/- since 1869.

Rheinisches Museum für Philologie, hrsg. O. Ribbeck + F. Bücheler [quarterly] *ann.* 14/- 8° *Frankfort* 27 *sqq.*, ,,

Ed. fr. 1827–29 by B. G. Niebuhr + C. A. Brandis, *Bonn*; fr. 1833–38 by F. G. Welcker + A. F. Näke, *ibid.*; fr. 1842 by Welcker, F. Ritschl, J. Bernays, A. Klette, O. Ribbeck, *Göttingen*.

Rundschau, Neue Philologische, hrsg. C. Wagener + E. Ludwig [fortnightly] *ann.* 12/- r 8° *Gotha* 80 *sqq.*, ,,
Studien zur griech. u. lat. Grammatik, hrsg. G. Curtius, *later* K. Brugmann, 10 vols.; *cont. as* Leipziger Studien, hrsg. O. Ribbeck + H. Lipsius *ann. v.p.* (7/- *to* 9/-) 8° *Leipzig* 68–78; 78 ,, ,,
Wiener Studien — hrsg. W. von Hartel + K. Schenkel [biennially; chiefly critiques] *ann.* 10/- 8° *Vienna* 79 ,, ,,
Wochenschrift für klass. Philologie, hrsg. Andresen + Heller [weekly] *ann.* 24/- 8° *Berlin* 84 ,, ,,

Italian.

Giornale Italiano di Filologia e Linguistica Classica, ed. Ceci + Cortese — 78 *sqq., in prog.*
Rivista di Filologia — ed. D. Comparetti + G. Müller + G. Flecchia — *Turin* 73 ,, ,,

Bibliographical Serials—*v.* K § 167.

174. HISTORY OF CLASSICAL STUDY AND BIOGRAPHY OF SCHOLARS.

History of Classical Study.

Comprehensive Periods.

Hirzel, C. — Grundzüge zu einer Geschichte der class. Philologie [46 pp only] 1/6 8° *Tübingen* [62] 73
Hübner, E. — Grundriss zu Vorlesungen üb. Gesch. u. Encycl. d. klass Philologie 4/- 8° *Berlin* 76
Reinach, S. — —*in his* Manuel de Philologie Classique, 2 vols. 12/6 8° *Paris* [ ] 83–85
Schmidt, K. E. A. — Beiträge zur Geschichte d. Grammatik d. Griech. u. Latein. 7/6 8° *Halle* 59
v. Urlichs, Dr. — Grundlegung u. Geschichte d. Philologie [Müller's Hdb. Klass. Alterth., pt. i.] 5/6 8° *Nördlingen* 85

France.

Egger, E. — L'Hellénisme en France, 2 vols. [influ. of Gk. study on Fch. lang. and liter.] 8° *Paris* 69

Germany.

Bursian, Conrad — Geschichte d. classischen Philologie in Deutschland, 2 vols. 14/6 8° *Munich* 83
Horawitz, A. — Griech. Studien: Beiträge z. Gesch. d. Griech. in Deutschld., pt. i. 2/- 8° *Berlin* 83

Holland.

Müller, Lucian — Geschichte der klassischen Philologie in den Niederlanden 5/- 8° *Leipzig* 69

Ancient.

Gräfenhan, A. — Geschichte d. klassischen Philologie in Alterthume, 4 vols. 21/- 8° *Bonn* 43–50
Lersch, L. — Die Sprachphilosophie der Alten, 2 vols. *o.p.* [*pb.* 8/6] 8° ,, 38; 40
Parthey, G. — Das Alexandrische Museum [Alexandrian scholars] 4/- 8° *Berlin* 38
Ritschl, Friedrich — Die Alex. Bibliotheka—*in his* Opuscula, vol. i. 17/6 8° *Leipzig* 66
Steinthal, H. — Geschichte der Sprachwissenschaft bei d. Griechen u. Römer 11/6 8° *Berlin* 63

With special reference to Logic.

Wegener, K. P. — De aula Attalica [of Crates and the other Pergamene scholars] 4/- 8° *Copenhagen* 36

Mediæval.

BAEBLER, J. J. Beiträge z. e. Geschichte d. lat. Grammatik im Mittelalter 4/- 8° *Halle* 85
BURSIAN, C. —*ut supra.*
HAASE, Fr. De Medii Aevi Studiis Philologicis disputatio *o.p.* 8° *Breslau* 56
HALLAM, Henry —*in his* View of the State of Europe in the Middle Ages, 3 vols. [*v.* F § 13] 12/- p 8° Murray [18] 71
HEEREN, A. H. L. Geschichte der class. Liter. im Mittelalter, 2 vols. [unfinished; = Wrks., v. iv.–v.] 8° *Berlin* [1797–1801] 22
LACROIX, Paul —*in his* Science and Literature in the Middle Ages; finely ill. 31/6 r 4° Virtue [78] 86

Renaissance —*v. also* F § 53, *s.v.* Renaissance.

BURCKHARDT, J. G. —*in his* Civilization of Period of Renaiss. in Italy, tr. S. G. C. Middlemore 15/- 8° Sonnenschein [78] 90
SYMONDS, J. Addington Revival of Learning in Italy [*v.* F § 53] 16/- 8° Smith & Elder [77] 82
VOIGT, G. Wiederlebung des classischen Alterthums, 2 vols. 16/- 8° *Berlin* [59] 80; 81

Germany.

SCHROEDER, J. F. Das Wiederaufblühen d. klass. Stud. in Deutschld. in 15–16 Jahrh. 4/- 8° *Halle* 64

Biography of Scholars.

Collectively.

Biographisches Jahrbuch für Alterthumskunde 1877–1887 [obituary notices of class. scholars] ea. 5/- 8° *Berlin* 78–88 *in prog.*
ECKSTEIN, F. A. Nomenclator Philologorum [short biogr. dict. of class. scholars] 6/- 8° *Leipzig* 71
NICOLL, H. J. Great Scholars [popular lives of Buchanan, Bentley, Porson, Parr] 1/- c 8° Ward & Lock [80] 88
PÖKEL, W. Philologisches Schriftsteller-Lexicon 6/- 8° *Leipzig* 82

Individually.

ALBERTI, Dr. Val. [1635–97] Life of Alberti, six times Rector of Univ. Leipzig. By Can. R. C. Jenkins 5/- s 4° Nutt 90
BENTLEY, Richard [1662–1742]—*v.* K § 24, *s.v.* Eighteenth Century.
CASAUBON, Isaac [1559–1614] Life of. By Rev. Mark Pattison 18/- 8° Longman 75
NIEBUHR, B. G. [1776–1831] Life and Letters of. By Mme. Hensler [tr.]; w. essays by Bunsen, Brandis and Löbell, 3 vols. *o.p.* [*pb.* 42/-; *w.* 15/-] 8° Bentley 51–52
RITSCHL, Friedrich Friedrich Ritschl: eine wissenschaftliche Biographie. By Lucian Müller [Calvary's Bibl.] 3/- 12° *Berlin* [77] 78
SCALIGER, Jos. [1540–1609] Life of. By Rev. Mark Pattison—*in his* Collected Essays 24/- 8° Clar. Press 89
" Joseph Justus [the younger] Joseph Justus Scaliger. By Prof. Jac. Bernays [in German] 5/6 8° *Berlin* 55

Printers: Early ALDUS and PAULUS MANUTIUS, *v.* K § 15; STEPHENS, *v* K § 13.

XXV. Greek Philology and Literature.

175. GREEK GRAMMAR (a): GENERALLY.

Generally —*v. also* K § 168: Greek and Latin: Comparatively.

ABBOTT + MANSFIELD, E. D. / E. Greek Grammar 3/6 p 8° Rivington 80
*BRUGMANN, K. Griechische Grammatik [= v. ii. of Iwan Müller's "Klass. Alterthumswiss."] 5/6 8° *Nördlingen* 85
BUTTMANN, Ph. Larger Greek Grammar, ed. Supf [tr.] [1st. edn. of orig. 1819–25] 13/6 8° Whittaker [ ] 48
CURTIUS, Prf. G. Student's Gk. Gr. [tr. 1st. edn. of orig. '52] 6/-; Elucid. to same [tr.; orig. '63] 7/6 p 8° Murray 67; 70
" " Griechische Schulgrammatik, bearb. v. W. v. Hartel 2/- 8° *Leipzig* 88
DONALDSON, Dr. J. W. Greek Grammar ["standard," but now antiquated] 16/- 8° Deighton, *Camb.* [ ] 62
GOODWIN, Prf. W. W. [Am.] Elementary Greek Grammar [Abgd. *sub tit.* School Grammar, 3/6] 6/- c 8° Macmillan [71] 80
HADLEY, Prf. J. [Am.] Greek Grammar, ed. Prf. F. de Forest Allen [Am.] 6/- c 8° " [ ] 84
JELF, W. E. Greek Grammar, 2 vols. [based on Kühner; now antiquated] 30/- 8° Parker [42–45] 66
KAEGI, Dr. Adolf Griechische Schulgrammatik 3/- 8° *Berlin* [84] 89
KOCH, Ernest Griech. Schulgrammatik [based on results of comp. philol.] 3/- s 8° *Leipzig* [66–69] 85
KRÜGER, K. W. Griechische Sprachlehre, 2 vols., 12/-; Small Edn. 2/6 8° *Berlin* [42–55] 71–79; 78
KÜHNER, R. Ausführliche Grammatik d. griech. Sprache, 2 v. 42/- 8° *Leipzig* [34] 69–72
" " Elementarbuch der griechischen Sprache 3/- 8° " [ ] 79
LATTMANN + MÜLLER J. + H. D. Griechische Grammatik für Gymnasien, 2 pts. ea. 2/- 8° " [70] 86; 87
*MEYER, Gustav Griechische Grammatik [Bibl. Indogerm. Grammatiken] 11/- 8° " [80] 86

* Represents the "New School" of comparative philology.

RUTHERFORD, W. G. First Greek Grammar, pt. i.: Accidence, 2/-; ii.: Syntax, 2/-; in 1 vol. 3/6 f 8° Macmillan [78] 88; 90
*TOURNIER + RIEMANN, E. + O. Premiers Éléments de Grammaire Grecque 8° *Paris* 82

Inscriptions: Grammar of—*v.* K § 184: Inscriptions.

New Testament Greek—*v.* A § 32: Biblical Language, *s.v.* Greek.

176. GREEK GRAMMAR (*b*): ACCIDENCE.

Generally.

RÖDER, Wilibald — Formenlehre der griechischen Sprache [comparative] 1/6 8° *Berlin* 67

Verb.

BAIRD, J. S. — Catalogue of Greek Verbs: irregular and defective 2/6 c 8° Bell [5–] 78

*CURTIUS, Prf. G. — The Greek Verb: struct. & develop., tr. Prf. A. S. Wilkins + E. B. England 12/– 8° Murray [80] 84

The first edn. of the original [*Bildung d. Tempora u. Modi*, 8° *Berlin* '46] treated also of the Latin verb.

FLEGEL, K. — Flexion des griechischen Verbums 1/6 8° *Leipzig* 79

JOHANSSON, K. F. — De Derivatis Verbis contractis Linguæ Graecæ Quæstiones 6/– 8° *Upsala* 86

MEYER, Leo — Griechische Aoriste 4/– 8° *Berlin* 79

*VEITCH, Dr. W. — Greek Verbs, Irregular and Defective: forms, meaning, quantity 10/6 c 8° Clar. Press [48] 88

Embracing all the tenses used by Greek writers, with reference to the passages in which they are found.

Tenses and Moods.

AKEN, A. F. — Grundzüge d. Lehre v. Tempus u. Modi im Griechischen 4/– 8° *Rostock* 61

DELBRÜCK, B. — Das Conjunctiv u. Optativ im Sansk. u. Griech. [orig. of the moods treated scientif.] 4/6 8° *Halle* 71

HARTMANN, F. — De Aoristo Secundo 1/6 8° *Berlin* 81

v. d. PFORDTEN, H. — Zur Geschichte des griechischen Perfectums 2/– 8° *Munich* 82

STENDER, J. — Beiträge zur Geschichte des griechischen Perfects 2/6 8° *Leipzig* 83

Verbal-Nouns.

BIRKLEIN, F. — Entwickelungsgeschichte des substantivierten Infinitivs 4/– 8° *Würzburg* 88

DELBRÜCK, B. — De Infinitivo Graeco 8° *Halle* 63

Noun.

Case.

RUMPEL, Theodor — Die Casuslehre, 4/–; Zur Casustheorie [w. spec. ref. to Greek] 3/6 8° *Halle* 45; *Gütersloh* 66

Gender.

LANGE, A. R. — De Substantivis femininis græc. secundæ declinat. cap. duo 1/– 8° *Leipzig* 85

Pronoun.

MIDDLETON, T. F. — The Doctrine of the Greek Article, ed. H. J. Rose [*good*] *o.p.* [*pb.* 13/–] 8° Rivington [08] 41

v. d. PFORDTEN, H. — Zur Geschichte der griechischen Denominativa 4/– 8° *Leipzig* 86

Particles.

ADAMS, F. A. [Am.] — Greek Prepositions: studied fr. the orig. meangs. as designatns. of space 3/6 8° *New York* 85

BÄUMLEIN, W. — Untersuchungen über die griechischen Partikeln 10/– 8° *Stuttgart* 61

DEVARIUS, M. — De Graecae Linguae Particulis, ed. R. Klotz, 2 vols. in 3 36/– 8° *Leipzig* [1527] 35–42

*HARRISON, Gessner [Am.] — Treatises on the Greek Prepositions and of cases of nouns w. wh. used $3.50 8° *Philadelphia* 58

HARTUNG, J. A. — Lehre von d. Partikeln der griechischen Sprache, 2 pts. 13/6 8° *Erlangen* 32; 33

KREBS, F. — Die Präpositionsadverbien in d. späteren histor. Gräcität, pts. i.–ii. ea. 3/– 8° *Munich* 84; 85

MOMMSEN, Tycho — Beiträge zu der Lehre v. den griechischen Präpositionen, pts. i.–iii. 7/6 4° *Frankfort* 79–87

PALEY, F. A. — Greek Particles and their Combinations 2/6 12° Bell [ ] 81

177. GREEK GRAMMAR (*c*): SYNTAX.

Bibliography and Introduction.

HÜBNER, Dr. E. — Grundriss zu Vorlesungen üb. die griech. Syntax [w. bibliograph.] 3/– 8° *Berlin* 83

Generally.

BERNHARDY, G. — Wissensch. Synt. d. gr. Spr. 12/– 8°; Paralipom. Synt. Graec. 2/6 4° *Berlin* 29; *Halle* 62

DELBRÜCK, B. — Die Grundlagen der griechischen Syntax [comparative] 4/– 8° *Halle* 79

FARRAR, Archd. F. W. — Brief Greek Syntax 4/6 f 8° Longman 67

HOLZWEISSIG, Dr. Fried. — Griechische Syntax 1/– s 8° *Leipzig* [78] 86

MADVIG, J. N. — Syntax, tr. [fr. Danish] by H. Browne + T. K. Arnold 8/6 c 8° Rivington [53] 80

SCHANZ, M. [ed.] — Beiträge zur hist. Syntax der griech. Sprache, vols. i.–iii. (1) 18/– 8° *Würzburg* 82–88, *in prog.*

SCHANZ promises a historical syntax from Homer to Aristotle.

SEYFFERT, Dr. Moritz — Hauptregeln d. griech. Syntax, bearb. v. R. v. Bamberg 1/– 8° *Berlin* [78] 85

THOMPSON, F. E. — Syntax of Attic Greek, 8/6; Elementary Syntax 2/– c 8° Rivington 83; 85

Verb.

GOODWIN, Prf. W. W. — Syntax of the Moods and Tenses of the Greek Verb 14/– 8° Macmillan [ ] 90

178. GREEK GRAMMAR (*d*) : PHONOLOGY.

Generally.

CHRIST, W. — Grundrüge der griechischen Lautlehre — 6/- 8° *Leipzig* 59
FOY, K. — Lautsystem der griechischen Vulgärsprache — 3/- 8° ,, 79
The changes of sound from Ancient to Modern Greek.

Accentuation.

BARRY, — Notes on Greek Accents — 11/- 8° Bell 77
BLOOMFIELD, M. [Am. — The Origin of the Recessive Accent in Greek [*repr. fr.* Am. Jl. Philol., vol. ix.] 8° *Baltimore* 88
*CHANDLER, H. W. — Practical Intro. to Gk. Accent., 10/6 ; Elements of Gk. Accent. 2/6 c 8° Clar. Press [62] 82 ; 67
DARBISHIRE, H. D. — Notes on the Spiritus Asper in Greek — 8° Trübner 89
GRIFFITHS, — The Laws of Accents — 6*d.* 12° Parker
HADLEY, J. [Am.] — Nature and Theory of the Greek Accent (fr. *Trans. Am. Phil. Ass.* 69-70] *o.p.* 8° *New York* 71
MEINGAST, A. — Ueber das Wesen des griechischen Accentes, 2 pts. 2/- 8° *Vienna* 80
MISTELI, F. — Ueber griechische Betonung, i.: Allgem. Theorie, 3/-; ii. : Erläutn. [comp.] 2/- 8° *Paderborn* 75 ; 77
THUMB, A. — Untersuchungen über d. Spiritus Asper im Griechischen — 2/6 8° *Strassburg* 88
WHEELER, B. I. [Am.] — Der griechische Nominalaccent : mit Wörterverzeichniss — 3/6 8° ,, 85

Digamma.

*KNÖS, O. W. — De Digammo homerico Quaestiones, pts. i.-iii. — 10/- 8° *Upsala* 72-78
MONRO, Dr. D. B. — *—in his* Grammar of the Homeric Dialect — 10/6 8° Camb. Press 82
PETERS, Johann — Quaestiones etymologicae et gramm. de usu et vi diagammatis [very good] 1/6 4° *Berlin* 64
SAVELSBERG, J. — De Digammo ejusque immutationibus — 2/- 4° ,, 68
TUDEER, O. E. — De Dialectorum Graecarum Digammo testim. inscripp. coll. et exam. 3/- 8° *Helsingfors* 79

ει.
SMYTH, H. W. [Am.] — Der Diphthong ει im Griechischen [comparative] 2/- 8° *Göttingen* 85

νυ.
DEVENTER, W. C. — De Littera N Graecorum Paragogica [a dissertation] 1/6 8° *Münster* 63

179. GREEK GRAMMAR (*e*) : PALÆOGRAPHY AND TEXTUAL CRITICISM.

Palæography.

British Museum — Catalogue of the Ancient MSS., pt. i. [Greek] ; autotype facss. 20/- f° British Museum 81
*GARDTHAUSEN, V. — Griechische Paläographie ; 72 pl. 18/6 4° *Leipzig* 79
Lehmann, O. — Die tachygraphischen Abkürzungen d. griech. HSS. ; 10 pl. [sup. to above] 6/- 4° ,, 80
An excell. bk., dealing w. the hist. and liter. as well as materials and characteristics of writing in all ages, giving lists of known writers, of dated MSS., of abbreviations, of interpretative chronolog. tables and (at end) elab. tables of forms of letters in all typical MSS.
,, ,, — Beiträge zur griechischen Paläographie ; 5 pl. 2/6 4° *Leipzig* 77
de MONTFAUCON, Bern. — Palaeographia Graeca : de ortu et progressu Literarum Graec. *o.p.* [*w.* 25/-] f° *Paris* 1708
The standard bk. fr. which all later writers have drawn much of their material.
OMONT, H. [ed.] — Facsimilés des MSS. Grecs de la Bibliothèque Nationale 50/- f° ,, 90
Palæographical Society's Publications : Greek and Latin [w. excellent historical introduction] f° Palæograph. Soc.
VITELLI + PAOLI [eds.] — Collezione Fiorentina di Facsimili palaeogr. Greci e Latini, pt. i. f° *Florence* 84
*WATTENBACH, W. — Anleitung zur griechischen Paläographie ; 12 pl. 5/- 4° *Leipzig* [67] 77
A reproduction of his *Schrifttafeln zur Gesch. d. griech. Schrift*, 2 pts. ; 20 pl. 10/- f° *Berlin* 76 ; 77.
,, ,, [ed.] — Scripturae Graecae Specimina [photolithographs] 16/- *Berlin* 83
,, + v. VELSEN, A. [eds.] — Exempla Codicum Graecorum litteris minusculis scriptorum ; 50 pl. 60/- f° *Heidelberg* 78

Abbreviations.

ALLEN, T. W. — Notes on Abbreviations in Greek MSS. 5/- r 8° Clar. Press 89
LEHMANN, Oskar — Die tachygraphischen Abkürzungen d. griechischen Handschriften [*v. sup.*] 6/- 4° *Leipzig* 80

Alphabet

—v. also K § 99, *s.v.* Palæography.

KIRCHHOFF, A. — Studien zur Geschichte des griechischen Alphabets ; 2 pl. and 1 col. map 6/- 8° *Berlin* [63] 77
An account of the forms of the Greek letters on inscriptions.
v. SCHÜTZ, A. — Historia Alphabeti Attici ; 1 pl. 2/- 8° ,, 75

Inscriptions

—v. K § 184.

Textual Criticism.

COBET, C. G. — Variæ Lectiones in Scriptores Græcos 14/- 8° *Ludg. Bat.* [54] 73
,, ,, — Novæ Lectiones in Scriptores Græcos *o.p.* [*pb.* 15/- ; *w.* 35/-] 8° ,, ,, 58
,, ,, — Collectanea Critica in Scriptores Græcos 14/- 8° ,, ,, 78
,, ,, — Miscellanea Critica [chiefly Homer and Demosthenes] 14/- 8° ,, ,, 76
DOBREE, P. P. — Adversaria, ed. Dr. W. Wagner, 2 vols. ea. 5/- c 8° Bohn's Lib. [31] 83
GOW, Dr. J. — *—in his* Companion to the School Classics [introductory]—*v.* K § 167.
MADVIG, J. N. — Adversaria Critica, 3 vols. [*v. also* K §§ 168, 199] 35/- 8° *Hauniae* [*Copenhagen*] 71-84
i. : Ad Scriptores Graec., with a thorough treatment of Textual Criticism consid. as a science, 15/- ; ii. : Ad Scriptores Lat., 15/- ; iii. : Ad Scriptores Graec. et Lat., 5/-.
RITSCHL, Friedrich — Opuscula Philologica, 5 vols. 99/- 8° *Leipzig* 67-79
i. : Ad Litteras Graec. spectantia, 17/6 '67 ; ii. : Ad Plautum et Gram. Lat. spect., 17/6 '68 ; iii. : Ad Litteras Lat. spect., 20/- '77 ; iv. : Ad Epigraphicam et Gram. Lat. spect., 23 pl., 26/- '78 ; v. : Varia, 18/- '79.
*RUTHERFORD, W. G. — The New Phrynichus [revised text, intro. and comm.] 18/- 8° Macmillan 81

K §§ 180–181

Bucolic Poets.

HILLIER, E. Die Textgeschichte der griechischen Bukoliker 3/6 8° *Leipzig* 88

Individual Greek Writers—*v.* K §§ 190–198, *passim.*

New Testament (Books useful also for general purposes; *v. also* A § 18).

*HAMMOND, Rev. C. E. Outlines of Textual Criticism applied to the New Testament 3/6 12° Clar. Press [72] 84
SCRIVENER, Dr. F. H. Plain Introduction to [textual] Criticism of N. T.; 40 facs. 18/- 8° Bell [61] 83
WARFIELD, Rev. B. B. Introduction to Textual Criticism of N. T. [Theolog. Educator; elementary] 2/6 12° Hodder 87
WESTCOTT + HORT, Can. B. F./Dr. F. J. Introd. *and* Appendix *to their* New Testament in Orig. Gk. [*ut* A § 17].

180. GREEK GRAMMAR (*f*): ORTHOGRAPHY AND PRONUNCIATION.

BARET, P. Essai historique sur la Prononciation du Grec 3/- 8° *Paris* 78
BLACKIE, Prf. J. S. On Greek Pronunciation 3/6 8° Douglas, *Edin.* 52
*BLASS, F. Ueber die Aussprache des Griechischen 3/6 8° *Berlin* [70] 88
DAWES, E. A. S. Pronunciation of Greek: w. suggestions f. reform in teaching Gk. 2/- 8° Nutt 89
ENGEL, E. Die Aussprache des Griechischen 2/6 8° *Jena* 87
RANGABÉ, A. R. Die Aussprache des Griechischen [advocates pron. like Mod. Gk.] 2/- 8° *Leipzig* [81] 82
ZACHER, K. Die Aussprache des Griechischen [a lecture] 1/6 8° ,, 88

181. GREEK GRAMMAR (*g*): ETYMOLOGY (LEXICOGRAPHY, DICTIONARIES, &c.)

Generally.

CLEMM, W. De Compositis Graecis quae a verbis incipiunt 2/6 8° *Giessen* 67
*CURTIUS, Prf. G. Princip. of Gk. Etymol., tr. Prf. A. S. Wilkins + E. B. England, 2 vols. 28/- 8° Murray [75–76] 86
FÜGNER, F. De Nominibus Graecis cum praepositione copul. 1/6 8° *Leipzig* 78
KUHL, J. Beiträge z. griech. Etymologie, i. [Δἰά bei Homer] 3/- 8° ,, 85
NECKEL, O. De Nominibus Graecis compositis 2/6 8° ,, 82
REGNIER, Ad. Traité de la Formation et de la Composition des Mots dans la langue Grecque 8° *Paris* [ ] 55
SCHÖNBERG, G. Ueber griechische Composita 2/- 8° *Mitau* 68
WEBER, H. Etymologische Untersuchungen, pt. i. 1/6 8° *Halle* 61
ZACHER, K. Zur griechischen Nominalcomposition [Bresl. Philol. Abhandl. I. (1)] 3/6 8° *Breslau* 86

Dictionaries: General—*Special Lexicons are classed under their subjects, or the authors w. wh. they deal.*

FRAEDERSDORFF, J. W. English-Greek Lexicon [tr.], ed. Arnold + Brown 21/- m 8° Rivington [68] 82
*LIDDELL + SCOTT, H. G./R. A. Greek-English Lexicon, 36/-; abridged 7/6 4° Clar. Press [3–]83; 84
* ,, ,, Intermediate Greek-English Lexicon 12/6 s 4° ,, 89
Based on the 1883 edn. of the larger work, but much fuller in references to authorities, etc.
PAPE, W. Handwörterbuch der griechischen Sprache, 4 vols. 47/- m 8° *Brunswick* [42–45] 88
Vols. i.–ii.: Greek-German, ed. M. SENGEBUSCH, 20/-; iii.: Proper Names, ed. G. E. BENSELER, 22/-; iv.: German-Greek, ed. SENGEBUSCH, 9/-.
SOPHOCLES, Prf. E. A. Greek Lexicon of Roman Byzantine Periods, ed. Prf. J. H. Thayer [Am.] $10 r 8° *New York* [70] 88
B.C. 146–A.D. 1100; Greek-English.
STEPHANUS, H. Thesaurus Graecae Linguae, ed. C. B. Hase + W. + L. Dindorf, 9 vols. [Gk.-Latin] £21 f° *Paris* [16–28] 34–66
By far the most important of the larger Thesauruses
YONGE, Prf. C. D. English-Greek Lexicon, 21/-; School Edn. of same 8/6 8° Longman 49; 64

Strictly Etymological.

BENFEY, Th. Griechisches Wurzellexicon, 2 vols. 18/- 8° *Berlin* 39; 42
PAPE, W. Etymologisches Wörterbuch der griech. Sprache [Gk. wds. acc. to termins.] 8/- 8° ,, 36
WHARTON, E. R. Etyma Graeca: etymological lexicon of classical Greek 7/6 8° Rivington 82
ZEHETMAYR, S. Lexicon Etymologicum Latino-Sanscritum comparativum 9/- r 8° *Vienna* 73

Loan-words

—*v.* K § 169: Greek and Latin Etymology, *s.v.* Loan Words.

Names.

Place-names.

ANGERMANN, C. Geographische Namen Altgriechenlands 2/6 4° *Meissen* 83
GRASBERGER, L. Studien zu den griechischen Ortsnamen 8/- 8° *Würzburg* 88

Proper-names.

FICK, A. Die griechischen Personen-Namen nach ihrer Bildung erklärt [comparative] 8/- 8° *Göttingen* 75
KLEINPAUL, R. —*in his* Menschen- und Völkernamen 8/- 8° *Leipzig* 85
PAPE, W. Wörterbuch der griechischen Eigennamen, ed. G. E. Benseler = vol. iii. *of his* Handwörterbuch, *ut supra.*

Synonyms

—*v. also* K § 171: Greek and Latin Synonyms comparatively.

*SCHMIDT, Dr. J. H. H. Synonymik der griechischen Sprache, 4 vols. 54/- 8° *Leipzig* 76–86

182. GREEK GRAMMAR (4): PROSODY.

Verse.

Gradus ad Parnassum.

BRASSE, J. — Greek Gradus — 15/- 8° Longman [27] 42
MALTBY, Bp. Edw. — Greek Gradus — *o.p.* [*pb.* 21/- ; *w.* 7/6] 8° Simpkin [15] 50

Metaphors.

HENSE, — Poetische Personifikation der griechischen Dichter — 2/6 8° *Halle* 68

183. GREEK METRICS.

Sources and Introduction—*v. also* K § 189.

v. LEUTSCH, Ernst — Grundriss zu Vorlesungen über d. griechische Metrik — 4/- 4° *Göttingen* 41

Generally.

BRAMBACH, W. — Rhythmische u. metr. Untersuchungen — 4/- 8° *Leipzig* 71
DINDORF, W. — Metra Aeschyli, Sophoclis, Euripidis et Aristophanis — 8/6 8° *Oxford* 42
HILBERG, J. — Princip. d. Silbenwägung u. d. Gesetze d. Endsilben in d. gr. Poes. — 8/- 8° *Vienna* 79
*ROSSBACH + WESTPHAL, A./R. —*in their* Theorie der musischen Künste d. Hellenen, vols. i.-ii. — 14/- 8° *Leipzig* [68 ; 78] 85 ; 86

The great authority on the metric systems of the ancients, w. full literary and musical illustrations. A thoroughly revised ed. of their *Metrik d. griech. Dram. u. Lyriker*, 1854-65.

" A. — Griechische Rhythmik — 7/6 8° *Leipzig* 85
RZACH, A. — Studien zur Technik d. nachhomer. heroischen Verses — 3/6 r 8° *Vienna* 80
" " — Neue Beiträge zur Technik d. nachhomer. Hexameters — 2/- r 8° " 82
SCHMIDT, J. H. H. — Die Kunstformen d. griech. Poesie und ihre Bedeutung — 51/- 8° *Leipzig* 68-72

i.: Die Eurhythmie in d. Chorgesängen, 8/- '68 ; ii.: Antike Compositionslehre, 12/- '69 ; iii.: Monodien u. Wechselgänge d. attisch. Tragöd., 12/- '71 ; iv.: Griechische Metrik, 15/- '72.

Metres of Æschylus, Pindar, Sophocles—*v.* K § 191, § 190, § 191 *respectively.*

Greek and Latin Metrics: Jointly—*v.* K § 172 : Greek and Latin Metrology.

184. GREEK INSCRIPTIONS.

Treatises, Introductions.

FRANZ, Johannes — Elementa Epigraphices Graecae ; 2 pl. [a good introduction] 14/- r 4° *Berlin* 40
HICKS, E. L. [ed.] — Manual of Greek Historical Inscriptions — 10/6 8° Clar. Press 82

Includes a great many inscriptions at Oxford, at Cambridge, and in the British Museum.

REINACH, S. — Traité d'Épigraphie grecque [w. essay by C. T. Newton] 17/- 8° *Paris* 85
ROBERTS, J. S. — Intro. to Gk. Epigraphy, vol. i. ; iii. [the Archaic Inscripp. & Gk. Alphab.] 18/- 8° Camb. Press 87

Grammar.

MEISTERHANS, K. — Grammatik der attischen Inschriften — 6/6 8° *Berlin* [85] 88

Collections.

*BOECKH + FRANZ, A./J. [eds.] Corpus Inscriptionum Graecarum ab A. Boeckh + J. Franz, coll. edd. E. Curtius + A. Kirchhoff, 4 vols. ; indices H. Roehl — £9 7/6 f° *Berlin* (Academy) 28-58 ; 77

Contains some 10,000 inscriptions. At least twice this number have been discovered since.

CAUER, P. [ed.] — Delectus Inscriptionum Graecarum — 7/- 8° *Leipzig* [77] 83

Intended to illustrate the dialects.

COLLITZ, H. [ed.] — Sammlung griechischer Dialekt-Inschriften — 8° *Göttingen* 84-89 *in prog.*

Vol. i., pt. i.: Griech.-Cypr. Inscripp. [W. DEECKE] 4/6 ; ii.: Aeolian [F. BECHTEL], Thessal. [A. FICK] 2/- ; iii.: Boeot. [R. MEISTER] 5/- ; iv.: Eleans [F. BLASS] 4/6. Index to vol. i., 5/- ; vol. ii., pt. i.: Epirot., Acarn., *etc.* [F. BECHTEL] 4/- ; ii.: Achaian, *etc.* [O. HOFFMANN] 5/-

DITTENBERGER, G. [ed.] — Sylloge Inscriptionum Graecarum, 2 vols. — 16/- 8° *Leipzig* 83

i.: Historical Inscriptions ; ii.: Antiquarian Inscriptions. With copious indices. A very good selection.

KAIBEL, G. [ed.] — Epigrammata Graeca ex lapidibus conlecta — 12/- 8° *Berlin* 78
LOEWY, E. [ed.] — Inschriften griechischer Bildhauer ; w. facss. — 20/- 4° *Leipzig* 85
NEWTON + HICKS, [Sir] C. T./E. L. [eds.] Collection of Ancient Greek Inscriptions in British Museum, 3 vols. ea. 20/- f° Brit. Mus. 74 ; 83 ; 86
ROEHL, H. [ed.] — Schedae Epigraphicae, 2/6 ; Imagines Inscr. Graec. Antiquiss. — 4/- 4° *Berlin* 76 ; 83

Attic.

*KIRCHHOFF + KOEHLER, A./U. [eds.] Corpus Inscriptionum Atticarum — £11 18/- f° *Berlin* (Academy) 73-90

i.: Inscr. Euclidis anno vetust. [KIRCHHOFF] 24/- '73 ; ii.: Inscr. aetat. inter Eucl. et August., 3 pts. [U. KOEHLER] 76/- '77-'83 ; iii.: Inscr. aetat. Romanae, 2 pts., 5 pl. [W. DITTENBERGER] 88/- '78-'82 ; iv.: Suppl., 2 pts., '77-'88. *Cf.* also Roehl, *infra*.

DROYSEN, H. [ed.] — Sylloge Inscriptionum Atticarum ; 2 pl. [school-bk.] 6/- 4° *Berlin* 78
ROEHL, H. [ed.] — Inscriptiones Graecae Antiquissimae praeter Attica repert. — 16/- f° " 82

Boeotian.

LARFELD, W. [ed.] Sylloge Inscriptionum Boeoticarum [showing popular dialects] 10/- 8° *Berlin* 83

Carthaginian —*v.* K § 113.

Cretan.

BÜCHELER + ZITELMANN, F. E. Das Recht von Gortyn [= spec. no. of *Rheinisches Museum*] 4/- 8° *Frankfort* 85
KLEEMANN, M. [ed.] Reliquiarum Dialecti Creticae, pt. i. 1/6 8° *Halle* 72

Cypriotic.

SCHMIDT, Moritz [ed.] Sammlung kyprischer Inschriften in epichorischer Schrift; 22 pl. 24/- f° *Jena* 76

Elean.

BLASS, F. [ed.] Die eleischen Inschriften, *etc.* 4/6 8° *Göttingen* 85

Euxine.

LATYSCHEW, B. [ed.] Inscripp. Antiq. Orae Septentr. Ponti Euxini graec. et lat., vol. i. 20/- *St. Petersburg* 86
A supplement to the *Corpus Inscripp. Graec.* [*ut supra*] and the *Corpus Inscripp. Latin.* [*ut* K § 208]

Ionic.

BECHTEL, F. [ed.] Die Inschriften des Ionischen Dialektes; 5 pl. 8/- 4° *Göttingen* 87
" " [ed.] Thasische Inschriften Ionischen Dialekts im Louvre 2/- 4° " 84

Lycian.

SCHMIDT, Moritz [ed.] The Lycian Inscriptions after Aug. Schönborn's copies; 13 pl. (4 col.) 18/- f° *Jena* 68
" " Neue lykische Studien; 2 pl. 12/- 8° " 69
SAVELSBERG, J. [ed.] Beiträge zur Entzifferung der lykischen Sprachdenkmäler, 2 pts. 10/- 8° *Bonn* 74; 78

185. GREEK DIALECTS.

Generally.

AHRENS, H. L. [ed.] Die griechischen Dialekte, ed. R. Meister, vol. i.–ii. [a thorough revision] 13/- 8° *Göttingen* [39–52] 82; 89
i.: Asiatic-Aeolic, Boeotian, and Thessalian dialects, 6/- '82; ii.: Elean, Arcadian, Cypriotic, 7/- '89.
COLLITZ, H. Die Verwandtschaftverhältnisse der griechischen Dialekte 1/- 8° " 85
MEISTER, Dr. R. —*v.* Ahrens, *supra.*
SMYTH, Dr. H. Weir The Greek Dialects Clar. Press *in prep.*

Aeolic.

AHRENS, H. L. De Dialectis aeolicis et pseudaeolicis [1839] —*new edn.* by Meister, *v. supra.*
BECHTEL, F. Die aeolischen Inschriften, *and* A. Fick: Die thessalischen Inschriften 2/- 8° *Göttingen* 83
BRAND, A. De Dialectis aeolicis quae dicuntur, pt. i. 1/6 8° *Berlin* 85
HINRICHS, G. De Homericae Elocutionis Vestigiis aeolicis 3/- 8° *Jena* 75
HIRZEL, Ludwig Zur Beurtheilung des aeolischen Dialekts 1/- 8° *Leipzig* 62
MUCKE, F. De Consonarum in Gr. ling. praeter dial. Aeol. geminatione, pt. i. 8° *Budissae* 83
VOLKMANN, R. Quaestionum de Dialecto aeolica capita ii. 8° *Halle* 79

Arcadian.

SPITZER, J. Lautlehre des arkadischen Dialektes 2/- 8° *Kiel* 83

Attic and Homeric—*v. also* K § 190, *s.v.* Homer (AIDS).

AHRENS, H. L. Griechische Formenlehre d. homer. u. attischen Dial 2/6 8° *Göttingen* [52] 69
HECHT, Max Orthographisch-dialektische Forschungen auf Grund attischer Inschriften, 2 pts. 2/- 4° *Königsberg* 85; 86
KRÜGER, K. W. Homerische und Herodotische Formenlehre 1/- 8° *Berlin* [49] 79
van LEEUWEN + da COSTA, J. *fun.* Mendes, Het Taaleiger der homer. Gedichten, 4/-; Germ. tr. by E. Mehler 2/6 8° *Leyden* 83; *Lpzg.* 86
MEISTERHANS, K. Grammatik der attischen Inschriften 6/6 8° *Berlin* [85] 88
*MONRO, D. B. Grammar of the Homeric Dialect 10/6 8° Clar. Press [82]
RUTHERFORD, Prf. W. G. History of the Attic Dialect—*in* the New Phrynichus [*v.* K § 177].
SAYCE, Prf. A. H. On the Language of the Homeric Poems 18/- 8° Macmillan 81

Boeotian —*v. also* K § 190, *s.v.* Pindar (AIDS).

FUHRER, A. De Dialecti Boeotica 1/- 8° *Göttingen* 71
LARFELD, W. De Dialecti Boeoticae imitationibus [repr. in his *Sylloge*, *ut* K § 93] 2/- 8° *Bonn* 81

Cretan.

HELBIG, Hugo Quaestiones de Dialecto Cretica 1/6 4° *Plauen* [69] 73
LÜBY, G. De Dialecto Cretica 2/- 8° *Dessau* 69

Cypriotic.

DEECKE, W. Die griechisch-kyprischen Inschriften in epichorischer Schrift 2/6 8° *Göttingen* 83
ROTHE, A. Quaestiones de Cypriorum Dialecto, pt. i. 2/- 8° *Leipzig* 75

Delphic.

HARTMANN, Th. — De Dialecto Delphica — *Breslau* 74

Doric.

AHRENS, H. L. — De Dialecto dorica [1843] —*new edn.* by Meister, *v. supra.*
WEBER, Hugo — Die dorische Partikel κα : ein Beitrag z. Lehre v. d. griech. Dial. 1/6 8° *Halle* 64

Elean.

DANIEL, C. — De Dialecto Eliaca 1/6 8° *Halle* 80

Ionic.

KARSTEN, W. — De Titulorum Ionicorum Dialecto 2/6 8° *Halle* 82
SMYTH, Dr. H. Weir — Vowel System of Ionic Dialects—*in* Trans. Am. Phil. Assoc., vol. xx.—a prelude to his larger wk., *supra.*

Laconic.

DAVID, E. — Dialecti Laconicae Monumenta Epigraphica [inaug. dissert.] 1/- 8° *Königsberg* 82
KRAMPE, A. — De Dialecto Laconica [dissertation] 1/- 8° *Münster* 67
MÜLLENSIEFEN, P. — De Titulorum Laconicorum Dialecto 1/6 8° *Strassburg* 82

Lesbian.

FÜHRER, A. — Ueber den lesbischen Dialekt 2/6 4° *Arnsberg* 81
WALD, — Additamenta ad Dial. et Lesb. et Thessal. cognoscendam 2/- 8° *Berlin* 71

Megaric.

SCHNEIDER, E. — De Dialecto Megarico 2/- 8° *Giessen* 82

Modern Greek —*v.* K § 186.

Phoenician —*v.* K § 213.

Rhodian.

BRÜLL, — Ueber den Dialekt der Rhodier 2/6 4° *Leobschütz* 75

Sicilian.

ARENS, J. — De Dialecto Sicula 1/- 8 *Münster* 68

Thessalian —*v. also* Lesbian, *supra.*

FICK, A. — Die Thessalischen Inschriften—*v.* Aeolic, *supra, s.v.* Bechtel.
v. d. PFORDTEN, H. — De Dialecto Thessalica 2/- 8° *Munich* 79
PRELLWITZ, W. — De Dialecto Thessalica 1/6 8° *Göttingen* 85
REUTER, E. — De Dialecto Thessalica 2/- 8° *Berlin* 85

Zaconic [a descendant of the Laconic].

DEFFNER, M. — Zakonische Grammatik, pt. i 6/- 8° *Berlin* 81

186. MODERN GREEK (ROMAIC) PHILOLOGY AND LITERATURE.

Grammar.

*GELDART, Rev. E. M. — Guide to Modern Greek [Key 2/6] 7/6 p 8° Trübner 83
Simplified Grammar of Modern Greek [Simplified Grammar Series] 2/6 c 8° " 83
*MULLACH, F. W. A. — Grammatik der griechischen Vulgär-Sprache *o.p.* [*pb.* 8/- ; *w.* 25/-] 8° *Berlin* 56
PSICHARI, Jean — Essais de Grammaire Historique Néo-Grecque, 2 pts. 8° *Paris* 86 ; 89
RANGABÉ, A. R. — Grammaire abrégé du Grec actuel 5/- 8° " [73] 86
SOPHOCLES, Prf. E. A. — Romaic or Modern Greek Grammar 10/6 8° *Boston* [66] 79
TIEN, Rev. Anton — Neo-Hellenic Manual [gram., vocab., dial., letters, etc.] 5/- f 8° W. H. Allen 89
*VINCENT + DICKSON, E./T. G. — Handbook of Modern Greek 6/- 12° Macmillan [79] 81
VLACHOS, A. — Neugriechische Grammatik 1/6 8° *Leipzig* [64] 82
ZOMPOLIDES, Dr. D. — Course of Modern Greek, pt. i. : Elementary Method 5/- c 8° Williams 87

Zaconic —*v.* K § 185 : Greek Dialects.

Serial.

Journal of Hellenic Studies, vols. i.–viii., w. pl. ea. vol. 30/- 8° Macmillan 80–87 *in prog.*

Chrestomathy.

VLACHOS, A. [ed.] — Neugriechische Chrestomathie 3/- s 8° *Leipzig* 70

Phonology.

BRADY, — Lautveränderungen d. neugriechischen Volksprache 1/6 8° *Göttingen* 86
FOY, K. — Lautsystem der griechischen Vulgärsprache 3/- 8° *Leipzig* 79

K § 187

Etymology.

Dictionaries.

CONTOPOULOS, N. Modern Greek-English and English-Modern Greek Lexicon, 2 vols. 27/- 8° *Athens* [67] 80

JANNARAKIS, A. Deutsch-neugriechisches Handwörterbuch, 2 pts. 8/- 8° *Hanover* 83

LASCARIDES, G. P. Phraseological English-Ancient-and-Modern Greek Lexicon, 2 vols. 30/- f 8° Trübner 82

Chios.

PASPATI, Dr. A. G. Τὸ Χιακὸν Γλωσσάριον· ἤτοι ἡ ἐν Χίῳ λαλουμένη γλῶσσα 8° *Athens* 89

Roman Byzantine Periods—v. K § 179.

Loan Words.

MIKLOSICH, F. Die slavischen Elemente im Neugriechischen 8° *Vienna* 70

History of Literature.

FAURIEL, C. —*his* Chants pop. de la Grèce Moderne *has an essay of 144 pp. contg. a complete survey of Romaic literature*, 2 vols. *o.p.* [w. 30/-] 8° *Paris* 24 | 25

GIDEL, A. Ch. Études sur la Littérature grecque moderne 7/6 8° „ 66

Greek imitations of French romances of chivalry from the twelfth century.

„ „ Nouvelles Études sur la Littérature grecque moderne 9 fr. 8° „ 78

NICOLAI, R. Geschichte der neugriechischen Litteratur 4/- 8° *Magdeburg* [66-67] 76

RANGABÉ, A. R. Histoire Littéraire de la Grèce Moderne, 2 vols. 8/- 12° *Paris* 77

„ „ Précis d'un Histoire de la Littérature Néo-hellénique, 2 vols. [Calvary's *Bibl.*] 8/- 12° *Berlin* 80

Collection.

LEGRAND, E. [ed.] Bibliothèque Grecque Vulgaire, 3 vols. 50/- 8° *Paris* 80-81

Folk-Literature —v. B § 13: Modern Greek Mythology and Folklore.

187. HISTORY OF GREEK LITERATURE: (a) GENERALLY.

General Histories.

BENDER, F. Geschichte d. griech. Litteratur [to Ptolemies] 12/- 8° *Leipzig* 86

BERGK, Theodor Griechische Literaturgeschichte, vol. i.; vols. ii.-iv. posthum. ed. G. Hinrichs 30/- 8° *Berlin* 72; 83-87

*BERNHARDY, G. Grundriss der griechischen Literatur, 2 vols. in 3 39/- 8° *Halle* [36-45] 72-80

Standard. Vol. i.: Innere Geschichte, 13/6 [36] 72; ii.: Epos, Elegie, Iamben, Melik, 11/- [45] 77; iii.: Drama, Alexandriner, Byzantiner, Fabel, 13/6 [45] 80.

BROWNE, Prf. R. W. History of Classical Literature, 2 vols. [Greece only] *o.p.* [*pb.* 28/-; *w.* 15/-] 8° Bentley 51

BURNOUF, E. Histoire de la Littérature Grecque, 2 vols. [popular] 6/- 12° *Paris* [69] 85

v. CHRIST, Prf. Griechische Literaturgeschichte; 16 pl. [Müller's *Hdb. Klass. Alterth.*] 12/- r 8° *Nördlingen* [88] 90

JEBB, Prf. R. C. Primer of Greek Literature [Macmillan's Literature Primers] 1/- 18° Macmillan 78

JEVONS, F. B. History of Greek Literature [to d. of Demosthenes; students' bk.] 8/6 c 8° Griffin [86] 90

MAHAFFY, Prf. J. P. History of Classical Greek Literature, 2 vols. [i.: Poetry; ii.: Prose] ea. 9/- c 8° Macmillan [80] 90

More descriptive and less critical than MÜLLER, *ut infra*. Vol. i. has an appendix on Homer by Prf. A. H. SAYCE.

MÜLLER + DONALDSON, K. O. / J. W., History of the Literature of Ancient Greece [tr.], 3 vols. *o.p.* [*pb.* 36/-; *w.* 21/-] 8° Parker 50-58

Vols. i.-ii. tr. (Sir) G. C. LEWIS + J. W. DONALDSON; v. iii. is a cont. by DONALDSON. The orig., posthum. ed. Ed. MÜLLER, [=vols. i.-ii. (?)] re-ed. Emil HEITZ, 12/- 8° Stuttgart [41] 82, was cont. by HEITZ (=ii. 2) 6/- 8° ib. 84. Still a very valuable source of information, but less full than MURE.

MUNK, Ed. Geschichte der Griechischen Literatur, ed. R. Volkmann, 2 vols. [popular] 12/- 8° *Berl.* [49] 79; [49] 80

A compendium, with numerous extracts.

Verrall, A. W. [ed.] The Student's Greek Tragedians: based on Munk; port. 3/6 c 8° 90

The extracts fr. the tragedies are Dr. PLUMPTRE'S trs.

MURE, Col. Wm. Critical History of Language & Literature of Anc. Greece, 5 vols. *o.p.* [*pb.* 69/-; *w.* 63/-] 8° Longman [50-57] 54-60

The Epic and Lyric poetry, and History, down to the death of Xenophon. Extremely full and scholarly: *not* good for popular reading.

NICOLAI, R. Geschichte der gesammten griechischen Literatur, 3 vols. 21/- 8° *Magdeburg* [65-67] 73-78

Contains elaborate bibliographical references.

PIERRON, Alois Histoire de la Littérature Grecque [a compendium] 3/- 12° *Paris* [50] 82

SITTL, K. Geschichte der griechischen Literatur, vol. i. 5/-; ii. 6/6; iii. 6/6 [to Alex. Great] 8° *Munich* 84; 86; 87

Collected Essays.

ABBOTT, Evelyn [ed.] Hellenica: essays on Greek poetry, philos., and literature 16/- 8° Rivington 80

Aeschylus E. MYERS. | The Theology and Ethics of Sophocles E. ABBOTT. | System of Education in Plato's Republic R. L. NETTLESHIP. | Aristotle's Conception of the State A. C. BRADLEY. | Epicurus W. L. COURTNEY. | The Speeches of Thucydides R. C. JEBB. | Xenophon H. G. DAKYNS. | Polybius J. L. S. DAVIDSON. | Greek Oracles F. W. H. MYERS.

Series.

Classical Writers, ed. J. R. Green [brief descriptions] ea. 1/6 f 8° Macmillan 79, *etc.*

Demosthenes (Prf. S. H. BUTCHER), Euripides (Prf. J. P. MAHAFFY), Sophocles (Prf. Lewis CAMPBELL).

Book-Writing.

*BIRT, Theodor Das antike Buchwesen in s. Verhältniss zur Literatur 12/- 8° *Berlin* 82

PALEY, Dr. F. A. Bibliographia Graeca [date and orig. of bk.-wtg. am. Gks.] 8° *London* 81

SCHMITZ, W. Schriftsteller und Buchhändler im Athen u. übrig. Griechenland 2/- 8° *Heidelberg* 76

188. HISTORY OF GREEK LITERATURE: (b) SPECIAL DEPARTMENTS (a) POETRY AND DRAMA.

Poetry: Comprehensive Works.

*BERNHARDY, G. — Grundriss, pt. ii.—*v.* K § 187.
BODE, G. H. — Geschichte der hellenischen Dichtkunst, 3 vols. in 5 [to Alex. Great] 18/- 8° *Leipzig* 38-40

Critical Essays, etc.

BIRT, Theodor — Elpides: eine Studie zur Geschichte d. griech. Poesie 2/- 8° *Marburg* 81
GIRARD, J. — Études sur la Poésie Grecque 3/- 12° *Paris* 84
Epicharmus, Pindar, Sophocles, Theocritus, Apollonius.
MYERS, F. W. H. — Essays: series i., Classical 4/6 c 8° Macmillan 83
NITZSCH, G. W. — Die Sagenpoesie der Griechen kritisch dargestellt 10/6 8° *Brunswick* 52-53
SCHMIDT, J. H. H. — Kunstformen der griechischen Poesie und ihre Bedeutung, 4 vols. [*v.* K § 92] 51/- 8° *Leipzig* 68-72
*SYMONDS, J. A. — Studies of the Greek Poets, ser. i.-ii. ea. 10/6 8° Smith & Elder [73] 88; [76] 88

Didactic Poetry, Fables, etc.

EHLERS, J. — Αἴνιγμα καὶ γρῖφοι, 2/-; De Graecorum aenigmatis et griphis 1/6 4° *Bonn* 67; *Prenzlau* 76
HAGEN, H. — Antike und Mittelalterliche Räthselpoesie 1/- 8° *Berne* [69] 77
JACOBS, Joseph — —*in his* Fables of Æsop, 2 vols. [Bibl. de. Carabas] 14/- s 8° Nutt 98
KELLER, O. — Untersuchungen über die Geschichte der griechischen Fabel 2/6 8° *Leipzig* 62
OHLERT, K. — Räthsel und Geschäftsspiele der alten Griechen 5/- 8° *Berlin* 86
OESTERLEY, H. — Romulus: d. Paraphrasen d. Phädrus u. d. Äsop. Fabel im Mittelalter 8° ,, 70

Bucolic Poetry.

FRITZSCHE, A. Th. H. — De Poetis Graecorum Bucolicis 1/6 8° *Giessen* 44
GEBAUER, G. A. — De Poetarum Graec. Bucolicorum carmin., vol. i. [Theocritus to Virgil] 4/- r 8° *Leipzig* 61

Dramatic Literature.

Generally.

DARLEY, J. R. — The Grecian Drama *o.p.* [*pb.* 12/-; *w.* 7/6] 8° Groombridge 40
GÜNTHER, G. — Grundzüge d. tragischen Kunst aus d. Drama d. Gr. entwickelt 10/- 8° *Leipzig* 85
KLEIN, J. L. — Geschichte des Dramas der Griechen und Römer, 2 vols. 21/- 8° ,, 65; 65
i.: Griechische Tragödie; ii.: Griechische Komödie und das Drama der Römer.
MOULTON, R. G. — The Ancient Classical Drama: study in literary evolution 8/6 c 8° Clar. Press 90
MYRIANTHEUS, L. — Die Marschlieder des griechischen Dramas 3/- 8° *Munich* 73
RAPP, Moritz — Geschichte des griechischen Schauspiels 6/- 8° *Tübingen* 62
v. SCHLEGEL, A. W. — Lectures on Dramatic Art and Literature [tr.] [1st. ed. *of orig.* 09-11] 3/6 c 8° Bohn's Lib. 46
A survey of the most remarkable dramatic compositions fr. the time of the Greeks to beginning of 19th century.
WALFORD, — Handbook of the Greek Drama *o.p.* [*pb.* 6/-; *w.* 4/6] 8° Longman 56

Tragedy.

CHAIGNET, E. A. — La Tragédie Grecque 3/- 12° *Paris* 77
HEIMSOETH, F. — Kritische Studien zu den griechischen Tragikern, pt. i. 7/- 8° *Bonn* 65
MUNK, Ed. — The Student's Greek Tragedians [tr.], ed. Dr. A. W. Verrall; port. 3/6 c 8° Sonnenschein 91
PATIN, H. J. G. — Études sur les Tragiques Grecs, 4 vols. 12/- 12° *Paris* [41-43] *v.y.*
SCHURÉ, E. — —*in his* Le Drame Musicale, 2 vols. 8° ,, 75
WELCKER, F. G. — —*v. infra, s.v.* Epic.

Comedy.

AGTHE, C. — Parabase u. Zwischenacte d. altatt. Komödie; 6 ill. 4/-; Suppl., 6 ill. 2/6 8° *Altona* 66; 68
BOTHE, F. H. — Die griechischen Komiker [critical] 2/- 8° *Leipzig* 44
CRAMER, G. — Die altgriechische Komödie u. ihre geschichtl. Entwickelung 1/6 4° *Köthen* 74
du MÉRIL, E. — Histoire de la Comédie Ancienne, 2 vols. ea. 7/- 8° *Paris* 64; 69
MEINEKE, A. — Historia Critica Comoediae Graecae—*in* vol. i. *of his edn. of* Comicorum Graec. Fragm.—*ut* K § 191.
MUHL, J. — Zur Geschichte der alten attischen Komödie 2/- 8° *Augsburg* 81
RIBBECK, O. — Alazon, 4/6; Kolax, 4/-; Agroikos, 2/- ["ethological studies"] r 8° *Leipzig* 82; 83; 85
ZIELINSKI, Th. — Die Gliederung der altattischen Komödie; 1 col. pl. 10/- 8° ,, 85
,, ,, — Die Märchen-Komödie in Athen 2/- r 8° *St. Petersburg* [85] 89

Stage.

BAUMEISTER, A. [ed.] — —*in his* Denkmäler d. klassischen Altertums; 3 vols.; ill. 69/- 4° *Munich* 84-88
DONALDSON, Prc. J. W. — The Theatre of the Greeks: hist. and exhib. of Gk. drama 5/- c 8° Bohn's Lib. [49] 75
DUMON, K. — Le Théâtre de Polyclète [tech. acc. of his théatre at Epidaurus] 8° *Paris* 90
FLACH, H. — Das griechische Theater; 2 ill. [a lecture; popular] 2/- 8° *Tübingen* 78
FREYTAG, Gustav — —*in his* Die Technik des Dramas 5/- 8° *Leipzig* [63] 81
*HAIGH, A. E. — The Attic Theatre: descrip. of stage and performances at Athens; ill. 12/6 8° Clar. Press 90
van HERWERDEN, H. — —*his* Studia Thucydidea, *contains also his* Analecta Scenica 4/- 8° *Utrecht* 69
MARGOLIOUTH, D. S. — Studia Scenica, pt. i., General Intro. and *Trachiniae* 1-300 2/6 8° Macmillan 83
OEHMICHEN, G. — Bühnenwesen d. Griechen u. Römer [Iwan Müller's *Hdb. Klass. Alterth.*, pt. xiv.] 6/6 8° *Nördlingen* 90
SOMMERBRODT, J. — Scaenica, 8/-; Das altgriechische Theater 1/- 8° *Berlin* 76; *Stuttgart* 65
STRACK, J. H. — Das altgriechische Theatergebäude [=9 pl. w. descriptive text] 11/6 f° *Potsdam* 43
WIESELER, F. — Theatergebäude u. Denkmäler d. Bühnenwesens b. d. Griechen u. Römern; 14 pl. (3 col.) 11/- f° *Göttingen* 51
WITZSCHEL, A. — The Athenian Stage, tr. Paul *o.p.* [*pb.* 4/-] c 8° Rivington 50

Epic Poetry.

NITZSCH, G. W. — Beiträge zur Geschichte der epischen Poesie d. Griechen — 9/- 8° *Leipzig* 62
" " — Die Sagenpoesie d. Griechen kritisch dargestellt, vol. i., bk. 1 (Homeric) 4/6 8° *Braunschweig* 52
WELCKER, F. G. — Der epische Cyclus, 2 vols. ; vol. i. 8/- ; ii. 10/- — 8° *Bonn* [35] 65 ; [49] 82
The Greek tragedies arranged with regard to the Epic Cycle.
v. WILAMOWITZ-MÖLLENDORFF, U.—Homerische Untersuchungen, pp. 328 *sqq.* : Der epische Cyklus 7/- 8° *Berlin* 84

Lyric Poetry.

FLACH, H. — Geschichte der griechischen Lyrik nach d. Quellen dargestellt, 2 vols. 13/- 8° *Leipzig* 83 ; 84
HARTUNG, J. A. — —Introduction *to his* Die griechischen Lyriker, *ut* K § 190.

189. HISTORY OF GREEK LITERATURE: (γ) SPECIAL DEPARTMENTS (β) PROSE.

Geographers

—*v. also* E § 9 : Manuals of Ancient Geography.
BUNBURY, E. H. — —*in his* Hist. of Anc. Geog. among Gks. & Romans, 2 vols. ; maps and ill. 21/- 8° Murray [79] 84
GÜNTHER, S. — Stud. z. Gesch. d. Geogr., pt. iii. : Aeltere u. neuere Hypothesen 2/6 8° *Halle* 78
HIRSCHFELD, Dr. — Bericht üb. unsere geograph. Kenntniss d. alten griech. Wolf, 2 pts. *o.p.*
de SAINT-MARTIN, Vivien — Étude sur la Géogr. grec. et lat. de l'Inde, 2 vols. 40/- 4° *Paris* 58 ; 61
Especially on PTOLEMY'S *India*.
" " — —*in his* Histoire de la Géographie et des Découvertes ; w. atlas 17/- r 8° " 73
THOMAS, G. M. — Der Periplus des Pontus Euxinus ; col. map [fr. Munich MSS.] 4/- 4° *Munich* 64

Grammarians.

FRESENIUS, A. — De Mξεων Aristophanearum et Suetoniarum excerptis Byzantis 4/- 8° *Wiesbaden* 76
SCHÖMANN, G. F. — Die Lehre von d. Redetheilen nach der Alten 4/6 8° *Berlin* 62

Historians.

CREUTZER, F. — Die historische Kunst der Griechen, hrsg. J. Kayser 7/- 8° *Darmstadt* [03] 45
ROSCHER, W. — Klio: Beiträge z. Geschichte d. historischen Kunst, v. i. [Proleg. & Thucydides] 8/- 8° *Göttingen* 42
SCHRÖDER, W. — De Primordiis Artis Historicae apud Graecos et Romanos 2/6 8° *Jena* 68
ULRICI, H. — Charakteristik der antiken Historiographie 5/6 8° *Berlin* 33
VOLLGRAFF, J. C. — Greek Writers on Roman History 2/6 8° *Leyden* 80
On the authority used by Plutarch and Appianus.
VOSS, G. J. — De Historicis Graecis, ed. A. Westermann 6/- 8° *Leipzig* [1623] 38

Letter-Writers.

BENTLEY, Richard — Dissertations on the Epistles of Phalaris, Themistokles, Sokrates, Euripides, and the Fables of Æsop, ed. W. Wagner [w. intro. and notes] 5/- c 8° Bohn's Lib. [1699] 83
The sheets of the German edn. (Calvary's *Bibl.*, 3 pts. 8/- *Berlin* '74) bound up with Messrs. Bell & Sons' title-page.
BOUCHÉ-LECLERQ, A. — De la Dignité des Lettres Anciennes 2/- 8° *Paris* 74
WESTERMANN, A. — De Epistolarum Scriptoribus Graecis, 8 pts. [reprints] 4° *Leipzig* 51–58

Military Science: Writers on.

RÜSTOW + KÖCHLY, W. + H. Gesch. d. griech. Kriegswesens : nach d. Quellen ; 134 ill. and 6 pl. [to Pyrrhos] 8/6 8° *Aarau* 52

Music and Metre: Writers on.

AMBROS, A. W. — —*in his* Geschichte der Musik, 3 vols. 33/- 8° *Breslau* 62–68
GEVAERT, F. A. — Histoire et Théorie de la Musique de l'Antiquité, 2 vols. ea. 25/- 8° *Gand* 75 ; 81
GUHRAUER, H. — Der Pythische Nomos [fr. *Jahrbb. Class. Philol.*] 1/6 8° Teubner, *Leipzig* 76
PAUL, Oscar — Die absolute Harmonik der Griechen 5/- 4° " 67
ROSSBACH + WESTPHAL, A. + R.—*v.* K § 183.
TIRON, Alix — Études sur la Musique Grecque 10/- 8° *Paris* 66
WESTPHAL, R. — Geschichte der alten. u mittelalterlichen Musik, pts. i. & iii. [pt. ii. not pub.] 9/- 8° *Breslau* 64 : 66
" " — Die Musik des griechischen Alterthumes 9/- 8° *Leipzig* 83

Modern Writers on Greek Metrics—*v.* K § 183.

Orators.

*BLASS, F. — Die Attische Beredsamkeit, 3 vols. 50/- 8° *Leipzig* 68–80
i.: Gorgias to Lysias, 13/-; ii.: Isocrates and Isaeus, 14/-; iii. (1): Demosthenes, 14/-; iii. (2): Demosthenes' Opponents and Companions, 9/-.
BRÉDIF, L. — L'Éloquence Politique en Grèce [on Demosthenes] 8° *Paris* 79
BROUGHAM, Henry, Ld. — —*in his* Contributions to the *Edinburgh Review* *o.p.* 8° Black 55
Gives a good idea of the general characteristics of the Attic orators.
GIRARD, J. — Études sur l'Éloquence Attique [Lysias, Hyperides, Demosthenes] 3/- 12° *Paris* [74] 84
*JEBB, Prf. R. C. — The Attic Orators from Antiphon to Isaeos, 2 vols. 25/- 8° Macmillan 76
For Prf. JEBB'S Texts, to accompany this critical work, *v.* K § 199.
PERROT, G. — L'Éloquence Politique et Judiciaire à Athènes, v. i. [precursors of Demosthenes] 8° *Paris* 73
VOLKMANN, R. — Rhetorik der Griechen u. Römer in systematischer Uebersicht 10/- 8° *Leipzig* [72] 74

Philosophers

—*v.* C §§ 2–3, 5–15.

Proverb-Writers.

CRUSIUS, O. Analecta Critica ad Paroemiographos Graecos 4/- 8° *Leipzig* 83
WARNKROSS, M. De Paroemiographis capita duo 1/6 8° *Griefswald* 81

Romance and Romances : Greek—*v.* K § 44 : Greek Romances, *s.v.* History.

Science.

Generally —*v. also* H § 1 (esp. Whewell).

GÜNTHER + WINDELBAND, Prfs. Geschichte d. antiken Naturwiss. u. Philos [Müller's *Hdb. Kl. Alt.*] 5/6 r 8° *Nördlingen* 88
HOEFER, Ferdinand Hist. d. l. Botanique, Minéral. et Geol. 3/- 12° *Paris* 72

Astronomy —*v. also* H § 21.

GRANT, R. —*in his* History of Astronomy from the Earliest Ages *o.p.* [*pb* 16/-] 8° Baldwin 52
GRUPPE, O. F. Die kosmischen Systeme der Griechen 3/- 8° *Berlin* 51
HOEFER, Ferdinand —*in his* Histoire de l'Astronomie depuis les Origines 3/6 12° *Paris* 73
LEWIS, Sir G. C. Historical Review of the Astronomy of the Ancients *o.p.* [*pb.* 15/- ; *w.* 30/-] 8° Parker 62
v. MÄDLER, J. H. —*in his* Geschichte d. Himmelskunde v. d. ältesten Zeiten, 2 v. 17/- 8° *Brunswick* 73
SCHIAPARELLI, G. V. Die Vorläufer d. Copernicus im Alterthum [tr. fr. Ital.] 3/- 8° *Leipzig* 76
WOLF, Rudolf —*in his* Geschichte der Astronomie [Gesch. d. Wiss. in Dtschld.] 12/- 8° *Munich* 77

Botany —*v. also* H § 48.

KOCH, Karl Die Bäume und Sträuche des alten Griechenlands 6/- 8° *Berlin* [79] 84
LENZ, H. O. Botanik der alten Griechen und Römer [tr. extracts, w. notes] 10/- 8° *Gotha* 59

Mathematics.

BRETSCHNEIDER, C. A. Die Geometrie und die Geometer vor Eukildes 4/- 8° *Leipzig* 70
CANTOR, Moritz —*in his* Vorlesungen über die Geschichte der Mathematik, vol. i. 20/- 8° Teubner, *Leipzig* 80
*GOW, Dr. J. A Short History of Greek Mathematics 10/6 8° Camb. Press 84
GÜNTHER, S. —*in his* Untersuchungen zur Geschichte d. mathem. Wissenschaften ; 4 pl. 9/- 8° Teubner, *Leipzig* 76
HANKEL, H. Zur Geschichte d. Mathematik im Alterthum u. Mittelalter 9/- 8° ,, ,, 74
HEATH, T. L. Diophantos of Alexandria : a study in the history of Greek algebra 7/6 8° Camb. Press 85
SUTER, H. —*in his* Geschichte der mathematischen Wissenschaften, 2 pts. 22/- 8° *Zürich* [71] 73 ; 75

Medicine.

ADAMS, Dr. Francis —*in his edn. of* Paulus Aegineta, *v.* H* § 3, *s.v.* Greek Writers on Medicine.
BAAS, J. H. —*in his* Grundriss der Geschichte der Medicin 20/- r 8° *Stuttgart* 76
HAESER, H. —*in his* Lehrbuch der Geschichte der Medicin, vol. i. [in 3 vols.] 18/- 8° *Jena* [ ] 75

Metrology (Weights and Measures).

BRANDIS, J. Münz-, Maass-, u. Gewichtswesen in Vorderasien 14/- 8° *Berlin* 66
FENNER v. FENNEBERG, L. Längen-, Feld. u. Wegemaase d. Völk. d. Alterth. 2/- 8° ,, 59
HULTSCH, F. Griechische und Römische Metrologie 2/6 8° ,, 62
MÜLLER, Hermann Die heiligen Maasse d. Alterthums [esp. Heb. and Gk.] 2/6 8° *Freiburg* 59

Mineralogy.

LENZ, H. O. Mineralogie d. alten Griechen und Römer 4/- 8° *Gotha* 61

Zoology —*v. also* H § 70.

HOEFER, Ferdinand —*in his* Histoire de la Zoologie dep. l. temps l. plus recul. 3/6 12° *Paris* 73
LENZ, H. O. Zoologie der alten Griechen und Römer [tr. extracts, w. notes] 8/6 8° *Gotha* 56

190. GREEK POETS.

Collections.

Didactic Poets —*v. also* K § 196 : Greek Writers on Natural Science.

Bucolic Poets.

Bucolici Poetae [Theocr., Bion, Moschus] rec. H. L. Ahrens 10*d.* p 8° Teubner, *Leipzig* [ ] 75
,, rec. H. L. Ahrens ; ed. crit., 2 vols. [vol. ii. = scholia] 22/- 8° *Leipzig* 55 ; 59
,, with German notes and tr. J. A. Hartung 7/- 12° ,, 58
,, et Didactici with Latin tr. C. F. Ameis + F. S. Lehrs + F. Dübner + A. Köchly 12/6 r 8° Didot, *Paris* [46–51] 62
Theocr., Bion, Mosch. (AHRENS) ; Nikander, Oppianus, Marcellus (LEHRS) ; Philet (DÜBNER) ; Aratus, Manetho, Maximus (KÖCHLY).

Eclogues.

Eclogae Poetarum Graecorum, rec. H. Stadtmüller 3/6 p 8° Teubner, *Leipzig* 83

Epic Poets.

Epicorum Fragmenta rec. J. Kinkel ; ed. crit. vol. i. 3/- p 8° Teubner, *Leipzig* 77
Cf. also Homeri et Cycli Epici Fragmenta, ed. w. lat. tr. W. Dindorf, [illegible] r 8° Didot, *Paris* 81.
,, Graec. Corpus cura A. Koechley 14/6 8° ,, ,, 52–74

K § 190

Elegiac Poets.

HARTUNG, J. A. [ed.] Elegiaci Graeci, w. German tr. and notes, 2 vols. 6/6 12° *Leipzig* 58 ; 59

Vide also Lyrici Poetae, *infra*. A selection *sub tit. Extracts fr. Gk. Elegiac Poets*, ed. H. KYNASTON 1/6 f 8° Macmillan 80.

Popular Songs —*for* Modern Greek Folk-songs, *v.* C § 13 : Mod. Gk. Mythology and Folklore.

LEGRAND, Ém. [ed.& tr.] Chansons Populaires Grecques [w. French trs.] 2/6 8° *Paris* 76

Paroedorum Graec. Corpus ed. H. S. toe Laer 8° *Amsterdam* 67

Scenici Poetae —*v.* K § 191 : Greek Dramatists.

Sillographi Poetae De Timone Phliasio ceterisque Syllog. Graec. By C. Wachsmuth [w. fragms.] 2/- r 8° Teubner, *Leipzig* 59

Gnomic Poets

Gnomici Poetae 1/- 16° Tauchnitz, *Leipzig* [15] 74

Lyric Poets.

BERGK, Theodor [ed.] Lyrici Poetae, 3 vols. 33/- 8° *Leipzig* [43] 78-82

i. : Pindar, 9/- ; ii. : Elegiaci et Iambographi, 10/- ; iii. : Melici, Scolia, Carm. pop., 14/-.

HARTUNG, J. A. [ed.] ,, ,, with German tr. and notes, 6 vols. 12° ,, 55-57

i.-iv. : Pindar, 10/6 ; v. : Archilochus and Doric Poets, 3/- ; vi. : Alkaeus, Sappho, Simonides of Keos, etc., 4/-.

POMTOW, J. [ed.] Poetae Lyrici Graeci Minores, 2 vols. [a choice little edn.] 5/- 16° ,, 85

Anthology.

BERGK, Theodor [ed.] Anthologia Graeca, rec. Ed. Hiller 3/- p 8° Teubner, *Leipzig* [54] 90

BUCHHOLZ, E. [ed.] Anthologie aus den griechischen Lyrikern, 2 vols. 3/6 p 8° ,, ,, [64-66] 83

KYNASTON, H. [ed.] Poetae Graeci [extracts from less-known poets, with notes] 3/6 p 8° *Eton* [ ] 79

NEAVES, Lord [ed.] Greek Anthology [trs. ; Anc. Class. for Eng. Readers ; popular] 2/6 12° Blackwood 74

THACKERAY, F. St. J. [ed.] Anthologia Graeca 4/6 12° Bell [70] 77

TYLER, Prf. H. M. [Am. ; ed.] Selection from the Greek Lyric Poets ; w. notes $1.10 12° *Boston* 8-

WILKINS, H. M. [ed.] Progressive Greek Anthology [school-book] 5/- c 8° Longman 65

*WRIGHT, R. S. [ed.] Golden Treasury of Ancient Greek Poetry, ed. Evelyn Abbott 10/6 f 8° Clar. Press [66] 89

Translations.

TOMLINSON, Graham R. [ed.] Selections from the Greek Anthology [Camelot Series] 1/- 16° Walter Scott 89

Translations by Dr. Garnett, Andrew Lang, Goldwin Smith, Alma Strettell, W. M. Hardinge, J. A. Symonds, Goldwin Smith, etc.

Æsop

—*v. also* Babrius, *infra*. *For* Avianus' [Flavius'] *version*, *v.* K § 214.

TEXTS : Fabulæ rec. C. Halm, 1/- p 8° ; Editio Tauchnitziana 9*d.* 16° Teubner [52] 74 ; *Leipzig* [21] 77

TRANSLATIONS : The fables now extant in prose under ÆSOP'S name are entirely spurious, as was proved by BENTLEY, in his *Diss. on Fables of Æsop* [*ut* K § 189], and are of Oriental (prob. Indo-Persian) origin.

AID : —*v.* Jos. Jacobs—*in his* Fables of Æsop, *etc.*, 2 vols. 14/- s 8° Nutt 98

Anacreon.

TEXTS : Carmina rec. V. Rose, 1/- p 8° ; rec. C. H. Weise, 6*d.* [*v. also* Poetae Lyrici, *supra*] 16° Teubner [68] 76 ; Tauchn. [44] 78

TRANSLATIONS :

Odes : tr. Thomas Moore (the poet) ; 54 ill. by G. de Roussy *o.p.* [*pb.* 12/6 ; *w.* 10/-] 16° Hotten [ ] 69

tr. T. J. Arnold (in original metres) *o.p.* [*pb.* and *w.* 3/6] 12° ,, 69

Apollonius Rhodius—Text : Argonautica.

rec. R. Merkel + H. Keil, ed. crit., pt. i. Text & Crit. App., 6/- ; ii. Prolegg. & Scholia 9/- 8° Teubner, *Leipzig* 53 ; 54

,, ,, —*as* vol. iv. of A. Köchly's *Corp. Poett. Epicorum* 1/- p 8° ,, ,, [52] 72

,, w. Lat. tr. F. S. Lehrs + F. Dübner [w. Hesiod, Musaeus, etc.] 12/6 r 8° Didot, *Paris* 78

TRANSLATION : tr. E. P. Coleridge [a prose tr. ; from Merkel's text] 5/- c 8° Bohn's Lib. 89

A narrative poem founded on the legends relating to the Argonautic expedition.

AIDS :

Hémardinquer. De Apollonii Rhodii Argonauticis 3/6 8° *Paris* 72

Linde, R. De diversis recensionibus Apollonii Rhodii Argonauticon 1/6 8° *Hanover* 85

Linsenbarth, O. De Apollonii Rhodii casuum syntaxi comparato usu homerico 1/- 8° *Leipzig* 87

Michaelis, J. J. De Apollonii Rhodii Fragmentis [dissert. inaug.] 1/- 8° *Halle* 75

Rzach, Alois Grammatische Studien zu Apollonius Rhodius [fr. *Sitzgsber. Wien. Akad.*] 3/- r 8° *Vienna* 78

Stender, Julius De Argonautarum ad Colchos usque exped. fabulae hist. crit. 2/- 8° *Kiel* 74

Babrius

—*for* Aesop, *v. supra* ; *for* Avianus' [Flavius'] *version*, *v.* K § 214.

TEXTS : Fabulae rec. A. Eberhard, 4/- p 8° ; *rec. M. Gitlbauer 4/- 8° Weidmann 75 ; *Vienna* 82

,, F. G. Schneidewin 9*d.* p 8° Teubner, *Leipzig* [53] 65

ANNOTATED TEXTS : *with English notes ; disserts., comm. and lex. Prf. W. G. Rutherford 12/6 8° Macmillan 83

,, German notes and tr. J. A. Hartung 3/- r 12° *Leipzig* 58

AIDS :

Dübner, Fr. Animadversiones Criticae de Babrii Μυθιάμβοις 1/6 r 8° *Paris* 44

Eberhard, A. Observationes Babrianae, 1/6 ; Verbesserungsvorschläge zu Babrius 2/- 8° *Berlin* 65

Piccolos, N. Quelques Observations sur Babrius [textual criticism] 1/6 8° *Paris* 45

*Rutherford, Prf. W. G. —*in his edition of* Babrius, *ut supra* : *of the greatest value*.

Bion

—*v. also* Bucolici, *supra*.

TEXT : Carmina rec. G. Hermann [contains also Moschus] 1/6 p 8° Weidmann, *Berlin* 49

TRANSLATIONS : —*v.* Theocritus, *infra*.

Hesiod.

TEXTS: Opera — rec. A. Köchly + G. Kinkel 5/- 8° Teubner, *Leipzig* 70
,, A. Rzach, 3/-; rec. A. Fick ["in urspr. Form wiederhergestellt"] 4/- 8° *Lpz.* 84; *Göttingen* 87
,, J. Flach, 6d.; rec. G. F. Schömann 1/6 p 8° Teubner, 78; Weidmann, 69

ANNOTATED TEXTS: with English notes F. A. Paley [Bibliotheca Classica] 10/6, *red. to* 5/- 8° Bell 61
,, Latin ,, C. Goettling, ed. H. Flach 8/- 8° *Leipzig* [31] 78
,, Latin tr. F. S. Lehrs + F. Dübner 12/6 r 8° Didot, *Paris* 78
,, ,, notes J. Flach 2/- p 8° Weidmann, *Berlin* 74

Opera et Dies: ,, Latin notes D. J. van Lennep 4/6 8° *Amsterdam* 47
,, English notes W. T. Lendrum [Classical Series] c 8° Macmillan *in prep.*

Theogonia: with German notes, intro. and essay F. G. Welcker 4/- 8° *Elberfeld* 65
Published as an Appendix to his *Griechische Götterlehre*, 3 vols. 30/- 8° *Göttingen* 57-62.
,, ,, ,, and explan. comm. G. F. Schömann 6/- 8° Weidmann, *Berlin* 68
,, Latin notes D. J. van Lennep 10/6 8° *Amsterdam* 43
,, ,, prolegomena H. Flach 4/- 8° Weidmann, *Berlin* 73

Eumeli, Cinaethonis, Asii et Carminis Naupactii Fragmenta: coll. et ed. W. Marckscheffel 7/6; *red. to* 2/- 8° *Leipzig* 40

TRANSLATION: tr. J. Banks [w. Callimachus and Theognis] 5/- c 8° Bohn's Lib. 56
The Hesiod and Theognis portions contain merely some proverbial and political "philosophy," respectively.

Hymnes Orphiques: trad. Leconte de Lisle [Theoc., Bion, Mosch., Tyrtaeus, Odes Anacréon.] 6/6 8° *Paris* 69
Works and Days: tr. Geo. Chapman, ed. Rev. R. Hooper [with Musaeus, etc.] 6/- c 8° J. R. Smith [1618] 58

AIDS:
Davies, Rev. J. — Hesiod and Theognis [pop. biogr. & acc. of wks.; Anc. Classics f. Eng. Readers] 2/6 f 8° Blackwood 73
Flach, H. — Das System der Hesiodischen Kosmogonie 3/- 8° Teubner, *Leipzig* 74
,, — Hesiodische Theogonie, 4/-; Hesiodische Gedichte 2/- 8° ,, ,, 73; 74
,, — Das dialektische Digamma des Hesiod 2/- 8° *Berlin* 76
,, ,, (ed.) — Glossen und Scholien zur Hesiodischen Theogonie [w. prolegg.] 8/- 8° Teubner, *Leipzig* 76
,, ,, — Die beiden ältesten Handschriften des Hesiod; 1 pl. 2/- 8° ,, ,, 77
Gruppe, Otto — Ueber die Theogonie des Hesiod 4/6 8° *Berlin* 41
Leitschuh, Fr. — Die Entstehung d. Mythologie nach Hesiod 2/- r 8° *Wurzburg* 67
Meyer, A. — De compositione Theogoniae Hesiodeae 2/- 8° *Berlin* 87
Petersen, Chr. — Ursprung und Alter der Hesiodischen Theogonie [sch.-progr.] 1/6 4° *Hamburg* 62
Rzach, A. — Der Dialekt des Hesiodos 3/- 8° Teubner, *Leipzig* 76
Schneider, Paul — De Elocutione Hesiodea Commentario, pt. I. [diss. inaug.] 1/6 8° *Berlin* 71
Schömann, G. F. — Die Hesiodische Theogonie ausgelegt und beurtheilt 6/- 8° ,, 68
Steitz, A. — Die *Werke und Tage* geprüft und erklärt 4/- 8° *Leipzig* 69
Welcker, F. G. — Die Hesiodische Theogonie 4/- 8° ,, 65

Illustrations.
Flaxman, J. — Compositions from the Works and Days, etc., of Hesiod 3/6 obl 4° Seeley [5-] 79

Homer.

Batrachomyomachia: rec. A. Baumeister: Ed. Crit. 1/6; rec. J. Draheim 1/- p 8° *Göttingen* 52; *Berlin* 74
Hymni: rec. A. Baumeister 9d.; rec. A. Gemoll 7/- p 8° Teubner, *Leipzig* [58] 74; 86
rec. Eug. Abel [w. Hymni and Batrachyom.] 2/- 8° *Prague* 86
Hymnus Cereris — rec. F. Bücheler [w. photolith. facs. of the Leyden MS.] 2/6 4° Teubner, *Leipzig* 69
,, in Venerem — ,, C. Goettling 2/- 4° *Jena* 65

Ilias. TEXTS: rec. J. La Roche; Ed. Crit., 2 vols. ea. 11/- 8° Teubner, *Leipzig* 73; 76
,, A. Nauck, 2/6; ex rec. W. Dindorf, cur. C. Hentze 2/6 p 8° Weidmann 74; Teubner [55] 85
,, W. Bäumlein 5/6 8°; 1/6 c 8°; 1/6 24° Tauchnitz, *Leipzig* 54
,, ed. J. van Leeuwen + J. F. + M. B. Mendes da Costa, 2 pts. [w. critical apparatus] 8° *Leyden* 89
Represents the advanced school of textual reformers in Homeric matters.
ex. rec. W. Dindorf, et Cycli Epici Reliquiae [with Latin tr.] 10/6 r 8° Didot, *Paris* 81
rec. W. Christ: Ed. Crit., 2 vols. ea. 8/- 8° Teubner, *Leipzig* 84; 84
,, A Fick, 2 vols. ["in d. urspr. Sprachform wiederhergestellt"] 20/- 8° *Göttingen* 86
bks. i.-xii.: ,, Dr. F. A. Paley [Cambridge Texts] 2/6 16° Bell 67
16 bks.: ,, A. Köchly 3/6 p 8° Teubner, *Leipzig*

ANNOTATED TEXTS:
Ilias bks. i.-xxiv.: *w. Eng. notes & intro. Walter Leaf: v. i. [bks. i.-xii.], ii. [xiii.-xxiv.] [Class. Lib.] ea. 14/- 8° Macmillan 86; 89
*,, ,, ,, intro. & brief gram. D. B. Monro: v. i. [i.-xii.]; ii. [xiii.-xxiv.] [bk. i. separ. 2/-] ea. 6/- f 8° Clar. Press [88] 89; 88
MONRO'S commentary is probably the best for school use, LEAF'S for scholar's use.
,, ,, ,, F. A. Paley, v. i. [i.-xii.] 12/-; *red. to* 8/-; ii. [xiii.-xxiv.] [Bibl. Class.] 14/-; *red. to* 6/- 8° Bell [73] 89
,, ,, ,, Dr. F. A. Paley [Grammar School Classics] 6/6 f 8° ,, 73
,, Germ. ,, J. La Roche, 6 pts. ea. 1/6 *or* 2/- p 8° Teubner [70-71] 78-86
*,, ,, ,, C. F. Ameis + C. Hentze, 8 pts. [separ. ea. 1/3 *or* 1/6] 9/6 f 8° ,, [68-78] 84-86
,, ,, ,, Appendix, 8 pts. [sep. ea. 1/- *or* 1/6] 11/- p 8° ,, [72-78] 82-86
,, ,, ,, J. U. Faesi, hrsg. F. R. Franke, 4 vols. ea. 2/- [ii. 1/6] p 8° Weidmann [51-52] 86-87
bks. i.-xii. — w. Eng. notes S. H. Reynolds [Catena Classicorum] 6/- f 8° Rivington 70
[,, i., ix., xi., xvi.-xxiv.] ,, ,, ,, J. H. Pratt + W. Leaf ["Story of Achilles"; Class. Ser.] 6/- f 8° Macmillan 80
,, i.-ii., xxi., xxii.: ,, ,, ,, A. Sidgwick, i.-ii. 2/6; xxi., xxii. ea. 1/6 f 8° Rivington [77-80] 85-87
,, i.-vi.: ,, ,, ,, J. R. Boise [Am.]; map $1.50 12° *Chicago* [69] 78
,, i.-iii.: ,, ,, ,, T. K. Arnold 3/6 c 8° Rivington 76
,, i.-iii.: ,, ,, ,, T. D. S. Hillhouse [Am.] [based in Ameis' edn.] $1.60 12° *Boston* 87

K § 190

bks. i. : w. Eng. notes J. Bond + A. S. Walpole [Elementary Classics] 1/6 18° Macmillan 84
" " " Dr. F. A. Paley 1/- f 8° Bell 81
" " " D. B. Monro [w. essay on grammar] 2/- p 8° Clar. Press 78
" iv., vi.–viii., xxi. : " " " H. Hailstone ea. 1/6 f 8° " 80 ; 81 ; 82
" vi. : " " " J. S. Philpotts 2/- f 8° Rivington 76
" xiii.–xxiv. : " " " D. B. Monro 6/- c 8° Clar. Press 89
" xviii. : " " " S. R. James [Elementary Classics] 1/6 f 8° Macmillan

Odysseia. TEXTS : rec. A. Nauck, 2 pts. ea. 2/- p 8° Weidmann, *Berlin* 74
" W. Bäumlein 4/- 8° ; 1/6 c 8° ; 1/6 24° Tauchnitz, *Leipzig* 54
" J. La Roche : Ed. Crit., 2 vols. : 11 pl. 13/- 8° *Leipzig* 67 ; 68
" W. Dindorf 2/6 ; re-ed. C. Hentze, 2 pts. ea. 9*d.* p 8° Teubner, *Leipzig* [56] 83
" P. Cauer, 2 pts. ea. 1/- 16° *Leipzig* 86 ; 87
" A. Ludwich, vol. i. 8/- 8° Teubner, *Leipzig* 89
" A. Fick ["in d. urspr. Sprachform wiederhergestellt"] 12/- 8° *Göttingen* 83
" H. Hayman, 3 vols. ; ill. 50/- 8° Nutt 66 ; 71 ; 82

ANNOTATED TEXTS : *with English notes W. W. Merry, i.–xii. 5/- ; xiii.–xxiv. 5/- c 8° Clar. Press [71] 88 ; 78
" German " C. F. Ameis + C. Hentze, 4 pts. ea. 1/6 ; Append. 4 pts. 1/- *or* 1/6 p 8° Teubner [56–68] 77–84
" " " J. U. Faesi + W. C. Kayser, i. 2/- ; ii.–iv. ea. 1/6 p 8° Weidmann [49–50] 78–87
Odyss. bks. i.–xii. : " English " Rev. W. W. Merry + J. Riddell 16/- 8° Clar. Press 76
" i. & ii. : " " " Rev. W. W. Merry ea. 1/6 f 8° " 87 ; 87
" i. : " " " J. Bond + A. S. Walpole [Elem. Classics] 1/6 f 8° Macmillan 83
" ix. : " " " Prf. J. E. B. Mayor [Classical Series] 2/6 f 8° " [73] 84
" ix. & x. " " " G. M. Edwards ea. 7/6 c 8° Camb. Press 89
" xxi.–xxiv. : Triumph of Odysseus, with English notes, S. G. Hamilton [Class. Ser.] 3/6 f 8° Macmillan 83

TRANSLATIONS :
Iliad and Odyssey : tr. W. C. Bryant [Am.] : Iliad, $2.50 ; Odyssey [both blank verse] $2.50 8° *Boston* [70] 7- ; [71] 7-
" Geo. Chapman, w. intro. & notes Rev. R. Hooper : ea. in 2 v. [verse] ea. *wk.* 12/- sq 8° J. R. Smith [1614] 65 ; [1615] 74
" " " ed. R. H Shepherd : in 1 v. [also Iliad in Univ. Lib. 1/- Rtl. 84] 6/- c 8° Chatto 75
" Alex. Pope, ed. Rev. H. J. Carey—in 1 vol. [verse] 2/6 c 8° Routledge [1720 ; 1725] 89
" A. S. Way : Iliad, 2 vols. ea. 9/- ; Odyssey, 7/6 [verse] s 4° Low 86–89 ; 86
In a new metre—a rhyming anapaestic hexameter : "the English equivalent of the Homeric line." The *Od.* was orig. issued *sub nom.* "Avia."
tr. P. S. Worsley + Prf. J. Conington : Iliad 21/- ; Odyss. [by Worsley alone] 12/- c 8° Blackwood 68 ; 77
übers. J. H. Voss, 2 v., 4/6 16° ; w. 25 ill. B. Genelli 9/- r 8° [also ea. 9*d.* Nat. Bibl.] *Stuttgart* [1793] 70 ; 76
Iliad : " Prf. J. S. Blackie—*in his* Homer and the Iliad, 4 vols. [verse] 42/- 8° Douglas, *Edin.* 66
" homometrically C. B. Cayley [verse] 12/6 8° Longman 76
" J. G. Cordery (blank-verse) 7/6 c 8° Paul [70] 90
" Lord Derby [blank verse] 10/- p 8° Murray [65] 76
" Andrew Lang + Walter Leaf + Ernest Myers [prose] 12/6 8° Macmillan 83
Similes of the Iliad : " W. C. Green ; with notes 12/- 4° Longman 77
Odyssey : *" Prf. S. H. Butcher + Andrew Lang [prose] 6/- c 8° Macmillan [79] 89
" Earl of Carnavon, bks. i.–xii. [blank verse] 7/6 c 8° " 87
" Sir Chas. du Caue [verse] 10/6 8° Blackwood 80
" Wm. Morris [in anapaestic hexameters] 6/6 8° Reeves & Turner [87] 88
An excellent tr., but marred—at least as a popular tr.—by use of many Chaucerian and archaic words and meanings of words.
" Gen. Schomberg, 2 vols. [verse] ea. 12/- 8° Murray 79–81
Hymns and Batrachomyomachia : tr. Geo. Chapman, ed. Rev. R. Hooper 6/- sq 8° J. R. Smith [161-] 57

Illustrated Translations.
Iliad and Odyssey w. Outline ill. by J. Flaxman [Pope's tr.] 6/- c 8° Warne [34] 90
Iliad Flaxman's Designs 2/6 8° Bell 80
Iliad w. 24 pl. by Henri Motte [photogravs. ; Chapman's tr. w. intro. H. Morley] 31/6 4° Low 87
w. 12 phototypes by F. Preller and Flaxman : Voss' German tr. 40/- f° *Munich* 82

AIDS :
Criticism, Commentaries, etc.
Bekker, Imm. Homerische Blätter, 2 vols. vol. i. 5/6 ; ii. 5/- 8° *Bonn* 63 ; 72
*Buchholz, E. Die Homerischen Realien, pts. i.–iii. ea. 6/- ; iv. 5/- ; v. 6/- 8° *Leipzig* 71–84
i. : Welt u. Natur ; ii. : Die Drei Naturreiche [Zoology, Botany, Mineralogy] ; iii. : Oeffentliches Leben ; iv. Privates Leben ; v. : Religion.
Collins, Rev. W. L. Homer, 2 pts. [pop. biogr. and acc. of works : Anc. Class. f. Eng. Rdrs.] ea. 2/6 12° Blackwood 69 ; 70
Düntzer, H. Homerische Abhandlungen, 9/- ; Die homerischen Fragen 4/- r 8° *Leipzig* 72 ; 74
Eustathius, Abp. of Thessal. Commentarii ad Il., 4 vols., 61/6 ; ad. Odyss., 2 vols. 30/- 4° " [ ] 27–30 ; 25–26
Freund, W. Präparationen zum Ilias, 14 pts. ; zum Odyssee, 13 pts. ea. pt. 6*d.* 16° *Leipzig* *n.d.*
Gladstone, W. E. Studies on Homer and the Homeric Age, 3 vols. ; maps *o.p.* [*pb.* 33/- ; w. £4] 8° Clar. Press 58
" " Juventus Mundi : the gods and men of the Heroic Age 10/6 8° Macmillan 69
" " Primer of Homer [Macmillan's Primers Series] 1/- 18° " 78
" " Homeric Synchronism 6/6 c 8° " 76
An inquiry into the time and place of Homer. *Cf.* also review of Gladstone on Homer in E. A. FREEMAN'S *Essays*, v. ii. 10/6 8° Macmillan 80.
*Jebb, Prf. R. C. Homer : a short introduction to the Iliad and Odyssey 3/6 c 8° MacLehose, *Glas.* [87] 89
Koblou, F. Questions Homériques [mythol., topograph., instits., etc.] 5/- 8° *Paris* 70
Widal A. Études Littéraires et Morales sur Homère [scenes fr. Iliad] 3/- 12° " [60] 63
Wilamowitz-Möllendorf, W. Homerische Untersuchungen 7/- 8° *Berlin* 84
Wolf, F. A. Prolegomena ad Homerum ; w. Imm. Bekker's notes [Calvary's *Bibliothek*] 2/- 16° " [ ] 86
Cf. also the essays by M. Arnold, H. COLERIDGE, G. GROTE [in his *Hist. of Greece*], and of J. A. SYMONDS [in his *Studies*].
Iliad.
Kammer, E. E. Aesthetischer Kommentar zu Homer's Ilias 4/- 8° *Paderborn* 89
Nägelsbach, C. F. Anmerkungen zum Ilias [philosophical] 7/6 8° *Nuremberg* [34] 64
Peppmüller, R. Commentar des 24ten Buches d. Ilias [w. general introduction] 10/- 8° *Berlin* 76
Odyssey.
Nitzsch, G. G. Erklärende Anmerkungen zur Odyssee, 3 vols. [bks. i.–xii.] 24/- 8° *Hanover* 26–40

Language.
Ahrens, H. L. — Griechische Formenlehre d. Homer. und Attischen Dialekten, pt. i. [Homer] 2/6 8° *Göttingen* [52] 69
Brugman, K. — Ein Problem d. homer. Textkritik und der vergleichenden Sprachwissenschaft 4/- 8° *Leipzig* 76
Buttmann, Ph. — Lexilogus: Beiträge z. griech. Worterklärung, 2 vols. [Homer and Hesiod] ea 3/6 8° *Berlin* [18] 65; [18] 60
" — The same, tr. J. R. Fishlake o.p. [pb. 12/-; w. 6/-] 8° Murray [3rd ed. 46] 61
Cobet, G. C. — Miscellanea Critica [emendations to Homer and Demosthenes] 14/- 8° *Leyden* 76
Delbrück, B. — Gebrauch d. Conjunct. u. Optativs—*in his* Syntakt. Forschh. 4/6 8° *Halle* 71
Ellendt, J. E. — Drei homerische Abhandlungen [w. notes on life of Homer] 3/- 8° *Leipzig* 61; 63; posth.] 64
Fulda, A. — Unters. üb. d. Sprache d. hom. Gedichte [ΘΥΜΟΣ, ΦΡΗΝ, *etc.*] 4/6 8° *Duisburg* 65
Goebel, A. — Lexilogus zu Homer u. den Homeriden, 2 v., i. 16/-; ii. 17/- 33/- 8° *Leipzig* 78; 80
Lange, Ludwig — Der homerische Gebrauch d. Partikel εἰ, 2 pts. 6/- 4° " 72; 73
La Roche, J. — Homerische Studien [accus. in Homer] 3/6; Homer. Untersuchungen 6/- r 8° *Vienna* 61; *Leipzig* 69
Lehrs, K. — De Aristarchi studiis Homericis 7/6 8° *Leipzig* [33] 65
Loebell, R. — Quaestiones de Perfecti Homer. forma et usu [diss. inaug.] 1/6 8° " 76
Ribbeck, Otto — Homerische Formenlehre 1/6 8° *Berlin* 73

Concordances.
Dunbar, Dr. H. — Concordance to the Odyssey and Hymns 21/- 4° Clar. Press 80
Prendergast, G. L. — Concordance to the Iliad, 2 pts. o.p. 4° Longman 69; 74

Dictionaries.
Autenrieth, G. — Homeric Dictionary, tr. R. P. Keep; 5 vols. [school-book] 6/- c 8° Macmillan [76] 81
Crusius, G. C. — Compl. Gk. and Eng. Lexicon for Homer and Homeridae, [tr.] ed. T. K. Arnold 9/- c 8° Rivington [65] 71
*Ebeling, H. [ed.] — Lexicon Homericum, By C. Capelle, A. & E. Eberhard, *etc.*; 3 vols. in 2 pts. 60/- i 8° Teubner, *Lps.* 71–85
" — Schulwörterbuch zu Homer's Odyssee und Ilias 2/- 8° *Leipzig* [67] 82
Seiler, E. E. — Griechisch-Deutsches Wörterbuch z. Homeros u. d. Homeriden 5/- r 8° " [56] 69

Grammars.
*Monro, D. B. — Grammar of the Homeric Dialect 10/6 8° Clar. Press 82
Vogrinz, G. — Grammatik des Homerischen Dialektes 7/- 8° *Paderborn* 89

Scholia.
Bachmann, L. [ed.] — Scholia in Homeri Iliadem qu. in Bibl. Paul. Lips. leguntur, 3 vols. 12/6 8° *Leipzig* 33; 36; 38
Bekker, Imm. [ed.] — Scholia in Homeri Iliadem, 2 vols. o.p. [pb. 9/-] 4° *Berlin* 25
*Dindorf + Maas, W. + E. [eds.] — Scholia Graeca in Iliadem Townleyana, 6 vols. 86/- 8° Clar. Press 75–84
" W. [ed.] — Scholia Graeca in Odysseam ex codd. aucta, 2 vols. 15/6 8° " 55

Origin of the Homeric Poems.
Bonitz, H. — Ueber den Ursprung der homerischen Gedichte 3/- r 8° *Vienna* [60] 81
Geddes, Prf. W. — The Problem of the Homeric Poems 14/- 8° Macmillan 78
Geppert, C. E. — Ueber den Ursprung der homerischen Gesänge, 2 pts. 8/- r 8° *Leipzig* 40
Wilkins, G. — The Growth of the Homeric Poems 6/- 8° Longman 85

Prosody and Metrology.
Hartel, W. — Beiträge zur homerischen Prosodie und Metrik 3/- 8° *Berlin* [72] 73

Stories from Homer.
Church, Rev. A. J. — Stories from Homer [w. 24 pl. after Flaxman's designs] 5/- c 8° Seeley [77] 82

Theology and Mythology.
Harrison, Jane E. — Myths of the Odyssey in Art and Literature; ill. 18/- 8° Smith & Elder 82
Nägelsbach, C. F. — Die Homerische Theologie, ed. G. Autenrieth 8/6 8° *Nuremberg* [40] 84
" — Die Nachhomerische Theologie d. griech. Volksglaubens [tr. Alexander] o.p. [pb. 8/-] 57
v. Sybel, Ludwig — Die Mythologie der Ilias 7/6 8° *Marburg* 77

Topography.
v. Baer, K. E. — Wo ist der Schauplatz d. Odyss. zu finden—*in his* Histor. Fragen 9/- r 8° *St. Petersburg* 73
" — Ueber die homerischen Lokalitäten in d. Odyssey; 3 pl. [posthum.] 6/- 4° *Brunswick* 78
Benjamin, S. G. W. [Am.] — Troy: its legend, history and literature; map $1 16° *New York* 80
An attempt to tell the Trojan story in a popular way, in the light of recent discoveries.
Brentano, L. — Alt-Ilion im Dumbrekthal; map 4/6 8° *Frankfort* 77
" — Zur Lösung d. Troianischer Frage; map, 3/6; Troia u. Neu-Ilion 2/- 8° *Heilbronn* 81; 82
Forchhammer, P. W. — Beschreibung der Ebene von Troja; map 12/- 4° *Frankfort* 50
Helbig, W. — Das homerische Epos aus den Denkmälern erläutert 13/- 8° *Leipzig* [ ] 87
Nicolaides, G. — Topographie et Plan Stratégique de l'Iliade: map 6/6 8° *Paris* 67
*Schliemann, Dr. H. — Troy and its Remains, ed. P. Smith: pl. and ill. 42/- 8° Murray 75
" — Ilios: city and country of Trojans: pl. and ill. [excavations, 1871–73, '78–'79] 50/- i 8° " 80
" — Troja: results of researches, etc.; maps and ill. [1882] 42/- r 8° " 83
Schuchhardt, C. — Schliemann's Ausgrabungen in Troja, Tiryns, Mykene, *etc*; 6 maps and 290 ill. 8/- 8° *Leipzig* 90
Stillman, W. J. [Am.] — On the Track of Ulysses; ill. [archæological cruise am. Gk. islands] $4 8° *Boston* 88
Repr. fr. the *Century* magazine. With an added article on the Venus of Melos.
v. Warsberg, Alex. — Odysseische Landschaften 10/- 8° *Vienna* 78

Translation of Homer.
Arnold, Matthew — On translating Homer; *and* Last Words on same 4 Oxf. lects.] o.p. [pb. 3/6 ea.; w. 35/-] c 8° Longman 61; 62

Moschus

—*v.* Poetae Bucolici, *supra.* TRANSLATION—*v.* Theocritus, *supra.*

Pindar.

TEXT: rec. Tycho Mommsen, 1/6; ed. crit. 2 vols. 16/- 8° Weidmann, *Berlin* 66; 64
" and Fragmenta: " W. Christ, 1/-; rec. F. G. Schneidewin 1/- p 8° Teubner *Leipzig* [69] 73; [50] 65
ANNOTATED TEXTS: * with English notes, intros. and essays Dr. C. A. M. Fennell, 2 vols. 18/- c 8° Camb. Press 79; 83
Olympian and Pythian Odes, 9/-; Isthmian and Nemean Odes, 9/-.
" " " Donaldson 16/- 8° Longman 41
" " " Cookesley, 2 vols. 28/- 8° Williams 51
" " " Prf. B. Gildersleeve [Am.] 7/6 c 8° Macmillan 85
" Latin " L. Dissen, ed. F. G. Schneidewin, 2 pts. 7/- 8° *Gotha* [30] 43; 47
i Text, 4/- 43; ii. (1) Commentarius in Olymp. et Pyth., 1/6 47 ii. (2) Commentarius in Nem. et Isth., 1/6 '47.
" German " J. A. Hartung, 4 vols. 10/6 12° *Leipzig* 55–56
Selection: " English " Prf. T. D. Seymour [Am.] $1.55 12° *Boston* 8-
Olymp.: " German " J. J. Schwickert 3/- 8° *Trier* 78

TRANSLATIONS:
Works: tr. T. C. Baring [verse] 7/- 16° Paul 75
* " E. Myers, with intro. and notes [prose] 5/- c 8° Macmillan [74] 84
" Dr. F. A. Paley: with notes and intro. [prose] 7/6 p 8° Williams 6-

Olymp. & Pyth.: tr. F. D. Morice [verse] 7/6 c 8° Paul 75

AIDS:

Criticism.

Buchholtz, E. Die sittliche Weltanschauung d. Pindaros u. Aeschylos 4/- 8° Teubner, *Leipzig* 69
Croiset, A. Poésie de Pindar et les Lois du Lyrisme Grec 6/6 8° *Paris* 80
Friederichs, K. Pindarische Studien 2/- 8° *Berlin* 63
van Herwerden, H. Pindarica 1/6 8° *Leipzig* 61
de Jongh, A. Pindarica 3/- 8° *Coblenz* 47
Metzger, Friedrich Pindar's Siegeslieder erklärt 8/- 8° Teubner, *Leipzig* 80
Villemain, A. F. Sur le Génie de Pindar 5/- 8° *Paris* 50

Language.

Bossler, C. De Praepositionum usu apud Pindarum [dissert. inaug.] 1/6 8° *Darmstadt* 62
Erdmann, H. T. O. De Pindari usu syntactico capita duo [" "] 1/6 8° *Halle* 67
Friese, Ernest De casuum singulari apud Pindarum usu [" "] 1/6 8° *Berlin* 66
Godofredus, M. De elocutione Pindari 2/6 8° *Susati* n.d. (65)
Grosse, Ed. De particulis copulativis τέ u. καί apud Pindarum 14/6 8° *Aschersleben* 58
Peter, W. A. De Dialecto Pindari [dissert. inaug.] 1/6 8° *Halle* 66

Concordance.

Bindseil, H. E. (ed.) Concordantiae omnium vocum carminum integr. et fragm. Pind. 18/-; *red. to* 10/- 4° *Berlin* 75

Lexica.

Duncan, J. M. Lexicon Graecum ex C. D. Dammii Lex Homer.-Pind. [1755, cur. V.C.F. Rost] 21/- 4° *Leipzig* [1763-74] 31-33
Rumpel, J. Lexicon Pindaricum 12/- 8° " 83

Scholia.

Abel, E. (ed.) Scholia Vetera in Pindari Nemea et Isthmia, vol. ii. (pts. 1-3) ea. 5/- [vol. i. to appear later] 8° *Berlin* 84
Lehrs, K. Die Pindarscholien [a critical account] 7/- 8° *Leipzig* 73
Mommsen, Tycho Parerga Pindarica [w. some fragm. to Nem. ix., x., xi.; schl.-progr.] 2/- 4° *Frankfort* 77
" (ed.) Scholia Germani in Pindari Olympia e cod. Caesar. Vindobonensi 2/6 8° *Kiel* 61
Semitelos, D. K. Πινδάρου σχόλια Πατμιακά 4/6 8° *Athens* 74

Life.

Bippart, Geo. Pindar's Leben, Weltanschauung und Kunst 3/- 8° *Jena* 48
Lübbert, E. Pindar's Leben und Dichtungen 1/6 4° *Bonn* 82
Mommsen, Tycho Pindaros: zur Geschichte d. Dichters u. d. Parteikämpfe s. Zeit 2/- 8° *Kiel* 45
Morice, F. D. Pindar [pop. biog. and acc. of works; Anc. Class. f. Eng. Rrs.] 2/6 12° Blackwood 78
Schmidt, Leopold Pindar's Leben und Dichtung 8/6 4° *Bonn* 82

Prosody.

Boeckh, Aug. Ueber die Versmaasse d. Pindaros [also repr. in his edn. of Pind., ii.] 3/- 8° *Leipzig* 09
Schmidt, J. H. H. —*in his* Die Eurhythmie in d. Chorgesängen d. Griechen 6/- 8° " 68
" Moriz Ueber den Bau der Pindarischen Strophen 4/- 8° " 82

Sappho.

Carmina et Fragmenta: rec. C. F. Neue 3/- 4° *Berlin* 27
Memoirs, Text and Translation. By H. T. Wharton, port. 7/6 f 8° Stott [85] 87

TRANSLATION: —*v. also* Wharton, *supra.*
FIELD, Michael Long Ago [short lyrics expanded fr. Sappho] 10/6 c 8° Bell 89
HIGGINSON, T. W. [Am.]—*his* Afternoon Landscape: poems and trs., *conts. trss. fr. Sappho* 5/- 8° Longman 89

AIDS:

Arnold, Bernhard Sappho [a lecture; Samml. gemeinverständl. Vortr.] 1/- 8° *Berlin* 71
Koch, Th. Alkäos und Sappho 2/- 8° " 62
Luniak, J. Quaestiones Sapphicae 8° *Kazan (Russia)* 90
Michaelis, A. Thamyris und Sappho auf einem Vasenbild; 1 pl. 2/6 4° *Leipzig* 65
Nagulewski, D. In Quaestiones Sapphicas observationes 2/- 8° " 90
Wharton, H. T. —*in his edn. of the text, etc., supra.*

Theocritus

—*v. also* Bucolici Graeci, *supra.*

TEXT: ex rec. A. T. A. Fritzsche, 9*d.*; rec. C. Ziegler 4/- 8° *Leip.* [69] 70; *Tübing.* [44] 69; 67

ANNOTATED TEXTS: with English notes Dr. H. Kynaston [new edn. of Snow (1869)] 4/6 f 8° Clar. Press 73
" Latin notes A. T. H. Fritzsche 9/- 8° Teubner, *Leipzig* [65-69] 70
" " " Dr. F. A. Paley 4/6 f 8° Bell [63] 69
" " " Bp. Chr. Wordsworth 7/- 8° " [44] 77
" German notes A. T. H. Fritzsche, ed. E. Hiller 3/6 p 8° Teubner, *Leipzig* [57] 69

TRANSLATIONS: by C. S. Calverley [verse] 7/6 c 8° Bell [69] 83
" Andrew Lang, w. intro. essay [w. Bion & Moschus; prose; Gold. Treas. Ser.] 4/6 18° Macm. [80] 89

AIDS:

Brinker, K. De Theocriti vita carminibusque subditiciis 2/- 8° *Leipzig* 84
Dübner, F. Scholia in Theocritum 12/6 r 8° Didot, *Paris* [42] 78
Rumpel, J. Lexicon Theocriteum 6/- 8° *Leipzig* 79

Theognis

—*v. also* Poetae Lyrici, *supra.*

TEXT: Elegiae: rec. Ch. Ziegler 2/- 8° *Tübingen* 80
" Reliquiae: " J. Sitzler 5/- 8° *Heidelberg* 80

TRANSLATION: tr. J. H. Frere—*in his* Collected Works, vol. ii. Chatto [39] *in prep.*

AIDS:

Davies, Rev. J. Hesiod and Theognis [pop. accounts; Anc. Class. f. Eng. Rrs.] 2/6 f 8° Blackwood [73] 80
van Herwerden, H. Animadversiones philolog. in Theognidem 2/- 8° *Cologne* 70
Jordan, H. Quaestiones Theognideae 1/6 4° *Königsberg* 85

191. GREEK DRAMATISTS.

Collections.

Comicorum Graec. Fragmenta, ed. Aug. Meineke, 5 v. in 9 [70/-; *red. to* 36/-]; Ed. Minor, 2 v. [15/-; *red. to* 9/-] 8° *Berlin* 39-57; 47
" " " ed. Aug. Meineke, re-ed. F. H. Bothe [w. Latin tr.] 12/6 r 8° Didot, *Paris* 55
" " " rec Th. Kock, vols. i.-ii. ea. 18/-; iii. 16/- r 8° *Leipzig* 80; 84; 89

Poetae Scenici — rec. W. Dindorf — 21/- i 8° Parker [46] 69

Aeschylus, Sophocles, Euripides, Aristophanes, Fabulae, Fragmenta.

Tragicorum Graec. Fragmenta, rec. A. Nauck — 17/- 8° Teubner, *Leipzig* 56

Selections: Fragments of Greek Comic Poets, ed. F. A. Paley [w. verse trss. *en regard*] 4/6 p 8° Sonnenschein 88

Selections from 15 poets. The last bk. edited by Dr. PALEY before his death in 1889.

" Selections from the Greek Tragedians, ed. Rev. E. D. Stone — 3/6 c 8° Rivington 90

Aeschylus.

TEXTS: *rec. N. Wecklein, 2 vols.: Ed. Crit. [i.: text, scholia, app. crit.; ii.: conject. emends.]. — 20/- c 8° *Berlin* 84
" R. Merkel — 21/- f° Clar. Press 71
" W. Dindorf, 1/6; rec. A. Kirchhoff — 3/6 p 8° Teubner [50] 82; Weidmann [ ] 80
" H. Weil — 1/6 8° Teubner, *Leipzig* 84
" F. A. Paley [Cambridge Texts] 3/- 16° Bell 60
" E. A. J. Ahrens, with Latin tr. — 17/- r 8° *Paris* 77

ANNOTATED TEXTS: with English notes F. A. Paley [Bibliotheca Classica] 18/-; *red. to* 8/- 8° Bell [47] 79
" Latin " H. Weil, 2 vols. [ea. play separately 2/- or 2/6] 14/6 8° *Giessen* 58–67
" German " and tr. J. A. Hartung, 8 vols. 13/6 [ea. play sep. 1/6 to 2/6] s 8° *Leipzig* 52–55

Agamemnon: *with English notes, intro. comm. & tr. A. W. Verrall [Class. Lib.] 12/- 8° Macmillan 89
" " " and tr. [verse] J. F. Davies — 3/- c 8° *Utrecht* 68
" " " and tr. [verse] B. H. Kennedy — 6/- c 8° Camb. Press [78] 82
" " " A. Sidgwick — 3/- f 8° Clar. Press [81] 88
" " " F. A. Paley [Camb. Texts w. Notes] 1/6 18° Bell 80
" Latin " D. S. Margoliouth [textual notes] 2/6 8° Macmillan 82
" German " R. Enger, hrsg. E. Gilbert — 3/- p 8° Teubner, *Leipzig* [55] 74
" " " F. W. Schneidewin + Hense — 2/6 p 8° Weidmann, *Berlin* [56] 83
" " " and tr. K. H. Keck, 9/-; C. F. v. Nägelsbach — 3/- p 8° *Leipzig* 63; *Erlangen* 63

Choephoroe: ed. crit. F. A. Paley — 7/6 c 8° Camb. Press 82
with English notes Prf. J. Conington — 6/- 8° Longman 57
*" " " A. Sidgwick — 3/- f 8° Clar. Press 84

Eumenides: with English notes & tr. [verse] D. Drake [Classical Lib.] 5/- 8° Macmillan 85
" " " " ["] J. F. Davies — 7/- 8° Longman 85
" " " Arthur Sidgwick — 3/- f 8° Clar. Press 88
" " " F. A. Paley [Camb. Texts w. Notes] 1/6 18° Bell 80
" German " and tr. G. F. Schömann — 2/6 45

Oresteia (= Agam., Choeph., Eum.) with English notes and tr. A. O. Prickard [Classical Library] c 8° Macmillan *in prep.*
" Latin " F. A. Paley — 7/6 8° Deighton, *Cambridge* 45
" German " N. Wecklein — 6/- 8° *Leipzig* 88

Persae: with English notes A. O. Prickard [Classical Series] 3/6 f 8° Macmillan 87
" " " F. A. Paley [Camb. Texts w. Notes] 1/6 18° Bell 80
" German " W. S. Teuffel, 1/6; L. Schiller — 1/6 p 8° Teubner [66] 86; Weidmann 69

Prometheus Vinctus: with English notes A. O. Prickard — 2/- f 8° Clar. Press [78] 82
" " " F. A. Paley [Camb. Texts w. Notes] 1/6 18° Bell 75
" " " North Pinder — 2/- 12° Longman 74
" " " M. G. Glazebrook — 2/6 c 8° Rivington 87
" German " L. Schmidt, 1/6; N. Wecklein — 2/- p 8° Teubner 70; [72] 78
" " " and tr. G. F. Schömann — 6/- 8° *Greifswald* 43

Septem contra Thebas: with English notes F. A. Paley [Camb. Texts w. Notes] 1/6 18° Bell 78
" " " J. F. Davies — 1/- 12° Lockwood [64] 78
*" " " intro. and comm. A. W. Verrall, with tr. [Class. Lib.] 7/6; School Edn. [+ M. A. Bayfield] 3/6 8° Macmillan 87; 88
" " " Prf. Isaac Flagg [Am.] $1.10 12° *Boston* 8-
" Latin life of Aeschylus, ed. Friedr. Ritschl — 3/- 8° Teubner, *Leipzig* 75

Supplices: with English notes, intro. comm. & tr. Prf. T. G. Tucker [Classical Lib.] 10/6 8° Macmillan 89
" Latin " F. I. Schwerdt, 2 pts. — 3/- 8° *Berlin* 58
" German " J. Oberdick — 4/- 8° " 69

TRANSLATIONS:

Works: tr. F. A. Paley, with short notes [prose] 7/6 8° Bell [64] 71
*" Dean E. H. Plumptre [verse] 7/6 c 8° Isbister [69] 73
*" E. D. A. Morshead [verse] 7/6 c 8° Paul [77] 81

Agamemnon, Libation-Bearers [Choephorae], Furies [Eumenides]. *Vide also* Supplices, *infra*.

tr. Robert Potter [verse; Morley's Univ. Lib.] 1/- c 8° Routledge [29] 86

Prometheus Bound, The Suppliants, Seven against Thebes.

tr. Anna Swanwick [verse] 5/- c 8° Bohn's Lib. [73] 81
übers. J. G. Droysen, 6/-; übers. J. J. C. Donner — 3/6 8° *Berlin* [32] 84; [54] 87

Agamemnon: tr. Rob. Browning [verse] 5/- f 8° Smith & Elder [77] 89
" Earl of Carnarvon [blank verse] 6/- c 8° Murray 79
" B. H. Kennedy [verse] 6/- c 8° Camb. Press [78] 82
" Dn. H. H. Milman [verse; w. Bacchae of Euripides] 9/- p 8° 65
*" A. W. Verrall—*with his edn. of text, ut supra* 12/- 8° Macmillan 89

Eumenides: " B. Drake—*with his edn. of text, ut supra* [verse] 5/- 8° " 85

Oresteia (= Agam., Choeph., Eum.) tr. C. N. Dalton [verse] 5/- f 8° J. R. Smith 68

K § 191

Persae: tr. W. Gurney [verse] 3/- 12° Bell 73
Prometheus: ,, Elizabeth Barrett Browning—*in her* Works, vol. ii. [verse] 5/- c 8° Smith & Elder [33] 89
,, Augusta Webster [verse] 3/6 c 8° Macmillan 66
Septem contra Thebas: ,, W. Gurney [verse] 3/- 12° Bell 79
* ,, A. W. Verrall—*with his edn. of text, ut supra* 7/6 8° Macmillan 87
[Supplices]: * The Suppliant Maidens, tr. E. D. A. Morshead [verse] 3/6 c 8° Paul 83
tr. Prf. T. G. Tucker—*with his edn. of text, ut supra* 10/6 8° Macmillan 89

Aids.
Criticism, Commentaries, etc.
Boyes, J. F. Illustrations to Aeschylus from Ancient and Modern Poets 9/- 8° Whittaker 44
Buchholz, E. Die sittliche Weltanschauung d. Pindaros u. Aeschylos 4/- 8° Teubner, *Leipzig* 69
Dronke, Gustav Die religiösen u. sittlichen Vorstellungen d. Aeschyl. u. Sophocles 2/6 8° *Leipzig* 61
Girard, Jules Le Sentiment Religieux en Grèce d'Homère à Eschyle 6/6 8° *Paris* 69
Klotz, Richard Studia Aeschylea 2/- 4° *Leipzig* 84
Ludwig, Alfred Zur Kritik des Aeschylus [a series of essays] 1/6 r 8° *Vienna* 60
Newman, Prf. F. W. Comments on the Text of Aeschylus 5/- 8° Trübner 85
*Patin, H. J. G. Études sur les Tragiques Grecs. : Eschyle 3/- 12° *Paris* [41-43] 71
Schmidt, F. W. Kritische Studien zu Aeschylos und Sophokles 6/- 8° *Berlin* 86
Sommerbrodt, J. De Aeschyli re scenica, 3 parts [school-programmes] 4/6 8° *Leipzig* 48; 51; 58
These are included in his *Scaenica*, 8/- 8° *Berlin* '76.
Wecklein, N. Studien zu Aeschylus 4/- 8° *Berlin* 72
Westphal, R. Prolegomena zu Aeschylus' Tragödien 3/- 8° Teubner, *Leipzig* 69
Choephorae.
Baumgarten, O. Quaestiones Scenicae in Aeschyli Choephoris [diss. inaug.] 1/6 8° *Halle* 78
Hense, Otto Kritische Blätter, pt. i. : Choephoroe 2/- 8° ,, 70
Eumenides.
Wieseler, F. Conjectanea in Aeschyli Eumenides 4/- 8° *Göttingen* 39
Persae.
Conradt, C. Die Abtheilung lyrischer Verse in griech. Drama, pt. i. [Prom. and Pers.] 5/- 8° *Berlin* 79
Hannak, E. Das Historische in den Persern d. Aeschylos [schl.-progr.] 1/6 8° *Vienna* 65
Keiper, Ph. Perser d. Aeschylos als Quelle f. altpers. Alterthumskunde 2/- 8° *Erlangen* 77
Prince, Charles Études Critiques et Exégétiques sur les Perses 4/6 8° *Neuchatel* 68
Prometheus Vinctus, and Orestia.
Foss, B. De loco in quo Prometheus ap. Aeschyl. Vinctus sit; 1 pl. 1/6 8° *Bonn* 62
Martin, Th. H. La Prométhéide : étude de cette trilogie 3/6 s 8° *Paris* 75
Teuffel, W. S. Ueber des Aeschylos Prometheus u. Orestie 1/6 4° *Tübingen* 61
Weiske, B. G. Prometheus und sein Mythenkreis [posthumous] 9/- 8° *Leipzig* 42
Wieseler, F. Adversaria in Aeschyli Prometheum Vinctum 2/- 8° *Göttingen* 43
Supplices.
Maass, E. De Æschyli Supplicibus commentatio 1/6 8° *Leipzig* 90
Textual Criticism.
Bamberger, F. Opuscula Philologica maximam partem Aeschylea 5/- 8° *Leipzig* 56
Heimsoeth, F. Wiederherstellung der Dramen d. Aeschylus : die Quellen 9/- 8° *Bonn* 61
,, ,, Die indirecte Ueberlieferung d. aeschylischen Textes 4/- 8° ,, 62
van Herwerden, H. Emendationes Aeschyleae 1/6 r 8° Teubner, *Leipzig* 78
Lexica.
Dindorf, W. Lexicon Aeschyleum, 2 vols. 16/- r 8° *Leipzig* 73; 76
Linwood, W. Lexicon to Aeschylus o.p. [pb. 12/- ; w. 7/6] 8° Walton [43] 47
Language.
Lalin, De Praepositionum usu apud Aeschylum commentatio academica 2/- 8° *Upsala* 85
Menge, H. De Praepositionum usu apud Aeschylum [diss. inaug.] 1/- 8° *Göttingen* 63
Life.
Copleston, R. S. Aeschylus (pop. biogr. and acc. of wks. ; Anc. Class. for Eng. Readers) 2/6 f 8° Blackwood 71
Schoell, F. De locis nonnullis ad Aesch. vitam epistula 2/- 8° *Jena* 76
Susemihl, Fr. De vita Aeschyli quaestiones epicriticae [diss. inaug.] 1/6 4° *Griefswald* 76
Metrica.
Dindorf, W. Metra Aeschyli, Sophoclis, Eurip. et Aristoph. descripta o.p. [pb. and w. 8/-] 8° *Oxford* 42
Schmidt, J. H. H. —*in his* Die Eurhythmie in d. Chorgesängen d. Griechen 8/- 8° *Leipzig* 68
Illustrations.
Flaxman, J. Compositions from the Tragedies of Aeschylus [36 plates] 3/6 obl 4° Seeley [31] 79

Aristophanes.

Texts: rec. Th. Bergk, 2 vols. 3/6 p 8° Teubner, *Leipzig* [52] 72
,, A. Meineke, 2 vols. 7/6 8° ; 3/- c 8° ; 2/6 24° Tauchnitz, ,, 60; 61
,, W. Dindorf [with Latin tr.] 12/6 r 8° Didot, *Paris* 77
,, A. v. Velsen p 8° *Leipzig* 69–83
Ecclesiazusae, 2/6 ; Equites, 2/6 ; Plutus, 2/ ; Ranae, 2/6 ; Thesmophoriazusae, 2/-.
* ,, F. H. M. Blaydes, 2 vols. 16/- 8° *Halle* 86
Annotated Texts: with Latin notes F. H. Bothe, 4 vols. [also ea. sep. at 1/- to 3/-] 18/- 8° *Leipzig* 45-58
Onomasticon: ,, ,, ,, H. A. Holden [also each play separate] 18/- 8° Bell (48) 63
Comoediae quatuor: ,, ,, ,, F. H. M. Blaydes [Eq., Nub., Vesp., Ran.] 12/- 8° [42] 82
Acharnenses: with English notes F. A. Paley 4/6 f 8° Bell 76
* ,, ,, ,, intro. and gloss. Rev. W. W. Merry 3/- f 8° Clar. Press (80) 88
,, Latin ,, F. H. M. Blaydes 3/6 8° Williams 71
,, German ,, and tr. W. Ribbeck 7/- 8° *Leipzig* 64
,, and Equites: ,, English ,, W. C. Green [Catena Classicorum] 4/- 12° Rivington [67] 80
Aves: with English notes F. H. M. Blaydes 10/- 8° *Halle* [42] 82
,, ,, ,, W. C. Green [Pitt Press Series] 3/6 12° Camb. Press [75] 79
,, ,, ,, intro. Rev. W. W. Merry 3/6 f 8° Clar. Press 90
English notes only Prf. B. H. Kennedy [no text] 1/6 c 8° Macmillan 74
with Latin notes F. H. M. Blaydes 10/- 8° *Leipzig* 82
* ,, German ,, Th. Kock 2/6 p 8° Weidmann, *Berlin* [64] 76
Ecclesiazusae: with Latin notes F. H. M. Blaydes 4/- 8° *Halle* 80
Equites: * ,, English ,, and intro. Rev. W. W. Merry [v. Acharn (Green), sup.] 3/- f 8° Clar. Press 87
* ,, German ,, Th. Kock 1/6 p 8° Weidmann, *Berlin* [53] 67

with English notes and tr. W. Ribbeck 6/6 8° *Berlin* 67
Extracts, ed. A. Sidgwick [elementary] 1/6 s 8° Rivington [72] 87
Text only: A. v. Velsen 3/- 8° Teubner, *Leipzig* 69

Lysistrata: with Latin notes F. H. M. Blaydes 6/- 8° *Halle* 80

Nubes: *with English notes and intro. Rev. W. W. Merry 3/- f 8° Clar. Press [79] 89
,, ,, ,, W. C. Green [Catena Classicorum] 3/6 12° Rivington [68] 80
,, ,, ,, Prf. M. W. Humphreys [Am.] $1.25 12° *Boston* 8-
,, ,, ,, A. Sidgwick [elementary] 1/6 s 8° Rivington [72] 85
,, Latin ,, W. S. Teuffel 1/6 p 8° Teubner, *Leipzig* [56] 63
,, German ,, W. S. Teuffel 3/- p 8° ,, ,, [67] 87
* ,, ,, ,, Th. Kock 2/- p 8° Weidmann, *Berlin* [52] 76

Pax: with English notes F. A. Paley 4/6 12° Bell 73
,, ,, ,, W. C. Green 3/6 c 8° Longman 73
,, ,, ,, and [verse] tr. B. B. Rogers 7/6 c 8° Bell 67
,, Latin ,, F. H. M. Blaydes 6/- 8° *Halle* 83

Plutus: with English notes W. C. Green [Pitt Press Series] 3/6 12° Camb. Press 86
,, ,, ,, A. Sidgwick [elementary] 1/6 s 8° Rivington [78] 87
,, Latin ,, F. H. M. Blaydes 6/- 8° *Halle* 84
,, ,, ,, Rev. H. A. Holden 2/- 8° Deighton, *Camb.* [ ] 85

Ranae: with English notes F. A. Paley 4/6 f 8° Bell 78
* ,, ,, ,, and intro. Rev. W. W. Merry 3/- f 8° Clar. Press [84] 87
,, ,, ,, W. C. Green [Pitt. Press Series] 3/6 12° Camb. Press 79
,, ,, ,, A. Sidgwick [elementary] 1/6 s 8° Rivington [74] 87
,, German ,, Th. Kock 1/6 p 8° Weidmann, *Berlin* [56] 68

Thesmophoriazusae: with Latin notes F. H. M. Blaydes 5/- 8° *Halle* 80

Vespae: *with English notes Rev. W. W. Merry 2/- f 8° Clar. Press 84
,, ,, ,, W. C. Green [Catena Classicorum] 3/6 12° Rivington 68
,, ,, ,, and [verse] tr. B. B. Rogers 7/6 c 8° Bell 76
,, Latin ,, A. v. Velsen 3/- p 8° *Leipzig* 81

TRANSLATIONS:

Comedies: Eight Comedies, tr. L. H. Rudd [rhymed metres] 15/- 8° Longman 67
,, übers. Joh. Minckwitz + J. E. Wessely, 5 vols. [verse] 13/6 16° *Stuttgart* 56-73
,, ,, J. J. C. Donner, 3 vols. ea. 5/- 8° *Leipzig* 61-62

Acharnenses, Knights and Clouds, tr. Walsh 5/- c 8° Bohn 48
* ,, Knights, Birds, Frogs and Peace, tr. J. H. Frere [Morley's Universal Lib.; metrical] 1/- c 8° Routledge [39-42] 86
,, tr. Prf. R. Y. Tyrrell [verse] 2/6 c 8° Hodges, *Dublin* 83
,, ,, C. J. Billson [verse] 3/6 c 8° Paul 82

Aves: tr. Prf. B. H. Kennedy, 6/- [verse]; Help-notes to same [Classical Lib.] 1/6 c 8° Macmillan 74

[Lysistrata]: Revolt of the Women, tr. B. B. Rogers 3/- 4° Bell 78

Pax, Vespae: tr. B. B. Rogers, *in his editions of these plays, supra.*

AIDS.

Criticism, etc.
v. d. Bakhuysen, W. H. De Parodia in Comoediis Aristophanis 2/6 8° *Coblenz* 77
Deschanel, E. Études sur Aristophane 3/- 12° *Paris* [67] 82
Dobree, P. P. Observationes Aristophaneae, ed. W. Wagner [Calvary's *Bibliothek*] 1/6 s 8° *Berlin* 75
Meineke, A. Vindiciarum Aristophanearum liber 5/6 8° *Leipzig* 65
Müller-Strübung, H. Aristophanes und die historische Kritik 16/- 8° Teubner, *Leipzig* 73
Schmidt, J. H. H. —*in his* Die antike Compositionslehre 18/- 8° *Leipzig* 69

Language.
Sobolewski, S. De Praepositionum usu Aristophaneo 4/- 8° *Leipzig* 90

Concordance.
Dunbar, Dr. H. Concordance to Comedies and Fragments of Aristophanes 21/- 4° Clar. Press 83

Scholia.
Dindorf, W. [ed.] Scholia Graeca in Aristophanem, 3 vols. 20/- 8° *Oxford* 19-38
Dübner, F. [ed.] ,, ,, cum prolegom. grammaticorum, etc. 12/6 r 8° Didot, *Paris* [42] 77

Life.
Collins, Rev. W. L. Aristophanes [pop. biogr. and acc. of wks.; Anc. Class. for Eng. Readers] 2/6 f 8° Blackwood 72
Ranke, C. F. De Aristophanis Vita comment. 6/- 8° *Leipzig* [30] 45

Euripides.

TEXTS: rec. Ad. Kirchoff, 3 vols. 5/- p 8° *Berlin* [55] 67-68
,, A. Nauck, vols. i.-ii., ea. 1/6; iii. [Fragmenta] 3/- p 8° Teubner, *Leipzig* [54] 71
,, F. A. Paley, 3 vols. [Camb. Texts] ea. 3/6 c 8° Bell 58; 59; 60
,, A. Prinz, vol. i. Medea, 2/-; ii. Alcestis 1/3 p 8° Teubner, *Leipzig* 78; 79
,, A. Witzschel, 3 vols. 10/6 8°; 3/- c 8° 3/- 24° Tauchnitz, ,, [10] 72

Fragmenta: ,, F. W. Wagner, ed. F. Dübner 12/- r 8° Didot, *Paris* [46] 78

ANNOTATED TEXTS: *with English notes F. A. Paley, 3 vols. [Bibliotheca Classica] ea. 16/-; *red. to* 8/- 8° Bell [58] 72; [58] 75; [60] 82
,, ,, ,, F. A. Paley [Camb. Texts with Notes] ea. 1/6 [one 2/-] f 8° Bell 75-83
Alcestis, Andromache, Bacchae, Hecuba, Hercules, Hippolytus, Ion (2/-), Iphigenia in Tauris, Medea, Orestes, Phoenissae, Troades.
,, ,, ,, A. Sidgwick [abbreviated; omits all choruses; quite elem.] ea. 1/6 f 8° Rivington [72-79] 84-86
Alcestis, Bacchae, "Cyclops" (Iphigenia in Tauris), Electra, Hecuba, Ion.
,, Latin ,, J. E. Pflugk + R. Klotz, 11 pts. [sep. 1/6 to 3/-] 15/- p 8° *Leipzig* [29-60] 42-77
,, German ,, and tr. J. A. Hartung, 19 pts. [sep. 1/6 to 3/-] 37/- p 8° ,, 48-53
* ,, French ,, H. Weil 10/- 8° *Paris* [68] 79

Alcestis: with English notes C. S. Jerram 2/6 f 8° Clar. Press [80] 85
,, ,, ,, J. E. C. Welldon [Classical Series] f 8° Macmillan *in prep.*

K § 191

Bacchae: with English notes [Prf.] R. Y. Tyrrell 6/- 8° Longman 71
A fresh edn. is in prep. by Prof. TYRRELL for Macmillan's Classical Series.
* „ „ „ and intros. Dr. J. E. Sandys [w. ill. fr. ancient art] 12/6 c 8° Camb. Press [80] 85
„ „ „ E. S. Shuckburgh [Classical Series] f 8° Macmillan
„ „ „ Prf. I. T. Beckwith [Am.] $1.15 12° *Boston* 8-
„ German „ G. F. Schöne 1/- p 8° Weidmann, *Berlin* [51] 58
* „ „ „ N. Wecklein 2/- p 8° Teubner, *Leipzig*

Hecuba: with English notes and intro. C. H. Russell 2/6 f 8° Clar. Press 89
„ German „ R. Prinz 2/- p 8° *Leipzig* 83

Helena: with English notes C. S. Jerram 3/- f 8° Clar. Press 82

Heraclidae: with English notes E. A. Beck [Pitt Press Series] 3/6 f 8° Camb. Press 81
„ „ „ and intro. C. S. Jerram 3/- f 8° Clar. Press 88
„ German „ N. Wecklein 1/- 8° *Munich* [ ] 85

Hercules Fur.: with English notes J. T. Hutchinson + A. Gray [Pitt Press Ser.] 2/- f 8° Camb. Press 76
„ German „ intro. & comm. U. von Wilamowitz-Moellendorff, 2 v. 22/- 8° *Berlin* 89
Vol. I. is devoted to a lengthy introduction to the Attic tragedy, 10/-; ii. =text and commentary, 12/-.

Hippolytus: with English notes Prf. J. P. Mahaffy + J. B. Bury [Classical Series] 3/6 f 8° Macmillan 82
„ „ „ and intro. W. S. Hadley [Pitt Press Series] 2/- f 8° Camb. Press 89
„ German „ Th. Barthold 2/6 p 8° Weidmann 80
„ „ „ N. Wecklein 1/6 p 8° Teubner, *Leipzig* 85
„ Latin „ and preface Rev. C. D. Badham 4/6 4° Parker 53

Ion: with English notes Rev. C. D. Badham [elementary] 4/6 8° Williams 62
„ „ „ and intro. M. A. Bayfield [Classical Ser.] 3/6 f 8° Macmillan 89

Iphigenia in Aulis: with English notes C. E. S. Headlam 2/6 f 8° Camb. Press 89
„ „ „ and tr. B. England [Classical Ser.] c 8° Macmillan *in prep.*

Iphigenia in Tauris: with English notes C. S. Jerram 3/- f 8° Clar. Press 85
„ „ „ E. B. England [Classical Series] 4/6 f 8° Macmillan 82
„ Latin „ Rev. C. D. Badham 7/- 8° Williams 51
„ German „ G. F. Schöne + H. Koechly + Th. Barthold 2/- p 8° Weidmann, *Berlin* [53] 72
„ „ „ N. Wecklein 1/6 p 8° Teubner, *Leipzig* 76
„ „ „ W. Bauer, hrsg. N. Wecklein 1/- 8° *Munich* [ ] 84

Medea: with English notes J. H. Hogan 3/6 c 8° Williams 73
„ „ „ M. G. Glazebrook 2/6 c 8° Rivington 86
* „ „ „ A. W. Verrall, 7/6 [Classical Series] Small Edn. 3/6 f 8° Macmillan 81; 82
„ „ „ C. S. Jerram 2/- f 8° Clar. Press
„ „ „ C. B. Heberden 2/- f 8° „ 86
„ „ „ Prf. F. A. Allen [Am.] $1.10 12° *Boston* 76
* „ German „ N. Wecklein 2/- p 8° Teubner, *Leipzig* 74

Phoenissae: with German notes G. Kinkel 9d. p 8° „ „ 71

Troades: *with English notes Prf. R. Y. Tyrrell 4/- c 8° Hodges, *Dublin* 82

TRANSLATIONS: übers. J. J. C. Donner, 3 vols. ea. 5/- 8° *Heidelberg* [41; 45; 52] 76
tr. J. Cartwright [Medea, Iph. in Aulis, Iph. in Tauris] 6/- 8° Nutt 66
„ H. Williams [Medea, Alcestis, Hippol.; blank verse] 5/- c 8° Longman 72

Alcestis, Electra, Orestes, *etc.* tr. [verse] Robert Potter [Morley's Universal Library] 1/- c 8° Routledge [ ] 87

[Alcestis]: Balaustion's Adventure, "transcribed" by Rob. Browning 5/- f 8° Smith & Elder [71] 89

[Bacchae]: Bacchanals, tr. Dn. H. H. Milman [w. *Agam.* of Aesch.] 9/- p 8° 65
tr. Prf. J. E. Thorold Rogers 3/- 12° Parker 72

Bacchanals, Ion, Medea, *etc.* tr. Michael Wodhull, w. intro. Prf. H. Morley [verse; Morley's Univ. Lib.] 1/- c 8° Routl. [1782] 87

Hecuba, Helen, Androm., *etc.* tr. Michael Wodhull, w. intro. Prf. H. Morley [verse; Morley's Univ. Lib.] 1/- c 8° „ [1782] 88

Hippolytus, The Crowned: tr. A. Mary F. Robinson 5/- s 8° Paul 82

Ion: tr. H. B. L. [orig. metres; with stage directions] 4/6 f 4° Williams 89

Medea: tr. Augusta Webster 3/6 f 8° Macmillan 68

AIDS:

Criticism, etc.

Barthold, T. Kritisch-exeget. Untersuchungen zu d. Eurip. *Medea and Hippolytus* 2/6 4° *Hamburg* 87
Haupt, Richard Die äussere Politik des Euripides, 2 pts. [school-programmes] 3/- 4° *Eutin* 70; *Plœn* 77
Kvicala, J. Studien zu Euripides, 2 pts. 7/- 8° *Vienna* 79; 80
Nauck, A. Euripideische Studien, 2 pts. 9/- 4° *St. Petersburg* 59; 62
I.: Hecuba, Orestes, Phoenissae, Medea, 4/-; ii.: Hippol., Alcestis, Andromache, Troades, Rhesus, 5/-.
Patin, H. J. G. Études sur les Tragiques Grecs: Euripides, 2 vols. ea. 3/- 12° *Paris* [43] 84
Wecklein, N. Studien zu Euripides 4/- 8° Teubner, *Leipzig* 74
v. Wilamowitz-Möllendorff, U. Analecta Euripidea 6/- 8° *Berlin* 75

Alcestis.

Bissinger, G. Dichtungsgattungen u. Grundgedanken d. Alcestis; 2 pts. 2/- 4° *Erlangen* 69; 71

Bacchae.

Pfander, Ed. Ueber Euripides Bakchen [school-programme] 2/- 4° *Berne* 68

Ion.

Fütterer, P. De Euripidis Ion [philological] 1/6 8° *Münster* 67
Hense, Otto De Ionis fabulae Euripideae partibus choricis 1/- 8° *Leipzig* 76

Iphigenia in Aulide.

Hennig, H. De Iphigeniae Aulidensis forma et condicione [diss. inaug.] 3/- 8° *Berlin* 70
Vitelli, Gir. Intorno ad alcuni luoghi della Ifigenia in Aul. 4/6 12° *Florence* 77

Iphigenia Taurica.

Köchly, H. Emendationes in Euripidis Iphig. Tauricam, pts i.-v. [diss. inaug.] 4/6 4° *Zürich* 60-61
Kvicala, J. Beiträge zur Kritik u. Exegese d. Taur-Iphig. 1/6 r 8° *Vienna* 58

Phoenissae.

Spiro, Fr. De Euripidis Phoenissis 2/- 8° *Berlin* 84
Zipperer, W. De Eurip. Phoen. versibus suspectis et interpol. 1/6 8° *Würzburg* 75

Rhesus.
Menzer, O. — De Rheso tragoedia [dissert. inaug.] 1/- 8° *Berlin* 67

Textual Criticism.
Scholia.
Dindorf, W. (ed.) — Scholia Graeca in Euripiden, 4 vols. [= vols. iv.–vii. of his edn. of text.] 36/- 8° Clar. Press 34–6
Schwartz, E. (ed.) — Scholia in Euripidem, vol. i. 9/- 8° *Berlin* 8

Language.
Roemheld, F. — De Epithetorum compositorum apud Eurip. usu et formatione 3/- 8° *Giessen* 77

Lexicon.
Matthiae, Aug. — Lexicon Euripideum, vol. i. (A–Γ) 12/6 8° *Leipzig* 41

Life, etc.
Donne, W. B. — Euripides [pop. biog. and acc. of wks.; Anc. Class. f. Eng. Rrs.] 2/6 12° Blackwood 72
Mahaffy, Prf. J. P. — Euripides [Classical Writers; introductory] 1/6 f 8° Macmillan 79

Metrology.
Arnold, R. — Die chorische Technik des Euripides 8/- 8° *Halle* 78

Menander

—*for* Texts, etc., *v.* Collections, *supra* (Comicorum Fragmenta).

AID:
Benoit, Charles — Essai historique et littéraire 4/6 8° *Paris* 54

Sophocles.

TEXT:
rec. W. Dindorf, 1/6; rec. A. Nauck 2/6 p 8° Teubner [25–49] 85, Weidmann 67
,, Prf. Lewis Campbell 4/6 12° Clar. Press 73
,, F. A. Paley [Camb. Texts] 3/6 16° Bell 82
,, Th. Bergk 4/6 8°; 2/- c 8°; 1/3 24° Tauchnitz 58

ANNOTATED TEXTS:
* with English notes Prf. Lewis Campbell, 2 vols. ea. 16/- 8° Clar. Press [73] 79; 81
i.: Oedip. Tyr., Oedip. Col., Antigone; ii.: Ajax, Elect., Trachin., Philoct., Fragm.
* with English notes by same, for school use, Text, 4/6; Notes, 6/- [*sep. inf.*] 8° ,, 86
* ,, ,, ,, comm. and prose tr. Prf. R. C. Jebb, pts. i.–iv. 8° Camb. Press [84–89] 88–89
i.: Oedipus Tyrannus, 12/6 ['84] '88; ii.: Oedipus Coloneus, 12/6 ['86] '89; iii.: Antigone, 12/6, '88; iv.: Philoctetes, 12/6, '89.
with English notes F. H. Blaydes + F. A. Paley, vol. i. 8/-; ii. 6/- [Bibl. Class.] 8° Bell 59–80
i.: (by BLAYDES) Oed. Tyr., Oed. Col., Ant., 18/-, *red. to* 8/-; ii.: (by PALEY) Philoct., Elect., Trachin., Ajax, 12/-, *red. to* 6/-. Separ. Plays, ea. 2/6.
w. Eng. notes Rev. W. Linwood [Oed. Tyr., Col., Ant. = "Theban Trilogy"] 7/6 c 8° Longman 78
,, ,, ,, Ed. Wunder [tr.], 2 vols. [ea. play separ. 3/-] 18/- 8° Nutt 54–64
,, ,, ,, F. A. Paley [Camb. Texts with Notes] ea. 1/6 f 8° Bell [81–82] 88, *etc.*
Antigone, Electra, Oedi us Col., Oed. Tyr., Philoctetes.
,, Latin ,, Rev. W. Linwood 16/- 8° Longman [48] 77
,, ,, ,, W. Dindorf, 2 vols. [i.: Text, 5/6; ii.: Notes, 4/6] 10/- 8° Parker, *Oxford* 32; 49
,, ,, ,, Ed. Wunder, 2 vols. [ea. play sep. 1/6 *or* 2/-] 8° *Leipzig* [31–37] 56–78
,, German notes and tr. J. Hartung, 8 vols. [ea. play separ. 2/6] 17/- r 12° ,, 50–51
,, ,, ,, ,, N. Wecklein, 7 pts. ea. 1/6; or in 1 vol. 9/- 8° *Munich* [*v.y.*] 86
,, French ,, E. Fournier 10/- 8° *Paris* [ ] 77

Ajax:
* with English notes Prf. R. C. Jebb [Catena Classicorum] 3/6 c 8° Rivington [68] 80
* ,, ,, ,, Prf. Lewis Campbell + Evelyn Abbott 2/- f 8° Clar. Press 76
,, ,, ,, F. H. M. Blaydes 6/- 8° Williams 75
,, Latin ,, C. A. Lobeck [for advanced students] 6/- 8° *Berlin* [09] 66
,, German ,, F. W. Schneidewin + A. Nauck 1/6 p 8° Weidmann, *Berlin* [49] 82
,, ,, ,, G. Wolff 1/6 r 8° Teubner, *Leipzig* [58] 75

Antigone:
* with English notes Prf. Lewis Campbell + Evelyn Abbott 1/9 f 8° Clar. Press 75
* ,, ,, ,, and (prose) tr. Prf. R. C. Jebb [*v. supra*] 12/6 8° Camb. Press 88
,, ,, ,, Prf. L. D'Ooge (Am.) $1.35 12° *Boston* 8–
,, ,, ,, J. Bond + A. S. Walpole [Classical Series] f 8° Macmillan *in prep.*
,, German ,, F. W. Schneidewin + A. Nauck 1/3 p 8° Weidmann, *Berlin* [52] 86
,, ,, ,, L. Bellermann, hrsg. G. Wolff 1/6 p 8° Teubner, *Leipzig* [65] 85

Electra:
* with English notes Prf. R. C. Jebb [Catena Classicorum] 3/6 c 8° Rivington [69] 80
* ,, ,, ,, Prf. Lewis Campbell + Evelyn Abbott 2/- f 8° Clar. Press 77
,, ,, ,, F. H. M. Blaydes 6/- 8° Williams 78
,, German ,, F. W. Schneidewin + A. Nauck 1/6 p 8° Weidmann, *Berlin* [53] 82
,, ,, ,, L. Bellermann, hrsg. G. Wolff 1/6 p 8° Teubner, *Leipzig* [63] 85
,, archæol. ill. and scholia O. Jahn, ed. A. Michaelis 4/- 8° *Bonn* [ ] 82

Oedipus Coloneus:
* with English notes and [prose] tr. Prf. R. C. Jebb [*v. supra*] 12/6 8° Camb. Press [86] 89
* ,, ,, ,, Prf. Lewis Campbell + Evelyn Abbott 1/9 f 8° Clar. Press 74
,, German ,, F. W. Schneidewin + A. Nauck 1/6 p 8° Weidmann, *Berlin* [51] 84
,, ,, ,, L. Bellermann, hrsg. G. Wolff 1/6 p 8° Teubner, *Leipzig* [70] 76; 85

Oedipus Rex (Tyrannus):
* with English notes and [prose] tr. Prf. R. C. Jebb [*v. supra*] 12/- 8° Camb. Press [84] 88
,, ,, ,, by the same [Pitt Press Series] 4/6 c 8° ,, 85
* ,, ,, ,, Prf. Lewis Campbell + Evelyn Abbott 2/- f 8° Clar. Press [73] 82
,, ,, ,, and tr. [prose] Prf. B. H. Kennedy, 8/-; School Edit. 5/- c 8° Camb. Press 82
,, ,, ,, Archd. W. Basil Jones [Dindorf's text] 1/6 18° Clar. Press 67
,, ,, ,, Prf. J. Williams White (Am.) $1.50 12° *Boston* [73] 75
,, German ,, F. W. Schneidewin + A. Nauck 1/6 p 8° Weidmann, *Berlin* [51] 86
,, ,, ,, L. Bellermann, hrsg. G. Wolff 1/6 p 8° Teubner, *Leipzig* [72] 86

Philoctetes:
* with English notes comm. and prose tr. Prf. R. C. Jebb [*v. supra*] 12/6 8° Camb. Press 89
,, ,, ,, Prf. Lewis Campbell + Evelyn Abbott 2/- f 8° Clar. Press 79
,, ,, ,, T. K. Arnold (based on Schneidewin) 3/- f 8° Rivington
,, ,, ,, F. H. M. Blaydes 6/- 8° Williams 70
,, German ,, F. W. Schneidewin + A. Nauck 1/6 p 8° Weidmann, *Berlin* [49] 82

K § 192

Trachiniae: * with English notes Prf. Lewis Campbell + Evelyn Abbott 2/- f 8° Clar. Press 77
" " " F. H. M. Blaydes 6/- 8° Williams 72
" " " A. Pretor 4/6 c 8° Bell 77
" German " F. W. Schneidewin + A. Nauck 1/6 p 8° Weidmann [54] 80

TRANSLATIONS: tr. Dn. E. H. Plumptre [verse] 4/6 c 8° Isbister [65] 90
" Sir George Young [dramatic and lyric verse] 12/6 8° Deighton, *Camb.* 89
* " Prf. Lewis Campbell [verse; Antig., Elect., Trachin.] 7/6 c 8° Paul [73] 83
* " " " [verse; Oedipus Rex, Philoctetes] 5/- 8° Blackwood 74
" Francklin [Morley's Universal Lib.] 1/- c 8° Routledge [ ] 87
" R. Whitelaw [verse] 8/6 c 8° Rivington 83
übers. J. C. Donner, 2 vols. 6/- 8° *Leipzig* [38–39] 83

Ajax: tr. Prf. Lewis Campbell, *sub tit.* Death and Burial of Aias [verse] 3/- 8° Blackwood 76
Antigone: " Prf. R. C. Jebb—*in his edn. of same* [prose] 12/6 8° Camb. Press 88
Oedipus Coloneus: " Prf. R. C. Jebb—*in his edn. of same* [prose] 12/6 8° " [86] 89
" Rex: " Prf. R. C. Jebb—*in his edn. of same* [prose] 12/6 c 8° " [84] 88
" Prf. B. H. Kennedy [prose] 1/- c 8° " 82
* " E. D. A. Morshead [verse] 3/6 c 8° Macmillan 85
" Dr. A. W. Verrall + E. Conybeare 1/6 f 8° Rivington 87
Philoctetes: " Prf. R. C. Jebb—*in his edn. of same* [prose] 12/6 8° Camb. Press 89

Aias:

Criticism, etc.

Heuse, O. Studien zu Sophocles 8/- 8° *Leipzig* 80
Kvicala, J. Beiträge zur Kritik und Erklärung d. Sophocles, 4 pts. [fr. *Sitzgber. Wien. Akad.*] 6/6 r 8° *Vienna* 64; 65; 65; 69
i.–iii. are chiefly on the *Electra*; iv. on *Oedipus Rex.*
Margoliouth, D. S. Studia Scenica, pt. i. [Gen. Intro. and text of *Trachin.* 1–300] 2/6 8° Macmillan 83
Patin, H. J. G. Études sur les Tragiques Grecs: Sophocle 3/- 12° *Paris* [41–43] 77
Schmidt, F. W. Kritische Studien zu Aeschylos und Sophokles 8/- 8° *Berlin* 86
Schmidt, J. H. H. —*in his* Die antike Compositionslehre 18/- 8° *Leipzig* 69
Schütz, Hermann Sophokleische Studien [explan. of the difficult parts] 6/- 8° *Potsdam* 90

Antigone.

Meineke, Aug. Beiträge zur Kritik d. Antigone [philological] 1/- 8° *Berlin* 61
Sligmann, L. Die Antigone des Sophocles 3/- 8° *Halle* 69

Oedipus Coloneus.

Mähly, J. Des Oedipus Coloneus des Sophocles 2/6 8° *Basle* 68

Philoctetes.

Richter, E. A. Beiträge zur Kritik u. Erklärung d. Philoktet. [sch.-progr.] 1/- 4° *Altenburg* 76

Textual Criticism.

Hellenic Society, Facsimile of the Laurentian MS. of Sophocles £6
Kennedy, B. H. Studia Sophoclea, pt. i. [= exam. of Lewis Campbell's edn. of text, *sup.* pt. ii. is also pub.] 3/- c 8° Bell 74
Müller, G. H. Emendationes et Interpretationes Sophocleae 9/- 8° Weidmann, *Berlin* 78
Wecklein, N. Ars Sophoclis Emendandi: accedunt analecta Euripidea 4/- 8° *Wurzburg* 69

Language.

Noyes, J. F. Illustrations to Sophocles from Ancient and Modern Poets 7/- 8° Whittaker 44
Escher, Ed. Der Accusativ bei Sophocles [dissert. inaug.] 2/- 8° *Zürich* 76
Krichauff, E. Quaestiones de Participii apud Sophoclem usu [dissert. inaug.] 2/6 4° *Kiel* 76
Schindler, C. F. De Soph. verborum inventore, pt. i.: De Nominum compositione 1/6 8° *Wratislaw* 77

Dictionaries.

Dindorf, W. Lexicon Sophocleum *o.p.* [*pb.* 13/-] 8° *Leipzig* 69
Ebeling, H. Griechisch-Deutsches Wörterbuch zu Sophocles 3/- 8° " 69
*Ellendt, F. Lexicon Sophocleum, ed. H. Genthe 22/- r 8° *Berlin* [34–35] 67–72
Genthe, H. Index Commentationum Sophocl. ab a. 1836 triplex [suppl. to above] 3/- 8° " 74

Life, etc.

Campbell, Prf. Lewis Sophocles [Classical Writers: Introductory] 1/6 f 8° Macmillan 79
Collins, C. W. Sophocles [pop. biog. and acc. of wks.; Anc. Class. for Engl. Readers] 2/6 f 8° Blackwood 71
Schöll, Adolf Sophokles: sein Leben und Wirken: nach d. Quellen 2/- 8° *Frankfort* [42] 70

Metrics, etc.

Bellermann, L. De Metris Sophoclis 2/- 4° *Berlin* 64
Brambach, W. Metrische Studien zu Sophokles 5/- 8° Teubner, *Leipzig* 69
" Die Sophokleischen Gesänge metrisch erklärt 2/6 8° *Leipzig* [70] 81
Gleditsch, H. Die Cantica d. Sophok. Tragödien u. ihrem rhythm. Bau 6/- 8° *Vienna* [67–68] 83
Hense, Otto Der Chor des Sophokles 2/6 8° *Berlin* 77
Muff, Christian Die chorische Technik des Sophocles 8/- 8° *Halle* 77
Schmidt, J. H. H. —*in his* Leitfaden in d. Rhythmik u. Metrik d. class. Sprachen 3/- 8° *Leipzig* 69
" Moritz Die Sophokleischen Chorgesänge rhythmirt 1/- 8° *Jena* 70

Illustrations.

Farren, R. [artist] The Oedipus Tyrannus of Sophocles: etchings obl 4° Macmillan, *Camb.* 87
Lachmann, F. Umrisszeichnungen zu Sophokles; 16 pl. by L. Schulz 12/- 4° *Leipzig* 73
Speed + Pryor, L. + F. R. [eds.] Sophocles' Oedipus Tyrannus; ill. [record of Camb. performances in Nov. '87] 12/6 s f° Macmillan, *Camb.* 88

192. GREEK HISTORIANS AND GEOGRAPHERS.

Collections.

Geographers.

MÜLLER, C. [ed.] Geographi Graeci Minores, w. Latin tr., v. i.–ii. [in 3 v.] 25/-; Atlas 12/6 r 8° Didot, *Paris* [55] 82 [61] 82

Historians.

DINDORF, L. [ed.] Historici Graeci Minores, 2 vols. [Bibliotheca Teuberiana] 4/6 and 4/- resp. p 8° Teubner, *Leipzig* 70; 71
MÜLLER, C. [ed.] Historicorum Graecorum Fragmenta, 5 vols. 72/- r 8° Didot, *Paris* [41–70] 68–83
NIEBUHR + BEKKER, $\frac{\text{B. C.}}{\text{[eds.]}}$ Byzantinae Historiae Scriptores, 49 vols. ea. 6/- to 15/- 8° *Bonn* [ ] 28–78

Africanus, S. Jul. Ὀλυμπιαδῶν ἀναγραφή, with Latin notes I. Rutgers 4/- 8° *Leyden* 62

K § 192

Anaximander Milesius: seu vetustissima quaedam rerum univers. conceptio restituta, rec. J. Neuhäuser 14/- 8° *Bonn* 83

Appian Historia Romana: rec. A. Mai 12/6 r 8° *Paris* [40] 77
rec. L. Mendelssohn, 2 vols. 10/6 p 8° 79; 81

AIDS:
Hannak, E. Appianus und seine Quellen 2/6 8° *Vienna* 69
Kratt, G. De Appiani elocutione 3/- 8° *Baden* 86
Krumbholz, P. De Praepositionum usu Appianeo 2/- 8° *Jena* 85
Wijnne, J. A. De fide et auctoritate Appiani in bellis Roman. civil. 2/6 8° *Groningen* 55

Aristotle —v. K § 194.

Arrian.

TEXTS:
Anabasis Alexandri: rec. C. Sintenis [w. geograph. plate] 1/6 c 8° Weidmann, *Berlin* 67
" " " C. Abicht, *sub tit.* Expeditio Alexandri 1/3 p 8° Teubner, *Leipzig* 76
Scripta Minora: " R. Hercher 1/- p 8° " " [54] 85
Anabasis et Indica: " F. Dübner; Reliquia, *etc.*, rec. C. Müller 12/6 r 8° Didot, *Paris* [46] 77
ANNOTATED TEXTS:
Expeditio Alexandri: with Latin notes C. W. Krüger, 2 vols. 6/6 8° *Leipzig* 35; *Berlin* 48
" German notes C. Sintenis, 2 vols. 4/- p 8° Weidmann, *Berl.* [49] 60; 63
" " " C. Abicht, 2 vols. 2/6 p 8° Teubner, *Leipzig* 71; 75
book v. " English " C. E. Moberly [*sub tit.* "Alex. in Punjaub."] 2/- f 8° Rivington 75
TRANSLATION. Anabasis of Alexander: tr. with comment. E. J. Chinnock 7/6 c 8° Hodder 84

Ctesias.

TEXT. Fragmenta: rec. W. Dindorf—*added to his edition of* Herodotus [w. Latin tr.] 12/6 r 8° Didot, *Paris* [45] 77
" A. Lion [with Latin tr.] 4/- 8° *Göttingen* 23
" J. Ch. F. Bähr 5/- 8° *Frankfort* 24
ANNOTATED Text:
Persika. Fragments of: with English notes and intro. J. E. Gilmore [Classical Library] 8/6 8° Macmillan 89

Dio Cassius. TEXT: Historia Romana, 4 vols. [Editio Tauchnitiana] ea. 1/6 16° *Leipzig* [18] 70–77

Diodorus Siculus.

TEXT: with Latin tr. L. Dindorf [1828–31], ed. C. Müller, 2 vols. 25/- r 8° Didot, *Paris* [42; 44] 55
ex. rec. L. Dindorf, 5 vols. [with his Latin notes] 8/6 p 8° " " 67–68

AIDS:
Pohler, J. Diodoros als Quelle zur Gesch. v. Hellas in d. Zeit v. Thebens Aufschwung 2/- 8° *Cassel* 85
Schneider, G. J. De Diodori fontibus 2/- 8° *Berlin* 80

Dionysius Halicarnassus.

TEXT: Antiq. Romanae: rec. A. Kiessling, 4 vols. 11/- p 8° Teubner 60; 64; 67; 70
" " " C. Jacoby, vol. i. 4/- 8° " 85
" " " A. Kiessling + V. Prou [w. Latin tr.] 12/6 r 8° Didot, *Paris* 86
De Imitatione Reliquiae, ed. Prf. Hermann Usener 3/- 8° *Bonn* 89

AIDS:
Cobet, C. G. Observationes criticae et palaeographicae ad Dionys. Halicarn. 6/- 8° *Leyden* 77
Vierck, H. Die Quellen d. Livius u. Dionysius f. d. älteste Gesch. d. Rom. Rep. 2/- r 8° *Strassburg* 77

Ephorus Fragmenta, ed. M. Marx 6/- 8° *Carlsruhe* 15

Eratosthenes Geograph. Fragmenta, ed. H. Berger 8/6 8° *Leipzig* 80

AID:
Maass, Ernst Analecta Eratosthenica 3/- 8° *Berlin* 83

Hecateus Fragmenta, ed. R. H. Klausen; map *red. to* 3/- 8° *Berlin* 31

Herodotus.

TEXT: rec. Dn. J. W. Blakesley, 2 vols. [Camb. Texts] ea. 3/6 16° Bell 61
" H. R. Dietsch, cur. H. Kallenberg, 2 vols. ea. 1/6 p 8° Teubner, *Leipzig* [74] 84
" H. Stein, 2 vols. ea. 3/- 8° Weidmann, *Berlin* [69; 72] 84
" C. Abicht, 2 vols. 6/- 8°, 3/- c 8° Tauchnitz, *Leipzig* 69
" W. Dindorf [w. Lat. tr., & fragm. of Ctesias, Castor, Eratosth., etc.] 12/6 r 8° Didot, *Paris* [45] 77
ANNOTATED TEXTS: with English notes Dn. J. W. Blakesley, 2 v. [Bibl. Class.] 32/-; *red. to* 12/- 8° Bell 54
" Latin " I. C. G. Baehr, 4 vols. 30/- 8° *Leipzig* [30–35] 56–61
" German " C. Abicht, 6 pts. 11/6 p 8° Teubner [61–66] 72–77
Separately: book i. 2/-; ii. 1/6; iii.–iv. 2/-; v.–vi. 2/-; vii. 2/-; viii.–ix. 2/-.
*with German notes H. Stein, 6 pts. 14/- 12° Weidmann, *Berlin* [\[illegible\]] \[illegible\]
Separately: book i. 2/6; ii. 2/-; iii. 1/8; iv. 1/8; v. vi. 2/-; vii. 2/-; viii.–ix. 2/6.
with German notes K. W. Krüger, 5 pts. [ea. pt. sep. 2/-] 8/6 p 8° *Leipzig* 55–75
bks. i. and ii. with English notes H. G. Woods, bk. i. 6/-; bk. ii. [Catena Class.] 5/- c 8° Rivington 73; 73
" ii. " German " A. Wiedemann 12/- 8° Teubner, *Leipzig* 90
" ii.–iii. " English " J. Kenrick *o.p.* [*pb.* 12/-; *w.* 6/-] 8° Fellows 41
" i. and iii. " " " Prf. A. H. Sayce 16/- 8° Macmillan 89
Useful as giving the latest views of English and Continental Egyptologists.

K § 192

bks. iv.–ix. with English notes R. W. Macan 8° Macmillan *in prep.*
„ v., vi., viii. (1–90); ix. (1–89) with English notes E. S. Shuckburgh, v., 3/–; vi., 4/–; others ea. 3/6 f 8° Camb. Press 90; 89; 87; 87
„ vii.–viii. with English notes Rev. A. H. Cooke [Class. Ser.] f 8° Macmillan *in prep.*
„ ix. „ „ „ E. Abbott 3/– f 8° Clar. Press 87
Selections: „ „ „ Rev. W. W. Merry 2/6 f 8° „ [80] 88
TRANSLATION: tr. G. C. Macaulay, w. notes and indices, 2 vols. 18/– c 8° Macmillan 90
„ G. + Sir H. Rawlinson + Sir J. G. Wilkinson, 4 vols. 48/– 8° Murray [58–60] 75
Embodying, with good notes, the results of cuneiform and hieroglyphic discovery up to 1875. *Vide also* K § 10.
bk. ii. Euterpe [= Herod. ii.]: Englished by B[arnaby] R[ich], ed. A. Lang 10/– c 8° Nutt [ ] 88

AIDS:
Bauer, Adolf — Die Entstehung der Herodotischen Geschichtswerkes 4/– 8° *Vienna* 78
Gompers, Theodor — Herodoteische Studien 2/6 8° „ 83
Heikel, I. A. — De Participiorum apud Herodotum usu 2/6 8° *Berlin* 84
Kallenberg, H. — Commentatio critica in Herodotum 1/– 4° „ 84
Schweighäuser, J. — Lexicon Herodoteum, 2 vols. 10/6 8° *Argent (Strassburg.)* 24
Swayne, G. C. — Herodotus [pop. biogr. and acc. of wks.; Anc. Class. f. Eng. Rrs.] 2/6 12° Blackwood 70
Turner, D. W. — Notes on Herodotus 5/– c 8° Bohn's Lib. 53
Wheeler, J. T. — Analysis and Summary of Herodotus 5/– c 8° „ 52
„ „ — The Geography of Herodotus [tr. selections, w. illustr. information] 12/– 8° Nuttall [54] 61
White, Dr. J. S. [Am.] — Herodotus for Boys and Girls, w. notes and intros.; 50 ill., 2 vols. 16° *or* 1 vol. 4° ea. $2.50 *New York* 84
Stories from Herodotus.
Church, Rev. A. J. — Stories of the East from Herodotus; col. pl. 5/– c 8° Seeley [80] 88
„ „ — Story of the Persian War from Herodotus; col. pl. 5/– c 8° „ [81] 89

Hipparchus

Geograph. Fragmenta, rec. H. Berger 3/– 8° *Leipzig* 69

Pausanias.

TEXT: rec. J. H. Schubart, 2 vols. 4/6 p 8° Teubner, *Leipzig* [53; 54] 75
„ L. Dindorf [with Latin tr.] 12/6 r 8° Didot, *Paris* [45] 82
TRANSLATIONS: Description of Greece; tr. w. notes A. R. Shilleto, 2 vols. ea. 5/– c 8° Bohn's Lib. 86
The same, tr. J. G. Frazer Macmillan *in prep.*

AID:
Hitzig, H. — Zur Pausaniasfrage 2/– 8° *Zürich* 87
Kalkmann, A. — Pausanias der Perieget 8/– 8° *Berlin* 86

Plutarch.

TEXTS: rec. Th. Böhmer + F. Dübner, 5 vols. [w. Latin tr.] 58/6 r 8° Didot, *Paris* [46–55] 62–77
Vitae, 2 vols. 25/–; Moralia, 2 vols. 25/–; Fragmenta et Spuria, 8/6.
„ C. Sintenis + R. Hercher, 3 pts. ea. 9*d.* p 8° Weidmann, *Berlin*
Vitae: rec. C. Sintenis, 5 vols. [also sep. 2/– and 2/6] 8/6 p 8° Teubner [52–55] 73–75
„ Imm. Bekker, 5 vols. [also in pts. ea. 1/–] 10/– c 8°; 7/6 24° Tauchnitz, *Leipzig* [[illegible]] [illegible]
ANNOTATED TEXTS:
Vitae: w. German notes C. Sintenis + R. Hercher, 3 pts. 1/– and 2/– p 8° Weidmann, *Berlin* [[illegible]] [illegible]
„ „ „ O. Siefert + F. Blass, 6 pts. ea. 1/– and 1/6 p 8° Teubner, *Leipzig* 59–75
„ English „ Rev. A. H. Holden, pts. i.–iv. 23/– c 8° Camb. Press [85] 88; 86–90
Gracchi, 4/– [85] '88; Nicias, 5/– '87; Sulla, 4/– '86; Timoleon, 4/– '90.
Galba and Otho: „ „ „ and intro. E. G. Hardy [Classical Series] 6/– f 8° Macmillan 90
„ Themistokles: „ „ „ Rev. H. A. Holden [Classical Series] 5/– f 8° „ 82
„ German „ A. Bauer 2/6 8° *Leipzig* 84

TRANSLATIONS:
Lives: tr. A. H. Clough, 18/– [also 3 vols. 30/– 8° *Edin.* 83] 8° Low [59] 77
„ A. Stewart + G. Long, 4 vols. ea. 3/6 c 8° Bohn's Lib. 80–82
„ J. + W. Langhorne, 2 vols. 10/6 [also 2/6 c 8° Routledge '90] 8° Chatto [1770] 75
„ Selected: Selections from North's tr., ed. Prf. W. W. Skeat 6/– c 8° Macmillan 75
A Selection of the Lives illustrating SHAKSPERE'S Plays.

AIDS: —*v. also* § K 194: Philosophers.
Bernardakis, G. N. — Symbolae criticae et palaeographicae in Plutarchum 4/– 8° *Leipzig* 79
Peter, H. — Die Quellen d. Plutarchs in d. Biographien d. Römer 3/– 8° *Halle* 65
Wyttenbach, D. — Lexicon Plutarcheum, 2 vols. 25/–; *red. to* 9/– 8° *Leipzig* [35] 43
A re-issue of the stock of the first edn., which bore the title *Index Graecitatis in Plutarchi Opera.*

Polybius.

TEXT: rec. F. Hultsch, 4 vols. i.–iii. ea. 3/–; iv. 4/6 p 8° Weidmann, *Berlin* 67–71
„ L. Dindorf, 4 vols. [v. i. ed. Büttner-Wobst] [sep. ea. 3/–] 11/– p 8° Teubner, *Leipzig* [66–68] 82
„ F. Dübner [with Latin tr.] 17/– r 8° Didot, *Paris* [65] 80
„ bks. ii.–iv.: Sel. fr.: w. Engl. notes Rev. W. W. Capes [Class. Ser.; *sub tit.* Hist. of Achaean League] 6/6 f 8° Macmillan 88
Selections *ed. J. L. Strachan-Davidson, w. notes, prolegomena, etc.; 3 maps 21/– 8° Clar. Press 88
TRANSLATION: *The Histories, tr. E. S. Shuckburgh, 2 v.; w. intros., etc. [fr. Hultsch's text] 24/– c 8° Macmillan 89

AIDS:
La Roche, P. — Charakteristik des Polybius 2/– 8° *Leipzig* 57
Markhauser, W. — Der Geschichtschreiber Polybius 2/6 8° *Munich* 58
Pichler, A. — Polybius' Leben, Philosophie und Staatslehre 3/6 8° *Landshut* 60
v. Scala, R. — Die Studien des Polybius, pt. i. 5/– 8° *Stuttgart* 90
Schweighäuser, J. — Lexicon Polybianum *o.p.* 4° *London* 22

Ptolemy

Geographiae libri viii., ed. C. Müller, vol. i., pt. i. [w. Latin tr.] 12/6 i 8° Didot, *Paris* 83
Reproduction of the Greek MS. at Mount Athos, ed. V. Langlois 63/– 4° *Paris* 67

AIDS:
Bunbury, E. H. — —*art.* Ptolemy, *in* Ency. Brit., vol. xx. [*also his art.* Pytheas, *in same vol.*] 30/– 4° Black 86
Winsor, Justin [Am.] — Bibliography of Ptolemy's Geography [1462–1867: 42 pp.] r 8° *Cambridge, Mass.* 84

Strabo.

TEXT: rec. A. Meineke, 3 vols. [separ. i. 2/–; ii. 2/–; iii. 2/6] 6/– p 8° Teubner, *Leipzig*, [52–53] 66
,, Paul Otto [Leipziger Studien, Suppl. to vol. xi.] 8/– 8° ,, 89
with Latin tr. F. Dübner+C. Müller 30/– r 8° Didot, *Paris* 53–57

Contains 15 coloured maps, which may be had separately for 12/6.

TRANSLATIONS: tr. W. Falconer+H. C. Hamilton, 3 vols. ea. 5/– c 8° Bohn's Lib. 54
* ,, E. S. Shuckburgh, 2 vols. c 8° Macmillan 90
Géographie de Strabo, trad. par A. Tardieu, 3 vols. 9/– 12° *Paris* 80

AIDS:
Bidder, H. De Strabonis studiis Homericis capita duo [dissert. inaug.] 1/6 8° *Gedani* 89
Hasenmüller, J. De Strabonis geographi vita [dissert. inaug.] 1/– 8° *Bonn* 63
Meineke, A. Vindiciarum Strabonianarum liber 4/– 4° *Berlin* 52
Miller, A. Die Alexandergeschichte nach Strabo, pt. i. 3/– 4° *Würzburg* 82
Vogel, A. De fontibus quibus Str. in lib. xv. usus sit 1/6 8° *Göttingen* 74
Wilkens, H. Quaestiones de Strabonis aliorumque rerum gallicarum auctorum fontibus 1/6 8° *Marburg* 86

Thucydides.

TEXTS: rec. G. Böhme, 3 vols. ea. 1/3 p 8° Teubner, *Leipzig* [50] 75
,, Imm. Bekker 3/– p 8° *Berlin* [32] 68
,, Dr. J. W. Donaldson, 2 vols. [Camb. Texts] ea. 3/6 16° Bell 59
,, J. M. Stahl, 2 vols. 6/– 8°; 3/– c 8° Tauchnitz, *Leipzig* 73; 74
,, bk. iv.: ed. Dr. W. G. Rutherford [Classical Library] 7/6 8° Macmillan 90

A revision of the text, w. 3 disserts. on T.'s style and diction, textual interpolations and MSS. emendation.

ANNOTATED TEXTS: with English notes and maps Dr. T. Arnold, 3 vols. [good, text obsolete] 36/– 8° Parker [48–51] 74
* ,, Latin ,, E. F. Poppo+J. M. Stahl [ea. bk. also separ.] *v.p.* Teubner, *Leipzig* [43–75] 88 *in pr.*
,, ,, ,, H. van Herwerden, vols. i.–iii. 6/– 12° *Cologne* 77–79
,, German ,, K. W. Krüger, 2 vols. 12/–; *or* 4 pts. ea. 3/– 8° *Berlin* [46–58] 84
* ,, ,, ,, J. Classen, 8 pts. ea. 2/6 and 3/– p 8° Weidmann, *Berlin* [62] 79
,, ,, ,, G. Böhme, 4 pts. ea. 1/6 p 8° Teubner, *Leipzig* [56] 85
,, French ,, A. Didot, 2 vols. [text and tr. *en regard*] 15/– 8° Didot, *Paris* 68; 78
,, bks. i.–ii. with English notes C. Bigg [Catena Classicorum] 6/– c 8° Rivington 68
,, ,, ,, T. K. Arnold i. 5/6; ii. 4/6 f 8° ,, 54
,, ,, ,, H. Broadbent [Classical Series] f 8° Macmillan
,, ,, ,, [and crit. appar.] R. Shilleto i. 6/6; ii. 5/6 8° Bell 72; 80
,, iii.–iv. ,, ,, ,, G. A. Simcox [Catena Classicorum] 6/– c 8° Rivington 75
,, ,, iv. ,, ,, ,, C. E. Graves [Classical Series; bk. v. *in prep.*] 5/– f 8° Macmillan
,, ,, ,, A. T. Barton+A. S. Chavasse 5/– 16° Longman 84
,, ,, vi. ,, ,, ,, Dougan 6/– Bell
,, ,, vi.–vii. ,, ,, ,, Rev. P. Frost [*sub tit.* "Sicilian Exped."; Class. Ser.] 5/– f 8° Macmillan [67] 81
,, ,, vii. ,, ,, ,, Prf. C. F. Smith [Am.] [based on Classen] $1 16° *Boston* 86
,, Selections: ,, ,, ,, E. H. Moore 3/6 c 8° Rivington 85

TRANSLATIONS: * tr. B. Jowett, 2 vols. [vol. i. = tr.; ii. = notes, essays and disserts.] 32/– 8° Clar. Press 81
,, Rev. H. Dale, 2 vols. ea. 3/6 c 8° Bohn's Lib. 48; 49
,, R. Crawley [*sub tit.* "Peloponnesian War"] 10/6 c 8° Longman [74] 75
Speeches from Thucyd. tr. H. M. Wilkins 6/– 8° ,, [70] 73

AIDS:
Criticism, Commentaries, etc.
Freund, W. Präparationen zu Thucydides, 9 pts. ea. 6d. 16° *Leipzig* n.dd.
Girard, Jules Essai sur Thucydide 3/– 12° *Paris* 60
van Herwerden, H. Studia Thucydidea 5/– 8° *Utrecht* 69
Müller-Strübung, H. Thukydideische Forschungen 7/– 8° *Vienna* 81
Sheppard+Evans, L. G. / L. Notes on Thucydides: original and compiled, books, i.–iii. 7/6 c 8° Longman [bk i.–ii. 57] 76
Steup, J. Thukydideische Studien, pt. i. 2/6; ii 4/– 8° *Freiburg* 81; 86
Wheeler, J. T. Analysis and Summary of Thucydides 5/– c 8° Bohn's Lib. 52
Textual Criticism.
van Herwerden, H. Analecta critica ad Thucydidem, Lysiam, Soph., etc. 2/– 8° *Utrecht* 68
Linwood, Rev. W. Remarks and Emendations on some Passages in Thucydides *o.p.* [*pb.* 4/6; *w.* 3/6] 8° Walton [5–] 60
Language.
Darpe, F. De verborum apud Thucydidem collocatione [diss. inaug.] 1/6 8° *Warendorf* 65
Herbst, L. Ueber ἄν beim Futur im Thucydides [school progr.] 1/6 4° *Hamburg* 67
Preibisch, C. De comparativi cum comparata re conjuncti usu Thuc. 1/– 8° *Wratislaw* 69
Stahl, J. M. Quaestiones Grammaticae ad Thucydidem pertinentes 2/– 8° *Leipzig* 86
Struve, O. De compositi operis Thucydidis temporibus [diss. inaug.] 1/– 8° *Halle* 78
Widmann, Simon Peter De finalium enuntiatorum usu Thucydideo [,, ,,] 2/6 8° *Göttingen* 75
Wisen, Theodore De vi et usu particulae ἄν apud Thucydidem [,, ,,] 1/– 8° *Copenhagen* 62
Dictionary.
Bétant, E. A. Lexicon Thucydideum, 2 vols. *o.p.* [*w.* 84/–] 8° *Geneva* 43; 47
v. Essen, M. H. N. Index Thucydideus ex Bekkeri edit. stereot. confectus 12/– 8° *Berlin* 87
Scholia.
Bernardakis, G. N. Σχόλια εἰς τὰς δημηγορίας τοῦ Θουκυδίδου συνταχθέντα 5/– 8° *Athens* 67
Life, etc.
Collins, Rev. W. L. Thucydides [pop. biog. and acc. of wks.; Anc. Class f. Eng. Rrs.] 2/6 f 8° Blackwood 78

K § 192

Xenophon.

TEXTS:

rec. A. Hug+L. Dindorf, 5 vols. p 8° Teubner, *Leipzig* [ ] 78-83

Anab. 1/6; ed. min. 1/-; Cyrop. 2/-; ed. min. 1/2; Hist. Graec. 1/2; Memor. 1d.; Scripta minora, 1/2.

rec. G. Sauppe, 5 vols. 10/- 8°; 4/6 c 8°; 4/- [also separ.] 24° Tauchnitz [65-67] 67-70
,, C. Schenkl, vol. i. 1/6, ii. 2/6 p 8° Weidmann, *Berlin* 69; 76

ANNOTATED TEXTS:

Agesilaus: with English notes, syntax and indices R. W. Taylor 2/6 c 8° Rivington 80
,, ,, ,, H. Hailstone [Pitt Press Series] 2/6 12° Camb. Press 79
,, Latin ,, L. Breitenbach 1/6 p 8° Teubner, *Leipzig* 43

Anabasis: with English notes J. F. Macmichael [Gram. Sch. Classics] 5/- f 8° Bell [ ] 83
,, ,, ,, A. Pretor, 2 vols. [ea. bk. sep. 2/- or 2/6; Pitt Press] 7/6 f 8° Camb. Press [75-79] 81
,, Latin ,, L. Breitenbach 6/- 8° *Halle* 67
,, German ,, F. Vollbrecht, 2 vols. ea. 1/6 p 8° Teubner [57] 77; [58] 75
,, ,, ,, C. Rehdantz+O. Carnuth, 2 vols. ea. 2/- p 8° Weidmann [63] 82; [64] 85
,, ,, ,, K. W. Krüger 2/6 p 8° *Leipzig* [30] 71
,, ,, ,, R. Kühner; map 4/6 p 8° Teubner, *Leipzig* 52
,, bk. i. with English notes A. S. Walpole [Elementary Classics] 1/6 18° Macmillan 81
,, bks. i.-ii. ,, ,, ,, H. Hailstone [Classical Series] 4/6 f 8° ,, 82
,, bks. i. and iii. ,, ,, ,, J. Marshall ea. 2/6 f 8° Clar. Press 85; 88
,, bks. i.-iv. ,, ,, ,, Prf. W. W. Goodwin+J. W. White [Am.] [Class. Ser.] 5/- f 8° Macmillan 77
,, ,, ,, R. W. Taylor, 2 vols. ea. 3/6 Rivington 78, 70
,, bk. ii. ,, ,, ,, C. S. Jerram 2/- f 8° Clar. Press 78
,, bk. iv. ,, ,, ,, North Pinder 1/- 18° Seeley 73

Cyropaedia: Text, rec. J. F. Macmichael [Camb. Texts] 2/6 16° Bell
,, ,, A. Hug, 1/6; Ed. Minor 1/- 8° Teubner, *Leipzig* 83; 83
with English notes G. M. Gorham [Gram. Sch. Classics] 6/- f 8° Bell [ ] 70
,, Latin ,, F. A. Bornemann 1/6 p 8° *Leipzig* 38
,, German ,, L. Breitenbach, 2 pts. ea. 1/6 p 8° Teubner, *Leip.* [58] 75; 78
,, ,, ,, F. K. Hertlein, 2 vols. 1/6 and 2/6 p 8° Weidmann, *Berl.* [53] 86; 76
,, bks. i.-ii., iii.-v. with English notes Rev. H. A. Holden [Pitt Press Ser.] i.-ii., 2 v. 6/-; iii.-v. 5/- c 8° Camb. Press 87; 87
,, bks. i., iv.-v. ,, ,, ,, Dr. C. Bigg, i. 2/-; iv.-v. 2/6 f 8° Clar. Press 88
,, bks. vii.-viii. ,, ,, ,, A. Goodwin [Classical Series] 5/- f 8° Macmillan 79

De Reditibus Libellus: Text, rec. A. Zurborg 2/- p 8° Weidmann, *Berlin*

Hellenica: ,, ,, C. G. Cobet 2/- 8° *Amsterdam* 62
,, ,, O. Keller [w. crit. appar. and index] 10/-; Ed. Minor, 1/- 8° Teubner, *Leipzig* 90; 89
with English notes T. K. Arnold 3/6 f 8° Rivington
,, Latin ,, L. Breitenbach 6/- p 8° Teubner, *Leip.* 53-63
,, German ,, R. Büchsenschütz, 2 pts. ea. 1/6 p 8° ,, [60] 84; 73
,, ,, ,, L. Breitenbach, 3 pts. 2/- and 2/6 p 8° Weidmann, *Berl.* [73] 84; 74; 76
,, bks. i.-ii. ,, English ,, H. Hailstone [Classical Series] 4/6 f 8° Macmillan 78
,, ,, ,, ,, ,, G. E. Underhill 3/- f 8° Clar. Press 88
,, ,, ,, Dr. I. J. Manatt [Am.] $1.60 sq 8° *Boston* 8-

Hiero: *with English notes Rev. H. A. Holden [Classical Series] 3/6 f 8° Macmillan [83] 88
,, ,, ,, R. Shindler 2/6 16° Sonnenschein 83
,, German ,, L. Breitenbach *o.p.* p 8° Teubner, *Leipzig* 44

Memorabilia: with English notes Rev. P. Frost [Gram. Sch. Classics] 4/6 f 8° Bell 67
,, ,, ,, A. R. Cluer [Classical Series] 6/- 12° Macmillan 80
,, Latin ,, R. Kühner 3/6 p 8° Teubner, *Leip.* [41] 58
,, German ,, L. Breitenbach 2/6 p 8° Weidmann, *Berl.* [54] 78
,, ,, ,, R. Kühner 1/6 p 8° Teubner, *Leip.* [62] 76
,, ,, ,, Mor. Seyffert 2/- 8° *Leipzig* [42] 83
,, ,, ,, E. Weissenborn, pts. i.-ii. 1/6 8° *Gotha* 84
,, bk. i. ,, English ,, C. E. Moberley 2/- 18° Rivington [75] 86

Oeconomicus: with English notes Rev. H. A. Holden [Classical Series] 6/- f 8° Macmillan 84
,, Latin ,, L. Breitenbach 1/6 p 8° Teubner, *Leipzig* 41

Selections: ,, English ,, J. S. Phillpotts; maps 3/6 f 8° Clar. Press [71] 81
,, ,, ,, ,, ,, +C. S. Jerram [elementary] 3/6 f 8° ,, [77] 82

TRANSLATIONS:

Works: tr. Ashley, Spelman, Smith, Fielding, etc. 12/- 8° Chatto [*v.y.*] 75
*,, H. G. Dakyns, w. intro. & notes, vol. i. [Gen. Intro.; Anab.; Hellen. i.-ii.] [in 4 vols.] 10/6 c 8° Macmillan 90 *in prog.*

Agesilaus: tr. H. Hailstone [prose] 1/6 12° Hamilton 79

Anabasis: tr. G. B. Wheeler [literal prose] 3/6 12° Low [66] 76

Economist: tr. A. D. O. Wedderborn+W. Gershom Collingwood, w. pref. J. Ruskin 7/6 8° G. Allen, *Orpington* 8-

AIDS:

Commentaries, etc.

Croiset, Alfred — Xénophon: son charactère et son talent 3/6 8° *Paris* 73
Freund, W. — Präparationen zu Xenophon, 21 pts. ea. [illegible] 16° *Leipzig* n.d.

Anabasis, 6 pts.; Cyropaedia, 6 pts.; Hellenica, 5 pts.; Memorabilia, 4 pts.

Hartmann, I. I. — Analecta Xenophontea — 10/- 8° *Leipzig* 87
Schambach, O. — Xenophontische Studien, 3 pts. [from *Sitzsber. Wien. Akad.*] 4/6 r 8° *Vienna* 69-76
L: Anabasis, 1/8 '69; II.: Apomnemoneumata, 2/- '73; Oikonomikos, Symposion and Apology, 1/6 '76.

Agesilaus.
Sachse, A. — Ueber Xenophon's Agesilaus [dissert. inaug.] 1/- 8° *Göttingen* 75
Anabasis.
Rehdantz, C. — Kritischer Anhang zu Xenophon's Anabasis [suppl. to his edn. of text, *supra*] 1/- 8° *Berlin* 65
Taine, Henri — Xénophon: l'Anabasie—*in his* Essais de Critique 3/6 12° *Paris* [58] 74
Cyropaedia.
Hémardinquer, — La Cyropédie: essai s. l. idées mor. et polit. d. Xén. 3/6 8° *Paris* 72
Nicolai, Adolf — Xenophon's Cyropædie und Ansichten v. Staate [sch.-progr.] 1/- 4° *Bernburg* 67
Hellenica.
Schambach, O. — Untersuchungen über Xenophon's Hellenika [dissert. inaug.] 1/6 8° *Jena* 71
Hiero.
Nicolai, Adolf — Ueber Xenophon's Hiero [schl.-program.] 1/6 4° *Dessau* 70
Memorabilia.
Krohn, A. — Sokrates und Xenophon 4/6 8° *Halle* 75
Ribbing, S. — Verhältniss zw. d. Xenoph. u. Platon. Berichten üb. Socr. 4/- 8° *Upsala* 70
Language.
Richter, E. A. — Krit. Untersuchungen üb. d. Interpol. i. d. Schriften X.'s. 5/- 8° Teubner, *Leipzig* [72] 73
Sauppe, G. A. — Lexilogus Xenophontis: seu index Xen. grammaticus 3/- 8° *Leipzig* 68
Schmidt, J. — Xenophon Studien, pts. i.-iv. 6/- 8° ,, 7-80
Taylor, R. W. — Syntax to Xenophon's Anabasis; with notes 9d. Rivington 78
Wilisch, E. G. — Das indirecte Reflexivpronomen in Anabasis u. Hellenika [sch.-prog.] 1/- 8° *Zittau* 71
Wiseman, F. O. — De genere dicendi Xenophonteo quaestiones selectae 1/6 8° *Leipzig* 88
Dictionaries.
Generally.
Sturz, F. W. — Lexicon Xenophonteum, 4 vols. o.p. [w. 21/-] 8° *Leipzig* 01-04
Anabasis.
Crosby, Alpheus [Am.] — Lexicon to Xenophon's Anabasis $1 12° *New York* 73
Krüger, C. W. — Wörterbuch zu Xenophon's Anabasis 2/- 8° *Berlin* 78
Marshall, J. — Vocabulary to the Anabasis 1/6 f 8° Clar. Press 88
Theiss, F. C. — Wörterbuch zu Xenophon's Anabasis, hrsg. H. Strack 2/6 f 8° *Leipzig* [41] 84
Vollbrecht, F. — Wörterbuch zu Xenophon's Anabasis; 75 ill. 2/6 8° Teubner, *Leipzig* [ ] 76
Cyropaedia.
Crusius, G. C. — Wörterbuch zu Xenophon's Kyropædie, hrsg. H. Strack 2/- 8° *Leipzig* [44] 81
Hellenica.
Thiemann, C. — Wörterbuch zu Xenophon's Hellenika 1/6 8° Teubner, *Leipzig* 83
Memorabilia.
Koch, G. A. — Wörterbuch zu Xenophon's Memorabilien 1/6 8° *Leipzig* 70
Life, etc.
Dakyns, H. G. — Xenophon's Life and Work—*in* Hellenica, ed. E. Abbott 16/- 8° Rivington 80
Grant, Sir Alex. — Xenophon [pop. biogr. and acc. of wks.: Anc. Class. f. Eng. Rrs.] 2/6 f 8° Blackwood 71
Roquette, A. — De Xenophontis vita 2/- 8° *Königsberg* 84

193. GREEK ORATORS.

Collections.

BAITER + SAUPPE, J. G. + H. [eds.] Oratores Attici [with Latin notes] 39/- 4°; small edn., 14 vols. [also separ.] 21/- 16° *Zürich* 38-50; 38-43
BLASS, F. [ed.] — Antiphon, Gorgias, Antisthenes, Alcidamas [texts only] 2/6 p 8° Teubner, *Leip.* [ ] 81
*JEBB, Prf. R. C. [ed.] — Selections from the Attic Orators, with English notes [Classical Series] 6/- f 8° Macmillan [80] 88
Selections from Antiphon, Andokides, Lysias, Isokrates, and Isaeus. For JEBB'S critical work on the Attic Orators, v. K § 189.
MÜLLER, C. [ed.] — Oratores Attici, 2 vols. [texts, with Latin trns., scholia and index] 25/- r 8° Didot, *Paris* [46-7] 77; 58
SPENGEL, L. [ed.] — Rhetores Graeci, 3 vols. [texts only] 9/- p 8° Teubner, *Leipzig*

Aeschines.

TEXTS: rec. Ferd. Schultz: Ed. Crit. 8/- 8° Teubner, *Leipzig* 65
,, F. Franke, 1/2; rec. A. Weidner 3/- p 8° Teubner [51] 73; Weidmann 72
ANNOTATED TEXTS: with Latin notes J. H. Bremi, 2 vols. 4/- c 8° *Zürich* 24
,, German ,, and tr. G. E. Bensler, 3 vols. ea. 1/6 12° *Leipzig* 55; 59; 60
In Ctesiphontem: with English notes T. K. Arnold 4/- c 8° Rivington 60
,, ,, ,, Rev. T. Gwatkin + E. S. Shuckburgh [Classical Series] f 8° Macmillan *in prep.*
,, ,, ,, G. A. + W. A. Simcox 12/- 8° Clar. Press 73
,, ,, ,, R. B. Richardson [Am.] [based on Weidner, *ut supra*] $1.50 12° *Boston* 89
,, Latin ,, A. Weidner 4/- 8° Teubner, *Leipzig* 72
,, German ,, A. Weidner 2/- p 8° Weidmann, *Berlin* 78

AIDS:
Criticism.
Castets, F. — Eschine: étude historique et littéraire 3/6 12° *Paris* 75
Marchand, G. — Charakteristik des Redners Aeschines [dissert. inaug.] 2/- 8° *Cassel* 70
Textual Criticism.
Büttner, R. — Quaestiones Aeschineae [De Codd. Aesch. auctor. et generibus; diss. inaug.] 1/6 4° *Gera* 78
Language.
Finsterwalder, C. — De conjunctivi et optativi in enunt. secund. usu Aesch. [diss. inaug.] 1/- 8° *Jena* 78
Trentepohl, V. — Observationes in Aeschinis usum dicendi [diss. inaug.] 1/6 8° *Strassburg* 77
Scholia.
Dindorf, W. [ed.] — Scholia Graeca in Aeschinem et Isocratem o.p. [pb. 4/-] 8° *Oxford* 51
Life.
Stechow, Ewald — De Aeschinis Oratoris Vita 2/6 4° *Berlin* 41

Andocides.

TEXT: rec. F. Blass [—*v. also* Oratores Attici, *supra*] 1/6 8° Teubner, *Leip.* [71] 80
ANNOTATED TEXT: De Mysteriis, with English notes W. J. Hickie [Classical Series] 2/6 f 8° Macmillan 82
,, ,, and De Reditu, w. English notes and intro. E. C. Marchant 5/- c 8° Rivington 89

K § 193

Antiphon.

TEXT: rec. F. Blass, 2/6 p 8°; rec. V. Jernstedt 3/6 8° Teubner, *Lps.* [71] 81; *St. Petersb.* 8c

AIDS:
Hartman, J. J. — Studia Antiphontea 2/6 8° *Leyden* [illegible]
Ignatius, F. — De Antiphontis elocutione commentatio 3/- 8° *Berlin* [illegible]
Pahle, F. — Die Reden des Antiphon: eine krit. Untersuchung [sch.-progr.] 1/- 8° *Jever* 6c
Sauppe, A. — Quaestiones Antiphonteae [,,] 1/- 8° *Göttingen* 61
Schäfer, H. — De nonnullarum particularum apud Ant. usu [diss. inaug.] 1/6 8° ,, 77

Antisthenes:

Fragmenta, rec. A. W. Winckelmann [*also in* Blass' Antiphon, *ut sup.*] 2/- 12° *Zürich* 42

AIDS:
Chappuis, C. — Antisthène [prize essay] 2/6 8° *Paris* [illegible]
Dümmler, F. — Antisthenica 2/- 8° *Halle* [illegible]

Aristotle. Rhetoric—*v.* K § 194.

Demosthenes.

TEXT: rec. W. Dindorf [3 vols.], vol. i. 2/6; Ed. Minor, vol. i. (2 pts.) ea. 1/- p 8° Teubner, *Lps.* [50-51] 85
,, Im. Bekker, 3 vols. 11/6 8°; 4/6 c 8°; 4/- 24° Tauchnitz ,, 54; 55; 55
,, J. Th. Voemel [w. Latin tr.] 17/- r 8° Didot, *Paris* [43-45] 78

ANNOTATED TEXT: with English notes R. Whiston, 2 vols. [Bibliotheca Classica] ea. 8/- 8° Bell 59; 68
,, German ,, and tr. G. E. Benseler, 10 vols. [also separ.] 14/- 8° *Leipzig* 56-76
,, French ,, H. Weil 7/- 8° *Paris* 77
Adversus Leptinem, in Midiam, de Falsa Legatione, in Coronam.

Adv. Aristocratem, In Cononem, Eubul.: w. German notes A. Westermann 2/- p 8° Weidmann, *Berl.* [ ] 65
,, Androt., adv. Timocratem: w. English notes and comm. W. Wayte 7/6 c 8° Camb. Press 83
De Corona: with English notes Rev. A. Holmes [Catena Classicorum] 5/- c 8° Rivington [71] 80
,, ,, ,, ,, B. Drake, rev. E. S. Shuckburgh [Classical Series] 4/6 f 8° Macmillan [5-] 89
,, & adv. Lept.: ,, German ,, A. Westermann + E. Rosenberg 2/6 p 8° Weidmann, *Berl.* [51] 86
,, & Aesch. Ctes. ,, English ,, G. A. + W. H. Simcox 12/- 8° Clar. Press 73
De Falsa Legatione: *with English notes R. Shilleto 6/- c 8° Bell [46] 74
,, ,, ,, G. H. Heslop [Catena Classicorum] 6/- c 8° Rivington 72
,, Latin ,, J. Th. Voemel 16/- 8° *Leipzig* 62
Adv. Leptinem: with English notes B. W. Beatson 3/6 c 8° Bell [64] 79
[*v. also* "De Coron.," *sup.*]
,, ,, ,, Rev. J. R. King [Classical Series] 4/6 f 8° Macmillan
* ,, ,, ,, and intro. Dr. J. E. Sandys 9/- 8° Camb. Press 90
,, Latin ,, J. Th. Voemel 4/- 8° *Leipzig* 66
In Midiam: with English notes A. Holmes [based on Buttmann] 4/6 c 8° Johnson, *Camb.* [63] 68
,, ,, ,, Prf. A. S. Wilkins + Dr. H. Hager [Classical Ser.] f 8° Macmillan *in prep.*
,, ,, ,, E. A. M. F. Fennel 5/- 12° *Edinburgh* [84] 88
,, Latin ,, Th. Buttmann [= new edn. of G. L. Spalding (1794)] 3/6 8° *Berlin* 64
Olynthiacs: *with English notes G. H. Heslop [Catena Classicorum] 2/6 c 8° Rivington 71
,, and Philipp. i. ,, ,, ,, Prf. A. S. Wilkins 4/6 12° Longman 70
,, ,, ,, Dr. Evelyn Abbott + P. E. Matheson—*v.* Philippics, *infra.*
,, and Philipp.: with German notes A. Westermann + E. Rosenberg 2/6 p 8° Weidmann, *Berl.* [50] 83
Philippics: with English notes G. H. Heslop [Catena Classicorum] 3/- c 8° Rivington [68] 80
,, German ,, C. Rehdantz, 2 pts. 1/6 and 3/6 p 8° Teubner, *Lps.* [65] 77; [65] 86
,, 1st: ,, English ,, Rev. T. Gwatkin [based on above; Class. Ser.] 2/6 f 8° Macmillan 83
,, ,, & Olynthiacs: ,, ,, Evelyn Abbott + P. E. Matheson 3/6 f 8° Clar. Press 87
,, ii.-iii. ,, ,, ,, the same 4/6 c 8° ,, 90
,, i.-iii. ,, ,, ,, Prf. F. B. Tarbell [Am.] $1.10 12° *Boston* 8-
Selections: "Private Orations": *w. Eng. notes and intros. F. A. Paley + J. E. Sandys, 2 vols. 13/6 8° Camb. Press [74] 86; [75] 86
i: Contra Phormionem, Lacritum, Pantaenetum, Boeotum, de Nomine, Boeotum de Dote, Dionysodorum, 6/-.
ii: Pro Phormione, contra Stephanum i-ii, Nicostratum, Cononem, Calliclem, 7/6.
,, "Public Orations" w. English notes G. H. Heslop [Catena Classicorum] 6/- c 8° Rivington 72
,, "Hellenic Orations" w. English notes Prf. Isaac Flagg [Am.] [*Symmories, Megalopol., Rhodians*] $1.10 12° *Boston* 8-

TRANSLATIONS:
Orations: *tr. C. R. Kennedy, with notes, 5 vols. ea. 5/- c 8° Bohn's Lib. 52-63
Orat. agst. Aeschines on the Crown, tr. Brandt 3/6 c 8° Longman 70

AIDS:
*Blass, F. — Die attische Beredsamkeit, vol. iii. [Demosthenes] 14/- 8° Teubner, *Leipzig* 77
Boullée, A. — Histoire de Démosthène [w. histor. and crit. notes] 4/6 8° *Paris* [34] 68
Brodribb, W. J. — Demosthenes [pop. biog. and acc. of wks.; Anc. Class. f. Eng. Readers] 2/6 12° Blackwood 77
Butcher, Prf. S. H. — Demosthenes [Classical Writers; introductory] 1/6 f 8° Macmillan 81
Desjardins, A. — Essai sur les Plaidoyers de Démosthène 2/6 8° *Paris* 6.
Dilges, Ph. J. — Philippische Reden des Demosthenes 3/6 8° *Cologne* 89
Fialon, E. — Démosthène et Eschine [anal. of and extr. (w. trs.) fr. princ. wks. w. notes] 3/- 12° *Paris* 69
Freund, W. — Präparationen zu Demosthenes' Philippische Reden, 6 pts. ea. 6d. 16° *Leipzig* n.d.
Hartel, W. — Demosthenische Studien, 2 pts. [fr. *Sitzber. Wiener Akad.*] 3/6 r 8° *Vienna* 77; 78
Schäfer, A. — Demosthenes und Seine Zeit, 3 vols. ea. 10/- 8° *Leipzig* [56; 58; 58] 8-
Swoboda, R. — De Demosthenis quae feruntur prooemiis 3/- 8° *Vienna* 87
Uhle, P. — Quaestiones de Orationum Demostheni falso addictarum scriptoribus, 2 pts. 3/6 8° *Leipzig* [illegible]; 86
Commentary.
Dindorf, W. — Adnotationes Interpretum, 3 vols. 15/- 8° Clar. Press 49
Textual Criticism.
Cobet, C. G. — Miscellanea Critica [emendations to Homer and Demosth.] 14/- 8° *Leyden* 76

Hyperides.

TEXTS: Orationes quattuor et Fragmenta, rec. F. Blass — 1/6 p 8° Teubner, *Lps.* [69] 81
,, duae, rec. C. G. Cobet — 2/6 c 8° *Leyden* [53–58] 77

AID:
Westermann, A. — Index Graecitatis Hyperideae, 8 pts. — 5/- 8° *Leipzig* 60–63

Isaeus.

TEXT: rec. C. Scheibe, 1/6; rec. H. Buermann — 3/- p 8° Teubner [60] 74; Weidmann 83
ANNOTATED TEXT: with English notes Prf. W. Ridgeway — [Classical Series] c 8° Macmillan *in prep.*
TRANSLATION: übers. G. F. Schömann — 1/- p 8° *Leipzig* [30] 09

AID:
Lincke, E. M. — De elocutione Isaei — 2/6 8° *Leipzig* 84
Röder, W. — Beiträge zur Erklärung und Kritik des Isaios — 2/6 8° *Jena* 80

Isocrates.

TEXT: rec. G. E. Benseler, re-ed. F. Blass, 2 vols. — ea. 1/6 p 8° Teubner, *Lps.* [52] 78
Demonicus, Panegyricus: with English notes Dr. J. E. Sandys — [Catena Classicorum] 4/6 c 8° Rivington [69] 72
,, Areop. Evag.: ,, German ,, O. Schneider — 1/6 p 8° Teubner, *Lps.* [59] 74
Evagoras: ,, English ,, H. Clarke — 2/6 16° Sonnenschein 82
Panegyr., Areopagiticus: ,, German ,, R. Rauchenstein + K. Reinhardt — 1/6 p 8° Weidmann, *Berl.* [49] 82
,, Philipp.: ,, ,, ,, O. Schneider — 2/- p 8° Teubner, *Lps.* [60] 86

AIDS:
Buermann, H. — Handschriftliche Ueberlieferung des Isokrates, 2 pts. — ea. 1/- 8° *Berlin* 86
Engel, W. H. — De tempore quo divulgatus sit Isoc. panegyricus — [schl.-prog.] 1/- 4° *Stargard* 61
Keil, B. — Analecta Isocratea — 4/- 8° *Prague* 85
Oncken, W. — Isocrates und Athen — 2/6 8° *Heidelberg* 62
Ponickau, R. B. — De Isocratis Demonicea — 1/6 8° *Leipzig* 90
Reinhardt, C. — De Isocratis aemulis — [dissert. inaug.] 1/6 8° *Bonn* 73
Sanney, P. — De Schola Isocratea, pt. i. — [dissert. inaug.] 1/6 8° *Halle* 67

Libanius Sophista: Orationes et Declamationes, rec. J. J. Reiske, 4 vols. in 5 — *red. to* 84/- 8° *Altenburg* [v. i. 1784] 1791–97

AIDS:
Förster, R. — Fr. Zambeccari und die Briefe d. Libanios — 10/- 8° *Stuttgart* 78
,, — De Libanii libris MSS. Upsal. et Lincop. commentatio — 2/6 4° *Rostock* 77
Sievers, G. R. — Das Leben des Libanius — 6/- 8° *Berlin* 68

Lysias.

TEXT: rec. A. Westermann — 3/- 8°; 1/6 c 8°; 1/- 24° Tauchnitz, *Leipzig* 54
,, and Fragments: ,, C. Scheibe, 1/6; rec. C. G. Cobet — 3/- p 8° Teub., *Lps.* [52] 74; *Amst.* 63

ANNOTATED TEXTS:
Selections: with English notes E. S. Shuckburgh — [Classical Series] 6/- f 8° Macmillan [82] 85
,, ,, ,, Dr. J. M. Whiton [Am.] — $1.10 12° *Boston* 8–
* ,, German ,, R. Rauchenstein, hrsg. K. Fuhr, pt. i. 2/-; ii. 1/6 p 8° Weidmann, *Berl.* [48] 83; [48] 86
Epitaphios: ,, ,, ,, H. Frohberger, pt. 4/6; ii.–iii. — ea. 1/6 p 8° Teubner, *Leipzig* 68
,, English ,, F. J. Snell — 2/- f 8° Clar. Press 87

AIDS:
*Blass, F. — Die attische Beredsamkeit von Gorgias bis Lysias [v. K § 189] — 13/- 8° Teubner, *Leipzig* 68
Franken, C. M. — Commentationes Lysiacae — 2/6 8° *Utrecht* 65
Hölscher, L. — De Vita et Scriptis Lysiae — 4/- 8° *Berlin* 37
Sachse, G. — Ueber die 30ste. Rede des Lysias — 1/6 4° *Leipzig* 86
Scheibe, C. F. — Vindiciae Lysiacae, 2/-; Lectiones Lysiacae — 1/6 8° ,, 45; 56
Schultze, P. — De Lysiae oratione xxx. — 1/- 8° *Berlin* 83
Thomaschik, P. — De Lysiae epitaphii authentia verisimili — 1/- 8° *Breslau* 87
Westermann, A. — Quaestiones Lysiacae, 3 pts. — 2/-; 1/- and 1/6 4° *Leipzig* 59; 64; 65

194. GREEK PHILOSOPHERS.

Collections.

*DIELS, H. [ed.] — Doxographi Graeci: with Latin proleg. — [Placita Philosophorum] 24/- 8° *Berlin* 79
MULLACH, F. G. A. [ed.] — Philosophorum Graecorum Fragmenta, 3 vols. — [w. Latin trs.] 37/6 r 8° Didot, *Paris*, 60; 67; 81
,, ,, — Eleaticorum Philosophorum Fragmenta — [w. Latin trs.] 3/- 8° *Berlin* 45
RITTER + PRELLER, H. + L. [ed.] — Historia Philosophiae Graecae, rec. F. Schultess — 10/- 8° *Gotha* [38] 88
A good collection of passages fr. anc. authors, ill. the history of ancient philosophy.

Antoninus, M. Aurelius.

TEXT: rec. J. Stich — 2/6 p 8° Teubner, *Leipzig* 82
,, F. Dübner, w. Latin tr. — [with Theophrast., Epictetus] 12/6 r 8° Didot, *Paris* 77
ANNOTATED TEXT: Bk. iv.: with tr. and notes Hastings Crossley — 6/- c 8° Macmillan 82
TRANSLATIONS, CRITICISM, ETC.—*v.* C § 11: Stoics.

Aristotle

—*v. also* K § 196.

TEXTS: rec. I. Bekker, 11 vols. — [ea. vol. separ. 5/6] 50/- 8° *Oxford* 37
Tauchnitz Edn., 11 vols. — [also separ.] 17/6 8° Tauchnitz, *Leipzig* 77
rec. F. Dübner + Aem. Heitz, 5 vols. — [w. Lat. trs., fragm. and indices] 67/- r 8° Didot, *Paris* 64–83
* ,, I. Bekker, 5 vols. — [w. Latin trs., fragm., scholia, index] 80/- 4° *Berlin* 31–70
The text alone is sold separately, as well as in separate parts.

De Anima: Text, rec. W. Biehl, 1/6; rec. Torstrik — 5/6 p 8° Teubner, *Lps.* [62] 84; ?
,, ,, *with English notes and tr. E. Wallace — 18/- 8° Camb. Press 82
,, ,, ,, Latin ,, F. A. Trendelenburg — 12/- 8° *Berlin* [33] 77

K § 194

Ethica Eudemia : Text, rec. F. Susemihl 2/- p 8° Teubner, *Leipzig* 85
w. Latin notes A. T. H. Fritzsche 7/6 8° *Ratisbonne* 51
Ethica Nicomachea : Text, rec. F. Susemihl, 2/- ; ex rec. I. Bekkeri 5/- c 8° Teubn. [80] 84 ; Macmillan 77
ed. J. E. Thorold Rogers : with references 4/6 c 8° Rivington [ ] 65
,, Ingram Bywater Clar. Press *in prep.*
with English notes and Essays Sir Alex. Grant, 2 vols. 32/- 8° Longman [58] 84
,, Latin ,, W. Ramsauer 12/- 8° Teubner, *Leipzig* 78
books i.–iv. ,, English ,, Edw. Moore [w. continuous analysis] 10/6 c 8° Rivington [71] 86
,, v. ,, ,, ,, H. Jackson 6/- 8° Camb. Press 79
,, v. & x. ,, ,, ,, and tr. F. A. Paley 4/- 12° Hall, *Cambridge* 72
Fragmenta : rec. V. Rose 4/6 p 8° *Leipzig* 86
Magna Moralia : Text, rec. F. Susemihl 1/6 p 8° Teubner, *Leipzig* 83
Metaphysica : Text, rec. W. Christ 2/6 p 8° ,, ,, 86
with Latin notes H. Bonitz, 2 vols. *o.p.* [scarce ; *pb.* 31/6, *w.* 42/-] 8° *Bonn* 48 ; 49
Oeconomica rec. F. Susemihl 1/6 p 8° Teubner, *Leipzig* 87
Organon : with Latin Notes Th. Waitz, 2 pts. pt. i. 9/- ; pt. ii. 10/- 8° *Leipzig* 44 : 46
Selections : ed. J. R. Magrath 3/6 c 8° Rivington [68] 77
Poetica : rec. F. Ueberweg, 1/- ; Ed. Crit., rec. J. Vahlen [w. Latin notes] 5/- 8° *Berlin* [70] 75 ; *Leipzig* [74] 85
,, W. Christ, 8*d.* ; rec. F. Susemihl 3/- p 8° Teubner, *Leipzig* 78 ; 80
with German notes and tr. F. Susemihl 4/- p 8° *Leipzig* [ ] 82
,, ,, ,, ,, ,, F. Frandscheid 4/- 8° *Wiesbaden* 82
Politica : rec. F. Susemihl 2/6 p 8° Teubner, *Leipzig* [72] 82
with English notes Dr. R. Congreve 18/- 8° Longman [55] 74
,, ,, ,, R. D. Hicks [based on Susemihl ; Classical Lib.] 8° Macmillan *in prep.*
,, ,, ,, & intro. W. L. Newman, 2 vols. [w. two import. prefat. essays] 28/- 8° Clar. Press 88
,, German ,, F. Susemihl 16/- 8° *Leipzig* 79
bks. i., ii., iv., (vii.) : ,, English ,, and tr. W. E. Bolland [w. intro. essays A. Lang] 7/6 c 8° Longman 77
,, i., ii., iii. : ,, German ,, ,, ,, Bernays 4/6 72
Sophistici Elenchi : with English notes and tr. E. Poste [Classical Library] 8/6 8° Macmillan
Rhetorica : rec. A. Roemer : ed. crit. 2/6 p 8° Teubner, *Leipzig* 85
*with English notes E. M. Cope + J. E. Sandys, 3 vols. 21/- 8° Camb. Press [67] 77
Introduction to : with English notes and analysis E. M. Cope 14/- 8° Macmillan 67
with Latin notes and an old Latin tr., ed. L. Spengel, 2 vols. ea. 8/- 8° Teubner, *Leipzig* 67

TRANSLATIONS : —*v.* C § 9 : Aristotle and Aristotelianism.
Aids —*for other* English Books, *v.* C § 9.
Criticism, Commentaries, etc.
Commentaria in Aristotelem Graeca, vols. i.–xxiii. *var. prices* 8° *Berlin* 82–89 *in prog.*
*Grote, Geo. Aristotle, ed. Prfs. A. Bain + G. Croom Robertson [posthumous] 18/- 8° Murray [72] 84
Contains Life of Aristotle, full acc. of the *Organon*, short acc. of *De Anima*, and abstract of six books of *Metaphys.*
Spengel, L. Aristotelische Studien, 4 pts. [fr. *Abhandl. d. Bayer. Akad.*] 12/- 4° *Munich* 63–67
i. : Nicom. Ethics, 1/6 '63 ; ii. : Eudem. Ethics, 3/- '65 ; iii. : Politics and Economics, 3/6 '66 ; iv. : Poetica, 3/- '67.
Supplementum Aristotelicum editum consilio academiae litterarum regiae Borussicae, vols. i.–ii. (1) 24/- 8° *Berlin* 87
Teichmüller, G. Aristotelische Forschungen, 3 vols. 18/6 8° *Halle* 67 : 69 : 73
i. : Poetics, 3/6 '67 ; ii. : Philosophy of Art, 9/- '69 ; iii. : Parousia, 4/- '73.
Vahlen, J. Aristotelische Aufsätze, 3 pts. [fr. *Sitzber. Wien. Akad.*] 2/6 r 8° *Vienna* 72 : 72 : 74
Ethics : Nicomachean.
Grant, Sir Alex. —*in his* Aristotle's "Ethics," with English notes, 2 vols. 32/- 8° Longman [58] 84
Hatch, W. M. The Moral Philosophy of Aristotle 18/- 8° Murray 79
Tr. of *Nicomachean Ethics* and *Paraphrase* attributed to ANDRONICUS, with analysis of each book.
Rassow, H. Forschungen über die Nikomachische Ethik 4/- 8° *Weimar* 74
Wilson, J. C. Aristotelian Studies I. : Nic. Eth. vii., chaps. 1–10 5/- 12° Clar. Press 79
Logic.
Prantl, C. Entwickelung d. Arist. Logik aus Plato [fr. *Abh. Bayer. Ak.*] 3/- 4° *Munich* 53
Trendelenburg, F. A. Elementa Logices Aristoteliceae [extracts, w. Lat. notes and tr.] 2/6 8° *Berlin* [36] 78
,, ,, Erläuterungen zu der Aristotelischen Logik 3/- 8° ,, [42] 76
Organon.
v. Kirchmann, J. H. Erläuterungen zum Organon [w. German tr. of text] 6/- 8° *Heidelberg* 83
Poetics and Theory of Art.
Döring, A. Die Kunstlehre des Aristoteles 6/- 8° *Jena* 76
Reinkens, J. Aristoteles über Kunst [espec. tragedy] 8/- 8° *Vienna* 70
Vahlen, J. Beiträge zu Aristoteles' Poetik, 4 pts. [fr. *Sitzber. Wien. Akad.*] 6/- 8° ,, 65 : 67 : 67 ; 67
Politics.
Bradley, A. C. —*essay* Aristotle's Conception of the State—*in* Hellenica [*v.* D § 3] 16/- 8° Rivington 80
Lang, Andrew The Politics of Aristotle : an introductory essay 2/6 c 8° Longman 86
Oncken, W. Die Staatslehre des Aristoteles in Umrissen, 2 pts. 14/6 8° *Leipzig* 70–73
Susemihl, F. De Politicis Aristoteleis quaestiones criticae 2/6 8° ,, 86
Psychology.
Brentano, F. Die Psychologie des Aristoteles [espec. νοῦς ποιητικός] 4/- 8° *Mayence* 67
Rhetoric.
Diels, H. Ueber das 3te. Buch der Aristotelischen Rhetorik 2/- 4° *Berlin* 86
Cope, E. M. Introduction to Aristotle's "Rhetoric," with analysis and notes 14/- 8° Macmillan 67
Textual Criticism, Lost Works.
Diels, H. Ueber die Berliner Fragmente der 'Ἀθηναίων πολιτεία 4/- 4° *Berlin* 85
Heitz, E. Die verlorenen Schriften des Aristoteles [prize essay] 6/- 8° *Leipzig* 65
Margoliouth, D. S. [ed.] Analecta Orientalia ad Poeticam Arist. [w. intro. (in Latin)] 10/6 8° Nutt 88
Müller, Aug. Das arabische Verzeichniss d. Arist. Schr.—*in his* Morgenl. Forsch. 12/- 8° *Leipzig* 75
Shute, Richard Hist. of Process by which the Arist. Writings arrived at Present Form 7/6 8° Clar. Press 80
Language.
*Bonitz, H. Index Aristotelicus [= vol. v. of Bekker's text, *ut supra*] 26/- 4° *Berlin* 70
,, ,, Aristotelische Studien, 5 pts. [fr. *Sitzber. Wien. Akad.*] 6/- r 8° *Vienna* 62 ; 63 ; 63 ; 66 ; 67
Mediaeval Study of Aristotle.
Hertz, W. Aristoteles in den Alexanderdichtungen des Mittelalters 4/- 8° *Munich* 90
Schneid, M. Aristoteles in der Scholastik 2/6 8° *Eichstätt* 74

K § 194

Epictetus.

TEXT: Dissert., rec. F. Dübner; w. Latin tr. [*conts. also* Theophr., M. Aurel.] 12/6 r 8° Didot, *Paris* [40] 77
TRANSLATIONS, AIDS, ETC.—*v.* C § 11: Stoics and Stoicism.

Epicurus.

[Fragments]: Epicurea, ed. Prf. Hermann Usener, w. Germ. intro., sug. rgs., etc. [good edn.] 16/- 8° Teubner, *Leipzig* 87
TRANSLATIONS, AIDS, ETC.—*v.* C § 12: Epicureans.

Heraclitus Ephesii.

Fragmenta: ed. I. Bywater 6/- 8° Clar. Press 77
,, Dr. G. T. W. Patrick [Am.] w. English notes and tr. Murray, *Baltimore* 89

Aids —*for* English Books, *v.* C § 5: Presocratic Schools.
Bernays, J. Die Heraclitischen Briefe 5/- r 8° *Berlin* 69
Lasalle, Ferd. Die Philosophie Herakleitos dargestellt, 2 vols. 21/- r 8° ,, 58
Matinée, A. Héraclite d'Éphèse 2/- 12° *Paris* 60
Mayer, G. Heraklit und Schopenhauer 1/- 8° *Heidelberg* 86
Patin, A. Heraklits Einheitslehre 1/6 8° *Leipzig* 86
Pfleiderer, Edm. Die Philosophie d. Heraklit v. Ephesus im Lichte der Mysterienidee 8/- 8° *Berlin* 86
Teichmüller, G. Neue Studien zur Geschichte d. Begriffe, pts. 1–2 (Herak.) ea. 6/- 8° *Gotha* 76; 78

Plato.

TEXTS: rec. J. G. Baiter + J. C. Orelli + A. G. Winckelmann: Ed. Crit., 2 pts. 30/- 4° *Zürich* 39–42
,, the same: small ed., 21 pts. [*also* separ. 1/- to 3/-] 30/- 12° ,, [38–41] 44–87
,, C. F. Hermann, 6 vols. [sep. 10*d.* to 2/- ea.] 10/6 p 8° Teubner [51–53] 73–74
ex rec. R. B. Hirschig + C. H. C. Schneider, 3 vols. [w. Latin trss.] 34/- r 8° Didot, *Paris* 77–82
*rec. M. Schantz: Ed. Crit., in pts. ea. 2/6 to 6/- 8° Tauchnitz, *Leipzig* 75–81

i. (Euth., Apol., Crito, Phaedo) 6/-; ii. (1) (Cratylus) 3/-; ii. (2) (Theaetetus) 3/-; v. (1) (Sympos.) 2/6; v. (2) (Phaedrus) 2/6; vi. (1) (Alcib., Hipparch., Amatores, Theages) 3/-; vi. (2) (Charm., Laches, Lysis) 2/6; vii. (Euthyd., Protag.) 4/6; viii. (Gorg., Meno) [illegible]; xii. (Leg. 1–6) 6/-; xiii. 4/6.

rec. G. Stallbaum, 1 vol. 13/6 i 8°; 8 vols. [sep. 1/- to 2/- ea.] 9/- 16° Tauchnitz [50] 73; [50] 66–74
ANNOTATED TEXTS: with Latin notes G. Stallbaum, 21 pts. [*also* separ. 3/- to 3/6 ea.] 90/- 8° Teubner, *Leipzig* 27–77
Four Dialogues on Trial and Death of Socrates, with English notes C. W. Moule [Class. Ser.] f 8° Macmillan *in prep.*

Euthydemus, Apologia, Crito, Phaedo.

Apologia: *with English notes J. Riddell [w. digest of Platonic idioms] 8/6 8° Clar. Press [67] 78
,, ,, ,, F. J. H. Jenkinson [Classical Series] f 8° Macmillan *in prep.*
,, ,, ,, and intro. J. Adam [Pitt Press Series] 3/6 f 8° Camb. Press 87
,, ,, ,, St. George Stock 2/- f 8° Clar. Press 87
,, and Crito: * ,, ,, ,, Dr. W. Wagner 2/6 f 8° Bell [69] 87
,, ,, ,, W. C. Green 3/- 12° ,, 79
,, ,, ,, W. Smith [incl. pt. of Phaedo] 3/6 c 8° Murray [ ] 72
,, ,, ,, Prf. J. W. White [Am.] $1 12° *Boston* 74
,, German ,, C. Schmelzer 1/6 p 8° Weidmann, *Berlin* 83
,, ,, ,, Ch. Cron 1/- p 8° Teubner, *Leipzig* [ ] 87
Convivium —*v.* Symposium, *infra.*
Crito [*v. also* Apol. *supra*]: with English notes and intro. J. Adam [Pitt. Press Series] 2/6 f 8° Camb. Press 88
Euthydemus and Laches: with English notes G. H. Wells 4/- Bell 81
,, Latin ,, Dr. C. D. Badham 4/- 8° Williams 65
Euthyphro [*v. also* Meno, *inf.*]: with English notes G. H. Wells 3/- 12° Bell 80
with English notes and intro. J. Adam 2/6 f 8° Camb. Press 90
,, German ,, M. Wohlrab 8*d.* p 8° Teubner, *Leipzig* [ ] 87
,, ,, ,, M. Schanz 9*d.* p 8° 87
Gorgias: *with English notes Dr. W. H. Thompson [Bibliotheca Class.] 7/6 8° Bell 71
,, German ,, C. Schmelzer 2/- p 8° Weidmann, *Berlin* 83
,, ,, ,, J. Deuschle, 2/6; Appendix 1/- p 8° Teubner, *Leipzig* [73] 87
,, ,, ,, R. B. Hirschig 7/- 8° *Utrecht* 73
Laches [*v. also* Euthyd., *sup.*]: with English notes M. T. Tatham [Classical Series] 2/6 f 8° Macmillan 88
with German notes Ch. Cron 1/- p 8° Teubner, *Leipzig* [ ] 87
,, ,, ,, C. Schmelzer 1/- p 8° Weidmann, *Berlin* 86
Meno: with English notes E. S. Thompson [Classical Series] f 8° Macmillan *in prep.*
,, ,, ,, ,, St. George Stock 2/6 f 8° Clar. Press 87
,, and Euthyphro: with German notes C. Schmelzer 1/6 p 8° Weidmann, *Berlin* 83
Parmenides: with English notes T. Maguire [Dublin Univ. Ser.] 8° Hodges, *Dublin* 82
Phaedo: ,, ,, ,, Dr. W. Wagner 5/6 f 8° Bell 70
* ,, ,, ,, and intro. R. D. Archer-Hind [Classical Library] 8/6 8° Macmillan 84

Contains a good introduction of Plato's psychology, etc.

,, ,, ,, W. D. Geddes [notes are philosophical; Class. Lib.] 8/6 8° ,, [63] 85
,, German ,, C. Schmelzer 1/6 p 8° Weidmann, *Berlin* 83
,, ,, ,, M. Wohlrab 1/6 p 8° Teubner, *Leipzig* [84] 87
Phaedrus: *with English notes Dr. W. H. Thompson [Bibliotheca Class.] 7/6 8° Bell 68
,, German ,, C. Schmelzer 1/- p 8° Weidmann, *Berlin* 82
Philebus: * with English notes Dr. C. D. Badham 4/- 8° Williams [55] 78
,, ,, ,, E. Poste 7/6 8° Clar. Press 60
,, ,, ,, H. Jackson 8° Macmillan *in prep.*
,, ,, ,, Dr. F. A. Paley 4/- c 8° Bell 73

K § 194

Protagoras :	with English notes W. Wayte	4/- c 8°	Bell	[ ] 71
	„ „ „ and tr. J. A. Towle [Am.]	75c. 12°	*Boston*	87
	„ German „ J. Deuschle + Ch. Cron	2/- p 8°	Teubner, *Leipzig*	[83] 87
	„ „ „ H. Sauppe	1/6 p 8°	Weidmann, *Berlin*	[ ] 85
Respublica :	with English notes and introd. essays Prfs. B. Jowett + Lewis Campbell		Clar. Press	*in prep.*
	„ „ „ tr. and intro. J. Adam, 4 vols. [i. : Intro. and Tr. ; ii.–iv. : Text and Notes]		Camb. Press	*in prep.*
bks. i.–ii. :	with English notes G. H. Wells	5/6 c 8°	Bell	82
„ i.–v. :	„ „ „ T. H. Warren [not very good ; Classical Series]	6/- f 8°	Macmillan	88
„ i. :	„ „ „ Hardy	3/- f 8°	Longman	82
„ x. :	„ „ „ B. D. Turner	4/6 c 8°	Rivington	89
	„ German „ C. Schmelzer, 2 pts.	ea. 2/6 p 8°	Weidmann, *Berlin*	84–85
Sophistes and Politicus :	with English notes Prf. Lewis Campbell	18/- 8°	Clar. Press	67
[Symposium] Convivium :	with Latin notes Dr. C. D. Badham	4/- 8°	Williams	66
	„ „ „ O. Jahn, ed. H. Usener ; 3 ill.	3/- 8°	*Bonn*	[64] 75
	„ German notes G. F. Rettig, 2 vols. i. [text], 2/6 ; ii. [comm.]	10/- r 8°	*Halle*	75 ; 76
	„ „ „ C. Schmelzer	1/- p 8°	Weidmann, *Berlin*	82
	„ „ „ A. Hug	3/- p 8°	Teubner, *Leipzig*	[82] 85
Theaetetus :	with English notes Prf. Lewis Campbell	10/6 8°	Clar. Press	[61] 83
	„ „ „ and tr. B. H. Kennedy	7/6 c 8°	Camb. Press	
	„ German „ Schmidt	6/6 8°	*Leipzig*	80
Timaeus :	* with English notes and tr. R. D. Archer-Hind [excellent edn. ; Class. Lib.]	16/- 8°	Macmillan	88
Selection :	„ „ „ J. Purves	6/6 c 8°	Clar. Press	83

* Includes the whole of the *Apology* and *Crito* ; has preface by JOWETT

TRANSLATIONS—*v.* C § 8 : Plato and the Older Academy.

AIDS	—*for* English Books, *v.* C § 8 : Plato and the Older Academy.			
Criticism, etc.				
Bonitz, H.	Platonische Studien [enlarged repr. fr. *Sitz. Wien. Ak.* 1851–60]	7/6 8°	*Berlin*	[75] 86
Chaignet, A. E.	Psychologie de Platon, 4/6 8° ; Vie et Écrits de Platon	3/6 12°	*Paris*	62 ; 71
Christ, W.	Platonische Studien	2/- 4°	*Munich*	85
Munk, Ed.	Die natürliche Ordnung d. Platon. Schriften	9/- 8°	*Berlin*	57
Peipers, D.	Erkenntnisstheorie Plato's, 17/- ; Ontologia Platonica	14/- 8°	*Leipzig*	74 ; 83
Susemihl, F.	Die genetische Entwickelung d. Platonischen Philosophie, 2 vols.	21/- 8°	„	55 ; 60
Teichmüller, G.	Die Platonische Frage [criticism of Zeller]	3/- 8°	*Gotha*	76
„ „	Zu Platon's Schriften, Leben und Lehre	10/- 8°	*Breslau*	84
Teuffel, W.	Uebersicht der Platonischen Literatur [school-programme]	2/- 4°	*Tübingen*	74
Ueberweg, F.	Echtheit und Zeitfolge Platonischer Schriften [and chiefly events of his life]	7/6 r 8°	*Vienna*	61
Zeller, Ed.	Platonische Studien	4/6 8°	*Tübingen*	39
Dialogues : Collectively.				
Day, A.	Summary and Analysis of the Dialogues of Plato	5/- c 8°	Bohn's Lib.	70
Schmidt, Hermann	Beiträge zur Erklärung Platonischer Dialoge	3/- 8°	*Wittenberg*	74
Gorgias.				
Cron, Chr.	Beiträge zur Erklärung d. Platonischen Gorgias	3/- 8°	*Leipzig*	70
Phaedo.				
Bischoff, Albert	Platon's Phaedon : Erklärung u. Beurtheilung d. Gesprächs	3/- 8°	*Erlangen*	66
Schmidt, Hermann	Kritischer Kommentar zu Plato's Phaedon, 2 pts.	3/6 8°	*Halle*	50 ; 52
Protagoras.				
Schöne, Richard	Ueber Platon's Protagoras	2/- 8°	*Leipzig*	62
Respublica.				
Krohn, A.	Studien zur Sokrat.-Platon. Liter., vol. i. : Der Platonische Staat	9/- 8°	*Halle*	75
Proclus	Commentariorum in Rempublicam Platonis partes ineditae	10/- 8°	*Berlin*	86
Rettig, G. F.	Prolegomena ad Platonis Rempublicam	7/6 8°	*Berne*	45
Theaetetus.				
Peipers, D.	Erkenntnisstheorie Plato's, *ut sup., has special refer. to Theaetetus.*			
Schmidt, Hermann	Kritischer Kommentar zu Plato's Theaetet [fr. *Jahrbb. Class. Phil.*]	4/- 8°	Teubner, *Leipzig*	77
Timaeus.				
WILSON, J. Cook	On the Interpretation of the Timaeus [w. spec. refer. to Archer-Hind's edn., *sup.*]	6/- 8°	Nutt	89
Textual Criticism.				
Schanz, Martin	Studien zur Geschichte des Platonischen Textes	5/- 8°	*Würzburg*	74
„ „	Ueber d. Platocodex d. Markusbibliothek in Venedig	4/- 8°	*Leipzig*	77
Language : Indexes.				
Abbott, Evelyn	Index to Plato [compiled for 2nd edn. of Jowett's Dialogues of P.]	2/6 8°	Clar. Press	75
Ast, G. A. F.	Lexicon Platonicum, sive vocum Platon. index, 3 vols.	20/- 8°	*Leipzig*	35–38
Hunziker + Dübner, F. [eds.]	Indices et Scholia	8/- 8°	„	74
Life.				
Teichmüller, F.	—*ut supra, s.v.* Criticism			
Weiper, E.	Platon und seine Zeit	4/- 8°	*Kassel*	65

Plutarch

—*for editions of his* Opera, *v.* K § 192 : Greek Historians.

TEXTS : Moralia	rec. G. N. Bernardakis, vol. i. 3/- ; vol. ii.	3/- p 8°	Teubner, *Leipzig*	88 ; 89
	„ R. Hercher, vol. i.	2/6 p 8°	„ „	72
	accurate edita [anonymously], 6 vols.	9/6 16°	Holtze „	71–75

TRANSLATIONS : Morals —*v.* C § 15 : Neo-Pythagoreans, *etc.*

AIDS	—*v also* C § 15 : Neo-Pythagoreans, *and* K § 192 : Greek Historians.			
Gréard, O.	De la Morale de Plutarch	3/- 12°	*Paris*	[66] 74
Larsen, S. C.	Studia Critica in Plutarchi Moralia	3/- 8°	*Copenhagen*	89
Volkmann, R.	Leben, Schriften und Philosophie Plutarchs, 2 vols. 15/- ; *red. to* 10/-	8°	*Berlin*	69

Theophrastus.

TEXT: rec. F. Wimmer, 3 vols. 7/- p 8° Teubner, *Leipzig* 54–62
,, F. Dübner, w. Lat. tr. [w. Epict., M. Aurelius, etc.] 12/6 r 8° Didot, *Paris* [40] 77
Characters: rec. H. E. Foss, 1/6; rec. E. Petersen 3/- p 8° Teubner, *Lpzg.* 58; *Lpzg.* 59
*with English notes and tr. Prf. R. C. Jebb 6/6 c 8° Macmillan 70

AIDS:
Boehme, J. De Theophrasteis quae feruntur περὶ σημείων excerptis 2/- 8° *Hamburg* 84
Diels, H. Theophrastea 1/- 4° *Berlin* 83

196. GREEK WRITERS ON GRAMMAR, METRICS AND MUSIC.

Grammarians.

Collections —*for* Modern Writers on Greek Grammar, *v.* K §§ 175–182.
BACHMANN, L. [ed.] Anecdota Graeca, 2 vols. 16/6; *red. to* 5/- 8° *Leipzig* 28; 29
BEKKER, I. [ed.] Anecdota Graeca, 3 vols. 10/6 8° *Berlin* 14; 16; 21
BOISSONADE, J. F. [ed.] Anecdota Graeca, 5 vols. £5 5*s*., *and* Anec. Graeca Nova 18/- 8° *Paris* 29–33; 44
CRAMER, J. A. [ed.] Anecdota Graeca e codd. Oxon., 4 v.; e codd. Paris, 3 v.; 7 v. *o.p.* [*w.* 45/-] 8° *Oxford* 35–37; 39–41
SCHNEIDER, R. [ed.]. Grammatici Graeci, vol. i., pt. i. [minor wks. of Apollonius Dyscol.] 10/- r 8° Teubner, *Lpzg.* 78 *in prg.*

Ammonios Alex. De Adfinium Vocab. Differentia, ed. L. C. Valckenaer, cur. G. H. Schäfer [*w.* 7/6] 4° *Leipzig* [1739] 22
Apollonius Dyskolos Vier Bücher üb. d. Syntax übers. u. erl. A. Buttmann [*v.* Schneider, *sup.*] 9/- 8° *Berlin* 78
,, ,, De Constr. Orationis, rec. J. Bekker, [*w.* 3/6]; Die Pronomine liber, ed. same [*w.* 2/6] 8° ,, 17; 13

AIDS:
Egger, E. Apollonius Dyscole: essai sur l. théories gramm. de l'antiquité 12/6 8° *Paris* 54
Lange, L. Das System der Syntax des Apollonius Dyskolos 1/- 8° *Göttingen* 52

Choeroboskos Dictata in Canones, ed. Th. Gaisford, 3 vols. *o.p.* 8° *Oxford* 42
Didymos Chalkenteros Opuscula, ed. F. Ritter, 3/-; Fragmenta, ed. Mor. Schmidt 9/- 8° *Cologne* 45; *Lps.* 51
Dionysios Thrax Ars Grammatica, rec. G. Uhlig 8/- 8° *Leipzig* 84
Dositheos Interpretatorum libri 3, ed. E. Böcking 2/6 12° *Bonn* 32
,, Ars Grammatica, ed. H. Keil 2/6 8° *Leipzig* 69–71
Gregorios Corinthios [et alii] De Dialectis Linguae Graecae, ed. G. H. Schäfer; 7 pl. [*w.* 13/6] 8° ,, 11
Herodianos Techn. Reliquiae, coll. disposuit emend. A. Lentz, 2 vols. 54/- r 8° ,, 67; 70
,, ,, Scripta Tria Emendatiora, ed. K. Lehrs 8/6; *red. to* 3/6 8° *Königsberg* 48
Philemon Grammat. quae supersunt, ed. Fr. Osann 6/-; *red. to* 3/- 8° *Berlin* 21
Phrynichus *The New Phrynichus: revised text of his *Ecloga*, ed. Dr. W. G. Rutherford 18/- 8° Macmillan 81
Theodosios Alex. Grammatica, ed. C. W. Göttling 4/6 8° *Leipzig* 22
Tryphon Fragmenta, coll. et disposuit A. von Felsen 2/6 8° *Berlin* 53

Greek Writers on Metrics—*for* Modern Writers on Greek Metre, *v.* K § 183.

Collections.
MANGELSDORF, W. [ed.] Anecdota Chisiana de re metrica: comment. instruxit 4° *Carlsruhe* 76
WESTPHAL, R. [ed.] Fragmente d. griech. Rhythmiker [Suppl. to Rossbach, *ut* K § 183] 2/- 8° *Leipzig* 61

Hephaestion Alex. Encheiridion, ed. Th. Gaisford, 2 vols. *o.p.* [*w.* 10/-] 8° *Oxford* [10] 56
,, ,, ,, ed. R. Westphal [= Scriptores Metrici, vol. i.] 3/- 12° *Leipzig* 66

AID:
Rombach, A. De Hephaestionis libris et reliquiis 3/- 4° *Breslau* 57–58

Music.

Aristides Quintilianus De Musica libri iii., ed. w. Latin notes A. Jahn; 2 pl. 6/- 8° *Berlin* 82

AIDS:
Caesar, J. Grundriss d. griech. Rhythmik in Anschl. an Arist. erläut. 4/- r 8° *Marburg* 61

Aristoxenos Harmonische Fragmente, ed. w. German tr. P. Marquard 8/- 8° *Berlin* 68
,, *Melik und Rhythmik, ed. w. German tr. R. Westphal 30/- 8° *Leipzig* 83
Athenaeos —*in* xiv. bk., *v.* K § 198.
Euclid *Εἰσαγωγὴ ἁρμονική*, *and* *Κατατομὴ κανόνος*—*in his* Opera.
Libanios *Ὑπὲρ τῶν ὀρχηστῶν*—*v.* K § 193: Greek Orators.
Plato —*in his* Laws, bk. vii.—*v.* K § 194: Greek Philosophers.
Plutarch De Musica, ed. R. Volkmann, 4/-; w. German notes R. Westphal 4/- 8° *Leipzig* 57; *Breslau* 65

AID:
Sassmann, J. F. Plutarchi Symp. Quaest. ultimam interpret. dissert. crit. 2/- 8° *St. Petersburg* 41

Pollux Onomasticum, iv. 94—ed. J. Bekker 9/- 8° *Berlin* 46

196. GREEK WRITERS ON PHYSICAL SCIENCE.

Collections —*v. also* K § 187 : Gk. Poets, *s.v.* Poetae Bucol. et Didact. (Aratus, Maneth. & Maxim. & others on astrology).

Anecdota Graeca et Graecolatina, rec. Valentin Rose, 2 pts. 15/- 8° *Berlin* 64 ; 70
i. : Adamantius on orig. of winds, Priscianus on winds, Apuleius on physiogn., *etc.* ; ii. : Aristoph. Byzant. ; Anthemus' *Diaetetica*, Gargilius Martialis, Hippocr. *de cibis*, Caelius Aurelianus, mechanics of Philo and Hero.
Metrologicorum Script. Reliquiae, rec. F. Hultsch, vol. i. [Scriptores Graeci] 3/- p 8° Teubner, *Leipzig* 64
Paradoxographi Graeci, rec. A. Westermann 4/6 8° *Brunswick* 39
,, Antigonus, Apollonius, Phlegon, etc., rec. O. Keller 3/- p 8° Teubner, *Leipzig* 77
Physici et Medici Graeci Minores, rec. J. L. Ideler, 2 vols. 6/- 8° *Berlin* 41 ; 42
Poetarum de Re Physica et Medica reliquias, coll. U. C. Bussemaker 8° *Paris* 51

Aelian De Natura Animalium—*in his* Opera, rec. R. Hercher [w. Latin tr.] 12/6 r 8° Didot, *Paris* 58
,, ,, ,, ,, ,, ,, same, vol. i. 4/- p 8° Teubner, *Leipzig* 64

Aratus.
TEXT : Phaenomena et Diosemeia, rec. Imm. Bekker 2/6 8° *Leipzig* 28
TRANSLATION :
[Diosemeia] The Skies and Weather, tr. with English notes E. Poste 3/6 c 8° Macmillan 80

Aristotle.
De Caelo, Generat. et Corrupt. : Text, rec. C. Prantl 1/6 p 8° Teubner, *Leipzig* 81
De Coloribus Audibil., Physiogn. : Text, rec. C. Prantl 8*d.* p 8° ,, ,, 81
De Partibus Animal. : Text, rec. B. Langkavel 2/- p 8° ,, ,, 68
Historia Animalium : with German tr. H. Aubert + F. Wimmer, 2 vols. ; 7 pl. 19/- 8° *Leipzig* 68
Physica : rec. C. Prantl 1/6 p 8° Teubner, *Leipzig* 79
AIDS :
Biese, F. Philosophie d. Aristoteles, vol. ii. : Die besonderen Wissenschaften 10/- 8° *Berlin* 42
Vol. i., on the Logic and Metaphysics, costs 9/- 8° *ib.* 35.
Lewes, G. H. Aristotle : a chapter from the history of science 15/- 8° Smith & Elder 64
An account of the physical treatises. Chapter i. is a life of Aristotle
Meyer, J. B. Aristoteles Thierkunde 6/- 8° *Berlin* 55
Sundevall, C. J. Die Thierarten des Aristoteles [Germ. tr. fr. the Swedish] 4/6 8° *Stockholm* 63
Mammalia, birds, reptiles, insects.

Theophrastus Historia Plantarum, rec. H. Wimmer [= Opera, vol. i.] 2/6 p 8° Teubner, *Leipzig* 54
AID :
Kirchner, O. Die botanischen Schriften d. Theophrastus [fr. *Jahrbb. Class. Phil.*] 2/6 8° Teubner, *Leipzig* 74

Medicine : Greek Writers on (ARETAEUS, GALEN, HIPPOCRATES, PAULUS ŒGINETA)—*v.* H* § 3.

197. GREEK WRITERS ON MILITARY SCIENCE.

Collections.
Militaris Rei Scriptores, rec. H. Köchly + W. Rüstow, 2 vols. ; 16 pl. [w. German notes and trss.] 19/- 12° *Leipzig* 53 ; 55
i. : Aeneas, Hero and Philo, 7/- '53 ; ii. (1) : Asklepiodotos, Aelian, 8/- '55 ; ii. (2) : Byzantine Anonymous Writers, 4/- '55.
Poliorcétique des Grecs : Textes restitués d'après les MSS., avec comment., rec. C. Wescher 34/- 4° *Paris* 67

Aeneas Tacticus.
Comm. Poliorceticus : rec. A. Hug, 1/6 ; rec. R. Hercher 1/6 p 8° Teubner74 ; Weidmann70
with Latin notes, R. Hercher 4/- 8° Weidmann, *Berlin* 70
AIDS :
Hug, Arnold Aeneas von Stymphalos 1/6 4° *Zürich* 77
Lange, A. C. De Aenea Commentario Poliorcetico 2/- 8° *Berlin* 79
Ries, J. De Aeneae Tactici commentario Poliorcetico 2/6 8° ,, 90

198. GREEK MISCELLANEOUS PROSE WRITERS AND WRITINGS.

Athenaeus Naucratita Dipnosophistae, rec. G. Kaibel, vol. i. 5/-, ii. 5/-, iii. 7/6 8° Teubner, *Lps.* 87 ; 87 ; 90

Lucian.
TEXTS : rec. J. Sommerbrodt, vol. i., pt. i. 3/-, pt. ii. 6/- p 8° Weidm., *Berl.* 86 ; 90
,, C. Jacobnitz, 3 vols. ea. 2/6 ; or 6 pts. ea. 1/3 p 8° Teubner [52-53] 71-74
,, W. Dindorf, 3 vols. 13/6 8° ; 5/6 c 8° Tauchnitz, *Leipzig* 58
,, F. Fritsche, 3 vols. [also in 6 pts., ea. 3/6 *to* 6/-] 34/- 8° *Rostock* 60-82
,, C. H. Weise, 4 vols. [Editio Tauchnitiana ; separ. 1/6 ea.] 5/- 16° *Leipzig* [19] 67-77
ex. rec. W. Dindorf, 2 pts. [with Latin tr.] 17/- r 8° Didot, *Paris* [40] 67

ANNOTATED TEXTS:
Selections: with English notes W. E. Heitland [Pitt Press Series] 3/6 f 8° Camb. Press [78] 82
Somnium, Charon, Piscator, De Luctu.
" " " Evelyn Abbott 3/6 s 8° Rivington [73] 84
" " " J. Bond+A. S. Walpole [Element. Class.] 1/6 18° Macmillan 86
" " " Rice 2/- 12° Hodges, *Dublin* 82
" " " C. S. Jerram 1/6 f 8° Clar. Press [79] 79
" " " W. R. Inge+H. Macnaghten 3/6 c 8° Rivington 88
" German " J. Sommerbrodt, 3 pts. i.–ii., ea. 1/6; iii. 3/- p 8° Weidmann[53–58]69–78
" " " C. Jacobitz, 3 pts. ea. 1/6 p 8° Teubner, *Leipzig*[ ]80–83
TRANSLATIONS: übers. Theodor Fischer, 4 vols. [also in 21 pts., ea. 4*d*.] 7/6 r 16° *Stuttgart*[66–67]85 *sqq.*
Selections: tr. Howard Williams: Dialogues of the Gods, the Sea-Gods and the Dead 5/- c 8° Bohn's Lib. 88
AIDS:
Bernays, J. Lucian und die Kyniker 3/- 8° *Berlin* 79
Blümner, H. Archäologische Studien zu Lucian 2/- 8° *Breslau* 67
Collins, Rev. W. L. Lucian [pop. biog. and acc. of wks.; Anc. Classics f. Eng. Rrs.] 2/6 f 8° Blackwood 73
Croiset, M. Essai sur la Vie et les Œuvres de Lucien 6/6 8° *Paris* 82
Friedrichsmeier, F. De Luciani re metrica 1/6 8° *Leipzig* 90
Rothstein, M. Quaestiones Lucianae 3/- 8° *Berlin* 89
Sommerbrodt, J. Lucianea [textual and other criticism] 4/- 8° *Leipzig* 72

Letter-Writers.

Epistolographi Graeci, ed. w. Latin notes R. Hercher 17/- r 8° Didot, *Paris* 73
SOCRATIS et SOCRATICORUM, Pythagorae et Pythagoreorum Epistolae, ed. w. Latin notes J. C. Orelli *o.p.* [*w.* 7/6] 8° *Leipzig* 15

Proverb-Writers.

GAISFORD, T. [ed.] Paroemiographi Graeci *o.p.* [*pb.* 5/6; *w.* 5/-] 8° *Oxford* 36
Proverbs fr. Bodl. Lib., Proverbs fr. Cod. Coislinian., Diogenianus, Zenobius.
LEUTSCH+SCHNEIDEWIN, E. V./F. W. [eds.] Corpus Paroemiographorum Graecorum, 2 vols. *o.p.* [n. 20/-] 8° *Göttingen* 39; 51
i.: Zenobius, Diogenianus, Plutarch, Gregorius Cyprius, 8/- 39; ii.: Diogenianus, Gregorius, Cyprius, Macarius, Aesop, 15/- 51.

Romance-Writers and Romances—*v.* K § 44: Greek Romances.

Wit: Greek (PROSE and VERSE).

PALEY, Dr. F. A. [tr.] Gk. Wit: collec. of smart sayings & anecdotes, transl.; 2 ser. in 1 v. [prose writers] 4/6 f 8° Bell [80; 84] 88
Trsld. Selns. fr. Aelian, Athen., Diodor. Sic., Diog. Laert., Herod., Lucian, Plutarch, Strabo, Stobaeus, etc.
" " [ed. & tr.] Fragments of the Greek Comic Poets [w. English verse trss. *en regard*] 4/6 p 8° Sonnenschein 88
Selns. (w. trss.) from Alexis, Anaxandrides, Anaxilas, Antiphanes, Apollodorus, Aristophanes, Aristophon, Axionicus, Clearchus, Cratinus, Diphilus, Eubulus, Euphron, Eupolis, Hegesippus, Hermippus, Menander, Metagenes, Pherecrates, Philemon, Philippides, Plato Comicus, Theopompus, Timocles, Xenarchus.

XXVI. Latin Philology and Literature.

199. LATIN GRAMMAR: (a) GENERALLY AND HISTORY OF THE LANGUAGE.

Grammar.

Bibliography and Introduction.
HÜBNER, Dr. E. Grundriss zu Vorlesungen üb. die lateinische Grammatik 3/- 8° *Berlin* [76] 81
Text-Books.
ALLEN+GREENOUGH, J. H./J. B. [Ams.] Latin Grammar for Schools and Colleges $1.25 12° *Boston* [84] 89
BRÉAL+PERSON, M.+L. Grammaire Latine Élémentaire 8° *Paris* 88
GILDERSLEEVE, B. L. [Am.] Latin Grammar $1.50 12° *New York* [ ] 73
HARRE, Dr. Paul Lateinische Schulgrammatik, pt. i. [Accidence] 1/6; ii. [Syntax] 2/- 8° *Berlin* 85; 88
HAVET, L. Abrégé de Grammaire Latine 8° *Paris* 86
HOLZWEISSIG, Dr. Fr. Lateinische Schulgrammatik in kürzer Fassung 2/6 8° *Hanover* [85] 89
KENNEDY, Dr. B. H. Public School Latin Grammar, 7/6; Revised Latin Primer 2/6 c 8° Longman [47] 83; 88
*KÜHNER, R. Ausführliche Grammatik der lateinischen Sprache, 2 vols. 25/- 8° *Hanover* [2 ed. 44] 77–79
" " Elementargrammatik der lateinischen Sprache 3/- 8° " [ ] 81
LATTMANN+MÜLLER, J./H. D. Kurzgefasste lateinische Grammatik 3/6 8° *Göttingen* [ ] 84
MADVIG, J. N. Latin Grammar [tr. fr. Danish] [1st edn. of orig. 1844] 12/- 8° Parker [49] 57
" " Latin Grammar for the Use of Schools [tr.] $2.50 s 8° *Boston* 80
POSTGATE+VINCE, J. P.+C. A. New Latin Primer 2/6 c 8° Cassell [88] 89
REINACH, Salomon Grammaire Latine à l'usage des classes supérieures 2/6 8° *Paris* 86
*ROBY, H. J. Grammar of the Latin Language fr. Plautus to Suetonius, 2 pts. 19/6 c 8° Macmillan [71] 87; [73] 82
i.: Sounds, Inflexions, Word-formation, 9/-; ii.: Syntax, Prepositions, etc., 10/6. With copious examples.
" " School Latin Grammar 5/- c 8° " [62] 82
SONNENSCHEIN, Prf. E. A. Latin Grammar: Accidence 1/6; Syntax 1/6—in 1 v. 3/- [Parallel Gram. Ser.] 16° Sonnenschein [88; 89] 90
STEGMANN, Dr. Carl Lateinische Schulgrammatik 2/6 8° *Leipzig* [85] 87
STOLZ+SCHMALZ, F./J. H. Lateinische Grammatik [comparative; Handb. d. kl. Alterthumswiss.] 5/6 8° *Nördlingen* [85] 89
Early Latin —*v.* K § 209: Ancient Dialects of Italy.

History of the Language and Critical Studies—*v. also* K § 168, *s.v.* Collected Essays.

ANTON, H. S. Studien zur lateinischen Grammatik, i. 3/6; ii. 4/-; iii. 10/- 8° *Erfurt* [69] 71; 71; 89
BÄBLER, J. J. Beiträge zu einer Geschichte d. lat. Grammatik im Mittelalter 4/- 8° *Halle* 85
EDON, G. Traité de Langue Latine Savant et Populaire; 9 pl. 8/6 8° *Paris* 84
HAASE, F. Vorlesungen über lateinische Sprachwissenschaft, 2 v. [struct. of sent., etc.] 11/6 8° *Leipzig* 74; 80
HEERDEGEN, F. Untersuchungen zur lateinischen Semasiologie, 3 pts. 4/- 8° *Erlangen* 75-81
JORDAN, H. Kritische Beiträge zur Geschichte der lateinischen Sprache 7/- 8° *Berlin* 79
LÜBBERT, E. Grammatische Studien, 2 vols. 7/- 8° *Breslau* 67; 70
MADVIG, J. N. Opuscula Academica; port. [*v. also* K §§ 169, 179] 20/- 8° *Copenhagen* [34; 42] 87
PAUCKER, C. Vorarbeiten zur lateinischen Sprachgeschichte, hrsg. H. Rönsch, 3 pts. in 1 v. 15/- 8° *Berlin* 83-84
QUICHERAT, L. Mélanges de Philologie 5/- 8° *Paris* 79
PROBST, A. Beiträge zur lateinischen Grammatik, pts. i.-ii. 5/-; pt. iii. (1-2) ea. 1/6 8° *Leipzig* 83; 84
i.: Zur Lehre vom Verbum, 3/-; ii.: Von den Partikeln Konjunktionen, 2/-; iii. Syntax, 2 pts. 2/6.
REISIG, K. Vorlesungen üb. lat. Sprachwiss., ed. H. Hagen, *etc.*, 3 vols. and Index. [Calvary's *Bibliothek*] 30/- s 8° *Berlin* [39] 79-90 *in prog.*
i.: Etymology, ed. H. HAGEN, 3 vols. 6/-; ii.: Semasiology, ed. F. HEERDEGEN, 4/-; iii.: Syntax, ed. J. H. SCHMALZ+G. LANDGRAF, 18/-; Index, 2/-.
SCHMITZ, Dr. W. Beiträge zur lateinischen Sprach- u. Literaturkunde 8/- 8° *Leipzig* 77
THUROT, Ch. [ed.] Notices et Extraits de divers MSS. Latins pour servir à l'histoire des Doctrines grammaticales au Moyen Age 15/- 4° *Paris* 69

200. LATIN GRAMMAR: (*b*) ACCIDENCE.

Generally.

BAUER, Friedrich Die Elemente der lateinischen Formenlehre, 2 pts. ea. 1/6 8° *Nördlingen* 65; 65
CORSSEN, W. Kritische Beiträge zur lat. Formenlehre, 18/6; Kritische Nachträge 7/- 8° *Leipzig* 63; 66
FUMI, F. G. Note Glottologiche, i.: Note Latine e Neo-latine 8° *Palermo* 82
MERGUET, H. Die Entwickelung der lateinischen Formenbildung; w. suppl. 6/- 8° *Berlin* 70; 71
" " —*in his* Einfluss d. Anal. u. Differenzierung a. d. Gestaltg. d. Sprachformen 1/- 4° *Königsberg* 76
*NEUE, F. Formenlehre der lateinischen Sprache, hrsg. C. Wagener, 2 vols. & index 44/- 8° *Berlin* [61-66] 75; 90
Vol. i.: Substantive, 18/-; ii.: Adject., Numerals, Pronouns, Adverbs, Prepos., Conjuncts., Interjects., 20/-; Index, 7/6. A storehouse of Latin forms, containing the result of late textual criticism.
SCHWEIZER-SIDLER+SURBER, Dr. H./Dr. A. Grammatik der lateinischen Sprache, pt. i. [latest philol. school] 4/- 8° *Halle* [69] 88
WAGENER, Carl Hauptschwierigkeiten der lateinischen Formenlehre [alphab. arrgmt.] 2/- 8° *Gotha* 88

Noun.

d'ARBOIS de JUBAINVILLE, H. La Declinaison Latine en Gaule à l'époque mérovingienne 8° *Paris* 72
BÜCHELER, F. Grundriss der lateinischen Declination, hrsg. J. Windekilde 4/- 8° *Bonn* [66] 79
" " The same, tr into French by C. Havet—in *Bibl. de l'École d. Hautes Études* 7/- 8° *Paris* 76

Case.

MICHELSEN, Conrad Kasuslehre d. lat. Sprache von causal-localen Standpunkt 4/- 8° *Berlin* 43

Gender.

APPEL, E. De Genere Neutro Intereunte in Lingua Latina 3/- 8° *Erlangen* 83
HEERDEGEN, F. Ueber lateinische Genus-regeln 1/- 4° " 73
MEYER, Wilhelm Die Schicksale des lateinischen Neutrums in Romanischen 4/- 8° *Halle* 83

Particles.

DAHL, B. Die lateinische Partikel *ut* 6/- 8° *Christiania* 82
HOFFMANN, Emanuel Die Construction der lateinischen Zeitpartikeln [*repr. fr.* Ztschr. Oesterr. Gymnas.] 2/- 8° *Vienna* 60
RIBBECK, O. Beiträge zur Lehre v. d. lateinischen Partikeln 1/6 8° *Leipzig* 69
TURSELLINUS, H. De Particulis Latinis Commentarii, ed. F. Hand, 4 vols. 40/- 8° " [1598] 29-45

Verb.

EISENLOHR, E. Das lateinische Verbum 1/- 8° *Heidelberg* 80
ENGELHARDT, M. Die lateinische Conjugation 2/6 8° *Berlin* 87
STOLZ, F. Zur lateinischen Verbalflexion, i. 2/- 8° *Innsbruck* 82
WESTPHAL, R. Die Verbalflexion der lateinischen Sprache 8/- 8° *Jena* 73

201. LATIN GRAMMAR: (*c*) SYNTAX.

Generally.

ANTOINE, F. Syntaxe de la langue Latine 7/- 8° *Paris* 84
*DRAEGER, A. Historische Syntax der lateinischen Sprache, 2 vols. i. 12/-; ii. 14/- 8° *Leipzig* [74] 78; [77] 81
HOFFMANN, E. Studien auf dem Gebiete der lateinischen Syntax 4/- 8° *Vienna* 84
HOLTZE, F. W. Syntaxis Priscorum Scriptorum Latinorum, 2 vols. [to Terence] ea. 7/- 8° *Leipzig* 61; 62
" " Syntaxis Fragmentorum Scenic. Romanorum qui post Ter. fuerunt adumbratio [*v. also* K § 214, *s.v.* Lucretius] 2/- 8° " 82
REISIG, Karl Vorles. üb. lat. Sprachwiss, vol. iii., ed. J. H. Schmalz+G. Landgraf [*v.* K § 199] 18/- s 8° *Berl.* [39] 90
RIEMANN, O. Syntaxe Latine d'après les principes de la gram. historique 3/6 8° *Paris* 86

"Cum" Constructions.

HALE, Prf. W. G. [Am.] The "Cum" Constructions: their history and functions, i. [Critical] 40c.; ii. [Construc.] 80c. [Cornell Studies] 8° *Ithaca, N.Y.* (Macm.) 87; 89

Position of Words.

ABEL, Karl	Grundzüge d. lat. Wortstellung—*repr. in his* Sprachw. Abhandl.	10/-	8°	*Leipzig* [2nd ed. 71]	85
CRAMER, A.	Ueber Wortstellung und Betonung d. lateinischen Sprache			*Cöthen*	42 *sqq.*
RASPE, F.	Die Wortstellung der lateinischen Sprache entwickelt	1/6	8°	*Leipzig*	44

Verb.

Tenses and Moods.

KLUGE, H.	Die Consecutio Temporum im Lateinischen	2/6	8°	*Cöthen*	83
LATTMANN, H.	Selbstständiger u. bezogener Gebrauch d. Tempora im Lateinischen	4/-	8°	*Göttingen*	90
LÜBBERT, E.	Beiträge zur Modus- und Tempuslehre d. älteren Latein	7/-	8°	*Breslau*	70
WEISSENBORN, W.	De Modorum apud Latinos natura et usu	2/-	4°	*Eisenach*	46

Verbal-Nouns.

GENBERG, P.	De Gerundiis et Supinis Latinorum, pts. i.–ix.			*Lund*	41
MÜLLER, Gustav	Zur Lehre vom Infinitiv im Lateinischen	1/6	4°	*Görlitz*	78
RICHTER, E. L.	De Supinis Linguae Latinae, 5 pts.		4°	*Königsberg*	56-60
ROTTER, H.	Ueber das Gerundium der lateinischen Sprache	2/-	4°	*Cottbus*	71
WEISSENBORN, W.	De Gerundio et Gerundivo Latinae Linguae	3/-	8°	*Eisenbach*	44

Participles.

HELM, F.	Quaestt. Syntacticae de Participiorum usu Tacit., Vell., Sallust.	3/-	8°	*Leipzig*	79
WEISWEILER, J.	Das lateinische Participium Futuri Passivi	3/-	8°	*Paderborn*	90

202. LATIN GRAMMAR: (*d*) PHONOLOGY.

Generally.

BENARY, A. A.	Die römische Lautlehre, vol. i. [comparative treatment]	4/-	8°	*Berlin*	37
*BIRT, Theodor	Lautlehre der lateinischen Sprache, 2 vols.		8°	*Leipzig*	87

Accent and Quantity.

BRANDIS, K. G.	De aspiratione Latina quaestiones selectae	2/-	8°	*Bonn*	81
MEYER, W.	Ueber d. Beobachtung d. Wortaccentes in d. altlatein. Poesie	4/-	4°	*Munich*	84
STADELMANN, J.	De Quantitate Vocalium Latinas Voces terminantium		8°	*Lucerne*	84
STOLZ, Dr. Friedr.	Lateinische Lautlehre—*in* Iwan Müller's *Hand. klass. Alterth.*, vol. ii. [*ut* K § 167].				
*WEIL + BENLOEW, H. L.	Théorie Générale de l'Accentuation Latine [an excellent work]	8/-	8°	*Paris*	55

Dentals.

BERGK, Theodor	Beiträge zur lat. Gramm., pt. i. [Auslautendes D im alten Latein]	3/-	8°	*Halle*	70

Gutturals.

BERSU, Ph.	Die Gutturalen und ihre Verbindung mit *v* im Lateinischen	5/-	8°	*Berlin*	85

203. LATIN GRAMMAR: (*e*) PALÆOGRAPHY AND TEXTUAL CRITICISM.

Palæography.

*ARNDT, W. [ed.]	Lateinische Schrifttafeln, 2 pts., 60 photolith., pl. and letterpress, i. 9/-; ii. 15/-		f°	*Berlin*	76; 78
British Museum	Catalogue of the Ancient MSS., pt. ii. [Latin]; w. autotype facss.	60/-	f°	British Museum	84
CHAMPOLLION, A. [ed.]	Paléographie des Classiques Latins [after MSS. at Bibl. Nat., Paris]	*o.p.*	4°	*Paris*	39
CHASSANT, A.	Paléographie des Chartes et des MSS. des 11 au 17 siècle	5/-	12°	"	[39] 76
CHATELAIN, E. [ed.]	Paléographie des Classiques Latins, 10 pts.; ea. 15 pl. [facss. of MSS.], ea.	8/6	f°	"	84 *sqq.*, *in prog.*
MABILLON,	De Re Diplomatica		f°	"	1681

The standard work fr. which all later writers have drawn much of their material: it deals, however, with Latin charters much more than with MSS. of classical writers.

Palæographical Soc.	Publications [w. excellent historical introduction]—*v.* K § 179.				
PROU, M.	Manuel de Paléographie Lat. et Franç. du 6. au 17. siècle	10/-	8°	*Paris*	90
SCHMITZ, W. [ed.]	Monumenta tachygraphica codicis Parisiensis latini 2718, pt. i. 22 pl.; ii. 15 pl. ea.	10/-	4°	*Hanover*	82; 85
WATTENBACH, W.	Anleitung zur lateinischen Paläographie	3/-	4°	*Leipzig*	[69] 86
* " + ZANGEMEISTER, C.	Exempla Codicum Lat. literis maiusculis scriptorum, & suppl.; 60 pl.	85/-	f°	*Heidelberg*	76; 80

Inscriptions

—*v.* K § 208 and K § 209: Ancient Dialects of Italy, *passim*.

Abbreviations.

CHASSANT, A.	Dictionnaire des Abbrév. usitées dans les MSS. [chiefly charters]	7/-	8°	*Paris* [2nd ed. 62]	84
RUESS, F.	Ueber die Tachygraphie der Römer	2/-	8°	*Munich*	79

K §§ 204–205

Alphabet.

MOMMSEN, Th. Die italischen Alphabete—*in his* Die unteritalischen Dialekte, *ut* K § 209.
RITSCHL, F. —*in his* Opuscula Philologica, vol. iv., w. Atlas 26/- 8° *Leipzig* 78

Textual Criticism —*v. also* K § 179, *s.vv.* Madvig, Ritschl.

HAGEN, H. Gradus ad Criticen [rules and exx. in conject. criticism (Latin only)] 3/- 8° *Leipzig* 79
HAUPT, Moritz Opuscula, 3 vols. 38/- 8° " 75–77
JORDAN, H. Kritische Beiträge zu Geschichte der lateinischen Sprache 7/- 8° *Berlin* 79
i.: Gk. Names in Latin; ii.: Rhotacismus; iii.: Oldest Latin Remains; iv.: *Ast, Absque, quidam, quod.*

Greek and Latin: Collectively—*v.* K § 179.

Individual Texts —*v.* K §§ 214–224, *passim.*

204. LATIN GRAMMAR: (*f*) ORTHOGRAPHY AND PRONUNCIATION.

Orthography.

BRAMBACH, W. Die Neugestaltung der lateinischen Orthographie 6/- 8° *Leipzig* 68
" " Hülfsbüchlein für lateinische Rechtschreibung 1/- 8° " [76] 83
MÜLLER, Lucian Orthographiæ et Prosodiæ Latinæ Summarium 1/4 p 8° " 78
OBERDICK, J. Studien zur lateinischen Orthographie 2/- 4° *Münster* 79

Pronunciation —*v. also* K § 202, *s.v.* Accent and Quantity.

BIRT, Theodor —*in his* Lautlehre der lateinischen Sprache, 2 vols. *Leipzig* 87
Camb. Philolog. Soc. Pronunciation of Latin in the Augustan Period 3*d.* 12° Trübner 87
*CORSSEN, W. Aussprache, Vokalismus u. Betonung d. lateinischen Sprache, 2 v. *o.p.* [*pb.* 84/-] r 8° *Leipzig* [58] 68–70
A standard work, but many of CORSSEN's theories of Latin Phonetics have found no acceptance with the best philologists.
ELLIS, A. J. Practical Hints on the Quantitative Pronunciation of Latin 4/6 f 8° Macmillan 74
FISHER, M. [Am.] The Three Pronunciations of Latin [advocates Engl. method] $1 12° *New York* [ ] 85
GEPPERT, C. Ueber die Aussprache des lateinischen im ältern Drama 2/- 8° *Leipzig* 58
MARX, A. Hülfsbüchlein f. d.Ausspr. d. lat. Vocale in positionslangen Silben 2/6 8° *Berlin* [83] 89
In new ed. changes as to pron. of vowels in syllab. long by position in ab. 150 words are given.
KING, D. B. [Am.] Latin Pronunciation [brief outline of Rom., Continent., & Eng. methods] 1/6 12° *Boston* 8-
PÖTZL, K. Die Aussprache des Lateinischen 3/- 8° *Leipzig* 88
SCHUCHARDT, Prf. H. Der Vokalismus des Vulgärlateins, 3 vols. 28/6 8° " 66–68
*SEELMANN, Emil Die Aussprache des Latein n. physiol.-histor. Grundsätzen 8/- 8° *Heilbronn* 85
WIGGERT, J. Studien zur lateinischen Orthoepie 2/6 4° *Stargard* 80

205. LATIN GRAMMAR: (*g*) ETYMOLOGY: LEXICOGRAPHY, DICTIONARIES, &c.

Lexicography.

NETTLESHIP, Prf. H. Contributions to Latin Lexicography 21/- 8° Clar. Press 89
Conts. the letter A, two-thirds of the book, and other articles. Part of a new Lat.-Eng. lex. undertaken by the author but abandoned.
v. PAUCKER, C. Beiträge zur lat. Lexicogr. u. Wortbildung, 3 pts. and Appendix 8/6 8° *St. Petersburg* 74–75
" Addenda Lexicis Lat., 2 pts., 6/- 8°; Addendorum Lex. Lat. subrelicta 4/- 4° *Dorpat* 72; 72
" Spicilegium Addendorum Lexicis Latinis 7/6 8° " 75
" Supplementum Lexicorum Latinorum, 8 pts. ea. 3/- 8° *Berlin* 82–87
" Kleinere Studien: Lexikalisches und Syntaktisches, pts. i.–iv. 7/6 8° " 83
Notes on the Latinity of, i.: Diomedes, 1/6; ii.: Orosius, 2/6; iii.: Sulpicius Severus, 2/-; iv.: Eustathius, 1/6.

Serial.

Archiv für lateinische Lexicographie u. Grammatik, hrsg. E. Wölfflin, vols. i.–vi. [quarterly] *ann.* 12/- 8° *Leipzig* 84–89 *in prog.*
Undertaken in view of an important new Latin lexicon to be pub. w. support of Bavarian Acad. of Sciences.

Glosses —*v. also* K § 219.

HILDEBRAND, G. F. [ed.] The Paris Glossary 54
LOEWE, Gustav Prodromus Corporis Glossariorum Latinorum [on sources and uses] 10/6 8° Teubner, *Leipzig* 76
* " " [ed.] Glossae Nominum, ed. G. Götz [Gloss. Amplon. 3, Erfurt; w. essays on glossography] 6/- 8° " " 84
* " + GÖTZ, G. eds.] Corpus Glossariorum Latinorum, vol. i. ; ii. 20/-; iii. ; iv. 20/- 8° " " 87–89
SWEET, H. [ed.] Facsimile of the Epinal Glossary [Gloss. Amplon. 1, Erfurt] 15/- 4° E. Eng. Txt. Soc. (Trübnr.) 83
WARREN, Minton [Am. ed.] The St. Gallen Glossary *Cambridge, Mass.* 85
For list of other earlier edited Glosses, *v.* Nettleship's *Contrib. to Latin Lexic.* *ut sup.*], pp. xvi.–xvii.

Dictionaries.

General.

Lexicons to special writers or subjects are classed under their names.

ANDREWS, Dr. E. A. [Am.] Latin Dictionary [Lat.-Eng.; based on Freund] 18/- 4° Low [54] 62
*FORCELLINI, Aeg. Totius Latinitatis Lexicon, ed. V. de Vit, 6 vols. [Latin-Latin] £8 8/- 4° *Prato* [1771] 58–79
* " " Idem, Pars altera: Onomasticon tot. Lat., ed. V. de Vit; pts. i.–xxxiii. ea. 2/6 4° " 59–88 *sqq.*
FREUND, W. Wörterbuch der lateinischen Sprache, 4 vols. 51/-; *red. to* 30/- 8° *Leipzig* 34–45
" " The same: French tr. by Theil, 3 vols. 70/- 4° *Paris* 35–65

K § 205

*GEORGES, K. E. Deutsch-Lat. & Lat.-Deutsch Handwörterb., 4 vols. 32/- ; Abridgd. 2 v. ea. 7/6 8° *Leipzig* [34] 80–82; 85
Based on SCHELLER, *ut infra*.

KEY, Thos. H. Latin-English Dictionary [posthumous] 31/6 4° Camb. Press 89
On the Crude-form system. Incomplete, omitting such words as to which the author thought he had no improvement to suggest. Chiefly valuable for its etymol. conjectures.

KLOTZ, R. Handwörterbuch d. lat. Sprache [good for examples] 18/- 8° *Brunswick* [53–57] 74
*LEWIS + SHORT, Dr. C. T./Dr. C. [Am.] Latin Dictionary [Latin-English] 25/- 4° Clar. Press [79] 81
Based on ANDREW'S edition of FREUND, *ut supra*.

„ (alone) Latin Dictionary for Schools 18/- s 4° „ 89
SCHELLER, J. J. G. Dictionary of the Latin Language, tr. J. E. Riddell 21/- f° Clar. Press 35
SMITH, Dr. Wm. Latin-English Dictionary, 16/- m 8° ; Abridged 7/6 sq 16° Murray [60] 88; [ ] 88
Based on FREUND; but omits the Proper Names, which ANDREWS (*ut supra*) gives.

„ „ + HALL, Prf. T. D. English-Latin Dictionary; 16/- m 8° ; Abridged 7/6 sq 12° Murray [70] 88 ; [ ] 88
WHITE + RIDDLE, J. T./J. E. Latin-English Dictionary, 2 vols. 42/- r 8° ; Abridged 7/6 p 8° Longman [38] 80 ; 65
English-Latin Dictionary 5/6 p 8° „ 70
WOELFFLIN, Prf. E (ed.) —*v. supra, s.n.* Archiv f. lat. Lexicogr.

Strictly Etymological Dictionaries.

BRÉAL + BAILLY, M + A. Dictionnaire Étymologique Latin 9/- 8° *Paris* [85] 86
INGRAM, Dr. J. K. Dictionary of Latin Etymology Murray *in prep.*
POSTGATE + VINCE, J. P./C. A. Dictionary of Latin Etymology Macmillan *in prep.*
VANICEK, Alois Etymologisches Wörterbuch der lateinischen Sprache 6/- 8° *Leipzig* [74] 81
Indo-European words in alphabetical order, with the Greek and Roman words derived from them. Suggestive; but to be used w. caution.

WHARTON, E. R. Etyma Latina 7/6 8° Rivington 90

Forms of Words.

*GEORGES, K. E. Lexikon der lateinischen Wortformen, pts. i.–iv. ea. 2/- [to occupy 5 or 6 pts.] r 8° *Leipzig* 89–90 *in prog.*
KOFFMAN, G. Lexicon lateinischer Wortformen 4/- 8° *Göttingen* 74

Mediæval Latin —*v.* K § 210.

Loan Words.

SAALFELD, G. A. Tensaurus Italograecus [Gk. loan and foreign words in Lat.] 20/- 8° *Vienna* 84
„ „ Index Graec. Vocab. in Ling. Lat. translatorum 3/- 8° *Berlin* 74–77
„ „ Lautgesetze d. griechischen Lehnwörter im Lateinischen 2/- 8° *Leipzig* 84
VANICEK, Alois Fremdwörter im Griechischen und Lateinischen 2/- 8° „ 78
WEISE, F. O. Die griechischen Wörter im Lateinischen 18/- r 8° „ 82

Names.

ELLENDT, F. De Cognomine et Agnomine Romano 1/6 8° *Königsberg* 53
FORCELLINI, Aeg. Onomasticon, ed. V. de Vit—*ut supra.*
HÜBNER, E. Quaestiones Onomatologicae Latinae *Bonn* 54
MOHR, W. Quaestiones Grammaticae ad Cognomina Romana pertinens 2/- 8° *Sondershausen* 77

Geographical.

GRAESSE, J. G. Th. Orbis Latinus [Latin names of modern towns] 4/6 8° *Dresden* 61
SAALFELD, G. A. Handbüchlein d. Eigennamen aus d. alt., mittl. u. mod. Geogr. [Germ.-Lat.] 4/- 8° *Leipzig* 85

Synonyms.

DÖDERLEIN, L. Lateinische Synonyme und Etymologien, 6 vols. 30/- 8° *Leipzig* 26–38
„ Handbuch der Lateinischen Synonymik 3/- 8° „ [40] 49
„ Handbook of Latin Synonyms, tr. Arnold 4/- c 8° Rivington 52
MEISSNER, C. Kurzgefasste lateinische Synonymik [school-bk.] 1/- 8° *Leipzig* [ ] 86
MENGE, H. Kurzgefasste lateinische Synonymik [school-bk.] 2/6 8° *Wolfenbüttel* [74] 78
SCHMALFELD, F. Lateinische Synonymik [school-bk.] 4/- 8° *Alterburg* [37] 69
SCHULTZ, Ferd. Lateinische Synonymik [school-bk.] 3/- 8° *Paderborn* [41] 79
SHUMWAY, Prf. E. S. [Am.] Handbook of Latin Synonyms [based on Meissner, *supra*] 60c. sq 16° *Boston* 8-
TEGGE, A. Studien zur lateinischen Synonymik, 10/- ; Lateinische Schulsynonymik 1/- 8° *Berlin* 86 ; 87

Miscellaneous Monographs.

ABBOTH, O. Die Umwandlungen der Themen im Lateinischen 2/- 8° *Göttingen* 75
BRÉAL, Michel Les Mots Latins
ERDENBERGER, G. E. De Vocalibus in altera compos. vocum lat. parte attenuatis 2/- 8° *Leipzig* 83
v. PAUCKER, C. Materialien zur lateinischen Wortbildungsgeschichte, pts. i.–vii. 9/6 8° *Berlin* 83–86
STOLZ, F. Die lateinische Nominalcomposition in formaler Hinsicht 2/6 8° *Innsbruck* 77
UNDOLPH, P. De Latinæ Linguæ Vocabulis compositis 2/- 8° *Breslau* 68

206. LATIN GRAMMAR: (*h*) STYLE.

HAACKE, A.	Lateinische Stilistik	4/-	8° *Berlin*	[ ] 75
HAND, F.	Lehrbuch des lateinischen Stils, hrsg. H. L. Schmitt	4/-	8° *Jena*	[33] 80
KLOTZ, Reinh.	Handbuch der lateinischen Stilistik, hrsg. Rich. Klotz [his son; posthum.]	5/-	8° *Leipzig*	74

Antibarbarus.

KREBS, J. Ph.	Antibarbarus, ed. J. H. Schmalz, 10 pts.	ea. 2/-	8° *Frankfort*	[37] 86-87

Metaphors.

NEUE, F.	—*in his* Formenlehre der lateinischen Sprache, 2 vols.	44/-	8° *Berlin*	[61-66] 75; 77

207. LATIN GRAMMAR: (*i*) PROSODY AND METRICS.

Generally —*v.* K § 172: Greek and Latin Metrology: Comparatively.

MÜLLER, Lucian	De Re Metrica Poetarum Latinorum [esp. Plautus and Terence]	8/-	8° Teubner, *Leipzig*	61
" "	Rei Metricae Poetarum Latinorum [" " " ; schl.-bk.]	2/-	8° *St. Petersburg*	78
" "	Orthographiae et Prosodiae Latinae Summarium	1/4 p	8° *Leipzig*	78
*NÄGELSBACH, C. F.	Lateinische Stilistik für Deutsche	12/-	8° *Nuremberg*	[46] 82

A thorough examination of the difference between Latin and German idiom; the noun, adjective, verb; metaphors, construction; dependent clauses, etc. A standard work.

RAMSAY, W.	Manual of Latin Prosody, 5/-; Elementary Manual of Latin Prosody	2/6 c	8° Griffin	[40] 70

Saturnian Verse.

BARTSCH, Karl	Der saturnische Vers und die altdeutsche Langzeile	2/-	8° *Leipzig*	67
*HAVET, L.	De Saturnio Latinorum Versu	12/6	8° *Paris*	80
KELLER, O.	Der saturnische Vers als rhythmisch erwiesen, 2 pts.	2/6	8° *Prague*	83; 86
KLOTZ, Richard	Grundzüge altrömischer Metrik	12/-	8° *Leipzig*	90
KORSCH, Th.	De Versu Saturnio	2/-	8° *Moscow*	68
*MÜLLER, Lucian	Der saturnische Vers und seine Denkmäler	4/-	8° *Leipzig*	85
PFAU, J. A.	De Numero Saturnio commentatio	2/-	8° *Quedlinburg*	[46-64] 64
RITSCHL, Fr.	Saturniae Poesis Reliquiae—*repr. in his* Opusc. Philolog., vol. iv.	26/-	8° *Leipzig*	[54] 78
THURNEYSEN, R.	Der Saturnier u. s. Verhältniss z. späteren röm. Volksverse	2/-	8° *Halle*	85

Metres of Plautus, Seneca, Terence—*v.* K § 215.

Latin Writers on Metrics—*v.* K § 219.

Gradus ad Parnassum.

CAREY, Dr. John	Gradus ad Parnassum [w. the English meanings]	7/- p	8° Stationers' Co.	[? 1-] 90
CONRAD, Julius	Gradus ad Parnassum sive Thesaurus Ling. Lat. prosodiacus	5/-	8° *Leipzig*	[29] 80
PESSONNEAUX, E.	Gradus ad Parnassum: dict. prosod. et poët. de la lang. lat.		8° *Paris*	[ ] 83
QUICHÉRAT, L.	Thesaurus Poeticus Linguae Latinae	10/6 r	8° "	[36] 82
SINTENIS+MÜLLER, C. H./O. M.	Gradus ad Parnassum, hrsg. G. A. Koch	5/-	8° *Leipzig*	[22] 79
de WAILLY, A.	Gradus ad Parnassum		8° *Paris*	[ ] 83
YONGE, Prf. C. D.	Gradus ad Parnassum	12/-	8° Longman	[50] 56

208. LATIN INSCRIPTIONS.

Bibliography and Introduction.

HÜBNER, E.	Grundriss zu Vorlesungen über d. röm. Epigraphie [w. bibliogr.]	*o.p.*	8° *Berlin*	77

Treatises, Manuals.

ARNOLD, W. T.	Handbook of Latin Epigraphy		Macmillan	*in prep.*
BORGHESI, B.	—*in his* Oeuvres Complètes, 9 vols. [3 vols. in epigraphy] 9 vols.	£9	4° *Paris*	62-84
CAGNAT, René	Cours élémentaire d'Epigraphie Latine	10/-	8° "	[86] 90
ZELL, C.	Handbuch der römischen Epigraphik, 3 pts.; 3 pl.	14/-	8° *Heidelberg*	74

Mechanical Copies.

HÜBNER, Dr. E.	Ueber mechanische Copieen von Inschriften	1/-	8° *Berlin*	87

Collections.

*Corpus Inscriptionum Latinarum — f° *Berlin* (Acad.) 62 *in prog.*

i.: Praes-Augustan. (TH. MOMMSEN) 48/- [63] *in prep.*
Priscae Latinitatis (F. RITSCHL) 90/- 62
ii.: Hispan. Latinae (E. HÜBNER) [illegible] 69
iii.: Asiae, Prov. Eur. Graec., Illyr. (MOMMSEN) [Suppl. I. 17/- 89] [illegible] 73
iv.: Pomp. Hercul. (K. ZANGEMEISTER) [illegible] 71
v.: Galliae Cisalp. (MOMMSEN), 2 vols. 10? - 72-77
vi.: Urbis Romae (W. HENZEN+J. de ROSSI), i. iii. 84/- 76-82; v. 94-75 [4 more parts *in prep.*]
vii.: Brit. (HÜBNER) 32/- 73
viii.: Afric. (G. WILMANNS), 2 vols. 96/- 81
ix.: Calabriae, Apuliae, Samnii, etc. (MOMMSEN) 90/- 83
x.: Bruttiorum, Sicil., Sardin., etc. (MOMMSEN), 2 vols. 124/- 83
xi.: Aemiliae, Umbriae, Etruriae (E. BORMANN), v. I. 60/- 88
xii.: Galliae Narbon. (O. HIRSCHFELD) 90/- 88
xiii.: Trium Galliarum et duarum German. (HIRSCHFELD+ZANGEMEISTER) *in prep.*
xiv.: Latii Antiqui (H. DESSAU) 64/- 87

Ephemeris Epigraphica: suppl. to above, vols. i.-vii.			r 8° *Berlin*	72-90 *in prog.*
Desiderata du Corp. Inscr. Latin., by E. Desjardins., 5 pts.; 16 pl.		60/-	f° *Paris*	74-75

K § 208

FABRETTI, A. — Corpus Inscript. Ital. et Glossarium Italicum, w. 3 suppl. and 4 pl. by J. F. Gamurrini — 130/– 4° *Turin* 67; 72–78; *Flor.* 80
From Umbrian, Sabine, Oscan, Volscian, Etruscan and other monuments. With 96 pl.
FINAZZI, G. [ed.] — Sylloge Inscrip. Lat. Aevi Rom. Rei publicae, 2 pts.; pl. [to Caesar] 12/– 8° *Turin* 77
GARRUCCI, R. [ed.] — Sylloge Inscriptionum Latinarum, 2 vols.; Addenda — ,, 77; 81
Down to Caesar. Chronological arrangement.
HÜBNER, E. [ed.] — Exempla Scripturae Epigraph. Latinae [Caesar to Justinian] 46/– f° *Berlin* 85
ORELLI, J. C. [ed.] — Inscriptionum Latinarum Select. Collectio, 2 v.; suppl. by G. Henzen, 1 v.; 3 v. 22/– 8° *Zürich* 28; 56
RITSCHL, Fried. [ed.] — Prisc. Lat. Monum.—*v.* Corp. Inscripp., v. i. *sup.* Five Suppl. *in his* Opusc. Philol. 26/– 8° *Leipzig* 78
WILMANNS, J. [ed.] — Exempla Inscriptionum Latinarum in usum Academicum, 2 vols. 30/– 8° *Berlin* 73
Down to late Empire. Arranged according to subjects. Copious indices.
ZVETAIEFF, J. [ed.] — Inscriptiones Italiae Mediae Dialecticae; w. f° Atlas 30/– 1 8° *Moscow* 84
,, ,, [ed.] — Inscriptiones Italiae Inferioris Dialecticae in usum acad. 8/– 8° *Leipzig* 86

Acta Fratrum.

HENZEN, W. [ed.] — Acta Fratrum Arvalium 12/– 8° *Berlin* 74
Edon, G. — Appendix on Fratr. Arval.—*in his* Traité de Lang. Latine 8/6 8° *Paris* 84

Early Roman Law.

BRUNS, C. G. [ed.] — Fontes Juris Romani Antiqui, ed. Th. Mommsen 8/6 8° *Freiburg* [60] 81
Legis XII. Tabularum Reliquiae, ed. R. Schoell [also in Bruns, *supra*] 3/6 8° *Berlin* 66

Monumentum Ancyranum.

MOMMSEN, Th. [ed.] — Res Gestae Divi Augusti 12/– 8° *Berlin* [65] 83

Euxine.

LATYSCHEW, B. [ed.] — Inscripp. Antiq. Orae Septentr. Ponti Eux. Graec. et Lat., vol. i. 20/– *St. Petersburg* 86
A supplement to the *Corpus Inscripp. Latin.* [*ut supra*] and the *Corpus Inscripp. Graec.* [*ut* K § 184]

France.

le BLANT, E. — Inscriptions Crétiennes de la Gaule, 2 vols. *Paris* 57; 65

Alpes Maritimes.

BLANK, E. — Epigraphie Antique der Départment des Alpes Maritimes, 2 vols. 8° *Nice* 80

Lyons.

de BOISSIEU, A. [ed.] — Inscriptions Antiques de Lyon d'après les monum. et l. auteurs 4° *Lyons* 46–54

Moselle.

ROBERT, Ch. [ed.] — Epigraphie Gallo-Romaine de la Moselle 4° *Paris* 69–73

Germany and Austria.

Baden.

RAPPENEGGER, Ph. W. [ed.] Die röm. Inschriften welche bisher in Baden aufgefunden wurden *Mannheim* 45

Rhine.

BRAMBACH, W. [ed.] — Corpus Inscriptionum Rhenanarum; w. pref. F. Ritschl 36/– 4° *Elberfeld* 67
STEINER, J. W. Ch. [ed.] Codex Inscriptionum Romanarum Rheni, 2 pts. *o.p.* *Darmstadt* 37
,, ,, ,, ,, ,, Danubii et Rheni, 5 pts. *o.p.* ,, 51–64

Vienna.

ALLMER + de TERREBASSE, A. A. [eds.] Inscriptions Antiques et du Moyen Âge de Vienne, 5 vols. and Atlas *Vienna* 75

Great Britain. —*for a fuller list, v.* G § 2 and F § 18.

BRUCE, J. C. — Lapidarium Septent.: descrip. of Roman monuments in N. of England f° 70–75
McCAUL, Rev. J. [ed.] — Britanno-Roman Inscriptions: w. critical notes 15/– 8° Longman 63
HÜBNER, E. [ed.] — Inscriptiones Britanniae Christianae; 2 maps [*v. also* Corp. Inscripp., vol. vii., *sup.*] 14/– 4° *Berlin* 76
Contains two supplements to his *Inscripp. Hispan. Christ.*, *ut infra*. The 7th vol. of *Ephem. Epigraph.* [*ut sup.*] conts. Mr. F. HAVERFIELD's coll. of Rom. inscripp. discovered in Britain since 1879, forming a suppl. to above.

Wales.

WESTWOOD, J. O. — Lapidarium Walliae; early inscribed and sculptured stones of Wales 80/– 4° Parker 80

Hungary.

ROMER, Fl. [ed.] — Inscriptiones Monumentorum Romanorum [= Acta Nova Mus. Nat. Hung.] *Pesth* 73

Italy.

GARRUCCI, R. [ed.] — Sylloge Inscripp. Lat. aevi romani usque ad Caesarem, 2 pts. and suppl. *Turin* 75; 77; 81

Naples.

MOMMSEN, Th. [ed.] — Inscriptiones Regni Neapolitani Latinae; 2 maps 75/–; *red. to* 42/– f° *Leipzig* 52

Rome —*v. also* A § 53: The Catacombs.

de ROSSI, J. B. [ed.] — Inscriptiones Christ. Urbis Romae vii. saec. Antiquiores, vol. i., pts. 1–2 ea. 63/– f° *Rome* 57; 87 *in prog.*

K § 209

Portugal.

JORDÃO, L. M. [ed.] Portugalliae Inscriptiones Romanae, vol. i. *Lisbon* 59

Spain.

HÜBNER, E. [ed.] Inscriptiones Hispaniae Christianae; map [*v. also* Corp. Inscrip., *sup.*] 9/- 4° *Berlin* 71

Switzerland.

HAGEN, H. [ed.] Prodromus Nov. Insc. Lat. Helv. Sylloges, tit. Aventic. et. vicin. 4/- 4° *Bern* 78
MOMMSEN, Th. [ed.] Inscriptiones Confoed. Helvet. Lat. [= Mitth. Ant. Ges., vol. x.] 16/6 4° *Zürich* 54

Africa —*v. also* Corp. Inscripp., vol. viii., *supra.*

Algeria.

RÉNIER, L. [ed.] Inscriptions Romaines de l'Algerie, vol. i. f° *Paris* 55-58

209. ANCIENT DIALECTS OF ITALY: ETRUSCAN, OSCAN, UMBRIAN; EARLY LATIN.

Collectively.

Dictionaries.

BÜCHELER, F. Lexicon Italicum [a list of words common to the dialects of Italy] 4° *Bonn* 81

Treatises, etc.

BUGGE, Sophus Altitalische Studien [Scientific Soc. of Christiania] 2/- 8° *Christiania* 78
CONWAY, R. S. The Italic Dialects, i.: Text of Inscripp. 8° Trübner *in prep.*
Oscan, Pelignian, Sabine, *etc.*; Oldest Latin and Faliscan; Volscian, Picentine and Umbrian.
CORSSEN, W. Beiträge zur italischen Sprachkunde 16/- r 8° *Leipzig* 76
FABRETTI, A. Le Antiche Lingue Italiche; osserv. pal. e gram. 5/6 4° *Turin* 74
Part of the *Corpus Inscripp. Ital.*, *ut* K § 210. Germ. tr. of same 9/- 8° *Leipzig* '77.
HUSCHKE, Ph. E. Zu den Altitalischen Dialecten 3/- 8° *Leipzig* 72
MOMMSEN, Th. Die unteritalischen Dialecte; 19 pl. [somewhat superseded] 28/- 4° " 50
PAULI, C. [ed.] Altitalische Studien, pts. i.–v. [esp. Etruscan; *v. also* Pauli, *infra*] i. 3/-; ii.–v. ea. 8/- 8° *Hanover* 83-87

Early Latin.

ALLEN, Prf. F. D. [Am.] Remnants of Early Latin [school-book] 80c. sq. 12° *Boston* 80
BELL, A. De Locativi in prisca Latinitate vi et usu 8° *Breslau* 90
BUCHHOLZ, H. Priscae Latinitatis Originum libri tres 10/- 8° *Berlin* 77
HOLTZE, F. W. Syntaxis Priscorum Scriptorum Latinorum, 2 vols. [to Terence] 13/6 8° *Leipzig* 61; 62
LÜBBERT, E. Beiträge zur Modus- und Tempuslehre des älteren Latein 7/- 8° *Breslau* 70
RITSCHL, Friedr. —*in his* Opuscula, *ut* K § 179; *and his edd.* of Fragm. Comic. *and* Fragm. Frag. [*ut* K § 215].
SCHNEIDER, E. [ed.] Dialectorum Italicarum aevi vetustioris exempla, pt. i. 4/- 8° *Leipzig* 86
" J. De Temporum apud Priscos Scriptores Latinos usu quaestt. selectae 1/- 8° *Breslau* 88
" E. [ed.] Dialectorum Italicarum aevi vetustioris exempla, vol. i., part i. 4/- 8° *Leipzig* 86
STUDEMUND, W. [ed.] Studia in Priscos Scriptores Latinos, vol. i. part i. 6/-; pt. ii. [posthum. ed. by pupils] 7/- 8° *Berl.* 73; 90
*WORDSWORTH, J. [ed.] Fragments and Specimens of Early Latin 18/- 8° Clar. Press 74

Ennius, Lucilius, Varro [*v.* K § 214]; *Accius, Livius Andron., Naevius, Plautus, Terence* [*v.* K § 215]; *Cato* [*v* K § 221].

Etruscan.

BUGGE, S. Beiträge zur Erforschung der etruskischen Sprache [= Etr. Forsch. iv. *ut inf.*] 12/- 8° *Stuttgart* 83
" " Etruskisch und Armenisch, pt. i. 3/- 8° " 90
CORSSEN, W. Ueber die Sprache der Etrusker, 2 vols.; 27 pl. 50/- r 8° *Leipzig* 74; 75
DEECKE, W. Corssen und die Sprache der Etrusker 1/6 8° *Strassburg* 75
" " Die etruskischen Bilinguen 6/- 8° " 83
" " Etruskische Forschungen, 4 pts. 31/- 8° *Stuttgart* 75-80
" +PAULI, W. Etruskische Forschungen und Studien, pts. i.–vi. [contin. of above] 40/- 8° " 81-84
DEECKE, who writes in antagonism to CORSSEN, holds Etruscan to be an Aryan lang.; PAULI takes the opposite view.
ELLIS, Dr. Robert Sources of Etruscan and Basque Languages 7/6 8° Trübner 86
Claims Etruscan as in main a Thraho-Armen. lang. w. Basque or Iber. and Afric. elements. Latter pt. of bk. is attempt to connect Basque w. Caucas. lang.
LINDSAY, A. W. C. [= E. of CRAWFORD] Etruscan Inscriptions Analyzed 12/- 8° Longman 72
MEYER, G. Die etrusk. Sprachfrage—*in his* Essays und Studien [*ut* K § 94].
MÜLLER, K. O. Die Etrusker, ed. W. Deecke, 2 vols. 32/- 8° *Stuttgart* [29] 77
PAULI, C. Etruskische Studien, 3 pts. [*v. also* Pauli, *supra*] 10/- 8° *Giessen* 79-80
" " Altitalische Forschungen, pt. i.: Inschriften nordetrusk. Alphabets; 7 pl. 9/- 8° *Leipzig* 85
POGGIO, V. Contribuzioni allo Studio della Epigraphia Etrusca *Genoa* 78
SCHMIDT, M. De Rebus Etruscis 2/- 4° *Jena* 77
STICKEL, J. G. Das Etruskische durch Erklär. v. Inschr. u. Namen [Semitic theory] 13/- r 8° *Leipzig* 58
TAYLOR, Rev. Isaac Etruscan Researches 14/- 8° Macmillan 74
Believes that Etruscan is a member of the Altaic (" Ugric ") family.

Messapian.

MAGGIULLI + CASTROMEDIANO Le Inscrizioni Messapiche raccolte 71

Oscan —*v. also* Umbrian, *s.v.* Lepsius, *infra.*

Bruppacher, H. Versuch einer Lautlehre der oskischen Sprache 1/6 8° *Zürich* 69
Enderis, E. Versuch einer Formenlehre der oskischen Sprache 3/- 8° „ 71
Grotefend, G. F. Rudimenta Linguae Oscae 3/- 4° *Hanover* 39
Huschke, Ph. E. Die Oskischen und Sabellischen Sprachdenkmale [explan., gram., gloss.] 9/- 8° *Elberfeld* 56
Mommsen, Th. Oskische Studien 2 pts., 4/6 8° *Berlin* 45-46
Zvetaieff, J. [ed.] Sylloge Inscriptionum Oscarum; w. f° atlas 40/- r 8° *St. Petersburg* 78

Umbrian.

Aufrecht + Kirchhoff, $\frac{Th}{A}$ [eds.] Die umbrischen Sprachdenkmäler, 2 vols.; 10 pl. 30/- 4° *Leipzig* 49; 51
Bücheler, F. Umbrica 6/- 8° *Bonn* 83
Grotefend, G. F. Rudimenta Linguae Umbricae, 8 pts. 10/- 4° *Hanover* 35-39
Jordan, H. Quaestiones Umbricae: cum appendicula praetermissorum 2/- 4° *Königsberg* 82
Lepsius, R. [ed.] Inscriptiones Umbricae et Oscae 30/- 4° *Leipzig* 41

Eugubine Tables.

Bréal, Michel [ed.] Les Tables Eugubines, w. French tr. and comm.; 13 photograph. pl. 25/- 8° *Paris* 75
Bücheler, F. Populi Iguvini Lustratio, 2/-; Interpretatio Tab. Iguv., 3 pts. 4° *Bonn* 76; 78-80
Huschke, Ph. E. [ed.] Die iguvischen Tafeln [w. other Umbr. inscripp. and gram. and gloss.] 15/- 8° *Leipzig* 59

Volscian.

Corssen, W. De Volscorum Lingua 1/6 4 *Naumburg* 58

210. POST-CLASSICAL AND VULGAR LATIN.

Berblinger, W. De Lingua Romana Rustica 2/- 8° *Glückstadt* 65
Böhmer, P. Die lateinische Vulgärsprache, 2 pts. ea. 1/- 4° *Oels* 66; 69
*Budinsky, A. Die Ausbreitung d. latein. Sprache über Italien u. d. Provinzen 6/- 8° *Berlin* 81
Rebling, O. Versuch einer Charakteristik der römischen Umgangssprache [sch.-progr.; good] 2/- 8° *Kiel* [73] 83
Sittl, K. Die lokalen Verschiedenheiten d. lat. Sprache [esp. African Latin] 3/- 8° *Erlangen* 82
Wölfflin, E. Bemerkungen über das Vulgärlatein—*in Philologus*, vol. xxxiv. [1876]
„ „ Ueber d. Latinität d. Cassius Felix—*in Abhandl. d. Bayer. Akad.* 1880, pt. iv.

Phonology.

*Schuchardt, Prf. H. Der Vokalismus des Vulgärlateins, 3 vols. 27/6 8° *Leipzig* 66-68
Shows the passage of Classical Latin into the Romance languages.

Sermo Plebeius of Petronius—*v.* K § 214.

Vulgate [Old-Lat. version of Scriptures].

Kaulen, F. Geschichte der Vulgata, 7/-; Handbuch der Vulgata 3/- 8° *Mayence* 69; 70
Rönsch, H. Itala und Vulgata 8/- 8° *Marburg* 69
The idioms of the primit. Xtn. *Itala* and the Catholic Vulgata, w. refer. to Roman popular speech.

Mediaeval Latin.

Boucherie, A. Mélanges Latins et Bas-latins 8° *Montpellier* 75

Dictionaries.

Diefenbach, L. Glossarium Latino-Germanicum [pub. as Suppl. to Ducange] 36/- 8° *Frankfort* 57
„ „ Novum Glossarium Lat.-German. mediae et infimae Latinitatis 12/- 8° „ 67
*Du Cange, C. D. Glossarium mediae et infimae Latinitatis, ed. G. A. L. Henschel, 10 vols. £12 4° *Niort* [1678] 82-88
Also his *Nov. Gloss. Lat.-Germ. med. et infim. aetatis*, 10/- 8° '67. Du Cange has been abridged by Maigne d'Arnis, *sub tit. Lexicon Manuale ad Script. Med. et Infim. Latinitatis*, 15/- r 8° *Paris* '66.
„ „ The same: Anastatic reprint, pt. i. 10/- 4° *Breslau* [1678] 90 *in prog.*

Relation of Latin to the Romance Languages.

Beger, F. A. Lateinisch und Romanisch, [posthum.] hrsg. J. H. Beger [especially French] 1/6 8° *Berlin* 63
Eyssenhardt, F. Römisch und Romanisch: Beitrag zur Sprachgeschichte 4/- 8° „ 82
Fuchs, A. Die romanischen Sprachen in ihrem Verhältniss zum Lateinischen [w. map] 8/- r 8° *Halle* 49
Cf. H. Steinthal: *Verh. d. Roman. zum Latein in d. Bedeutungen d. Wörter* in Herrig's *Archiv* [*ut* K § 196] vol. xxxvi., pp. 109-142.
Gröber, G. Vulgär-lateinische Substrate romanischer Worte—*in* Archiv f. lat. Lexicogr., pt. ii., *sqq.* [*ut* K § 205]
An important contribution, with a long list of new derivations of Romance words from Vulgar Latin.
Steinthal, H. Verhältniss der romanischen Sprache zum Latein *o.p.* 8° *Leipzig* 64
Thomsen, V. Lateinisch und Romanisch—*in his* Opuscula Philologica ad Madvigium 8° *Copenhagen* 76

Declension.

d'Arbois de Jubainville, La Déclinaison Latine en Gaule à l'époque Mérovingienne 8° *Paris* 72
Scheler, A. Exposé des Lois qui régissent la Transform. franç. d. Mots Latins 8° *Brussels* 75
Wölfflin, E. Lateinische und romanische Comparation 2/- 8° *Erlangen* 79

Etymology.

Darmesteter, A. Formation des Mots composés dans l. lang. Française *Paris* 74
Compared with other Romance Languages and especially Latin.

Neuter.

Meyer, Wilhelm Die Schicksale d. lateinischen Neutrums im Romanischen 4/- 8° *Halle* 83

Syntax.

Clairin, P. Du génetif latin et de la préposition *de* 6/6 8° *Paris*

211. HISTORY OF LATIN LITERATURE: (a) GENERALLY.

Bibliography.

HÜBNER, E. — Grundriss zu Vorlesungen über d. röm. Literaturgeschichte — 8/- 8° *Berlin* [69] 78

MAYOR, Prf. J. E. B. — Bibliographic Clue to Latin Literature [based on HÜBNER] 10/6 c 8° Macmillan 75

TEUFFEL, Prf. W. S. — *—in his* History of Roman Literature, *ut infra.*

General History.

ALBERT, P. — Histoire de la Littérature Romaine, 2 vols. — 6/- 2 8° *Paris* [71] 85

*BÄHR, J. C. F. — Geschichte der römischen Literatur, 3 vols. — 24/- 8° *Leipzig* [28-32] 68-70

Vol. iv. [Supplement] conts. pt. i.: Christl.-röm. Dichter u. Geschichtschreiber, 4/6 ['36] '72; pt. ii.: Christl.-röm. Theologie, 7/6 '37.

*BERNHARDY, G. — Grundriss der römischen Literatur — 13/6 8° *Halle* [30] 74

BROWNE, R. W. — History of Roman Classical Literature — 9/- 8° Bentley [53] 84

CRUTTWELL, C. T. — History of Roman Literature [to time of Antonines; popular] 8/6 c 8° Griffin [77] 88

Cruttwell, + Banton, C. T. P. [eds.] Specimens of Roman Literature [„ „] 10/6 c 8° „ [79] 81

Also in 2 pts: i.: Roman Thought, 4/-; ii.: Roman Style, 5/-; Key to pt. ii, § a, 2/6.

*MUNK, Ed. — Geschichte der römischen Literatur, ed. O. Seyffert, 2 v. [scholarly & pop.] 10/- 8° *Berlin* [58-61] 75-77

Fausset, W. Y. [tr.] — The Student's Cicero; port. [tr. of part of Munk's *Geschichte*] 3/6 c 8° Sonnenschein 90

NICOLAI, R. — Geschichte der römischen Literatur — 12/- 8° *Magdeburg* 79-81

PIERRON, Alois — Histoire de la Littérature Romaine — 3/6 12° *Paris* [ ] 81

SCHANZ, Prf. M. — Geschichte der römischen Literatur, pt. i. [Müller's *Hdb. Klass. Alterth.*] 5/6 r 8° *Nördlingen* 90

SIMCOX, G. A. — History of Latin Literature, 2 vols. [Ennius to Boethius] 32/- 8° Longman 83

*TEUFFEL, Prf. W. S. — History of Roman Literature, tr. Dr. W. Wagner, 2 vols. — 21/- 8° Bell 73

A fifth edn. of the original [1870], ed. L. SCHWABE, was pub. pt. i. 7/6 8° *Leipzig* '90. New edn. of Eng. tr., ed. by Prf. WARR, *in prep.*

WILKINS, Prf. A. S. — Roman Literature [Macmillan's Primer Series; elementary] 1/- 18° Macmillan 90

Early Christian Literature—*for* Patristics, *v.* A § 55: Patristics.

BAEHR, J. C. F. — *—ut supra*, vol. iv.

CRUTTWELL, Rev. C. T. — History of Early Christian Literature — Griffin *in prep.*

*EBERT, A. — Geschichte der christlich-lateinischen Literatur, 2 vols. — 21/- 8° *Leipzig* 74-80

Vol. i. to Charlemagne 12/-, '74; vol. ii. to Chas. the Bald, 9/- '80 [=vol. i.-ii. of his *Litteratur d. Mittelalters*]; French tr. of latter by AYMERIC+CONDAMIN, 2 vols. 15/- 8° *Paris* '83-'84.

KRUMBACHER, K. — Abriss d. Byzant. Litteraturgesch. [Müller's *Hdb. Klass. Alterth.* vol. ix., pt. 2] 5/6 r 8° *Nördlingen* 90

TEUFFEL, Prf. W. S. — *—ut supra.*

Mediaeval Latin Literature.

TRAUBE, Dr. — Abriss d. Gesch. d. lat. Lit. im. M.-A. [Müller's *Hdb. Kl. Alt.*, vol. ix., pt. 3] 5/6 r 8° *Nördlingen* 90

Series.

Ancient Classics for English Readers, ed. Rev. W. L. Collins—*each volume entered separately, infra, v.* §§ 214-224, *passim.*

Classical Writers, ed. J. R. Green [brief accounts] ea. 1/6 f 8° Macmillan 79 *sqq.*

Latin vols.: Livy (Rev. W. W. CAPES); Tacitus (Prf. A. J. CHURCH+W. J. BRODRIBB); Vergil (Prf. H. NETTLESHIP).

Collective Essays, etc.

BURN, Rev. Rob. — Roman Literature in relation to Roman Art; ill. — 14/- 8° Macmillan 88

An attempt to show the similarity 'tween Rom. liter. and art by pointing out the national traits fr. wh. both sprang.

CONINGTON, Prf J. — Miscellaneous Writings, 2 vols. — 30/- 8° Longman 70

NETTLESHIP, Prf. H. — Lectures on Subjects connected w. Latin Literature and Scholarship — 7/6 c 8° Clar. Press 85

Book-writing, Book-selling, etc.

ARBENZ, E. — Die Schriftsteller in Rom zur Zeit der Kaiser [a lecture] 1/- 8° *Basle* 77

*BIRT, Theodor — Das antike Buchwesen in s. Verhältniss zur Literatur — 12/- 8° *Berlin* 82

With contributions to the textual criticism of Theocritus, Catullus, Propertius, etc.

HAENNY, L. — Schriftsteller und Buchhändler im alten Rom — 2/6 r 8° *Leipzig* [84] 85

RITTER, G. — Das litterarische Leben in alten Rom — 2/- 8° *Prague* 78

212. HISTORY OF LATIN LITERATURE: (b) SPECIAL DEPARTMENTS: (a) POETRY AND DRAMA.

POETRY.

Critical Essays, etc.

CORSSEN, W. — Origines Poesis Romanae — 3/6 8° *Berlin* 46

MARTHA, Const. — Les Moralistes sous l'Empire Romaine [philosophers and poets] 3/- 12° *Paris* [64] 66

NISARD, D. — Études de Moeurs et de Critique sur les Poètes Latins de la Décadence, 2 v. 6/- 12° „ [34] 78

PATIN, H. S. G. — Études sur la Poésie latine, 2 vols. — 6/- 12° „ [69] 75

RIBBECK, O. — Geschichte der römischen Dichtung, vol. i. 7/-; vol. ii. — 10/- 8° *Vienna* 87; 89

*SELLAR, Prf. W. Y. — The Roman Poets of the Republic — 10/- 8° Clar. Press [63] 89

* „ „ — The Roman Poets of the Augustan Age: Virgil — 9/- c 8° „ [77] 83

„ „ — Horace and the Elegiac Poets — „ *in prep.*

ZINGERLE, A. — Zu den späteren lateinischen Dichtern, pts. 1-2 — 5/6 8° *Innsbruck* 73; 78

Didactic Poetry. Fables, etc.

HAGEN, H. — Antike und Mittelalterliche Räthselpoesie — 1/- 8° *Berne* [69] 77
HERVIEUX, L. — Les Fabulistes Latins, 2 vols. [Augustus to end of Mid. Ages] 8° *Paris* 84
KNOBLOCH, R. — Das römische Lehrgedicht bis zum Ende der Republik — 2/- 4° *Halle* 81

Bucolic Poetry.

HUNGER, C. — De Poesi Romanorum Bucolica — 1/6 8° *Halle* 41

Epic Poetry.

BRIZZI, Domin. — De Diversis Rationibus ac Viis quas Latini epicorum poematum Scriptores iniverunt — 42/- 8° *Batavia* 78
KÖNE, J. R. — Ueber die Sprache der römischen Epiker [w. chap. on metrics] 4/- 8° *Münster* 40
KUNZ, F. — Die älteste römische Epik [in relation to Homer] 1/6 8° *Leipzig* 90
SOUPÉ, Philibert — Étude sur le Charactère National et Relig. de l'Epopée Latine — 2/6 8° *Paris* 53

Lyrical Poetry.

Elegiac Poetry.

GRUPPE, O. F. — Die römische Elegie, 2 vols. — 8/- and 4/6 8° *Leipzig* 38 ; 39
i.: Conts. general critical researches; ii.: deals with Tibullus, Propertius, and Ovid's *Amores*.

Erotic Poetry.

PALDAMUS, H. — Die römische Erotik — 1/6 8° *Greifswald* 33

Popular Songs.

DU MÉRIL, E. — Poésies Populaires Latin. Antérieures au 12° siècle — 7/- 8° *Paris* 43
" " — Poésies Populaires Latin. au Moyen Âge — 7/- 8° " 47

Satirical Poets.

BENECKE, — Études sur les Classiques Lat., ser. i.: Les Satiriques — 3/6 8° *Paris* 53
GRUBEL, B. — De Satirae Romanae origine et progressu — 2/- 4° *Posen* 83
LINGUITI, A. — De Satirae Romanae ratione et natura — 1/6 8° *Salerno* 75
MACEWEN, A. R. — Origin and Growth of the Roman Satiric Poetry — *Oxford* 77
METTE, B. — De Satira Romana et Satira Graecorum Poesi — 4° *Brilon* 68
NETTLESHIP, Prf. H. — The Roman Satura: its orig. form in conn. w. its develop. — *Oxford* 78
ROTH, C. L. — Zur Theorie und innern Geschichte der römischen Satire — 1/- r 8° *Stuttgart* [43-44] 48
SCHNITZLER, J. P. J. — De Satirae Romanae Novae natura et forma [diss. inaug.] 1/6 8° *Rostock* 70
SCHULTZ, Julius — De Prosodia Satiricorum Romanorum capita duo [diss. inaug.] 1/- 8° *Regimonti* 64

Saturnian Verse — *v.* K § 207: Latin Metrics.

DRAMATIC LITERATURE.

Generally.

GRYSAR, — Der römische Mimus [repr. fr. *Sitzgsber. d. Wien. Akad.*] 2/- r 8° *Vienna* 54
KLEIN, J. L. — Geschichte des Dramas d. Griechen u. Römer—vol. ii. pt. 2 conts. Roman 12/- 8° *Leipzig* 65
MEYER, Maurice — Études sur le Théâtre Latin — 5/- 8° *Paris* 47
v. SCHLEGEL, A. W. — *in his* Lectures on Dramatic Art & Literature [tr.] [1st ed. of orig. '09-'11] 3/6 c 8° Bohn's Lib. 46

Tragedy.

RIBBECK, O. — Die römische Tragödie im Zeitalter d. Republik — 18/- 8° *Leipzig* 75
SCHURÉ, E. — *in his* Le Drame Musicale, 2 vols. — 8° *Paris* 75

Comedy.

DU MÉRIL, E. — Histoire de la Comédie Ancienne, 2 vols. — ea. 7/- 8° *Paris* 64 ; 69
RIBBECK, O. — *v.* K § 188: Greek Drama, *s.v.* Comedy.
SPENGEL, A. — Ueber die lateinische Komödie [Festrede d. bayer. Akad.] 1/- 4° *Munich* 78

Atellan Farces.

MEYER, Maurice — Des Atellanes — 8° *Dijon* 42
MUNK, Ed. — De Fabulis Atellanis — 3/- 8° *Leipzig* 40

Stage — *v. also* K § 188: Greek Drama, *s.v.* Stage.

MOULTON, R. G. — The Ancient Classical Drama: study in literary evolution — 8/6 c 8° Clar. Press 90
OEHMICHEN, G. — Bühnenwesen d. Griechen u. Römer [Iwan Müller's *Hdb. Klass. Alterth.*, v. xiv.] 6/6 8° *Nördlingen* 90

213. HISTORY OF LATIN LITERATURE: (c) SPECIAL DEPARTMENTS: (β) PROSE.

Agricultural Writers.

BEHEIM-SCHWARZBACH, H. — Beitrag zur Kenntniss des Ackerbaues der Römer — 2/6 8° *Cassel* 66
DAUBENY, Charles — Lectures on Roman Husbandry *o.p.* [*pb.* 12/-; *w.* 7/6] 8° Parker 57
DEBAINS, A. — Aperçu Hist. sur l'Agricult. en Italie sous la domin. Romaine — 8° *Versailles* 62
MAGERSTEDT, A. F. — Bilder aus der römischen Landwirthschaft, 6 pts. — 27/- r 8° *Sondershausen* 58-63
i.: Viticulture, 4/6 '58; ii.-iii.: Cattle, 8/6 '59-'60; iv.: Fruit-culture, 4/- '62; v.: Grain and Flower-culture, 8/- '62; vi.: Bees, 4/- '63.

K § 214

Oemler, Paul — Antike Landwirthschaft — 1/6 r 8° *Hamburg* 72

Walmer, W. — Die Obstlehre der Griechen und Römer — 4/6 r 8° *Reutlingen* 45

Theophrastus, Cato, Varro, Palladius, Columella.

Surveying: Writers on.

Cantor, Moritz — Die römischen Agrimensoren, 5 pl. [histor.-mathem. investigation] 6/- 8° *Leipzig* 75

Steuber, E. — Die römischen Grundsteuervermessungen [fr. text of *Gromat. Codex*] 4/- r 8° *Münich* 77

Grammarians, etc.

Keil, H. — Quaestiones Grammaticae [on the Latin grammarians, etc.] 8° *Leipzig* 60

Steinthal, H. — Geschichte der Sprachphilosophie bei den Griechen und Römern, 2 vols. 11/6 8° *Berlin* 63

With special reference to logic.

Historians.

de Beaufort, Louis — Diss. sur l'Incertitude des cinq premiers Siècles de l'Hist. Rom. 6/- 8° *Paris* [*Utrecht* 1738] 66

de Closset, Leon — Essai sur l'Historiographie des Romains [to Augustus] 8° *Brussels* 50

Gerlach, F. D. — Die Geschichtschreiber der Römer bis auf Orosius 2/- 16° *Stuttgart* 55

Lewis, Sir G. C. — Enquiry into the Credibility of Early Roman History, 2 vols. [*v.* F § 12] *o.p.* [*pb.* 30/-; *w.* 50/-] 8° Parker 55

Nisard, D. — Les quatre grands Historiens Latins [Cæsar, Sallust, Livy, Tacitus] 3/- 12° *Paris* 74

Nitzsch, K. W. — Die römische Annalistik bis auf Valerius Antias 6/- 8° *Berlin* 73

Peter, C. — Zur Kritik d. Quellen der älteren römischen Geschichte *Halle* 79

" H. — Die Quellen Plutarch's in den Biographien der Römer " 65

Schmitz, M. — Quellenkunde d. römischen Geschichte bis auf Paulus Diaconus *Gütersloh* 81

Schröder, W. — De Primordiis Artis Historici apud Graecos et Romanos 2/6 8° *Jena* 68

Ulrici, H. — Charakteristik der alten Historiographie 5/6 8° *Berlin* 33

Augustan Historians.

Dirksen, H. E. — De Scriptt. Historiae Augustae [textual criticism] 4/6 8° *Leipzig* 42

Paucker, C. — De Latinitate Scriptorum Historiae Augustae melemata 4/- 8° *Dorpat* 70

Peter, H. — Historia Critica Scriptorum Historiae Augustae [philological] 1/6 4° *Leipzig* 60

" " — Exercitationes Criticae in Scriptores Historiae Augustae 1/- 4° *Posen* 63

Plew, J. — Marius Maximus als Quelle d. Scriptores Hist. August. 2/- 4° *Strassburg* 78

Panegyrists.

Baehrens, Aem. [ed.] — Panegyrici xii. Latini 4/- p 8° Teubner, *Leipzig* 74

Philosophers —*v.* O §§ 2-3, 11, 12, 14.

Rhetorical Literature.

Berger, A. — Histoire de l'Eloquence Latine [posth.], ed. V. Cucheval, 2 v. [to Cicero] 6/- 12° *Paris* [72] 81

Demarteau, J. — L'Eloquence Republicaine de Rome d'après les Fragments authentiques 4/6 8° *Mons* 70

Volkmann, R. — Die Rhetorik d. Griechen u. Römer in systemat. Uebersicht 10/- 8° *Leipzig* [72] 74

Science —*v.* K § 189.

214. LATIN POETS.

Collections.

Generally.

Walker, W. S. [ed.] — Corpus Poetarum Latinorum 18/- r 8° Bell [48] 81

Anthologies.

Thackeray, F. St. J. [ed.] — Anthologia Latina [poetry; w. brief English notes] 6/6 c 8° Bell [65] 69

Wilkins, H. M. [ed.] — Progressive Latin Anthology [school-book] 4/6 12° Longman 64

Mediaeval Poetry.

Corpus Script. Eccles. Latin., vol. xvi.: Poetae Christiani Minores, pt. i. *Vienna* (Acad.) 88

The vol. includes Robinson Ellis' edition of Orientius.

Du Meril, E. — Poésies Populaires Latines antérieures au 12° siècle *Paris* 45

" " — " " " du Moyen Âge " 47

" " — " inédites du Moyen Âge " 54

Dümmler, E. [ed.] — Poetae Latini Aevi Carolini, vol. i. 17/- l 4° *Berlin* 81

Hagen, H. [ed.] — Carmina Medii Aevi max. part. inedita [fr. MSS. in Swiss libs.] 4/- 8° *Berne* 77

Minor Poets.

Baehrens, Aem. [ed.] — Poetae Latini Minores, 5 vols. [also separately] 19/- p 8° Teubner, *Lpz.* 79-83

Pinder, North [ed.] — Selections from the less known Latin Poets 15/- 8° Clar. Press 69

Lyrical Poetry.

Eclogues.

BRANDT, S. [ed.] Eclogae Poetarum Latinorum 1/4 p 8° Teubner, *Leipsig*

Elegiac Poets.

VOLZ, B. [ed.] Die römische Elegie [sel. fr. the elegiac poets, w. German notes] 2/- p 8° Teubner, *Lps.* [71] 76

Hymns: Christian —*v.* A § 115: Hymnology, *s.v.* Collections: Latin.

Satirical Poets.

DESPOIS, E. [tr.] Satiriques Latins: trad. [Juvenal, Persius, Lucilius, Turnus, Sulpicia] 3/- 12° *Paris* [64] 73

Avianus [= Flavius] [elegiac version of 42 Aes. fables]

Fabulae, rec. Karl Lachmann 6*d.* 8° *Berlin* 45
*ed. Prf. Rob. Ellis [w. proleg., crit. app., comm., etc.] 8/6 8° Clar. Press 87

AIDS:
Jacobs, Joseph —*in his* Fables of Aesop, *etc.*, 2 vols. [Bibl. de Carabas] 20/- s 8° Nutt 90
Müller, Lucian De Phaedri et Aviani Fabulis libellus 1/- 8° Teubner, *Leipsig* 75
Unrein, O. De Aviani Aetate 2/- 8° *Jena* 85

Catullus, Tibullus, and Propertius.

TEXT: rec. M. Haupt, cur. J. Vahlen 2/6 16° *Leipsig* [3rd ed., 68] 85
,, Lucian Müller 3/- p 8° Teubner, *Lps.* [70] 74
Contains also the fragments of Laevius, Calvus, Cinna, and other poets.
,, J. P. Postgate c 8° Bell 90

ANNOTATED TEXT:
Selections: with English notes H. A. Wratislaw + F. N. Sutton [Gram. Sch. Classics] 3/6 f 8° Bell 69
,, German ,, K. P. Schulze 2/6 p 8° Weidmann, *Berlin* 79

AID.
Davies, Rev. J. Catullus, Tibullus, and Propertius [pop. biogr. and acc. of wks.; Anc. Class. f. E. Rrs.] 2/6 12° Blackwood 76

Catullus.

TEXT: rec. Aem. Baehrens: ed. crit., 2 vols. vol. i. 4/-; ii. [= Comment.] 12/6 8° Teubner, *Lps.* 76; 85
,, Lucian Müller 8*d.* p 8° ,, ,, [77] 83
,, Ludwig Schwabe 1/6 p 8° Weidmann, *Berlin* 86
Selections: Carmina Selecta, rec. Prf. Robinson Ellis 3/6 f 8° Clar. Press [66] 72

ANNOTATED TEXT: with English notes and intro. Dr. J. P. Postgate 3/- f 8° Bell 89
* ,, crit. app. and proleg. Prf. Robinson Ellis: ed. crit.; 2 pl. [*v. also inf.*] 16/- 8° Clar. Press [67] 78
,, German ,, A. Riese 4/- 8° Teubner, *Leipsig* 84
,, French ,, E. Benoist, and French tr. E. Rostand, 2 vols. 17/- 8° *Paris* 82; 90
Selections: with English notes F. P. Simpson [Classical Series] 5/- f 8° Macmillan [79] 80
,, ,, ,, Prf. H. A. Strong 5/- c 8° *Melbourne* 79

TRANSLATIONS:
Works: tr. Prf. Robinson Ellis [in orig. metres] 5/- 16° Murray 71
,, Dr. J. Cranstoun, with notes [verse] 7/6 c 8° Nimmo 67
* ,, [Sir] Theodore Martin, with intro. and notes [verse] 7/6 c 8° Blackwood [61] 76
,, T. Hart Davies [verse] 6/- c 8° Paul 79
übers. Rud. Westphal 2/6 8° *Leipsig* 84
trad. E. Rostand [verse]—*v.* Annot. Texts, *supra.*

AIDS.
Baehrens, Aem. Analecta Catulliana 2/- 8° *Jena* 74
Couat, A. Étude sur Catulle [a thesis] 4/6 8° *Paris* 74
*Ellis, Prf. Robinson Commentary on Catullus 18/- 8° Clar. Press [76] 89
Hupe, C. De Genere Dicendi C. Valerii Catulli Veronensis 2/- 8° *Münster* 71
*Munro, H. A. J. Criticisms and Elucidations of Catullus 7/6 8° Deighton, *Cambridge* 78
Overholthaus, G. Syntaxis Catullianae capita duo [dissert. inaug.] 1/- 8° *Papenburg* 75
Peiper, R. Catullus: Beiträge zur Kritik seiner Gedichte 2/- 8° *Breslau* 75
Ribbeck, O. C. Valerius Catullus: literar.-histor. Skizze [a lecture] 1/6 8° *Kiel* 63
Richter, R. Catulliana 1/6 4° *Leipsig* 80
Weber, H. Quaestiones Catullianae 4/- 8° *Gotha* 90

Ennius.

TEXT: rec. J. Vahlen *o.p.* [*pb.* 6/-; *w.* 21/-] 8° *Leipsig* 54
Carmina Reliq., rec. Lucian Müller 8/- 8° *St. Petersburg* 84

AIDS.
*Müller, Lucian Ennius: Einleitung in d. Studium d. lateinischen Poesie 8/- 8° *Petersburg* 83
Roeper, G. De Q. Ennii Scipione 1/6 4° *Danzig* 68
Vahlen, J. Ueber die Annalen des Ennius 2/- 4° *Berlin* 86

Horace.

TEXTS: rec. M. Haupt, cur. J. Vahlen 3/- 16° *Leipsig* [ ] 81
,, O. Keller + A. Holder, 2 vols. 21/-; Ed. Minor 4/- 8° ,, 64–70; 78
,, Rev. A. J. Macleane [Camb. Texts] 2/6 16° Bell
,, Lucian Müller 1/4; Ed. Minor, 1/- p 8° Teubner, *Lps.* [69] 79; 85
,, R. W. King; w. ill. fr. antique gems and intro. by H. A. J. Munro 21/- 8° Bell 69
,, G. Stallbaum 3/- 8°; 1/4 c 8°; 1/- 24° Tauchnitz, *Leipsig* 54
,, C. Schenkel 2/6 p 8° Weidmann, *Berlin*

K § 214

Éditions de Luxe.

CORNISH, F. A. [ed.] Q. Horati Flacci Opera; w. front. by Alma Tadema [Parchment Lib.] 6/- f 8° Paul 78
ECKSTEIN, F. A. [ed.] Q. Horati Flacci Carmina 12/- 8° *Bielefeld* 76
MÜLLER, Lucian [ed.] Q. Horati Flacci Carmina [a miniature edn.] 2/6 16° Teubner, *Leipzig* 74

ANNOTATED TEXTS: with English notes Prf. J. B. Greenough [Am.] $1.35 12° *Boston* 8-
" " " A. J. Macleane, ed. G. Long (Bibl. Class.) 18/-; *red. to* 8/- 8° Bell [53–60] 69
" " " " " [Gram. Sch. Classics] 6/6 f 8° " [ ] 79
Also separately, Odes, 3/6; Satires, 3/6. The above two and YONGE'S edn. *infra*, are now rather antiquated.
" " " F. W. Cornish, 2 pts. (Odes, Epodes, Carmen, Saec.) 6/- c 8° Murray 88
" " " Prf. J. E. Yonge, 21/- 8°; School Edition 4/6 c 8° Longman 67; 68
* " Latin " J. G. Orelli, vol. i. cur. W. Hirschfelder; ii. cur. W. Mewes ea. 20/- 8° *Berlin* [37–44] 85; 90
* " " " " " " Ed. Minor, 2 vols. 9/- p 8° " [68] 82; 84
" " " W. Dillenburger 6/- 8° *Leipzig* [43] 81
" " " and full Index F. Ritter, 2 vols. 19/6 8° " 56–57
" " " R. Bentley and index C. Zangemeister, 2 vols. 16/- 8° *Berlin* 69
* " German " A. Kiessling: Odes and Ep. 3/-; Satires, 2/6; Epp. 3/- 8° Weidmann 84; 86; 89
" " " H. Schütz, 3 pts. ea. 3/- p 8° " [75] 80; 82; 83

Odæ: *with English notes E. C. Wickham, 12/- 8°; School Edn. 6/- c 8° Clar. Press [74] 77; [81] 87
Includes also the *Carmen Seculare* and *Epodes*. A 2nd vol., incl. *Satires, Epp.* and *Ars Poet.*, is in prep.
" " " J. M. Marshall (also sep. 1/6 ea.; Catena Class.) 7/6 c 8° Rivington 75
" " " T. E. Page [ea. bk. separ. 2/-; Class. Ser.] 6/- f 8° Macmillan 83
" German " C. W. Nauck, 2/6; H. Schütz 3/6 p 8° Teub., *Lps.* [ ] 89; Weidm., *Berl.* [74] 80
" " " Lucian Müller 3/- 8° *Giessen* 82

Satiræ: *with English notes A. Palmer [Classical Series] 6/- f 8° Macmillan 83
* " Latin " and German tr. C. Kirchner [+W. S. Teuffel], 2 vols. 16/6 8° Teubner, *Leipzig* 54; 57
Vol. i.: Text, Trs. and Crit. App., 6/- '54; ii. pt. 1: Comm. to bk. i., 6/- '55; ii. pt. 2: Comm. to bk. ii. [by TEUFFEL] 6/- '57.
" German " [full] L. F. Heindorf, cur. L. Döderlein 6/- 8° *Leipzig* [15] 59
" " " A. Th. H. Fritzsche, 5/6; H. Schütz 3/6 p 8° Teubner, 75–76; Weidm. 81
" and Epistolae: " " " G. T. A. Krüger 3/- p 8° Teubner, *Lps.* [ ] 85
" " " Life and Character, by R. H. Hovenden [= epitome of Sat. and Epist.] 4/6 f 8° Macmillan 82

Epistolæ: with German notes H. Schütz 3/- p 8° Weidmann, *Berl.* 83
" Latin " [full] S. Obbarius + Th. Schmidt, 2 vols. 14/- r 8° *Leipzig* 37–47
" and Ars Poet.: * " English " Prf. A. S. Wilkins [Classical Series] 6/- f 8° Macmillan 85
" " " " " German " O. Ribbeck 5/- 8° *Berlin* 69

Ars Poetica [*v. also* Epist., *sup.*]: w. translations Dn. D. Bagot [prose and verse] 5/- sq 8° Blackwood [ ] 80
Selection: with English notes Beere 3/- c 8° Hodges, *Dublin* 82

TRANSLATIONS:

Works: *tr. J. Lonsdale + S. Lee [prose; Globe Editions] 3/6 gl 8° Macmillan 73
" Prf. J. Conington, 2 vols. [verse] 12/- f 8° Bell [63] 77; 69
Odes and Carmen Seculare, 5/6; Satires, Epistles, and Art of Poetry, 6/6.
" Sir Theodore Martin: w. life and notes, 2 vols. [verse] 21/- c 8° Blackwood [60] 88
" by the most eminent hands [Jonson, Dryden, Lytton, Martin, etc.; Chandos Lib.] 1/6 c 8° Warne [*v.y.*] 89

Odes: tr. R. H. Hovenden [metrical paraphrase] 4/6 f 8° Macmillan 74
" and imitated by various hands, ed. C. W. F. Cooper 1/6 f 8° Bell [80] 89
" F. W. Newman [unrhymed metre] 4/- p 8° Trübner [53] 76

Satires: tr. R. M. Millington [rhythmic prose] 4/- c 8° Longman 70
" Andrew Wood [verse] 4/- 8° Nimmo, *Edin.* 70
übers. C. Kirchner—*v.* Annotated Texts, *supra.*
" L. Döderlein [with the text] 7/- r 8° Teubner, *Leipzig* 60
" Epistles & Art of Poetry: trad. A. Dethon, 2 vols. [in verse; w. text *en regard*] 8/6 8° *Marseilles* 67
" " " trad. A. Rey [w. text and bibliogr. by E. de Porry] 5/- 12° " 68

Since the tr. of the *Odes* and *Satires* by the EARL OF ROCHESTER [1715], there have been about 40 trs. of the Odes, with or without other works, into English; and since S. DUNSTER'S tr. of the *Satires* [1709], about 12 of them.

AIDS.

Criticism, Commentaries, etc.

Bobrik, R. Horaz: Entdeckungen und Forschungen, pt. i. 28/- 4° *Leipzig* 85
Currie, Joseph Notes on Horace: explan., critical and grammat. 4/- 12° Griffin 60
Düntzer, H. Kritik u. Erklärung der Horazischen Gedichte, 5 vols. [also separ.] 21/6 12° *Braunschweig* 40–44
Gebhardi, W. Aesthetischer Kommentar zu den lyrischen Dichtungen d. Horaz 4/- 8° *Paderborn* 85
Keller, Otto Epilegomena zu Horaz, 3 vols. 24/- 8° *Leipzig* 79–80
Oesterlen, Theodor Komik und Humor bei Horaz, pt. i. (*Sat.* and *Epodes*); ii. (*Odes*); pt. iii. ea. 3/- 8° *Stuttgart* 85; 86; 87
" " Studien zu Vergil und Horaz 2/6 8° *Tübingen* 85
Plüss, H. Th. Horaz-studien 6/- 8° *Leipzig* 82
Poiret, Jules Horace: étude psychologique et littéraire 8° *Paris* 89
Rosenberg, E. Die Lyrik des Horaz 3/- 8° *Gotha* 83
Sellar, Prf. W. Y. Horace and the Elegiac Poets 8° Clar. Press *in prep.*
*Verrall, A. W. Studies, Literary and Historical, in the Odes of Horace 8/6 8° Macmillan 85
Weissenfels, O Horaz's Bedeutung für das Unterrichtsziel des Gymnasiums 3/- 8° *Berlin* 85
" " Loci disputationis Horatianae 2/6 " 85

Language.

Bentley, Richard Notae atque Emendationes in Hor. integrae 3/6 8° *Quedlinburg* [1711] 25
Ernesti, J. H. M. Clavis Horatiana: indd. rer. et verb. phil.-crit., 3 vols. 7/- 8° *Leipzig* [02–04] 23
Unger, Rob. Emendationes Horatianae 4/- 8° *Halle* 77

Dictionary.

Koch, G. A. Wörterbuch zu Horaz [school-book] 4/6 8° *Hannover* [69] 79

Life.
Arnold, August — Das Leben d. Horaz, u.s. philos., sittl. u. dichter. Charakter — 2/6 r 8° *Halle* 60
Detto, W. A. — Horaz und seine Zeit — 3/- 8° *Berlin* 83
Hovenden, R. H. — Horace: his life and character [= epitome of *Satt.* and *Epp.*] 4/6 12° Macmillan 77
Jacob, Fr. — Horaz und seine Freunde, 2 vols. — 5/6 8° *Berlin* 52; 53
Martin [Sir] Theod. — Horace [pop. biog. and acc. of works; Anc. Class. f. E. Rrs.] 2/6 12° Blackwood 70
Milman, Dn. H. H. — Life of Horace *o.p.* [*pb.* 9/-; *w.* 6/-] 8° Murray 53
Müller, Lucian — Quintus Horatius Flaccus: eine Biographie — 3/- 8° *Leipzig* 80
Walckenaer, — Histoire de la Vie et des Poésies d'Horace, 2 vols. — 9/- 12° *Paris* [ ] 58

Juvenal.

TEXT: rec. C. F. Hermann, 8*d.*; rec. A. Weidner — p 8° Teubner [54] 73; Weidmann 86
,, O. Ribbeck — 1*s.* 6*d.* 8°; 6*d.* c 8°; 6*d.* 24° Tauchnitz, *Leipzig* 59
* ,, O. Jahn, cur. F. Bücheler [w. Persius and Sulpiciæ Saturæ] 3/- 8° Weidmann, *Berlin* [68] 86
,, A. J. Macleane [Camb. Texts] 1/6 18° Bell 65

ANNOTATED TEXTS: w. Eng. notes A. J. Macleane, ed. G. Long [w. Persius; Bibl. Class.] 12/-; *red. to* 6/- 8° ,, [57] 67
,, ,, ,, H. Prior [expurg. text; Gram. Sch. Class.] 4/6 f 8° ,,
,, ,, ,, G. A. Simcox [omits Sat. 2, 6, 9; Catena Class.] 5/- c 8° Rivington [67] 73
* ,, ,, ,, J. E. B. Mayor, 2 vols. [13 Sat.—v. good] ea. 10/6 c 8° Macmillan [48] 88
,, ,, ,, School Edn. of same [Class. Ser.] 5/-; Sat. 10–11, 3/-; Sat. 12–16, 3/6 c 8° ,, 84; 79; 79
,, ,, ,, E. G. Hardy [Classical Series] 5/- c 8° ,, 81
,, ,, ,, C. H. Pearson + H. A. Strong, 2 pts. [13 Satires] 6/6 c 8° Clar. Press 87
Pt. I.: Intro. and Text, 3/-; Pt. II.: Notes, 3/6.
,, German notes A. Weidner — 4/- p 8° Teubner, *Leipzig* 73

TRANSLATIONS: tr. W. Gifford [verse; w. a prose tr. by L. Evans] 5/- c 8° Bohn's Lib. [02] 52
,, J. D. Lewis [with text and notes; literal prose] 14/- 8° Trübner 73
,, S. H. Jeyes [spirited and free tr.; w. anal. and brief notes] 3/6 c 8° Thornton, *Oxon.* 85
,, Prf. H. A. Strong + A. Leeper — 3/6 c 8° Macmillan 82
übers. W. Hertzberg + W. S. Teuffel, 3 pts. — ea. 6*d.* 16° *Stuttgart* 64; 65; 67

AIDS:
Dürr, — Das Leben Juvenals — 1/6 4° *Leipzig* 88
Hosius, C. — Apparatus Criticus ad Juvenalem — 3/- 8° *Bonn* 88
Naguiewski, M. D. — De Juvenalis Vita Observationes — 3/6 8° *Riga* 83
Ribbeck, O. — Der echte und der unechte Juvenal — 4/- 8° *Berlin* 65
Scholte, Andreas — Observationes Criticae in Saturas Juvenalis — 3/6 8° *Utrecht* 73
Spicilegium Iuvenalianum, scripsit Rud. Beer — 3/- 8° *Leipzig* 88
An examination of the Codex Pithoeanus [*Montpellier*] of Juvenal, w. facs. of Pithou's MS.
Walford, Edward — Juvenal [pop. biog. and acc. of wks.; Anc. Class. f. E. Rrs.] 2/6 12° Blackwood 78
Widal, Auguste — Juvénal et ses Satires: études littéraires et morales — 3/- 12° *Paris* [66] 70

Lucan

Text — 1/6 p 8° Tauchnitz, *Leipzig* [34] 78
Pharsalia: with English notes C. E. Haskins, and intro. W. E. Heitland — 14/- 8° Bell 87
bk. i.: ,, ,, ,, W. E. Heitland + C. E. Haskins — 1/6 f 8° Camb. Press 75
,, Latin ,, C. H. Weise — 12/- 8° *Quedlinburg* 35
,, ,, ,, Hug. Grotius + Ric. Bentley, ed. C. F. Weber, 3 vols. 33/-; *red. to* 10/- 8° *Lpz.* 21–31

TRANSLATIONS: by H. T. Riley [prose] 5/- c 8° Bohn's Lib. 53
trad. J. Demogeot — 6/6 8° *Paris* 66

AID:
Usener, H. (ed.) — Scholia Bernensia in Lucani bellum civile: 1 pt. — 8/- 8° *Leipzig*

Lucilius, Caius

Saturarum Reliquiae emend. et adnot. Lucian Müller — 9/- 8° Teubner, *Leipzig* 72
,, ,, ,, C. Lachmann — 6/- 8° *Berlin* 76

TRANSLATION: by L. Evans [prose; w. Juvenal and Persius] 5/- c 8° Bohn's Lib. 52

AIDS:
Gerlach, F. D. — Lucilius und die römische Satura — 1/- 4° *Basle* 44
Harder, F. — Index Lucilianus [suppl. to Lachmann's text, *supra*] 1/- 8° *Berlin* 78
van Heusde, I. A. C. — Studia Critica in C. Lucilium poetam — 3/- 8° *Utrecht* 42
Kleinschmidt, M. — De Lucilii genere dicendi — 3/- 8° *Marburg* 83
Marx, F. — Studia Luciliana — 2/- 8° *Berlin* 82
Müller, Lucian — Leben und Werke des Caius Lucilius — 1/6 8° *Leipzig* 76
,, ,, — Luciliana — 1/6 8° *Berlin* 84

Lucilius Junior (Corn. Severus)

Aetna: revised, emended, and explained, H. A. J. Munro 3/6 12° Deighton, *Camb.* 67

Lucretius.

TEXTS: rec. H. A. J. Munro [Camb. Texts] 2/6 16° Bell 60
,, J. Bernays — 1/6 p 8° Teubner, *Leipzig* [52] 74

ANNOTATED TEXTS: * w. English notes and tr. H. A. J. Munro, ed. J. Duff, 3 vols. — 24/- 8° Bell [64] 86
,, Latin ,, C. Lachmann, vol. i. [text] 4/-; vol. ii. [comm.] 7/- 8° *Berlin* [50] 71
,, German ,, F. Bockemüller, 2 vols. — 14/- 8° *Leipzig* 73; 74
bks. i.–iii.: with English notes J. H. Warburton Lees [Classical Series] 4/6 f 8° Macmillan 84
v.: ,, French ,, Benoist + Lantoine — 3/6 12° *Paris* 84
Selections: with English intro. Prf. A. J. Church — 2/6 c 8° Rivington 89

K § 214.

TRANSLATIONS: —*for* English Tra., *v.* O § 12: Epicureans.
trad. André Lefèvre [verse] 6/6 8° *Paris* 76

AIDS —*v. also* O § 12 *for English books.*
Bruns, I. Lucrez-Studien 2/- 8° *Freiburg* 84
Holtze, F. W. Syntaxis Lucretianae lineamenta 3/6 8° *Leipzig* 68
Kraetsch, E. De abundanti dicendi genere Lucretiano 1/- 8° *Berlin* 81
Lachmann, C. In Lucretii de rer. nat. Commentarius 7/- 8° „ [50] 66
Martha, C. Le Poème de Lucrèce: morale, religion, science 3/- 8° *Paris* [69] 73
Montée, P. Étude sur Lucrèce considéré comme moraliste 2/6 8° „ 60
Städler, C. G. L. De Sermone Lucretiano 2/- 8° *Jena* 69
Susemihl, F. De Carminis Lucretiani prooemio 2/- 4° *Berlin* 84
Woltjer, I. Lucretii philosophia cum fontibus comparata 6/- 8° *Groningen* 77

Martial.

TEXT: rec. F. G. Schneidewin 2/- p 8° Teubner, *Leipzig* 71
„ „ „ ed. crit., 2 vols. 15/- 8° *Grimma* 42
• „ L. Friedländer, 2 vols. 18/- 8° *Leipzig* 86
„ W. Gilbert 2/6 p 8° Teubner, *Leipzig* 86

ANNOTATED TEXTS: with Latin notes J. Flach [not a very good book] 3/- 8° *Tübingen* 81
„ German notes L. Friedländer 2/- 8° *Königsberg* 84
Epigrams: bk. i.: „ English notes Prf. J. E. B. Mayor Macmillan *in prep.*
Selections: „ „ „ Rev. H. M. Stephenson [Class. Lib.] 6/6 c 8° „ [80] 88
„ „ „ F. A. Paley + W. H. Stone [Gram. Sch. Cl.] 6/6 f 8° Bell 68
• with intro. Prfs. W. Y. Sellar + G. G. Ramsay 3/6 c 8° *Edinburgh* 84

TRANSLATIONS from various sources [verse; w. prose versions] 7/6 c 8° Bohn's Lib. 59
Select Epigrams: for English Readers, tr. Prf. W. T. Webb 4/6 f 8° Macmillan 80

AID:
Gilbert, W. Ad Martialem quaestiones criticae 1/- 4° *Dresden* 83
Stephani, A. De Martiale verborum novatore [an index; Breslauer Philol. Abhandl.] 8° *Breslau* 89
Zingerle, A. Martial's Ovid-Studien: Untersuchungen 2/- r 8° *Innsbruck* 77

Ovid.

TEXTS: rec. R. Merkel, 3 vols. ea 1/- p 8° Teubner, *Leipzig* [50-52] 73-75
„ A. Riese, 3 vols. 8/6 8°; 3/- c 8° Tauchnitz, „ 71; 72; 74
„ O. Korn: Epistles, 5/-; Metamorphoses 3/- 8° *Berlin* 68-
Ibis • „ Prf. Robinson Ellis: ed. crit. 10/6 8° Clar. Press 81
Tristia • „ S. G. Owen; w. facss. of Marsianus and Turonensis MSS., and proleg. 16/- 8° „ 89

ANNOTATED TEXTS:
Epistolae-Selections: with English notes E. S. Shuckburgh [Elementary Classics] 1/6 f 8° Macmillan 82
Fasti: „ „ „ F. A. Paley, 3 pts. [Gram. Sch. Class.] ea. 2/- f 8° Bell [54] 88
„ „ „ T. H. Hallam [Classical Series] 5/- f 8° Macmillan 82
„ German „ H. Peter, 2 pts. 4/- p 8° Teubner, *Leipzig* [74] 79
„ bk. vi.: „ English „ A. Sidgwick [Pitt Press Series] 1/6 f 8° Camb. Press 78
Heroides: • „ „ „ A. Palmer 6/- c 8° Bell 74
„ „ „ E. S. Schuckburgh [Classical Series] 4/6 f 8° Macmillan 79
Ibis: Selections: „ English „ R. W. Taylor 2/6 f 8° Rivington
Libellus de Medicamine Faciei: ed. A. Kunz 3/- 8° *Vienna* 81
Metamorphoses: • with German notes M. Haupt, ed. O. Korn, 2 vols. ea. 2/6 p 8° Weidmann, *Berlin* [52] 85; 85
„ „ „ J. Siebelis + F. Polle, 2 vols. ea. 1/6 p 8° Teubner, *Leipzig* [53] 85
bks. xiii.-xiv.: „ English „ C. Simmons [Classical Series] 4/6 f 8° Macmillan 87
„ Selections: „ „ „ Marriott 4/6 c 8° Williams 68
„ „ „ Bradley + J. T. White 4/6 f 8° Longman
„ „ „ W. Ramsay, ed. G. G. Ramsay 5/6 f 8° Clar. Press 68
Tristia: bk. i. & iii.: „ „ „ S. G. Owen i. 3/6; iii. 2/- f 8° „ 85; 89
Selections: „ „ „ Prfs. J. H. Allen + J. B. Greenough [Am.] $1.25; with Vocabulary $1.55 12° *Boston* 8-
„ „ „ A. J. Macleane [Camb. Texts w. Notes] 1/6 f 8° Bell [56] 75
„ „ „ R. W. Taylor [*sub tit.* Stories in Elegiac Verse] 3/6 c 8° Rivington [76] 78
„ „ „ R. W. Taylor [*sub tit.* Stories in Hexameter Verse] 2/6 c 8° „ [80] 86
„ German „ Günther 1/6 p 8° Teubner, *Leipzig* 85

TRANSLATIONS:
Works: tr. H. T. Riley: Metam. 5/-; Fasti, etc. 5/-; Heroides and Minor Wks. 5/- c 8° Bohn's Lib. 51-52
Metamorphoses: • „ H. King [blank verse] 10/6 c 8° Blackwood 71

AIDS:
Birt, Theodor De Halieuticis Ovidio Poeta falso adscriptis 6/- 8° *Berlin* 78
Church, Alfred J. Ovid [pop. biog. and acc. of wks.; Anc. Class. f. E. Rrs.] 2/6 f 8° Blackwood 76
Eichert, O. Wörterbuch zu Ovid's *Verwandlungen* 2/6 8° *Hanover* [ ] 86
Gruppe, O. F. Die römische Elegie. vol. ii.—*v.* K § 212.
Nageotte, Eug. Ovide: sa vie, ses oeuvres 3/6 8° *Paris* (*Mâcon* 72) 73
Petersen, W. Quaestiones Ovidianae 1/6 4° *Kiel* 77
Sedlmayer, H. S. Prolegomena Critica ad Heroides Ovidianas 3/- 8° *Vienna* 78
„ „ Kritischer Commentar zu Ovid's *Heroiden* 2/- 8° „ 80
Siebelis, J. Wörterbuch zu Ovid's *Metamorphosen* 3/- 8° *Leipzig* [74] 85
Washietl, J. A. De Similitudinibus Imaginibusque Ovidianis 6/- 8° *Vienna* 83
Zingerle, A. Ovid und sein Verhältniss zu den Vorgängern und Gleichzeitigen römischen Dichtern, 3 pts 7/- r 8° *Innsbruck* 69-71

Persius.

TEXT: rec. C. F. Hermann 6*d.* p 8° Teubner, *Leipzig* [62] 79
* ,, O. Jahn, cur. F. Bücheler [w. Juvenal and Sulpic. Sat.] 3/- 8° Weidmann, *Berlin* [68] 86
ANNOTATED TEXT: *with English notes and tr. Prf. J. Conington, ed. Prf. H. Nettleship 7/6 p 8° Clar. Press [72] 74
,, ,, ,, A. Pertor [Catena Classicorum] 3/6 8° Rivington 68
,, Latin ,, O. Jahn [full commentary] *o.p.* [*pb.* 9/- ; *w.* 36/-] 8° *Leipzig* 43
,, ,, ,, and life Isaac Casaubon. cur. F. Dübner 6/- 8° ,, [*Leyden* 1695] 33
TRANSLATION: *by Prf. J. Conington—*in his edn. of* Works, *supra.*
,, W. Gifford [verse; w. a prose version by L. Evans] 5/- c 8° Bohn's Lib. [21] 52

AID:
Hermann, C. F. Lectiones Persianae 3/- 4° *Marburg* 42
Liebl, H. Beiträge zu den Persius-scholien 2/- 8° *Strassburg* 83

Petronius.

TEXT: *rec. F. Bücheler, 10/- ; Ed. Minor 3/6 p 8° *Berlin* [62] 71 : 82
ANNOTATED TEXT: w. French Notes and tr. J. Marchena, and intro. G. B[runet] + P. L[acroix] 3/6 16° *Brussels* 65
TRANSLATIONS: by W. K. Kelly [prose] 5/- c 8° Bohn's Lib. 54
trad. Héguin de Guerle [w. text, & "recherches sceptiques s. l. *Satyricon*"] 3/- 12° *Paris* [35] 62

AIDS:
v. Guericke, A. De Linguae vulgaris Reliquiis apud Petronium et Inscripp. Pompeian. 1/6 8° *Gumbinnen* 75
Ludwig, Ernest De Petronii Sermone Plebeio [dissert. inaug.] 1/- 8° *Marburg* 69
Pétrequin, J. E. Recherches historiques et critiques sur Pétrone 4/- 8° *Lyons* 69
Segebade, J. Observationes grammat. et criticae in Petronium 2/6 8° *Halle* 80
Wehle, W. Observationes Criticae in Petronium [dissert. inaug.] 1/6 8° *Bonn* 61

Phaedrus.

TEXT: rec. Lucian Müller, 6*d.*; Ed. Crit. [w. Latin notes] 3/- 8° *Leipzig* [68] 73 ; 77
,, C. Th. Dressler, 6*d.*; rec. A. Riese 6*d.* p 8° Teubner [50] 66 ; Tauchn. 86
,, F. Eyssenhardt 9*d.* p 8° Weidmann, *Berlin* 67
ANNOTATED TEXTS: with English notes and vocabulary Schmitz 1/6 16° Chambers
,, German ,, J. Siebelis + F. A. Eckstein 1/- p 8° Teubner, *Leipzig* [51] 54
,, ,, ,, F. E. Raschig + R. Richter 1/- p 8° Weidmann, *Berlin* [ ] 71
TRANSLATION: tr. C. Smart [verse; w. a prose version by H. T. Riley] 5/- c 8° Bohn's Lib. [1765] 53

AIDS:
Hartman, J. J. De Phaedri fabulis commentatio 2/6 8° *Leyden* 89
Müller, Lucian De Phaedri et Aviani Fabulis libellus 1/- 8° Trübner, *Leipzig* 75
Oesterley, H. Romulus: Paraphrasen d. Phaed. u. d. Æsop. Fab. im Mittelalt. 2/- 8° *Berlin* 70

Propertius —*v. also* Catullus, Tibullus and Propertius, *supra*, and Tibullus, *infra*.

TEXT: rec. H. Keil 10*d.* p 8° Teubner, *Leipzig* [50] 80
,, L. Müller 10*d.* p 8° ,, ,, [70] 90
,, Aem. Baehrens: ed. crit. 6/- 8° *Leipzig* 80
ANNOTATED TEXTS: with English notes F. A. Paley 9/- 8° Bell [53] 72
,, Latin ,, G. A. B. Hertzberg, 3 vols. in 4 15/- 8° *Halle* 43–45
bk. iv.: *with English notes A. Palmer 5/- 8° Bell 80
,, v.: ,, ,, ,, F. A. Paley, w. tr. [verse] 3/- ,, 66
Selections: * ,, ,, ,, Prf. J. P. Postgate [Classical Series] 6/- f 8° Macmillan [81] 82
TRANSLATIONS: tr. Dr. J. Cranstoun [with life and notes] 7/6 c 8° Blackwood 76
,, P. J. J. Gantillon [verse] 3/6 c 8° Bell 85
,, E. R. Moore 2/6 12° Rivington 70
übers. F. Jacob, ed. W. Binder [verse] 2/6 16° *Stuttgart* [59] 68

AIDS:
Frahnert, Zum Sprachgebrauch des Propers 1/- 4° *Halle* 74
Gruppe, O. F. Die römische Elegie, vol. ii.—*v.* K § 212.
Heydenreich, Ed. Quaestiones Propertianae [dissert. inaug.] 1/- 8° *Dresden* 75
Kuttner, B. De Propertii Elocutione Quaestiones [dissert. inaug.] 1/6 8° *Halle* 78
Lütjohann, C. Commentationes Propertianae 2/- 8° *Kiel* 69
Mallet, F. Quaestiones Propertianae 1/6 8° *Göttingen* 82
Marx, A. De S. Propertii vita et librorum ordine temporibusque 1/6 8° *Leipzig* 84
Rossberg, C. Lucubrationes Propertianae 1/6 8° *Stade* 77
Sandström, C. E. Emendationes in Propert., Lucan., Valer. Flaccum 2/6 8° *Upsala* 78
Unger, Robert Analecta Propertiana 2/6 4° *Halle* 50

Prudentius.

ANNOTATED TEXT: ed. w. Latin notes and crit. appar. Albert Dressel 7/6 8° *Leipzig* 60
& TRANSLATION: Translations from Prudentius: a selection. By F. St. John Thackeray [verse] 7/6 16° Bell 90
Hymns: tr. Geo. Morison, 3 pts., 3/6, 5/6, 5/6 ; or in 1 vol. 14/- 8° Macmillan & Bowes, *Camb.* 89
BROCKHAUS' book [*vid. infra*] conts. a German tr. of the *Apotheosis*.

AIDS:
Breidt, H. De Aurelio Prudentio Clemente Horatii imitatore 2/- 8° *Heidelberg* 87
Brockhaus, Clem. Aurel. Prudentius in seiner Bedeutung für die Kirche 5/6 8° *Leipzig* 72
Kantecki, A. E. De Aurelii Prudentii Clementis genere dicendi quaestiones [dissert. inaug.] 1/- 8° *Munster* 74
Puech, Aimé Étude sur Prudence *o.p.* 8° *Strassburg* 68

K § 214

Statius.

TEXTS: rec. G. Queck: i. Silvae, Achill. 1/6; ii. Theb. 2/6 p 8° Teubner, *Leipzig* 54; 54
,, Aem. Baehrens + P. Kohlmann, i. Silvae, 2/-; ii. (1) Achill., 1/-; (2) Theb. 5/- p 8° ,, ,, 76; 79; 84
Achilleis and Thebais: ed. crit. rec. Otto Müller, vol. i. [= Thebaidos i.-vi.] 8/- 8° *Leipzig* 70
[Silvae, i. 2]: Epithalamium, ed. A. Herzog [with Latin notes] 2/6 8° ,, 81
[,, iii. 5]: Ecloga ad uxorem, rec. Alb. Imhof 1/- 4° *Halle* 63
[,, v. 5]: Ecloga ultima, rec. Rob. Unger 6/- 8° *Neustrelitz* 68
TRANSLATION: übers. K. W. Bindewald, pts. i.-vi. [= Thebaidos i.-viii.; orig. metre] ea. 6*d.* 16° *Stuttgart* 68-75

AIDS:
Goetz, G. De Statii silvis emendandis disputatio 6*d.* 4° *Jena* 84
Gronovius, J. F. In Statii Silvarum libros v. diatribe, 2 vols. 15/-; *red. to* 5/- 8° *Leipzig* [*Hague*, 1637] 12
Imhof, Albert De Silvarum Statianarum condicione critica 1/- 4° *Halle* 59
Kohlmann, Phil. Neue Studien zur Thebais [fr. a Paris MS.] 1/- 4° *Posen* 73
Moerner, F. De P. Papinii Statii Thebaide quaestiones criticae, grammaticae, metricae 1/6 8° *Königsberg* 90
Müller, Otto Quaestiones Statianae 1/- 4° *Berlin* 61
Sandström, E. Studia Critica in Statium 2/- 8° *Upsala* 78
Waller, W. Excursus criticus in P. Papinii Statii Silvas 1/- 8° *Breslau* 85

Tibullus —*v. also* Catullus, Tibullus and Propertius, *supra.*

TEXTS: rec. Lucian Müller, 6*d.*; rec. Ed. Hiller, 9*d.* p 8° Teubner [70] 75; Tauchnitz 86
,, Aem. Baehrens: ed. crit. 3/- 8° *Leipzig* 78
Selections: with English notes Frost [*sub tit.* Florilegium Poeticum] 3/- f 8° Bell
,, ,, ,, Prf. J. P. Postgate [Classical Series] f 8° Macmillan *in prep.*
and Ovid ,, ,, ,, W. Ramsay 5/- c 8° Griffin 59
and Propertius ,, ,, ,, Prf. G. G. Ramsay 6/- f 8° Clar. Press 87
TRANSLATION: Elegies of Tibullus, tr. Dr. J. Cranstoun [verse; w. life and notes] 6/6 c 8° Blackwood 72
übers. W. Binder, 1/6 16°; übers. A. Eberz 2/6 [both verse; orig. metre] 16° *Stuttg.* 62; *Frankf.* 65

AIDS:
Bährens, Aem. Tibullische Blätter 2/6 8° *Jena* 76
Delegrise, J. H. E. Propylaeen zu den 4 Büchern Elegien d. Tibullus 1/6 8° *Helmstedt* 72
Ehrlich, B. De Tibulli elocutione quaestiones 1/- 8° *Leipzig* 83
Fabricius, B. Die Elegien Tibullus u. einiger Zeitgenossen erklärt 3/- 8° *Berlin* 81
Gruppe, O. F. Die römische Elegie, vol. ii.—*v.* K § 212.
Kleemann, Selmar De libri tertii carminibus q. Tib. nomine circumferuntur 1/- 8° *Argentorati* 76
Protzen, Ernest De Excerptis Tibullianis [dissert. inaug.] 1/6 8° *Greifswald* 69
Rothstein, M. De Tibulli Codicibus 2/6 8° *Berlin* 80
Streifinger, J. De Syntaxi Tibulliana [dissert. inaug.] 1/6 8° *Würzburg* 81
Wisser, W. Quaestiones Tibullianae (diss. inaug.) 1/- 8°; Ueber Tibull. ii. 5 1/- 4° *Leipzig* 69; *Eutin* 74

Valerius Flaccus.

TEXT: rec. G. Thilo 7/6 8° *Halle* 63
,, Aem. Baehrens, 1/6; rec. C. Schenkl 2/6 p 8° Teubner 75; Weidmann 71
TRANSLATION: trad. J. J. A. Caussin de Perceval 6/- 8° *Paris* 28

AIDS:
Braun, Phil. Observationes Crit. et Exeget. in *Argonautica* [dissert. inaug.] 1/- 8° *Fulda* 69
Damsté, P. H. Adversaria critica ad C. Valerii Flacci *Argonautica* 2/- 8° *Leipzig* 85
Gebbing, H. De C. Valerii Flacci tropis et figuris [dissert. inaug.] 1/6 8° *Marburg* 78
Peters, J. De Valerii Flacci vita et carmine 1/6 8° *Leipzig* 90
Schenkl, Karl Studien zu den *Argonautica* [fr. *Sitzsber. Wiener Akad.*] 2/- r 8° *Vienna* 71

Varro.

Saturae Menippae: rec. A. Riese 6/- 8° *Leipzig* 65
Eumenidum Reliquiae: ,, et adnot. Th. Roeper, 3 pts. 4/- 4° *Danzig* 58; 61; 62

AIDS: —*v. also* K § 216: Latin Historians, *and* K § 221: Latin Writers on Agriculture.
Reiter, Hugo Quaestiones Varronianae grammaticae, 2 pts. [dissert. inaug.] 2/- 8° *Königsberg* 81
Vahlen, J. Varronis Saturarum Menippearum reliq. conjectanea 4/6 8° *Leipzig* 58

Vergil.

TEXTS: Opera: rec. Prf. Conington [Camb. Texts] 3/6 16° Bell
,, B. H. Kennedy: with proleg. and crit. commentary 5/- 12° Camb. Press 76
,, H. Paldamus 4/6 8°; 1/6 c 8°; 1/3 24° Tauchnitz 54
*,, O. Ribbeck; ed. crit., 5 vols. 36/- 8° Teubner, *Leipzig* 59-68
i.: Bucol. and Georg., 5/- '59; ii.: Aen. i.-vi., 8/- '60; iii.: Aen. vii.-xii., 8/- '62; iv.: Append. Vergiliana; 1 pl. 5/- '68: Proleg. Crit.; 3 pl. 10/- '66.
,, O. Ribbeck [separ.; Buc. and Georg., 6*d.*; Aen., 1/-] 1/6 p 8° ,, ,, [72] 81
,, Th. Ladewig [separ.; Buc. and Georg., 9*d.*; Aen., 1/-] 1/6 p 8° Weidmann, *Berlin* 66
,, M. Haupt 5/- 16° *Leipzig* [58] 73
ANNOTATED TEXTS: *with English notes Prf. J. Conington, ed. Prf. H. Nettleship, 3 vols. [Bibl. Class.] ea. 14/-; *red. to* 10/6 8° Bell [58-62] 71-76
*Abridged Edn. [Gram. Sch. Class.]: Bucol., Georgics, Aeneid i.-iv. [by J. G. Sheppard], 5/6; Aeneid v.-xii., 5/6. Or in 9 pts., ea. 1/6 or 2/-.
with English notes J. B. Greenough [Am.] $1.75 12° *Boston* 8-
,, ,, ,, B. H. Kennedy; w. 2 maps 10/6 c 8° Longman 76
,, ,, ,, T. L. Papillon, 2 vols. 10/6 c 8° Clar. Press 82
,, ,, ,, Prf. C. D. Yonge *red. to* 7/6 c 8° Bentley 62
,, ,, ,, A. Sidgwick, 2 vols.: vol. i. [Text]. 3/6; ii. [Notes]. 4/6 [Pitt Press Series] c 8° Camb. Press 90; 90

ANNOTATED TEXTS: *with Latin notes A. Forbiger, 3 vols. ea. 24/- 8° *Leipzig* [36–39] 72–75
i: Bucol. and Georg. [w. prol. diss.] 7/- [36] 72; ii.: Aen. i.–vi. 8/- [37] 73; iii.: Aen. vii.–xii., Carm. Minora ascr. to Vergil, 9/- [39] 75.
,, French ,, E. Benoist, 3 vols. ea. 6/6 8° *Paris* [66] 76; 69; 72
,, German ,, Th. Ladewig + C. Schaper: Buc. and Georg. 2/-; Aen. i.–vi. 2/-; vii.–xii. 2/6 p 8° Weidmann [50; 51; 82; 84; 86]
,, ,, ,, K. Kappes: Bucol. and Georg. 2/-; Aen., 4 pts. ea. 1/6 p 8° Teubner [76; 73, 74, 74, 74; 96; 84, 87, 87, 87]
Aeneid: ,, Latin ,, G. W. Gossrau 13/- 8° *Quedlinburg* [46] 76
,, ,, ,, P. H. Peerlkamp, 2 vols. 8/- 8° *Leyden* 43
*,, English ,, A. Sidgwick [Pitt Press Series] ea. bk. 1/6 f 8° Camb. Press 76–83
bk. i.: ,, ,, ,, C. S. Jerram [also ed. A. S. Walpole 1/6 (Macmillan)] 2/6 f 8° Clar. Press 87
,, i.–iii.: ,, ,, ,, T. L. Papillon + A. E. Haigh [new edn. of pt. of Papillon's ed. *ut sup.*] 3/- c 8° Clar. Press 90
,, ii., v.: ,, ,, ,, F. Storr 1/- and 1/6 12° Rivington [78] 88; 89
,, i.–vii.: ,, ,, ,, J. T. White ea. bk. 1/6 12° Longman 72–85
,, ,, ,, ,, ,, Dr. L. Schmitz 3/6 c 8° Collins 79
[,, ii.:] ,, ,, ,, Bradley [*sub tit.* Troy Taken, also ed. J. H. Skrine 1/6 (Macm.)] 2/6 f 8° Longman
,, ii.–iii.: ,, ,, ,, E. W. Howson [Classical Series] 3/- f 8° Macmillan 81
,, v.: ,, ,, ,, Rev. A. Calvert [*sub tit.* the Funeral Games; Elem. Class.] 1/6 18° ,, 79
,, vi.: ,, ,, ,, Rev. A. J. Church 8d. 18° Seeley 73
,, ix.: ,, ,, ,, A. E. Haigh: Text 1/-; Notes 1/-; Introd. 1/6 f 8° Clar. Press 87
,, xi.–xii.: ,, ,, ,, F. Storr 2/6 12° Rivington 76
,, ,, ,, ,, ,, abdgd. fr. J. Conington [Gram. School Class.] 3/- c 8° Bell 76
Bucolics:* with English notes C. S. Jerram 2/6 f 8° Clar. Press 87
,, ,, ,, A. Sidgwick [Pitt Press Series] 1/6 f 8° Camb. Press 87
,, and Georgics: ,, ,, ,, T. Keightley 4/6 Whittaker 48
Georgics: bks. i.–ii. and iii.–iv.: *with English notes A. Sidgwick [Pitt Press Series] ea. 2/- f 8° Camb. Press 85; 86
bk. iv.: with English notes C. G. Jepp, 1/6; J. T. White 1/- f 8° Rivington; Longman 72

TRANSLATIONS:
Works: tr. Prf. J. Conington [prose] 6/- c 8° Longman [72] 87
,, John Dryden [a strong, robust verse tr.; Morley's Univ. Lib.] 1/- c 8° Routledge [1697] 84
,, C. R. Kennedy [blank verse] *o.p.* [*pb.* 9/-; *w.* 5/-] 8° Bohn [50] 61
*,, J. Lonsdale + S. Lee [prose; Globe Edns.] 3/6 8° Macmillan [71] 82
*,, J. W. Mackail: Aeneid, 7/6 c 8°; Eclogues and Georgics 5/- r 16° Macmill. 85; Rivington 90
trad. E. Pessonneaux, 2 vols. [w. the text] 6/- 18° *Paris* [58] 74
Aeneid: tr. Prf. J. Conington [verse; scholarly] 6/- c 8° Longman [66] 88
,, Wm. Morris [verse] 14/- p 8° Ellis (Reeves & T.) [76] 82
,, Rev. R. C. Singleton [verse] 7/6 16° Bell [55–59] 71
,, W. J. Thornhill [blank verse] 7/6 c 8° Hodges, *Dublin* 86
,, Sir Chas. [Ld. Just.] Bowen [Eclogues & Aeneid i.–vi.; Eng. hexameters, scholarly and graceful] 12/- 8° Murray [88] 89
,, Bp. Gavin Douglas, ed. Geo. Dundas, 2 vols. *o.p.* [*w.* 25/-] 4° Bannatyne Club [1553] 39
Of interest as being the first tr. of a Roman classic executed [1513] in the English language.
Eclogues: by C. S. Caverley [verse] 7/6 c 8° Bell [66] 86
,, E. J. L. Scott [heroic verse] 3/6 f 8° Paul 84
,, and Georgics: by Wilkins 3/6 c 8° Longman 73
Georgics: ,, R. D. Blackmore [verse] 1/- s 8° Low [71] 86
,, J. Rhoades [verse] 5/- s 8° Paul 81

AIDS:
Criticism, Commentaries, etc.
Eichhoff, F. G. Études Grecques sur Virgile, 3 vols. *o.p.* [*w.* 20/-] 8° *Paris* 25
A collection of all the passages fr. Gk. poets imitated in the *Bucolics, Georgics,* and *Æneid.*
Lersch, L. Antiquitates Vergilianae ad vitam populi Rom. descriptae 3/6 r 8° *Bonn* 43
Miscellanea Virgiliana *o.p.* [*pb.* 10/6; *w.* 7/6] 8° Grant, *Cambridge* 28
Conts. E. HOLDSWORTH'S notes on *Georg.* and *Aen.* i.–vi. [1749–68], Jas. SPENCE'S *Char. of Virg.* [fr. his *Polymetis* 1747], Bp. W. WARBURTON on *Aen.* vi. [first *pb.* in his *Divine Legation of Moses* 1737 *sqq.*] and J. JORTIN'S *Crit. Remarks on Virgil* [1790].
Plüss, H. T. Vergil und die epische Kunst 8/- 8° *Leipzig* 84
Ste. Beuve, C. A. Étude sur Virgile [w. a study of Quintus of Smyrna] 2/6 18° *Paris* [57] 70
*Sellar, Prf. W. Y. Poets of the Augustan Age: Virgil 9/- c 8° Clar. Press [77] 84
Servius, Maurus Honoratus Commentarii in Virgilium, rec. G. Thilo + H. Hagen, vols. i.–iii. (1) 34/6 8° *Leipzig* 78–84
Spitta, Ph. Quaestiones Vergilianae 1/6 4° *Sonderhausen* 67
Tissot, P. F. Études sur Virgile, 2 vols. [Vergil compared w. other anc. poets] 10/- 8° *Paris* [25; 30] 41
Weidner, Andreas Commentar zu Virgils Aeneis, lib. i.–ii. 8/- 8° Teubner, *Leipzig* 69
Aeneid.
Henry, James Aeneidea: critical, exeget. and æsthet. remarks on Aen., 2 v. [bks. i.–iv.] 8° Williams 73; *Dublin* 78–79
Magnier, L. Analyse Critique et Littéraire de l'Énéide 4/- 12° *Paris* [ ] 44
*Nettleship, Prf. H. Suggestions introductory to the Study of the Aeneid 1/6 f 8° Clar. Press 75
Eclogues.
Büttner, Ernst Ueb. d. Verhältn. v. V's. Eklogen zu Theok. Idyllen 1/6 4° *Insterburg* 73
Changuion, F. D. Virgil und Pollio [on *Eclogues* ii.–v.] 1/- 8° *Basle* 76
Georgics.
Bockemüller, Fr. Virgil's *Georgica* nach Plan und Motiven erklärt 2/- 8° *Stade* 74
Bosson, A. Études Agronomiques sur les *Géorgiques* 2/6 18° *Paris* 66
Textual Criticism.
Ek, J. G. [ed.] Ad Verg. ex cod. membran. bibl. Lund coll. 3/- 4° *Lund* 47
Hagen, H. [ed.] Scholia Bernensia ad Verg. Bucol. et Georg. 6/- 8° *Leipzig* 76
Hermann, Arn. [ed.] Die Veroneser Vergilscholien 3/6 8° *Donaueschingen* 69; 70
Kvicala, J. Virgil-Studien [w. collation of Prague MS.] 4/- r 8° *Prague* 78

K § 215

Perts, G. H. — Ueb. d. Berl. u. Vatic. Blätter d. ältest. HS. d. Virgil; 3 pl. — 4/6 4° *Berlin* 63
Ribbeck, Otto — Appendix Vergiliana *and* Prolegomena Critica [= vols. iv. and v. of his ed. of text, *ut supra*] 3/- *and* 10/- 8° *Leipzig* 68; 66

Georgics.
Schafer, Carl — De Georgicis a Vergilio emendatis — 2/- 4° *Berlin* 73

Language.
Antoine, F. — De Casuum Syntaxi Vergiliana — 3/- 8° *Paris* 83
Krause, H. — De Vergilii usurpatione infinitivi [dissert. inaug.] 1/6 8° *Halle* 78

Dictionary.
Greenough, J. B. [Am.] — Vocabulary to Virgil's Complete Works — $1 12° *Boston* 8-
Koch, G. A. — Wörterbuch zu den Gedichten d. Virgil, 4/-; Schulwörterbuch zur Aeneid — 2/6 8° *Hanover* [55] 85; 80

Grammar.
Reid, J. S. — A Grammar of Vergil — Macmillan *in prep.*

Life.
Bobrik, R. — Studien zu Vergil und Horaz — 1/6 8° *Tübingen* 83
Collins, Rev. W. L. — Virgil [crit. biog. and acc. of wks.: A. C. f. E. Rrs.—pop.] 2/6 f 8° Blackwood 70
Nettleship, Prf. H. — Vergil [Classical Writers; introductory] 1/6 f 8° Macmillan 79

Mediæval.
*Comparetti, N. — Virgilio nel Medio Evo, 2 vols. *o.p.* [*pb.* 12/6; *w.* £1] 8° *Livorno* 72
" " — Virgil im Mittelalter, übers. H. Dütschke — 6/- 8° Teubner, *Leipzig* 75
Nettleship, Prf. H. — Ancient Lives of Vergil [w. essay on the Poems] 2/- 8° Clar. Press
Tunison, Jos. S. [Am.] — Master Vergil: a series of studies — $2 8° *Cincinnati* 89

A *résumé* of the many mediæval anecdotes of Virgil in the light of a poet, mechanical inventor, lover, magician, etc. To some extent based on *Comparetti*, *ut supra*.

Zappert, Geo. — Virgil's Fortleben im Mittelalter — 4/- f° *Vienna* 51

Topography.
de Bonstettin, L. — Voyage sur l. scène des 10 dern. livres de l'Énéide — *o.p.* 8° *Geneva* [04] 13
Henry, Jas. — Notes of 12 years' Voyage of Discov. in first 6 bks. of *Aeneis* — 6/- 8° *Dresden* 33

Stories from Virgil.
Church, Rev. A. J. — Stories from Virgil [w. 24 ill. after Pinelli] 3/- c 8° Seeley [76] 87

215. LATIN DRAMATISTS.

Collections.

*Ribbeck, O. [ed.] — Comicorum Romanorum praeter Plautum et Terentium Reliquiae — 14/- 8° *Leipzig* [55] 73
* " " — Tragicorum Romanorum Reliquiae, rec. O. Ribbeck — 9/- 8° " [52] 71

Accius.

Texts: —*in* Lucilius, rec. L. Müller [*v.* K § 214]; *in* Wordsworth's *Fragments* [*v.* K § 209].

Aid:
Müller, Lucian — De Accii Fabulis — 2/- 8° *Leipzig* 90

Livius Andronicus and Cn. Naevius

Fabularum Reliquiae, emend. et adnot. Lucian Müller 2/- 8° *Berlin* 85

Plautus.

Texts:
rec. C. H. Weise, 4 vols. [rather antiquated] ea. 1/- 16° Tauchnitz, *Leipzig* [21] 75-79
" A. Fleckeisen, 2 vols. ea. 3/- [ea. play separ., 6*d.*] p 8° Teubner [50-51] 72-90
i: Amphit., Capt., Mil. Glor., Rud., Trin.; ii: Asin., Bacch., Curc., Pseud., Stich.
* rec. F. Ritschl.: ed. crit., cur. G. Goetz + G. Loewe + F. Schoell 8° Teubner, *Leipzig* [48-52] [illegible]

Amphitruo	[Goetz+Loewe]	4/-	Captivi	[Schoell]		Menaechmi	[Schoell]		Rudens	[Schoell]	
Asinaria	[" + "]	4/-	Casina	["]	6/-	Mercator	[Goetz]	4/-	Stichus	[Goetz]	4/-
Aulularia	["]	2/6	Curculio	[Goetz]	2/6	Poenulus	[" +Loewe]	5/-	Trinummus	[Schoell]	6/-
Bacchides	[Goetz+Loewe]	4/-	Epidicus	["]	3/-	Pseudolus	[Goetz]		Truculentus	[Schoell]	4/6

w. Latin Notes J. L. Ussing, 5 vols. 8° *Copenhagen* 75-89
i: Amphit., Asin., 11/6 75; ii: Aulul., Bacch., Capt., Curc., 14/- 78; iii: (1) Cas., Cist. 13/6 87; iii: (2) Epidicus, Mostell., Menaech., 11/6 80; iv: (1) Mil. Glor., Mercator, 10/- 82; iv: (2) Pseudolus, Poenulus, 10/- 85; v: Pers., Rud., Stich., Trin., Truc. 13/6 86.
rec. F. Leo, vol. i. [Amph., Asin., Aulul., Bacch.] 2/- p 8° *Berlin* 85

Annotated Texts:

Amphitruo: with English notes Prf. A. Palmer [Classical Series] 5/- f 8° Macmillan 90
Aulularia: with English notes Dr. W. Wagner [w. intro. on Plaut. prosody] 4/6 12° Bell [66] 76
ed. P. Langen: w. crit. appar. 1/- 8° *Münster* 89
Captivi: *Ed. Crit.; w. English notes Prf. E. A. Sonnenschein 6/- 8° Sonnenschein 80
An Appendix contains Bentley's Plautine emendations fr. his copy of Pareus [the 2nd ed., *Frankf.* 1623] now in Brit. Mus.
*with English notes Prf. E. A. Sonnenschein [schl. edn. of above] 3/6 8° " [80] 83
" " " W. M. Lindsay 2/6 f 8° Clar. Press 87
* " German " J. Brix 1/- p 8° Teubner, *Leipzig* [70] 84
Menaechmi: with English notes Dr. W. Wagner 4/6 12° Bell 78
" Latin " [textual] J. Vahlen 2/- 8° *Berlin* 82
* " German " J. Brix 1/- p 8° Teubner, *Leipzig* [73] 80
Miles Gloriosus: *with English notes Prf. R. Y. Tyrrell [Classical Series] 5/- f 8° Macmillan [81] 85
" Latin " O. Ribbeck 3/- 8° Teubner, *Leipzig* 81
* " German " A. O. F. Lorenz 3/- 12° Weidmann, *Berl.* [69] 86
* " " " J. Brix 1/6 p 8° Teubner, *Leipzig* [75] 82
Mostellaria: with English notes W. Ramsay, ed. Prf. G. G. Ramsay 14/- 8° Macmillan 69
* " " " Prf. E. A. Sonnenschein 5/- f 8° Bell 85
* " German " A. O. F. Lorenz 3/- p 8° Weidmann, *Berlin* [66] 86
Pseudolus: *with German notes A. O. F. Lorenz 2/6 p 8° " " [76] 83
Trinummus: " English " C. E. Freeman + A. Sloman 3/- f 8° Clar. Press 83
" " " " Dr. W. Wagner 4/6 12° Bell 72
* " German " J. Brix, rec. Max Niemeyer 1/6 p 8° Teubner, *Leipzig* [64] 88
Truculentus: with Latin notes A. Spengel [w. Studemund's crit. appar.] 3/- 8° *Göttingen* 68

Translations:

Comedies: literally tr. H. T. Riley, 2 vols. [prose] ea. 5/- c 8° Bohn's Lib. 52
" " " [Trinumm., Men., Aulul., Captivi] 1/- c 8° " [52] 88
übers. W. Binder, 4 vols. [verse; also in 46 pts. ea. 35 pf.] 16/6 16° *Stuttgart* 61–69
" J. J. C. Donner, 3 vols. [verse] ea. 5/- 8° *Leipzig* 64
trad. E. Sommer, 2 vols. [w. intro. and notes] 6/- 12° *Paris* [65] 76
[Captivi]: The Captives of Plautus, tr. Prf. H. A. Strong 2/6 c 8° Bentley [73] 82
[Mostellaria]: The Haunted House, tr. Prf. H. A. Strong 2/- c 8° " 71

Aids —*v. also* K § 209, *s.v.* Early Latin.

Criticism, Commentaries, etc.

Abraham, W. Studia Plautina 2/- 8° *Leipzig* 84
v. Bagnato, Plautus in s. Verhältn. z. s. griech. Originalen 1/6 4° *Ehingen* 78
Crain, M. Ueber die Composition der plautinischen Cantica 2/6 8° *Berlin* 65
Dziatzko, C. De Prologis Plautinis et Terentianis [dissert. inaug.] 2/- 8° *Bonn* 63
Geppert, C. E. Plautinische Studien, pt. i., 3/-; ii. 2/6 8° *Berlin* 70; 71
Hubrich, Th. De Diis Plautinis Terentianisque 2/- 8° *Regensburg* 83
Jahresbericht über T. M. Plautus [*repr. fr.* Jahresb üb. d. Fortschr. d. klass. Alterth.] 8° *Berlin*
1880–1881 by A. Lorenz; (1882) 1883–1885 by Prf. O Seyffert; 1886–1 *not pub. yet* (Sept., 1890).

*Langen, P. Beiträge zur Kritik u. Erklärung des Plautus 6/- 8° *Leipzig* 80
" " Plautinische Studien [Berliner Studien] 13/- 8° " 86
v. Reinhardstoettner, C. Plautus: spätere Bearbeitungen plautinischer Lustspiele 18/- 8° " 86
Schnoor, H. Quaestiones Plautinae [dissert. inaug.] 2/- 4° *Kiel* 78
Weise, C. H. Die Komödien d. Plautus: Krit. n. Inhalt u. Form beleuchtet 3/- 8° *Quedlinburg* 66

Aulularia.

Benoist, L. E. Lettre à M. Egger sur div. passages de l'*Aulularia* 2/6 8° *Lyons* 63
Claus, W. De *Aulularia* fabula iisque script. q. eam imit. sunt 1/6 8° *Stettin* 62
Lorenz, A. O. F. Collationen d. Cod. vet. Camerarii et Cod. Ursinianus 1/6 4° *Berlin* 72
Collations of two Vatican MSS. of the *Aulularia*.
Wagner, W. De Plauti *Aulularia* [dissert. inaug.] 1/- 8° *Bonn* 64

Epidicus.

Müller, Richard De Plauti Epidico [dissert. inaug.] 1/6 8° *Bonn* 65

Miles Gloriosus.

Gandino, G. B. Osservazioni critiche intorno del *Mil. Glor.* 1/6 8° *Turin* 73
Goetz, G. Emendationes *Militis Gloriosi* Plautinae 6d. 8° *Jena* 90
Schmidt, Fritz Untersuchungen über d. *Miles Gloriosus* 2/- 8° *Leipzig* 77

Poenulus.

Hasper, Theodor De Poenuli Plautinae duplici exitu 1/- 8° *Leipzig* 68
Movers, F. C. Punische Texte in *Poenulus* kritisch erklärt 2/6 8° *Breslau* 45
Schröder, Paul —*his* Phöniz. Sprache *has append. cont. expl. of the Punic passages* 12/- 8° *Halle* 69

Proverbs.

Schneider, J. De Proverbiis Plautinis Terentianisque [dissert. inaug.] 1/6 8° *Berlin* 78

Language.

Ballas, Aem. Grammatica Plautina, 2 pts. 2/- 8° & 4° *Berlin* [68; 72] 84
Biese, Alfred De objecto interno apud Plaut. et Terent. 2/- 4° *Kiel* 78
Kloss, Richard Zur Alliteration u. Symmet. b. Plautus [esp. *Mil. Gl.* act 1] 1/6 4° *Zittau* 76
Köhler, H. De verborum accentus cum numer. ratt. in Pl. 1/6 8° *Halle* 77
Lübbert, E. —*in his* Grammatische Studien, 2 pts. pt. i. 7/-; ii. 2/6 8° *Breslau* 67; 70
Rassow, H. De Plauti Substantivis 3/6 8° *Leipzig* 81
Ribbeck, Otto —*in his* Beiträge zur Lehre v. d. lat. Partikeln 1/6 8° " 69
Rothe, Carl Quaestiones Gramm. ad us. Plaut. et Terent. [dissert. inaug.] 1/6 8° *Berlin* 76
Schmidt, Fritz Quaestiones de Pronomin. Demonstr. formis Plautinis [" "] 2/6 8° " 75
Seyffert, Oscar Studia Plautina [school-programme] 1/6 4° " 74
Studemund, W. Studia in Priscos Scriptores Latinos—*v.* K § 209.
Walder, E. Der Infinitiv bei Plautus 1/6 8° " 74

Lexicons.

Pareus, Ph. Lexicon Plautinum *o.p.* [w. 7/6] 8° *Nuremberg* 1645
Weise, C. H. Lexicon Plautinum [repr. fr. his edn. of text, *ut sup.*] 4/- 8° *Quedlinburg* [38] 86

Textual Criticism.

Baier, B. De Plauti Fabularum recensionibus Ambrosiana et Palatina 3/- 8° *Breslau* 85
Geppert, C. E. Ueb. d. Codex Ambros. u. s. Einfluss a. d. Plaut. Kritik 2/- 8° *Leipzig* 47
Kloss, Reinh. Emendationum Plautinarum libellus 1/- 4° " 68
Niemeyer, Maxim. De Plauti Fabularum recensione duplici [dissert. inaug.] 1/- 8° *Berlin* 77
*Ritschl, Friedrich Parerga zu Plautus und Terenz, vol. i.; 1 pl. 10/- 8° *Leipzig* 45
* " " Neue Plautinische Excursen, pt. i. 3/- 8° " 69
" " Prolegomena de rationibus criticis gram. prosod. metricis 4/- 8° " 80
A reprint of his Introduction to his edition of the Trinummus.
* " " Opuscula, vol. ii.: ad Plaut. et grammat. lat. spectans 17/6 8° " 68
Schoell + Goetz + Loewe, F. + G. + G. Analecta Plautina 6/- 8° Teubner, *Leipzig* 77
Divinationes in *Trnc.*; Symbola Crit. ad priores fabulas; Conjectanea Plaut.
Sonnenschein, Prf. E. A. Bentley's Plautine Emendations [Anecdota Oxon.] 2/6 f 4° Clar. Press 83
Edited fr. Bentley's annot. copy of Gronovius in the Bodleian; *v. also* same writer's ed. of *Captivi, supra.*
Spengel, L. Reformvorschläge—*ut infra, s.v.* Metrica. 8-
*Studemund, W. (ed.) Plauti Fabularum Reliquiae Ambrosianae cod. rescripti Ambros. Apographum 70/- f 4° *Berlin* 89

Life.

Collins, Rev. W. L. Plautus and Terence [pop. biog. and acc. of wks.; Anc. Class. for Eng. Rrs.] 2/6 f 8° Blackwood 73

Metrics.

Müller, C. F. W. Plautinische Prosodie, 16/-; Nachträge zur Plaut. Prosodie 4/- 8° *Berlin* 69; 71
" Lucian De Re Metrica Poetarum Latin. [esp. Plautus and Terence] 12/- 8° *Leipzig* 61
" " Rei Metricae Poetarum Lat. Summarium [esp. Plautus and Terence] 2/- s 8° " 78
Ritschl, Friedrich —*in* Prolegomena *to* vol. i. *of his edn. of* Plautus (1848); *also in his* Opuscula, vol. ii. [*ut supra*], *and* Neue Plautinische Excursen [*ut sup.*].
*Seyffert, Oscar Quaestionum Metricarum Particula [dissert. inaug.] 1/- 8° *Berlin* 64
*Spengel, Andr. Reformvorschläge zur Metrik bei Plautus u. d. übrigen Scenikern 10/- 8° " 82
" " De Versuum Creticorum usu Plautino [dissert. inaug.] 1/- 8° " 61
" " T. Maccius Plautus: Kritik, Prosodie, Metrik 3/- 8° *Göttingen* 65
*Studemund, W. De Canticis Plautini 2/- 4° *Halle* 64

K § 216

Seneca, Luc. Annaeus.

TEXT: Tragoediae: rec. R. Peiper+G. Richter 5/6 p 8° Teubner, *Leipzig* 67

ANNOTATED TEXT: ,, F. Leo; vol. i. [Observv. crit.] 3/-; ii. [Text, w. *Octavia*] 6/- p 8° Weidmann, *Berlin* 78; 79

TRANSLATION: übers. W. A. Swoboda, 3 vols. [w. German notes] 12/- s 8° *Vienna* [21-25] 28-30

,, Ed. Sommer, pts. i.-iv., vi., vii. [verse; no more pub.] ea. 9*d.* 12° *Dresden* 34

i.: Hercul. Fur.; ii.: Thyestes; iii.: Phoenissae; iv.: Hippol.; vi.: Troades; vii.: Medea. The last Eng. tr. was by Ed. SHERBURNE, 1702 [Medea, Phaedra, Hippol., Troades].

AIDS:

Braun, W. — Die Tragödie *Octavia* u. die Zeit ihrer Entstehung 1/6 8° *Kiel* 63

Richter, Gustav — De Seneca trag. auctore comment. philolog. [dissert. inaug.] 1/- 8° *Bonn* 62

Sandström, C. E. — De Senecae tragediis commentatio 2/6 8° *Upsala* 72

Schmidt, Bernh. — Observationes Criticae in Senecae tragoedias 2/- 8° *Jena* 65

Smith, R. M. — De arte rhetorica in L. A. Senecae tragoediis perspicua 2/- 8° *Leipzig* 85

Weil, Henri — La Règle des Trois Acteurs trag. de Sén. 1/6 8° *Paris* 65

Widal, Aug. — Études sur trois Trag. d. Sénèque [imit. fr. Eurip.] 2/6 18° *Aix* 64

Metrics.

Hoche, Max — Die Metra des Tragikers Seneca 1/6 8° *Halle* 62

Schmidt, Bernh. — De emendand. Sen. trag. rationibus prosod. et metr. 2/- 8° *Berlin* 60

Terence.

TEXTS: rec. A. Fleckeisen 1/6 p 8° Teubner, *Leipzig* [57] 74

,, Dr. W. Wagner [Camb. Texts] 3/- 12° Bell 69

* ,, F. Umpfenbach: ed. crit. 10/- 8° Weidmann, *Berlin* 70

* ,, C. Dziatzko 1/6 8° Tauchnitz, *Leipzig* 84

ANNOTATED TEXTS: with English notes Dr. W. Wagner 10/6; *red. to* 7/6 8° Bell 69

,, ,, ,, E. St. John Parry [Bibliotheca Class.] 18/-; *red. to* 9/- 8° ,, 57

Adelphi: with English notes H. Preble [Am.] [= tr. of Dziatzko] 30c. 12° *Boston* 8-

,, ,, ,, Rev. A. Sloman 3/- f 8° Clar. Press 86

,, ,, ,, Dr. W. Wagner 1/6 f 8° Bell

,, German ,, A Spengel 2/- p 8° Weidmann, *Berlin* 79

* ,, ,, ,, C. Dziatzko 2/- p 8° Teubner 81

Andria: with English notes Dr. W. Wagner 1/6 f 8° Bell 82

,, ,, ,, C. E. Freeman + Rev. A. Sloman 3/- f 8° Clar. Press 85

,, German ,, R. Klotz 5/6 8° *Leipzig* 65

,, ,, ,, A. Spengel 2/- p 8° Weidmann, *Berlin* 75

,, and Eunuchus: with English notes T. L. Papillon [Catena Classicorum] 4/6 c 8° Rivington [70] 78

Heauton Timorum.: ,, ,, ,, E. S. Shuckburgh [w. tr. 4/6; Classical Ser.] 3/- f 8° Macmillan 77

,, ,, ,, Dr. W. Wagner 1/6 f 8° Bell [72] 82

Phormio: with English notes J. Bond + A. S. Walpole [Class. Ser.] 4/6 f 8° Macmillan [79] 89

,, ,, ,, Dr. W. Wagner 1/6 f 8° Bell 82

,, ,, ,, Rev. A. Sloman 3/- 12° Clar. Press 87

* ,, German ,, C. Dziatzko 1/6 p 8° Teubner, *Leipzig* [74] 85

TRANSLATIONS:

Comedies: tr. H. T. Riley [literal prose; w. Phaedrus] 5/- c 8° Bohn's Lib. 53

übers. Joh. Herbst, 12 pts. ea. 35 pf. s 8° *Berlin* [55] 85 *sqq.*

,, J. J. C. Donner, 2 vols. [verse] 9/- 8° *Leipzig* 64

Heauton Timorum.: tr. E. S. Shuckburgh—*in his edn. of same, ut supra.*

AIDS:

Braun, Konrad — Quaestiones Terentianae [dissert. inaug.] 1/- 8° *Göttingen* 77

Engelbrecht, A. G. — Studia Terentiana 3/- 8° *Vienna* 83

Franke, Otto — Terenz und die lat. Schulcomödie in Deutschld. 3/- 8° *Weimar* 77

Kohl, A. — Didaskaliae Terentianae explicatae [dissert. inaug.] 1/6 8° *Halle* 66

Umpfenbach, F. — Analecta Terentiana [schl.-progr.] 1/- 4° *Mayence* 74

Adelphi.

Zimmermann, F. G. — Terenz und Menander [on the *Adelphi*; schl.-progr.] 1/- 4° *Clausthal* 42

Language.

Goetz, G. — Glossarium Terentianum 6*d.* 4° *Jena* 85

Henrichs, A. — De Ablativi apud Terent. usu et ratione [schl.-progr.] 1/- 4° *Elbing* 58-60

Hoffer, Chr. — De Personarum usu in Terentii comoediis [dissert. inaug.] 1/- 8° *Halle* 77

Life.

Collins, Rev. W. L. — Plautus and Terence [pop. biog. and acc. of wks.; Anc. Class. f. Eng. Rrs.] 2/6 f 8° Blackwood 73

Metrics.

Conrad, C. — Die metrische Composition d. Comödien des Terenz 5/- 8° *Berlin* 76

McCaul, J. — Remarks on the Terentian Metres *o.p.* [*pb.* 4/-; *w.* 2/6] c 8° Longman 28

Meissner, C. — Die Cantica d. Terenz und ihre Eurhythmie 3/- 8° Teubner, *Leipzig* 81

,, ,, — De iambico apud Terentium septenario 2/- 8° ,, ,, 84

Müller, Lucian — —*v.* Plautus, *supra.*

216. LATIN HISTORIANS AND GEOGRAPHERS.

Collections.

Geographi Latini Minores, coll. et rec. A. Riese 6/- 8° *Heilbronn* 78

Historicorum Romanorum Reliquiae, rec. H. Peter, vol. i., Vet. Hist. Reliq., 16/- 8°; Ed. Min., v. i. 5/6 p 8° Teubner 70; 83

Augustan Historians.

Historiae Augustae Scriptores, rec. H. Jordan + F. Eyssenhardt, iterum rec. H. Peter, 2 vols. 5/6 p 8° *Leipzig* [64] 65

Ammianus Marcellinus.

TEXTS: rec. F. Eyssenhardt, 11/-; Editio Minor 5/- 8° *Berlin* 71; 72
Fragmenta Marburgensia: rec. H. Nissen; w. photolith. pl. 4/- 4° ,, 76
ANNOTATED TEXT: *with Latin notes V. Gardthausen, 2 vols. ea. 4/- p 8° Teubner, *Leipzig* 74:75
TRANSLATION: tr. Prf. C. D. Yonge 7/6 c 8° Bohn's Lib. 62

AIDS:
Criticism, etc.
Hudemann, E. E. Quaestiones Ammianae [schl.-program.] 1/- 4° *Landsberg* 64
Michael, Hugo De Ammiani studiis Ciceronianis [dissert. inaug.] 1/- 8° *Wratislaw* 74
Möller, E. A. W. De Ammiano Marcellino [dissert. inaug.] 6d. 8° *Regensburg* 63
Reinhardt, G. De Praepositionum usu apud Ammianum 1/- 8° *Cöthen* 87
Reiter, A. De Ammiani Marcellini usu orationis obliquae 1/6 8° *Regensburg* 87
Textual Criticism
Gardthausen, V Conjectanea Ammianea cod. adhibito Vaticano 1/- 8° *Kiel* 69
Topography.
Gardthausen, V. Die geographischen Quellen des Ammian [*repr. fr.* Jahrbb. Class. Phil.] 1/6 8° *Leipzig* 73
Unger, Robert De Amm. Marc. locis controversis epistola [to Th. Bergk] 1/- 8° *Neu-Strelitz* 68

Caesar.

TEXTS: rec. B. Dinter, 3 v. [w. Suppls. of A. Hirt & others] ea. 1/-; Ed. Min. 2/- p 8° Teub. [64;70;76]80; [64-70]73-5
,, A. Holder: Ed. Crit. 15/- 8° *Freiburg* 82
,, F. Kraner [w. Suppls. of A. Hirt and others] 4/6 8°; 1/6 c 8°; 1/3 24° Tauchnitz, *Leipzig* 61
,, E. Hoffmann, 2 vols. 4/6 p 8° 90
ANNOTATED TEXT: *with English notes A. G. Peskett. i.-iii., 3/-; iv., v., vii., ea. 2/-; vi., viii., ea. 1/6 [Pitt Press] f 8° Camb. Press 78-85
De Bello Civili: with English notes C. E. Moberly [bk. i. separ. 2/-] 3/6 f 8° Clar. Press [72] 77
,, German ,, F. Kraner + F. Hoffmann; 2 maps 2/6 p 8° Weidmann, *Berlin* [56]85
,, ,, ,, A. Doberenz, ed. C. Dinter 2/6 p 8° Teubner, *Leipzig* [54]84
De Bello Gallico: with English notes C. E. Moberly 4/6 f 8° Clar. Press [71] 82
,, ,, ,, Dr. L. Schmitz 3/6 c 8° Collins 78
,, ,, ,, A. K. Isbister 4/- c 8° Longman [64] 66
,, ,, ,, Geo. Long [Gram. Sch. Class.] 5/6 f 8° Bell [61] 68
,, ,, ,, J. Bond + A. S. Walpole [after Kraner, Cl. Ser.] 6/- f 8° Macmillan 87
,, ,, ,, Prf. W. F. Allen + J. H. Allen + Prf. H. P. Judson [Ams.] $1.35 12° *Boston* 8-
,, German ,, F. Kraner + W. Dittenberger 2/6 p 8° Weidmann, *Berlin* [53]86
,, ,, ,, A. Doberenz, ed. B. Dinter 2/6 p 8° Teubner, *Leipzig* [52]77
,, ,, ,, H. Rheinhard; col. map, 9 pl., geog. and topic. index 3/- 8° *Stuttgart* [60] 86
bks. i.-iii.: ,, English ,, J. H. Merryweather + C. C. Tancock: i. 2/-; ii.-iii. 2/-; in 1 v. 3/6 f 8° Rivington [79] 89
,, i.-vii.: ,, ,, ,, *in* Macmillan's Elementary Classics ea. 1/6 18° Macmillan 79-87
Bk. i. [A. S. Walpole] 79; ii.-iii. [W. G. Rutherford] 79; iv. [C. Bryans] 86; v. [C. Colbeck] 87; vii. [J. Bond + A. S. Walpole] 87.
bks. i.-ii.; iii.-v.: ,, ,, ,, C. E. Moberly 2 vols.: ea. vol. 2/6 f 8° Clar. Press 89
,, vii.: ,, ,, ,, W. C. Compton; w. ill. of fortif., weapons, etc., & maps 4/6 c 8° Bell 89

TRANSLATION:
Commentaries on Gallic and Civil Wars, literally tr. 5/- c 8° Bohn's Lib. 51

AIDS:
Criticism, etc.
Freund, W. Präparationen zu Cäsar, 10 pts. ea. 6d. 12° *Leipzig* [ ] n.dd.
Köhler, Albrecht De auctorum belli Africani et Hisp. latinitate 2/- 8° *Erlangen* 77
Landgraf, G. Untersuchungen zu Caesar u. s. Fortsetzern [chfly. on *Bell. Alex.* and *Bell. Africum.*] 3/- 8° ,, 88
Procksch, Albrecht Gebrauch der Nebensätze bei Caesar [schl.-progr.] 1/- 4° *Bautzen* 70
Schlitte, Fr. De Gaio Julio Cesare grammatico [dissert. inaug.] 1/- 8° *Halle* 65
Wichert, Geo. Das Wichtigste a. d. Phraseol. bei Nepos u. Caesar 2/- 8° *Berlin* 72
Dictionaries.
Creak, Alb. Dictionary to Caesar's Gallic War 2/6 c 8° *Hodder* 71
Eichert, Otto Wörterb. zum Gall. Krieg. 1/6; zu Caes. u. s. Fortsetzer 2/- p 8° *Bresl.* [60]85; *Hanov.* [60]87
Menge + Preuss, R. + S. Lexicon Caesarianum, pts. i.-x. 18/- r 8° Teubner, *Leipzig* 85-90
*Merguet, H. Lexicon Caesareum, 3 vols. 53/- r 4° *Jena* 77-86
Preuss, S. Lexicon zu d. Pseudo-Caesarianischen Schriften 8/- 8° *Erlangen* 84
Names: Critic.
Glück, C. W. Die bei Caesar vorkommenden keltischen Namen 3/- 8° *Munich* 57
Life.
Delorme, S. César et ses Contemporains 3/-; übers. E. Döhler 3/6 8° *Paris* 68; *Leipzig* 73
*Froude, J. A. Caesar; a sketch [very eulogistic; popular] 6/- 8° Longman [79] 86
van Limburg-Brouwer, P. Cesar en zijne Tijdgenooten, 4 pts. 25/- 8° *Groningen* 44-46
Merivale, Dn. C. —*in his* History of the Romans [v. F § 12]
Napoleon iii. History of Julius Caesar (tr.); 2 vols., w. valuable maps and ill. 25/- 8°; 1 vol. 5/- c 8° Cassell 66
Written, as the author declares, "to prove that when Providence raises up such men as Caesar, Charlemagne, and Napoleon, it is to trace out to people the path they ought to follow," etc. In reality an apology for Napoleonic absolutism; but of some value, notwithstanding.
Fallue, L. Études Archéol. sur *César* par Napoléon 2/- 12° *Paris* 67
Rüstow, W. Geschichte Caesar's von Napoleon commentirt; maps 8/6 8° *Stuttgart* 65-67
Trollope, A. Caesar [pop. biog. and acc. of wks.; Anc. Class. f. E. Rrs.] 2/6 f 8° Blackwood 70
Williams, Archd. J. Life of Caesar 2/6 c 8° Routledge [54] 78
Ariovistus.
Schlumberger, J Caesar u. Ariovist [attempt to locate pl. of A.'s defeat] 3/- 8° *Colmar* 77
Vercingetorix.
Chappe, L. Vercingétorix: étude 1/- 8° *Paris* 66
Girard, M. A. Histoire de Vercingétorix, roi des Arvernes 2/6 8° *Clermond Ferrand* 64
"de Lyvron, L." [= L. de Lestoille] Vercingétorix 3/- s 8° *Paris* 69
Mathieu, P. P. Vercingétorix et César à Gergovia chez les Arvernes; 3 pl. 2/6 8° *Clermond Ferrand* 62
Monnier, Francis Vercingétorix et l'Indépendence Gauloise 2/- 12° *Paris* [74] 75

K § 216

Military.
Judson, Prf. H. Pratt (Am.) Caesar's Army; study of the military arts of Romans in last days of the Republic; maps 75c. 12° *Boston* 8-
[v.] Klöckeritz], F. Unters. üb. d. Kriegführung d. Römer in d. Feldz. d. Caesar, *etc.* 2/- 8° *Mayence* 6-
Prevost, Ferd. Dissert. sur le Pont constr. p. César, p. passer le Rhin; maps 1/- 8° *Saumur* 65
Rüstow, W. Heerwesen u. Kriegführung C. Jul. Caesars; 4 pl. 3/- 8° *Nordhausen* [55] 62
de Saulcy, Ferd. Les Campagnes de César dans les Gaules (military) 6/- 8° *Paris* 62
Naval.
Jal, Auguste La Flotte de César: études s. l. marine antique 3/6 12° *Paris* 61
Campaigns.
Bellum Africanum.
Fröhlich, Franz Das Bellum Africanum sprachlich u. histor. behandelt 2/- 8° *Brugg* 72
Bellum Civile.
v. Göler, Aug. Die Kämpfe bei Dyrrhachium u. Pharsalus; 4 pl. and plans 4/- 8° *Carlsruhe* 54
" " Der Bürgerkrieg zwischen Caesar und Pompeius; 2 pl. 2/6 r 8° *Heidelberg* 61
Hofmann, Fr. De Origine belli civilis Caesar commentarius 4/- 8° *Berlin* 58
Bellum Gallicum.
Fallue, L. Conquête des Gaules [analysis of the Commentaries] 6/- 8° *Paris* 62
v. Göler, A. Caesar's Gallischer Krieg; B.C. 58–53, 10 pl., 6/-; 52, 3 pl., 2/6; 51, 2 pl. 2/6 r 8° *Stutt.* 58; *Carlsr.* 59; *Heidelb.* 60
Köchly + Rüstow, H. + W. Einleitung zu Caesar's Gallisch. Krieg *o.p.* [*pb.* 2/-] r 8° *Gotha* 37
" H. Caesar und die Gallier [a lecture] 1/- 8° *Berlin* 71
Wagler, F. A. Hülfsbüchlein zu Caesar's *Bellum Gallicum* 6d 8° " [62] 77
Maps.
v. Kampen, A. [ed.] Maps to illustrate Caesar's Gallic War 6/- obl 4° Sonnenschein 79
Rüstow, W. [ed.] Atlas zu Caesar's Gallischem Krieg 2/6 r 8° *Stuttgart* 68
Bellum Hispanicum.
Degenhart, J. De auctoris belli Hispan. elocut. et fide histor. 2/6 8° *Würzburg* 77
Moléro, J. M. Sanchez Résumé d. Campagnes d. César en Espagne (tr. fr. Span.) 3/- 8° *Paris* 68

Topographical Monographs.
Britain —*for* Romans in Britain, *v.* F § 18.
Appach, F. H. Caesar's Brit. Expeds. and the subseq. geology of Romney Marsh 4/6 8° J. R. Smith 68
Lewin, Thos. The Invasion of Britain by Julius Caesar 10/- 8° Longman [59] 62
de Saulcy, Ferd. Les Expéditions de César en Grande-Bretagne 2/6 8° *Paris* 60
Vine, Rev. F. T. Caesar in Kent; maps [account of his landing and battles] 5/- s 4° Stock [87] 88
Wainwright, J. Julius Caesar: did he cross the channel? 4/- f 8° J. R. Smith 69
France.
Bréan, A. C. Jules César dans la Gaule 2/6 8° *Orléans* 64
" " Itinéraire de César d'Agendicum à Gergovia-Boiorum et Avaricum 2/- 8° " 65
Creuly + Jacobs, C. + A. Géographie Histor. de Gaule (inq. into sit. of Uxellodunum) 2/6 8° *Paris* 60
" " " Carte de Gaule sous le proconsulat de César 2/6 8° *Lyons* 64
Houssaye, H. Le Premier Siège de Paris 4/6 16° *Paris* 76
Maissiat, J. César en Gaule, vols. i.–ii. ea. 8/6 8° " 65; 76
Rouby, Ed. Le Siège de Marseilles par César; map 2/6 8° " 75
Alesia (7th Campaign).
Cucherat, Fr. Alésia et les Aulerci Brannovices 2/6 8° *Lyons* 64
Dejardins, E. Alésia [reply to art. in *Revue d. 2 Mondes*, 1 May, '58] 2/6 8° *Paris* 59
Fivel, Théod. L'Alésia près de Novalaise sur l. Rhône (Savoy) 4/6 8° *Arras* 66
Gouget, G. Mémoire s. l. Lieu d. l. bataille livrée d. l. siège d'Alésia 3/- 4° *Paris* 63
Gravot, A. Étude sur l'Alésia de César, Alise Izernore (Ain) 4/6 8° *Nantua* 62
Quicherat, Jules L'Alésia de César, 1/-; Conclusion pour Alaise 2/6 8° *Paris* 57; 58
Germany.
v. Cohausen, A. Caesar's Rheinbrücken philol., milit. u. techn. untersucht; 22 ill. 2/- 8° *Leipzig* 67
Eichheim, M. Caesar's Feldzüge gegen d. german. Belgier 1/- 8° *Neuburg* 64
v. Poellnitz, C. Römische Rheinbrücke bei Mainz 2/- 8° *Mayence* 84
Switzerland.
Eichheim, M. Die Kämpfe d. Helvetier gegen Caesar 1/6 8° *Neuburg* [66] 76
Fazy, H. Genève sous la Domination Romaine [archæological] 1/6 4° *Geneva* 68
Guillemot, P. Excursions archéol. dans les montagnes d. l. Côte-d'Or 3/- 8° *Dijon* 61

Curtius, Quintus.

TEXT: rec. H. E. Foss, 1/6; rec. Th. Vogel 1/6 p 8° Teubner, *Lps.* [51] 74; 80
" E. Hedicke 1/6 p 8° Weidmann, *Berlin* 67
with English notes C. T. Zumpt [tr. fr. Latin (1846)] 3/- 12° Chambers 52
" German " and intro. Th. Vogel, 2 vols. 2/6 and 2/- p 8° Teubner, *Lps.* [70] 75; [72] 85
" " " J. Mützell, 2 vols. 14/- 8° *Berlin* 75; 41
Selections: " English " W. E. Heitland + T. E. Raven [*sub tit.* Alex. in India; Pitt Press Ser.] 3/6 c 8° Camb. Press 79
TRANSLATION: übers. J. Siebelis, 9 pts. 3/6 p 8° *Stuttgart* [60] 66–73
" A. H. Christian, 4 pts. ea. 6d. 16° " [55] 73–75
AIDS:
Criticism, etc.
Alan, Henry Observationes in Q. Curtium Rufum 1/6 f 8° *Dublin* 65
Foss, H. E. Quaestiones Curtianae [schl.-programm.] 1/6 4° *Altenburg* 58
Krah, Ed. Curtius als Schullectüre, 2 pts. [schl.-program.] ea. 1/6 4° *Insterburg* 70; 71
Petersdorff, R. Neue Hauptquelle des Q. Curtius Rufus 2/- 8° *Hanover* 84
Textual Criticism.
Ling, M. Bericht üb. d. Curtius HSS. d. ungar. National-museums 1/6 4° *Pesth* 73
Schuessler, O. De Q. Curti Rufi codice Oxon. A. (schl.-progr.) 1/- 4° *Nordhausen* 74
Language.
Adams, W. De ablativi absoluti apud Q. Curtium Rufum usu 1/- 8° *Arnsberg* 86
Dictionary.
Eichert, Otto Wörterbuch zu Q. Curtius Rufus 2/6 8° *Hanover* 71
Schmidt, M. C. P. Schulwörterbuch zu Curtius Rufus 1/6 8° *Prague* 87
Life.
Hirt, Adolf Ueber d. Leben d. Geschichtschreibers Q. Curtius Rufus 2/- 8° *Berlin* 80

Ennius.

AID —*v.* K § 214.

Eutropius.

TEXTS: rec. R. Dietsch, 6*d.*; rec. F. Ruehl — 6*d.* p 8° Teubner, *Lps.* [50] 75; 87
,, W. Hartel, 9*d.*; rec. H. Droysen — 1/- p 8° Weidmann, *Berlin* 72; 78
cum vers. Graeca, etc., rec. H. Droysen — 16/- 4° *Berlin* 76
ANNOTATED TEXTS: with English notes C. Bradley + J. T. White — 2/6 c 8° Longman [2-] 66
,, ,, ,, W. Welch + C. G. Duffield [Elem. Class.] 1/6 f 8° Macmillan 83
TRANSLATION: tr. J. S. Watson [w. Justin and Nepos; w. notes] 5/- c 8° Bohn's Lib. 53
AIDS:
Hartel, W. — Eutropius und Paulus Diaconus [repr. fr. *Sitzsber. Wien. Akad.*] 1/6 r 8° *Vienna* 72
Pirogoff, W. — De Eutropii breviarii ab. u.c. indole ac fontibus 2/- 8° *Berlin* 73
Dictionary.
Eichert, Otto — Wörterbuch zu Eutropius 6*d.* 8° *Hanover* [50] 71

Florus

rec. C. Halm [w. Ampelius, rec. E. Wölfflin] 1/- p 8° Teubner, *Lps.* [54] 79
TRANSLATION: by J. S. Watson [w. Sallust and Velleius] 5/- c 8° Bohn's Lib. 58
AIDS:
Köhler, F. E. — Observationes Criticæ in Flavium [dissert. inaug.] 6*d.* 8° *Göttingen* 65
Reber, Jos. — Das Geschichtswerk d. Florus [schl. progr.] 1/6 8° *Freising* 65
Spengel, Leonh. — Ueber d. Geschichtsbücher d. Florus [fr *Abh. Bayer. Akad.*] 2/- 4° *Munich* 61

Livy.

TEXTS: rec. J. N. Madvig + J. L. Ussing, 8 pts. [ea. 2/- to 4/-] 22/6 8° *Copenhagen* 61–75
,, W. Weissenborn, 6 pts. ea. 1/- p 8° Teubner [50–51] 87
,, H. J. Müller bks. i.–xxvi. in 6 pts., ea. 1/- p 8° Weidmann, *Berlin* 81 *sqq.*
,, Martin Hertz, 4 vols. 24/- 8°; 7/- c 8°; 6/- 24° Tauchnitz, *Leipzig* 57–64
,, A. Luchs, 3 vols. ea. 3/- 8° Weidmann, *Berlin* 88, *etc.*
ANNOTATED TEXTS: *w. German notes W. Weissenborn + H. J. Müller, 10 v. 37/- [ea. 2/6 to 5/6] p 8° ,, [53–66] 75–86
,, ,, ,, M. + H. J. Müller + E. Wölfflin, 6 vols. ea. 1/6 to 2/- p 8° Teubner [ ] 86, *etc.*
Book i.: with English notes and [valuable] intro. Prf. J. R. Seeley 6/- 8° Clar. Press [71] 81
,, i.–iii.: ,, ,, ,, H. M. Stephenson: i. [Elem. Classics] 1/6; ii.–iii., 5/- [Class. Ser.] f 8° Macmillan 83
,, iv.: ,, ,, ,, the same [Pitt Press Series] 2/- f 8° Camb. Press 90
,, i.–v.: ,, ,, ,, Prendeville, bks. i.–iii., 3/6; iv.–v. 3/6 Bell 78
,, ii.: ,, ,, ,, H. Belcher 3/6 f 8° Rivington 82
,, ii.–iii.: ,, ,, ,, Rev. H. M. Stephenson [Class. Series] 5/- f 8° Macmillan 82
,, v.: ,, ,, ,, A. R. Cluer, rev. P. E. Matheson 2/6 f 8° Clar. Press [82] 89
,, xxi.–xxii.: ,, ,, ,, W. W. Capes [Classical Series] 5/- f 8° Macmillan 78
,, ,, ,, M. S. Dimsdale [Pitt Press Series] ea. 2/6 f 8° Camb. Press 89
,, xxi.–xxiii.: ,, ,, ,, M. T. Tatham [xxi., xxii. separ., ea. 2/6] 5/- c 8° Clar. Press [86] 88; 90
,, xxiii.–xxiv.: ,, ,, ,, G. C. Macaulay [Classical Series] 5/- f 8° Macmillan 85
Selections: (fr. Bks. viii.–ix.) with English notes E. Calvert + R. Saward 2/- 18° Rivington
w. English notes H. Lee-Warner, 3 parts ea. 1/6 f 8° Clar. Press 73–75
sub tit. Seven Kings of Rome, w. Eng. notes and vocab. J. Wright 3/6 f 8° Macmillan 87
Scenes fr. iv.–v. Decades of Livy, w. Eng. notes F. H. Rawlins [Class. Ser.] 3/6 f 8° ,, 87
TRANSLATIONS.
History of Rome: tr. Spillan + Edmonds + Devitte, 4 vols. ea. 5/- c 8° Bohn's Lib. 49–50
Bks. i.–iv.: tr. Rev. H. M. Stephenson Macmillan *in prep.*
,, xxi.–xxv.: Second Punic War, tr. A. J. Church + W. J. Brodribb 7/6 c 8° ,, 83
AIDS:
Criticism, Commentaries, etc.
Böttcher, C. — Kritische Untersuchungen üb. d. Quellen d. Livius [bks. 21–22] *o.p.* [*pb.* 2/-] 8° *Leipzig* 69
Freund, W. — Präparationen zu Livius Römischer Geschichte, 21 pts. ea. 6*d.* 16° ,, *n.d.*
Frigell, A. — Epilegom. ad Liv. lib. xxi.; Proleg. in libros xxii.–xxiii. ea. 1/6 8° *Upsala* 81; *Gotha* 83; 85
Kaestner, E. — Quaestiones Livianæ 2/- 8° *Celle* [41] 43
Keller, L. — Der zweite Punische Krieg u. seine Quellen 4/6 8° *Marburg* 75
Klinger, G. — De Decimi Livii libri fontibus 2/- 8° *Leipzig* 84
Koehler, U. — Qua rat. Liv. annalib. usi sint hist. Lat. et Græci 2/6 4° *Göttingen* 60
Kreyssig, J. Theoph. — Annotationes ad T. Livii libr. xli.–xlv. 4/- 4° *Meissen* 49
Machiavelli, N. — Discourses on 1st Decade of Livy, tr. N. Hill Thomson [1st edn. of orig. 1531] 12/- c 8° Paul 83
Müller, Mor. — Beiträge zur Kritik und Erklärung d. Livius [sch.-progr.] 1/- 4° *Stendal* 66
Nissen, H. — Kritische Untersuchungen üb. d. Quellen d. 4 u. 5 Dekade 5/- 8° *Berlin* 63
Perthes, H. — Quaestiones Livianæ [dissert. inaug.] 1/- 8° *Bonn* 63
Peter, C. — Ueber die Quellen d. 21–22 Buchs d. Livius [sch.-progr.] 2/- 4° *Naumburg* 63
Virck, H. — Quellen d. Liv. u. Dionysios f. d. älteste Gesch. d. röm. Rep. 2/- 8° *Strassburg* 77
Walker, John — Supplementary Annotations on Livy *o.p.* [*pb.* 12/-; w. 5/-] 8° Longman 22
Language.
Ballas, E. — Die Phraseologie des Livius 4/6 8° *Posen* 85
Güthling, C. E. — De Titi Livii Oratione, 2 pts. [schl.-progr.] ea. 1/- 4° *Lauban* 67; *Liegnitz* 72
Kühnast, L. — Hauptpunkte der livianischen Syntax 8/- 8° *Berlin* 72
Müller, Mor. — Zum Sprachgebrauch des Livius [schl.-program.] 1/6 4° *Stendal* 77
Riemann, O. — Etudes sur la Langue et Grammaire de Live 8° *Paris* [79] 84
Wölfflin, E. — Livianische Kritik und Livianischer Sprachgebrauch [schl.-progr.] 1/6 4° *Winterthur* 64
Dictionary.
Ernesti, A. W. — Glossarium Livianum, ed. I. T. Kreyssig 4/- 8° *Leipzig* [1784] 27
*Fügner, F. — Lexicon Livianum, pt. i. 2/6 r 8° Teubner, *Lps.* *in prog.* 85
Textual Criticism.
Alan, Henry — Emendationes Livianæ, 4 pts. ea. 2/- 12° *Dublin* 64; 67; 71; 74
Frigell, A. — Collatio codicum Livianorum atque editt. antiquiss., pt. i. 3/- 8° *Upsala* 78
Gitlbauer — De Codice Liviano vetustissimo Vindobonensi [dissert. inaug.] 5/- 8° *Vienna* 76
Luchs, A. — Emendationum Livianarum particulae, i.–iv. 3/6 4° *Erlangen* 81–90
Madvig, J. N. — Emendationes Livianae iterum auctiores editae 10/6 8° *Hauniae* [60] 77
Mommsen + Studemund, T. + G. — Analecta Liviana 12/- 4° *Leipzig* 73
Walker, John — Supplementary Annotations on Livy *o.p.* [*pb.* 12/-; w. 5/-] 8° Longman 22

K § 216

Life, etc.

Capes, Rev. W. W. — Livy [Classical Writers; introductory] 1/6 f 8° *Leipzig* 79

Collins, Rev. W. L. — Livy [pop. biogr. and acc. of wks.; Anc. Class. f. Eng. Rrs.] 2/6 12° Blackwood 76

*Taine, Henri — Essai sur Tite Live 3/- 12° *Paris* [60] 66

Topography.

Ellis, R. — Treat. on Hannibal's Passage of Alps over Mt. Cenis [v. Law, *inf.*] *o.p.* [*pb.* 7/6] 8° Parker 54

" " — Inquiry into the Ancient Routes 'tween Italy and Gaul 6/- 8° Bell 67

Conts. an exam. of the theory of Hannibal's passage of Alps by the Little St. Bernard.

Höfler, — Ueber Hannibal's Zug nach Etrurien [fr. *Sitzuber. Wien. Ak.*] 6d. r 8° *Vienna* 90

Law, W. J. — Criticism of Mr. Ellis' new theory of Route of Hannib. *o.p.* [*pb.* 3/-] c 8° Upham 55

" " — The Alps of Hannibal: exam. of the old controversy, 2 v. 21/- 8° Macmillan, *Camb.* 66

Maissiat, J — Annibal en Gaule 6/6 8° *Paris* 74

Replat, J. — Le Passage d'Hannibal dans les Alpes 2/- 12° *Annecy* 51

de Verneuil, R. — Étude sur le Passage du Rhône et d. Alpes [military] 2/- 8° *Paris* 73

Whitaker, John — The Course of Hannibal over the Alps ascertained, 2 v. *o.p.* 8° *London* 1794

Stories from Livy.

Church, Rev. A. J. — Stories from Livy; col. pl. 5/- c 8° Seeley [82] 87

Goldschmidt, P. — Geschichten aus Livius; 3 pl. (1 col.) 3/- 8° *Leipzig* 71

Nepos, Cornelius.

TEXT:

rec. C. Halm, 6d.; mit Wbch. H. Haacke, 1/6; rec. R. Dietsch p 8° Teubner, *Lps.* [71] 75; [ ]73; 59 [69]

" " " ed. crit. 2/6 8° *Leipzig* 71

" G. A. Koch 1/6 8°; 6d. c 8°; 6d. 24° Tauchnitz, *Lps.* 55

" C. Nipperdey 8d. p 8° Weidmann, *Berlin* 67

with English notes O. Browning, rev. W. R. Inge 3/- f 8° Clar. Press [68] 88

" " " Rev. J. F. Macmichael. [Gram. Sch. Cl.] 2/6 f 8° Bell 74

" " " J. T. White [new edn. of C. Bradley's edn.] 3/6 12° Longman [66] 72

" German " C. Nipperdey cur. B. Lupus: Ed. Minor 1/6 p 8° Weidmann, *Berlin* [51] 85

" " " " " Ed. Major 3/- 8° " " [49] 79

" " " J. Siebelis, ed. M. Jancovius 1/6 p 8° Teubner, *Leipzig* [51] 86

" " " H. Ebeling, 9d.; mit Wörterbuch 1/6 8° " " 71

" French " Monginot 5/- 8° *Paris* " [ ] 82

TRANSLATION:

tr. J. S. Watson [with Justin and Eutropius] 5/- c 8° Bohn's Lib. 53

trad. E. Sommer [w. the text] 2/6 12° *Paris* 75

AIDS:

Freund, W. — Präparationen zum Cornelius Nepos, 5 pts. ea. 6d. 16° *Leipzig* n.d.

Unger, G. F. — Der sogenannte Cornelius Nepos 3/6 4° *Munich* 81

Language.

Hölzer, V. — Beiträge zu einer Theorie der lateinischen Semasiologie [on Nepos] 6/6 8° *Berlin* 89

Ignatius, W. — De verb. c. praepos. compos. ap. Nep., Liv., Curt. c. dativo struct. 3/- 8° " 77

Lupus, Bernh. — Der Sprachgebrauch des Cornelius Nepos 6/6 8° " 76

Dictionaries.

Eichert, Otto — Schulwörterbuch zu Cornelius Nepos 1/- 16° *Breslau* [47] 82

Haacke, H. — Wörterbuch zu Nepos [also w. Halm's text, *supra*] 1/- p 8° Teubner, *Leipzig* [68] 87

Koch, G. A. — Erklärendes Wörterbuch zu d. Cornelius Nepos 1/- 8° *Hanover* [68] 85

White, J. T. — Vocabulary to Nepos 9d. 18° Longman 71

Pollio, C. Asinius.

De Bello Africo Commentarius: rec. E. Wölfflin + A. Miodonski 7/- 8° *Leipzig* 89

Sallust.

TEXTS:

rec. R. Dietsch: ed. crit., 2 vols. ea. 7/6 12° *Leipzig* 59

" R. Dietsch, 8d.; rec. H. Jordan 1/6 p 8° Teub. [43] 74; Weidm. [66] 87

" G. Long [Camb. Texts] 1/6 18° Bell 60

" F. D. Gerlach 2/6 8°; 1/- c 8°; 9d. 24° Tauchnitz, *Leipzig* 56

ANNOTATED TEXTS:

Catiline & Jugurtha: with English notes Profs. J. H. Allen + J. B. Greenough [Ams.] 65c. 12° *Boston* 8-

" " " W. W. Capes 4/6 f 8° Clar. Press 84

" " " G. Long [Grammar Sch. Class.] 5/- f 8° Bell 81

" " " Dn. C. Merivale, 2 pts. [Class Ser.] ea. 2/6 f 8° Macmillan [52] 82

" " " " Fraser, 2 pts. ea. 2/6 f 8° Bell

" Latin " R. Dietsch: Catiline *o.p.* [*pb.* 3/-; *w.* 7/6]; Jug. 4/6 12° Teubner, *Leipzig* 43; 46

" " " F. D. Gerlach 15/- r 8° *Basle* 52

" German " R. Jacobs + H. Wirz 2/6 p 8° Weidmann, *Berlin* [ ] 81

" " " R. Dietsch *o.p.* [*pb.* 2/6] p 8° Teubner, *Leipzig* 64

Catiline: " English " A. M. Cook [Classical Series] 4/6 f 8° Macmillan 84

" " " " B. D. Turner 2/- f 8° Rivington 87

Jugurtha: " " " A. M. Cook [Classical Series] f 8° Macmillan *in prep.*

Histor. Fragmenta: " Latin " F. R. Kritz, 3 pl. 9/ 8° *Leipzig* 53

KRITZ has also edited the Catiline and Jugurtha, with Latin notes, 2 vols. 4/6 and 9/- 8° *Leipzig*, 28; 34.

TRANSLATION:

Catiline & Jugurtha: tr. A. W. Pollard [Catiline *separ.* 3/-] 6/- c 8° Macmillan 82; 87

AIDS:

Criticism, etc.

Alan, Henry — In Sallustii Catilinam et Jugurth. curae secundae 2/6 c 8° *Dublin* 69

Freund, W. — Präparationen zu Sallust, 5 pts. ea. 6d. 16° *Leipzig* n.d.

de Gerlache — Études sur Sallust [and other historians] 4/6 8° *Brussels* [47] 76

John, Const. — Die Entstehungsgeschichte d. Catalin. Verschwörung 3/- 8° Teubner *Leipzig* 76

Jordan, H. — De C. Sallustii historiarum libri reliquiis 66

Teuffel, W. S. — Ueber Sallustius und Tacitus [schl.-progr.] 1/- 4° *Tübingen* 68
Textual Criticism.
Boese, Gustav — De fide et auctoritate cod. Sallust. Vat. 3864 [dissert. inaug.] 1/- 8° *Göttingen* 74
Clason, O. — Eine Sallust Handschrift aus d. Rostocker Univ.-Bibl. 2/- 8° Teubner, *Leipzig* 74
Kuhlmann, L. — Quaestiones Sallustianae Criticae 1/6 4° *Leipzig* 87
Language.
Badstübner, — De Sallustii dicendi genere commentatio [school-progr.] 1/6 8° *Berlin* 63
Braun, R. — Beiträge zur Statistik d. Sprachgebrauches Sallusts 1/- 8° ,, 85
Christ, O. — De Ablativo Sallustiano 2/- 8° *Jena* 83
Constans, L. — De Sermone Sallustiano 6/6 8° *Paris* 80
Nitschner, A. — De Locis Sallustianis qui apud scriptores et grammaticos veteres leguntur 2/6 8° *Göttingen* 84
Rohde, P. — Adjectivum quo ordine apud Sallustium conjunctum sit cum substantivo 2/6 4° *Hamburg* 87
Uber, F. — Quaestiones aliquot Sallustianae grammaticae et criticae 2/- 8° *Göttingen* 82
Dictionary.
Eichert, Otto — Vollständiges Wörterbuch zu C. Sallustius Crispus 2/6 8° *Hanover* [64] 71

Suetonius.—Texts.

Quae Supersunt : rec. C. L. Roth 1/6 p 8° Teubner, *Leipzig* [58] 75
Praeter Caes. libr. reliq.: rec. A. Reifferscheid ; 1 pl. 14/- 8° ,, ,, 60
De Gramm. et Rhet. lib.: rec. F. Osann : ed. crit. 3/- 8° *Giessen* 54
Transl.: Twelve Cæsars: tr. Dr. Alex. Thomson, rec. T. Forester 5/- c 8° Bohn's Lib. [1796] 55
,, ,, ,, ,, ,, ; w. 24 good ports. $3.75 m 8° *Philadelphia* 88

Aids:
Becker, Gust. — Quaestiones Criticae de Suet. de vit. Caesarum [sch.-progr.] 1/- 4° *Memel* 62
Ruhnken, D. [ed.] — Scholia in Suetonii vitas Caesarum 7/6 8° *Leyden* 88
Thimm, H. R. — De usu atque elocutione C. Suetonii Tranquilli [dissert. inaug.] 1/6 8° *Regensburg* 67

Tacitus.

Text: rec. C. Halm, 3 v. 8*d*. & 1/6 ; rec. C. Nipperdey, 4 v. 1/4 & 2/- p 8° Teub. [50-1] 80-3 ; Weidm. [71-2] 76
,, F. Haase, 2 vols. 7/6 8° ; 3/- c 8° ; 2/6 24° Tauchnitz, *Leipzig* 55
Agricola : ,, A. E. Schoene 2/- 8° *Berlin* 89
Germania : ,, A. Holder 2/- 8° Teubner, *Leipzig* 78
De Oratoribus : ,, Aem. Baehrens 2/6 8° *Leipzig* 81
Annot. Texts: * w. Lat. notes J. C. Orelli [v. ii. cur. H. Schweizer-Sidler + G. Andresen + C. Meiser
r 8° *Zürich & Berlin* [46-59] 59-84
i. [Annales] *o.p.* [*pb.* 10/- ; w. 19/-] *Zürich* [46-48] 59 ; ii. 1. [Germania] 4/6 *Berl.* [59] 77 ; ii. 2. [De Orat.] 3/- [59] 77 ; ii. 3. [Agricola] 4/6 [59] 80 ; ii. 4. [Hist. 1] 4/6 [59] 84.

with German notes [& tr.] F. Ritter, i.-ii. [Ann.] ea. 2/6 ; iii.-iv. [Hist., Agr.] 2/6 & 2/- 8° *Leipzig* 64-68
,, French ,, E. Jacob, 4 vols. ea. 6/6 8° *Paris* 75-77
Agricola & Germania : with English notes Prf. W. F. Allen [Am.] $1.10 12° *Boston* 8-
* ,, ,, ,, A. J. Church + W. J. Brodribb [Classical Ser.] ea. 2/-, or in 1 vol. 3/6 f 8° Macmillan [69] 82
,, ,, ,, Rev. P. Frost [Grammar Schl. Classics] 3/6 f 8° Bell 61
,, Latin ,, F. C. Wex 7/6 8° *Brunswick* 52
,, ,, ,, Fr. Kritz 2/- 8° *Berlin* [59] 74
* ,, German ,, A. A. Draeger 10*d*. p 8° Teubner, *Lpzg.* [ ] 84
* ,, ,, ,, C. Nipperdey + G. Andresen, vol. i. 3/6 ; ii. 3/- p 8° Weidmann, *Berl.* [ ] 79 ; [ ] 80
Annales : with English notes Rev. P. Frost [Bibliotheca Class.] 15/- ; *red. to* 8/- 8° Bell 72
,, ,, ,, Prf. G. O. Holbrooke [Am.] ; maps 16/- 8° Macmillan 82
* ,, ,, ,, H. Furneaux, vol. i. [= bks. i.-vi.] 18/- 8° Clar. Press 83
,, German ,, A. A. Draeger, 2 vols. ea. 2/6 p 8° Teubner, *Leipzig* [68] 87 ; [69] 87
* ,, ,, ,, K. Nipperdey, 2 vols. 3/- and 2/6 p 8° Weidmann, *Berl.* [51] 79 ; [52] 73
,, French ,, E. Jacob 2/6 12° *Paris* 77
,, bks. i.-ii. : with English notes A. H. Beesley 5/- f 8° Longman 69
,, ,, ,, J. S. Reid [Classical Series] f 8° Macmillan *in prep.*
,, ,, i.-iv. : ,, ,, ,, H. Furneaux [bk. i. separ. 2/- '87] 5/- f 8° Clar. Press 85
,, ,, vi. : ,, ,, ,, A. J. Church + W. J. Brodribb [Class. Ser.] 2/6 f 8° Macmillan 78
Germania [*v. also* Agric. *sup.*]: with English notes [and ethnogr. dissert.] Dr. R. G. Latham *o.p.* [*pb.* 12/6] 8° Walton 51
* with German notes Fr. Kritz, ed. W. Hirschfelder 2/6 8° *Berlin* [64] 78
,, ,, ,, [and tr.] A. Holtzmann, hrsg. A. Holder 8/- 8° *Leipzig* 73
,, ,, ,, Schweizer-Sidler 2/- 8° *Halle* [ ] 84
Historiae : with English notes W. H. Simcox, 2 vols. [Catena Class. ; Orelli's text] ea. 6/- c 8° Rivington 75 ; 76
,, ,, ,, Rev. W. A. + H. M. Spooner 8° Macmillan *in prep.*
,, ,, ,, ,, A. D. Godley [Classical Series] i.-ii. 5/- ; iii.-v. 5/- f 8° ,, 87 ; 90
* ,, German ,, C. Heraeus, 2 vols. ea. 2/- p 8° Teubner [64] 85 ; [70] 85
,, ,, ,, E. Wolff, vol. i. [= bks. i.-ii.] 2/6 p 8° Weidmann, *Berlin* 86
De Oratoribus : with German notes C. Peter 3/- 8° *Jena* 77
,, ,, ,, G. Andresen 1/- p 8° Teubner, *Leipzig* 72

Translations:
Agricola and Germany : tr. A. J. Church + W. J. Brodribb [w. dialogue on Oratory] 4/6 c 8° Macmillan [69] 77
Annals ,, A. J. Church + W. J. Brodribb [w. notes and maps] 7/6 c 8° ,, [76] 77
,, bks. i.-vi. : übers. A. Stahr [*sub tit.* Geschichte d. K. Tiberius ; w. notes] 8/- 8° *Berlin* 71
History : tr. A. J. Church + W. J. Brodribb [w. notes and map] 6/- c 8° Macmillan [64] 73

Aids:
Hochart, P. — De l'Authenticité d. Annales et d. Hist. de Tacite 7/- 8° *Paris* 84
Müller, Joh. — Beiträge zur Kritik u. Erklärung des Tacitus, 4 pts. ea. 1/3 8° *Innsbruck* 69-74
i.: Hist. i.-ii. 69 ; ii.: Hist. iii.-iv. 69 ; iii.: Ann. i.-vi. 73 ; iv.: Ann. xi.-xvi. and Index to the 4 pts. 74.

K § 216

Agricola.
Urlichs, L. — Commentatio de vita et honoribus Agricolae — 1/6 4° *Würzburg* 68

Annals.
de Meilhan, G. S. — Préface aux Annales de Tacite — 3/- 16° *Paris* 68
Pfitzner, W. — Die Annalen des Tacitus kritisch beleuchtet, v. i. [=bks. i.-iv.] 4/- 8° *Halle* 69
S., E. — Notes to the Annals of Tacitus, 2 vols. — 5/- 16° Parker 70

Germany.
Baumstark, A. — Urdeutsche Staatsalterthümer z. Erläuterung d. *Germania* — 22/- r 8° *Berlin* 71
" " — Ausführl. Erläut. d. Germania, 2 pts. — 22/- 8° *Leipzig* 75 : 80
i. Allgemeiner Theil, 15/-; ii. Besonderer völkerschaftlicher Theil, 7/-.
" " — Taciti *Germania* erläutert; w. map by H. Kiepert — 1/6 8° *Leipzig* [ ] 81
Böttger, H. — Wohnsitze d. Deutschen in d. v. Tacit. beschrieb. Lande; 1 col. pl. — 10/- 8° *Stuttgart* 77
Geffroy, Aug. — Rome et les Barbares [on the *Germania*] 3/- 12° *Paris* [74] 76
Keferstein, C. — Ansichten üb. d. celtischen Alterthümer [=edn. of *Germ.*, iii., pt. i.] 3/- 8° *Halle* 51
Müllenhoff, C. — Germania Antiqua — 3/- 8° *Berlin* 73
Schierenberg, G. A. B. — Die Römer im Cheruskerlande; 1 map — 3/- 8° *Frankfort* 62
Schweizer-Sidler, H. — Tacitus' Germania erläutert — 1/6 8° *Halle* [74] 84
Völker, C. C. C. — Der Freiheitskampf d. Bataver unter Claudius Civilus, 2 pts. — 4/- 8° *Elberfeld* 61 : 63
Waitz, Geo. — *in his* Deutsche Verfassungsgeschichte, vol. i. — 10/- 8° *Kiel* 65
v. Wietersheim, E. — Der Feldzug d. Germanicus an d. Weser; 1 map — 3/- r 4° *Leipzig* 50
Wormstall, Jos. — Ueber die Tungern und Bastarnen — 1/- 8° *Münster* 68

Textual Criticism.
Heraeus, C. — Studia Critica in Mediceos Tacit. codices, pt. i. (dissert. inaug.) 2/- 8° *Marburg* 46
Annals.
Tacitus und Bracciolani: the Annals forged in the XV. Century — 21/- r 8° Diprose & Bateman 78

Language.
*Dräger, A. — Ueber Syntax und Styl des Tacitus — 3/- 8° Teubner, *Leipzig* [69] 82
Gerber, A. — De Partic. quadam in serm. Tacit. proprietate [sch.-progr.] 2/- 4° *Leutschau* 63
" " — Dissert. de part. *an*, 1/6; De usu praepos. ap. Tac., 2/- [sch.-progr.] 4° *Perth* 65; *Glückst.* 71
" " — De Conjunctionum temporis usu Taciteo [sch. progr.] 2/- 4° *Glückstadt* 74
Hahn, Herm. — De Particularum *quasi* et *velut* usu Tacit. [dissert. inaug.] 2/- 8° *Göttingen* 77
Hüttermann, F. — De usu Subjunct. relat. et absol. ap. Tac. [" "] 1/- 8° *Münster* 64
Ihm, G. — Quaestiones syntacticae de elocutione Tacitea (compar. w. Caesar, Sallust, Velleius, etc.) 2/- 8/- *Giessen* 82
Maué, H. C. — De Praepositionis *ad* usu Taciteo [" "] 1/6 8° *Frankfort* 70
Sirker, C. — Taciteische Formenlehre — 2/- 8° *Berlin* 71
Zernial, U. — Capita ex Genit. usu Tac., 1/6; De Eloc. Tacit. — 1/- 4° *Göttingen* 64; *Burg* 68

Dictionary.
*Gerber + Greef, F. + A. — Lexicon Taciteum, pts. i.-viii. — ea. 4/- r 8° Teubner, *Leipzig* 77-90 *in prog.*

Grammar.
Reid, J. S. — A Grammar of Tacitus — 8° Macmillan *in prep.*

Life, etc.
Church + Brodribb, A. J. + W. J. — Tacitus [Classical Writers; introductory] 1/6 f 8° Macmillan 81
Clason, O. — Tacitus und Suetonius: eine vergleich. Untersuchung — 2/6 8° *Breslau* 70
Donne, W. B. — Tacitus [popular biog. and acc. of wks.; Anc. Class. f. E. Rrs.] 2/6 f 8° Blackwood 73
Dubois-Guchan, E. P. — Tacite et son Siècle, 2 vols. — 13/6 8° *Paris* [in pt., *Nantes*] 59 : 60
Freytag, L. — Tiberius und Tacitus — 7/6 8° *Berlin* [in pt., *Marburg* 68] 71

Valerius Maximus.

Factorum et Dict. Memorab.: rec. C. Halm, 4/6; rec. C. Kempf — 4/- p 8° Teubner, *Leipzig* 65 ; 89
Selections: with English notes W. R. Inge — 3/6 c 8° Rivington 90

AIDS:
Blaum, R. — Quaestionum Valerianarum Specimen (schl.-progr.) 2/- 4° *Strassburg* 76
Gelbcke, C. F. — Quaestiones Valerianae [dissert. inaug.] 1/- 8° *Berlin* 65
Zschech, F. — De Cicerone et Livio Valerii Maximi fontibus [dissert. inaug.] 1/- 8° " 65

Varro.

TEXTS:
Antiquitates: rec. R. Merkel—*in* Ovid's *Fasti* — 5/- 8° *Berlin* 41

AIDS — *v. also* K § 214: Latin Poets, K § 219: Latin Writers on Grammar, *and* § 221: Latin Writers on Agriculture.
Boissier, G. — Études sur la Vie et les Ouvrages de Varron — 6/6 8° *Paris* [61] 75
Mashly, Jac. — Varroniana — 1/- 4° *Basle* 65
Sanio, F. D. — Varroniana in d. Schriften d. röm. Juristen — 6/- 8° *Leipzig* 67
Language.
Müller, Aug. — De Priscis Verborum formis Varronianis [dissert. inaug.] 1/6 8° *Halle* 77
Stuenkel, L. — De Varroniana Verborum formatione [dissert. inaug.] 1/- 8° *Argentorati* 75

Velleius Paterculus.

TEXT: rec. C. Halm — 1/- p 8° Teubner, *Leipzig* 76
TRANSLATION: by J. S. Watson [with Florus and Sallust] 5/- c 8° Bohn's Lib. 52

AIDS:
Fechter, D. A. — Die Amerbachische Handschrift d. Velleius Paterculus — 1/6 8° *Basle* 44
Fritsch, — Ueber den Sprachgebrauch des Velleius Paterculus, pt. i. [schl.-program.] 2/- 4° *Arnstadt* 76
Georges, H. — De Elocutione M. Velleii Paterculi [dissert. inaug.] 1/6 8° *Leipzig* 77
Kaiser, P. — De fontibus Velleii Paterculi — 1/- 8° *Berlin* 84
Koch, G. A. — Quaestiones Velleianae [schl.-program.] 1/6 4° *Leipzig* 66
Stanger, Jos. — De M. Velleii Paterculi fide commentatio [dissert. inaug.] 1/- 8° *Munich* 83
Wilhelm, Eug. — Quaestiones Velleianae — 1/- 8° *Jena* 66
Dictionary.
Koch, G. A. — Wörterbuch zu Velleius Paterculus — 1/6 12° *Leipzig* 57

217. LATIN ORATORS.

Collection.

HALM, C. [ed.] Rhetores Latini Minores 17/- r 8° *Leipzig* 63

Cicero.

TEXT : Opera : *rec. J. G. Balter + C. L. Kayser, 11 vols. [separ. 1/6 and 2/- ea.] 22/- 8° Tauchnitz, *Leipzig* 60-69
,, J. C. Orelli + J. G. Baiter, 11 vols. 80/- r 8° *Zürich* [26-37] 45 63
* ,, R. Klotz + A. S. Wesenberg + C. F. W. Müller, rec. W. Friedrich 11 v. 22/6 p 8° Teubner, *Lpz.* [50-57] 80 *sqq.*
Also separately in vols., ea. 2/6 (vol. xi. : Indices), or in parts, 6*d.* to 1/6 each.
rec. C. F. A. Nobbe 22/6 r 4° Tauchnitz, *Leipzig* [28-50] 69
,, ,, ,, ; with Latin notes, 11 vols. [separ. 1/6 and 2/- ea.] 24/- i 8° ,, *Lpz.* [49-50] 66-73
Epistolæ : ,, A. S. Wesenberg, 2 vols. ea. 3/6 p 8° Teubner 72 ; 73
* ,, with English notes and proleg. Prf. R. Y. Tyrrell, 3 vols. ea. 12/- 8° Hodges, *Dublin* [79] 85 ; 86 ; 90
The "Correspondence of Cicero," arranged in its chronological order, with revised text. Mr. L. C. Purser is joint edr. of vol. iii.
ad Atticum : rec. et ill. J. C. G. Boot, 2 vols. vol. i. 7/6 ; ii. 8/6 8° *Amsterdam* 65 ; 66
,, bk. i. : with English notes A. Pretor 4/6 c 8° Bell 73
Selectae : rec. R. Dietsch, pt. i. 1/- ; ii. 1/6 [after Klotz's text] p 8° Teubner, *Leipzig* [54] 74
*with English notes Albert Watson [Text only, 4/-, '74] 18/- 8° Clar. Press [70] 81
,, ,, ,, E. St. John Parry 6/- c 8° Longman 67
,, ,, ,, J. H. Muirhead 6/- f 8° Rivington 85
,, ,, ,, C. E. Pritchard + E. R. Bernard 3/- f 8° Clar. Press [72] 82
,, ,, ,, G. Long, 1/6 ; J. E. Jeans [Elem. Class.] 1/6 f 8° Bell 80 ; Macmillan 84
,, Latin ,, A. Matthiae 4/- 8° *Leipzig* [16] 49
* ,, German ,, K. Supfle + E. Boeckel 3/6 8° *Carlsruhe* [36] 80
,, ,, ,, J. Frey 2/6 p 8° Teubner, *Leipzig* [64] 73
,, ,, ,, F. Hofmann + G. Andresen, 2 vols. ea. 2/6 p 8° Weidmann [60] 84 ; [78] 85
Orationes : rec. C. Halm, 2 vols. 16/- 8° *Leipzig* 45 ; 48
with English notes Geo. Long, 4 vols. [Bibl. Class.] 64/- ; *red. to* 32/- 8° Bell i. [51] 62 ; ii.-iv. 55-58
Also separately, i. 8/-, ii. 8/-, iii. 8/-, iv. 8/-. Useful for Roman Law.
Selectae : xi. rec. Otto Heine 2/6 8° *Halle* [ ] 83
xiii. with English notes Prf. W. F. Allen [Am.] ; ill. $1.40 12° *Boston* 8-
xxi. rec. R. Klotz, 2 pts. 1/6 p 8° Teubner, *Leipzig* [53] 74
*xviii. ,, K. Halm, 2 pts. ea. 1/- p 8° Weidmann, *Berlin* [38] 87
xviii. ,, A. Eberhard + W. Kirschfelder 2/- p 8° Teubner, *Leipzig* 74
Pro Archia : *with English notes Prf. J. S. Reid [Pitt Press Series] 2/- f 8° Camb. Press [78] 84
,, French ,, and new collation E. Thomas 2/6 8° *Paris* 82
,, German ,, F. Richter + A. Eberhard 6*d.* p 8° Teubner, *Leipzig* [ ] 84
and in Catil. : ,, ,, ,, C. Halm + G. Laubmann 1/6 p 8° Weidmann, *Berlin* [51] 82
and p. Licin. : * ,, English ,, Prf. J. S. Reid 1/6 f 8° Camb. Press 77
Pro Balbo : *with English notes Prf. J. S. Reid [Pitt Press Series] 1/6 f 8° ,, 78
In Caecilium : with German notes F. Richter + A. Eberhard 6*d.* p 8° Teubner, *Lps.* [70] 84
and Verrem iv.-v. : * ,, German ,, C. Halm + G. Laubmann 2/6 p 8° Weidmann, *Berlin* [52] 82
,, i. : ,, English ,, W. E. Heitland + H. Cowie [Pitt Press Series] 3/- f 8° Camb. Press 76
,, i. : ,, ,, ,, J. R. King 1/6 f 8° Clar. Press 87
Pro Caecina : * ,, Latin ,, C. Halm 6/- 8° *Leipzig* 47
In Catilinam : * ,, English ,, Prf. A. S. Wilkins [based on Halm ; Class. Series] 3/6 f 8° Macmillan [71] 85
,, ,, ,, E. A. Upcott 2/6 f 8° Clar. Press [87] 89
* ,, German ,, C. Halm + G. Laubmann 1/6 p 8° Weidmann [51] 86
,, ,, ,, F. Richter, hrsg. A. Eberhard 1/- p 8° Teubner, *Leipzig* [ ] 82
Pro Cluentio : * ,, English ,, W. Y. Fausset [an excellent edn.] 6/- c 8° Rivington 87
* ,, ,, ,, W. Ramsay, ed. Prf. G. G. Ramsay 3/6 f 8° Clar. Press [59] 69
Pro Deiotaro : — *v.* Pro Ligario, *infra*.
Pro L. Flacco : with German notes A. Du Mesnil 4/6 8° Teubner, *Leipzig* 83
De Lege Agraria : ,, Latin ,, A. W. Zumpt 2/6 8° *Leipzig* 61
Pro Lege Manilia : [Imper. Cn. Pomp.] *w. Eng. notes Prf. A. S. Wilkins [based on Halm ; Class. Ser.] 2/6 f 8° Macmillan [79] 85
*with Latin notes C. Halm 3/6 8° *Leipzig* 48
with German notes Fr. Richter 1/- p 8° Teubner, *Lps.* [ ] 83
and p. Roscio : with German notes C. Halm + G. Laubmann 1/6 p 8° Weidmann, *Berlin* [54] 81
Pro Archia : *with English notes Prf. J. S. Reid 1/6 f 8° Camb. Press 77
Pro Ligario, Deiotaro, and Marcello : with German notes F. Richter, hrsg. A. Eberhard 1/- p 8° Teubner, *Leipzig* [70] 86
,, ,, *and Milone, ,, ,, ,, C. Halm + G. Laubmann 1/6 p 8° Weidmann, *Berlin* [50] 86
Pro Marcello : —*v.* Pro Ligario, *supra*.
with German notes F. Richter, hrsg. A. Eberhard 1/- p 8° Teubner, *Lps.* [ ] 86
Pro Milone : with English notes J. S. Purton [Pitt Press Series] 2/- f 8° Camb. Press [73] 75
Vide also Pro Ligario, Deiotaro and Milone, *supra*.
Pro Murena : with English notes W. E. Heitland [Pitt Press Series] 3/- f 8° Camb. Press [75] 76
,, Latin ,, C. Zumpt 2/- 8° *Berlin* 59
,, German ,, C. Halm + G. Laubmann 1/6 p 8° Weidmann, *Berlin* [66] 83
,, ,, ,, H. A. Koch, hrsg. G. Landgraf 1/- p 8° Teubner, *Leipzig* [66] 85

K § 217

Philippicae: with English notes Rev. J. R. King 10/6 8° Clar. Press [68] 79
" German " C. Halm + G. Laubmann 1/6 p 8° Weidmann, *Berlin* [56] 86
" " " H. A. Koch, hrsg. A. Eberhard 1/- p 8° Teubner, *Leipzig* [70] 78
ii.: * " English " Prf. J. E. B. Mayor [based on Halm; Class. Series] 5/- f 8° Macmillan [61] 82
" " " G. A. Peskett, 2 vols. 3/6 12° Camb. Press 87
Pro Plancio: " " " H. A. Holden [Pitt Press Series] 4/6 f 8° " [81] 81
" German " E. Köpke 1/6 p 8° Teubner, *Leipzig* [56] 73
Pro Rabirio: " English " W. E. Heitland 7/6 8° Camb. Press 82
Pro Roscio Amerino: " " " E. H. Donkin [tr. of Halm; Class. Series] 4/6 f 8° Macmillan 79
" " " St. George Stock 3/6 f 8° Clar. Press 90
" German " G. Landraf: ed. crit. 6/- 8° *Erlangen* 84
" " " F. Richter, hrsg. A. Fleckeisen 1/- p 8° Teubner, *Leipzig* [64] 77
" and p. Lege Man: * " " " C. Halm + G. Laubmann 1/6 p 8° Weidmann, *Berl.* [54] 86
Pro P. Sestio: " English " H. A. Holden [Classical Series] 5/- f 8° Macmillan 83
* " Latin " C. Halm 5/6 8° *Leipzig* 45
" German " H. A. Koch, hrsg. A. Eberhard 1/- p 8° Teubner, *Leipzig* [63] 77
" " " C. Halm + G. Laubmann 1/6 p 8° Weidmann [53] 86
Pro Sulla: * " English " Prf. J. S. Reid [Pitt Press Series] 3/6 f 8° Camb. Press 82
* " Latin " C. Halm 3/- 8° *Leipzig* 45
" German " F. Richter, hrsg. G. Landraf 9d. p 8° Teubner, *Leipzig* [69] 85
" and p. Murena: * " " " C. Halm + G. Laubmann 1/6 p 8° Weidmann, *Berlin* [66] 83
In Vatinium: * " Latin " C. Halm 2/6 8° *Leipzig* 46
In Verrem, i.: " English " H. Cowie [Pitt Press Series] 1/6 f 8° Camb. Press 76
iv.; v.: " German " F. Richter, hrsg. A. Eberhard ea. 1/6 p 8° Teubner, *Leipzig* [66] 76–86
iv.–v. & in Caec.: * " " " C. Halm + G. Laubmann 3/- p 8° Weidmann, *Berlin* [52] 82
Selections: Extracts from Cicero, with English notes H. Walford, 3 pts. ea. 1/6 f 8° Clar. Press 79
Chrestomathia Ciceroniana, with German notes C. F. Lüders 3/- p 8° Teubner, *Leipzig* [67–68] 78

TRANSLATIONS —*v. also* O § 14: Eclectics.
Orations: [literally] tr. Prf. C. D. Yonge, 4 vols. ea. 5/- c 8° Bohn's Lib. 51–52
übers. C. Halm, w. German notes, 7 pts. ["Ausgewählte Reden"] ea. 1/3 p 8° Teubner, *Lps.* [ ] 83–86
In Catilinam: The Catiline Orations, tr. W. C. Green 2/6 12° Bell 76
Pro Cluentio: tr. W. C. Green 3/- f 8° Hall, *Cambridge* 71
Epistolae: —*in* Life and Letters of Cicero, by Rev. G. E. Jeans 10/6 c 8° Macmillan [80] 88
A tr. of the Letters is incl. in Watson's edn. [*ut supra*] with notes.
Philippics (14): tr. Rev. J. R. King 6/-; New Transl. of i.–ii. (only) 2/6 c 8° Thornton, *Oxon.* 78; 80

AIDS:
Bibliography.
Deschamps, P. Essai Bibliographique sur Cicéron [w. pref. Jules Janin] 5/- 8° *Paris* 63
Criticism, etc.
Munk, Ed. —*ut infra*; contains a digest of Cicero's writings.
Wallies, M. De Fontibus Topicorum Ciceronis [dissert. inaug.] 1/- 8° *Halle* 78
Letters.
Klotz, Reinh. Adnotat. ad Cic. epist. ad Pomponium, 2 pts. 2/- 4° *Leipzig* 69
Nake, Bruno Hist. Crit. Cicer. epist., 1/- 8°; De Planci et Cic. epp. 2/- 4° *Bonn* 61; *Berlin* 66
" " Der Briefwechsel zwischen Cicero und Decimus Brutus 2/- 8° Teubner, *Leipzig* 76
Nisard, Charles Notes sur les Lettres de Cicéron 4/6 8° *Paris* 82
Textual Criticism.
Krauss, J. M. Ciceronis Epistolarum Emendationes 1/- 8° Teubner, *Leipzig* [66] 63
Lectiones Variae ex M. T. Cic. edit. Oxon. et Neapol. descriptae, 3 vols. 12/- 8° *Halle* 25–30
Seyffert, Moritz Palaestra Ciceroniana 4/- 8° *Leipzig* [ ] 83
Thurot, Chas. Cicéron *Epistolae ad familiares* [notice of 12 cent. MS. in Paris] 2/- 8° *Paris* 74
Wesenberg, A. S. Emendationes [alterae]: sive annot. crit. ad Cic. epistol. 3/- 8° Teubner, *Leipzig* 73
Wrampelmeyer, H. Codex Wolfenbuttelanus No. 205, 4 pts. [Caeliana, Murena] 5/- 4° *Hanover* 72; 73; 76; 78
Language.
Frohwein, E. Die Perfectbildungen auf *vi* bei Cicero 2/- 8° *Gera* 74
Hellmuth, H. De Serm. Proprietatibus quae in prioribus Cic. oratt. inveniuntur 1/- 8° *Erlangen* 78
Landgraf, G. Ciceronis Elocutione in orationibus pro P. Quinctio et pro Sex. Rosc. Am. 1/- 8° *Würzburg* 78
Lieven, H. Die consecutio temporum des Cicero 2/- 4° *Riga* 72
Nieländer Der factitive Dativus in d. Ciceron. Schriften 1/6 4° *Krotoschin* 74
Stinner, A. De eo quo Cicero in Epistolis usus est sermone 2/- 8° *Oppeln* 79
Thielmann, Ph. De Sermonis Proprietatibus quae leguntur ap. Cornificum et in primis Ciceronis libris [diss.] 2/- 8° *Strassburg* 79
Wetzel, M. De consecutione temporum Ciceron. capita duo [dissert. inaug.] 1/6 8° Teubner, *Leipzig* 77
Dictionaries.
*Merguet, H. [ed.] Lexicon zu den Reden des Cicero, 4 vols., £9 10/-; Lex. z. d. Schriften Cic., pts. i.–viii. ea. 4/- 1 8° *Jena* 77–84; 87 *in prog.*
Nizoli, M. [ed.] Lex. Cicer. ex rec. Alex. Scoti, cur. J. Facchiolati, 3 vols. *o.p.* [*pb.* 30/6] 8° Priestley (1734) 20
Orelli + Baiter, J. C. + J. G. Onomasticon Tullianum, 3 pts. [= vols. vi.–viii. of their *edn.* of Cic. works] 27/- 8° *Zürich* 36–38
Life, etc.
Abeken, B. R. Account of the Life and Writings of Cicero, tr. Chas. Merivale *o.p.* [*pb.* 9/-; *w.* 5/-] c 8° Longman 54
Boissier, G. Cicéron et ses Amis: étude s. l. soc. rom. d. temps de Cés. 3/- 12° *Paris* [65] 77
Brückner, C. A. F. Leben des M. Tullius Cicero, pt. i. [civil and priv. life] 10/- 8° *Göttingen* 52
Collins, W. L. Cicero [pop. biog. and acc. of wks.: A. C. f. E. Rrs.] 2/6 f 8° Blackwood [72] 85
Forsyth, Wm. Life of Marcus Tullius Cicero [champions Cicero; mainly drawn fr. his letters] 10/6 8° Murray [64] 71
Froude, J. A. —*in his* Caesar: a sketch [a temperate condemnation of Cicero] 6/- c 8° Longman [79] 80
d'Hugues, G. Une Province Romaine sous la Républ. [proconsulat of Cic.] 3/- 12° *Paris* 76
Jeans, Rev. G. E. Life and Letters [tr.] of Cicero [w. historical and critical notes] 10/6 c 8° Macmillan [80] 88
Middleton, Rev. C. Life of Cicero ["standard"] *o.p.* [*pb.* 9/-; *w.* 3/-] c 8° Bohn [1741] 48
Muirhead, J. H. Cicero: Intro. to Study of his Life and Works 1/6 c 8° MacLehose, *Glasg.* 83
Munk, Ed. The Student's Cicero, tr. and ed. W. Y. Fausset; port. 3/6 c 8° Sonnenschein 89
An able vindication of Cicero fr. the fierce attacks of MOMMSEN, with tr. extracts.
Trollope, Anthony Life of Cicero, 2 vols. 24/- c 8° Chapman 89
A defence of Cicero's political course agst. the views held by MOMMSEN, FROUDE, MERIVALE, and others.

Quintilian —*v.* K § 220.

Seneca, M. Annaeus [father].

TEXT: rec. A. Kiessling 4/6 p 8° Teubner, *Leipzig* 72
,, Conrad Bursian 7/6 8° *Leipzig* 57

AIDS:
Buschmann, Charakteristik d. griech. Rhetoren bei Seneca [sch.-progr.] 1/6 4° *Parchim* 78
Gruppe, Otto Quaestiones Annaeanae [dissert. inaug.] 1/- 8° *Sedini* 73
Sander, M. Der Sprachgebrauch Seneca's, 2 pts. 3/- 4° *Waren* 77: 80

218. LATIN PHILOSOPHERS.

Cicero.

Opera: —v. K § 217: Latin Orators.
Academica: *with English notes Prf. J. S. Reid 15/- 8° Macmillan [74] 85
De Amicitia (Laelius): * ,, ,, ,, Prf. J. S. Reid [Pitt Press Series] 3/6 f 8° Camb. Press [79] 84
,, ,, ,, A. Sidgwick 2/- 12° Rivington [78] 83
,, ,, ,, Geo. Long 1/6 f 8° Bell 80
,, ,, ,, E. S. Shuckburgh [Elem. Class.] 1/6 18° Macmillan 85
* ,, German ,, M. Seyffert, hrsg. C. F. W. Müller 9/- 8° *Leipzig* [*Brandenb.* 74] 76
,, ,, ,, C. W. Nauck, 9d.; J. Sommerbrodt 9d. p 8° Weidmann [52] 84; [ ] 84
,, ,, ,, G. Lahmeyer 9d. p 8° Teubner, *Leipzig* [62] 75
,, ,, ,, C. Meissner 9d. p 8° ,, ,, 87
,, & De Senec. (Catomaj.): ,, English ,, W. Heslop 2/- f 8° Clar. Press 84
De Finibus: * ,, ,, ,, Prf. J. S. Reid, 3 vols.: i. and ii. *in prep.*; iii. = tr. 8/- 8° Camb. Press *in prep.*; 83
* ,, Latin ,, J. N. Madvig 22/6 8° *Copenhagen* [38] 76
,, German ,, H. Holstein 3/- p 8° Teubner, *Leipzig* 73
bks. i.-ii.: ,, ,, ,, D. Boeckel 1/6 p 8° Weidmann, *Berlin* 72
De Legibus: ex. rec. J. Vahlen 4/- 8° *Berlin* [71] 83
with German notes A. Du Mesnil 5/- 8° *Leipzig* 79
De Natura Deorum: ,, English ,, Prf. J. B. Mayor: Ed. Crit., i. 10/6; ii. 12/6; iii. 10/- 8° Camb. Press 80-85
,, ,, ,, of G. F. Schömann, tr. A. Stickney [Am.] $1.55 12° *Boston* 8-
,, German ,, G. F. Schömann 2/6 p 8° Weidmann, *Berlin* [50] 76
,, ,, ,, A. Goethe 2/6 p 8° Teubner, *Leipzig* 87
De Officiis: with English notes H. A. Holden [w. intro. and analysis] 9/- c 8° Camb. Press [54] 84
,, German ,, O. Heine 2/6 p 8° Weidmann [57] 85
,, ,, ,, J. v. Gruber 1/6 p 8° Teubner, *Leipzig* [56] 74
,, ,, ,, C. Tücking 2/6 8° *Paderborn* 79
,, ,, ,, C. F. W. Müller 2/6 p 8° Teubner, *Leipzig* 82
De Republica: with German notes C. Meissner 6d. p 8° Teubner *Lpz.* [*Berlin* 69] 78
,, French ,, and intro. J. E. Vignon 2/6 12° *Paris* [76] 78
Somnium Scipionis: with English notes W. D. Pearman [Pitt Press Ser.] 2/- f 8° Camb. Press 83
,, German ,, C. Meissner 6d. p 8° Teubner, *Leipzig* [70] 86
De Senectute (Cato maj.): *with English notes Geo. Long [Camb. Texts with Notes] 1/6 f 8° Bell 80
[*v. also* De Amic. *supra*.]
,, ,, ,, Prf. J. S. Reid [Pitt Press Ser.] 3/6 f 8° Camb. Press 79
,, ,, ,, E. S. Shuckburgh [Elem. Class.] 1/6 18° Macmillan 82
,, ,, ,, A. Sidgwick 2/- 12° Rivington 78
,, ,, ,, J. H. Allen + J. B. Greenough [Ams.] 65c. 12° *Boston* 8-
,, German ,, G. Lahmeyer, 9d.; C. Meissner 8d. p 8° Teubner [57] 77; [70] 85
,, ,, ,, J. Sommerbrodt 1/- p 8° Weidmann, *Berlin* [51] 77
Tusculanae Disputationes: rec. Mor. Seyffert 6/- 8° *Leipzig* 64
with Latin notes R. Kühner 9/6 8° *Jena* [ ] 74
* ,, German ,, G. Tischer + G. Sorof, 2 pts. ea. 1/6 p 8° Weidmann, *Berlin* [50] 84-86
,, ,, ,, O. Heine 2/6 p 8° Teubner, *Leipzig* [64] 73

TRANSLATIONS: —v. C § 14: Eclectics.

AIDS —v. *also* K § 217, K § 220.
Desjardins, A. Les Devoirs: essai sur la morale de Cicéron [prize essay] 3/- s 8° *Paris* 65
Hirzel, R. Untersuchungen zu Cicero's Philosoph. Schriften, 3 vols. 35/- 8° *Leipzig* 77-83
i: De Nat. Deor., 5/-; ii., De Fin., De Off., 18/-; iii: Acad., Tusc. Disp., 12/-.
Levin, T. W. Six Lectures Introductory to the philosophical writings of Cicero 7/6 8° Deighton, *Camb.* 71
Mayor, Prf. J. E. B. Sketch of Ancient Philosophy from Thales to Cicero 3/6 12° Camb. Press 81
Intended mainly for students reading CICERO.
*Zeller, Prf. Ed. History of Eclecticism in Greek Philosophy, tr. S. F. Alleyne 10/6 c 8° Longman 83
ZELLER'S & LEVIN'S books are the only two of the above which deal directly or at all extensively with CICERO'S philosophy.

De Natura Deorum.
Klotz, Reinh. Adnotat. crit. ad Cic. *de nat. deorum*, 4 pts. 2/6 4° *Leipzig* 67-68
De Officiis.
Leitmeir, D. Apologie d. christl. Moral. [compar. of *de off.* and Ambrose] 2/- 8° *Munich* 66
De Oratore.
Piderit, K. W. Zur Kritik und Exegese von Cicero *de oratore* 2/- 8° *Hanau* 57-58
De Republica.
Macrobius, Comm. in Somnium Scipionis [one of the chief sources for the *Repub.*]—v K § 224.

Lucretius —v. K § 214: Latin Poets.

Seneca, Luc. Annaeus.

Opera quae supersunt: rec. F. Haase, 3 vols. 8/- p 8° Teubner, *Lpz.* [52-53] 72-74

i.: Dialogi, Epigrammata super Exilio, Ludus de Morte Claudii, De Clementia, 2/6 [52] 74; ii.: De Benefic., Natur. Quaestt., 2/6 [52] 73; iii.: Epistt. moral., Fragm., De Remed. fort., Supposita, 4/- [53] 72.

5 vols. [Editio Tauchnitiana] ea. 1/3 16° *Leipzig* [32] 73-78

i.-ii.: Scripta Moral; iii.-iv.: Epist. ad Lucil.; v.: Nat. Quaestt., Apocolocyntosis, Fragm., Indices.

rec. H. J. Müller 14/- 8° *Prague* 87

Dialogorum lib. xii.: *rec. M. C. Gertz 8° *Copenhagen* 87

,, H. A. Koch + J. Vahlen: ed. crit. 5/- 8° *Leipzig* 79

De Benef. et Clement.: ,, M. C. Gertz 4/6 p 8° Weidmann, *Berlin* 76

TRANSLATIONS:

De Beneficiis: On Benefits, tr. Aubrey Stewart 3/6 c 8° Bohn's Lib. 87

Minor Dialogues: tr. Aubrey Stewart [with his dialogue on Clemency] 5/- c 8° ,, 89

Morals: ,, W. Clode [a selection of his prose; Camelot Series] 1/- 16° Walter Scott 88

AIDS —*for* English Books, *v.* O § 11: Stoics.

Life and Philosophy.

Aubertin, Chas. Sénèque et S. Paul 3/- 12° *Paris* [57] 70

Doergens, Armin. Senecae disciplinae moralis cum Antoniniana comparatio 2/6 8° *Leipzig* 57

Fleury, A. S. Paul et Sénèque, 2 vols. 10/6 8° *Paris* 53

Haas, Jac. De L. Annaei Senecae Philosoph. monitis [dissert. inaug.] 2/- 8° *Munich* 78

Holzheer, Der Philosoph. Seneca, 2 pts. [school-program.] 3/6 8° *Rastatt* 58: 59

Martens, Alfred De L. Annaei Senecae vita et tempore 1/6 8° *Altona* 71

Science.

Marx, K. F. H. Anordnung der d. Medic. betreff. Aussprüch. Senecas 3/- 4° *Göttingen* 77

Nehring, A. Die geologischen Anschauungen d. Seneca, 2 pts. [sch.-progs.] 2/- 4° *Wolfenbüttel* 73: 76

Textual Criticism.

Gertz, M. C. Studia Critica in Senecae Dialogos 3/6 8° *Copenhagen* 74

Matthiae, Otto Observationes Criticae in L. Annaeum Senecam [dissert. inaug.] 1/- 8° *Berlin* 65

Language.

Hoppe, A. Ueber die Sprache des Philosoph. Seneca, 2 pts. [schl.-progrs.] *Lauban* 73: 77

Rauschning, O De Latinitate L. Annaei Senecae [dissert inaug.] 1/- 8° *Regensburg* 76

Varro.

Logistorici: rec. A. Riese—*in his edn of* Saturae Menippeae 6/- 8° Teubner, *Leipzig* 65

Curio de Cultu Deorum: fragm., coll., et adnot. L. Krahner [sch.-progr.] 2/6 4° *Friedland* 51

219. LATIN WRITERS ON GRAMMAR, LEXICOGRAPHY, METRICS, &c.

Collectively.

KEIL, H. [ed.] Grammatici Latini, 7 vols. and Supplement 158/6 8° *Leipzig* 55-80

i.: Charisius. Diomedes 19s. | ii.-iii.: Priscianus £1 11s. | iv.: Probus, Donatus, Servius, Sergius 19s. | v.: Cledonius, Pompeius, Julianus, Consentius, Phocas, Eutyches, Augustinus, Palaemon, Asper, Macrobius 19s. | vi.: Victorinus, Caesius, Bassus, Fortunatianus, Terentianus Maurus, Plotius, Rufinus, Mallius Theodorus £1 3s. | vii.: Scaurus, Velius Longus, Caper, Agroecius, Cassiodorus, Martyrius, Beda, Albinus, Audax, Dositheus, Arusianus, Messius, Corn. Fronto £1 11s. 6d. | *Suppl.* Anecdota Helvetica, ed. H. Hagen 19s.

Metrology.

GAISFORD, Thomas [ed.] Scriptores Latini Rei Metricae *o.p.* [*pb.* 12/-; *w.* 4/6] 8° *Oxford* 37

Marius Victorinus | Marius Plotius Sacerdos | Caesius Bassus | Atilius Fortunatianus | Servius *de centrum metris* | Rufinus | Censorinus | Priscianus *de metr. comic.* | Diomedes | Mallius Theodorus | Julius Severus *de pedibus* | Isidori glossarium; *etc.*

Festus, S. Pompeius

De Verborum Significatione, ed. A. Dacer, 2 vols. [Delphine edn.] *o.p.* [*w.* 10/-] r 8° Valpy 26

*,, ,, ,, ,, A. Thewrewk de Ponor, pt. i. 7/6 8° *Leipzig* 90

Loci [metrologici] e Festi lib. de verb. signif., rec. F. Hultsch—*in* Metrol. Reliq., vol. ii. 2/6 p 8° Teubner, *Leipzig* 66

TRANSLATION: trad. A. Savagner [Collection Panckoucke] *o.p.* 8° *Paris* 46

Nonius Marcellus & Fulgentius

ed. F. D. Gerlach + C. L. Roth [w. crit. appar.] 4/- r 8° *Basle* 42

ed. Lud. Quicherat 12/6 8° *Paris* 72

ed. J. H. Onions Clar. Press *in prep.*

Mr. ONIONS, who pub. a collat. of the Harl. MS. of Nonius in 1882, has just died (in 1889), and it is doubtful if the above will appear.

AIDS:

Quicherat, Lud. Introduction à la lecture de Nonius Marcellus 1/- 8° *Paris* 72

Schmidt, Paul De Nonii Marcelli auctoribus grammaticis; 1 f° pl. 3/- 8° *Leipzig* 68

Vahlen, J. Analectorum Nonianorum libri duo 1/6 8° ,, 59

Macrobius

—*v.* K § 224: Miscellaneous Writers.

Priscian.

Opera: rec. emaculavit A. Krehl, 2 vols. 16/6; *red. to* 6/- 8° *Leipzig* 19; 20

Varro.

De Lingua Latina: rec. L. Spengel, rec. A. Spengel 8/- 8° *Berlin* [26] 85

,, ,, ,, ,, F. Hultsch—*in* Metrolog. Reliq., vol. ii. 2/6 p 8° Teubner, *Leipzig* 66

,, ,, ,, emend. et adnot. C. O. Müller *o.p.* [*pb.* 6/-; *w.* 15/-] 8° *Leipzig* 33

AIDS —*v. also* K § 214.

Spengel, Leonh. Ueb. d. Kritik d. Varron. Bücher *de ling. lat.* 2/- 4° *Munich* 55

Wilmanns, A. De Varronis libris grammaticis 4/- 8° *Berlin* 64

220. LATIN WRITERS ON ORATORY.

Cicero.

De Claris Oratoribus (Brutus): rec. F. Ellendt 7/- 8° *Berlin* [25] 44
*with English notes Prf. Martin Kellogg [Am.] $1.20 12° *Boston* 89
„ German „ K. W. Piderit, hrsg. w. Friedrich 2/6 p 8° Teubner, *Lpz.* [62] 89
„ „ „ O. Jahn, hrsg. A. Eberhard 2/- p 8° Weidmann, *Berl.* [49] 77
De Inventione: —*v.* Rhetorica, *infra*.
De Oratore: with English notes Prf. A. S. Wilkins bk. i. 7/6; bk. ii. 5/- f 8° Clar. Press [79] 88; 81
„ Latin „ F. Ellendt, 2 vols. 18/- 8° *Berlin* 40
„ German „ G. Sorof, 3 vols. ea. 2/- p 8° Weidmann, *Berlin* 75
„ „ „ K. W. Piderit, hrsg. F. T. Adler 5/6 p 8° Teubner, *Lps.* [59] 86
Orator: rec. F. Heerdegen 3/6 8° „ „ 84
*with English notes Dr. J. E. Sandys 16/- 8° Camb. Press 85
„ German „ O. Jahn 1/6 p 8° Weidmann, *Berl.* [51] 69
„ „ „ K. W. Piderit 2/- p 8° Teubner, *Lps.* [65] 76
Rhetorica (Ad Herennium & De Invent.): rec. W. Friedrich 1/- p 8° „ „ 84
ed. crit. A. Weidner 4/- 8° Weidmann, *Berl.* 78

TRANSLATION:
De Oratore: tr. F. B. Calvert 7/6 c 8° Hamilton 72

AID:
Piderit, K. W. Zur Kritik und Exege v. Cicero's Brutus, 2 pts. 2/- 4° *Copenhagen* 60; 62

Cornificius.

Rhetoricorum ad C. Herennium libri iv. w. Latin comment. C. L. Kayser 8/- 8° *Leipzig* 54
Also cont. in Cicero's *Opera* (complete edns.) and *in his Rhetorica ut supra.*

AIDS:
Baiter, J. G. Varietas Lectionis ad Rhetor. ad Herenn. e 6 codd. 3/- 4° *Zürich* 44
v. Destinon, J. De Codicum Cornificianorum ratione 2/- 8° *Kiel* 74
Giambelli, C. De Rhetoricorum ad Herennium auctore 2/- 8° *Turin* 78
Kröbnert, R. De Rhetoricis ad Herennium [dissert. inaug.] 1/6 8° *Regensburg* 73

Quintilian.

De Institutione Oratoria: rec. E. Bonnell, 2 vols. ea. 1/6 p 8° Teubner [54] 72; 74
„ C. Halm: ed. crit., 2 vols. 16/6 8° *Leipzig* 68; 69
lib. x.: „ C. Halm 6*d*. p 8° Teubner, *Leipzig* 78
Declamationes quae supersunt, rec. C. Ritter 5/- 8° „ „ 84
ANNOTATED TEXTS: with Latin notes G. L. Spalding + C. T. Zumpt, 6 vols. *o.p.* [*w.* 32/-] 8° *Leipzig* 1798–1834
lib. i.: „ French „ Ch. Fierville 8/6 8° *Paris* 90
lib. x.: * „ English „ Prf. J. E. B. Mayor, pt. i. 10/- 8° Deighton, *Camb.* 72
„ German „ E. Bonnell + F. Meister 1/- 12° Weidmann, *Berl.* [51] 84
„ „ „ G. T. A. Krüger 1/- p 8° Teubner, *Lps.* [61] 74
TRANSLATION: [literally] tr. Rev. J. S. Watson, 2 vols. ea. 5/- c 8° Bohn's Lib. [55; 56] 82

AIDS:
Claussen, J. D. D. Quaestiones Quintilianae 2/- 8° Teubner, *Leipzig* 73
Morawski, C. Quaestiones Quintilianae [dissert. inaug.] 1/6 8° *Posen* 74
Ritter, C. Die Qu. Declamationen: Art u. Herkunft derselben 8/- 8° *Freiburg* 81
Teichert, P. De fontibus Quintiliani rhetoricis 1/6 8° *Königsberg* 84
Textual Criticism.
Chatelain + le Coultre, E. + J. Quint. Inst. Oratoire [collat. of 10 cent. MS. in Paris] 2/- 8° *Paris* 75
Fierville, Ch. De Quint. codd. et praecip. de cod. Carcassonensi 4/6 8° „ 74
Language.
Bonnell, E. Lexicon Quintilianum [= vol. vi. of ed. of Spalding + Zumpt, *sup.*] 10/- 8° *Leipzig* 34
Törnebladh, R. De usu particul. ap Quint., 1/-; Quaestt. Crit. Quint., 1/-; De Eloc. Quintil. 1/- 8° *Stockholm* 61; *Calmar* 60; *Upsala* 58
Life.
Pils, Karl Quintilianus: ein Lehrerleben aus d. römischen Kaiserzeit 4/- 8° *Leipzig* 63

221. LATIN WRITERS ON AGRICULTURE AND SURVEYING.

AGRICULTURAL WRITERS.

BLUME + LACHMANN + RUDORFF, F. + K. A. [eds.] Die Schriften der römischen Feldmesser, vols. i.–ii. 19/6 r 8° *Berlin* 48; 52
i.: Gromatici Veteres, rec. LACHMANN; 40 pl., 12/- '48; ii.: German notes, etc., to same, 7/6 '52.
GIRAUD, C. [ed.] Rei Agrariae Scriptorum Nobiliores Reliquiae 8/6 8° *Paris* 42
NISARD, C. [ed.] Les Agronomes Latins [w. French trs.] 10/- r 8° Didot, *Paris* 44
Cato, Varro, Columella, Palladius.

Cato, M. Porcius De Agricultura liber, & Varro: Res Rust., rec. H. Keil, v. i. (1) 2/6, i. (2) 6/- r 8° Teubner, *Leipzig* 81; 84
Praeter Librum de Re Rustica quae extant, rec. H. Jordan 5/- „ „ 60

Varro De Re Rustica, rec. H. Keil, 6/- *ut sup.* (Cato); rec. F. Hultsch—*in* Metrol. Reliq., v. ii. [*ut* K § 219].

AIDS —*v. also* K § 214: Latin Poets, & K § 216: Latin Historians.
Riecke, Adolf M. Terentius Varro, der römische Landwirth; 1 plan 1/6 8° *Stuttgart* 61

222. LATIN WRITERS ON PHYSICAL SCIENCE.

METEOROLOGICAL WRITERS.

HULTSCH, F. [ed.] Scriptorum Meteorologicum Reliquiae, vol. ii. [Scriptores Romani] 2/6 p 8° Teubner, *Leipzig* 66

NATURAL SCIENCE: GENERALLY.

Plinius (major).

Historia Naturalis: rec. D. Detlefsen, 5 vols. 11/-; vol. vi. [Indices] 4/6 p 8° Weidmann, *Berlin* 66-73; 82
,, L. Jan + C. Mayhoff; 5 vols.; vol. vi. [Indices] 13/6 p 8° Teubner, *Leipzig* 54-75
Selection: ,, C. L. Urlichs 3/- p 8° Weidmann, *Berlin* 57
TRANSLATION: with English notes J. Bostock + H. T. Riley, 6 vols. ea. 5/- c 8° Bohn's Lib. 55-57

AIDS:
Brieger, Ad. De Fontibus libr. xxxiii.-xxxvi. nat. hist. Plin. [dissert. inaug.] 1/6 8° *Greifswald* 57
Furtwängler, A. Plinius und s. Quellen üb. d. bildenden Künsten 2/- 8° *Leipzig* 77
Mayhoff, C. Lucubrationes Plinianae, 2/6; Novae Lucub. Plin. [disserta. inaug.] 2/6 8° *Wratisl.* 65; *Dresden* 74
Nolten, D. Quaestiones Plinianae [dissert. inaug.] 1/- 8° *Bonn* 66
Oemichen, G. Plinianische Studien zur geogr. u. kunsthist. Literatur 4/- 8° *Erlangen* 80
Urlichs, C. L. Vindiciae Plinianae, 7/-; Quellenregister z. d. letzten Bücher 1/- 8° *Erlangen* [53;66] 66; *Würzb.* 78
White, Dr. J. S. [Am.] Pliny for Boys and Girls; 52 ill. $2.50 4° *New York* 89

Language.
Grasberger, L. De usu Pliniano [dissert. inaug.] 2/6 8° *Würzburg* 60
Müller, J. Der Stil des älteren Plinius 4/- 8° *Innsbruck* 83

Index.
Schneider, Otto Indices in Plinii *Historia Naturalis*, 2 vols. 24/-; *red. to* 12/- 8° *Hamburg* 57

Seneca, Luc. Annaeus Naturales Quaestiones—*v.* K § 218: Latin Philosophers.

Medicine: Latin Writers on—*v.* H § 3, *s.v.* Roman Writers on Medicine.

223. LATIN WRITERS ON ARCHITECTURE AND MILITARY SCIENCE.

Frontinus.

De Aquis Urbis Romae, rec. F. Buecheler 2/- p 8° Teubner, *Leipzig* 58
Strategematum libri iv. & De Aquis Rom., rec. A. Dederich 1/6 p 8° ,, ,, 55

AID:
Alan, Henry Observationes in S. Jul. Frontini *Strategemata* 6d. c 8° *Dublin* 73

224. LATIN MISCELLANEOUS PROSE WRITERS.

Gellius.

Noctes Atticae: rec. Marc. Hertz, 2 vols. 4/6; Ed. Crit., vol. i. 10/-, ii. 15/- 8° *Lps.* [53] 86; *Berlin* 83; 85
TRANSLATION:
Attic Nights: Die attischen Nächte, übers. Fritz Weiss, 2 vols. [w. German notes] 18/- 8° *Leipzig* 75; 76

There was an English tr. of the *Attic Nights* by Wm. BELOE, 3 vols. 8° *London* 1795.

AIDS:
Hertz, Martin Opuscula Gelleiana: lateinisch und deutsch 7/- 8° *Berlin* 86
" " Vindiciae Gellianae alterae [a letter to J. N. Madvig] 2/- 8° *Leipzig* 73
Kretzschmer, J. De Auli Gellii fontibus, pt. i. [grammat.] (dissert. inaug.) 2/- 4° *Posen* [60] 60
Mercklin, L. Die Citiermethode u. Quellenbenutzung d. Gell. i. d. Noct. Att. 2/- 8° *Leipzig* 60

Macrobius

Opera: rec. L. Jan: Ed. Crit., 2 vols. 16/- [*red. to* 6/-, Calvary, *Berl.* '89] 8° *Quedlinburg* 48; 52

Vol. i.: Comment. in Ciceronis Somnium Scipionis et Excerpta de Differentiis et Societatibus Graeci Latinique verbi; Prolegg. et Cic. *Somnium Scipionis*; Fragm. de Verbo, 2 pl. 6/- 48; ii.: Saturnalia, 10/- 52.

rec. F. Eyssenhardt, 1 pl. 5/6 p 8° Teubner, *Leipzig* 68

AIDS:
Linke, H. Quaestiones de Macrobii Saturnalium Fontibus 2/- 8° *Breslau* 80
Schoemann, G. F. C. Commentatio Macrobiana [dissert. inaug.] 1/- 8° *Greifswald* 71
Wissowa, G. De Macrobii Saturnalium Fontibus 2/- 8° *Breslau* 80

Plinius (minor).

Epistolae: rec. W. Keil 1/6 p 8° Teubner, *Leipzig* [53] 73
,, W. Christ 1/4 ,,
,, Th. Mommsen 1/6 p 8° Weidmann
,, H. Keil + Th. Mommsen: ed. crit. 11/- 8° *Leipzig* 70
bks. i.-ii.: with English notes J. Cowan [Classical Series] f 8° Macmillan *in prep.*
bk. iii.: *with English notes J. E. B. Mayor + J. H. Rendall [Classical Series] 5/- f 8° ,, 80
Letters to Trajan: ,, ,, ,, and introd. essays E. G. Hardy [Classical Lib.] 10/6 8° ,, 89
Selections: ,, ,, ,, A. J. Church + W. J. Brodribb 6/- c 8° Longman 71
,, ,, ,, C. E. Prichard + E. R. Bernard 3/- f 8° Clar. Press [72] 87
,, ,, ,, H. R. Heatley; maps 3/- c 8° Rivington 89

TRANSLATIONS: by W. Melmoth, ed. F. C. T. Bosanquet 5/- c 8° Bohn's Lib. [1746] 78
,, J. D. Lewis 5/- 8° Trübner 78

AIDS:
Bender, H. Der jüngere Plinius nach seinen Briefen [schl.-progr.] 2/- 4° *Tübingen* 73
Church + Brodribb, A. J. + W. J. Pliny [pop. biog. and acc. of wks.: A. C. f. E. Rrs.] 2/6 12° Blackwood 71
Mommsen, T. Étude sur Pline le jeune, trad. C. Morel 3/6 8° *Paris* 73
The original from wh. this is tr. appeared in *Hermes*, vol. iii. (1869).

Language.
Ess, F. Quaestiones Plinianae: de praepositionum cum ablativo usu [diss.] 2/- 4° *Leipzig* 88
Holstein, H. De Plinii Minoris Elocutione, 2 pts. [schl. progr.] ea. 1/- 4° *Naumbg.* 62; *Magdebg.* 69
Kraut, K. Ueber Syntax und Styl. jüngeren Plinius [schl. progr.] 2/- 4° *Tübingen* 72

XXVII. Teutonic Philology.

225. GENERALLY.

Bibliography, Encyclopædia and Methodology.

v. BAHDER, K. Die deutsche Philologie im Grundriss 6/- 8° *Paderborn* 83
HERRMANN, C. H. Bibliotheca Germanica [German bks. fr. 1830 to 1875] 6/- 8° *Halle* 78

Current Literature —*v. infra, s.v.* Magazines and Serials [*esp.* Jahresbericht *and* Litteraturblatt].

History of the Languages of the Teutonic Branch.

BEHAGHEL, O. Geschichte der deutschen Sprache—*in* Paul's Grundriss, vol. i., pt. 3 [*ut infra*].
,, ,, Die deutsche Sprache [a good and *very* cheap bk.; 231 pp.] 1/- s 8° *Prague* 86
FÖRSTEMANN, E. W. Geschichte des deutschen Sprachstammes, 2 vols. [full of material] 18/- *Nordhausen* 74; 75
GRIMM, Jacob Geschichte der deutschen Sprache, 2 vols. 13/- 8° *Berlin* [48] 80
KELLE, Johannes Vergleichende Grammatik der germanischen Sprachen 10/- 8° *Prague* 63
*PAUL, Prf. H. [ed.] Grundriss der germanischen Philologie, vol. i., pt. 1–3, 4/-; il. 1–4 ea. 2/- 8° *Strassb.* 89–90 *in prog.*
General Principles (by Editor); Phonetics, Gothic, O.-G. and Scand. (Prf. E. SIEVERS); Hist. of Germ. Lang. (O. BEHAGHEL); English and A.-S. (Prf. F. KLUGE); English Dialects (Dr. J. WRIGHT); Mid. Eng. Liter. (Prf. A. BRANDL); English Metre (Prf. J. SCHIPPER), and other departs. by eminent Germ. philologians.
SCHERER, W. Zur Geschichte der deutschen Sprache 12/- 8° *Berlin* [68] 90
A very valuable work for advanced students, involving an acquaintance with Compar. Grammar and Sanskrit.
SCHLEICHER, A. Die deutsche Sprache, hrsg. J. Schmidt 7/- 8° *Stuttgart* [60] 88
STRONG + MEYER, Prf. H. A. / Dr. Kuno History of the German Language [based on recent German research] 6/- 8° Sonnenschein 86

Relation of Lithuanian to the Teutonic Branch.

HASSENCAMP, R. Ueber d. Zusammenhang d. lettoslav. u. german. Sprachstammes 3/- r 4° *Leipzig* 76

Grammar: Generally.

GRIMM, Jacob Deutsche Grammatik, hrsg. W. Scherer + G. Roethe + E. Schröder, vols. i.–iii. 51/- 8° *Berlin* [19–37] 70; 78; 89
Gothic, O.-H. Germ., O.-Saxon, A.-S., O.-Frisian, O.-Norse, Mid.-H. Germ., Mid.-Low Germ., Swed., Dan., Germ., Dutch, English
Made an epoch in Comparative Philology, and is even now of very great use to the advanced student.
HELFENSTEIN, Dr. J. Comparative Grammar of the Teutonic Languages—*v.* K § 237.
HEYNE, Moritz Kurze Grammatik d. altgermanischen Dialekte, pt. i. 5/- 8° *Paderborn* [62] 80
Phonology and Inflection of Gothic, Old-High German, Old-Saxon, Anglo-Saxon, Old-Frisian, Old-Norse.
HOLTZMANN, A. Altdeutsche Grammatik, vol. i., pts. 1–2 [to occupy 3 vols.] 7/- 8° *Leipzig* 70; 75
Gothic, Old-Norse, Old-Saxon, Anglo-Saxon, and Old-High German. Vol. i. is devoted to phonology.

Phonology.

HOLTZMANN, A. —*ut supra.*
PAUL, Hermann Zur Geschichte d. german. Vokalismus—*in* Paul + Braune's *Beiträge*, vol. vi. (1879), pp. 1–261 [*ut inf.*]

Grimm's Law, Verner's Law—*v.* K § 120: Aryan Philology, *s.v.* Phonetics.

Palæography: Runes.

BURG, F. Die älteren nordischen Runeninschriften 4/- 8° *Berlin* 85
DIETRICH, Waldemar Runen-Sprachschatz [= dict. of Runes] *o.p.* [*w.* 5/-] 8° *Stockholm* 44
GRIMM, Wilhelm Ueber deutsche Runen; 11 pl. 8° *Göttingen* 21
HENNING, Rudolf Die deutschen Runendenkmäler; 4 pl. and 20 ill. 25/- f° *Strassburg* 89
KIRCHHOFF, Ad. Das gothische Runenalphabet [w. essay on orig. of Runes] 8° *Berlin* [51] 54
LILJEGREN, J. G. Run Lära, 9 pl. [*w.* 3/6] 8°; Run-Urkunder; ill. [*w.* 5/-] 12°; Monum. Runica [*w.* 7/6] 4° *Stockholm* 32; 33; 34
MITCHELL, J. M. The Runic Literature of Scandinavia 10/6 4° J. R. Smith 63
*STEPHENS, Prf. Geo. Old Northern Runic Monum. of Scand. and Eng., v. i.–iii.; ill. ea. 50/- f° *Copenh.* (Williams) 66; 68; 84
* ,, ,, Handbk. of Old Northern Runic Monum. [epitome of above; w. all the ill.] 40/- 4° *Copenhagen* 84
,, ,, Ruthwell Cross, Northumbria, A.D. 680: with its Runic verses 10/- f° J. R. Smith 68
,, ,, Thor the Thunderer, carved on a Scandinavian font of ab. year 1000 6/- 4° *Copenh.* (Williams) 78

K § 226

TAYLOR, Rev. Isaac — Greeks and Goths: a study of the Runes — 9/- 8° Macmillan 79
THORSEN, — Danske Runemindesmærker forklarede, pt. i. [Schleswig]; pl. — 25/- r 8° *Copenhagen* 64
WIMMER, Prf. L. F. A. — Die Runenschrift; 3 pl. and ill. — 14/- 8° Weidmann, *Berlin* 87

A revised and expanded edition of his *Om Runeskriftens Oprindelse*, pub. at *Copenh.* 1874; written to confirm A. KIRCHHOFF'S view, that the Runes were derived fr. the Roman alphabet.

ZACHER, Julius — Das gothische Alphabet Vulfilas u. das Runenalphabet; 1 pl. — 8° *Leipzig* 55

Etymology.

Dictionaries.

GRAFF, Dr. E. G. — Althochdeutscher Sprachschatz—*v.* K § 228: Old-High German.
*GRIMM, J.+W. — Deutsches Wörterbuch, fortg. v. Heyne+Hildebrand+Weigand, vols. i.–vii. [A–N.], viii. 1–4, xi. 1, xii. 1–3 £10 4/- r 8° *Leipzig* 54–90 *in prog.*

The great authority on German philology: gives etymol., history, mod. development, with illus. of every word from the time of Luther down to that of Goethe. Being cont. (very slowly) in parts at 2/- to 3/- ea.

MÜHLHAUSEN, A. — Geschichte des Grimm'schen Wörterbuchs [a lecture] 1/- 8° *Berlin* 88
*WEIGAND, F. L. K. — Deutsches Wörterbuch, 2 vols. [new edn. of F. Schmitthenner] 34/- r 8° *Giessen* [57–71] 8-

A sort of minor GRIMM; gives comparative etymologies from Gothic, Latin, Greek, and Sanscrit.

Accidence.

v. BAHDER, K. — Bildung d. Verbalabstracta im Germanischen [Preisschrift] 5/- 8° *Halle* 80
KLUGE, Friedr. — Nominale Stammbildungslehre d. altgermanischen Dialekte 3/- 8° ,, 86

Verb.

KLUGE, Friedr. — Beiträge z. Geschichte d. german. Conjugation [Quellen u. Forsch.] 4/- 8° *Strassburg* 79
SIEVERS, E. — Paradigmen zur deutschen Grammatik 3/- r 4° *Halle* 74

Gothic Old-Norse, Anglo-Saxon, Old-Saxon, Old-High German, Middle-High German.

Noun.

JACOBI, — Untersuchungen üb. d. Bildung d. Nomina in d. german. Sprachen, pt. i. *Breslau* 76
SÜTTERLIN, L. — Geschichte der *Nomina agentis* in Germanischen 3/- 8° *Strassburg* 87
ZIMMER, H. — Die Nominalsuffixe *a* und *â* in d. germ. Sprachen [Quellen u. Forsch.] 7/- 8° ,, 75

Adjective.

MEYER, Leo — Ueber d. Flexion des Adjectiva im Deutschen 1/6 8° *Berlin* 63

Syntax: *Pronoun.*

KÖLBING, E. — Unters. üb. d. Ausfall d. Relativpronomens in d. germ. Sprach. 1/6 8° *Strassburg* 72

Magazines and Serials—*v. also* K § 119.

Germania — vols. i.–xiii. [1856–68] ed. F. Pfeiffer; xiv. [1869] & onwards, ed. Karl Bartsch. [quarterly] *ann.* 15/- 8° *Vienna* 56; 59 *sqq.*, *in prog.*
Göttinger Beiträge zur deutschen Philologie, hrsg. Mor. Heyne+Wilh. Müller, pts. i.–iv. 8/- 8° *Paderborn* 87–88 ,,
Jahresbericht über die Erscheinungen auf d. Gebiete d. german. Philologie ea. vol. of 4 pts. 12/- 8° *Halle* 80 *sqq.* ,,
Literaturblatt für germ. und roman. Philologie, ed. O. Behaghel+F. Neumann [monthly] *ann.* 10/- 4° *Heilbronn* 80 ,, ,,

The best critical journal, consisting of reviews of new books.

PAUL+BRAUNE, H./W. [eds.] Beiträge z. Geschichte d. deut. Sprache u. Litter., vols. i.–xv. [Index to i.–xii. 2/- '88] *per vol.* 15/- 8° *Halle* 74–89 ,,
Quellen und Forschungen z. Sprache u. Culturgesch. d. germ. Völker, ed. B. ten Brink+W. Scherer+E. Martin, pts. i.–lxvii. ea. 1/- to 7/- 8° *Strassburg* 74 *sqq.* ,,
Wiener Beiträge zur deutschen u. englischen Philologie, hrsg. R. Heinzel+J. Minor+J. Schipper, pts. i.–iii. 12/- 8° *Vienna* 85–87 ,,
Zeitschrift für deutsches Alterthum, vols. i.–xvi. [1841–73] ed. F. Müllenhoff; xvii.–xviii. [1874–75] ed. E. Steinmeyer; xix.–xxxiii. [1876–81] ed. Steinmeyer+Müllenhoff+W. Scherer *per vol.* [=4 pts.] 15/- 8° *Berl.* 41–89 *in prog.*
,, für deutsche Philologie, ed. E. Höpfner+J. Zacher *per vol.* [=4 *pts.*] 12/- 8° *Halle* 68 *sqq.* ,,
,, für deutsche Sprache, hrsg. Prf. Daniel Sanders [monthly] *ann.* 12/- 8° *Hamburg* 87 ,, ,,

226. GOTHIC PHILOLOGY AND LITERATURE.

Grammar: Generally.

BALG, G. H. [Am.] — Comparative Grammar of Gothic Lang., pts. i.–ii. [in 8 pts.; w. spec. ref. to Eng. and Germ.] ea. 50c. r 8° *New York* 86–89 *in prog.*
*BRAUNE, W. — Gothic Grammar: w. selections and glossary, tr. G. H. Balg [Am.] 3/6 8° Low 83

The original edition [2/6 8° *Halle* 80; 87] forms one of the series *Grammatiken germanischer Dialekte*.

DOUSE, T. Le Marchant — Introduction to the Gothic of Ulfilas 10/6 c 8° Taylor & Francis 86
MEYER, Leo — Gothische Sprache [esp. in rel. to Sansc., Gk. and Lat.] 14/- 8° *Berlin* 69
RAMSAY, W. M./C. D. — Gothic Handbook: intro. to hist. of Goths and study of Gothic Language 6/- c 8° Wells Gardner 89
WRIGHT, Dr. Joseph — Gothic Primer Clar. Press. *in prep.*
ZIMMER, H. — Repetitorium und Examinatorium über d. gotische Grammatik 1/6 8° *Leipzig* 90

Accidence.

Adjectives.

BERNHARDT, E. Ueber die Flexion der Adjectiva in Gotischen *Erfurt* 77

Participles.

LÜCKE, Absolute Participia im Gotischen u. ihr Verhält. z. Griech. *Göttingen* 76

Syntax.

Article.

BERNHARDT, E. Der Artikel in Gotischen [school-programme] 1/6 4° *Erfurt* 74

Verb.

BURKHARDT, Der Gebrauch d. Conjunctivs bei Ulfilas [dissert.] *Grimma* 72
SCHIRMER, Carl Ueber d. syntakt. Gebrauch d. Optativus im Gotischen [dissert.] 1/6 8° *Marburg* 74

Noun.

KÖHLER, Arthur Ueber d. syntakt. Gebrauch d. Dativs im Gotischen [dissert.] 8° *Dresden* 64
SCHRADER, Karl Ueber d. syntakt. Gebrauch d. Genetivs in d. got. Sprache [dissert.] 1/6 8° *Göttingen* 75

Pronoun.

ECKARDT, Ueber d. Syntax d. gotischen Relativpronomens [dissert.] *Halle* 75

Palaeography.

EWALD+LOEWE, P.+G. [eds.] Exempla Scripturae Visigothicae [40 plates] 50/- f° *Heidelberg* 83

Phonology.

WEBSTER, H. L. Zur Gutteralfrage im Gotischen 4/- 8° *Leipzig* 90

Etymology.

FEIST, G. Grundriss der gotischen Etymologie 5/- 8° *Strassburg* 88

Dictionaries.

DIEFENBACH, L. Vergleichendes Wörterbuch der gothischen Sprache, 2 vols. 27/- r 8° *Frankfort* 47-51
SCHULZE, E. Gotisches Wörterbuch 5/- 8° *Züllichau* [48] 67
The first edition was published *sub tit. Gothisches Glossar.*

SKEAT, Prf. W. W. Mœso-Gothic Glossary [w. an outl. of the grammar] 9/- s 4° Asher 68
Contains a list of A.-S. and English words etymologically connected with the Mœso-Gothic.

Roots.

BYRNE, Rev. J. Origin of the Greek, Latin and Gothic Roots 18/- 8° Trübner 88

Particles and Adverbs.

BEZZENBERGER, A. Untersuchungen üb. d. gotischen Adverbien und Partikeln 2/6 8° *Halle* 73
DORFELD, C. Das Präfix *ga-* [Gothic *ga-*] bei Ulfilas und Tatian 1/6 8° „ 85
SCHWAHN, Die gotischen Adjectiv-Adverbien [dissert. inaug.] *Bonn* 73

Prepositions.

NABER, F. Gotische Präpositionen [schl.-programme] 1/- 8° *Detmold* 79

Chrestomathy.

WACKERNAGEL, W. [ed.] Gothische und altsächsische Lesestücke [w. vocabulary] 2/- 4° *Basle* 71

Literature.

History.

SIEVERS, Prf. E. Geschichte d. gotischen Litteratur—*in* Paul's Grundriss, vol. ii., pt. 1 [*ut* K § 225] 2/- 8° *Strassburg* 90

Gospels.

(a) *Manuscripts.*
Codex Argenteus [?4 cent.]: ed A. Uppström [fragm. of Gothic Gospels at Upsala] 19/6 f° *Upsala* 54-5
Codices Gotici Ambrosiani: ed. same [Epp. Paul, Esra, Nehem.] 15/- 4° *Stockholm* 68
(b) *Editions.*
Anglo-Sax., Gothic, Wiclf. and Tynd. Gospels, ed. J. Bosworth+G. Waring [in parallel cols.] 12/- 8° J. R. Smith [65] 73
ULPHILAS, Bp. [4 cent.] Vet. et Nov. Test. Fragmenta, ed. H. C. v. Gabelentz+J. Löbe, 2 vols. 40/- 4° *Leipzig* 43; 60
„ „ „ hrsg. E. Bernhardt [w. Greek text and comm.] 13/6 8° *Halle* 75
* „ „ „ H. F. Massmann 10/- 8° *Stuttgart* 57
With parallel Greek and Latin versions; notes, dictionary and historical introduction in German.
* „ „ „ F. L. Stamm [text, dict. and gram. (in Germ.) ed. M. Heyne] 5/- 8° *Paderborn* [58] 79
Gospel of S. Mary ed. Prf. W. W. Skeat 4/- c 8° Clar. Press 78

AIDS —*for* Language of Ulfilas, *v. supra.*
SCOTT, Rev. C. A. —*article* Ulfilas, *in* Encyclo. Brit., vol. xxiii. 30/- 4° Black 88
WAITZ, G. Leben und Lehre des Ulfilas 8° *Hanover* 40

227. FRISIAN PHILOLOGY AND LITERATURE.

History of the Language.

SIEBS, Theodor — Zur Geschichte der englisch-friesischen Sprache, pt. i. — 10/- 8° *Halle* 89

Dictionaries.

HALBERTSMA, J. — Lexicon Frisicum, vol. i. [A–Feer] — 16/- r 8° *The Hague* 74

HETTEMA de HAAN, M. — Idioticon Frisicum [Frisian-Latin-Dutch] — 18/- s 4° *Leeuwarden* 74

East-Frisian.

ten DOORNKAAT-KOOLMAN, J. — Wörterbuch der ostfriesischen Sprache, 3 vols. — 44/- r 8° *Norden* 77–84

Old Frisian.

v. RICHTHOFEN, K. — Altfriesisches Wörterbuch — 10/- 4° *Göttingen* 40

Grammars.

North-Frisian.

BENDSEN, B. — Die Nordfriesische Sprache nach der Moringer Mundart — 10/6 8° *Leyden* 60

Old Frisian.

CUMMINS, A. H. — Grammar of Old Friesic Lang. [w. readg.-bk. and vocab.] — 6/- c 8° Trübner [81] 87

GÜNTHER, Curt — Die Verba im Altostfriesischen [dissert. inaug.] — 2/- 8° *Leipzig* 80

van HELTEN, W. L. — Altostfriesche Grammatik — 8/6 8° *Leeuwarden* 90

Literature.

History.

HEWETT, W. T. [Am.] — Frisian Language and Literature; an historical study — 75c. 12° *New York* 79

Text.

Oera Linda Book [MS. 13 cent.]: text and tr. ed. W. R. Sandbach [a fraud] — 5/- 8° Trübner 76

228. GERMAN PHILOLOGY (a): OLD-HIGH AND OLD-LOW GERMAN.

Grammar: Generally—*v. also* K § 225: Teutonic Philology: Generally (GRIMM, HEYNE, HOLTZMANN).

*BRAUNE, W. — Althochdeutsche Grammatik [Samml. Gramm. germ. Dial.] — 5/- 8° *Halle* 86

HAHN, K. A. — Althochdeutsche Grammatik, ed. A. Jeitteles [w. selns. and glossary; antiquated] — 3/- 8° *Prague* [52] 75

Etymology.

Dictionaries —*v. also* K § 225: Teutonic Philology: Generally.

GRAFF, Dr. E. G. — Althochdeutscher Sprachschatz: W'buch d. altdeutschen Sprache, 7 vols. — 50/- 4° *Berlin* 34–46
Conts. all the O.-H. G. words used bef. 12 cent., comp. w. M.-H. G., Indian dialects, Gk., Lat., Old Pruss., Goth., A.-S., Old Dutch, Icel., Scand., Sansc., etc., and showing the roots w. the High and Low Germ., Engl., Dutch, Danish and Swed. langs. have in common. Vol. vii. is an Index, by H. F. MASSMANN.

SCHADE, Oskar — Altdeutsches Wörterbuch [= Lesebuch, pt. ii. (*ut inf.*)] — 30/- 8° *Halle* [66] 73–83

WACKERNAGEL, W. — Altdeutsches Handwörterbuch — 8/- r 8° *Basle* [ ] 78

Glosses.

*STEINMEYER + SIEVERS, $\frac{E.}{E.}$ [eds.] Die althochdeutsche Glossen, vol. i. 15/-; ii. 20/-; iii. ? — l 8° *Berlin* 79; 82; 89

Names.

*FÖRSTEMANN, E. — Aldeutsches Namenbuch, vol. i. [Personal-names] 27/-; ii. [Place-names] 30/- — 8° *Nordhausen* 54; 56–59

" " — Die deutschen Ortsnamen [conts. a bibliography] — 6/- 8° " 63

Chrestomathies and Collections.

BRAUNE, W. [ed.] — Althochdeutsches Lesebuch — 4/- 8° *Halle* [75] 88

HATTEMER, H. [ed.] — Denkmahle des Mittelalters, 3 vols. [still useful] *o.p.* [*pb.* 52/6] — r 8° *St. Gallen* 44–49

MÜLLENHOFF, K. [ed.] — Altdeutsche Sprachproben, hrsg. M. Roediger — 4/- 8° *Berlin* [64] 85

* " + SCHERER, W. [eds.] Denkmäler deutscher Poesie u. Prosa aus d. 8–12 Jahrh. — 14/- 8° " [63] 73

SCHADE, Oskar [ed.] — Altdeutsches Lesebuch, pt. i. [texts] 4/6; ii. [dict. *ut sup.*] — 30/- 8° *Halle* 62; [66] 73–83

SIMROCK, Karl [ed.] — Altdeutsches Lesebuch in neudeutscher Sprache — 5/- 8° *Stuttgart* [51] 84

WACKERNAGEL, W. [ed.] — Deutsches Lesebuch, i.: Altdeutsch; ii.–iii. [since 1500] — 30/- r 8° *Basle* [35–36] 73

WRIGHT, Dr. Joseph [ed.] — An Old High German Primer [w. grammar, notes and gloss.] — 3/6 f 8° Clar. Press 90

Manuscripts.

v. KELLER, H. A. — Verzeichniss altdeutscher Handschriften, hrsg. E. Sievers — 5/- 8° *Tübingen* 90

Romance Elements in Old-High German.

FRANZ, W. — Die lateinisch-romanischen Elemente im Althochdeutschen — 2/- 8° *Strassburg* 84

Metrics.

SCHNEIDER, J. I. Systemat. u. geschichtl. Darstellung d. d. Verskunst v. ihrem Ursprung 4/- 8° *Tübingen* 61
VILMAR, A. F. C. Die deutsche Verskunst nach ihrem geschichtl. Entwickelung 3/- 8° *Marburg* 70
Forms the second part of his *Anfangsgründe der deutschen Grammatik*.

Old-Low German.

Grammar.

HEYNE, Moritz Kleine altsächsische und altniederfränkische Grammatik 1/6 8° *Paderborn* 73
Mr. NIEMEYER, the Halle publisher, has announced an O.-Low Germ. Gram. as in prep. ? author's name.

Phonology.

GALLÉE, J. H. Altsächsische Laut- u. Flexionslehre, pt. i. [kleinere westfäl. Denkmäler] 8° *Haarlem* 78

Etymology: Dictionary.

HEYNE, Moritz Altsächsisches Glossar—*appended to his edn. of the* Heliand [*ut* K § 248].

Names.

ALTHOF, H. Grammatik altsächs. Eigennamen in westfäl. Urkunden [9-11 cent.] 1/6 8° *Paderborn* 79

Literature.

HELIAND, —*v.* K § 248.

Middle-Low German—*v.* K § 231: German Dialects, *s.v.* Platt.

229. GERMAN PHILOLOGY (*b*): MIDDLE-HIGH GERMAN.

Grammar: Generally—*v. also* K § 225: Teutonic Philology: Generally.

HAHN, K. A. Mittelhochdeutsche Grammatik, hrsg. F. Pfeiffer 3/6 8° *Basle* [42-47] 84
MARTIN, Ernst Mittelhochdeutsche Grammatik [elementary] 1/- 8° *Berlin* [3rd edn. 67] 89
PAUL, Hermann Mittelhochdeutsche Grammatik [Samml. Gramm. germ. Dial.] 3/- 8° *Halle* [81] 84
SCHACHINGER, Rudolf Die Congruenz in der mittelhochdeutsche Sprache 3/6 r 8° *Vienna* 90
*WEINHOLD, K. Mittelhochdeutsche Grammatik 8/- 8° *Paderborn* [77] 83
" " Kleine Mittelhochdeutsche Grammatik 2/6 8° *Vienna* [81] 89
ZUPITZA, J. Einführung in das Studium des Mittelhochdeutschen 2/- 8° *Oppeln* [68] 84

Phonology.

BERNHARDT, E. Abriss der mittelhochd. Laut- u. Flexionslehre [sch.-bk.] 6*d.* 8° *Halle* [79] 81
KÖHLER, E. Mittelhochdeutsche Laut- u. Flexionslehre [w. metrology; sch.-bk.] 1/- 8° *Dresden* 80

Pronunciation.

BECHSTEIN, R. Die Aussprache des Mittelhochdeutschen 2/- 8° *Halle* 58

Etymology —*v. also* K § 225: Teutonic Philology: Generally.

Dictionaries.

BENECKE, G. F. Mittelhochdeut. Wörterbuch, ausgearb. W. Müller+F. Zarncke, 3 vols. 51/- r 8° *Leipzig* 54; 63-66; 68
DIEFENBACH+WÜLCKER, L/E Hoch- und Nieder-Deuts. Wörterb. der Mittleren und Neueren Zeit 17/6 r 8° *Basle* 74-85
Intended specially as a supplement to GRIMM's great dictionary.
*LEXER, Dr. M. Mittelhochdeutsches Handwörterbuch, 3 vols. 66/- r 8° *Leipzig* 72-78
" " Mittelhochdeutsches Taschenwörterbuch [w. gram. intro.] 5/- 16° " [81] 85

Chrestomathy.

ENGLMANN, Lor. [ed.] Mittelhochdeutsches Lesebuch, hrsg. O. Brenner [w. gram. and vocab.] 3/6 8° *Munich* [63] 87
WEINHOLD, K. [ed.] Mittelhochdeutsches Lesebuch [w. grammar and glossary] 4/- 8° *Vienna* [50] 75
WRIGHT, Dr. Joseph [ed.] Middle-High German Primer [60 pp. of texts, w. gram., notes, gloss.] 3/6 f 8° Clar. Press 88

Metrics.

v. MUTH, R. Mittelhochdeutsche Metrik 3/- 8° *Vienna* 82

Middle-Low German—*v.* K § 231: German Dialects, *s.v.* Platt.

230. GERMAN PHILOLOGY (*c*): MODERN HIGH GERMAN.

History of the Language—*v. also* K § 225, *s.v.* Hist. of Lang.

v. BAHDER, Karl Grundlagen der neuhochdeutschen Schriftsprache 90
KLUGE, Friedrich Von Luther bis Lessing 8° 89

Linguistic Geography.

BERNHARDI, K. Die Sprachgrenze zwischen Deutschland und Frankreich [w. a col. map] 1/- r 8° *Cassel* 71
BOECKH, R. Der Deutschen Volkszahl und Sprachgebiet in d. europ. Staaten 8/- 8° *Berlin* 69
Cf. also his *Sprachkarte vom preuss. Staate* (acc. to census of 1861), plate 2: as also H. KIEPERT'S *Die Sprachgrenze in Elsass-Lothringen* (w. map)—in *Ztschr. d. Gesellsch. f. Erdkunde zu Berlin*, vol. ix. (1874) (of wh. a reduction is given in PETERMANN'S *Mittheilungen* 1875), and map 10 in R. ANDREE+O. PESCHEL'S *Physik.-statist. Atlas d. deut. Reiches*.

K § 230

Grammar : Generally.

Becker, K. F. Handbuch der deutschen Sprache 6/- 8° *Prague* [28–29] 76
Heyse, J. C. A. Deutsche Grammatik, hrsg. Otto Lyon 4/- 8° *Hanover* [14] 86
Schulz, B. Die deutsche Grammatik in ihren Grundzügen 5/- 8° *Paderborn* [69] 86
Whitney, Prf. W. D. [Am.] Compendious German Grammar 4/6 p 8° Macmillan 79
Wilmanns, W. Deutsche Grammatik für die Unter- u. Mittelklassen 2/- 8° *Berlin* [77] 83

Accidence : *Adjective.*

Osthoff, Prf. H. Zur Gesch. d. schwachen deutsch. Adjectivums [Osthoff's Forsch., pt. ii.] 6/- 8° *Jena* 76

Verb.

Kluge, F. Beiträge zur Geschichte der deutschen Conjugation [Quellen u. Forsch.] 4/- 8° *Strassburg* 79

Syntax.

Erdmann, O. Grundzüge der deutschen Syntax, pt. i. [in its histor. devel.] 3/6 8° *Stuttgart* 86

Sentence.

Kern, Friedr. Die deutsche Satzlehre : Untersuchung ihrer Grundlagen 2/- 8° *Berlin* [83] 88

Phonology

—*v. also* K § 120 : Aryan Philology, *s.v.* Phonetics.

v. Bahder, Karl Grundlagen d. neuhochdeutschen Lautsystems [15–16 centuries] 6/- 8° *Strassburg* 90
Soames, L. Introduction to English, French and German Phonetics 6/- c 8° Sonnenschein 90

Orthography and Pronunciation.

Andresen, K. G. Sprachgebrauch und Sprachrichtigkeit 5/- 8° *Heilbronn* [80] 80
Duden, Konrad Neue Schulorthographie, 1/- ; Verschiedenheiten d. amtl. Regelbücher üb. Orthogr. 1/- 8° *Munich* [81] 86 ; [86] 86
" " Orthographischer Wegweiser, 1/6 ; Orthographisches Wörterbuch 2/- 8° *Leipzig* [81] 84 ; [80] 87
Saalfeld, G. A. Die neue deutsche Rechtschreibung 1/- 8° *Heilbronn* 85
Sanders, Daniel Katechismus der deutschen Orthographie [Weber's Katechismen] 1/6 8° *Leipzig* [ ] 86
" " Orthographisches Wörterbuch 3/- 8° " [75] 76
Rocca, O. Die richtige Aussprache des Hochdeutschen 2/- 8° *Rostock* 86
Vietor, W. German Pronunciation : practice and theory 1/6 8° *Heilbronn* 85

Historical.

Michaelis, G. Beiträge zur Geschichte der deutschen Rechtschreibung, 2 pts. 2/6 8° *Berlin* 77 ; 80

Etymology.

Dictionaries.

Flügel, J. Pract. Dictionary of Eng. and Germ. Langs., 2 vols., 17/6 8° ; Abgd. 6/- c 8° *Leipzig* [43] 83
Grieb, Chr. F. Dictionary of the English and German Languages, 3 vols. 20/- r 8° *Stuttgart* [63] 85
*Grimm, J. + W. —*v.* K § 225.
Heyne, Moritz Deutsches Wörterbuch, vol. i. [A–G] 10/- r 4° *Leipzig* 90 *in prog.*
*Kluge, Friedrich Etymologisches Wörterbuch der deutschen Sprache 10/- r 8° *Strassburg* [82–83] 88
Janssen, V. F. Gesammtindex *to same* 7/- 8° " 90
Köhler, F. German and English Dictionary [both parts] 6/- 8° *Leipzig* [59–61] 81
*Lucas, N. J. Dictionary of English and German Langs., 4 vols. *o.p.* [*w.* £6 6/-] i 8° *Bremen* 54–68
A new edn. of this—by far the most important—dictionary has been said to be in preparation for several years.
*Muret Encyclopædic Dictionary of the English and German Languages *Berlin* *in prep.*
Likely to be a very important work : has been in preparation since 1869.
Sanders, Daniel Wörterbuch der deutschen Sprache, 2 vols. 72/- 4° *Leipzig* [59–65] 8-
" " Handwörterbuch der deutschen Sprache 7/6 r 8° " [69] 88
" " Ergänzungswörterbuch der deutschen Sprache 30/- 4° *Berlin* [79 *sqq.*] 8-
" " Wörterbuch der Hauptschwierigkeiten in der deutschen Sprache 3/- 8° " [72] 88
Thieme, F. W. Critical Dictionary of Engl. and Germ. Langs., ed. E. Preusser [both parts] 11/- 8° *Hamburg* [46] 85
*Weigand, F. L. K. —*v.* K § 225.
Weir, Elizabeth Cassell's German Dictionary [best smaller wk. ; both pts.] 7/6 8° Cassell 89
Whitney, Prf. W. D. [Am.] Compendious German and Eng. Dictionary [w. etymols.] 7/6 c 8° Macmillan 77

Foreign Elements.

Ebel, H. Ueber die Lehnwörter der deutschen Sprache 4° *Berlin* 56
Heyse, J. C. A. Fremdwörterbuch, hrsg. Carl Böttger 5/- r 8° *Leipzig* [ ] 87
Kehrein, Jos. Fremdwörterbuch : mit etymologischen Erklärungen 8° *Stuttgart* 77
Kiesewetter, L. Neuestes vollständigstes Fremdwörterbuch 8° *Glogau* [ ] 69–71
Meyer, Leo Ueber Fremdwörter, insbesondere d. slavischen, im Deutschen [lecture] 8° *Dorpat* 73
Sanders, Daniel Fremdwörterbuch, vols. i.–ii. 8° *Leipzig* 71

Folk-Etymology.

Andresen, K. G. Ueber deutsche Volksetymologie [excellent popular book] 5/6 8° *Heilbronn* [76] 88
Pogatscher, Prf. A. Zur Volksetymologie [addns. to above ; school-progr.] 1/6 8° *Graz* 84

Names	—*v. also* K § 120: Aryan, *and* K § 228: Old High German.				
ABEL, H. F. O.	Die deutschen Personennamen, hrsg. W. Robert-tornow	2/-	8°	*Berlin*	89
ANDRESEN, K. G.	Konkurrenz in der Erklärung der deutschen Geschlechtsnamen	3/-	8°	*Heilbronn*	83
DEECKE, W.	Die deutschen Verwandtschaftsnamen	4/-	8°	*Weimar*	70
Synonyms.					
EBERHARD, J. A.	Synonymisches Handwörterbuch d. deutschen Sprache, ed. O. Lyon	11/-	8°	*Leipzig*	[02] 88
MÜLLER, Ed.	Sinn und Sinnverwandtschaft deutscher Wörter	6/6	8°	,,	86
SANDERS, Daniel	Deutscher Sprachschatz geordnet nach Begriffen	25/-	r 8°	*Hamburg*	73-77
,, ,,	Bausteine zu e. Wörterbuch d. sinnverwandt. Ausdrucke im Deutschen	6/-	8°	*Berlin*	90
SCHÖPPER, Jacob	Synonyma [*Dortmund* 1550].				
Schröder, Edw.	Jacob Schöpper v. Dortmund und seine Synonymik	1/6	4°	*Marburg*	90
Metrics					
BRÜCKE, E.	Die physiologischen Grundlagen d. neuhochdeutschen Verskunst	2/-	8°	*Vienna*	71
WESSELY, J. E.	Das Grundprincip des deutschen Rhythmus d. 19. Jahrhunderts 7/- [*red. to* 3/-, Weigel, *Lpz.*]		8°	*Leipzig*	68
WESTPHAL, R.	Theorie der neuhochdeutschen Metrik		8°	*Jena*	[70] 77
Miscellanea.					
SANDERS, Daniel	Deutsche Sprachbriefe	20/-	8°	*Berlin*	[79] 89

231. GERMAN PHILOLOGY (*d*): GERMAN DIALECTS.

Generally.					
FROMMANN, G. K. [ed.]	Die deutschen Mundarten, vols. i.-vi. & N. S. vol. i. [all pub.] *o.p.* [*w.* 50/-]		8°	*Nuremb.* 53-59; *Halle*	77
HEYNE, Moritz	Kurze Grammatik der altgermanischen Sprachstämme, vol. i.	4/6	r 8°	*Paderborn*	[70] 74
PIPER, P. H. E.	Verbreitung der althochdeutschen Dialekte; w. col. map [to A.D. 1300]	1/-	8°	*Lahr*	80
SOCIN, Adolf	Schriftsprache und Dialekte im Deutschen	10/-	8°	*Heilbronn*	88
WEINHOLD, K.	Grammatik der deutschen Mundarten, 2 pts. i.: Alemannische Grammatik, 11/6; ii.: Bairische Grammatik, 9/6.	22/-	8°	*Berlin*	63; 67
Specimens.					
WELCKER, Hermann [ed.]	Dialekt-gedichte [coll. of dialect songs of North and South]	5/-	8°	*Leipzig*	[8-] 89
Bavaria.					
SCHMELLER, J. A.	Bayerisches Wörterbuch von Wörtern und Ausdrücken, 2 vols.	30/-	4°	*Munich*	[27]69; [37]78
Carinthia.					
LEXER, Dr. M.	Kärntisches Wörterbuch	8/-	r 8°	*Leipzig*	62
Egerländer.					
NEUBAUER, J. [ed.]	Altdeutsche Idiotismen der Egerländer Mundart	3/-	8°	*Vienna*	87
Frisian	—*v.* K § 227.				
Hesse.					
VILMAR + v. PFISTER, A. F. C. / H.	Idiotikon von Hessen, 7/-; Suppl. No. 1 5/-; Suppl. No. 2	3/-	8°	*Marburg*	68; 86; 89
Livonia.					
v. GUTZEIT, W.	Wörterschatz d. deutschen Sprache Livlands, v. i. (1-4), ii. (1-4), iii. (1-2), iv. (1)	22/-	8°	*Riga*	59-89 *in pr.*
Mecklenburg.					
"MI" [=F. G. SIBETH]	Wörterbuch der Mecklenburgischen Vorpommerschen Mundart	3/-	8°	*Leipzig*	76
NERGER, K.	Grammatik des mecklenburgischen Dialektes älterer u. neuerer Zeit	*o.p.*	8°	,,	69
Old Saxon	—*v.* K § 228.				
Platt.					
BERGHAUS, H.	Sprachschatz der Sassen, pts. i.-xxi.	*ea.* 1/6	8°	*Berlin*	78-84
DANIELL, J. F.	Wörterbuch d. Altmarkisch-Platt-Deutschen Mundart	6/-	8°	*Salzwedel*	59
LÜBBEN + WALTHER, A. / CH.	Mittelniederdeutsches Handwörterbuch, 2 pts.	10/-	8°	*Norden*	85; 89
MOLEMA,	Wörterbuch der groningenschen Mundart in 19 Jahrh., vols. i.-iii.	28/-	8°	,,	87-89 *in prog.*
SCHILLER + LÜBBEN, K. / A.	Mittelniederdeutsches Wörterbuch, 5 vols.	72/-	8°	*Bremen*	75-81
Serial.					
Jahrbuch des Vereins für niederdeutsche Sprachforschung, vol. i.-xiv.		*ann.* 4/-	8°	*Norden*	76-89 *in prog.*
Korrespondenzblatt des Vereins für niederdeutsche Sprachforschung, vols. i.-viii.		*ann.* 2/-	8°	,,	77-89 ,,

Specimens.

Niederdeutsche Denkmäler, vols. i., iii. (1) and iv. 17/- 8° *Norden* ?-84 *in prog.*

REUTER, Fritz — Sammtliche Werke: 15 v. 45/-; "Volks-Ausg." 7 v 21/-; separ. ea. 2/- to 5/6 8° *Wismar* [*v.y.*] *v.y.*

Saxony.

ALBRECHT, K. — Die Leipziger Mundart: Grammatik und Wörterbuch 4/- 8° *Leipzig* 81

LIESENBERG, F. — Die Stieger Mundart [a dialect of the Lower Harz] 5/- 8° *Göttingen* 90

Slang, Thieves' Language, etc.

AVE-LALLEMENT, F. C. B. —*in his* Das deutsche Gaunerthum, 4 pts.; ill. 30/- 8° *Leipzig* 58–62

Vols. iii.–iv. deal with the Thieves' Language; and pt. iv. [pp. 318–603] conts. a Jewish-German dictionary.

Swabia.

BIRLINGER, Ant. — Schwäbisch-augsburgisches Wörterbuch 8/- 8° *Munich* 64

KAUFFMANN, F. — Geschichte der schwäbischen Mundart im Mittelalter u. Neuzeit 8/- 8° *Strassburg* 90

v. SCHMID, J. C. — Schwäbisches Wörterbuch: mit. etymolog. u. histor. Anmkgn. 11/- 8° *Stuttgart* 61

Switzerland.

*STAUB + TOBLER, F. + L., *etc.* [eds.] Schweizerisches Idiotikon, pts. i.–xvi. [a dictionary] ea. 2/- 4° *Frauenfeld* 81 *in prog.*

WYSS, Bernhard [ed.] — Schwyzer-dütsch, pts. i.–xl. ea. 6*d.* 8° *Zürich* 63–87 *in prog.*

Specimens.

SUTERMEISTER, O. [ed.] — Dichtungen in Baseler Mundart, 6/-; in Berner Mundart 3/6 8° *Zürich* 85; 85

" " [ed.] — Dichtungen in Graubündner Mundart, 4/-; in Luzerner Mundart 4/- 8° " 85; 85

" " — Dichtungen in Züricher Mundart 6/- 8° " 85

Tyrol.

SCHÖPF, J. B. — Tirolisches Idiotikon, 9 pts. 13/6 8° *Innsbruck* 62–66

Westphalia.

JELLINGHAUS, Hermann — Westphälische Grammatik: Laute u. Flexionen d. Ravensbergischen Mundart 4/- 8° *Norden* 77

232. DUTCH AND FLEMISH PHILOLOGY AND LITERATURE.

Grammar.

AHN, F. — Concise Gram. of Dutch Lang., ed. Dr. J. M. Hoogvliet + Dr. Stern 3/6 c 8° Trübner [54] 87

HOOGVLIET, Dr. J. M. — Elements of Dutch Grammar [w. chrestomathy, exx., and key] *The Hague* [ ] 89

SNELL, A. L. — Dutch Grammar 3/6 12° Trübner 85

TRAUT + v. d. JAGT — Niederländische Grammatik, 5/-; Key to same [in German] 1/6 8° *Leipzig* 88; 88

VAN DER PYL — Practical Dutch Grammar 4/- 12° *Rotterdam* [19] 62

Middle Dutch.

FRANCK, J. — Mittelniederländische Grammatik [w. selns. and vocab.] 7/- 8° *Leipzig* 83

Etymology.

Dictionaries.

BOMHOFF, D. — Dutch-English and English-Dutch Dictionary, 2 pts. in 1 vol. 10/6 12° *Arnhem* [32] 77

CALISCH, T. M. + N.S. — Complete Dictionary of Eng. and Dutch Langs., 2 vols. [both pts.] 9/- p 8° *Leyden* [75] 90

PICARD, A. — Pocket Dictionary of English-Dutch and Dutch-English Languages 10/- 16° *Gouda* [ ] 77

SCHUERMANS, L. W. — Algemeen Vlaamsch Idioticon 19/- 8° *Leuven* 56–70

de VRIES + WINKEL, M. + L. Woordenboek d. Nederlandsche Taal, in pts. [26 pub. to '80] ea. 2/- 4° *The Hague* 64 *sqq. in prog.*

WINKLER, J. — Algemeen Nederduitsch en Friesch Dialecticon, 2 vols. 18/- r 8° " 74

Middle and Old Dutch—v. also K § 229, *s.v.* Diefenbach + Wülcker; *and* K § 231, *s.v.* Platt.

OUDEMANS, A. C. — Middel- en Oud- Nederl. Woordenb., pts. i.–vii. £4 8° *Arnhem* 69–80

West-Flemish.

DE BO, L. L. — West-Vlaamsch Idioticon 30/- 4° *Bruges* 70–73

Synonyms.

HENDRIKS, J. V. — Proeve van een Woordenboek van Nederlandsche Synoniemen 8° *Deventer* 80

Foreign Elements.

DOZY, R. — Lijst v. Nederl. Woorden d. uit Arab., Hebr., Perz. en Turk. afkom. zijn 8° *The Hague* 67

Dialogues.

WILLIAMS + LUDOLPH [eds.] Dutch and English Dialogues 3/- 12° Williams 69

Literature.

History —*for* English Books, *v.* K § 32 : History of Dutch Literature.

HOFFMANN v. FALLERSLEBEN Horae Belgicae, 11 pts. in 4 vols. *o.p.* [*w.* 30/-] 8° *Hanover* 36–57
A valuable coll. of ancient Dutch poems. Pt. i. conts. a survey of the liter., pt. vii. [1856] a *Glossarium Belgicum*.
JONCKBLOET, W. J. A. Geschiedenis der Middennederlandsche Dichtkunst, pts. i.–iii. *o.p.* 8° *Amsterdam* 51–55
" " Geschiedenis der Nederlandsche Letterkunde, pts. i.–ii. 8° *Gröningen* [68] 73 ; [70] 74
" " Geschichte d. niederländ. Literatur, übers. W. Berg, 2 vols. 21/- 8° *Leipzig* 70 ; 72
MONE, F. J. Uebersicht der niederländischen Volksliteratur 7/- 8° *Tübingen* 38
SCHNEIDER, L. Geschichte der niederländischen Litteratur 8° *Leipzig* 87
van VLOTEN, J. Schets van de geschiedenis d. Nederlandsche Letteren 8° *Tiel* [71] 79

233. SCANDINAVIAN : (*a*) ICELANDIC AND OLD NORSE PHILOLOGY.

Grammar, Introduction, etc.

BAYLDON, Rev. G. Elem. Grammar of Old Norse, or Icelandic, Language 7/6 8° Williams 70
BRENNER, O. Altnordisches Handbuch [gram., texts, gloss., survey of liter.] 7/- 8° *Leipzig* 82
MÖBIUS, Theodor Ueber die altnordische Sprache [now somewhat antiquated] 1/- 8° *Kiel* 72
NOREEN, A. Altnordische Grammatik [Samml. Gram. germ. Dial. ; *Altschwed. Gramm.* to follow] 4/- 8° *Halle* 84
" " —*in* Paul's Grundriss, vol. i., pts. 2–3 [*ut* K § 225] *is a hist. of the Scandin. languages* ea. 2/- 8° *Strassburg* 89
" " —*article* Scandinavian Languages, *in* Encyclo. Brit., vol. xxi. 30/- 4° Black 87
POESTION, J. C. Einleitung in das Studium des Altnordischen, pt. i. [gram.] 3/- ; ii. [chrestom. and vocab.] 4/- 8° *Hagen* 85 ; 87
RASK, R. K. Grammar of Icelandic Tongue, tr. [Sir] G. W. Dasent *o.p.* [*w.* 12/6] r 8° Trübner 43
" " Easy Method of Learning Old Norse, tr. Lund [new vers. of above] 4/- s 8° " 69
SWEET, Henry Icelandic Primer : w. grammar, notes and glossary 3/6 c 8° Clar. Press 86
VIGFUSSON, G. Origines Islandiæ, ed. Prf. F. York Powell [posthumous] *in prep.*
*WIMMER, Prf. L. F. A. Altnordische Grammatik, übers E. Sievers 2/- 8° *Halle* 71

Modern Icelandic.

CARPENTER, W. H. Grundriss der Neu-Isländischen Grammatik 4/- 8° *Leipzig* 80

Etymology : *Dictionaries.*

*CLEASBY, R. Icelandic-English Dictionary, (posth.) ed. G. Vigfusson 67/- 4° Clar. Press 69–74
Appendix by Prf. W. W. SKEAT : *List of English Words, the Etymology of which is illustrated by Icelandic*, 2/- 4° *id.* '76
EGILSSOHN, S. Lexicon Poeticum Antiq. Linguae Septentrionalis *o.p.* [*w.* 84/-] r 8° *Copenhagen* 60
MOEBIUS, Theodor Altnordisches Glossar [*to his* Analecta, *infra*] 12/- 8° *Leipzig* 66

Chrestomathies.

BRENNER, O. —*in his* Altnordisches Handbuch, *ut supra.*
DIETRICH, F. E. C. [ed.] Alt-Nordisches Lesebuch [w. grammar and vocab.] 7/- 8° *Leipzig* [43] 64
ETTMÜLLER, L. [ed.] Altnordisches Lesebuch 5/6 4° *Zürich* 61
*MOEBIUS, T. [ed.] Analecta Norraena : extracts fr. 20 Old-Norse Works, ed. G. Vigfusson 8/- 8° *Leipzig* [50] 77
PFEIFFER, F. [ed.] Altnordisches Lesebuch [w. gram. and dict. in German] 7/6 r 8° " 60
UNGER, C. R. [ed.] Oldnorsk Laesebog : mit Glossarium 5/- 8° *Christiania* 63
*VIGFUSSON + POWELL, F. Y. [G. ; eds.] Icelandic Prose Reader [w. notes, gram., gloss.] 10/6 c 8° Clar. Press 79
*WIMMER, Prf. L. F. A [ed.] Altnordisches Lesebuch, übers.
WISEN, Th. [ed.] Carmina Norraena, vol. i. [texts and Latin notes], ; ii. (dict.) 8/- 8° *Lund* ? ; 89

234. SCANDINAVIAN : (*b*) ICELANDIC AND OLD NORSE LITERATURE.

Bibliography.

MOEBIUS, Theodor Catalogus Librorum Islandicorum, 2 pts. 7/6 8° *Leipzig* 56–80

Collections.

—*v. also* K § 233 : Icelandic Philology, *s.v.* Chrestomathies.

ASMUNDARSON, V. [ed.] Fornaldarsögur Nordrlanda, vols. i.–ii 12/- 8° *Reykjavik* 86 *in prog.*
GERING, Hugo [ed.] Islendzk Aeventyri, 2 vols. [legends, novels, folk-tales] 13/- 8° *Halle* 84
MÜLLER, [ed.] Sagabibliothek, 3 vols. [w. descrip. and anal. of the Sagas] *o.p.* [*w.* 25/-] 12° *Copenhagen* 17–20
*VIGFUSSON, Prf. Gudbrand [ed.] Icelandic Sagas, vols. i.–ii. ea. 10/- r 8° Rolls Series 88
i. : Orkneyinga Saga, Magnus Saga, w. addns. fr. Flatey Book [xiv. cent.].
ii. : Sturla the Lawman's Lives of Kings Hacon and Magnus [xiii. cent.], w. glossaries ; vols. iii.–iv. (trns. by G. W. DASENT) *in prep.*
" + *MOEBIUS, Th. [eds.] Vatnsdaelnsaga, Hallfredasaga and Flóamannasaga 8° *Leipzig* 60
*POWELL, F. York [eds.] Corpus Poeticum Boreale, 2 vols. 42/- 8° Clar. Press 83
Classified text, w. trs. of the whole body of existing ancient Icelandic liter. fr. the earliest times to 13 cent. ; w. intro., excursus and notes. A stupendous and very important work.

Faroese.

HAMMERSHEIB, V. U. [ed.] Farsk Anthologi, 2 pts. [w. brief liter. hist., gram. and vocab.] 5/- 8° *Copenhagen* 88

K § 234

Translations.

ANDERSON, Prf. R. B. [tr.] Viking Tales of the North : translated [popular] $2 12° *Chicago* [77] 89

Translations of the Sagas of Thorstein Viking's son and Fridthiof the Bold ; with G. W. STEVENS' tr. of Tegner's Fridthiof's Saga.

CAPPEL, E. S. [tr.] Old Norse Sagas : translated ; ill. [popular] 3/6 c 8° Sonnenschein 82

MAGNUSSON + MORRIS, E./W. [trs.] Three Northern Love Stories, etc. : translated 10/6 c 8° Reeves & Turner 75

Individual Sagas (Texts and Translations).

Are's Isländerbuch ; ed. Th. Möbius [w. German tr.] 3/- 8° *Leipzig* 70

Biskupa Sögur, ed. Prf. G. Vigfusson, 2 series [lives of Icel. bishops 1056–1331] 8° Icel. Liter. Soc. 58 ; 61

Vide also *Laurentius Saga*, a part of this collection, *infra*.

Blomstrvalla Saga : ed. Th. Möbius 2/6 8° *Leipzig* 55

Didriks Saga : ed. C. R. Unger 10/- r 8° *Christiania* 53

Edda Saemundar [verse] w. Latin trans. and gloss., 3 vols. *o.p.* [*w.* 90/-] 4° *Copenhagen* 27–28

ed. Sophus Bugge

" S. Grundtvig 6/- 8° *Copenhagen* [68] 74

" Karl Hildebrand 6/- 8° *Paderborn* 76

" w. German notes and gloss. H. Lüning 24/- 8° *Zürich* 59

Translations : tr. Benj. Thorpe 7/6 8° Trübner 66

" Bp. P. H. Mallet—*in his* Northern Antiquities 5/- c 8° Bohn's Lib. [1770] 47

*übers. Karl Simrock [w. Edda Sturlusonar] 8/- 8° *Stuttgart* [51] 88

" A. Holtzmann [w. German notes] 14/- 8° *Leipzig* 75

Selections : —*some of the* Songs *are tr.* W. Morris, *in his* Sigurd the Volsung and Niblungs 6/- sq 8° Reeves [77] 87

Edda Snorri Sturlusonar, [prose] ed. J. Sigurthsson, 2 vols. [w. Latin tr.] 24/- 8° *Copenhagen* 48 ; 52

*ed. F. Jónsson 7/6 r 8° " 76

*" E. Wilken ; w. German intro. [108 pp.] and notes, vol. i. [text] 6/- 8° *Paderborn* 78

Translations : tr. [Sir] G. W. Dasent *o.p.* [*w.* 7/6] 8° *Stockholm* 42

übers. Karl Simrock [w. Edda Saemundar] 8/- 8° *Stuttgart* [51] 88

AIDS TO THE EDDAS —*v. also* B § 20 : Scandinavian Mythology.

BERGMANN, F. W. Die Edda-Gedichte kritisch hergestellt, übersetzt und erläutert 8/- 8° *Strassburg* 79

HOFFORY, Julius Eddastudien, pt. i. ; 3 pl. 4/- 8° *Berlin* 89

MEYER, E. H. Völuspa : eine Untersuchung 6/6 8° " 90

WILKEN, E. Untersuchungen zur Snorra Edda 5/6 8° *Paderborn* 78

Egils Saga ed. [in Danish] F. Jónsson, 3 pts. 16/- 8° *Copenhagen* 88–89

Elis Saga ok Rosamund : ed. [for the first time] E. Kölbing [w. intro. notes and tr. in Germ.] 8/6 8° *Heilbronn* 81

Eyrbyggja Saga : ed. w. Latin tr., var. lectt. and index C. J. Thorkelin *o.p.* [*w.* 6/6] 4° *Copenhagen* 1787

ed. G. Vigfusson 6/- 8° *Leipzig* 64

tr. Sir Walter Scott—*in* P. H. Mallet's Northern Antiquities [tr.] 5/- c 8° Bohn's Lib. [1770] 47

Faereyinga Saga : ed. C. C. Rafn ; map. and facs. [w. Danish tr.] *o.p.* [*w.* 5/-] r 8° *Copenhagen* 32

Fagrskinna korfattet Norsk Konge Saga, ed. Munch + Unger 6/- 8° *Christiania* 57

Finnboga Saga : ed. H. Gering 4/- 8° *Halle* 79

Flateyjarbok : Samling af Norske Konge-Sagaer, 3 vols. 20/- r 8° *Christiania* 66–68

Fornaldar Sagan : Islenzkud og Aukin af Páli Melsted 5/- 8° *Reykjavik* (*Iceland*) 64

Forn Manna Sögur : 12 vols. [historic sagas of extra-Icelandic events] 70/- 8° *Copenhagen* 25–37

Fornsogur : ed. G. Vigfusson + Th. Möbius 5/- 8° *Leipzig* 60

Vatnsdaelasaga, Hallfredarsaga, Flomannasaga.

Gisli, the Outlaw, Story of : tr. [Sir] G. W. Dasent ; ill. *o.p.* [*pb.* and *w.* 7/6] s 4° Douglas, *Edin.* 66

Grettis Saga [by G. ASMUNDARSON] : ed. G. Magnusson + Thordarson, 2 pts. 3/6 8° *Copenhagen* 59

" " tr. E. Magnusson + W. Morris [prose] 8/- c 8° Reeves & Turner [69] 82

" " popular version by Rev. S. Baring-Gould ; 10 pl. and map 6/- c 8° Blackie 89

Gull-Thoris Saga, or Thorskfirdhinga Saga : ed. K. Maurer 2/6 r 8° *Leipzig* 58

Gunnlaug Schlangenzunge, übers. E. Kölbing [text is in Wimmer's *Leseb.*, *ut* K § 20] 1/- 16° *Heilbronn* 78

Hakonar Saga : ed. G. Vigfusson—*v.* Collections, *supra.*

Heimskringla ella Norge's Kongesagaer, ed. C. R. Unger 15/- 8° *Christiania* 68

" tr. S. Laing, *sub tit.* Chron. of Kgs. of Norway, ed. R. B. Anderson, 4 vols. 63/- 8° Nimmo [44] 89

Written by Snorri STURLUSON [12th cent.], consisting chiefly of historical sagas.
An abridgment is contained in CARLYLE'S *Early Kings of Norway*, 1/- 16° Chapman [75] 89.

Islendinga Sögur : efter gemle Haandskrifter, 2 vols. [*v. also Sturlunga, inf.*] 24/- 8° *Copenhagen* 43–47

Karlamagnus Saga : ed. C. R. Unger [13 cent. vers. of Charlemagne, *v.* K § 48] 6/- 8° *Christiania* 60

Kormaks Saga : ed. Th. Möbius 4/- r 8° *Halle* 86

Kristni Saga :

Brenner, O. Ueber die Kristnisaga : kritische Beiträge z. altnord. Lit. 3/- 8° *Munich* 78

Laurentius Saga [pt. of *Biskupa Sögur*] : Life of Laurence, Bp. of Hólar, tr. O. Elton [well tr.] 5/- 16° / 8° Rivington 90

Landnáma Bóc [" Bk. of Taking of the Land "], ed. G. Vigfusson + F. York Powell Clar. Press *in prep.*

The fullest of the old Icelandic chronicles.

Lilja (" The Lily ") : ed. w. tr. and notes E. Magnusson [relig. poem of 4 cent.] 10/6 c 8° Williams 70

Magnus Saga [hist. and miracles of Earl Magnus, Patron Saint of Kirkwall Cathedral] : ed. Vigfusson, *v.* Collections, *sup.*

Nials Saga [by N. THORGEIRSSON] : udgivet efter gamle Handskriften, vols. i.–ii. 22/6 8° *Copenhagen* 75–89 *in prog.*

" " tr. [Sir] G. W. Dasent, 2 vols. ; maps *o.p.* [*pb.* 28/- ; *w.* 20/-] 8° Douglas, *Edin.* 61

Olafs Saga : udgivet Munch + Unger [*w.* 15/-] 8° *Christiania* 53

Orkneyinga Saga [hist. of men of Orkney] : ed. G. Vigfusson—*v.* Collections, *supra.*

" " tr. J. A. Hjaltalin + G. Goudie, ed. J. Anderson ; maps and pl. 10/6 8° *Edinburgh* 73

Sturlunga and Islendinga Sagas: ed. G. Vigfusson, 2 vols. [v. also Islendinga, supra] 42/- 8° Clar. Press 78
With prolegomena wh. revolutionized knowledge of Icelandic historical literature.

Thomas Saga: ed. C. R. Unger [Thos. à Becket] 14/- r 8° *Christiania* 69
" " ed. M. E. Magnússon, 2 vols.; w. tr., notes and glossary, vols. i.-ii. ea. 10/- r 8° Rolls Series 75; 84

Tristan Saga: Norse & Eng. version, ed. w. Germ. trs., intros. & notes E. Kölbing, 2 pts. ea. 12/- 8° *Heilbronn* 78; 82
I: Tristrams Saga ok Isondar, 12/- '78; II.: Sir Tristrem [English text], 12/- '82.

Vapnfirdinga Saga: ed. G. Vigfusson 61

Viga Glum Saga: tr. w. notes and intro. Sir Edm. Head 5/- f 8° Williams 66
" " übersetzt F. Kh—— 2/- r 8° *Graz* 88

Völsunga Saga: tr. E. Magnusson + W. Morris [Camelot Series] 1/- 16° Walter Scott [76] 88

Folk-tales and Legends—*v.* B § 20: Scandinavian Mythology, *etc.*, *s.v.* Icelandic.

Treatises, etc., on the Sagas Generally.

DÖRING, Bemerkungen üb. Typus u. Styl. d. isländ. Saga [schl.-programme] 2/6 8° *Leipzig* 77; 78
GOULD, Rev. S. Baring- Iceland: its scenes and sagas 10/6 c 8° Smith & Elder [63] 64
METCALFE, Fred. The Oxonian in Iceland: with folklore and sagas *o.p.* [*pb.* 2/6] 12° Hotten [61] 67
" " —*in his* Englishman and Scandinavian: A.-S. and Old Norse Literature 18/- 8° Trübner 80

History of the Literature—*v.* K § 41: Scandinavian Literature.

235. SCANDINAVIAN: (*c*) SWEDISH AND DANISH & MODERN NORWEGIAN PHILOLOGY.

Collectively.

Serial.

Arkiv for nordisk Filologi, ed. S. Bugge + N. Lindner + A. Noreen + L. F. A. Wimmer + G. Storm, vols. i.-vi. *ea. vol.* 8/- 8° *Christiania* 83-89 *in prog.*

Swedish.

Grammars.

MAY, A. Practical Grammar of the Swedish Language 6/- p 8° *Stockholm* [*n.d.*] 73
OTTÉ, [Miss] E. C. Simplified Grammar of the Swedish Language 2/6 c 8° Trübner 84

Etymology: Dictionaries.

DALIN, A. F. Svensk Ordbog [a good book] 20/- r 8°; Hand Ordbog 7/6 12° *Stockholm* 50-55; 68
Pocket Dictionary of English and Swedish Languages 3/6 16° *Leipzig* [47] 87
NILSSON + WIDMARK + BOLLIN, $\frac{\text{L. G.}}{\text{F. P.; A. Z.}}$ Engelsk-Svensk Ordbok 16/- 8° *Stockholm* [75] 89
OMAN, V. E. Svensk-Engelsk Hand-Ordbok 8/- c 8° " [72] 89

Dialogues.

MAY, A. [ed.] Swedish and English Conversation 2/6 p 8° *Stockholm* [49] 55

Danish and Modern Norwegian.

Grammars.

BOJESEN, M. Guide to the Danish Language 5/- 12° Trübner 63
FRAEDERSDORFF, T. W. Practical Introduction to Danish, or Norwegian 4/- 12° Norgate 60
OTTÉ, [Miss] E. C. How to Learn Danish. 7/6 [Ollendorff System] Key 3/- c 8° Trübner [79] 84; 79
" " Simplified Grammar of the Danish Language 2/6 c 8° " 84
PETERSON, C. J. P. [Am.] Norwegian-Danish Grammar and Reader [w. vocabulary] 6/6 8° *Chicago* 75
RASK, Dr. E. C. Danish Grammar: w. extracts, ed. Repp 5/- 12° *Copenhagen* [ ] 46

Etymology: Dictionaries.

Danske Ordbog udgiven under Videnskabernes Selskabs Bestyrelse, vols. i.-vii. [-U] 63/- 4° *Copenhagen* 1793-1865
FERRALL + REPP + ROSING Danish-English and English-Danish Dictionary 4/- 16° " [61-63] 73
GEELMUYDEN, J. English Norwegian Dictionary, ed. J. Brynildsen 10/6 p 8° Nutt [ ] 87
LARSEN, A. Danish-Norwegian-English Dictionary 7/6 c 8° *Copenhagen* [80] 84
Pocket Dictionary of the English and Dano-Norwegian Languages 3/6 16° *Leipzig* [48] 87
ROSING, S. English-Danish Dictionary 8/6 c 8° [ ] 74

Dialogues.

BOJESEN, M. Danish Speaker 3/6 12° Trübner 65

236. ENGLISH PHILOLOGY: (*a*) GENERALLY, HISTORY OF THE LANGUAGE, &c.

Encyclopædia, Methodology, Introduction.

EARLE, Prf. J. The Philology of the English Tongue [purely linguistic] 7/6 c 8° Clar. Press [71] 87
ELZE, Karl Grundriss der englischen Philologie 8/- 8° *Halle* [87] 89
Hermeneutics, Geography, History, Antiquities.
*KÖRTING, Dr. Gustav Encyklopädie und Methodologie der englischen Philologie 8/- 8° *Heilbronn* 88
" " Grundriss d. Geschichte d. englischen Sprache und Literatur 5/- 8° *Münster* 87

SCHMITZ, B. Encyklopädie d. philol. Stud. d. neueren Sprachen, 4 pts. [esp. Fch. & Eng.] 15/- 8° *Leipzig* [59] 75-76

Three *Supplements* were pub., 3/- [60] 79; 2/6 [61] 81; 3/- [64] 81; and 3 pamphlets compl. them, *sub tit. Neueste Fortschritte d. franz.-engl. Phil.* 2/-; *Greifswald* [66] 73; 2/6 *ib.* 70; 3/- *ib.* 72. None of these were incorporated in the second edn. of the *Encyklopädie*. The chief value of the work is a strictly pedagogic one.

*STORM, Johann Englische Philologie, vol. i. [tr. by author fr. his own Danish original (*Christiania* 78)] 9/- 8° *Heilbronn* 81

This first volume deals entirely with the Living Language: Phonetics, Pronunc., Synonyms, Dialects, American Liter., Americanisms, Literature, etc.

VIETOR, W. Einführung in das Studium der englischen Philologie 2/- 8° *Marburg* 88

History of the English Language.

CRAIK, Prf. G. Lillie —*in his* History of English Liter. and Lang. [fr. Norm. Conq.] 7/6 c 8° Griffin [61] 80

FIEDLER + SACHS, E. C. Wissensch. Gramm. d. engl. Sprache, vol. i.: ed. E. Kölbing—*v.* K § 237: English Grammar.

LATHAM, Dr. R. G. History and Etymology of the English Language, 2 vols. [antiquated, but not useless] *o.p.* [*pb.* 28/-; *w.* 9/6] 8° Walton 55

LOUNSBURY, T. R. [Am.] History of the English Language $1 12° *New York* 79

MARSH, G. P. [Am.] Lectures on the English Language [rather obsolete] 15/- 8° Low [62] 72

" " The same: abridged Dr. W. Smith [" "] 7/6 c 8° Murray [62] 88

MARSHALL, W. The Past, Present and Future of England's Language 5/- c 8° Longman 78

MORSBACH, Dr. Lorenz Ueber den Ursprung der neuenglischen Schriftsprache 4/- 8° *Heilbronn* 88

OLIPHANT, T. L. K. The Old and Middle English [to 14th cent.] 9/- f 8° Macmillan [73] 90

The first edition (1873) of this book was pub. under the title, *The Sources of Middle English*.

ROEMER, J. Origins of the Eng. People and Language [a compil. of no great value] 18/- 8° Bell 88

SHEPHERD, H. E. [Am.] History of the English Language [to Georgian era] $1.50 12° *New York* 79

TRENCH, Abp. R. C. English, Past and Present 5/- f 8° Paul [55] 88

WEISSE, B. [Am.] Origin, Progress and Destiny of English Language and Literature $5 8° *New York* 78

Since 1300.

HALL, Fitzedward Modern English 10/6 c 8° Trübner 70

MORSBACH, Lor. Ueber den Ursprung der neuenglischen Schriftsprache 4/- 8° *Heilbronn* 88

OLIPHANT, T. L. K. The New English, 2 vols. [ill. of growth of lang. fr. 1300-1811] 21/- c 8° Macmillan 86

Miscellanea.

ALFORD, Dn. H. The Queen's English: a manual of idiom and usage 1/- f 8° Bohn's Lib. [64] 88

A series of ingenious lectures, unpretentious and semi-humorous, sarcastically and smartly replied to by G. W. MOON, *The Dean's English*, 1/6 c 8° Hatchard [64] 78.

HODGSON, Dr. W. B. Errors in the Use of English 3/6 c 8° Douglas, *Edin.* 81

WHITE, R. Grant [Am.] Every-day English 10/6 c 8° Low 80

Magazines and Permanent Serials—*v. also* K § 95: Comparative Philology, and K § 225: Teutonic Philology.

*Anglia Vols. i.-viii., ed. R. Wülker + M. Trautmann; ix. by R. Wülker alone, x.-xii. by E. Flügel + G. Schirmer *per vol.* [= 4 pts.] 20/- 8° *Halle* 78-89 *in prog.*

Vols. i.-iii., ea. in 3 pts.; iv.-viii. ea. in 4 pts., of wh. pts. 2 and 4 are called *Anzeiger* (consisting of reviews, etc.); ix. *sqq.* ea. in 3 pts.

Archiv. für das Studium der neueren Sprachen, vols. i.-lxxxiv. ed. L. Herrig; lxxxv. Prf. J. Zupitza ea. vol. [= 4 pts.] 6/- 8° *Brunswick* 46-89 *in prog.*

Beiträge, Erlangener, zur englischen Philologie, ed. H. Varnhagen, pt. i. 5/6 8° *Erlangen* 90 *in prog.*

*Englische Studien ed. Prf. E. Kölbing, vols. i.-xiii. [pts. also separ. at higher rates] *per. vol.* [= 3 pts.] 15/- 8° 77-89 *in prog.*

Jahrbuch für roman. u. eng. Sprache u. Litter.; vols. i.-v. ed. A. Ebert., vi.-xii. *and* N. S. i.-ii. ed. L. Lemcke *per. vol.* [= 4 pts.] 12/- [N. S. i.-ii. ea. 16/-] 8° *Berl.* 59-71; *Lpz.* 74-76 *not con.*

Vols. i.-xii. (1859-1871) were pub. *sub tit. Jahrb. f. rom. u. eng. Litteratur.* New Series, under above title, commenced 1874.

Mittheilungen aus d. gesammt. Gebiete d. englischen Sprache u. Litteratur, ed. Dr. E. Flügel [monthly] 90 *in prog.*

A *Beiblatt* to *Anglia*, *ut supra*.

*Modern Language Notes, ed. A. Marshall Elliott [Am.] [eight pts. annually] *Baltimore* 86 *sqq. in prog.*

Transactions of the Modern Language Association, vol. i. [1884-1886] 8° *Baltimore* 86 *in prog.*

Wiener Beiträge zur deutschen und englischen Philologie—*v.* K § 225.

The *Academy* and the *Athenæum*, often contain valuable articles on English philological subjects.

237. ENGLISH PHILOLOGY: (*b*) GRAMMAR: GENERALLY. PHONETICS.

Grammar: Generally.

FIEDLER + SACHS, E. C. Wissenschaftliche Grammatik d. engl. Sprache, 2 vols. *Leipzig* [50] 77; [55] 61

Vol. i. (Hist. of Lang., Phonol., Accid.) ed. E. KÖLBING 6/- [50] 77; vol. ii. (Syntax, Metrol.) ed. C. SACHS, 6/- [50] 61. Second vol. obsolete.

HELFENSTEIN, Dr. J. Comparative Grammar of the Teutonic Languages 18/- 8° Macmillan 70

English comparatively with Gothic, Old Norse, Danish, Swedish, German, Old Saxon, Dutch, etc.

*KOCH, C. F. Historische Grammatik der englischen Sprache, 3 vols. 28/- 8° *Cassel* [63] 82; [65] 78; 68

Vol. i. Laut- u. Flexionslehre [unalt. fr. 1st ed.] 10/-; ii. Satzlehre, hrsg. J. Zupitza, 10/-; iii. Wortbildung u. Fremde Elemente. An Engl. tr. by Dr. Rich. MORRIS has been announced by Trübner as in prep. for several years, but has not appeared yet (August, 1890).

*MÄTZNER, Ed. Englishe Grammatik, pt. i. 11/-; ii. 11/-; iii. 14/- 8° *Berlin* [60] 80; [64] 82; [65] 85

" " English Grammar: method., analyt., histor. [tr.], 3 vols. 36/- 8° Murray 74

The second and third edns. of the original do not differ much fr. the first, so the Engl. tr. is still representative.

*MORRIS, Dr. R. Historical Outlines of English Accidence 6/- c 8° Macmillan [72] 89
The *Historical Outlines of English Syntax* by Morris and Dr. L. Kellner is in preparation.
SCHMIDT, Immanuel Englische Grammatik [a very good school-bk.] 2/- 8° *Berlin* [76] 83

Grammar of Individual Writers—*v. also* K § 240: English Metrology, *s.v.* Individual Writers.

CHAUCER, Geoffrey [1328–1400]
ten BRINK, Prf. B. Chaucer's Sprache und Verskunst 5/- 8° *Leipzig* 84
ELLIS, Alex. J. —*in his* On Early English Pronunciation [*ut infra*].
EINENKEL, Eugen Streifzüge durch d. mittelengl. Syntax [esp. Chaucer] 4/- 8° *Münster* 87
SCHRADER, Das altengl. Relativpronomen mit besond. Berücksicht. Chaucer's [diss.] 1/6 8° *Kiel* 80
LANGLAND, William [14 cent.]
BERNARD, Emil William Langland: a grammatical treatise 2/- 8° *Bonn* 74
MILTON, John [1608–1674]
GOTTSCHALK, Ueber d. Gebrauch d. Artikels in Milton's *Paradise Lost* [diss. inaug.] 1/6 8° *Halle* 83
SHAKSPERE, Wm. [1564–1616]
ABBOTT, Dr. E. A. Shakespearian Grammar [ill. differ. 'tw. Shaksp. and mod. English] 6/- c 8° Macmillan [69] 73
CRAIK, G. L. The English of Shakespeare [a philolog. comm. on *Julius Caesar*] 5/- p 8° Chapman [57] 64
ELLIS, A. J. —*in his* On Early English Pronunciation [*ut infra*].
KELLNER, Dr. L. Zur Syntax d. engl. Verbums [w. spec. ref. to Shakspere] 3/- 8° *Vienna* 84
SPENSER, Edmund [1552–1599]
BOHNE, Bemerkungen zur Grammatik Spenser's [schl.-programme] 1/6 8° *Geestemünde* 84
HOFFMANN, M. Ueber die Allegorie in Spencer's *Faerie Queene* [diss.] 1/6 4° *Leipzig* 87
WAGNER, G. On Spencer's use of Archaisms 2/- 8° *Halle* 79
WICLIF, John [1324–84]
FISCHER, Ueber die Sprache J. Wyclifs [dissert.] 1/6 8° " 80

Anglo-Saxon Writers and Works—*v.* K §§ 247–253.

Phonetics and Pronunciation—*v. also* K § 120: Aryan Philology, *s.v.* Phonetics.

BELL, A. M. —*in his* Visible Speech: the science of universal alphabetics 15/- 4° Simpkin 67
ELLIS, Alex. J. —*in his* Princ. of Speech and Vocal Physiol., 5/-; —*in his* Sounds and their Relations f 8° Hamilton [ ]65; 82
" " —*in his* On Early English Pronunciation, pts. i.–iv., ea. 10/-; pt. v. 25/- [w. spec. ref. to Chaucer and Shaksp.] 8° E. Eng. Text Soc. 69–75; 89
Vide also his abridgment of pt. v. of this work, *English Dialects: their Homes and Sounds*, *ut* K § 241.
POGATSCHER, Prf. A. Lautlehre d. griech., lat. u. roman. Lehnworte im Altengl. [Quellen u. Forsch.] 5/- 8° *Strassburg* 88
SIEVERS, E. —*v.* K § 120.
SOAMES, L. Introduction to English, French and German Phonetics 6/- c 8° Sonnenschein 90
SWEET, H. —*in his* Primer of Phonetics 3/6 f 8° Clar. Press [77] 90
With special reference to English, French, German, Latin and Greek.
" " Primer of Spoken English 3/6 f 8° " 90
A tr. of his *Elementarbuch d. gesprochenen Englisch*, orig. written in German, 2/6 8° Leipzig [85] 86
* " " History of English Sounds from the Earliest Period 14/- 8° " [72] 88
TRAUTMANN, M. Sprachlaute im Allgem. u. Eng., Franz. u. Deut. im Besond.; 10 ill. 7/- 8° *Leipzig* 84–86
VIETOR, W. Elemente d. Phonetik u. Orthoepie d. Deutschen, Engl. u. Französischen 5/- 8° *Heilbronn* [84] 86
" " Aussprache d. Englischen [acc. to Germ.-Eng. dicts. before 1750] 6d. 8° *Marburg* 87
WESTERN, August Englische Lautlehre fur Studirende und Lehrer 2/- 8° *Heilbronn* 85
WEYMOUTH, Dr. R. F. On Early English Pronunciation [in opposition to A. J. Ellis] 10/6 c 8° Asher 74

Spelling Reform —*v. also* D § 167.

238. ENGLISH PHILOLOGY: (c) ETYMOLOGY.

Principles.

SKEAT, Prf. W. W. Principles of English Etymology, Ser. I [The Native Elements] 9/- c 8° Clar. Press 87
Series ii. will deal with foreign element.

Dictionaries: General.

ANNANDALE, C. Concise Dictionary of the English Language 10/6 sq 8° Blackie 86
*CASSELL & Co. [pubs.] Encyclopædic Dictionary, 7 vols. ea. 21/- 4° Cassell 79–88
An excellent piece of work, with useful Appendices of lists of phrases and quots. [Gk., Lat., etc., w. explans.], Scripture and other anc. names, abbreviations (over 1,000), acc. of English lexicography, list of dicts. and encyclopædias, etc.
CHARNOCK, Dr. R. S. Nuces Etymologicae [omitted words fr. the etymol. dicts.] 10/- c 8° Trübner 89
Century Dictionary: an encyclop. lexicon of the Eng. lang., pts. i.–iv.; ill. ea. 10/6 4° Unwin 89–90 *in prog.*
To comprise 24 monthly pts. at 10/6 ea., making 6 vols. at 42/- ea. in all. Elaborate and showy, but not very good. Intended to occupy an intermediate place between MURRAY'S and OGILVIE'S dictionaries.
JOHNSON, Dr. Sam. Dict. of English Lang., ed. H. J. Todd, re-ed. Dr. R. G. Latham, 4 vols. £7 4° Longman [1755] 82
" " The same, edited by the same: Abridged Edn. 14/- r 8° " [1755] 76
MILNE, David Readable English Dictionary: etymologically arranged 7/6 c 8° Murray 89
*MÜLLER, Ed. Etymologisches Wörterbuch der englischen Sprache, 2 vols. 18/- 8° *Cöthen* [64–67] 78; 79

K § 238

*MURRAY, Dr. J. H. H. [ed.] New English Dictionary, pts. i.–v. [to Clivy] [on materials of Philol. Soc.; in 24 pts.] ea. pt. 12/6 i 4° Clar. Press 84–90 *in prog.*

NUTTALL, P. A. Standard Pronouncing English Dictionary [good popular book] 3/6 c 8° Warne [63] 90

*OGILVIE, Dr. John Imperial Dictionary of Eng. Lang., ed. C. Annandale, 4 vols., 3000 ill. £5 i 8° Blackie 82

Literary, etymological, scientific and pronouncing.

" " Comprehensive Eng. Dictionary; ill. 32/–; Student's Dictionary 7/6 r 8° 16° " [63] 80; [65] 74

RICHARDSON, Dr. C. Dictionary of English Language: explan., etymol., quotats., 2 vols. 94/6 4° Bell [37] 63; 64

" " The same: with the quotations omitted 15/– 8° " [38] 56

Does not profess to contain every word; intended for philologists and chiefly valuable for etymol.; in larger edn. the quotations are arranged chronologically.

*SKEAT, Prf. W. W. Etymological Dictionary of the English Language 44/– 4°; Abridged 5/6 c 8° Clar. Press [79] 84; [81] 87

WEDGWOOD, H. Contested Etymologies in Skeat's Dictionary 5/– c 8° Trübner 82

STORMONTH, Rev. Jas. Etymol. and Pronounc. Dict. of the Eng. Lang., ed. Rev. P. H. Phelp 7/6 c 8° Blackwood [71] 88

WEBSTER, Noah [Am.] Dictionary of English Lang., ed. Goodrich + Porter + Mahn 21/– 4° Bell [28] 80

" " The same: with appendices [70 pp. of literary illustrations] 31/6 4° " [28] 69

WEDGWOOD, Hensleigh Dictionary of English Etymology 21/–m 8° Trübner [62–65] 88

Considerably antiquated, and never entirely sound; but nevertheless useful.

WORCESTER, J. E. [Am.] Quarto Dictionary; ill. 31/6 4° *Philadelphia* [46] 81

There have been pub. in England and America more than 150 Dictionaries of general English since Dr. JOHNSON'S time alone.

Folk Etymology.

HARE, J. C. Fragments of two Essays in English Philology, ed. Prf. J. E. B. Mayor 3/6 8° Macmillan 73

1. Words derived from names of places; 2. Words corrupted by false analogy or false derivation.

*PALMER, Rev. A. Smythe Folk Etymology: dictionary of corrupted words 21/– 8° Bell 81

An elaborate and important work.

Foreign Elements in the English Language.

Generally.

Stanford's Dictionary of Anglicized Words Camb. Press *in prep.*

A collection of foreign words imperfectly naturalized and ill understood. Mr. STANFORD left a sum of £5,000 for its compilation and publication.

Anglo Indian.

WHITWORTH, G. C. Anglo-Indian Glossary: glossary of Indian terms used in English 12/– 8° Paul 78

*YULE + BURNELL, Col. H. / A. C. Hobson-Jobson: glossary of Anglo-Indian words 36/– 8° Murray 86

Anglo-Norman —v. *also* K § 275.

French.

BEHRENS, Dietrich Beiträge zur Geschichte der französischen Sprache in England, pt. i. 8/– 8° *Heilbronn* 86

This first pt. is on the phonology of Fch. loan-words in Middle-English. It forms pt. 2 of vol. v. of the *Französ. Studien.*

Gaelic.

MACKAY, Chas. Gaelic Etymology of Langs. of W. Europe [esp. English and Lowland Scotch] 42/– i 8° Trübner 78

Not trustworthy, but contains a good deal of useful material.

Icelandic.

SKEAT, Prf. W. W. List of Eng. Words whose etym. is ill. by Icel. [suppl. to Cleasby's *Icel. Dict.*] 2/– 4° Clar. Press 77

Names.

Place-Names —*for* General Treatises, v. K § 120.

HOPE, R. C. Dialectical Place-Nomenclature 83

Wales and West of England.

MORGAN, Rev. Thos. Handbk. of Origin of Place-names in Wales and Monmouthshire 8° Author, *Merthyr* 87

PULMAN, G. P. R. Names of Places, chiefly in W. of England: etym. and histor. consid. 12° *Crewkerne* 57

Scotland.

MAXWELL, Sir H. E. Studies in Topography [= toponymy] of Galloway 14/– 8° Douglas, *Edin.* 87

A list of 4,000 names of places. Etymol. equivalents appended to Gaelic words untrustworthy.

Ireland.

*JOYCE, Dr. P. W. Irish Names and Places: origin and history, 2 series 10/– c 8° *Dublin* (Whittaker) [69–75] 83

" " Irish Local Names explained 1/– f 8° *Dublin* (Simpkin) [ ] 83

Words derived from Place-Names —v. J. C. Hare's Fragments, essay i. [*ut supra*].

Plant-Names —v. K § 241: English Dialects.

Surnames —v. G § 24: Christian Names and Surnames.

Words derived from Proper Names —v. *also* Hare, *supra.*

CHARNOCK, Dr. R. S. Verba Nominalia 14/– 8° Trübner 82

Synonyms.

CRABBE, G. English Synonyms Explained [Popular Library] 3/6 c 8° Routledge [23] 89

DRESER, W. Englische Synonymik, 6/–; School Edition [= abridgment] 2/6 8° *Wolfenbüttel* 81; 83

FALLOWS, S. [Am.] Complete Handbook of Synonyms and Antonyms $1 16° *Chicago* [83] 89

*ROGET, Dr. P. M. Thesaurus of English Words and Phrases [classified] 10/6 c 8° Longman [52] 79

SMITH, Archd. C. J. Synonyms Discriminated: ill. w. quotations [a dictionary] 14/– 8° Bell [71] 82

" " Synonyms and Antonyms: kindred words and their opposites 5/– c 8° Bohn's Lib. [ ] 68

Words: History of.

PALMER, Rev. A. Smythe Leaves from a Word-Hunter's Note Book 7/6 c 8° Trübner 76

TRENCH, Abp. R. C. English Past and Present, 5/–; On the Study of Words 5/– f 8° Paul [55] 88; [51] 90

WHITE, R. Grant [Am.] Words and their Uses: past and present 5/– c 8° Low [70] 86

Obsolete Words and Meanings.

DAVIES, T. L. O. Supplementary English Glossary [12,000 words, w. quots.] 16/– 8° Bell 81

A supplement to the dictionaries of JOHNSON ed. LATHAM RICHARDSON [w/ K § 238], NARES [w/ inf.], HALLIWELL [w/ K § 240]

*HALLIWELL[-PHILLIPS], J. O. Dictionary of Archaic and Provincial Wds., Phrases, etc., fr. 14 cent., 2 v. 15/– 8° Reeves & Turner [44; 47] 89

HOPPE, A. Englisch-Deutsches Supplementlexicon, pts. i.–ii. [to occupy 4 parts] ea. 8/– r 8° *Berlin* [71] 88 *in prog.*

*NARES, Archd. R. Glossary of Words, Phrases, Customs, etc., ed. J. O. Halliwell + T. Wright, 2 vols. [16–17 cent.] 21/– 8° J. R. Smith [22] 76

*SCHMIDT, Alex. —*in his* Shakespeare Lexicon, 2 vols. 24/– r 8° *Berlin* [74; 75] 86

SMITH, H. P. Glossary of Terms and Phrases 3/6 8° Paul [83] 89

TRENCH, Abp. R. C. Glossary of Eng. Words used former. in Senses differ. fr. present 5/– f 8° " [59] 90

WRIGHT, Thos. Dictionary of Obsolete and Provincial English, ed. S. J. Herrtage, 2 vols. ea. 5/– c 8° Bohn's Lib. [57] 86

Obsolete Agricultural Words, etc. —v. K § 241: English Dialects.

Bible English.

Authorized Version.

DAVIES, T. L. O. Bible English [old and disused expressions] 5/6 c 8° Bell 75

LUMBY, Rev. J. R. Glossary of Difficult, Ambiguous or Obsolete Bible Words 8*d.* 12° S.P.C.K. 80

*WRIGHT, W. Aldis Bible Word-Book: glossary of archaic words, etc. 7/6 c 8° Macmillan [84] 85

Revised Version.

MOON, G. Washington Ecclesiastical English [criticism of English of the new Revision] 3/6 c 8° Ward & Downey [86] 87

239. ENGLISH PHILOLOGY: (*d*) ACCIDENCE AND SYNTAX.

Accidence and Syntax: Collectively.

Verb.

BANDOW, C. Der Conjunctiv in der neuenglischen Prosa [schl.-progr.] 1/6 8° *Berlin* 69

BLUME, Rud. Ursprung u. Entwickelung d. Gerundiums im Englischen [diss. inaug.] 1/6 8° *Bremen* 80

HOLZ, Gerold On the Use of the Subjunctive Mood in the A.-S. and Old English [diss. inaug.] 2/– 8° *Zürich* 82

KASTEN, Inquiry into the Use of the Subjunctive Mood: Elizab. period [diss. inaug.] 2/– 8° *Rostock* 74

KELLNER, Dr. L. Zur Syntax d. engl. Verbums [w. spec. refer. to Shakspere] 3/– 8° *Vienna* 84

KUJACK, On the Use of the Auxiliary Verbs in Old English [schl.-progr.] 1/6 8° *Lauenberg* 76

RUSTEBERG, Historical Development of the Gerund in the English Lang. [diss. inaug.] 2/– 8° *Leipzig* 74

Noun.

WEGENER, Gebrauch d. Accusativs im Englischen [schl.-progr.] 2/– 8° *Königsberg* 52

Pronoun.

BAHRS, Ueber d. Gebrauch d. Anrede-Pronomina im Altenglischen [schl.-prog.] 2/– 8° *Vegesack* 86

BÖTHKE, Der Gebrauch d. Pronomina im Englischen [schl.-prog.] 1/6 8° *Thorn* 68

BREITKREUZ, O. Beitrag z. Gesch. d. Possessiv-pronomina in d. engl. Sprache [diss. inaug.] 1/6 8° *Göttingen* 82

NOACK, Paul Geschichte d. relativen Pronomina in d. engl. Sprache [diss. inaug.] 1/6 8° " 82

PENNING, History of the Reflective Pronouns in the English Language [diss. inaug.] 1/6 8° *Leipzig* 75

SCHMIDT, On the Use of the Relative Pronouns in the English Language [schl.-prog.] 1/6 8° *Memel* 62

Particles: *Adverbs and Prepositions.*

SATTLER, W. Die adverbialen Zeitverhältnisse [illustr. by examples] 1/– 8° *Halle* 76

The same author has contrib. a series of interesting papers on the use of prepositions in *Englische Studien*, vols. i.–x. [v. K § 236].

Syntax.

BRINKMANN, F. Syntax des Französischen und Englischen, vol. i. 12/–; vol. ii. 17/6 2° *Brunswick* 84; 85

EINENKEL, E. Streifzüge durch die mittel-englische Syntax [espec. Chaucer] 5/– 8° *Münster* 88

KELLNER, Dr. L. History of English Syntax—to form vol. ii. of Morris' *Histor. Outl.* [ut K § 237] *in prep.*

Position of Words.

VERRON, Construction or arrangmt. of words and sentence in Engl. Lang., 3 pts. [sch.-progr.] ea. 1/6 8° *Münster* 76; 78; 79

Syntax of Special Writers and Writings —v. K § 237.

240. ENGLISH PHILOLOGY: (c) METRICS.

Generally —v. also K § 62: Theory, etc., of Poetry.

ELLIS, Alex. J. —in his On Early English Pronunciation [ut K § 237].
" " Chapters on Metre 86
GUEST, E. History of English Rhythms, ed. Prf. W. W. Skeat 18/- 8° Bell [38] 82
There are no very material changes in the text of this second edn., and the work is therefore to a large extent obsolete
GUMMERE, Dr. F. B. [Am.] Handbook of Poetics [a school-book] $1.10 12° *Boston* 88
LANIER, S. [Am.] The Science of English Verse [mainly popular] $2 12° *New York* 80
MAVOR, Prf. J. B. Chapters on English Metre 7/6 8° Clay 86
*SCHIPPER, J. Englische Metrik in histor. u. systemat. Entwickelung, vols. i. 13/6; ii. (1) 10/- 8° *Bonn* 82; 88
Vol. i.: Old-English Metres. An English tr. is announced.
SKEAT, Prf. W. W. Essay on Alliterative Poetry—in Bp. Percy's Folio MS., vol. iii. [ut K § 65].
WITCOMB, On the Structure of English Verse 8° *Paris* 84

Practical Guide and Rhyming Dictionaries.

HOOD, Tom [*jun.*] Practical Guide to English Versification 2/6 f 8° Hogg [69] 88
LONGMUIR, J. Rhythmical Index to the English Language *o.p.* [*pb.* and *w.* 2/6] c 8° Tegg 77
WALKER, John Rhyming Dictionary of the English Language, ed. J. Longmuir 3/6 c 8° Routledge [1775] 88
Conts. a chap. explaining the use of the dict. in deciphering errors in telegrams!

Elizabethan Writers on Rhythm (DRYDEN [1667], LODGE [1580], PUTTENHAM [1589], Sir Pp. SYDNEY [1595], WEBBE [1586])—v. K § 62.

Individual Writers.

CHAUCER, Geoffrey [1328-1400]
*ten BRINK, Prf. B. Chaucer's Sprache und Verskunst 5/- 8° *Leipzig* 84
LINDNER, F. The Alliteration in Chaucer's *Canterbury Tales* [diss. inaug.] 1/- 8° *Rostock* 76
JONSON, Ben [1574-1637]
WILKE, W. Metrische Untersuchungen zu Ben Jonson [diss. inaug.] 1/6 8° *Halle* 85
MARSTON, John [1575-1633]
v. SCHOLTEN Metrische Untersuchungen zu Marston's Trauerspielen [diss. inaug.] 1/6 f 8° *Halle* 86
MARLOWE, Christopher [1564-1593]
SCHIPPER, J. De Marlovii versu 2/- 8° *Bonn* 67
SHAKSPERE, Wm. [1564-1616]
*ABBOTT, Dr. E. A. —in his Shakespearian Grammar [ut K § 237].
BROWNE, G. H. Notes on Shakespere's Versification: w. appendix on the verse tests 40c. 12° *Boston* 84
Vide also the Introductions, etc., of FURNIVALL, FLEAY, and INGRAM, to the pubns. of the Early Eng. Text Society.
WYATT, Sir Thos. [1503-1542]
*ALSCHER, R. Sir Thos. Wyatt u. s. Stellung in d. Entwickelungsgesch. d. eng. Lit. 4/- 8° *Vienna* 86

241. ENGLISH DIALECTS.

Bibliography.

Catalogue of the English Dialect Society's Library, pt. i. [to 1879], 1/-; ii. [1880-88] 1/- 8° Eng. Dialect Soc. (Tbnr.) 80; 88
SKEAT + NODAL, W. W. / J. H. [eds.] Bibliographical List of Books illustrative of Eng. Dialects, 3 pts. 15/- 8° " " " 73; 75; 77
i.: Dictionaries [W. W. SKEAT], 4/6; ii.: County Literature [SKEAT], 6/-; iii.: Scottish, Anglo-Irish, Cant, Slang [J. H. NODAL], 4/6.

Collectively.

ELLIS, Alex. J. English Dialects: their homes and sounds [abdgmt. of pt. v. of his E. Eng. Pronunc., ut K § 237] 8° E. Eng. Text Soc. (Tbnr.) 90

Dictionaries.

BROCKETT, J. T. Glossary of North County Words, 2 vols. [fr. MS. of J. G. Lambton] *o.p.* 8° *Newcastle-on-Tyne* [25] 46
English Dialect Dictionary: Provisional editor, Rev. A. Smythe Palmer Eng. Dialect Soc. (Tbnr.) *in prep.*
This project is on foot, and may be commenced during 1890. It is proposed to collect all the dialect material from published works, magazines, etc., and to illustrate it by quotations from the best books written in dialect.
Five Original Glossaries: by various writers 7/6 8° Eng. Dialect Soc. (Tbnr.) 81
Isle of Wight, Oxfordshire, Cumberland, North Lincolnshire, Radnor.
GROSE, Francis Glossary of Provincial & Local Words, w. S. Pegge's Suppl. [1814] *o.p.* [*w* 4/6] 8° J. R. Smith [1787] 39
*HALLIWELL [-PHILLIPS] J. O. Dict. of Archaic & Provincial Wds., Phrases, etc., fr. 14 cent., 2 v. 15/- 8° Reeves & Turner [44-47] 89
MARSHALL + WILLAN, W. / R. Glossary of North of England Words [7 glossaries] 7/6 8° Eng. Dialect Soc. [14, *etc.*] 73
RAY, John Collection of English Words not generally used, ed. Prf. W. W. Skeat 8/- 8° " " " [1674] 74
The above is a reprint of the *second* edition, 1691.
SAYWELL, Rev. J. L. New Popular Handbook of County Dialects [specs., w. prelim. notes] 3/- c 8° Trübner 90

K § 241

SKEAT, Prf. W. W. [ed.] Five Original Provincial English Glossaries 7/- 8° Eng. DialectSoc.(Tbnr.)76

Cleveland, Kent, Surrey, Oxfordshire, South Warwickshire.

" " [ed.] Seven Provincial English Glossaries from various sources 8/- 8° " " " " 74

" " [ed.] Five Reprinted Glossaries [Wilts, E. Anglia, Suff., Yorks., etc.] 7/- 8° " " " " 79

Surtees Society A Glossary of Northern Words 8° Surtees Soc. *in prep.*

Intended chiefly to illustrate and explain the words occurring in the existing pubns. of the Society. Has been in preparation 30 years!

WRIGHT, Thos. Dictionary of Obsolete & Provincial English, ed. S. J. Herrtage, 2 v. ea. 5/- c 8° Eng. Dialect Soc. (Thnr.) [57] 86

Miscellaneous Articles, etc.

GOMME, G. L. [ed.] Dialects and Popular Sayings [repr. fr. *Gentleman's Mag.*] 7/6 8° Stock 83

Obsolete Words, etc. —*v.* K § 238 : English Etymology, *s.v.* Obsolete Words.

Specimens.

ELWORTHY + SKEAT, F. T./W. W. [eds.] Specimens of English Dialects 8/6 8° Eng. DialectSoc. (Tbnr.)79

Contents: *Exmoor Scolding and Courtship* [ELWORTHY]: *A Bran New Wark* [SKEAT].

MORRIS, Dr. Richard [ed.] Alliterative Poems in West Midland Dialect of 14th cent. [about 1360] 16/- 8° " " " " 64

Agricultural Words.

BRITTEN, Jas. [ed.] Old Country and Farming Words [fr. agricultural books] 10/6 8° Engl. DialectSoc. (Thnr.)80

FITZHERBERT, "Master" Book of Husbandry, ed. Prf. W. W. Skeat 8/6 8° " " " "[1534]82

TUSSER, Thos. Five Hundred Pts. of Good Husbandry, ed. W. Payne + S. J. Herrtage 12/6 8° " " " "[1580]78

PALLADIUS, On Husbondrie, pt. i. ed. Rev. B. Lodge, ii. ed. S. J. Herrtage [fr. unique MS.] 15/- 8° " " " " 72; 79

Bird Names.

SWAINSON, Rev. Chas. English Provincial Bird Names 12/- 8° Eng. Dialect Soc. 85

Plant Names.

*BRITTEN + HOLLAND, J. + R. Dictionary of English Plant Names, 3 pts. 8/6, 8/6 and 10/- 8° Eng. DialectSoc. 78; 79; 84

EARLE, Prf. J. English Plant Names 5/- 16° Clar. Press 80

From the Tenth to the Fifteenth cents.; chiefly taken fr. WRIGHT'S *A.-S. and O.-E. Vocabularies* [*v.* K § 240].

FRIEND, Rev. Hilderic —*in his* Flowers and Flower Lore ; ill. [*v. also infra, s.v.* Devon] 7/6 8° Sonnenschein [84] 89

HOOPS, Joh. Ueber die altenglischen Pflanzennamen [good] 8° *Freiburg* 89

PRIOR, Dr. R. C. The Popular Names of British Plants [good, but etymology weak] 7/6 p 8° Norgate [63] 79

SMITH, John Dict. of Popular Names of Plants in Domestic and General Economy 14/- 8° Macmillan 81

TURNER, W. The Names of Herbs : w. intro. and index Jas. Britten 6/6 8° Eng. DialectSoc. [1548] 81

Slang and Cant —*for* Americanisms, *v. infra.*

BARRÈRE + LELAND, Prf. A./C. G. Slang, Jargon and Cant, 2 vols. [a dictionary] ea. 31/6 f 4° Whittaker 88

BAUMANN, H. Londonismen: Slang und Cant [dictionary; useful but not wholly trustworthy] 4/- 8° *Berlin* 87

FARMER, J. S. Slang and its Analogues : past and present, 3 vols. [a dictionary] 105/- f 4° Watt 90

HERRTAGE, S. J. Dictionary of Slang *in prep.*

HOTTEN, J. C. Slang Dictionary : vulgar words, street phrases and fast expressions 6/6 c 8° Chatto [59] 73

Specimens.

AWDELEY, John Fraternitye of Vacabondes [1565], Harman's Caveat [1566], *etc.*, ed. E. Viles + F. J. Furnivall 7/6 8° E. Eng. Text Soc. 66

NON-EUROPEAN ENGLISH DIALECTS.

Americanisms.

BARTLETT, J. R. [Am.] Dictionary of Americanisms 20/- 8° Trübner [48] 77

Admits a large number of words which are, strictly speaking, not "Americanisms."

FARMER, J. S. Americanisms, Old and New [a dictionary] 31/6 i 4° Poulter 89

LELAND, C. G. [Am.] Dictionary of Americanisms Whittaker *in prep.*

de VERE, Prf. Schele [Am.] Americanisms : the English of the New World $2 8° *New York* 71

Pennsylvanian Dutch.

HALDEMANN, Prf. S. S. [Am.] Pennsylvania Dutch : a dial. of S. Germany w. infusion of Engl. $1.25 12° *Philadelphia n.d.* (7-)

Creolese-English —*v.* K § 161.

Pidgin-English —*v.* K § 153.

Gipsy-English —*v.* K § 166.

ENGLISH DIALECTS : ACCORDING TO COUNTIES.

Vide also E § 17 : English Topography, *passim.*

Berkshire.

LOWSLEY, Maj. B. Glossary of Berkshire Words and Phrases 10/- c 8° Eng. DialectSoc. (Tbnr.)88

Cheshire.

DARLINGTON, Thos. Folk-speech of South Cheshire 15/- 8° Eng. DialectSoc. (Tbnr.)87

HOLLAND, R. Glossary of Cheshire Words, 3 pts. 7/-, 9/- and 6/- 8° " " " 84; 85; 86

LEIGH, Egerton Glossary of Cheshire Words [based on Wilbraham (1820) 26] 10/6 8° Hamilton

K § 241

Cornwall.

BANNISTER, J. Glossary of Cornish Names [20,000 anc. & mod. local, family & personal names] 12/- 8° *Truro* 71
COURTNEY + COUCH, M. A. / T. Q. Glossary of Words and Phrases in Cornwall 6/- 8° Eng. Dialect Soc. (Tbnr.) 80
JAGO, F. W. P. English-Cornish Dictionary 21/- 8° *Plymouth* 87

Cornish Philology —*v.* K § 280.

Cumberland.

DICKINSON, W. Glossary of Words and Phrases of Cumberland 6/-; Supplement 1/- 8° Eng. Dialect Soc. (Tbnr.) 78;79
FERGUSON, R. Dialect of Cumberland [w. chapter on place-names] 5/- c 8° *Carlisle* (Williams) 73

Devonshire —*v. also* Westmoreland, *infra.*

FRIEND, Rev. Hilderic Devonshire Plant Names 5/- 8° Eng. Dialect Soc. (Tbnr.) 82
PENGELLY, W. Words Current in Devon in the Fifteenth Century 82
WEYMOUTH, Dr. R. F. Devon Words—*in* Philolog. Soc. Transactions 1854.

Dorsetshire.

BARNES, Rev. W. Grammar and Glossary of the Dorset Dialect 6/- 8° *Berlin* (Trübner) 63

Specimens.

BARNES, Rev. W. —*for his* Poems of Rural Life [in Dorset dialect], *v.* K § 68, *s.v.* Nineteenth Century.

Gloucester.

ROBERTSON, J. D. Glossary of Words in use in the County of Gloucester, ed. Lord Moreton 8° Eng. Dialect Soc. (Tbnr.) 90

Essex.

CHARNOCK, Dr. R. S. Glossary of the Essex Dialect 3/6 8° Trübner 80

Hampshire.

COPE, Rev. Sir W. H. Hampshire Words and Phrases 6/- 8° Eng. Dialect Soc. (Tbnr.) 83

Herefordshire.

DUNCUMB, J. Glossary of Words used in Herefords. [1804]—*in* Seven Provinc. Gloss. 7/- 8° E. Dialect Soc. (Tbnr.) 74
HAVERGAL, Preb. F. T. Herefordshire Words and Phrases: colloquial and archaic 5/- 4° Robinson, *Walsall* 87

Isle of Man —*v. infra.*

Isle of Wight.

LONG, W. H. Dictionary of the Isle of Wight Dialect 3/6 f 8° *Newport, I. o. W.* 86

Kent.

PARISH + SHAW, Rev. W. D. / Rev. W. F. Dictionary of the Kentish Dialect and Provincialisms 10/- 8° Eng. Dialect Soc. 87

Isle of Thanet.

LEWIS, J. Glossary of Words used in the I. of Thanet [1736]—*in* Seven Provinc. Gloss. 7/- 8° E. Dialect. Soc. (Tbnr.) 74

Lancashire.

CUNLIFFE, Henry Glossary of Rochdale-with-Rossendale Words and Phrases 7/6 c 8° Heywood, *Manc.* 86
NODAL + MILNER, J. H. / G. Glossary of the Dialect of Lancashire, 2 pts. 9/6 8° E. Dialect Soc. 75;82
PEACOCK, M. The North-Lancashire Dialect 2/- c 8° Bell 86

Specimens.

"BOBBIN, Tim" [= John COLLIER] Works in Prose and Verse; w. glossary 10/6 c 8° *Manc.* [19] 62
HARLAND + WILKINSON, J. / T. T. [eds.] Ballads & Songs of Lancashire: ancient & modern [chfly. bef. 19 cent.] 3/6 c 8° Heywood, *Mcr.* [65] 75
WAUGH, Edwin Poems and Lancashire Songs [and many other similar works] 6/- f 8° *Manchester* [*n.y.*] 76

Leicestershire.

EVANS, Rev. A. B. The Dialect of Leicestershire, ed. Sebastian Evans 10/6 8° Eng. Dialect Soc. (Tbnr.) 81

Lincolnshire.

COLE, Rev. R. E. Glossary of Words used in Wapentake of Graffoe 7/6 8° Eng. Dialect Soc. (Tbnr.) 86
PEACOCK, Edw. Glossary of Wds. used in Wapentakes of Manley & Corringham, 2 v., ea. 12/6 8° " " " [77] 89

Norfolk.

*FORBY, Robert Vocabulary of East Anglia [Norfolk and Suffolk], ed. W. Rye [30] *in prep.*

Specimen.

CAPGRAVE, John Chronicle of England, ed. Hingeston [written in Norfolk dial.] 10/- r 8° Rolls Ser. 58

Northamptonshire.

BAKER, Anne Eliz. Glossary of Northamptonshire Words and Phrases, 2 vols. 16/- p 8° J. R. Smith 54
STERNBERG, T. Dialect and Folklore of Northamptonshire 5/- p 8° " 51

Shropshire.

*JACKSON, Georgina — Shropshire Word Book: archaic and provincial words 31/6 8° Trübner 79-81

Somersetshire.

ELWORTHY, Rev. F. T. — Dialect of West Somerset, 3/6; Gram. of Dialect of W. Somerset 5/- 8° E. Dialect Soc. 75; 77
* " " — Glossary of West Somerset Words [a very excellent work] 25/- 8° " " " 88
JENNINGS, James — On the Dialect of Somersetshire: w. glossary and poems 4/6 f 8° J. R. Smith [25] 69

Specimens.

HALLIWELL [-PHILLIPS], J. O. [ed.] Collection of Pieces in the Dialect of Zummerset *o.p.* [*pb.* 2/-; *w.* 3/6] 8° J. R. Smith 43

Suffolk

—*v.* Norfolk, *supra.*

Surrey.

GOWER, G. Leveson — Surrey Provincialisms—*in* Five Original Glossaries 7/- 8° Eng. Dialect Soc. (Tbnr.) 76
KEMBLE, — Surrey Woods—*in* Philolog. Soc. Transactions 1854

Sussex.

COOPER, W. D. — Glossary of the Provincialisms in use in the County of Sussex 3/6 p 8° J. R. Smith [36] 53
PARISH, Rev. W. D. — Dictionary of the Sussex Dialect 8° *priv. prin. Lewes* 75

Westmoreland.

Specimens.

ELWORTHY + SKEAT, F. T./W. W. [eds.] Specimens of E. Dialects [Devon, Westmoreland] 8/6 8° Eng. Dialect Soc. 79
WHEELER, Ann [ed.] — Westmoreland Dialect (dialogues, with glossary) 3/6 p 8° J. R. Smith [2nd ed. 02] 40

Wiltshire.

AKERMAN, J. Yonge — Glossary of Provincial Words and Phrases in Use in Wiltshire 3/- f 8° J. R. Smith 42
BRITTON, J. — Wiltshire Words—*in* Five Reprinted Glossaries 7/- 8° Eng. Dialect Soc. (Tbnr.) 79

Specimens.

AKERMAN, J. Yonge [ed.] Wiltshire Tales [in dialect] 2/6 f 8° J. R. Smith 53

Worcestershire.

CHAMBERLAIN, Mrs. — Glossary of West Worcestershire Words, w. glossic notes T. Hallam 4/6 8° Eng. Dialect Soc. 82
LAWSON, Can. — Upton-on-Severn Words 2/6 8° " " " 84

Yorkshire.

ADDY, S. O. — Glossary of Words used in the Neighbourhood of Sheffield 15/- 8° Eng. Dialect Soc. 88
ATKINSON, Rev. J. C. — Glossary of the Cleveland Dialect 24/- 4° J. R. Smith 68
Additions to same—*in* Five Original Glossaries 7/- 8° Eng. Dialect Soc. (Tbnr.) 76.
EASTER + LEES, Rev. A./Rev. T. — Glossary of Dialect of Almondbury and Huddersfield 8/6 8 Eng. Dialect Soc. (Tbnr.) 83
HARLAND, Cpt. J. — Glossary of Words used in Swaledale 4/- 8° " " " " 73
NICHOLSON, John — Folk-Speech of East Yorkshire 3/6 c 8° Brown, *Hull* 89
ROBINSON, C. Clough — Glossary of Mid-Yorkshire Words [w. outline of grammar] 9/- 8° Eng. Dial. Soc. [62] 76
" F. K. — Glossary of Words used in Neighbourhood of Whitby, 2 vols. 7/6 and 6/6 8° " " [55] 75; 76
ROSS + STEAD, F. + R. — Glossary of Holderness Words 7/6 8° " " " 77

SCOTLAND.

DUNCAN, A. — Early Scottish Glossary [sel. fr. Duncan's *Appendix Etymologiae*]—*in* Seven Provinc. Gloss. 8/- 8° Eng. Dial. Soc. 74
*JAMIESON, Dr. J. — Etymolog. Dict. of Scottish Lang., ed. J. Longmuir + D. Donaldson, 4 v. £7 10/-; Suppl. 27/6 8° Gardner, *Paisley* [08-25] 79-87
MACKAY, Dr. Charles — Dictionary of Lowland Scotch 7/6 p 8° Whittaker 89
MURRAY, Dr. J. A. H. — Dialect of the Southern Counties of Scotland [Philol. Soc.] [*w.* 12/6] 8° Trübner 73

Specimens.

Buik of Chroniclis of Scotland, ed. W. B. Turnbull, 3 vols. [metrical, 16 cent.] ea. 10/- r 8° Rolls Series
Legends of the Saints in Scottish Dialects of 14 cent., ed. W. M. Metcalfe, pt. i. 8° Scot. Text Soc. 88 *in prog.*

Proverbs, Folk-songs, etc.—*v.* B § 15, *s.v.* Scottish; Poetry—*v.* K § 68, *passim.*

Banffshire.

GREGOR, Rev. W. — Dialect of Banffshire [Philolog. Soc.] 5/- 8° Trübner 66

Shetland and Orkneys.

EDMONSTON, T. — Etymological Glossary of the Shetland and Orkney Dialect [Philolog. Soc.] 5/- 8° Trübner 66

ISLE OF MAN.

Specimens.

BROWNE, Rev. T. H. — Fo'c's'le Yarns [= "forecastle yarns"] [1st edn. pub. anonymously] 7/6 c 8° Macmillan [73] 89
" " — The Doctor, and other Poems in the Manx Patois 6/- f 8° Sonnenschein 87
" " — The Manx Witch, and other Poems 7/6 c 8° Macmillan 89

IRELAND.

Antrim and Down.

PATTERSON, W. H. Gloss. of Words and Phrases used in Antrim and Down 7/- 8° Eng. Dialect Soc. 80

Wexford.

POOLE, J. Glossary of Forth and Bargy, ed. w. notes W. Barnes [w. some specimens] 4/6 f 8° J. R. Smith 67

242 ANGLO-SAXON PHILOLOGY (WITH OLD WEST-SAXON).

Grammar: Generally.

GREIN, C. W. M. Kurzgefasste angelsächsische Grammatik [posthumous; not v. good] 2/- 8° *Cassel* 80
KÖRNER, Karl Einleit. in d. Stud. d. A.-S., pt. i. [Gram.], 2/-; ii. [Chrestom.] 9/- 8° *Heilbronn* [78] 87; 80
MARCH, F. A. [Am.] Comparative Grammar of Anglo-Saxon Language 10/- 8° Trübner [70] 77
Illustrated by the forms of Sanscrit, Greek, Latin, Gothic, O.-Sax., O.-Fris., O.-Norse, and O.-High-German.
MÜLLER, Theodor Angelsächsische Grammatik, hrsg. H. Hilmer [posthum.; more elem. than Sievers] 4/6 8° *Göttingen* 83
RASK, E. Grammar of the Anglo-Saxon Tongue [tr. fr. Danish] 5/6 c 8° Trübner [30] 75
*SIEVERS, Prf. Ed. Angelsächsische Grammatik [Samml. Gramm. germ. Dial.] 4/6 8° *Halle* [82] 86
" " The same, tr. Prf. A. S. Cook [Am.], *sub tit.* Old English Grammar $1.25 12° *Boston* [86] 88
Contains only the Phonology and Accidence.
SWEET, H. Grammatical Introduction—*prefixed to his* A.-S. Reader [*ut infra*].
The first Anglo-Saxon Grammar published was by George HICKES: *Institutiones Anglo-Saxonicae et Maeso-Gothicae*, Oxford, 1689.

Grammar [and Departments of Grammar] of Individual Writers and Writings—v. K §§ 247–253.

Old West-Saxon.

COSIJN, P. J. Kurzgefasste altwestsächsische Grammatik, pt. i. [Vocale d. Stammsilben] 8° *Leyden* 81
" " Altwestsächsische Grammatik 12/- 8° *The Hague* 88

Etymological Grammar.

LOTH, J. Etymologische angelsächsisch-englische Grammatik 8/- 8° *Elberfeld* 70
A unique and useful work, but to be used with caution.

Dictionaries —*v. also the* Glossaries *in the* Chrestomathies, *infra.*

BOSWORTH, Prf. J. Anglo-Saxon Dict., ed. [fr. MS.] Prf. T. N. Toller, pts. i.–iii. [to Sar.] ea. 15/- 4° Clar. Press [38] 82–87 *in prog.*
" " Compendious Anglo-Saxon & English Dictionary [extr. fr. 1st ed. of above] 12/- 8° Reeves & Turner [52] 88
GREIN, C. W. M. Kleines angelsächsisches Wörterbuch, bearb. F. Groschopp 5/- 8° *Cassel* 83
" " Handy Anglo-Saxon Dictionary, ed. F. Groschopp, tr. Prf. J. A. Harrison + Prf. W. M. Baskerville [Ams.] $3 8° *Boston* [85] 88
" " Sprachschatz der A.-S. Dichter [= Bibl. A.-S. Poesie, v. iii.–iv. *ut infra*].
LEO, H. Angelsächsisches Glossar, 2 vols. [arrgd. acc. to stems] 15/- r 8° *Halle* 72–77

Early Lexicography.

WRIGHT, Thos. [ed.] Anglo-Saxon and Old-English Vocabularies, ed. Dr. R. Wülcker, pt. i. [texts] ii. [indices] 28/- 8° Trübner [57; 73] 84

Syntax.

MÜLLER, Theodor —*in his* Angelsächs. Grammatik [*ut supra*].
SWEET, H. —*in his* A.-S. Reader [*ut infra*].

Noun.

KRESS, Gebrauch d. Instrumentals in d. A.-S. Poesie 2/- 8° *Marburg* 64

Metrics.

GUEST, Edwin —*in his* History of English Rhythms [*ut* K § 240].
HIRT, Hermann Untersuchungen zur westgermanischen Verskunst, pt. i. [Anglo-Sax.] 3/- 8° *Leipzig* 89
MERBOT, R. Aesthetische Studien zur angelsächs. Poesie 1/6 8° *Breslau* 83
RIEGER, Max Die alt- und angelsächs. Verskunst [repr. fr. *Ztschr. deutsche Philol.*] 1/6 r 8° *Halle* 76
*SCHIPPER, Dr. J. —*in his* Englische Metrik, *ut* K § 240: English Metrics; & *in* Paul's Grundriss [*ut* K § 225].
SCHUBERT, Hermann De Anglo-Saxonum re metrica [diss. inaug.] 1/6 8° *Berlin* 70
*SIEVERS, E. Zur Rhythmik d. german. Alliterationsverses—*in* Paul + Braune's Beiträge, vol. x. [*ut* K § 225].
SKEAT, Prf. W. W. Essay on Alliterative Poetry—*in* Bp. Percy's Folio MS., vol. iii [*ut* K § 65].
VETTER, Ferd. Zum Muspilli u. zur altgerman. Alliterationslehre [good] 4/- 8° *Vienna* 72

Chrestomathies.

BRENNER, O. [ed.] Angelsächsische Sprachproben [useful elem. bk.; w. glossary] 2/- 16° *Munich* 79
EARLE, Prf. J. [ed.] Book for Beginners in Anglo-Saxon [texts, w. gloss and grammar] 2/6 f 8° Clar. Press [77] 84
ETTMÜLLER, L. [ed.] Engla and Seaxna Scopas and Boceras [Bibl. deut. Natl. Litter.] 5/- 8° *Quedlinburg* 50
A collection of pieces and portions of pieces in verse and prose.

*GREIN, C. W. M. [ed.] Bibliothek der angelsächsischen Poesie, 4 vols. 8° *Göttingen* 57–64

i. 8/-, ii. 9/-, Texts; iii.-iv. Dictionary. New edn. by R. WÜLCKER, vol. i. [Beowulf and minor pieces] 12/- *Cassel* '83; ii. (1) 8/- '88; ii. (2) 4/- '88; iii. 10/- '89.

* ,, ,, Bibliothek der A.-S. Prosa, hrsg. R. Wülcker, vol. i. [Aelfric], 8/–; ii. (pt. 1) 4/– [texts and gloss.] 8/– 8° *Cassel* [72] 85; 85

Library of Anglo-Saxon Poetry —ea. ent. separ. K §§ 247–251 [texts, notes, and gloss.] 12° *Boston*[83*sqq.*]88, *etc.*

i.: Beowulf and Fight at Finnsburgh, $2.25; ii.: CAEDMON'S Exodus and Daniel, 65c.; iii.: Andreas, etc.; ZUPITZA'S Old and Mid.-Eng. Reader.

KLUGE, Friedrich [ed.] Angelsächsisches Lesebuch 4/6 8° *Halle* 88

KÖRNER, Karl [ed.] Angelsächsische Texte [w. Germ. trss., notes, & gloss; = pt ii. of *Einleit.*, *sup.*] 9/– 8° *Heilbronn* 80

MARCH, F. A. [Am.; ed.] Anglo-Saxon Reader: w. notes, brief grammar and vocabulary 7/6 8° Low 71

*SWEET, H. [ed.] Anglo-Saxon Reader in Prose and Verse: w. notes and glossary 8/6 f 8° Clar. Press [76] 89

* ,, ,, [ed.] Second Anglo-Saxon Reader: archaic and dialectical 4/6 f 8° ,, 88

,, ,, [ed.] Old English Reading Primers, w. glossaries, pt. i. 1/6; ii. 1/6 f 8° ,, 85; 86

i.: Selected Homilies of AELFRIC; ii.: Extracts from ALFRED'S OROSIUS.

THORPE, Benj. [ed.] Analecta Anglo-Saxonica [prose and verse, w. glossary] 7/6 p 8° J. R. Smith [34] 68

WÜLCKER, Dr. R. [ed.] Kleinere Angelsächsische Dichtungen [w. vocabulary] 4/– s 4° *Halle* 82

Since 1885 Dr. WÜLCKER has omitted the C from his name.

*ZUPITZA, Prf. J. [ed.] —*in his* Old and Middle English Reader [*ut* K § 244] *are 27 pp. of A.-S. texts.*

Old Saxon and Anglo-Saxon.

GALLÉE, Prf. J. H. [ed.] Old Saxon Texts *subscr.* 35/–; *to be raised to ?* 50/– f° *Leyden* *in prep.*

To form a critical edn. of all the documents wh. exist in the Low-German dialect known as Old-Saxon. Will contain a new edn. of the *Heliand* (incl. refer. to a 3rd fragmentary MS. discov. by Prf. H. LAMBEL). A phototype facs. of ea. MS., preceded by critical and palaeograph. information and a general introd. essay, are to be given. Text in English and German.

HEYNE, Moritz [ed.] Kleinere altniederdeutsche Denkmäler; w. glossary [Bibl. ältest. deut. Litt.-Denkm.] 4/– 8° *Paderborn* [ ] 77

RIEGER, Max Alt- u. Angelsächs. Lesebuch, nebst altfries. Stücken [w. good vocab.] 8/– r 8° *Giessen* 61

Later Anglo-Saxon —*some specimens in the* Chrestomathies, *ut* K § 242.

243. LATER ANGLO-SAXON PHILOLOGY (Norman Conquest to middle XIII. Cent.).

Grammars.

MÜLLER, Theodor —*in his* Angelsächsische Grammatik [*ut* K § 242].

Grammar of Orrm —*a short treatise in* Sweet's Middle English Primer [*ut infra*].

Dictionaries

—*cont. to some extent in* Mätzner's Wörterbuch [*ut inf.*], *and* Stratmann's *O.-E. Dict.* [*ut* K § 244].

Chrestomathies.

*MÄTZNER, E. [ed.] Alt-Englische Sprachproben: nebst Wörterbuch: in 2 pts. r 8° *Berlin* 67–89 *in prog.*

i. (Texts and notes) (1) Poetry; (2) Prose, 24/- '67-'69; ii.: Dictionary, pts. 1-10 65/- *in prog.* From the *Ormulum* and the *Ancren Riwle* to Chaucer. An indispensable collection.

*MORRIS, Dr. R. [ed.] Specimens of Early English, pt. i.: w. intro., notes, and gloss. 9/– f 8° Clar. Press [74] 79

Old English Homilies to King Horn (1150-1300) 9/-. For pt. ii., v. K § 244.

SWEET, H. [ed.] First Middle English Primer: w. grammar and gloss. 2/– 8° Clar. Press 84

Extracts from the *Ancren Riwle* and the *Ormulum*.

,, ,, Second Middle English Primer 2/– f 8° ,, 87

244. OLD [1250–1350] AND MIDDLE [1350–1500] ENGLISH PHILOLOGY.

Grammar, etc.: Generally.

BÖDDEKER, Karl Gramm. d. Mittelengl.—*in his* Alteng. Dicht. d. MS. Harl. 2253 [*ut infra*].

BRANDL, Prf. Altenglische Grammatik—*to appear in* Paul's Grundriss [*ut* K § 225].

Early English Text Soc. *Many of their pubns. contain, in their Introductions, grammatical matter or materials.*

MORRIS + SKEAT, Dr. R. / Prf. W. W. —*in the* Introductions *to their* Specimens of Early English, *ut infra.*

MORSBACH, Dr. L. Mittelenglische Grammatik *in prep.*

STRATMANN, F. H. Mittelenglische Grammatik 2/– 8° *Crefeld* 85

Grammar of Langland, Chaucer, and Shakspere —*v.* K § 237.

Phonology.

POGATSCHER, Prf. Alois Zur Lautlehre d. griech., lat. u. roman. Lehnworte im Altengl. [Quell. u. Forsch.] 5/- 8° *Strassburg* 88

Pronunciation

—*v.* K § 237 (espec. *ELLIS, A. J.).

Etymology.

Dictionaries.

*MÄTZNER, E. — Wörterbuch—*accompanying his* Alt-Englische Sprachproben [*ut* K § 243].

MAYHEW+SKEAT, Rev. A. L./Prf. W. W. Concise Dictionary of Middle English [1150–1580] 7/6 c 4° Clar. Press 88

MORRIS+SKEAT, Dr. R./Prf. W. W. Glossaires—*to their* Specimens of Early English [*ut* K § 243, *et infra*].

*STRATMANN, F. H. — Dictionary of the Old English Language, ed. H. Bradley [12, 13, 14 cent]. 8° Clar. Press [64–67] *in prep.*

WÜLCKER, Dr. R. — Wörterbuch—*to his* Altenglisches Lesebuch—*ut infra.*

ZUPITZA, Prf. J. — Vocabulary [tr.]—*to his* Old and Middle English Reader [tr.]—*ut infra.*

Accidence.

BRÜCK, F. — Consonantendoppelung in d. mittelengl. Comparativen u. Superlativen 1/6 8° *Leipzig* 86

Syntax.

EINENKEL, Eugen — Streifzüge durch die mittelenglische Syntax [w. spec. ref. to Chaucer] 5/- 8° *Münster* 87

Caxton's Language and Style.

KELLNER, Dr. L. — —*his edn. of* Blanchardyn and Eglantine [*ut* K § 47] *conts. a very import. treatise of this, of over* 100 *pp., w. illust. quotations.*

Chaucer's Language —*v.* K § 237.

Gower's Language.

MEYER, Karl — John Gower's Beziehungen zu Chaucer und König Rich. II. [diss. inaug.] 2/- 8° *Bonn* 90

TIETE, Georg — Zu Gower's *Confessio Amantis*, pt. i. [Lexikalisches] [diss. inaug.] 1/6 8° *Breslau* 89

Metrics.

*SCHIPPER, Dr. J. — —*in the latter chaps. of his* Englische Metrik, [*ut* K § 240]; *& in* Paul's Grundriss [*ut* K § 225].

SKEAT, Prf. W. W. — —*in his* Essay on Alliterative Poetry—*in* Bp. Percy's Folio MS., vol. iii. [*ut* K § 65].

Chaucer's Metres —*v.* K § 240: English Metrology, *s.v.* Chaucer.

Chrestomathies and Collections.

Altenglische Bibliothek — hrsg. E. Kölbing, vols. i.–iii. 17/6 8° *Heilbronn* 83–85

Amis and Amiloun [E. KÖLBING] 7/- 84 | Octavian Sage [SARRAZIN] 4/6 85 | Osbern Bokenam's Legenden [C. HORSTMANN] 6/- 89.

BÖDDEKER, Karl — Altenglische Dichtungen d. MS. Harl. 2253 [w. gramm. and gloss.] 8/- 8° *Berlin* 78

This MS. is a very miscellaneous and interesting one; it conts. also many French and Latin pieces. Date about 1300.

Early English Text Society: Publications of, 147 v.—*the most import. entered separ. infra* 8° E. Eng. Text Soc. (Tbnr.) 64–89 *in prog.*

The Original Series—92 vols., 1864–89; Extra Series—55 vols., 1867–89. A complete set to 1889 is worth about £20.

*MÄTZNER, E. — —*v.* K § 243.

*MORRIS+SKEAT, Dr. R./Prf. W. W. [eds.] Specimens of Early Eng.: w. intro., notes and gloss., pt. ii. 7/6 f 8° Clar. Press [ ] 79

Robert of Gloucester to Gower (1298–1393). For pt. i., v. K § 243. Cont. by SKEAT, *infra.*

*SKEAT, Prf. W. W. — Specimens of English Literature: w. intro., notes, and glossary 7/6 f 8° Clar. Press [72] 79

From LANGLAND'S *Piers Ploughman* to SPENSER'S *Shepheardes Calendar* (1394–1579).

WÜLCKER, Dr. R. [ed.] — Alt-Englisches Lesebuch, 2 vols. in 3 pts. 12/6 8° *Halle* 74; 79; 80

From *Genesis and Exodus* to *History of Merlin*, vol. i. [Texts 1250–1350] 4/-; ii. (1) [texts 1350–1500] and notes 7/-; ii. (2) Glossary, 2/-.

ZUPITZA, Prf. J. [ed.] — Alt- und mittelenglisches Uebungsbuch [w. vocabulary] 5/- 8° *Vienna* [74] 84

" " — Old and Middle English Reader, tr. Prf. G. E. MacLean [Am.] 12° *Boston* 86

A good little selection, from CAEDMON'S *Hymn* to John LYDGATE'S *Guy of Warwick*. With specimens, in parallel columns, for study of West Saxon, Northumbrian and Mercian dialects.

245. ANGLO-SAXON AND EARLY AND MIDDLE ENGLISH LITERATURE: (*a*) HISTORY OF.

ANGLO-SAXON.

Bibliography, Encyclopædia and Methodology.

KÖRTING, Gustav — —*in his* Encyklop. u. Methodol. d. englischen Philologie 8/- 8° *Heilbronn* 88

*WÜLKER, Dr. R. — Grundriss zur Geschichte der angelsächsischen Litteratur 10/- 8° *Leipzig* 85

Indispensable to students of Anglo-Saxon Literature.

History of Literature.

*ten BRINK, Prf. B. — Geschichte der englischen Litteratur, vols. i.–ii., (pt. 1) 14/6 8° *Berlin* 77; 89

Vol. i. [to Wiclif] 8/- '77; vol. ii. (pt. 1) [to accession of Elizabeth] 6/6 89.

" " — Early English Literature [Am. tr.] [= Hist. of Eng. Lit., vol. i.] 3/6 c 8° Bohn's Lib. 87

EARLE, Prf. J. — Anglo-Saxon Literature [Dawn of Liter. Series; popular, but good] 2/6 f 8° S.P.C.K. 84

EBERT, Adolf — —v. iii. *of his* Allg. Gesch. d. Litt. d. Mittelalters—*deals fully w. A.-S. liter.* 12/- 8° *Leipzig* 87

HAIGH, Rev. D. H. — The Anglo-Saxon Sagas: exam. of their value as aids to history 8/6 8° J. R. Smith 61

A sequel to his *Conquest of Britain by the Saxons* 15/- 8° *id.* 61—wh. is itself a harmony of the *Historia Britonum* of GILDAS, the *Brut* and the Saxon Chronicle.

METCALFE, Rev. F. — Englishman and Scandinavian [compar. of A.-S. and Old-Norse Lit.] 18/- 8° Trübner 80

MORLEY, Prf. H. — English Writers, vols. i.–iii. [*v.* K § 18; popular] ea. 5/- c 8° Cassell 87; 88; 88

SWEET, Henry — Sketch of Hist. of Ang.-Sax. Liter.,—*in* Warton's Hist. of Eng. Poetry, ed. W. C. Hazlitt, 3 v. [*v.* K § 21].

Latin Literature of the Anglo-Saxons.

EBERT, Adolf — vol. i. *of his* Litt. d. Mittelalters [*ut* K § 221] *is a hist of Xtn. Lat. Liter. to Charlemagne.*
TEUFFEL, W. S. — *—in his* History of Roman Literature [*ut* K § 221].

Biography.

WRIGHT, Thomas — Biographia Britannica Literaria, v. i. [A.-S. per.]; v. ii. [A.-Norm.] 2 v. 24/- 8° Parker 42; 46

EARLY AND MIDDLE ENGLISH.

Bibliography.

COLERIDGE, H. — Glossarial Index to Printed English Literature of 13 century 2/6 8° Trübner 59

History.

BÖDDEKER, Karl — Einleitung—*to his* Alteng. Dichtungen d. MS. Harl. 2253 [13 cent.; w. gram. and gloss.] 8/- 8° *Berlin* 78
HORSTMANN, C. — *—his* Altenglische Legenden, ser. ii. [*ut* K § 254] *conts. a good sketch.*

246. ANGLO-SAXON LITERATURE: (*b*) COLLECTIONS.

Collections.

*Codex Exoniensis: collection of Ang.-Sax. Poetry, ed. Benj. Thorpe [w. trss. in par. cols.] *o.p.* [*pb.* 20/-; *w.* 15/-] r 8° Soc. of Antiq. 42
" " ed. I. Gollancz: w. new tr. 8° E. Eng. Text Soc. *in prep.*
*Codex Vercellensis, Anglo-Saxon Poetry of the, ed. J. M. Kemble, 2 pts. [w. trss. in par. cols.] *o.p.* 8° Aelfric Soc. 43-56
i.: Legend of Saint Andrew. ii.: CYNEWULF'S Elene, and Minor Poems. For other editions of the Elene, v. CYNEWULF, *infra*.
*SWEET, H. [ed.] — The Oldest English Texts [texts only] 20/- 8° E. Eng. Soc. (Tbnr.) 85
Incl. all the extant Old-English texts up to ab. 900, which are preserved in contemp. MSS., w. the exception of the *Chronicle* and the wks. of Alfred. With an intro. of 34 pp., an exhaustive glossary of 190 pp., and alphab. Index to the Glossary (14 pp.).

Translations: German.

GREIN, C. W. M. [tr.] — Dichtungen der Angelsächsen: stabreimend übersetzt, 2 vols. 6/- 8° *Göttingen* [57; 59] 63
Vol. i.: CAEDMON'S *Genesis, Exodus, Daniel, Judith, Christ and Satan*; CYNEWULF'S *Christ, Harrowing of Hell, Phoenix, Panther, Whale*; BEOWULF—vol. ii.: *Andreas, Juliana, Guthlac, Elene, Dream of Holy Rood, Departed Soul's Address to the Body, Doomsday, Endowments & Pursuits of Men, Various Fortunes of Men*; ALFRED'S *Metres of Boethius, Riddles, The Wanderer, The Exile's Complaint, Botschaft d. Gemahls an seine Frau* [=Cod. Exon. "Riddle 88 and "A Fragment."]

Chrestomathies —*v.* K § 242.

247. ANGLO-SAXON LITERATURE: (*c*) POPULAR EPICS.

Battle of Brunnanburg ed. Grein—*in his* Bibl.; ed. Körner *in his* Einleit., pt. ii. [*ut* K § 242]; ed. Zupitza—*in his* Reader [*ut* K § 244].
" " ed. Dr. T. R. Price [Am.] [w. *Battle of Maldon*; Lib. A.-S. Poetry] 12° *Boston* *in prep.*

Battle of Maldon —*v.* Byrhtnoth's Death—*infra.*

Beówulf [8 cent.]

Facsimile: [autotype] and Transliteration of the MS., ed. J. Zupitza 25/- f° E. Eng. Text Soc. (Tbnr.) 82
The text is also cont. in GREIN'S *Bibliothek d. A.-S. Poesie*, ed. WÜLCKER (*ut* K § 242).

Annotated Edition: ed. w. English tr., notes, and glossary Thos. Arnold 12/- 8° Longman 76
" " notes & [Heyne's] gloss. Prf. J. A. Harrison + R. Sharp [Ams.] $1.25 12° *Boston* [82] 83
" " tr. and notes Benj. Thorpe 7/6 p 8° J. R. Smith [55] 75
" " intro. and glossary Prf. G. Zupitza 8° E. Eng. Text Soc *in prep.*
*" German notes and glossary Moritz Heyne 5/- 8° *Paderborn* [63] 88
" " " " " R. Wülker—*in* Grein's *Bibl.* [*ut* K § 242].
" " " " " A. Holder [Germanist. Bücherschatz] 5/6 8° *Freiburg* 84

Selections: ed. in the chrestoma. of Ettmüller, March and Rieger [*ut* K § 242], of Sweet [*ut* K § 243].

TRANSLATIONS: tr. Prf. J. Earle Clar. Press *in prep.*
" Prf. J. M. Garnett [Am.] [w. Fight at Finnsburg; blank verse] $1.10 12° *Boston* [82] 89
" Lt.-Col. H. W. Lumsden [in 7-ft. iambics] 5/- c 8° Paul [81] 82
übers. C. W. M. Grein [repr. fr. his *Dicht. d. Angelsachsen*] 2/- 8° *Cassel* [57] 83
" Moritz Heyne [in 5-ft. iambics] *Paderborn* 63
" Karl Simrock [w. German notes] *Stuttgart* 59
trad. L. Botkine [prose; not quite the whole poem] 8° *Havre* 77

AIDS:
General and Miscellaneous Criticism and Illustration.

BOTKINE, L. — Beówulf: analyse historique et géographique 8° *Paris* 76
*ten BRINK, Prf. B. — Beówulf: Untersuchungen [Quellen und Forschungen] 6/- 8° *Strassburg* 88
DEDERICH, H. — Historische u. geograph. Studien zum Beówulf 2/- 8° *Cologne* 77
DISRAELI, Isaac — Beówulf: the hero-life—*in his* Amenities of Literature 3/6 c 8° Routledge [41] 81
FAHLBECK, — Beówulf-qvädet sasom källa for nordisk fornhistoria 2/0 8° *Lund* 86
HARRISON, J. [Am.] — Old Teutonic Life in Beówulf—*in The Overland Monthly* for July, 1894.
HEYNE, Moritz — Ueber Lage u. Konstruksion d. Halle Heorot in Beówulf 1/- 8° *Paderborn* 64
LEHMANN, H. — Brünne und Helm im angelsächs. Beówulf [diss. inaug.] 2/6 8° *Leipzig* 85
MARCH, F. A. [Am.] — The World of Beówulf—*in Proceedings of Amer. Philolog. Assoc.* 1882.

K § 248

MÖLLER, H. — Das altenglische Volksepos — pt. i. [Abhandlungen] 3/- ; ii. [Texts] 2/- 8° *Kiel* 83 : 83
MÜLLENHOFF, K. — Beówulf — 3/- 8° *Berlin* 88
" " — Beówulfstudien — 8° " 89
MÜLLER, Nathanael — Mythen im Beówulf in ihrem Verhältniss z. germ. Mythologie — [diss. inaug.] 2/- 8° *Leipzig* 78
SARRAZIN, Gregor — Beówulf-Studien : Beitrag zur Geschichte altgermanischer Sage — 5/- 8° *Berlin* 88
SCHULTZE, Martin — Altheidnisches in der A.-S. Poesie — [espec. in Beówulf : sch.-progr.] 2/- 8° " 77

The *Mythology* in *Beowulf* is also treated largely in *e.g.* GRIMM'S *Teut. Mythol.*, in SIMROCK'S *Deut. Myth.* [*ut* B § 20]; and in L. UHLAND'S *Schriften z. Gesch. d. Dichtung u. Sage*, vol. viii, 18/- 8° *Stuttg.* '73.

Composition.
ETTMÜLLER, L. — Carmen de Beów. quale fuerit antequam in manus interpol. inciderit. — *Zürich* 75
HORNBURG, — Die Komposition des Beówulf — [school programme] 1/6 8° *Metz* 77
RÖNNING, T — Beówulfs-Kvadet : en literaer-historisk undersögelse — 3/- 8° *Copenhagen* 83
SCHEMANN, Karl — Die Synonyma im Beówulf mit Rücks. auf Komp. u. Poetik — [diss.] 1/6 8° *Hagen* 82

Language.
BANNING, — Die epischen Formeln im Beówulf, pt. i. : Die verbalen Synonyma — [diss. inaug.] 1/6 8° *Marburg* 86
*HEINZEL, R. — —*in his* Ueber den Stil d. altgerm. Poesie — [Quellen u. Forsch., vol. x.] 2/- 8° *Strassburg* 74
KÖHLER, W. — Syntakt. Gebrauch d. Infinitivs u. d. Participien im Beówulfslied — [diss. inaug.] 1/6 8° *Münster* 88
NADER, E. — Zur Syntax des Beówulfliedes ; Genetiv im Beówulf — [sch.-progr.] 5/- 8° *Brünn* 79 : 80 : 82
" " — Dativ und Instrumental im Beówulf — [schl.-progr.] 2/6 *Vienna* 82 ; 83
SCHEMANN, Karl — Die Synonyma im Beówulfslied—*ut supra.*
SCHULZ, Fr. — Die Sprachformen des Hildebrand-Liedes im Beówulf — 1/6 8° *Königsberg* 82

Byrhtnoth's Death (Battle of Maldon) ed. Grein—*in his* Bibl., v. i., ed. Körner—*in his* Einleit., pt. ii. [w. tr.], ed. Sweet—*in his A.-S. Reader* [*ut* K § 242].
" " — ed. Dr. T. R. Price [Am.] — [w. Brunaburgh ; Lib. A.-S. Poetry] 12° *Boston* *in prep.*
TRANSLATION : — tr. Prf. J. M. Garnett [Am.] — " 89

AIDS :
ten BRINK, Prf. B — —*his* Hist. of Engl. Liter. [tr.], vol. i., *conts. a detailed synopsis of its contents* — 3/6 c 8° Bohn's Lib. 87
ZERNIAL, U. — Das Lied von Byrhtnoth's Fall — [school-programme] 1/- 4° *Berlin* 82

Fight at Finnsburg—*in edns. of* Beówulf by Harrison, Heyne [*ut sup.*]—*in chrestoms.* by Ettmüller, Grein, Rieger, Wülcker [*ut* K § 242].
TRANSLATIONS : — tr. Garnett, Thorne ; übers. Simrock—*in their tr. and edns. of* Beówulf, *supra.*

AIDS
— —*many of those entered under* Beówulf *deal with the* Fight at Finnsburg *also.*
MÖLLER, H. — —*his* Altenglisches Volksepos, vol. ii. [*ut sup.*] *contains a strophic reconstruction of the poem.*

Waldere's Lay, King ed. Prf. Geo. Stephens : w. Engl. tr., comm. and glossary ; 1 photo. facs. 6/6 8° *Copenhagen* 60
" " " ed. J. V. Scheffel + A. Holder, *sub tit.* Waltharius : lat. Gedicht d. 10 Jahrh. [conts. A.-S. vers. and Germ. tr.] 10/- 4° *Stuttgart* 74

Also ed. in Wülcker's edn. of Grein's *Bibl.*, vol. i. and WÜLCKER'S *Kleinere A.-S. Dichtungen* [*ut* K § 242].

AIDS :
FISCHER, J. — Zu den Waldere-Fragmenten — [dissert. inaug.] 1/- 8° *Breslau* 86
HAIGH, D. — —*in his* Anglo-Saxon Sagas [*ut* K § 245 ; conts. text also].
MÖLLER, H. — —*his* Altenglisches Volksepos [*ut sup.*] *conts. a strophic reconstruction of the poem.*

249. ANGLO-SAXON LITERATURE : (*d*) CHRISTIAN EPICS.

Caedmon [*d.* 680] — Metrical Paraphrase of Scripture, ed. w. tr. and notes B. Thorpe — *o.p.* r 8° *London* 32
" — The same, ed. K. W. Bouterweck, 2 vols. — [w. glossary] 22/- r 8° *Elberfeld* 54 : 51
Christ and Satan : ed. C. W. M. Grein—*in his* Bibliothek, A.-S. Poesie, vol. i. [*ut* K § 242].
Genesis, Exodus & Daniel: ed. C. W. M. Green—*in his* Bibliothek, A.-S. Poesie, vol. i. [*ut* K § 242].
Exodus and Daniel : ed. Prf. Theod. W. Hunt [Am.] — [Lib. Anglo-Sax. Poetry] 65*c.* 12° *Boston* [86] 88

These poems, together with *Christ and Satan*, are, it has been almost finally decided, *not* by CAEDMON.

Holy Rood, Dream of the : ed. J. M. Kemble [w. tr. in par. cols.]—*in* Cod. Vercell. [*ut* K § 246].
" " " Grein—*in his* Bibl. A.-S. Poesie, vol. ii. ; ed. Sweet—*in his* A.-S. Reader [*ut* K § 242].

Conts. several passages answering closely to the Runic inscription on Ruthwell Cross [v. *infra*].

Hymn : ed. Rieger—*in his* Lesebuch ; ed. Zupitza—*in his* Reader [*ut* K § 244].
photolithographed in the Facsimiles of Ancient MSS., pt. ix., plate 140 — f° Palaeograph. Soc. 79
TRANSLATION : tr. Lindsay + Napier—*in* Modern Language Notes, 1889, No. 5 [*ut* K § 236].

The question of the authenticity of this *Hymn*, supposed to be CAEDMON'S first work, is discussed in ten BRINK'S *Early English Literature*, appendix A. [*v.* K § 245]

Judith : ed. Prf. A. S. Cook [Am.] w. intro., gloss. and tr. [Lib. Ang.-Sax. Poetry] $1 s 4° *Boston* 88
" *in the chrestoms. of* Ettmüller, Grein, Körner, Rieger [*ut* K § 242].
tr. Prf. J. M. Garnett [Am.] — 75*c.* c 8° *Boston* 89
Ruthwell Cross [a Runic inscrip. of 21 lines at Ruthwell, Northumb.—attrib. to CAEDMON].
" ed. Prf. Geo. Stephens [*repr. fr. his* Old North. Runic. Mons., *ut* G § 7] 10/- f° J. R. Smith 69
" *ed. J. Zupitza—*in his* Old and Middle-English Reader [*ut* K § 244].
" ed. H. Sweet—*in his* The Oldest English Texts [*ut* K § 246].

AIDS :
Generally.
BALG, H. — Der Dichter Cädmon und seine Werke — [diss. inaug.] 1/6 8° *Göttingen* 82
BEDE, Ven. [*d.* 672] — Historia Eccles. gentis Anglorum [*ut* A § 62].

The solitary source for CAEDMON'S life : acc. to ten BRINK very trustworthy on the whole.

BOUTERWECK, C. W. — De Cädmon poeta (diss.) 1/- ; Ueber Cädmon d. ältesten A.-S. Dichter — [sch.-prog.] 1/- 8° *Elberfeld* 45 : 45
ten BRINK, Prf. B. — —*appendix A to his* Early Engl. Liter. [tr.] *discusses authenticity of Caedmon Poems* — 3/6 c 8° Bohn's Lib. 85
GÖTZINGER, Dr. Ernst — Ueber die Dichtungen d. Cädmon u. deren Verfasser — [diss. inaug.] 1/- 8° *Göttingen* 67
SANDRAS, S. G. — De Carminibus anglo-sax. Caedmoni adjudicatis disquisitio — 8° *Paris* 59
WATSON, R. S. — Caedmon, the first English poet — [popular] 3/6 c 8° Longman 79

Language.
Hofer, O. — Der syntaktische Gebrauch d. Dativs u. Instrument. in d. Caedmon beigelegten Dichtungen — 84
Ziegler, H. — Der poet. Sprachgebrauch in d. Cädmonschen Dichtungen [diss. inaug.] 1/6 8° *Munster* 83
Christ and Satan.
Groschopp, F. — Das angelsächs. Gedicht *Christ u. Satan* [diss. inaug.] 1/6 8° *Halle* 83
Kühn, A. — Dissertatio über d. angelsächs. Gedichte von Christ u. Satan 1/- 8° *Jena* 83
Genesis.
Heinze, — Zur altenglischen *Genesis* 8° *Berlin* 89
Sievers, Prf. E. — Der Heliand und die angelsächsische *Genesis* 3/- 8° *Halle* 75
Hymn.
Wülcker, Prf. R. — Ueber d. Hymnus Caedmons—*in* Paul and Braune's Beiträge, vol. iii., pp. 348–357 [*ut* K § 225].
Attempts to disprove the authenticity of the Northumbrian poem. Replied to by Prf. J. Zupitza in *Ztschr. f. deut. Alterth.*, vol. xxii., pp. 210 *sqq.*
Ruthwell Cross —*also in* Stephens' and Zupitza's *edns.*, *supra.*
Bugge, Sophus — —*in his* Studies over de nord. Gude-og Helte-sagns Oprindelse 8° *Christiania* 81–87
" " — The same, tr. O. Brenner, pts. i.–ii. [denies its antiquity] 6/- 8° *Munich* 81 ; 82
Dietrich, Franc — Disputatio de Cruce Ruthwellensi [univ. programme] 1/- 4° *Marburg* 65

Cynewulf [? 8 cent.]—with some of the Pseudo-Cynewulfian Poems.
Andreas : [authorship very doubtful ; *part of* Codex Vercell., *q.v.* K § 246 (w. tr.)].
ed. C. W. M. Grein—*in his* Bibl. A.-S. Poesie, i. [*ut* K § 242].
" " Jacob Grimm [with the *Elene*] 8° *Cassel* 40
" " Prf. W. M. Baskerville [Am.] ; w. English notes [Lib. of A.-S. Poet.] 25*c.* 12° *Boston* [86] 88
" " Prf. Richard Wülker 89
Translation : übers. C. W. M. Grein—*in his* Dichtungen der Angelsächsen [*ut* K § 246].
Christ [*part of* Codex Exon., *q.v.* K § 246 (w. tr.)]—*also* ed. C. W. M. Grein—*in his* Bibl. d. A.-S. Poesie, vol. ii. [*ut* K § 242].
*Elene [*part of* Codex Vercell., *q.v.* K § 246 (w. tr.)].
ed. C. W. M. Grein—*in his* Bibl. A.-S. Poesie, vol. ii. [*ut* K § 242].
" " Jacob Grimm [with the Andreas] 2/- 8° *Cassel* 40
" " Prf. C. W. Kent [Am.] [w. Latin text, notes and gloss. after Zupitza, *inf.* ; Lib. A.-S. Poetry] 65*c.* 12° *Boston* 89
* " J. Zupitza : w. German notes and glossary 2/- 8° *Berlin* [77] 88
Translations : tr. Prf. J. M. Garnett [Am.] 75*c.* c 8° *Boston* 89
übers. C. W. M. Grein—*in his* Dichtungen der Angelsächsen [*ut* K § 246].
Later versions of the legend (the miraculous discovery of the Holy Cross through the Empress Helena) have been ed. by Dr. Rich. Morris, *sub tit.* *Legends of the Holy Rood, etc.* 10/- 8° E. Eng. Text Soc. 71.

Guthlac, Legend of : [doubtful ; *pt. of* Codex Exon., *q.v.* K § 246 (w. tr.)]—*also ed.* C. W. M. Grein, *in his* Bibl. A.-S. Poesie, vol. ii. [*ut* K § 242].
Translation : übers. C. W. M. Grein—*in his* Dichtungen der Angelsächsen [*ut* K § 246].
Goodwin, C. W. [ed.] The Anglo-Saxon Version of the life of Saint Guthlac [w. tr.] *o.p.* 8° J. R. Smith 48
An Anglo-Saxon tr. of the Latin *Vita Guthlaci* of Felix of Croyland. From the Cotton MS.

Harrowing of Hell [*pt. of* Codex Exon., *q.v.* K § 246 (w. tr.) ; *also ed.* C. W. M. Grein, *in his* Bibl. A.-S. Poesie, vol. i. [*ut* K § 242].
Translation : übers. C. W. M. Grein—*in his* Dichtungen der Angelsächsen [*ut* K § 246].
Juliana, St., Legend of : [*part of the* Codex Exon., *q.v.* K § 246 (w. tr.)]—*also ed.* C. W. M. Grein, *in his* Bibl. A.-S. Poesie [*ut* K § 242].
Translation : übers C. W. M. Grein—*in his* Dichtungen d. Angelsachsen [*ut* K § 246].
Phoenix [*part of the* Codex Exon., *q.v.* K § 246 (w. tr.)]—*also ed.* C. W. M. Grein, *in his* Bibl. A.-S. Poesie, vol. ii., and E. Ettmüller's *Scopas* [*ut* K § 242].
" ed. Prf. W. S. Currell [Am.] : w. English notes [Lib. of Anglo-Saxon Poetry] 12° *Boston* 89
" " Grundtvig, *s.v.* Phœnix-Fugeln [w. Danish intro. and tr.] 8° *Copenhagen* 40
Riddles [*part of* Codex Exon., *q.v.* K § 246 (w. tr.)]
" ed. C. W. M. Grein [w. tr.]—*in his* Bibliothek A.-S. Poesie, vol. i. [*ut* K § 242].
" " Prf. B. W. Wells [Am.] : w. English notes [Library of A.-S. Poetry] 12° *Boston* *in prep.*

Aids :
Generally.
Dietrich, Franc. — De Kynewulfi Poetae aetate—*v. infra, s.v.* Riddles.
Hammerich, Fr. — —*in his* Aelteste Christliche Epik der Angelsachsen (tr. fr. Danish) 4/6 8° *Gutersloh* 74
Leiding, H. — Die Sprache d. Cynewulf. Dichtungen *Christ, Juliana, Elene* 2/- 8° *Marburg* 88
Leo, H. — Quae de se ipso Cynevulfus poeta anglo-saxonicus tradiderit 2/- 8° *Halle* 57
d'Ham, O. — Der gegenwärtige Stand der Cynewulffrage 1/6 8° *Limburg* 83
Language.
Hotlburr, F. — Synt. Gebrauch d. Genetivs in Cyn. [Andr., Guthl., Phoen., and Hell ; diss.] 1/6 8° *Leipzig* 84
Jansen, — Beiträge zur Synonymik u. Poetik d. Cynewulf [diss. inaug.] 1/6 8° *Munster* 83
Rössger, R. — Syntact. Gebrauch d. Genetivs in Cynewulf [Elene, Christ, Jul. ; diss.] 1/6 8° *Leipzig* 83
Schürmann, J. — Darstellung der Syntax in Cynewulf's *Elene* [diss. inaug.] 1/6 8° *Paderborn* 84
Andreas.
Hinze, W. — Zum altenglischen Gedicht *Andreas*, pt. i. [programme] 1/- 8° *Berlin* 90
Kent, C. W. — Teutonic Antiquities in *Andreas* and *Elene* 2/6 8° *Leipzig* 87
Ramhorst, Fr. — Das altenglische Gedicht vom heiligen Andreas [diss. inaug.] 1/6 8° *Berlin* 86
Elene.
Glöde, O. — Cynewulf's *Elene* und ihre Quelle [dissert. inaug.] 1/6 8° *Rostock* 86
Schürmann, Jos. — Darstellung der Syntax in Cynewulf's *Elene* (= Neuphilolog. Studien, pt. iv.) 2/6 8° *Paderborn* 84
Harrowing of Hell [an A.-S. *poem in close relationship to the* Christ].
Kirkland, J. — Study of the Anglo-Saxon Poem, *The Harrowing of Hell* [diss.] 1/6 8° *Halle* 85
Claims the authorship of it for Cynewulf.
Juliana.
Conradi, B. — Syntax in Cynewulf's *Juliana* 2/- 8° *Halle* 86

K § 249

Riddles.

*DIETRICH, Franc. — De Kyn. aetate, aenigmatum fragm. e cod. Lugdun., ill. [univ. prog.] 1/6 4° *Marburg* 59
MÜLLER, Ed. — Die Räthsel des Exeterbuches [schl. programme] 1/6 8° *Cothen* 61
PREHN, Aug. — Komposition und Quellen d. Räthsel d. Exeterbuchs [Neuphil. Studien] 2/- 8° *Paderborn* 83
Sources — *These are the Latin riddles of Aldhelm, Symphosius, Eusebius, and Tatwine.*
ALDHELM [Abbot of Malmesb.; *d.* 709] Opera, ed. Dr. J. A. Giles *o.p.* 8° *Oxford* 44
EUSEBIUS and Tatwine [Abp. Canterb., 8 cent.] Riddles, ed. A. Ebert—*in* Berichte d. Ges. d. Wiss., Phil.-hist. Kl., 23 Apl. 77.
SYMPHOSIUS — Riddles, rec. A. Riese—*in* Anthol. Lat. [*v.* K § 214], and ed. w. Germ. notes Wernsdorff—*in his* Poet. Lat. Min., vol. vi. [*v.* K § 214].

Heliand [an Old-Saxon poem on Gospel history, having import. relations to CAEDMON, and in a less degree to CYNEWULF. Comp. *circa* 830].

" ed. Otto Behaghel [Altdeutsche Textbibliothek] 2/6 8° *Halle* 82
" * " Moritz Heyne [with glossary] 6/- 8° *Paderborn* [66] 83
" * " E. Sievers [Germanistische Handbibliothek] 8/- 8° *Halle* 78
" " Karl Simrock 8/- 1 8° *Berlin* [56] 82
" " Prf. J. H. Gallée—*in his* Old-Saxon Texts [*ut* K § 242] *in prep.*

AIDS:
BEHRMANN, — Die Pronomina Personalia u. ihr Gebrauch in Heliand [diss. inaug.] 1/6 8° *Marburg* 80
MÖLLER, H. — Ueber d. Instrumentalis im Heliand u. d. homer. Suffix φι [sch. progr.] 1/6 8° *Danzig* 74
PIPER, — Ueber d. Gebrauch d. Dativs im Ulfilas, Heliand und Otfrid [" "] 1/- 4° *Altona* 74
PRATJE, H. — Dativ und Instrumentalis in Heliand [compar. treatment] 1/6 8° *Sobernheim* 80
" " — Accusativ im Heliand: syntaktisch dargestellt 1/6 8° " 82
RIES, J. — Stellung v. Subject u. Prädicatsverbum im Heliand [Quellen u. Forsch.] 3/- 8° *Strassburg* 80
*SIEVERS, Prf. E. — Der Heliand und die angelsächsische Genesis 3/- 8° *Halle* 75
*WINDISCH, W. O. E. — Der Heliand und seine Quellen [important] 2/6 8° *Leipzig* 68

249. ANGLO-SAXON LITERATUTE: (*c*) DIDACTIC POETRY.

Be Domes Dæge ed. J. R. Lumby [w. tr. *en regard*] 2/- 8° E. Eng. Text. Sc. (Tbnr.) 76
From MS. at C. C. C. Camb.; first 2 verses also in ETTMÜLLER'S *Scopas* [*ut* K § 246]. Not to be confused w. the poem in the *Cod. Exon.* of same title [*ut infra*]. This Camb. poem is a tr. of a Latin original [? by BEDE or ALCUIN].

AID:
HÖFER, J. — Die syntactischen Erscheinungen in *Be Domes Dæge* [diss. inaug.] 2/- 8° *Halle* 90

Codex Exoniensis [*v.* K § 246] *The following pieces:*

† ‡ Be Domes Dæge.
† Bi manna cræftum ["Endowments and Pursuits of Men"].
† ⊙ ‡ Bi manna wyrdum ["The Various Fortunes of Men"; also tr. H. Morley—*in his* Lib. Eng. Lit., vol. i., *v.* K § 19].
† ⊙ ‡ Bi manna mode ["Monitory Poem"].
† ⊙ Departed Soul's Address to the Body—*also in* Cod. Vercell. [*v.* K § 246] THORPE'S *ed. of* Cod. Exon. *conts. corrns. fr.* Cod. Vercell., *w. prose trs. of both texts*; KEMBLE'S *ed. of* Cod. Vercell. *conts. prose trs. of both texts.* LONGFELLOW *has tr. vv.* 1–21 *in his* Translations, *and vv.* 15–21 *in his* Poets and Poetry of Europe, *v.* K § 17].
ed. Rich. Buchholz *fr.* 2 MSS. [at Worcester and Oxon.], w. Germ. tr. and treatise 2/- 8° *Erlangen* 90
† ⊕ ⊙ Father's Instructions to his Son.
Physiologus [a Bestiary].
† ‡ *The Panther*; † ⊙ ‡ *The Whale*; † *The Partridge* (in Cod. Exon. as "a fragment."
⊕ † ⊙ Gnomic Verses
TRANSLATIONS: tr. B. ten Brink—*in his* Early English Literature, tr. Prf. H. M. Kennedy [Am.] 3/6 c 8° Bohn's Lib. 87
† Wonders of Creation.

AIDS:
Physiologus.
DIETRICH, Fr. — —*in his* Commentatio de Kynewulfi poetae aetate (univ. progr.) 1/6 4° *Marburg* 59
LAUCHERT, Dr. F. — Geschichte des *Physiologus* [Quellen und Forschungen] 8° *Strassburg* 90
Departed Soul's Address to the Body.
BUCHHOLZ, Richard — —*in his edn. of the text, ut supra.*
KLEINERT, G. — Ueber den "Streit zwischen Leib und Seele" [diss. inaug.] 1/6 8° *Halle* 80

Codex Vercellensis —[*v.* K § 246]. *The following pieces:*

† Bi manna lease [named "a Fragment" in Cod. Verc.].
Departed Soul's Address to the Body—*also in* Cod. Exon., *q.v. supra.*
† Fates of the Twelve Apostles.

Exhortation to a Christian Life, ed. J. R. Lumby *in his edn. of* Be Domes Dæge [w. tr.] 2/- 8° E. Eng. Text Soc. (Tbnr.) 76

†‖⊙ Gnomic Verses [Brit. Mus., Cott. MS.]
TRANSLATION tr. Sharon Turner—*in his* History of the Anglo-Saxons, vol. iii. pp. 195 *sqq.*

† Menologium [Brit. Mus., Cott. MS.; end 11 cent.], ed. Earle—*in his* Two Saxon Chronicles [*ut* K § 251].

†⊕⊙‡ Runa gerim ["Song of the Runes"; Brit. Mus., Cott. MS.]
ed. L. Botkine, *sub tit.* La Chanson des Runes [w. Fch. tr. and notes] 8° *Havre* 79

AIDS:
KIRCHHOFF, Adolph — Das gotische Runenalphabet 1/6 8° *Berlin* [51] 54
ZACHER, Julius — Das gotische Alphabet Vulfila's und das Runenalphabet *Leipzig* 55

†Salomon and Saturnus, Dialogue of: ed., w. hist. intro. and tr., J. M. Kemble [fr. MS. at C. C. C. Camb.] 8° Aelfric Soc. 48
Conts. the alliterative as well as the prose version, the A.-S. prose of Adrian and Ritheus, the Latin of Adrian and Epictus, together with *The Master of Oxford's Catechism*, and, as Append., *Anglo-Sax. Apophthegms* [the A.-S. Cato], *Proverbs of Alfred, Proverbs of Hending, etc.*

AIDS:
HOFMANN, K. — Einleitung—*to his edn. of* [Amis et Amiles *and*] Jourdain de Blaives *Erlangen* [70] 82
SCHAUMBERG, W. — Untersuch. üb. d. deut. Spruchged. Sal. u. Morolf [= Paul and Braune's *Beitr.*, ii. *ut* K § 223] 8° *Halle* 76
VOGT, Friedrich [ed.] — —*in his* Die deutschen Dichtungen von Salomon und Morolf 10/- 8° " 80

‡=ed. GREIN—*in his* Bibl.; ⊕=ed. WÜLKER—*in his new ed. of* GREIN; ‡=ed. SWEET—*in his* A.-S. Reader, ⊙=ed. ETTMULLER—*in his* Scopas [*ut* K § 246]; †=tr. GREIN—*in his* Dichn. d. A.-S. [*ut* K § 246]

250. ANGLO-SAXON LITERATURE: (*f*) LYRICAL POETRY.

A. RELIGIOUS.

Psalter: A.-S. Translation, fr. MS. [? 11 cent.] at Bibl. Nat. Paris; I—L in prose, LI—CL in allit. verse; L also in Brit. Mus. Bibl. Cott. [Kent dialect, ? 10 cent.].
,, ed. B. Thorpe, *sub tit.* Libri Psalm. vers. ant. Lat. cum paraphras. Anglosax. *o.p.* 8° *Oxford* 35
,, ed. C. W. M. Grein—*in his* Bibl. d. Angelsächs. Poesie, vol. ii. [*ut* K § 242].

Prayers, Hymns, the Paternoster, the Gloria, etc., ed. C. W. M. Grein—*in his* Bibl. d. A.-S. Poesie [*ut* K § 242].

B. SECULAR.

Codex Exoniensis [*v.* K § 246]. *The following pieces:*

†⊕☉‡ The Exile's Complaint.
†⊕☉‡ Message of the Husband to his Wife [as "Riddle lii." and "A Fragment"].
†⊙ Riming Poem — ed. B. Thorpe—*in sec. edn. of his* Analecta [*ut* K § 242], *sub tit.* Paraphrase of Job xxix.-xxx.
TRANSLATIONS: Latin tr. by Ettmüller—*in his* Scopas [*ut* K § 242].
Thorpe in his edn. of *Cod. Exon.* trs. (in the notes) only portions of this poem. "My endeavours to give a version of the 'Riming Poem' have failed."
†⊙ Ruin, The — ed. Prof. J. Earle, *sub tit.*, An Anc. Saxon Poem of a city . . . supposed to be Bath, w. tr., notes, etc. *Bath* 72
,, H. Leo, *sub tit.* Carmen Anglo-Saxon in Cod. Exon.: w. notes, etc. [univ. progr.] 1/6 8° *Halle* 65
†⊕☾‡ Sea-farer, The
⊙⊕‡ Traveller's Song ["Widsið"]—*also* ed. H. Möller—*in* pt. ii. *of his* Altengl. Volksepos [*ut infra*].
⊙ TRANSLATION: —*also* tr. Gummere (Am.)—*in* Modern Language Notes, 1889, No. 7 [*ut* K § 236].
AID:
MÖLLER, H. — *in his* Das altenglische Volksepos, pt. i. [Abhandlungen], ii. [Texte] 5/- 8° *Kiel* 83
†⊕‡⊙ Wanderer, The — also ed. H. Sweet—*in his* Anglo-Saxon Reader [*ut* K § 240].

251. ANGLO-SAXON LITERATURE: (*g*) PRINCIPAL PROSE WORKS.

Alfred the Great [849 (?)–901] Whole Works of: with preliminary essays, 3 vols. *o.p.* r 8° Parker 52–53
AUGUSTIN'S, St., *Soliloquias*, tr. King Alfred: ed. O. Cockayne—*in* The Shrine: a coll. of occas. papers *o.p.* 64–69
BEDE'S Ven., *Historia Ecclesiastica*, tr. King Alfred: *There have been 2 edns.*—by A. Wheloc, *Cambr.* 1643; by J. Smith, *Cambr.* 1722
Specimens —*in the chrestoms. of* Ettmüller, Körner, March, Sweet [*ut* K § 242]; *of* Zupitza [K § 244].
Translations tr. E. Thomson—in Whole Wks. of Alfred, *ut sup.*; Latin tr. in Wheloc's edn., *ut sup.*
BOETHIUS' *De Consolat. Philosophiae*, tr. Kg. Alfred: ed. Rev. Sam. Fox [w. Engl. tr., notes and gloss.] 5/- c 8° Bohn's Lib. 64
Specimens —*in the chrestoms. of* Ettmüller, March, Sweet, Thorpe [*ut* K § 242].
Translation Fox's tr., cont. in his edn. of text [*sup.*], is repr. in full in *Whole Works* (*ut sup.*)
"Metres" [rhythmic passages; prob. not Alfred's]. *Text* and *Tr.* are in Fox's ed. [*sup.*]; *Specimens* in Ettmüller, Körner, March [*ut* K § 242].
GREGORY'S *Cura Pastoralis*: West-Sax. vers. by Kg. Alfred, ed. H. Sweet, 2 pts. [w. Lat. orig., and Eng. tr.] ea. 10/- 8° E. Eng. Text Soc. (Tbnr.) 71; 72
ed. Thos. Wright—*in his* Biographia Britann., vol. i. [*ut* K § 245; A.-S. text and Eng. tr.]
Extracts ed. Körner—in his *Einleitung*, pt. ii.; ed. Sweet—in his *A.-S. Reader* [*ut* K § 242]; ed. Zupitza—in his *Uebungsb.* [*ut* K § 244].
Handboc [Enchiridion] —*lost*.
Laws [*v. also* D § 5] ed. Dr. Reinhold Schmid—*in his* Gesetze der Angelsachsen [w. Germ. trns., etc.] r 8° *Leipzig* [pt. i. 32] 58
ed. B. Thorpe—*in his* Ancient Laws and Institutes of Eng. [w. Eng. trns. etc.] 1 v. f°. and 2 v. r 8° 70/- r 8° Rolls Series 40
Extracts ed. Alb. Cook (Am.)—*in his* Extracts fr. the Anglo-Saxon Laws [selns. also in Körner, *ut* K § 242] 50c. 12° *New York* 80
OROSIUS tr. King Alfred, ed. Dr. J. Bosworth; 14 facss. & col. map *o.p.* [*pb.* 16/-; *w.* 10/-] r 8° Longman 59
*ed. H. Sweet, pt. i. [text, w. Latin original] 13/- 8° E. Eng. Text Soc. (Tbnr.) 83
Specimens —*in the chrestoms. of* Brenner, Körner, Sweet, Thorpe [w. notes] [*ut* K § 242].
Translations tr. Thorpe in his *Analecta* [*ut* K § 242]; tr. Bosworth *in his* ed. of text [*sup.*], and in *Whole Works* [*sup*].
,, McCubbin + D. T. Holmes, *sub tit.* Orosian Geography, w. maps 2/- c 8° Clive 88
Voyages of Ohthere and Wulfstan [with Hakluyt's Muscovy] [Nat. Lib.] 6*d.* 18° Cassell 89
The orig. text of OROSIUS, a Spanish priest (5 cent.), has been ed. B. v. HAVERCAMP: *Historiarum libri vii.* 5/- 8° *Thorn* 57. It is also in MIGNE'S *Patrol.*, vol. xxxi. 12/6 r 8° *Paris*.

Proverbs [metrical; certainly *not* by Alfred]—*v.* K § 253: Later Anglo-Saxon Literature.
Psalms, tr. King Alfred [very doubtful]—*v.* K § 250: Anglo-Saxon Lyrical Poetry.

AIDS:
Life.
ASSER [9 cent.] Life of Alfred (tr.)—*in* Six Old Eng. Chronicles, tr. Dr. J. A. Giles 5/- c 8° Bohn's Lib. 48
This, and the *Anglo-Saxon Chronicle* (esp. the latter), form our only really trustworthy sources for ALFRED'S life.
FREEMAN, Prf. E. A. —*in his* Old English History [*ut* F § 18] *and* Hist. of Norman Conquest, vol. i. [*ut* F § 19].
HUGHES, Thos. Alfred the Great [Sunday Library; popular; good] 6/- c 8° Macmillan [70] 78
*PAULI, D. Rr. Life of Alfred the Great [tr.], ed. B. Thorpe [best short life] 5/- c 8° Bohn's Lib. 53
Language.
PRISER, O. Die Sprache d. Alfred d. Grossen und König Ine's [diss.] *Strassburg* 83
Article.
HÜLLWECK, Ueber d. Gebrauch d. Artikels in d. Werken Alfred's [diss.] 1/6 8° *Berlin* 87
Boethius: The "Metres."
LEICHT, A. Ist König Alfred d. Verfasser d. allitter. Metra d. Boethius [diss. inaug.] 1/- 8° *Leipzig* 82
ZIMMERMANN, O. Ueber den Verfasser d. altengl. Metren d. Boethius [diss. inaug.] 1/6 8° *Greifswald* 82

K § 252

Gregory's Cura Pastoralis.
DEWITZ, A. Untersuchungen üb. Alfred's *Cura Pastoralis* [diss. inaug.] 2/- 8° *Bunzlau* 82
SWEET, Henry Introduction to his edn. of the text, *supra.*
Language.
COSIJN, P. J. —*in his* Altwestsäch. Gramm., *and his* Kurzgefasste altwests. Gramm.—*ut* K § 242.
FLEISCHHAUER, W. Ueber d. Gebrauch d. Konjunctivs in Alfred's *Cura Pastoralis* 1/6 8° *Erlangen* 85
WÜLFING, E. Darstellung d. Syntax in Alfred's *Cura Pastoralis*, pt. i. 1/6 8° *Leipzig* 87
Orosius.
BOCK, K. Syntax d. Pronomina und Numeralia in Alfred's Orosius [diss. inaug.] 1/- 8° *Göttingen* 87
HAMPSON, R. T. Essay in the Geography of King Alfred—*appended to* Bosworth's edn. of text, *ut sup.*
SCHILLING, H. Alfred's Bearbeitung der Weltgeschichte des Orosius [diss. inaug.] 2/- 8° *Halle* 86
Proverbs —*v.* K § 253: Later Anglo-Saxon Literature.

Aelfric, Abbot [955–? 1020–25].

BEDE'S, Ven., *De Temporibus*: ed. T. Wright—*in his* Pop. Treatises on Science during Middle Ages [*ut* K § 252].
ed. Rev. O. Cockayne—*in his* Saxon Leechdoms, etc.—[w. tr.; *ut* K § 252].
Canones [to Bp. Wulfsine] ed B. Thorpe—*in his* Ancient Laws and Institutes of England [*ut supra*; w. Eng. tr.]
Colloquium ed. Thorpe—*in his* Analecta [*ut* K § 242]; ed. T. Wright—*in his* A.-S. and O.-E. Vocabs. [*ut* K § 242].
Grammar and Glossary [Sax.-Lat.-Eng.] ed. J. Zupitza, pt. i. [text & variants] [Samml. engl. Denkm.] 7/- 8° *Berlin* 80
Glossary ed. Thos. Wright—*in his* Anglo-Saxon and Old-English Vocabularies, *ut* K § 242.
Epinal Glossary: facsimile, ed H. Sweet 15/- f° E. Eng. Text Soc. 83
Homilies: 1st and 2nd Ser. [*Homiliae Catholicae*], ed. Benj. Thorpe, 2 vols. [w. trs.] 8° Aelfric Soc. 44; 46
Selections —*in the chrestoms. of* Brenner, Ettmüller, Sweet [A.-S. Rr. and O.-E. Rg. Pr.], Thorpe [*ut* K § 242].
A new edition by F. HORSLEY is in preparation.
Passiones Sanctt. ed. Prf. W. W. Skeat, pts. i.–iii. 22/- 8° E. Eng. Text Soc. 81; 85; 90
Selections —*in the chrestoms. of* Körner, Sweet, Thorpe [*ut* K § 242]; ed. R. Morris in his *Old Eng. Homilies* [*ut* K § 254].
On the Old and New Test.—*in the chrestoms. of* Ettmüller, Grein, Sweet ["Preface to O. T."]—*ut* K § 242.
Pentateuch, w. Joshua, Judges and Job: ed. C. W. M. Grein—*his* Bibl. A.-S. Prosa, vol. i. 8/- 8° *Cassel* 72
Specimens —*in the chrestoms. of* Brenner, Ettmüller, Körner, Thorpe [*ut* K § 242]; *of* Zupitza [*ut* K § 244].
Sermo ad Sacerdotes ed. B. Thorpe—*in his* Ancient Laws & Instit. of Eng., vol. ii. [w. tr.] 1 v. f° & 2 v. 70/- r 8° Rolls Series 40
Translation of Alcuin on Genesis, ed. G. E. MacLean: w. var. rgs., notes and Lat. orig. [diss.] 2/- 8° *Halle* 83
AIDS:
DIETRICH, Ed. [*alias* Franz] Abt. Ælfrik—*in the* Zeitschrift für historische Theologie, 1855–56.
In 4 parts: on ÆLFRIC'S writings, doctrine of the church, character and culture, life. An epoch-making contribution in its department, adopting views of ÆLFRIC'S personality since generally accepted.
Language.
KOHN, F. Theodor Die Syntax d. Verbums in Ælfrik's "Heiligenleben" [diss.] 1/- 8° *Leipzig* 90
SCHRADER, B. Studien zur Aelfricschen Syntax 2/- 8° *Jena* 87
WOHLFAHRT, Th. Die Syntax d. Verbums in Ælfrik's Heptateuch u. Hiob. [diss.] 1/6 8° *Munich* 85

Anglo-Saxon Chronicle.

EARLE, Prf. J. E. Two of the Saxon Chronicles Parallel [A. and E.] 16/- 8° Clar. Press 65
PLUMMER, C. [ed.] Two of Saxon Chronicles Parallel [781–1001]: revis. text. w. intro. 3/- c 8° ,, 89
*THORPE, Benj. [ed.] The Anglo-Saxon Chronicles; vol. i.: texts; ii.: translation ea. 10/- r 8° Rolls Series 61
THORPE'S edn. conts. 6 diff. texts fr. 6 MSS. (parallel); EARLE'S has the Parker MS. (*Corp. Chr. Camb.*) and the Laudian (*Bodleian*), w. full notes, an important Preface and Glossary. Six MSS. and fragments of a seventh are extant; they terminate at various dates, the latest at 1154. Each has been identified with one or other of the great religious houses of the South, viz.: A. (*Winch.*), B. (*Canterbury*), C. (*Abingdon*), D. (*Worcester*), E. (*Peterborough*), F. (*Canterbury*). A. is in C. C. Camb., B., C. and D. are in *Brit. Mus.* (*Cotton Lib.*), E. is in *Bodl. Oxon.*, F. and G. in *Brit. Mus.* (*Cott. Lib.*).
Extracts —*in the chrestoms. of* Brenner, Ettmüller, Körner, Marsh, Sweet, Thorpe [*ut* K § 242].
AIDS:
BEHM, Language of the Later Part of Peterborough Chronicle [= E.: diss.] 2/- 8° *Upsala* 84
GRUBITZ, E. Kritische Untersuchung üb. die angelsächs. Annalen [diss.] 1/6 8° *Göttingen* 68
KUBE, Die Wortstellung in der Sachsenchronik [diss.] 1/6 8° *Jena* 86

Wulfstan, Abp. [11 cent.]

Homilies ed. Prf. Arthur Napier, pt. i. [text and variants] [Samml. eng. Denkm.] 7/- 8° *Berlin* 83
Sermo Lupi Episc. ed. H. Sweet—*in his* Anglo-Saxon Reader [*ut* K § 242].
Laws ed. B. Thorpe—*in his* Ancient Laws and Institutes of England, vol. ii. [*ut supra*].
AIDS:
DIXON, W. Henry Fasti Eboracenses: lives of Archbps. of York, ed. Can. J. Raine, vol. i. 15/- 8° Longman 63
MOHRBUTTER, Darstellung d. Syntax in d. 4 ächten Pred. d. Wulf. [diss.] 1/6 8° *Münster* 85
NAPIER, Prf. A. Ueber die Werke des altengl. Erzbischofs Wulfstan [diss.] 1/6 8° *Weimar* 82

253. ANGLO-SAXON LITERATURE: (*b*) MINOR PROSE WORKS.

RELIGIOUS.

Gospels.

BOSWORTH + WARING, J.; G. [eds.] Four Versions of the Gospels 12/- 8° J. R. Smith [65] 74
Gothic, A.D. 360; Anglo-Saxon, A.D. 995; Wiclif, A.D. 1389; Tyndale, A.D. 1526—in parallel columns.
SKEAT, Prf. W. W. [ed.] A.-S. Northumbrian & Old Mercian Gospels: synoptically arranged 30/- 4° Camb. Press [58; 71; 74; 78] 90
1st edn. in 4 pts. Pt. i. prepared by J. M. KEMBLE; completed and (after his d. 1857) pub. by C. HARDWICK.

Gregory's Dialogues, tr. Bp. Werfrith [at request of Kg. Alfred; previously ascribed to Alfred].

,, ,, ed. Krebs + Prf. W. W. Skeat + H. Johnson *in prep.*
Preface to same —*in* Earle's Anglo-Saxon Literature: w. English tr. 2/6 f 8° S.P.C.K. 84
AIDS:
JOHNSON, Henry Gab es zwei v. einander unabhäng. Uebers. d. Dial. Greg? [negat. reply: diss.] 1/6 8° *Berlin* 84

Homilies : Collections of.

Blickling Homilies : ed. Dr. Rich. Morris, pt. i. 8/– ; ii. 4/– ; iii. 8/– [A.D. 971] 8° E. Eng. Text Soc. (Tbnr.) 74 ; 76 ; 80
A coll. of 19 homilies fr. MS. of end 10 cent. belonging to Marq. of LOTHIAN (Blickling Hall, Norfolk).

AID:
FLAMME, Syntax der Blickling Homilies [dissert. inaug.] 1/6 8° *Bonn* 85
NAPIER, Prf. A. [ed.] Anglo-Saxon Homilies : hitherto unprinted 8° E. Eng. Text Soc. (Tbnr.) *in prep.*

Hymnarium Anglo-Saxon : from MSS. of Eleventh Century 8° Surtees Soc. (Whittaker) 52

Leofric Missal ed. F. E. Warren [as used in Exeter Cathedral 1050–72] 35/– 8° Clar. Press 83

MISCELLANEOUS.

Laws, Documents, etc.

EARLE, Prf. J. [ed.] Collection of Anglo-Saxon Documents : w. intro., notes and gloss 8° Clar. Press *in prep.*
KEMBLE, J. M. [ed.] Codex Diplomaticus Ævi Saxonici, 6 vols. Histor. Soc. of Science (J. R. Smith) 39–48
THORPE, Benj. [ed.] Ancient Laws and Institutes of England 1 vol. f° & 2 vols. r 8° 70/– Rolls Series 40

Science and Medicine.

COCKAYNE, Rev. T. O. [ed.] Leechdoms, Wortcunning and Starcraft, 3 vols. ea. 10/– r 8° Rolls Series 64–66
A collection of Anglo-Saxon medical treatises, with English trs. and two Prefaces. Form valuable illus. of A.-S. orthography.
WRIGHT, Thos. [ed.] Popular Treatises on Science 6/– c 8° Hist. Soc. of Sc. (J. R. Smith) 41
Conts. one A.-S. piece : *Anglo-Saxon Manual of Astronomy, i.e.* the A.-S. version of BEDE'S *De Temporibus*.

Vocabularies.

HESSELS, Dr. J. H. [ed.] An Eighth Century Latin-Anglo-Saxon Glossary 10/– 8° Camb. Press 90
WRIGHT, Thos. [ed.] Anglo-Saxon & Old-English Vocabularies, ed. R. Wülcker, 2 vols. 28/– 8° Trübner [57 ; 73] 84
Illustrating the condition, manners, etc., of the English from the 10th to the 15th centuries.

253. LATER ANGLO-SAXON LITERATURE.

Collections.

MORRIS, Dr. Richard [ed.] Old-English Miscellany [a Bestiary, Kentish sermons, "Prov. of Alfred," Relig. Poems of 13 cent.] 10/– 8° E. Eng. Text Soc. (Tbnr.) 72
WRIGHT, Thos. [ed.] Anecdota Literaria [Eng., Lat. and Fch. poems of 13 cent.] 7/6 8° J. R. Smith 44
Chrestomathies —*v.* K § 242 and § 243.

POETRY.

Didactic Poetry.

Bestiarium ed. E. Mätzner—*in his* Sprachproben, pt. i. [*ut* K § 243].
,, Dr. Rich. Morris—*in his* Old-English Miscellany [*ut supra*].
,, T. Wright + J. O. Halliwell [-Phillips]—*in their* Reliquiae Antiquae, vol. i.
2 v., *red. to* 24/– 8° J. R. Smith 41 ; 43
A N.-E. English poem of 800 verses of middle 13 cent. A fabulous allegor. nat. hist. of the lion, eagle, serpent, ant, stag, wolf, spider, whale, siren, elephant, turtle-dove, panther.

Owl and the Nightingale ed. Rich. Morris—*in his* Specimens, pt. i. [*ut* K § 243].
,, J. Stevenson *o.p.* 4° Roxburghe Club 38
,, F. H. Stratmann 2/– 8° *Crefeld* 68
,, Thos. Wright *o.p.* p 8° Percy Society 43
Selection (*v.* 701 to end) ,, E. Mätzner—*in his* Sprachproben, i. [*ut* K § 243].

AIDS:
BORSCH, Ueber Metrik u. Poetik d. *Owl and Nightingale* [dissert.] 1/6 8° *Münster* 83
EGGE, —*in* Modern Language Notes, 1887, No 1 [*ut* K § 236]
NÖLLE Die Sprache d. altengl. Eule und Nachtigall [dissert.] 1/– 8° *Göttingen* 90
A southern English poem of 1792 lines (only ab. 20 words of O.-F. origin) of middle 13 cent.

Proverbs of King Alfred ed. J. M. Kemble—*in his edn.* of Salomon and Saturnus [*ut* K § 249].
,, Dr. Rich. Morris—*in his* Old English Miscellany [*ut supra*].
,, T. Wright + J. O. Halliwell [-Phillips]—*in their* Reliquiae Antiquae, vol. i. [*ut supra*].
Extracts ,, Dr. Rich. Morris—*in his* Specimens, vol. i. [*ut* K § 243].

AID:
GROPP, On the Language of the Proverbs of Alfred [dissert.] 1/6 8° *Halle* 99

Historical.

LAYAMON [13 cent.] Brut, ed. w. tr. notes and gloss. Sir F. Madden [both MSS.] r 8° Soc. of Antiquaries 47
Specimen ed. E. Mätzner—*in his* Sprachproben, pt. i. ed. Dr. R. Morris—*in his* Specimens, pt. i. [*ut* K § 243].

AIDS:
CALLENBERG, Layamon und Orm nach ihren Lautverhältnissen verglichen [dissert.] 1/6 8° *Jena* 76
KRAUTWALD, H. Layamon's *Brut* verglichen mit Wace's *Roman de Brut* [dissert.] 1/– 8° *Breslau* 87
A fabulous history of England from the destruction of Troy to A.D. 689, a poetical semi-Saxon paraphrase of the *Roman de Brut* of WACE, the Norman *trouvère* [ed. Le Roux de LINCY, 2 v. 8° *Rouen* 36 ; 38]—itself a translation of GEOFFREY OF MONMOUTH'S *Hist. Regum Brit.* [ed. San Marte 8° *Halle* 54 ; tr. J. A. Giles—in his *Six O.-E. Chrons.* 5/- c 8° Bohn's Lib. 48].

K § 254

Lives of the Saints.

Catherine, St., [of Alexandria], Life of; ed. Dr. E. Einenkel [w. Latin original] 15/- 8° E. Eng. Text Soc. (Tbnr.) 84
Juliana, St., Life of ed. Rev. O. Cockayne + E. Brock [2 versions; w. trns.] 2/- 8° ,, ,, ,, ,, 72
,, ,, Dr. R. Morris—*in his* Specimens, pt. i. [2 texts; *ut* K § 243]
Marherete, St. ,, Rev. O. Cockayne [3 texts, *c.* 1200, 1310, 1330] *o.p.* 8° ,, ,, ,, ,, 66

Lyrical Poetry: Collections of Miscellaneous Pieces.

Morris, Dr. Richard (ed.)—*in his* Old English Miscellany [*ut supra*].
Wright + Halliwell [-Phillips], T./J.O. [eds.]—*in their* Reliquiæ Antiquæ [*ut supra*].

Religious Poetry.

Genesis and Exodus, Story of: ed. Dr. Richard Morris [about 1250] 8/- 8° E. Eng. Text. Soc. (Tbnr.) 65
Extracts —*in the chrestoms. of* Mätzner, pt. i. [*ut* K § 243]; *of* Wülker, *of* Zupitza [*ut* K § 224].

Aids:
Fritzsche, Ist d. angels. *Story of Genesis and Exod.* d. Werk *eines* Verfassers—*in* Anglia, vol. v. [good; *ut* K § 236].
Hilmer, Die Sprache von *Genesis and Exodus* [school-progr.] 1/6 4° *Sondershausen* 76

The *Story of Genesis and Exodus* is a metrical paraphrase of the two O. T. bks., of 2536 and 1642 verses resp. Date *c.* 1250.

Hali Maidenhad ["holy state of Maidenhood"] ed. Rev. O. Cockayne [*c.* 1200] *o.p.* 8° E. Eng. Text. Soc. (Tbnr.) 66

An alliterative homily of the 13th century.

Orrm [a monk of early 13 cent.]
Ormulum ed. R. M. White, w. notes and glossary, ed. Holt, 2 vols. 21/- 8° Clar. Press [52] 78
Extracts —*in the chrestoms. of* Mätzner (pt. i.), Sweet (pt. i.), Zupitza [*ut* K § 243.]

Aids:
Effer, Einfache und doppelte Kons. im *Ormulum* [dissert.] 1/6 8° *Bonn* 85
Sachse, R. Das unorgan. *e* im *Ormulum*; Untersuch. üb. d. Flexionsweise [,,] 1/6 8° *Halle* 81
Sweet, H. Grammar and Glossary—*in his* First Middle English Primer—*ut* K § 243.

The *Ormulum* is a rhythmical paraphrase of the Gospels, consisting of Preface, Intro., etc., and 32 homilies based on the theolog. wks. of Bede, Gregory I. and Isidor's Comm.

Poema Morale ed. F. J. Furnivall—*in his* Early Engl. Poems and Lives of the Saints [Egerton MS.] *o.p.* 8° *London* 62
,, H. Lewin [crit. edn.] 2/- 8° *Halle* 81
,, Rich. Morris—*in his* Old English Homilies, vol. i. [Lambeth and Egerton MSS.] 7/- 8° E. Eng. Text. Soc. (Tbnr.) 67
,, ,, ,, ,, vol. ii. [Trin. Coll. Camb. MS.] 8/- 8° E. Eng. Text. Soc. (Tbnr.) 73
,, ,, ,, Old English Miscellany [Jesus Coll. Oxon. MS.] 10/- 8° 72
,, ,, ,, Specimens, pt. i. [*ut* K § 243] [conts. reprs. of Jesus and Trin. MSS.]

A South-Eastern English homily in 397 verses of considerable force.

Dame Siris ed. E. Mätzner—*in his* Sprachproben, pt. i. [*ut* K § 243].
,, Thos. Wright—*in his* Anecdota Litteraria [*ut supra*].

Aids:
Elsner, W. Untersuchungen zum mittelenglischen *Dame Siris* 1/6 8° *Berlin* 87

A Southern-English poem of 450 verses, of *c.* 1250–1258. Undoubtedly of Oriental origin.

PROSE.

Ancren Riwle [Anachoretarum Regula] ed. E. Kölbing: critical edn. [Altenglische Bibl.] 8° *Heilbronn* *in prep.*
ed. Rev. Jas. Morton *o.p.* [*w.* 4/-] s 4° Camden Soc. 53
Extracts —*in the chrestomathies of* Mätzner (pt. ii.) *and* Morris (pt. i.) [*ut* K § 243].

A prose-wk. in 8 pts. written prob. by Bp. Rich. le Poor [*d.* 1237]: on devot. services, govt. of the senses, temptations, confession, penance, charity, etc., written for a society of anchoresses. Afterwards tr. into Latin.

254. OLD [1250-1350] and MIDDLE [1350-1500] ENGLISH LITERATURE: (*a*) POETRY.

Chaucer, Geoffrey [1328–1400]—*v.* K § 68.
Gower, John [1325–1408]—*v.* K § 68.
Hoccleve [*or* Occleve; 1370–1454], Thos.—*v.* K § 68.
Langland, William [14 cent.]—*v.* K § 68.
Lyndsay, Sir David [1490–1568]—*v.* K § 68.
Minot, Laurence [14 cent.]—*v.* K § 68.

Didactic Verse.

Bernard, St. De Cura Rei Famuliaris: ed. Prf. J. R. Lumby 2/- 8° E. Eng. Text. Soc. 70

Contains also some early Scottish Prophecies.

Cursor Mundi [*c.* 1320] ed. Dr. Rich. Morris, pt. i. 10/6; ii. 15/-; iii. 15/-; iv. 10/-; v. 25/- [4 texts] 8° E. Eng. Text. Soc. 74; 75; 76; 77; 78

The *Introduction* to this edn. has not been pub. yet.

Specimens: ed. Dr. R. Morris—*in his* Specimens, pt. ii.; ed. Zupitza—*in his* Reader [*ut* K § 244].

Aids:
Haenisch, Dr. Inquiry into the Sources of the *Cursor Mundi* [dissert.] 1/6 8° *Breslau* 82
Hupe, Dr. H. Genealogie u. Ueberlieferung d. HSS. d. *Cursor Mundi* [dissert.] 1/- 8° *Erlangen* 86

A N. of Eng. metrical paraphrase of the O. and N. Test. history fr. the Creation to Doom's-day, w. many mediæv. legends and romances intermingled. About 24,000 lines.

How the Good Wife Taught her Daughter: ed. Prf. W. W. Skeat—*in his edn. of* Barbour's Bruce, pt. iii. [*v. infra*] 21/- 8° E. Eng. Text Soc. (Tbnr.) 77

Proverbs of Hendyng [end 13 cent.] ed. K. Böddeker—*in his* Altenglische Dichtungen [*ut* K § 244].
„ J. M. Kemble—*in* Appendix *to his* Salomon and Saturn [*ut* K § 249].
„ T. Wright + J. O. Halliwell [-Phillips]—*in their* Reliquiæ Ant. [*ut* K § 253].

Extracts ed. Mätzner—*in his* Sprachproben, pt. i. [*ut* K § 243]; ed. Morris—*in his* Specimens, pt. ii. [*ut* K § 244].

Ratis Raving ed. Prf. J. R. Lumby, *sub tit.* R. R. & other Moral & Relig. Pieces 3/- 8° E. Eng. Text. Soc. (Tbnr.) 70

Instructions of a Father to his Son; 1731 verses. MS. in Camb. Univ. Lib.

ROLLE, Richard, of Hampole [? 1280-? 1349] Pricke of Consciense, ed. Dr. Richard Morris; w. intro., notes and index [in verse] 8° Philological Soc. 63

Extracts —*in the chrestoms. of* Mätzner (pt. i.) [*ut* K § 243]; *of* Morris (pt. ii.), of Wülker [*ut* K § 244].

A Northumbrian poem. For HAMPOLE'S *Prose Treatises*, v. K § 253.

Thewies of Gud Women ed. Prf. J. R. Lumby—*in his edn. of* Ratis Raving [*ut supra*] 8° E. Eng. Text. Soc. (Tbnr.) 70

WILLIAM of Shoreham [beg. 14 cent.] Poems, ed. Thos. Wright [scarce; but a bad edn.] p 8° Percy Society 49

Specimens —*in the chrestoms. of* Mätzner (pt. i.) [*ut* K § 243]; *of* Morris (pt. ii.), *of* Wülker [*ut* K § 244].

Poems on the Seven Sacraments, their Ceremonies, the Ten Commandments, the Seven Sins, tr. of Rob. GROSSETESTE'S Hymn to the Virgin, treatise on original sin, etc.

AIDS:

DANKER, O.	—*in his* Laut- u. Flexionslehre der mittelkentischen Denkmäler	[dissert.]	2/-	8° *Strassburg*	79
KONRATH, M.	Beiträge zur Erklär. u. Textkritik d. Wm. v. Schoreham [*sic*]		2/6	8° *Berlin*	78

Fables [Fabliaux].

Fox and the Wolf, ed. T. Wright—*in* Percy Soc. Pubs., vol. viii.; *also* + J. O. Halliwell [-Phillips]—*in their* Reliq. Ant. [*ut* K § 253]
„ E. Mätzner—*in his* Sprachproben, pt. i. [*ut* K § 243].

Probably written dur. reign of Edw. i. and based on the *Roman du Raynard*.

HENRYSON, Robert [1430-1507] Fables, ed. Diebler—*in Anglia* [*v.* K § 236] [13 Fables after Aesop].

AIDS:

DIEBLER	Die Fabeldichtungen Robert Henryson's	[dissert.]	1/6	8° *Halle*	85
IRVING, Dr. David	—*in his* History of Scottish Poetry, ed. Dr. J. A. Carlyle	*o.p.* [*pb.* 16/-; *w.* 7/6]		8° Edmonston, *Edin.*	61
SCHIPPER, J.	—*in his* William Dunbar		7/-	8° *Berlin*	84

Land of Cockaigne [13 cent.] ed. Dr. F. J. Furnivall—*in his* Early English Poems & Lives of Saints 6/- 8° *Berlin* 62
„ E. Mätzner—*in his* Sprachproben, pt. i. [*ut* K § 243].

A satire on the corruptions of the court, painting a "Land of the Kitchen,"—a fool's paradise.

Gospels —*v.* K § 252: *s.v.* Gospels.

Historical Poems and Chronicles—*v. also* F § 35 and § 36: History of Scotland, *s.vv.* Sources.

BARBOUR, Bp. J. [1316-96] The Bruce [1375-77], ed. Cosmo Innes; w. intro. and notes [*w.* 12/6] 4° Spalding Club 57
„ „ „ „ „ „ Dr. Jamieson 6/- c 8° *Edinburgh* [20] 69
„ „ * „ „ „ „ Prf. W. W. Skeat, pt. i. 12/-; ii. 4/-; iii. 2/-; iv. 8° E. Eng. Text Soc. 70; 74; 77; 89

Extracts —*in the chrestoms.* of Mätzner (pt. ii.) [*ut* K § 243]; *of* Morris (pt. ii.); *of* Wülker [*ut* K § 244].

AIDS:

HENSCHEL, F. H.	Darstellung d. Flexionslehre in Barbour's *Bruce*	[dissert.]	1/6	8° *Leipzig*	86
SCHIPPER, J.	—*in his* William Dunbar		7/-	8° *Berlin*	84

An epic poem, extending fr. d. of Alex. iii. to d. of Robert i., relating the adventures of Robert in his struggles for freedom against the English [1286-1332].

Chronicle of England to 1327, ed. M. L. Perrin [about 1350] 8° E. Eng. Text Soc. *in prep.*

Crowned King ed. Prf. W. W. Skeat—*in his ed.* of Piers Plowman, Text C. 18/- 8° E. Eng. Text Soc. (Tbnr.) 73

Early Scottish Prophecies and Fragm. of Allit. Poem on Beckett's Proph.: ed. Prf. J. Lumby—*in his edn. of* Bernard's *De Cur. Rei fam.* 2/- 8° „ „ 70

Libell of English Policye [A.D. 1436]: ed. W. Hertzberg [w. metr. tr. and hist. intro. by R. Pauli—in Germ.] 4/- 8° *Leipzig* 78

Richard Coeur de Lion: ed. Weber—*in his* Metrical Romances, 3 vols. *o.p.* 8° *London* 11

Extract ed. R. Wülcker—*in his* Altenglisches Lesebuch [*ut* K § 244].

Prose Analysis by G. Ellis—*in his* Specimens of E. Eng. Metrical Romances 5/- c 8° Bohn's Lib. [05] 48

Richard the Redels ed. Prf. W. W. Skeat—*in his edn. of* Piers Plowman, Text 3 18/- 8° E. Eng. Text Soc. (Tbnr.) 73
* „ „ „ —*in his edn. of* the same, 2 vols. 31/6 8° Clar. Press 86
„ T. Wright—*sub tit.* Poem of the Deposition of Richard *o.p.* [*w.* 2/6] s 4° Camden Soc. 38
„ „ —*in his* Political Poems and Songs, 2 vols. [*v.* F § 21] ea. 10/- r 8° Rolls Series 59; 61

AID:

ZIEPEL, C.	Reign of Rich. ii., and Comments. on the Poem of his Deposition	1/6	4° *Berlin*	74

ROBERT OF BRUNNE [Rob. Manning; 13-14 cent.] Chronicles, ed. Dr. F. J. Furnivall, 2 v. [Cadwalader to Edw. i. (1272)] ea. 10/- r 8° Rolls Series 87

A contemp. tr. of the Chronicle of Peter LANGTOFT. Dr. FURNIVALL has another edn. in prep. for the E. E. Text Soc. The French orig has been ed. T. WRIGHT in *Rerum Brit. med. aevi script.*, 2 vols. [66] 68.

Extracts ed. Mätzner—*in his* Sprachproben (pt. i.) [*ut* K § 243]; ed. Wülker—*in his* Lesebuch [*ut* K § 244].

AID:

HELLMERS, G.	Ueb. d. Sprach R. M.'s u. Autorschaft d. *Medns. on Supper of our Lord*	[diss.]	2/6	8° *Goslar*	85

ROBERT OF GLOUCESTER [? 12 cent.] Metrical Chronicle, ed. W. Aldis Wright, 2 vols.; w. intro. & gloss. ea. 10/- r 8° Rolls Ser. 87

Of no great literary value, but of high philological importance. No notes by the editor.

AID:

PABST, Felix	Die Sprache d. Reimchronik d. Rob. v. Glouce., pt. i. [Lautlehre]	[diss. inaug.]	2/6	8° *Berlin*	90

Thomas of Erceldoun: Romance and Prophecies of, ed. Alois Brandl [Samml. engl. Denkmäler] 4/- 8° *Berlin* 80
„ Dr. J. A. H. Murray [from 5 MSS.] 10/6 8° E. Eng. Text Soc. (Tbnr.) 75

A poem of the beg. 15 cent., consisting of 700 verses of *post factum* prophecies on Scot. hist. of 14 cent.

Ballads —*v.* K § 65, *passim.*

K § 254

Homilies [Metrical] : Collections.

FURNIVALL, Dr. F. J. [ed.]—*there are a few in his* Early English Poems and Lives of Saints 6/- 8° *Berlin* 62
MORRIS, Dr. Richard [ed.] O. Eng. Homilies, pt. i. 7/-; ii. 8/-. Series II., 8/- [12 & 13 cents.; w. trs.] 8° E. Eng. Text Soc. 67; 68; 73
,, ,, [ed.] —*his* O.-E. Miscellany, *conts. some* Kentish Sermons [before 1250] 10/- 8° ,, ,, ,, (Tbnr.) 72
,, ,, [ed.] Early English Homilies [13 cent.] 8° ,, ,, ,, *in prep.*
SMALL, J. [ed.] English Metrical Homilies : from MSS. of 14 century; w. notes 12/- s 4° *Edinburgh* 62
Specimens —*in the chrestoms. of* Mätzner (pt. i.), *and* Morris (pt. i.) [*ut* K § 243].

AIDS:
COHN, Sprache d. mittelengl. Predigten-samml. d. HS. Lambeth 487 [dissert.] 1/6 8° *Berlin* 80
KRÖGER, A. Sprache d. Dialect d. mittelengl. Homilien in HS. B. 14, 52 Tr. Coll. Camb. [,,] 1/6 8° *Erlangen* 85

Lais

Lai de Fresne [beg. 14 cent.] ed. Weber—*in his* Metrical Romances, vol. i., 3 vols. *o.p.* 8° *London* 11
,, [in modern form] Ellis—*in his* Specimens of E. E. Metrical Romances 5/- c 8° Bohn's Lib. [05] 48
An English tr. of the French original of MARIE of FRANCE.

Sir Orfeo [? beg. 14 cent.] ed. J. O. Halliwell [-Phillips]—*in his* Illns. of Fairy Myth. of *Mids. Nts. Drm.*
This, orig. pub. 1845, has been repr. by W. C. HAZLITT in his edn. of J. RITSON'S *Fairy Tales, etc.* 10/- c 8° Pearson [31] 75
,, Dr. S. Laing *o.p.* 4° Abbotsford Club 57
* ,, O. Zielke [w. intro. and notes in German] 4/- 8° *Breslau* 80
A travesty of the myth of Orpheus and Eurydice, after a French original.

Legends and Lives of the Saints.

The Great Collections.

A Southern Collection [end 13 cent.] *ed. [in part] C. Horstmann, *sub tit.* Altenglische Legenden 4/- 8° *Paderborn* 75
Barlaam and Josaphat [Bodl. MS.] | Birth of Jesus [MS. Ashmol.; MS. Egert.] | Childhood of Jesus [MS. Laud] | St. Patrick's Purgatory [MSS. Ash., Egert., Ld.]

B Northern Collection [beg. 14 cent.] *ed. [in part] C. Horstmann, *sub tit.* Samml. alteng. Legg., Neue Folge [for conts., *v. infra*] 21/- 8° *Heilbronn* 81

C BARBOUR'S Scottish Collection, Barbour's Legendensammlung, ed. C. Horstmann, 2 vols., i. 8/-; ii. 10/- 8° ,, 81; 82
Here ed. for the first time. Contains also the fragments of his *Trojan War*. Legend of *Machor* is missing here, as it was printed in the editor's *Samml. altengl. Legg.* Neue Folge [*ut sup.*]. The coll. is based on the *Legenda Aurea*, but utilizes also the *Vitae Patrum* and *Speculum historiale* of VINCENT of BEAUVAIS.

D Johannes MIRKUS' Festial [prose; *c.* 1400]—*there have been* 18 *edns. of this:* 1st by Caxton [*Westminster* 1483], last by W. de WORDE [*Lond.* 1532].
Sermo in Festum ed. C. Horstmann—*in his* Samml. altengl. Legenden, Neue Folge [*ut supra*].
Conts. some 40 legends, based on the *Legenda Aurea*, as well as on the *Gesta Romanorum* and English sources.

E OSBERN BOKENAM'S Lives of the Saints [1443-6] ed. E. Kölbing [Altenglische Bibliothek] 6/- 8° *Heilbronn* 83
ed. for the Roxburghe Club 4° Roxburghe Club 35
Legend of S. Elizabeth ed. Wülcker—*in his* Altenglisches Lesebuch [*ut* K § 244].
Conts. thirteen lives of female saints, drawn from the *Legenda Aurea*.

F Legenda Aurea: Translation of [prose; 1438]—*there have been* 2 *edns. of this:* Caxton 1484, Caxton 1487.

AID:
*HORSTMANN, C. Einleitungen *to* [*and throughout*] *his* 3 *works, supra, and his* Samml. altengl. Legg. [ser. i., 1878], *infra*.

Single Legends.

Collectively.

FURNIVALL, Dr. F. J. [ed.] Early English Poems and Lives of the Saints 6/- 8° *Berlin* 62
HORSTMANN, C. [ed.] Early English Lives of Saints [Laud MS.; earliest version] 20/- 8° E. Eng. Text Soc. (Tbnr.) 87
Supplementary Early English Lives of Saints, *in prep.* Early Engl. Verse Lives of Saints [Harl. MS.] *in prep.* Both E. E. T. S.
* ,, ,, Sammlung altenglischer Legenden, 7/6; The same, Neue Folge 21/- 8° *Heilbronn* 78; 81

(a) Canticum de Creatione [Tr. Coll. Oxon. MS.] | Childhood of Jesus [Harl. MS.] | Christine [Arundel MS.] | Disputacioun bytw. a cristene mon and a Jew [Vernon MS.] | Dorothea [Harl. MS.] | Erasmus [Harl. MS.] | Euphrosyne [Vernon MS.] | Magdalena [Laud and Auchinl. MSS.] | Marina [Harl. MS.] | Robert of Cisyle [Vern. and Tr. Coll. Ox. MS.]

(b) Child of Bristowe [Harl. MS.] | Christopher, S. [Thornton MS.] | Coment le sauter noustre dame [Dig. MS.] | De Principio Creationis [Ashm. MS.] | De Erkenwalde [Harl. MS.] | Edmund, S. and Fremund [,, ,,] | Ethelreda, S., Vita [Cott. MS.] | Eustas [Digby MS.]; *also repr. of Lond.* 1566 | Giles, S., of Lydgate [Harl. MS.] | Hell, Two Tales of, *i.e. Complaint of a Soul and Punishm. of Adultery* [Ashm. MS.] | Ipotis [Vernon MS.] | John the Evangelist, S. [Thornton MS.] | Kateryne, S. [Camb. MS.] | Legend of Crucifix [Ashmole MS.] | Margarete of Lydgate, S. [Bp. Cosin's Lib.] | Mary Legg. of Good Knight and Wife [Ashm. MS.] | Margrete, S. [Auchin. and Ashm. MS.] | Sacred Blood at Hayles [Royal MS.] | Stacyons of Jerusalem [Ashm. MS.] | Tale of Incestuous Daught. [Camb. & Ashm. MSS.] | ,, ,, Smyth and his Dame [*repr. fr.* Copland] | Wolfade and Ruffyn, SS. [Cott. MS.]

MORRIS, Dr. Rich. [ed.] Legends of the Holy Rood, etc. [O.-E. poems of 11, 14 & 15 cents.] 10/- 8° E. Eng. Text Soc. (Tbnr.) 71

Individually.

Alexius-Legenden ed. J. Schipper, pt. i. [14 and 15 cent. versions; Quellen u. Forsch.] 2/6 8° *Strassburg* 77
Celestin ed. C. Horstmann—*in Anglia*, vol. i. [*v.* K § 236].
Childhood of Jesus ed. C. Horstmann—*in his* Samml. alteng. Legenden; *ut supra* [pt. i. previously ed. 2/- 8° *Münster* 73]
AID:
REINSCH, Rob. Die Pseudo-Evangelien v. Jesu u. Maria's Kindheit 4/- 8° *Halle* 79
Editha: sive chronicon Vilodunense, ed. C. Horstmann [in Wilts dialect; Cott. MS.] 4/- 8° *Heilbronn* 83
AID:
HEUSER, Die mittelenglischen Legenden von St. Editha u. S. Ethelreda 8° *Erlangen* 87

Euphrosyne — ed. C. Horstmann—*in Englische Studien*, vol. i. [*v.* K § 236]—*et supra*, *s.v.* Samml. alteng. Legg.

Gregory — ed. C. Horstmann—*in* Herrig's *Archiv*, vol. lvi. [*v.* K § 236] [from the Vernon MS.]
,, Fritz Schulz [from the Auchinleck MS. ; w. notes and gloss.] 4/- 8° *Königsberg* 76
,, Turnbull—*in his* Legendae Catholicae [from the Auchinleck MS.] *o.p.* *Edinburgh* 40

AID:
HOLTERMANN, Ueber Sprache, Poetik u. Styl. d. Gregory-leg. d. Auch. MS. (dissert.) 1/6 8° *Munster* 82

Katharine, St.
CAPGRAVE, J. [1393–1464] Life of S. Katharine, ed. C. Horstmann [*v. also his* Samml., N. F., *supra*] 8° E. Eng. Text Soc. (Tbnr.) *in prep.*

Magdalen
AID:
KNORK, O. Untersuchungen über d. Magdalenelegende d. MS. Laud 108 (dissert. inaug.) 2/- 8° *Berlin* 90

Marina — ed. K. Böddeker—*in his* Altenglische Dichtungen [*ut* K § 244].

Margarete
AID:
KRAHL, Ernst Untersuchungen über vier Versionen d. mittelenglischen Margaretenlegende (diss. inaug.) 2/- 8° *Berlin*. 89

Patrick, St. — ed. C. Horstmann—*in his* Alteng. Legenden [ser. i., 1875; *ut sup.*] [Ashm., Egert., Laud MSS.]
,, E. Kölbing—*in Englische Studien*, vol. i. [*v.* K § 236] [fr. Cotton Calig. A ii.]
,, Toulmin Smith—*in Englische Studien*, vol. ix. [*v.* K § 236] [fr. 15 cent. MS.]
,, Turnbull + Dr. S. Laing—*in* Owain Miles and other Fragments *o.p.* *Edinburgh* 37

AIDS:
de VERE, Aubrey Legend of St. Patrick (a poem) 5/- c 8° Paul 72
WRIGHT, Thomas St. Patrick's Purgatory: essay on legends of purgat, hell and parad. of mid. ages 6/- c 8° J. R. Smith 44

Susanna ["Pystyl of Swete Suswane"] ed. Dr. S. Laing—*in his* Select Remains of Ancient Scottish Poetry 42/- 4° Gardner, *Paisley* [22] 84
ed. C. Horstmann—*in Anglia*, vol. i. [*v.* K § 236].

Theophilus — ,, E. Kölbing—*in Englische Studien*, vol. i. [*v.* K § 236] [the later Engl. version]

AID:
KÖLBING, E. —*in his* Beiträge z. vergl. Gesch. d. romantischen Poesie u. Prosa im M.A. 7/6 8° *Breslau* 76

Thomas à Becket — ed. Black, *sub tit.* Life and Martyrdom of Thomas Becket *o.p.* 8° *London* 45
,, Dr. J. A. Giles, *sub tit.* Vita S. Thomas Cantuar., 7 vols. [several lives] *o.p.* 8° Parker 45
,, C. Horstmann—*in Englische Studien*, vol. iii. [*v.* K § 236] [fr. C. C. C. Camb. MS.]

Vision of S. Paul — ed. C. Horstmann—*in* Herrig's *Archiv*, vol. lii. [*v.* K § 236] [Laud MS.]
,, ,, ,, —*in Englische Studien*, vol. i. [*v.* K § 236] [Vernon MS.]
,, Dr. R. Morris—*in his* Old English Miscellany [Jes. Coll. Oxon. MS.] 10/- 8° E.E.Text Soc. (Tbnr.) 72
,, ,, ,, —*in the same:* Appendix [Bodl. MS. Douce] 10/- 8° ,, ,, 72

Visions of Tundale: w. other metrical moralizations, etc., ed. Turnbull *o.p.* *Edinburgh* 43
ed. R. Wülker—*in his* Altenglisches Lesebuch [*ut* K § 244]

Werburghe, St. — Life of, By Henry Bradshaw [*d.* 1513], ed. C. Horstmann 10/- 8° E.E.T.Soc. [Pynson 1521] 87

Lyrical Verse.

MORRIS, Dr. Richard [ed.] —*his* Old English Homilies [*ut supra*] *conts. several religious songs.*

WRIGHT, Thomas [ed.] Specimens of Lyric Poetry *o.p.* p 8° Percy Society 42

,, ,, [ed.] —*in his* Political Songs of England from reign of John to Edward ii. 2 vols. [*v.* F § 21] ea. 10/- r 8° Rolls Series 59; 61

Specimens —*in the chrestoms. of* Morris (pt. ii.), *and of* Wülker [*ut* K § 244].

Psalter.

Anglo-Saxon and Early-English Psalter, 2 vols. [ed. Rev. Jos. Stevenson] ea. 10/- 8° Surtees Soc. (Whittaker) 43; 47
,, ,, ed. F. Harsley 8° E. Eng. Text Soc. (Tbnr.) *in prep.*

Single Psalms ,, —*in the chrestoms. of* Mätzner (pt. i.) [*ut* K § 242]; *of* Morris (pt. ii.); *of* Wülker [*ut* K § 244].

AID:
WENDE, Ueberlieferung und Sprache d. Mittelenglischen Psalters 1/- 8° *Breslau* 84
A Northumbrian tr. of the Psalms after the Vulgate of ab. middle of rn. of Edw. Prose Tr., *v.* K § 255

Romances —*v.* K § 46: British Romances, & K § 47: English Romances.

255. OLD AND MIDDLE ENGLISH LITERATURE: (*b*) PROSE.

DAN MICHEL [14 cent.] Ayenbite of Inwyt ["again-bite (remorse) of conscience"] *ed. Dr. Richard Morris [1340] 10/6 8° E. Eng. Text Soc. (Tbnr.) 66
ed. Rev. Jos. Stevenson 4° Roxburghe Club 55

Extracts —*in the chrestoms. of* Mätzner (pt. ii.) [*ut* K § 242] *of* Morris (pt. ii.); *of* Wülcker [*ut* K § 244].

A moral treat. on the 10 Commandments, Apostles' Creed, 7 Deadly Sins, *etc., etc.* Tr. in Kentish dialect fr. La Somme des Vices et des Vertus (1279).

AID:
VARNAGEN, H. Beiträge zur Erklärung u. Text-Kritik d. *Ayenbite—in Englische Studien*, vol. i. [*v.* K § 236].

K § 255

MAUNDEVILLE, Sir J. [? 1300–1371 or 2] Voiage and Travaile of [1356], ed. J. O. Halliwell (-Phillips); w. facs. ill. 7/6 8° Reeves & T. [39] 83
The same, ed. John Ashton; w. facs. ill. [—v. E § 6] 10/6 8° Pickering 88
Extracts —*in the chrestoms. of* Mätzner (pt. ii.) [*ut* K § 242]; *of* Morris (pt. ii.), *of* Wülcker [*ut* K § 244].

AIDS:
SCHÖNBORN, Bibliographische Untersuchungen üb. d. Reisebeschreibung des Maundeville *o.p.* 8° *Breslau* 40
TOBLER, Titus —*in his* Bibliographia Palaestinae 8/- 8° *Leipzig* [67] 71
VOGELS, Die ungedruckten lateinischen Versionen Maundeville's 8° *Crefeld* 86
A tr. fr. a Fch. original. First English edition 1725 [*see* 1727].

ROLLE, Richard, of Hampole [? 1280–? 1349] English Prose Treatises, ed. Rev. G. G. Perry [nine moral treatises] 1/- 8° E. Eng. Text Soc. (Tbnr.) 66
A tenth Treatise has been ed. ULLMANN in *Englische Studien*, vol. vii. v. K § 256]—from Camb. Univ. Lib. MS.
Extracts —*in the chrestoms. of* Mätzner (pt. ii.) [*ut* K § 242] *of* Wülcker [*ut* K § 244].
For his *Myrour of Life* (*Speculum Vitae*) and *Pricke of Conscience*, v. K § 254.

TREVISA, John [1398–1408; of Cornwall] Translation of Higden's *Polychronicon*—*v.* F § 21: History of England, *s.v.* Sources.
Extracts —*in the chrestoms. of* Mätzner (pt. ii.) [*ut* K § 242]; *of* Morris's (pt. ii.), *of* Wülcker [*ut* K § 244].
TREVISA continued HYGDEN'S *Chronicle* from 1342 to 1357; and CAXTON, who first printed it in 1482, further continued it to 1460.

WICLIF, John [1324–1384]—*for his* Works, *v.* A § 3; *for* Transl. of Bible, *v.* A § 17.

AID:
FISCHER, Ueber die Sprache Wyclif's: Laut u. Flexionslehre (dissert.) 1/6 8° *Halle* 80

Agriculture.

PALLADIUS, On Husbandrie, pt. i. ed. Rev. B. Lodge, 10/-; ii. ed. S. J. Herrtage, 5/- [fr. MS. of ab. 1420] 8° E. Eng. Text Soc. (Tbnr.) 72; 79

Astronomy.

CHAUCER, Geoffrey Treatise on the Astrolabe, ed. Prf. W. W. Skeat [A.D. 1391] 10/- 8° E. Eng. Text Soc. (Tbnr.) 72

Books of Courtesy, etc.

CAXTON, William Book of Curtesye: three versions, ed. Dr. F. J. Furnivall 5/- 8° E. Eng. Text Soc. 68
" " Bk. of Ordre of Chyualry, ed. W. Bayne [about 1484] 8° " *in prep.*
Queene Elizabethes Achademy: a Book of Precedence, ed. Dr. F. J. Furnivall 13/- 8° " 69
Conts. essays on early Italian and German Books of Courtesy by W. M. ROSSETTI and Dr. E. OSWALD.

Chronicle.

CAPGRAVE, John Chronicle of England, ed. Rev. F. C. Hingeston 10/- r 8° Rolls Series 58
Valuable as a record of the language spoken in Norfolk in 15th century.

Deeds and Documents.

MORSBACH, Dr. Lorenz [ed.] Early English Deeds and Documents 8° E. Eng. Text Soc. *in prep.*
Gilds, English: their Statutes and Customs, ed. Toulmin Smith + Lucy T. Smith [A.D. 1389] 8° " " (Tbnr.) 70
Wills, The Fifty Earliest English, in the Court of Probate, ed. Dr. F. J. Furnivall [A.D. 1387–1439] 7/- 8° " " " 82

Devotional Manuals, etc.

BOETHIUS, De Consolatione Philosophiae: Chaucer's Tr. [A.D. 1321], ed. Dr. Rich. Morris 12/- 8° E. E. Text Soc. 68
Extracts ed. Wülker—*in his* Altenglische Lesebuch [*ut* K § 244].
Lay-Folks' Catechism [by Abp. THORESBY], ed. Can. Simmons + F. D. Matthew 8° " *in prep.*
" Mass-Book: 4 texts, ed. Can. Simmons 25/- 8° " 79
Legenda Aurea —*v.* K § 254, *s.v.* The Great Collections, F.

Language.

Catholicon Anglicum ed. S. J. Herrtage [an Eng.-Lat. word-bk., A.D. 1483] 20/- 8° E. Eng. Text Soc. (Tbnr.) 81
LEVINS, Peter Manipulus Vocabulorum: a rhyming dict., ed. H. B. Wheatley [1570] 12/- 8° " " " " 67
Orthographie and Congruitie of the Britan Tongue; ed. H. B. Wheatley [by Hume; about 1617] 4/- 8° " " " " 65

Lives of the Saints.

HORSTMANN, Dr. C. [ed.] Prose Lives of Woman Saints [about A.D. 1610] 12/- 8° E. Eng. Text Soc. (Tbnr.) 86

Manners.

Early English Meals and Manners, ed. fr. Harleian and other MSS., F. J. Furnivall 12/- 8° E. Eng. Text Soc. (Tbnr.) 68
The Babee's Book, Aristotle's A B C Urbanitatis, Stans Puer ad Mensam, etc.

Psalter.

HEREFORD, Nic. Translation of the Psalms [*etc.*], ed. Rev. J. Forshall + Sir W. Madden, re-ed. Prf. W. W. Skeat [A.D. 1380] 3/6 c 8° Clar. Press [50] 79
Single Psalms ed. Dr. R. Morris—*in his* Specimens, pt. ii. [*ut* K § 244].
A versified tr. fr. above edn. *sub tit. Paraphrase of the Seven Penitential Psalms*, *o.p.* p 8° Percy Soc. 42. *Selections* herefrom in WÜLCKER'S *Altengl. Lesb.* [*ut* K § 244].

Romances —*v.* K §§ 46, 47.

XXVIII. Romance Philology and Literature.

256. ROMANCE PHILOLOGY: GENERALLY.

Bibliography, Encyclopædia and Introduction.

Bibliographischer Anzeiger für romanische Sprachen und Literaturen, ed. E. Ebering [bi-monthly] *ann.* 12/- 8° *Leipzig* 83 *sqq. in prog.*

*GRÖBER, G. Grundriss der romanischen Philologie pt. i. 4/-; ii. 4/-; iii. 6/- 8° *Strassburg* 86; 87; 88

Very comprehensive, dealing with all parts of the study of Romance Philology.

Jahrbuch f. roman. u. engl. Spr. u. Litt. [*ut infra*]—*conts. bibliogrs.* 1858–1874.

*KÖRTING, G. Encyclopædie und Methodologie der romanischen Sprachen, i. 4/-, ii. 7/-, iii. 10/-; Indices 3/- 8° *Leipzig* 84; 84; 86; 88

MORF, H. Das Studium der romanischen Philologie 1/6 8° *Zürich* 90

NEUMANN, F. Die romanische Philologie [*repr. fr.* Schmid's Encycl. d. Erzieh.] 2/- 8° *Leipzig* 86

Zeitschrift für roman. Philologie [*ut infra*]—*conts. annually a survey of the Romance liter. of preceding year.*

Magazines and Serials.

Anzeiger, Bibliographischer, für romanische Sprachen u. Literaturen, ed. E. Ebering [bi-monthly] *ann.* 12/- 8° *Leipzig* 83 *sqq. in prog.*

Archiv für das Studium d. neueren Sprachen, vols. i.–lxxxv., hrsg. L. Herrig; since Oct., '89 J. Zupitza, ea. vol. [=4 pts.] 6/- 8° *Brunswick* 46–89 *in prog.*

Ausgaben und Abhandlungen aus d. Gebiete d. roman. Philol., hrsg. E. Stengel, pts. 1–79 [also separ.] £10 8/- 8° *Marburg* 80–88 *in prog.*

Giornale di Filologia Romanza, ed. E. Monaci, vols. i.–viii (?) 8° *Rome* 78 *sqq. in prog.*

Formerly [1872–1876] pub. at Imola *sub tit. Rivista di Filologia Romanza*, ed. MANZONI + MONACI + STENGEL.

Jahrbuch für romanische und englische Sprache u. Litt., v. i.–v., ed. A. Ebert; vi.–xii. and New Ser. i.–ii., ed. L. Lemcke ea. vol. [of 4 pts.] 12/- N. S. i.–ii. ea. 16/- 8° *Berl.* 59–71; *Lps.* 74–76 *not cont.*

Literaturblatt zur germanische und roman. Philologie, ed. O. Behaghel + F. Neumann [reviews of new books; monthly] *ann.* 10/- 4° *Heilbronn* 80 *in prog.*

Neuphilologische Studien, hrsg. G. Körting, pts. i.–v. [conts. Romance articles] 8/6 8° *Paderborn* 83–86 *in prog.*

Revue des Langues Romanes, par la Soc. pour l'étude des Langues Rom., vols. i.–xxxi. [monthly] 8° Montpelier 70–89 *in prog.*

Formerly pub. quarterly. Devoted chiefly to Modern Provençal, and of no great *general* interest.

*Romania, publ. Paul Meyer + Gaston Paris, vols. i.–xvii. [Index to vols. i.–x. 7/-] *ann.* 20/- m 8° *Paris* 72–89 *in prog.*

Romanische Forschungen, hrsg. K. Vollmöller, vols. i.–vii. *var. prices* 8° *Erlangen* 82–89 *in prog.*

Romanische Studien, hrsg., E. Boehmer, pts. i.–xxv. *var. prices* 8° *Bonn* 71–88 *sqq. in prog.*

Studij di Filologia Romanza, ed. E. Monaci 8° *Rome* 84 *sqq. in prog.*

*Zeitschrift für romanische Philologie, hrsg. G. Gröber, vols. i.–xiii. ea. vol. [of 4 pts.] 20/- 8° *Halle* 77–89 *in prog.*

History of the Romance Languages.

BRUCE-WHITE, A. Histoire des Langues Romanes et de leur Littér., 3 vols. 21/- r 8° *Paris* 41

Of no scientific value.

DIEZ, F. Kleinere Arbeiten und Recensionen, hrsg. Prf. H. Breymann; port. 6/- 8° *Munich* 83

LEWIS, Sir G. C. Essay on the Origin and Formation of the Romance Languages 7/6 8° Parker [35] 62

A poor compilation, based on good, bad, and indifferent authorities.

Relation of Romance to Latin—*v. also* K § 310.

SCHOLLE, F. Ueber d. Begriff "Tochtersprache" 2/- 8° *Berlin* 69

An excellent little work on the conception of "daughter-language" and its correct application to the Romance languages, espec. French.

Relation of Romance to Celtic.

THURNEYSEN, R. Keltoromanisches [the Celtic etymols. of Diez's Etym. W'bch.] 4/- 8° *Halle* 84

WINDISCH, Prf. E. —*article* Keltische Sprachen, *in* Gröber's Grundriss, pp. 283–312 [*ut supra*].

Grammar.

*DIEZ, F. Grammatik der romanischen Sprachen, hrsg. K. Vollmöller, 3 vols. ea. 8/-; *or* in 1 vol. 21/- 8° *Erlangen* [36–42] 75; 77; 87

The last (fourth) edn. has the *Romanische Wortschöpfung* as an appendix, first added to this edn. Includes all the Romance languages, excepting Rhæto-Romansch. Vol. i.: Intro. and Phonology; ii.: Accidence and Etymology; iii.: Syntax. The 3rd edn. [*Bonn* 70–72] contained numerous changes which are objected to by some scholars, who consider the 2nd. edn. [*Bonn* 1856–60] the best. The 4th edn. [*Bonn* 76–77] is a repr. of the 3rd., and the 5th edn. [in 1 vol., *Bonn* 82] has the vols. and pp. of the 4th in the margin. An Eng. tr. was pub. in 1863 [4/6 8° Williams] but it is next to worthless now.

" " Grammaire des langues Romanes, trad. A. Brachet + A. M. Fatio + G. Paris, 3 vols. 34/- 8° *Paris*

*MEYER-LÜBKE, W. Grammatik der romanischen Sprache

" " Grammaire de la langue Romane [trad.] 8° *Paris* 90

NOTLEY, E. A. Comparative Grammar of French, Italian, Spanish, and Portuguese [not much use] 7/6 obl. 8° Trübner 68

Phonology.

BOEHMER, E. Klang, nicht Dauer—*in* Roman. Studien, vols. iii.–iv. [*ut supra*].

ten BRINK, B. Dauer und Klang [called forth by Boehmer, *ut supra*] 1/6 8° *Strassburg* 79

BRACHET, A. Rôle d. Voyelles latins atones d. l. langs. romanes 8° *Paris* 66

HORNING, A. Zur Geschichte des lateinischen *C* vor *e* und *i* im Romanischen 4/- 8° *Halle* 83

JORET, C. Du *C* dans les Langues Romanes 10/- 8° *Paris* 74

K § 257

Etymology.

CAIX, N. Studi di Etimologia Ital. e Romanza [crit. of and addns. to Diez's *W'buch*] 8° *Florence* 78
DIEZ, Fr. Romanische Wortschöpfung [a suppl. to his *Gramm.*]. 8° *Bonn* 75
DIEZ'S last work, written in his 81st year and one year before his death. Of no great value.
EGGER, E. Les Substantifs Verbaux formés p. l'apocope de l'infinitif, *etc.* 8° *Paris* 75
MAHN, A. Etymol. Untersuch. a. d. Gebiete d. roman. Philol., spec. 1–24 [chfly. Fch.] 8° *Berlin* 53-76
MICHAELIS, Fräul. C. Studien zur romanischen Wortschöpfung [chfly. Span. and Portug.] 4/- 8° *Leipzig* 76
MIRISCH, M. Geschichte d. Suffixes *-olus* in d. roman. Sprachen [dissert.] 2/- 8° *Bonn* 82
*OSTHOFF, H. Das Verbum in d. Nominalcomposition in Deut., Griech., Slav., Roman. 11/6 8° *Jena* 78

Compound Words —*v.* K § 270, *s.v.* Compound Words (*DARMESTETER, MEUNIER).

Dictionaries.

*DIEZ, F. Etymologisches Wörterbuch der romanischen Sprachen, hrsg. A. Scheler 18/- 8° *Erlangen* [53] 87
Jarnick, J. V. Index zu Diez's Etymolog. Wörterbuch 3/- 8° *Berlin* 78
An Eng. tr. of above was made by J. C. DONKIN in 1864 [15/- 8° Williams] and a French by Gaston PARIS in 1863 [8° *Paris*]; but both are superseded by the new edn. of the original. *Vide also* CAIX, *supra.*
KÖRTING, Gustav Lateinisch-Romanisches Wörterbuch, pts. i.–iii. ea. 2/- 8° 90 *in prog.*

Accidence.

Verb.

FOTH, Karl Verschiebung d. latein. Tempora in d. rom. Sprachen [Rom. Stud. viii.] 2/- 8° *Strassburg* 76
FUCHS, A. Die unregelmässigen Verben in den romanischen Sprachen *o.p.* 8° *Halle* 40
*TOBLER, A. Darstellung d. latein. Conjugation u. ihrer roman. Gestaltung 8° *Zürich* 57

Participle.

ULRICH, J. Die formelle Entwickelung d. Partic. Präteriti in d. roman. Sprachen *Halle* 79

Tense.

MUSSAFIA, A. Zur Präsensbildung im Romanischen *fr.* Abhandl. Wien. Akad.] 1/6 8° *Vienna* 83

Noun.

Gender.

*MEYER, W. Die Schicksale d. lateinischen Neutrums im Romanischen 4/- 8° *Halle* 83

History of Romance Philology.

DIEZ, Fr. [1794–1876]
Breymann, Prf. H. Fr. Diez: sein Leben, seine Werke u. ihre Bedeutung [an address] 1/- 8° *Munich* 78
Sachs, K. Diez und die romanische Philologie [lecture] 1/- 8° *Berlin* 78
Stengel, E. Erinnerungsworte an Fr. Diez [an extended address] 1/6 8° *Marburg* 83
GRÖBER, G. —*in his* Grundriss [*ut supra*].
KÖRTING, G. Geschichte der romanischen Philologie *in prep.*
MEYER, Paul Report on the Philol. of Rom. Langs. dur. last few years—*in* Proc. Philol. Soc. 1873–74 [*ut* K § 95].
STENGEL, E. Report on the Philol. of Rom. Langs.—*in same* 1874–75 *sqq.*
" " Beiträge zur Geschichte der romanischen Philologie in Deutschland [Ausg. u. Abh. lxiii.] 1/6 8° *Marbg.* 86

Collected Essays.

BARTSCH, Karl Gesammelte Vorträge und Aufsätze 8/- 8° *Freiburg* 83
SCHUCHARDT, Prf. Hugo Romanisches und Keltisches [collection of miscell. essays] 7/6 8° *Berlin* 86

257. MODERN ITALIAN PHILOLOGY (*a*): GRAMMAR, &c.

Introduction and Bibliography.

BREITINGER, H. Das Studium des Italienischen 3/6 8° *Zürich* 79

History of the Language.

*CAIX, N. Le Origini della Lingua Poetica Italiana 8° *Florence* 80
" " La Formazione degli idiomi litterari [*repr. fr.* Nuova Antologia] 8° " 74
DEMATTIO, F. Origine, Formazione ed Elementi della Lingua Italiana 2/- 8° *Innsbruck* [ ] 78
MAHN, A. Ueb. d. Entstehung d. ital. Spr. aus d. lat., griech., deut. u. kelt. Elem. 1/- 8° *Berlin* 81
MORANDI, Luigi Origine della Lingua Italiana 8° *Città di Castello* 83
v. REINHARDSTÖTTNER, C. Die italienische Sprache: ihre Entstehung aus d. Latein, *etc.* 8° *Halle* 69
TOSELLI, Origine della Lingua Italiana, 3 vols. [w. Gallo-Italic dict.] 8° *Bologna* 81

Grammar.

BARAGIOLA, A. Italienische Grammatik [w. refer. to Lat. and Rom. langs.] 5/- 8° *Strassburg* 80
DANTE, Alighieri [1265–1321] De Vulgari Eloquentia—*in his* Opere Latine, ed. Giuliani, vol. i. 8° *Florence* 78
Böhmer, E. Ueber Dante's Schrift *De Vulgari Eloquentia* 1/- 8° *Halle* 68
d'Ovidio, F. —*in* Archivio Glottologico, vol. ii., pp. 59 *sqq.* [*ut* K § 256].
*MEYER-LÜBKE, W. Italienische Grammatik 12/- 8° *Leipzig* 90
MUSSAFIA, A. Italienische Sprachlehre in Regeln u. Beispielen [a good bk.] 4/- 8° *Vienna* [60] 88
v. REINHARDSTÖTTNER, C. Theoretisch-practische Grammatik d. italienischen Sprache 3/- 8° *Munich* [ ] 80
SAUER, C. M. Italian Conversation Grammar [Key, 2/-; Otto's system] 5/6 c 8° *Heidelbg.* (Dulau) [6-] 79
VOCKERADT, H. Lehrbuch d. ital. Gramm., i. [Gram.], 6/-; ii. [Reader] 5/- [espec. good in syntax] 8° *Berlin* 78; 78

Phonology.

BAMBELLI, R. R. Studj filologico-crit. sulle lettere dell' Alfabeto Italiano 8° *Rome* 66
CAIX, N. Osservazione sul Vocalismo Italiano [*extr. fr.* Rivista Europaea] 8° *Florence* 75

Etymology.

*CAIX, N.	Studi di Etimologia Italiana e Romanza		8° *Florence*	78

Dictionaries.

Academia della Crusca	Vocabolario della Lingua Italiana, vols. i.–v.		r 8° *Florence* [1612] 63–85	*in prog.*
FANFANI, P.	Il Vocabolario Novello della Crusca		8° *Florence*	77
BARETTI, J.	Ital.-Eng. & Eng.-Ital. Dict., ed. J. Davenport + E. Comelati, 2 vols.	21/–	8° Simpkin	[ ] 77
FANFANI,	Vocabolario della lingua italiana		8° *Florence*	[ ] 82
JAMES + GRASSI, W. G.	Dictionary of English and Italian Languages	[both parts] 5/– s	8° *Leipzig*	[54] 84
MELZI, B.	Nuovo Vocab. Universale della Ling. Ital. [combined dict. & cyclo.; *very* cheap]	7/–	8° *Turin*	80
MICHAELIS, H.	Vollständiges Wörterbuch d. ital. u. deutschen Sprachen	[both pts.] ea. 6/–	8° *Leipzig*	[79] 85
	Good for technological words and phrases.			
MILLHOUSE, J.	New English and Italian Pronouncing Dictionary, 2 vols.	[both parts] 12/– sq	8° Hirschfeld	[5–] 89
*PETROCHI, P.	Novo Dizionario universale della lingua italiana		8° *Milan* 85 *sqq.*	*in prog.*
	Includes also, in a separate section, Old-Italian.			
*RIGUTINI + FANFANI	Vocabolario Italiano della Lingua Parlata	[1775 pp.] 20/–	8° *Florence*	[ ] 83
	An excellent and very cheap book.			
*TOMMASEO, N.	Dizionario della Lingua Italiana, 4 vols.	£15	4° *Rome*	65–79
ZAMBALDI, Fr.	Vocabolario Etimologico Italiano	6/6	8° *Turin*	89

Loan Words.

ALLARIO, C.	I principali Francesismi da evitarsi nella ling. parl. e scritta		8° *Turin*	79
CENTONZA, R.	I più comuni Vocaboli e modi errati della ling. Ital.		8° *Naples*	79
GATTA, M.	Dizionario Etimologico delle Voci di Orig. Greca più usitate		8° *Milan*	67
NARDUCCI, E.	Saggio di Voci Ital. derivate dall' Arabo		8° *Rome*	61

Synonyms.

FANFANI, P.	Nuovo Vocabolario dei Sinonimi della Lingua Italiana	[schl.-bk.] s	8° *Milan*	79
FISCHER,	Streifzüge in das Gebiet der italienischen Synonymik	[schl.-progr.]	*Magdeburg*	81
GRASSI, G.	Saggio intorno ai Sinonimi della lingua Italiana		8° *Turin*	[21] 79
MESCHIA, A.	Dei Sinonimi della Lingua Italiana		8° *Foligno*	[ ] 78
*TOMMASEO, N.	Dizionario dei Sinonimi della Lingua Italiana		8° *Milan*	[35] 67

Accidence.

DEMATTIO, F.	Morfologia Italiana	2/–	8° *Innsbruck*	76

Verb.

COMPAGNONI,	Teorica dei Verbi Italiani, ed. P. Fanfani		8° *Florence*	65

Noun.

d'OVIDIO, Fr.	Sull' Origine dell' unica forma fless. del nome ital.		8° *Pisa*	72

Syntax.

DEMATTIO, F.	Sintassi della Lingua Italiana	2/–	8° *Innsbruck*	72
FORNACIARI, R.	Sintassi Ital. del uso moderno		*Florence*	81
PESAMENTO,	Sintassi comparativa del Latino e dell' Italiano		"	67

Verb.

GÜTH, A.	Lehre vom Conjunctiv mit Anwendung auf d. ital. Sprache	1/–	8° *Berlin*	76

Pronoun.

KNUTH, O.	Sull' Uso del Pronome Personale delle Ling. Franc. ed Ital.	1/–	8° *Dressen*	78

Prosody and Metrics.

KURZWEIL, E.	Traité de la Prosodie de la Langue Italienne		8° *Paris*	64
PICCI, G.	Compendio della Guida allo studio delle belle lettere		8° *Milan*	[ ] 65
SCHUCHARDT, Prf. H.	—*in his* Ritornell und Terzine	8/–	8° *Halle*	74
ZAMBALDI,	Il Ritmo dei Versi Italiani		8° *Turin*	74

Chrestomathies and Collections.

d'ANCONA + COMPARETTI, A. D. [eds.]	Le Antiche Rime Volgare sec. Cod. Vat. 3793, vols. i.–iv.		8° *Bologna*	73–86
BARAGIOLA, A. [ed.]	Crestomazia Italiana Ortofonica	[incl. also dialects] 7/–	8° *Strassburg*	81
BARTOLI, [ed.]	Crestomazia della Poesia Ital. del periodo delle origini		8° *Turin*	82
Collezione di Opere inedite e rare dei primi tre secol. d. ling. ital.			8° *Bologna* 63 *sqq.*	*in prog.*
	Pub. by the R. Commissione pe' testi di lingua.			
" di Operette inedite o rare			8° *Florence* 82 *sqq.*	*in prog.*
EBERT, A. [ed.]	Handbuch d. ital. Nationallitteratur		8° *Frankfort*	[54] 74
MONACI, E. [ed.]	Crestomazia Italiana dei primi secoli		8° 89	*in prog.*
NANNUCCI, V. [ed.]	Manuale della Lett. del primo secolo d. ling. ital., 2 vols.		8° *Florence*	[ ] 74
Scelta di Curiosità letter. inedite o rare del sec. xiii.-xvii.			8° *Bologna* 61 *sqq.*	*in prog.*
TALLARIGO + IMBRIANI, C. V. [eds.]	Nuova Crestomazia Italiana, vol. i.	[to occupy 3 vols.]	8° *Naples*	82
TOZZETTI, O. T. [ed.]	Antologia della Poesia Italiana		8° *Livorno*	83
ULRICH, J. [ed].	Altitalienisches Lesebuch	[of no great value] 3/–	8° *Halle*	86

258. MODERN ITALIAN PHILOLOGY (*b*): DIALECTS.

Generally.

ARBOIT, A. Dei dialetti Italiani 8° *Parma* 80
*ASCOLI, G. J. —*article* Italian Dialects—*in* Encyclo. Brit., vol. xiii. 30/- 4° Black 82
CAIX, N. —*in his* Origine, *ut* K § 257: Italian Philology (*a*).
" " Saggio sulla Storia della ling. ital. e dei dialetti ital. 8° *Parma* 72
With an introduction on the origin of Neo-Latin.
MUSSAFIA, A. Beitrag zur Kunde d. nordital. Mundarten im 15 Jahrh. [*repr. fr.* Denkschr. Wien. Akad.] 6/6 4° *Vienna* 73
RAJNA, P. On the Dialects of Italy—*in* Eighth Annual Address to Philolog. Soc. 8° Trübner

Magazine.

Archivio Glottologico Italiano, ed. G. J. Ascoli, vols. i.–xi. [almost entirely on dialects] 8° *Rome* 73 *sqq. in prog.*

Specimens.

BIONDELLI [ed.] I Dialetti Gallo-Italici [Lomb., Piedm., Emilian.] 8° *Milan* 53
PAPANTI [ed.] I Parlari Ital. in Certaldo alla festa del centenario di Boccaccio *Livorno* 75
Gives the 9th novel of the first day of the *Decameron* in several hundred Ital. dialects.
ZUCCAGNI-ORLANDINI, [ed.] Raccolta dei Dialetti Ital. con illustr. etnologiche 8° *Florence* 44

Folk-Literature —*v.* B § 17: Italian Folklore.

Abruzzi.

FINAMORE, G. Vocabolario dell' Uso Abruzzese 8° *Milan* 80

Bergamo.

TIRABOSCHI, A. Vocabolario dei Dialetti Bergam., 18/-; Append. vol. i. 8/- 8° *Turin* 73; *Bergamo* 79

Bologna.

CORONEDI-BERTI, C. Vocabolario Bolognese-Italiano, 2 vols. 54/- 8° *Bologna* 69: 74
GAUDENZI, A. I Suoni: le forme, etc. dell' odierno dial. di Bologna 6/6 8° *Turin* 90

Brescia.

ROSA, G. Vocabolario Bresciano-Italiano 8° *Brescia* 78

Como.

MONTI, P. Vocabolario dei Dialetti di Como 12/- r 8° *Milan* 45

Ferrara.

FERRI, L. Vocabolario Ferrarese-Italiano 5/- 8° *Ferrara* 90

Florence.

ARLÍA, Linguaggio degli Artigiani Fiorentini 8° *Florence* 76
FRIZZI, Gius. Dizionario dei frizzetti popolari Fiorentini 2/6 8° *Città di Castello* 90
GARGIOLLI, Il Parlare degli Artigiani di Firenze 8° *Florence* 76
GIACHI, P. Dizionario del Vernacolo Fiorentino, *etc.* 8° " 78

Judikarian (border-land of Lombard and Venet. dialects).

GARTNER, Th. Die Judikarische Mundart [*extr. fr.* Sitzber. Wien. Akad.] 2/- 8° *Vienna* 82

Lombardy.

MEYER, Carl Sprache und Sprachdenkmäler der Longobarden [sources, gramm., gloss.] 4/6 8° *Paderborn* 77

Mentone.

ANDREWS, Essai de Grammaire du Dialecte Mentonais 8° *Nice* 75

Milan.

BANFI, G. Vocabolario Italiano-Milanese 8° *Milan* [ ] 70
CHERUBINI, Fr. Vocabolario Milanese-Italiano, 4 vols. and Suppl. 40/- 8° " 56–61
MUSSAFIA, A. Darstellung d. altmail. Mundart nach Bonvesin's Schriften [13 cent.] [extr.] 1/- r 8° *Vienna* 68
SALVIONI, Fonetica del Dialetto Moderno della città di Milano 8° *Turin* 84

Mirandola.

MESCHIERI, E. Vocabolario Mirandolese-Italiano 8° *Bologna* 76

Naples.

de AMBRA, R. Vocabolario Napol.-Italiano 8° *Naples* 73
MACHT, C. Der Neap. Dialekt theoret. u. prakt. erläutert [schl.-progr.] 2/- 8° *Hof* 78
ROCCO, E. Vocabolario del dialetto Napolitano 8° *Naples* 82

Otranto.

MOROSI, G. Studj sui Dialetti della Terra d'Otranto 8° *Lecce* 69

Parma.

MALASPINA, C. Vocabolario Parmigiano-Ital., 4 vols. 8° *Parma* 56–59
" " Aggiunte al Vocabolario Parmigiano-Italiano 8° " 80

Pavia.

GAMBINI, C. Vocabolario Pavese-Italiano 8° *Milan* 79

Piedmont.

del Pozzo Glossario Etimologico Piemontese 5/- 8° *Turin* 88
di SANT' ALBINO, V. Gran Dizionario Piemontese-Italiano 25/- 4° „ 59

Romagna.

MATTIOLI, A. Vocabolario Romagnolo-Italiano 8° *Imola* 79
MUSSAFIA, A. Darstellung der romagnolischen Mundart [extract] 1/- r 8° *Vienna* 71

Sardinia.

DELIUS, N. Der sardinische Dialect des 13 Jahrhunderts 1/- 8° *Bonn* 68
HOFMANN, G. Die logudoresische und campidanesische Mundart [dissert.] 1/6 8° *Marburg* 85
*SPANO, G. Ortografia Sarda nazionale 8° *Cagliari* 40
* „ Vocabolario Sardo-Ital. et Ital.-Sardo, 2 vols. 8° „ 51; 52

Sicily.

AVOLIO, C. Introduzione allo Studio del Dial. Siciliano 8° *Moto* 82
BIUNDI, G. Dizionario Siciliano-Italiano 6/- 12° *Palermo* 57
HÜLLEN, Vocalismus des Alt- und Neu-Sicilianischen [dissert.] 1/6 8° *Bonn* 84
MORTILLARIO, V. Nuovo Dizionario Siciliano-Italiano 24/- 4° *Palermo* [38] 79
VIGO, L. [ed.] Raccolta amplias. di Canti popolari Siciliani 12/- r 8° *Catania* [ ] 70-74
Contains 6000 songs. The *Prolegomini* [150 pp.] conts. a full bibliography of Sicilian dialects.
WENTRUP, Beiträge zur Kenntniss des sicilianischen Dialectes 8° *Halle* 80

Tuscany.

FANFANI, P. Vocabolario dell' Uso Toscano, 2 vols. 9/- 12° *Florence* 63

Venice.

BOERIO, G. Dizionario del Dialetto Veneziano 34/- 4° *Venice* 61

259. ROUMANIAN (WALLACHIAN) PHILOLOGY.

Ethnography (Linguistic).

CANTIMIR, Descriptio Moldaviæ 8° *Bucharest* 72
DIEFENBACH, Lor. Völkerkunde Ost-Europa's, insbes. Hämushalbinsel u. untere Donaugeb., 2 v. 15/- 8° *Darmstadt* 80
„ „ Die Volkerstämme der europäischen Türkei 2/6 8° *Frankfort* 77
HOMFALOY, P. Le Peuple Roumain ou Valaque 8° *Tours* 81
JUNG, S. Römer und Romanen in den Donauländern *Innsbruck* 77
*KANITZ, F. Donaubulgarien und der Balkan, 3 vols.; 20 pl. & 383 ill. [travels, 1860-1876] 40/- r 8° *Leipzig* [76-79] 82-83
NYROP, K. Romanske Mosaiker 8° *Copenhagen* 85
PIC, J. L. Ueber die Abstammung der Rumänen 5/- 8° *Leipzig* 80
*PICOT, E. Les Roumains de la Macédoine 8° *Paris* 75
RÖSLER, Robert Romänische Studien: Beitr. z. älteren Gesch. Romäniens 8/6 8° *Leipzig* 71

History of the Language.

*HASDEU [*or* HÂJDEU] Cuvente den bătrâni, 2 vols. and Supplement 8° *Bucharest* 78; 79; 8-
PASCUTIU Origin' a Româilor si latinitâteă limbei Române 8° *Arad.* 81

General Philology.

KOPITAR, Kleinere Schriften, hrsg. F. Miklosich *Vienna* 75
*MIKLOSICH+IVE, E. Rumänische Untersuchungen—*in* Denkschriften d. Wien. Akad., vol. xxxii. [1882].
TITKIN, H. Studien zur rumänischen Philologie, pt. i. 3/- 8° *Leipzig* 84

Grammar.

CIPARIU, T. Gram. Limb. Roman., v. i. [Analitica], ii. [Sintetica] [pubn. of Acad. Soc of Buch.] 8° *Bucharest* 70; 77
„ „ Principii de Limbă si de Scriptură 8° *Blasiu* 64
JARNIK, U. Sprachliches aus rumänischen Volksmärchen [schl.-progr.] *Vienna* 77
MASSIMU, J. Practische Grammatik d. rom. Sprache (Ollendorf's method) *Hermannstadt* [71]
MIRCESCO, V. Grammaire de la Langue Romaine 3/6 12° *Paris* 63
PUMNUL, A. Grammatik der rumänischen Sprache, ed. Isopescul 2/6 8° *Czernowitz* [64] 82
STRAJAN Manuel de Gramm. Limb. Roman. 8° *Bucharest* 81
TORCEANU, R. Grammar of the Roumanian Language [Simplified Grammars Series] 5/- p 8° Trübner 83
WOITKO, B. Grammatik der romanischen Sprache 4/- 8° *Vienna* 83

Phonology.

GASTER, M. Zur rumänischen Lautgeschichte: die Gutturalen [*repr. fr.* Zeitschr. f. rom. Phil.] 2/- 8° *Halle* 78
*MIKLOSICH, F. Beiträge zur Lautlehre rumän. Dialekte, pts. i.-v. [*repr. fr.* Sitgsb. Wien. Akad.] 5/6 8° *Vienna* 81-83
TITKIN, H. —*ut supra.*

K § 280

Orthography.

FROLLO, G. L. — O noŭa incercare de solutiune a problemului ortograficu — 8° *Bucharest* 75
MAIORESCU, — Despre scrierea limbei rum. — 8° *Jassi* 66
SCHUCHARDT, Prf. H. — De l'Orthographie du Roumain—*in* Romania, vol. ii. [*ut* K § 256].

Etymology.

Dictionaries.

BARCIANU, S. P. — Wörterb.d.román.u.deut.Sprache[i. Roum.-Germ.] 5/-; ii. [Germ.-Roum.] 8/- 12° *Hermannst.*[68]86; 88
FROLLO, — Dizionario Rumeno-Italiano-Francese — 8° *Pesth* 75
FRUNDESCU, — Dictionariu Topograficu si Statisticu alu României — *Bucharest* 72
An excellent and very useful book for ethnographical and linguistic studies.
*HASDEU, — Etymologicum magnum Romaniæ, pts. i. *sqq.* [a very important wk.] 8° ,, 85 *sqq. in prog.*
*LAURIANU+MASSIMU, A. T. / J. C. Dictionariulu limbei romane, 2 vols. ,, 76; 79
de PONTBRIANT, R. — Dictionaru Romano-Franscescu 15/- 8° ,, 62

Loan Words.

*de CIHAC, A. — Dictionnaire d'Etymologie Daco-Romane, 2 vols. 28/- 8° *Frankfort* 70; 79
Vol. i.: Latin elements, 8/-; vol. ii.: Slav, Magyar, Turkish, Modern Greek, and Albanian elements, 20/-.
MIKLOSICH, F. — Die slavischen Elemente im Rumänischen—*in* Denkschr. d. Wien. Akad., vol. xii. [1862].

Syntax.

CIPARIU, T. — Suppliment la Sintactică: Despre limba română — 8° *Blasiu* 77
STOICESCU+CALINESCU — Manual de Sintaxa Română — 8° *Bucharest* 79

Chrestomathy.

CIPARIU, T. [ed.] — Crestomazia sau analecte literare — 8° *Blasiu* 58
PICOT, Emile [ed.] — Documents p. servir à l'étude des dialectes Roumains — 8° *Paris* 73
POPU, ? [ed.] — Conspect asupra literaturei române, 2 vols. — 8° *Bucharest* 75; 76

History of the Literature.

CIPARIU, T. — *in his* Crestom. [*ut sup.*] *gives a good sketch of devel. of Rouman. literature.*
,, ,, — *in his* Principii [*ut sup.*] *gives a bibliogr. of old-Rouman. literature.*
DENSUSIANU, — Istoria limbei si literaturei române — 8° *Jassi* 85
GASTER, M. — Literatura pupulara romána — 8° *Bucharest* 83
POPPIU, — Poeiĭ si Prosă, 2 vols.—*conts. brief notes on the liter. of end 18 cent.* 8° *Libenburg* 68 *sqq.*
Short biographical and bibliographical sketches, with specimens of writings.

260. RHÆTO-ROMANIAN.

Ethnography (Linguistic).

ALTON, I. — Beiträge zur Ethnologie von Ostladinien — 8° *Innsbruck* 80
BIDERMANN, J. — Die Romanen und ihre Verbreitung in Oesterreich — *Graz* 77
,, ,, — Die Italiener im tiroler Provinzialverbande — *Innsbruck* 74
BUDINSKY, A. — Ausbreitung d. lat. Sprache üb. Ital. u. d. Provinzen d. röm. Reichs — *Berlin* 81
*v. CZÖRNIG, C. — Die alten Völker Oberitaliens: eine ethnographische Skizze — *Vienna* 85
GARTNER, Th. — *in his* Grammatik, *ut infra.*
KÄMMEL, O. — Die Entstehung des österreichischen Deutschthums, vol. i. — *Leipzig* 79
PLANTA, — Das alte Rätien staatlich u. kulturhist. dargestellt; 2 pl. 14/- r 8° *Berlin* 72

History of the Language.

ANDEER, Justus — Ueber Ursprung und Geschichte d. räto-romanischen Sprache 2/- 8° *Chur* 62
RUFINATSCHA, P. — Ueber Ursprung und Wesen d. roman. Sprache [schl-progr.] *Meran* 53

Grammar.

ANDEER, Justus — Rätoromanische Elementargrammatik 3/- 8° *Zürich* 80
*ASCOLI, G. J. — Saggi Ladini—*in* Archivio Glott. Ital., vol. i.; Saggio di Morfol. e Lessicolog. Soprasilvan. *ib.* vol. vii.
*GARTNER, Th. — Rätoromanische Grammatik [Sammlung romanischer Grammatiken] 5/- 8° *Heilbronn* 83
A very valuable and comprehensive work, probably the most important hitherto written on Rhæto-Romanian lang.

Phonology

—*v. also* ASCOLI, *ut supra*, GARTNER *and* ALTON, *ut infra.*
SCHUCHARDT, Prf. H. — Ueber einige Fälle bedingten Lautwandels im Churwälschen [diss.] 1/- 8° *Gotha* 70
STENGEL, E. — Vocalismus des lat. Elementes in d. Dial. v. Graubünden u. Tirol [diss.] 1/6 8° *Bonn* 68

Orthography and Pronunciation.

CARIGIET, B. — Ortografia gienerala speculativa Ramontscha — 8° *Dissentis* 58
PALLIOPPI, Z. — Ortografia ed Ortoëpia del idiom Romauntsch d'Engiadin'ota 1/6 16° *Chur* 57

Etymology.

Dictionaries.

CARIGIET, B. — Räto-romanisches Wörterbuch: Surselvisch-deutsch 6/- 8° *Bonn* 82
CARISCH, O. — Taschen-Wörterbuch d. rhätoromanischen Sprache in Graubünden 5/- 12° *Chur* [48-52] 87

Loan Words.

MISCHI, J. — Deutsche Worte im Ladinischen [school-programme] 1/6 8° *Brixen* 82

Chrestomathy.

DECURTINS, C. [ed.] Rhätoromanische Chrestomathie, vol. i., part i. 8/- 8° *Erlangen* 88 *in prog.*

ULRICH, J. [ed.] Rätoromanische Chrestomathie, 2 pts., 11/-: pt. i., 5/-; ii., 6/- [texts, notes, gloss.] 8° *Halle* 82; 83

" " [ed.] Rätoromanische Texte, pt. i., 4/-; ii. 4/- 8° *Halle* 83; 84
i.: Vier Nidwaldische Texte, 4/-; ii.: BIFRUN'S tr. of New Testament: (Intro., Matthew, Mark).

Accidence.

CARISCH, O. Grammatische Formenlehre d. deutsch. u. räto-rom. Sprache [schl.-bk.] 3/- 8° *Chur* 52

Verb.

STÜRZINGER, J. Ueber die Conjugation im Räto-Romanischen [dissert.] 2/- 8° *Winterthur* 79

Literature.

BÖHMER, E. Verzeichniss d. räto-roman. Litteratur—*in* Romanische Studien, vol. vi. ['83—*v.* K § 256].

RAUSCH, F. Geschichte der Literatur des räto-romanischen Volkes [untrustworthy] 3/- 8° *Frankfort* 70

SCHNELLER, Chr. Ueb. d. volksmündl. Liter. d. Romanen in Tirol [sch.-progr.] 2/- 8° *Innsbruck* 69

Dialects.

*ALTON, J. Die ladinischen Idiome in Ladinien, Gröden, Fassa, *etc.* 6/- 8° *Innsbruck* 79

MARTINEAU, Russell Romonsch Lang. in the Grisons and Tirol—*in* Tracts. Philol. Soc. 1880–81, pt. 3 [*vi.* K § 95].

MITTERRUTZNER, J. C. Die rätoladinischen Dialecte in Tirol u. ihre Lautbezeichnung *o.p.* 8° *Brixen* 56

ROSENKRANTZ, Rhaetoromanska Språkets Dialekter 8° *Upsala* 53

*SCHNELLER, Chr. Roman. Volksmundarten in Südtirol etym. u. gramm. dargestellt, vol. i. 6/- 8° *Gera* 70

Gredner Dialect.

GARTNER, Th. Die Gredner Mundart 11/- 4° *Linz* 79

Sulzberg Dialect.

GARTNER, Th. Sulzberger Wörter [repr. of a schl.-progr.] 2/- 8° *Leipzig* 83

261. SPANISH PHILOLOGY.

Grammar.

FOERSTER, P. Spanische Sprachlehre 10/- 8° *Berlin* 80

FRANCESON, C. F. Grammatik der spanischen Sprache 8° " [22] 82

HARVEY, W. F. Simplified Grammar of the Spanish Language [Simplified Grammars Ser.] 3/6 c 8° Trübner 90

HARTZENBUSCH + LEMMING, Practical Guide to Spanish Conversation 5/- c 8° " [ ] 77

KNAPP, Prf. W. I. [Am.] Grammar of the Modern Spanish Language $1.15 12° *Boston* 8-

d'OVIDIO, F. Kurzgefasste spanische Grammatik 8° *Naples* 79

SAUER, C. M. Spanish Conversation Grammar [Key, 2/-] 5/- 8° *Heidelberg* [70] 88

SCHILLING, J. Spanische Grammatik, 4/- Key 1/6 8° *Leipzig* [82] 86; [83] 87

VELASQUEZ + SIMONNÉ, M./T. Method of Learning to Read, Write and Speak Spanish [Key, 4/-] 6/- c 8° Trübner [75] 80

WIGGERS, J. Grammatik der Spanischen Sprache [w. a good syntax] 4/6 8° *Leipzig* [60] 84

Etymology.

Lexicography.

MICHAELIS, Carolina —*in her* Studien zur romanischen Wortschöpfung [espec. Spanish & Port.] 4/- 8° *Leipzig* 76

Dictionaries.

Academia Española Diccionario de la Lengua Castellana 8° *Madrid* [1726–39] 84

BOOCH-ARKOSSY, F. Spanish-Deutsches und Deutsch-Spanisches Handwörterbuch, 2 vols. 12/- 8° *Leipzig* [ ] 87

CALANDRELLI, M. Diccion. Filol. Comparado de la Lengua Castellana, vols. i.–v. ea. 10/- r 8° *Buenos Ayres* 80–83 *in prog.*

COVARRUVIAS, Tresoro de la Lengua Castellana [etymological] 8° *Madrid* 74

*CUERVO, R. J. Diccionario de Construction y Regimen de la Lengua Castellana, vols. i.–ii. 8° *Paris* 84; 88

de EGUILAZ Y YANGUAS, L. Glosario etimológico de las palabras españolas 21/- r 8° *Granada* 86

FRANCESON, C. F. Spanisch-Deutsches und Deutsch-Spanisches Wörterbuch, 2 pts. ea. 6/-; in 1 v. 6/- 8° *Leipzig* [49] 84

LOPEZ + BENSLEY, J. M./E. R. New Dictionary of Spanish and English Languages [both parts] 16/- r 8° *Paris* 78

NEUMAN + BARETTI, J. Dictionary of the Spanish and English Langs., ed. Sevane, 2 vols. 28/- 8° Dulau [2-] 74

SALVA, Diccionario de la lengua castellana 8° *Paris* [ ] 57

" Novisimo Diccionario de la lengua castellana 8° " 78

TOLHAUSEN, Louis Spanisch-deutsches und deutsch-spanisches Wörterbuch, 2 vols. 15/- i 8° *Leipzig* 86–89

VELASQUEZ, M. Pronouncing Dictionary of Spanish and Eng. Langs., ed. Cadena, 2 vols. 24/- r 8° Hirschfeld [73] 89

" " Dictionary of the Spanish and English Langs.; Abridged Edn. 6/- c 8° Trübner [78] 89

Loan Words.

*DOZY + ENGELMANN, R. P./W. H. Glossaire des Mots Espagnols et Portug. derivés de l'Arabe 10/6 8° *Leyden* [62] 69

LOPEZ, J. F. Filologia Etymol. y Filosof. de las Palabras Griegas d. l. leng. Cast. 8° *Paris* [ ] 84

Idioms.

BECKER + MORA, Sarah C. [Am.]/Frederico Spanish Idioms: with their English equivalents [ab. 10,000 phrases] $2 8° *Boston* 87

K § 262

Prosody.

TRACIA, Diccionario de la Rima 8° *Barcelona* 58

Chrestomathy.

BAIST + MORF, [eds.] Altspanische Chrestomathie *in prep.*
VELASQUEZ + SIMONNEI, M. + T. New Spanish Reader : prose and verse, ed. Cadena 6/- c 8° Trübner 80.

Dialects.

Aragon.

BORAO, G. Diccionario de Voces Aragonesas 8° *Saragossa* 59

Bascongado.

de SALCEDO, P. N. Diccionario Etimologico del Idioma Bascongado, pts. i.–? [to comprize about 50 pts.] ea. 1/6 8° *Leipzig* 87 *sqq. in prog.*

Basque —*v.* K § 140 : Basque Philology.

Bogotan [NEW GRANADA].

CUERVO, R. J. Apuntaciones Criticas sobre el Lenguage Bogotano 8° *Chartres* [76] 85

Creolese.

SCHUCHARDT, Prf. H. Creolische Studien, pt. iv. : Das Malaiospanische d. Philippinen [*v.* K § 161] 1/- 8° *Vienna* 83

Gallega.

MARGUIA, Man. Diccionario de Escritos Gallegas [w. an anthology] 8° *Vigo* 64
SACO ARCE, A. Gramatica Gallega 8° *Lugo* 68

Nalmatl-Spanish (NICARAGUA).

BRINTON, Prf. D. G. [Am. ; ed.] The Güergüence : a comedy ballet : text and tr. ; w. intro. and notes [Lib. Abor. Lit.] $2 12° *Philadelphia* 84

Old Leonese.

GESSNER, Das Altleonesische : Beitrag zur Kenntniss des Altspanischen 8° *Berlin* 67

Manuscripts.

British Museum Catalogue of the Spanish MSS., vol. i. 15/- ; ii. 15/- ; iii. 15/- 8° British Museum 75 ; 77 ; 81

Literature (English Books only) —*v.* K §§ 42, 58, 78.

Folk Literature —*v.* B § 18.

282. PORTUGUESE PHILOLOGY.

Grammar.

BARATA, A. F. Estudos da Lingua Portugueza 8° *Lisbon* 73
BROU, F. P. Grammatica particular sobre as princip. difficuldades Portug. 8° ,, 75
*BRAGA, Th. Grammatica Portugueza Elementar : methodo historico-comparativo 8° *Oporto* 77
*COELHO, Prf. F. A. Questões da Lingua Portugueza, pt. i. [lexicogr., consonants ; v. important] 8° ,, 74
*CORNU, J. tudes de Grammaire Portugais—*in* Romania, vols. x.–xi. [*v.* K § 256].
d'ORSEY, A. J. D. Practical Grammars of Portuguese and English [Ollendorf System] 7/- 12° Trübner [ ] 88
*JOÃO RIBEIRO Grammatica Portugueza 8° *Rio de Janeiro* [ ] 89
The best scientific Portuguese grammar. A great feature of the bk. is the continuous reference to differences between the Portuguese proper and Brazilian Portuguese.
KINLOCH, A. Compendium of Portuguese Grammar, ed. A. J. Dos Reis 4/6 8° Williams [ ] 76
*v. REINHARDSTÖTTNER, C. Grammatik der portug. Sprache [on basis of Lat. & Romance research] 10/- 8° *Strassburg* 79
SCHMITZ, F. J. Portugesische Grammatik, 4/6 ; Key, 1/6 8° *Leipzig* 84 ; 85
VIEYRA, A. Grammar of the Portuguese Language, ed. Fuente 7/- p 8° Dulau [12] 90

Accidence.

*COELHO, Prf. F. A. Theoria da Conjugação em Latim e Portuguez 8° *Lisbon* 70

Dialects.

Generally.

COELHO, Prf. F. A. Os Dialectos Romanicos o Neolatinos na Africa, Asia e America 8° *Lisbon* 81

Brazilian.

LEITE DE VASCONCELLOS, J. O Dialecto Brazileiro 8° *Oporto* 84
PLATZMANN, Jul. Grammatik der brasilianischen Sprache 8/- 8° *Leipzig* 74

Creolese.

SCHUCHARDT, Prf. H. Kreolische Studien, pts. i.–iii. [*extr. fr.* Sitzungsber. d. Wien. Akad.] 1/6 r 8° *Vienna* 82 ; 83 ; 83
i. : Negerportugiesisches v. S. Thomé (West Africa) 6d. ; ii. : Indoportugies. v. Cochim, 6d. ; iii. : Indoportugies. v. Diu, etc., 6d. Cont. in *Ztschr. f. rom. Phil.* 188) *sqq.*

Mirandes.

LEITE DE VASCONCELLOS, J. O Dialecto Mirandez 8° *Oport* 83

Etymology.

MICHAELIS, Carolina —*in her* Studien zur romanischen Wortschöpfung [much on Portuguese] 4/- 8° *Leipzig* 76

Dictionaries.

*COELHO, Prof. F. A. Diccionario manuel etymologico da lingua Portugueza 14/- 8° *Leipzig* 90

ELWES, A. Portuguese-English and English-Portuguese Dictionary 6/- c 8° Lockwood [ ] 88

de FLORIA, F. Diccionario da Lingua Portugueza, 2 vols. 8° *Lisbon* 58

JOÃO RIBEIRO Diccionario Grammatical 8° *Rio de Janeiro*

de LACERDA, José New Dict. of Portuguese and English Languages, 2 vols. 84/- 4° *Lisbon* 66; 71

MICHAELIS, H. Wörterbuch der portugesischen und deutschen Sprache, 2 pts. ea. 7/6 8° *Leipzig* 87; 87

*de SANTA ROSA, Fr. Joachim Elucidario das Palavras, Termos o Frasas Portug., ed. F. da Silva, 2 vols. 8° *Lisbon* [1798–99] 65

VALDEZ, J. F. Portuguese-English and English-Portug. Pronouncing Dictionary, 2 vols. 15/- 12° *Rio de Janeiro* [76] 79

*VIEIRA, Grande Diccionario Portuguez, 5 vols. £6 10/- 4° *Oporto* 73–75

„ (VIEYRA) New Pocket Dictionary, 2 vols. [abrgd. fr. above] 10/- 12° *Paris* (Trüb.) [78] 90

WOLLHEIM DA FONSECA Handwörterbuch der deutschen u. portugesischen Sprache [both parts] 9/- *Leipzig* [ ] 83

Loan Words.

DOZY + ENGELMANN, $\frac{R. P.}{W. H.}$ Glossaire des Mots Espagn. et Portug. derivés de l'Arabe 10/6 8° *Leyden* [62] 69

de SOUSA, João Vestigios da Lingua Arabica em Portugal [a dictionary] *o.p.* 8° *Lisbon* [ ] 30

Synonyms and Epithets.

ROQUETTE + da FONSECA, $\frac{L.}{J.}$ Dicc. dos Synonymos e de Epithetos Portuguez 8° *Paris* 58

Chrestomathy.

*BRAGA, Th. [ed.] Antologia Portugueza [w. a short hist. of Port. poetry] 8° *Oporto* 76

Literature (English Books only)—*v.* K §§ 42, 58, 78.

Folk-Literature —*v.* B § 18.

263. CATALANIAN PHILOLOGY.

Sources, etc.

ALART, B. J. [ed.] Documents a. la Langue Catalan d. anc. comtés de Roussillon et Cerdagne 5/- 8° *Paris* 81

BALAGUER Y MERINO [ed.] Ordinacions y Bans del comtat d'Empurias [Cat. text, w. notes] 8° *Montpellier* 79

de BOFARULL Y MASCARÓ, P. [ed.] Documentos literarios en antigua lengua Catalana [14–15 cents.] *Barcelona* 57

Forms vol. xiii. of the Coleccion de Documentos inéditos del Archiv. Gen. de la corona de Aragon.

History of the Language, and Grammar.

de BOFARULL, P. La Lengua Catalana considerada historicamente [lecture (1857); *repr. in his* Estudios, *inf.*

„ „ Estudios: sistema gramatical y crestomatía de la leng. Catal. 8° *Barcelona* 64

CAMBOULIU, F. R. Recherches sur les Origines étymologiques de l'Idiome Catalane 8° *Montpellier* 63

DIEZ, F. —*v. his notes to his* Grammatik [*ut* K § 256].

FARRÉ Y CARRIÓ Gram. hist. de la Lenguas Castil. y Catalan. 8° *Madrid* 84

„ „ Gram. Catalan. Estudis sobre le matexa 8° *Barcelona* 74

*MILÁ Y FONTANALS Estudios de Lengua Catalana 8° „ 75

*MUSSAFIA, A. —*his* Einleitung *to his edn. of* Seven Sages [*ut* K § 264] *gives excell. sketch of O.-Cat. lang.*

Grammars in Catalanian—*v.* K § 264 (MEYER).

Orthography.

Acad. Real de Buenas Letras: Ortographia de la Lengua Catalana 8° *Barcelona* 84

Etymology.

Dictionaries.

FERRIER, P. Diccionario Catalan-Castellano 8° *Barcelona* [36–39] 47

LABERNIA, P. Diccionario Catalan-Castellano-Latino, pts. i.–xxvi. 35/- 8° „ [48] 88 *sqq. in prog.*

SAURA, J. A. Novíssim Diccionario Manual de la Lenguas Catalana-Castellana, 2 vols. 20/- 8° „ [ ] 83; 84

264. CATALANIAN LITERATURE.

History.

BALAGUER, V. De la Litteratura Catalana [lecture before Real Academia de la Historia] 8° *Madrid* 75

CAMBOULIU, F. R. Essai sur l'Histoire de la Littérature 8° *Paris* [ ] 58

CARDONA, E. Della antica Lett. Catalan. 2/6 8° *Naples* 80

*EBERT, A. Zur Geschichte der catalan. Litteratur—*in* Jahrb. f. rom. u. eng. Lit. vol. ii. [*ut* K § 256].

HELFFERICH, A. Raymond Lull u. die Anfänge d. catal. Litteratur 4/- 8° *Berlin* 58

JOAQUIN MARIA BOVER Biblioteca de Escritores Baleares 8° *Palma* 60

MILÁ Y FONTANALS De los Trovadores en España [linguistic and literary] *o.p.* [*w.* 15/-] 8° *Barcelona* 61

„ „ Katalanische Dichter [14 to beg. 15 cent.]—*in* Jahrb. f. rom. Lit., vol. v. [*ut* K § 256].

„ „ Notes sobre la Influencia de la lit. ital. en la catalana 8° *Barcelona* 77

K § 265

Modern Literature.

FASTENRATH, J. Uebersicht d. catalan. Liter.—*in his* Catal. Troubadoure [*ut infra*].
de MOLINS, A. E. Diccionario biográfico e bibliográf. de escritores y artistas Catal. del. siglio 19; pts. i.–x. 4° *Barcelona* ?–90 *in prog.*
RUBIO Y ORS, J. Breve Reseña del actual Renacimiento d. L leng. y. lit. Catal. 8° *Barcelona* 77
" " The same, tr. into Fch. by Ch. Boy s 8° *Lyons* 79
SAVINE, —*in his tr. of* J. Verdaguer's Atlantida [*ut infra*].
*TUBINO, F. M. Historia del Renacimiento liter. contemp. en Cat., Baleares y Valenc. 8° *Madrid* 80
VOGEL, E. —*his* Neucatal. Studien *conts. a survey of Mod. Cat. Lit., bas. on Turbino* [= Neuph. Stud. pt. v.] 3/- *Paderb*

Collections.

Coll. de Documentos Inéditos del Archivo de la Corona de Aragon—*conts. many Old Catal. chronicles, etc.*
Llibre d'Or de la Moderna Poesía Catalana 8° *Barcelona* 78
MARIAN AGUILÓ Y FUSTER [ed.]
Biblioteca Catalana de les mes principals y eletes obres en nostra llengua *in monthly pts.* [62 pub. to '88] 8° *Barcelona* 71 *sqq. in prog.*
MATHEU Y FONTANELLS [ed.] Llibre del Amor [coll. of modern poems] 8° " 82
" " Llibre de la Patria [" " "] 8° " 82
MILÁ Y FONTANALS [ed.] Poëtes Lyriques Catalans [*repr. fr.* Rev. d. Lang. Rom. (*ut* K § 256)] 2/6 8° *Montpellier* 78
" " [ed.] Poëtes Catalans : les noves rimades, la codolada [Soc. p. étude lang. rom.] 3/- 8° " 76
" " [ed.] Romancerillo Catalan [a critical edn.] 9/- 8° *Barcelona* [ ] 82

Folk-literature —*v.* B § 18.

Language.

*MEYER, Paul [ed.] Traités Catalans de Grammaire et de Poétique—*in* Romania, vols. vi., viii., ix. [*ut* K § 256].

Individual Writers and Texts.

Old Catalanian.

ARNALDO DE VILANOVA. AID : Menendez Pelayo, Arn. de Vilanova : médico catalan del siglo xiii. [essay] 8° *Madrid* 79
AUSIAS MARCH Obras, ed. F. Pelayo-Briz 8° *Barcelona* 64
CARBONELL, Opúsculos inéditos de Cronista Catal., ed. A. de Bofarull 8° " 64
DESCLOT, B. Crónica, ed. C. Buchon—*in* Chroniques Étrangères rel. a. Expéd. Francs. *Orleans* [40] 76
New edns. are to appear in the Bibl. Catalana and in the Bibl. de Escritores Aragoneses.
James i. of Aragon : Libre dels Feyts Esdevenguts en la Vida, ed. Aguiló y Fuster [Bibl. Cat.] 8° *Barcelona* 73–80
" " Chronicle of, tr. J. Forster ; w. histor. intro. P. de Gayangos, 2 vols. 28/- 8° Chapman 83
MULET, Obres Festives compostes segons antiga, ed. C. Llombart 8° *Madrid* 76
Peter iv. of Aragon : Crónica, ed. A. de Bofarull 8° *Barcelona* 50
LULL, Rámon Obras Rimadas, ed. Gerónimo Rosselló, pts. i.–xix. 20/- 8° *Palma* [59] 87 *sqq. in prog.*
Libre del Orde de Cavayleria, ed. Aguiló y Fuster 8° *Barcelona* 79
Libre de Maravelles, ed. J. Rosselló [Bibl. Catalan.] 8° "
" " " K. Hofmann, *sub tit.* Ein katal. Thierepos. [*fr.* Denkschr. Akad. Wiss.] 8° *Munich* 72
MUNTANER, Ramon Crónica d. Don Jaume i., ed. K. Lanz [Bibl. d. Litt. Vereins] [*w.* 7/6] 8° *Stuttgart* 44
" " ed. C. Buchon—*in* Chroniques Étrangères *Paris* 27
" " " A. de Bofarull 8° *Barcelona* 60
" " übers. K. Lanz, 2 vols. 11/6 8° *Leipzig* 42
Saint Amador, Vida de [14 cent.] ed. V. Lieutaud 8° *Marseilles* 79
*Seven Sagas : Catalan. Metrische Version, hrsg. A. Mussafia [*fr.* Denkschr. Wien. Akad.] 4/- 4° *Vienna* 76

Modern Catalanian : A few specimens.

Prose.

CARETA Y VIDAL Brosta, aplech de quentos, novelas, fabulas, *etc.* 8° *Barcelona* 78
FELIN Y CODINA Lo Rector de Vallfogona [a historical novel] s 8° " 77
RIERA Y BERTAN Escenas de la Vida Pagesa [novelettes] s 8° " 78

Poetry, etc.

BALAGUER, V. Tragedies ; w. Spanish tr. 8° *Madrid.* 78
FASTENRATH, J. [tr.] Catalanische Troubadoure d. Gegenwart : verdeutscht [w. histor. intro.] 8/- 8° *Leipzig* 90
LLOMBART, C. Niu d'Abeilles : epigrams llemosins s 8° *Valencia* [ ] 76
VERDAGUER, Jascinto La Atlantida ; w. Spanish tr. 8° *Barcelona* 78
" " " French tr. A. Savine 8° *Paris* 83
" " Idilis y Cants Mistichs ; Caritat [poems] 8° *Barcelona* [ ]82 ; 85

265. OLD PROVENÇAL (LANGUE D'OC) PHILOLOGY.

Introduction.

CHABANEAU, C. La Langue et la Littérature Provençale : leçon d'ouverture 8° *Paris* 79
" " Sur la Langue Romane du Midi de la France [= Hist. de Languedoc, vol. x.] 8° *Toulouse* 85
MAHN, A. Ueber das Studium der provenz. Sprache und Litteratur 8° *Berlin*]74
MEYER, P. —*article* Provençal Language—*in* Encyclo. Brit., vol. xix. 30/- 4° Black 85

Grammar.

BARTSCH, Karl —*in his* Chrestomathie [*ut* K § 267].
DEMATTIO, Grammatica della lingua provenzale 3/6 8° *Innsbruck* 80
DIEZ, F. —*in his* Grammatik d. roman. Sprachen [*ut* K § 256], espec. vols. i.–ii.
KITCHIN, Darcy B. Introduction to the Study of Provençal [liter., gram., texts, gloss.] 4/6 c 8° Williams 87
MAHN, A. Grammatik und Wörterbuch der altprovenzalischen Sprache, pt. i. 6/- 8° *Köthen* 85
Pt. i. devoted to phonology: far behind the times.
RAYNOUARD, F. J. M. —*his* Lexique [*ut inf.*] conts. gram. remarks, *and his* Choix de Poesies, vol. vi. [*ut* K § 267] *ii* a Gramm. Comp.
R.'s theory was that Prov. was the orig. general Romance lang. from the Lat., and that the other Rom. langs. were derived fr. it.
STENGEL, Prf. E. [ed.] Die beiden ältesten prov. Grammatiken 6/- 8° *Marburg* 78
Contains *Lo Donatz Proensals* by UC FAIDIT (13 cent.), and *Las Rasos de Trobar*, by RAIMON VIDAL (13 cent.), w. a Prov.-Ital. glossary.

Phonology —*v. also* Mahn, *ut supra.*

MEYER, P. Phonétique Provençale—*in* Mém. Soc. Linguist.
NEUMANN, Fr. Die german. Elemente in d. prov. u. frz. Sprache; pt. i. [vowels & diphthongs; diss.] *Heidelberg* 76
SABERSKY, H. Zur provenzalischen Lautlehre 3/- 8° *Berlin* 88

Orthography and Pronunciation.

ARBAUD, D. De l'Orthographie Provençale *o.p.* 8° *Aix* 65
PFÜTZNER, F. Ueber die Aussprache des provenzalischen *a* [dissert.] *Halle* 85
WIECHMANN, E. Ueber die Aussprache des provenzalischen *e* [dissert.] 8° „ 81

Etymology.

Dictionaries.

HONNORAT, S. J. Dictionnaire Prov.-Frç.: ancienne et moderne, 3 vols. in 4 *o.p.* [*w.* 75/-] 4° *Digne* 46–49
RAYNOUARD, F. J. M. Lexique Roman: Dictionnaire de la Langue des Troubadours, 6 vols. [w. selns.] *o.p.* [*w.* £5] 8° *Paris* 36–38
Modern —*v.* K § 266: Provençal Dialects.

Accidence.

Verb.

Present and Imperfect.
HARNISCH, A. Die altprov. Präsens- u. Imperf.-bildung [Ausgaben u. Abhandl. xl.] 8/- 8° *Marburg* 86
MUSSAFIA, A. Zur Präsensbildung im Romanischen—*in* Berichte Berl. Akad. 1883.
Perfect.
MEYER, K. Prov. Gestaltung d. vom Perfectstamme gebild. Tempora d. Lat. [Ausg. u. Abhand xii.] 2/- 8° *Marburg* 83
SCHENCKER, F. Ueber die Perfektbildung im Provenzalischen [dissert.] *Zürich* 83
Future.
WOLFF, C. F. Futur u. Conditional II. im Altprovenzalischen [Ausgaben u. Abh. xxx.] 1/6 8° *Marburg* 84
Infinitive.
FISCHER, A. Der Infinitiv im Provenz. nach d. Reimen d. Trobadors [Ausgaben, u. Abhand. vi.] 1/6 8° *Marburg* 83
Participle.
MANN, P. Das Partizip Präteriti im Altprovenzalischen [Ausg. u. Abhandl. xli.] 3/- 8° *Marburg* 86

Noun.

LOOS, Th. Die Nominalflexion im Provenzalischen [Ausg. u. Abhandl. xvi.] 1/6 8° *Marburg* 84
Declension.
REIMANN, P. Die Declination der Subst. u. Adj. in d. Langue d'Oc zum J. 1300 [dissert.] *Danzig* 82
Vocative.
BEYER, A. Die Flexion d. Vocativs im Altfrz. u. Prov. [diss.; *repr. in* Ztschr. rom. Phil. vii.] *Halle* 83

Pronoun.

BAUQUIER, À travers la Langue d'Oc: double forme de quelqu. pronoms 8° *Montpellier* 79
BOHNHARDT, W. Der Personalpronomen im Altprovenzalischen 4/- 8° *Marburg* 88
v. ELSNER, A. Form und Verwendung d. Personalpronomens im Altprovenzal. 2/- 8° *Kiel* 86

Syntax.

PAPE, Die Wortstellung in der provenzalischen Prosalitteratur [dissert.] *Jena* 84

Chrestomathies —*v.* K § 267.

266. PROVENÇAL DIALECTS.

Collectively.

*AZAÏS, G. Dictionnaire des Idiomes Romans du Midi de la France, vols. i.–iii. 37/- 8° *Montpellier* 77–82
BOUCOIRAN, L. Dictionnaire d. Idiomes mérid. dep. Nice jusq. Bayonne, 5 pts. (complete) 30/- 8° *Nîmes* 75–86
JOUBERT, Glossaire du Centre de la France, 2 vols. 8° *Paris* [56] 64; [58] 64
MISTRAL, F. Lou Tresor dou Felibrige: dictionn. Prov.-Français, 2 vols. 110/- r 4° *Aix-en-Prov.* 79–86
Magazine —*v.* K § 256 (Revue des Langues Romanes).
Folk-Literature —*v.* B § 15: French Mythology and Folklore.

Auvergne.

DONIOL, H. Les Patois de la Basse Auvergne: leur grammaire et leur litterature 5/- 8° *Montpellier* 77

K § 269

Aveyron.

DURAND, J. P.	Études de Philologie et Linguistique Aveyronnaises [family and place-names]		8°	*Paris*	79
VAYSSIER,	Dictionnaire Patois-Français du departement de l'Aveyron		8°	*Rodez*	79

Béarn.

*LESPY + RAYMOND, V. + P.	Grammaire Béarnaise : avec vocab. Français-Béarnais, 2 vols.	8/6	8°	*Montpellier* [2nd ed. 80]	86
* „ „	Grammar and Vocabulary of Bearn, tr. and abdgd. R. G. Molyneux	5/-	r 8°	Frowde	88
* „ „	Dictionnaire Béarnais : ancien et moderne, 2 vols.	17/-	8°	*Montpellier*	87

Bordeaux.

DELEINGUT, G.	Essai grammatical sur le Gascon de Bordeaux		8°	*Bordeaux*	67

Burgundy.

MIGNARD, Th. J. A. P.	Vocabulaire raisonné et comparé du dialecte et du patois de Burgundie		8°	*Paris*	65

Creuse.

*THOMAS, A.	Rapport s. une Miss. Philol. dans la Creuse—*in* Archives Miss. Scient., ser. III., vol. v.				

Dauphiné.

COLOMBE DE BATINES	Bibliographie du Patois de Dauphiné	*o.p.*	8°	*Grenoble*	35
MONTIER, L.	Grammaire Dauphinoise : dialecte de la vallée de la Drôme		8°	*Paris*	83

Forez

—*v. also* Lyons (ONOFRIO), *infra.*

GRAS, L. P.	Dictionnaire du Patois Forézien		8°	*Paris*	64
NOËLAS, M.	Dictionnaire du Patois Forézien		8°	*Lyons*	65

Gascony.

DUBUISSON,	Glossaire Gascon—*in his* Historia Monast. S. Severi in Vasconia		8°	*Villeneuve*	78
de GRATELOUP,	Grammaire Gasconne et Française, publ. C. Chabaneau [fr. MS. of 1734]	3/6	8°	*Paris*	87
LUCHAIRE, Achille [ed.]	Recueil de Textes Gascons de l'ancien dialecte Gascon [to 14 cent.; w. gloss.]	5/-	8°	„	81

Languedoc.

AZAÏS, G.	Dictionnaire des Idiomes Languedociens : etymol., compar. et technologique		8°	*Béziers*	67
BARTHÈS, M.	Glossaire Botanique : languedocien, français, latin [w. a study of the dial.]	4/6	8°	*Montpellier*	73-76
„ „ [ed.]	Flourétos de Mountagno, 2 v. [Langued. poetry, w. Fch. trs. *en regard*]	8/6	8°	„	78; 85
d'HOMBRES, M.	Dictionnaire Languedocien-Français, 2 vols.	34/-	4°	*Alais* 72; *Aix*	79
*MUSHACKE, W.	Geschichtl. Entwickelung d. Mundart v. Montpellier—*in* Frz. Stud., vol. iv. 5 [*ut* K § 268]	6/-	8°	*Heilbronn*	84

His *Einleitung* to this essay contains a survey of the literature of the dialect.

Limousin.

*CHABANEAU, Ch.	Grammaire Limousine : phonétique; parties du discours	12/6	8°	*Paris*	76

Lyons.

MONIN,	La Genèse des Patois : en partic. du roman ou patois Lyonnais		8°	*Paris*	73
ONOFRIO, S. B.	Essai d'un Glossaire des Patois de Lyonnais, Forez et Beaujolais	10/6	8°	*Lyons*	61
du PUITSPELU, N.	Dictionnaire Étymologique du Patois Lyonnais, in pts.	ea. 4/6	8°	*Basle*	87 *in prog.*
ZACHER, A.	Beiträge zur Lyoner Dialect	[dissert.]		*Bonn*	84

Mentone.

ANDREWS, J. B.	Vocabulaire du Patois Mentonais	3/6	12°	*Nice*	77

Nice.

SARDOU, A. L.	L'Idiome Niçois		8°	*Paris*	78
„ „	Exposé d'un Système rationel d'Orthographie Niçoise		8°	„	81
„ + CALVINO	Grammaire de l'Idiome Niçois		8°	*Nice*	83

Provence.

SAVINIAN,	Grammaire Provençale : sous-dialecte Rhodanien		8°	*Avignon*	82

Pyrenees.

*LUCHAIRE, Achille	Études sur les Idiomes Pyrénéens de la région française	7/-	8°	*Paris*	79

Rouergue.

*AYMERIC, J.	La Dialecte Rouergat—*in* Zeitschr. f. roman. Philologie, vol. iii. [*ut* K § 256]				
*CONSTANS, L.	Essai sur l'Hist. du sous-dialecte du Rouergue	4/6	8°	*Paris*	80
„ „ [ed.]	Le Livre de l'Épervier, capitulaire de la commune de Millau (Aveyron)	8/6	8°	*Montpellier*	82

Savoy.

BRACHET, F.	Dictionnaire du Patois Savoyard : canton d'Albertville		8°	*Albertville*	83

267. PROVENÇAL LITERATURE: OLD AND MODERN.

Manuscripts.

*BARTSCH, Karl —*in his* Grundriss, *ut infra, is a list and descript. of Prov. MSS.*
CHABANEAU, C. Notes sur quelques MSS. Provençaux perdus ou égarés 4/6 8° *Paris* 86
CONSTANS, L. Les MSS. Provençaux de Cheltenham 3/- 8° ,, 82
NOULET + CHABANEAU, $\frac{J.B.}{C.}$ [eds.] Deux Manuscrits Provençaux du XIVe siècle [Soc. p. étude langs. rom.] 12/6 8° *Paris* 88
Poems by RAIMON DE CORNET, PEIRE DE LADILS and other poets of the Toulouse school.
TODD, J. H. [ed.] The Books of the Vaudois [Waldensian MSS. at Trin. Coll. Camb.] 6/- c 8° Macmillan 65

General History. Troubadours.

BALAGUER, V. De la Poesia Provenzal en Castilla y en Leon 8° *Madrid* 77
" " Historia Politica y Literaria de los Trovadores, 6 vols. 8° ,, 77–80
*BARTSCH, Karl Grundriss der Geschichte der provenzalischen Litteratur 5/- 8° *Elberfeld* 72
" " Ueber d. roman. u. deutschen Tagelieder—*in his* Vorträge [*ut* K § 256].
BIRCH-HIRSCHFELD, Prf. A. Ueber die den Troubadours bekannten epischen Stoffe 2/6 8° *Leipzig* 78
BÖHMER, E. Die provenzalische Poesie der Gegenwart [good] 1/6 8° *Halle* 70
Estimates the number of Provençals in 1870 at about two millions.
BREYMANN, [Prf.] H. Provençal Literature in Ancient and Modern Times [pamphlet] 1/- 8° *Manchester* 75
CHABANEAU, C. [ed.] Biographies des Troubadours en langue Provençale [= Hist. de Languedoc, vol. x.] 8° *Toulouse* 86
With the Latin, Provençal, Italian and Spanish Texts, introduction and notes, and bibl. of Prov. writers to end 13 cent.
" " Origine et Établissement de l'Acad. des Jeux Floraux [= Hist. de Languedoc, vol.? 8° ,, 85
*DIEZ, F. Die Poesie der Troubadours, hrsg. Karl Bartsch 1/6 8° *Leipzig* [26] 83
* " " Leben und Werke der Troubadours, hrsg. Karl Bartsch 10/- 8° ,, [29] 82
*FAURIEL, C. Histoire de la Poésie Provençale, 3 vols. *o.p.* [*w.* 20/-] 8° *Paris* 46–48
" " The same, tr. Adler [Am.], *sub tit.* History of Provençal Poetry $3 8° *New York* 47
GRÖBER, G. Unters. üb. d. Liedersammlungen d. Troubad.—*in* Rom. Stud., vol. ii., pp. 337–670 [*ut* K § 256].
HUEFFER, Dr. Francis The Troubadours: hist. of Prov. life and literature in Middle Ages 12/6 8° Chatto 78
MAHN, A. [ed.] Biographien der Troubadours [in Provençal language] 2/- 8° *Berlin* [53] 78
" " Ueber die epische Poesie der Provenzalen [espec. Jaufre. & Girartz de Rossilho] ,, 79
" " Die epische Poesie der Troubadours, vol. i., pts. i.–iii.: Girartz de Rossilho ea. 1/6 8° ,, 83–86 *in prog.*
MERAY, A. Vie au temps d. Trouvères; Vie au temps d. cours d'Amour 8° *Paris* 73; 76
MEYER, P. —*article* Provençal Literature—*in* Encyclo. Brit., vol. xix. 30/- 4° *Black* 85
" Les Derniers Troubadours de la Provence *Paris* 71
MICHEL, F. Heinrich von Morungen u. d. Troubadours [Quellen u. Forschh.] 6/- 8° *Strassburg* 80
MILÁ Y FONTANALS De los Trovadores en Espagna *o.p.* [*w.* 15/-] 8° *Barcelona* 61
NOSTRADAMUS, J. Vie des plus célèbres Poètes Provençaux, ed. C. Chabaneau [1575] *in prep.*
NOUBLET, J. B. Essai s. l'hist. littér. des Patois d. Midi d. Fr. aux 16–17 siècles 8° *Toulouse* 79
PRESTON, H. W. [Am.] Troubadours and Trouvères: new and old $2.50 c 8° *Boston* 76
RUTHERFORD, J. The Troubadours: their lives and their lyrics [w. trs.] 10/6 c 8° Smith & Elder 73
SCHELER, A. Untersuchungen üb. d. Trouvères belges d. 12–14 Jahrh. [Ausg. u. Abh. xvii.] 1/6 8° *Brussels* 84

Collections and Chrestomathies.

APPEL, C. [ed.] Provenzalische Inedita 8/- 8° *Leipzig* 90
*BARTSCH, Karl [ed.] Chrestomathie Provençale [1st edn. *sub tit.* Provenz. Lesebuch] 8/- 8° *Elberfeld* [55] 80
" " [ed.] Denkmäler der provenzalischen Litteratur [Publ. Litt. Vereins] 8° *priv. prin. Stuttgart* 56
BAYLE, A. [ed.] Anthologie Provençale [Troub. 10–15 cent., w. Mod. Fch. tr. *en regard*] *Aix* 79
Bibliothèque Provençale 9 vols. 8° ,, 59–79
MAHN, A. [ed.] Die Werke der Troubadours: in Provençal, 4 vols. 27/- 12° *Berlin* 46–85
" " [ed.] Gedichte der Troubadours, 4 vols. ,, 56–73
" " Commentar und Glossar zu den Werken der Troubadours ,, 71–78
MEYER, Paul [ed.] —*v.* K § 273.
RAYNOUARD, F. J. M. [ed.] Choix de Poésies orig. des Troubadours, 6 vols. [w. gram.] *o.p.* [*w.* 126/-] 8° *Paris* 16–21
SUCHIER, H. [ed.] Denkmäler provenzalischer Literatur und Sprache, vol. i. 20/- 8° *Halle* 83

Individual Writers, Texts, and Aids.

Agnes [myst. play; 14 cent.] Facsimile in heliotype, ed. E. Monaci [19 pl., w. 8 pp. of text] 20/- f° *Rome* 80
" ed. Karl Bartsch *Berlin* 69
" ,, L. Clédat [w. Fch. tr. *en regard* and notes by A. L. Sardou] 15/- 8° *Nice* 77–78
AID:
Clédat, L. La Mystère de Sainte Agnès [an exam. of the MS.]—*in* Bibl. de l'École d'Athènes, vol. i.
Aigar et Maurin [chans. d. geste]: ed. A. Scheler 5/- 8° *Brussels* 77
ALBERY OF BESANÇON Alexander-fragment
AID:
Flechtner, H. Die Sprache des Alexander-fragmentes [dissert.] *Strassburg* 80
ARNAUT DANIEL [*c.* 1180–1200]
AID:
Canello, V. La Vita e le Opere del Trovatore Arnaut Daniello 9/- 8° *Halle* 83
ARNAUT VIDAL DE CASTELNOUDARI [beg. 14 cent.] Guillem de la Barra, ed. P[aul] M[eyer] 8° *Paris* 68
BERNART DE VENTADORN [*c.* 1148–95] Provenzalische Lieder, hrsg. N. Delius *o.p.* 8° *Bonn* 53
AIDS:
Belsch, F. Die Syntax des Bernart von Ventadorn—*in* Symbolae Joachimicae, 2 pts. 15/- 8° *Berlin* 8[illegible]
Bischoff, Hans Biographie des Troubadours Bernart von Ventadorn [dissert.] 2/- 8° [illegible]
Hofmeister, R. Sprachl. Untersuchungen d. [illegible] Bern. v. Vent's. = Stengel's Ausgaben u. Abh., pt. [illegible] 1/6 8° *Marburg* [illegible]

K § 267

Bertolomeu Zorgi [*or* Zorzi; *fl.* 1250–70]
Aid:
Levy, E. — Der Troubadour Bertolomeu Zorgi [Habilit.-Schrift.] 2/- 8° *Halle* 83

Bertran de Born [*fl.* 1180–95] Leben und Werke, hrsg. A. Stimming; w. German notes and glossary 10/- 8° *Halle* 79
Aids:
Clédat, L. — Du Rôle historique de Bertran de Born 8° *Paris* 78
Laurens, V. — Le Tyrtée du Moyen-âge [history of Bertran de Born] 8° „ [61] 75

Boëthius, ed. K. Bartsch—*in his* Chrest. Prov. [*ut* K § 267]; ed. F. Renouard—*in his* Choix de Textes [*ut* K § 267].
„ F. Diez—*in his* Altroman. Sprachdenkmäler [*ut* K § 277]; ed. P. Meyer—*in his* Recueil d'Anc. Textes [*ut* K § 277].
„ F. Hündgen, *sub tit.* Das alt-prov. Boëthius [w. Germ. tr., notes, essays & gloss.] 6/- 8° *Oppeln* 84

Breviari d'Amour —*v.* Matfre, *infra.*

Croisade d'Albigeoise [13 cent. chanson] ed. P. Meyer, 2 vols. [w. French tr.] 15/- 8° *Paris* 75:79
Notes additionnelles were pub. by Meyer in the Bulletin de la Soc. de l'Hist. de France, vol. xvi.
French Translation: trad. Mary-Lafon, *sub tit.* La Croisade contre les Albigeois [also tr. Meyer, *sup.*] 8° „ 68
Aid:
Kraack, L. — Ueber d. Entstehung u. die Dichter d. *Crois. c. l. Albig.* [Ausg. u. Abhand. xv.] 1/6 8° *Marburg* 84
Supposed to be written by the authoress Dorimunda. For the prose version of this poem v. *Guerre des Albigeois, infra.*

Daude de Pradas [early 13 cent.] Li Auzel Cassador, ed. C. Sachs [only pt. i.; schl.progr.] 2/6 4° *Brandenburg* 65
Romance of D. d. P. on the Four Cardinal Virtues, ed. P. Stickney 3/6 8° *Florence* 79

Daurel et Beton [chans. de geste] ed. Paul Meyer [Soc. des Anciens Textes; *v.* Girartz de Rossilho, *infra*] 8/6 8° *Paris* 80

Esther [a tragedy] ed. E. Sabatier; w. French intro. and notes 8° *Nimes* [1774] 77

Favre, Abbé [1727–1782] Oeuvres Complètes, 3 vols. 8° *Montpellier* 85

Fierabras [chans. de geste] ed. J. Bekker—*in* Abhandl. Berl. Akad. Wiss. 1829 7/- 4° *Berlin* 30
„ E. Stengel 2/6 4° *Marburg* 80

Flamenca, Roman de ed. Paul Meyer 10/- 8° *Paris* 65

Folquet de Lunel [1244–?] ed. Eichelkraut 10/- 8° *Göttingen* 72

Folquet de Marseilles [1180?–1231]
Aid:
Pratsch, S. — Biographie des Troubadours Folquet von Marseille [dissert.] 1/6 8° *Göttingen* 79

Francesco da Barberino.
Aid:
Thomas, A. — Franc. da Barberino et la Littérature Prov. en Italie au moyen-âge 4/6 8° *Paris* 83

Gaucelm Faidit [1190 (?)–1240]
Aid:
Meyer, Paul — Das Leben des Troubadours Gaucelm Faidit [dissert.] 1/6 8° *Heidelberg* 79

Girartz de Rossilho [9 cent.]
Manuscripts: Bodleian, Oxon.: ed. Prf. W. Foerster—*in* Romanische Studien, vol. v. [*ut* K § 256].
ed. A. Mahn [first 3190 verses only]—*in his* Gedichte der Troubadours [*ut* K § 267].
„ Bibl. Nat., Paris: ed. C. Hofmann, 2 vols. 4/6 8° *Berlin* 55:57
For a revision of this edn. v. F. Appelstedt in *Romanische Studien*, vol. v. [*ut* K § 256].
ed. Fr. Michel *o.p.* [*pb.* 10/-; w. 8/] 8 *Paris* 56
„ Bibl. Harl., ed. J. Stürzinger—*in* Romanische Studien, vol. v. [*ut* K § 256; *also in* Michel's edn., *sup.*].
French Translation: trad. Paul Meyer [fr. the Oxford MS.] 2/- 8° *Paris* 84
Aids:
Breuer, G. M. — Sprachliche Untersuchung zu Girarts de Rossilho, hrsg. Mignard [dissert.] 1/6 8° *Bonn* 84
Hentschke, G. — Die Verbalflexion im Oxforder *Roland* [dissert.] 1/6 8° *Halle* 83
Mahn, A. —*v. supra, s.v.* History.
Schweppe, K. — Études sur Girartz de Rossilho [w. part of Bodl. MSS.; diss.] 3/- 8° *Stettin* 78
The Romance serials and journals have many important articles on Girartz de Rossilho.
The only undoubtedly original *chansons de geste* in Provençal. Only two others exist: *Fierabras* and *Betonnet d'Hanstone*, both of which are prob. trs. fr. O.-F. originals. [*v. Fierabras* and *Daurel et Beton, supra.*] There is also a fragm. *Aigar et Maurin.*

Guerre des Albigeois [*v.* Croisade, *sup.*] ed. par un Indigène [w. glossary, etc.] 3/- 8° *Toulouse* 63
French Translation: tr. F. P. G. Guizot—*in the* Collection des Mémoires, vol. xv. 1.

Guillem Anelier Histoire de la Guerre de Navarre, ed. Fr. Michel; w. Fch. tr. and notes [Coll. de Docum. Inédits] 8° *Paris* 56
Vier provenzalische Gedichte [Rügelieder], hrsg. A. Gisi 1/6 4° *Solothurn* 77
Aid:
Diehl, R. — Guillem Anelier de Toulouse, Dichter d. zweiten Theiles d. Alb. Chronik [Ausg. u. Abhand.] [diss.] 1/- 8° *Marburg* 83

Guillem de Berguedan Lieder, hrsg. A. Keller *Mitau* 49

Guillem de Cabestaing [*d.* 1181–96] Chansons, ed. Fr. Hueffer, *ut infra.*
Aids:
Beschnidt, E. — Die Biographie des Troubadours Guillem de Cabestaing u. ihr histor. Werth [dissert.] 1/6 8° *Marburg* 79
Hueffer, Fr. — Der Trobadour Guillem de Cabestaing: sein Leben u. seine Werke [dissert.] 1/6 8° *Berlin* 69

Guillem Figueira
Aid:
Levy, E. — Guillem Figueira: ein provenzal. Trobadour [w. text of his *chansons*; diss.] 1/6 8° *Berlin* 80

Guillem IX. de Poito [reigned 1087–1127] Chansons, hrsg. Holland + A. Keller *Tübingen* 50
Aids:
Bartsch, Karl — Ueber das Leben und die Werke Wilhelms ix., Grafen v. Poitiers *Hildesheim* 79
Palustre, L. — Histoire de Guillem ix. dit le troubadour [*extr. fr.* Mém. Soc. Antiq. de l'Ouest] 8° *Paris* 82
Sachse, M. — Ueber das Leben und die Lieder d. Wilhelm ix., Grafen v. Poitou [dissert.] *Leipzig* 80

Guiot de Provins Oeuvres, hrsg. F. Wolfart + San Marte (= A. Schulz) [w. Germ. tr., intro. & notes] 9/- 8° *Halle* 61
Aid:
Eisentraut, L. — Grammatik zu Guiot de Provins *Cassel* 79

Honorat, St. Vida de ed. A. L. Sardou; w. Fch. notes *Nice* 75
Aid:
Hosch, S. — Quellen u. Verhältniss d. prov. u. lat. Lebensbeschreibung d. H. [dissert.] 1/6 8° *Berlin* 77

Infantia Mariae et Christi: ed. O. Schade *Halle* 69
Aid:
Reinsch, — Die Pseudo-Evangelien v. Jesu u. Maria's Kindheit in roman. u. germ. Litteratur *Halle* 79

Istoria Petri et Pauli [Prov. mystery of 15 cent.]: ed. P. Guillaume 6/6 8° *Paris* 87

JAUFRE DE PONS.
 AID:
 Chabaneau, C. Les Troubadours Renaud et Geoffrey de Pons [extr. fr. Courier litt. de l'Ouest] 1/6 8° Paris 81
 Mahn, A. —v. supra, s.v. History.
JAUFRE RUDEL [fl. 1140–1170].
 AID:
 Stimming, A. Jaufre Rudel: sein Leben und seine Werke 1/6 8° Kiel 73
LAMBERT, Bethelehem, ed. W. Kreiten [a selection of Mod.-Prov. chansons, w. Germ. trs.] 1/6 8° Freiburg 82
Leys d'Amors.
 AID:
 Lienig, P. Die Grammatik der Leys d'amors: verglichen mit d. Sprache d. Troubadours, pt. i. (phonol.) 3/- 8° Breslau 90
Li Chantari di Lancelloto: ed. W. De Gray Birch [troubad. poem of 14 cent.] 7/- r 8° Roy. Soc. of Lit. (Trübner) 74
MARGUERITE d'OYNOT Oeuvres, ed. E. Philipon 8° Lyons 77
MATFRE ERMENGAUD Breviari d'Amor, ed. G. Azaïs, 2 vols. 8° Paris 62; 81
 AID:
 Mussafia, A. Handschriftl. Studien, pt. iii.: Mittheilungen aus 2 Wiener HSS. d. Brev. d'Am. 1/- 8° Vienna 64
MATHIEU, A. La Farandulo: poésie provençale, ed. F. Mistral; w. Fch. tr. 3/6 8° Avignon [ ] 68
MISTRAL, Frédéric [19 cent.] Mirèio [Mireille (1859)] [an epic poem w. Fch. prose tr.] 2 8° Paris [ ]
 Mirèio: English tr. Harriet W. Preston; front. 3/6 c 8° Unwin 90
 ,, French tr. E. Rigaud 8° Paris [ ] 81
 ,, ,, C. Hennion 8° Tours 79
 ,, German tr. [Frau] B. M. Dorieux-Brotbeck 5/- 8° Heilbronn 80
 Calendu [1867], übers. J. Westenhöffer [only the first song] Mühlhausen 83
MONTAUDON, Moine de [fl. 1180–1200] ed. O. Klein [= Stengel's Ausgaben u. Abhandl., pt. vii.] 4/- 8° Marburg 85
 ed. E. Philippsohn; w. Germ. notes, life, etc. [dissert.] 1/6 8° Halle 73
 AID:
 Sabatier, E. Le Moine de Montaudon 8° Nîmes 70
N'AT DE MONS Werke, hrsg. W. Bernhard [Altfrz. Bibliothek] 5/6 8° Heilbronn 87
Nobla Leyczon ed. C. Dühr; w. German tr. and notes (chiefly etymological) [schl.-progr.] 1/6 8° Friedland 69
 ,, E. Mätzner; w. German tr., intro. and notes [,,] o.p. 8° Berlin 45
PEIRE CARDENAL.
 AID:
 Maus, F. W. Peire Cardenal's Strophenbau in Verh. z. anderen Trolnd. [= Ausg. u. Abhand. v.] 3/- 8° Marburg 84
PEIRE DE CORBIAC Trésor, en vers provençale, ed. C. Sachs [schl.-progr.] 1/6 8° Brandenburg 59
PEIRE ROGIER [fl. 1160–1180] AID: Appel, C. Leben und Lieder des Peire Rogier [dissert.] 1/6 8° Berlin 82
PONS DE CAPDOILL [1150–1190] AID: Napolsky, M. Leben und Werke d. Pons der Capdoill 4/- 8° Halle 80
Prise de Damiette [in 1219] Provençal version, ed. Paul Meyer [extract] 4/- 8° Paris 77
 AID:
 Meyer, Paul De Captione Damiatae fragment. provinciale [w. Fch. tr.] Geneva 79
Prise de Jérusalem: ed. C. Chabaneau 8° Paris 90
RAMBAUT DE VAGUEIRAS [1180–1207] Bonifaz de Montferrat u. Ramb. de Vaqueiras, ed. L. Streit Berlin 77
 ,, ,, Les Frevols Venson le plus fort, etc., hrsg. A. T[obler] ,, 82
RAIMON FÉRAUT —v. Honorat, supra.
RAINAUT DE PONS —v. Jaufre de Pons, supra.
RAMBERTINO BUVALELLI [13 cent.] Le Rime Provenzali di Ramb. Buvalelli [anon. edited] 8° Florence 85
 AID:
 Casini, T. La Vita e le Poesie di Rambertino Buvalelli 8° Bologna 80
Renard, Lou Renard provenc.: rouman en douge cant 8° Aix 78
ROUMANILLE, José [b. 1818] Li Margarideto, 3/6; Le Campano Mountado 2/- Avignon 47; 57
 Lis Oubreto en vers, 3/6; The same in prose, 3/6; Lou Mège de Cucagnan 8° Avignon [59] 64; 59 1 63
 Lis Entarro chin galejado boulegarello 74
 [ed.] Contes Provençaux Avignon 83
SABOLY, Nicolas [1614–1675] AID: Faury, P. Saboly: étude littéraire et historique 8° Charpentras 76
Saint Amador, Vida de [14 cent.] ed. V. Lieutaud [v. also K § 264: Catal. Liter.] 8° Marseilles 78
 ,, André [mystery] by Marcellin Richard, ed. J. Fazy; w. French intro. 8° Aix 83
 ,, Bénézet, Vie de [13 cent.] ed. J. H. Albanès; w. Fch. tr. and notes o.p. [m. £5] 8° Marseilles 76
 ,, Douzeline, Vie de [13 cent.] ed. J. H. Albanès; w. Fch. tr. and hist. and crit. intro. 8° ,, 79
 ,, Enimie, Vie de ed. C. Sachs 8° Berlin 57
 ,, George Viede: poème Provençal, ed. C. Chabaneau 2/6 8° Paris 87
Sainte Marguerite, Vie de, en vers romans, ed. Moulet [extr. fr. Mém. Acad. Toulouse, ser. vii. vol. vii.] 8° Tours 75
 ,, Marie Vie des Saintes Marie Jacobé et Marie Salomé, ed. Abbé Moreau 8° Montpellier 79
 ,, ,, Madeleine dans la litt. Provençale: texts in prose and verse, ed. C. Chabaneau 10/- 8° Paris 87
Sermons du 12 Siècle en vieux Provençale, ed. F. Armitage 3/- 8° Heilbronn 84
VIDAL, Peire [fl. 1175–1215] Lieder, hrsg. Karl Bartsch 6/- 8° Berlin 57

268. FRENCH PHILOLOGY (a): INTRODUCTION. MAGAZINES. HISTORY OF THE LANGUAGE.

Introduction and Methodology—v. also D § 167, s.v. Languages, Modern.

BREITINGER, H. Studium und Unterricht des Französischen 3/- 8° Zürich [77] 85
MEISSNER, A. L. The Philology of the French Language 3/- 12° Hachette [74] 83
WENDT, O. Encyklopädie des französischen Unterrichts 3/- 8° Hanover 88

Magazines and Serials.

Französische Studien, hrsg. G. Körting + E. Koschwitz [a Suppl. to the Ztschr., infra] 8° Heilbronn 81–88 in prog.
 Vol. i. (3 pts.) 7/6; ii. 10/-; iii. (7 pts.) 18/-; iv. (5 pts.) 15/-; v. (4 pts.) 19/-; vi. (4 pts.) 13/-.
Revue de Philologie Française et Provençale
Zeitschrift für neufranz. Sprache und Litter., vols. i.–vi., ed. G. Körting + E. Koschwitz, vii.–xi., ed. H. Körting [died 1890] + D. Behrens ea. vol. [of 8 pts.] 15/- 8° Oppeln 79–89 in prog.

K § 268

History of the Language.

AUBERTIN, Ch. — Histoire de la Langue et Littér. franç. au moyen-Age, 2 vols. 12/6 8° *Paris* [78–79] 85
" " — Origine et Formation de la Langue et Métrique franç. " 82
de CASSAGNAC, Granier — Les Origines de la Langue Française 8° " 72

Maintains that the French is directly descended fr. the Celtic;—but is readable and full of useful material.

COCHERIS, H. — Entretiens sur la langue française 8° *Paris* 77
GÉNIN, F. — Des Variations du langage franç. depuis le 12e siècle *o.p.* [*scarce; w.* 12/–] 8° " 46
*LITTRÉ, E. — Histoire de la Langue Française, 2 vols. 6/– 8° " [62] 78

Not a history, but a good coll. of essays on the orig., etymol., gram., etc., of the Fch. lang. to Mid. Ages.

" " — Études et Glanures p. servir à l'histoire de la langue française 8° *Paris* 80
LOISEAU, A. — Histoire de la Langue Française [to end of 16 cent.] 6/6 8° " 81

French Language in England.

BEHRENDS, D. — Beitr. z. Geschichte d. frz. Sprache in Engl., pt. i. [= Franz. Stud., vol. v.] 8/– 8° *Heilbronn* 86
SCHEIBNER, O. — Die Herrschaft d. Franzosen in England [11–14 cent.; schl.-progr.] *Annaberg* 80

A good paper, by a "Neuphilologue."

Sixteenth Century —v. K § 274: Middle-French Philology.

Modern French (17th cent. to present time).

Malherbe's Position, Grammar, etc. [1555–1628].

BASSOT, L. — Un Réformateur de la Poésie française [on Malherbe] 8° *Paris* 81
BECKMANN, F. A. — Étude sur la Langue et la Versification de Malherbe [dissert.] *Bonn* 72
HOLFELD, H. — Ueber die Sprache des F. de Malherbe [dissert.] 2/– 8° *Posen* 75
NAUENDORF, — De l'Influ. opérée de M. sur la poés. et lang. franç. [progr.] *Marburg* 71

The Hôtel de Rambouillet and the Précieux.

*BERBLINGER, — Das Hotel Rambouillet u. s. culturgeschichtl. Bedeutung [progr.] 1/6 4° *Rendsburg* 75
COUSIN, Victor — La Société franç. au 17 siècle d'après Mlle. de Scudéry 8° *Paris* 55
FISCHER, F. A. — Das Hotel Rambouillet und die Précieux 1/6 8° *Jena* 68
KALLSEN, B. — Die französische Salonlitteratur im 17 Jahrhundert 62
*LIVET, C. L. — Précieux et Précieuses [the standard work] 8° *Paris* 59
ROEDERER, — Mémoire p. servir à l'hist. de la Société polie 8° " 57
SOMAIZE, — Dictionnaire des Précieuses, ed. C. L. Livet " [ ] 60

A dictionary of the Précieux language by a Précieux.

TIBURTIUS, G. — Molière und das Précieusenthum [dissert.] 1/– 8° *Neumark* 73

Vide also infra, s.v. Molière. Most other works on Molière deal more or less fully with the Précieux—*cf.* K § 35.

WEISSER, Emile — L'Hôtel de Rambouillet: essai d'histoire littéraire 2/– 4° *Breslau* 73

The Academy.

LUCAS, H. — De Academiae quam vocant Francogallicam originibus *Rheine* 79
" " — Essai sur la littérature française du 17 siècle [on the wks. of the "40 Immortals"] " 79
PELISSOT + d'OLIVET, — Histoire de l'Académie Française, ed. C. L. Livet 8° *Paris* [ ] 58
*VAUGELAS, — Remarques sur la Langue Française, ed. A. Chassang, 2 vols. 8° " [ ] 80

Classical Language of the 17th Century.

CHASSANG, A. —*in the* Introduction *to his edn. of* Vaugelas, *ut supra.*
MÜLLER, J. — Remarques s. l. lang. d. Classiques Fr. au 17 siècle [dissert.] 1/6 8° *Leipzig* 71
SCHÄFER, C. — Die syntakt. Alterthümlichkeiten d. fr. Spr. d. 17 Jahrh. [dissert.] 1/6 8° *Jena* 82

Boileau, Nicolas [1636–1711]

BORNGESSER, F. — L'Art Poétique de Boileau [schl.-progr.] 1/6 8° *Bayreuth* 83
KAULEN, E. — Die Poetik Boileau's [dissert.] 1/6 8° *Münster* 81

Corneille [1606–1684]

GODEFROY, F. — Lexique Comparé de la lang. de C. et du 17 siècle, 2 vols. *o.p.* [*w.* 15/–] 8° *Paris* 62
MARTY-LAVEAUX, — Lexique—*to his edn. of* Corneille's *Oeuvres* " 68
RICKEN, W. — Unters. üb. d. metrische Technik Corneille's, pt. i. 3/– 8° *Berlin* 84

Lafontaine [1631–1697]

LORIN, — Vocabulaire pour les Oeuvres de Lafontaine *o.p.* 8° *Paris* 52

Molière [1622–1673]

GÉNIN, F. — Lexique Comparé de la langue de Molière, *etc.* *o.p.* [*w.* 7/6] 8° *Paris* 46
HEIDKAMP, W. — Remarques sur la langue de Molière [schl.-progr.] *Münstereifel* 82

de Sévigné, Mme. [1626–1696]

SOMMER, E. — Lexique de la langue de Mme. de Sévigné 8° *Paris* 67

269. FRENCH PHILOLOGY (*b*): GRAMMAR: GENERALLY. PALÆOG., ORTHOG., PHONOL.

Grammar —*mere school-books are omitted.*

Bibliography.

STENGEL, E. Verzeichniss französischer Grammatiken [chronologically arrgd.; fr. end of 14th to beg. 18th cent.] 4/6 8° *Oppeln* 90

Text-Books, etc.

AYER, C. Grammaire comparée de la Langue Française [strong in syntax] 8° *Paris* [76] 85
BASTIN, J. Étude phil. de la lang. franç.; ou grammaire comparée 8° *St. Petersburg* 79
BRACHET, A. Historical Grammar of the French Tongue, tr. Dn. G. W. Kitchin 3/6 f 8° Clar. Press [68] 88
BREYMANN, Prf. H. French Grammar based on Philological Principles 4/6 f 8° Macmillan [74] 81
BRUNOT, F. Grammaire historique de la langue française 8° *Paris* 87
CHASSANG, A. Nouvelle Grammaire Française: cours supérieur 8° " [ ] 82
LÜCKING, G. Französische Schulgrammatik [a very good bk.] 2/- 8° *Berlin* [80] 83
MARTY-LAVEAUX Grammaire historique de la Langue Française 8° *Paris* 75
MÄTZNER, E. Französische Grammatik [w. spec. refer. to Latin] 10/- 8° *Berlin* [56] 84
Still the most scientific work, but in many parts antiquated. The new edns. are mere reprts. of the 1st.
PLATTNER, Ph. Französische Schulgrammatik [a very good bk.] 2/- 8° *Carlsruhe* 83
TOBLER, A. Vermischte Beiträge zur französischen Grammatik 5/- 8° *Leipzig* 86

Palaeography.

CHASSANT, A. Paléographie des Chartes et des MSS. des 11 au 17 siècle 5/- 12° *Paris* [39] 76
" " Dictionnaire des Abbréviations usitées dans les MSS. [chfly. Latin and Fch. charters] 7/- 8° *Paris* [2nd ed. 62] 84
L'École des Chartes Recueil de Facsimiles, 4 pts.; pl. f° " 80–87
PROU, M. Manuel de Paléographie Latine et Française [6–17 cent.] 10/- 8° " 90

Orthography and Pronunciation.

BENECKE, A. Darstellung der Lehre v. d. französischen Aussprache 2/- 8° *Potsdam* [75] 80
DIDOT, A. F. Observations sur l'orthographie française [w. a hist. of the reform since 15 cent.] 8° *Paris* 68
*LESAINT, M. A. Traité complet et méthod. de Prononciation française 9/- 8° *Leipzig* [62] 71
EBERS, E. Ueber d. verschiedenen Systeme *etc.* d. französ. Orthographie [schl. progr.] 1/6 8° *Osnabrück* 83
MENDE, A. Étude sur la Prononciation de l'*e* muet à Paris 8° *London* 80
NIEMER, G. Ueber d. orthogr. Reformversuche d. fr. Phonetiker d. 19 Jahrh. 2/- 8° *Greifswald* 82
PARIS, Gaston Étude sur le rôle de l'accent Latin dans la langue Française 3/6 8° *Paris*
PLÖTZ, C. Systematishe Darstellung der französischen Aussprache 1/6 8° *Berlin* [ ] 84
STÜRZINGER, J. [ed.] Orthographia Gallica [Altfranzösische Bibl.] 2/6 8° *Heilbronn* 84
A good edn. of the oldest treatise (anonymous) on French pronunciation and orthography.
*THUROT, Ch. De la Prononciation franç. depuis le 16e siècle, 2 vols. and Index *o.p.* [*scarce*; w. 45/-] 8° *Paris* 81; 83; 84

Phonology —*v. also* K § 120: Aryan Philology, *s.v.* Phonetics.

AYER, Ch. Phonologie de la Langue Française 8° *Paris* [74] 75
BEYER, F. Das Lautsystem des Neufranzösischen 2/- 8° *Köthen* 87
" " Französische Phonetik für Lehrer 4/- 8° " 88
KÖRITZ, W. Ueber das *s* vor Cons. im Französischen 8° *Strassburg* 85
LINDNER, F. Grundriss d. Laut- u. Flexionsanalyse d. neufrz. Schriftsprache [not v. good] 3/- 8° *Oppeln* 81
*PASSY, Paul Le Français parlé 8° *Paris*
" " Sons de Français 8° "
SCHELER, A. Exposé des Lois qui régissent la transform. fr. d. Mots Latins 3/- 12° *Brussels* 78
SOAMES, L. Introduction to English, French and German Phonetics 6/- c 8° Sonnenschein 90
*TRAUTMANN, M. Die Sprachlaute im allgemeinen [esp. Eng., Fch. and German] 7/- 8° *Leipzig* 84

270. FRENCH PHILOLOGY (*c*): ETYMOLOGY.

Generally.

NISARD, Ch. Curiosités d'Etymologie Française 8° *Paris* 63
MAHN, A. Etymologische Untersuchungen—*v.* K § 256: Romance.
ROTHENBERG, I. De Suffixorum Mutatione in Lingua Francogallia [written in German; diss.] 2/- 8° *Göttingen* 80
SCHÖTENSACK, H. A. Beitrag z. e. wiss. Grundlage f. etym. Unters. d. frz. Sprache 10/- 8° *Bonn* 83
A by no means scientific book—*e.g. échapper* deriv. fr. *ex champ*—from the (battle) field.

History of French Lexicography.

COURTAT, Monographie du Dictionnaire de l'Académie Française 8° *Paris* 80
FELS, A. Das Wörterbuch d. französischen Akademie, pt. i. [on the 1st edn.] [sch.-prog.] 1/6 8° *Hamburg* 84
KERVILER, Essai d'une Bibliographie raisonnée de l'Académie Française 8° *Paris* 77
SCHWARTZE, R. Die Wörterbücher d. fr. Sprache vor d. Erscheinen d. Dict. de l'Acad. [1350–1694; diss.] 1/- 8° *Jena* 75

Compound Words.

*DARMESTETER, A. Formation des Mots composés dans la lang. franç. [comparative] 8° *Paris* 75
MEUNIER, L. F. Les Composés qui contiennent un verbe à un mode personnel [in Latin, French, Italian and Spanish] 8° " 73
SCHMIDT, Joh. Ueber die französische Nominalzusammensetzung [sch.-progr.] 1/- 4° *Berlin* 72

K § 270

Creation of New Words.

*DARMESTETER, A. De la Création des Mots nouveaux dans la langue française 8/6 8° Paris 77

Dictionaries.

l'Académie Française, Dictionnaire histor. de la langue française, 2 vols. 30/- 4° Paris [1694] 84

The most complete dictionary; but quite thrown into the shade by LITTRÉ'S great work. For hist. of the Dict., v. K § sq.

BEAUJEAN, A. Dictionnaire de la Langue Franç.: abrégé de Littré 13/- 8° Paris [75] 86
BELLOWS, John Pocket Dict., French.-Eng. and Eng.-French [an excellent pocket-dict.] 10/6 32° Trübner [73] 77
CLIFTON + GRIMBAUD New Eng.-French and French-Eng. Dict., 2 vols. 30/- r 8° Hachette
GASC, F. E. A. English-French and French-English Dictionary 10/6 8° Bell [73] 89
HAMILTON + LEGROS, H. + E. Dict. Internat., Fr.-Angl. et Angl.-Fr., 2 vols. 24/- r 8° Paris 76
HATZFELD + DARMESTETER, A. + A. Dictionnaire général de la lang. franç. du commencem. du xvii. siècle jusqu'à nos jours, 30 pts. ea. 1/- 8° Paris 90 in prog.
*LITTRÉ, E. Dictionnaire de la Langue Française, 4 vols. and Supplément by M. Devic 90/- l 4° ,, [63–72] 74–84

Contains examples, synonyms, etymology and history of words to 11th century. A monumental work: one of the finest, if not the finest, dictionary in any language ever produced by a single man. Abridged by A. BEAUJEAN, one of LITTRÉ'S collaborateurs, ut supra.

Littré, E. Comment j'ai fait mon *Dictionnaire—in his* Études et Glanures [ut K § 268].
Pétrequin, J. E. Étude littéraire et lexicologique sur le Dictionnaire de M. Littré Lyons 75
MASSON, Gustave Dict. of the French Language [both pts.; based on Elwall] 6/- c 8° Macmillan 74
*SACHS + VILLATTE, C. E. Encyklopädisches Wörterbuch d. franz. u. deutschen Sprache, 2 vols. 66/- 4°; small edn. 2 v. in 1, 13/6 8° [an excellent work] Berlin [69–75] 87; [74–80] 88
SPIERS, Dr. French Dictionary, 2 vols. 21/- r 8° Hachette [ ]

Etymological Dictionaries.

*BRACHET, A. Etymological French Dictionary, tr. Dn. G. W. Kitchin 7/6 c 8° Clar. Press [73] 78
*SCHELER, Auguste Dictionnaire d'Etymologie Française 15/- r 8° Brussels [73] 80
SCHÖTENSACK, H. A. Französisch-Etymologisches Wörterbuch, pts. i.–iv. 13/6 8° 90 in prog.
STAPPERS, H. Dictionnaire Synoptique d'Etymologie Française 8° Brussels 85
TOUBIN, Ch. Dictionnaire Étymolog. et Explic. de la lang. Fr. [esp. popular lang.] 12/6 r 8° Paris 86

Mediæval Glossaries.

Cassel and Reichenau [8 cent.] Glossaries—v. K § 277, s.v. "Earliest Monuments."
CHASSANG, A. [ed.] Petit Vocabulaire Latin-franç. du 13° siècle [fr. Evreux MS.] Paris [ ]
FOERSTER + KOSCHWITZ, W. + E. [eds.]—*their* Altfranz. Uebungsb. [*ut* K § 273] *conts. the Reich. and Cass. glosses and another.*
SCHELER, A. [ed.] Lexicographie Latine du 12 et du 13 siècle [*repr. fr.* Jahrb. f. rom. Phil.] 3/6 8° Leipzig 67

Three works by JEAN GARLANDE, Alex. NECKAM, and ADAM DU PETIT-PONT.

,, ,, Olla Patella: vocab. latine versifié avec gloss. franç. [fr. Lille MS.] Brussels 79

The most important mediæval gloss. is the Latin-Fch. Dict. of FIRMIN LE VER [FIRMINIUS VERRIS, comp. betw. 1420–1440], upon wh. cf. SCHWARTZE, ut supra.

Doublets.

BRACHET, A. Dictionnaire des Doublets ou doubles formes de la lang. franç.; w. Suppl. 2/6 8° Paris [68] 83

Foreign Elements.

Generally.

LOUBENS, Recueil des Mots français tirées des Langues Étrangères 8° Paris 83

Celtic.

GRÜNEWALD, M. Ueber die keltischen Elemente im Französischen Brunswick 74
LÜCKE, Grammaire d. Idiomes Celtiques en rapp. av. la lang. franç. [progr.] Schleswig 76
THURNEYSEN, R. Keltoromanisches [the Celtic Etymols. in Diez's Etymol. W'bch.] 4/- 8° Halle 84

Greek.

LOUBENS, Recueil de Mots français dérivé de la Langue Grecque 8° Paris 80

Latin

—v. K § 210: Post-Classical Latin.

Oriental.

DEVIC, M. Dictionnaire Étymologique des Mots franç. d'origine oriental 7/6 s 8° Paris 76

Teutonic.

*ATZLER, F. Die germanischen Elemente in der französischen Sprache 3/- 8° Cöthen 67
HOTTENROT, Germanische Wörter im Französischen [programme] 1/6 8° Cologne 76
MACKEL, E. Die germanischen Elemente in d. französ. u. provenzal. Sprache [= Frz. Stud. vi. 1] 7/- 8° Heilbronn 87
NEUMANN, F. Die germ. Elemente in d. provenzal. u. franz. Spr. [phonetical; diss.] 1/6 8° Berlin 76
SCHECK, M. 500 german. Wörter u. 1,600 germ. Vocabeln in d. franz. Sprache 1/- 16° Stuttgart 75
SCHULTZE, M. Die germanischen Elemente der französischen Sprache 1/- 8° Berlin 76
SCHWEISTHAL, Rôle de l'élément franc de la langue française 8° Paris 83
WALTEMATH, W. Die fränkischen Elemente in der französischen Sprache [dissert.] 1/6 8° Paderborn 85

Names.

Personal Names.

FREYBERG, E. Französische Personennamen aus Guiman's Urkundenbuch v. A.ras [diss.] 1/6 8° *Halle* 82
LARCHEY, L. Dictionnaire des Noms [20,200 names] *Nancy* 80
MOISY, D. Études philologiques d'Onomatologie Normande *Paris* 75
RIGOLLOT, Essai d'Onomastique [family names of Vendôme in 16 cent.] 80
RITTER, E. Les Noms de Famille *Paris* 75

Place-Names.

de CHABAN, Essais sur l'Origine d. Noms Locaux de Touraine et Vendômois *Vendôme* 81
ESSER, Q. Ueber gallische Ortsnamen in der Rheinprovinz 1/6 8° *Andernach* 74
GLÜCK, E. Die bei Cäsar vorkommenden keltischen Ortsnamen 3/- 8° *Munich* 57
LITTRÉ, F. Noms de Lieu en France—*in his* Études et Glanures [*ut* K § 268].
MAUNIER, E. Études étymol., *etc.*, sur les noms de villes, bourgs, *etc.* 8° *Paris* 62
QUICHERAT, J. De la Formation fr. des anciens Noms de Lieux 8° ,, 67

Synonyms.

BOURGNIGNON + BERGEROL, E. Dictionnaire des Synonymes Français *Paris* 84
HERZ, J. Französische Synonyma 1/- 4° *Heilbronn* 79
*LAFAYE, Dictionnaire de Synonymes Français [the standard work] *Paris* [ ] 78
SARDOU, A. L. Nouveau Dictionnaire des Synonymes Français ,, 84
SCHMITZ, B. Französische Synonymik 4/6 8° *Leipzig* [68] 83

Synonyms in Individual Texts—*v.* K § 277, *s.vv.* Amis, Chanson de Roland.

271. FRENCH PHILOLOGY (*d*): ACCIDENCE.

Generally.

KOSCHWITZ, E. Neufranzösische Formenlehre 2/- 8° *Oppeln* 88

Verb.

BREYMANN, Prf. H. Die Lehre vom französischen Verb 2/6 8° *Munich* 82
*CHABANEAU, C. Histoire et Théorie de la Conjugation Française 4/6 8° *Paris* [68] 78
MOSEN, C. Das französische Verb 3/- 1 8° *Vienna* 87
THURNEYSEN, R. Ueber die Conjugation des Verbums *estre* *Jena* 82
WIGAND, A. Formation et Flexion du Verbe franz. basées sur le Latin 2/6 8° *Hermannstadt* 82

Participle.

BASTIN, Le Participe Passé Français et son Histoire 8° *St. Petersburg* 81
DOMKE, Ueber die französischen Participien [schl.-progr.] 8° *Greifenberg* 75
MERCIER, A. Histoire des Participes Français 3/6 8° *Paris* 80

Noun.

Gender.

MERCIER, A. De Neutrali genere quid factum sit in Gallica Lingua 2/- 8° *Paris* 79

Pronoun.

GESSNER, E. Zur Lehre vom französischen Pronomen, 2 pts. 2/6 8° *Berlin* [73-74] 85
SCHULZE, O. Zur Entwickelung des französ. Demonstrativpronomens [schl.-progr.] *Vegesack* 76

Particles.

Preposition.

CLAIRIN, P. Du Génetif Latin et de la Préposition *de* [good] 8° *Paris* 80

272. FRENCH PHILOLOGY (*e*): SYNTAX, PROSODY, STYLE, METRICS.

Syntax: Generally—*for* Syntax of Verb, Noun, etc., *v.* K § 271, *s.vv.* Verb, Noun, *etc.*

BRINKMANN, F. Syntax des Französischen und Englischen, vol. i. 12/- ; vol. ii. pts. i.-ii. 17/6 8° *Brunswick* 84; 85
*MÄTZNER, E. Syntax d. neufranz. Sprache, 2 vols. [standard ; still valuable] *o.p.* [*w.* 18/-] 8° *Berlin* 43; 45

Position of Words.

HABICHT, F. Beitr. z. Begründung d. Stellung v. Subj. u. Pred. im Neufranz. *Jena* 82

Prosody and Style.

BEAUVAIS, A. E. Deutsch-Französische Phraseologie, 2 vols. 8° *Wolfenbüttel* 84
FRANKE, E. Französische Stilistik, pts. i.-ii. ea. 3/- 8° *Oppeln* 86

K § 273

*PLOETZ, Karl — Vocabulaire Systématique et Guide de Conversation Française — *Berlin* — [ ]

ROCHE, A. — Du Styl et de la Composition littéraire — s 8° *Paris* — *n.d.*

*SCHMITZ, B. — Deutsch-Französische Phraseologie in systematischer Ordnung — *Berlin* — [72] 82

WILCKE, R. — Der französische Aufsatz [a good little book] 1/6 — 8° *Hamm* — 83

Metrics

—*v. also* K § 277, *s.vv.* Amis, Chans. de Roland.

*BECQ DE FOUQUIÈRES, L. — Traité Général de Versification Française — 6/6 — 8° *Paris* — 79

A very important work, the first really scientific and philosophical treatise on Fch. metrics.

BENLOEW, L. — Précis d'une Théorie des Rhythmes — ,, — 62; 63

FOTH, K. — Die französische Metrik in ihren Grundzügen [school book] 1/6 — 8° *Berlin* — 79

*LUBARSCH, E. O. — Französische Verslehre — 12/- — 8° ,, — 79

PIERSON, P. — Métrique naturelle du langage [w. prel. notice by Gaston Paris] 8/6 — 8° *Paris* — 84

QUICHERAT, L. M. — Traité de Versification Française — *o.p.* — 8° ,, — [28] 58

TOBLER, A. — Vom französischen Versbau alter u. neuer Zeit [Fch. tr., 4/6 8° *Paris* 85] 3/- — 8° *Leipzig* — [80] 83

History.

BELLANGER, L. — Études histor. et philolog. sur la Rime Franç. [15 cent. to pres. time] — 8° *Paris* — 76

273. OLD FRENCH [A.D. 842-14TH CENT.] PHILOLOGY (LANGUE D'OIL).

Geographical Limit.

de TOURTOULON + BRINGUIER, $\frac{Ch.}{O.}$ Étude s. l. limite géogr. de l. lang. d'Oc et l. d'Oïl, pt. i. [w. map] 5/- 8° *Paris* — 76

Grammar

—*v. also the* Introductions *to* Editions of Texts in K § 277, *passim.*

*BURGUY, G. F. — Grammaire de la Langue d'Oïl, 3 vols. [12-13 cent.; w. glossary] 25/- — 8° *Berlin* — [53-56] 82

CLÉDAT, L. — Grammaire élémentaire de la vieille langue française [a good element. bk.] — 8° *Paris* — 85

HORNING, A. — Grammaire de l'ancien français—*in his edn. of* Bartsch's Chrestom., *ut infra.*

LÜCKING, Gustav — Die ältesten französischen Dialekte [*ut* K § 275] 7/- — 8° *Berlin* — 77

Practically a treatise on the French language to middle of 11th cent. (*Alexis*).

ROGET, F. F. — Introduction to Old French — 6/- c 8° Williams — 87

History, grammar, chrestomathy of 100 pp. [fr. Bartsch *ut infra*], glossary.

SCHWAN, E. — Grammatik des Altfranzösischen — 3/- — 8° *Leipzig* — 88

Phonology

—*v. also the* Intros. *and* Notes *to edns. of* Texts in K § 277, esp. those by Andresen, Foerster, Koschwitz, Mall, Paris, Suchier, Vollmöller.

LENCER, — Versuch e. Parallele zwischen d. Entwickelung d. Altfranz. u. d. Englischen — *Schleiz* — 67

MATZKE, J. E. — Dialect. Eigenthümlichkeiten in d. Entwick. d. mouillierten *l* in Altfrz. — 2/6 — 8° *Paris* — 90

NEUMANN, F. — Laut- und Flexionslehre d. Altfranzösischen — 3/6 — 8° *Heilbronn* — 78

Dialects: Ancient —*v.* K § 275.

Etymology.

Lexicography.

JENSCH, — Beiträge zur Lexicographie d. Altfranzösischen [schl.-programme] 1/6 — 8° *Magdeburg* — 58

Dictionaries —*v. also the* Glossaries *appended to* Editions of Texts *in* K § 277.

BARTSCH, Karl — —*his* Chrestomathie de l'Anc. Franç. [*ut infra*] *conts. a good glossary.*

BURGUY, G. F. — —*in vol. iii. of his* Grammaire [*ut supra*] *is a convenient glossary, tho' its etymols. are untrustworthy.*

DUCANGE, C. — —*vol. iii. of his* Glossarium [*ut* K § 210] *contns. an extensive O.-F. dictionary.*

GODEFROY, F. — Dict. de l'anc. Lang. Franç. vols. i.-v. [Quantel] [9-15 cent.; to occupy 10 v.] ea. vol. 42/- — 4° *Paris* 79-89 *in prog.*

HIPPEAU, C. — Dictionnaire de la Langue Française aux 12e-13e siècles [not good] 10/- — 8° ,, — 66-72

LA CURNE SAINTE-PALAYE — Dictionn. histor. de l'anc. lang. franc., ed. L. Favre + M. Pajot, 10 v. ea. 25/- — 4° *Niort* — 75-84

Of no great value now. The author of the MS., now first pub., died in 1781, and the editing is meagre.

Accidence.

Verb.

BEHRENS, A. — Endung d. 2 Person Pluralis d. altfrz. Verbums — 1/6 — 8° *Leipzig* — 90

FREUND, H. — Verbalflexion d. ältesten franz. Sprachdenkmäler [dissert.] 1/- — 8° *Heilbronn* — 79

SPOHN, — Ueber die Conjonctif im Altfranzösischen — *Schrimm* — 82

Adjective.

EICHELMANN, L. — Flexion u. attrib. Stellung d Adj. i. d. ältest. frz. Sprachdenkm. [dissert.] 1/6 — 8° *Heilbronn* — 79

HAMMESFAHR, A. — Zur Comparation im Altfranzösischen [dissert.] 1/6 — 8° *Strassburg* — 81

Noun.

v. LEBINSKY, C. — Declination d. Substant. in d. Oil-sprache [diss.; *suppl. by* Horning *in* Ztsch. rom. Phil. vi.] 1/6 8° *Breslau* 78

SCHNEIDER, R. — Flexion d. Substantivs in d. ält. fr. Denkmäler [dissert.] 1/6 — 8° *Marburg* — 83

Pronoun.

GANZLIN, K. — Pronomina demonstrativa im Altfranzösischen — 1/6 — 8° *Leipzig* — 88

GENGENAGEL, K. — Kürzung d. Pronomina hinter vocalisch. Auslaut im Altfz. [dissert.] 1/- — 8° *Halle* — 82

NISSEN, P. — Nominativ d. verbund. Personalnomina i. d. ält. frz. Sprachdenkm. [dissert.] 1/6 — 8° *Kiel* — 82

PIETZCH, C. — Beiträge zur Lehre vom altfranzösischen Relativum — 2/- — 8° *Halle* — 88

Numerals.

KNÖSEL, K. — Das altfranzösische Zahlwort [dissert.] 1/6 — 8° *Erlangen* — 84

Syntax.

BOURCIEZ, E. Syntaxe de l'ancien Français [a sketch] 1/- 8° *Bordeaux* 85
KLAPPERICH, J. Histor. Entwickelung d. syntakt. Verhältn. d. Bedingungssätze im Altfrz. [= Frz. Stud. iii. 3] 2/6 8° *Heilbronn* 82
SCHÄFER, W. Die altfranzösischen Doppelrelativsätze [dissert.] 1/6 8° *Marburg* 84
SCHNEIDER, A. Die ellipt. Verwendung d. partitiv. Ausdrucks in Altfranz. [dissert.] 1/6 8° *Breslau* 83

Verb.

KÖRNIG, F. Der syntaktische Gebrauch d. Impf. u. hist. Perf. im Altfrz. [dissert.] 1/6 8° *Berlin* 83

Participle.

BONNARD, J. Le Participe Passé en vieux Français 2/6 8° *Lausanne* 77
BUSSE, J. Die Congruenz d. Part. Prät. in activ. Verbalconstr. im Altfr. [dissert.] 1/6 8° *Göttingen* 82
KLEMENZ, Paul Syntaktischer Gebrauch d. Part. Präs. u. d. Gerundium im Altfrz. 1/- 8° *Breslau* 84
SCHLUTTER, H. Gesch. d. syntakt. Gebrauch d. Passé déf. u. Imparf. im Franz. 1/- 8° *Halle* 84

Interrogative Sentence.

SCHULZE, A. Der altfranzösische direkte Fragesatz 5/- 8° *Leipzig* 88

Particles: Prepositions—*v. also* K § 277: *s.v.* Joinville.

DICKHUT, W. Form u. Gebrauch d. Präpos. i. d. ält. fr. Sprachdenkm. [dissert.] 1/6 8° *Münster* 83
GESSNER, E. Sur l'Origine des Prepositions Françaises *Berlin* 58
RAITHEL, G. Die altfranz. Präpositionen, pt. i. [dissert.] 1/- 8° „ 75
SCHLENNER, Die Präposition *de* und ihr adnominal. Gebrauch [dissert.] 1/6 8° *Halle* 81

Position of Words —*v. also* K § 277: *s.vv.* Aucassin, Chanson de Roland, Crestien.

KRÜGER, P. Wortstellung in d. frz. Prosalitteratur d. 13 Jahrh. [dissert.] 1/6 8° *Berlin* 76
VÖLCKER, B. Wortstellung in d. ältesten franz. Sprachdenkmalen [= Frz. Stud. iii. 7] 2/- 8° *Heilbronn* 82
WAGNER, R. Stellung d. attributiven Adjectivs in altfrz. Prosatexten [13–15 cent.] 2/6 8° *Leipzig* 90

Prosody —*v. also* K § 277: *s.vv.* Amis, Chans. de Rol., Crestien.

TOLLE, K. Betheuern u. Beschwören in d. altrom. [= Fch.] Poesie *Erlangen* 83
ZUTAVERN, K. Ueber die altfranzösische epische Sprache *Heidelberg* 85

Metrics.

PARIS, Gaston —*his introduction to his edn. of* Vie de St. Alexis [*ut* K § 277].

Chrestomathies.

*BARTSCH, Karl [ed.] Chrestomathie de l'Ancien Français [8–15 cent.; w. glossary] 10/- 8° *Leipzig* [66] 84
" " The same; w. a grammar of Old French by A. Horning 12/6 8° *Paris* 87
CONSTANS, L. [ed.] Chrestomathie de l'Ancien Français, 4/6; Supplement [11–15 cent.; schl.-bk.] s 8° „ 84; 86
FOERSTER + KOSCHWITZ, W. K. [eds.] Altfranzösisches Uebungsbuch, pt. i. 3/-; Supplement, pt. i. 3/- 8° *Heilbronn* 84; 86
Pt. i.: Die ältesten Sprachdenkmäler, w. a facs.; pt. ii.: Rolandmaterialien.
LIDFORSS, E. [ed.] Choix d'anciens textes français 5/- 4° *Paris*
MEYER, Paul [ed.] Recueil d'anciens Textes, pts. i.–ii. ea. 5/- 8° „ 74 77
i.: Vulgar-Latin, Provençal; ii.: Old-Fch. Poetry; iii.: Old-Fch. Prose, w. glossary *in prep.*
TOYNBEE, Paget [ed.] Specimens of Mediæval French Clar. Press *in prep.*

274. MIDDLE-FRENCH [15TH TO BEGINNING 17TH CENT.] PHILOLOGY.

History of the Language.

*DARMESTETER + HATZFELD, A. A. Le Seizième Siècle en France: tableau de la littér. et langue, 2 pts. 8° *Paris* 78
A good piece of wk.: one of the best histories of a brief period of literary history extant in small compass.

Orthography and Pronunciation—*v.* K § 269: (esp. STÜRZINGER [ed.] *and* THUROT).

Phonology.

LANGE, Der vocalische Lautstand in d. frz. Sprache d. 16 Jahrh. *Elbing* 83
THÖNE, O. Die lautl. Eigenthümlichkeiten d. fr. Spr. d. 16 Jahrh. [dissert.] *Marienburg* 83

Chrestomathies.

BRACHET, A. [ed.] Morceaux choisis d. Grands Écrivains fr. du 16e siècle [w. gram. and vocab.] 8° *Paris* [74] 81
DARMESTETER + HATZFELD [*ut supra*]—*conts., as appendix, a seln. of 16th cent. prose and verse.*
MERLET, G. [ed.] Les Grands Écrivains du 16e siècle [Extr. d. Class. Fr.: w. notes] s 8° *Paris* 7-
MONNARD, Ch. [ed.] Chrestomathie des Prosateurs Franç. du 14–16 siècle [w. gram. and voc.] *Geneva* 62

Pronoun.

LAHMEYER, Das Pronomen in d. frz. Sprache d. 16. u. 17. Jahrhunderts 2/6 8° *Göttingen* 86

Syntax.

*BENOIST, A. De la Syntaxe franç. entre Palsgrave et Vaugelas 8° *Paris* 76
PALSGRAVE, an Englishman, was the first author of a proper French Grammar (pub. 1530; re-ed. GÉNIN 8° *Paris* 52): VAUGELAS was a Fch. grammarian (1585–1650).
GRÄFENBERG, S. Beiträge zur franz. Syntax des xviten. Jahrhunderts 2/- 8° *Erlangen* 85
HAASE, A. Französische Syntax des xviiten. Jahrhunderts 7/- 8° *Oppeln* 88
SCHÄFER, C. Die wichtigsten syntakt. Alterthümlichkeiten d. frz. Spr. d. 17. Jahrh. [diss.] 1/6 4° *Jena* 82

275. FRENCH DIALECTS (a): ANCIENT: WITH A FEW SPECIMENS OF LITERATURE.

Collectively —*v. also the* Introductions *and* Notes *appended to edns. of Texts, ut* K § 277 : *passim.*
BURGUY, G. F. —*in his* Grammaire [*ut* K § 273].
DIEZ, F. —*in his* Grammatik [*ut* K § 256].
LÜCKING, Gustav — Die ältesten französischen Dialekte 7/- 8° *Berlin* 77
PARIS, Gaston —*in his* Introduction *to his edn.* Alexis [*ut* K § 277].
Monographs.
FLECK, A. — Der betonte Vocalismus einiger altostfr. Sprachdenkmäler [dissert.] 1/6 8° *Marburg* [illegible]
ZEMLIN, J. — Der Nachlaut *i* in d. Dialekten Nord- u. Ostfrankr. [dissert.] 1/6 8° *Halle* [illegible]
The Introductions and notes to edns. of O.-F. texts (K § 277) often cont. much important dialectical matter.

Central Dialect (ISLE OF FRANCE and pt. of CHAMPAGNE).
METZKE, E. — Der Dialekt von Isle de France im 13 u. 14 Jahrhundert *Breslau* 81
Literature.
CRESTIEN DE TROIES —*v.* K § 277, *s.v.* Arthurian Romances.
GARNIER DE PONT ST. MAXENCE —*v.* K § 277, *s.v.* Chronicles in Verse.
de JOINVILLE, Sire —*v.* K § 277, *s.v.* Prose : Chronicles.

Eastern Dialects.

Burgundian (NIVERNAIS, BERRY, ORLÉANAIS, TOURAINE, etc.).
Literature.
Ysopet, Der Lyoner — hrsg. Prf. W. Foerster [Altfranzös. Bibl., vol. v.] 3/6 8° *Heilbronn* 82

Lothringian (LOTHRINGEN).
FLECK, Aug. — Der betonte Vocalismus einiger altfrz. Sprachdenkmäler 2/- 8° *Marburg* 77
Literature.
BERNARD, St. —*v.* K § 277, *s.v.* Prose : Sermons.
Psalter, Der lothringische — hrsg. E. Apfelstedt [= Altfranzös. Bibl., vol. iv.] 6/- 8° *Heilbronn* 81

Western Dialects.
GÖRLICH, Ewald — Die südwestlischen Dialekte d. Langue d'Oïl [= Franz. Stud. iii. 2 (*ut* K § 256)] 5/- 8° *Heilbronn* 82
" " — Die nordwestlischen Dialekte d. Langue d'Oïl [= Franz. Stud. v. 3 (*ut* K § 256)] 4/- 8° " 86

Anglo-Norman (ENGLAND)—*v. also* K § 268, *s.v.* French Lang. in England.
KLOPPE, — Recherches sur le dialecte de Wace, 2 pts. *Marburg* 53 : 54
LE HÉRICHER, L. — Glossaire Étymol. Anglo-Normand : ou l'Anglais ramené à la lang. franç. 6/6 8° *Avranches* 84
A curious book, as may be judged from the title.
SKEAT, Prf. W. W. — Rough List of Eng. Words fd. in Anglo-Fch. [13–14 cents.]—*in* Trans. Philol. Soc. 80–81, pt. iii., Append. v., pp. 91–168.
VISING, J. — Étude s. le dialecte Anglo-Normand du 12 siècle [dissert.] *Upsala* 82
" — Sur la Versification Anglo-Normande " 84
Literature.
ADGAR's Legends of Mary —*v.* K § 277, *s.v.* Religious and Moral Poetry.
Auban, St., Life of —*v.* K § 277, *s.v.* Religious and Moral Poetry.
BENOÎT DE STE. MORE —*v.* K § 277, *s.v.* Other Romances.
Brandan, St., Voyage of —*v.* K § 277, *s.v.* Religious and Moral Poetry.
CHANDOS HERALD — Le Prince Noir [14 cent.], ed. Fr. Michel ; w. Engl. tr. 50/- 4° *Quaritch* 83
CHARDRY, —*v.* K § 277, *s.v.* Religious and Moral Poetry.
Charlemagne : Anglo-Norman poem of 12 cent., ed. Fr. Michel *o.p.* [*w.* 6/-] 8° *London* 36
Chroniques Anglo-Normands —*v.* K § 277, *s.v.* Chronicles in verse.
GAYMAR, Geoff. [*c.* 1146] —*v.* K § 277, *s.v.* Chronicles in verse.
Horn, Ritter : ed. R. Brede + E. Stengel, fr. Camb., Oxon. and Lond. MSS. : [Ausgaben u. Abhandl. viii.] 6/- 8° *Marburg* 83
ed. F. Wissmann ; w. notes and gloss. [Quellen u. Forsch.] 3/6 8° *Strassburg* 81
MARIE OF FRANCE [13 cent.] —*v.* K § 277, *s.vv.* Indiv. Lyric Writers and Didactic (*b*) : Lais.
PHILIPPE DE THAÜN —*v.* K § 277, *s.v.* Early Poetry : Didactic (*c*).
WACE, Robert —*v.* K § 277, *s.v.* Chronicles in Verse.

Franco-Norman (MAINE, BRITTANY, PERCHE, POITOU, ANJOU).
BOUCHERIE, — Le Dialecte Poitevin au 13° siècle 8° *Montpellier* 73
HOTZEL, — Der norman. Dialekt und die französische Schriftsprache [schl.-progr.] *Eisenach* 69
ROETH, C. — Ueber d. Ausfall des intervocalen *d* im Norman. [dissert.] *Halle* 82
SCHULZKE, P. — Betontes *e*+*i* und *o*+*i* in d. norman. Mundart [dissert.] " 79
STRAUCH, M. — Lat. *o* in der norman. Mundart [dissert.] " 81
THIERKOPF, P. — Der stammhafte Wechsel im Norman. [dissert.] " 8[illegible]
Literature.
Bibliotheca Normannica : Denkmäler normann. Litteratur u. Sprache, hrsg. H. Suchier, vols. i.–iii. 18/6 8° *Halle* 79–87
i. : Reimpredigt, hrsg. H. SUCHIER, 4/6 ; ii. : Judenknabe [5 Gk., 14 Lat., 8 Fch. texts], hrsg. E. WOLTER, 4/- ; iii. : Lais d. Marie de France, hrsg. K. WARNKE [w. notes Reinh. KÖHLER], 10/-.

Picardian (ARTOIS, FLANDERS, BAS-MAINE, pt. of CHAMPAGNE, HENNEGALL, NAMUR, LÜTTICH, BRABANT).

HAASE, H. Das Verhalten d. picard. u. wallon. Denkmäler d. Mittelalt. [*a* & *e* bef. *n*; diss.] *Halle* 80
JENRICH, C. Die Mundart d. *Münchener Brut* [diss.; attributes poem to Namur dial.] ,, 81
SIEMT, O. Ueber lat. *c* vor *e* und *i* im Pikardischen [dissert.] ,, 81

Literature

Alexis, St., Vie de —*v.* K § 277, *s.v.* "Earliest Monuments."
Aucassin et Nicolete —*v.* K § 277, *s.v.* Fiction.
Chevalier as deus espees —*v.* K § 277, *s.v.* Romans d'Aventures.
Dit dou vrai aniel —*v.* K § 277, *s.v.* Didactic Poetry (*a*): Dits.
MOUSKES, Philippe —*v.* K § 277, *s.v.* Chronicles in Verse.
PHILIPPE DE RÉMY —*v.* K § 277, *s.v.* Romans d'Aventures.
RAOUL DE HOUDENC —*v.* K § 277, *s.v.* Lyric Poets.

278. FRENCH DIALECTS (*b*): MODERN.

Bibliography.

SCHEFFLER, W. —*in his* Die französische Volksdichtung und Sage *Leipzig* 83; 84

Anjou.

MENIÈRE, Glossaire Angevin étymologique comparé avec différents dialectes 8° *Angers* 81

Aunis.

MEYER, L. E. Glossaire de l'Aunis 3/- 8° *Paris* 71

Breton —*v.* K § 280: Celtic Philology (*b*): Cymric Branch.

Champagne: *Rheims.*

SAUBINET, E. Vocabulaire du bas langage Rémois 8° *Rheims* 45

Lille.

DESROUSSEAUX DU BUC, L. Nouveau Glossaire Lillois [w. histor. and gramm. intro.] 8° *Lille* 67
VERMESSE, L. Vocabulaire du Patois Lillois 8° ,, 60

Lorraine.

ADAM, Lucien Les Patois Lorrains [gram., gloss., texts] 8/6 8° *Nancy* 81
MICHEL, Dict. d. expressions vicieuses [esp. Lorraine] 8° ,, 81

Maine.

CHARDON, Études sur les dialectes et les patois [spec. Maine] 8° *Le Mans* 69

Metz.

HORNING, A. Die ostfranzösische Grenzdialekte zwischen Metz und Belfort 4/6 8° *Heilbronn* 87

Normandy.

Bibliography.

FRÈRE, E. Manuel du Bibliographe Normand *o.p.* 8° *Rouen* 59

Dictionaries.

du BOIS, L. Glossaire du Patois Normand, augmenté par Travers 8° *Caen* 50
LITTRÉ, E. Histoire et Glossaire du Normand—*in his* Études et Glanures [*ut* K § 268].
du MÉRIL, A. + E. Dictionnaire du Patois Normand 8° ,, 50
MÉTIVIER, G. Dictionnaire Franco-Norman [Guernsey, etc.] 12/- 8° *London* 70
MOISY, D. Dictionnaire du Patois Normand, 2 vols. 12/6 8° *Caen* 87
ROMDAHL, A. Glossaire du Patois du Val de Saire 8° *Linkoeping* 81
VASNIER, Petit Dictionnaire du Patois Normand 8° *Rouen* 62

History, etc.

JORET, Ch. Des Charactères et de l'Extension du Patois Normand 5/- 8° *Paris* 83
,, ,, Essai sur le Patois Normand du Bessin 5/- 8° ,, 81

Phonology.

JORET, C. Mélanges de Phonétique Normande 2/6 8° *Paris* 85

Parisianisms —*v. also* Slang, *infra* (espec. LARCHEY).

BOTZON, L. Sur le Langage Actuel de Paris [school-programme] *Frankfort* 73
NISARD, Ch. Étude sur le Langage Populaire de Paris 6/6 8° *Paris* 72
,, ,, De quelques Parisianismes Populaires expliq. d. 17–19 siècles 2/6 12° ,, 76
VILLATTE, C. Parisismen [alphab. dict. of Parisianisms] 5/- 8° *Berlin* [84] 90

Picardy.

*CORBLET, T. Glossaire Étymol. et comp. du Patois Picard [anc. and mod.; w. bibliogr.] 7/6 8° *Paris* 51

K § 277

Poitou.

Dreux du Radier — Essai sur le Langage Poitevin — 2/6 8° *Niort* 66
Favre, L. — Glossaire du Poitou, de la Saintonge et de l'Aunis [w. bibliogr.] 8° *Poiters* 68
Levrier, G. — Dictionnaire Étymologique du Patois Poitevin 8° *Niort* 78
Rousseau, Abbé — Glossaire Poitevin — 3/6 8° *Paris* 69

Provençal

—*v.* K § 266.

Saintonge.

Eveille, A. — Glossaire Saintongeais — 12/6 8° *Bordeaux* 88
Jonain, P. — Dictionnaire du Patois Saintongeais — 7/6 8° *Royau* 69

Slang

—*v. also* Parisianisms, *supra.*

Barrère, Albert — Argot and Slang [French-English Dictionary, with intro.] 10/6 p 8° Whittaker [87] 89
Delvau, A. — Dictionnaire de la Langue Verte — 5/– 8° *Paris* [ ] 83
Larchey, L. — Dictionnaire Historique, Etymolog. et Anecdot. de l'Argot Parisien; ill. 5/– r 8° ,, [ ] 80
Michel, F. R. — Études de Philologie comparée de l'Argot [of Europe and Asia] *o.p.* [*w.* 10/–] r 8° ,, 56
Rigaud, L. — Dictionnaire de l'Argot Moderne — 5/– s 8° ,, 81
Vitu, A. — De Jargon et Jobelin: avec un dictionnaire du jargon — 10/– 8° ,, 90

Switzerland

—*v. also* K § 231.

Ayer, Ch. — Introduction à l'étude d. Dialectes du pays romand [not v. good] 8° *Neuchâtel* 78
Bridel, D. — Glossaire du Patois de la Suisse Romande, ed. Favrat — 8/– 8° *Basle* 67

Fribourg.

Grangier, L. — Glossaire Fribourgeois 8° *Fribourg* 64-68
Häfelin, F. — Recherches sur les Patois Romans du canton de Fribourg [gram., chrest., gloss.] 8° *Leipzig* 79

Geneva.

Gaudy-Lefort, — Dictionnaire Genévois *o.p.* 8° *Geneva* 27

Vosges.

Haillant, N. — Essai sur un Patois Vosgien, pt. i. [phonology] 10/– 8° *Epinal* 83
Jouve, L. — Coup d'œil sur les Patois Vosgiens [*repr. fr.* Echo des Vosges] 8° ,, 64

Walloon.

Altenburg, W. — Versuch einer Darstellung d. wallon. Mundart, 3 pts. [sch.-progr.; phonetical] 8° *Eupen* 80; 81; 82
Chansons et Poésies Wallonnes [Pays de Liège] 4/6 8° *Liège*
Chavée, H. — Français et Wallons [a parallel] 7/– 8° *Brussels* 57
Dejardin, J. [ed.] — Dictionnaire des Spots [proverbs] 8/6 8° *Liège* 63
Grandgagnage, C. — Dictionnaire etymol. de la Langue Wallonne vols. i.–ii. pt. 1 *o.p.* [*w.* 15/–] i 8° ,, 45; 50
,, ,, — The Same, vol. ii. pt. 2 [end], ed. w. suppl. and glossary, A. Scheler — 10/– i 8° *Brussels* 80
,, ,, — Vocab. des Noms Wallons d'Animaux, de Plantes et de Mineraux 8° ,, 57
M[ichiels], L. — Grammaire élémentaire Liègeoise *o.p.* [*w.* 7/6] 8° *Liège* 63
Remacle, L. — Dictionnaire Wallon-Français, 2 vols. — 21/– 8° ,, [ ] 53
Sigart, J. — Glossaire étymologique Montois — 8/6 8° *Brussels* 70

Extra-European Dialects.

Canadian.

Dun, O. — Glossaire Franco-Canadien et Vocab. de Locutions Vicieuses usitées au Canada 8° *Quebec* 80
Elliott, Prf. [Am.] — On a Philological Expedition to Canada [Johns Hopkins Univ. Circ., Dec. '84] 8° *Baltimore* 84

Creolese

—*v. also* K § 161.

Baissac, E. — Étude sur le patois Créole-Mauricien 8° *Nancy* 80

277. OLD FRENCH LITERATURE.

Collections: Modern.

Altfranzösische Bibliothek, hrsg. W. Foerster, vols. i.–xi. — 67/6 8° *Heilbronn* 79–87 *in prog.*
Excellent edns. by prominent German Romance scholars, of Old-French and Provençal texts. The more import. ent. separ.
Bibliothèque Française du Moyen-âge, ed. P. Meyer + Gaston Paris 8° *Paris* 84 *in prog.*
i.-ii.: Recueil d. Motets franc. des 12-13 siècles, by G. Raynaud.
Französische Neudrucke hrsg. K. Vollmöller, pts. i.–viii. — 20/6 8° *Heilbronn* 80–88 *in prog.*
Société des Anciens Textes. Publications of, vols. i.–xxiii. [the more import. ent. separ.] 8° *Paris* 75–86 *in prog.*

Chrestomathies —*v.* K § 273.

"The Earliest Monuments."

DIEZ, F. [ed.] Altromanische Sprachdenkmale [Eide, Eulalia, Boethius] 8° *Bonn* 46

With German notes and an Introduction on French epic verse.

,, [ed.] Altromanische Glossare berichtigt u. erklärt [Reichenau & Cassel glosses] 2/6 8° ,, 65

FOERSTER + KOSCHWITZ, W. + E. [eds.]—pt. i. *of their* Altfrz. Uebungsbuch [*ut* K § 273] *conts.* the "*Earliest Monuments*" 3/- 8° *Heilbronn* 84

KOSCHWITZ, E. [ed.] Les plus anciens Monuments de la Langue Française 1/- s 8° ,, [79] 86

PARIS, Gaston [ed.] Les plus anciens Monuments d. l. lang. fr.: Album [Soc. Anc. Textes] 8° *Paris* 75

STENGEL, Prf. E. [ed.] Die ältesten frz. Sprachdenkmäler—*in* Ausgaben und Abhandlungen, pts. i. and xi. 8/- & 1/- *Marburg* 84

AIDS:

Koschwitz, E. Commentar zu d. ältesten frz. Sprachdenkm., pt. i. [Altfrz. Bibl.] 6/- 8° *Heilbronn* 86

Commentaries to (1) (2) (3) (7) and (9).

Schneider, R. Flexion d. Substantive in d. ält. Denkm. u. im *Charlemagne* [dissert.] *Marburg* 83

Individual Texts.

Alexis, Vie de St. [12 cent.] ed. Gaston Paris + L. Pannier *o.p.* [*w.* 24/-] 8° *Paris* 72

A methodical reconstruction of the oldest text, with an important introduction on the language and metre of the poem. The *text* (only) was repr. 1/6 8° *Paris* 85.

Cambridge Psalter ed. Fr. Michel [Coll. de Docum. Inédits] 8° *Paris* 76

AIDS:

Fichte, E. Die Flexion im Cambridge Psalter *Halle* 79

Schumann, W. Vocalismus und Consonantismus d. Cambridge Psalter—*in* Frz. Studien, vol. iv, 4 [*ut* K § 268] 2/6 8° *Heilbronn* 84

Cassel Glossary [8 cent.] [Teutonic and Romance gloss.; came from Fulda]—*v.* Diez's Altroman. Glossare, *supra*.

Oxford Psalter ed. Fr. Michel 8° *Oxford* 60

AIDS:

Harseim, Vocalismus und Consonantismus im Oxford Psalter - *in* Roman. Studien., vol. iv. [*ut* K § 256].

Meister, J. H. Die Flexion im Oxford Psalter *Halle* 77

Reichenau Glossary [8 cent.], ed. Hoffmann [Latin and Romance gloss.; MS. at Carlsruhe] 63

ed. F. Diez—*in his* Altromanische Glossare—*ut supra*.

The "Earliest Monuments" comprise: (1) The Strassburg Oaths, (2) Song of St. Eulalie; (3) Jonah-fragment (at Valenciennes); (4) Leodegar (separ. ed. Gaston PARIS); (5) Poem on *Passion*; (6) *Alexius* (*v. supra*); (7) *Solomon's Song*; (8) *Alexander-fragm.* of AUBERI of BESANÇON [*v.* K (*sub*: Provençale)]; (9) *Epistle of S. Stephen*; (10) *Sponsus*—to wh. may be added the prose wks.; (11) *Tr. of Bks. of Kings* ("*Quatre Livres*"); (12) Oxford *Psalter* (*v. sup.*); (13) Cambridge *Psalter* (*v. sup.*). KOSCHWITZ includes (1) (2) (3) (4) (5) (10); PARIS gives photogr. facsm. of (1) (2) (3) (4) (5); STENGEL gives (1) (2) (3) (4) (5) (6) (7) (8) and (9).

Chansons de Gestes.

History.

CASTETS, F. Recherches sur l. rapports d. chans. d. g. et. de l'ep. chev. ital. 5/- 8° *Paris* 87

GAUTIER, Léon Les Épopées Françaises, 4 vols. [vol. ii. not pub. yet] 33/6 8° ,, [65–68] 78–82

PARIS, Gaston Histoire poétique de Charlemagne *o.p.* [*pb.* 21/-; *w.* 25/-] 8° ,, 65

On the origins and ramifications of the legend. Of much importance for the hist. of the O.-F. chanson-de-geste.

PERSCHMANN + REIMANN + RHODE, H. + W. + A. Beiträge zur Kritik d. frz. Karlsepen [= Ausg. u. Abhand. iii.] 5/- 8° *Marburg* 82

RAJNA, Pio Le Origini dell' Epopea Francese 8° *Florence* 84

For English versions and texts of the Carlovingian Romances, *v.* K § 48.

Texts.

ADENÈS LI ROIS [13 cent.] Roumans de Berte aux grans pies, ed. A. Scheler 3/6 8° *Brussels* 74

AID:

Feist, A. Zur Kritik der Bertasage [Ausg. u. Abhandl. lix.] 1/6 8° *Marburg* 86

AIMERI DE NARBONNÈ Chanson de Geste, ed. L. Demaison [Soc. Anc. Textes] 8° *Paris*

Aiol et Mirabel *and* Elie de St. Gille, ed. Prf. W. Foerster; w. Germ. notes and gloss. [w. glossary] 21/- 8° *Heilbronn* 76–82

,, ,, ,, ed. F. Normand + G. Raynaud [Soc. Anc. Textes] *Paris* 78

Aliscans [12 cent. chans. d. geste]; ed. F. Guessard + A. de Montaiglon 70

,, ed. Dr. Jonckbloet—*in his edn. of* Guillaume d'Orange, 2 vols. 8° *The Hague* 54

Amis et Amiles and Jourdains de Blaives, ed. C. Hofmann 4/- 8° *Erlangen* [52] 82

,, and Amiloun [Eng. vers.]: W. O.-Fch. source, hrsg. E. Kölbing [Altengl. Bibl.] 7/- 8° *Heilbronn* 84

Jourdains de Blaives is a continuation of the chanson de geste *Amis et Amiles*.

AIDS:

HÖLLEN, J. Stil. u. Compos. d. *Amis et Amiles* u. *Jourd. de Blaives* [dissert.] 1/6 8° *Münster* 83

KLEIN, H. Sage, Metrik u. Grammatik d. *Amis et Amiles* [dissert.] 1/6 8° *Bonn* 75

KOCH, J. Ueber *Jourdains de Blaives* 1/6 8° *Königsberg* 75

KÖLBING, Prf. E. Ueberlieferung d. Sage v. *Amis et Amiles*—*in* Paul and Braune's Beiträge [*ut* K § 223].

LAUSBERG, Die Verbalen Synonyma in *Amis et Amiles* u. *Jourdains de Blaives* [dissert.] 2/- 8° *Münster* 84

LINK, Th. Eine sprachliche Studie über die agn. Version der *Amis-Sage* 1/6 8° *Munich* 83

MODERSOHN, Die Realien in *Amis u. Amiles* u. *Jourdains de Blaives* [dissert.] 2/6 8° *Münster* 86

SCHOPPE, J. Metrum u. Assonanz d. *Amis et Amiles* [= Franz. Stud. iii. i. (*ut* K § 268)] 2/6 8° *Heilbronn* 8-

Aquin [chans. d. geste] ed. Jollon des Longrais 8° *Nantes* 80

Aspremont [chans. de geste] ed. F. Guessard + L. Gautier 8° *Paris* 55

Auberi [chans. d. geste] ed. P. Tarbé; ed. A. Tobler 8° *Rheims* 49; *Lps.* 70

Aye d'Avignon [chans. d. geste] ed. F. Guessard + P. Meyer 8° *Paris* 61

Aymon, Quarte Fils —*v.* Renaus de Montauban, *infra*.

BODEL, Jean Les Saisnes, ed. Fr. Michel [Charlemagne's wars w. Witekind] *o.p.* 8° ,, 39

,, ,, ,, ,, Four Pastourelles are ed. K. Bartsch—*in his* Altfrz. Rom. u. Pastourellen [*ut infra*].

K § 277

Chanson de Roland.

Texts.

(*a*) *Reprints and Facsimiles:* ed. Prf. W. Foerster fr. Châteauroux and Venetian (vii.) MSS. [Altfrz. Bibl.] 10/- 8° *Heilbronn* 83
" " " fr. Paris, Lyons, and Cambr. MSS. and Lothr. fragm. [Altfrz. Bibl.] 10/- 8° " 87
" Prf. E. Kölbing; w. German notes fr. Venetian MS. (iv.) 5/- 8° " 77
" Prf. E. Stengel, fr. Cod. O., Digby 23 MS. 3/- 8° " 78

(*b*) *Editions:* ed. Karl Bartsch; w. German notes, intro. and index 3/- 12° *Leipzig* 74
" Prf. E. Böhmer, *sub tit.* Rencesval [Oxford Text] 2/- 8° *Halle* 72
" L. Clédat [a good working edn., w. glossary] 2/6 8° *Paris* 86
" Léon Gautier; w. Mod. Fch. tr., comm. and gloss. [a classical edn] 5/- 8° *Tours* [72] 87
" " " ; smaller edn. 3/6 s 8° " [ ] 84
" Fr. Michel *Paris* [37] 69
" Th. Müller, pt. i. [text and notes] [the best scientific edn., Oxford MS.] 8° *Göttingen* [63] 78

The second part was to have been a Glossary, but MÜLLER has died since.

Translations.

(*a*) *Modern French:* trad. A. d'Avril 8° *Paris* [ ] 80
" Léon Gautier—*in his edn. of text, ut supra.*
" P. Jônain 8° *Bordeaux* 62
" Petit le Julleville; w. French notes 9/- 8° *Paris* 78

(*b*) *German:* übers. W. Hertz 2/6 8° *Stuttgart* 61

(*c*) *English:* —*v.* K § 48.

AIDS:

Bibliography.

BANQUIER, J. Bibliographie de la *Chanson de Roland* 1/- 8° *Heilbronn* 77
*SEELMANN, Emil Bibliographie des Rolandliedes 3/- r 8° " 88

General Criticism.

DIEHL, Die Rolandssage in der altfranzösischen Poesie *Marienwerder* 67
FOERSTER, Prf. W. Roland-Materialien [=Suppl. pt. i. *of his* Altfrz. Uebungsbuch, *ut* K § 273] 3/- 8° *Heilbronn* 86
GRÄVELL, Die Charakteristik der Personen im Roland 8° " 80
MEYER, H. Abhandlung über Roland (schl.-progr.) *Bremen* 68

Dictionaries

—*in edns. by* CLÉDAT, GAUTIER, *supra.*

Language.

BEYER, E. Die Pronomina im Rolandlied [dissert.] 1/6 8° *Halle* 75
BOCKHOFF, H. Der syntaktische Gebrauch der Tempora im Roland [dissert.] *Münster* 80
CARLBERG, Étude sur l'Usage Syntactique dans la Chanson de Roland *Lund* 75
KELLER, A. Die Sprache des Venezianer Roland V[4] 8° *Calw* 85
LEMBERG, D. D. Die Synonyma im Rolandslied [Oxford text; dissert.] 1/- 8° *Münster* 86
LÖSCHHORN, H. Zum normanischem Roland [dissert.] 1/- 8° *Göttingen* 73
MORF, H. Wortstellung im Rolandslied = Roman-Studien iii. pp. 199 *sqq.* [*ut* K § 256].
NIEBUHR, C. Syntaktische Studien zum altfrz. Rolandsliede, pt. i. 2/- 8° 88
REISSERT, O. Syntaktische Behandlung d. Verses im Alexius- u. Rolandliede [Ausg. u. Abhand. xiii.] 2/6 8° *Marburg* 84
RIECKE, Construction d. Nebensätze im Rolandsliede [dissert.] *Münster* 83
SIMON, M. Ueb. d. flexivischen Verfall d. Substantivs im Rolandslied [dissert.] 1/- 8° *Bonn* 67
TRAUTMANN, M. Tempora und Modi im Rolandslied [dissert.] *Halle* 71

Rhythm.

HILL, F. Ueber d. Metrum in der *Chanson de Roland* [dissert.] 1/6 8° *Strassburg* 73
RAMBAU, A. Ueber d. als ächt nachweisb. Assonanzen des Rolandsliedes [Oxford text] 6/- 8° *Halle* 78

Style.

DEKKES, H. Gebrauch d. Epitheta Ornantia im altfrz. Rolandsliede [dissert.] *Münster* 83
ZILLER, F. Der epische Styl des altfrz. Rolandsliedes [schl.-progr.] *Magdeburg* 83

Textual Criticism.

DÖNGES, E. Die Baligantepisode im Roland [dissert.] 1/6 8° *Heilbronn* 80
LAURENTIUS, G. Zur Kritik der *Chanson de Roland* *Leipzig* 76
PAKSCHER, A. Zur Composition und Kritik des Rolands 3/- 8° *Berlin* 85

Manuscripts.

OTTMANN, H. Die Stellung v. Venet (v) in d. Ueberlieferung d. *C. de R.* 2/6 4° *Marburg* 79
PARSCHMANN, H. Die Stellung von O in d. Ueberlieferung d. *C. de R.* [dissert.] 1/- 8° " 80

The Romance [K § 256] and French [K § 268] philological journals contain very many—often very important—monographs on *Roland.*

Charlemagne's Reise nach Jerusal. u. Constantinopel, ed. E. Koschwitz [Altfrz. Bibl.; w. gloss.] 4/6 8° *Heilbronn* [80] 83
" " " Sechs Bearbeitungen d. Gedichts, ed. E. Koschwitz 5/6 8° " 79

Cymric, Eng., 3 O.-F. and Norse versions of the *chanson*, semi-burlesque in character, wh. w. *Antioche*, forms two of the earliest instances of the appearance of the "*Esprit Gaulois.*"

Chevalerie Ogier de Danemarche, ed. Barrois *o.p.* 8° *Paris* 42
Chevalier au Cynge *and* Godefroid de Bouillon, ed. C. Hippeau, 2 vols. [only 300 printed] 14/- 8° " 74; 77

This group of *Chansons de gestes* comprises *Antioche, Les Chétifs, Les Enfances, Godefroy, Baudoin de Sebourc, Bastars de Bouillon*, and others.

Antioche [chans. d. geste; ? by GRAINDOR DE DOUAI] ed. Paulin Paris, 2 vols. 8° *Paris* 48
Modern Fch. Trsl. trad. Mme. de Sainte-Aulaire 8° " 48-68

AID:

PARIS, Paulin Nouvelle Étude sur la Chanson d'Antioche 8° *Paris* 74

Bastars de Bouillon [sequel to below]
Baudoin de Sebourc } —*v.* Romans d'Aventures. [extract] 2/- 8° *Brussels* 74

Doon de Maience ed. St. Bormans 8° *Paris* 59
Elie de St.-Gille ed. Prf. W. Foerster—*with* Aiol et Mirabel, *supra.*
" " " G. Raynaud [Soc. Anc. Textes] 8° *Paris* 79
Fierabras ed. F. Guessard—*in his* Anciens Poètes de la France [*ut supra*].
" " A. Kroeber + G. Servois 8° *Paris* 60

Italian Version: El cantare di Fierabraccia et Uliuieri, ed. E. Stengel [= Ausg. u. Abhand. ii.] 6/- 8° *Marburg* 81

For the English text (*Sir Ferumbras*), *v.* K § 48; for the Provençal, *v.* K § 269.

AID:

GRÖBER, G. Die handschriftl. Gestaltungen d. "Fierabras" und ihre Vorstufe 1/6 8° *Leipzig* 69

An excellent example of the best German "higher criticism"—*cf.* also his *Unters. üb. d. Troubad.* [*ut sup.*].

GÉRARD DE ROUSSILLON —*v.* K § 267 Provençal Literature, *s.v.* Girartz de Rossilho.
GÉRARD DE VIANE . ed. P. Tarbé *o.p.* 8° *Rheims* 50
Guillaume d'Orange Chansons de Geste, ed. Dr. W. J. A. Jonckbloet, 2 vols. *o.p.* [*w.* 24/-] 8° *Hague* 54
" " The same, mis en nouveau lang., p. Jonckbloet 6/- 8° *Amsterdam* 67

Conts. *Le Couronnement Loys, Prisl d'Orange, Charroi de Nimes, Moniage Guillaume* and others—entire or in extract.

Hugues Capet ed. de la Grange 8° *Paris* 64
Huon de Bordeaux ed. F. Guessard + C. Grandmaison 8° " 60

AIDS:
KOCH, M. Das Quellenverhältniss in Wieland's *Oberon* *Marburg* 80
LINDNER, F. Ueber d. Beziehungen d. *Ortnit* z. *Huon de Bordeaux* *Rostock* 73

The source fr. wh. SHAKSPERE drew some of his characters in *Mids. Nt's. Dream*, and WIELAND and WEBER the plots of their *Oberons*.

JEAN LE FLAGY Garin le Lohérain, ed. Paulin Paris, 2 vols. *o.p.* 8° *Paris* 35-37
" " " " ed. [in part] Rhode—*in* Stengel's Ausgaben u. Abhandl. iii. [*ut* K § 256].
Jourdains de Blaives —*sequel to* Amis et Amiles, *q.v.*, *supra*.
Macaire ed. F. Guessard 8° *Paris* 66
" ed. A. Mussafia [*with* Prise de Pamp.]—*in his* Altfrz. Gedichte a. Venez. Hss. [*ut inf.*, *s.v.* Early Poetry].
Prise de Pampelune ed. A. Mussafia [*with* Macaire]—*in his* Altfrz. Gedichte aus Venez. Hss. [*ut infra*, *s.v.* Early Poetry].
RAOUL DE CAMBRAI ed. E. le Glay *o.p.* 8° *Paris* 40
German Translation: übersetzt L. Settegast—*in* Archiv f. neuere Sprachen, vol. lxx. [*ut* K § 256].
Analysis: Analyse des Romans de R.de. C. et de Bernier. By J. Deligne *o.p.* 8° *Lille* 50
Renaus de Montauban [Quatre Fils Aymon] ed. H. Michelant [Bibl. d. litt. Vereins] 8° *Stuttgart* 62
" P. Tarbé 8° *Rheims* 61

The source of one of the most popular French chap-books. For the English text, *v.* K § 48.

Arthurian Romances [and their sources].

Collections.

HUCHER, E. [ed.] Romans de la Table Ronde, 3 vols. [w. full and valuable notes] 8° *Le Mans* 72-79

Contains (1) Rob. de BORRON'S *Joseph d'Arimathie*, in its prose version. There is also a verse version [ed. Fr. MICHEL 8° *Paris* 41]: neither have any reference to ARTHUR. (2) Walter MAP'S *Great Saint Graal*, wh. was based on de BORRON'S wk., but still has no direct connection with ARTHUR. (3) The *Romance of Percivale* [original form by de BORRON], wh. represents the quest for the Graal by a Knight *not* of the Round Table. The connecting link 'tween the two last is *Merlin* [attrib. to de BORRON], showing the Welsh influence; and this leads to *Artur*, thence *Lancelot du Lac*, *Quest of San Graal*, *Mort Artus*.

PARIS, Paulin [ed.] Les Romans de la Table Ronde, 5 vols. [abstract and commentary] 5 8° *Paris* 68-77

Individual Texts.

*CRESTIEN DE TROIES Percival le Gallois, ed. Ch. Potvin, 6 vols. 8° *Mons* 65-72

Includes also a previously unknown prose version of the romance, unquestionably older than CHRESTIEN'S and quite different fr. de BORRON'S.

" " Le Chevalier à la Charrette, ed. [fr. Map's *Lancelot du Lac*] Dr. Jonckbloet *The Hague* 50
" " " " " " ed. P. Tarbé *o.p.* 8° *Rheims* 49
" " Le Chevalier au Lyon, ed. W. L. Holland 5/- 8° *Hanover* [62] 86
" " The same, hrsg. Prf. W. Foerster [= vol. ii. of a cpl. edn. of Chr. d. Troies] 8° *Halle* 90
" " Erec et Énide, ed. M. Haupt *Berlin* 60
" " The same, ed. Prf. W. Foerster [= vol. iii. of a cpl. edn. of Chr. d. Troies] 6/- 8° *Halle* 90

The legend on which TENNYSON has based his *Enid*.

" " Cligès, ed. Prf. W. Foerster; w. German notes [= vol. i. of a cpl. edn. of Chr. d. Troies] 10/- 8° *Halle* 84

AIDS:
BISCHOFF, F. Der Conjunctiv bei Crestien von Troyes [a good essay] 3/6 8° *Halle* 81
GÄRTNER, G. Der *Iwein* Hartmanns von Aue u. der *Chevalier au Lyon* 1/6 8° *Breslau* 75
GOOSSENS, Dr. H. Ueber Sage, Quelle u. Kompos. des *Chevalier au Lyon* [= Neuphil. Stud. pt. i.] 1/- 8° *Paderborn* 83
GROSSE, R. Der Stil Crestien's von Troies [= Franz. Stud. i. 2 [*ut* K § 268] 6/6 8° *Heilbronn* 8-
HOLLAND, W. L. Ueber Crestien de Troies und zwei seiner Werke 8° *Tübingen* 47
" " Crestien de Troies: eine litterargeschichtliche Untersuchung 5/6 8° " 54
LE COULTRE, J. L'Ordre des Mots dans Crestien de Troyes [dissert.] 2/6 8° *Dresden* 75
POTVIN, Ch. Bibliographie de Crestien de Troyes, *etc.* 8° *Brussels* 63
SCHILLER, H. Der Infinitiv bei Crestien [dissertation] 1/- 8° *Breslau* 83

Tristan, ed. Fr. Michel, 2 vols. [not the entire text] *London* 35; 39

Other Romances.

Athis et Prophilias [= Porphyrias], ed. A. Weber [the siege of Athens] 8° *Berlin* 81
BENOÎT DE STE. MORE [1154-89] Roman de Troie, ed. A. Joly, 2 vols. [w. glossary] *o.p.* [*w.* 40/-] 8° *Paris* 70; 71

AIDS:
Dunger, Hermann Die Sage vom Trojanerkrieg in d. Bearbeitungen des Mittelalters 2/- 8° *Leipzig* 69
" " Dictys Septimius [schl.-progr.: on sources, etc., of *Ephemeris Belli Trojani*] 1/6 8° *Dresden* 78
Fischer, C. Ueb. d. altfranz. Rom. de Troie als Vorbild d. mittelhochd. Trojadichtn. [= Neuphil. Stud. ii.] 1/6 8° *Paderborn* 83
Greif, W. Die mittelalterl. Bearbeitungen d. Trojanersage [Ausg. u. Abhandl. lxi.] 8/- 8° *Marburg* 86
Joly, A. —vol. i. of his edn. (*ut supra*) conts. *a history of the legend in the Middle Ages*.
Körting, G. Dictys und Dares: Beitrag z. Geschichte d. Trojasage 3/- 8° *Halle* 74
Lüigen, E. Quellen und historischer Werth der fränkischen Trojasage 1/- 8° *Bonn* 76
Settegast, F. Benoit de Ste.-More *Leipzig* 76

A philological discussion on the identity of the author of the *Roman de Troie* and the *Chronique des Ducs de Normandie*. This poem contains the undoubted original of SHAKSPERE'S Cressida (Briseida). For the English text, *v.* K § 47.

LAMBERT LI TORS + ALEX. OF BERNAY [12 cent.] Li Romans d'Alexandre, ed. H. Michelant 8° *Stuttgart* 46
" " " " " " " ed. F. Le Court de la Villethassetz + E. Talbot 61
" " " " " " " ed. P. Meyer: ed. crit. *in prep.*

K § 277

Sources.

PSEUDO-CALLISTHENES [7 cent.] Selns. fr. ed. Römheld, *s.v.* Beitr. z. Gesch. d. Alexandersage [progr.] *Hersfeld* 73
A tr. from the Syriac version of PSEUDO-CALLISTHENES.

QUINTUS CURTIUS tr. into Latin verse by Gauthier of Châtillon

AID:
BLUMRR, F. Alexander der Grosse in Jerusalem [schl.-progr.] *Büdingen* 71

Octavian, Roman de; hrsg. K. Vollmöller [from Bodleian MS.; Altfr. Bibl.] 4/6 8° *Heilbronn* 83

Roman de Thèbes [12 cent.]—ed. Constans, *infra* (next line) [based on Statius]

AID:
Constans Légende d'Oedipe étudiée: en partic. d. R. de Thèbes 81

Fabliaux.

Collections.

KELLER, A. [ed.] Zwei Fabliaux aus einer Neuenburger Handschrift *o.p.* [*w.* 3/6] 8° *Stuttgart* 40

LEGRAND d'AUSSY [ed.] Fabliaux ou Contes du 12 et du 13 siècles, 4 vols. *o.p.* [*w.* 20/-] 8° *Paris* 1779–81
The standard collection, consisting of extracts, abstracts and translations into Modern French.

de MONTAIGLON + RAYNAUD, A. G. [eds.] Fabliaux des 13e et 14e Siècles, 6 vols. ea. 9/- 8° ,, 72–86

RENOUARD [ed.] Fabliaux du Moyen Âge, 5 vols. [w. other mediæval romances] *rare* 8° ,, 29
An enlargement and revision of LEGRAND d'AUSSY, *ut supra.*

Translations: English.

HAZLITT, W. C. [tr.] . Feudal Period, ill. by a series of tales [prose trss. fr. Legrand] *o.p.* [*pb.* 3/6; *w.* 5/-] c 8° Reeves & Turner 78

WAY + ELLIS, G. L. G. [trs.] Fabliaux or tales fr. the French, 3 v. [a seln. fr. Legrand d'Aussy; verse trss.] *o.p.* c 8° *London* [1796–1800] 15

Individual Texts.

Gautier d'Aupais, le Chevalier à la Corbeille, ed. Fr. Michel [two 13 cent. fabliaux] 35

Roman de Renart [13 cent.] ed. Méon, 4 vols.; Supplément by Chabaille [the standard edn.] *o.p.* [*w.* 25/-] 8° *Paris* 26; 35
Includes not merely the *Ancien Renart*, but also the *Couronnement Renart*, and *Renart le Nouvel*, w. meagre extracts fr. the very lengthy *Renart Contrefait* [14 cent.].

,, ,, ed. Ernest Martin, 2 vols. [excell. crit. edn.] 18/- 8° *Strassburg* 82; 83

,, Mod. Fch. Translation: trad. Paulin Paris, *sub tit.* Aventures de Maître Renard et d'Ysengrin 8° *Paris* 61

,, Mis en vers C. Potvin 8° *Brussels* 60

AIDS:
JONCKBLOET, Dr. W. J. A. Étude sur le Roman de Renart 10/- 8° *Groningen* 63
MARTIN, E. Examen Critique des MSS. du Roman de Renart 2/- 8° *Basle* 72
,, ,, Le Pèlerinage de Renart—*in* Romanische Studien, vol. i. [*ut* K § 256].
PARIS, Gaston Nouvelle Étude sur le Roman de Renart 8° *Paris* 60
POTVIN, C. Introduction *and* Bibliographie—*in his transl. of text, ut supra.*
ROTHE, A. Les Romans du Renart examinés, analysés et comparés *o.p.* [*w.* 3/-] 8° *Paris* 45
WOLF, Ferd. Roman de Renart le Contrefait [*fr.* Denkschr. d. Wien. Akad.] 1/- 4° *Vienna* 61
Text and account of a new variant from a Vienna MS.

Ysopet [diminutive of Aesop]

Lyoner Yzopet [13 cent.] ed. Prf. W. Foerster; w. Germ. intro., notes and gloss. [Altfranz. Bibl.] 5/6 8° *Heilbronn* 82
In the dialect of the Franche-Comté. Conts. the original Latin text also.

MARIE OF FRANCE [13 cent.] Ysopet—*in vol. ii. of her* Oeuvres, ed. Roquefort, 2 vols. *o.p.* 8° *Paris* 20

AID:
HERLET, B. Studien über die sogenannte Yzopets 2/6 8° *Leipzig* 92

Early Poetry.

Bibliography of Lyric Poetry.

RAYNAUD, G. Bibliographie des Chansonniers Français des 13 et 14 siècles, 2 vols. 12/6 8° *Paris* 84

History.

BARTSCH, Karl Die lateinischen Sequenzen des Mittelalters [music and rhythm] 5/- 8° *Rostock* 68

LAVOIX, Étude sur la musique au siècle de St. Louis—*in* Raynaud's Motets, vol. ii. [*ut supra*].

WOLF, Ferdinand Ueber die Lais, Sequenzen und Leiche 11/- 8° *Heidelberg* 41

Collections of Lyric Poetry—*for* Folk Songs, *v.* B § 16: French Mythology and Folklore.

BARTSCH, Karl [ed.] Altfranzösiche Romanzen und Pastourellen 7/6 8° *Leipzig* 70
A delightful and extensive coll. of specimens of the two earliest forms of French lyrical poetry (12 cent. Northern tongue).

DINAUX, A. [ed.] Trouvères, Jongleurs et Ménestrels, 4 vols. ea. 7/6 r 8° *Brussels* 37; 39; 43; 63
i.: Trouvères Cambrésiens; ii.: Trouvères de la Flandre; iii.: Trouvères Artésiens; iv.: Trouv. Belges d. 12–14 siècle.

GUESSARD, F. [ed.] Les Anciens Poëtes de la France, 10 vols. 48/- 12° *Paris* 59–70
Conts. the following *chansons de geste:*
Gui de Bourgogne. Otinel. Floovant. | Doon de Mayence. Gaufrey. | Fierabras. Parise la Duchesse. | Huon de Bordeaux. Aye d'Avignon. | Gui de Nanteuil. Gaydon. | Hugues Capet. Macaire. | Aliscans.

de MONTAIGLON + de ROTHSCHILD, A. Jas. [eds.] Recueil de Poésies fr. des 15 et 16 siècles, 13 v. [Bibl. Elzév.] ea. 5/- 8° *Paris* 55–78
Two more vols., containing the Glossary, are to follow.

MUSSAFIA, A. [ed.] Altfranz. Gedichte aus Venezianischen Handschriften 6/- 8° *Vienna* 64
La Prise de Pampelune; Macaire.

PARIS, Gaston [ed.] Chansons du 15e Siècle [with the music; Soc. Anc. Textes] 12/6 8° *Paris* 75

RAYNAUD, G. [ed.] Rondeaux et autres Poésies du 15e siècle 7/- 8° ,, 90

SCHELER, A. [ed.] Trouvères Belges du 12 au 14 siècle, 6/-; New Series 6/- m 8° *Brussels*, 76; *Louv.* 79

Troubadours — *v.* K § 267: Provençal Literature.

Individual Lyric Writers.

ADAM DE LA HALLE [trouvère and dram.; 13 cent.] Oeuvres Complètes, ed. Coussemaker 72

MARIE OF FRANCE [13 cent.] Oeuvres, ed. Roquefort, 2 vols. *o.p.* [w. 12/-] 8° *Paris* 20

Transl. Selections: —*some of her* lais *are paraphrased by* A. W. O'Shaughnessy—*in his* Lays of France 10/6 c 8° Ellis 72

RAOUL DE HOUDENC [early 13 cent.] Songe d'Enfer, ed. M. L. A. Jubinal; Voie de Paradis, ed. same.

RUTEBOEUF [1230 (?)–1285 (?)] Oeuvres Complètes, ed. A. Jubinal, 3 vols. 10/6 8° *Paris* [39] 74

,, Gedichte, hrsg. A. Kressner 10/- 8° *Wolfenbüttel* 85

THIBAUT DE CHAMPAGNE [1201–53] Poésies, ed. P. Tarbé [chiefly *chansons d'amour*] *o.p.* 8° *Rhiems* 51

,, ,, Li Romans de la Poire, hrsg. F. Stehlich 8° *Halle* 81

Chronicles in Verse.

Chronique Ascendante du Mont-St. Michel, ed. S. Luce

Chroniques Anglo-Normandes, ed. Fr. Michel, 3 vols. *o.p.* [w. 18/-] *Rouen* 36–40

Chroniques de Normandie, ed. Fr. Michel ,, 39

GARNIER DE PONT ST. MAXENCE [12 cent.] St. Thomas, ed. J. Bekker; w. Supplement [*fr.* Abhandl. Berl. Akad.] 4° *Berlin* 39; 45

,, ,, ,, ,, ed. E. Etienne 5/- 8° *Paris*

A life of Becket, in verse.

GAYMAR, Geoffrey [*c.* 1146] Estoire des Engles, ed. Thomas Wright Caxton Society 50

Pt. i. is also ed. in PETRIE + SHARPE'S *Monum. Hist. Brit.* [*ut* F § 18]; pt. ii. in MICHEL'S *Chron. Anglo-Norm.*, vol. i. [*ut sup.*].

GODFREY OF MONMOUTH Der Münchener Brut in französ. Versen, ed. K. Hoffmann and K. Vollmöller [12 cent. version] 8° *Halle* 77

AID:
Jenrich, K. Die Mundart des Münchener Brut [dissert.] 1/6 8° ,, 87

MOUSKES, Philippe Chronique Rimée, ed. de Reiffenberg, 2 vols. [Coll de Chron. Belges] *o.p.* [*pb.* 45/-] 4° *Brussels* 36; 38

AID:
Link, Theodor Ueber die Sprache der *Chronique Rimée* de Phil. Mouskes [dissert.] 1/6 8° *Erlangen* 81

WACE, Robert [1120–1174] Roman de Brut [1155], ed. Leroux de Lincy, 2 vols. *o.p.* 8° *Rouen* 36; 38

*Roman de Rou et de Ducs de Normandie [1160], ed. Dr. Hugo Andersen, 2 vols. 34/- 8° *Heilbronn* 77; 79

Chronique Ascendante, ed. Dr. H. Andersen—*in* vol. ii. *of his edn. of* Roman de Rou—*ut supra.*

AIDS:
Language.
KLOPPE, Recherches sur le dialecte de Wace, 2 pts. [programmes] *Marburg* 53; 54
KOWALSKI, R. Der Conjunctiv bei Wace [dissert.] *Göttingen* 80
Chronique Ascendante.
HORMEL, Untersuchung über die *Chronique Ascendante* [dissert.] *Marburg* 80
Roman de Rou.
KÖRTING, G. Ueber die Quellen de Rou [contained in *Jahrb. f. rom. u. eng. Phil.*] 1/6 8° *Leipzig* 67
POHL, Th. Untersuchung der Reime im *Roman de Rou* *Erlangen* 85
RAYNOUARD, F. J. M. Observations philologiques et grammaticales sur le *Roman de Rou* *o.p.* 8° *Rouen* 29

Didactic Poetry (a): Dits.

CONDÉ, Jean Gedichte, hrsg. A. Tobler [Bibl. Litter. Verein; *v. also* Scheler, *infr.*] 8° *priv. prin. Stuttgart* 60

Dit de Jean le Rigolé ed. G. Raynaud—*in* Romania, vol. vii. [*ut* K § 256].

Dit de l'Unicorne et del Serpent, ed. J. Wollenberg *Berlin* 49

Dit du Vrai Aniel ed. A. Tobler 2/- 8° *Leipzig* [71] 84

RUTEBOEUF —*v. supra, s.v.* Lyric Poets.

SCHELER, A. [ed.] Dits et Contes de Baudoin de Condé, Jean de Condé et W. de Couvin, 4 vols. 20/- 8° *Brussels* 66–68

Didactic Poetry (b): Lais (narrative poems).

MARIE OF FRANCE [13 cent.] Oeuvres, ed. Roquefort [*ut sup.*]—vol. i. conts. the lais, ii. the fables.

,, ,, Lais, hrsg. K. Warnke; w. notes Reinhold Köhler [Bibl. Normann., v. iii.] 10/- 8° *Halle* 87

Didactic Poetry (c): Miscellaneous.

PHILIPPE DE THAÜN [Englishman, early 12 cent.] Bestiaire, ed. Thos. Wright—*in his* Pop. Treats. on Science 6/- 8° Hist. Soc. of Sc. 41

,, ,, Li Compoz, hrsg. E. Mall [a chronology] 4/6 8° *Strassburg* 73

WALTER OF METZ [13 cent.] Image du Monde: Selections in Le Roux de Lincy's Livre d. Légendes [a *trésor* or pop. encyclo.] *o.p.* 8° *Paris* 36

AIDS:
FRITSCHE, F. Ueber die Quellen der *Image du Monde* *Halle* 80
HAASE, Ueber die Reime in der *Image du Monde* [dissert.] 1/6 8° ,, 79

Didactic Poetry (d): Religious and Moral Poetry. Lives of Saints.

ADGAR's Marien-Legenden ed. Carl Neuhaus [fr. Egerton MS.; Altfrz. Bibl.] 8/- 8° *Heilbronn* 86

Auban, St., Vie de ed. Rob. Atkinson [w. 21/-] 4° *priv. prin. London* 76

AID:
SUCHIER, H. Ueber die Mat. Paris zugeschriebene *Vie de St. Auban* 2/- 8° *Halle* 7

Brandan, St., Voyage ed. H. Suchier—*in* Roman. Studien, i. pp. 553 sqq. [*ut* K § 256].

,, ,, ,, Fr. Michel 78

AIDS:
BIRKENHOFF, R. Ueber Metrum und Reim d. altfrz. Brandanlegende [Ausg. u. Abhand. xix.] 2/- 8° *Marburg* 84
BREKKE, K. Étude sur la Flexion dans le *Voyage de S. Brandan*, poème Ang. Norm. du 12 siècle 2/6 8° *Paris* 85
HAMMER, W. Die Sprache der anglo-normann. Brandanlegende 2/6 8° *Halle* 85

K § 277

CHARDRY [Eng. trouvère; 13 cent.] Josaphat, Set Dormanz, Petit Plet, ed. J. Koch; w. notes and gloss. [Anglo-Norm. dial.; Altfranzös. Bibliothek] 7/- 8° *Heilbronn* 79

AID: REINBRECHT, Die Legende v. d. Siebenschläfern [dissert.] 1/6 8° *Göttingen* 81

Psalter, Lothringischer [14 cent.] ed. F. Apfelstedt [Bibl. Mazarin; Altfranz. Bibl.] 6/- 8° *Heilbronn* 81

With a Grammar of the Old-Lothringian Dialect, and a Glossary.

Psautier de Metz [14 cent.] ed. F. Bonnardot: ed. crit. [supplements Apfelstedt's bk., *ut sup.*] 7/6 8° *Paris* 85

From Paris, London and Epinal MSS. For Cambridge and Oxford Psalters, v. "Earliest Monuments," *supra*.

RAYNAUD, G. [ed.] Recueil de Motets français des 12 et 13 siècles, 2 vols. [w. intro. and notes] 15/- 8° *Paris*

WACE, Robert [1120–1174] La Vie de Sainte Marguerite, ed. A. Joly 8° *Caen* 79

" " La Vie de la Vierge Marie, ed. V. Luzarche *o.p.* 8° *Tours* 59

Previously ed. MANCEL + TREBUTIEN, *sub tit.* *L'Établissement de la Fête de la Conception de Notre Dame*, o.p. 8° Caen 42.

" " St. Nicolas, hrsg. R. Delius 8° *Bonn* 50

AID: UHLEMANN, F. Grammat. u. Krit. Studien üb. Wace's *Conception* und *St. Nicholas* [dissert.] 1/6 8° *Bremen* 78

Allegorical Poetry.

Roman de la Rose ed. J. Croissandeau, 5 vols. [w. notes and glossary] 8° *Orleans* 81

" Jean Dupré [verse 1490] *Paris* [ ] 78

" Fr. Michel, 2 vols. 7/- 8° " 64

* " P. Marteau, 5 vols. [w. intro., notes, tr. and gloss.] 45/- 8° *Orléans* 78–79

AIDS:

BEKKER, J. Ueber die Handschriften des *Roman de la Rose* in d. Königl. Bibl. *o.p.* *Berlin* 50

HEINRICH, F. Ueber d. Stil Guill. de Lorris u. Jean de Meung [Ausg. u. Abhand. xxix.] 1/6 8° *Marburg* 85

The poem was commenced by WILLIAM of LORRIS, *c.* 1260, and contin. by JEAN DE MEUNG, *c.* 1300. It was tr. into English by CHAUCER, though the authorship of the English tr. we have is denied by some.

Roman de la Poire ed. Stehlich 8° *Halle* 81

An obvious imitation of the *Roman de la Rose*.

Venus la Déesse d'Amor [13 cent.] ed. Prf. W. Förster 3/- 8° *Bonn* 80

Romans d'Aventures.

ADENÈS LI ROIS [13 cent.] Bueves de Commarchis, ed. A. Scheler, 3/6; Enfances Ogier, ed. same 4/6 8° *Brussels* 74; 74

" " Li Roumans de Cléomadès, ed. A. van Hasselt, 2 vols. 10/- 8° " 65–66

Amades et Idoine ed. C. Hippeau 8° *Paris* 63

Baudoin de Sebourc ed. Bocca, 2 vols. [*v.* also *sup.* Chans d. Gestes, *s.v.* Chev. au Cynge] *o.p.* 8° *Valenciennes* 41

Bastars de Bouillon [sequel to above and a very late *chanson*]: ed. A. Scheler 5/- 8° *Brussels* 77

Blancandin et l'Orgueilleuse d'Amour: ed. Michelant 10/- 8° *Paris* 67

Brun de la Montaigne, ed. P. Meyer [Soc. d. Anciens Textes] 4/6 8° " 76

Chevalier as deus Espees, Li: ed. Prf. W. Förster [belongs to the Round Table series] 15/- 8° *Halle* 77

AID: Schulze-Veltrup, Der syntakt. Gebrauch d. Conj. in *Li Chevr. as 2 Espees* [dissert.] 1/6 8° *Münster* 85

Dolopathos ed. H. Oesterley, *sub tit.* Johannis de Alta Silva Dol. 4/6 8° *Strassburg* 73

" " Brunet + A. de Montaiglon *o.p.* [*w.* 7/6] 8° *Paris* 56

AID: MUSSAFIA, A. Ueber die Quellen des altfranzös. *Dolopathos* *Vienna* 65

Vide also *Sept Sages*, *infra*, *s.v.* Fiction.

Durmars li Gallois ed. E. Stengel [Bibl. d. Litter. Vereins] 8° *priv. prin. Stuttgart* 73

Flore et Blanchefleur ed. J. Bekker [Berlin. Acad.] *w.* 2/- 4° *Berlin* 44

" " " Edéléstand du Méril *o.p.* [*w.* 9/-] 8° *Paris* 56

AIDS:

Schwalbach, Verbreitung d. Sage v. *F. u. B.* in d. europ. Litteratur *Krotoschin* 69

Sommer, E. —*intro. to his* Konrad Fleck's *Flor und Blanscheflur* 8° *Quedlinburg* 46

Sundmacher, H. Die altfranz. u. mittelhochd. Bearbeitung v. *Flor u. Blanscheflur* *Göttingen* 72

Gerard de Nevers [*or* La Violette]: ed. Fr. Michel 34

Guillaume de Palerne ed. H. Michelant [Soc. des Anciens Textes] 8/6 8° *Paris* 76

GUILLAUME, le CLERC Fergus, ed. E. Martin 6/- 8° *Halle* 72

Joufrois de Poitiers ed. Hofmann + Muncker " 80

PHILIPPE DE RÉMY [Rheims; 13 cent.] Romance of Blonde of Oxford and Jehan of Dammartin, ed. Le Roux de Lincy 2 4° Camden Soc. 58

Roman de la Manekine, ed. F. Michel Bannatyne Club 40

Oeuvres, ed. H. Suchier, 2 vols. 21/- 8° *Paris* 84; 85

AIDS:

BORDIER, H. L. Philippe de Rémi, sire de Beaumanoir [w. extr. fr. *Blonde* and *Manekine*] 8° *Paris* 69

SCHWAN, E. Philippe de Rémi und seine Werke—*in* Roman. Studien, vol. iv. [*ut* K § 236].

PYRAMUS, Denis Parthenopex de Blois, ed. Crapelot *o.p.* 8° *Paris* 34

A kind of modernized *Cupid and Psyche*.

RAOUL DE HOUDENC [early 13 cent.] Méraugis de Portlesquez, ed. H. Michelant [Round Table legend] 8° *Paris* 69

" " Roman des Eles [Ailes], ed. A. Scheler 3/6 8° *Brussels* 68

" " Vengeance de Raguidel, ed. Hippeau [episode of *Perceval*]

AID: ZINGERLE, W. Ueber Raoul de Houdenc und seine Werke [dissert.] 1/6 8° *Erlangen* 80

RENAUS DE BEAUJEAU Le Bel Inconnu ou Giglain, ed. C. Hippeau [append. is the Middle-Eng. vers.] 5/- 8° *Paris* 60

AID: MEBES, Der Wigalois v. Wirnt v. Gravenberg u. s. altfrz. Quelle [progr.] *Neumünster* 79

The Engl. form of this romance is *Libius Disconius*, a corruption of *Li [illegible] [illegible] [illegible]*

Violette, La —*v.* Gerard de Nevers, *supra*.

Later Poetry.

Collections.

QUEUX DE ST. HILAIRE, Marq. de [ed.] Livre de Cent Ballades 8° *Paris* 68

A coll. of poems believed to have been composed by the famous knight-errant BOUCIQUALT and his companions on their way to the battle of Nicopolis.

Individual Writers.

CHARLES D'ORLEANS [1391–1465; father of Louis XII.] Poésies, ed. d'Héricault, 2 vols. 8° *Paris* 74; 75

AID:
Stähle, W. Ueber die Sprache des Herzogs Charles von Orleans *Parchim* 66

CHARTIER, Alain [1390(?)–1458]—*the only edn. is that by* A. Duchesne *Paris* 1617

AIDS:
Hannappel, Die Poetik Alain Chartier's—*in* Französische Studien, i. 3 [*ut* K § 268] 7/6 8° *Heilbronn* 79
Höpfner, E. Die Wortstellung bei Alain Chartier u. Gerson [dissert.] 1/6 8° *Leipzig* 83

DESCHAMPS, Eustache [1328–1415] Oeuvres, ed. Marq. de Queux de St. Hilaire, vols. i.–ii. [Soc. d. Anc. Textes] 8° *Paris* 80

AID:
SARRADIN, A. Eustache Deschamps: sa vie et ses oeuvres 8° *Paris* 80

FROISSART, Jean [1337–1410] Poésies, ed. A. Scheler, 3 vols. 8° *Brussels* 70–72
de LESCUREL, Jehannot [14 cent.] Poésies, ed. A. de Montaiglon *o.p.* 8° *Paris* 55
de MACHAULT, Guill. [1284 (?)–1377 (?)] Prise d'Alexandrie, ed. L. de Mas-Latrie [Soc. de l'Orient Latin] 8° *Geneva* 77
" Voir Dit, ed. Paulin Paris [Soc. des Bibliophiles] s 8° *Paris* 75

Early Drama.

History.

CHASSANG, Les Essais dramatiques imités de l'antiq. au 14–15 siècle *o.p.* 8° *Paris* 52
COUSSEMAKER, Drames Liturgiques du Moyen-âge 8° *Rennes* 80
MILCHSACK, G. Die Oster- und Passionsspiele, pt. i. [Lat. Osterfeiern] 8/- 8° *Wolfenbüttel* 80
du MERIL, Origines Latines du Théâtre moderne *o.p.* 8° *Paris* 49
PARFAICT, F. + C. Histoire générale du Théâtre français, 15 vols. *o.p.* 8° *Paris* 1734–49

A standard work on which most subsequent books have been based.

PICOT, Em. La Sottie en France—*in* Romania, vol. vii. [*ut* K § 256]: *on the Old French Comic Drama.*
SEPTET, Marius Les Prophètes de Christ [on the liturgical drama] 8° *Paris* 78

General Collections.

FOURNIER, E. [ed.] Théâtre Français avant la Renaissance [myst., moral., farces, 1450–1550] 8° *Paris* *n.d.* (72)
MONMERQUÉ + MICHEL [eds.] Théâtre François au Moyen Age 7/6 8° " [39] 79
VIOLLET-LE-DUC [ed.] Théâtre Français Ancien, 10 vols. [to Corneille, vol. x. = gloss.; Bibl. Elzévir.] s 8° " 54–57

Mystery and Miracle Plays.

Adam ed. Lusarches *o.p.* 8° *Tours* 56
" " L. Palustre 8° *Paris* 77
BODEL D'ARRAS, Jean [13 cent.] Jeu de Saint Nicolas, ed. Monmerqué + Michel, *ut supra.*

AID:
HEITHECKER, F. Bodel's St. Nicolas: Beitrag z. altfrz. Drama *Münster* 85

GREBAN, A. [15 cent.] Mystère de la Passion, ed. G. Paris + G. Raynaud [fr. Paris MSS.] 21/- 8° *Paris* 78
MIGNE, Abbé Dictionnaire d. Mystères [coll. of mysteries, moral, etc.] r 8° " 54
Miracles de Nostre Dame par personnages, ed. Gaston Paris + U. Robert, 7 vols. [Soc. Anc. Textes] 56/- 8° " 76–80

From a MS. containing 40 Miracle Plays of the Virgin dating from the 14th cent.

AIDS:
SCHNELL, H. Untersuchungen üb. d. Verfasser d. *Miracles de N.-D. par personnages* [Ausg. u. Abhandl. xxxiii.] 2/- 8° *Marburg* 85
" " Ueber d. Abfassungszeit d. *Miracles d. N.-D. p. personnages* [" "] 1/- 8° " 86

Mystère du Vieil Testament, ed. J. de Rothschild, 3 vols. [Soc. d. Anc. Textes] 8° *Paris* 79–82
RUTEBOEUF [1230(?)–85(?)] Miracle de Théophile, ed. A. H. Klient [w. Mod. Fch. tr.] 8° *Upsala* 69

Farces.

JACOB, P. L. [ed.] Recueil de Farces Françaises du 15 siècle 8° *Paris* [59] 76
PICOTT + NYROP, [eds.] Nouveau Recueil de Farces Franç. des 15 et 16 siècles 8° *Copenhagen* 80

Secular Dramatists.

ADAM DE LA HALLE [trouvère and dram.; 13 cent.] Oeuvres Complètes; ed. Coussemaker [also in Monmerqué + Michel, *ut sup.*] 72
Li Jus du Pelerin, Li Gieus de Robin et de Marion, Li Jus Adan: facs. repr. of MSS., ed. A. Rambeau
[Ausg. u. Abhandl. lviii., *ut* K § 256] 3/- 8° *Marburg* 86

AID:
BAHLSEN, Leopold Adam de la Hale's Dramen u. das *Jus du Pelerin* [Ausg. u. Abhandl. xxvii., *ut* K § 256] 5/6 8° *Marburg* 85

Mystère du Siège d'Orléans ed. F. Guessard + E. de Certain 8° *Paris* 64

AID:
TIVIER, H. Étude sur le Mystère du *S. d'O.* et Jacques Milet (supposed author) 8° *Paris* 68

This is a profane mystery, versifying and dramatizing fr. the Chronicles. The actual events shortly after their occurrence.

Pathelin, Farce de [mid. 15 cent.] ed. P. L. Jacob ["Bibliophile Jacob"] s 8° *Paris* [59] 76

AIDS:
DICKMANN, A. Maistre Pierre Pathelin [schl.-programme] 1/6 4° *Hamburg* 75
STÄHLE, W. *Pathelin* in litter., gramm. u. sprachl. Hinsicht [dissert.] 1/6 8° *Marburg* 64

K § 277

Prose.

Chronicles.

Chronique de Rains [Rheims].

AID:
NYTROP, K. — Notice sur un Nouveau MS. de la *Chr. d. R.*—*in* Romania, vol. viii. [*ut* K § 256].

Chroniques de France, Grands, [*or* Chr. de St. Dénys] ed. Paulin Paris, 6 vols. — *Paris* 36-39

de COMMINES, Philippe [1447 (?)–1511] Mémoires—*v.* Miscellaneous Prose, *infra*.

FROISSART, Jean [1337–1409] Chroniques, ed. Buchon, 3 vols. [best edn. for general use] 8° *Paris* [24–26] 55

" " " " S. Luce: Ed. crit., vols. i.–? [to occupy several vols.] 8° " *in prog.*

" " " " Kervyn de Lettenhove, 20 vols. 8° *Brussels* 63 *sqq.*

AIDS:
JAHN, P. — Ueber das Geschlecht d. Substantiva bei Froissart [dissert.] 1/6 8° *Halle* 81
RISSE, J. — Recherches sur l'Usage Syntactique de Froissart [dissert.] 1/6 8° " 80

GUILLAUME DE TYR [13 cent.] Guillaume de Tyr, et ses Continuateurs, ed. Paulin Paris, 2 vols. 28/- 8° *Paris* 79; 80

de JOINVILLE, Sire [1224–1319] Oeuvres [Hist. de St. Louis, etc.], ed. Natalis de Wailly; w. Fch. tr. 12/6 8° " 74

AIDS:
ENGEL, E. — Gebrauch d. Präpositionen bei Joinville [programme] 1/- 4° *Heidelberg* 84
HAASE, A. — Ueber d. Gebrauch d. Conjunctif bei Joinville [sch.-programme] 1/6 8° *Köslin* 81-82
" " — Syntaktische Untersuchungen zu Villehardouin und Sire de Joinville 3/6 8° *Oppeln* 84
NEBLING, R. — Der Subjonctif bei Joinville [dissert.] *Kiel* 81
PFAU, C. — Gebrauch u. Bildungsweise d. Adverbien bei Joinville [dissert.] *Jena* 85
SEPTET, M. — Jean, Sire de Joinville [histor. and literary analysis] 8° *Paris* 74
de WAILLY, Natalis — Sur la Langue de Joinville—*in* Bibl. de l'école des Chartes, vol. xxix. [1868].

TURPIN, Abp. of Rheims [8 cent.] Historia Caroli Magni et Rotholandi, ed. S. Ciampi *o.p.* 8° *Florence* 22

" " " " " " " F. Castets 8° *Montpellier* 80

" " " " " " " F. Wulff, *sub tit.* Chronique dite de Turpin [fr. 2 Paris MSS.] *Lund* 81

" " " " " " " Th. Auracher [fr. Munich MS.; schl.-progr.] *Munich* 76

AIDS:
AURACHER, Th. — Der sogenannte poitevinische Turpin—*in* Ztschr. f. Roman. Philol., vol. i. [*ut* K § 256].
GAUTIER, Léon — —*in his* Epopées Françaises 8° *Paris* 78
*PARIS, Gaston — De Pseudo-Turpino 8° " 65

An O.-F. tr. of a Latin original, certainly *not* by TURPIN, and prob. compos. about middle 11 cent. Of the smallest literary importance.

de VILLEHARDOUIN, Geoff. [1160–1213] Conquête de Constanti [= Fourth Crusade], ed. Natalis de Wailly 8° *Paris* [74] 82

AID:
HAASE, A. — Syntaktische Untersuchungen zu Villehardouin und Sire de Joinville 3/6 8° *Oppeln* 84

Glossaries —*v.* K § 270.

Sermons.

BERNARD, St. [12 cent.] Li Sermon de, ed. Le Roux de Lancy —*in his edn. of* Quatre Livres des Rois 42

" " " " Prf. W. Foerster—*in* vol. ii. *of* Romanische Forschungen [*ut* K § 256] 20/- 8° *Erlangen* 85

AIDS:
CLÉDAT, F. — La Flexion dans les Sermons de St.-Bernard 1/6 s 8° *Paris* 84
FOERSTER, Prf. W. — Zu den altfrz. Predigten de St. Bernard—*in* Romanische Studien, vol. iv. [*ut* K § 256].
KUTSCHERA, O. — Le MS. des Sermons Franç. du St. B. trad. du Latin de 1207 [dissert.] 1/6 8° *Halle* 78

de SULLY, Maurice [1160–96; Bp. of Paris].

AID:
MEYER, P. — Les MSS. des Sermons Français de Maurice Sully—*in* Romania, vol. v. [*ut* K § 256].

Moral Treatises.

BOZON, Nicole [14 cent.] Contes Moralisés, ed. Lucy Toulmin Smith + P. Meyer; w. intro., notes and vocab. [Soc. d. Anc. Textes] 8° *Paris* 90

Chevalier de la Tour Landry [14 cent.] ed. Prf. A. de Montaiglon 8° " 54

Bible stories, moral tales, precepts for conduct, etc.; written for the author's three daughters.

Legal Treatises.

Laws of William the Conqueror, ed. R. Schmid—*in his* Gesetze d. Angelsachsen, pt. i. [texts, Germ. tr. & notes] 8° *Leipzig* 32

AID:
HOTZEL, F. — Die altfrz. Gesetze Wilh. d. Eroberers: grammatische Abhandlung [schl.-progr.] 1/6 4° *Eisenach* 59

Livre de Justice et de Plet, ed. Rapetti; w. glossary by Chabaille 40

Travels.

MARCO POLO [1256–1323] Le Livre de Marco Polo, ed. Bar. A. E. Nordenskiöld [for Engl. trss., *v.* E § 6] *Stockholm* 82

The same, ed. G. Pauthier, 2 vols. [after Rusticien de Pise (1298)] 33/6 8° *Paris* 65

Saint Voyage de Jherusalem du Sgr. d'Anglure [1358], ed. F. Bonnardot + A. Longnon [Soc. Anc. Textes] 9/- 8° " 78

Miscellaneous Treatises.

BRUNETTO LATINI [1220–94; the master of Dante] Li Livres de Trésor [*c.* 1270], ed. P. Chabaille [an encyclopædia] 63

Italian Translation: trad. R. Rennier 8° *Florence* 84

Livre des Mestiers [14 cent.] ed. H. Michelant 75

Gives a complete idea of the organization of Guilds and Trades of Paris in 14 cent.

Fiction.

History.

PARIS, Gaston — Les Contes Orientaux dans la Littér. franç. du Moyen-Âge [a lecture] 8° *Paris* 75

Collections.

MOLAND + HÉRICAULT [eds.] Nouvelles des 13ᵉ et du 14ᵉ Siècle, 2 vols. [Bibl. Elzévirienne] 10/- s 8° *Paris* 56; 58

i.: (13 cent. tales): *L'Empereur Constant* [W. MORRIS' *Man born to be a King*]; a prose vers. of *Amis et Amiles*; *Le Roi Flore et la belle Jehanne*; *La Comtesse de Ponthieu*; *Aucassin et Nicolete*. | ii.: (14 cent. tales): *Asseneth*; *Troilus* [prose vers. of BENOIT de STE. MORE'S legend of *Troilus and Cressida*]; English story of the Rebel Fulk Fitzwarine.

Individual Writers and Pieces.

Aucassin and Nicolete [13 cent.] ed. w. [verse] tr., intro., essays and gloss. F. W. Bourdillon 7/6 f 8° Paul 87

Contains a bibliogr. (after BRUNNER and SUCHIER). The essays are on the music, words, Beaucaire, Mediæval hours of the day, the fabled country *Torelore* and the *convade*.

" " tr. Andrew Lang; ill. Jaccomb Hood *o.p.* [*pb.* 5/-; *w.* 15/-] f 8° Nutt 87
" " ed. H. Suchier; w. intro. and gloss. in German 2/6 s 8° *Paderborn* [78] 81
" " ed. Gaston Paris; w. A. Bida's modern Fch. tr. and 9 ill. *o.p.* [*w.* 18/-] 4° *Paris* 78

AIDS:
BRUNNER, H. — Ueber *Aucassin et Nicolette* [dissert.] 1/6 4° *Halle* 80
SCHLICKUM, J. — Wortstellung in *Aucassin et Nicolete* [= Franz. Stud. iii. 3. (v. K § 268)] 2/- 8° *Heilbronn* 85

Written in mingled prose and verse. The finest prose tale of the French Middle Ages.

Sept Sages, Li Romans des: ed. Ch. Brunet + A. de Montaiglon 8° *Paris* 56
ed. A. Keller [fr. Paris MS.] 12/- 8° *Tübingen* 36
" Gaston Paris [two versions; Soc. d. Anc. Textes] 8° *Paris* 76

AID:
MUSSAFIA, A. — Beiträge zur Litteratur der Sieben Weisen Meister 8° *Vienna* 68

Vide also *Dolopathos*, *supra*, s.v. Romans d'Aventures.

de TUIM, Jehan [13 cent.] Roman de Jules César, ed. F. Settegast 8° *Halle* 81

A free version of LUCAN.

278. MIDDLE-FRENCH LITERATURE (15TH TO BEGINNING OF 17TH CENTURY).

Poetry.

Collection of Songs.

PARIS, Gaston [ed.] — Chansons du 15ᵉ Siècle [Soc. des Anc. Textes] 8° *Paris* 76

A coll. of 15th cent. *pastourelles*, war-songs, love-songs, a few patriotic songs, folk-songs, etc.

Individual Writers.

d'AUBIGNÉ, Theod. Agrippe [1550–1630] Oeuvres, ed. Réaume + de Caussade, 4 vols. [to occupy 5 vols.] 8° *Paris* 72–77

AID:
RÉAUME, — Étude historique et littéraire sur Agrippe d'Aubigné 8° " 83

d'AUVERGNE [*or* de PARIS], Martial [1420 (?)–1508] Amant rendu Cordelier, ed. Prf. A. de Montaiglon [Soc. d. Anc. Textes] 8° "

There is no other modern ed. of his works. The last pub. were *Vigilles de Char. vii.* 1724, and *Arrêts d'Amour* 1731.

de BAIF, Jean Ant. [1532–89] Poésies Choisies, ed. Becq de Fouquières 8° " 74
BAUDE, Henri [1430–1495] Oeuvres, ed. J. Quicherat [only part of the works] 8° " 56
*BELLAY, Joachim du [1524–60] Oeuvres, ed. Martyr-Laveaux, 2 vols. 8° " 66; 67

AIDS:
PERSON, E. — Introduction—*to his edn. of* Deffence et Illustration de la lang. frç. *Paris* *n.d.* (?80)
PLÖTZ, G. — Étude de J. du B. et son rôle d. l. réformes de Ronsard [not good] 1/6 8° *Berlin* 74

The Deffence et Illustration [1549] was the manifesto of the Pléiade, an association of seven men [RONSARD, du BELLAY, BELLEAU, BAIF, DAURAT, JODELLE and PONTUS de TYARD], whose object was the reformation of the Fch. language. RONSARD'S *Odes* [on the Horatian pattern] [1550] was the first practical illustr. of their method.

BELLEAU, Rémy [1528–77] Oeuvres, ed. Gouverneur, 3 vols. [Bibl. Elzévirienne] s 8° *Paris* 66–67
de COLLÉRYE, Roger [15 cent.] Oeuvres, ed. C. d'Héricault 8° " 55
COQUILLART, [1421 (?)–1510] Oeuvres, ed. C. d'Héricault, 2 vols. 8° " 57
DESPORTES, Philippe [1546–1606] Oeuvres, ed. A. Michiels 8° " 58

AID:
GRÖBEDINKEL, P. — Der Versbau Desportes u. Fr. de Malherbe—*in* Französ. Studien, vi. pt. i. 4/6 8° *Heilbronn* 80

JEAN le MAIRE de BELGES [1475–1448 (?)] Oeuvres [poetical and historical] Belgian Acad. *in prep.*

His principal work is the *Illustrations des Gaules*, incorporating many of the mediæval legends.

JODELLE, Étienne [1532–73]—*v.* Drama, *infra.*
LABÉ, Louise ["la belle Cordière"; 1526–66] Poésies, ed. Tross 8° *Paris* 71
de MAGNY, Olivier [?–1560 (?)] Poésies, ed. E. Courbet, 5 vols. s 8° " 81 *sqq.*
" " " Sonnets inédits, ed. T. de Larroque s 8° " 8
MARGUERITE d'ANGOULÊME [Qu. of Navarre; 1492–1549] Les Marguerites de la Marguerite des Princesses, ed. F. Franck, 4 vols. 8° " 73–7[illegible]
" " Deux Farces inédites, ed. C. Lacour [authorship v. doubtful] 8° " 56
MAROT, Clément [1497 (?)–1544] Oeuvres, ed. P. Jannet + C. d'Héricault, 4 vols. 8° *Paris* [68–72] 73
" ed. Guiffrey—*now pub. in pts.* [a fine edn.]
" Choisis, ed. C. d'Héricault [w. a good intro.] 3/- s 8° "

AID:
GLAUNING, F. — Syntaktische Studien zu Marot [dissert.] 1/6 8° *Erlangen* 73

K § 27B

REGNIER, Mathurin [1573–1613] *Oeuvres, ed. E. Courbet 8° *Paris* 75
" " E. Poitevin 8° " 60
" " Viollet-le-Duc [Bibl. Elzévirienne] s 8° " [22] 53
Satires, 3 Epistles, 5 Elegies, odes, stanzas, epigrams, *etc.*

AID:
LAFE, Analyse et Critique des Satyres de Regnier [schl.-progr.] 1/6 4° *Königsberg* 60

*de RONSARD, Pierre [1524–85] Oeuvres, ed. P. Blanchemain, 2 vols. [Bibliothèque Elzèvir.] ea. 5/– s 8° *Paris* 57

AIDS:
*Berdes, J. Étude littéraire de Ronsard [life, works, influence; schl.-progr.] 1/6 8° *Dessau* 75
Büscher, La Versification de Ronsard [schl.-programme] 1/6 4° *Weimar* 67
Dor, C. Rons. quam habuerit vim ad ling. fr.-gall. excolendam [dissert.] 1/6 8° *Bonn* 67
Erkelenz, H. Ronsard und seine Schule [dissert.] 1/6 8° *Würzburg* 68
Felgner, G. Ueb. Eigenthümlichkeiten d. Ronsard'schen Phraseologie [sch.-progr.] 1/6 4° *Gotha* 60
Scheffler, W. Essai sur Ronsard et sa réforme littéraire [dissert.] 1/6 8° *Rostock* 73
Stötzer, O. Étude sur Ronsard et son école *Bützow* 74

de SAINT GELAIS, Mellin [1491–1558] Oeuvres, ed. Blanchemain, 3 vols. 8° *Paris* 73
TAHUREAU, Jacques [1527–55] Poésies, ed. Blanchemain, 2 vols. 8° *Geneva* 69
*VILLON, François [1431–(?)] Oeuvres Complètes, ed. P. Jannet *Paris* 66
" " ed. P. Lacroix " [54] 77
" " ed. L. Moland " 79

AIDS:
Bijvanck, W. G. C. Essai critique sur les Oeuvres de Villon, pt. i. [*Petit Testament*] *Leyden* 83
*Longnon, A. Étude biographique sur François Villon 8° *Paris* 77
Nagel, François Villon: Darstellung s. Lebens nach s. Gedichten *Berlin* 77
Stimming, A. François Villon " 69
Tamm, R. Bemerkungen zur Metrik und Sprache Villon's [schl.-progr.] *Freiberg* 79

Fiction.

BEROALDE DE VERVILLE [1558–1612] Le Moyen de Parvenir, ed. P. L. Jacob 8° *Paris* 68
des PÉRIERS, Bonaventure [1500–44] Oeuvres, ed. C. Lacour, 2 vols. 8° " 66
Incl. the *Nouvelles Récréations et Joyeux Devis* [a coll. of 129 short tales, in style of *Cent Nouvelles*] and *Cymbalum Mundi* [in dialogue].
BOUCHET, Guillaume [early 17 cent.] Serées [soirées], ed. Roybet *Paris* *in prog.*
Cent Nouvelles Nouvelles, ed. Thos. Wright, 2 vols. 10/– 8° " 58
de CHOLIÈRES, Sieur [16 cent.] Les Matinées, *and* Les Après-Dinées, ed. Tricotel, 2 vols. " 79
Gesta Romanorum —*v.* B § 3.
Jean le Paris [end 15 cent.], ed. Prf. A. de Montaiglon 8° *Paris* 74
A cross 'tween a *roman d'aventures* and a folk-tale, telling how the King, as "Jean de Paris," outwitted the King of England, in suit for hand of Infanta of Spain.

MARGUÉRITE d'ANGOULÊME [Qu. of Navarre; 1492–1549] Heptameron, ed. Le Roux de Lincy, 3 v. 8° *Paris* 53–55

AIDS:
Génin (ed.) Lettres de Marguérite d'Angoulême, 2 vols. *Paris* 41; 42
Lotheissen, M. Margarethe von Navarra: ein Cultur- u. Litteraturbild 5/– 8° *Berlin* 85

NICHOLAS DE TROYES [16 cent.] Grand Parangon de Nouvelles Nouvelles
Based on the *Decameron* and *Gesta Romanorum* with some original tales.
NOEL DU FAIL [1520–91] Propos Rustiques, ed. La Borderie *Paris* 78
" " Contes d'Eutrapel, ed. C. Hippeau, 2 vols. [crit. and satir. dialogues] 8° " 75
Quinze Joyes du Mariage, ed. P. Jannet [a satire] 8° " [53] 57
RABELAIS, Fr. [1495–1553] Oeuvres, ed. Bourgaud Desmarets + E. J. B. Ratberg, 2 v. [a good. edn.] 8° " [57] 73
" ed. P. Jannet + L. E. D. Moland, 7 vols. [Bibl. Elzév.] 8° " [ ] 73
" ed. C. Marty-Laveaux, vols. i.–iv. 8° " 70–81
" ed. Prf. A. de Montaiglon + L. Lacour, 3 vols. 8° " 68–73

AIDS:
Beiträge zur Geschichte d. französischen Sprache aus Rabelais Werken, 3 pts. [schl.-progr.] *Breslau* 61; 66; 74
*FLEURY, J. Rabelais, 2 vols. [best general commentary] 8° *St. Petersburg* 76; 77
LIGIER, H. La Politique de Rabelais 8° *Paris* 80
MAYSARGUES, A. Rabelais: étude sur le 16e siècle 8° " 69
NOEL, E. Rabelais et son Oeuvre 8° " 80
SÉBILLOT, P. Gargantua dans les Traditions populaires [Littér. Populaires] 6/6 s 8° " 73
VALLÉT, C. La Génie de Rabelais 8° " 60

de la SALLE, Antoine [1398–1461 (?)] Petit Jean de Sainté, ed. Guichard 8° *Paris* 43
For *Cent Nouvelles Nouvelles*, *Pathelin* and *Quinze Joyes du Mariage* [all three attributed to Antoine de la SALLE] *v. supra*, K § 277 and *supra*, resp.
Violier des Histoires Romaines ed. Gustave Brunet 8° *Paris* 58
A Fch. tr. of the *Gesta Romanorum* [*v.* B § 3] wh. first appeared in early pt. of 16 cent. and went thro many edns.

Drama.

History.

*EBERT, Ad. Entwickelungsgeschichte d. frz. Tragödie vornehmlich im 16ten. Jahrh. [standard] 8° *Gotha* 56
FAGUET, La Tragoedie française au 16e siècle 8° *Paris* 83

Individual Writers.

GARNIER, Robert [1545–1601] Tragédies, ed. Prf. W. Foerster; w. German notes, 4 vols. 4/–, 3/–, 3/–, 3/– [Samml. frz. Neudr.] 8° *Heilbronn* 82–83

AIDS:
BERNAGE, M. S. Étude sur Robert Garnier 2/6 8° *Paris* 80
HAASE, A. Zur Syntax Robert Garniers [= Franz. Stud. v. I: *v.* K § 268] 3/6 8° *Heilbronn* 81
JENSEN, A. Syntaktische Studien zu Robert Garnier *Kiel* 83

GRINGO(I)RE, Pierre [1475–1534] Oeuvres, ed. C. d'Héricault + A. de Montaiglon + J. de Rothschild, 2 vols. [Bibl. Elzév.] 10/- s 8° *Paris* 58; 77
JODELLE, Étienne [1532–73] Oeuvres, ed. Marty-Laveaux, 2 vols. ,, 68; 70

AIDS:
HERTING, A. Der Versbau Étienne Jodelle's [dissert.] *Kiel* 84
KAHNT, P. Jodelle's u. Garnier's Tragoedien u. Seneca's Einfluss [dissert.] *Marburg* 85

de LARIVEY, Pierre [1540–1612] ed. Paul Jannet—*in* vols. v.–vii. *of* Théâtre Frçs. Anc. [Bibl. Elzév.; *ut* K § 277, *s.v.* Early Drama].
VOGELS, J. Der syntakt. Gebrauch d. Tempora u. Modi bei P. de Larivey—*in* Rom. Stud. v. [*ut* K § 256].

Miscellaneous Prose.

de la BOËTIE Étienne [1530–63] Oeuvres, ed. Feugère [political] 8° *Paris* 46
,, ,, Remarques s. l'Eroticus d. Plutarque, ed. R. Dezeimeries 8° *Bordeaux* 68
BRANTOME, Pierre [1540–1614] Oeuvres, ed. Buchon, 2 vols. [a standard edn.] 8° *Paris* 38; 39
,, ed. Lalanne [pubs. of Soc. de l'Hist. de France] ,, *in prog.*
,, ed. Mérimée + Lacour, 7 vols. 8° ,, 58–79
Biographical essays: *Vies des Grands Capitaines, Des Rodomontades Espagnols, Vie des Dames Galantes*, etc.
CHASTELLAIN, Georges [1403–1475] Chronique de Messire Jacques de Lalaing, ed. Kervyn de Lettenhove, 8 vols. 40/- 8° *Bruss.* 63–66
A biography.
de COMMINES, Philippe [1447 (?)–1511] Mémoires, ed. Chantelauze 8° *Paris* 81
,, ,, ,, ed. Kervyn de Lettenhove, 1 vol.; Lettres et Négotiations, 2 vols. 8° *Brussels* 67; 74

AIDS:
ARNOLD, W. Die ethisch-politische Grundanschauung d. Philippe v. Commines *Dresden* 73
FIERVILLE, Documents inédits sur Philippe de Commines 8° *Paris*
TÖNNIES, Paul La Syntaxe de Commines 1/6 8° *Berlin*

Gregoire lo Pape, Li Dialogue [O.-F. tr., 12 cent.]; ed. Prf. W. Förster 10/- r 8° *Halle* 76
MARGUÉRITE DE VALOIS [Qu. of Navarre; 1552–1615] Mémoires, ed. F. Guessard [pubs. of Soc. de l'Hist. d. Frce.] *Paris* 42
,, ,, ,, ed. F. Guessard [Bibl. Elzévirienne] s 8° *Paris* 58
MEIGRET, Louis Tretté de grammère frc. [1550], hrsg. Prf. W. Foerster [Samml. frz. Neudr.] 4/- 8° *Heilbronn* 87
de MONTAIGNE, M. E. [1533–92] Oeuvres, ed. J. V. Le Clerc, 4 vols. [a standard edn.] 8° ,, 65–66
,, ed. Louandre [Bibliothèque Charpentier] s 8° ,,
,, ed. Courbet + Roger ,, *in prog.*

AIDS:
BIGORIE DE LASCHAMPS, F. Michel de Montaigne: sa vie, ses oeuvres et son temps 8° *Paris* [ ] 60
DEZEIMERIES, R. Recherches s. l. recension d. texte posthume des *Essais* de Montaigne 8° *Bordeaux* 66
WENDELL, H. Étude sur la Langue des *Essais* de Montaigne [dissert.] 8° *Stockholm*

Orthographia Gallica ed. J. Stürzinger [Altfranz. Bibl.] 2/6 8° *Heilbronn* 84
Satyre Ménipée [1594] ed. J. Franck [a political satire] *Oppeln* 84
,, Labitte 8° *Paris* 69
,, Charles Read ,, 76

AID:
FRANK, J. *Zur Satyre Ménipée*: eine kritische Studie [schl.-progr.] 1/6 8° *Nikolsburg* 80

XXIX. Celtic Philology and Literature.

279. CELTIC PHILOLOGY (a): GENERALLY.

The Early Celtic Race.

BRANDES, H. B. C. Die ethnographischen Verhältnisse der Kelten und Germanen 6/- 8° *Leipzig* 57
DIEFENBACH, L. —*in his* Origines Europaeae: die alten Volker Europa's mit ihren Sippen und Nachbaren 20/6 8° *Frankfort* 61
,, Celtica: sprachliche Documente zur Geschichte der Kelten, 3 vols. 8° *Stuttgart* 39–40
HOLTZMANN, A. Kelten und Germanen 8° ,, 55
LEMIÈRE, P. L. Étude sur les Celtes et les Gaulois 8/6 8° *Paris* [74; 76] 81
RHYS, Prf. J. —*in his* Lectures on Welsh Philology [*ut* K § 280].
ROGET DE BELLOQUET, Bar. Ethnogénie Gauloise, 4 vols. 25/- 8° ,, 68–75
Vol. i.: Glossaire Gaulois, 7/6 ('68) '72; ii.: Preuves Physiologiques, 7/- ('68) '75; iv.: Les Cimmériens, posthum. ed. A. MAURY + H. GAIDOZ, 3/-; iii. *not sold separ.*

Grammar, etc.

ARBOIS DE JUBAINVILLE Études Grammaticales sur les Langues Celtiques 7/- 8° *Paris* 81
EBEL, Dr. H. Celtic Studies, tr. w. intro. Prf. W. K. Sullivan [a bad tr.] 10/- 8° Williams 63
SCHUCHARDT, Prf. H. Romanisches und Keltisches [collection of miscell. essays] 7/6 8° *Berlin* 86
WINDISCH, Prf. E. Keltische Sprachen—in Ersch + Gruber's *Encyklopädie*, Sect. II., pt. 35 13/6 4° *Leipzig* 84
*ZEUSS, J. C. Grammatica Celtica e Monumentis Vetustis, ed. H. Ebel [in Latin] 30/- r 4° *Berlin* [53] 68–71
The standard authority: holds to the Celtic language the same sort of position that GRIMM does to the Teutonic, DIEZ to the Romance, and MIKLOSICH to the Slavonic.
Güterbock + Thurneysen B. + R. Indices Gloss. et Vocabul. Hibern. quae in [Zeuss] explanatur 7/- r 8° *Leipzig* 81
Molloy, J. O. Index Nominum et Vocab. Hibern. quae in [Zeuss] reperiuntur 10/- 8° *Eblanae* 78
ZIMMER, H. Keltische Studien, pt. i., 3/-; ii. [Altirische Betonung] 6/- 8° *Berlin* 81; 84

Magazines and Serials.

Archivio Glottologico — *has contd. and conts. valuable Celtic articles.*

Revue Celtique — ed. H. Gaidoz, and subsequently d'Arbois Jubainville, vols. i.–vi. ea. 20/- m 8° *Paris* 70 *sqq.*

Celtic Element in Romance, *v.* K § 256; in French, *v.* K § 270.

Inscriptions: Ogham—*v.* G § 14.

280. CELTIC PHILOLOGY (*b*): CYMRIC BRANCH.

Old Gallic.

GLÜCK, Chr. W. — Die bei Cäsar vorkommenden keltischen Namen [by a pupil of Zeuss] 3/- 8° *Munich* 57

MONE, F. — Die gallische Sprache u. ihre Brauchbarkeit für d. Geschichte *o.p.* 8° *Carlsruhe* 57

MONIN, H. — Monuments des anciens Idiomes Gaulois 8 *Paris* 72

Endeavours to establish the influence of Celtic on Gallic Latin.

Chrestomathy — —*v.* K § 282 (*sub voc.* HOLDER).

Breton (Armoric).

Grammar.

HINGANT, Abbé J. — Éléments de la Grammaire Bretonne 3/- 8° *Tréguier* 69

LEGONIDEC, J. F. M. — Grammaire Celto-Bretonne, ed. Brizeaux 21/- 8° *Paris* [sec. ed. 36] 50

Dictionaries.

LEGONIDEC, J. F. M. — Dictionnaire Breton-Franç. et Fr.-Bret., ed. Villemarqué, 2 v. *o.p.* [*pb. & w.* 42/-] 4° *Saint Brieuc* 47; 50

LOTH, J. — Vocabulaire Vieux Breton 8/6 8° *Paris*

TROUDE, A. E. — Dictionnaire Français et Breton 10/- 8° *Brest* 43

Welsh.

History of the Language, etc.

BRADSHAW, Henry — —*papers in his* Collected Papers [*ut* K § 3] 16/- 8° Camb. Press 89

JAMES, Ivor — The Welsh Language in the xvi. and xvii. Centuries [repr. fr. *Red Dragon*] 2/- 8° Owen, *Cardiff* 87

*RHYS, Prf. John — Lectures on Welsh Philology 15/- c 8° Trübner [77] 81

Grammar.

NETTLAU, Dr. Max — Studies in Welsh Grammar *in prep.*

ROWLAND, Th. — Grammar of the Welsh Language, 4/6 Exercises 4/6 p 8° *Bala* [67] 76; [71] 78

SATTLER, E. — *Y Gomeryd:* Grammatik d. Kymraeg 10/- 8° *Zürich* 86

SPURRELL, W. — Grammar of the Welsh Language 3/- f 8° *Caerfyrddin* [48] 70

" " — Practical Lessons in Welsh on Natural Method 2/6 12° *Carmarthen* 81

Dictionaries.

*EVANS, Rev. D. Silvans — *Geiriadur Cymraeg:* Dictionary of Welsh Language, pt. i. 10/6; ii. 5/- r 8° Spurrell, *Carmarthen* 87; 88

PUGHE, W. Owen — Dictionary of the Welsh Language expl. in English, 2 vols. *o.p.* [*w.* 60/-] r 8° *Denbigh* [03] 32

The first edn. was pub. under name of WM. OWEN, after which the author changed his name.

SPURRELL, W. — Dictionary of the Welsh Language [both parts] 8/6 f 8° *Caerfyrddin* [48–49] 89

Cornish — —*for* Modern Dialect, *v.* K § 241.

Grammar.

NORRIS, E. — Sketch of Cornish Grammar 3/- 12° Parker 59

Dictionaries.

BANNISTER, Dr. J. — Glossary of Cornish Names—*v.* K § 241, *s.v.* Cornwall.

JAGO, F. W. B. — An English-Cornish Dictionary 21/- 4° Simpkin 87

POLWHELE, Rev. R. — Cornish-English Vocab. and Provincial Glossary, pl. *o.p.* [*w.* 25/-] 4° *Truro* [08] 36

*WILLIAMS, Rev. R. — Lexicon Cornu-Britannicum, w. examp. and tr., 3 pts. in 1 vol. 42/- 4° *Llandovery* 62–65

Cont. Welsh, Armoric, Irish, Gaelic and Manx synonyms, w. illus. fr. Sanscrit, Gk., Lat., German, etc.

281. CELTIC PHILOLOGY (*c*): IRISH-GAELIC BRANCH.

Irish.

Grammar.

BOURKE, Can. U. J. — College Irish Grammar, 2/6; Easy Lessons in Irish 2/6 s 8° *Dublin* 79; [67] 77

JOYCE, Dr. P. W. — Grammar of the Irish Language 1/- s 8° Gill, *Dublin* 79

O'DONOVAN, Dr. J. — Grammar of the Irish Language [scholarly] *o.p.* [*pb.* 21/-; *w.* 10/6] 8° *Dublin* 45

*WINDISCH, Prf. E. — Grammar of the Irish Language, tr. Dr. N. Moore 7/6 c 8° Camb. Press 82

" " — Compendium of Irish Grammar, tr. McSwiney 6/- 8° Gill, *Dublin* 83

" " — Grammatik der Altirischen [Indogerm. Grammatiken] *Leipzig* *in prep.*

WRIGHT, C. H. H. — Grammar of the Modern Irish Language 2/6 12° Williams [55] 60

Phonology and Metrics.

ZIMMER, H. — Ueber altirische Betonung und Verskunst 6/- 8° *Berlin* 84

K § 282

Etymology.

Dictionaries.

Ascoli, Prf. Lexicon Palaeo-Hibernicum—*in his ed.* of Old Irish Codex in the Ambros. Lib. *Milan* *in prog.*
O'Reilly, E. Irish-English Dictionary, ed. J. O'Donovan 21/- 4° *Dublin* [17] 64

Glosses.

Sanas Chormaic: Cormac's Glossary, tr. J. O'Donovan, ed. W. Stokes 52/6 4° *Calcutta*(Trübner) 68
Stokes, Whitley [ed.] Goidelica: Old and Early Middle Irish Glosses [prose and verse] 18/- r 8° Trübner [62] 72

Loan Words.

Güterbock, B. Bemerkungen üb. d. latein. Lehnworte in Irischen [dissert.] 1/6 8° *Königsberg* 82

Place-Names.

Joyce, Dr. P. W. Origin and History of Irish Names of Places, 2 vols. ea. 5/- c 8° Gill, *Dublin* [69-75] 71
" " Irish Local Names Explained [arrgd. in alphab. order] 1/- f 8° " "

Gaelic.

History of the Language, etc.

Blackie, Prf. J. S. The Language and Literature of the Scottish Highlands 6/- c 8° Douglas, *Edin.* 81
Michel, Francisque Crit. Inquiry into the Scottish Language 63/- 4° Blackwood 82

Grammar.

Stewart, Rev. Alex. Elements of Gaelic Grammar, ed. McLauchlan 3/6 12° McLachlan, *Edin.* [80] 86

Etymology.

Mackay, Dr. Chas. Gaelic Etymology of the Languages of West. Europe [of no great value] 42/- r 8° Trübner 77

Dictionaries.

McAlpine, N. Pronouncing Gaelic Dictionary, with Grammar [both pts.] 9/- 8° *Edinburgh* [63] 81
Macleod + Dewar, Dr. Norman / Dr. D. Dictionary of the Gaelic Language [both pts.] 12/6 8° McLachl. *Ed.* [66] 87

Manx.

Grammar.

Kelly, John Practical Grammar of Ancient Gaelic or Manx, ed. Rev. W. Gill 7/6 8° Manx Soc. [05] 70

Dictionary.

Kelly, John Manx and English Dictionary, ed. Mosley + Gill, 2 vols. [both parts] 21/- 8° Manx Soc. [08] 66

Names.

Moore, Rev. A. W. Manx Names [place-names and surnames; w. phonet. intro. by Prf. J. Rhys] 10/6 8° Stock 90

283. CELTIC LITERATURE (*a*): CYMRIC BRANCH.

History and Study of Literature.

d'Arbois de Jubainville Introduction à l'Étude de la Littérature Celtique 8° *Paris* 83
Arnold, Matthew On the Study of Celtic Literature 8/6 c 8° Smith & Elder 67

Chrestomathy.

*Holder, Prf. Alfred Alt-Celtischer Sprachschatz [to be cpl. in 18 quarterly pts.] ea. 8/- r 8° *Leipzig*(Nutt) 90 *in prog.*
To form a complete coll. of materials for study of Old-Celtic—*i.e.* contemp. inscripp. (monumental and numismatic), Gk. and Lat. writers, itineraries and glossaries. Words alphab. arrgd., illustr. quots. chronolog., inscripp. locally. "Old-Celtic" is here intended to designate Gaulish and the basis common to both Gaelic and Kymric.

Breton.

Loth, J. [ed.] Chrestomathie Bretonne, pt. i. [Breton-Armoricain] 8/6 8° *Paris* 90
Stokes, Whitley [ed.] Middle-Breton Hours, w. tr. and gloss. index 6/- 8° *Calcutta*(Williams) 76
" " ["] The Breton Glosses at Orleans 10/6 8° " " 80
de la Villemarqué, H. Poëmes Bretons du Moyen-age, text and trs. 6/6 8° *Paris* 79
" " " [ed.] Poëmes des Bardes Bretons du 6me Siècle, text and trs. 8/- " [50] 60
" " " [ed.] Le Grand Mystère de Jésus [Breton Mystery] 6/- 8° " 65
" " " [ed.] Barzaz-Breiz [collection of Breton folk-songs] 6/6 8° " [40] 46

Folk-Literature —*v.* B § 15.

Welsh.

Bibliography.

Goossens, H. —*in his* Ueber Sage *etc.* d. Chev. au Lyon *gives a good list of works on the earlier Welsh literature* [= Neuphil. Stud., pt. i.] 1/- 8° *Paderborn* 83
Rowlands, Rev. W. Cambrian Bibliography [in Welsh—bks. from 1546-1799] 15/- 8° *Llanidloes* 69

History of the Literature.

Rhys, Prf. John —*in his* Lectures on Welsh Philology—*ut* K § 280.
*Stephens, Thos. Literature of the Kymry, ed. Rev. D. Silvan Evans [12-14 cents.] 15/- 8° Longman [49] 76
Wilkins, Charles History of the Literature of Wales [1300-1650] r 8° *Cardiff* 84

Modern Collections.

*JONES + WILLIAMS + PUGHE, $\frac{O.IE.}{W.O.}$ [eds.] Myvyrian Archæology of Wales, coll. from ancient MSS. [pith of Welsh literature from 6 to 15 cent.] r 8° WelshMSS.Soc., *Llandov.* [04–07] 61–70
MENZIES, Louisa J. [tr.] Legendary Tales of Ancient Britons [tr. fr. Chronicles; popular] 3/- f 8° J. R. Smith 64
NASH, D. W. [tr.] Taliesin: trs. of Remains of Welsh Bards 14/- 8° " 57
SKENE, W. F. [ed.] Four Ancient Books of Wales, 2 vols. [Bardic poems of 6 cent.] 36/- 8° Douglas, *Edin.* 68

Early Collections and Pieces.

Black Book of Carmarthen: text, ed. J. Gwen Evans [autotype facsimile of the oldest Welsh MS.] r 8° *priv. prin. Oxford* 88
Previously edited in JONES' *Myvyrian Arch. of Wales*, and in Skene's *Four Ancient Books—ut supra.*
Brut y Tywysogion [" Chron. of the Princes "] ed. w. Eng. tr. Williams ab Ithel; facs. 10/- r 8° Rolls Series 60
Bruts [histor. chronicles of Wales]: text, ed. Prf. J. Rhys + J. Gwen Evans [Welsh Texts Ser.] r 8° *priv. prin. Oxford* 90
Edeyrn ["Golden-tongued"] Dosparth Edeyrn Davod Aur: anc. Welsh Grammar [13 cent.], w. "Rules of Welsh Poetry," by D. ddu Athraw [14 cent.]: text, trs. and notes by Williams ab Ithel 8° Welsh MSS. Soc. 56
Elucidarium ed. Prf. J. Rhys + J. M. Jones [Anecdota Oxon.; fr. 14 cent. MSS.] 4° Clar. Press *in prep.*
Iolo MSS. ed. w. English trs. Taliesin Williams ab Iolo; pl. *o.p.* [*w.* 50/-] r 8° WelshMSS.Soc., *Llandov.* 48
A selection of anc. MSS. in prose and verse, fr. the coll. made by A. Williams Iolo Morganwg.
LEWIS GLYN COTHI Poetical Works, ed. w. notes, etc., Rev. W. Davies + Rev. J. Jones [*w.* 12/6] 8° Cymrodorion Soc. 37
The works of a celebrated bard, who flourished in the rns. of Henry vi., Edw. iv., Rich. iii. and Henry vii.
Liber Landvensis [register of Llandaff cathedral]: ed. P. B. Davies-Cooke [Welsh Texts Ser.] r 8° *priv. prin. Oxford in prep.*
Lyfr yr Ancr ["the Anchorite's bk."], ed. Prf. J. Rhys + J. M. Jones [Anecd. Oxon.; lives of Welsh saints] f 4° Clar. Press *in prep.*
Mabinogion, The fr. Anc. Welsh MSS., w. tr. & notes Lady C. Guest, 3 v.; facs. & ill. *o.p.* [*w.* £5] i 8° Longman 38–49
" " The same, tr. only 21/- r 8° Quaritch [49] 77
" " Text, ed. Prf. J. Rhys + J. Gwen Evans [facsimile reproduction of MS.] 21/- r 8° *Oxford* 87
" " traduit en entier J. Loth 13/6 8° *Paris* 90
Meddygon Myddfai ed. Williams ab Ithel, w. tr. and notes J. Pughe *o.p.* [*w.* 10/-] 8° WelshMS.Soc., *Llandov.* 62
The Medical Practice of Rhiwallon and his sons, w. the Llyn-y-Fan ("Legend of the Lake").
Morte d'Arthure —*v.* K § 46.
Y Gododin [poem on battle of Cattraeth, by Aneurin, 6 cent.] with tr. Williams ab Ithel *o.p.* [*w.* 7/6] 8° *Llandovery* 52
Prudau Padric [S. Patrick's Purgatory]: Early Versions of, ed. w. tr. & gloss. Rev. R. Williams, 2 pts. 30/- 8° 78; 80

Folk-Literature —*v.* B § 15.

Cornish.

NORRIS, E. [ed. and tr.] The Ancient Cornish Drama, ed. and tr., 2 vols. 21/- 8° Clar. Press 59
Three dramas, constit. a very important relic of the ancient Cornish dialect has a gram. [50 pp.] and vocab. [128 pp.].
STOKES, Whitley [ed.] Beunans Meriasek: Life of St. Meriasek [drama]; text, tr. and notes 15/- r 8° Trübner 72
" " ["] Creation of the World, w. tr. and notes [a Cornish Mystery] 6/- 8° *Berlin* (Williams) 64

Folk-Literature —*v.* B § 23.

283. CELTIC LITERATURE (*b*): IRISH-GAELIC BRANCH.

Irish.

Bibliography.

d'ARBOIS DE JUBAINVILLE Essai d'un Catal. de la Lit. épique de l'Irlande 8° *Paris* 83

History of Literature —*v. also* K § 282: Cymric Branch, *s.v.* Hist. and Study of Literature.

O'GRADY, S. Early Bardic Literature [of no great value] 1/- c 8° Low 79

Inscriptions.

PETRIE, Dr. G. [ed.] Christn. Inscript. in Irish Lang., ed. M. Stokes, 2 vols.; pl. 60/- 4° Hodges, *Dubl.* 72; 78

Manuscripts.

GILBERT, J. T. [ed.] Facsimiles of National Manuscripts of Ireland, 4 vols; illum. pl. [a magnificent work]—vol. i. *o.p.* [*w.* £5]; ii.–iii. ea. 42/-; iv. (1) 105/-, (2) 90/- Irish Rec. Off. 74 *sqq.*

Modern Collections.

BROOKE, Miss [ed. & tr.] Reliques of Irish Poetry: texts in Irish char. w. verse and trs. *o.p.* [*w.* 12/6] 8° *Dublin* [1789] 16
Celtic Soc. & Irish Archaeolog. Soc.—*for lists of their pubns.*, *v.* F § 41.
HARDIMAN, Jas. [ed. & tr.] Irish Minstrelsy: Bardic Remains of Irel., w. verse trs., 2 vols. *o.p.* [*w.* 30/-] 8° *London* 31
The trs. are from the pens of FURLONG, Hy. GRATTAN, CURRAN, and others. The notes are learned and largely philological.
O'CURRY, Eug. Appendix *to his* Lects. on MS. Materials, pp. 463–664, *conts. several old texts and trs.* 14/- 8° *Dublin* [61] 74
Ossianic Society's Transactions, 6 vols. *o.p.* [*w.* 40/-] *Dublin* 53–61
Cont. wks. of early Irish liter., w. trs. and notes by O'KEARNEY, CONNELLAN O'GRADY, and other scholars.

STOKES, Dr. Whitley [ed.] Three Middle-Irish Homilies on Lives of Saints (Patrick, Briget, & Columba), text and tr. 10/6 c 8° *Calcutta*(Trübner) 77
„ „ [ed.] Old Irish Glossaries; w. intro. 10/6 8° Williams 62

Cormac's Glossary, O'Davoran's Glossary. Glossary to the Calendar of Oingus.

„ „ [ed.] Old Irish Glosses [4; 9th cent.; at Würzburg & Carlsruhe, w. tr. & gloss. index] 8° Philol. Soc. (Trübner) 87
„ „ [ed.] The Tripartite Life of Patrick: w. other documents rel. to that saint, 2 vols. 20/- r 8° Rolls Series 88
WINDISCH, Prf. E. [ed.] Irische Texte, mit Wörterbuch 24/- 8° *Berlin* 81
„ +STOKES, Whitley The same: series ii., pts. i.–ii. *Leipzig* 87; 89

Ancient Collections, and Pieces—*v. also* F § 41.

ADAMNAN, St. [624–704] Life of Saint Columbia, ed. Dr. W. Reeves 40/- 4° Irish Archæol. Soc. 57
„ „ The same, ed. Bp. Forbes+W. F. Skene [Historians of Scotland] 21/- 8° Paterson, *Edin.* 74

Both admirable edns., w. valuable notes and disserts. For popular lives of St. Columba, v. F § 37.

Annals of the Kingdom of Ireland, ed. J. O'Donovan: text and tr. *en regard*, 7 vols. *o.p.* [*w.* £6 10/-] 4° *Dublin* 56
Banquet of Dun Na n-Gedh: and Battle of Magh Rath [Moira], tr. and notes J. O'Donovan 10/- s 4° Irish Archæol. Soc. 42
Battle of Magh Lena: ed. E. Curry [see also line *supra*] 10/- r 8° Celtic Soc. 53
Book of Ballymote: coll. of pieces [prose and verse], w. intro. etc. Prf. R Atkinson: [facs. of MS.] 105/- i f° Roy. Irish Acad. 87
„ Leinster: Irish MS. of 12 cent., ed. Prf. R. Atkinson: facs. of MS. [*v. infra, s.v.* Togail] £6 6/- f° „ „ 80
„ Lismore: Lives of the Saints from the; ed. Dr. Whitley Stokes; w. trss. [Anecdota Oxon.] 31/6 4° Clar. Press 89

Bk. of Lismore, called after the Dke. of Devonshire's castle of Lismore, where it was found in 1814 in a walled-up passage, is a MS. of 1490–1500, consisting of a coll. of compositions of many subjects, periods and authors. STOKES' intro. gives a full acc. of its contents. The lives here are of Patrick, Columba, Briget, Senan, Finian, Finchua, Brendan, Ciaran of Clonmacnois, Mochua.

„ Rights: ed. w. tr. and notes J. O'Donovan [Celtic Soc. pubs.] *o.p.* [*w.* 8/6] c 8° *Dublin* 47

A guide to Irish ceremonial and taxation.

Calendar of Oengus: ed. Whitley Stokes; w. tr., notes and glossarial index 14/- 4° *Dublin* 80
Cath Finntraga, or Battle of Ventry, ed. Kuno Meyer, w. tr. [Anecdota Oxon.] 6/- 4° Clar. Press 85
KEATING, Rev. Geof. The Three Shafts of Death, ed. Prf. R. Atkinson [Irish MS. Series] 3/6 8° Williams 90
Leabhar Breac, the Speckled Book [in Lat. and Ir.]: facs. of MS. 2 v. 84/- f° R. Irish Acad. 72–76
Atkinson, Dr. R. [ed.] Leabhar Breac: Passions & Homilies from, w. tr. & gloss. [Todd Lect. Ser.] 30/- 8° Williams 87
Leabhar Na h-Uidhri: coll. of pieces in Irish [*c.* 1100 A.D.]: facs. of MS. 63/- f° R. Irish Acad. 79
Merugud Uilix Maicc Leirtis, ed. w. tr. Dr. Kuno Meyer [a prose "Irish Odyssey" of 13 cent.] 3/- 8° Nutt 86
Mesca Ulad: ed. w. tr. and notes W. M. Hennessy [Todd Lecture Series] 4/- 8° Williams 89
Peredur ab Efrawc: ed. w. notes and glossary Dr. Kuno Meyer 3/- 8° *Leipzig* 87
Pursuit after Diarmuid and Grainne, ed. S. O'Grady 8° Ossianic Society 57
Saltair na Rann: ed. W. Stokes [coll. of Irish Poems; Anecd. Oxon.] 7/6 4° Clar. Press 83
Togail Troi [Destruction of Troy, from Book of Leinster]: text, tr., and gloss. W. Stokes 18/- 8° „ 81

Folk-Literature —*v.* B § 15.

Gaelic.

Bibliography.

REID, J. Bibliotheca Scoto-Celtica: acc. of all bks. pub. in Gaelic lang. *o.p.* 8° *Glasgow* 32

Manuscripts.

National MSS. of Scotland, Facss. of; pts. i.–iii. (photozincos in gold & colours) *o.p.* [*pb.* 63/-; *w.* £5] f° Scot. Rolls Ser. 67 *sqq.*

Collections.

CAMPBELL, J. F. [ed.] Leabhar na Féinne, v. i. [texts] [coll. of anc. heroic ballads, chiefly 1512–1871] 10/- f° McLachlan, *Ed.* 72
Dorn and Deorg: Gaelic Poems, with trss. and notes 2/6 c 8° Simpkin 74
McGREGOR, Dn. Sir J. Book of Ancient Gaelic Poetry [fr. 16th century MS. coll.], w. tr. and notes Rev. T. McLauchlan+W. F. Skene ["Dean of Lismore's Book"] 12/- 8° *Edinburgh* 62
McKELLAR, Mrs. [ed]. Gaelic and English Poems 3/6 c 8° Simpkin 80
MACKENZIE, J. [ed.] Beauties of Gaelic Poetry, with notes 12/- 8° *Edinburgh* 72
NICOLSON, Alex. [ed.] Collect. of Gaelic Proverbs [based on Macintosh (1785)] 9/- c 8° McLachlan, *Ed.* [81] 82
OSSIAN, Poems of, in orig. Gaelic, w. tr. Arch. Clark, 2 v. [conts. also Macpherson's tr.] 31/6 8° Blackwood 70
„ „ „ tr. J. McPherson 3/6 18° Longman [1773] 76

Folk-Literature —*v.* B § 15.

Manx.

Prayer-Book, Early Manx: MS. ed. Rev. F. J. Moore+Prf. J. Rhys [pub. for the Manx Soc.] Clar. Press *in prep.*

K §§ 284–285

XXX. Slavonic Philology and Literature.

284. GENERALLY AND COLLECTIVELY.

Introduction.

MORFILL, W. R. — Essay on the Importance of Study of Slavonic Lang. [inaug. lecture] 1/- 8° Frowde 90

Philology: Generally.

ABEL, Dr. Carl — Slavic and Latin: [Ilchester] Lects. in Comp. Lexicogr. 5/- p 8° Trübner 83
" " — The same, German tr. by R. Dielitz, *sub tit.* Gross- und Kleinrussisch 6/- 8° *Leipzig* 85
LESKIEN, A. — Quantität und Betonung in der slavischen Sprachen " 85 *sqq.*
" " — Die Declination im Slavisch-Litauischen und Germanischen " 76
MIKLOSICH, F. — Dictionnaire abrégé de six langues slaves 30/- 8° *Vienna* 85
Russian, Old-Slavonic (Cyrillic), Bulgarian, Servian, Chech, Polish. In both French and German.
" " — Vergleichende Grammatik d. slavischen Sprachen 4 vols. £4 8° " [illegible]
i. Lautlehre, 20/-; ii. Stammbildung, 15/-; iii. Wortbildung, 18/-; iv. Syntax, 30/-
" " — Etymologisches Wörterbuch der slavischen Sprachen 20/- 8° " 89
SCHAFARICK, P. J. — Gesch. d. Slav. Sprache u. Lit nach allen Mundarten 8/- 8° *Prague* 69

Magazine.
Archiv für slavische Philologie, ed. Jagic, vols. i.–x. [ea. vol. = 4 pts. (at 6/-)] ea. vol. 20/- 8° *Berlin* 75–87 *in prog.*

Foreign Elements.

SCHUCHARDT, Prf. H. — Slawo-Deutsches und Slawo-Italienisches 10/- 4° *Graz* 84

Pronunciation.

LESKIEN, A. — Untersuchungen üb. Quantität u. Betonung in d. slavischen Sprachen, pt. i. 5/- 8° *Leipzig* 85

History of the Literature: Generally.

GASTER, Dr. M. — Greeko [*sic*]-Slavon. Liter. & its rel. to Folkl. of Mid. Ages [Ilchester Lects.] 7/6 c 8° Trübner 87
KREK, G. — Einleitung in die slavische Literaturgeschichte 21/- 8° *Graz* [ ] 87
MORFILL, W. R. — Slavonic Literature ["Dawn of Liter." Series; popular] 2/6 8° S.P.C.K. 83
PYPIN + SPASOVIC, A. H./W. D. — Istorija Slavjanskich Literatur, 2 vols. 8° *St. Petersburg* 79; 81
" " " — Geschichte der slavischen Literaturen, übers. T. Pech, 2 vols., vol. i. 11/-; ii. 19/- 8° *Leipzig* 81; 83
An important work, but omits Russian Literature in both the original and the German tr.
SCHAFARICK, P. J. — Geschichte der südslawischen Literatur, 2 vols. 17/6 8° *Prague* 64
Folk-Literature —*v.* B § 19.

285. INDIVIDUAL SLAVONIC LANGUAGES AND LITERATURES.

Albanian.

BENLOEW, Louis — Analyse de la langue Albanaise: étude de grammaire comparée 5/- 8° *Paris* 79
BOPP, Friedr. — Das Albanesische in seinen verwandtschaftlichen Beziehungen *Berlin* 55
DOZON, — Manuel de la Langue Chkipe [Albanian] 8° *Paris* 78
GEITHER, L. [ed.] — Die albanesischen und slavischen Schriften; 20 pl. 28/- 4° *Vienna* 83
JARNIK, U. — Zur albanesischen Sprachkunde 8° *Leipzig* 81
MEYER, G. — Kurzgefasste Albanesische Grammatik [Indogerm. Grammatiken] 2/6 s 8° " 88
" " — Albanesische Studien, pts. i.–ii. 3/- r 8° *Vienna* 83; 84
i.: On plural-formations of Alban. nouns, 2/-; ii.: Alban. numerals, 1/6.
" " — Sprache u. Literatur der Albanesen—*in his* Studien und Essays 7/- 8° *Berlin* 85
MIKLOSICH, F. — Albanesische Forschungen—*in* Denkschriften d. Wiener Akad., vols. xix.–xx.
[*cf. also* H. SCHUCHARDT—*in* Ztschr. f. vergl. Sprachf., xx.]
W[ASSA] P[ASHA] — Grammaire Albanaise [Simplified Grammars] 7/6 c 8° Trübner 89
Folk-Literature —*v.* B § 19.

Bohemian (Czech).

CENSKY, F. — Grammatik der böhmischen Sprache 3/6 8° *Prague* 83
JONAS, Ch. — Dictionary of English and Bohemian Languages, 2 pts. 11/- 8° " 76
JUNGMANN, — Bohemian-Latin-German Dictionary, 5 vols. £6 10/- 4° R. Ac. of *Prague* 35–39
KOTT, Fr. — Czech-German Dictionary, 3 vols. 60/- 8° *Prague* 78–82
MOUREK, V. E. — Dict. of Eng. and Bohemian Langs. Pt. i. Eng.-Boh. 10/- 8° " 79
SCHAFARIK, P. J. — Elemente der altböhmischen Grammatik 1/6 8° " [ ] 67
TIEFTRUNK, W. — Böhmisches Lesebuch, with German Dictionary, 2 pts. 4/6 8° " [ ] 72
VYMAZAL, Fr. — Böhmische Grammatik 3/- 8° *Brünn* 81

Literature —*for* Folk-Literature, *v.* B § 19.

WRATISLAW, Rev. A. H. Native Liter. of Bohemia in xiv. cent. [Ilchester Lects.] 5/- 16° Bell 78
" " [tr.] Bohemian Poems: ancient and modern, translated, with essay 49
" " [tr.] The Queen's Court MS. and other anc. Bohemian poems, translated *Camb.* 52
" " [tr.] Baron Wratislaw's Adventures, translated 65

Bulgarian, Modern.

Dictionaries.

BOGOROFF, V. A. Dictionnaire Bulg.-Franç. and Franç.-Bulg. 2 vols. ea. 16/- 8° *Vienna* 71–73
MORSE + VASILIEF, English and Bulgarian Dictionary, 2 pts. *o.p.* [*w.* 15/-] *Constantinople* 60

Grammars, etc.

CANKOF + KYRIAK, A. + D. Grammatik der bulgarischen Sprache 5/- 8° *Vienna* 52
CLEBORAD, F. L. Bulgarische Grammatik 4/6 8° " 88
MORSE + VASILIEF, Grammar of Bulgarian Language, w. vocabulary *o.p.* [*w.* 10/-] *Constantinople* 59

Phonology.

MIKLOSICH, F. Geschichte der Lautbezeichnung im Bulgarischen 2/6 4° *Prague* 83

Folk-Literature —*v.* B § 19.

Bulgarian: Old (Cyrillic, Palæo-Slavonic).

LESKIEN, A. Handbuch der altbulgarischen [altkirchenslawischen] Sprache [gram., texts, gloss.] 7/6 8° *Weimar* [71] 86
MIKLOSICH, F. Lexicon Palaeoslovenico-Graeco-Latinum 27/- r 8° *Vienna* [50] 62–65
" " Radices Linguae Slovenicae veteris Dialectae 3/6 8° *Leipzig* 45
" " Lautlehre und Formenlehre d. Altslov. Sprache, 2 pts. 6/- r 8° *Vienna* 50–54
" " Altslovenische Formenlehre in Paradigmen " 74
WIEDEMANN, O. Beiträge zur altbulgarischen Conjugation 2/6 8° *Dorpat* 86

Literature.

MIKLOSICH, F. [ed.] Monumenta Linguae Palaeoslovenicae 12/- r 8° *Vindob.* 51
Monumenta Linguae Palaeoslovenicae, ed. A. Kaluzniacki, vol. i.: Evang. Putnanum 20/- 8° *Teschen* 88

Hungarian —*v.* K § 142.

Illyrian.

BERLIC, A. T. Grammatik d. Illyr. Spr. d. Serben, Kroaten, etc. 5/- 8° *Agram* 50
RICHTER, A. F. Illyrisch-Deutsch u. Deutsch-Illyr. Wörterb., 2 vols. 15/- r 8° 39

Lithuanian: Lettish, Old Prussian.

Bibliography.

LESKIEN, —*in his* Report on Lith., Lettish and Pruss. *in the* Trans. Philolog. Soc., 1877.

Philology and Literature.

BEZZENBERGER, Prf. A. [ed.] Littauische u. Lettische Drucke d. 16 u. 17 Jahrhunderts, pts. 1–4. 25/- 8° *Göttingen* 74–87
" " Littauische Forschungen 10/- 8° " 82
" " Ueber die Sprache der preussischen Letten 4/- 8° " 85
" " Geschichte der litauischen Sprache [16–17 cent.] 16/- 8° " 77
KURSCHAT, F. Wörterbuch der lithauischen Sprache, vol. i. 27/-; ii. 12/- 8° *Halle* 74; 83
" " Grammatik der lithauischen Sprache [w. map of Lith. languages] 12/- 8° " 76
LESKIEN, A. Der Ablaut der Wurzelsilben im Litauischen 7/- 8° *Leipzig* 84
" " Die Declination im Slavisch-litauischen und Germanischen 5/- r 4° " 76
NESSELMANN, Die Sprache der alten Preuszen 8° *Berlin* 45
SCHLEICHER, August Handbuch d. litauische Sprache, 2 vols. [i.: gram.; ii.: texts and gloss.] 12/- 8° *Prague* 56–57
WEBER, Litauische Grammatik [Indogerman. Grammatiken] *in prep.*

Relation to the Teutonic Branch—*v.* K § 225: Teutonic Philology: Generally.

Folk-Literature —*v.* B § 19.

Polish.

Dictionaries.

BARANOWSKI, J. J. Anglo-Polish Lexicon 12/- f 8° Trübner 84
BOOCH-ARKOSSY, F. Polnisch-Deutsches u. Deutsch-Polnisches Wörterbuch, 2 vols. 20/- 8° *Leipzig* [68] 83
CHODGKI, Polish-English and English-Polish Dictionary 22/- r 8° *Berlin* 74
Dictionnaire Polonais-Français et Français-Polonais, 3 pts in 1 vol. *o.p.* [*w.* 42/-] r 8° " [ ] 58
LINDE, S. B. Slownik Jezyka Polskiego, 6 vols. [Dict. of Polish Lang.] 84/- 8° *Lwów* 54–61
LUKASZEWSKI + MOSBACH, H. A. Polnisches-Deutsches u. Deutsch-Poln. Taschenwörterbuch, 2 v. in 1 4/6 12° *Berlin* [81] 85
SCHMIDT, J. A. E. Nouv. Dict. Portatif: Franç.-Polon. and Polon.-Franç. 3/6 16° *Leipzig* 70

Folk-Literature —*v.* B § 19.

K § 288

Grammars.

JOEL, M. — Anleitung zur Polnischen Sprache, 4/6; Key, 1/6 [Ollendorfian meth.] 4/6 8° *Frankfort* 66; 69
ORDA, N. — Grammaire Analyt. et Prat. de la Langue Polonaise 10/6 8° *Warsaw* 74
POPLINSKI, T. — Grammatik der Polnischen Sprache 2/6 8° *Thorn* [ ] 81

Literature, etc.

History.

NITSCHMANN, H. — Geschichte der polnischen Litteratur 9/- 8° *Leipzig* [83] 88

Specimens.

NEHRING, [ed.] — Altpolnische Sprachdenkmäler 8/- 8° *Berlin* 87

Old Polish.

Phonology.

LECIEJEWSKI, J. — Der Lautwerth der Nasalvocale im Altpolnischen 2/6 8° *Vienna* 86

Russian.

Dictionaries.

ALEXANDROW, A. — Complete English-Russian Dictionary, 2 vols. 24/- 8° *Petersburg* 79
BANKS, — Russko-Angliiskii Slovar, 2 vols. 36/- 8° *Moscow* 40
FREY, — Russisch-Deutsch u. Deutsch-Russisches Handwörterbuch, 2 vols. *Leipzig* *n.d.* (71)
MAKAROFF, N. — Dictionnaire Russe-Français & Français-Russe, 4 vols., 34/- 8°; 2 vols. 17/- 12° *St. Petersbg.* 84; 87–88
PAWLOWSKY, J. — Deutsch-Russisches Wörterbuch, 2 vols. ea. 17/- r 8° *Riga* [ ] 86
Pocket Dictionary of the English and Russian Languages [both pts.] 5/- 12° *Leipzig* 74
REIFF, C. P. — Parallel Dictionaries: Russ., French, German and English ea. 8/- r 12° *Carlsruhe* [53] 74–76

Lexicography.

ABEL, Dr. C. — Gross- u. Klein-Russisch, übers. R. Dielitz [tr. fr. the Ilchester Lectures; on compar. lexicography] 6/- 8° *Leipzig* 85

Grammars, Chrestomathies, etc.

ASBOTH, Oskar [ed.] — Russische Chrestomathie für Anfänger 2/6 8° *Leipzig* 90
CORNET, J. — Manual of Russian and English Conversation 3/6 12° " [ ] 75
DNEPROVSKIJ, K. — Russian Chrestomathy 4/- 8° *Prague* 73
FREETH, F. — Condensed Russian Grammar 3/6 c 8° Trübner 87
GOWAN, Maj. W. E. [tr.] — Ivanoff's Russian Grammar 6/- 8° Paul
KINLOCK, A. — Russian Conversation Grammar: w. exercises and vocab. 9/- c 8° Trübner 90
*MORFILL, W. R. — Grammar of the Russian Language 6/- c 8° Clar. Press 89
REIFF, C. P. — English-Russian Grammar, for the use of Englishmen 6/- c 8° *Paris* (Williams) [53] 83
RIOLA, H. — How to Learn Russian [Key, 5/-; Ollendorff System] 12/- c 8° Trübner [78] 90
" " — Graduated Russian Reader, with Vocabulary 10/6 c 8° " 79
SCHNURMANN, I. Nestor — Russian Manual [gram., exx., dialogues, etc.] 7/6 f 8° W. H. Allen [ ] 88
" " — Aids to Russian Composition [exx., vocabs., extracts, etc.] 7/6 f 8° " " 88
SOBOLEVSKI, Prf. — Lectures on the History of the Russian Language [in Russian]
THOMPSON, A. R. — Russian and English Dialogues 5/- c 8° " " 82
WASSILIJEWITSCH, A. — Chrestomathie Russe, avec un Vocabulaire 4/- 8° *Frankfort* 80

History of Literature—*for* Novels, *v.* K § 56; *for* Poetry, *v.* K § 77; *for* Folk-Literature, *v.* B § 19.

HALLER, K. — Geschichte der russischen Literatur 8° *Riga* 82
v. REINHOLDT, A. — Geschichte der russischen Literatur 13/6 8° *Leipzig* 86

Servian.

Dictionaries.

DANICIC, D. — Wörterbuch der altserbischen Sprache, 3 vols. *Belgrade* 64
" " — Kroato-Servian Dictionary, vol. i., pt. i. [A–Bes] 8/6 8° *Zagreb* 80
FILIPOVIC, J. — Wörterbuch der Kroat. u. Deutsch. Sprache, 4 vols. 36/- s 8° *Agram* 69–75
" " — Kroatisch-Deutsches Wörterbuch, 2 vols. 21/- s 8° " 77
*KARADSCHITSCH, — Lexicon Serbico Germanico-Latin; Deutsch.-Serb. Wörterbuch *Vienna* 52; 77
POPOVIC, G. — Wörterb. der Serbischen u. Deutschen Sprache, 2 vols. [both parts] 18/- 8° *Pancova* [79] 86; 81

Loan Words.

POPOVIC, G. — Türkische und andere orientalische Wörter in d. serbischen Sprache 8° *Belgrade* 84

Grammars, etc.

BOSKOVIC, S. — Lehrbuch der Serbischen Sprache 3/- 8° *Budapesth* 78
LESKIEN, A. — Die Quantität im Serbischen 5/- 8° *Leipzig* 85
MORFILL, W. R. — Simplified Grammar of the Serbian Language [Simplified Grammars] 4/6 c 8° Trübner 87
PARCIC, C. A. — Grammaire de la Langue Serbo-Croate, tr. Feavrier 9/- 8° *Paris* 77
SCHAFARICK, P. J. — Geschichte des Serbischen Schriftthums 10/6 8° *Prague* 65

Folk-Literature —*v.* B § 19.

Slovakic.

Author	Title	Price	Size	Place	Date
Loos, J.	Wörterbuch d. Deutsch, Ungar. u. Slovak. Sprache, 2 vols.	14/-	8°	*Pesth*	70
Pastrnek, F.	Beiträge zur Lautlehre der slovakischen Sprache	2/6	8°	*Vienna*	88
Sket, J.	Grundriss der slovenischen Grammatik	2/-	8°	*Klagenfurt*	88
,, ,, [ed.]	Slovenisches Sprachbuch	3/-	8°	,,	[ ] 88
Victoria, J.	Grammatik der Slovakischen Sprache	3/6	8°	*Pesth*	[ ] 78

Slovenic.

Author	Title	Price	Size	Place	Date
Cornel, A.	Praktische Grammatik der Slovenischen Sprache	3/6	8°	*Klagenfurt*	76
Janezic, A.	Taschenw'b. : Slowen.-Deutsch, 5/- ; Deutsch.-Slowen.	6/-	16°	,, 50 ;	[51] 67

Wendic (Sorbic).

Author	Title	Price	Size	Place	Date
Haupt + Schmaler	Volkslieder der Wenden [Lausitz], 2 vols.	21/-	4°	*Grimma*	44-4-
Jordan,	Grammatik der wendischserbischen Sprache	2/6	8°	*Prague*	41
Liebsch, G.	Syntax d. wendischen Sprache [lang. in the Oberlausitz]	4/-	8°	*Bautzen*	84
Zwahr, F. G.	Niederlausitz-Wendisch-Deutsches Handwörterb., 5 pts.	6/-	8°	*Spremberg*	46-47
Folk-Literature	—v. B § 19.				

XXXI. Artificial (Universal) Languages.

286. VOLAPÜK. WORLD-ENGLISH.

Volapük.

Dictionaries.

Author	Title	Price	Size	Place	Date
Kerckhoffs, Aug.	Wörterbuch : Deutsch-Volapük und Volapük-Deutsch	7/6	8°	*Paris*	87
Krause, G.	Volapük Dictionary [Volapük-English and English-Volapük]		8°	Sonnenschein	*in prep.*
Linderfelt, K. A. [Am.]	Complete Volapük Dictionary [Volapük-English and English-Volapük]	$2	24°	*Milwaukee*	88
Pflaumer, Prf. W.	Wörterbuch der Volapük	4/-	8°	*Halle*	88
Schleyer, J. M.	Grosses Weltsprache Wörterbuch [about 20,000 words]	8/-	8°	*Constance*	[87] 88
Wood, M. W. [Am.]	Dictionary of Volapük [Volapük-English and English-Volapük]	$2	c 8°	*New York*	89

Grammars, etc.

Author	Title	Price	Size	Place	Date
Harrison, I. H.	Complete Course of Volapük [based on Kerckhoffs]	2/6	f 8°	Hachette	[87] 89
Kerckhoffs, Aug.	Grammar of Volapük, abridged K. Dornbusch	2/-	16°	*Paris*	87
Kirchhoff, Prf. Alfred	Grammar of Volapük, 2/6 ; Key to same	2/6	c 8°	Sonnenschein	[88] 88 : 88
Linderfelt, K. A. [Am.]	Volapük : an easy method of acquiring the language	50c.	16°	*Milwaukee*	[88] 88
Schleyer, J. M.	Grammar with Vocabularies of Volapük, tr. A. Seret [by the inventor]	6/6	c 8°	Whittaker	[ ] 87
Schneid, Augustus	Vereinfachtes Volapük	2/-	8°	*Brünn*	87
Seret, W. A.	Grammar and Vocabulary and Volapük	5/6	c 8°	Whittaker	87
Sprague, C. E. [Am.]	Handbook of Volapük	5/-	c 8°	Trübner	[88] 88

Commercial Correspondence.

Author	Title	Price	Size	Place	Date
Kniele, Dr. B.	The Volapük Commercial Correspondent, ed. G. Krause	3/6	c 8°	Sonnenschein	89

World-English.

Author	Title	Price	Size	Place	Date
Bell, A. Melville	World-English	1/-	8°	Trübner	89

Butler & Tanner, The Selwood Printing Works, Frome, and London.

PHILOLOGY AND ANCIENT LITERATURE

WITH SPECIMENS OF THE MODERN LITERATURES OF NON-EUROPEAN LANGUAGES.

It has been deemed desirable to include throughout the remainder of this CLASS *the more important modern* FOREIGN *works and editions. Where thoroughly good English books, however, exist, covering the same ground, this has not always been done quite systematically.*

XIV. The Philological Sciences and Oriental Philology Generally.

92. BIBLIOGRAPHY.

Generally.

BONAPARTE, Prce. Louis-Lucien Attempt at a Catalogue of his Library. By Victor Collins—*ut* K § 4.
Orientalische Bibliographie [*ut* B.B. K § 92]: ed. R. Garbe + Th. Gleiniger, *etc.*, v. i.–vii. [quarterly] *ann.* 10*m.* [*subscr.* 8*m.*] 8° Reuther, *Berl.* 87–93 *in prg.*
ZIEMER, Prf. H. Kurze Philol. Uebersicht üb. d. sprachwiss. Litter. d. letzt. 2 Jahre r 8° a/o Orient. Inst., *Woking* 94

Oriental Incunabula.

SCHWAB, M. [ed.] Les Incunables Orientaux et les Impress. Orient. au commenc. d. 16 siècle 6*fr.* 8° Techener, *Paris* 83

School-Programmes, Dissertations, etc.—*for* Greek and Latin *v.* K § 167; Romance and English *v.* K § 256.

German.

Jahres-Verzeichniss d. a. deut. Schulanst. erschienenen Abhdgn., vols. i.–v. [1889–93] ea. 2*m.* or 2*m.*40 8° Asher, *Berl.* 90–94 *in prg.*
" " d. a. deut. Universit. ersch. Schriften, vols. i.–iv. [1885–89] ea. 5*m.* to 9*m.* 8° " " 87–89 ? *in prg.*
KLÜSSMANN, R. System. Verzeichniss d. Abhgn.…in Schulschriften: 1876–85; w. 2 indexes 5*m.* 8° Teubner, *Lps.* 89

Swedish and *Finnish.*

JOSEPHSON, A. G. S. Avhandlingar ock Program. utgiv. vid Svenska och Finska Acad. ock Skolor: 1855–90 6*kr.*50 8° Lundequist, *Upsala* 91–93

93. ORIGIN AND PHILOSOPHY OF LANGUAGE.

CURTI, Theod. Die Sprachschöpfung: Versuch einer Embryologie d. menschl. Spr. 1*m.*50 8° Stuber, *Würzbg.* 90
DILLMANN, C. —*in his* Mathematik als Fackelträgerin e. neuer Zeit 3*m.* 8° Kohlhammer, *Stuttgart* 89
Conts. an interesting chap. on Orig. of Lang., fr. the pt.-of-view of the natural sciences.
GIESSWEIN, A. Die Hauptprobleme der Sprachwissenschaft 5*m.* 8° Herder, *Freiburg* 92
On some of the relations of the science of language to theology, philosophy and anthropology.
GREG, R. P. Comparative Philology of the Old and New Worlds in rel. to Archaic Speech 31/6 r 8° Paul 93
An attempt to show, by a series of words and their cognates, that an archaic substratum underlies all langs. now in existence, and is therefore also visible in the langs. of Amer. and Africa. Elaborate introd. (73 pp.) in favour of common origin of human race.
KLEINPAUL, Dr. Rud. Das Leben der Sprache u. ihre Weltstellung, 3 vols. ea. 10*m.*, *or together* 24*m.* 8° Friedrich, *Lps.* [88; 92; 90] 93
i. *Sprache ohne Worte* [idea of a general science of lang.]; ii. *Strombgebiet der Sprache* [origin, developmt., physiology]; iii. *Rätsel der Sprache* [words and meanings]. Interesting bks., intended for the educated laity rather than for specialists. The "Second Edn." is merely a reissue of the First, w. a new title-page.
KRAUSE, K. Ch. F. Zur Sprachphilosophie, hrsg. Aug. Wünsche [posthumously pub.] 3*m.* 8° Schulze, *Lps.* 91
LEFEVRE, André F. Race and Language [Internat. Scient. Ser.] c 8° 5/- Paul; $1.50 Appleton, *N.Y.* 94
MÜLLER, Prf. F. Max [and criticism of his views]—*v.* K § 96.
POLLE, F. Wie denkt das Volk üb. d. Sprache? [good popular bk.] 2*m.* 8° Teubner, *Lps.* 89
REGNAUD, Prf. Paul Origine et Philosophie du Langage—*ut* K § 120.
ROSENSTOCK, Paul E. Plato's Kratylos u. d. Sprachphilos. d. Neuzeit, pt. i. [to W. v. Humboldt] [progr.] 4° *Strassb.* 93
RUNZE, G. Studien z. vergl. Religionsgesch., vol. i.: Sprache u. Religion 6*m.* 8° Gaertner, *Berlin* 89
Conts. a good estimate of results of philol. research mainly for treatmt. of theolog. problems, and other matter of interest to the philologist.

SAINEANU, Prf. Lazar   Raporturile intre Grammatica si Logica   8° Socecu, *Bucharest* 91
A lucid and methodical little bk. on the "Relations betw. Grammar and Logic." Suggestive and up-to-date.

STEYRER, Joh.   Der Ursprung der Sprache der Arier   5*m*.20   8° Hölder, *Vienna*   91

Onomatopœia.

TIMMERMANS, A.   Traité dell' Onomatopée : clef etymol. p. l. racines irréducibles   4*fr*.   8° Bouillon, *Paris*   91

94. COLLECTED PHILOLOGICAL ESSAYS AND WRITINGS.

BENFEY, Prf. Theod.   Gesammelte kleinere Schriften, hrsg. Prf. A. Bezzenberger, pts. iii.–iv.   20*m*.   8° Reuther, *Berl*.   91
Also a reissue. w. new title-page, 4 pts., 29*m*., '93. i. *Kleinere sanskritphilolog. Schr.*, 11*m*.; ii. *Kleinere sprachwiss. Schr.*, 8*m*.; iii. *Kleinere Schr. zur Märchenforschung*, 6*m*.; iv. *Kleinere Schr. vermischten Inhalts*, 4*m*.

COOK, Can. F. C.   The Origins of Religion and Language [*ut* 𝔅.𝔅. K § 93]   15/-   8° Murray   84
Five essays on (1) *Rig Veda* (spec. relig. syst.); (2) Pers. Cuneiform Inscrps. and *Zend-Avesta*; (3) *Gâthâs* of Zoroaster; (4) Languages, anc. and mod.; (5) Egyptian comp. w. Semit., Aryan and Turanian words.

CUST, R. N.   Linguistic and other Oriental Essays from 1847 to 1890, ser. iii.   21/-   8° Paul   91

DARMESTETER, Prf. Arsène   Reliques Scientifiques, recueillies p. son frère [Jas. Darmesteter], 2 v.; port. 40/*fr*. 8° Cerf, *Paris* 90

" Prf. Jas.   Essais Orientaux—*ut* B § 2.

DUMONT, Alb.   Mélanges d'Archéologie et d'Épigraphie, ed. Th. Homolle   25*fr*.   8° Thorin, *Paris*   92

GRIMM, Jakob   Kleinere Schriften, 8 vols.   80*m*. 8° Bertelsmann, *Gütersloh* 64–90
i. *Reden u. Abhandlungen*, 9*m*. ['64] '79; ii. *Abhandl. z. Mythol. u. Sittenkunde*, 9*m*. '65; iii. *Abh. z. Litter. u. Grammatik*, 9*m*. '66; iv.–vii. *Recensionen u. vermisch. Aufsätze*, 9*m*., 10*m*.50, 9*m*., 12*m*. '70, '71, '72, '84; viii. *Vorreden, Zeitgeschichtliches u. Persönliches*, 12*m*.50, '90. Vols. i.–vi. were pub. by Dümmler, *Berlin*.

" Wilh.   Kleinere Schriften, hrsg. Gust. Hinrichs, 4 vols.   47*m*.50 8° Bertelsmann, *Gütersloh* 82–87
Vols. i.–ii. were pub. by Dümmler, *Berlin*.

v. GUTSCHMID, A.   Kleine Schriften, hrsg. v. Frz. Mühl, vols. i.–v.   102*m*.   8° Teubner, *Lpz*. 89–92
i. *Schr. zur. Ägyptol. u. Gesch. d. griech. Chronographie*, 24*m*. '89; ii. *Schr. z. Gesch. u. Liter. d. semit. Völker u. z. älteren Kirchengesch.*, 24*m*. '90; iii. *Schr. z. Gesch. u. Liter. d. nicht-semit. Völker v. Asien*, 20*m*. '92; iv. *Schr. z. Griech. Gesch. u. Liter.*, 20*m*.; '93; v. 24*m*. '94.

Mélanges Orientaux : textes et tradns., p. les Profrs. d. l'Ecole d. Langs. Orient. Vivantes   25*fr*.   8° Leroux, *Paris*   83
Miscellaneous Arabic, Pers., Gk., Jap., Bulgar., Chinese texts and trs.; w. *Notice Histor. sur l'Ecole des Langues*.

Mélanges Renier : recueil de travaux publ. p. l'Ecole d. Haut. Etudes   15 *fr*. 8° Vieweg (Bouillon) *Paris* 87
A series of papers, pub. in memory of L. RENIER, pres. of Ec. Haut. Etud., by AMIAUD: *Cyrus, roi de Perse*; BERGAIGNE: *Syntaxe des compar. védiq.*; HALÉVY: *Notes Sémit.*, *etc*.

MERLO, P.   Saggi Glottologici é Letterari, [posthum.] ed. F. Ramorino, 2 vols.   16° Hoepli, *Milan*   90

MEYER, Prf. Gust.   Essays und Studien zur Sprachgeschichte u. Volkskunde 7*m*. 8° Oppenheim. *Berl*. (*now* Trübner, *Strsb*.) 85
The Philol. Essays are (1) *Das indogerm. Urvolk*, (2) *Die etrusk. Sprachfrage*, (3) *Sprache u. Litter. d. Albanesen*, (4) *Das heutige Griechisch*, (5) *Constantin Sathas u. d. Slavenfrage in Griechenland*. For Folklore contents *v*. B § 3.

" " "   The same, ser. ii.   6*m*.   8° Trübner, *Strassbg*. 93

Nouveaux Mélanges Orientaux : p. les Professeurs de l'Ecole d. Langs. Orient. Vivantes; 1 facs.   15/*fr*.   8° Leroux, *Paris*   86
Miscellaneous Persian, Turkish, Annamitic, Chinese, Tamil, Armenian etc. texts and trs.

Recueil de Textes et de Traductions : p. les Professeurs de l'Ecole d. Langs. Orient. Vivantes, 2 vols. 30/*fr*. 8° Leroux, *Paris*   89
Miscellaneous Arabic, Turkish, Malayan, Tcheremiss, Chinese, Roumanian *etc*. texts and trs.

RÖNSCH, Herm.   Collectanea Philologica, [posthum.] ed. Carl. Wagener   7*m*.   8° Heinsius, *Bremen* 91

THOMSEN, Prf. Vilhelm   Festskrift—*on his 25 yrs'. jubilee*   [368 pp.]   8° *Copenhagen*   94
22 papers, by as many of his former pupils; on Philol., General, Classical, Teutonic *etc*.—all but one in Danish.

Study of Languages.

WALSHE, Dr. W. H.   The Colloquial Faculty for Languages   5/-   Churchill   [85] 86
Tho' written fr. a medical pt.-of-view (author is a M.D.) will be read w. great interest and advantage by linguists.

Classical —*v*. K § 168.

95. SERIES AND PERMANENT SERIALS.

Anecdota Oxoniensia : 4 Series : (i.) *Classical*, *v*. K § 173; (ii.) *Semitic*, *v*. K § 105; (iii.) *Aryan*, *v*. K § 119.

Series iv. *Mediæval and Modern* [vi.–ix. not pb. yet]:
i. *Sinonoma Bartholomei* ....ed. J. L. G. MOWAT 3/6 (90*c*. *nt*.)
ii. *Alphita* ....ed. J. L. G. MOWAT 12/6 ($3.25 *nt*.)
iii. *Saltair Na Rann* [*ut* 𝔅.𝔅. K § 283]....ed. Dr. Whitley STOKES 7/6 ($1.90 *nt*.) 83
iv. *Cath Finntrága* [*ut* 𝔅.𝔅. K § 283] ....ed. Dr. Kuno MEYER 6/- ($1.50 *nt*.) 85
v. *Lives of Saints*, fr. Bk. of Lismore [*ut* 𝔅.𝔅. K § 283] ed. Whitley STOKES, w. tr. 31/6 ($8 *nt*.) 89
x. *Old Test. : Earliest Basque Transl.* [*ut* K § 140] ......ed. Llew. THOMAS 18/6 94

Annales du Musée Guimet : vols. i.–xxx. ; pl.   4° Leroux, *Paris* 80–92 *in prg*.
Pubns. of the Ministère de l'Instrn. Publ. et des Beaux Arts, the outcome of Emile GUIMET'S scientific mission, consisting of texts and trs. of Oriental bks. w. comms. *etc*. by eminent scholars.

i., ii., iv. *Mélanges* ....ea. 15/*fr*. 80 ; 80 ; 82
iii. *Bouddhisme au Tibet*......SCHLAGINTWEIT [tr., *v*. 𝔅.𝔅. A § 14] 20/*fr*. 81
v. *Fragmts. extr. du Kandjour* [*ut* K § 155] ..Léon FEER, 20/*fr*. 83
vi. *Lalita Vistara*, pt. i. [*ut* K § 124]..trad. P. E. FOUCAUX, 15/*fr*. 83
vii. *Mélanges* 20/*fr*. 84
viii. *Yi King*, pt. i. [*ut* K § 154]..trad. P. L. F. PHILASTRE, 15/*fr*. 85
ix. *Hypogées Royaux de Thèbes*, pt. i. [*ut* K § 102] ..E. LEFEBURE, 75/*fr*. 86–89
x. *Mélanges* [*ut* K § 125] 30/*fr*. 87
xi.–xii. *Réligion Popul. des Chinois* ....J. J. M. de GROOT, 40/*fr*. 87
xiii. *Le Ramayana* [*ut* K § 124]............Ch. SCHOEBEL, 12/*fr*. 87
xiv. *Essai s. l. Gnosticisme Egypt.* [*ut* A § 11] ......E. AMELINEAU, 15/*fr*. 88
xv. *Siao-Hio* [*ut* K § 154] ....trad. C. de HARLEZ, 15/*fr*. 88
xvi. *Hypogées Royaux de Thèbes*, pt. ii.–iii. [*ut* K § 102] ....E. LEFEBURE, 60/*fr*. 89
xvii. *Pakhome, St., Hist. de* [*ut* K § 115] ..E. AMELINEAU, 60/*fr*. 89
xviii. *Avadana Cataka* [*ut* K § 127]...... trad. Leon FEER, 20/*fr*. 90
xix. *Le Lalita Vistara*, pt. ii. [*ut* K § 127]..trad. FOUCAUX, 15/*fr*. 90
xx. *Textes Taoristes* [*ut* K § 154] ......trad. C. de HARLEZ, 20/*fr*. 92
xxi., xxii., xxiv. *Le Zend Avesta*, v. i.–iii. [*ut* A § 13] ..trad. Prf. J. DARMESTETER, ea. 20/*fr*. 92–93
xxiii. *Yi-King*, pt. ii. [*ut* K § 154]..trad. P. L. F. PHILASTRE, 15/*fr*. 93
xxv. *Hist. des Monast. d. l. Basse Egyp.* [*ut* K § 102]....ed. and tr. AMELINEAU, 40/*fr*. 94
xxvi. *Le Siam Ancien*; ill. [*ut* K § 156] ..L. FOURNEREAU, *in prep*.
xxvii.–viii. *Hist. d. l. Sépulture en Egypte*, 2 v.; ill. [*ut* K § 102] .. AMELINEAU, *in prep*.
xxix.–xxx. *Mélanges* ....*in prep*.

Berlin, Königl. Museen : Mittheilungen aus d. Orient. Sammlungen ; pl. f° Spemann, *Berlin* 89–9 *in prg.*

Ausgrabungen zu Sendschirli, pt. i. [*ut* K § 105*] 25*m.* 93
El Amarna, Thontafelfund, i.–ii. (1–2) [*ut* K § 107] .. H. Winckler, 70*m.* 89–90
Himjarische Inschr. u. Alterthümer 26*m.* 93
Märchen d. Papyrus Westcar [*ut* K § 102] .... Ad. Erman, 41*m.* 91
Suaheli Schriftstücke [*ut* K § 161] ...... ed. C. G. Büttner 22*m.* 92

Bibliothèque de l'Ecole des Hautes Etudes : Sciences Philol. et Hist., fasc. i.–lxxxiv. *v.p.* 4° Bouillon, *Paris* 69–91 *in prg.*

Contains many valuable texts and treatises, many entered separately under their subjects. A *Section des Sciences Religieuses* (vols. i.–iv., to 1894) is also pub.

Columbia Univ. : Studies, vol. i. 8° Macmillan 94 *in prg.*

A series of papers on Classical and Oriental philology and archæology.

Ecole de Langues Orientales Vivantes : ser. I.–III., ea. 20 vols.; IV. (i.–iv.) 8° Leroux, *Paris* 76–93 *in prg.*

I. i.–ii. Mir abdul Kerim Boukhari, *Asie Centrale* [*ut* K § 136] .. Ch. Schefer, 30*fr.* 76 ; 79
iii.–iv. Risa Qouly Khan, *Ambassade au Kharezm* [*ut* K § 134] .. Ch. Schefer, 30*fr.* 76 ; 79
v. *Poèmes histor. en Grec. Vulgaire* [*ut* K § 186] .. E. Legrand, 15*fr.* 77
vi. de St.-Priest, Cte., *Mémoires sur l'Ambassade de Frce. près la Porte Ottomane* .. Ch. Schefer, 12*fr.* 77
vii. *Recueil d'Itinéraires et de Voyages dans l'Asie Centr. et l'Extrême Orient* .. Ch. Schefer *etc.*, 15*fr.* 78
viii. *Bagh-o-Bahar* [*ut* B.B. K § 128] .. Garcin de Tassy, 12*fr.* 78
ix. Urechi, G., *Chronique de Moldavie* [*ut* K § 259] .... Em. Picot, 25*fr.* 78
x.–xi. Cordier, H., *Bibliotheca Sinica* [*ut* K § 154 and B.B. K § 154] .. 137*fr.* 78–94
xii. Bretschneider, *Recherches sur Pekin* .... trad. V. Collin de Plancy, 10*fr.* 79
xiii. Devéria, G., *Relatns. d. Chine av. Annam* [*ut* K § 156] 7*fr.*50 80
xiv.–xv., xx. Daponte̊s, C., *Ephemerides Daces* [*ut* K § 186] .... E. Legrand, 27*fr.*50 80–88
xvi. *Recueil d. Documns. s. l'Asie Centr.* [*ut* K § 154] .. C. Imbault-Huart, 10*fr.* 81
xvii. *Tam-tu'-Kinh* [*ut* B.B. K § 156] .... A. Des Michels, 20*fr.* 82
xviii. de Daron, Et Açoghih, *Hist. Universelle*, pt. i. [*ut* K § 130] .. E. Dulaurier, 10*fr.* 83
xix. *Luc vân tiên ca diên* [*ut* B.B. K § 156] ...... A. Des Michels, 20*fr.* 83
II. i. Nassiri Khosrau, *Voy. en Perse etc.* [*ut* K § 134] .... Ch. Schefer, 25*fr.* 87
ii.–iii. Machéras, L., *Chronique de Chypre* [*ut* K § 186] .. E. Miller, 40*fr.* 81
iv.–v. Barbier de Meynard, *Dict. Turc-Frs.* [*ut* K § 144 and B.B. K § 144] .. 80*fr.* 85 ; 90
vi. *Miradj-Nameh* [*ut* B.B. K § 144] Pavet de Courteille, 15*fr.* 82
vii.–viii. *Chrestomathie Persane* [*ut* B.B. K § 133] .... Ch. Schefer, 30*fr.* 83 ; 85
ix. *Mélanges Orientaux* [*ut* K § 94] 25*fr.* 83
x.–xi. *MSS. Arabes d. l'Escurial* [*ut* B.B. K § 114] .... Hartw. Derenbourg, 15*fr.* 85 ; *i.p.*
xii. Ousama Ibn Mounkidh, 2 pts. [*ut* K § 115] .... Hartw. Derenbourg, 45*fr.* 85 ; 89
xiii. *Chronique dite de Nestor* .... [fr. Russ.] L. Leger, 15*fr.* 84
xiv.–xv. *Kim van Kieu tan truyen* [*ut* K § 156] .. A. Des Michels, 40*fr.* 84 ; 85
xvi.–xvii. *Hist. d. Dynast. Divines* [*ut* B.B. K § 151] .. L. de Rosny, 30*fr.* 85
xviii. Abulqâsem b. Ahmed Ezziâni, *Maroc* [*ut* K § 115] ...... O. Houdas, 15*fr.* 86
xix. *Nouveaux Mélanges Orientaux* [*ut* K § 94] 15*fr.* 86
xx. du Mans, Ralph., *L'Estat de la Perse en* 1660 .... Ch. Schefer 20*fr.* 90
III. i. Devéria, G., *Frontière Sino-Annamite* [*ut* K § 156] .. 20*fr.* 86
ii.–iii. Esseghir b. Elhadj [*ut* K § 115] ... O. Houdas, 30*fr.* 88 ; 89
iv. Nalivkine, *Hist. d. Khanat d. Khokand* ... [fr. Russ.] A. Dozon, 10*fr.* 89
v.–vi. *Recueil d. Textes et Traductions* [*ut* K § 94] 30*fr.* 89
vii.–viii. Nizam oul Moulk, *Siasset Nameh* [*ut* K § 134] ...... Ch. Schefer, 30*fr.* 91
ix.–x. El Nesawi, *Djelal-Eddin Man* [*ut* K § 115] .... O. Houdas, 15*fr.* 91 ; *i.p.*
xi. Chin Loun Kouoh Kiang Yuh Tchi, pts. i.–ii. [*ut* K § 154] .. A. Des Michels, 15*fr.* 91
xii. Filelfe, F. *Lettres Grecques* [*ut* K § 186] .. E. Legrand, 20*fr.* 92
xiii.–xiv. Moham. Nerchakhy, *Boukhara* [*ut* K § 134] .... Ch. Schefer, 15*fr.* 92 ; *i.p.*
xv. *Les Français dans l'Inde* [1736–61] .... J. Vinson, 15*fr.* 92
xvi.–xvii. Khalil Ed-Dahiry, *Egypte et Syrie* [*ut* K § 115] .... Ravaisse, 12*fr.* 93 ; *i.p.*
xviii. *Tableau Genealog. d. Princes d. Moldavie* .... Em. Picot, *i.p.*
xix.–xx. Courant, Maur., *Bibliogr. Coréenne* [*ut* K § 150] ...... *i.p.*
IV. i.–iv. Lambrecht, E., *Catal. d. l. Bibl. de l'Ecole* .... *i.p.*

By the Librarian of the School.

Harvard Univ. : Studies and Notes in Philology and Literature, vols. i.–ii. 8° ea. $1.50 Ginn, *Boston* / ea. 6/- *nt.* Arnold 93 ; 94 *in prg.*
Helsingfors : Mémoires de la Société Néo-philologique, vol. i. 6/- 8° *Helsingfors* 93 *in prg.*
Lehrbücher des Seminars für Orientalische Sprachen in Berlin Spemann, *Berl.*, *in prg.*

Ephe [=Ewe]-*Sprache : Lehrbuch* [*ut* K § 161] .. Ernst. Heinrich 91
Japan. Umgangssprache : Lehrbuch [*ut* K § 150] R. Lange, 24*m.* 90
Osmanische Spr. : Lehrbuch [*ut* K § 144] .... J. J. Manissadjian 93
Suaheli-Handbuch [*ut* K § 161] W. v. Saint Paul Illaire, 10*m.*50, 90
Suaheli Wörterbuch [*ut* K § 161] .... C. G. Büttner, 13*m.* 90

A very useful Series as a whole ; excellently, even sumptuously, produced.

Oriental Club, Phila. : Oriental Studies : a selection of papers read bef. the Club $2.50 8° *Boston* 94
Oriental Translation Fund : New Series ea. 10/- c 8° Orient. Tr. Fd. (Luzac) 91–94 *in prg.*

Bānabhatta *Srī Harsha Charita* [*ut* K § 124 xii.*] ...... tr. E. B. Cowell + Thomas, *in prep.*
Jawini *Nigaristan* [=" Picture Gallery "] .. tr. Edw. Rehatsek, *in prep.*
Mirkhond *Rauzat-us Safā*, vols. i.–ii. [*ut* K § 134] .... tr. Edw. Rehatsek 91 ; 92
Mirkhond *Life of Mohammed*, 2 vols. [*ut* K § 134] .... tr. Edw. Rehatsek 93
" *Lives of Abu Bakr, etc.* [*ut* K § 134] .... tr. Edw. Rehatsek 94

Porta Linguarum Orientalium, sive Elementa Linguarum Orient. 8° Reuther, *Berlin* 37–94 *in prg.*

Ægypt. Gramm. [*ut* K § 101] .... Prf. Ad. Erman, 16*m.* 94
" " [*ut* K § 101] .. Prf. Ad. Erman, tr. Breasted, 18/- 94
Æthiop. Gramm. [*ut* B.B. K § 116] .... F. Praetorius, 6*m.* 86
Arab. Bibel-Chrestom .... G. Jacob, 2*m.*25, 88
" " [*ut* B.B. K § 114] .... G. Jacob, tr. 2*m.*40, 88
Arab. Gramm. .... A. Socin, 6*m.* [40] 89
Arab : Veterum Carmin. Delectus [*ut* B.B. K § 114] Th. Nöldeke, 7*m.* 90
Armen. Gramm. [*ut* B.B. K § 139] .. J. H. Petermann, 4*m.* [37] 73
Assyr. Gramm. .... F. Delitzsch, 12*m.* 89
" " [*ut* B.B. K § 106] F. Delitzsch, tr. Kennedy, 14/- 89
Chald. Gramm. [*ut* B.B. K § 108] .. J. H. Petermann, 4*m.* [41] 72
Hebräische Gramm. .... Herm. L. Strack, 3*m.*60 [64] 90
" " [*ut* B.B. K § 117] .... Herm. L. Strack, tr. Kennedy 4/6 [ ] 89
Koptische Gram. [*ut* K § 101] .... G. Steindorff, 13*m.*20, 94
Persische Gramm. [*ut* B.B. K § 133] C. Salemann + V. Shukovski, 7*m.* 89
Samarit. Gramm. [*ut* B.B. K § 117] .... J. H. Petermann, 4*m.* 72
Syrische Gramm. .... E. Nestle, 7*m.* [81] 88
" " [*ut* B.B. K § 109] .. E. Nestle, tr. Kennedy, 8/- [ ] 89
Targum. Chrestom. [*ut* B.B. K § 109] .... A. Merx, 7*m.*50 88
Türk. Gramm. [*ut* B.B. K § 144] .... A. Müller + H. Gies, 8*m.* 89

Sacred Books of the East, tr. by various scholars and ed. Prf. F. Max Müller 8° Clar. Press / Macmillan, N.Y. 79–94 *in prg.*

SERIES I.
i., xv. *Upanishads* [ut B.B. K § 124] .... F. MAX MÜLLER, ea. 10/6 79 ; 84
ii., xiv. *Sacr. Laws of Aryas* [ut B.B. K § 124] ..Geo. BÜHLER, ea. 10/6, 79 ; 82
iii., xvi., xxvii., xxviii. *Sacr. Bks. of China* [ut B.B. K § 154] ..Jas. LEGGE, 12/6, 10/6, 25/-, 79 ; 82 ; 85
iv., xxiii., xxxi. *Zend-Avesta* [ut B.B. K § 131] ..J. DARMESTETER, 10/6, 10/6, 12/6, 80 ; 85 ; 87
v., xviii., xxiv., xxxvii. *Pahlavi Texts* [ut A § 14 and B.B. K § 132] E. W. WEST, 12/6, 12/6, 10/6 ; 80 ; 82 ; 83 ; 92 *i.p.*
vi., ix. *Qur'ân* [ut B.B. K § 115] ...... E. H. PALMER, 21/-, 80 ; 82
vii. *Instits. of Vishnu* [ut B.B. K § 124]......Julius JOLLY, 10/6, 80
viii. *Bhagavadgîtâ, etc.* [ut B.B. K § 124] ..K. T. TELANG, 10/6, 82
x. *Dhammapada* and *Sutta Nipâta* [ut B.B. K § 127] ....Max MÜLLER + V. FAUSBÖLL, 10/6, 81
xi. *Buddhist Suttas* [ut B.B. K § 127] T. W. Rhys DAVIDS, 10/6, 81
xii., xxvi., xli. *Satapatha Brâhm.* [ut K § 124 and B.B. K § 124] Jul. EGGELING, ea. 12/6, 82 ; 85 ; 93
xiii., xvii., xx. *Vinaya Texts* [ut B.B. K § 127] .... Rhys DAVIDS + OLDENBERG, ea. 10/6, 81 ; 82 ; 83
xix. *Fo-sho-hing-tsan-king* [ut B.B. K § 154] ....Sam BEAL, 10/6, 83
xxi. *Saddharma-pundarîk* [ut B.B. K § 124] ....H. KERN, 12/6, 84
xxii. *Gaina-sûtras*, pt. i. [ut B.B. K § 125] .... Herm. JACOBI, 10/6

SERIES II.
xxv. *Manu* [ut B.B. K § 124] .... Geo. BÜHLER, 21/-, 86
xxix., xxx. *Grihya-sûtras* [ut B.B. K § 124]......HOLDENBERG, ea. 12/6, 87 ; 89
xxxii. *Vedic Hymns*, pt. i. [ut A § 14] ....F. MAX MÜLLER, 18/6, 92
xxxiii. *Narada* [ut B.B. K § 124] ....Jul. JOLLY, 10/6, 90
xxxiv., xxxviii. *Vedânta sûtras* [ut K § 124 and B.B. K § 124] .. G. THIBAUT, 12/6, 90 ; 12/6 92
xxxv., xxxvi. *King Milinda* [ut K § 127 and B.B. K § 127] ..T. W. Rhys DAVIDS, 10/6, 90 ; 12/6 91
xxxix., xl. *Texts of Tâoism* [ut K § 154] ...... Jas. LEGGE, 21/-, 92
xlii. *Hymns of Arthav.Veda* [ut K § 124] ....Prf. M. BLOOMFIELD, *in prep.*
xliii., xliv. *Sathapatha Brâhm.*, pts. iv., v. ..J. EGGELING, *in prep.*
xlv. *Gaina-sûtras*, pt. ii. .... Herm. JACOBI, *in prep.*
xlvi. *Vedanta-sûtras*, pt. iii. ....G. THIBAUT, *in prep.*
xlviii. *Vedic Hymns*, pt. ii. .... Prf. Max MÜLLER, *in prep.*
xlix. *Buddh. Mahayana Texts* [ut K § 127] .... E. B. COWELL, *etc.* 12/6, 94

Amer. prices 10/6=$2.75; 12/6=$3.25; 21/-=$5.25.

A Third Series will be undertaken, if sufficient support is offered, in response to an appeal issued.

96. COMPARATIVE PHILOLOGY (*a*): GENERAL TREATISES.

*v. d. GABELENTZ, Geo. Die Sprachwissenschaft 14*m.* 8° Weigel, *Leipzig* 91
On the problems, the methods and the results so far achieved in the science of language.

GILES, P. A Short Manual of Philology for Classical Students c 8° Macmillan *in prep.*
An intro. to the methods and conclusions of recent philology. Sound and inflexion, w. consid. attention given to general principles and a short acc. of the compar. syntax of the noun and verb.

MÜLLER, Prf. F. Max The Science of Language, 2 vols. 21/- ($7) c 8° Longman [61–64] 91
A new edn. (the 15th) of his *Lects. on the Science of Lang.* [ut B.B. K § 96], orig. deliv. at the Royal Institn. in 1861 and 1863. The lecture-form has been eliminated, and many addns. have been made. A new Germ. tr. of this edn. has been made by Drs. R. FICK + WISCHMANN [8° Engelmann, *Lpz.*], the former tr. by Prf. BÖTTINGER [*id. ib.*] being suppressed.

" " Three Lectures on the Science of Language 50*c.* 8° Open Ct. Pb. Co., *Chicago* 93
Achelis, Th. Max Müller und die vergleichende Sprachwissenschaft 80*pf.* 8° Verlagsanstalt, *Hambg.* 93
Böhtlingk, Prf. F. Max Müller als Mythendichter *St. Petersburg* 91
An exposure of some astounding statements made in the author's *Natural Religion*, ut A § 4.

Whitney, Prf. W. D. [Am.] Max Müller and the Science of Language 50*c.* 12° Appleton, *N.Y.* 92
A lively criticism of the new edn.

STEINTHAL, H. Abriss der Sprachwissenschaft, hrsg. F. Mistelli, pt. ii. 11*m.* 8° Dümmler, *Berlin* [61] 93
Charakteristik der hauptsächlichsten Typen des Sprachbaues. Conts. good, if somewhat abstruse and rather "philosophical" summaries of the distinguishing features of many languages.

STRONG + LOGEMAN + WHEELER, Prf. H. A. / W. S. / B. I. [Am.] Intro. to Study of History of Language 10/6 ($3.50) 8° Longman 91
In 1888 Prf. STRONG issued a tr., more or less well done, of PAUL'S *Principien d. Sprachgeschichte* [ut B.B. K § 96]: here he has reproduced a large part of that bk.

Aryan : comparatively—*v.* K §§ 119, 120.

Classification.

DE LA GRASSERIE, Raoul De la Classification des Langues 2*fr.* 8° Maisonneuve, *Paris* 90

Polyglott.

Lord's Prayer in Three Hundred Languages ; w. pref. Dr. Reinold Rost [pp. 86] 10/6 r 8° Gilbert & Rivington 91

Hamitic, Semitic and Aryan : Comparatively.

ABEL, Dr. Carl Ægypt. indoeur. Sprachverwandtschaft [Einzelbeitr. z. allg. u. vergl. Spr.] 2*m.* 8° Friederich, *Lpz.* 90
" " Offener Brief an Prf. G. Meyer 1*m.* 30 ; Nachtrag 1*m.* 30 8° " ,,91 ; 91
" " Ægyptisch und Indogermanisch [a popular lecture] 1*m.* 8° Krauer, *Frkft.* 93
WINKLER, H. —*in his* Zur Sprachgeschichte, 6*m.*; *and* Weiteres zur Sprachgeschichte 4*m.* 8° Dümmler, *Berl.* 87 ; 89
Seeks to establish a relationship betw. the Uralaltaic and Egypto-Semitic-Indogerm. langs.

Slang —*v.* K § 277, *s.v.* Slang (MICHEL).

97. COMPARATIVE PHILOLOGY (*b*): BIOGRAPHY OF THE STUDY.

BERGAIGNE, Abel
Henry, Prf. Victor L'Oeuvre d'Abel Bergaigne [pp. 24] 8° Thorin, *Paris* 89

BOPP, Franz. [1791–1867].
Lefmann, Prf. S. Franz Bopp : sein Leben und seine Wissenschaft, pt. i. 8*m.* 8° G. Reimer, *Berlin* 91
An interesting memoir of the founder of Indo-german. compar. philology, w. refs. to his contemps. (Wilh. v. HUMBOLDT, A. W. SCHLEGEL, *etc.*). This vol. ends at 1833, the date of pubn. of vol. i. of *Vergl. Gramm.* [ut B.B. K § 120]. Selected correspondence is added.

BURNOUF, Eug. [1801–52] Choix de Lettres : 1825–52, ed. Mons. + Mme. Delisle [dau.] ; port. & facs. 12*fr.* r 8° *Paris* 91
Supplies a good deal of material towards the hist. of oriental studies in France during the present century. Bibliography added.

98. COMPARATIVE PHILOLOGY (c): GRAMMAR. ETYMOLOGY. PHONOLOGY. METRICS.

Etymology.

BLOOMFIELD, Prf. Maur. [Am.] Adaptation of Suffixes in Congeneric Classes of Substantives 8° 91

A valuable contrib. tow. an explan. of origin of terminatns. of certain nouns by help of analogy. Repr. fr. *Amer. Jl. of Philol.*

Onomatopoieia —*v.* K § 93.

Syntax.

BERSANETTI + ALLAN, P. E. Affinità Sintattiche tra el Greco et l'Italiano [comparative] 2*l.* 16° Zanichelli, *Bologna* 92

DE LA GRASSERIE, Raoul Etudes de Grammaire Comparée: Du verbe *être* 3*fr.* 8° Maisonneuve, *Paris* 87

" " Etudes de Grammaire Comparée: De la Catégorie du Nombre 2*fr.* 8° " " 88

" " Etudes de Grammaire Comparée: De la Categorie du temps 5*fr.* 8° " " 88

" " Etudes de Gram. Comp.: De la Conjugaison Objective [pp. 39] 2*fr.* 8° Impr. Nat., *Paris* 88

" " Etudes de Gram. Comp.: Des Divisions de la Linguistique [pp. 164] 5*fr.* 8° Maisonneuve, *Paris* 88

" " Etudes de Gram. Comp.: De la veritable Nature du Pronom [pp. 50] 2*fr.* 50 8° Lefever, *Louvain* 88

" " Etudes de Gram. Comp.: De la Psychologie du Langage [pp. 108] 4*fr.* 8° Maisonneuve, *Paris* 89

" " Etudes de Gram. Comp.: De la Categorie des Cas [pp. 351] 15*fr.* 8° " " 90

" " Etud. de Gram. Comp.: Relatns. Gramm. dans leur concept et expressn. [pp. 357] 15*fr.* 8° " " 90

" " Etudes de Grammaire Comparée: De la catégorie des modes [pp. 111] 4*fr.* 8° Bouillon, *Paris* 91

" " Et. de Gr. Comp.: Recherches récentes d. l. Linguist. rel. a. langs. d. l'Extrème Orient 8° Impr. Nat., *Paris* 91

Deals principally w. the researches of Prf. TERRIEN DE LACOUPERIE [v. B.B. K § 152].

MIDDLETON, G. An Essay on Analogy in Syntax 3/- ($1) c 8° Longman 92

Attempt to classify the differ. branches of the infln. of analogy in syntax, following the *Junggrammatiker* in distinguishing betw. phonetic change, wh. is purely physiolog., and syntactical change, wh. is psycholog. Mainly Gk. and Lat., w. illns. fr. mod. langs., incl. English.

RECHA, Carl Zur Frage üb. d. Ursprung d. perfectivierenden Functn. d. Verbalpräfixe 2*m.* 80 8° *Dorpat* 93

RIES, Jno. Was ist Syntax?: ein kritischer Versuch 3*m.* 8° Elwert, *Marburg* 94

Phonology.

BORINSKI, K. Grundzüge d. Systems d. artikulierten Phonetik 1*m.* 50 8° Göschen, *Stuttgt.* 91

CLARK, Jno. Manual of Linguistics 7/6 c 8° Thin, *Edin.* 93

A concise, useful and up-to-date sketch of Indo-European and espec. English phonology, serving as an Introduction to the wks. of BRUGMANN, PAUL, SWEET, etc., but unfortunately not very systematically arranged. Good index.

DE LA GRASSERIE, Raoul Etudes de Grammaire Comparée: Essai de Phonétique Générale 12*fr.* 8° Maisonneuve, *Paris* 90

" " The same: Essai de Phonétique Dynamique ou Historique Comparée 8*fr.* 8° " " 91

MASCKE, H. Ueb. d. Bedeutungen d. Sprachlaute u. d. Bildg. d. Wortbegriffe 3*m.* 8° Calvör, *Göttingen* 93

Diseases of Language: Aphasia.

JAMES, Prf. Wm. [Am.] *treats fully and v. well of Aphasia in his* Principles of Psychol., *ut* O § 71.

Other psychologists and mental pathologists deal w. the subject, but JAMES' treatment is the best and likely to be the most fruitful.

Magazine.

Neueren Sprachen, Die: Ztschr. f. d. neusprachl. Unterricht, hrsg. Prf. W. Vietor, 10 pts. *ann.* 12*m.* Elwert, *Marbg.* 93 *in prg.*

With a Beiblatt entitled *Phonetische Studien*, superseding the journal under that title [*ut* B.B. K § 98].

Metrics. Prosody.

DE LA GRASSERIE, Raoul Etudes de Grammaire Comparée: Analyses Métriques et Rhythmiques 10*fr.* 8° Maisonneuve, *Paris* 93

KAWCZYNSKI, Max Essai Comparatif sur l'Origine et l'Histoire des Rhythmes 6*fr.* 8° Bouillon, *Paris* 89

PIERSON, P. La Métrique Naturelle du Langage [Bibl. Ecole Htes. Etud.] 10*fr.* 8° " " 83

*WESTPHAL, Dr. Rud. Allgemeine Metrik d. Indogerm. u. semit. Völker [Calvary's Bibl.] 10*m.* 8° Calvary, *Berlin* 92

An important wk., on the basis of comparative philology; w. an excursus *Der griech. Hexameter in d. deut. Nachbildung* by Dr. H. KRUSE.

99. RELATION OF LANGUAGE TO WRITING (a): PALÆOGRAPHY.

Origin and History of Writing.

BERGER, Ph. Histoire de l'Ecriture dans l'Antiquité; 9 pl. and 7 ill. *o.p.* [*w.* 10/-] 8° *Paris* 92

KETTLE, D. W. Pens, Ink and Paper: discourse on caligraphy, anc. and mod. [*w.* 21/-] 16° Sette of Odde Vols. 85

DE LACOUPERIE, Terrien Beginnings of Writing in Central and Eastern Asia—*ut* K § 152.

Generally.

GIRY, Prf. A. Manuel de Diplomatique 20*fr.* 8° Hachette, *Paris* 94

Diplômes et Chartres: Chronologie Technique; Eléments Critiques et Parties Constitutives de la Teneur des Chartres; Les Chancelleries; Les Actes Privés.

MADAN, Falconer [Bodl. Lib.] Books in Manuscript—*ut* I § 111.

MIDDLETON, Prf. J. H. Illuminated MSS. in Classical and Mediæval times—*ut* I § 111.

REUSENS, Eléments de Paléographie et Diplomatique d. Moy. Age; 118 pl. 8*fr.* 1 4° Author, *Louvain* 91

SCOTT + DAVEY, Rev. Dr. Sam. Guide to the Collector of Historical Documents—*ut* G § 26.

*THOMPSON, E. Maunde [Brit. Mus.]—*in his* Manual of Greek and Latin Palæography—*ut* K § 179.

THOYTS, E. E. How to Decipher and Study Old Documents; facss. 4/6 c 8° Stock 93

A useful guide for the beginner; quite elementary and popular. With Introd. by C. Trice MARTIN, of H.M. Public Record Office, and short bibliogr. of Engl. and foreign bks. Conts. an irrelevant and worthless chap. on *Character by Handwriting.*

WRIGHT, Andr. Court Hand Restored: assistant in reading deeds, charters, etc. 21/- 4° Chatto [1776] 79

Illuminated [and other] *MSS.*—*v.* I § 111.

Water-marks.

BRIQUET, C. M. Valeur d. Filigranes du Papier d. déterm. l'age d. docums. [pp. 13] 8° Romet, *Geneva* 92

100. RELATION OF LANGUAGE TO WRITING (*b*): STENOGRAPHY (SHORTHAND).

Bibliography.

MANCS. Public Free Libs.: The Shorthand Coll. in Free Reference Lib. [44 pp.; Occasional Lists, no. 3] r 8° Blacklock, *Manc.* 91

History.

FAULMANN, Prf. K. Geschichte und Litteratur der Stenographie 6*m.* 8° Bermann, *Vienna* 94

INNES + MÄRES, Hugh W. / Geo. C. [Ams.]—*are publishing in* The Natl. Stenographer, 1892 *sqq.* [Chicago, U.S.A.] *a voluminous hist. of shorthd.*

MOSER, Hans Allgemeine Geschichte d. Stenographie, vol. i.; 21 pl. 4*m.* 8° Klinkhardt, *Lpz.* 89

Commences w. classical times, and is to bring the history down to present day.

PENDLETON, Jno. Newspaper Reporting in Olden Time and To-day—*sut* K § 26.

Illustrates the growth of newspaper enterprise in Engl., and gives an acc. of birth and devel. of shorthand—dealing chiefly, however, with the life and work of the reporter.

PITMAN, [Sir] Is. A History of Shorthand [*repr. fr. Phonetic Journal*, 1884] 2/- c 8° Pitman [84] 91

A very one-sided performance, ignoring the mere existence of many other excellent recent (and rival) systems wh. are doing good work in Parliament, the Law Courts and among pressmen. Much space is given to demolishing defunct and worthless systems. Pitman's is still no doubt the best, however; but not the only good one.

Biography.

BORDLEY, Sim. Geo. [*author of* Cadmus Britannicus, 1787, *the 1st script syst. of shorthd.*]

Gibson, John W. Memoir of Samuel Bordley

PITMAN, Sir Is. [1813; *living*].

Baker, Alf. The Life and Work of Sir Isaac Pitman; ill. 1/- f 8° Simpkin 94

Reed, Thos. Allen Life of Sir Isaac Pitman; ill. and facss. 3/6 c 8° „ 94

Sir Isaac PITMAN still (Aug., 1894) presides over the Phonetic Institute at Bath, wh. he has superintended for over half a century.

Systems.

BROWNE, Walt. T. The "Simplex" Shorthand 1/- f 8° Heywood, *Manc.* 91

CALLENDAR, H. L. Manual of Orthographic Cursive Shorthand [the Cambridge System] c 8° 1/- Camb. Press / 90c. *net*, Macmillan, *N.Y.* 91

The best of the "one-slope" systems.

GABELSBERGER, Fr. Xav. Anleitung zur deutschen Rede-Zeichen-Kunst, 2 vols. 4° *Munich* 34

Conts. a very interesting account of English shorthand, w. an Engl. bibliogr. to 1834, briefly recorded.

Celestial Writing: or the Norman Script. Phonetic Writing 3/- 8° Eyre & Spottiswoode 94

An abbreviated script phonetic system, based on a modified form of the Consonant Alphabet of GABELSBERGER.

HAY, W. Shorthand Simplified and Improved 1/6 c 8° Sonnenschein 92

A new and simple syst. somewhat on the lines of the 18th cent. methods of BYROM and LEWIS, but w. a much more exact represn. of vowels.

JANES, Alf. Phonetic Shorthand: a new and complete system 1/- 12° Author [85] 87

MARES, G. Carl Rational Shorthand f 8° „ 87

PITMAN, [Sir] Isaac Shorthand Instructor 3/6 c 8° Pitman 93

RUNDELL, Jos. Benj. —*has pub. several sheets and magazine articles on his system.*

SPENCER, Wm. Geo. System of Lucid Shorthand; w. pref. Herb. Spencer [son] 1/- c 8° Williams 94

An ingenious syst. of abbreviated longhand, orig. written in 1843. A pamphlet of 10 pp. entitled *Scientific Shorthand, the Briefest, Simplest, and most Natural System in the world*, by "Herbert SPENCER," 2/6, stated to be ent. at Stats.' Hall, but bearing no printer's or publr's. name, is to be avoided—except as a curiosity. It has no relation to SPENCER'S system, and does not emanate fr. the only Herb. SPENCER known to fame.

SWEET, H. Manual of Current Shorthand, Orthographic and Phonetic 4/6 c 8° Clar. Press 92

Abbreviated longhand, on the "script" basis, and the words all written at one level: two systems (1) orthographic, (2) phonetic.

TAYLOR, Sam. System of Stenography [of consid. historical importance] 3/- f 8° Simpkin [1786] 65

XV. Hamitic Philology, Inscriptions, etc.

101. ANCIENT EGYPTIAN AND COPTIC (*a*): PHILOLOGY.

Ancient Egyptian: Hieroglyphic, Demotic, Hieratic.

History of the Language.

HOMMEL, Fritz Der babylon. Ursprung d. ägypt. Kultur = Aufsätze u. Abhgn., pt. i.—*sut* K § 105.

Claims to shew that Egyptn. was orig. merely a dialect of the North-Babylon. Semitic. The argumt. is contin. in his paper *Die Identität d. ältesten babyl. u. ägypt. Göttergenealogie*—in *Transns. of 9th Congress of Orientalists.*

Grammar, etc.

BRUGSCH, H. Die Ægyptologie, pt. ii. 14*m.*, both pts. in 1 v. 24*m.* 8° Friedrich, *Lpz.* 90; 89-90

A good outline of the entire science of Egyptology, by one of the leading Egyptologists of the age.

ERMAN, Prf. Adolf Ægyptische Grammatik [Porta Ling. Orient.] 16*m.* 8° Reuther, *Berlin* 94

„ „ Egyptian Grammar, tr. Prf. Jas. Hy. Breasted [Am.] 18/- 8° Williams 94

LORET, Victor Manuel de la Langue Egyptienne [*ut* B.B. K § 101]: new edn 20*fr.* 8° Leroux, *Paris* [88] 92

MASPERO, G. Formes d. l. Conjugaison en Egypt. anc. Démot. et Copte [Bibl. Ec. Ht. Etud.] 10*fr.* 8° Bouillon, *Paris* 71

Etymology.

Dictionary.

CHARDON + DENISSE, D. / L. Dictionnaire Démotique, pt. i. [to occupy *c.* 8 pts.] 5*fr.* 8° Leroux, *Paris* 93

Names.

LIEBLEIN, J. Hieroglyphisches Namenwörterbuch, pts. i.; ii.; iii. 30*m.*; iv. 18*m.* Hinrichs, *Lpz.* 91; 91; 91; 92

From the monuments. Genealogically and alphabetically arranged.

Plural Formation.

ERMAN, Prf. Adolf — Die Pluralbildung des Ægyptischen : ein grammatischer Versuch 6*m.* 4° Engelmann, *Lpz.* 78

Magazine and Permanent Serials.

Recueil de Travaux rel. à la Philol. et à l'Archéol. Egypt. et Assyr., ed. G. Maspero—*ut* K § 107
Revue Egyptologique [*now*] ed. E. Revillout, vols. i.–vii. [ea. 4 pts.] ea. vol. 30*fr.* 4° Leroux, *Paris* 80–94 *in prg.*

Coptic : *Grammar.*

STEINDORFF, G. — Koptische Grammatik [Porta Ling. Orient.; w. chrestom. & vocab.] 13*m.*20 8° Reuther, *Berlin* 94

102. ANCIENT EGYPTIAN AND COPTIC (*b*): INSCRIPTIONS, TEXTS, ETC.

Bibliography.

AMÉLINEAU, Prf. E. — Rapports s. l. Travaux faits en Egyptologie : 1889–91 [19 pp.] 3/6 r 8° Orient. Inst., *Woking* 93

History of Research—*v.* G § 9.

Inscriptions and Papyri—*v. also* G § 9.

AMÉLINEAU, E. [ed. & tr.] Monums. p. serv. à l'hist. de l'Egypte Chrét. au 4 siècle, vol. i. 30*fr.* 4° Leroux, *Paris* 89
Inéd. Copt. and Arab. docum. on hist. of St. Pakhôme and his communities; w. Fch. trs. *Annals du Musée Guimet, vol. xvii.* (Also Mission Arch., *ut inf.*)
" " Hist. du Patriarche Copte Isaac : étude critique [w. Coptic text & Fch. tr.] 6*fr.* 4° Leroux, *Paris* 90
" " Des Actes des Martyrs de l'Eglise Copte [a critical study] 10*fr.* 8° " " 90
" " La Morale Egypt. quinze siècles avant notre ère 10*fr.* 4° " " 92
A study of the Boulaq papyrus, no. 4.
" " Géographie de l'Egypte à l'Epoque Copte 35*fr.* 8° Welter, *Paris* 93
" " [ed.] Hist. d. Monastères de la Basse-Egypte [Ann. d. Mus. Guimet] 40*fr.* 4° Leroux, *Paris* 94
Coptic texts of lives of SS. Paul, Antoine, Macaire, *etc.*; w. Fch. trs.
" " Hist. d. l. Sépulture et d. Funérailles en Egypte, 2 v.; ill. [Ann. Mus. Guimet] 4° " " *in prep.*
BÉNÉDITE, G. [ed.] Temple de Philæ, pt. i. : Textes Hieroglyphiques [Mission Arch. Frç.] 40*fr.* 4° Leroux, *Paris* 93
Berlin Royal Museums. Ægyptische Urkunden aus den königl. Museen, pts. i.–xi. ea. 2*m.*40 8° Weidmann, *Berlin* 92–94 *in prg.*
Bibliothèque Egyptologique : ed. Prf. G. Maspéro, vols. i.–viii. 8° Leroux, *Paris* 93–94 *in prg.*
i.–ii. MASPÉRO, G. *Etudes de Mythol. et d'Archéol. Egypt.* [*ut* A § 11]....ea. 12*fr.*
iii. de ROCHEMONTEIX, Marq., *Œuvres Diverses*; pl. ....15*fr.*
iv. DEVÉRIA, Th., *Mémoires Divers* ....*in prep.*
v.–viii. de ROUGÉ, E., *Mémoires Divers* ....*in prep.*
Book of the Dead : [*v. also* GUIEYSSE *inf.*] ed. Dr. Chas. H. S. Davis ; w. Introd., tr., and comm. $5 (25/- *nt.*) r 4° Putnam 94
BOURIANT, U. —*v.* Mission Archéol. Frçse. au Caire, *infra.*
BRUGSCH, Dr. H. [ed.] Thesaurus Inscriptionum Ægypticarum, pt. v. 100*m.*, vi. [last] 90*m.* r 8° Hinrichs, *Lpz.* 90; 91
v.: Historic–biographical inscriptions; vi.: Miscellaneous inscr. in hierog., hierat. and demot. characters. Complete wk. costs £20 *s.*
" " [ed.] Drei Festkalender d. Tempels v. Apollinopolis Magna; 10 pl. [w. Germ. trs.] 20*m.* 4° Hinrichs, *Lpz.* 77
" " [ed.] La Tente Funéraire de la Princesse Tsimkheb; map and pl. [Deir el-Bahari] 15/- r 4° *Cairo* 89
Brucianus, Codex : Gnostische Schriften in kopt. Sprache, hrsg. C. Schmidt 22*m.* 8° Hinrichs, *Lpz.* 92
Forms pts. 1 and 2 of vol. viii. of the *Texte u. Untersuchungen zur Geschichte d. altchristl. Litteratur.*
Catalogue des Monuments et Inscripp. de l'Egypte Antique, vol. i. [Nubia to Kom Ombos]; ill. 42*m.* i 4° *Vienna* 94
Corpus Papyrorum Ægypti : ed. R. Revillout + A. Eisenlohr, pt. iii. 18*fr.* 4° Leroux, *Paris* 94 *in prg.*
Vol. III. *Le Plaidoyer d'Hypéride contre Athénogène*, ed. Eug. Revillout, 25*fr.* '92.
DÜMICHEN, Dr. Joh. [ed.] Die monatl. Opferfestlisten d. grossen Theban. Festkalenders v. Medinet-Habu 30*m.* 4° Hinrichs, *Lpz.* 81
EBERS, G. [ed.] Papyrus Ebers—*ut* B.B, K § 102.
Joachim, H. [tr.] Papyros Ebers : zum erstenmal vollständig übersetzt 4*m.* 8° G. Reimer, *Berlin* 90
Egyptian Exploration Fund : Publications—*ut* G § 9.
Etudes Egyptologiques : vols. i.–xvi.; pl. 420*fr.*; *red. to* 300*fr.* 4° Bouillon, *Paris* 73–80
GAYET, Alb. J. [ed.] Stèles de la xiie. Dynastie au Musée Egyp. d. Louvre; 60 pl. [Bibl. Ec. Ht. Et.] 17*fr.* 4° " " 86
" " [ed.] Monumts. Coptes d. Boulaq; *and* Temple d. Louxor—*v.* Mission Archéol. Frçe., *infra.*
GRÉBAUT, Eug. [tr.] Hymme à Ammon-Ra du Mus. d. Boulaq [Bibl. Ec. Ht. Etud.] 22*fr.* 8° " " 75
" " + BRUGSH-BEY + DARESSY, $\frac{E.}{G. (eds.)}$ Le Musée Egyptien : recueil de monuments *Cairo* 91
GUIEYSSE + LEFÉBURE, $\frac{P.}{E.}$ [eds.] Le Papyrus Funéraire de Soutimes; w. Fch. tr. and notes 50*fr.* f° Leroux, *Paris*
Facs. reprodn. fr. a hierogl. copy of *The Bk. of the Dead* in the Bibl. Nat., Paris.
HAMDY BEY + REINACH, T. [eds.] Une Nécropole Royale à Sidon 200*fr.* 92
HESS, J. J. [ed.] Der gnostische Papyrus v. London; 11 pl. [Introd., text., and Demotic-Germ. gloss.] 30*m.* 8° Friesenhahn, *Freibg.* 92
HYVERNAT, Prf. Henri [ed.] Les Actes des Martyres d'Egypte *Paris* 85
The Coptic texts, ed. chiefly fr. MSS. in the Vatican and Borgian Libraries, w. French trs.
" " [ed.] Album de Paléographie Copte pour servir à l'Introd. Paléographiques des "Actes des Martyres;" pts. 1–4 25*fr.* r f° Leroux, *Paris* 88
Conts. 57 large f° photo. pl., on wh. are reprod. about 100 examples of Coptic writing, fr. 6 cent. A.D. to end 18th cent.
LEDRAIN, Eug. [ed.] Les Monumts. Egyp. d. l. Bibl. Nat., pt. i. 12*fr.*; ii.–iii. 25*fr.*; pl. [Bibl. École Ht. Etud.] 8° Bouillon, *Paris* 80; 81
LEFÉBURE, E. [ed.] Les Hypogées Royaux de Thèbes, pl.; 3 pts. [Ann. Musée Guimet] 75*fr.* 4° Leroux, *Paris* 86; 89; 89
Vide also Mission Archéol. Frçse., *infra.*
" " [ed.] Rites Egyptiens : constrn. et protectn. d. édifices [Ec. d. Lettres d'Alger] 3*fr.* 8° Leroux, *Paris* 89

LEGRAIN [ed.] Livre des Transformations [fr. MS. in Louvre] *Paris* 9-
LEPSIUS, Dr. R. [ed.] Denkmäler—*ut* 𝔅.𝔅. K § 102.
Wiedemann, A. [ed.] Index d. Götter- u. Dæmonennamen zu Lepsius Denkmäler 6*m*. 8° 92
Leyden: Ægypt. Monumenten van het Nederl. Mus. v. Oudheden, ed. C. Leemans, pts. i.–xxx. *o.p.* [*w.* £50] r f° Brill, *Leyden* 39–89
Also pub. w. French text *sub tit. Monumens égyptiens du Musée d'Antiq. des Pays-Bas à Leyde.*
LORET, Victor La Flore Pharaonique d'après les Documts. hiéroglyphiques 3*fr*. 8° Baillière, *Paris* 87
" " L'Egypte au Temps d. Pharaons: vie, science, art; 18 ill. 3*fr*.50 12° " " 89
MALLET, D. La Culte de Neit à Sais: étude d. mythol. égyptienne [Ec. d. Louvre] 15*fr*. 8° Leroux, *Paris* 88
MARIETTE, Aug. [ed.] L'Album du Musée de Bulâq; 40 photogr. pl. [*w.* £15] f° *Cairo* 72
A fine work; very scarce, nearly the whole stock having perished in the fire which destroyed the premises of M. Mourès at Cairo.
" " [ed.] Deir-el-Bahari: documa., topog., hist. et ethnog. dans ce temple; 16 pl. 80*m*. r 4° Hinrichs, *Lpz*. 77
" " Voyage dans l'Haute-Egypte, entre le Cairo, *etc.*, 2 vols.; 83 heliogr. pl. 300*fr*. f° Welter, *Paris* [ ]93
Second edn. of this important archæological journey. First edn. used to fetch ab. £40 by auction.
MARUCCHI, Hor. [ed.] Monumenta Papyracea Ægyptiaca 12*l*. 8° Loescher, *Rome* 92
MASPÉRO, G. [ed.] Etudes Egyptiennes, vol. ii., pt. 2 15*fr*. 8° Maisonneuve, *Paris* 91
" " [ed.] Monums. divers d'Egyp. et de Nubie p. Mariette [*ut* 𝔅.𝔅. K § 102]: Texte, pts. i.-ii. [*v. also* Mission Arch., *inf.*] f° *Chalons-sur-Saône* 89 *in prg.*
Mélanges d'Archéologie Egyptienne et Assyrienne, vols. i.–iii.—*ut* K § 107.
Mission Archéologique Française au Caire, vols. i.-xv.; col. pl. and fine ill. 4° Leroux, *Paris* 85–94 *in prg.*

I. (i.–iii.) Miscellanies .... 25*fr*., 40*fr*., 30*fr*.
(iv.) MASPÉRO, G. *Momies Roy. d. Déir-el-Bahari* .... 50*fr*.
II.–III. (ii.) LEFEBURE, E. *Hypogées de Thèbes*, 3 pts. [*v. sup.*] 135*fr*.
(iii.) GAYET, Alb. J. *Monums. Coptes d. Boulaq* .... 40*fr*.
(iv.) RAVAISSE, P. *Hist. et Topog. d. Caire d'après Makrizi*.. 20*fr*.
Pt. ii. Pt. i. is contained in i. (iii.).
IV. (i.) AMÉLINEAU, E. *Monuments, etc.*, pt. i. [*ut supra*] .... 60*fr*.
V. (i.) VIREY, Ph. *Tombeau d. Rekhmara* .... 40*fr*.
(ii.) " " *Tombeaux Thébains* .... 40*fr*.
(iii.) BÉNÉDITE, BOURIANT, *etc.* *Tombeaux Thébains* .... 50*fr*.
(iv.) SCHEIL, Père, *Tombeaux Thébains* .... *in prep.*
VI. (i.) MASPÉRO, G. *Fragms. d. l. Vers. théb. d. l'Anc. Test.*... 20*fr*.
(ii.) Do., Continuation; and Miscellanies .... 25*fr*.
(iii.) CASANOVA, *Catal. d. Verres d. l. Coll. Fouquet* .... 16*fr*.
(iv.) " *La Citadelle d. Caire d'apr. Makrizi*.... *in prep.*

VII. BOURGOIN, J. *Précis de l'Art Arabe*; 300 pl. .... 150*fr*.
VIII. (ii.) Miscellanies .... [(iii.) in prep.] 15*fr*., 20*fr*.
IX. (i.) BOURIANT, U. *Texte Grec. d. Livre d'Hénoch* .... 30*fr*.
(ii.) SCHEIL, Père *Deux Traités d. Philon* .... 16*fr*.
(iii.) BOURIANT, U. *L'Evang. et l'Apoc. d. Pierre; Le Texte Grec. d. Livre d'Hénoch*; facs. of MS. [*ut* A § 19] .... 40*fr*.
X.–XI. DE ROCHEMONTEIX, *Le Temple d'Edfou*, pt. i. .. 30*fr*. *in prg.*
XII. MALLET, D. *Premiers Etabls. d. Grecs e. Egyp.* .... 30*fr*.
XIII.–XIV. BÉNÉDITE, G. *Le Temple d. Philae*, pt. i. [*ut inf.*] 40*fr*. *in prg.*
XV. GAYET, Alb. J. *Le Temple d. Louxor*, pt. i. ...... 40*fr*. *in prg.*
XVI. BOURIANT, U. *Le Temple d. Médinet Abou*, pt. i. .... *in prep.*
XVII. " " [tr.] *Descr. Topog. d. l'Egyp. p. Makrizi*, *in prep.*

Papyrus Prisse:
Virey, Ppe. Etudes sur le Papyrus Prisse [Bibl. Ecole Htes. Etudes] 8*fr*. 8° Bouillon, Paris 87
Papyrus Rainer: Mittheilungen aus d. Sammlung, ed. J. Karabacek, vols. i.-v.; pl. and ill. 50*m*. 4° Hofdruckerei, *Vienna* 86–89
Conts. *inter alia* extensive papers on wrg. materl. used for the MSS. cont. in the Erzherzog Rainer colln., by J. KARABACEK and J. WIESNER.
Papyrus Westcar:
Erman, Prf. Adolf [ed.] Märchen des Papyrus Westcar, 2 pts.; 12 pl. [Mittheil. Orient. Samml. d. Mus. Berl.] 41*m*. f° Spemann, *Berl.* 91
A photographic reprodn. of the MS. (275 lines—many fragmts.), w. hieroglyphic transcriptn., and 22 pp. of autographed notes. Pt. ii. conts. a glossary, and an import. chap. on hieroglyphic palæography, the first of its kind. The papyrus is a colln. of strange stories of the semi-mythical kings of the iii. and iv. Dynasties.
" " Die Sprache des Papyrus Westcar 4° Dieterich, *Göttingen* 91
A special grammar of the best example we have of what may be called "Middle-Egyptian."
PETRIE, Prf. W. M. Flinders Papyri
Crum, W. E. [ed. and tr.] Coptic MSS. brought from the Fayum, ed. w. notes; 4 pl. 7/6 *nt*. 4° Nutt 93
Copies of 55 texts (2 Biblical, 4 patristic, 2 liturg., 35 letters, rent lists and accounts), belonging chiefly to period fr. A.D. 560–900. In some cases trs. in full are given. 5 indexes.
Mahaffy, Prf. J. P. [ed.] The Flinders-Petrie Papyri—*ut* K § 179.
PIEHL, K. [ed.] Inscriptions hiéroglyphiques rec. en Egypte, Ser. ii., pt. 2: Commentary 24*m*. Hinrichs, *Lpz*. 92
PLEYTE, W. [ed.] Le Papyrus de Turin, facs. p. F. Rossi, pt. vii. [complete, 7 pts. 140*fl*.] 4° Brill, *Leyden* 76
Recueil de Travaux rel. à la Philol. et Archéol. Egypt. et Assyr., ed. G. Maspéro—*ut* K § 107.
REVILLOUT, Eug. [ed.] —*v.* Corpus Papyrorum Ægypti.
DE ROCHEMONTEIX, Marq. Le Temple d'Edfou—*v.* Mission Archéol. Frçse., *supra*.
SCHACK-SCHACKENBURG, H. Ægyptologische Studien, pts. i.–ii. 4*m*.; 5*m*. 4° Hinrichs, *Lpz*. 93; 94
i. *Zur Grammatik d. Pyramidentexte*; ii. *Die Sternentabellen u. d. sonnl. Relationen d. theban. Stundentafeln.*
SCHEIL, Père Tombeaux Thébains—*v.* Mission Arch. Frçse., *supra*.
VIREY, Ppe. [ed.] Le Tombeau d. Rekhmara; *and* Tombeaux Thébains—*v.* Mission Arch. Frçse., *supra*.

Translated Specimens.

Records of the Past: Engl. trs. of Anc. Monum. of Egypt and W. Asia—*ut* F § 6.

103. LIBYAN PHILOLOGY.

Berber. Kabail (Tamachek) [ALGERIA, TUNISIA, MOROCCO].

Bibliography.

BASSET, Prf. René Rapport s. l. Etudes Berbères, Ethiop. et Arabes: 1887–1891—*ut* K § 116.

History of the Language: Relation to Basque.

v. d. GABELENTZ, H. C. Verwandtschaft d. Baskischen m. d. Berber-Sprachen—*ut* K § 140.

Grammar. Etymology.

BASSET, Prf. René — Le Dialecte de Syouah — [Ecole d. Lettres d'Alger] 4*fr.* 8° Leroux, *Paris* 90

Together w. his *Notes de Lexicogr. Berbère*, pts. i.–iv. [*ut* B.B. K § 103], forms a compar. vocab. of the Berber dialects. Author has also in prep. a Compar. Gram. of the Berber Dialects, a Berber-French Dict. (classif. in order of roots), and a French-Zouaoua (or Kabail) Dict.

BISSUEL, Cpt. H. — Les Touaregs de l'Ouest ; 2 maps — 3*fr.*50 12° *Algiers* (Libr. Mérid., *Montpellier*) 87

BRICCHETTI-ROBECCHI — Sul Dialetto di Siuwah — 4° *Rome* 89

BRINTON, Prf. Dan. G. [Am.]—*in his* Ethnologic Affins. of Anc. Etruscans ; *and* Etrusc. and Libyan Names, *ut* K § 209.

Seeks to attach Berber to Etruscan, the key to wh. he claims it to be.

DE GUIRAUDON, Th. G. — Vocabulary of the Jebilee Dialect — *in prep.*

*MASQUERAY, Em. — Dictionnaire et Textes Touaregs — *in prep.*

MOTYLINSKI, Calassanti — On the Dialect of the Djebel-Nefousa — *in prep.*

QUEDENFELD — Eintheilg. u. Verbreitg. d. Berber-Völkerung in Marokko — 8° *Berlin* 89

RINN, Louis — Les Origines Berbères — 10*fr.* 8° Jourdan, *Algiers* (Challamel, *Paris*) 89

Linguistic and ethnological studies. Derives Gk., Lat., French, and many other langs. fr. the Berber!

Literature.

Aradh Ir'ounath : trad. Rev. Mayor — *Lucerne* 88

*BASSET, Prf. René [ed.] Loqmân Berbère—*ut* B.B. K § 103.

* ,, ,, [ed.] Recueil d. Textes et d. Documts. rel. à l. Phil. Berb. — 8° *Algiers* 87

,, ,, [ed.] Contes Populaires Berbères—*ut* B.B. B § 3.

HANOTEAU, Cpt. [Gen.] [ed.] Poésies populaires de la Kabylie du Jurjura [1867]—*ut* B.B. B § 34.

Kera imouren bouaoual Rebbi ; trad. Rev. Mayor — *Lucerne* 88

MOULIÉRAS, Prf. Aug. [ed.] Les Fourberies de Si Djeh'a : contes Kabyles, vol. i. — 12° *Oran* 91

,, ,, [tr.] Les Fourberies de Si Djeh'a : trad. et annot. [Bibl. Colon. d. Linguist.] 3*fr.*50 18° Leroux, *Paris*

,, ,, [ed.] Légendes et Contes d. l. Grande Kabylie, pts. i.–ii. [Ec. d. Lettres d'Alger] ca. 3*fr.* 8° ,, ,, 9–

New Test., Gosp. of St. Matthew : Injil in Sidi Iesoû ir Masih — 16° Bible Society 87

Poème de Çabi en Dialecte Chelha, ed. Prf. René Basset — 8° Leroux, *Paris* 79

Relation de Sidi Brahim de Massat, trad. Prf. René Basset ; w. notes — 1*fr.*50 8° ,, ,, 83

104. KUSHITIC PHILOLOGY.

Bedauye [NORTH-EAST AFRICA].

REINISCH, Prf. Leo — Die Bedauye-Sprache, pt. i. ; ii. ; iii. 1*m.*50 ; iv. 90*pf.* [*extr. fr.* Sitzber. Wien. Akad.] r 8° Tempsky, *Vienna* 92 ; 93 ; 94 ; 94

Galla, Somali, Hariri [EAST AFRICA].

BRICCHETTI-ROBECCHI — Lingue parlate Somali, Galla e Harari — 8° *Rome* 90

FERRAND, G. — Le Çomal ; Notes de Grammaire Çomalie — 8° *Algiers* 84 ; 86

PAULITSCHKE —*in his* Beiträge z. Ethnogr. u. Anthrop. d. Somâl, Galla u. HarIri ; 40 pl., *etc.* 24*m.* 4° Baldamus, *Lps.* [86] 88

,, —*in his* Harâr-Forschungsreise nach d. Somâl- u. Galla-Ländern ; 2 maps & 50 ill. 15*m.* 8° Brockhaus, *Lps.* 88

PRAETORIUS, F. — Zur Grammatik der Gallasprache — 22*m.* 8° Peiser, *Berlin* 93

VITERBO, Prf. — Grammatica e. Dizionario della Lingua Oromonica — Hoepli, *Milan* 92

A Galla-Ital. and Ital.-Galla dict., w. sketch of grammar, both based on the wks. of CHIARINI and Leon des AVANCHERS. Repr. fr. CECCHI'S *Da Zeila alle Frontiere de Caffa*.

Kunama [NORTH-EAST AFRICA].

REINISCH, Prf. Leo — Die Kunama-Sprache in Nord-Ostafrika, pt. iii. [W'buch.] 2*m.*, iv. [Deut.-Kun. W'verzeich.] 3*m.* 8° Tempsky, *Vienna* 90 ; 91

Nubia : *Literature.*

DE ROCHEMONTEIX, Marq. [ed.] Quelques Contes Nubiens ; w. [accurate] interlinear trs. — 8° *Cairo* 88

Quara [Agaw people of KWARA].

REINISCH, Prf. Leo — Die Quarasprache : Deutsch-Quar-Wörterverzeichniss — 80*pf.* r 8° Tempsky, *Vienna* 87

XVI. Semitic Philology and Literature.

105. SEMITIC PHILOLOGY GENERALLY AND COLLECTIVELY.

Grammar.

HOMMEL, Fritz — Aufsätze u. Abhandlungen arabistisch-semitolog. Inhalts, pt. i. — 8*m.* 8° Franz, *Munich* 92

Pt. i. *Der babylon. Ursprung d. ägypt. Kultur nachgewiesen.*

WINCKLER, H. — Altorientalische Forschungen, pts. i.–ii. — ea. 6*m.* 8° Pfeiffer, *Lps.* 93 ; 94

i. *D. syr. Land Jaudi, D. nordarab. Land Musri, Die Gideoneradkin., Phönic. Glossen, Polit. Entwickg. Altmesopot.* ; ii. *D. babylon. Kassitendynastie, Babyl. Herrschaft in Mesopot.* [a cont.], *Bisra u. Bronze b. d. Babyl. in Assyr., D. Maler, Semit. Inschriften, etc.*

WRIGHT, Prf. Wm. — Lectures on the Comparative Grammar of the Semitic Languages — 14/- 8° Camb. Press 90

Posthumously ed. by Prf. W. Robertson SMITH, his successor in the chair of Arabic at Cambridge, and A. Ashley BEVAN, one of his pupils. The first systematic attempt to found a comparative grammar of the Semitic dialects, RENAN'S promised work never having got beyond the introductory volume [*ut* B.B. K § 106], incl. Assyr. and Babylon, wh. RENAN omits. Edm. CASTLE, also an Englishman, was the compiler of the first compar. dictionary of the Semitic languages.

K § 105*

Accidence.

HAUPT, Paul — Abriss der Assyrischen Formenlehre — Hinrichs, *Lps.* 90

Nouns.

BARTH, J. — Die Nominalbildung in den Semitischen Sprachen, pt. ii. 10*m.* 8° Hinrichs, *Lps.* 91

DE LAGARDE, Paul A. — Register u. Nachträge z. d. "Uebersicht üb. d. Bildg. d. Nomina" [*ut* B.B. K § 105] 8*m.* 8° Dieterich, *Göttingen* 91

Palæography.

Alphabet —*v. also* K § 109 (EUTING).

EUTING, Dr. Julius — Table of the Semitic Characters—*in* Bickell's *Outlines of Hebr. Grammar*, *ut* B.B. K § 117 [also separ. prin. (Author, *Strassb.*)]

" " — Semitische Schrifttafeln [one leaf] f° Author, *Strassb.* 77

Epigraphy.

*Corpus Inscriptionum Semiticarum [photograph. facss., w. Fch. trs. and notes] f° Acad., *Paris* (Klincksieck) 81–93 *in prg.*

Part I. [*Inscr. Phœnic.*, ed. E. RENAN] tom. i., fasc. 1–4, 112*fr.* '81–'87; tom. ii., fasc. 1, 25*fr.* '91—*ut* K § 113.
Part II. [*Inscr. Aramaic.*] tom. i., fasc. 1, 50*fr.* '90; 2, 50*fr.* '93—*ut* K § 108.
Part IV. [*Inscr. Himyarit. et Sabææ*] tom. i., 32*fr.*50 '89.

Magazines.

Revue Sémitique d'Epigraphie et d'Histoire Ancienne, ed. Jos. Halévy [quarterly] *ann.* 20*fr.* 8° Leroux, *Paris* 92 *sqq.*, *in prg.*

Semitische Studien, ed. Prf. Karl Bezold, pts. i.–iii. 24*m.* 8° Felber, *Berlin* 94 *in prg.*

Started by the founder and edr. of the *Ztschr. f. Assyr.* (*ut* B.B. K § 106) for the pubn. of Semitic texts other than Cuneiform.

Series.

Anecdota Oxoniensia: Semitic Series — s 4° Clar. Press / Macmillan, *N.Y.*

Vol. I., pt. i. SAADIAH, Rabbi, *Comm. on Ezra and Nehem.*, ed. H. J. MATHEWS, 3/6 (90c. *nt.*); ii. *Book of the Bee*, ed. E. A. Wallis BUDGE, 21/- ($5.25 *nt.*) '86 [*ut* B.B. K § 119]; iii. JEPHET IBN ALI, *Comm. on Bk. of Daniel*, ed. Prf. D. S. MARGOLIOUTH, 21/- ($5.25 *nt.*) '89 [*ut* A § 30]; iv. *Mediæval Jewish Chronicles*, ed. Dr. Ad. NEUBAUER, 14/- ($3.25 *nt.*) '87 [*ut* B.B. F § 7]; v. *Palestin. Vers. of Holy Scripp.*, ed. and tr. Rev. G. H. GWILLIAMS, 6/- ($1.90 *nt.*) '93 [*ut* A § 17].

Studia Sinaitica: *prices nt.* Camb. Press 94 *in prg.*

i. *Syriac MSS. in Conv. of St. Kather., Mt. Sinai* [*ut* K § 109] Agnes Smith LEWIS, 10/6 '94
ii. *Arab. Vers. of St. Paul's Epp.* [*ut* K § 115] ...... Marg. Dunlop GIBSON, 5/- 94
iii. *Arab. MSS. in Conv. of St. Kather., Mt. Sinai* [*ut* K § 114] Marg. Dunlop GIBSON, 6/- 94
iv. *Tract of Plutarch on a Man's Enemies* .... Dr. Eberh. NESTLE 2/- 94

105.* HITTITE [PROB. NON-SEMITIC] INSCRIPTIONS AND HISTORY.

Ausgrabungen zu Sendschirli [N. Syria], pt. i. [Mittheiln. a. d. Orient. Samml. Berl.] 25*m.* f° Spemann, *Berlin* 93 *in prg.*

Contribns. by Dr. von LUSCHAN, the director of the expedns., Prf. SCHRADER, Prf. SACHAU. The lang. of the inscripp. has been the subj. of discussn., and seems to be a mixture of Aramaic and Hebr.

CAMPBELL, Prf. Jno. [Canad.] The Hittites: their inscriptions and their history, 2 vols.; pl. 21/- *nt.* 8° Nimmo 91

Acc. to author, Hittite civilization has been ubiquitous. He surveys mankind "fr. China to Peru," and finds traces of it everywhere.

DE CARA, F'r. C. A. — Della Identità degli Hethei e dei Pelasgi dimonstrata 8° *Rome* 91

The author has an important wk. on the Hittites and Pelasgians *in prep.*

CONDER, Cpt. [Maj.] C. R. Altaic Hieroglyphs: a memoir, w. tr. of all known Hittite Inscrs.; ill. 5/- c 8° A. P. Watt 87

Seeks to show that the symbols are the prototypes whence the Cuneiform system has developed; that they have possibly a common origin w. the hieroglyphic syst. of Egypt; and that perhaps even the Chinese characters may have also developed fr. the original Altaic picture-writing. Author has also a wk. on the Tell el-Amarna tablets in prep. for Pal. Expl. Fd., in which he deals w. their importance for reconstructing the hist. and condition of Pal. in 14 cent. B.C. He believes that the Abiri referred to in them were the Hebrews. To cont. maps and 2 pl. of the Lachish inscription.

DELITZSCH, Prf. Fried. — Beiträge z. Entkiffg. u. Erklärg. d. Kappad. Keilschrifttafeln—*in* Abhgn. d. Sächs. Ges. xiv. (4) [1893].

GOLÉNISCHEFF, W. [ed.] — 24 Tablettes Cappadociennes d. l. Collection Golen *St. Petersburg* 91

HALÉVY, Jos. [ed.] — Les Deux Inscriptions Hétéennes de Zindjirli [N. Syria] 6*fr.* 8° Leroux, *Paris* 94

See also his art. on the 2 inscripp. (7 and 8 cent.: now in Berlin Museum) in *Revue Sémitique*, no. 1 [*ut* K § 105]. Their lang. is either Hebr. tinged w. Aramaic, or Aram. tinged w. Hebr.; and HALÉVY thinks their authorship was Hittite, the Hatti of the Assyr. inscripp.

HIRSCHFELD, G. — D. Felsenreliefs in Kleinasien u. d. Volk d. Hethiter; 2 pl. and 15 ill. 4*m.*50 4° G. Reimer, *Berl.* 87

An important work. Extr. fr. *Abhandgn. d. Berl. Akademie.*

HUMANN + PUCHSTEIN, C. O. —*in their* Reisen in Kleinasien u. Nord-Syrien; 3 maps and 53 pl. 60*m.* f° D. Reimer, *Berl.* 90

JENSEN, Prf. Peter — The Solution of the Hittite Question [*repr. fr.* Sund. Schl. Times] 93

Author regards the Hittite as an Indo-Europ. lang., w. espec. close rels. to the Armenian of to-day—a combination of the views of SAYCE and PEISER.

DE LANTSHEERE, Léon — De la Race et de la Langue des Hittites 8° Goemaere, *Brussels* 92

A clear and compreh. acc. of all that was known or conjectured up to 1891; well arrgd. and w. careful refs. to authorities. The arguments seeking to show that the authors of the Hittite monumts. were the Hittites of the O.T., and of the Egypt., Assyr., and Vannic inscripp., are set forth w. great lucidity. Enlarged fr. his *Hittites et Amorites*, 8° *Brussels* '87.

LENORMANT, Fr̨çois. [ed.] Sceaux à Légendes en Ecriture Hamathéenne

MÜLLER, Prf. D. H. [ed.] Die altsemit. Inschriften v. Sendschirli in d. kgl. Mus. z. Berlin 5*m.* 8° Hölder, *Vienna* 93

Text in Hebrew transcription, Germ. tr., commentary, grammat. outline and vocabulary.

" Max [son of Prf. F. Max]—*in his* Asien und Europa nach altägyptischen Denkmälern 8° *Leipzig* 93

Agrees w. HIRSCHFELD in regarding Cappadocia as the home of the entire civilizn. of Asia Minor.

PEISER, F. E. — Die hetitischen Inschriften: ein Versuch ihrer Entzifferung 6*m.* 8° Peiser, *Berlin* 92

Pennsylvania Univ.: —*an edn. of the 30 Cappadoc. inscripp. in possessn. of the Univ. is in prep.*, ed. Prf. H. V. HILPRECHT.

PERROT + CHIPIEZ, Georges/Chas. The Hittites—*in their* History of Ancient Art, *ut* I § 85.
RAMSAY Syro-Cappadocian Monuments in Asia Minor—*in* Athen. Mittheilgn. XIV. (2) [1889].
„ + HOGARTH Prähellenische Denkmäler aus Kappadocien—*in the* Recueil de Travaux rel. à la Philologie et à l'Archéol. égypt. et assyr. 1893, *ut* K § 107.
SAYCE, Prf. A. H. —*in the* Recueil de Travaux; *also in* Sitzbg. Berl. Akad., 1892, pp. 43-53.
Refutes the theory of the Semitic origin of the Hittite language. *Cf.* the discussn. betwn. him, CHEYNE, TYLER and others in *The Academy*, 1893 (Nos. 1094-99).

106. ASSYRIAN, BABYLONIAN AND CUNEIFORM PHILOLOGY.

Grammar.

HAUPT, Prf. Paul Prolegomena to a Comparative Assyr. Grammar—*in* Jl. Amer. Orient. Soc., v. xiii., pp. 249-270.
„ „ The Assyrian E Vowel [*extr. fr.* Jl. Amer. Orient. Soc., vol. viii.] 8° *Baltimore* 87

Etymology: *Dictionary.*

DELITZSCH, Prf. Fried. Assyrisches Handwörterbuch, pt. i. 14*m.* 4° Hinrichs, *Lpz.* 94
MUSS-ARNOLT, W. Assyrisch-Englisch-Deutsches Glossar, pt. i. 5*m.* Reuther, *Berlin* 94 *in prog.*

Names.

LOTZ, Wilh. Eigennamenlexikon zur babylon.-assyrischen Keilschriftliteratur 8° Hinrichs, *Lpz.* 91

Metrology.

AURÈS, A. Traité de Métrologie Assyrienne 6*fr.* 8° Bouillon, *Paris* 91
A learned and elaborate discussion of the ancient Assyrian weights and measures.

Inscriptions.

DELITZSCH, Prf. Fried. Beitr. z. Entzifferg. u. Erklär. d. kappad. Keilinschrifttafeln 3*m.* 8° Hirzel, *Lpz.* 93
FRIEDRICH, Thom. Kabiren und Keilinschriften [pp. 94] 8*m.* 8° Pfeiffer, *Lpz.* 93

Magazines and Permanent Serials.

Babylonian and Oriental Record, ed. Prf. Terrien de Lacouperie + Th. G. Pinches *ann.* 12/6 8° Editor (Luzac) 86 *sqq.*, *in prg.*
Revue d'Assyriologie et d'Archéologie Orientale: ed. J. Oppert + E. Ledrain, vols. i.-iii. [ea. 4 pts.] ea. vol. 30*fr.* 4° Leroux, *Paris* 91-94 *in prg.*
Society for Biblical Archæology: Proceedings.

107. ASSYRIAN, BABYLONIAN AND CUNEIFORM INSCRIPTIONS AND LITERATURE.

History of Assyriology.

BEZOLD, Dr. Chas. Fortschritte d. Keilschriftforschg. in neuester Zt. [Samml. gemeinverst. Vortr.] 60*pf.* 8° Verlagshdg., *Hambg.* 88
DELATTRE, P. Alf. Louis L'Assyriologie depuis onze ans [chiefly philology] 8° Leroux, *Paris* 91
V. GUTSCHMID, A. Neue Beiträge zur Gesch. d. alt. Orients: Assyriol. in Deutschld. 4*m.* 8° *Leipzig* 76
LINCKE, Dr. Arth. A. Bericht üb. d. Fortschritte d. Assyriol.: 1886-1893 [chiefly hist. & civilizn.] 8° Bär, *Lpz.* / 3/6 Orient. Inst., *Woking* 94
SCHRADER, Prf. Eberh. Keilinschriften und Geschichtsforschung 14*m.* 8°
An important contribution to geography, history and chronology, derived *fr.* cuneiform inscriptions.
WINCKLER, H. Ein Beitrag zur Geschichte d. Assyriologie in Deutschland 1*m.* 50 8° Pfeiffer, *Lpz.* 93

Texts and Translations. Treatises.

Series.

Assyriologische Bibliothek: hrsg. Friedr. Delitzsch + Paul Haupt; pl. r 4° Hinrichs, *Lpz.* 90-92 *in prg.*
New Vols.:
viii. *Samassumukin* [*ut infra*] .... C. F. LEHMANN, 40*m.* 92
ix. *Achämenideninschr. zter Art* [*ut inf.*] F. H. WEISSBACH, 30*m.* 90
x. (1) *Altpers. Keilinschrn.*, i. [*ut* K § 130] .... F. W. WEISSBACH + W. BANG, 10*m.* 93
xi. *Beitr. zum altbabyl. Privatrecht* [*ut infra*] B. MEISSNER, 30*m.* 93
Beiträge zur Assyriologie u. vergleich. Sprachwiss., hrsg. F. Delitzsch + P. Haupt, v. i. pt. 2, 17*m.*, ii. 1, 17*m.*, 2, 20*m.*, 3, 5*m.* r 8° Hinrichs, *Lpz.* 90; 91; 92; 93
Johns Hopkins Univ.: Contributions to Assyriology, *etc.*, vol. i., pt. 1 $6 8° Johns Hopk. Univ., *Baltimore*, *in prg.*
*Keilinschriftliche Bibliothek, hrsg. Prf. Eberhard Schrader, vol. iii. pt. 1, 8*m.*; 2, 6*m.*; 3, 18*m.* 8° Reuther, *Berl.* 92; 90; 91 *in prg.*
The series, as far as pub., forms a valuable, if not indispensable, storehouse of Assyr. and Babyl. texts in transcriptions, w. trs. and in some cases notes. It is the latest wk. of the founder of Assyriology in Germy., who ab. 1870 commenced his career as an Assyriologist, and for a long time fought single-handed agst. heavy odds, the new study being not only ignored in Germy. but regarded by many eminent scholars as little better than charlatanism. His zeal was, however, in 1875 rewarded by the first chair in Assyriology.
Mélanges d'Archéologie Egyptienne et Assyrienne, vols. i.-iii.; pl. 30*fr.*; *red. to* 15*fr.* 4° Bouillon, *Paris* 72-78
Palestine Exploration Fund: Publications—*ut* A § 47.
Records of the Past: Series ii., ed. Prf. A. H. Sayce, vols. i.-vi. c 8° ea. 4/6 Bagster / ea. $1.75 Pott, *N.Y.* 89; 90; 91; 92
A new series of tr. inscripp., docums., *etc.*, w. notes. It is—at present, at least—not to be continued, owing to lack of public support. As a series, the pubs. is a very useful one, almost indispensable as an aid to the critical study of the Bible.
Recueil de Travaux rel. à la Philol. et Archéol. Egypt. et Assyr., ed. G. Maspéro, vols. i.-x.; pl. 310*fr.*; *red. to* 200*fr.* xi.-xv. ea. 30*fr.* 4° Bouillon, *Paris* 70-88; 89-93 *in prg.*
Transactions of the Society of Biblical Archæology, vols. i.-xvi. *ann.* 21/- in 8° Soc. of Bibl. Archæol. 72-94 *in prg.*

K § 107

Individually.

*ABEL + WINCKLER, $\frac{L.}{H.}$ [eds.] Der Thontafelfund v. El-Amarna, 2 vols.; *c.* 170 pl. [Mittheil. a. d. orient. Samml. d. Mus. z. Berl.] 70*m.* f° Spemann, *Berl.* 89; 90; 90

Vide Tell el-Amarna, *infra* (note).

" " [eds.] Keilinschrifttexte zum Gebrauch bei Vorlesungen [100 pp.] 15*m.* 4° Spemann, *Berlin* 90

AMIAUD + SCHEIL, $\frac{A.}{V.}$ [eds. and trs.] Inscriptions de Salmanasar ii. [Kg. of Assyr., 860–824] [transcr., tr. and notes] 12*fr.* 50 8° Welter, *Paris* 90

Asaph Psalms:

King, Dr. E. G. The "Asaph" Psalms in their conn. w. the Early Religion of Babylonia—*sub* A § 12.

BEZOLD, Dr. Chas. [ed.] Catal. of Cuneiform Tablets in the Kouyunjik Collection, vols. i.–ii. ea. 15/- 8° Brit. Mus. 89; 91

Descrns. of thousands of tablets and fragments. The 2nd vol. is devoted to those fr. the famous clay library founded by ASSURBANIPAL B.C. 668–626, and preserved by the kings of Assyria at Nineveh, and conts. also a classifcn. of omen and astrolog. texts—a wk. hitherto unattempted.

" " [ed.] Oriental Diplomacy; w. vocab., grammat. notes, *etc.* 18/- *net.* p 8° Luzac 92

The transliter. text of cuneif. despatches betw. the kings of Egypt and W. Asia in 15 cent. B.C., discov. at Tell el-Amarna, and now in Brit. Mus. A useful supplt. to the Brit. Mus. vol. on the Tell el-Amarna tablets.

BLACKDEN + FRASER, $\frac{M. W.}{G. W.}$ [eds.] Graffiti of Hat-Nub [pp. 15] obl *priv. prin.* (10/- Luzac) 93

Copies of graffiti of great hist. and palæogr. importce. ranging fr. vi.–xii. Dynasty; discov. at Alabaster Quarry of Hat-Nub, nr. Tell el-Amarna.

BOISSIER, Alf. Recherches sur quelques Contrats Babyloniens [Leipzig dissert.] 4*fr.* 8° Leroux, *Paris* 91

A sketch of Babyl. law of contract, ill. by trns. of docum., incl. the famous Michaux Stone. Interesting as showing the independ. position of women, and how even a slave could make a contract w. a banker.

" " [ed.] Documents Assyriens relatifs aux Présages, vol. 1, pt. 1 12*fr.* 8° Bouillon, *Paris* 94

BONAVIA, Dr. E. The Flora of the Assyrian Monuments and its Outcomes [digressive] 10/- *net.* 8° Constable 93

CONDER, Cpt. [Maj.] —*sub* K § 105.*

EPPING + STRASSMAIER, $\frac{J.}{J. N.}$ [eds.] Astronomisches aus Babylon; w. copies of inscripp. 4*m.* 8° Herder, *Freibg.* 89

Texts fr. 3 tablets of lunar ephemerides for yrs. 188, 189 and 201 of era of SELEUCUS (wh. began B.C. 312), w. long astronom. commentary and remarks on Babyl. ephem. of planets in general.

GOLÉNISCHEFF, W. [ed.] Vingt-quatre Tablettes Cappadociennes de la coll. W. Golénischeff [w. intro.] *St. Petersburg* 92

HARPER, Prf. Rob. Fcs. [Am.; ed.] Assyrian and Babylonian Letters belonging to K Colln. in Br. Mus., pts. i.–ii.; pl. ea. 25/- c 8° Luzac 92; 94

Part. of a colln. of letters fr. governors of cities in Mesopotamia addressed to SARGON, SENNACHERIB, ESARHADDON and ASSURBANIPAL. To occupy 6 Pts., last 2 of wh. are to be devoted to a general descrn. of the contents of the letters, a vocab., *etc.* Printed by Univ. of Chicago Press.

HAUPT, Paul [ed. and tr.] Die sumerischen Familiengesetze: eine assyr. Studie [text, transcr. & tr.] 12*m.* 4° Hinrichs, *Lpz.* 79

HILPRECHT, Prf. H. V. —*v.* Pennsylvania Univ., *infra.*

JENSEN, Prf. Peter Die Kosmologie der Babylonier: Studien u. Materialien; 3 maps 40*m.* 8° Trübner, *Strassbg.* 90

Almost every word wh. occurs in pubd. cuneiform texts conc. Babyl. cosmology is here collected, explained and critically examined. In 1st pt. he treats of the *Universe and its Parts* (sky, Zodiac, Mountain of Sunrise, abodes of blessed and damned, the Oceanos), in 2nd of *Creation and Formation of World* (Creation and Deluge).

JEREMIAS, Dr. Alf. Izdubar-Nimrod: eine altbabylon. Heldensage; 4 autotype pl. 2*m.* 80 r 8° Teubner, *Lpz.* 91

Conts. a long. intro. to the anc. Chaldean Epic, wh. recounts the Twelve Labours of Gilgames, and a tr. or paraphrase of its contents as far as preserved. The tr. is based on HAUPT'S text, *sub* 𝔅.𝔊. K § 107. The first rendering of the Epic was given in SMITH'S *Chald. Acc. of Genesis*, *sub* 𝔅.𝔊. K § 107. A good piece of wk.

KNUDTSON, Dr. J. A. [ed.] Assyr. Gebete an d. Sonnengott f. Stadt u. königl. Haus, 2 v. 40*m.* Pfeiffer, *Lpz.* 93

Temp. ESARHADDON and ASSURBANIPAL. Edr. has in prep. a complete edn. of the cuneif. texts of that series of tablets wh. have commonly—but erroneously—been said to be inscribed w. texts referring to the downfall of the Assyr. Empire.

LEHMANN, C. F. Samassumukin, König von Babylonien [B.C. 668–648] [Assyr. Bibl.] 40*m.* r 8° Hinrichs, *Lpz.* 92

A large and handsome vol., one of the most exhaustive monographs wh. have appeared since OPPERT'S famous *Expédition Scientifique* [*sub* 𝔅.𝔊. K § 107]. The inscripp. of SAMAS-SUM-YUKIN (who was hf.-bro'. to ASSURBANIPAL, and who, after d. of his father ESARHADDON, received the anc. kingdom of Babyl. as his share) are the immed. subj. of the bk., but form a starting-pt. for a very full discussn. of histor. and linguist. questns. of much importance to the Assyr. student. A consid. pt. of bk. is occupied w. a clear and cogent refutation of the paradox wh. sees in the Sumerian lang. of anc. Chaldæa an elabor. syst. of Cabbalistic writing. Vocabulary added.

LOTZ, Wilh. [ed. and tr.] Inschriften Tiglath-Pilesers i. [transcriptn., w. Germ. tr.] 20*m.* r 8° Hinrichs, *Lpz.* 80

MEISSNER, B. [ed. and tr.] Beiträge zum altbabylon. Privatrecht; 55 litho. pl. [Assyr. Bibl.] 30*m.* 8° " " 92

55 pl. of cuneif. texts, the greater pt. copied fr. the "envelope" or case tablets in Brit. Mus. (others fr. Berlin Mus.), w. sign-list of forms of Babyl. characters occurring in texts, Introd., trs., and notes.

" " + ROST, Paul [eds.] Die Bauinschriften Sanheribs [w. transcrn., tr., gloss. & comm.] 10*m.* 8° Pfeiffer, *Lpz.* 93

MOLDENKE, Dr. Alf. B. [Am.; ed. & tr.] Cuneiform Texts in the Metropol. Museum of Art: ed. & tr. $1.25 8° *New York* 93

PEISER, F. E. [ed.] Babylonische Verträge des Berliner Museums [autographed, transcr., transl.] 28*m.* 4° W. Peiser, *Berlin* 90

Ninety texts from the colln. purchased by Berl. Mus. in 1889, w. 2 Appendx. contg. the Brit. Mus. texts belonging to them. Introd., treatise, commentary, and lists of words and proper names by Prf. KÖHLER.

" " Jurisprudentiae Babylonicae quae supersunt: Commentatio 2*m.* 8° W. Peiser, *Berlin* 90

Pennsylvania Univ.: The Babylonian Exped. of: Series A: Cuneiform Texts, ed. Prf. H. V. Hilprecht, vol. i. pt. i.; 50 pl. 4° $\frac{\text{Partridge, } \textit{Phila.}}{\text{som, Merkel, } \textit{Erlangen}}$ 93

The Amer. Exped., under command of Dr. PETERS, conducted its excavns. at Niffer (or Nuffar), and their results are of great importance. Thousands of inscripp. and clay-bks. have been found, forming an almost continuous histor. series fr. the dawn of Babyl. civilisn. to the age of the Pers. kings. HILPRECHT accomp. the expedn.

ROST, Paul [ed. and tr.] Die Keilschrifttexte Tiglat-Pilesers iii. n. d. Orig. in Br. Mus., vols. i.–ii. 20*m.* 8° & 4° Pfeiffer, *Lpz.* 93

i. German Introd., transcription, tr., vocab. and comm.; ii. Autographed text.

DE SARZEC, Ern. Découvertes en Chaldée, ed. Léon Heuzey, 3 vols. (5 pts.); heliograv. pl. 90*fr.* f° Leroux, *Paris* 85–92

Pb. under auspices of Fch. Minister of Publ. Instrn. Of great value for palæography, philology, history, and art. Trs. of the inscripp. of Urbau and Gudea by AMIAUD. A transcriptn. and tr. of the texts by HALÉVY, are given in vol. xi. of *Recueil de Travaux* (*sub* K § 107).

Price Introduction to the Inscriptions discovered by Sarzec [dissert. inaug.] 8° *Leipzig* 87

SCHEIL, V. [ed.] Inscription Assyrienne de Samsi-Ramman iv. [kg. of Assyria 824–811] 8*fr.* 4° Welter, *Paris* 89

SCHRADER, E. [ed. & tr.] Höllenfahrt der Istar: ein altbabyl. Epos [w. tr., comm. and gloss.] 4*m.* 8° Ricker, *Giessen* 74

STRASSMAIER, J. N. [ed.] Babylonische Texte, pts. vi. (B) *and* viii.–xi. ea. 12*m.* 8° Pfeiffer, *Lpz.* 92; 90–94 *in prg.*

TALLQVIST, H. L. [ed. & tr.] Babylonische Schenkungsbriefe [transcribed, tr. and annot.] 2m.60 8° *Helsingfors* 91
" " Die Sprache d. Contracte Nabû-Nâ'ids [555–538 B.C.] 5m. 8° " (Pfeiffer, *Lps.*) 90
Tell el-Amarna Tablets, The, in the British Museum; autotype pl. 28/- 8° British Museum 92

Discov. in 1888 by a Tell el-Amarna woman, digging at the foot of the hills for small antiquities. Of this "find" the Brit. Mus. secured 82 tablets, the Gizeh Museum in Egypt c. 60 and the Berlin Mus. c. 160 pieces, of wh. a large no. are fragments giving no connected sense. The Berlin texts with those of Gizeh added were pub. in lithography by Drs. ABEL + WINCKLER [*ut sup.*]. These tablets, written c. 1500–1450 B.C., are unique as a means of weaving together the threads of the histories of 2 or 3 of the greatest nations of antiquity. With a Summary of Contents, Introd., notes and bibliogr.

Petrie, Prf. W. M. Flinders Tell el-Amarna; w. chaps. by Prf. A. H. Sayce, F. Ll. Griffith, F. C. J. Spurrell—*ut* G § 9.

Vide also ABEL, BEZOLD, *supra*, and K § 105* (CONDER, note).

TIELE, Prf. C. P. —*in his* Babylon.-Assyr. Geschichte, 2 vols. [Handbb. d. Alten Gesch.] 13m. 8° F. A. Perthes, *Gotha* 86; 88

An indispensable text-bk. for Assyriologists, giving a compreh. histor. criticism of the inscripp. of Babyl. and Ass. kings, w. regard to their compilation and trustworthiness. Vol. i., Earliest Times to Death of SARGON II., 6m.; ii. Accession of SENNACHERIB to Conquest of Babel by CYRUS, 7m.

WEISBACH, F. H. [ed.] Achämenideninschriften zweiter Art [Elamitisch-Neususisch-Anzanisch]; 16 pl. [Assyr. Bibl.] 30m. r 4° Hinrichs, *Lps.* 90

The texts, transcrns., trs., comm., vocab., notes and bibliography.

WINCKLER, Dr. Hugo [ed.] Altbabylonische Keilschrifttexte z. Gebrauch b. Vorlesungen 10m. 8° Pfeiffer, *Lps.* 92

[*v. also* ABEL, *sup.*]

" " [ed.] Der Thontafelfund v. El-Amarna—*v.* ABEL, *supra.*
" " [ed.] Keilinschriftliches Textbuch zum Alten Testament, pt. i. 2m.; ii. 3m. 8° " " 91; 92 *in prg.*
" " [ed.] Sammlung von Keilinschriften, vol. i. pt. 1, 5m.; 2, 8m.; ii., pt. 1, 6m., 2, 8m. " " 93; 93; 93; 93

i. (1) *Die Inschriften Tiglat-Pilesers I.*; (2) *Texte verschiedenen Inhalts.*

" " Alt-testamentliche Untersuchungen

A colln. of studies and notes on O.T. hist. and difficult passages, only some of wh. have to do with the cuneiform inscripp.

108. CHALDEE [WEST OR BIBLICAL ARAMAIC] PHILOLOGY.

Grammar.

DALMAN, Galiläisch-Aramäische Grammatik 8° Hinrichs, *Lps.*, *in prep.*

Accidence.

Nouns.

DE LAGARDE, P. —*v.* K § 105, *s.v.* Nouns.

Verb.

ROSENBERG, J. Das aramäische Verbum im babylonischen Talmud 2m. 8° Elwert, *Marburg* 89

Etymology: Dictionary.

SCHWALLY, F. Idioticon d. christlich-palästinischen Aramäisch 6m.40 8° Ricker, *Giessen* 93

Plant-names —*v.* B § 7 (Löw).

Epigraphy.

*Corpus Inscriptionum Semiticarum, Pars ii.: Inscripp. Aramaicæ—*ut* K § 105.
EUTING, Dr. Julius [ed.] Sinaitische Inschriften; 40 autogr. pl. 24m. 4° G. Reimer, *Berl.* 91

Facs. and transcripts of betw. 600 and 700 specs. of the celebrated inscriptions on the rock-faces of the Sinaitic peninsula, wh. have for the most pt. (espec. in Engl.) been regarded as relics of the wandergs. of Israel in the Wilderness of Horeb [*e.g.* Chas. FORSTER, in his *Israelitish Authorship of the Sinaitic Inscripp.*, 1856]. They are short benedictory or memorial formulas, in Aramaic, the proper names nearly always pure Arabic—the wk. of the Arabic-spkg. but Aram.-wrtg. Nabatæans who held the N.-sect. of the great trade route fr. Aden to Petra and Bosra. Three are dated. EUTING attribs. them all to the period of 1st to 6th cent.

" " [ed.] Altaramäische Inschriften aus Teimâ [Arabia]—*in* Sitzgsber. Berl. Akad. 1884, no. 35; w. 2 pl.
" " [ed.] Nabatäische Inschriften aus Arabien; 29 pl. 4° G. Reimer, *Berl.* 85

Alphabet.

EUTING, Dr. Julius Tabula Scripturae Aramaicae [a repr.; one leaf] f° Author, *Strassbg.* 90

Literature.

BEDJAN [ed.] Manuel de Piété [prayers, meditns. and offices in Chaldee] 16m. 8° Harrassowitz, *Lps.* 93

109. SYRIAC [EAST-ARAMAIC] PHILOLOGY (a): CLASSICAL.

Bibliography.

DE LAGARDE, P. Bibliothecae Syriacae a P. de L. coll. quae ad Philol. Sacram pertinent 50m. 4° Dieterich, *Göttgn.* 92

Grammar.

Abp's. Mission to Assyr. Christians: Syriac Grammar [72 pp.] 10/6 8° Mission Press, *Urmi* (S.P.C.K) 9-

Founded partly on Eastern copies of BAR-HEBRÆUS and BAR-ZOBAI, and gives the Eastern Syrian traditions fr. wh. the Jacobite grammars often differ. In E. Syr. (Nestorian) type.

Etymology.

Dictionary.

BAR BAHLULE, Hassan Lexicon Syriacum: voces Syr. et Graec., ed. R. Duval, pts. i.–iii., ea. 20fr. 4° Bouillon, *Paris* 88; 90; 92
BROCKELMANN, Dr. Carl Lexicon Syriacum, fasc. i.–ii. s 4° ea. 4m. Reuther, *Berl.* / ea. 4/- nt. Clark, *Edin.* 94 *in prg.*

A new Syriac dict., by a pupil of Prf. Theod. NÖLDEKE, to be completed in 10 pts. (c. 800 pp.). For the root-words, LAGARDE'S Syriac type is used, and for the derivatives a smaller size of the same mould has been prepared.

K §§ 110-112

BRUNN, F'r. J. Syriac-Latin Dictionary 16/- Catholic Press, *Beyrout*, *in prep.*
SMITH, Dr. R. Payne [ed.] Thesaurus Syriacus, pt. ix. s f° 25/- Clar Press / Macmillan, *N.Y.* 93
The wk. is expected to be soon finished. Miss Payne SMITH is preparing a compendium of it in English, wh. will be a boon to Syriac students.

Manuscripts.

LEWIS, Agnes Smith [ed.] Catal. of Syriac MSS. in Convent of St. Katherine on Mt. Sinai [Studia Sinait.] 10/6 *nt.* Camb. Press 94

110. SYRIAC PHILOLOGY (*b*): MANDAITIC [a corrupt Syriac] LITERATURE.

Literature

Genzá [Sidrâ Rabbâ]: Mandäische Schriften aus, übers. u. erlaut. W. Brandt 8*m.* 8° Vandenhoeck, *Göttgn.* 93
POGNON, H. [ed.] Une Incantation contre les Génies malfaisants en Mandaïte 2*fr.*50 8° Bouillon, *Paris* 93

111. SYRIAC PHILOLOGY (*c*): MODERN SYRIAC.

Grammar.

Abp's. Mission to Assyrian Christians: Modern Syriac Grammar 10/6 8° Mission Press, *Urmi* (S.P.C.K.)

Accidence.

Verbs.

Abp's. Mission to Assyrian Christians: Vocabulary of Modern Syriac Verbs 5/- 8° Mission Press, *Urmi* (S.P.C.K.)

Literature.

KAYSER, K. [tr.] Das Buch v. d. Erkenntniss d. Wahrheit: übersetzt 15*m.* r 8° Trübner, *Strassbg.* 93
New Testament:
Gwynn, Rev. Jno. On a Syriac MS. of N.T. belong. to E. of Crawfd.; 1 pl. [Trans. R. Irish Acad.] 3/6 4° Williams 94
NÖLDEKE, Prf. Theod. Die v. Guidi hrsg. syrische Chronik übers. u. commentirt 1*m.*10 8° Freytag, *Lpz.* 93
Patrologia Syriaca, ed. Abbé R. Graffin ca. 20*fr.* r 8° *Paris* *in prep.*
An important new series, to comprehend the wks. of the Syriac Fathers, w. Latin trs., commencing w. APHRAATES' *Homilies* [based on WRIGHT'S edn., *ut* B.B. K § 112] and JOHN OF EPHESUS. Uniform w. MIGNE'S *Patrologia* [*ut* B.B. A § 55].
PHILOXENUS, Bp. of Mabbôgh [460–?523] Discourses, A.D. 485–519, ed. and tr. Dr. E. A. Wallis Budge, v. i.: Text; 4 pl. 21/- Asher 94
Pub. for Roy. Soc. of Liter. Many of the discourses, wh. treat of the Xtn. life and character, are here pub. for first time. Author is best known for his version of the N.T.
PRYM + SOCIN, E./A. [eds. and trs.] Der neu-aramäische Dialekt d. Tûr 'Abdin, 2 pts. 16*m.* Vandenhoeck, *Göttgn.* 81
Pt. i. conts. the Texts, ii. the tr.: Syrian legends and folktales, orally collected.
PSEUDO-CALLISTHENES, [7 cent.] Hist. of Alex. the Gt., ed. & tr. Dr. E. A. Wallis Budge; w. notes 25/- 8° Camb. Press 89
A good edn. and tr. of the Syriac version of the PSEUDO-CALLISTHENES.
RAABE, R. [tr.] Gesch. d. Dominus Mâri, e. Apostels d. Orients: übers. u. untersucht 2*m.* 8° Hinrichs, *Lpz.* 93
A legendary acc. of the missionary activity of the Apostle Dominus Mâri (a monk of the convent of Dorkonai), who was sent by his teacher ADDAI, one of the 70 disciples of the Lord, to preach the Gospel in "the region of the East, the land of Babylon." The text has been ed. by ABBELOOS.
Sindban: oder die Sieben Weisen Meister, hrsg. Friedr. Baethgen [Syriac w. Germ. tr.] 2*m.* 8° Hinrichs, *Lpz.* 70

112. SYRIAC LITERATURE AND INSCRIPTIONS.

History, Criticism, etc.

NESTLE, Dr. Eberh. Marginalia und Materialien 10*m.* 8° Heckenhauer, *Tübingen* 93
WRIGHT, Prf. Wm. Syriac Literature [repr. of article in Encyclo. Brit., ed. 9] 6/- *nt.* c 8° Black *in prep.*

Texts and Translations.

Acta Martyrum et Sanctorum, Syriace ed. Bedjan, vol. i. 25*fr.*, ii. 30*fr.*, iii. 30*fr.*, iv. 30*fr.* 8° Harrassowitz, *Lpz.* 90; 91; 92; 94
,, Mar Kardaghi [Assyr. Prefect] qui sub Sapore ii. martyr occubuit, ed. J. B. Abbeloos [w. Lat. tr.] 3*m.*50 8° *Lpz.* 90
Alexis, St.:
Amiaud, A. La Légende Syriaque de St. Alexis [Bibl. Ecole Haut. Etudes] 7*fr.*50 8° Bouillon, *Paris* 89
APHRAATES:
Funk, S. Die Haggadischen Elemente in d. Homilien d. Aphraates 2*m.* 8° 91
Apocrypha of Old Test.: Libri Vet. Test. Apocryphi syriace e rec. Paul A. de Lagarde 20*m.* 8° Brockhaus, *Lpz.* 61
Book of the Governors: —*v.* Thomas, *infra.*
CHWOLSON, D. [ed.] Syrisch-nestorianische Grabinschriften aus Semirjetschie; 4 pl. 10*m.*50 4° *St Petersburg* 90
CLEMENT OF ROME Recognitiones, ed. Paul A. de Lagarde 20*m.* r 8° Brockhaus, *Lpz.* 62
De Sancta Cruce: Syriac text and Germ. tr. Dr. Eberhard Nestle 4*m.* 8° Reuther, *Berlin* 9-
Based on a Lond. MS. dated 1196 and a tr. by Dudley LOFTUS [from *An Ancient Aramean Biography*, Dubl. 1686]. A Syrian story of a double discov. of Christ's Cross, one *temp.* Peter and John by Spouse of Emp. CLAUDIUS, the other by HELENA, mother of CONSTANTINE.
EPHRAEM THE SYRIAN:
Grimme, H. Der Strophenbau in d. Gedichten Ephraems d. Syrers 4*m.* 8° Beith, *Frbg.* 93
EPIPHANIUS:
Nestle, Dr. Eberh. Die dem Epiphanius zugeschriebenen Vitæ Prophetarum 3*m.* 8° 93
GEORGE, Bp. [*c.* 640–724] Gedichte und Briefe, übers. u. erläut. Prf. V. Ryssel 7*m.* 8° Hirzel, *Lpz.* 91
A tr. of the important *Letter to the Presbyter Jesus* and all the learned Bp's. known writings, except his trs. of Gk. writers (notably ARISTOTLE)—the letters distrib. under heads of Church Hist., Exegesis, Hist. of Doctrine, etc. The notes occupy half the bk., and are of great value. A sketch of the life of the "Bp. of the Arabs" is prefixed. None of the wrgs. now tr. have been hitherto pb. in the orig., except the *Letter to Presb. Jesus or Yeshua*, wh. was pb. by LAGARDE in his *Analecta Syriaca* [1858, *ut* B.B. K § 112]. The greater pt. of the tr. of the epistol. remains first appeared in *Theolog. Studien u. Kritiken*, 1883.

HARRIS, Prf. J. Rendel [ed.] Some Interesting Syrian and Palestinian Inscriptions 4/- r 8° Camb. Press 91
JOHN OF EPHESUS Third Part of his Eccles. Hist., tr. Dn. R. Payne Smith 10/- 8° Clar. Press 60
" " Comm. de Beatis Orient. et Hist. Eccl. Fragm., ed. W. J. van Douwen + J. P. N. Land 5/- 4° *Amsterdam* 89
JOSHUA ben ŠIRA Book of Wisdom
KAATZ, S. [ed. and tr.] Die Scholien d. Gregorius Abulfaragius Bar Hebraeus z. Josh. b. Sira 1m.25 8° Kauffmann, *Frankft.* 92
Edited fr. 4 MSS. of the *Horreum Mysteriorum*, w. German Introd., tr. and notes.

JULIANOS der Abtrünnige: Syrische Erzählungen, hrsg. J. G. E. Hoffmann 12fl. 4° Brill, *Leyden* 80
STEPHEN BAR SUDAILI: the Syrian mystic and the bk. of Hierotheos, ed. w. Eng. tr. A. L. Frothingham, *jun.* [Am.] 2fl.50 8° Brill, *Leyden* 86
THOMAS, Bp. of Margâ The Book of the Governors, ed. Dr. E. A. Wallis Budge, 2 vols. 40/- *nt.* 8° Paul 93
A learned ed. of the *Historia Monastica* of THOMAS fr. MSS. in Brit. Mus., Vatican and elsewhere. Vol. I. Syriac text in Nestorian character, Introd., Index of Proper Names, etc.; ii. Engl. tr. The Introd. deals w. the rise and progress of Xtn. monasticism and asceticism in Mesopotamia and neighbouring countries. The period covered by the *Hist.* is A.D. 580–850.

Folktales, etc. —*v.* B § 27* and B.B. B § 27.*

113. PHŒNICIAN AND CARTHAGINIAN PHILOLOGY AND INSCRIPTIONS.

Grammar.

Etymology: Dictionary.

BLOCK, A. Phönizisches Glossar 2m.50 8° Mayer & Müller, *Berl.* 91

Epigraphy.

Inscriptions.

*Corpus Inscriptionum Semiticarum, Pars i.: Inscripp. Phœnic., ed. E. Renan—*ut* K § 105.
An extremely important collection of Phœnician inscriptions.

EUTING, Prf. Julius Phönikische Inschrift v. Gebâl (Byblus): lithograph [1 leaf] f° Author, *Strassbg.* 76
" " Erläuterung einer zweiten Opferverordnung aus Carthago; 1 pl. [9 pp.] Trübner " 74
PELLEGRINI, Astorre Studii d'Epigrafia Fenicia—*extr. fr.* Atti dell' Acad. di Scienze, *etc.*, di Palermo 93.
A series of valuable notes on Phœnician epigraphy, and on the inscripp. pub. by RENAN in the *Corp. Inscr. Semit.* *ut supra*.

114. ARABIC PHILOLOGY: CLASSICAL AND MODERN.

Grammar.

EL KOURY EL CHARTOUNI Exercises sur la Grammaire Arabe, 2 vols. 12° *Beyrout* 90
FREUND, S. Die Zeitsätze im Arabischen [comparative] 3m. 8° Jacobsohn, *Breslau* 93
*GREEN, Maj. A. O. A Practical Arabic Grammar, pt. ii. c 8° 10/6 Clar. Press / $2.60 *nt.* Macmillan, *N.Y.* [ ] 93
VERNIER, D. [S.-J.] Grammaire Arabe 14fr. 8° Jesuit Coll., *Beyrout* 91

Algeria.

BELKASSEM BEN SEDIRA Cours pratique de Lange Arabe 12° *Algiers* [ ] 91
" " Dialogues Français-Arabes 32° " [ ] 89
MOULIÉRAS, Prf. Aug. Manuel Algérien [gram., chrestom., lexicon] 5fr. 12° Maisonneuve, *Paris* 88

Egypt.

SEIDEL, A. Prakt. Handbuch d. arab. Umgangspr. ägypt. Dialekts [w. vocab.] 10m. 8° Gergonne, *Berlin* 94
VOLLERS, Dr. Karl Lehrbuch d. ägypto-arab. Umgangssprache [w. exx. and vocab.] 7fr. s 8° Imprim. Cathol., *Beyrouth* 91

Morocco.

MEAKIN, J. E. B. An Introduction to the Arabic of Morocco 6/- f 8° Paul 91
SOCIN, A. Zum Arabischen Dialekt von Marokko 3m. 8° Hirzel, *Lpz.* 93

Etymology.

DE LAGARDE, Paul A. Register und Nachträge—*ut* K § 105.
GUIDI Alcune Osservazioni di Lessicografia Araba 8° *Vienna* 87

Dictionaries.

CAMERON, D. A. Arabic-English Vocabulary [Modern Egyptn. Arabic] 7/6 8° Quaritch 92
CARDAHI, Abbé P. G. [S.-J.] Dictionnaire Syrique-Arabe—*ut* B.B.K § 109.
GASSELIN, Ed. Dictionnaire Français-Arabe, pts. xli.–xlviii. [last] ea. 3fr. [compl., 2 vols. 150fr.] 4° Leroux, *Paris* 80–91
*LANE, E. W. Arabic-Engl. Lexicon, der. fr. Eastern sources, ed. S. Lane-Poole, pt. viii. [last] 25/- r 4° Williams 93
The completion of this important wk., vol. i. of wh. was issued in 1863. It is the only *English* Arab. dict. wh. is printed in artistic and beautiful Arab. type.
MARCEL, J. J. Dict. Frçs.-Arabe d. Dialectes vulg. d'Algér., Tunisie, Maroc. et Egyp. 6fr. 8° Maisonneuve, *Paris* [37] 85
STACE, Col. E. N. English-Arabic Vocabulary [colloquial Arabic] 7/6 8° Quaritch 93
Sammlung v. Wörterverzeichnisse als Vorarbeiten z. e. Wb. d. alt-arab. Poesie, vol. i.—*v.* K § 115 (Mu'allakât).
WORTABET, Prf. Arabic-English Dictionary 18/- p 8° Luzac [88] 93
A concise dict. of the more common words found in Arab. classical writers, intended for students' use.

Loan Words.

FRAENKEL, S. Die Aramäischen Fremdwörter im Arabischen [Prize Essay] 5fl.25 8° Brill, *Leyden* 86

K § 115

Epigraphy.

Corpus Inscriptionum Arabicarum : Part I.: Egypt, fasc. i.: Cairo 25*fr.* Leroux, *Paris* 94
*DOUGHTY, C. M. —*in his* Travels in Arabia Deserta, 2 vols. [1882-88—*ut* 𝔅.𝔅. 32].
*HOMMEL, Prf. F. [ed.] Südarabische Chrestomathie—*ut infra.*
*HUBER, Chas. —*in his* Journal d'un Voyage en Arabie : 1883–1884 4° Leroux, *Paris* 93

With many inscripp., Sabäan, Minæan, Proto-Arabic, Nabathæan (Aramaic mostly excl., because incl. in *Corp. Inscripp. Semit.*—*ut* K § 109). Of considerable epigraphic value.

MÜLLER, Dav. H. [ed.] Epigraphische Denkmäler aus Arabien ; 12 pl.[Denkschr. d.k. Akad. Vienna] 4° Akad., *Vienna* 89

Palæography. Manuscripts. Papyri.

Berlin, Königl. Bibl. : Verzeichniss d. arab. HSS., v. W. Ahlwardt, vols. ii.–v. 111*m.* r 4° Asher, *Berl.* 89–93
Bodleian Lib., Oxford : Arabic Papyri : collotype reprod., w. transcr. and tr. Prf. D. S. Margoliouth ; 2 facss. [50 copies] 5/- *nt.* f° Luzac 94
British Museum : Catalogue of the Arabic MSS. [*ut* 𝔅.𝔅. K § 114] : Supplement 42/- 4° British Museum 94
Gotha, Herzogl. Bibl. : Die arabischen Handschriften, v. W. Pertsch, vols. i.–v. 4° F. A. Perthes, *Gotha* ?–93
Katherine, Convent of St., Mt. Sinai : Catal. of MSS., ed. Marg. Dunlop Gibson 6/- *nt.* Camb. Press 94
MERX, Alb. [ed.] Documents de Paléographie hébraique et arabe—*ut* K § 117.
Specimens of 122 Various Handwritings : old and new Arab. MSS. reprod. in facs. [w. Key] 5/- 8° Paul [ ] 91

Prosody. Synonyms.

EL KHOURY EL CHARTOUNI Petit Manuel de Style épistolaire 12° *Beyrout* 89
LAMMENS, Père Synonymes Arabes [a good book] 12° ,, 87

Chrestomathies.

ALLAOUA [ed.] Recueil de Thèmes et Versions [tales, sayings, enigmas, *etc.*] 8° *Mostaganem* 90
BELKASSEM BEN SEDIRA [ed.] Cours de Littérature Arabe 12° *Algiers* 91
BRÜNNOW, Rud. E. [ed.] Arabische Prosa-Chrestomathie Reuther, *Berlin, in prep.*
[CHEÏKO, Père (ed.)] Chrestomathie Arabe : recueil d. morceaux d. anc. auteurs, 2 vols. 8° *Beyrouth* (15*fr.* Maisonn., *Paris*) 79–81
DELPHIN [ed.] Recueil de Textes p. l'Etude de l'Arabe parlé 12° *Paris* 91

A good colln. for a knowl. of the life and language of the Algerians, espec. of province of Oran.

DERENBOURG, H. [ed.] Anthologie de Textes arabes inédits 6*fr.* 8° *Paris* 93
,, ,, [ed.] Chrestomathie élém. d. l'Arabe Littéral [w. gloss. ; Bibl. Colon. d. Ling.] 7*fr.*50 18° Leroux, *Paris* 92
ESH-SHINGITI [ed.] Fuhúl esh-shi'r [a poetical chrestomathy] *Boulak, in prep.*
FAIZULLAH-BHAI [ed.] A Moslem Present : anthol. of Arab. poems, pt. i. 2/- 8° Williams 93

A coll. of Arab. poems ab. the Prophet and Faith of Islam, w. Engl. trs. and notes.

GREEN, Maj. A. O. [ed.] Collection of Modern Arabic Stories, Ballads, Poems and Proverbs 3/6 c 8° Clar. Press 92
HIRSCHFELD, Dr. Hartwig [ed.] Arabic Chrestomathy in Hebrew Characters ; w. gloss. 7/6 8° Paul 92

A good selection fr. the vast Jewish Arabic literature, little-known to students, but of considerable interest, intrinsically and for the linguistic peculiarities of its dialects.

*HOMMEL, Prf. F. [ed.] Südarabische Chrestomathie, pt. i. 16*m.*50 4° Lu Kaschik, *Munich* 93

A full and complete introd. to the inscripp. of Southern Arabia, the importance of wh. has recently been revealed by Dr. GLASER. This Part gives acc. of the Minæan and Sabæan texts, their alphabet and phonology, followed by a grammar of the 2 dialects, w. Appendices and exhaustive Bibliogr. [fr. NIEBUHR in 1774 to 1892], to wh. are added a sln. of the Minæan inscripp., w. notes and gloss. of words and proper names. Autographed, not printed.

HOUDAS, Prf. Oct. [ed.] Chrestomathie Maghrebine : recueil de textes arabes inédits ; w. vocabs. 6*fr.* 8° Leroux, *Paris* 91
MORITZ, B. [ed.] Sammlung arab. Schriftstücke aus Zanzibar u. Oman ; w. gloss. and 23 facss. 16*m.* 8° *Berlin* 92

Forms the 9th vol. of the *Lehrbücher des Seminars für Orientalische Sprachen in Berlin.*

MOULIÉRAS, Prf. Aug. [ed.] Nouvelle Chrestomathie Arabe, pt. i. 3*fr.*75 8° Heim, *Constantinople* 89
,, ,, [ed.] Cours gradué de Thèmes Français-Arabes 5*fr.* 8° Maisonneuve, *Paris* 90
NÖLDEKE, Th. [ed.] Delectus Veterum Carminum Arabicorum ; w. gloss. [Porta Ling. Orient.] 7*m.* 8° Reuther, *Berlin* 90
THORNTON, F. du Pré Elementary Arabic : Texts and Glossary 3/6 c 8° W. H. Allen 93

A useful little bk. for the Engl. student who wd. know something of book-lore as well as of the spoken lang. of the bazaar in mod. Egypt.

115. ARABIC LITERATURE.

Bibliography.

BASSET, Prf. René Rapport s. l. Etudes Berbères, Ethiop. et Arabes : 1887–1891—*ut* K § 116.
British Museum : Catalogue of the Arabic Books [by A. G. Ellis] 45/- 4° British Museum 94
CHAUVIN, Prf. Victor Bibliographie des Ouvrages Arabes, pt. i. 6*fr.* 8° Vaillant-Carmanne, *Liège* 92 *in prg.*

A contin. of the 2nd. edn. of the *Bibliotheca Arabica* [1799–1804] r1. of SCHNURRER (whose libr. was purchased by All Souls Coll., Oxon.), covering the yrs. 1810 to 1885, when the task is taken over by FRIEDERICI'S *Bibl. Orient.* [*ut* 𝔅.𝔅. K § 92] and MÜLLER'S *Orient. Bibliogr.* [*ut ib.*]. Limited to wks. pub. in Christian Europe. To occupy 15 to 20 vols., arrgd. acc. to subjects. Pt. i. conts. Preface (40 pp.), Alphab. Index of Names of Authors, etc., in SCHNURRER [whose arrgmt. was chronolog. only], (3) spec. of his own wk., dealing w. Proverbs.

Strassburg Univ. u. Landesbibl. : Catalog der arabischen Literatur [by Prf. Julius Euting] 7*m.*50 4° Trübner, *Strassbg.* 77

History of Literature—*v. also* A § 13.

BASSET, Prf. René —*in his* Mélanges d'Histoire et de Littérature Orientales, 2 pts. 8° *Louvain* ? ; 88
BROCKELMANN, C. Das Verhältniss v. Ibn al Athirs Kâmil z. Tabaris Ahbâr errusul wa'l mulûk 1*m.*80 8° Trübner, *Strassbg.* 90

Traces the relns. of IBN AL ATHIR to his model TABARI. The Arab. historians habitually reproduced each other : IBN AL ATHIR, TABARI ; ABULFEDA, IBN AL ATHIR ; IBN OUARDI, ABULFEDA ; and so on—the orig. pt. commencing where the predecessor left off.

v. KREMER, A., Freih. Ueb. das Budget d. Einnahmen unter d. Reigerg. d. Harûn al Raschid 8° Tempsky, *Vienna* 87
,, ,, Ueb. d. Einnahmebudget d. Abbasiden-Reiches v. Jahre 306 ; 3 pl. 5*m.*40 4° ,, ,, 87

Extr. fr. *Denkschriften d. Wiener Akademie.*

SALMONÉ, Prf. Muhammedan Dominion, Past and Present *in prep.*

Stated to contain a crit. study of the liter., hist., character and customs of the Arabic-speaking subjects of Turkey, and of the govt. and condn. of the country.

Geographers.

JACOB, G. Studien in arabischen Geographen, pt. i. 1*m.*50 ; ii. 1*m.*20 ; iii. 2*m.* ; iv. 1*m.*80 8° Mayer & Müller, *Berl.* 91 ; 92 ; 92 ; 93

Philosophers.

DE BOER, T. Widersprüche d. Philos. nach Al-Gazzali u. i. Ausgleich d. Ibn Rosa 5*m*.50 8° Trübner, *Strassb.* 94
MEHREN, Aug. Ferd. Averroès dans ses Rapports av. celle d'Avicenne et de Ghazzali 8° Brill, *Leyden* 88
" " Les Rapports de la Philosophie d'Avicenne avec l'Islam 1*fr*.50 8° " " 83
MUNK, S. Mélanges de Philosophie Juive et Arabe—*ut* K § 118.
WÜSTENFELD, F. Der Imâm el-Schâfi'î u. seine Anhänger, pt. i. 5*m*.; ii. ; iii. 7*m*. 4° Dieterich, *Gött.* 90; 91; 91

Poets.

FAIZULLAH BHAI Essay on Pre-Islamitic Arabic Poetry 8° Educ. Soc. Press, *Bombay* (Williams) 93
With spec. refer. to the poems known as the *Seven Suspended Poems*. Repr. fr. the Introd. to Cpt. F. E. JOHNSON'S tr. of the *Seven Poems*.

GUIDI Sui Poeti citati nell' Opera Khazânut el Adab 4° *Roma* 87
A useful suppl. to the large wk. of EL BAGHDADI, pupil of the celebrated EL KAFADJI, in 4 quarto vols.; w. excellent index.

JACOB, G. Studien in arabischen Dichtern, pt. i. 2*m*.80 8° Mayer & Müller, *Berl.* 93
This 1st Pt. is a criticism of Dr. L. ABEL'S new edn. of MU'ALLAQÂT (*ut infra*).

SALANI, P. Biographie des Poètes Arabes Chrétiens, pts. i.–iii. 8° *Beyrout* 90 *in prg.*
Every Arabic poet who has made any allusion to Xtianity., however slight, is regarded as "Christian"—a technical error, but one wh. greatly increases the scope and utility of the bk.

SCHWARTZ, P. 'Umar Ibn Abî Rebî'a: ein arabischer Dichter der Umajjadenzeit 2*m*.40 8° Harrassowitz, *Lpz.* 93

Biography.

ALFARADHI, Aben Historia Virorum doctorum Andalusiæ, ed. Fr. Codera, vol. i. [Bibl. Arab. Hispan.] 20/- 4° *Madrid* 91
In Arabic, fr. the Codex Tunicensis; w. indexes. Here edited for the first time, forming vol. vii. of the Bibliotheca Arabico-Hispana.

FISCHER, Dr. Aug. Biographien v. Gewährsmännern d. Ibn Ishâg, hptschl. aus Ad-Dahabi 5*m*. 8° Brill, *Leyden* 90
Edited from Berlin and Gotha MSS.

HAMADÂNI [poet] Lettres, ed. Ibrahim el Ahdab 8° *Beyrout* 90
IBN EL ABBAR Completum libri Assilah, 2 vols. [Bibl. Arabo-Hispanica] 8° *Madrid* 87; 89
Completes the *Silah* of IBN BACHKOUAL, a biogr. dict. of famous writers of Spain.

Encyclopædia.

HAJI KHALFA Lexicon Encyclopædicum et Bibliographicum, ed. w. Lat. tr. Gust. Flügel, 7 vols. *o.p.* [*w.* 95/-] 4° *Leipzig* 35-58
A standard work, containing much information about Arabic literature.

Fiction, Proverbs, etc.

AMÉLINEAU, Prf. E. [tr.] Contes et Légendes de l'Egypte chrétienne—*ut* 𝕭.𝕭. B § 27.
Many have been preserved only in an Arabic version, here tr. One of these, *Comment le Royaume de David passa aux Mains du Roi d'Abyssinie* is a résumé of some chaps. of the *Fetha Nagast*, the Ethiop. national romance.

Barlaam and Josaphat:
Hommell, Fritz Die älteste arabische Barlaam Version 8° *Vienna* 88
" " —*in his* Append. *to* N. Weisslovits' Prinz u. Derwisch—*ut* K § 126.
Kuhn, E. Baarlam und Joasaph: eine bibliograph.-literargesch. Studie—*v.* B § 3.
DIETERICI, Friedr. [ed.] Thier u. Mensch vor d. König der Genien, aus d. Schr. d. lauteren Brüder in Basra 4*m*.50 8° Hinrichs, *Lpz.* [ ] 81
GROFF, Florence [ed.] Contes Arabes extraits des MSS. de la Bibl. Nat.; map [autographed] 5*fr*. 8° Leroux, *Paris* 88
GRÜNBAUM, Dr. M. [ed.] Neue Beiträge zur semitischen Sagenkunde—*ut* B § 26.
A coll. of tales and myths attaching to the persons of the Old Test. patriarchs by Jewish and Arabic Haggadah, arrgd. under names fr. ADAM to DAVID and SOLOMON. Mainly of Jewish origin, tho' some of the Arabic traditions are genuinely old. Of interest to the philologist rather than the folklorist. Of no value to the historian or Biblical student.

Kalilah i Dimnah; Russian tr., ed. Attal; w. Introd. Riabnin 8° *Moscow* 89
DE LANDBERG, Carlo [ed. & tr.] Proverbes et Dictons du Peuple Arabe—*ut* 𝕭.𝕭. B § 27.*
Thousand and One Nights [Alif Lailat wa Lailat]:

Texts.

Groff, Florence [ed.] Zein el Asnam: conte d. M. e. U. N.; w. Arab. vocab. [fr. MSS. at Bibl. Nat.] 6*fr*. 8° Leroux, *Paris* 89
Salhani, P. A. [S.-J.; ed.] Alf Lailat wa Lailat, vols. iii.–v. ea. 6*fr*. p 8° Imprim. Cathol., *Beirut* 89-90

Translations.

Aldine Edn. fr. the text of Dr. J. Scott; tinted process ill. S. L. Wood, 4 vols. [*L.P.* (100)] 24/- f 8° Pickering 90
Lane, E. W. [tr.] Stories from the Arabian Nights: a selection, ed. S. Lane-Poole, 3 vols., ea. w. front. [Knickerbocker Nuggets] ea. $1 (2/6) 18° Putnam 91
Conts. a new tr. of the story of *Aladdin*, discov. by ZOTENBERG in the Paris MS., *ut* 𝕭.𝕭. K § 115. A good seln., w. interesting Intro.

Geography.

AL-BELÂDSORI Liber Expugnationis Regionum, ed. J. de Goeje 17*fl*. 4° Brill, *Leyden* 63-66
AL-HAMDÂNÎ Geographie d. Arab. Halbinsel, ed. D. H. Müller, 2 vols. 14*fl*.50 8° " " 84; 91
Edited for the first time: fr. MSS. at Berlin, Constantinople, London, Paris, and Strassburg. Vol. i. Arab. text; ii. Notes and Indexes.

Bibliotheca Geographorum Arabicorum, ed. J. de Goeje, pt. vi. 9*fl*.50, vii. 7*fl*.50; viii. 22*fl*. 8° Brill, *Leyden* 89; 92; 94
KHALIL ED-DAHIRY Description d. l'Egypte et d. l. Syrie, ed. M. Ravaisse [Ec. Langs. Or. Viv.] 12*fr*. 8° Bouillon, *Paris* 93
" " The same, tr. M. Ravaisse [Ec. Langs. Orient. Viv.] 8° " " *in prep.*

K § 115

Grammarians.

ABU BEKR IBNO 'L ANBARI Kitabo-l'-Adhdad, ed. Th. Houtsma 4*fl.*20 8° Brill, *Leyden* 81

A bk. of Arabic words wh. have more than one meaning. From Leyden MS.

ABU BEKR EZ ZOBAÏDI Il Kitâb al Istidrâk, ed. Guidi [suppl. to Sibawaihi] 4° *Rome* 90

ABU 'L-WALID MERWAN IBN DJANAH Livre d. Parterres Fleuris, ed. J. Derenbourg [Bibl. Ecole Ht. Etud.] 25*fr.* 8° Bouillon, *Paris* 86

" " " The same, tr. into French by Moïse Metzger [a Hebr. Gram. in Arabic] [Bibl. Ecole Ht. Etud.] 15*fr.* 8° " " 89

HARIRI Molhat el Irab [Grammatical Recreations]: trad. Léon Pinto, 3 pts. 12° Challamel, *Paris* 8-

IBN MÂLEK L'Alfiyyah, trad. A. Goguyer [followed by tr. of his Lamiyyat] 8° *Beyrout* 88

A minutely faithful tr. of the grammatical poem, almost as obscure as its original.

" " L'Alfiyyah, ed. Léon Pinto; w. Fch. tr. *en regard*, and notes; 2 pts. ea. 1*fr.*25 4° Poulet, *Constant.* 87

Liber as-Sojutii de Nominibus Relativis, ed. P. J. Veth, 3 vols. in 2 12*fl.*70; *red. to* 6*fl.* 4° Brill, *Leyden* 40-51

SIBAWAIHI [*d.* 787–809] Kitab Sibouya, ed. H. Derenbourg, vol. ii., pt. 2 12/- r 8° *Paris* 89

The text of a treatise on Arabic grammar, ed. fr. MSS. at Cairo, The Escorial, Oxford, Paris, St. Petersburg, and Vienna.

" Buch üb. d. Grammatik, tr. G. Jahn; w. notes, 14 pts. ea. 4*m.* 8° Reuther, *Berl.* 94 *in prg.*

Based on DERENBOURG'S edn. [*ut sup.*] and SIRAFI'S *Commentary*, w. extracts fr. other commentaries.

ZAINUD-DÎN IBN IL-WARDÎ Donum Wardianum, hrsg. R. Abicht 2*m.* 8° Preuss, *Breslau* 91

A didactic poem on Arabic grammar.

History —*v. also* A § 13.

ABD 'AL DJALILAL-TENESSY Complémt. d. l'hist. des Beni-Zeiyan, rois d. Tlemcen, ed. Abbé J. J. L. Bargès 12*fr.* 8° Leroux, *Paris* 87

ABD EL QÂDER Réglements Militaires, ed. Patorni, w. Fch. tr.; 2 pts. 8° *Algiers* 90

ABOU HANIFAH ED DINAWERI [*d.* 895] Kitab ab Ahbâr at tiwal, ed. Guirgass 8° Brill, *Leyden* 88

Editor died before completion of the work, wh. was effected by DE ROSEN.

AL-BERUNI [*b.* 971] Chronology of Ancient Nations, Engl. tr. Dr. C. E. Sachau; w. notes 42/- 1 8° 79

ALBOULQÂSEM BEN AHMED EZZIÂNI Le Maroc de 1631 à 1812, ed. Prof. Oct. Houdas; w. Fch. tr. [Bibl. Ec. Ht. Etud.] 15*fr.* 8° Leroux, *Paris* 86

AL-HARIRI [1084–1122] The Last Twenty-four Mukâmât ["Assemblies"], tr. Dr. Steingass 8° Orient. Transl. Fd., *in prep.*

The first 26 Assemblies were tr. Thos. Chenery in 1867 [*ut* B. K § 115]. For over seven centuries this wk. has been esteemed, next to the *Koran*, as the chief treasure in the Arabic lang. It consists of 50 oratorical, poetical, moral, encomiastic, and satirical discourses.

BAR HEBRÆUS ABOU'L FARADJ Tarikh Mokhtasar eddoual, ed. P. Salhani 8° *Beyrout* 90

BASSET, Prf. René [ed.] Documents Musulmans sur l. Sièges d'Alger en 1541 2*fr.*50 8° Leroux, *Paris* 90

ELDAD HAD-DÂNÎ: Die Recensionen u. Versionen d. Eldad had-Dânî, hrsg. Prf. Dan. H. Müller 4*m.*40 8° Tempsky, *Vienna* 92

Extr. fr. *Denkschr. d. Wien. Akad.* A crit. edn. of the diary of the so-called Eldad of the tribe of Dan, who pretended to have visited the Ten Tribes in 880 A.D. The diary (first prin. 1480, and several times reprin.) is fully investigated by GRAETZ'S in his *Hist. of the Jews*, vol. v. [*ut* F § 7], and espec. by A. EPSTEIN, of Vienna, who has pub. an edn. of the var. texts fd. in MSS., and a monograph on the subject.

EN-NESAWI Histoire du Sultan Djelal ed-din Mankobirti, ed. Prf. Oct. Houdas, vol. i. [Text]; ii. [tr. & notes; *in prep.*] [Ecol. Langs. Orient. Viv.] 15*fr.* 8° Leroux, *Paris* 91

ESSEGHIR BEN ELHADJ (EL OUFRANI) Nozet-Elhâdj: Hist. de la Dynastie Saadienne au Maroc: 1511–1670, ed. Prf. Oct. Houdas [Ecole d. Lang. Orient. Viv.] 15*fr.* 8° Leroux, *Paris* 88

" " The same, trad. Prf. Oct. Houdas [Ecole d. Lang. Orient. Viv.] 15*fr.* 8° " " 89

IBN EL QOUTYA [10 cent.] Hist. d. l. Conquète de l'Andalousie, ed. Prf. Oct. Houdas; w. Fch. tr.; 2 v. 8° " " 89

Imâd Ed-din El-Katib El-Isfahani. Conquête d. l. Syrie et Palest., ed. Ct. C. de Landberg, v. i. [text] 15/- *Leyden* 88

IBN-KHALDOUN Prolégomènes Historiques, ed. Quatremère, 3 vols. in 4 35*fr.* 4° Maisonneuve, *Paris* 58

MAÇOUDI [9–10 cent.] Prairies d'Or, ed. et trad. C. Barbier de Meynard + Pavet de Courteille, 9 vols. [Soc. Asiatique] ea. 7*fr.*50 8° Impr. Impér., *Paris* 62–78

A universal hist. and geograph. description of the then-known globe, as well as a hist. of the Arabs fr. estab. of Caliphate to A.D. 944.

'Omârah Al-Hakami Yaman: its early mediæval history, ed. Hy. C. Kay; w. tr. and notes 17/6 *nt.* 8° India Off. (Arnold) 92

Ed. fr. MSS. in Brit. Mus. (apparently *c.* 700 yrs. old), acquired in 1886, a work long believed to be hopelessly lost. It covers a period of *c.* 350 yrs., fr. beg. 9 cent. to nearly end 12 cent., and is the sole orig. authority for the hist. of its period, fr. wh. later writers have largely borrowed. It conts. many curious pictures of life and manners among the sedentary inhabitants of Arabia, and is of considerable value.

NÖLDEKE, Theod. Die Ghassânischen Fürsten aus d. Hause Gafnas [*extr. fr.* Abhgn. Berl. Ak.] 4*m.* 4° G. Reimer, *Berl.* 87

OUSAMA BEN MONQUIDZ: Livre des Exemples, ed. Prf. Hartwig Derenbourg, vols. i.–ii. [Ec. Langs. Orient.] 30*fr.* 8° Leroux, *Paris* 85; 89

Vol. i. conts. chaps. 1–5 of a Life of OUSAMA (bas. on his autob., discov. by DERENBOURG in Escorial Lib.); ii. conts. the text (fr. author's orig. MS. in Escorial). A valuable contrib. to hist. of Crusades: 1095–1188.

de Landberg, Cte. Ousama ben Monqidz—*in his* Critica Arabica, pt. ii. 8° Brill, *Leyden* 88

PEISER, F. E. [ed.] Der Gesandtschaftsbericht d. Hasan ben Ahmed el-Haimî 5*m.* r 8° Peiser, *Berlin* 94

SALAH ED-DIN Imâd ed-din el Katib-el-Isfahâni, ed. Cte. de Landberg, v. i. [Text] 19*fr.* 8° Brill, *Leyden* 88

On the conquest of Syria and Palestine: important for history of the Crusades.

SHIHÂB AD-DIN Conquest of Abyssinia, ed. S. Arth. Strong *in prep.*

Based on the unique MS. in Brit. Mus., and NERAZZINI'S detailed analysis of the wk. [pub. *sub tit.* "*La Conquista Musul. dell' Ethiopia nel secolo xvi.*," *Rome* '91.]

STIFÂN ED DOUAIHI EL DUHDOUNI [*d.* 1704] Histoire des Maronites, ed. Rachid el Khouri 8° *Beyrout* 91

TABARI Annales, ed. J. Barth + Nöldeke + Goeje + Loth, *etc.*, Ser. I., vii. (1) 7/-; III., viii. 7/6 8° Brill, *Leyden* 90; 91

Law.

ABD EL QÂDER, Moham. Der überfliess. Strom i. d. Wissensch. d. Hanefiten u. Schafaiten, übers. Hirsch 8° *Leipzig* 91

ABU ISLÂK AS-SHÎRÂZÎ At Tanbîh, ed. A. W. T. Juynboll [fr. Leyden and Oxford MSS.] 5*fl.*25 8° Brill, *Leyden*

ECH CHENCHOURI Traité d. Successions Musulm. (Ab Intestat), ed. Zeys, trad. Luciani [*extr. fr. his* Comm. d. l. Rahbia] 10*fr.* 8° *Paris* 91

IBN ACEM Toh-fah: Traité de Droit Musulman, ed. Prf. Oct. Houdas + F. Martel; w. Fch. tr. and notes, 8 pts. ea. 2*fr.*50 8° Gavault St. Lager, *Algiers* 82–93

MINHÂDJ AT-TÂLIBÎN Guide des zelés croyants, ed. L. W. C. van den Berg, 3 vols. 42/- r 8° *Batavia* 82–84

A manual of jurisprudence, acc. to the rite of Châfi'î. With French tr. and notes.

Philosophy and Religion—*v. also* A § 13.

ABÛ ALÎ AL-HOSAIN B. ABDULLA = AVICENNA, *infra*.
AL-FÂRÂBI — Philosophische Abhandlungen, übers. F. Dieterici — 5*m.* 8° — 92
AL-FAYYOÛMÎ, Josef [tr.] Version arabe du Pentateuque, ed. J. Derenbourg, vol. i. — 10*fr.* 8° *Paris* — 93
AVICENNA [980 *or* 78–1036 *or* 7] Kitâbu 'l-ishârât wa 't-tanbîhât, ed. Prf. J. Forget, pt. i. — 6*fl.*50 8° Brill, *Leyden* — 92
An excellent critical edn. of the text of AVICENNA'S "Book of Theorems," of capital importance for the study of Moham. logic and metaphysic; based on 9 MSS. at Berl., Leyden, and Oxford, the oldest (Leyden; imperfect) dating fr. A.H. 408 (=A.D. 1017–18), 20 yrs. before AVICENNA'S death. French tr. to follow.
" Traités Mystiques: Arab. text, w. Fch. comm. A. F. Mehren, pt. i. 1*fl.*75; ii. 2*fl.*; iii. 3*fl.* f° Brill, *Leyden* 89; 93; 94
Koran:

Chrestomathy.
Nallino, C. A. [ed.] Chrestomathia Qorani Arabica — 4*m.*50 8° Gerhard, *Lps.* — 92

Commentary.
Fell, Dr. Winand — Indices ad Beidhawii Commentarium in Coranum [*ut* 𝕭.𝕸. K § 115] 10*m.* r 4° Vogel, *Lps.* — 78
Margoliouth, Prf. D. S. [tr.] Chrestomathia Baidawiana: comm. of El-Baidawi on Sura iii.: tr., w. notes 12/6 *nt.* p 8° Luzac — 94
MAIMONIDES, Moses [1131–1204] Guide to the Perplexed: Arabic orig. text, w. Fch. tr. & notes S. Munk, 3 vols. *o.p.* 8° *Paris* — 55–66
The tr. was also issued separ., *sub tit.* "*Le Guide des Egarés.*" For Engl. tr. v. 𝕭.𝕸. K § 118 (should be K § 115).
" " Commentar z. Tractat Berachoth: Arab. text and Hebr. tr., ed. E. Weile 2*m.* 8° Mayer & Müller, *Berl.* 91
" " Commentar. z. Tractat Kitajim: Arab. text, ed. S. Bamberger 2*m.*50 8° Kauffmann, *Frankft.* 91
" " Commentar z. Tractat Peah: Arab. text, ed. D. Herzog 2*m.*20 8° Calvary, *Berl.* 94
" " Commentar d. Michnah: Seder Tohoroth, ed. J. Derenbourg; w. Hebr. tr.; 2 vols. 8° *Berlin* 87
" " Kiddusch Hachodesch: übers. u. erläut. Ed. Mahler 2*m.*50 8° Lippe, *Vienna* 89
MUCHIR B. ABBA MARI [12 cent.] The Yalkut on Isaiah, ed. J. Spira; w. notes 10/6 8° Luzac — 94
New Test.: Arabic Version of St. Paul's Epistles, ed. Marg. Dunlop Gibson [Studia Sinait.] 5/- *nt.* Camb. Press — 94
Arab. vers. of Epp. to Romans, Corinth., Gal., and pt. of Ephes., ed. fr. 9 cent. MS. in Convent of St. Katherine on Mt. Sinai.
" : Gospels
Ciasca, A. — Evangeliorum Harmonicae Arabicae — 4° *Rome* — 88
Guidi — Le Traduzione degli Evangelii in Arabo e in Etiopico — 4° " — 88
Tatian [latter hf. 2 cent.] Diatattaron—*ut* A § 55.
Oiseau: traité mystique, ed. Aug. Ferd. Mehren — 8° Brill, *Leyden* — 87
Old Test., Daniel: Commentary on, by Jephet Ibn Ali, ed. and tr. Prf. D. S. Margoliouth—*ut* A § 30.
" " Job: Arabic Translation by Rabbi Sadia Gaon, w. comm. Cohn — 4° *Altona* — 89
Pakhôme, St., Histoire de, et de ses Communautés, ed. Prf. E. Amelineau: w. Fch. tr. [Ann. Mus. Guimet] 60*fr.* 4° Leroux, *Paris* — 89
The first title is *Monuments pour servir à l'hist. de l'Egypte chrét. au 4e. siècle.* S. PAKHÔME was virtually the founder and organizer of monastic life in Egypt, and the creator of the band of monks wh. played so important (often so disgraceful) a part in the evangeliz. of Egypt—in whose persecutions at first the Xtns. and afterw. the orthodox were the victims.
SADIA GAON — Œuvres, ed. Prf. Jos. Derenbourg, 12 vols.; w. Fch. trs. [Millenary Edn.] ea. 10*fr.* 8° Leroux, *Paris* 94 *in prg.*

- i. *Le Pentateuch* ... 10*fr.* 94
- ii. *Fragmt. d. Comm. Arab. s. l. Pentat.* ... *in prep.*
- iii. *Isaie* ... "
- iv. *Les Psaumes* ... "
- v. *Job* ... *in prep.*
- vi. *Les Proverbes* ... 10*fr.* 94
- vii. *Daniel* ... *in prep.*
- viii. *Œuvres Philosophiques* ... "
- ix. *Traité des Héritages* ... "
- x. *Siddour: ou Rituel* ... *in prep.*
- xi. *Mémoire de Saadia* ... "
- xii *Glossaire d. l. Langue d. Saadia* ... "

" " Commentaire sur la Sefer Yesira, ed. Mayer-Lambert; w. Fch. tr. — 8° *Paris* — 93
SAADIA BEN JOSEF AL-FAYYOÛMÎ Œuvres, ed. J. Derenbourg, v. i. [Arab. vers. of Pentateuch] 10*fr.* 8° Leroux, *Paris* — 91

Poetry.

ABUL ALA EL MA'ARRI.
v. Kremer, A., Freih. — Ueber die philosophischen Gedichte d. Abul Ala Ma'arri [extr.] 1*m.*60 8° Tempsky, *Vienna* 88
ABÛ-L-HASAN JEHUDA HALEWI Buch Al-Chazari, ed. Hartwig Hirschfeld, 2 pts. — 8° Schulze, *Lps.* ?; 88
Arabic text and the Hebrew tr. of JEHUDA IBN TIBBON.
" " Divan: Auswahl, übers. Gust Karpeles — 3*m.*50 8° *Berlin* — 93
ABÛ MIHGÂN — Carmina, ed. Ludwig Abel; w. Latin tr. and notes — 1*fl.*20 8° Brill, *Leyden* — 87
ABU OBEYD [10 or 11 cent.] The Celebrated Romance of the Stealing of the Mare, tr. Lady Anne + W. S. Blunt — 5/- *nt* sq p 8° Reeves & Turner — 93
L.P. (100) 10/6 *nt.* A charming spec. of Arabic mediæval poetry, redolent of Arab life and sentiment, said to have been known in Egypt over 800 yrs. ago. Tr. fr. Arab. Lady Anne BLUNT, and done into verse W. S. BLUNT.
AKHTAL — Diwân, ed. P. Salhani, pt. i. — 8° *Beyrout* — 91
AL HANSA [TOMADHIR; poetess] Anis el Djolasa, ed. Père Cheikho — 12° " — 88
" " Diwan, trad. Père de Coppier ["Sappho Arabe"] 12° " — 88
AL-HARIRI [1084–1122] —*v. supra, s.v.* History.
'AUS AL-HUTEJ'A — Diwân des Garwal b. Aus Al-Hutej'a, ed. Ignaz Goldziher [*extr. fr.* Zts. Deut. ML. Ges.] 6*m.* 8° Brockhaus, *Lps.* — 93
'AUS IBN HAJAR — Gedichte und Fragmente, ed. R. Geyer — 3*m.* 8° Friedrich, *Lps.* — 92
CHEIKHO, Père [ed.] —edn. of the Christian poets of Arabia, 6 pts. — 8--93
HAMADÂNI — Les Séances: Paraphrase by Cheikh 'Abdo — 8° *Beyrout* — 89
A mixture of a paraphrase and commentary on HAMADÂNI, the model of HARIRI.
IBN ZAIDUNI [*d.* 1070–71] Epistola ad Ibn Dschahwarum, ed. Besthorn [in verse]—*in his* Vita, *ut infra.*
Besthorn — Ibn Zaiduni Vita — 8° *Copenhagen* — 89
A good life of the vizier, followed by his Letter, written after his disgrace, to ABUL WALID, w. crit. appar. and copious comm.
JOHNSON, Cpt. F. E. [tr.] The Seven Poems suspended in the Temple at Mecca; w. Introd. Shaikh Taizullabhai 7/6 *nt.* 8° Luzac — 94
*Kitâb al Aghani: vols. i.–xx.; vol. xxi. ed. Rud. E. Brünnow, pt. 1 [Text] 12/- 8° *Bulâq*?; Brill, *Leyd.* 88
The most important *corpus* of Arab. poetry (pre-Islamitic and early post-Islam.) we have.
Salhani, P. A. [ed.] Choix d. Narrations tirées du Kitab al Aghâni, 2 vols. — 8° *Beyrout* — 88

DE LANDBERG, Ct. Carlo [ed.] Primeurs Arabes, fasc. i.–ii. 9fr. 16° Brill, *Leyden* 86 ; 89

Pt. i. contn. edn. of ABU MINGÂN, w. comm.: ii. ZOHAIR, w. comm. of ABUL HADDJÂDJ YOUSOF BEN CHANTAMARI [EL 'ALAM].

*LEBID [= LABÎD] Diwan, ed. Prf. Al-Khâlidî *Vienna* 80
„ „ Gedichte, ed. Dr. A. Huber, hrsg. Carl Brockelmann Brill, *Leyden* 92

Consists of a (1) prose tr. of AL-KHALIDI'S text (10 poems), (2) a text, (3) a tr. of the rest of the poets *Dîwan* bas. on 2 MSS. of modern date (at Leyden and Strassbg.), (4) a coll., w. tr., of all fragm. attrib. to LABID. An admir. piece of wk. on one of the best of the old classical poets of Arabia.

v. Kremer, Bar. Alf. Ueber die Gedichte d. Labyd—*in* Sitzungsber. d. Wiener Akad., 1881.
MU'ALLAKÂT Die Sieben Mu'allakât, hrsg. Dr. L. Abel; w. Germ. and Arab. comm., & vocab. 18m. 8° Spemann, *Berl.* 91

Forms vol. i. of the *Wörterverzeichnisse als Vorarbeiten z. e. Wb. d. alt. arab. Poesie.* For criticism of it v. JACOB, *ut supra.*

SIDI AHMED BEN YOUSOF Dictons Satiriques, ed. Prf. René Basset 3fr.50 8° Leroux, *Paris* 90

Folk Songs.

BOURIANT, U. [ed.] Chansons Populaires Arabes en dial. d. Caire 10fr. 8° Leroux, *Paris*

Forms vol. i. of the 8vo series of *Mémoires* d. l. Mission Archéol. Fçse. au Caire.

Rhetoric.

ARISTOTLE Rhetoric: Arabic tr., ed. Prf. D. S. Margoliouth; w. notes—*ut* K § 194.
'OBEID ALLAH MOHAMMED BEN 'IMRÂN L'Arte Poetica, ed. Schiaparelli 8° Brill, *Leyden* 90

Science.

NASSIRUDDIN EL-TOUSSY Traité du Quadrilatère, trad. Al Pacha Caratheodory 12m. 8° Harrassowitz, *Lps.* 92

116. ETHIOPIC PHILOLOGY AND LITERATURE (GEEZ, AMHARIC, TIGRÊ, TIGRIÑA).

Ethiopic (GEEZ).

Bibliography.

BASSET, Prf. René Rapport s. l. Etudes Berbères, Ethiop. et Arabes: 1887–91 [41 pp.] 3/6 r 8° Orient. Inst., *Woking* 92
FUMAGALLI, Gius. Bibliografia Etiopica: catal. degli scritti dalla Invenz. d. Stampa il 1891 12l. 8° Hoepli, *Milan* 92
GOLDSCHMIDT, L. Bibliotheca Æthiopica 6m. 8° Pfeiffer, *Lps.* 93

Grammar. Phrases.

DILLMANN, Aug. Bemerkungen z. Gramm. der Geez u. z. alt. Gesch. Abessiniens 8° *Berlin* 90
PIANO [ed.] Raccolta delle Frasi piu usuali [for use of the Ital. expedn.] 18° *Rome* 87
PRAETORIUS, F. Beiträge zur äthiopischen Grammatik u. Etymologie 8° *Leipzig* 88

Chrestomathy.

BACHMANN, J. [ed.] Æthiopische Lesestücke: inedita æthiopica [for students' use] 3m. 8° Hinrichs, *Lps.* 93

Epigraphy.

GALLINA Iscrizioni ethiopiche ed arabe in S. Stefano dei Mori 8° *Rome* 88

Literature.

Amda-Sion [King] Histoire des Guerres d'Amda Syon, ed. J. Perruchon; w. Fch. tr. [an import. text] 8° Leroux, *Paris* 90
„ „ Kriegsthaten gegen d. Muslim, übers. Aug. Dillmann 4° G. Reimer, *Berl.* 80
„ „ Victorias de Amda-Sion, ed. Pereira + Perruchon; w. Fch. tr. and notes 8° *Lisbon* 91
Apocryphal Scriptures —*v.* A § 19 *and* B.B. A § 19.
BASSET, Prf. René [ed.] Deux Lettres Ethiopiennes du 16e. Siècle 8° *Rome* 89

Letters fr. SAGA ZAAB to the Negouch LEBNA-DENGEL, and of Negouch GALÂOUDÊOUOS, attesting to the services of CATANHOSO.

Bible: Æthiopic Translation.
Bachmann, J. [ed.] Dodekapropheten Æthiopum, pt. i ; ii. [Malachi] 20m. 8° Niemeyer, *Halle* ; 93
„ „ [ed.] Die Klagelieder Jeremiæ in der Æthiop. Bibelübersetzung 2m.40 8° „ „ 93
„ „ [ed.] Der Prophet Jesaia nach d. Æth. Bibelübersetzung, pt. i. [text] 20m. 8° Felber, *Berlin* 94
GUIDI [ed.] Le Canzoni Gheez-Amariña [from Paris and Oxford MSS.] 4° *Rome* 89

Relate to the wars against the hereditary enemy, the Musulmans.

Lalibala, Vie de, Roi d'Ethiope, ed. J. Perruchon; w. Fch. tr. [Ecole de Lettres d'Alger] 10fr. 8° Leroux, *Paris* 92

Edited fr. Brit. Mus. MS., w. a *résumé* of the hist. of the Zagûés and descrn. of the Monolithic churches of Lalibala.

New Test.: Æthiopic Translation.
Guidi Le Traduzioni degli Evangelii in Arabo e in Etiopico—*ut* K § 115.
SECUNDUS [Neo-Pythag.] Philosophy: Æthiopic version, autograph. ed. Joh. Bachmann 9m. 8° Mayer & Müller, *Berl.* 88
„ „ „ Latin tr. Joh. Bachmann 1m.20 8° „ „ „ 87
Bachmann, Joh. Das Leben u. d. Sentenzen d. Secundus d. Schweigsamen [diss. inaug.] nn. 8° *Halle* 87
Weddâsê Mârjâm: ein äthiop. Lobgesang an Maria, hrsg. u. übers. R. Fries 3m. 8° Fock, *Lps.* 92
Zar'a Yâ'eqôb et Ba'eda Mâryân, rois d'Eth. 1434–78; ed. J. Perruchon; w. Fch. tr. 13fr. 8° Bouillon, *Paris* 93

Amharic (Abyssinia).

Grammar.

GUIDI — Grammatica elementare della Lingua Amariña — 8° *Rome* 89

MONDON-VIDAILHET, C. — Manuel Pratique de Langue Abyssine — 8/*fr.* 8° 92

Epigraphy.

MÜLLER, Prf. Dan. H. [ed.] Epigraphische Denkmäler aus Abessinien; 4 pl. and 1 table — 5*m.* r 4° Tempsky, *Vienna* 94

Fr. rubbings taken by J. Theod. BENT, to whose *Sacr. City of Ethiopns.* (*ut* E § 44) MÜLLER has contrib. a chap. on the inscripp. Exc. fr. *Denkschr. Wien. Akad.*

Etymology: Plant-names.

SCHWEINFURTH, Dr. G. — Abyssinische Pflanzennamen: alphab. Aufzählg. v. Namen — 6*m.* 4° G. Reimer, *Berlin* 93

Literature.

GUIDI [ed.] — Documenti Amariña — 4° *Rome* 91

Letters of the Negousch YOHANNES, of TAKLA HAIMÂNOT, King of Gojjam and of Menilik.

Tigré and Tigriña [Modern Ethiopic].

New Test., Gosp. of St. Mark: Evang. enligt Markus pä Tigre-Spräkel — *M'Kullo* 89

NÖLDEKE, Theod. [ed.] Tigre-Texte—*in* Wiener Ztschr. f. Kunde d. Morgenlandes, 1890.

SCHREIBER, J. — Manuel de la Langue Tigraï, pt. ii. [texts and vocab.] 8*m.* 8° Hölder, *Vienna* 93

117. HEBREW AND SAMARITAN PHILOLOGY.

Bibliography.

MONTET, Prf. E. — Aperçu d. Progrès depuis 1886 d. l'Hébraïque et Araméenne [18 pp.] 2/6 r 8° Orient. Inst., *Woking* 93

History of the Language.

BACHER, W. — Die hebräische Sprachwissenschaft von 10ten. bis zum 16ten. Jahrhundert 2*m.* 25 8° 92

EDKINS, Dr. Jos. — The Evolution of the Hebrew Language — 5/- 8° Trübner (Paul) 89

POZNANSKI, Sam. [ed.] Beiträge zur Geschichte der hebr. Sprachwissenschaft, pt. i. — 2*m.* 20 8° Calvary, *Berlin* 94

The 1st Pt. is an edn. of *Eine hebräische Grammatik aus d. xiii. Jahrhundert*; w. introd. and notes.

Grammar.

Accidence: Noun.

DE LAGARDE, Paul — Register und Nachträge—*ut* K § 105, *s.v.* Noun.

Prepositions.

[illegible]ERWECK, N. — Die hebräische Präposition *min* — 3*m.* 8° Faber, *Lps.* 93

Syntax.

H[illegible]MANN, H. — Beiträge zur Syntax der hebräischen Sprache — 2*m.* 92

H[illegible]ER, S. — Syntax der Zahlwörter in Alten Testament — 4*m.* 50 8° Möller, *Lund* 93

Etymology.

BARTH, J. — Etymologische Studien z. semit. insbesondere z. hebr. Lexicon — 4*m.* 50 8° Hinrichs, *Lps.* 93

Dictionaries.

CASSEL, D. — Hebräisch-Deutsches Wörterbuch — 4*m.* r 8° *Breslau* [ ] 91

A good short dictionary; w. a brief grammar.

FÜRST, Dr. Julius — Glossarium Græco-Hebraicum, pts. i.-iv. — 7*m.* m 8° Trübner, *Strassbg.* 90-91

A monum. of Jewish learning, w. abundant refs. to the ancient *Midrashim* and to mod. commentators.

*GESENIUS, W. — Hebr. u. Aram. Handwb. zum A.T., bearb. F. Mühlau + W. Volck — 15*m.* r 8° Vogel, *Lps.* [ ] 90

For the edn. of his great thesaurus by Prf. Fcs. BROWN, *etc.*, *v.* A § 22.

*SIEGFRIED + STADE, Prf. Carl / Prf. Bernh. Hebräisches Wörterbuch zum Alten Testamente — 20*m.* 8° Veit, *Lps.* 92

A compact and scholarly wk.; alphab. arrgd., w. a large no. of references. An excellent student's dictionary. With 2 Appendices (1) lex. to Aram. passages in O.T., (2) Germ.-Engl. vocab.

Dictionaries to Talmud, Targums, and Midrash—v. K § 118.

Synonyms.

LEVIN, S. — Versuch einer hebräischen Synonymik, pt. i. [Intrans. Verbs of Motion] 1*m.* 20 8° Calvary, *Berlin* 94

Palæography.

Alphabet.

EUTING, Dr. Julius — The Hebrew Alphabet—extr. fr. Palæograph. Soc., Orien. Ser., pt. vii.; 1 pl. f° Palæontograph. Soc. 82

" " — Tabula Scripturæ Hebraicæ delineata — Author, *Strassbg.* 82

MERX, Adalbert [ed.] Documents de Paléographie hébraïque et arabe; 7 pl. — 18*m.* 4° Brill, *Leyden* 94

K § 118

Phonology: *Accentuation.*

ACKERMANN, A. — Die hermeneut. Elemente d. bibl. Accentuation — 2m.50 — 8° Calvary, *Berlin* 93

BÜCHLER, Dr. Adolf — Untersuchn. zur Entstehung u. Entwickg. d. hebr. Accente, pt. i. — 3m.60 — 8° Freytag, *Lpz.* 92

The 1st pt. of a ser. of crit. researches on orig. and devel. of the Hebr. accents, dealing w. orig. of the vertical lines in accentuatn. and their true Massoretic significance. Accurate and learned.

DAVIS, Arth. — The Hebrew Accents of the 21 Bks. of the Bible—*ut* A § 22.

Gives the anc. Massoretic rules of the Hebr. accents in the Engl. lang.

Metrics.

BICKELL, Gust. — —*in his* Carmina Vet. Test. metrice — 6m.40 — 8° Wagner, *Innsbruck* 82

Conts. critical notes and a dissertation on Hebrew metrics.

" " — Metrices biblicæ regulæ exemplis illustratæ, and Suppl. — 1m.60 — 8° Wagner, *Innsbruck* 79; 79

GIETMANN, P. G. — De re metrica Hebræorum — 2m.40 — 8° Herder, *Freiburg* 80

HARTMANN, Mart. — Die hebräische Verskunst nach d. Werken jüdischen Metriker — 2m.50 — 8° Calvary, *Berlin* 94

LEY, J. — Grundzüge d. Rhythmus, d. Vers- u. Strophenbaues in d. Hebr. Poesie — 9m. — 8° Waisenhaus, *Halle* 75

Abbreviations.

LEDERER, Ph. [ed.] — Hebräische u. chaldäische Abbreviaturen gesammelt u. erläutert — 1m. — 8° — 94

Chrestomathy —*v.* K § 118, *s.v.* Hist. of Literature (WINTER + WÜNSCHE).

Serials.

Central-Anzeiger für jüdische Litteratur, ed. Dr. N. Brüll — [bi-monthly] *ann.* 8m. — 8° Office, *Frankfort* 90 *sqq.*, *in prg.*

Jahrbücher für jüdische Geschichte und Litteratur, ed. Dr. N. Brüll — *ann.* 7m. — 8° Reitz, *Frankft.* 80 *sqq.*, *in prg.*

Revue des Etudes Juives — *Paris* *in prg.*

118. HEBREW AND SAMARITAN LITERATURE.

Bibliography.

British Museum: Catalogue of Hebrew Bks. acquired since 1867 — [by van Straalen] 60/- — 4° British Museum 94

A supplement to ZEDNER'S Catalogue, *ut* 𝔅.𝔐. K § 118.

" " Descriptive List of the Hebrew and Samaritan MSS. [by Rev. G. Margoliouth] 6/- — 8° British Museum 94

About 1,300 MSS., arrgd. acc. to subjects, Bibl. MSS., Midrashim, Talmud and Halakhah, Liturgies, Kabbalah, Philosophy, Poetry, Philology, Mathem. and Astron. Medicine, Miscell. MSS., Charters. A detailed catal. to follow.

Corporation of City of Lond.: Catalogue of Hebraica and Judaica. By Dr. A. Löwe — 8° Libr. Committee 91

A very useful catalogue, well arrgd., w. Subjects Index and many cross-refs. Hebr. titles followed by concise Engl. explanations.

KAYSERLING, Dr. M. — Biblioteca Española-Portugueza-Judaica — 6m. — m 8° Trübner, *Strassbg.* 90

A bibl. dict. of Jewish authors, their wks. in Span. and Portug., and wks. on and against the Jews and Judaism. Conts. also a coll. of Span. proverbs quoted mostly fr. collections past and pres. in Amsterdam, and a list of periodicals in Spanish (printed in Rom. and Hebr. characters). Authors and Titles Indexes.

MENDELSSOHN — Bibliotheca Hebraica — [cont. by Zeitlin, *ut infra*]

MICHAEL, H. J. — Or Ha-Chajim: Bibliog. W'b. d. rabbin. Schriftthums [posthum. ed. hisson; in Hebr.] 6m. — 8° *Frankft.* 91

*ZEITLIN, W. — Bibliotheca Hebraica post-Mendelssohniana, pt. i. [A.-M.] — 7m.50 — 8° Köhler, *Lpz.* [ ] 91

A bibliography of modern-Hebrew literature since the beg. of Mendelssohn to the year 1890; alphab. arrgd., w. index of Hebr. titles.

History of Literature —*v. also* A § 12, *s.v.* Judaism.

BRANN, M. — Geschichte der Juden u. ihrer Litteratur, pt. i. — 2m. — 8° 93 *in prg.*

RENAN, Prf. Ern. — Les Ecrivains juifs frç. du 14 siècle — 4° Impr. Nat., *Paris* 94

Extr. fr. *Hist. littér. d. l. France*, vol. xxxi.

STEINSCHNEIDER, M. — Die hebr. Uebersetzungen d. Mittelalt. u. d. Juden als Dolmetscher 30m. — 8° Bibliog. Bureau, *Berl.* 93

WINTER + WÜNSCHE, Dr. J. / Prf. A. [eds.] Die jüdische Litteratur seit Abschluss d. Kanons, vol. i. — 11m. — 8° Mayer, *Trier* 94

A prose and verse anthology, w. biograph. and liter. Intros. This vol. deals w. Jewish-Hellen. and Talmudic liter.

Philosophy.

*MUNK, Salomon [tr.] — Mélanges de Philosophie Juive et Arabe, 2 pts. — *o.p.* [*pb.* 15*fr.*; *w.* 20/-] — 8° Franck, *Paris* 57; 59

Extracts ill. the life of Avicebron, w. notes and memoir, and a histor. essay on Arab and Jewish philosophy, esp. in Spain.

Poetry.

SULZBACH, A. — Die relig. u. weltl. Poesie d. Juden v. 7 bis 16 Jahrh. — 3m.75 — 8° Mayer, *Trier* 93

Texts and Translations.

Modern Collections and Series.

Auswahl hebräischer Classiker, pts. i.-ii. — [in Hebrew] 3m.20 — 8° Lippe, *Vienna* 88; 89 *in prg.*

i: ABÛ-L HASAN JEHUDA HALEWI *Sämmtl. Gedichte*, hrsg. Sam. PHILIPP, pt. i. sm.; ii. Hai GAON, *Sämmtl. Gedichte*, hrsg. Sam. PHILIPP, sm.m.

Bibliotheca Samaritana: hrsg. Dr. Heidenheim — *in prg.*

HALÉVY, J. [ed.] — Recueil de Compositions hébraiques en Prose et en Vers — 10*fr.* — 8° Leroux, *Paris* 94

NEUBAUER, Dr. — Mediæval Jewish Chronicles and Chronological Notes [Anecd. Oxon.]—*ut* 𝔅.𝔅. F § 7.

WRESCHNER, Dr. Leop. — Samaritanische Traditionen — 3m. — 8° Mayer & Müller, *Berl.* 88

An important monograph, by a new recruit for Samar. liter., on a Berlin Arabico-Samar. MS. comm. on Pentateuch, w. Germ. tr.

Individual Texts and Translations.

Agada: —*v.* A § 12.
Bible, Hebrew: —*v.* A § 12
Kabbala: —*v.* A § 12.
Massorah: —*v.* A § 12.
Midrash: —*v.* A § 12.
Mishna: —*v.* A § 12.
Talmud Jerusalim: —*v.* A § 12.

XVII. Aryan (Indo-Germanic) Philology.

FICK, in the new ed. of his *Vergleich. Wb. d. indogerm. Spr.* [*ut* K § 120], proposes the word "Teutarian" as a substitute for "Indo-Germanic" or "Indo-European"; but it is too late to hope for its general acceptance now.

119. COMPARATIVE ARYAN PHILOLOGY (*a*): GENERALLY.

Bibliography.

Anzeiger für indogermanische Sprach- u. Altertumskunde, red. Wilh. Streitberg
A useful bibliography, publd. as a *Beiblatt* to the *Indogermanischen Forschungen* [*ut infra*], but not sold separately.

History of the Language—*v. also* K § 96.

BARTHOLOMAE, Dr. Ch. Studien zur indogermanische Sprachgeschichte, pts. i. 5*m.*; ii. 7*m.* 8° Niemeyer, *Halle* 90; 91
This Pt. conts. (1) *Indogermanisch "Sh" und "Shh,"* (2) *Altindisch "asis"* (=Latin *eris*).

" " Arisches und Linguistisches [*extr. fr.* Beitr. Kunde Ind. Spr.] 5*m.* 8° Vandenhoeck, *Götti.* 91

Origin of Aryan Language—*v.* K § 93.

Aryan Peoples —*v. also* F § 5: Primitive Society.

D'ARBOIS DE JUBAINVILLE, H. Les Premiers Habitants de l'Europe, vol. ii. 12*fr.* 8° Thorin, *Paris* [77] 94
This vol. conts. the Indo-Europeans, viz. Ligurians, Hellenes, Italiots, Celts.

BEDDOE, Dr. J. Anthropological History of Europe—*ut* E § 3.

BRUNNHOFER, Herm. Urgeschichte d. Arier in Vorder- u. Centralasien, 3 vols. 16*m.* 8° Friedrich, *Lps.* [89; 90; 92] 93
Historico-geographical researches on the most ancient home of the *Rigveda* and *Avesta*. i. *Iran u. Turan* [*ut* B.B. K § 119]; ii. *Vom Pontus bis z. Indus*; iii. *Vom Aral bis z. Gangâ*.

van den GHEYN, Père L'Origine Européenne des Aryas 3*fr.* 8° *Paris* 89

KRAUSE, E. Tuisko-Land, der arischen Stämme u. Götter Urheimat 10*m.* 8° *Giessen* 91
Deals with the myths and legends of the *Vedas*, *Edda*, *Iliad* and *Odyssey*.

MUCH, Matth. Die Kupferzeit in Europe u. i. Verhältn. z. Kultur d. Indogerm. 10*m.* 8° Costenoble, *Jena* [ ] 93

PENKA, Karl Die Heimat der Germanen [*extr. fr.* Mittheiln. d. anthr. Ges. Wien.] 2*m.* 4° *Vienna* 93

REINACH, Salomon L'Origine des Aryens: histoire d'une controverse [pp. 128] 8° Leroux, *Paris* 92

SCHMIDT, Joh. Die Urheimath d. Indogermanen u. d. europ. Zahlsyst. [extr. fr. Preuss. Akad.] 2*m.* 50 4° G. Reimer, *Berlin* 90

Magazines, Serials and Series.

Anecdota Oxoniensia: Aryan Series s 4° Clar. Press / Macmillan, *N.Y.* *in prg.* 87–93

i.-iii. *Buddhist Texts fr. Japan* [*ut* K § 127] ed. F. MAX MÜLLER, *etc.* 3/6 (90c. *nt.*), 7/6 ($1.90 *nt.*), 10/- ($2.50 *nt.*)
iv. KATYAYANA'S *Sarvanukramani of Rig Veda* [*ut* B.B. K § 124 I] ed. A. A. MACDONELL, 16/- ($4 *nt.*)
v. *Dharma Samgraha* [*ut* K § 124 VIII.] ..ed. KENJIU KASAWARA, *etc.* 7/6 ($1.90 *nt.*)
vi. *not published yet.*
vii. ASVAGHOSHA, *Buddha Karita* [*ut* K § 127] ed. E. B. COWELL 12/6 ($3.25 *nt.*) 93

Beiträge zur Kunde der indogermanischen Sprachen, hrsg. v. A. Bezzenberger, vol. xvi.-xx. [ea. 4 pts.] *per vol.* 10*m.* 8° Vandenhoeck, *Göttingen* 90–94 *in prg.*

Bibliothek indogermanischen Grammatiken 8° Breitkopf, *Lps.* [76–92] 86–92 *in prg.*

i. SIEVERS, Prf. E. *Grundzüge d. Phonetik* [*ut* K § 120].. 5*m.* [76] 93
ii. WHITNEY, Prf. W. D. (Am.) *Sanskrit Gram.* [*ut* B.B. K § 121].. 10*m.* [79] 89
Germ. tr. H. Zimmer, 10*m.*, '80.
iii. MEYER, Gust. *Griech. Gram.* [*ut* K § 175] 9*m.* 50 81
iv. DELBRÜCK, B. *Einleit. i. d. Sprachstud.* 3*m.* 81
Engl. tr. [*ut* B.B. K § 119], 4*m.* '82.
v. HATZIDAKIS, G. N. *Einleit. i. d. neugriech. Gram.* [*ut* K § 186].. 10*m.* 92

Indogermanische Forschungen: Ztschr. f. indog. Sprach- u. Altertumsk. per vol. [5 pts.] 16*m.* r 8° Trübner, *Strassb.* 91 *sqq.* *in prg.*
Edited by Prfs. Karl BRUGMANN + Wilh. STREITBERG. The *Anzeiger* [*ut sup.*; separately paged] is given gratuitously with it, but not sold separately. Conts. important orig. articles and good criticisms over the whole field of Indogerm. philology.

Sammlung indogermanischer Wörterbücher 8° Trübner, *Strassb.* 87 *sqq.*, *in prg.*

i. HÜBSCHMANN, H. *Etymol. u. Lautlehre d. osset. Spr.* [*ut* B.B. K § 138] 4*m.* 87
ii. FEIST, Dr. S. *Grundriss d. gotischen Etymol.* [*ut* B.B. K § 226] 5*m.* 88
iii. MEYER, Gust. *Etym. Wb. d. alban. Sprache* [*ut* K § 185] 12*m.* 90

120. COMPARATIVE ARYAN PHILOLOGY (*b*): GRAMMAR. PHONOLOGY.

General Treatises. Collected Essays.

*BRUGMANN, Prf. Karl Grundriss d. vergl. Gram. d. indogerm. Sprachen, 2 vols. & Indices 56*m.* r 8° Trübner, *Strassbg.* 86–93
Vol. I. *Einleit., Lautlehre*, 14*m.* '86. Vol. II. *Wortbildungslehre*, pt. i. 12*m.* '89; pt. ii. (1) *Zahlwortbildg., Casusbildg. d. Nomina, Pronomina*, 10*m.* '90; pt. ii. (2) *Verbale Stammbildg. u. Flexion*, 14*m.* '92. *Indices*, 6*m.* '93. For vol. iii. *v.* *Delbrück, Vergleich. Syntax, infra.*

" " Compar. Grammar of the Indo-Germ. Langs. [tr.] 8° Paul 91
Vol. II. *Morphology (Stem-Formation and Inflexion)*, pt. i. 16/- '91; pt. ii. 12/6 '92. Well tr. by R. Seymour CONWAY + W. H. D. ROUSE. The previous vol. [*ut* B.B. K § 120] was tr. by Dr. Joseph WRIGHT much more literally and therefore less intelligibly. It is an indispensable work, extremely thorough and accurate—an extraordinary performance for a "one-man" book.

HENRY, Prf. Vict. Compar. Grammars of Gk. & Lat [*ut* B.B. K § 168], of Germ. & Engl. [*ut* K § 225].
Together form an excellent Introd. to Comparative Indogermanic Philology.

REGNAUD, Prf. Paul Principaux généraux d. Linguistique Indoeurop. [for students] 2*fr.* 12° Hachette, *Paris* 90
Interesting and suggestive, but to be taken *cum grano salis*: regards philology purely as a natural science.

" " Les Grandes Lignes d. Vocalisme et Dérivn. d. l. langs. indoeur. Leroux, *Paris*

" " Mélanges de Philologie indoeuropéenne [Bibl. Faculté Lettres à Lyon] 7*fr.* 50 8° " " 89

" " Origine et Philosophie du Langage 2*fr.* 12° Fischbacher, *Paris* [87] 89

K § 121

Accidence.

MERINGER, Rud. Beitr. z. Gesch. d. indogerm. Declination [*extr. fr.* Sitzb. Wien. Akad.] 1*m.* r 8° Tempsky, *Vienna* 91

Etymology.

TOUBIN, Chas. Essai d'Etymologie Historique et Géographique [pp. 467] 16° Picard, *Paris* 92

Dictionaries.

*FICK, Aug. Vergleichendes Wörterbuch d. indogerm. Sprachen [*ut* B.B. K § 120], 4th edn. hrsg. A. Bezzenberger + A. Fick + Whitley Stokes, v. i. 14*m.*; ii. 8*m.*60 l 8° Vandenhoeck, *Gött.*[68]91; 94

A dict. of roots and words supposed to have existed in the Indoeur. tongue, w. corresp. words and derivatives in the various languages. The best dict.; in the prev. (3rd) edn. not always trustworthy. Vol. i. conts. *Wortschatz d. Grundsprache d. arischen u. d. west-europ. Spracheinheit*, by FICK; vol. ii. *Urkelt. Sprachschatz*, by STOKES, tr. and ed. by BEZZENBERGER.

Personal Names —*v.* K § 181 (*FICK).

Place-Names.

KÖPPEN, W. Die Schreibung Geographischer Namen 1*m.*20 8° Seitz, *Hamburg* 93
WISNAR, T. Untersuchungen zur geographischen Namenkunde 1*m.*50 8° Fournier, *Znaim* 91

Roots.

PERSSON, P. Studien z. Lehre v. d. Wurzelerweiterung und Wurzelvariation 8*m.*80 8° Akad. Buchhg., *Upsala* 91

Pronoun.

TORP, A. Beiträge zur Lehre v. d. geschlechtslosen Pronomen i. d. indog. Sprachen [pp. 51] 8° Dybwad, *Christiania* 89

Syntax —*v. also* K § 98.

*DELBRÜCK, B. Vergleichende Syntax d. indogerman. Sprachen, vols. i. 20*m.*; ii. 12*m.*50 8° Trübner, *Strassbg.* 93; 92

A continuation [=vol. iii.] of BRUGMANN'S *Grundriss d. indogerm. Sprachen*, *ut supra.*

Phonology —*v. also* K § 98.

BECHTEL, Fritz Die Hauptprobleme der indogerman. Lautlehre seit Schleicher 9*m.* 8° Vandenhoeck, *Göttgn.* 91

A valuable Introd. to Indogerm. phonology, and at same time a hist. of research in the departmt., w. references to chief literature.

CLARK, Jno. Manual of Linguistics—*ut* K § 98.
SIEVERS, Prf. Ed. Grundzüge der Phonetik [*ut* B.B. K § 120]: 4th edn. [Bibl. Indogerm. Gramm.] 5*m.* 8° Breitkopf, *Lpz.* [76]93
SOAMES, (Miss) Laura Introduction to Phonetics: English, French and German c 8° 6/- Sonnenschein / $1.50 Macmillan, *N.Y.* 91

An excellent introductory manual, w. *Reading Lessons* and *Exercises.*

VIETOR, Prf. Wilh. Elemente d. Phonetik d. Deutschen, Englischen u. Französ. [*ut* B.B. K § 120: 3rd ed., pt. i.] 3*m.* 8° Reisland, *Lpz.* [84]93

121. INDIC PHILOLOGY AND LITERATURE (*a*): SANSKRIT PHILOLOGY.

Bibliography —*v.* K § 122.

Introduction.

OLDENBERG, Prf. H. The Study of Sanskrit—*in* Epitome of Three Sciences 75*c.* 12° Open Ct. Pb. Co., *Chicago* 90

Sansk. Research; From Jones to Lassen; Discov. of Veda; Interpret. of Veda; History of Vedic Epoch.

History of the Language.

LUDWIG, A. Die Genesis d. grammat. Formen d. Samskrit 4*m.*80 8° Rivnac, *Prague* 91

Grammar. Chrestomathies.

ABREU, G. de Vasconcellos [ed.] Curso de Literatura e Lingua sanscrita 8° *Lisbon* 83–91

A chrestomathy of Classical and Vedic texts, w. exercises.

BERGAIGNE + HENRY, Abel / Victor Manuel pour étudier le Sanscrit Védique 12*fr.* r 8° Bouillon, *Paris* 90

Conts. a short grammar, a chrestomathy and a glossary.

BOPP, Frz. [1791–1867] Kritische Grammatik der Sanskrita-Sprache 9*m.* 8° Nicolai, *Berlin* [29–32]68
GELABERT Y GURDIOLA, J. Manuel de Lengua Sanskrita [gram. and chrestom.] 16/- 8° *Madrid* 90

Intensitives.

BURCHARDI, G. Die Intensiva d. Sanskrit und Avesta, pt. i. 1*m.* 8° Harrassowitz, *Lpz.* 92

Nouns and *Verbs.*

JOHNSTON, Chas. Useful Sanskrit Nouns and Verbs: in English [*sic*] characters 2/6 s 4° Luzac 92

Paradigms of the simple declensions and conjugations, for learning by heart.

Etymology: Dictionaries —*for* Native Lexicography *v.* K § 124 XII.

APTE, Vaman Shivaram Student's Sanskrit-English Dictionary 18/- r 8° *Poona* 90
CAPPELLER, Prf. Carl Sanskrit-English Lexicon: tr. 21/- *nt.* r 8° Luzac 91

A tr. of his *Sansk. Wb.* [15*m.* r 8° Trübner, *Strssb.* '87], wh. is based on BÖHTLINGK'S two dictionaries, *ut* B.B. K § 121. Well adapted for use of beginners, dealing as it does specially w. the texts usually read in commencing Sanskrit. It also includes most Vedic words, and will be of use to philological students.

LAKSHMAN RAMCHANDRA VAIDYA Standard Sanskrit-English Dictionary [school-bk.] 10/6 s 4° (*India*) 8-
MACDONELL, Prf. Arth. A. Sanskrit-English Dictionary 42/- ($10.50 *nt.*) 4° Longman 92

A useful and practical bk., w. transliteration, accentuation and etymolog. analysis throughout, supplying the vocab. of post-Vedic liter. in general, and those portions of Vedic liter. wh. are readily accessible in good edns. Technical terms (other than legal and philosoph.) are excluded.

Palæography. Epigraphy—*v. also* G § 10.

Texts and Translations.

Bower MS.: ed. Dr. A. F. Rudolf Hoernle; w. translit., Engl. tr. and notes; pt. i. Govt. of India 93 *in prg.*

The MS. consists of a colln. of strips of birch-bark, brought fr. Cent. Asia by Cpt. Bower in 1890, and is of great palæogr. importance, bg. written in a peculiar kind of Nagari, of the N.-W. type, of ab. 4th to 6th cent., *i.e.* some 900 yrs. older than any previously known Sansk. MS. Its contents are of small interest: charms and medical nostrums, of a Buddhistic character. The 1st pt. deals w. 5 leaves (out of 56).

Epigraphia Indica: ed. Dr. Jas. Burgess, vol. ii.; 3 facs. pl. 3*rs.* r 4° Govt. Press, *Calcutta* 92

An important serial pubn., printing a variety of inscriptions coll. by the Archæol. Survey of India, supplementary to the *Corpus Inscripp. Indicarum* [*ut* 𝔅.𝔅. K § 121]. Issued in pts. at 18/- *per ann.*

HULTZSCH, Dr. E. [ed. & tr.] South Indian Inscriptions: Tamil and Sanskrit, vols. i.–ii. (1 & 2) 4° Govt. Press, *Madras* (Paul) 90–92

A good colln. of inscriptions, the Tamil generally of less histor. value than the Sanskrit.

RICE, Lewis [ed.] Inscriptions at Sravana Belgola; 26 pl. of facss. [over 400 pp.] 4° *Mysore* 89

A very valuable work, w. photo. and descr. of the colossal statue of Gomata and copies of 144 inscriptions in Rom. char., w. translitn., tr. *etc.*

Treatises.

BÜHLER, Prf. G. Die indischen Inschriften [reprint] 2*m.* 8° Tempsky, *Vienna* 90

A brilliant essay on the rel. of the inscriptions to the antiquity of Indian poetry.

SENART, E. Notes d'Epigraphie Indienne, pts. i.–iii. [*repr. fr.* Jl. Asiatique] ea. 3/*fr.* 8° *Paris* 88; 89; 90

Alphabet.

HOLLE, K. F. Table v. Oudh-en Nieuw-Indische Alphabetten [*w.* 15/-] r 8° *Batavia* 82

Greeks.

LEVI, Dr. Sylvain Quid de Græcis veterum Indorum Monumenta tradiderint [thesis] 2/*fr.* 8° Bouillon, *Paris* 90

Numismatics —*v.* G § 20.

Manuscripts.

Berlin, Königl. Bibl.: Verzeichniss d. Sanskrit- u. Prâkrithandschriften, vol. ii. [by Prf. A. Weber] r 4° Asher, *Berlin* 92

The index conts. c. 30,000 entries, showing its extent. There are 1,000 quarto pages of text, of wh. no less than 787 deal w. Jain literature, constituting an invaluable aid to the study of that religion.

BHANDARKAR, Ramkrishna Gopal Report on Search for Sansk. in Bomb. Presidy.: 1883–84 *Bombay* 87

Deccan College Lib.: Catalogue of collns. deposited in Deccan Coll. Lib. [by Shridhar R. Bhandarkar] " 88

A useful list of all the Sansk. MSS. purchased for Govt. of Bombay fr. 1868 to 1888; w. 81 pp. General Index.

Florence: Florentine Sanskrit MSS. examined. By Dr. Th. Aufrecht 8*m.* 8° Kreysing, *Lpz.* 92

India Office Library: Catalogue of Sanskrit MSS., pt. ii., 10/6; pt. iii., 10/6 4° Paul 90; 91

[i. *Vedic MSS.*—*ut* 𝔅.𝔅. K § 120]; ii. *Sansk. Gramms., Dicts., etc.*, iii. *Scientif. and Techn. Liter., Rhetoric, Law*; iv. *in prep.*]

Jammû: Catalogue of 5000 Sanskrit MSS. found at Jammû. By Dr. Stein 91

Oudh: Catal. of Sansk. MSS. existing in Oudh Province for 1887 [by Devi Prasâda] 8° *Allahabad* 88

Chronology, *etc.*

JACOBI, H. Methods & Tables for Verifying Hindu Dates, Eclipses, etc. [extr.] 4*m.* 8° Haeseler, *Kiel* 91

Prosody. Composition.

APTE, V. Sh. Student's Guide to Sansk. Composition: treat. on Sansk. syntax [pp. 466] 5/- s 8° *Poona* [ ] 91

Collected Essays.

v. BÖHTLINGK, Otto Festgruss zum Doktor-Jubiläum v. Seinen Freunden 2*m.* r 8° Kohlhammer, *Stuttgt.* 88

A series of valuable papers by ROTH, DELBRÜCK, BRADKE, WINDISCH, JACOBI, LUDWIG, AUFRECHT, GELDNER, HILLEBRANDT, *etc.*

v. ROTH, Prf. Rud. Festgruss an, zum Dr. Jubil. 1893, v. sein. Freunden u. Schülern 12*m.* 8° Kolhammer, *Stuttgt.* 93

122. INDIC (*b*): SANSKRIT LITERATURE (*a*): BIBLIOGRAPHY. HISTORY OF LITERATURE.

Bibliography.

ABREU, G. de Vasconcellos Summario d. Investigações em Samscritologia: 1886–91 [56 pp.] r 8° Impr. Nacional, *Lisbon* / 3/6 Orient. Inst., *Woking* 91

*AUFRECHT, Prf. Theod. Catalogus Catalogorum 36*m.* r 4° Brockhaus, *Lpz.* 91

An alphab. register of Sansk. works and authors, consisting of 800 quarto pp. in double cols. Indispensable to all Sansc. scholars as a work of constant reference. The expenses of production have been paid by the Germ. Orient. Soc., w. a handsome subsidy fr. the English India Office.

British Museum: Catal. of Sansk., Pali and Prakrit Bks. acqd. 1876–92 [by Prf. C. Bendall] 36/- 4° Brit. Museum 94

History of Literature.

BÜHLER + KIRSTE, Prf. G./J. Indian Studies, pts. i.–ii. 3*m.* 30 8° Tempsky, *Vienna* 92; 93

i. *The Jagaddûcharita of Sarvânanda*, 1m.80; ii. *Contribs. to Hist. of Mahâb.* [*ut* K § 123 II.] 1m.50.

REED, Elizab. A. [Am.] Hindu Literature: the ancient books of India $2 12° Griggs, *Chicago* 91

A good popular survey of anc. Sansk. liter. so far as it presents a picture of the earlier phase of Hindu religion, mythol. and legendary lore. Based on the best available materials, trustworthy and readable.

SCHERMAN, L. Materialien zur Gesch. d. indischen Visionslitteratur 10*m.* 8° Twietmeyer, *Lpz.* 93

Poetry.

PISCHEL, Prf. R. Die Hofdichter des Laksmanasena [12 cent.] 3*m.* 80 8° Dieterich, *Göttingen* 94

123. INDIC (c): SANSKRIT LITERATURE (β): SERIES AND COLLNS. OF TEXTS AND TRANSLATIONS

Series.

Ânandâśrama Sanskrit Series, nos. i.–xxv. ea. *rs.* 2 r 8° *Poona* 88 *sqq.*, *in prg.*
Edns. of MSS. collected and preserved by MAHÂDEO CHIMNÂJI APTE, a barrister of Poona, in a public edifice, wh. he has named the Ânandâśrama ["Hermitage of Delight"]. Subscrn. price is *rs.* 1½ if the whole series be taken.

Benares Sanskrit Series, ed. Prfs. Griffith + Thibaut [*c.* 50 pts. pub. to 1892] *Benares*
Bibliotheca Indica —the most important entered separately [Asiatic Soc. of Bengal] 8° *Calcutta* 47 *sqq.*, *in prg.*
Under the control of the Asiatic Soc. of Bengal, wh. receives a Govt. grant of 3,000 rupees a yr. for pub. of Sansk. liter. When the Soc.'s Centenary Review was pub. in 1883, 140 Sansk. wks. had been completed in the series.

Bombay Sanskrit Series, ed. Prfs. G. Bühler + F. Kielhorn—the most import. contents entered separately 8° Bombay 66 *sqq.*, *in prg.*
Under patronage of Govt. of Bombay. Orig. started in 1866, w. the aim of providing critical edns. of a certain no. of plays, poems and prose wks. for use of Univ. students; but, after supplying that want, it has launched out into deep waters.

Harvard Sanskrit Series: ed. Prf. Chas. Lanman [Am.] r 8° Ginn, *Boston* / Arnold 92 *in prg.*
Vol. i. *Jataka-Mala*, ed. Prf. Hendrik KERN (*ut* K § 127). $1.50 (6/- *nt.*) '91.

Nirnayasâgasa Press Sanskrit Series [excellently prtd. w. type founded at the Press owned by Jâvji Dâdâji] *Bombay* 86 *sqq.*, *in prg.*
The wks. first run thro' the *Kâvyamâlâ*, a mthly. serial devoted to pub. of wks. on rhetoric, dramas and minor poems. Portions of several appear ea. month, w. their pagination for separate binding when cpl.

VIDVÂSÂGARA, Jibânanda [ed.] Series of Sanskrit Texts *Calcutta*
Very cheap texts, but not accurate as a whole.

Vizianagram Sanskrit Series: ed. Prf. Arth. Venis—*v.* K § 124 IX.

Proverbs.

BÖHTLINGK, Otto [ed.] Indische Sprüche—*ut* B.B. K § 123.
Blau, A. [ed.] Index zu Otto Böhtlingk's 'Indische Sprüche' [Abh. f. Kunde d. ML.] 4*m.* 8° Brockhaus, *Lps.* 93

Translated Selections.

DUTT, Romesh Chunder [tr.] Lays of Ancient India: [verse] translns. [Trübner's Oriental Series] 7/6 8° Paul 94
WILLIAMS, Sir Monier Monier- [tr.] Indian Wisdom [*ut* B.B. K § 123]: new (4th) edn. 21/- 8° Luzac [75] 93
A series of tr. extrs. ill. the relig., philos. and ethical doctrines of the Hindus, preceded by a sketch of the hist. of Sansk. liter., and a short acc. of the past and pres. condn. of India, moral and intellectual. Forms a compendious and very interesting summary of Sansk. liter.

124. INDIC (d): SANSKRIT LITERATURE (γ): TEXTS, TRANSLATIONS AND AIDS.

I. THE VEDAS.

I. RIG-VEDA [*c.* 1500 B.C.; Hymns].

Samhitâ.

Texts.

MÜLLER, Prf. F. Max [ed.] Sacred Hymns of Brâhmans, w. Sâyana's [14 cent.] Comm. [*ut* B.B. K § 124]: new ed., 4 v. 4° ea. 42/- *nt.* Clar. Press / ea. $10 Macmillan, *N.Y.* [47–74] 90–92
The best, if not the only, critical edn. of the text and commentary. This new edn., based on a collatn. of new MSS. is pub. under patronage of the Maharajah of VIZIANAGRAM. The subscr. price for the 4 vols. was £5 5/- *nt.*

RÂJÂTÂMA SHASTRI [ed.] Rig-Veda, w. Commentary of Sâyânâ, 8 vols. 105/- r 8° Tatya, *Bombay* 91
A well-printed edn., the cheapest hitherto available. Added are the sûtras of PANINI, UNADI and Phit-sûtras Brihadrigvidhana and the Parisishtha.

Translations.

GRIFFITH, Ralph T. H. [tr.] The Hymns of the Rig-Veda, tr. w. a popular commentary, 4 vols. 45/- r 8° *Benares* 89–92
MÜLLER, Prf. F. Max [tr.] Vedic Hymns, pt. i.—*ut* A § 14.
PETERSON, Prf. Peter [tr.]—*in his* Handbook to the Study of the Rig-Veda, *ut infra.*

Upanishads.

Upanishads [ten]: w. the bhâshya of Sankarâchârya and other comms. [Ânandâsrama Series] *rs.* 2 r 8° *Poona*

Sûtras.

Siksâ [pronunciation].
Bhâradvâjaçîkshâ: ed. E. Sieg; w. Latin tr. and crit. and exeget. notes (in Latin) 4*m.* 8° Speyer, *Berlin* 92

Vyâkarana-sûtras [grammar].
Riktantravyâkarana: ed. Dr. A. C. Burnell, vol. i. [w. tr. of the sûtras] 10/- p 8° Trübner

Kalpa-sûtras [ritual].
Grihya-sûtras [rules of domestic ceremonies].
OLDENBERG + MÜLLER, Prf. Herm. / Prf. F. Max [trs.] The Grihya-Sûtras—*ut* A § 14.

Aids to Rig Veda [*and the Vedas collectively*].

BERGAIGNE, Abel Recherches sur l' Hist. de la Samhita du R.-V., pts. i.–iv. [*extrs. fr.* Jl. Asiat.] 7*fr.* 8° Leroux, *Paris* 87–87
" " Recherches sur l'Hist. de la Liturgie Védique [" "] 3/*fr.* 50 8° " " 89
" " Observations sur les Figures de Rhétorique dans le R.-V. [" "] 2/*fr.* 8° Vieweg, *Paris* 80

BLOOMFIELD, Prf. Maur. [Am.] Contribs. to the Interpretation of the Veda, ser. i.-v. 90-93 *in prg.*

Deals with all the Vedas. Ser. i. in *Am. Jl. of Philol.*, vol. X., pp. 465-88; ii. in same, XI. 319-56; iii. in *Jl. Amer. Orient Soc.*, XV. 143-188; iv. in *Am. Jl. Phil.*, XII. 414-43; v. in *Jl. Am. Or. Soc.*, XIII.; a sixth is to appear in *Am. Jl. Phil.* Extrs. of II.-V. (i. *o.p.*) may be had of Johns Hopkins Univ. Pub. Agency, *Baltimore*, about 5s. each.

LUDWIG, Prf. Alf. Ueber die Kritik des Rgveda-Textes [*extr. fr.* Abhgn. Böhm. Ges.] 1m.80 4° Calve, *Prague* 89
" " Ueber Methode bei Interpretationen des Rgveda [" "] 3m. 4° Rivnac, *Prague* 90
" " Ueber d. neuesten Arbeiten a. d. Gebiete d. Rgveda-Forschung 3m.20 8° " " 93

The two first are extracts fr. the *Abhandln.* the last fr. the *Sitzber.* of the *Böhm. Gesellsch. der Wissensch.*

OLDENBERG, Dr. H. —*has a work on the* Vedic Mythology *in prep.*

PETERSON, Prf. Peter Handbk. to the Study of the Rig-Veda, pts. i.-ii. [Bombay Sansk. Series] 7/6 8° *Bombay* 90; 92

Pt. i. conts. Sayana's Preface to his commentary on the R.V., the Comm. itself on the first 3 *Hymns* and tr. of the Preface into English. Pt. ii. conts. text of the Seventh Mandala of R.V., w. Sayana's Comm. (based on a collation of the *editio princeps*), and 40 pp. of critical notes. Pt. iii. will cont. notes to the whole work, a tr. of the *Hymns* and a full glossary.

SANDER, F. Rigveda und Edda 2m.50 8° Friedländer, *Berl.* 93

SIMON, R. Beiträge zur Kenntniss der vedischen Schulen 4m.50 8° Haeseler, *Kiel* 89

Upanishads.

Concordance.

JACOB, Col. G. A. Concordance to principal Upanishads and the Bhagavad-gitâ [Bombay Sansk. Ser.] [1082 pp.] 15/- 8° *Bombay* 91

Sûtras.

WEBER, Dr. Albrecht Ueber die Königsweihe, den Rajâsûya [*extr. fr.* Abhgn. Berl. Akad.] 10m. 4° G. Reimer, *Berlin* 94

II. SAMAVEDA [Songs].

Brâhmanas.

Sadvimçabrâhmana: hrsg. Kurt Klemm; pt. i. [w. specs. of Sâyana's Comm. and Germ. tr.] 2m.40 8° Bertelsmann, *Gütersloh* 94

Sâmavidhâna: eingeleitet u. übersetzt S. Konow 4m. 8° Niemeyer, *Halle* 93

Upanishads.

Chandogya-Upanishad: ed. Kâsinâtha Sâstri Agâse; w. comm., 2 pts. [Ânandâsrama Series] ea. *rs.*2 8° *Poona* 91; 93

Concordance —*v. supra, s.v.* Upan. of Rig-Veda (JACOB).

Sûtras.

Kalpa-sûtras.

Grihya-sûtra.

Gobhila-grihya-sûtra: tr.—*in* Oldenberg + Müller's Grihya-Sûtras, *ut* A § 14.

III. YAJURVEDA [Prayers].

A. BLACK YAJUS (TATTIRÎYA; text of the school of ÂPASTAMBA).

SURESVARA Vârtika on the Taittirîya-bhâshya 8° Ânandâsrama Press, *Poona*

Taittirîya Samhitâ: ed. Râjâram Shâstri Bodas + Shivram Shâstri Gore 9/- r 8° *Bombay* 88

Upanishads.

Concordance —*v. supra, s.v.* Upan. of Rig-Veda (JACOB).

Sûtras.

RÂMÂNUJA [11 cent.] Sûtra Bhâshyam: in Grandha characters, 2 vols. 25/- 4° *Madras* 89

Apparently a reprint of the edn. by the late CHENGALROYA NAIK.

Kalpa-sûtras.

Grihya-sûtras.

ÂPASTAMA-grihya-sûtra: tr.—*in* Oldenberg + Müller's Grihya-Sûtras, *ut* A § 14.

Hiranyakesi-grihya-sûtra: tr.—*in* Oldenberg + Müller's Grihya-Sûtras, *ut* A § 14.

Aid.

WINTERNITZ, M. Das altind. Hochzeitsrituel nach. d. Apastambiya-Grihyasûtra 6m. 8° Freytag, *Lpz.* 92

B. WHITE YAJUS (VÂJASANEYI).

Brâhmana.

Satapatha-brâhmana: tr. Prf. Julius Eggeling, pt. iii. [= bks. 5-7] [Sacred Bks. of East] 8° 12/6 Clar. Press / $3.25 *nt.* Macmillan, *N.Y.* 93

Upanishads.

Concordance —*v. supra, s.v.* Upan. of Rig-Veda (JACOB).

IV. ATHARVA [OR BRAHMA]-VEDA [Incantations].

PANDIT, S. P. [ed.] Âtharva-Véda [Bombay Sanskrit Series] 8° *Bombay* *in prep.*

Translation.

HENRY, Prf. Victor [tr.] Livre vii. de l'Atharva-Véda [w. notes] 6 *fr.* 8° Maisonneuve, *Paris* 92

Upanishads.

Asuri-Kalpa: a witchcraft practice, ed. H. W. Magoun [Am.]; w. Introd., tr. & comm. 30*c.* 8° Johns Hopkins Univ., *Baltim.* 89

JACOB, Col. G. A. [ed.] Âtharvana Upanishads, w. comms., notes and crit. appar. [11 Upans.; Bombay Sansk. Ser.] 6/- 8° *Bombay* 91

Mândûkyopanishad: ed. A. V. Kâthavate; w. Kârikâs of Gaudapâda and comm. [Ânandâsrama Ser.] *Poona* 91

Concordance —*v. supra, s.v.* Upanishads of Rig-Veda (JACOB).

Of spec. importance here towards settling the reading in the minor Atharv. Upan., the text of which is often corrupt.

K § 124

II. NATIONAL EPICS.

(1) **Mahâbhârata** [ascribed to VYÂSA].

Text and *Translation: German.*

BOPP, Prf. Frz. [ed. and tr.] Ardschuna's Reise z. Indra's Himmel u. and. Episoden d. Mahâb. 8*m.* 4° Nicolai, *Berl.* [24] 68

The 1st edn. of the orig. text, w. a (German) Metrical tr. and critical notes. Transl. separately 2*m.*50.

Aids.

BÜHLER + KIRSTE, Prf. G. / Prf. J. Indian Studies, no. ii.: Contribs. to Hist. of Mahâbhârata, pt. i. 1*m.*50 8° Tempsky, *Vienna* 92

Extr. fr. *Sitzungsber. d. Wien. Akad.* Its obj. is to estab. that the *Mahâb.* in the earlier cents. of our era did not materially differ in size, character and extent fr. the text now current; texts are quoted fr. 5th to 8th cent. writers, showing the opinions they held of the poem, wh. KIRSTE compares w. its oldest known abstract, the *Bhâratamanjari* of the Kashmirian poet KSHEMENDRA [mid. 11 cent.], wh. he finds "did not differ fr. the *Mahâb.* as we at pres. have it in any other way than two classes of MSS. differ from one another."

DARMESTETER, Prf. Jas. Points de Contact entre le Mahâb. et le Shâh-Nâmeh 2 *fr.* 8° Leroux, *Paris* 87

HOLTZMANN, Adolf Das Mahâbhârata und seine Theile, 3 vols. 34*m.*20 8° Haeseler, *Kiel* 92; 93; 93

Vol. i. *Gesch. u. Kritik. d. Mahâbhârata*, 12*m.*60; ii. *Die Theile des Gedichtes*, 12*m.*

" " Agni: nach den Vorstellungen des Mahâbhârata 1*m.* 8° Trübner, *Strassbg.* 78

" " Arjuna: ein Beitrag zur Reconstruction des Mahâbhârata 1*m.*60 8° " " 79

OMAN, Prf. Jno. Campbell [tr.] The Great Indian Epics: stories of Râmâyana and Mahâb.; w. notes and appends. p 8° 5/- Bell / Macmillan, *N.Y.* 94

A very readable analysis of the two poems.

SAUER, W. Mahâbhârata und Wate: eine indogermanische Studie 2*m.* 8° Wildt, *Stuttgt.* 93

Bhagavad-Gitâ [episode of Mahâbhârata].

Text and *Translations.*

GOSWANI, P. D. [ed. and tr.] Bhagavad-Gitâ; w. Sansk. and Engl. notes, and Engl. tr. and comm., pts. i.–ii. ea. 2/6 8° *Calcutta* 89 *in prg.*

HARTMANN, F. [ed. and tr.] Die Bhagavad-Gitâ: übersetzt u. erläutert 1*m.*50 8° Schwetschke, *Brunsw.* 93

Contains illustrative and corresponding quotations from leading German mystics.

Aids.

Commentary —*v.* K § 128, *s.v.* Marâthi (Dnyâneshvari).

Concordance.

JACOB, Col. G. A. Concordance to the Principal Upanishads and the Bhagavad-Gitâ [1,082 pp.]—*ut supra, s.v.* § 1.

Râmâyana [ascribed to VÂLMÎKI].

Text and *Translation.*

Râmâyana of VALMÎKI: with Commentary of Rama., pts. i.–ii. 24/- r 8° *Bombay* [ ] 89 *in prg.*

A republication of a well-known edition.

Aids.

BAUMGARTNER, A. Das Râmâyana u. d. Râma-Liter. d. Inder [Stim. a. Maria-Laach, Ergänz.-Hfte.] 2*m.*30 8° Herder, *Freibg.* 94

JACOBI, Prf. H. D. Râmâyana: Geschichte u. Inhalt, mit Concordanz 15*m.* 8° Cohen, *Bonn* 93

A valuable crit. study on the hist. of the *Râmâyana* and its place in Sansk. liter., contg. an exam. of the existing recensions in respect of interpolations and later addns.: fixes the time of its compositn. betw. 8th and 6th cent. B.C., when the *Mahâb.* had not taken shape and Buddhism was still in its infancy. Appendices give a summary of the epic acc. to Bombay edn., Alphab. List of Proper Names, etc. Concordance covers the Bombay and so-called Bengali recensions.

OMAN, Prf. Jno. Campbell—*in his* The Great Indian Epics, *ut supra, s.v.* Mahâbhârata.

SCHOEBEL, Chas. Le Ramayana a. pt. d. vue relig., philos. et moral [Ann. Mus. Guimet] 12 *fr.* 4° Leroux, *Paris* 87

III. Puranas and Tantras.

[Bhâgavata-Purâna]: Prem Sagar ["Ocean of Love"], tr. Edw. B. Eastwick *o.p.* [*pb.* 21/-; *w.* 15/-] 4° Madden 51

Tr. fr. the Hindi versn. of the *Braj Bhakha* tr. of the *Bhâgavata-Purâna.*

" " Prem Sagar: océan d'amour, trad. E. Lamairesse 6 *fr.* 8° *Paris* 93

Brahma-Baibasta-Purâna: ed. Jibananda Vidyasagara, 2 vols. 30/- 8° *Calcutta* 88; 88

A Purana describing the evolution from Brahma.

Kalki-Purâna: ed. Pandit Jibananda Vidyasagara 4/- 8° " 90

Saura-Purâna: [Ânandâsrama Series] r 8° *Poona*

Vishnu-Purâna: by Vyás 9/- obl *Bombay* [ ] 89

V. Drama.

Collectively.

LÉVI, Sylvain Le Théatre Indien [Bibl. Ecole Haut. Etud.] 18 *fr.* 8° Bouillon, *Paris* 91

An elabor. supplemt. to WILSON'S *Theatre of Hindus* [*ut* 𝔅.𝔅. K § 124 V.]. The two wks. together afford a *précis* of all extant Sansk. dramas of any importce. at all. Besides accs. of the plays, LÉVI gives chaps. on orig. of drama, and refutatn. of Prf. WINDISCH'S thesis that Hindus were largely influenced by Greeks in constru. of their drama-system; and sections on drama in several mod. langs.

Individually.

KÂLIDÂSA [6 cent.] Raghuvamsa, ed. G. R. Nandargikar; w. Engl. tr. and notes in Sansk. 9/- r 8° *Bombay* [ ] 91

With the Commentaries of MALLINATHA and copious extracts fr. the Comms. of HEMADRI, CHARRITRAVARDDHANA SUMATIVIJAYA and others.

" " Sakuntala, ed. Narayan Balkrishna Godbole + Kashinath Pandurang Parab 5/- 8° *Bombay* 89

" Acts 1–8: ed. Parshuram Narayan Patankar; w. Engl. tr., notes, etc. 6/- 8° *Poona* 89

A useful and well-equipped edn. for students. The tr. is close.

Translation: German.

LOBEDANZ, Edm. [tr.] Sakuntala: indisches Schauspiel [metrically tr.] 2*m.*40 8° Brockhaus, *Lps.* [ ] 91

SÛDRAKA, King [5 cent.] Vasantesenâ: oder d. irdene Wägelchen, übers. [freely] M. Haberland 1*m.* 8° Liebeskind, *Lps.* 93

VI. Poetry.

AMARU Sataka

Simon, R. Das Amarusataka in seinen Beziehungen dargestellt 9*m.* 8° Haeseler, *Kiel* 92

BHOJA RAJA Champuramayana, ed. Jibananda Vidyasagara [poem in prose and verse] 3/6 8° *Calcutta* [ ] 88

HARICHANDRA Dharmasarmâbhudaya [Nirnasâgara Press Series] 8° *Bombay* 90

JAGADDHARA Stutikusumânjali [Nirnasâgara Press Series] 8° ,, 90

KÂLIDÂSA [6 cent.] *Meghadûta ["Cloud-Messenger"], ed. Kâsinâth Bâpu Pâtbak, w. Engl. tr. *Poona* 94

An important edn. of the text, w. MALLINÂTHA'S Commentary, var. rgs. fr. 5 other comm., tr. and notes.

,, ,, ,, ,, ed. T. B. Pânabokke; w. Singhalese paraphrase (*Ceylon*) 94

,, ,, Shrutabodha: a poem, ed. Jibananda Vidyasagara; w. comm. 6*d.* 8° *Calcutta* [ ] 88

KSHEMENDRA Dasâvatâracharitra [Nirnasâgara Press Series] 8° *Bombay* 91

RATNÂKARA [Kashmir poet; 9 cent.] Chandoratatnâkara, ed. G. Huth; w. Thibetan tr. 2*m.* 8° Dümmler, *Berl.* 90

,, Haravijaya, ed. Durgâprased + Kâshinâth Pândurang Parab [Nirnasâg. Pr. Ser.] 14/- 8° *Bombay* 91

SÂTANÂHANA Gûthâsaptasatî; w. index [Nirnayasâgara Press Series] 8° ,, 9-

VII. Fables, Tales and Novels.

Hitopadesa ["Salutary Counsel"; summary of *Panchatantra*].

Translations.

English.

Arnold, Sir. Edwin [tr.] The Book of Good Counsels; ill. Gordon Browne 7/6 c 8° W. H. Allen [61] 93

A tr. of the *Hitopadesa*, orig. pub. in pt. in his edn. of the text (w. 3/6, 8° Bombay '59).

German.

Fritze, L. [tr.] Hitopadeça: Lehrbuch d. Lebensklugheit: übersetzt 2*m.* 8° Wigand, *Lps.* 88

KSHEMENDRA [11 cent.] Brihat Kathâmanjarî, hrsg. M. S. Levi, pts. i.-ii. 86; 92

An abstract or abbrevn. of GUNÂDHYA'S (lost) *Brihatkathâ*, one of the earliest and most extensive collns. of fables, composed in 1st or 2nd cent. A.D.

Pancatantra: Auszug in Kshemendras Brihat Kathâmanjarî, hrsg. L. v. Mankowski 6*m.* 8° 92

Suka-saptati ["70 (stories) by the Parrot"] Die Çukasaptati: textus simplicior, hrsg. R. Schmidt 9*m.* 8° Brockhaus, *Lps.* 93

Forms no. 1 of vol. 2. of the *Abhandl. f. d. Kunde d. Morgenlandes.*

,, ,, Die Çukasaptati, übers. R. Schmidt 4*m.*50 8° Haeseler, *Kiel* 93

Fairy Tales and Romances.

BANA [7 cent.] Kâdambarî, w. comms. of Bhânuchandra and his disciple Siddhachandra, ed. Prf. Peterson 14/- r 8° *Bombay* 90

DANDIN [6 cent.] Dasâkumâracharita, ed. Dr. Peterson, pts. i—ii. [Bombay Sanskrit Ser.] 8° *Bombay*

,, ,, Dasâkumâra Charita; w. Engl. tr. Jânakî Nâth Bhattâchâryya 3/- 12° *Calcutta* 89

VIII. Law —*v. also* D § 111.

Dharma Samgraha: ed. Kenjiu Kasawara + F. Max Müller + H. Wenzel [Anecd. Oxon.] 4° 7/6 Clar. Press / $1.90 nt. Macmillan, *N.Y.* 85

MANU Smriti: Instits. of Manu, ed. Pandit Gangâdhar Pushkarlâl 15/- r 4° *Bombay* 88

With a tr. in Hindi.

,, ,, ed. in Skt. and Mâgadhi Venkratraman Suri + Krishnâji Bishto Bhâgvat 18/- r 8° *Bombay* 88

Strehly, G. Les Lois de Manou 15*fr.* 8° *Paris* 93

PARÂSERA Smriti: w. Sâyana's comm., ed. Vâman S'âstri Islâmpurkar [Bombay Sansk. Ser.] 8° *Bombay*

IX. Philosophy.

History.

DEUSSEN, Prf. P. Allgemeine Geschichte d. Philosophie, 2 vols. 8° Brockhaus, *Lps.*, *in prep.*

Announced by Author at the Ninth Oriental Congress (Lond. 1892) as in prep. by him. The 1st vol. will be devoted to East Asiatic philos., the 2nd to that of West. Asia and that of Europe. Seeing that hitherto we know practically only one side of the thought of the intellectual world—the developmts. of occidental philos. fr. THALES to KANT and SCHOPENHAUER—a compreh. treatise by so learned a specialist as the author shd. prove highly valuable, affording us a view of a philos. quite independent of our own: the only real parallel to it obtainable.

GARBE, Dr. Rich. Die Samkhya-Philosophie: Darstellg. d. ind. Rationalismus nach d. Quellen 12*m.* 8° 94

Texts and *Translations.*

Series.

Vizianagram Sanskrit Series: ed. Arth. Venis 8° *Benares* 90 *in prg.*

A coll. of rare philosoph. treatises in Sanskrit, w. intros. and indices (Engl. trs. to follow in separate pts.) Wks. of the Vedânta school predominate. Edr. is Principal of the Sanskrit College, Benares.

1. MÎMÂMSÂ.

KRISHNA DVAIPÂYANA Brahmasûtras, ed. Nârâynna Sâstrî Eksâmbekara; w. comm., 2 pts. [Ânandâsrama Ser.] ea. *rs.* 2 8° *Poona* 91

KUMÂRILA [7 cent.] Tantravârtika r 8° *Benares*

MÂDHAVA ÂCHÂRYA Sarva-darsana-samgraha, tr. Prf. E. B. Cowell + A. E. Gough 10/6 p 8° Paul [ ] 94

A review of the different systems of Hindu philosophy.

SÂYANA Jaiminîya-nyâya-mâlâ-vistara [Ânandâsrama Series] 8° *Poona* 91

,, ,, ,, ed. Prfs. Goldstücker + E. B. Cowell

2. VEDÂNTA.

APPAYADÎKSHITA Siddhântalesa [Vizianagram Series] 4/6 8° *Benares* 91

A valuable Vedantic treatise, full of Vedic and non-Vedic quotations.

BÂDARÂYANA Çârîraka-Mîmânsâ, übers. Prf. P. Deussen [sûtras of Vedânta] 18*m.* 8° Brockhaus, *Lps.* 87

BRUINING, A. Bijdrage tot de Kennis van den Vedânta [a short but good monograph] 71

NISCHAL DASJEE [early 19 cent.] Vicharsagar, tr. Lala Sri Ram *sub tit.* Metaphysics of the Upanishads; w. notes r 8° rs.8 Heeralal Dhole, *Calc.* / $5.50 *Open Ct. Pb. Co., Chic.* 85

Panchadasi: tr. Prf. Arth. Venis [partial tr.; Vizianagram Series] 8° *Benares* 9-

" tr. Nandalal Dhole, *sub tit.* Hdbk. of Hindu Pantheism [Sansk. text, rs.4 84] r 8° rs.8 Heeralal Dhole, *Calc.* / $5.50 *Open Ct. Pb. Co., Chic.* 86

PRAKAS'ANANDA Vedânta Siddhântamuktâvali: ed. Prf. Arth. Venis; w. Eng. tr., Intro., notes, and index [Vizian. Ser.] 7/6 8° *Benares* 90

SADÂNANDA Vedânta-sara, tr. Nandalal Dhole; w. Introd. and notes 8° rs.3 Heeralal Dhole, *Calc.* / $5.50 *Open Ct. Pb. Co., Chic.* 88

SURÉSVARA Brihadâranyaka-bhâshya: Vârtika on [2075 pp. and 144-p. Index] 8° Ânandâsrama Press, *Poona* ?-93

The 144-p. Index to First Lines is a valuable adda., as every writer of the advaitavâdin schl. has drawn fr. the wk. and quotns. can now be readily traced.

Utharamimânsâ: ed. Uddhavâchârya Ainâpure; w. comm. and notes 25/- r 8° *Bombay* 88

The *Uttaramimânsâ*, or *Brahma Mimânsa*, is a comm. on the *Dnyânakânda*, or second portion of the Vedas, founded on the Upanishads.

Vedântaparibhâshâ: tr. Prf. Arth. Venis [Vizianagram Series] 8° *Benares* 9-

Vedânta-sûtras: w. bhâshya, comm. and adhikaranamâlâ [Anandâsrama Series] r 8° *Poona*

" " tr. G. Thibaut; vol. li. [Sacred Books of the East] 8° 12/6 Clar. Press / $3.25 *ol. Macmillan, N.Y.* 92

Vicharmala: tr. Lala Sri 8° rs.2 Heeralal Dhole, *Calc.* / $1.85 *Open Ct. Pb. Co., Chic.* 86

Treatise.

MÜLLER, Prf. F. Max Three Lectures on the Vedânta Philosophy 5/- 8° Longmans 94

Deliv. at Roy. Instim., Mch. '94, contg. a lucid acc. of the Vedânta philos. as set forth in the Upanishads, w. an interesting compar. of its teaching w. that of Eur. systs.

3. SÂNKHYA.

SANKARA

MANILAL DVIVEDI The Advaita Philosophy of Çankara—*in* Wiener Ztschr., 1888.

VIDYÂRANYA Srî Sankaradigvijayal, ed. Bâbâji Nârâyan Fadake [Life of Sankara] [Ânandâsrama Ser.] 18/- r 8° *Poona* 91

VACASPATIMISRA Sâmkhyattvakaumudî, übers. Dr. Rich. Garbe, *sub tit.* Mondschein d. Sâmkhya-Wahrheit 3*m*.40 Franz, *Munich* 92

VIJNÂNA BHIKSHU [16 cent.] Comm. z. den Sâmkhyasûtras, übers. Dr. Rich. Garbe; w. notes [Abh. K. d. ML.] 10*m*. 8° Brockhaus, *Lpz.* 89

4. YOGA.

MARKUS, P. Die Yogaphilosophie nach dem Râjamârtanda *Halle* 86

PATANJALI Yogo-sûtra: Engl. tr. by Manilal Nabhubhai Dvivedi; w. Intro. and notes 4/6 8° 90

Yoga Sûtras: ed. Mahâmahopâdhyâya Rajâram Shâstri Bodâs [Bombay Sansk. Ser.] 8° *Bombay*

Mimansas **[bringing the doctrines enunc. in the Brahmans into accord w. one another].**

KUMÂNLA BHATTA Tantravârtika, pts. 1-10 [gloss. on *bhâshya* on the *Mîmânsâsûtras* [Benares Sanskr. Ser.] 8° *Benares* 82 *sqq., in prg.*

LAWGÂKSHI BHÂSKARA Arthasangraha; w. tr. [elem. treatise on *Mîmânsâ*] [Benares Sansk. Ser.] 8° *Benares*

Shiva Samhita: Esoteric Science and Philos. of Tantras, tr. Srish Chunder Basu rs.2.12 8° Heeralal Bhole, *Calc.* 89

Treats of Evolution and Cosmogony, Anat. and Psychol., Psychometry and Clairvoyance, Yoga and Emancipation, etc.; w. Intro. on Yoga Philosophy.

5 & 6. NYÂYA and VAISESHIKA [Logic].

BHÎMÂCHÂRYA [*living*] Nyâyakosa [Bombay Sanskrit Series] 8° *Bombay* [ ]

A second edn., pract. a new wk., occupying 1096 pp. as agst. 267 of the first edn.

HARSHA Khandana-khandkâdyam 18/- 8° *Benares* 88

KANADA Aphorisms, ed. Vindhyeçvari Prasada Dube; w. comm. of Praçastapâda 85

TARKALANKARA Sabdasakiprakasika, ed. Jibananda Vidyasagara 2/6 8° *Calcutta* 78

TARKARATNA [16 cent.] Blaktiratnakar ["Sea of Devotion"], 14 pts. 8° -89

Regarded by the Vaishnavs as one of their standard relig. bks.

WINDISCH, Ernst Ueber das Nyâyabhâshya *Leipzig* 88

X. Heretical Systems.

Lalita Vistara: hist. d Bouddha, trad. Ph.-Ed. Foucaux, 2 pts. [Annales du Musée Guimet] ea. 15*fr*. 4° Leroux, *Paris* 83; 90

Mahâ-vastu: ed. E. Sénart, vol. ii.; w. (French) Intros. and comm. 25*fr*. 8° " " 90

The 1st edn. of the Skt. text, Vol. i. [*v.* B.B. K § 124 X.] was pub. in 1882.

Treatise.

RAM CHANDRA BOSE Hindu Philosophy popularly explained: the Heterodox Systems 6/- 16° *Calcutta* 88

With chaps. on Buddhism, Jainism, Charbakism, the Doctrines of Ramanuja, *etc.*

XI. Grammarians.

Kâsikâ-vritti: Zwei Kapitel der Kaçika, ed. Dr. B. Liebich 4*m*. 8° Preuss, *Breslau* 92

Krishnadâsa:

Weber, Prf. Albrecht Ueber d. Pârasîprakâça d. Krishnadâsa [*extr. fr.* Abhgn. Berl. Akad.] 8*m*. 4° G. Reimer, *Berl.* 87

" " Ueber d. zweiten grammat. Pârasîprakâça d. Krishnadâsa [*extr. fr.* Abhgn. Berl. Ak.] 6*m*. 4° G. Reimer, *Berl.* 89

PÂNINI [?3 cent].

LIEBICH, Dr. B. Pânini: ein Beitrag zur Kenntniss d. indischen Liter. u. Grammatik 10*m*. 8° Haessel, *Lpz.* 91

Treats PANINI in relat. to the other anc. grammarians, forming a fresh attempt to determine his place in Sansk. liter. by the help of materials made accessible since GOLDSTUCKER'S essay of 1861 [*v.* B.B. K § 124 xi.].

SIBAWAIHI Buch üb. Grammatik, übers. u. erlaut. G. Jahn, pts. i.-iii. ea. 4*m*. 8° Reuther, *Berl.* 93-94 *in prg.*

VÂMANA [?13 cent.] Stilregeln, bearb. Prf. Carl Cappeller 1*m*.50 l 8° Trübner, *Strassbg.* 80

XII. Lexicographers.

DURGASINHA — Dhatuvrittisara: material portion of the Katantra; w. extrs. fr. Ramanathas Manorama 6/6 8° (*India*) 87

HEMACHANDRA [12 cent.] Anekârthasamgraha, ed. Prf. Th. Zachariae; w. extrs. fr. Comm. of Mahendra 8° 10m. Holder, *Vienna* / Educ. Soc. Press, *Bombay* 93

Forms the 1st vol. of the *Quellenwerke der altind. Lexicogr.*, a small series of orig. Sansk. glossaries wh. the Impl. Acad. of Sciences of Vienna has undertaken to publish. It is a colln. of homonyms, giving the meanings of over 4,000 words.

TÂRÂNÂTHA TARKAVÂCHUSPATI [16–17 cent.] Mahâvyutpatti [5442 pp.] r 4° *Calcutta*

XII.* Historians.

BÂNABHATTA — Srî Harsha Charita, tr. Prf. E. B. Cowell + Thomas 8° Orient. Transl. Fd. *in prep.*

A history of King HARSHA, contg. acc. of the dynasty founded by PUSHYABHUTI at Thânesar, and partic. the beg. of career of the 2nd Mahârâjâdhirâja of this family called SRI HARSHA, who conquered the whole of N., Cent. and W. India fr. 606–648 A.D.

KAHLANA PANDITA — Râjatarangini, ed. Dr. M. A. Stein, w. crit. appar. and notes; vol. i. [text] 8° Byculla Press, *Bombay* 92

An important edn. of a valuable history of Kashmir, based on the *codex archetypus* (17 cent.) wh. the Edr. has discovered.

,, ,, — Râjatarangini, tr. into English J. Chunder Dutt, 2 vols. c 8° *Calcutta* (8/- Paul) 79; 87

XIII. Rhetoric, Poetics, etc.

ÂNANDAVARDHANA [9 cent.] Dhvanyâloka; w. comm. by Abhinavagupta [Nirnayasâgara Press] 8° *Bombay*

APPADÎKSHITA — Chitra-Mîmâmsâ [Nirnayasâgara Press] 8° ,,

GOVINDA — Kâvyâprâdipa; w. comm. [Nirnayasâgara Press] 8° ,,

JAGANNÂTHA — Rasagangâdhara, w. comm. [Nirnayasâgara Press] 8° ,,

With copious extracts fr. the Udâharana-chandrikâ [Nirnayasâgara Press] 8° *Bombay*.

RUDRATA [11 cent.] Kâvyâlankâra; w. comm. of Namisâdhu [Nirnayasâgara Press] 8° *Bombay*

,, — Çrncârâtilaha, ed. Dr. R. Pischel; w. Intro. and notes [w. Ruyyaka's Sahrdayalîlâ] 6*m.* 8° *Kiel* 90

RUYYAKA [12 cent.] Alankârasarvava [Nirnayasâgara Press] 8° *Bombay*

,, — Sahrdayalîlâ, ed. Dr. R. Pischel—*v.* Rudrata, *supra.*

VÂMANA [? 13 cent.] Kâvyâlankârasûtras, w. comm. [Nirnayasâgara Press] 8° *Bombay*

XIV. Astrology and Astronomy.

Account.

THIBAUT, Dr. G. —*in his edn. of* Varâha-Mihira, *ut infra.*

Texts.

VARÂHA-MIHIRA — Brihat Jataka, tr. N. Chitambaram Iyer [rectifies entry in B.B. K § 124, xiv.] 15/- 8° *Madras* 85

,, ,, — Panchasiddhântikâ, ed. Dr. G. Thibaut; w. Engl. tr. and intro. 16/- 4° *Benares* 89

A compend. of the 5 systs. of astronomy in vogue in the author's time. Conts. an Intro. Essay on Hindu astron., espec. val. as showing the kind of influence wh. the Gks. exerted on it.

XVI. Medicine.

Brihat Nighanta Ratnâkara: ed. Datharam, pt. i. ?; ii. 9/- r 8° *Bombay* ?; 89

A medical lexicon, compiled fr. other works; gives Sansk. names of plants and drugs, qualities, effects, etc., in Sansk. and Hindi.

Charaka Samhitâ: tr. Avinash Chandra Kaviratna, pts. i.-vi. ea. 4/- p 8° *Calcutta* 90–93 *in prg.*

VÂGBHATTA — Ashtânga-Rhidaya, ed. Ravidatta; w. Hindu tr. 28/- r 8° *Bombay* 90

,, — Rasaratnasamuchchaya, ed. Krishnarâva Vinâyaka Bâpata [Ânandâsrama Series] 8° *Poona* 91

A compendium of the treasures of medical preparations containing mercury.

VÂTSYÂYANA [6 cent.] Kamasutra, ed. Pandit Durgaprâsâda; w. commentary 14/- 8° *Bombay* 91

,, — Kama Soutra: règles de l'amour, trad. E. Lemairesse 6*fr.* 8° *Paris* 91

,, — Kama Sutra: transl. fr. the Sanscrit [*w.* 35/-] c 8° Kama Shastra Soc., *Cosmopoli* (= *London*) 83

Yogaratnâkarah: ed. Dr. Anna Moreshvarkunte [Ânandâsrama Series] 15/- r 8° *Poona* 89

A treatise on Hindu medicine published by several pandits.

125. INDIC (*e*): PRAKRIT PHILOLOGY AND LITERATURE.

[Prakrit has been defunct as a spoken language for about seven centuries.]

Jain Literature.

Bibliography. Manuscripts.

*Berlin, Königl. Bibl.: Verzeichniss d. Sansk.- u. Prâkrithandschriften —*ut* K § 121.

KLATT, J. — Specimen of a Literary-bibliogr. Jaina-Onomasticon 3*m.* r 8° Harrassowitz, *Lpz.* 93

History of Literature.

BÜHLER, Prf. G. — Ueb. d. Leben d. Jaina Mönches Hemachandra [extract] 4*m.* 50 4° Tempsky, *Vienna* 87

PADMARAJA PANDIT — Biographical History of Jain Authors Author's Priv. Press, *Bangalore*, *in prep.*

From the period of VARDHAMANA, the last of the Tirthankaras, whom tradition places in 7th cent. B.C.

WARREN, S. J. — Les Idées philos. et relig. d. Jaïnas, trad. [fr. Dutch (1875)] J. Pointet—*in* Mélanges *of* Musée Guimet, x. [*ut* K § 95].

Serial.

PADMARAJA PANDIT [ed.] [monthly] Author's Priv. Press, *Bangalore* 93 *in prg.*

Inscriptions.

RICE, B. Lewis [ed.] Inscriptions at Sravana Belgoda —*ut* K § 121.

An important wk., of over 400 pp. of text, giving the texts of the inscripp. in Rom. char., translitern., translation, etc.

K §§ 126–127

Texts: *Series.*

Jain Religious Book Soc. *Ajimganj (Murshidabad) in prg.*

Achârânga Sûtram; with comm. and *Balav bodha Dipika* .. 37/6
Antagadadashâ Sûtram; w. explan. 8/-
Anuttaropapâdika Sûtram; w. explan. 22/6
Anuyogdwâr Sûtram; w. *Vritti* and *Balav bodha Dipika* .. 20/-
Bhagwati Sûtram; w. *Vritti*, in Gujarati 150/-
Dynâtâdharmkathânga Sûtram; w. *Vivritti*, in Gujarati.... 26/-
Dashapennâ Sûtram; w. comm. and notes 5/-
Jain Râmâyanam; w. comm. and *Balav bodha Dipika* 4/-
Jivâbhigama Sûtram; w. *Vivritti* 45/-
Kalpa Sûtram Atmanindâbhâvnâch; w. *Balav bodha Dipika* 46/-
Nandi Sûtram; w. comm. and *Balav bodha Dipika*.......... 15/-
Niryavali Sûtram; w. *Balav bodha* explan. comm. and notes 5/-
Pâlarâso 2/-
Pradnyâpanâ Sûtram; w. comm. and notes, and *Vivritti*.... 80/-
Prishna Vyâkarana Sûtram; w. *Vivritti* & notes in Gujarati 10/-
Râjprashni; w. *Balavâ bodha Vritti*, in Gujarati.......... 15/-
Samavâyâng Sûtram; w. *Vritti*, in Gujarati.......... 22/6
Shrâddhadinkrityam Atmanindâbhâvnâch; w. *Balav bodha Dipika* 46/-
Sthânâng Sûtram; w. notes and comm. in Gujarati.......... 30/-
Sûtra Kritânga Sûtram; w. comm. and *Balav bodha Dipika* 37/6
Upapâtik Sûtram; w. *Balav bodha Vritti*, in Gujarati 10/-
Upâsakdnshâ Sûtram; w. explan. 7/6
Uttarâdhyana Sûtram; w. *Balav bodha Dipika* 30/-
Vipâk Sûtram; w. *Vivritti* and notes in Gujarati 7/6

Rao Bahadur Dhanapatisinha [promoter] Series of Jain Books [*v. also* 𝔅.𝔅. K § 125] *v.s. Calcutta, in prg.*

Acharangasûtra; w. comm. and *Balav bodha Dipika*........
Antagadadasharûtra; w. explan. ....
Anuttaropapa-dikasûtra; w. explan. ....
Anuyogdwârsûtra; w. *Vivritti* and *Balav bodha Dipika* ....
Bhagwatisûtra; w. *Vivritti* in Gujarati ....
Dashapennasûtra; w. comm. and notes..........
Jainaramayana; w. comm. and *Balav bodha Dipika* ....
Jivâbhigamasûtram; w. *Vivritti* ....
Nandisûtra; w. comm. and *Balav bodha Dipika* ....
Niryavalisûtra; w. *Balav bodha* explan. comm. and notes ..
Phishnâvyakaranasûtra; w. *Vivritti* and notes, in Gujarati..
Pradnyâpanâsûtra; w. comm., notes and *Vivritti* ....
Rashprashni; w. *Balav bodha* Gujarati..........
Samavâyâng-sûtra; w. *Vivritti* in Gujarati ....
Sthânângsûtra; w. notes and comm. in Gujarati ....
Sutrakritangasûtra; w. comm. and *Balav bodha Dipika* ....

126-7. INDIC (*f*)–(*g*): PALI AND SINGHALESE PHILOLOGY AND LITERATURE INCLUDING EARLY BUDDHISTIC SANSKRIT LITERATURE.

Grammar.

GUNASEKARA, A. M. Comprehensive Grammar of the Sinhalese Language 8° Skeen, Colombo / 12/6 Paul 91

Etymology: *Dictionary.*

CARTER, Chas. New English-Sinhalese Dictionary, pts. ii.-v. [last] ea. 5/- c 8° *Colombo* 90 *sqq.*

Literature.

History.

GRAY, Prf. Jas. The Niti Literature of Burma

Texts and Translations.

Abhidhamma Atthasâlini Atthayojanâ: ed. K. Pannâsekhara Thera 90
Abhidhammasangaho: ed. Nanadaramatissa Thero; w. Singhalese explan. 90
ASVAGHOSKA Buddha-Karita [Anecdota Oxoniensia] 4° 12/6 Clar. Press / $3.25 *net* Macmillan, *N.Y.* 93
Avadâna Çataka: Cent Légendes Bouddhiques, trad. Léon Feer [Ann. Musée Guimet] 20*fr.* 4° Leroux, *Paris* 91
BUDDHAGHOSA: Visuddhimaggo, w. Parakramabahu's comm., pts. i.-xvi. 87–91 *in prg.*
,, the hist. romance of the rise & career of Buddhaghosa, ed. Prf. Jas. Gray; w. tr. 6/- 8° Luzac 92
Introd. gives a good acc. of the vernacular wks. bearing on the subject.

Buddhist Mahayana Texts: tr. E. B. Cowell + F. Max Müller + J. Takakusu [Sacr. Bks. of East] 8° 12/6 Clar. Press / $3.25 *net* Macmillan, *N.Y.* 94
Buddhist Texts from Japan, ed. Prf. F. Max Müller + Bunyio Nanjio; pts. i.–iii. [Anecdota Oxoniensia] s 4° 21/- Clar. Press / $5.30 *net* Macmillan, *N.Y.* 87–93
i. *Vagrakkhedikâ*, 3/6 (90c. *net*); ii. *Sukhâvati Vyûha*, 7/6 ($1.90 *net*); iii. *Ancient Palm-leaves contg. Pragna-Pâramitâ-hridaya-sûtra, and Ushnisha-Vigaya-Dhârani*, 10/- ($2.50 *net*).

Dhammapadatthakathâ: *in prg.*
Jataka, The: w. its commentary: tales of the anterior births of Gotama Buddha, ed. Viggo Fausböll, vol. v. 28/- 8° Paul 92 *in prg.*
The Pali text. Two or three more vols. will complete the work.

,, Engl. tr., ed. Prf. E. B. Cowell [to occupy 7 or 8 vols.] 8° Cambr. Press / Macmillan, *N.Y.* *in prep.*
Vol. i., tr. R. CHALMERS, will contain the 40 stories given in Prf. RHYS-DAVIDS' discontinued tr. [*nt* 𝔅.𝔅. K § 127], and tr. of remainder of the 1st vol. of FAUSBÖLL'S edn. of text; and the other vols. will cover the vols. of the text. Vols. ii. tr. W. H. D. ROUSE; iii. R. A. NEILL + H. F. FRANCIS.

Ummagga Jataka; tr. T. B. Yatawara [edn. of text in prep.] 8° (*Ceylon*) 93
Jätäkä-Mälä ["Garland of Birth Stories"], ed. Prf. Hendrick Kern [of Leyden]; w. var. rgs. [Harvard Sansk. Ser.] r 8° Ginn, *Boston* / 6/- *net* Arnold 93
Critical edn. of the *Sanskrit* text, 34 in no., w. a 35th story (the Tortoise Tale), not in Sansk. but in perhaps the curious Gâthâ dialect (wh. is closer to Sansk. than Pali), added in the appendix. *No* introd. An acc. of the present colln. of tales (repres. the Northern tradition of the master's previous births) will be found in the late RAJENDRALALA MITRA'S *Nepalese Buddhist Literature*, pp. 49 *sqq.* [*nt* K § 128].

Mahâbodhivamso: ed. Pedinnoruwe Sobhita 90
Mahâvamsa: Pt. II. [= ch. xxxix.–c.] tr. L. C. Wijesinha; w. tr. of Pt. I. by G. Tournour [*nt* 𝔅.𝔅. K § 127] prefixed 8° *Colombo* 89
Snyder, E. N. Der Commentar u. d. Textüberlieferung d. Mahâvamsa 1*m.* 8° Mayer & Müller, *Berl.* 91
Milinda Panho: Questns. of King Milinda, tr. Prf. T. W. Rhys Davids, pt. ii. [Sacred Bks. of East] 8° 12/6 Clar. Press / $3.25 *net* Macmillan, *N.Y.* 91
Moggallâyana Vyâkarana: ed. Devamitta Thera 90
NEUMANN, K. E. (tr.) Der Wahrheitpfad: ein buddhist. Denkmal [in orig. metres] 3*m.*50 8° Veit, *Lpz.* 93
Pali Text Soc. Journal *and* Publicns., ed. Prf. T. W. Rhys Davids 8° Pali Text Soc. 82 *sqq.*
The 12 yrs.' issues (1882–93; 34 vols.) cont. 34 texts, ed. by var. edrs.—in all, some 7,000 pp., an invaluable series.

Prince and Dérvish.
Weisslovits, Nath. Prinz u. Derwisch: in hebräisch. Darstellg. a. d. Mittelalter 5*m.*40 8° Ackermann, *Munich* 90
An Indian romance, contg. hist. of early yrs. of Buddha. With compar. of Arab. and Gk. parallel texts.

Samantakûtavannâ : ed. W. Dhammânanda Sthavira + M. Nânissara ; w. Singhal. explan. 90
Sutta Nipâta : ed. Pannânandra Thera, pt. i. 90
" " übers. Dr. Arth. Pfungst, pt. i. [tr. *vid* Fausböll's Engl. tr., *ut* B.B. K § 127] 1m. 50 8° Trübner, *Strassbg.* 90
Suttasangaho : ed. M. Varâpitiya Sugatapâla 90
Tathâgata-udâna [or uppattipâtha] : Burmese versn., *sub tit.* Malalankara vatthu [*c.* 400 pp.] 8° *Rangoon* 91

The wk. of wh. Bp. P. BIGANDET'S *Life or Legend of Gaudama* [*ut* B.B. A § 14] is a tr. ; prev. tr. Rev. Chester BENNETT (Am.).

128. INDIC (*A*): MODERN ARYAN LANGUAGES OF INDIA: PHILOLOGY AND LITERATURE.

History of Vernacular Literature.

HARAPRASAD SHASTRI Vernacular Literature of Bengal [pp. 16] s 4° Hare Press, *Calcutta, n.d.* (91)

Repr. of a paper read bef. Cumbullatola Club, dealing w. native litr. of Bengal before introd. of Engl. education.

Bengali.

Grammar.

BEAMES, Jno. Grammar of the Bengali Language ; literary and colloquial 7/6 c 8° Clar. Press 94

Literature.

BISHVÁS, R. L. Upanyas Málá : a collection of stories 7/6 8° *Calcutta* 90
Hitopadesa [*ut* K § 124 VII.] : tr. into Bengali by Jogendra Chandra Chatterji [verse tr.] 8° " 89

Bihari.

GRIERSON + HOERNLE, Gen. A. / Dr. Comparative Dictionary of the Bihari Language, pts. i.–ii. 8° *Calcutta*?; 90 *in prg.*

Literature.

CHRISTIAN, John [tr.] Behar Proverbs : classified, arrgd., and tr. ; w. folklore notes—*ut* B § 4.

Gujarâti.

Grammar.

DÁLÁL, D. D. Manual of Gujarati Grammar [for use of Englishmen] 3/6 8° *Surat* 89
Prâchîna Gujerâti Sâhityâ Ratnamâlâ ["Garland of Gems of Old Guj. Lit."]: First Gem [Gram.], ed. H. H. Dhruva 8° *Bombay* 89
TISDALL, W. St. C. Simplified Grammar of the Gujarati [Trübner's Simplified Grammars] 10/6 c 8° Paul 92

Literature.

Alf Lailat [*ut* K § 115] : The Arabian Nights, tr. into Gujarati by Jehângir Bejanji Karâni, 2 vols. ea. 6/- r 8° *Bombay* 89 ; 91
Avesta [*ut* K § 131] : translit. and tr. into Gujarâti by Kâvasji Edalji Kangâ ; w. notes 6/- 8° " [ ] 88
Bhagavadgitanum Shuddha Gujaráti Bháshántar 7/6 8° *Ahmadabad* 90

A tr. of or rather comment. on the *Bhagavad Gîtâ* in Gujarâti by MUKHIÁJI MULJI MEGHÁJI + MUTSHIÁJI BÁPÁLÁL NATHUBHÁL

BORRADAILE [ed.] Gujurât Caste Rules, vols. i.–ii. [in Gujurâti] ea. 2/6 r 8° *Bombay* 88

Rules of Castes and other Analogues, Customs, and Usages of Hindus of Surat and Broach Districts. The colln. was made soon after 1827.

DÁLÁL, D. D. [ed.] Gujarati Proverbs: w. their Engl. equivalents [400 provbs., in alphab. order] 2/- 8° *Surat* 89
LILADHAR, Ghelábhái [ed.] Jain Kathá Sangraha Bhág Pahelo, pt. i. 4/- 8° *Bombay* 90 *in prg.*

A collection of short Jain tales, ill. the virtues encouraged and vices denounced by Jainism, in Gujarati.

MANILÁL NABHUBLÁI DVIVEDI Siddhânta Sâra ["The Established Truth"] 9/- r 16° *Bombay* 89

A review of relig. and philos. thought in India, advancing the claims of the advaita syst. of philos.—the doctr. of identity of universal spirit and matter.

Hindi.

Grammar.

*KELLOGG, Dr. G. H. A Grammar of the Hindi Language [*ut* B.B. K § 128] : sec. edn. 21/- 8° Paul [*Allahabad* 76] 93

An excellent book, of high scholastic value.

Literature.

Bhâgavata-Purâna [*ut* K § 124 III.] : Bhâgavat Ekâdashaskandha Bhâshâ, tr. Chaturdâs 3/- r 8° *Bombay* 88

A free version in Hindi of bk. xi. of *Bhâgwat.*, chiefly a dialogue betw. Krishna and his friend Uddhava.

MACKENZIE, Sir Don. Rûski Târikh [" History of Russia "], tr. into Hindi Munshi Nawal Kishor 30/- r 8° *Lucknow* 88
Mahâbhârata [*ut* K § 124 II.] : Hindi tr. by Pandit Kali Charan r 8° " 88 ; 88 ; 88

Mahâb. Anusâsan Parb ["Gt. War-bk. the Anusâsan"] 7/6 ; *Mahâb. Dron Parb* [" the Dron "] 8/- ; *Mahâb. Karn Parb* [" the Karn "] 4/-.

MALIK MOHAMMAD Padumawati [the oldest known poem in Hindi] :
Grierson, G. A. On the Padumwati [*repr. fr.* Journal Bengal Asiat. Soc.] 8° *priv. prin.* 93

Hindustani [Urdu].

Grammar.

KEMPSON, M. Syntax and Idioms of Hindustani 6/- c 8° W. H. Allen [90] 94

Progressive exercises in gram., reading and tr., of colloq. and liter. Hindustani, w. vocabularies.

PHILLIPS, Col. A. N. Hindustani Idioms ; w. vocab. & notes [for candidates for Higher Standard] 5/- c 8° Paul 93

Literature.

ALÂDIN GULÂM HUSEN [ed.] Gulistâne Panjatan ["Garden of the 5 Personages"] 16/- 4° *Bombay* 88
A collection of various Mohammedan religious songs; in Urdu.

AMÂNAT Indarsabhâ, neuind. Singspiel: lithog. text, w. Germ. tr. & notes F. Rosen 8*m*. 8° 92
Conts. an Introd. on the Indian drama of to-day.

Bágh o Bahár: abstract fr. the original text, ed. [Miss] Edith F. Barry 2/- f 8° W. H. Allen 90
The *Bagh e Bahâr*, or *Tale of the Four Dervishes*, has for generations been one of the textbks. for both the higher and lower standards of proficiency in Hindostani.

HAKIM AHMAD ALI-SAHIB Ma'mûl-i-Ahmadi; ill. [a manual of surgery] 8° Narayan Press, *Lahore* 90

Khassa.

ROBERTS, Rev. H. Grammar of the Khassi Language [Trübner's Simplified Grammars] 10/6 c 8° Paul 91
A competent grammar of one of the most interesting of the sub-Himalayan langs., spoken in the very centre of Assam.

Marâthi.

Literature.

Arya Chânakya: tr. Vámam Shástri Islámpurkar 3/6 8° *Bombay* 90
A free tr. of the *Mûdrârâkshasa* ["*The Minister Rakshasa and the Signet Ring*"] a Sansk. drama by VISHÂKHADATA.

[Bhagavatgita; *ut* K § 124 II.]: Dnyâneshvar Dnyâneshvari 2/6 8° *Bombay* 90
Perhaps the oldest Marathi bk. in existence. It is a commentary on the *Bhagavadgita*. DNYÂNESHVAR was both a poet and a saint, and his book is held in great veneration by the Hindus.

SADI [*ut* K § 134] Bostán, tr. [fr. Persian] Mádhavráv Vyankatesh Lele 5/- 12° *Bombay* 90
Thousand and One Nights [*ut* K § 115]: tr. Krishna Shástri Chiplunkar and others; ill. [1030 pp.] 16/- r 8° ,, [ ] 90
SARASVATI GANGÂDHAR Guru Charitra 10/- r 8° ,, [ ] 89
A popular bk., held in much veneration, contg. mytholog. stories and descrns. of Brahmanical duties.

Mikir.

NEIGHBOR, Rev. R. E. Vocabulary in English and Mikir 8/- r 8° *Calcutta* 78

Nepali: *Literature.*

Hariccandranrityam: ein altnepales. Tanzspiel, hrsg. A. Conrady [w. gram. Introd.] 1*m*.50 8° Koehler, *Lpz.* 92
RAJENDRALALA MITRA Nepalese Buddhist Literature

Somali.

SCHLEIDER, A. W. Die Somali-Sprache, pt. i. 6*m*. Fröhlich, *Berlin* 92

130. IRANIC (*b*): ZEND (OLD BACTRIAN) AND OLD PERSIAN (*a*): PHILOLOGY.

Epigraphy.

WEISSBACH + BANG, $\frac{\text{F. W.}}{\text{W. [eds.]}}$ Die altpersischen Keilinschriften, pt. i. [Assyriol. Bibl.] 10*m*. 4° Hinrichs, *Lpz.* 93

Alphabet.

EUTING, Dr. Julius [ed.] Drei Tafeln des Pehlevi- und Zend-Alphabets f° Author, *Strassbg.* 78
" " Uebersicht des Pehlevi-Alphabets [a reprint, one leaf] f° " " 91
JACKSON, Prf. A. W. Williams [Am.] The Avestan Alphabet and its Transcription; w. appendices 80*pf*. 8° *Stuttgt.* 91

Grammar.

JACKSON, Prf. A. V. Williams [Am.] Avesta Grammar in Comparison w. Sanskrit, pt. i. 8° $\frac{\text{9m. Kohlhammer, Stuttg.}}{\text{7s. Ginn, Boston}}$ 92
Intended for the general student of philology as well as the Orientalist. This Pt. incl. Acc. of Lang., Phonetic Laws and Accidence: a Syntax and Metre to follow.

KANGA, Kavasji Edalji Pract. Grammar of Avesta Lang., comp. w. Sanscrit 12/6 8° *Bombay* 91
Conts. a chapter on syntax, and another on the Gâthâ dialect.

TOLMAN, Dr. H. C. [Am.] A Grammar of the Old Persian Language $\frac{\text{Ginn, Boston}}{\text{4/6 Arnold}}$ 92
With vocabulary, and inscriptions of the Achaemenian kings.

Dictionary.

MILLS, Dr. L. H. [ed.] Zend-Sanskrit Dictionary of the Gâthâs *in prep.*
To be followed, probably, by a succinct dictionary to all the *Avesta*.

STEIN, Dr. —*has a* Zend Dictionary *in prep.*

Pronouns.

CALAND, W. Zur Syntax der Pronomina im Avesta [*repr. fr.* Trs. R. Acad. of Sc. Amst.] 1/6 4° *Amsterdam* 91

Chrestomathy.

JACKSON, Prf. A. V. Williams [Am.; ed.] Avesta Reader, pt. i.: Easier Texts; w. vocab. and notes $1.75 8° Ginn, *Boston* 93

131. IRANIC (*c*): ZEND LITERATURE.

Zend-Avesta.

Text.

*GELDNER, Prf. Karl F. [ed.] Avesta: die heiligen Bücher d. Parsen, pt. vi. 12*m*., vii. 8*m*. 4° Kohlhammer, *Stuttg.* 89; 93
A very important edn., w. var. readings fr. every accessible MS. of any authority. Also an Engl. tr. by same, pt. vi. 18*s*. '89; vii. 1'93.

Gâthâs [the earlier pt. of the *Avesta*, contg. the purest theology].

*MILLS, Dr. L. H. [ed. and tr.] Study of the Five Zarathushtrian Gâthas 30/- 8° *priv. prin.* Clar. Press / (Brockhaus, *Lpz.*) 90–94

With the Zend, Pahlavi, Sanskrit and Persian texts, free metr. English trs. of Pahl. and Sansk., and comm. to each. Auth. is also at wk. on tr. into Sansk. of the *Gâthas*, a spec. of wh. [*Yasna* 28] is cont. in ROTH'S *Festgruss*, *ut* K § 122.

Translations.

English.

JACKSON, Prf. A. V. Williams [Am.; tr.] A Hymn of Zoroaster [pp. xii. 62] 8° Ginn, *Boston* / 5/- Arnold 9-

A tr. of *Yasna* 31, with comments.

*MILLS, Dr. L. H. [tr.] —*in his* Study of the Five Zarathushtrian Gâthas, *ut supra.*

French.

*DARMESTETER, Prf. Jas. [tr.] Le Zendavesta : traduction nouvelle—*ut* A § 15.

Aids —*v. also* A § 15.

GELDNER, Karl Studien zum Avesta, pt. i. 5*m.* 8° Trübner, *Strassbg.* 82

132. IRANIC (*d*): MIDDLE PERSIAN [PHILOLOGY AND] LITERATURE.

Literature.

Gujastak Abalish : relation d. confér. presid. p. Calife Mâmoun; w. Fch. tr., notes & gloss. A. Barthélemy 3*fr.* 50 8° Bouillon, *Paris* 87

In the *Bibliothèque de l'École des Hautes Études.*

Pahlavi Texts : tr. E. W. West, pt. iv. [Contents of the Nasks]—*ut* A § 14.

Yasna : Collotype Reproduction of the Ancient MS. [J2]; w. its Pahlavi tr. [A.D. 1323] 210/- *nt.* r 4° Clar. Press 91

A wonderfully faithful facs. of the orig. MS., reprodg. all the peculiarities and traces of vicissitudes thro' wh. it has passed dur. the 570 yrs. of its life. Written at Cambay in A.Y. 692 [=A.D. 1323] it disappeared till 1720, before wh. it was brought fr. Broach to Naosari by DASTOR JÂMÂSP ÂSÂ [d. 1753]. In 1865 it was found by DASTOR JÂMÂSP MINOCHEHRJI. In the eighties it was sent to Tübingen [Prf. GELDNER for use in his edn. of the Avesta texts (*ut* K § 131)] and to Oxford [Dr. MILLS, for his *Gâthas* (*ut* K § 131)]. In 1889 it was pres. to Univ. Oxon., and is now in Bodl. Lib. Only 200 copies pubd. The entire Zend text of the MS. is tr. by Dr. L. H. MILLS in *Sacr. Bks. of East*, xxxi., and the Pahlavi text of its *Gâtha* portion is ed. and tr. in MILLS' edn. of the *Gâthas*, *ut* K § 131.

133. IRANIC (*e*): MODERN PERSIAN. PHILOLOGY.

Grammar.

GEITLIN, G. Principia Grammatices Neo-Persicæ [w. dialogues] 6/- 8° *Helsingfors* 90

PIZZI, Italo Manuale della Lingua Persiana [gram., chrestom., vocab.] 15*m.* 8° Gerhard, *Lpz.* 83

PLATTS, J. T. Grammar of the Persian Language, pt. i. [Accidence] 10/6 16° Williams 94

Etymology.

HORN, P. Grundriss der neupersischen Etymologie 15*m.* 8° Trübner, *Strassbg.* 93

Dictionary.

Bahâr-i 'Ajam : [a valuable Persian dict. compiled in India]

Faranghi Nâsiri : [a native Persian dictionary; lithographed] *Teheran* 71

SCHLIMMER Terminologie Medico-pharmaceutique Française-Persane [lithographed] " 74

*STEINGASS, Dr. F. A Comprehensive Persian and English Dictionary 76/- 4° W. H. Allen 92

A revised and reconstructed edn. of Johnson's enlargemt. [1852] of WILKINS-RICHARDSON'S *Pers., Arab. and Eng. Dict.* [1806-10], reducing the Arab. and increasing the Pers. element. Full use has been made of VULLERS' *Lex. Pers.-Lat.* [*ut* 無 K § 131], the *Bahâr-i 'Ajam* [*ut sup.*] MIRZA JA'FAR'S trs. of Turkish plays repr. in Engl., Frce. and Germy., and the Shah's orig. diaries of Europ. travel in 1873 and 1878. A useful bk., of value to the student of Pers. liter. rather than of the mod. colloq. lang.

Dialogues.

KAZIMIRSKI Dialogues Français-Persans [a very good bk.]

Translations into Modern Persian.

TALBOT, Maj. A. C. [tr.] Translations into Persian, vol. i.: Engl. Text; ii. Pers. Transl. [of some service to studts.] 15/- 8° *Calcutta* 90

134. IRANIC (*f*): PERSIAN LITERATURE.

History of Literature.

BARBIER DE MEYNARD, A. C. La Poésie en Perse [Bibl. Orient. Elzévirienne] 2*fr.* 50 18° Leroux, *Paris* 78

REED, Elizab. A. [Am.] Persian Literature : ancient and modern [a good pop. survey] $2.50 12° Griggs, *Chicago* 93

Drama.

QARAGADAGI Mons. Jourdan im Qarabeg : Pers. text, w. Germ. tr. and vocab. A. Wahrmund [modern comedy] 4*m.* r 8° Hölder, *Vienna* 89

ROGERS, Alex. [ed. & tr.] Three Persian Plays; w. tr. and vocabulary 7/6 c 8° W. H. Allen 91

Fiction.

CLOUSTON, W. A. [ed.] Some Persian Tales : translated; w. notes 1/3 32° Bryce, *Glasgow* 92

8 stories, 5 of wh. are selns. fr. the *Mahbub al-Kulub* ("Delight of Hearts"), a very large Pers. colln., tr. by Edw. REHATSEK [d. 1892]. Includes *The Kazi of Emessa*, an anc. versn. of SHAKSPERE'S "pound of flesh" story.

McCARTHY, Justin H. [tr.] The Thousand and One Days, 2 vols.; fronts. c 8° 12/- Chatto / $4 Lippincott, *Phila.* 92

Tr. fr. the Fch. *Les Mille et Un Jours*, Garnier, *Paris* '83, not so complete a colln. as *Les Mille et Un Jours* [Panthéon Littéraire] Delagrave, *Paris*. Two prev. Engl. versns. have appeared, (1) by Dr. KING, 1714, (2) by Ambrose PHILIPS, 1738, both of wh. have been more than once repr.

K § 134

Geography and History.

ABU'L HASAN, J. M. E. Das Mujmil et Târîkh-i-Ba'dnâdirîje, hrsg. Oskar Mann, pt. i. 3*fl.* Brill, *Leyden* 91

A hist. of Persia in the yrs. 1747-50, the anarchical period immed. following the assassination of Nádir shah (wh. forms the 1st portion of this bk.). Ed. fr. Berlin MS. w. an Intro. (in Germ.) and indices.

ARMENO, Christof. [tr.] Peregrinaggio di tre Giovani, figliuoli del re di Serendippo [tr. fr. Pers., 1557], hrsg. H. Gassner; w. Prf. Herm. Varnhagen [Erlanger Beiträge] 2*m*.50 8° Junge, *Erlangen* 91

HOUTSMA, Th. [ed.] Recueil de Textes relatifs à l'histoire des Seldjoucides, vol. iii. 5*fl.* 8° Brill, *Leyden* 86; 89

Vol. i. *Hist. des Seldjoucides du Kermân*, by MUHAMMED IBRAHÎM [Pers. text] 5*fl*.50; ii. *Hist. des Seldj. de l'Irâq*, by AL BONDARI [Arab. text; *ut* B.B. K § 115] 5*fl*.25; iii. A Turkish tr. of a (lost) Pers. original by IBN BIBI [15 cent.], covering the period 1190-1295 A.D., fr. death KILIJ-ARSLAN to rn. of ALA-ED-DIN KEIKUBAD. '92.

Makála-i-shakhsí sayyáh ki dar kaziyya-i-Bab navishta-ast—*v.* A § 13, *s.v.* Bábí-ism.

MIR ABDOUL KERIM BOUKHARY Hist. de l'Asie Centrale: Pers. text, ed. Ch. Schefer, 2 vols. ea. 15*fr.* f° *Paris* 76; 78

A history of Afghanistan, Bokhara, Khiva and Khokand, 1740-1818. *Ecole des Langues Orient. Vivantes.*

MIRKHOND [1432-98] Rauzat-us-Safâ ["Garden of Purity"], tr. Edw. Rehatsek, ed. F. F. Arbuthnot, Pt. I., vol. i.-ii. ea. 10/- 8° Orient. Tr. Fd. (Luzac) 91; 92

The first vol. of a New Series of the old Oriental Transl. Fund, but pub. at the expense of Mr. ARBUTHNOT. This pt. conts. a tr. of the Intro. and pt. of Book I. of MIRKHOND'S vast history. The rest of Bk. I. will not be tr. as it was done by David SHEA [1832], but 6 vols. are to appear, giving the hist. of the world as known to the Muslims fr. the creation of genii before Adam to the assass. of Ali, 4th Caliph of the Sunnis and 1st Imám of the Shi'ites: represents rather less than one-third of MIRKHOND'S whole wk. Vol. i. ends w. d. of Aaron, and consists largely of the hist. of the earlier prophets and the most extravagant fables: never before tr. Vol. ii. conts. Moslem version of our Bible stories fr. death of Moses to mission of I'sa (Jesus), of whose birth, life and d. many details are given.

" " Life of Muhammad the Apostle, tr. Edw. Rehatsek, 2 vols. 20/- 8° Orient. Transl. Fd. 93

Forms vols. i.-ii. of Pt. II. of the tr. of *Rauzat-us-Safâ*. A very full biography of the Prophet, not as he appeared in the eyes of his early converts and followers, but in all legends, accretions, miraculous interpositns., deliverances and manifestns. wh. poetry and piety have assoc. w. his career.

" " Lives of Abu Bakr, O'Mar, O'thmân and Ali, tr. Edw. Rehatsek, ed. F. F. Arbuthnot 10/- 8° Orient. Transl. Fd. 94

Forms vol. iii. of Pt. II. of *Rauzat-us-Safâ*. Lives of the four immediate successors of MOHAMMED.

NASSIRI KHOSRAU Voyage [1043-49] en Perse, Syrie, Palest. *etc.*, ed. Ch. Schefer 25*fr.* 8° Leroux, *Paris* 8-

The text, with Fch. tr. and notes. *Ecole des Langues Orient. Vivantes.*

NERCHAKHY, Moham. Descriptn. topogr. et hist. de Boukhara, vol. i. 15*fr.*; ii. [Tr., *in prep.*] [Ec. Langs. Or. Viv.] 8° Leroux, *Paris* 92

NIZAM OUL-MOULK Siasset Namèh, ed. C. Schefer, 2 vols. [Ecole Langs. Or. Viv.] ea. 15*fr.* 8° " " 91

A treatise on government, composed for the Sultan MELIK CHÂH by his vizier NIZAM OUL-MOULK.

RAVERTY, Maj. H. G. [tr.]

Has in prep. a tr., w. notes, of an old Pers. MS. of 1500 f° pp., contg. a hist. of 1000 yrs. fr. d. of MOHAMMED, A.D. 632.

RIZA QOULY KHAN Relation de l'Ambassade au Kharezm [Khiva], ed. Ch. Schefer, w. Fch. tr., 2 vols.; map [Ecole d. Langs. Orient. Vivantes] ea. 15*fr.* 8° Leroux, *Paris* 76; 79

Târîkh-i-Jadid ["The New History"]: tr. E. G. Browne, *and his* Traveller's Narrative—*ut* A § 13.

Târîkh-i-Zendiyyé ed. Ernst Beer Brill, *Leyden* 88

Forms a useful complement to ABUL HASAN, *ut supra*.

Philosophy.

CHEREF-EDDÎN-RÂMI Anis-el-'Ochchâq: traité d. termes figurés rel. à la beauté, trad. C. Huart; w. notes [Bibl. d. l'Ecole d. Haut. Etud.] 5*fr*.50 8° Bouillon, *Paris* 75

Poetry.

FERDUSI [10 cent.] Shah Nameh, tr. Jas. Atkinson [Lubbock's 100 Best Bks.] 3/6 c 8° Routledge [32] 92

An abridged tr. in prose and verse, originally (1832) pubd. in the *Oriental Transl. Fund* series of bks.

HÂFIZ of Shiraz [14 cent.] Diwan.

*Clarke, Lt.-Col. H. W. [tr.] The Diwan-i-Hâfiz: translated, 2 vols. [*w.* 35/-] 4° *priv. prin., Calcutta* 91

A good prose tr., w. life of the poet, Introd. and copious crit. and explan. notes, forming a perfect mine of Sûfic lore (no index, however). It is the first Eng. tr. of the entire *Diwan* of "the Persian Anacreon." The Introd. gives a compreh. list of prev. translators.

Education Soc. [pubs.] Odes of Hafiz: translated [75 odes, w. notes] *Bombay* 91

Hormasji Temulji Dadachanji [tr.] Fifty Odes of Hafiz; w. notes 5/- 8° " 89

McCarthy, Justin H. [tr.] Selection fr. the Diwan of Hafiz: translated 7/6 16° Nutt 93

Only 500 printed. Japan. vell. edn. (50) 21/- *nt.*

Payne, Jos. [tr.] —*metrical tr. of the whole* Diwan Villon Society, *in prep.*

JAMI [1414-1492].

Behâristân ["Abode of Spring"] tr. [F. F. Arbuthnot]; w. notes [unexpurgated] [*w.* 21/-] c 8° Kharma Shastra Soc., *Benares* [= *Lond.*] 87

Joseph and Zuleikha: tr. Alex. Rogers 16/- *nt.* 8° Nutt 92

The first complete literal Engl. tr.—in rather poor Engl. rhyme (7000 couplets). Only 250 printed.

Schmidt, R. Das Kathâkântukam des Çrîvara vergl. m. Jos. u. Zul. 2*m.* 8° Haeseler, *Kiel* 93

MU'IN-UDDIN JAWÎNI Nigaristân ["Picture Gallery"], tr. Edw. Rehatsek 8° Orient. Transl. Fd., *in prep.*

A work written in imitation of SA'DI'S *Gulistan*.

NIZAMI [12 cent.] Loves of Laili & Majnum, tr. Jas. Atkinson, ed. Rev. J. A. Atkinson [son] 3/6 12° Nutt [36] 94

A much abgd. paraphrase rather than a tr., giving a fair idea of the sense and spirit of the poem.

OMAR KHÂYYAM [11 cent.] *Rubaiyât, tr. Edw. Fitzgerald [*ut* B.B. K § 134]: new edn. [verse] 10/6 c 8° Macmillan [58] 90

SA'DI of Shiraz [*c.* 1193-1291].

Bostan: photogr. fr. MS. prepared J. T. Platts, collated *etc.* Alex. Rogers; w. notes 18/- r 8° W. H. Allen 91

Reprod. by photolithogr. fr. a MS. prepared in India on basis of best Indian edns., collated w. GRAF'S Vienna edn. (*ut* B.B. K § 135) and copied by a good calligraphist.

" trad. A. C. Barbier de Meynard [Bibl. Orient. Elzev.; 1st Fch. tr.] 10*fr.* 18° Leroux, *Paris* 80

Gulistân ["Rose Garden"]: tr. [Edw. Rehatsek]; w. notes [unexpurgated] [*w.* 21/-] c 8° Kharma Shastra Soc., *Benares* [= *Lond.*] 88

Translation: German.

Rückert, Friedr. [tr.] Saadi's Politische Gedichte, [posthum.] hrsg. E. A. Bayer; w. Life of Sa'di and notes 3*m*.60 8° Mayer & Müller, *Berl.* 94

135. IRANIC (*g*): BALOCHI PHILOLOGY.

Phonology.

GEIGER, W. Lautlehre der Balochi [extract] 2*m.* 8° Franz, *Munich* 91

136. IRANIC (*h*): PUSHTO (AFGHAN) PHILOLOGY AND LITERATURE.

Linguistic Ethnology.

BELLEW, Surg.-Gen. H. W. Inquiry into the Ethnography of Afghanistan [208 pp.] 7/6 8° Orient. Inst., *Woking* 91

Grammar.

BIDDULPH, C. E. —*in his* Afghan Poetry of the Seventeenth Century, *ut infra.*

Etymology. Phonology.

GEIGER, W. Etymologie und Lautlehre des Afghanischen 1*m.*70 8° Franz, *Munich* 93

Epigraphy.

DARMESTETER, Prf. Jas. La Grande Inscription de Quandahâr Imprim. Nat., *Paris* 91

An important essay on the inscrip. mentioned by H. W. BELLEW in his *Jl. of a Polit. Mission to Afgh. in 1857* (*ut* E.E. F § 31).

Literature.

*DARMESTETER, Prf. Jas. [ed. and tr.] Chants Populaires des Afghans [Soc. Asiatique] 20*fr.* 8° Leroux, *Paris* 88–90

An excellent wk., w. valuable Introd. on the language, history and literature of the Afghans.

Khush-Hal Khan Khatak: selns. fr.: ed. C. E. Biddulph, w. trs., *sub tit.* Afghan Poetry of 17th Cent. 10/6 4° Paul 90

Literal trs., contg. also a short but practical and well-considered grammatical introduction.

137-138. IRANIC (*i*)–(*k*): KURDIC AND OSSETIC PHILOLOGY AND LITERATURE.

Kurdic.

Literature —*for* Folk-Literature, *v.* B § 27* and B.B. B § 27.*

Ossetic.

Literature.

MILLER + v. STACKELBERG, W./R. [eds.] Fünf osset. Erzählungen in digorischem Dialect 1*m.*50 8° Voss, *Lpz.* 91

139. IRANIC (*l*): ARMENIAN PHILOLOGY AND LITERATURE.

Epigraphy.

MÜLLER-SIMONIS, P. —*in his* Du Caucase au Golfe Persique à travers l'Arménie, le Kurdistan et la Mésopotamie 4° *Paris* 92

Conts. a list of Vannic (Armenian) cuneiform Inscriptions, 68 so far pubd., their discoverers and localities; also 30 new inscripp. wh. he has himself seen or heard of.

WÜNSCH, Prf. Jos. D. [ed.] Die Keilinschrift von Asrut Darga; w. comm. [w. descr. by H. D. Müller] 2*m.*80 4° Gold, *Vienna* 86

Manuscripts.

Berlin Königl. Bibl.: Verzeichniss der Armenischen Handschriften, v. N. Karamianz; 5 pl. 6*m.* r 4° Asher, *Berlin* 88

Vienna Mechitharisten Congreg.: Haupt-Catalog d. armen. HSS., vol. i. pt. 1, and ii. pt. 1 3*m.*50 8° Gerold, *Vienna* 92

Literature.

DE DARON, Et. Açoghih Histoire Universelle, trad. E. Dulaurier, pt. i. [Ecole d. Langs. Or. Viv.] 10*fr.* 8° Leroux, *Paris* 83

XVIII. Non-Aryan and Non-Semitic Philology (Europe and Asia).

140. BASQUE.

Bibliography.

*VINSON, Prf. Julien Essai d'une Bibliographie de la langue Basque 30*fr.* 8° Maisonneuve, *Paris* 91

Mentions all Basque bks. and bks. on the Basque lang., w. re facss. of the rarest and most interesting titles. A suppl. dealing w. newspaper articles and quotations fr. Basque bks. is to follow.

Dodgson, Edw. Spencer —*has pb.* a Supplement *to above*, in 2 pts. 8° *priv. prin.* 92; 93

Lists of *errata*, bks. pub. since the main wk., and notes, some of value.

History of the Language: *Relation to Berber.*

DE CHARENCY De la Parenté du Basque [*extr. fr.* Mém. Acad. Nat. de Caen] 8° Delesques, *Caen* 94

V. D. GABELENTZ, H. C. Verwandschaft des Baskischen m. d. Berber-Spr., hrsg. v. Schulenburg 8*m.* 8° Sattler, *Brunsw.* 94

K §§ 141-142

Epigraphy.

WEBSTER, Rev. Wentworth [ed.] Sur Quelques Inscripp. du Pays Basque et d. Environs 8° 92

A pamphlet. repr. fr. the *Bulletin de la Société Historique de Bayonne.*

Grammar.

DE AZCUE, Prf. Resurreccion Maria Euskal Izkindea ó Gramática Euskara 12*fr.*50 8° *Bilbao* 91

400 pp. in double col., one of Basque, the other of Spanish tr. By the first Prf. of Basque in Biscay.

Verb.

VAN EYS, W. J. Les Verbes Auxiliares d. l. Nouv. Test. de Liccarague [60 pages] 4*fr.* 8° Nijhoff, *The Hague* 90

A contribution of some importance for Basque students.

SCHUCHARDT, Prf. Hugo Entstehung d. Bezugsformen d. bask. Zeitworts 3*m.*50 4° Tempsky, *Vienna* 93

Forms pt. i. of his *Baskische Studien*, reissued fr. the *Abhandl. d. Wiener Akad.* A monument of patient and thorough method. *Bezugsformen* appears to mean the relations to each other of the pro-nominal forms cont. in the Basque verb.

Literature.

CHARLES-BORDES [ed.] Cent Chansons Populaires Basques; w. Fch. tr. & music [orally collected] 5*fr.* 8° *priv. prin.* 94

Old Testament:

Earliest Transltn. of Old Test. into Basque, by Pierre D'Orte; ed. Llew. Thomas, facs. [Anecd. Oxon.] 4° 18/6 Clar. Press / Macmillan, *N.Y.* 94

Edited from the MS. in Library of Shirburn Castle, Oxfordshire. Conts. *Genesis* and part of *Exodus.*

RIPALDA'S [Span.] Catechism: Basque tr. of Capenaga [*Bilboa* 1656]: facs. edn. by Edw. S. Dodgson 8° *Viseu* (Quaritch) 94

St. Julien d'Antioche: ed. Prf. J. Vinson + Vict. Stempf [Coll. de Pastor. Basques, i.] 10*fr.* 16° Moquet, *Bordeaux* 91

A Basque pastoral, ed. fr. a MS. in the Bordeaux Library.

141. URAL-ALTAIC PHILOLOGY (*a*): GENERALLY. FINNISH. LAPPONIC. LIVIAN.

Generally.

BANG, Willy Uralaltaische Forschungen [Einzelbeitr. allg. u. vergl. Spr.] 2*m.* 8° Friedrich, *Leipzig* 90

WINKLER, H. —*in his* Sprachgeschichte, *and* Weiteres zur Sprachgeschichte, *ut* K § 96.

Bibliography.

Bibliotheca Zrinyiana: Bibliothek d. Dichters Nic. Zrinyi; port. 2*m.* 8° Kende, *Vienna* 93

Esthonian: *Dictionary.*

WIEDEMANN, Ferd. Ehstnisch-Deutsches Wörterbuch, hrsg. Jac. Hurt, pt. i. 5*m.*75 r 4° *St. Petersbg.* (Voss, *Lpz.*) 91 *in prg.*

Finnish.

Grammar.

ELIOT, C. N. E. A Finnish Grammar c 8° 10/6 Clar. Press / $2.75 *net.* Macmillan, *N.Y.* 91

To have simplified the study (as Mr. ELIOT has here done) of one of the most difficult languages of the world—not excl. Hungarian or even Turkish w. its initial impediment of the Arabic alphabet—is no mean feat of scholarship. The lang. possesses 15 distinct cases, 24 differentiated infinitive forms and a syntax at once elaborate and obscure. It is the first Finn. gram. in English, and conts. the only Syntax (exc. brief sketches) in any lang. more generally accessible than Swedish.

History of Literature —*for* Specimens, *etc.*, *v.* B § 33.

KROHN, J. Finska Litteraturens Historia, pt. i. [Kalevala], tr. E. Nervander [*ut* B § 33] 6*kr.*50 8° Weilin, *Helsingfors* 91

Lapponic.

QVIGSTAD, J. K. Nordische Lehnwörter im Lappinischen [extract] 6/- 8° Dybwad, *Christiania* 94

Livian —*for* German lang. of Livonia *v.* 𝕭.𝕭. K § 231.

SJÖGREN, Joh. Andr. Livische Grammatik [w. specimens of literature] 4° *St. Petersbg.* (15*m.* Voss, *Lpz.*) 61

" " Livisch-Deutsches u. Deutsch-Livisches Wörterbuch, hrsg. F. J. Wiedemann 4° *St. Petersbg.* (10*m.*50 Voss, *Lpz.*) 61

Mordwinic: *Phonology.*

PAASONEN, H. Mordvinische Lautlehre [pp. 123] r 8° *Helsingfors* 93

142. URAL-ALTAIC (*b*): MAGYAR (HUNGARIAN) PHILOLOGY AND LITERATURE.

Grammar.

KÖRÖSI, Aless. Grammatica teorico-practica della lingua Ungherese, pt. i. 8° Univ. Press, *Budapesth* 92

Etymology: *Dictionaries.*

BALAGI, Mor. Ungarisches u. Deutsches Wörterbuch, 2 v. [both parts] ea. 14*m.* m 8° *Budapesth* (Haessel, *Lpz.*) [2nd ed. 62-64] 91

BUDENZ, J. Magyar-Ugor összehasonlító Szótár [compar. Ugrian dict.] *Pesth* 73-81

FASTER, G. Dictionnaire Tchèque-Français et Français-Tchèque, 2 vols. 10*m.* 8° *Prague* 78

SZARVAS + SIMONYI, Gabr. / Sigism. Lexicon Linguæ Hungaricæ Aevi Antiquioris, pts. 1-3 r 8° ea. 2*m.* Hornyansky, *Pesth* 88-93 *in prg.*

A notable bk. even in this age of dictionaries: dealing w. the lang. fr. earliest period till the orthographic reforms of end of 18th cent. Appended is a list of bks. used in prep. of the dicty. forming a useful Hungarian bibliography.

Foreign Elements.

SCHUCHARDT, Prf. Hugo A Magyar Nyely Román Elemeihez [Romance elements] *Pesth* 89

Literature.

SALMEN, Ch. Quelques Réflexions sur la Littérature Hongroise [*extr. fr.* Revue Universitaire] 1*fr.*50 8° Lamertin, *Brussels* 93

144. URAL-ALTAIC (*d*): OSMANLI-TURKISH PHILOLOGY AND LITERATURE.

Bibliography.

HUART, Clément — Sommaire des Etudes Turques pendant 1886–91 [11 pp.] 2/6 r 8° Orient. Inst., *Woking* 93

Grammar.

DALMEDICO, Moise M. — Méthode Théor. et Prat. de la Langue Turque, 2 pts. ea. 9/- 8° *Constantinople* ? 88

MANISSADJIAN, J. J. — Lehrbuch der modernen osmanischen Sprache 16*m.* 8° Spemann, *Berl.* 93

A good practical grammar, handsomely produced, but w. many misprints. Forms vol. xi. of *Lehrbb. d. Semin. f. Orient. Spr. in Berlin.*

Etymology.

MEYER, Prf. Gust. — Türkische Studien, pt. i. : Griech. u. roman. Bestandtheile in Osm.-Türk. 2*m.* 8° Freytag, *Lps.* 93

Dictionaries.

*BARBIER DE MEYNARD, A. — Dictionnaire Turc-Française, pt. viii. [last] [Ecole Langs. Or. Viv.] 10*fr.* 4° Leroux, *Paris* 90

A Suppl. to other dicts., contg. (1) words of Turk. origin, (2) Arab. and Pers. wds. used in Turk., (3) provbs. and pop. phrases.

LÖBEL, D. Theophil — Deutsch-türkisches Wörterbuch [for popular daily use] 8*m.* 16° Keil, *Constantinople* [ ] 94

RADLOFF, Dr. W. — Versuch eines Wörterbuches der Türk-Dialekte, pt. iv. 3*m.* 4° *St. Petersburg* 91

*REDHOUSE, Sir Jas. W. — Turkish and English Dictionary, pts. v.–viii. [last] ea. 9/- i 8° Amer. Miss., *Constant.*; cpl. 60/- Quaritch 88–90

A wk. of stupendous learning, and ranking with LITTRÉ'S great French Dict. It occupies 2,224 double-col. pages, w. 70,000 separate articles, in 1 vol. of manageable size; and may be regarded as a Turkish or an Arabic or Pers. dict., all the usual and necessary words of the two subsid. langs. being comprised in the alphabet.

YOUSSOUF, R. — Dictionnaire Portatif Turc-Français [in Rom. and Turk. characters] 9/- 22° *Constantinople* 90

Foreign Elements.

MEYER, G. — Türkische Studien, pt. i. [Griech. u. rom. Bestandth. d. Osman.-Türk] 2*m.* 8° Tempsky, *Vienna* 93

Chrestomathy.

WELLS, Dr. Chas. [ed.] — Turkish Chrestomathy [w. interlinear trs.] 16/- 8° Quaritch 91

Extracts fr. the best Turkish historians, novelists, dramatists, etc.; w. biograph. and gram. notes, interlin. trs., and a few facs. MSS. ! the first Turkish Reading-book ever pubd.

Manuscripts.

Berlin Königl. Bibl. : — Verzeichniss der Türkischen Handschriften, v. W. Pertsch 25*m.* r 4° Asher, *Berlin* 89

Literature.

History of Poetry.

"DORA D'ISTRIA, Mme." [= Helène GHIKA, P'cess KOLZOFF-MASSALSKY] La Poésie chez les Ottomans 3*fr.*50 12° Maisonneuve, *Paris* [ ] 76

Specimens.

Fables Turques : — recueillies et trad. J. A. Decourdemanche [Bibl. Orient. Elzévirienne] 5*fr.* 18° Leroux, *Paris* 82

Livre des Femmes [Zenan-Nameh] : trad. J. A. Decourdemanche [Bibl. Orient. Elzévirienne] 2*fr.*50 18° " " 79

Miradj-Nameh : — L'ascension de Mahomed au ciel; ed. w. Fch. tr. and notes Pavet de Courteille ; w. col. facss. of the MS. [Ecole d. Langues Orient. Vivantes] 15*fr.* 8° Leroux, *Paris* 82

NASR-EDDIN-HODJA — Plaisanteries, trad. J. A. Decourdemanche [Bibl. Orient. Elzévirienne] 2*fr.*50 18° " " 76

" " — Sottisier ; suivi d'autres facéties Turq., trad. J. A. Decourdemanche 15*fr.* 16° Gay, *Brussels* 78

145. URAL-ALTAIC (*e*): TURKI (TATAR-TURKISH) PHILOLOGY.

Generally : *Etymology.*

MIKLOSICH, Frz. — Die türk. Elemente in d. südost.- u. osteurop. Sprachen, Suppl., pt. ii. 10*m.* 8° Freytag, *Lps.* 90

On the Turk. element in Gk., Alban., Rouman., Bulg., Serv., Russ. and Polish. Extr. fr. *Denkschr. d. Wiener Akad.*

RADLOFF, Dr. W. — Versuch eines Wörterbuches der Türk-Dialecte, pts. iv.–vi. 10*m.*10 4° *St. Petersbg.* (Voss, *Lps.*)

Palæography.

EUTING, Prf. Julius [ed.] — Tabula Scripturæ Uiguricæ, Mongolicæ, Mandschuricæ [a reprint, one leaf] f° Author, *Strassbg.* 91

Literature.

Thousand and One Quarters of an Hour ["Tartarian Tales"] : "edited" Leon. C. Smithers 6/- *nt.* 8° Nicols 94

L.P. (75) 21/- *nt.* An unacknowledged repr. fr. H. W. WEBER'S *Tartarian Tales* [Ballantyne 1812]—itself an unacknowl. repr. of Thos. FLLOYD'S tr. [sub tit. *Tartarian Tales* (*Dublin* 1764: repr. in *Novelists' Mag.*, 1785)] of Thos. GUEUL(L)ETTE'S wk., orig. pub. 1715—not 1723 (as stated by the "editor"), wh. is the date of the 2nd edn. "revue, corrigée, et augmentée," and also of GUEUL(L)ETTE'S *Contes Chinois* (his *Contes Mongols* appeared 1732, not 1723 (as stated by "edr.")). The tr. is a good and faithful one, tho' not suitable for children.

146. URAL-ALTAIC (*f*): MONGOLIC PHILOLOGY.

Generally.

v. SCHRENK, L. — Reisen in Amur-Lande : 1854–56.

Grube, W. — Anhang zur 3ten. Bande, pt. I. : Linguist. Ergebnisse, no. 1 [Giljak. dict., *etc.*] 5*m.*15 8° Voss, *Lps.* 93

Palæography

—*v.* K § 145 (EUTING).

147. URAL-ALTAIC (g): TUNGUSIC AND MANTSHOU PHILOLOGY.

Tungusic : *Etymology.*

CZEKANOWSKI, A. — Tungusisches Wörterverzeichniss, hrsg. A. Schiefner — [extract] 2m.50 — 8° *St. Petersbg.* — 77

Mantshou : *Palæography*—*v.* K § 145 (EUTING).

148. CAUCASIAN PHILOLOGY.

Generally.

ABERCROMBY, Jno. — —*his* Trip thro' East. Caucas. [*ut* E § 39] *has a chap. on the languages.*

Linguistic Ethnology.

DE MORGAN, J. — Mission Scientifique au Caucase, 2 vols. ; maps and ill. — 25*fr.* — 8° Leroux, *Paris* — 90

Vol. I. *Les Premiers Ages des Métaux dans l'Arménie russe* ; II. *Origines des Peuples du Caucase.*

Georgian : *Literature.*

SCHOLA RUSTAWELI — Der Mann im Tigerfelle, übers. Arthur Leist — Pierson, *Dresden* — 91

A verse tr. of the National Epic of the Georgians.

Sulkhan-Saba Orbeliani — tr. Oliver Wardrop, *sub tit.* Book of Wisdom and Lies — [Kelmscott Press] — Quaritch — *in prep.*

149. DRAVIDIAN (SOUTH INDIAN) PHILOLOGY AND LITERATURE.

Brahui : *Grammar.*

TRUMPP, Dr. E. — Essay on Brahui Grammar, tr. Th. Duka — [extract] 3/6 — 8° *London* — 87

Tamil.

Grammar.

POPE, Dr. Geo. Uglow — First Lessons in Tamil : intro. to the common dialect — 7/6 c 8° Clar. Press — [ ] 91

100 lessons on the ordinary dialect, w. exx. for tr. fr. Tamil and *vice versâ*. Last 73 pp. comprise an easy Catechism in Tamil of both class. and colloq. dials.

Native.

Ilakkana Vilakkam : — ed. C. W. Dámodaram Pillai ; w. commentary — 16/- s 8° *Madras* — 90

A comprehensive work in Tamil on the five divisions of Tamil grammar.

Epigraphy.

HULTZSCH, Dr. E. [ed. and tr.] South Indian Inscriptions : Tamil and Sanskrit—*ut* K § 121.

Literature.

Kurral, *or* Tiruvalluva-Nâyanâr : ed. Dr. G. U. Pope ; w. intro., grammar, notes, lexicon and concord., and interlin. tr. — 24/- — 8° W. H. Allen — 86

The notes cont. repr. of Fr. C. J. BESCHI'S and F. W. ELLIS' versions.

,, ,, — ed. M. Murugêça ; w. tr. Jno. Lazarus — *Madras* — 85

Nâladiyar : — ed. Dr. G. U. Pope ; w. tr., Intro. and notes — 8° 18/- Clar. Press / $6 *nt.* Macmillan, *N.Y.* — 93

L.P. £2. A good edn. of the famous old Tamil poem. Last 150 pp. are devoted to a lexicon and concord., w. authorities fr. oldest Tamil writers.

Selections.

DE DUMAST, P. G. [tr.] — Maximes traduites des Courals de Tirou Vallouvar — [pamphlet] *o.p.* — 8° *Nancy* — 54

GRAUL, Dr. Ch. [tr.] — Indische Sinnpflanzen und Blumen — [Bibl. Tamulica ; *ut* B.B. K § 149] 6*m.* — 8° Brockhaus, *Lpz.* — 65

Conts. metrical trs. into Germ. of the choicest couplets of the "Gnomen-Dichter TIRUVALLUVA."

ROBINSON, Rev. E. J. [tr.] — Tales and Poems of South India : translated — [scholarly trs. fr. *Kurral*] 5/- c 8° — Wesl. Conf. Off. — 85

Telugu.

Grammar.

MORRIS, Hy. — Simplified Gram. of the Telugu Lang. ; map of Telugu dist. [Simplified Gram.] 10/6 c 8° — Paul — 91

Etymology : Dictionary.

SANKARANARAYANA, P. — English-Telugu Dictionary — 10/6 — 8° (Luzac) — 92

Pt. of the Introd. is devoted to suggestns. (also repr. as a pamphlet) as to a common alphabet for the differ. langs. of India.

Literature.

POTTANA MATYNDU — Srimat Andhra Bhagavatam — 4/6 — 4° *Madras* — 90

A standard classical poem in Telugu on the story of the Bhâgavata.

Tulu : *Etymology : Dictionary.*

MANNER, Rev. E. — English-Tulu Dictionary — [pp. 657] — 8° *Mangalore* — 89

150-151. JAPANESE AND COREAN PHIL Y AND LITERATURE.

Collectively.

Serial —*v.* K § 152, *s.v.* Serial.

Corean.

Bibliography.

COURANT, Maur. Bibliographie Coréenne, 3 vols. [to r. Viv.] 8° Leroux, *Paris*, *in prep.*

Grammar.

SCOTT, Rev. Jas. Corean Manual [*nt* 𝔐.𝔐. K § 150]: seco 8° *Shanghai* [87] 94
Introd. gives a hist. of orig. of Corean alphabet, based on some anc. Buddh. records wr 'd cols. Author is H. B. M. Vice-Consul at Sha...

UNDERWOOD, H. G. Introduction to the Corean Language [i. Gram. notes, ... c 8° *Yokohama* / 18/- Quaritch 90

Etymology: Dictionary.

SCOTT, Rev. Jas. Dictionary of the Corean Language 8° *Shanghai* 92
The dict. hitherto used by Corean scholars is the *Ok Pyen*, a Chin. dict. wh. gives the Corean translitn. of sounds of Chin. characters w. their meanings in Chinese.

UNDERWOOD, H. G. Concise Dictionary of the Korean Language [Corean-Engl. and Engl.-Corean] c 8° *Yokohama* / 18/- Quaritch 90

Japanese.

Bibliography.

DE LA VINAZA, Conde Escritos d. los Portug. y Castell. ref. á l. lengs. d. Chin. y Jap. 9/- 8° *Lisbon* 92
A bibliogr. acc. of 250 bks. on Chin. or Japanese philol. printed or MS. by Span. and Portug. missionaries dur. 16 and 17 cents.

Grammar.

LANGE, R. Lehrbuch d. japan. Umgangssprache [Lehrbb. d. Sem. f. Or. Spr.] 24*m.* 8° Spemann, *Berlin* 90

Chrestomathy.

*PLAUTH, H. [ed.] Japanisches Lesebuch: Märchen und Erzählungen 20*m.* r 8° *Berlin* 91
An important chrestomathy, in Jap. colloq. lang., w. Lat. transcr. and Germ. notes. *Lehrbb. d. Semin. f. Orient. Spr. in Berlin.*

Literature.

Selections: translated. Drama.

LEQUEUX, A. [tr.] Le Théâtre Japonais [Bibl. Orient. Elzévir.] 2*fr.*50 12° Leroux, *Paris* 89

Individual Texts and Translations.

M., A. Ayame-Sam: Jap. romance of 23rd yr. of Meiji [=1890]; photos. 30/- *nt.* i 8° Walter Scott 92
A handsome vol., produced in Japan, w. good photos. by Prf. W. K. BURTON, of Impl. Univ. of Japan: interesting as repres. the evol. phase thro' wh. mod. Japan is passing.

Tchou-Chin-Goura: une vengeance Japan., tr. into Eng. F. Dickins & in Fch. A. Donsdebes; ill. 12*fr.* 8° *Paris* 90

Aino.

BATCHELOR, Rev. Jno. Aino-English-Japanese Dictionary & Grammar [*v. also* Chamberlain, *inf.*] 21/- r 8° *Tokio* 89
CHAMBERLAIN, B. H. Language, Mythol. and Geograph. Nomenclature of Japan 7/6 i 8° ,, 87
In the light of Aino studies. Incl. an Aino Gram. by Rev. Jno. BATCHELOR. *Jap. Imper. Univ. Memrs.*, no. 1.

152. MONOSYLLABIC LANGUAGES (*a*): CHINESE PHILOLOGY (*a*): GENERALLY.

Bibliography

—*v. also* K § 150 (VINAZA).

CORDIER, Prf. Henri Half a Decade of Chinese Studies: 1886–91 [*repr. fr.* T'oung Pao] [36 pp.] r 8° Brill, *Leyden* / 36 Orient. Inst., *Woking* 93
,, ,, Bibliotheca Sinica: Supplément, fasc. i., 12*fr.*, ii. 12*fr.* [Ecol. Lang. Or. Viv.] 8° Leroux, *Paris* 91; 94

Grammar.

Spoken Language.

DES MICHELS, Prf. Abel Manuel de la Langue Chinois écrite 25*fr.* 8° Leroux, *Paris* 88
IMBAULT-HUART, C. Cours éclectique de la Langue Chinoise Parlée, 4 vols. 110*fr.* 4° ,, ,, 90
KAINZ, K. Die Kunst d. chin. Sprache d. Selbstunterr. zu erlernen 2*m.* 8° *Vienna* 90
LAMING, Prf. Rich. Méthode p. apprendre les princ. génér. d. l. Lang. Chinoise 6*fr.* 18° Leroux, *Paris* 89

Etymology: *Dictionaries.*

BILLEQUIN, A. Dictionnaire François-Chinois 75*fr.* 92
*GILES, Herb. A. Chinese-English Dictionary [*c.* 1,500 pp.] 136/6 4° *Shanghai* (Quaritch) 92
Projected by the author in 1874, and in course of composition and printing ever since. The no. of characters given, ea. under a separate heading, is 13,848, ea. numbered for the purpose of easy reference by means of the Radical Index. Numerous illustr. entries, fr. both bks. and conversation (author maintaining that there is no real distinction betw. class. and colloq. Chinese). All the entries are tr. into Engl.

K'ang Hai
A famous native lexicon, said to cont. over 40,000 characters, tho' it is stated that a Chin. newsppr. can be printed w. a fount of 6000.

KWONG KI CHIU   English and Chinese Dictionary   8° *Shanghai* [ ]87
POLETTI, O.   Wan tzu tien   [Chinese dict. of 10,000 characters] 6/– 8° " 8–
" "   Pocket Chinese-English Vocabulary   6/– 12° " 89
SCHLEGEL, G.   Nederlandsch Chineesch Woordenboek, vols. i.–iv.   80*fl.* 1 8° Brill, *Leyden* 84–91

Characters. Writing.

BALL, J. Dyer   How to write Chinese; How to write Radicals   8vo; 12° Kelly & Welsh, *Hong Kong* 88; 88

Correspondence.

KWONG KI CHIU   Manual of Correspondence and Social Usages   8° Wah Cheung, *Shanghai* 85

Dialogues.

COUVREUR, Père   Guide de la Conversation Frç.-Anglais-Chinois [w. vocab.] 12*fr.* 8° *Ho-Hien-Fou* (Maisonneuve, *Paris*) 86
HAAS, Cons.-Gen. Ritter Jos.   Deutsch-Chinesisches Conversationsbuch   15*m.* 8° Hiersemann, *Lps.* [ ]86
KWONG KI CHIU   First Conversation-Book; Second Conversation Book   8° Wah Cheung, *Shanghai* 85; 85

Documentary Chinese.

HIRTH, Dr. F.   Textbook of Documentary Chinese, 2 vols.   [pb. for Insp. Gen. of Customs]   4° *Shanghai* 85; 88
" "   Notes on the Chinese Documentary Style   8° Shanghai / 4*m.* Hirth, *Munich* 88

Phrases.

KWONG KI CHIU   Dictionary of English Phrases, w. illustrative sentences   21/– 8° Low 81

Collected Essays.

HIRTH, Dr. F.   Chinesische Studien, vol. i.   15*m.* r 8° Hirth, *Munich* 90
Conts. some good articles (repr. fr. mags.) on the hist. of anc. orient. commerce, Eastern trade in Mid. Ages, porcelain industry in mid. ages, *etc.*

Serial.

T'oung Pao: Archives p. servir à l'Etude de l'Hist. d. Langues, de la Géogr. et de l'Etnographie de l'Asie Orientale, ed. Prfs. Gustave Schlegel + Henri Cordier [5 pts. ann.] r 8° ann. 12*fl.* Brill, *Leyden* / ann. 20/- Luzac 90 *in prg.*
Devoted to China, Japan, Corea, Indo-China, Central Asia and Malay.

Pre-Classical Language of China.

DE LACOUPERIE, Terrien [1844–94]   Beginnings of Writing in Central and Eastern Asia   21/– *nt.* 8° Nutt 94
Notes on 450 embryo-writings and scripts. 210 pages.
UHLE, Dr. Max   Beiträge z. Gram. d. vorklass. Chin., pt. i. [particle *wêih* in *Shoo-king* & *Shi-king*] 4*m.* 8° Weigel, *Lps.* 81

153. MONOSYLLABIC (*b*): CHINESE PHILOLOGY (*β*): DIALECTS.

Cantonese. Tung-Kwún. San Wûi.

BALL, J. Dyer   Cantonese-made-easy Vocabulary   [*v.* 𝔅.𝔅. K § 153] 8° *China Mail* Off., *Hong Kong* 86
" "   An English-Cantonese Pocket Vocabulary   8° " " 86
" "   The Tung-Kwún Dialect; The San-wui Dialect [*both repr. fr.* China Review] 8° " " 90; 90
Compar. syllabaries of Tung-Kwún and Cantonese, and Tung-Kwún and Cantonese pronunciations.

154. MONOSYLLABIC (*c*): CHINESE LITERATURE.

Quotations.

LOCKHART, J. H. S. [tr.]   Manual of Chinese Quotations—*ut infra, sub tit.* Ch'êng Yü K'ǎo.

Texts and Translations.

Collections.

DOUGLAS, Prf. Roh. K. [tr.]   Chinese Stories—*ut* B § 36.
*DE HARLEZ, C. [tr.]   Textes Taoristes: traduits d. orig. chinois et commentés [Ann. Mus. Guimet] 20*fr.* 8° Leroux, *Paris* 91
*LEGGE, Prf. Jas. [tr.]   The Sacred Bks. of China: the texts of Taoism, tr., 2 v. [Sacred Bks. of the East] 8° 21/- Clar. Press / $5.25 *nt.* Macmillan, *N.Y.* 92
Vol. i. conts. *The Tao Teh King* (the writings of KWANG-TZE, bks. i.-xvii.); vol. ii. the writings of KWANG-TZE, bks. xviii.-xxxiii., *The Thai-Shang Tractate of Actions and their Retributions*. Vols. not sold separately. Forms a companion series to Legge's *Texts of Confucianism* [*ut* 𝔅.𝔅. A § 10], of wh. a new and revised edn. is appearing (vol. i. contg. *Confucian Analects*, the *Great Learning*, and the *Doctr. of the Mean*, 30/- r 8° Clar. Press [61] 93).
SMITHERS, Leon. C. [ed.]   The Transfigurations of the Mandarin Fum-Hoam: transl.   [tales] 6/– *nt.* c 8° Nichols 94

Individual Texts and Translations.

Chan-Hai-King: antique géographie Chinoise, ed. Léon de Rosny, vol. i.   30*fr.* 8° Maisonneuve, *Paris* 91
Ch'eng Yü K'ào ["Quotns. Examined"]: tr. J. H. Stewart Lockhart *s. tit.* Manual of Chinese Quotations 8° Kelly & Walsh *Shanghai* 93
Tr. of a wk. wh. has been very popular in China in 4 or 5 centuries. The author of it was CH'IO CHÜN, styled CHUNG-SHĀN, and honoured after his death with the title of WAN CHWANG, "the Cultured and Serious."
CHIA LOUH KOUOH KIANG YUH TCHI   Geogr. d. Seize Royaumes fondés en Chine par des Chefs tatares [302–433], trad. Prf. A. des Michels, pts. i.–ii. [pt. iii. *in prep.*] [Ecole Langs. Orient. Viv.] ea. 7*fr.* 50 8° Leroux, *Paris* 91; 91
Hiao-king: Livre de la Piété filiale, ed. Léon de Rosny; w. Fch. tr. and notes   20*fr.* 8° Maisonneuve, *Paris* 89
HONG-LIANG-KIH   Chih Loub Kouoh Yuh Sché, trad. Prf. Abel des Michels, pt. i.   7*fr.* 50 8° *Paris* 91
A "geographical history of the sixteen kingdoms," here first translated. With notes.

*I-li : cérémonial de la Chine Antique, trad. Prf. C. de Harlez [never before tr.] 15*fr.* 8° Maisonneuve, *Paris* 90

This wk. completes the tr. of the 3 rituals of China the 2 others being the *Tcheou-li*, tradd. BIOT [*ut infra*] and the *Li-ki*, tr. J. LEGGE [*ut* S.B. K § 154]. In contradistinction to the *Tcheou-li* wh. concerns the duties of officials, and to the *Li-ki* wh. is an irregular coll. of fragments concerning the rites and the state compiled for the Han dynasty, the *I-li* is the true ritual of anc. China, dealing w. the prin. ceremonies and events of life in elabor. detail.

IMBAULT-HUART, C. [ed.] Recueil d. Documts. sur l'Asie Centrale ; 2 maps [Ecole Langs. Or. Viv.] 10*fr.* 8° Leroux, *Paris* 81

Shi King :

Allen, Clem. F. R. [tr.] The Book of Chinese Poetry known as the Shih Ching 16/– 8° Paul 91

A metrical paraphrase (in very modern Engl.) rather than a tr. of the *Shi King*. With Introd. disc. many histor. refs. in the colln.

Jennings, Wm. [tr.] The Shi King: the old poetic classic of the Chin. [Lubbock's 100 Best Bks.] 3/6 c 8° Routledge [ ] 91

Siao Hio : on Morale de la Jeunesse, tr. Prf. C. de Harlez; 2 maps [Annales d. Musée Guimet] 15*fr.* 4° Leroux, *Paris* 88

Suh-Ki-Li-Lih-Kiu ; or Friendly Letter of Lung shu to Kg. Sadvaha, ed. Rev. Sam. Beal ; w. tr. 5/– 8° Luzac 92

TCHOU-HI Kia-li : livres d. rites domest., trad. Prf. C. de Harlez [Bibl. Or. Elzév.] 2*fr.* 50 12° Leroux, *Paris* 89

Yi King : trad. P. L. F. Philastre, pt. i. 15*fr.* ; ii. 20*fr.* [the first Fch. tr.] [Ann. Mus. Guimet] 8° „ „ 85; 93

de Lacouperie, Prf. A. Terrien The Oldest Book of the Chinese, vol. I. : History & Methods 10/6 *nt.* 8° Nutt 93

On the *Yi King* and its authors. Repr. fr. *Journal of Royal Asiatic Society*. Only 150 printed.

155. MONOSYLLABIC (*d*) : TIBETAN PHILOLOGY.

Etymology : *Dictionaries.*

RAMSAY, Cpt. H. Western Thibet : a pract. dict. of the lang. and customs of Ladák Wazarat *Lahore* 90

Includes a mass of valuable information on the religion and social habits of the Hadákés.

SARAT CHANDRA DAS Tibetan Dictionary (Govt. of Bengal) *in prep.*

The most compreh. Tibet. dict. hitherto attempted. Author, who is bg. assisted by several coadjutors, is a Bengali pandit, who lived for some time in a Buddh. monastery at Lhasa, and now Tibetan translator to the Govt. The Tibet. word is first given (alphabet.), w. pronunc., then its Sansk. equivalent (if any), followed by (1) literal tr. acc. to its etymol., (2) sense or senses in speech or liter., (3) illustr. examples fr. liter., use bg. made of the Tibet.-Sansk. vocabs., *e.g.* the *Vyutpatti* and the *Mahâvyutpatti* (some of wh. have been tr. into Fch. by RÉMUSAT and into Engl. by CSOMA), of Sansk. wks. like the *Kalpalatâ Kavyâdarsâ*, w. their faithful Tibet. trs., of the *Kahgyur* (coll. of Buddh. scriptures in 108 vols.) and the *Tangyur* (a cyclo. of Indo-Tibet. liter. in 225 vols.) *etc.*

Palæography.

DE LACOUPERIE, Prf. Terrien The Beginnings of Writing in Thibet *in prep.*

Examines the existing systs. of writing in Cent. Asia, and seeks to show they are conn. thro' China w. cuneiform wrtg. of Euphrates Valley.

Literature.

Bibliotheca Indica [*ut* K § 123] *incl. several recent Thibetan texts*, ed. Babu Chandra Das and Babu Pratâp Chandra Ghosh.

Kandjour : Fragments extraits du, trad. Léon Feer [*ut* B.B. K § 155] : new ed. [Annales du Musée Guimet] 20*fr.* 4° Leroux, *Paris* 82

Naîhsargikaprayaçcittikadharmâs : Thibetan version, ubers. Georg Huth [81 pp.] 2*m.* 8° Trübner, *Strassb.* 90

Buddhistic rules of penance, etc., fr. the *Prâtimokshasûtram*, comp. w. Pali and Chin. versions ; w. notes.

156. MONOSYLLABIC (*e*) : ANNAMITIC, KHAMPTI, MIRI, SIAMESE, SINGPHO.

Annamitic.

Linguistic Ethnology.

AYMONIER, Etienne Notes sur l'Annam, pts. i.–ii. ea. 5*fr.* 8° *Saigon* (Leroux, *Paris*) 85 ; 86

i. *La Binh-Thuân* ; ii. *La Khanh-Hoa* (extr. fr. *Excursions et Reconnaissances*, a mag. devoted to Indo-Chinese matters, no longer pub.).

BOUINAIS + PAULUS Le culte des Morts dans l'Annam, *etc.* ; ill. [Bibl. de Vulg., Mus. Guim.] 3*fr.* 50 18° Leroux, *Paris* 93

DEVÉRIA, G. [tr.] La Frontière Sino-Annamite: docums. Chinois traduits [Ecole Langs. Or. Viv.] 20*fr.* 8° „ „ 86

„ „ Histoire des Relatns. d. l. Chine av. l'Annam-Vietnam d. 14–15 siècle [Ecole Langs. Or. Viv.] 7*fr.* 50 8° „ „ 80

DUMOUTIER, G. Les Symboles, Emblèmes et Accessoire du Culte chez les Annamites ; 35 ill. [Bibl. de Vulgaisatn. Mus. Guimet] 3*fr.* 50 8° „ „ 91

FREY, Col. [Gén.] L'Annamite, mère des Langues ; 3 maps 5*fr.* 8° Hachette, *Paris* 92

On the community of origin of the Celtic, Semitic, Soudanese and Indo-Chinese races.

„ Gén. Annamites et Extrême Occidentaux : recherches sur l'orig. d. langues 6*fr.* 8° „ „ 94

PAVIE + LEFÈVRE-PONTALIS, A. F. Exploration de l'Indo-Chine: Mémrs. et Docums., v. i. (1)–ii. (1) ea. 15*fr.* 4° Leroux, *Paris* 9–

To occupy 4 vols., w. many maps, pl., *etc.*, i. is archæological and histor., ii. is linguistic.

Grammar.

DIRR Grammatik der annamit. Sprache f. Selbstunterricht 2*m.* 8° Hartleben, *Vienna* 94

LAUNE, Henri Notions Pratiques de Langue Annamite [w. fables, *etc.*] 10*fr.* 8° Challamel, *Paris* 90

Literature.

Annales Imperiales de l'Annam : trad. [fr. Chinese text] Prf. Abel Des Michels, pt. i. 10*fr.* r 8° Leroux, *Paris* 89

Chuyen Do'i Xu'a ; trad, Prf. Abel Des Michels [folk-tales] 15*fr.* 8° „ „ 88

Code Annamite, Le : trad. P. L. F. Philastre, 2 vols. ; w. notes, *etc.* 50*fr.* 8° „ „ 76

Cambodian.

Aymonier, Etienne Grammaire de la Langue Chame 7*fr.* 50 8° *Saigon* (Leroux, *Paris*) 89

„ „ L'Epigraphie Kambodjéenne 2*fr.* 50 8° „ „ „ 85

„ „ Dictionnaire Khmêr-française 40*fr.* 4° „ „ „ 78

„ „ Quelques Notions sur les Inscriptns. en vieux Khmêr [*extr. fr.* Jl. Asiat.] 8° Impr. Nat., *Paris* 84

„ „ [ed.] Textes Khmêrs, ser. i. [w. condensed Fch. trs.] 25*fr.* 4° *Saigon* (Leroux, *Paris*) 78

FOURNEREAUX, Luc. Les Ruines Khmêres ; 110 pl. [Cambodia and Siam] 50*fr.* r 8° Leroux, *Paris* 91

„ + PORCHER, J. Les Ruines d'Angkor ; 100 pl. [Cambodia] 50*fr.* 4° „ „ 90

Khampti.

NEEDHAM, J. F. Grammar of the Khampti Language *in prep.*

Miri.

NEEDHAM, J. F.

Siamese: *Linguistic Ethnology.*

FOURNEREAU, L. Le Siam Ancien; fully ill. [Annales d. Musée Guimet] 4° Leroux, *Paris, in prep.*

Singpho [Chingpau].

NEEDHAM, J. F. Outline Grammar of the Singpho Lang. [gram., phrases, vocab.] 7/6 8° Secretariat Press, *Rangoon* 89

157. MONOSYLLABIC (*f*): BURMESE PHILOLOGY.

Linguistic Ethnology. Grammar.

CHASE, D. A. Anglo-Burmese Handbook: pract. guide to Burmese lang., ed. F. D. Phinney c 8° *Rangoon* (Paul) [ ]90

HOUGHTON, B. Essay on the Lang. of the Southern Chins and its Affinities 8° Govt. Press, *Rangoon* 93

Author, who is Dep.-Commr. at Sandoway, has reduced to writing the lang. of the Chins, who are of Tibet. descent. Favours theory of a connection betw. the Burmo-Tibetan and the Dravidian languages of S. India. Incl. Phonology, Grammar, a few conversational exercises and Chin-Engl. and Engl.-Chin vocab.

VOISION, L. Grammaire Franco-Birmane [*w.* specs.; bas. on Judson] [Bibl. Colon. d. Ling.] 12*fr.* 8° Leroux, *Paris* 87

Chrestomathy.

ST. JOHN, R. F. St. Andrew [ed.] A Burmese Reader c 8° roll Clar Press / Macmillan, *N.Y.* 94

A good Introd. to the written language, designed as a compan. to JUDSON'S *Gram. of Burm. Lang.* [*ut* B.B. K § 157]. Very well printed.

History of Literature.

GRAY, Prf. Jas. The Nîti Literature of Burma *Rangoon*

Text and Translation.

Buddhaghosuppatti: rise and career of Buddhaghosa, ed. and tr. Prf. Jas. Gray—*ut* K § 127.
Malalankara vatthu: —*ut* K § 127, *sub nom.* Tathâgata-udâna.

XIX. Malayo-Polynesian Philology.

158. MALAIC PHILOLOGY.

Collectively.

Bibliography.

VAN DER CHIJS, J. A. Proeve eener Nederl.-Indische Bibliografie 1659–1870; w. Suppl.; 2 v. [*w.* 5*fl.*] 4° *Leyden* 75; 79

MEYER, J. J. Aperçu d. Etudes Philol. d. Langues Malaises: 1886–91 2/6 r 8° Orient. Inst., *Woking* 93

Serial —*v. also* K § 152, *s.v.* Serial.

Bijdragen tot de Taal-, Land- en Volkenkunde van Nederlandsch-Indie, vols. i.-v. 8° *The Hague* ?–90 *in prg.*

Bornese. Malayan.

Grammar.

KLINKERT, H. C. Opstellen ter Vertaling in het Maleisch, 2 pts. 1*fl.*50 8° Brill, *Leyden* 79; 82

VAN WIJK, Prf. Gerth. Spraakleer der Maleische Taal 8° *Batavia* 90

A purely philological work, taking the same place in Malay philol. that PLATT'S *Hindust. Gram.* [*ut* B.B. K § 118] has occup. for many yrs. as the standard Urdu gram.

Etymology: Dictionary.

COWIE, Andson Engl.-Sulu-Malay Vocab., ed. W. Clark Cowie [w. gram. Introd., fables, *etc.*] 21/- *nt.* 8° Brit. N. Borneo Co. 93

KLINKERT, H. C. Nieuw Nederlandsch-Maleisch Woordenboek 11*fl.* 8° Brill, *Leyden* 85

ERRINGTON DE LA CROIX, J. Vocabulaire Français-Malais et Malais-Français [w. grammar] 10*fr.* 18° Leroux, *Paris* 89

Pronunciation.

Traveller's Malay Pronouncing Hand-Book 8° *Singapore* [ ] 89

Characters.

KLINKERT, H. C. [ed.] Facsimiles van eenige Maleische Handschriften 2*fl.*50 s 4° Brill, *Leyden* 85

Chrestomathy.

KLINKERT, H. C. [ed.] Kitáb Boenga Rampai: Bloemlezing uit de Maleische 3*fl.*50 8° Brill, *Leyden* 90

Literature.

GONGGRIJP, J. R. P. F. [ed.] Hhikajat Kalila dan Dawina [colln. of Malay tales] 6*m.*50 8° Sijthoff, *Leyden* 92

KLINKERT, H. C. [ed.] Drie Maleische Gedichten of de Sjaïrs Ken Tamboehan 3*fl.*50 8° Brill, *Leyden* 86

Bugis (CELEBES).

MATTHES, R. F. Boegineesch-Hollandsch Wordenboek [*sub* B.B. K § 158]: Supplement 5/- 8° Nijhoff, *The Hague* 89

Galilla.

VAN BAARDEN, Rev. M. J. On the Language of Galilla [in Dutch] *Utrecht* 91

The author classes the lang. spoken in the district of Galilla, in the northernmost pt. of the Islands of Halmaheira (or Jilolo) w. the langs. spoken in the Ternate and the rest of the Moluccas Archip.

Javanese.

Manuscripts. History of Literature.

Leyden Univ. Libr.: Catalogus van d. Javaansche en Madoereesche HSS. [by A. C. Vreede] 7fl.50 8° *Leyden* 92

With bibliogr. of the MSS., extracts, etc., of consid. value for the hist. of Javanese literature.

Chrestomathy. Specimens of Literature.

POENSEN, Prf. C. [ed.] Bloemlezing uit Javaansche Prosa-Geschriften; w. notes 7/- 8° Brill, *Leyden* 92

An excellent reading-bk., great variety of subject and style being offered, in progressive arrangement.

ROORDA, T. [ed.] Rădjă: het boek of de geschiedenis v. Nabi Moesă; re-ed. J. Memsma 2fl.50 8° Brill, *Leyden* [ ]81

Sĕrat Kantjil: het boek van den Kantjil, Javaansch Dierenepos 8° Nijhoff, *The Hague* 89

The 1st edn. of this colln. of Jav. fables was made fr. 4 MS. copies by late Dr. W. Palmer van den BROEK, and appeared under auspices of Dutch Asiatic Soc. 1878.

Sunda.

Grammar.

GRASHUIS, G. J. Bijdrage tot de kennis van het Soendaneesch 3m. 8° Brill, *Leyden* 91

Dictionary.

COOLSMA, S. Soendaneesch-Hollandsch Woordenboek 17/6 r 8° *Leyden* 84

Chrestomathy.

GRASHUIS, G. J. [ed.] Soendaneesche Bloemlezing [a chrestomathy of Moslim legends] 6/- 8° *Leyden* 91

159. MELANESIAN AND POLYNESIAN PHILOLOGY.

Collectively.

BRANDSTETTER, R. Malaio-polynesische Forschungen, pts. i.-ii. ea. 1m.50 8° Doleschal, *Lucerne* 93; 94

i. *Der Natursinn in d. ältr. Litteraturwerken d. Malaien*; ii. *Beziehn. d. Malagasy z. Malaiischen.*

Fiji.

KERN, H. De Fidjitaal vergeleken m. h. verwandt. in Indonesië 10/r. 4° *Amsterdam* 85

Murray Island.

v. D. SCHULENBURG, A. C., Graf Grammatik, Vocab. u. Sprachproben d. Spr. v. Murray Insel 4m. 8° Friedrich, *Lps.* 92

Samoa.

FUNK, B. Kurze Anleitung zum Verständniss der samoanischen Sprache [gram. & vocab.] 4m.50 8° Mittler, *Berlin* 93

160. AUSTRALIAN PHILOLOGY AND LITERATURE.

Australian.

Grammar.

THELKELD, Rev. T. E. [Austral.] Australian Grammar, ed. Dr. Jno. Fraser; w. Introd. N. S. W. Govt. [30] *in prep.*

To incl. also THRELKELD'S tr. of the Gospel of St. Luke into native Australian.

TREGEAR, Edw. [Austral.] Maori-Polynesian Comparative Dictionary 21/- r 8° Lyon, *Wellington, N.Z.* 91

Incl. the dialects of N.Z., the Navigator, Sandwich, Friendly, Society and Hervey Groups, the Paumotu Archipel., Malay Archip., Gambier Isl., Madagasc., Formosa, Micronesia, Melanesia, etc. It conts. 9,000 words, w. their meanings; a dict. of names etc. of Maori gods, heroes etc. of battles, events, etc.; the scient. nomencl. of native animals and plants.

Maori (NEW ZEALAND).

COLENSO, Rev. W. Maori-English and English-Maori Dictionary *in prep.*

*TREGEAR, Edw. The Maori-Polynesian Comparative Dictionary r 8° Lyon & Blair, *Welln.* / 21/- Petherick 91

An excellent wk., fuller than any prev. wk., many illustr. examples bg. given, and comparisons w. other allied Polyn. and Melan. langs.

Literature.

WHITE, Jno. [Austral.] —*in his* Ancient History of the Maori, *sub* B.B. B § 29.

New Guinea or **Papua.**

RAY + HADDON, Std. H. / Prf. A. C. A Study of the Languages of Torres Straits 8° Hodges, *Dublin* 93

The 3 Papuan langs. dealt w. are the Miriam, the Saibai, and the Daudai.

K § 161

XX. African Philology.

161. GENERAL AND SPECIAL TREATISES.

Bibliography.

DE GUIRAUDON, Cpt. Th. G. Report on Progress in Study of African Langs. in last few yrs. [12 pp.] 2/6 r 8° Orient. Inst., *Woking* 91

Collectively.

SCHLEICHER, A. W. Afrikanische Petrefakten 3*m.* 8° Fröhlich, *Berl.* 91

An attempt to establish, by the comparative method, the gram. formatns. and roots of the Afric. langs.

Bantu (purely an ethnolog. term, invented by Dr. W. H. J. BLEEK: covers whole of Cent. Africa).

Linguistic Ethnology and Grammar

HAARHOFF, B. J. Die Bantu-Stämme Süd-Afrikas 2*m.* 8° Fock, *Lps.* 90

*TORREND, Rev. J. [S.-J.] Comparative Grammar of the S. African Bantu Languages 25/- r 8° Paul 91

Comprises the langs. of Zanzibar, Mozambique, the Zambesi, Kafirland, Benguela, Angola, the Congo, the Ogowe, the Cameroons, *etc.* Introd., 2 Appendices (one of Ethnogr. Notes), and Index, and a chap. on Bantu liter., w. a long list of bks. in the lang. In the val. Introd. the author specifies and discusses the materials on wh. his labours are based, espec. dealing w. what Gk. and early Arab geographers have recorded of the Bantu tribes, whose orig. and spread he also traces.

Phonology.

DE GREGORIO, G. Cenni di Glottologia Bantu 4*l.* 8° Loescher, *Turin* 83

Serial.

Zeitschrift für afrikanische Sprachen, hrsg. C. G. Büttner [quarterly] *ann.* 12*m.* 8° Asher, *Berl.* 87–94 *in prg.*

Amharic (ABYSSINIA)—*v.* K § 116: Ethiopic.

Akra or **Ga** (GOLD COAST).

CHRISTALLER + BOHNER, J. G. / H. Uebungen in der Akra-Sprache [gram. and dialogues] 2*m.* 8° Missions-Buchhg., *Basle* 90

Asante [Fanti] (ASHANTE and GOLD COAST).

ELLIS, Maj. [Lt.-Col.] A. B.—*in his* The Tshi-Speaking Peoples of the Gold Coast, *ut* B.B. E § 46.

ZABALA, A. O. Vocabulary of the Fan Language [w. Spanish interpretation] 3/6 f 8° *London* 87

Bambara (KAARTA and BELEDOUGOU).

BINGER, Cpt. Louis Gust. Essai sur le Langue Bambara; map 4*fr.* 12° Maisonneuve, *Paris* 86

MONTEL, Rev. P. E. Eléments de la Grammaire Bambara [w. exx. and Bambara-Fch. dict.] 8° *St. Joseph d. Ngasobil* 87

Bedauye [NORTH-EAST AFRICA]—*v.* K § 104: Kushitic.

Berber (ALGERIA, TUNISIA, MOROCCO)—*v.* K § 103: Libyan.

Bubi (ISLAND OF FERNANDO PO).

JUANOLA, Rev. P. Joaq. Primer Paso á la Lengua Bubi *Madrid* 90

Bushman.

BERTIN, Geo. The Bushmen and their Language [an accurate summary] 8° *London* 86

Congolese.

BARFIELD, Jno. The Concords of the Congo Language *London* 84

CAMBIER, Le P. Essai sur la Langue Congolaise 3*fr.*50 8° *Brussels* 91

Fiote (French equivalent for Congolese).

CARRIE, Mgr. Grammaire de la Langue Fiote, dialecte du Kakongo *Loango* 90

" " [ed.] Histoire Sainte, Française et Fiote " 89

" " Dictionnaire Français-Fiote, dialecte du Kakongo *Paris* 90

JOHNSTON, H. H. —*in his* The River Congo [1884; *ut* B.B. E § 47].

Conts. a careful chap. on the Kongo, Ki-teke, Ki-buma and Ki-yansi langs.; w. short grammat. Introd.

USSEL, Rev. P. Petite Grammaire de la Langue Fiote, dialecte du Loango *Loango* 88

VISSEQ, Rev. P. Alex. Dictionnaire Fiot *Paris* 89

Dahomey.

DELAFOSSE Dictionnaire Dahoméen-Français et Frç.-Dahom. [Bibl. Colon. d. Ling.] 18° Leroux, *Paris, in prep.*

Ewe-speaking Peoples (DAHOMEY and SLAVE COAST).

ELLIS, Maj. [Lt.-Col.] A. B.—*in his* The Ewe-Speaking Peoples of West Africa, *ut* E § 46.

HENRICI, Ernst Lehrbuch der Ephe-Sprache: Anlo-Anecho- u. Dahom. Mundart 16*m.* 8° Spemann, *Berlin* 91

With a glossary. *Lehrbb. d. Seminars für Orient. Sprachen in Berlin*, vol. vi.

Fan (Pámue).

NASSAU, Rev. R. H. [Am.] Fañwe Primer and Vocabulary 8° *New York* 81

ZABALA, Amado Osorio Diccionario Pámue-Espagnol 8° *London* 87

Fiote —*v.* Congolese, *supra.*

K § 161

Fulah (West Africa).

de Sanderval, A. Ol. Victe — De l'Atlantique au Niger par le Foulah-Djallon — 8° *Paris* 83
Tautain, Dr. — Contribution à l'Étude d. l. Langue Foule — [not important] 8° „ 89–90

Galla [North-East Africa]—*v.* K § 104: Kushitic.

Giryama.

Taylor, Rev. W. E. — Grammar of the Giryama Language — [a good book] 9-

Hariri [North-East Africa]—*v.* K § 104: Kushitic.

Haussa.

Dirr, A. — Manuel prat. d. l. Langue Haoussa [w. chrestom. & vocab.] [Bibl. Colon. d. Ling.] 5*fr.* 18° Leroux, *Paris* 93
Schön, Rev. J. F. [ed. and tr.] Magana Haussa; w. Eng. tra. — [native provbs., fables, etc.] 6/- f 8° 85

Kabail —*v.* K § 103: Libyan.

Kaguru.

Last, J. T. — Grammar of the Kaguru Language — [w. Engl.-Kaguru vocab.] 8° *London* 86

Kamba.

Last, J. T. — Grammar of the Kamba Language — *London* 85

Kavirondo [South of Equator].

Wakefield, Rev. M. — Vocabulary of the Kavirondo Language — [list of 150 to 200 words] 8° *London* 87

Kibangi (Kiyansi).

Sims, A. — Vocabulary of the Kibangi — *London* 87

Kiteke.

Sims, A. — Vocabulary of the Kiteke: English-Kiteke — [w. gramm. preface] 8° *London* 86

Kunama [North-East Africa]—*v.* K § 104: Kushitic.

Kunbi (Mossamedes).

Nogueira, A. F. — O Lun Kumbi — 8° *Lisbon* 85

Makua.

Rankin, Dan. J. [ed.] — Arab Tales, tr. fr. Swahili into Telugu Dialect of Makua — *London* 87
With comparative vocabs. of 5 dialects of the Makua language.

Mang'anja [British Central Africa].

Scott, Rev. Dav. Clement — Cyclopædic Dict. of the Mang'anja Language, pt. I. — 8° *Edinburgh* 92
Pub. by the Foreign Missionary Comm. of Church of Scotl., by one of its missionaries. A very interesting bk., every word bg. ill. by sentences taken fr. actual native speech, or complete legends, thus giving glimpses of Mang'anja life, customs and thought. No Engl.-Mang'anja section, but a short vocab. at end serving as a guide in finding words. A short grammar is prefixed.

Masai.

Johnston, H. H. — —*in his* The Kilima-Njaro Expedn. [1886; *at* 𝔅.𝔅. E § 48].
Contains 2 chaps. on anthrop. and linguistics of the district explored, w. a compar. vocab. of *c.* 800 words of Masai lang. (closely allied to the Bari).

Mavia.

Da Cunha, Joaq. d'Almeida — Vocabulario de Lingua Mavia — *Loango* 86

Musuk.

Müller, Dr. Friedr. — Die Musuk-Sprache — [*extr. fr.* Sitzb. Wiener Akad.] r 8° Tempsky, *Vienna* 86

Negro-English (Creolese).

Hearn, Lafcadio — Gombo Zhebès: little dict. of Creole proverbs, w. notes [fr. 6 Creole dialects] $1 8° Coleman, *New Orleans* 85
Schuchardt, Prf. Hugo — Kreolische Studien, pt. ix. — [*extr. fr.* Sitzber. d. Wien. Akad.] 4*m.*50 8° Tempsky, *Vienna* 91

Nika.

Krapf + Rebmann, [Dr. L. / Rev. J.] Nika-English Dictionary — 8° *London* 87
Many words are inserted without their meanings, and the great majority of the phrases are untranslated.

Quara [Agaw People of Kwaar]—*v.* K § 104: Kushitic.

Ruganda.

Missions d'Afrique: — Essai de Grammaire Ruganda — [a useful grammar] 8° *Paris* 85

Sechuana (Bechuana, Sotho).

Crisp, Rev. Wm. — Notes towards a Secoana Grammar — [compl. gram. of Serolong dial.] 8° *London* [ ] 86

Somali [North-East Africa]—*v.* K § 104: Kushitic.

Swahili.

Grammar.

Black, C. — Introduction to Swahili — [useful for travellers only] 1/6 f 8° Simpkin 91
Büttner, C. G. — Hülfsbüchlein f. d. ersten Unterricht in d. Suaheli-Sprache — 2*m.* 8° Weigel, *Lpz.* [87] 91

K § 162

DELAUNAY, Père — Grammaire Kiswahili — 8° *Paris* 85

Avowedly based on STEERE (*ut* 𝔅.𝔅. K § 161), but containing much original matter.

ILLAIRE, Walt. v. St. Paul — Suaheli-Handbuch [Lehrbb. d. Sem. f. Or. Spr.] 10*m*.50 r 8° Spemann, *Berlin* 90
SEIDEL, A. — Praktische Grammatik d. Suaheli Sprache [Kunst d. Polyglottie] 2*m*. 8° Hartleben, *Vienna* 90

Etymology: Dictionaries.

BÜTTNER, C. G. — Wörterbuch der Suaheli-Sprache [both pts.] [Lehrbb. d. Sem. f. Or. Spr.] 13*m*. r 8° Spemann, *Berlin* 90
SHAW, A. Downes — Pocket Vocabulary of Ki-swahili, Ki-nyika, Ki-taita and Ki-Kamba — *London* 85
MADAN, A. C. — English-Swahili Dictionary [f. use of Universities Mission to Cent. Afr.] 7/6 *nt*. c 8° Clar. Press *and* S.P.C.K. 90

Chrestomathies. Specimens of Literature.

BÜTTNER, C. G. [ed.] — Anthologie aus der Suaheli-Litter. [poems and hists., w. Germ. trs.] 18*m*. 8° Felber, *Berlin* 93
" " [ed.] — Suaheli Schriftstücke in arab. Schrift, m. lat. Schr. umschr.; w. Germ. trs. 22*m*. 8° Spemann, *Berlin* 93

Lehrbb. d. Semin. f. Orient. Sprachen in Berlin. A valuable colln. of 61 pieces in facs., w. Appendices on (1) applicn. of Arab. alphab. to Swah. wrg., (2) Swah. epistolography, (3) notes to the facs. docums.

STEERE, Bp. E. [ed. and tr.] Swahili Tales as told by Natives of Zanzibar; w. trs. 5/- c 8° S.P.C.K. 90

Dialogues.

v. NETTELBLADT, F. Freiherr — Suaheli-Dragoman: Gespräche, W'buch u. Anleitungen; map 5*m*. 8° *Leipzig* 91

Teneriffe.

BUTE, Jno., Marquess of — On the Ancient Language of the Natives of Tenerife 2/6 8° Masters 91

Reprint of a paper contrib. to the Anthropological Section of the British Association, 1891.

Umbundu.

SANDERS + FAY, $\frac{\text{Rev. W. H.}}{\text{Rev. W. E.}}$ [Ams.] Vocabulary of the Umbundu Language [c. 3000 wds. in Engl. & Umb.] 8° *Boston* 85
STOVER, Rev. Wesl. M. [Am.] Observns. upon the Grammatical Structure and Use of the Umbundu 8° " 85

West Africa.

JOHNSON + CHRISTALLER, $\frac{\text{I. T.}}{\text{J.}}$ [eds.] Vocabularies of the Niger and Gold Coast 3/6 f 8° *London* 85

Wolof (SENEGAMBIA).

Dictionnaire Wolof-Français [by the Rom.-Cath. missionaries] *St. Joseph d. Ngasobil* 75
FAIDHERBE, Gen. L. L. C. — Langues Sénégalaises: gramm., vocabs., phrases [Bibl. Colon. d. Ling.] 7*fr*.50 18° Leroux, *Paris* 87

Wolof, Arabe-Hassania, Soninké, Sérère. All but "Arabe-Hassania" are reprts.

Guide de la Conversation en Quatre Langues [Fch., Wolof, Engl., Sérèr] *St. Joseph d. Ngasobil* 80

Yalulema.

SIMS, A. — Vocabulary of the Yalulema Language — *London* 87

Yoruba-speaking Peoples (GOLD COAST).

ELLIS, Lt.-Col. A. B. — —*in his* The Yoruba-Speaking Peoples of West Africa, *ut* E § 46.

Appendix (pp. 305-402) conts. in tabular form a compar. of Tshi, Ga, Ewhe and Yoruba langs., the 3 first of wh. assigned to the Volta group, the last to the Niger langs.

Zulu (Kafir and Xosa-Kafir).

Grammar.

AMBROSIUS, Père [= TRAPP] Grammatik der Zulu-Kaffirschen Sprache 8/- 8° *Mariannhill (S. Afr.)* 91

By one of the Trappist missionaries in Zululand.

CECCHI, Antonio — Da Zeila alle Frontiere del Caffa — 8° *Rome* 87
REINISCH, Prf. Leo — Die Kafa-Sprache: Grammatik, 1*m*.50; Wörterbuch, 2*m*. 8° Tempsky, *Vienna* 88; 88
TORREND, J. — Outline of a Xosa-Kafir Grammar, *etc.* 8° *Grahamstown* 87

XXI. American Aboriginal Philology and Literature.

162. GENERAL WORKS—*v. also* E § 53.

Bibliography.

LECLERC, Ch. — Bibliotheca Americana: hist., géog., archéol., linguistique 15*fr*. 8° Maisonneuve, *Paris* 78
*PILLING, Jas. C. [Am.] Bibliographies of the Indian Languages—*ut* E § 53.

Since entry in E § 53 have been pub. *Athapascan Langs.*, '93; *Chinookian Langs.*, '93; *Salishan* [= *Flathead*] *Langs.*, '93.

Classification.

BRINTON, Prf. Dan. G. [Am.] The American Race $2 12° Hodges, *N.Y.* 91

The first serious attempt at a systematic classif. of the whole of the Amer. race (N. and S.) on the basis of lang. (not excepting Dr. LATHAM'S attempt in 1859), following the precepts and examples of the Aryan and Semit. stocks.

*POWELL, Maj. J. W. [Am.] Indian Linguistic Families of America North of Mexico; map—*in* Seventh Annual Report of Amer. Bureau of Ethnology 4° Govt. Press, *Washington* 91

A very important contribn., based on the author's own researches, and on PILLING'S bibliogs. [*ut supra* and E § 53]. Conts. a list of 58 linguist. families wh. he believes to be specially distinct, w. synonyms of family names, enumern. of princ. tribes incl. in the family, geogr. area occupied and estimate of numbers: the results clearly shown in the map.

Serial.

Amer. Dialect Soc.: Dialect Notes — Cushing, *Boston* 90 *sqq.*, *in prg.*

President Prf. J. M. Hart, of Cornell Univ.; Sec. Edw. S. Sheldon, 17, Hurlbut St., Cambridge, Mass. The soc. has in prep. a work to be entitled *Contribs. to the Vocabulary of New England*, wh. is likely to be of some consid. value.

Etymology. Dictionaries.

DOUAY, L. Etudes étymologiques sur l'Antiquité américaine 8*fr.* 8° Maisonneuve, *Paris* 91
GATSCHET, A. S. [Am.; ed.] Forty Vocabularies of Western Languages $1 8° (*U.S.A.*) 91
ZEISBERGER, D. Indian Dictionary 4° *priv. prin.* (*Cambr.*, *Mass.*) 87
English-German-Iroquois; Onondaga and Algonquin; Delaware. Printed fr. orig. MS. in Harvard Coll. Lib.

Grammar.

PLATZMANN, J. Weshalb ich Neudrucke d. alt. Amer. Grammatiken veranlasst habe 5*m.* 8° Teubner, *Lpz.* 93

163. NORTH-AMERICAN AND CANADIAN PHILOLOGY AND LITERATURE.

Alaska.

TEWKES, J. Walt. [Am.; ed.] Zuñi Ceremonials and Melodies

Canadian Indian.

Literature.

PETITOT, E. [ed. and tr.] Traductions Indiennes du Canada Nord-Ouest; texts and trs.—*ut* **B.B.** B § 35.

Chiapanek.

DE ALBORNOZ, Juan Arte de la Lingua Chiaponeca, publ. A. L. Pinart 4° *Paris* 75

Chinook [COLUMBIA RIVER].

BOAS, Dr. Franz —*has a Grammar, Dictionary and Texts in prep.* Smithson. Inst., *Washn.*, *in prep.*

"Chinook Jargon."

HALE, Horatio Manual of the Oregon Trade Language [vocab., hist. sketch, specs.] 3/- c 8° Whittaker 90

The Chinook Jargon is of peculiar interest as affording the only known example of the evolution of a new lang. in quite recent times. Little more than 100 yrs. ago it was still unborn; at pres. moment many people speak it as their native tongue, and Mr. HALE (who in 1846 thought the Jargon would disappear) is now of opin. that it will continue to be medium of intercourse (the *lingua franca*) betw. the differ. races of N.-W. The orig. nucleus of the vocab. was formed by English-speaking traders and Indians of Nootka Sound, who mutually learned a few words of each other's lang.; the Chinooks, taking it up, added over 200 words; and intercourse w. the Canad. *voyageurs* led to introd. of Fr. words. The vocab. was further augm. by onomatopoetic formations (*e.g.* *tiptip* to boil; *tumtum* heart). The "root-stage" postulated for the prehist. periods of inflect. langs. is here an actual reality (tho' the "roots" are mostly polysyllabic); and, as in Chinese, almost any word may serve for noun, verb, adj. or adv. There are abt. 500 wds. in all, to wh. must be added compounds (*e.g.* *ship-stick*, a mast; *stick-skin*, bark of tree). The orig. of many words is v. amusing, *e.g.* *Kintshautsh* = English (fr. "King George"). At present there is no grammat. system. Will one be developed? [Author has resided since 1856 in Clinton, Ontario].

Chippeway [OJEBWAYS].

WILSON, Rev. E. F. [Am.] Manual of the Ojebways $1.50 12° 91

Creolese

—*v.* K § 161.

Dakota.

RIGGS, Rev. Steph. R. [Am.] Dakota-Engl. Dict. [*ut* **B.B.** K § 163]: new edn., ed. Jas. O. Dorsey [Am.] 4° Smithson. Inst., *Washn.* [52] 93

Inca.

FALB, R. Das Land d. Inca in s. Bedeutg. f. d. Urgesch. d. Spr. u. d. Schrift 18*m.* 8° *Leipzig* 83

Mississaga.

CHAMBERLAIN, A. F. [Canad.] The Language of the Mississaga Indians [scholarly; w. bibliogr.] McCalla, *Phila.* 92

Mosquito.

ACLAM, Lucien La Langue Mosquito 12*fr.* 8° Maisonneuve, *Paris* 91

Zimshian [NORTH-WEST AMERICA].

v. D. SCHULENBURG, A. C., Graf Die Sprache der Zimshian-Indianer 60*m.* 4° Sattler, *Brunsw.* 94

164. CENTRAL AND SOUTH AMERICAN INDIAN PHILOLOGY AND LITERATURE.

Collectively.

COUDREAU, H. [ed.] Vocabs. méthod. d. Langs. Ouayana, Aparai, Oyampi, Emérillon (Guyane) 12*fr.* 8° Maisonneuve, *Paris* 92

Andes.

FALB, Rud. Die Andessprachen in ihrem Zusammenhange m. d. semit. Sprachstamme 3*m.* 8° Friedrich, *Lpz.* 88

Araucanian [CHILE].

FEBRÉS, P. Andrès Gramática Araucana [1765], ed. Juan M. Lársen 16/- s 4° *Buenos Ayres* 84
" " Diccionario Araucano-Español [1765], ed. Juan M. Lársen [200 printed] 21/- s 4° " 82

Brazil.

ECKART, Anselm [ed.] Specimen Linguæ Brasil. vulg., ed. J. Platzmann 1*m.* 8° *Lpz.* 90

Bakaïrí [CENTRAL BRAZIL].

v. D. STEINEN, K. [ed.] Die Bakaïrí-Sprache 18*m.* 8° Koehler, *Lpz.* 92
A vocab., sentences, tales and grammar; w. valuable remarks on phonology of Karaïb langs., of a branch of wh. Bakaïrí is a member.

Guarani [very wide in extent].

RESTIVO, Paulo — Arte de la Lengua Guarani, ed. C. F. Seybold — 10*m.* 8° *Stuttgart* 92

SEYBOLD, Ch. F. — Brevis Linguæ Guarani Grammatica — 10*m.* 8° Kohlhammer, *Stuttg.* 90
Based on the works of A. Ruiz de MONTOYA [*ut* B.B. K § 164] and Sim. BANDINI.

" " — Lexicon Hispano-Guaranicum [bas. on P. Restiv, ed. Montoya] 15*m.* 8° " " 93

Maya [YUCATAN].

Palæography: Manuscripts.

FÖRSTEMANN, E. — Zur Entzifferung der Mayahandschriften, pt. i.; ii. 1*m.*; iii. 1*m.*; iv. 1*m.* 8° Berthing, *Dresden* 91; 92; 94

Literature.

RADA Y DELGADO+DE AVALA Y DEL HIERRO [eds.] Codex Maya [fine col. photogr. reprod.] 100*fr.* f° *Paris* 93

Mexican (Aztec, Nahuatla).

Grammar.

BUSCHMANN, J. C. E. — Grammatik der sonorischen Sprachen, pt. iii.: Das Zahlwort — 8*m.* 4° Dümmler, *Berlin* 67
Accid. omitted in B.B. K § 164. The wk. deals mainly w. the Tarahumara, Tepeguana, Cora and Cahita languages.

Literature.

Cacique MS.: — ed. H. de Saussure [= *his* Antiquités Mexicaines, fasc. i.] 24*m.* f° Georg, *Basle* 92

Libro de Tributos, Zapotecan Codex, *etc.*—*v.* Monuments of Mexican Art, ed. Dr. A. Peñafiel, *ut* G § 11.

Mexican Pictorial Chronicle: 31 leaves, reprod. fr. the orig. — 63/- f° Quaritch 90
The original was written on maguey paper soon after the date of the Spanish conquest.

Moxa.

MARDAN, P. — Arte de la Lengua Moxa: facs. ed. J. Platzmann — 30*m.* 4° Teubner, *Lps.* 94

Puquina.

DE LA GRASSERIE, Dr. Raoul [ed.] Langues Américaines: Langue Puquina — 2*m.*50 8° Köhler, *Lps.* 94
Texts cont. in the *Rituale seu Manuale Peruanum* of Geronimo de Ore (*Naples* 1607); w. Span. text *en regard*, interlin. Fch. tr., vocab. and gramm. notes.

Quichna [PERU].

Bibliography —*v.* E § 58. (ICAZBALCETA).

Linguistic Ethnology.

v. TSCHUDI, J. J. — Culturhistor. u. sprachliche Beiträge zur Kenntniss d. alten Peru — 11*m.*30 8° Freytag, *Lpz.* 91

Grammar.

DOMINGO DE SANCTO THOMAS — Arte de la lengua Quichua, publ. J. Platzmann — 10*m.* 8° Teubner, *Lps.* [ ] 91

*MIDDENDORF, Dr. E. W. Die einheimischen Sprachen Perus, 6 vols. — 129*m.* 8° Brockhaus, *Lps.* 90–92

Vol. i. *Das Runa Simi* [Quichua] ... 16*m.* 90
ii. *Wörterbuch d. Runa Simi* ... 48*m.* 90
iii. "*Ollanta*" [Germ. tr of the drama, w. notes] ... 18*m.* 90
Vol. iv. *Dram. u. lyr. Dichtungen d. Keshua Sprache* [w. Germ. tr.] 15*m.* 91
v. *Die Aimará-Sprache* ... 29*m.* 91
vi. *Die Mucik oder Chimu Sprache* ... 12*m.* 92
A compreh. and important series, now complete.

Literature.

Ollanta [drama]: — Germ. tr.—*v. supra, sub nom.* Middendorf, vol. iii.

Popol Vuh: livre sacré et les mythes des Quichés, ed. Brasseur de Bourbourg; w. Fch. tr.; pl. *o.p.* [*pb.* 25*fr.*; *w.* 24/-] r 8° Bertrand, *Paris* 61

XXII. Hyperborean Philology.

165. ALEUTIC AND ESQUIMAUX PHILOLOGY.

Asia.

Ainos —*v.* K § 150.

America.

Esquimaux.

BOAS, F. D. — Eskimo-Dialekt d. Cumberland-Sundes, pt. I. — 3*m.* 94

SCHULTZE, A. — Grammar and Vocabulary of Eskimo Language of N.-W. Alaska — $1.50 8° *Bethlehem* 94

WELLS+KELLY, Rog., *jun.* Jno. W. [Ams.] English-Eskimo and Eskimo-English Vocabularies [w. ethnog. notes; 72 pp.] 8° Govt. Prtg. Off., *Washgtn.* 90

166. GYPSY PHILOLOGY AND LITERATURE.

Folk-Literature —*v.* B § 39.

166.* UNCLASSED ASIATIC PHILOLOGY.

Hunza and Nagyr.

LEITNER, Dr. G. W. — Hunza Nagyr Handbook, pt. i. [*ut* B.B. K § 166*]: reissue, w. Suppl. 42/- f° Orient. Instit., *Woking* 93

" " — On the Sciences of Language and Ethnography — 1/- 8° Sonnenschein 90
With special reference to the language and customs of the people of Hunza—*v.* B.B. K § 166.*

XXIV. Greek-and-Latin Philology: Jointly.

167. GREEK-AND-LATIN BIBLIOGRAPHY. ENCYCLOPÆDIA. INTRODUCTION.

Bibliography.

HÜBNER, Dr. E. — Bibliographie d. klass. Altertumswiss.: Grundr. z. Vorlesungen — 15*m*. 8° Hertz, *Berlin* [76] 89
A second edn. of this admirable systematic *bibliographie raisonnée* [*ut* B.B. K § 167].

VALMAGGI, L. — Manuale Storico-bibliografico di Filologia Classica — 8*l*. 8° Clausen, *Turin* 94

Dissertations: *German*.

FOCK, Gust. [bkslr.] — Catalogus Dissertationum Philoldgicarum Classicarum — 2*m*.50. 8° Fock, *Lps*. 93
A classified list of some 18,300 dissertations, pub. on the Continent (except France), on class. philol. and antiqs. No Author's Index.

Early and *Rare Editions*.

CRAWFORD, Earl of — Hand List to Early Edns. of Gk. & Lat. writers [Bibliotheca Lindesiana] (*w*. 21/–) 8° *priv. prin.*, *Lond.* 85
Incl. also mediæval times; also a few of the rarer vocabs. and grammars. Only 50 copies printed.

DIBDIN, Dr. Thos. F. — Intro. to Knowl. of Rare & Valuable Edns. of Gk. & Lat. Class., 2 vols. [*w*. 40/–] 8° *London* [02] 27

Introduction.

BONNET, Max — La Philologie Classique — 3*fr*.50 s 8° Klincksieck, *Paris* 91
GILES, P. — A Short Manual of Philology for Classical Students —*ut* K § 96.
INAMA, Vigilio — Filologia Classica Greca et Latina — 16° Hoepli, *Milan* 94
SCERBO, Fr. — Caratteristiche del Greco e del Latino — 4*l*. 8° Loescher, *Florence* 93

Encyclopædia.

*v. MÜLLER, Prf. Iwan [ed.] Handbuch d. klassischen Altertums-Wissenschaft — r 8° Beck, *Munich* [85–94] 90–94

New Vols. and New Edns.
i. (1) *Grundlegung u. Gesch. d. Philol.* [*ut* B.B. K § 168]: new ed. 6*m*.50 [85] 91
i. (2) *Einleit. u. Hilfs-Disziplinen* [*ut* B.B. K § 168]: new ed. 8*m* 50 [85] 92.
Grundleg. u. Gesch. d. klass. Altertumswiss. [L. v. URLICHS, posth. ed. H. L. URLICHS]; *Hermeneutik u. Kritik* [Fr. BLASS]; *Paläog., Buchwesen u. HSS.-kunde* [*id.*]; *Griech. Epigraphik* [Wilh. LARFELD; 7 pl.]. *Röm. Epigr.* [Em. HÜBNER]; *Zeitrechng. d. Gr. u. Röm.* [G. F. UNGER]; *Gr. u. Röm. Metrologie* [Heinr. NISSEN].
iv. (1) *Griech. Staats u. Rechtsaltertümer* [*ut* B.B. K § 168] new ed. Geo. BUSOLT, 6*m*.50 [86] 92
iv. (2) *Griech. Privataltertümer* [I. v. MÜLLER], *Gr. Kriegsalt.* [Ad. BAUER] [*ut* B.B. K § 167]: new ed. ....[86] 93
iv. (2) *Röm. Staats- u. Kriegsaltert.* [*ut* B.B. K § 168] HERM. SCHILLER]; *Röm. Privataltert.* [Mor. VOIGT] 8*m* [87] 93
v. (1) *Gesch. d. alt. Philos.* [for tr. *v.* C § 2] Prf. W. WINDELBAND, 5*m*.50, 93.
Appended is 2nd ed. of *Gesch. d. Mathem. u. Naturwiss. im. Altertum* [*ut* B.B. K § 168] by Siegm. GÜNTHER.
v. (3) *Griech. Kultusaltert. u. antikes Bühnenwesen* [*ut* K § 188] P. STENGEL + G. OEHMICHEN, 6*m*.50, 90
vi. (1–2) *Klassische Kunstarchäologie*, Prf. SITTL, ea. 5*m* 50. 94
viii. (2) *Gesch. d. Röm. Litter.*, pt. ii. [*ut* K § 211] Prf. Mart. SCHANZ 8*m*. 92
ix. (1) *Gesch. d. Byzant.-Litter.* [*ut* K § 187] Dr. K. KRUMBACHER, 8*m*.50, 91

Problems.

HECHT, Max — Die greich. Bedeutungslehre: eine Aufgabe d. Klass. Philol. — 4*m*.40 8° Teubner, *Lps*. 88
LIPSIUS, Herm. — Die Aufgaben d. Class. Philol. in d. Gegenwt. [lecture] — 4° *Leipzig* 91

Translation.

CAUER, Paul — Die Kunst des Uebersetzens — [Gk. and Latin] 2*m*.40 8° Weidmann, *Berlin* 94

168. GREEK-AND-LATIN: COLLECTED ESSAYS.

by Single Writers —*v. also* K § 94.

AHRENS, Heinr. Ludolf [*d.* 1891] — Kleine Schriften, hrsg. Carl Haeberlin, vol. i. — 16*m*. 8° Halm, *Hanover* 91
This vol. is entitled *Zur Sprachwissenschaft*, and conts. papers, fr. 1829 onwards, on classical philology.

BAUNACK, J. + Th. — Studien auf d. Gebiete d. griech. u. d. arischen Sprachen, vol. i., pt. 2 — 7*m*. 8° Hirzel, *Lps*. 88
CURTIUS, Prf. Ern. — Gesammelte Abhandlungen, vol. i., 11*m*.; ii. [last] 12*m*.; ill. — 8° Besser, *Berlin* 93; 94
DROYSEN, Joh. Gust. — Kleine Schriften zur alten Geschichte, vol. i.; port. — [in 2 vols.] 10*m*. 8° Veit, *Lps*. 93
Griech. Beitrchr. v. § ägyp. Papyren u. Berl., Zur Gesch. d. Ketten, Päanien u. Dardanien, Demosthenes, Zur Gesch. d. Hellenismus, Die attische Communalverfassung.

GILDERSLEEVE, Bas. L. [Am.] — Essays and Studies — $3.50. 8° Murray, *Baltimore* 90
v. GUTSCHMID, Alf. — Schriften zur griech. Gesch. u. Liter. = Kleine Schriften, vol. iv.—*ut* K § 94
PATER, Walt. — Greek Studies — [posthumously pubd.] Macmillan *in prep.*

by Several Writers—*v. also* K § 95.

BERLIN, (Prf. Theod. MOMMSEN) — Commentationes Philologicæ in hon. Th. M. scripserunt Amici, 40*m*. 4° Weidmann, *Berlin* 77
" " " — Festschrift Th. Mommsen überreicht P. Jörs + E. Schwartz *etc.* 3*m*.60 8° Elwert, *Marbg*. 94
BONN (Prf. Reinh. KEKULÉ): Bonner Studien an R. Kekulé v.s. Schülern gewidmet — 20*m*. r 8° Spemann, *Berlin* 90
DRESDEN (Prf. K. F. W. Alf. FLECKEISEN): Commentationes Fleckeisenianae; port — 6*m*. 8° Teubner, *Lps*. 90

Graz: Analecta Graeciensia. von. Professoren d. Karl-Frz.-Univ. Graz 10*m.* 8° *Graz* 93
Greifswald [Prf. W. Studemund]: Commentationes in hon. G. S. conscrip-erunt Discipuli 10*m.* 4° Heitz, *Strasburg* 89
Leipzig [Prf. Herm. Lipsius] Griechische Studien Herm. Lipsius z. 60 Geburtstag dargebracht 6*m.* 8° Teubner, *Lpz.* 94
,, [Prf. Otto Ribbeck] Commentationes Philologae quibus O. R. congrat. Discipuli 12*m.* 8° ,, ,, 88
Leyden [C. Conto] Sylloge Commentationum quam C. Conto obtul. Philologi Batavi 5/- 8° Brill, *Leyden* 93
Munich [Prf. Wilh. v. Christ]: Abhandl. a. d. Gebiete d. class. Altertumswiss., v. seinen Schülern 10*m.* 8° Beck, *Munich* 92
,, (Prf. Ed. Woelfflin): Commentationes Woefflinianae; port. 8*m.* 8° Teubner, *Lpz.* 91
92 dissertns. by var. writers on pts. of Gk. and Lat. philol., lexicography bg. largely repres., as is natural in a work designed to honour a great lexicographer.
New York, Columbia Coll. (Dr. Hy. Drisler): Classical Studies in Honour of, by his Students; port. and ill. $4 (18/- *nt.*) 8° Macmillan 94
Zürich [Prf. H. Schweizer-Sidler] Philol. Abhdgn., z. Feier d. 50-j. jubil. s. Docentthät'kt. 4*m.* 4° Höhr, *Zürich* 92

169–170. GREEK-AND-LATIN GRAMMAR (*b* and *c*): ACCIDENCE. SYNTAX.

Nouns.

Torp, Alf. Den graeske Nominalflexion sammenlignende fremstillet 4*kr.* 50 r 8° Cammermeyer, *Christiania* 90

Case.

Krebs, Frz. Zur Rection der Casus in d. späteren histor. Gräcität, 3 pts. 3*m.*40 8° Lindauer, *Munich* 87–90
Pratje, H. Der altepische Casus mit d. Suffixe -φι syntact. dargestellt [progr.] 4° *Sobernheim* 90

Syntax.

Generally.

Brownrigg, C. E. A Classical Compendium [elementary Gk. and Lat. constructions] 2/6 c 8° Blackie 94
Middleton, G. An Essay on Analogy in Syntax—*ut* K § 98.
Ill. chiefly fr. Gk. and Lat.; w. Appendix contg. the form of syntact. analogy peculiar to Herodotus.
Miles, Eust. Hamilton Comparative Syntax of Greek and Latin, pt. i. 8° 2/6 Macmillan & Bowes, *Camb.* / $1.60 Macmillan, *N.Y.* 93
This Pt. deals w. Original and Early Meanings, and Principles of Syntax; w. Appendices. To occupy 2 Pts.

Verb.

Enault, E. Du Parfait en Grec et en Latin [Bibl. Ecole Htes. Etudes] 6*fr.* 8° Bouillon, *Paris* 86

172. GREEK-AND-LATIN GRAMMAR (*d*): METRICS—*v.* K § 183: Greek Metrics.

172.* GREEK-AND-LATIN: PALÆOGRAPHY—*v.* K § 179: Greek Palæography.

173. GREEK-AND-LATIN MAGAZINES AND PERMANENT SERIALS.

Magazines —*v. also* B.B. K § 173.

Philologische Untersuchungen, hrsg. A Kiessling and Ulr. v. Wilamowitz-Moellendorff, pts. i.–xiii. *v.p.* (2 to 16*m.*) 8° Weidmann, *Berl.* 80–92 *in prg.*
Revue des Etudes Grecques: ed. Théod. Reinach, vols. i.–vii. [*qrtly.*] *ann.* 10*fr.* [vols. i.–vi. for 50*fr.*] 8° Leroux, *Par.* 88–94 *in prg.*

University Serials.

Berlin: Berliner Studien f. class. Philol. u. Archäol. [*ut* B.B. K § 173], v. xi.–xv. *v.p.* (5.20–18*m.*) 8° Calvary, *Berl.* 90–94 *in prg.*
Breslau: Breslauer philologische Abhandlungen, hrsg. R. Förster, vols. i.–vii. *v.p.* (9.60–14*m.*) 8° Koebner, *Bresl.* 86–94 *in prg.*
Chicago: Studies in Classical Philology, vol. i. 8° Univ. Press, *Chicago* 93 *in prg.*
Cornell Univ.: Studies in Class. Philology: ed. Is. Flagg + Wm. G. Hale + Benj. I. Wheeler [Ams.], vol. i., pts. 1–2; ii. 48*c.*, 80*c.*, 30*c.* 8° Cornell Univ., *Ithaca* 89
Erlangen: Acta Seminarii philologici Erlangensis, vols. i.–v. *v.p.* 8° Deichert, *Lpz.* 80–91 *in prg.*
Halle: Dissertationes philologicæ Halenses, vols. i.–xii. *v.p.* (5–20*m.*) 8° Niemeyer, *Halle* 73–91 *in prg.*
Harvard: Harvard Studies in Classical Philology, vols. i.–iv.; pl. 8° ea. $1.50 Ginn, *Boston* / ea. 6/- *nt.* Arnold 90–93 *in prg.*
Jena: Commentationes Philologae Ienenses, edd. Ien. profess., v. i.–iv. *v.p.* (5–6*m.*) 8° Teubner, *Lpz.* 81–94 *in prg.*
Leipzig: Leipziger Studien z. cl. Phil., hrsg. O. Ribbeck + H. Lipsius + C. Wachsmuth, v. i.–xv. *v.p.* (7–19*m.*) 8° Hirzel, *Lpz.* 83–94 *in prg.*
Munich: Commentationes philologicæ, vol. i. 4*m.* 8° Kaiser, *Munich*
Oxford: Anecdota Oxoniensia: Classical Series s 4° Clar. Press / Macmillan, *N.Y.* *in prg.*

i. [Aristotle] *English MSS. of the Nicomach. Ethics* [*ut* K § 194] J. A. Stewart 3/6 (90c. *nt.*)
ii. Nonius Marcellus, *De Compendiosa Doctr.* [Harl. MS. 2719] ed. J. H. Onions 3/6 (90c. *nt.*)
iii. Aristotle's *Physics*, *bk. vii.* [*ut* K § 194] ed. R. Shute; w. Introd. 2/- (50c. *nt.*)
iv. Bentley, Rich. *Plautine Emendatns.* [*ut* B.B. K § 215] ed. Prf. E. A. Sonnenschein 2/6 (60c. *nt.*) 83
v. *Harleian MS.* 2610; Ovid, *Metam.* i.–iii. (1–622) *etc.* [*ut* K § 214] ed. Prf. Robinson Ellis 4/-
vi. Aristotle's *Categories*, *etc.*, *Collatn. w. Anc. Armen. Versions* [*ut* K § 194] ed. F. C. Conybeare 14/- 92
vii. Cicero *Collatns. fr. Harl. MS.* 2682 [*ut* K § 217] ed. Alb. C. Clark 7/6 91

Prague: Prager Studien aus d. Gebiete d. class. Alterthumswiss., pts. i.–iv. 7*m.*80 8° Dominicus, *Prague* 94 *in prg.*
Strassburg: Dissertationes philologicæ Argentoratenses selectæ. vols. i.–xi. *v.p.* (5–7*m.*) 8° Trübner, *Strassb.* 79–94 *in prg.*
Vienna: Dissertationes Philologicae Vindobonenses, vols. i.–iv. *v.p.* (4–8*m.*) 8° Tempsky, *Vienna* 87–93 *in prg.*

Archæological. Epigraphical.

Abhandlungen d. archäolog.-epigraph. Seminars d. Univers. Wien, hrsg. O. Benndorf + E. Bormann, v. i.–xi. ; ill. *v.p.* (3.60–9 60m.) 8° Gerold, *Vienna* 80–94 *in prg.*
Bolletino della Commissione Archæol. Communale di Roma [Latin only] (*qrtrly.*) 15/– r 8° *Rome*
" dell' Instituta di Correspondenza Archeologia [Lat. only] German Institute, *Rome*
Bulletin de Correspondance Hellénique, vols. i.–xvi. [Greek only] 8° Thorin, *Paris* ?–93 *in prg.*
Comptes Rendus de l' Académie des Inscriptions
ΕΦΗΜΕΡΙΣ ΑΡΧΑΙΟΛΟΓΙΚΗ [Greek only] *ann.* 21/– *Athens*
Mittheilungen d. deutsch. archäol. Institut zu Athen [Greek only] r 8° Wilberg, *Athens* 75–94 *in prg.*
Museo Italiano di Antichita Classica, ed. Comparetti [Latin only] *Rome*
Notizia degli Scavi di Antichita [Latin only] (*mthly.*) *ann.* 24/– "
Revue Archéologique ed. Bertrand + Perrot : ill. [Greek and Latin] *ann.* 25/– r 8° *Paris*
Winckelmannsprogramme : Programme zum Winckelmannsfeste pts. i.–liii. ; pl. and ill. *v.p.* r 4° G. Reimer, *Berlin* ?–94 *in prg.*

174. HISTORY OF CLASSICAL STUDY AND BIOGRAPHY OF SCHOLARS.

Generally.

Biographisches Jahrbuch für Altertumskunde, Jahrgang i.–xvii. *v.p.* (3–10m.) 8° Calvary, *Berlin* 78–94 *in prg.*
GUDEMANN, Prf. Alf. [Am.] Syllabus on the History of Classical Philology 8° $\frac{\text{\$1. Ginn, Boston}}{\text{s/6 Arnold}}$ 92

A surv. of class. research fr. time of Sophists to pres. day, contg. names (classif. under epochs) of most celebr. scholars and critics, w. biogr. notes, their chief contribns. (complete for anc. period) and bibliogr. Added are lists of import. scholia, explan. of critical signs employed in these lists of MSS. and *editiones principes*.

HOFFMANN, Friedr. Ueb. d. Entwickg. d. Begriffs d. Gram. b. d. Alten [sch.-progr.] 80*pf.* 4° Gräfe, *Königsb.* 91
NEBBLICH, Paul Das Dogma v. klass. Altertum in s. geschichtl. Entwickelung 7*m.*50 8° Hirschfeld, *Lpz.* 94

Mediæval.

CONRAD HIRSAUGENSIS [11 cent.] Dialogus super Auctores sive Didascalon, hrsg. Dr. G. Schepss 1*m.*60 8° Stuber, *Würzbg.* 90

Hitherto unedited. The author lived under Abbot GEBHARD [1091–1105] and his successors BRUNO and VOLMAR [1105–57] as a monk of the Benedict. Abbey of Hirschau in Würtembg. The *Dialogus* is a short colloquy on the classical writers then habitually read: ÆSOP, ARATUS, AVIANUS, BOETHIUS, CATO, CICERO, DONATUS, HOMER [the Lat. hexam. poem], HORACE, JUVENCUS, LUCAN, OVID, PERSIUS, PROSPER, PRUDENTIUS, SALLUST, SEDULIUS, STATIUS, VERGIL (to wh. should be added THEODOLUS).

Fourteenth Century.

PLANUDES, Maximus Epistulæ, ed. Max. Treu [*v.* K § 190, *s.v.* Gk. Anthol., Mackail (note)] 6*m.* 8° Koebner, *Breslau* 90

Modern.

Sixteenth Century.

CASAUBON, Isaac [1559–1614].
*Pattison, Rev. Mark Life of Isaac Casaubon [*ut* 𝔅.𝔅. K § 174]: new edn., by Prf. Hy. Nettleship; port. 8° $\frac{\text{16/- Clar. Press}}{\text{\$4 net. Macmillan, N.Y.}}$ [75] 92

An excellent and learned biography of the last of the great scholars of the sixteenth century, giving a wonderful picture of a great scholar's life in days when polemical theology had extinguished humanism. Notes by Ingram BYWATER + CHRISTIE; index by C. E. DOBLE.

Nineteenth Century.

BONITZ, Herm. [1814–88].
Gompertz, Theod. Hermann Bonitz : ein Nachruf [*extr. fr.* Biogr. Jahrb. f. Altert.] 2*m.* 8° Calvary, *Berlin* 89
COBET, Prf. G. C. Briven aan Geel uit Parijs en Italië, Nov. 1840–Jul. 1845 ; port. 7*fl.*50 8° Brill, *Leyden* 92

Written to Geel when Cobet, then only 27 yrs. of age, but of extraord. promise, was sent on a mission to collect materials for an edn. of Simplicius fr. the chief Europ. libraries. They bear witness to his immense knowl. of Gk. even at that early age.

DUNCKER, Max
Haym, R. Das Leben Max Dunckers erzählt ; port. 10*m.* 8° Gaertner, *Berlin* 91
GRIMM, $\frac{\text{Jacob}}{\text{Wilh.}}$ $\left[\frac{\text{1785–1863}}{\text{1876–1854}}\right]$ —*v.* K § 225 : Teutonic Philology.
HAUPT, Prf. Moriz [1808–74] Karl Lachmann's Briefe an M. H., hrsg. Prf. Joh. Vahlen 4*m.* 8° G. Reimer, *Berlin* 92
HEHN, Victor
Schiemann, Theod. Viktor Hehn : ein Lebensbild 5*m.* 8° Cotta, *Stuttgart* 94
Schrader, Dr. Osc. Victor Hehn : ein Bild seines Leben u. seiner Werke 3*m.* 8° Calvary, *Berlin* 91
JOWETT, Dr. Benj. 1817–1893] Life : may be undertaken by Dr. Evelyn Abbott
LEWIS, Rev. Sam. Savage [Librn. and Fellow of Corp. Chr. Coll., Camb.].
Lewis, Agnes Smith Life of Rev. Samuel Savage Lewis—*ut* G § 30.
LINCOLN, Jno. Larkin [Am. ; Prf. in Brown Univ.].
Life of John Larkin Lincoln ; w. extrs. fr. Diary and Letters ; 2 ports. *c.* \$4 8° *Boston* 94
LONSDALE, Rev. Jas. [1816–1892 ; tr. of Vergil and of Horace. *ut* 𝔅.𝔅. K § 214].
Duckworth, Russell Memoir of Rev. James Lonsdale ; w. Introd. G. C. Brodrick 6/– c 8° Longman 93

A modest biography of a modest but admirable scholar of the old type, who had no belief in the "gospel of getting-on.

MANUTIUS, Paul [Paolo MANUZIO ; 1511–74]—*v.* K § 15.
NAUCK, Prf. Joh. August [1822–? 1893].
Zielinski, Dr. Theod. Aug. Nauck : Bild s. Lebens u. s. Werke [*extr. fr.* Jahr. Forts. Cl. Alt.] 2*m.* 8° Calvary, *Berlin* 94
TEUFFEL, W. S
Teuffel, S. W. S. Teuffel : ein Lebensabriss 2*m.* 4° Fues, *Lpz.* 89

XXV. Greek Philology and Literature.

175. GREEK GRAMMAR (a): GENERALLY.

Grammars.

KÜHNER, R. Ausführliche Grammatik d. griech. Sprache [ut B.B. K § 175]: new edn., Pt. I., hrsg. F. Blass, vol. i. 12m. 8° Hahn, *Hanover* [34] 90
MEYER, Gust. Griechische Grammatik [Bibl. Indogerm. Gramm.] 9m.50 8° Breitkopf, *Lpz.* 81
MULLER, H. C. Historische Grammatik. d. hellenischen Sprache, 2 pts. 4fl.25 8° Brill, *Leyden* 91; 92
Forms the first 2 Pts. of the *Hellenische Bibliothek. Samml. v. Arbeiten a. d. Geb. d. alt-, mittel- u. neugriech. Spr. u. Litter.*, ed. H. C. MULLER + A. J. FLAMENT.
SONNENSCHEIN, Prf. Edw. A. Greek Gram.: Accidence 2/- (60c.); Syntax 2/6 (75c.) [Parallel Gram. Ser.] i 16° Sonnenschein / Macmillan, *N.Y.* 92; 94
v. WILAMOWITZ-MOELLENDORFF, Ulr. Commentariolum Grammaticum, I.–iv. ea. 80pf. 8° Dieterich, *Göttingen* 88–89

Collective Essays.

JOHANSSON, K. F. Beiträge zur griechischen Sprachkunde 6m. 8° Landström, *Upsala* 91
KRETSCHMER, Paul Beiträge zur griechischen Grammatik [*extr. fr.* Zts. f. vergl. Sprachforschg.] 1m. 8° Bertelsmann, *Gütersloh* 89
LA ROCHE, J. Beiträge zur griechischen Grammatik, pt. i. 6m. 8° Teubner, *Lpz.* 93

Magazines —*v.* K § 173.

176. GREEK GRAMMAR (b): ACCIDENCE; (c): SYNTAX.

Generally.

Syntax.

SCHANZ, M. [ed.] Beiträge zur historischen Syntax d. griech. Sprache, vols. iii. (2)–iv. (1) 19m. 8° Stuber, *Würzbg.* 89–93 *in prg.*
iii. 2, *Ursprung d. Substantivsatzes m. relat. Partikeln* [P. SCHMITT] 3m. '89; iii. 3–4 (i. ii), *Gesch. d. Pronomen Reflexivum*, 2 pts. [Ad. DYROFF], ea. 4m. '92, '93. iv. 1–2, *Hist. Synt. d. gr. Comparation*, pts. 1–2 [Otto SCHWAB], 4m., 3m. '93, '94.

Adverbs.

LUTZ, Leonh. Die Casus-Adverbien bei den attischen Rednern 1m.20 8° *Würzbg.* (Fock, *Lpz.*) 91

Article.

KALLENBERG, Herm. Studien über den griechischen Artikel, 2 pts. [schl.-progr.] 2m. 4° Gaertner, *Berlin* 90; 91
SCHMIDT, Carl De Articulo in nominibus propriis ap. Attic Scriptt. pedestres [diss.] 1m.50 8° *Kiel* (Fock, *Lpz.*) 90

Conditional Sentences.

SMITH, Rich. Horton The Theory of Conditional Sentences in Latin and Greek 21/- *nt.* ($.) 8° Macmillan 94
A curious specimen of a philological treatise: the fruit of nearly 50 yrs'. study of the subject—and many other subjects to boot. Intended "for the use of students (who will find it full of instructn. and learning); but it conts. a multitude of *obiter dicta* on other matters of general literary interest and occns. of amusement. Like BERKELEY, who began to write on Tarwater and ended w. a disquisn. on the Trinity, Mr. Horton SMITH has not known where to stop.

Noun, Pronoun.

DYROFF, Adolf Gesch. d. Pronomen reflexivum in d. älter. attisch. Prosa, *etc.* [diss.] 1m. 8° Stuber, *Würzbg.* 93
FLENSBURG, Nils Ueber Ursprung und Bildung des Pronomens αὐτός 1m.40 8° Möller, *Lund* 93
HASSE, Ernst Der Dual in Attischen [w. Preface by F. Blass] 1m.40 8° Hahn, *Hanover* 93
LELL, F. Der absolute Accusativ in Griech. bis z. Aristoteles [diss.] 8° *Würzburg* 93
LORENTZ, Paul Observv. de Pronominum Personal. apud Poetas Alexandrinos usu 1m.50 8° Heinrich, *Berl.* 92
REICHELT, C. De Dativis in οις et ᾳις (αις) exeuntibus [school-programme] 8° *Breslau* 93
SCHMIDT, Herm De Duali Graecorum et emoriente et reviviscente [diss. inaug.] 8° " 93

Particles.

POLASCHE, R. A. Beiträge zur Erkenntniss d. Partikeln ἄν u. κέν [schl.-progr.] 8° *Czernowitz* 91
WEHMANN, Max De ὥστε Particulae usu Herodot., Thucyd., Xenoph. [diss. inaug.] 1m.50 8° Trübner, *Strassb.* 91

Preposition.

LAMBERTON, W. A. [Am.] Πρός with the Accusative [*also note on* Antigone] 50c. 8° Hodges, *N.Y.* 91

Pronoun, Conjunction.

BARON, Chas. Le Pronom Relatif et la Conjonction en Grec [chfly. Homeric] 8° Picard, *Paris* 91

Relative Clause.

FRENZEL, Jos. Die Entwickelung des relativen Satzbaues im Griechischen 1m.20 8° Schöningh, *Paderborn* 89

Verb.

GROSSE, Herm. Beiträge z. Syntax d. griech. Mediums u. Passivums, 2 pts. [schl.-progr.] 1m.75 8° Fock, *Lpz.* 91: 91
HAMMERSCHMIDT, Karl Ueb. d. Grundbedeutg. v. Konjunktiv u. Optativ [diss.] 8° *Erlangen* 92
HOGUE, Addison [Am.] Irregular Verbs of Attic Prose [w. related wds. and Eng. derivatives] 12° $1.60 Ginn, *Boston* / 7/6 Arnold 89
KRAPP, F. D. substantivierte Infinitiv abh. v. Präpos. u. Präpos.-Adv. i. hist. Gräc. 3m. 8° Winter, *Heidelb.* 92
MUTZBAUER, Carl Grundlagen d. griech. Tempuslehre u. d. homer. Tempusgebrauch 15m. 8° Trübner, *Strassb.* 93
A good contribution to the historical syntax of Greek.
SÜTTERLIN, L. Zur Gesch. d. Verba denomin. in Altgr., pt. i. [obs. in -άω, -έω, -όω] 3m. 8° Trübner, *Strassb.* 91
WAGNER, Rich. Der Gebrauch des imperativ. Infinitivs im Griechischen [progr.] 8° *Schwerin* 91

178. GREEK GRAMMAR (*d*): PHONOLOGY.

Dialects.

SMYTH, Prf. Herb. Weir [Am.] The Sounds and Inflections of the Greek Dialects: Ionic—*ut* K § 185.

Accentuation.

SMITH, F. Darwin — Plain Guide to Greek Accentuation — 1/- 8° Blackwell, *Oxford* 91

WACKERNAGEL, K. — Beiträge zur Lehre vom griechischen Accent — [progr.] 1*fr*.50 4° Georg, *Basle* 94

WITRZENS, Joh. — Betonungssystem der griechischen Sprache — 3*m*.60 8° *Teschen* (Fock, *Lps*.) 89

179. GREEK GRAMMAR (*e*): PALÆOGRAPHY, MSS., AND TEXTUAL CRITICISM.

Generally —*v. also* I § 111, *s.v.* Illuminated MS.

BAST, F. J. Commentatio Palæographica—*in* Append. *to* Gregorius Corinthius de dial., ed. G. H. Schäfer *o.p.* [*pb.* 9*m*.] 8° Weigel, *Lps*. 11

Of considerable historical value.

MIDDLETON, Prf. J. H. —*in his* Illuminated Manuscripts in Classical and Mediæval Times—*ut* I § 111.

The first 2 chaps. are devoted to methods and materls. of wrg. in classical times, incl. selling and preserving bks. (the least satisfactory pt. of the work).

THOMPSON, Edw. Maunde — Manual of Greek and Latin Palæography; facss. [Internat. Scient. Ser.] c 8° 5/- Paul / $1.75 Appleton, *N.Y.* [93] 94

An excellent and concise manual of Gk. and Lat., and to some extent of English, writing. Chaps. 1-7 are devoted to external points conn. w. wrg. (history of classical alphabs.; math., implements, and forms of bks.; abbrevns. and contractns.); 8-12 deal w. Gk. palæogr. (majuscule and minuscule, and that of the papyri); 13-19 w. Lat. palæogr., following its course in differ. countries. Tables of cursive Gk. and Lat. alphabs. fr. B.C. 250 to A.D. 750; Bibliogr.; Index. By Prc. Librn. of Brit. Mus., author of article *Palæography* in *Encyclo. Brit.* (9th edn.).

WILCKEN, Ulr. [ed.] — Tafeln zur älteren griechischen Paläographie; 20 pl. — 10*m*. i 4° Giesecke, *Lps*. 91

Biblical Codices: Greek—*v.* A § 17 *and* B.B. A § 17.

Latin Words in Gk. Inscripp.—*v.* K § 204 (ECKINGER).

Magical.

WESSELY, C. [ed.] — Neue griechische Zauberpapyri — [*extr. fr.* Densksch. Wien. Ak.] 5*m*. r 4° Tempsky, *Vienna* 93

Tachygraphy.

GITLBAUER, Dr. Mich. — Die drei Systeme d. griechischen Tachygraphie — 3*m*.60 8° Freytag, *Lps*. 94

England.

British Museum:

*Kenyon, F. G. [ed.] — Catal. of Gk. Papyri in Brit. Mus., vol. i. [Texts] 42/- 4°; ii. [Autotype Facs.] 145/- f° Brit. Mus. 93; 93

A complete and luxurious catalogue of all the Gk. papyri acquired by Brit. Mus. up to end of 1890, with full texts of all those that are not of a literary character. The texts are revised by KENYON, who has added Intros. and notes, as well as a valuable introd. sketch of the hist. of Gk. cursive writing on papyrus, and elaborate Indices. The texts range fr. 3rd cent. B.C. to 8th A.D., and are of value as evidences of private life and manners in Greek Egypt, illustrating the business habits, occupations, legal formulæ, handwriting, arithmetic, *etc*., of a very important Hellenistic society. The facss. are most excellently prepared by the Autotype Co., and form the finest series of palæograph. reprodns. wh. has yet appeared anywhere.

* ,, ,, [ed.] — Classical Texts from the Papyri in Brit. Mus.; 9 autotype facss. — 7/6 4° British Museum 91

Conts. 10 MSS. of class. authors, *viz*., portions of *Iliad*, of 3rd Ep. of DEMOSTHENES [prob. 2 cent. A.D.], and of ISOCRATES' *On the Peace*; and 3 "new" works, a fragmt. of a speech of th HYPERIDES against one PHILIPPIDES, a portn. of a grammat. treat. bearing name of TRYPHON, the great Alexandrian scholar, and the *Mimiambi* of HERONDAS, occupying nearly half the vol. [*v*. K § 190].

Commentarii notarum Tironianarum cum prolegg. adnot. crit. et exeg. ed. Wilh. Schmitz; 132 pl. 40*m*. f° Teubner, *Lps*. 94

Monopoly Papyrus: ed. B. P. Grenfell *in prep.*

Acquired by Prf. W. M. Flinders PETRIE in Egypt in winter 1893-94. Written *c*. 264-260 B.C., it is a series of ordinances regarding the control of State monopolies, and the condns. under wh. they were to be let to tax-farmers, w. reservatns. protecting State fr. loss, the farmer and the publican fr. over-reaching.

Mahaffy, Prf. Jno. P. —*on reln. of Monopoly Pap. to documts. in Petrie Papyri*—*v. inf.*, *s.n.* Petrie Papyri (note).

Oxford Philological Soc.: Photographs of Eighty-two Herculanean Papyri [fr. Bodl. Lib. and Clar. Press] *priv. prin.* 89

Palæographic Soc.: Facsimiles of Ancient Greek Writing; 10 pl. f° Palæograph. Soc. 92

Ten plates, sel. fr. papyri ranging fr. 3rd and 4th cent. B.C. to 3rd cent. A.D.

Petrie Papyri:

Mahaffy, Prf. Jno. P. [ed.] The Flinders Petrie Papyri, pt. i., 30 autotyp. pl.; ii., 18 pl. ea. 42/- *nt*. r 4° R. Irish Acad., *Dubl.* (Williams) 91/93

From the *Cunningham Memrs.* viii.-ix. A colln. of fragmts. of classical texts fr. the Petrie papyri, discov. by Prf. W. M. Flinders PETRIE in the cartonnages of the mummy-cases of Tell Gurob—the most important bg. fragmts. of the lost *Antiope* of EURIPIDES [*ut* K § 191], of PLATO [*ut* K § 191], and of HOMER [*ut* K § 190]. The whole is of very great palæogr., liter., and histor. value, the papyri forming the earliest known chap. in hist. of Gk. palæogr. Excellently ed., w. transcriptns., commentaries, index, and Introd. contg. a sketch of Gk. life in Egypt. An Appendix is to appear, contg. facs. of the histor. narrative of the Syrian soldier, an interesting fragm., and a discussn. of relns. of *Monopoly Papyrus* [*ut sup.*] to the documts. in pt. ii. of above.

Egypt.

Corpus Papyrorum Ægypti, vol. iii.: Papyrus Grecs, facs. 1.: Hyperides in Athenogenem, publ. p. Eug. Revillout, *ut* K § 193.

France.

*OMONT, Henri [ed.] — Facsimiles de MSS. Grecs datés de la Bibl. Nat. du 9 au 14 siècle — 60*fr*. f° Leroux, *Paris* 90; 91

100 good facss., on 100 pl., ranging fr. 890 to 1590; w. short Introd. and Bibliogr. of printed bks. *etc*. since MONTFAUCON.

,, ,, [ed.] — Facsimiles de plus anciens MS. Grecs en onciale et en minuscule de la Bibl. Nat. du 4 au 12 siècle; 50 pl. — [suppl. to above] 32*fr*. f° Leroux, *Paris* 92

,, ,, [ed.] — Facsimiles de MSS. Grecs de la Bibl. Nat. des 15 et 16 siècles [50 facss.] 12*fr*.50 4° Picard, *Paris* 87

,, ,, [ed.] — Demosthenes Codex Σ [Bibl. Nat.]—*ut* K § 193; Aristotle's Poetica—*ut* K § 194.

,, ,, [ed.] — Catals. des MSS. Grecs de Fontainebleau sous François i. et Henri ii.; pl. 30*fr*. r 4° Picard, *Paris* 89

,, ,, [ed.] — Les MSS. d. l. Bibl. Nat. et d'autres Collns: MSS. Grecs, p. H. Omont; 60 pl. 60*fr*. 8° Leroux, *Paris*

,, ,, [ed.] — Inventaire sommaire des MSS. Grecs d. l. Bibl. Nat., 3 vols. 30*fr*. 8° Leroux, *Paris* 86; 87; 88

Germany.

Berlin Roy. Museum : Griechische Urkunden, pts. i.–vi.—*in* Ægyptische Urkunden a. d. kön. Mus. z. Berl., *ut* K § 102.

Greece.

SAKELLION, J. [ed.] Πατμιακὴ Βιβλιοθήκη *Athens* 90

Catalogue of Greek MSS. of Patmos; by the Keeper of the Athen. Natl. Lib.

Italy.

ALLEN, T. W. Notes on Greek Manuscripts in Italian Libraries 3/6 c 8° Nutt 91

BATIFFOL, Abbé Pierre La Vaticane de Paul iii. à Paul v. d'après des Documents nouveaux 3/*fr.* 18° Leroux, *Paris* 90

Gives a short descr. of the Gk. MSS. acquired fr. 1535 to 1621. The library possesses as many as 3,614 Gk. MSS., wh. are known as six collections, the Palatinus (471 MSS.), that of the Queen (190), the coll. of Ottoboni (471), that of Pius ix. (55), the Urbano coll. (165), the Vaticana [=Pontifical coll.] (2,302 MSS.).

MARTINI, Em. [ed.] Catalogo di MSS. greci esistenti nelle Biblioteche Italiene, vol. i., pt. i. 8/.50 8° Hoepli, *Milan* 93

Spain.

GRAUX + MARTIN, Chas. A. [eds.] Notices Sommaires de MSS. Grecs d'Espagne et de Portug. 8° Leroux, *Paris* 92

" " " Facsimilés de Manuscrits Grecs d'Espagne; 18 pl. [w. transcriptns.] 25/*fr.* 8° Hachette, *Paris* 91

180. GREEK GRAMMAR (*f*): PRONUNCIATION.

BLASS, Dr. F. Pronunciation of Ancient Greek, tr. W. J. Purton 8° 6/- Camb. Press / $1.90 *nt.* Macmillan, *N.Y.* 90

A tr. of the best book on the subject, careful and learned. For original German edn. v. 𝕭.𝕭. K § 180. Author rejects the idea that anc. Gk. was pronounced w. a stress accent, like the modern, and maintains that the literary tradition is more likely to be correct than the oral.

TÉLFY, Iwán Chronologie u. Topographie der griechischen Aussprache 2*m.* 8° Friedrich, *Lpz.* 93

Based on the testimony afforded by Greek inscriptions.

181. GREEK GRAMMAR (*g*): ETYMOLOGY.

Lexicography.

DURAY, Gust. Contributions à l'Etude de la Lexicographie Grecque 1/*fr.*50 12° Retaux-Bray, *Paris* 88

Dictionaries.

PRELLWITZ, Dr. Walth. Etymologisches Wörterbuch der griechischen Sprache 8*m.* 8° Vandenhoeck, *Göttgn.* 92

With special reference to Modern High German.

ROST, Val. Chr. Fr. Deutsch-Griechisches Wörterbuch, bearb. Dr. E. Albrecht 8*m.* 8° " " [18] 89

Personal Names. Names of Gods.

*FICK, Prf. Aug. Die griechischen Personennamen nach ihrer Bildung erklärt 12*m.* 8° Vandenhoeck, *Göttgn.* [75] 94

A new edn. of this epoch-making bk. [*ut* 𝕭.𝕭. K § 181], wh. was the first to explain the orig. and character of Indogermanic proper names, and to shew that (with a exceptions), all the Indogerm. langs. agreed in the nature of their formatn., that they were in fact pt. of the heritage wh. had descended fr. the days when the dialects that were devel. into the several langs. still existed side by side. This new edn. has been prep. w. help of Dr. Fr. BECHTEL, who has revised the illustrative quotns. and added many others, refs. bg. in each case given to the epigraphic authority on wh. a name rests.

PERFECKI, R. Versuch einige class. Götternamen etymologisch z. deuten [progr.] 8° *Kolomea* 91

Thrace —*v.* K § 185, *s.v.* Thrace (TOMASCHEK, vol. ii., 2).

Place-Names.

MUCHAU, Herm. Zur Etymologie griechischer Städtenamen [schl.-progr.] 4° *Brandenbg.* (Fock, *Lpz.*) 91

Loan Words: *Semitic.*

MUSS-ARNOLT, Rev. W. On Semitic Words in Greek and Latin $1 *nt.* 8° Westermann, *N.Y.* 93

Summarises the researches of LAGARDE and others

182-183. GREEK GRAMMAR (*h-i*): PROSODY. METRICS. STYLE.

Prosody.

CONSBRUCH, Max De Veterum περὶ ποιήματος Doctrina [Bresl. Philol. Abhgn.] 5*m.*40 8° Koebner, *Breslau* 90

Metaphors.

BLÜMNER, Hugo Studien zur Gesch. der Metapher im Griechischen, pt. i. [in Attic comedy] 8*m.* 8° Teubner, *Lpz.* 91

Metrics.

CHAIGNET, A. E. Essais sur la Métrique Grecque: le vers iambique 6/*fr.* 8° Bouillon, *Paris* 87

DINGELDEIN, Otto Der Reim bei den Griechen und Römern 2*m.* 8° Teubner, *Lpz.* 92

MEYER, Wilh. Anfang u. Ursprung d. latein. u. griech. rhythmischen Dichtung 5*m.*60 4° Franz, *Munich* 85

GIESEMANN, Paul De Metro paeonico sive cretico ap. poetas graecos [diss.] 1*m.*60 8° Preuss, *Breslau* 92

RIEMANN + DUFOUR, Othon Méd. Traité de Rhythmique et de Métriques grecques [158 pp.] 8° Colin, *Paris* 93

REICHENBERGER, Sigm. Die Entwickelg. d. metonymisch. Gebrauchs v. Götternamen in d. griech. Poesie [to end of Alexandr. age] 2*m.*40 8° Braun, *Carlsruhe* 91

STEIGER, Karl De Versuum paeonicorum et dochmiacorum ap. Poetas graec. usu, pts. i.-v. [progrs.] 6*m.* 4° *Wiesb. & Rinteln* 87-91

USENER, Dr. Herm. Altgriechischer Versbau [comparative] 2*m.*80 8° Cohen, *Bonn* 87

USSING, Prf. J. L. Graesk og Romersk Metrik 3*kr.* 8° Gyldendal, *Copenhagen* 93

Style.

Invectives. Oaths.

HOFFMANN, Gust. Schimpfwörter der Griechen und Römer [progr.] 1*m.* 4° Gaertner, *Berlin* 92
MEINHARDT, P. De Forma et Usu Juromentorum 1*m.*50 Pohle, *Jena* 92
As found in the Greek Comedians, in PLATO, XENOPHON, and LUCIAN

Metaphors.

THOMAS, Rob. Zur histor. Entwickelung d. Metapher in Griech. [diss. inaug.] 8° *Erlangen* 93

184. GREEK EPIGRAPHY.

Bibliography.

Jahresbericht über die Griechischen Inschriften, ed. Wilh. Larfeld : 1886–90, by Fr. Back, 3 pts. ea. 3*m.*60 8° Calvary, *Berl.* 91
Forms pts. 1–3 of the *Supplement-Band* to the New Series of the *Jahresber. üb. d. Fortschr. d. class. Altertumswiss.*

REINACH, Salomon Chroniques d'Orient : 1883–1890 15*fr.* 8° Didot, *Paris* 90
Supplements the entry in G § 5, wh. conts. a misprint. The 1890 *Chronique* is the 8th (not 24th) of the series. Excellent Index.

Collections.

British Museum : Coll. of Anc. Gk. Inscripp. ; ed. Sir C. T. Newton+E. L. Hicks, vol. iii., pt. 2 [Ephesus] 20/–; iv. (1) 10/– f° Clar. Press 90 ; 93

*COLLITZ+BECHTEL, H. F. [eds.] Sammlung der griechischen Dialekt-Inschriften, vols. ii.(3–4)–iv. (1–2) 25*m.*60 8° Vandenhoeck, *Göttgn.* 88–92 *in prg.*
New Pts. Vol. ii. (3–4) *Die delphischen Inschrn.*, 2 pts. (Joh. BAUNACK) 8*m.* '92, '92 : Vol. iii. (1) *Megarisch* (BECHTEL) 2*m.*40, '88; iii. (2) *Inschrn. v. Korinth., Kleonai, Sikyon, Phleius u. Korinth. Colonien* (F. BLASS), 2*m.* '88; iii. (3) *Die argiv. Inschrn.* (W. PRELLWITZ) 2*m.*40 '89, (4, pt. 1) *Die Inschrn. v. Aigina, Pholegandros, Anaphe, Astypalaia, Telos, Nisyros, Knidos* (F. BECHTEL) 3*m.*20, '89; Vol. iv. (Index), pt. 1 [covers vol. i.] 5*m.* 81; pt. 2 (1) [covers vol. ii. (1)] 2*m.*60, '88.

*Corpus Inscriptionum Graecarum Graeciae Septentrion., vol. i. 85*m.* f° G. Reimer, *Berl.* 92 *in prg.*
Vol. i. *Inscriptiones Graecae Megaridis, Oropiae, Boeotiae*, ed. Wilh. DITTENBERGER.

DE RUGGIERO, Prf. Ett. [ed.] Sylloge Epigraphica Orbis Romani—*ut* K § 208.

Abbreviations.

CARINI, Isid. Piccolo Manuale di Sigli ed Abbrev. d. Epigr. Class. [schl.-bk.] 8° Rome 86

Index to Proper Names.

FICK, Prf. Aug. —*in his* Die griechischen Personennamen, *ut* K § 181.
The lists of names in the epigraphic authorities adduced form practically an index to the proper names of the Gk. inscripp.

Magazines —*vi* K § 173.

Juridical.

DARESTE+HAUSSOULLIER+REINACH, R.+B. Th. (eds.) Recueil des Inscripp. Juridiques Grecques ; pt. i.–ii. ea. 7*fr.*50 8° Leroux, *Paris* 91 ; 92 *in prg.*
Texts, trs. and commentaries. To consist of 3 pts. Spec. prep. for students of jurisprudence ; but of great value to the epigraphist also.

Metrical Inscriptions. Epigrams.

KAIBEL, Prf. Geo. [ed.] Epigrammata Graeca ex lapidibus conlecta—*ut* K § 190, *s.v.* Greek Anthology.
PREGER, Th. [ed.] Inscriptiones Graecae Metricae ex scriptoribus praeter Anthologiam collectae—*ut* K § 190, *s.v.* Gk. Anthology.

Popular Decrees.

SWOBODA, Heinr. Die griechischen Volksbeschlüsse : epigraphische Untersuchungen 8*m.* 8° Teubner, *Lpz.* 90

Vase-inscriptions.

HARRISON+MACCOLL, Jane E. D. S. [eds.]—*in their* Greek Vase Paintings—*ut* I § 113.
KLEIN, Wilh. [ed.] Die griech. Vasen mit Lieblingsinschriften ; pl. and 37 ill. [Denkschr Wien. Akad.] 7*m.* r 4° Tempksy, *Vienna* 90
KRETSCHMER, P. Die griechischen Vaseninschriften ihrer Sprache nach untersucht 5*m.*50 8° Bertelsmann, *Güterst.* 94

Attic.

CONZE [ed.] Die attischen Grabreliefs, pt. i. ; 25 pl. and 16 pp. [a very dear bk.] 60*m.* r f° Spemann, *Berlin* 90
*Corpus Inscriptionum Atticarum, ed. A. Kirchhoff+U. Koehler, vol. ii. (4), iv. Suppl. 1 (3) and i. (3) 18*m.* f° Reimer, *Berlin* 91–93 *in prg.*
Vol. II., pt. iv. *Inscripp. attic. inter Euclidis ann. et Augusti temp.*, ed. U. KOEHLER, pt. iv. (=Indices, by Joh. KIRCHNER) 11*m.* '93; Vol. IV., Suppl., pt. i., fasc. 3, and i., pt. iii., 7*m.* '91.

GUTSCHER, Dr. Hans [tr.] Die attischen Grabschriften : chronologisch geordnet 2*m.* 8° *Leoben* (Fock, *Lpz.*) 90
Carefully tr. into Germ. after the orig. metres (but no text given) ; w. explanations and classification.

Cos.

*PATON+HICKS, W. R. Rev. E. L. The Inscriptions of Cos ; w. a map of Cos r 8° 28/- Clar. Press / $7 *nt.* Macmillan, *N.Y.* 91
A *corpus* of all known Coan inscripp., incl. many hitherto unpub., coll. and ed. by PATON. HICKS contributes an admirable introd., giving a consecutive hist. of the island fr. dawn of hist. in Greece. The cursive text, wh. in all cases accompanies the uncial, is the wk. of both edrs. Partial trs. are added, and there are to Appendices (*Sepulchr. Inscripp. w. Fines : Theocritus, Was he a Coan?* etc.).

Crete.

HALBHERR, Prf. —*has a complete corpus of Gk. inscripp. belonging to Crete in prep.*

K §§ 185-188

Epidaurus.

BAUNACK, Jos. Aus Epidauros: eine epigraphische Studie 6m. r 4° Hirzel, *Lpz.* 90

Euxine.

LATYSCHEW, B. [ed.] Inscripp. Antiq. Orae Septentr. Ponti Eux. graec. et lat., vol. ii. 30m. 4° *St. Petersburg* 91

Lycian.

BENNDORF, Prf. Otto [ed.]

Has in prep. for Austr. Acad. of Science a compl. coll. of Lycian Inscripp. (c. 140, of wh. 133 are in the old Lyc. lang., at present untranslatable), to form the 1st vol. of a compl. coll. of the anc. inscripp. of Asia Minor.

Pergamus.

FRÄNKEL, Max [ed.] Die Inschriften von Pergamon, vol. i. 50m. r 8° Spemann, *Berlin* 90

Sicily, Italy, etc.

KAIBEL, Geo. [ed.] Inscripp. graecae, Sicil., Ital., Gall. Hispan., Britann., German. 90m. f° G. Reimer, *Berlin* 90

The Gallic section edited by Alb. LEBEGUE.

185. ANCIENT GREEK DIALECTS.

Collectively.

HOFFMANN, Dr. Otto Die griechischen Dialekte in ihrem historischen Zusammenhange mit den wichtigsten ihrer Quellen, vols. i.–ii. 22m. 8° Vandenhoeck, *Göttgn.* 91; 93

i. *Der süd-achäische Dialekt*, 8m., '91; ii. *Der nord-achäische Dialekt*, 14m., '93. Opposes Dr. R. MEISTER [*ut* B, K § 185, *s. nom.* Ahrens, vol. ii.]. By "south Achaean" HOFFMANN denotes only Arcadian and Cyprian, identifying Æoli and Achæan, and thus altering the scheme of Gk. dialects somewhat, Ionic and Doric remaining as they did, but Æolic extending over pt. of Pelopon. and Cyprus. To avoid confus. w. Æolic of Asiatic coast, he calls this Achaean, and his Achaean falls into N. and S. divisions.

" " De mixtis graecae Linguae Dialectis 1m.60 8° Vandenhoeck, *Göttingen* 88

PEZZI, Dom. La Lingua greca antica 12l. 8° Loescher, *Turin* 88

An excellent short treatise, comparative and historical.

SCHNEIDER, R. [ed.] Excerptum περὶ διαλέκτων [fr. Cod. Barocc. lxxii. and Bodl. ciii.] 60pf. 8° Teubner, *Lpz.* 94

Sounds and Inflections.

SMYTH, Prf. Herb. Weir [Am.] The Sounds and Inflections of the Greek Dialects: Ionic 8° 24/- Clar. Press / Macmillan, *N.Y.* 94

Achæan.

HOFFMANN, Dr. Otto Die griechischen Dialekte, pts. i.–ii.—*ut supra.*

Æolic.

MUCKE, E. De Consonarum in Graec. ling. praeter Asiat. dial. aeol. geminatione, 2 pts. ea. 1m.50 [sch. prg.] 4° *Freibg.* (Fock, *Lpz.*) 92; 93

Attic and Homeric.

KALINKA, Ern. De Usu Coniunctionum quarundam ap. Scriptt. Attic. antiquiss. [diss.] 8° Tempsky, *Vienna* 90

VOGRINZ, Gottfr. Grammatik des homerischen Dialektes 7m. 8° Schöningh, *Paderborn* 86

Laut-Formen-, Bedeutungs- und Satzlehre.

Cretan.

SKIAS, A. N. Περὶ τῆς κρητικῆς διαλέκτου 3/- 8° Beck, *Athens* 92

Ionic

—*v. supra, sub nom.* Smyth.

Laconic: *Linguistic Ethnology.*

WIDE, S. —*in his* Lakonische Kulte, *ut* B § 12.

Megaric.

KÖPPNER, Friedr. Der Dialekt Megaras und der megarischen Colonien 1m. 8° Teubner, *Lpz.* 92

Thracian: *Linguistic Ethnology.*

SCHOETENSACK, Prf. Heinr. A. Ueb. d. Thraker als Stammväter d. Gothen, *etc.* 1m.25 4° Franzen, *Stendal* 61

Conts. a brief colln. of passages fr. class. writers in support of the Germanic kinship of the Thracians.

TOMASCHEK, Wilh. Die alten Thraker: eine ethnolog. Untersuchung, pt. i. 2m.60; ii. (1) 1m.40; ii. (2) 2m. r 8° Tempsky, *Vienna* 93; 94; 94

Pt. ii. deals w. *Sprachreste*, the 1st half giving *Glossen aller Art u. Götternamen*, and *Personen- u. Ortsnamen*. Extr. fr. *Sitzber. Wien. Akad.*

186. MIDDLE AND MODERN GREEK (ROMAIC) PHILOLOGY AND LITERATURE.

History of the Language.

GELDART, Rev. Edm. Mart. Mod. Gk. in relation to Ancient Gk. [mainly philological] *o.p.* [*pb.* & *w.* 4/6] f 8° Macmillan 70

PSICHARI, J. Études de Philologie néo-grecque 22fr.50 8° Bouillon, *Paris* 92

Researches on the historical development of Greek. *Bibl. de l'École d. Hautes Études.*

Dictionary of Middle Greek.

DU CANGE, C. Du Fresne Glossarium ad Script. Mediae et Infim. Graecit., 10 pts. ea. 9m.60 f° Koebner, *Breslau* [1688] 90-91

Anastatic reprint. Pt. X. is Appendices and *Etymologicum Vocabulorum.*

Introduction.

CONSTANTINIDES, Prf. Mich. Neohellenica: intro. to Mod. Gk. in form of dials., tr. Maj.-Gen. H. T. Rogers 6/- *nt.* ($1.90) c 8° Macm. 92

Serves as an introd. to Mod. Gk. Lang. and literature. Two imaginary scholars, a Greek and an Engl. Prof. of Gk., travel together in Greece, and the bk. records their conversns., wh. are on ordinary travellers' topics—the railway, steamer, hotels, vehicles, *etc.*; into them are worked other topics, rel. to Greece, the Gk. people and language, and specs. dating fr. 3rd cent. B.C. to pres. day are given, w. append. of examples of Cypriot dialect.

Grammar.

GARDNER, [Mrs.] Mary — Short Modern Greek Grammar [adapted fr. Wied, *nt inf.*] 4/6 c 8° Nutt 92

HATZIDAKIS, G. N. — Einleitung in die neugriechische Grammatik [Bibl. Indogerm. Gram.] 10*m.* 8° Breitkopf, *Lpz.* 92

JANNARIS, Prf. A. N. — Wie spricht man in Athen? 3*m.*; Comment parle-t-on à Athènes? 3*m.* 8° Giegler, *Lpz.* 90; 93

MITSOTAKIS, J. K. — Prakt. Gram. d. neugriech. Schrift u. Umgangsspr. 12*m.* r 8° Spemann, *Berlin* 91

Lehrbücher des Seminars für Orient. Sprachen zu Berlin, vol. v. With exercises and dialogues.

MULLER, H. C. — Historische Grammatik d. hellen. Sprachen, vols. i.–ii. [Hellen. Bibl.] ea. 4*m.* 8° Brill, *Leyden* 91; 92

A survey of the transition of Class. Gk. into Mod. Gk., w. sketch of mod. liter. Vol. ii. is a chrestom. fr. HOMER to pres. day (w. occas. trs.).

WIED, Carl — Ὁμιλεῖτε Ἑλληνικά; : Sprechen Sie Neugriechisch? 2*m.*50 8° Koch, *Lpz.* [82] 86

Seventeenth Century Grammar.

PORTIUS, Simon [17 cent.] Grammatica Ling. Graec. Vulg. [1638], ed. Wilh. Meyer; w. Introd. Jean Psichari 12*fr.*50 8° Bouillon, *Paris* 90

With grammatical and historical commentary. *Bibl. d. l'Ecole des Hautes Etudes.*

Etymology.

Dictionaries.

JANNARIS, Prf. A. N. — Pocket Dict. of Modern-Gk. and English Langs. as written and spoken sq f 8° Murray *in prep.*

LEGRAND, Emile — Dictionnaire Grec Moderne-Français; Franç.-Grec. Mod. ea. 6*fr.* 32° Garnier, *Paris* 83; 85

Loan-Words.

MEYER, Gust. — Die slav., alban. u. rumän. Lehnworte im Neugriech. 2*m.* 8° Tempsky, *Vienna* 94

Forms Pt. ii. of his *Neugriechische Studien*; extr. fr. *Sitzungsberichte d. Wiener Akademie.*

Dialects: *Bibliography.*

MEYER, Gust. — Versuch einer Bibliogr. d. neugriech. Mundartenforschung 2*m.* 8° Tempsky, *Vienna* 94

Forms Pt. i. of his *Neugriechische Studien*; re-issued fr. *Sitzungsberichte d. Wiener Akademie.*

THUMB, Alb. — Beiträge z. neugr. Dialektkunde, pt. i. [Vokale v. Amorgos] [*extr. fr.* Indog. Forsch.] 8° Trübner, *Strassb.* 92

Magazine.

Byzantische Zeitschrift: hrsg. Karl Krumbacher, vols. i.–ii. [quarterly] ea. vol. 20*m.* 8° Teubner, *Lpz.* 92–93 *in prg.*

Literature.

Bibliography.

LEGRAND, E. — Bibliographie Neo-Hellénique, 2 vols. 60*fr.*; *red. to* 30*fr.* m 8° Welter, *Paris* 85

A *catalogue raisonné* of books pub. in Mod.-Gk. in 15th and 16th cents.

Collections. Series.

Bibliothèque Grecque Elzévirienne: 18° Leroux, *Paris* 83-88

- BASILIADIS *Galatée* [a drama] Bar. d' ESTOURNELLES DE CONSTANT, w. Fch. tr., 5*fr.* [78] 86
- METAXAS, Const. *Souvenirs d. l. Guerre de l'Indépce.* tr. J. BLANCHARD, 5*fr.* 88
- PHARMACOPOULOS, *L'Indépce. d. Hellènes* .... w. Fch. tr., 2*fr.*50 84
- TERZETTI, *La Grèce Ancienne et Moderne* 2*fr.*50 84
- VALAORITIS, *Athanase Diakos; Phrosine* [2 poems] tr. J. BLANCHARD + Marq. QUEUX D. ST.-HILAIRE, 5*fr.* 86
- " *Poèmes Patriotiques* .... tr. the same, 5*fr.* 83
- VLASTO, E. *Les Giustiniani, dynastes de Chio*, tr. Karl HOPF, 2*fr.*50 88

Bibliothèque Grecque Vulgaire: ed. Emile Legrand, vols. iv.–vi. 110*fr.* 8° Welter, *Paris* 88–92 *in prg.*

- iv. *Epistolaire Grec* .... 20*fr.* Maisonneuve, *Paris* 88

  Letters mostly addressed to CHRYSANTHOS NOTARAS, patriarch of Jerus., by the princes of Wallachia and of Moldavia.
- v. HERMANIACOS, Const. *La Guerre de Troie* .. 20*fr.* Maisonneuve 90

  A 14 cent. poem in octosyll. verse, ed. fr. Leyd. and Paris MSS.
- vi. *Exploits de Basile Digénis-Acritas* ...... 15*fr.* Welter, *Paris* 92

LEGRAND, Emile [ed. and tr.] Recueil de Poèmes Historiques en grec vulgaire [Ecole Lang. Orient. Viv.] 15*fr.* 8° Leroux, *Paris* 77

Relate to Turkey and the Danubian principalities. Texts, French trs. and notes.

Folktales and Folksongs —*v.* B § 13 *and* B.B. § 13.

Proverbs.

KRUMBACHER, Dr. K. [ed.] Mittelgriechische Sprichwörter [*extr. fr.* Sitzber. Bayer. Akad.] 3*m.* 8° Franz, *Munich* 93

Romances —*v.* K § 44, *and* B.B. K § 44.

Individual Texts and *Translations.*

DAPONTÈS, C. Ephemerides Daces, ed. Em. Legrand, w. Fch. tr.; vols. i.–ii., 20*fr.*; vol. iii., 7*fr.*50 [Ecole Langs. Or. Viv.] 8° Leroux, *Paris* 80; 81; 88

FILELFE, François — Cent-dix Lettres grecques, ed. Emile Legrand [Ec. Lang. Or. Viv.] 20*fr.* 8° Leroux, *Paris* 92

Here pubd. for the first time, from the Codex *Trivulzianus* 873.

MACHERAS, Leonce — Chronique de Chypre; ed. w. Fch. tr. and notes E. Miller + C. Sathas, 2 v. [Ecole Lang. Orient. Viv.] 40*fr.* 8° Leroux, *Paris* 81

SHAKSPERE, Wm. — Hamlet, tr. into Mod. Gk. by M. N. Damiralis 91

There have been 3 previous trs. (1) by PHRBANOGLOUS, 1858, (2) by BIKELAS, 1882, (3) by POLULAS, 1889.

SOMMER, J.; GRAZIANI, A. M. Deux Vies de Jacques Basilicos, seign. de Samos, ed. Em. Legrand 20*fr.* 4° Maisonneuve, *Paris* 89

Forms vol. i. of the *Collection de Documents concernant l'Histoire polit. et littér. d. l. Grèce méd. et mod.*

THERIANOS, D. — Adamantios Korais, 3 vols. [life of Coray, in mod. Gk.] 21/- 8° *Tergeste* (= *Trieste*) 88–90

187. HISTORY OF GREEK LITERATURE (*a*): GENERALLY.

General Histories.

*BERNHARDY, G. Grundriss d. Griech. Litter. [*ut* B.B. K § 187]: new ed., bearb. Rich. Volkmann, pt. i. 15*m.* 8° Anton, *Halle* [36] 92

An entirely new edn. of this standard wk. Pt. i. conts. *Innere Geschichte der griech. Litteratur.*

CROISET, Alf. + Maur. Histoire de la Littérature Grecque; 3 vols. ea. 8 *fr.* 8° Thorin, *Paris* 87; 90; 91

PERRY, T. Sergeant [Am.] History of Greek Literature; well ill. [890 pp.] $7.50 8° Holt, *N.Y.* 91

A good *popular* hist. fr. the pre-Homeric songs down to HELIODORUS and ACHILLES TATIUS. Based on Alb. WOLFF'S *Pantheon d. klass. Alterth.* in the series known as *Classiker aller Zeiten u. Nationen* [1 8° Hempel, *Berl.* 63 *sqq.*].

Alexandrian.

SUSEMIHL, Fr. Geschichte d. Griech. Literatur in d. Alexandrinerzeit, vol. i. 16*m.*; ii. 14*m.* 8° Teubner, *Lpz.* 91; 92

An excellent and comprehensive wk., w. full literary references at foot of page.

Attic Writers.

SCHMID, Wilh. Der Atticismus in seinen Hauptvertretern, vols. i.-iii. 18*m.*20 8° Kohlhammer, *Stuttg.* 87; 89; 93

From DIONYSIUS of Halicarnassus to PHILOSTRATUS the Second.

Byzantine.

*KRUMBACHER, Dr. K. Geschichte d. Byzantinischen Literatur [Müller's Hdb. Kl. Altert.] 8*m.*50 8° Beck, *Nördlingen* 91

An excellent and thorough piece of wk., descr. the differ. branches of liter. severally (hist., philos., rhetoric, philology in its widest sense, poetry sacred and profane, prose romances—to name only the chief heads), tracing them in their devel. or decline fr. earliest to latest stage. Commences w. 6th cent., instead of 7th or early 8th as FINLAY and others have fixed on for the beginning of Byz. Emp., since CHRIST'S *Griech. Litteraturgesch.* [*ut* B.B. K § 187] in same series ends w. JUSTINIAN'S time. Most valuable lists of authorities and sources are appended to each section, rendering it altogether a mine of informn. for the period.

Early Christian —*v.* K § 17 (CRUTTWELL, *HARNACK).

Collective Essays.

*BUTCHER, Prf. S. H. Some Aspects of Greek Genius 7/- *nt.* ($2.50) c 8° Macmillan [92] 93

Very interesting, suggestive and stimulating essays, mostly deliv. to his Gk. class at Edinb. Univ. on *What we owe to Greece*, *The Gk. Idea of the State*, *Sophocles*, *The Melancholy of the Gks.*, *The Written and the Spoken Word*, *The Unity of Learning*, and a treatise [160 pp.] on *Aristotle's Conception of Fine Art and Poetry* [*ut* C § 9], the last replaced in 2nd edn. by *The Dawn of Romanticism in Gk. Poetry* (a fine study). The whole affords a very vivid picture of Gk. life, thought, aspiration and art.

Book Dedication [Greek and Roman].

GRÄFENHAIN, Rud. De More libros dedicandi ap. Graec. et. Rom. obvio [diss.] 8° *Marburg* 92

188. HISTORY OF GREEK LITERATURE (*b*): SPECIAL DEPARTMENTS (*a*): POETRY AND DRAMA.

Collectively.

CHURCH, Rev. Alf. J. Stories from the Greek Tragedians; ill. c 8° 5/- Seeley; $1 Scribner, *N.Y.* [79] 80

" " Stories from the Greek Comedians; 16 ill. c 8° 5/- Seeley; $1 Macmillan, *N.Y.* 92

Adaptations from the Greek dramatists *virginibus puerisque*, the argumt., descrn. of scene and explans. bg. combined into a narrative, and snatches of dialogue and verse trs. introduced.

*JEBB, Prf. R. C. The Growth and Influence of Classical Greek Poetry c 8° 7/- *nt.* Macmillan; $1 Houghton, *Boston* 93

Eight Lects. deliv. in 1892 in Johns Hopkins Univ., showing the chief characteristics of Gk. poets fr. the Homeric to the Alexandrian period (MENANDER) dwelling fully on the 5 poets whom the author regards as the most typical of the true Hellenic age—HOMER, PINDAR and the 3 Attic tragedians—and less fully on post-Euripidean poetry; and luminously illustrating the place of anc. Greece in the general hist. of poetry.

SYMONDS, Jno. Addington Studies of the Greek Poets [*ut* B.B. K § 188]: 3rd edn., 2 vols. 8° 25/- Smith & Elder; $6 *nt.* Macmillan, *N.Y.* [73; 76] 93

This 3rd edn. is rearrgd., the order of the studies bg. now chronological, and a study on the *Mimiambi* of HERONDAS, w. a prose tr. of it [*ut* K § 190] and addl. trs. of notably THEOGNIS, MENANDER and THEOCRITUS bg. added. The bk. does not represent the author's most mature, tho' it is his best known, work; but it has the saving merit of enthusiasm, and does for the budding student of Gk. poetry what MACAULAY'S *Essays* do for him w. respect to Engl. liter. and hist.

Muses in Greek Poetry.

MOCKER, Gust. Bruno De Musis a poet. Graec. in compon. carminn. invocatis [diss.] 8° *Leipzig* 93

Didactic Poetry.

Bucolic Poetry.

HILLER, Ed. Beiträge zur Textgeschichte d. griech. Bukoliker 3*m.*20 8° Teubner, *Lpz.* 88

TRIBUKEIT, Pp. De Proverbiis vulgaribusque locution. ap. Bucol. Graec. obviis [diss.] 1*m.* 8° Koch, *Königsb.* 89

Drama.

Generally. Stage.

BODENSTEINER, E. Szenische Fragen über den Ort des Auftretens und Abgehens von Schauspielern und Chor im griechischen Drama 4*m.* 8° Teubner, *Lpz.* 93

CAPPS, Edw. [Am.] The Stage in the Greek Theatre acc. to the extant Dramas [diss. inaug.] 2*m.*40 8° Calvary, *Berlin* 93

Extracted fr. the *Transactns. of the Amer. Philolog. Assocn.*, vol. xxii.

" " Vitruvius and the Greek Stage—*ut* K § 224.

DÄHN, Hans Scenische Untersuchungen, pt. i. [school-programme] 4° *Danzig* 92

DINGELDEIN, Otto Haben d. Theatermasken d. Alten d. Stimme verstärkt? [Berl. Stud.] 1*m.*50 8° Calvary, *Berlin* 90

FRANZ, Rud. Der Aufbau der Handlung in den klass. Dramen 4*m.*50 8° Velhagen, *Bielefeld* 92

HECHT, Rud. Die Darstellung fremder Nationalitäten im Drama d. Griech. [schl.-prog.] 4° *Königsberg* 92

MÜLLER, Alb. Die neueren Arbeiten a. d. Gebiete d. griech. Bühnenwesens [*extr. fr.* Philologus] 2*m*.50 8° Dieterich, *Götlgn.* 91
PICKARD, J. Standort d. Schausp. u. Chors im griech. Theat. d. 5 Jahrh. 1*m*. 8° Ackermann, *Munich* 92
ROEMER, A. Die Notation der alexandrinischen Philologen bei d. griech. Dramatikern 1*m*.60 8° Franz, *Munich* 92
STENGEL + OEHMICHEN, P. G. Griechische Kultusaltertumer u. antikes Bühnenwesen ; 8 pl. 6*m*.50 8° Beck, *Munich* 90
Iwan MÜLLER'S *Hdb. d. klass. Altertumswiss.*, vol. v. (3). Rectifies entry in B. B., K § 188.
STURMHÖFEL, A. Scene d. Alten u. Bühne d. Neuzeit : Lösung d. Volkstheaterfrage ; 15 pl. 8*m*. 8° Ernst, *Berlin* 89
WEISSMANN, K. Scenische Aufführung d. griech. Dramen d. 5 Jahrh. 1*m*.80 8° Kaiser, *Munich* 93
WHITE, J. W. [Am.] The Stage in Aristophanes—*in* Harvard Studies in Class. Philol., vol. ii., *ut* K § 173.

Tragedy.

BRUNS, Prf. Ivo Die griech. Tragödien als religionsgeschichtliche Quellen 1*m*. 8° Univ. Buchhg., *Kiel* 94
CAMPBELL, Prf. Lewis A Guide to Greek Tragedy c 8° 6/- Percival [Riv. & Perc.] / $1.50 Putnam, *N.Y.* 91
On Tragedy, its orig. and growth, subjects, condns. of representation, dram. construction, lives of tragic poets, fragments of lost plays, etc. Full of information and trenchant criticism ; w. some excellent trs. of selected fragmts.
HARRIES, Herm. Tragici Graeci qua arte usi sint in describ. insania [diss.] 1*m*. 8° *Kiel* (Fock, *Lpz.*) 91
MUNK, Dr. Ed. The Student's Manual of Greek Tragedy, ed. Dr. A. W. Verrall, port. c 8° 3/6 Sonnenschein / $1.50 Macmillan, *N.Y.* 91
A tr., w. notes and intro., of the pts. of his *Gesch. d. griech. Lit.* [*ut* B. B., K § 187] wh. deal with Æschylus, Sophocles and Euripides, w. tr. extracts fr. Dr. PLUMPTRE'S versions ; to wh. are added an Intro. on *Euripides and Modern Criticism* (24 pp.) and *Notes* (at end of bk.). A useful bk., well adapted to the beginner in Æsch. or Sophocles.
WECKLEIN, N. Ueber die Stoffe u. Wirkung der griech. Tragödie 1*m*.40 8° Franz, *Munich* 92
v. WILAMOWITZ-MÖLLENDORFF, Ulr. De Tragicorum graecorum Fragmentis Commentatio [Index Scholl.] 8° *Göttingen* 93

Comedy.

POPPELREUTER, Jos. De Comœdiæ atticæ primordiis Particulæ duo [diss.] 1*m*.20 m 8° Heinrich, *Berl.* 93
ROSENBUSCH, Hugo Quaestt. de Parodi in Comœd. Attic. antiquissima Compos. [diss.] 8° *Marburg* 92

Epic Poetry.

SCHULZE, Wilh. Quaestiones Epicæ 12*m*. 8° Bertelsmann, *Gütersloh* 92

Gnomic Poetry.

ELTER, Ant. De Gnomologiorum graec. Historia atq. Origine, 3 pts. [Index Scholl.] 4° *Bonn* 92-93

Lyric Poetry.

Convivial Songs.

GASTÉ, Prf. Armand De Scoliis, sive de Carminibus Convivalibus apud Graecos 3*fr*. 8° *Caen* (Thorin, *Paris*) 73

Epigrammatists.

FENGLER, Mart. De Graecorum Epigramm. qu. in lapidd. extant Dialecto [diss.] 8° *Kiel* 92
MAYER, Jos. Studia in Epigrammata graeca [dissert.] 8° *Münster* 93
REITZENSTEIN, R. Epigramm und Skolion [Alexandrian] 6*m*. 8° Ricker, *Giessen* 93

189. HISTORY OF GREEK LITERATURE (c) : SPECIAL DEPARTMENTS (β) : PROSE.

Astronomers.

TANNERY, Paul —*in his* Recherches sur l'Histoire de l'Astronomie Ancienne 8° Gauthier-Villars, *Paris* 93

Geographers.

BERGER, Hugo Gesch. d. wissenschaftl. Erdkunde d. Griechen, pt. i. 4*m*. ; ii. 4*m*. ; iii. 4*m*.40 ; iv. 4*m*.80 [end] 8° Veit, *Lpz.* 87 ; 89 ; 91 ; 92

Historians.

PETER, Herm. Die Scriptores historiae Augustae [6 liter. and histor. papers] 6*m*.40 8° Teubner, *Lpz.* 92

Mathematicians.

CANTOR, Mor. —*in his* Vorlesungen üb. d. Geschichte d. Mathematik, vol. i. 20*m*. 8° Teubner, *Lpz.* 80
ZEUTHEN, H. G. —*in his* Forelæsning over Mathematikens Historie [anc. and mediæv.] 5 *kr*. 8° Høst, *Copenhagen* 93

Medical Writers.

ALBERT, Maur. Les Médecins grecs à Rome 3*fr*.50 s 8° Hachette, *Paris* 94
COSTOMIRIS, Geo. A. Etudes sur les Ecrits inédits des Anciens Médecins Grecs, 2 pts. 8° Klincksieck, *Paris* 90 ; 92
Also on the Gk. medical writers, the texts of whose wks. are lost but extant in Lat. or Arabic. Extrs. fr. *Revue des Etudes Grecques*.

Music Writers.

GRAF, Ern. De Graecorum veterum re musica Quaestt. capita duo 2*m*. 8° Elwert, *Marburg* 89

Proverb Writers. Proverbs.

COHN, L. Zu den Paroemiographen : Mittheilungen aus HSS. [Bresl. Philol. Abhgn. ii. (2)] 1*m*.80 8° Koebner, *Breslau* 87
CRUSIUS + COHN, O. L. Zur hs. Ueberlieferung u. Quellenkunde d. Paroemiographen 2*m*.50 8° Dieterich, *Gött.* 92
Conts. as an Appendix the Proverbs of EUSTATHIOS. Extr. fr. *Philologus, Suppl. Band.*
HOTOP, A. De Eustathii Proverbiis [*extr. fr.* Jahrbb. f. Class. Philol.] 1*m*.60 8° Teubner, *Lpz.* 88
KOCH, Hans Quaestion. de Proverbiis ap. Aesch., Soph., Eurip., 2 pts. [progrs.] 4° *Bartenstein* 91 ; 92
SCHNECK, Bernh. Quaestt. Paroemiogr. de Codice Coisliniano 177 et Eudemi lexicis [diss.] 8° *Breslau* 92

Scientific Writers.

MILHAUD, Gast. Leçons sur les Origines de la Science grecque [316 pp.] 5*fr*. 8° Alcan, *Paris* 93

190. GREEK POETS.

Collections.

Generally.

STOBÆUS, Ioannes [A.D. *fl.* 500] Anthologium, rec. Curt Wachsmuth + O. Hense, v. i, 11*m.*; ii. 7*m.*; iii. 20*m.* 8° Weidmann, *Berl.*, 84; 84; 94

This anthology, orig. composed by STOBÆUS, for the education of his son, is of great value, as including numerous fragms. of wks. of Gk. philosophers, poets and especially dramatists, otherwise lost.

Translations.

APPLETON, Prf. W. H. [Am.; ed.] Greek Poets in English Verse; w. Introd. and notes 12° $1.50 Houghton, *Boston*; 6/- *net* Gay & Bird 93

375 selected trs. of specs. of Gk. poetry, incl. Homer, Hesiod, Pindar, Aesch., Soph., Eurip., Aristoph., Theocrit., Sappho, *etc.*

Epic Poets.

Corpusculum Poesis epicae graecae ludibundae, pts. i.–ii. ea. 3*m.* Teubner, *Lps.* 88; 85

Pt. i. *Parodorum epic. graec. et Orchestrali Reliquiae, ed. et enarr.* Paul BRANDT, '87; ii. *Sillographorum graec. Reliquiae, rec. et enarr.* Curt WACHSMUTH, '85.

VAN LEEUWEN, Prf. J. F. [ed.] Enchiridium Dictionis Epicae, pt. i. 8*m.*25 8° Sijthoff, *Leyden* 94

Epitheta Deorum —*v.* B § 12 (BRUCHMANN).

Gnomic Poets.

Gnomica: ed. Ant. Elter, 2 pts. [programme] 4*m.* 4° Teubner, *Lps.* 92; 93

i. SEXT. PYTHAG., CLITARCH., EUAGR. PONTICI *Sententiae*, 2*m.*40; ii. EPICTET., MOSCH. *Sententiae*, 1*m.*60.

Gnomologium Parisinum Ineditum: Appendix Vaticana, rec. Leo Sternbach [Sitzb. Krak. Ak.] 3*m.* r 8° Poln. Verl.-Ges., *Cracow* 93

Incantations.

HEIM, R. [ed.] Incantamenta Magica graeca latina 2*m.*80 8° Teubner, *Lps.* 93

Lyric Poets.

Texts.

BIESE, Alf. [ed.] Griechische Lyriker in Auswahl, 2 pts. [school-book] 1*m.*35 8° Freytag, *Lps.* 91; 92

Conts. a good many gems of Gk. poetry; some rather difficult (*e.g.* a Pythian ode on pp. 47-50). Pt. ii. consists of Introd. and notes.

*FARNELL, Geo. S. [ed.] Greek Lyric Poetry; w. intros. and notes; 5 pl. 16/- ($5) 8° Longman 91

A complete collection of all surviving fragments of Gk. lyric poetry, omitting only single words or half lines. With separ. accounts of each poet prefixed to his fragments; a long Intro.; and notes telling where each poem or fragm. is found and dealing w. their difficulties. No elegiac poems included, but some of the more important fragm. of PINDAR placed at end of the vol.

ZAMBALDI, F. [ed.] Lyricorum graecorum Reliquiae selectae 1*l.*80 16° Paravia, *Turin* [ ] 93

Translations.

POLLARD, Alf. W. [ed.] Odes from the Greek Dramatists; transl.—*ut* K § 191.

The Greek Anthology. Epigrams.

Anthologia Palatina Epigrammatum, ed. Fred. Dübner [i.–ii.] + Ed. Cougny [iii.], w. Lat. trs.: vols. i.–iii. ea. 15*fr* r 8° Didot, *Paris* 64; 72; 90

" Planudeæ.

Sternbach, Leo [ed.] Anthologiae Planudeae Appendix Barberino-Vaticana 4*m.* 8° Teubner, *Lps.* 90

HOFFMANN, Ern. [ed.] Sylloge Epigrammatum Graecorum quae ante medium saec. a Chr. n. tertium incisa ad nos pervenerunt 6*m.* 8° Kaemmerer, *Halle* 93

*KAIBEL, Prf. Geo. [ed.] Epigrammata Graeca ex lapidibus conlecta [*v. inf.*, Mackail, *note*] 12*m.* 1 8° G. Reimer, *Berlin* 78

Ut B.B. K § 184. Conts. at least 1,000 new epitaphs or dedics. in verse, derived fr. results of recent excavations.

*MACKAIL, J. W. [ed. and tr.] Select Epigrams from the Greek Anthology 16/- ($5.50) 8° Longman 90

A seln., in revised texts, w. elabor. and very valuable Introd. (68 pp.), prose trs. (at ft. of page) and some notes, of ab. 500 of the best pieces fr. the *Greek Anthology*, wh., as pub. in the monumental edn. of Friedr. JACOBS [13 vols. r 8° Dyk, *Lps.* 1794-1814 (*pub.* 66*m.*50)] is a *corpus* deriv. fr. many collns. and selns. by var. compilers in differ. ages contg. over 4,000 epigrams or "occasional poems" of all dates fr. B.C. 700 to A.D. 1000. Most of JACOBS' text is founded on a single Palatine (Heidelb.) MS., wh. represents (tho' not completely) the anthol. of CONSTANTINUS CEPHALAS, a Byzant. grammarian of ? 10 cent. Much of the Palat. anthol. belongs also to the shorter compiln. of MAXIMUS PLANUDES, who was ambassr. fr. Gk. Emp. to Venice in 1327; but there are ab. 400 epigrs. in the Planudean colln. which are not in the Palat., and ab. as many more preserved only by ATHENÆUS, DIOG. LAERT. and other gossips or grammarians. The *Gk. Anthol.*, owing to recent discovs., is of much wider scope to-day than in the days of JACOBS.

PREGER, Th. [ed.] Inscriptiones Graec. Metricae ex Scriptoribus praeter Anthologiam collectae 8*m.* 8° Teubner, *Lps.* 91

STADTMÜLLER, H. [ed.] Anthologia Graeca Epigramm. Palat. cum Planud., vol. i. 6*m.* 8° " " 94

Translations.

GARNETT, Dr. Rich. [tr.] A Chaplet from the Greek Anthology [Cameo Series] f 8° 3/6 Unwin; $1.50 Stokes, *N.Y.* 92

A short collection of graceful trs.

*MACKAIL, J. W. [ed.] —*in his edn. of the text, ut supra.*

SEIDENADEL, Karl [tr.] Altgriech. Epigramme, Tisch- u. Volkslieder: übers. [sch.-prg.] 4° *Rastadt* 92

Aids.

DILTHEY, Carl Coniectanea critica in Anthologiam graecam [228 pp.] 4° *Göttingen* 91

HERWERDEN, H. Studia Critica in Epigrammata graeca 1*fl.*75 8° Brill, *Leyden* 92

Notes to the 3rd vol. (by COUGNY) of the *Anthol. Palat.* (Didot) *ut supra*, w. Appendix of addit. epigrams.

SAKOLOWSKI, P. De Anthologia Palatina Quaestiones 2*m.*60 8° Gräfe, *Lps.* 94

Æsopus [B.C. *c.* 600] —*v. also* Babrius, *infra* (on whose *Fables* ÆSOP's were prob. founded).

Fabularum Æsopiarum Sylloge: ed. L. Sternbach [*fr.* Paris Cod. Gr. N. 690 suppl.] 3*m.* 8° 94

Aids —*v. also* B § 1, *s.v.* Migration of Fables.

HAUSRATH, A. Untersuchgn. z. Ueberlieig. d. äsop. Fabeln [*extr. fr.* Jahrb. Cl. Ph.; too late for insertn. in B § 1] 2*m.* 8° Teubner, *Lps.* 94

Alcaeus [B.C. 7th cent.].

GERSTENHAUER, Arth. De Alcæi et Sapphonis Copia Vocabulorum [dissert.] 8° *Halle* 92
TINCANIUS, Carl De Alcaei Carmine xviii., ed. a Theod. Bergk cur. 16° Zanichelli, *Bologna* 93

Anacreon [B.C. *c.* 550–*c.* 464].

Anacreontea : ed. A. H. Bullen; w. tr. of Thos. Stanley (*en regard*) [(1647) 1652]: 11 ill. J. R. Weguelin s 4° 21/- *n.* Lawrence & Bullen; $7.50 *n.* Scribner, *N.Y.* 93
Also 110 copies on Jap. vellum, w. an addl. pl. *o.p.* [*pb.* and w. 42/- *n.*]. A sumptuous edn. of the "elegant trifles"—for the book-lover rather than the student.
Anacreontea : ed. A. Delboulle ; and w. trs. and imitations of 16 cent. poets 16° Lemale, *Havre* 92
PELLEGRINO, Giov. Anacreonte Teio : Studio critico 16° Garibaldi, *Lecce* 91

Apollonius Rhodius [B.C. *c.* 260–? 190].

Argonauticon : trad. H. de La Ville de Mirmont ; w. Fch. notes and 2 indexes [pp. 480] 4° Rouam, *Paris* 92
" trad. H. de La Ville de Mirmont 3*fr.* 16° Hachette, *Paris* 93
" tr. Arth. S. Way [verse] *in prep.*
GOODWIN, Chas. J. [Am.] Apollonius Rhodius : his figures, syntax and vocab. [diss.] 8° Johns Hopk. Univ., *Baltimore* 91
KOFLER, Joh. Die Gleichnisse bei Apollonius Rhodios [school-programme] 8° *Brixen* 90
MOLTZER, M. N. J. De Apollonii Rhodii et Valerii Flacci Argonauticis—*ut* K § 214, *s.v.* Valerius Flaccus.
WÅHLIN, Laur. P. O. De Usu Modorum apud Apollonium Rhodium [comm. acad.] 8° *Lund* 92

Babrius [A.D. ? 3rd cent.].

Fragmenta : rec. Dr. Hesseling [of Leyden] ; w. facss. *in prep.*
The fragmts. of the *Fables* cont. in wax tablets found at Palmyra, 13 of wh. are at Leyden and 7 in Brit. Mus.
Translation : tr. Rev. Jas. Davies, *sub. tit.* The Fables of Babrius 5/- f 8° Lockwood 66
Aids.
CRUSIUS, Prf. Otto De Babrei Aetate 79
WERNER, Jul. Quaestiones Babrianae [= Berl. Stud. xiv. (2)] 1*m.* 50 8° Calvary, *Berlin* 92

Bion and **Moschus.**

STERN, Wald. De Moschi et Bionis Aetate (Tübingen dissert. inaug.] 8° *Münster* 93

Hero(n)das.

Mimiamboi

Assigned to 3 or 2 cent. B.C. Consist of 700 ll., divided in 7 distinct poems, in choliambic or Scazon iambic metre, and forming a kind of dramatic idyll, dealing w. scenes of ordin. domest. life, mostly humorous and all but one in dialogue form, entitled (1) *The Match-Maker*, (2) *The Pander*, (3) *The Schoolmaster*, (4) *A Visit to Æsculapius*, (5) *A Jealous Woman*, (6) is on women's dress, (7) dance, a visit to a cobbler's shop, and (8) *The Dream* is a small fragmt.] Discovered in 1891.

*British Museum : Herodas : autotype facs. of Pap. cxxxiv. 15/- 4° British Museum 92
" " Greek Classical Texts from Papyri : Herodas etc.—*v.* Kenyon, *infra.*
*Bücheler, Frz. [ed. and tr.] Herondae Mimiambi [w. Latin tr. and notes] 2*m.* 40 8° Cohen, *Bonn* 92
*Crusius, Otto [ed.] Mimiambi Herondae, accedunt Phoenicis Coronistae Mattii Mimiamb. fragm. 3*m.* 20 8° Teubner, *Lpz.* [92] 94
CRUSIUS has also pub. an Italian edn., 1894.
Headlam, Walt. [ed.] The Mimiamboi of Herondas ; w commentary Camb. Press; Macmillan, *N.Y.* *in prep.*
Herwerden, —*in* Mnemosyne [w. a commentary (not very good)].
Kenyon, F. J. [ed.] Mimiamboi of Herondas ; w. Introd.—*in his* Class. Texts fr. Brit. Mus., *ut* K § 179.
Mekler, Siegfr. [ed.] Herondas' Mimiamben [w. Germ. Introd., tr. and notes] 1*m.* 60 8° Konegen, *Vienna* 94
*Meister, Rich. [ed.] Herondas' Mimiamben [w. Germ. notes and Append. on the poet and dialect] 10*m.* 8° Hirzel, *Lpz.* 93
Extract fr. the *Abhandlgn. d. Sächs. Akad., Lpz.*
Rutherford, Dr. W. G. [ed.] Herondae Mimiambi : a first recension [w. short com.] 2/- *nt.* (60c.) 8° Macmillan 91
Edr. promises a complete edn., w. archæol. illns., and probably an Engl. tr.

Translations.

Boisacq, E. [tr.] Hérondas : les Mimiambes—Traduction française 2*fr.* 50 8° Thorin, *Paris* 93
Crusius, Otto [tr.] Herondas' Mimiamben : Deutsch, mit Einleitung u. Anmerkungen [blank verse] 2*m.* 8° Dieterich, *Gött.* 93
Dalmeyda, Geo. [tr.] Les Mimes d'Hérondas : traduction française, avec introduction 3*fr.* 8° Hachette, *Paris* [93] 94
Ristelhuber, P. [tr.] Les Mimes d'Hérodas : trads. en français, avec introd. et notes 2*fr.* 50 8° Delagrave, *Paris, n.d.* (93)
Setti, G. [tr.] I Mimi di Heroda ; 12 ill. fr. antiques [prose ; w. good Introd. of 65 pp.] 3*l.* 50 s 8° Sarasino, *Modena* 93
Symonds, Jno. Addington—*his* Studies of Gk. Poets, 3rd ed. [*ut* K § 188] *conts. a complete Engl.* (*prose*) *tr.*
Aids.
*CRUSIUS, Prf. Otto Untersuchungen zu den Mimiamben d. Herondas 6*m.* 8° Teubner, *Lpz.* 92
An elaborate commentary, taking ea. poem in succession and giving the doubtful or difficult passages w. explanations and more or less copious illns. from many sources, a tr. into Germ. bg. occas. added. Pp. 14–17 cont. a list of the recent contribs. to Heron(n)das literature.
SYMONDS, Jno. Addington —*chap. on* Herondas, *in his* Studies on Gk. Poets, 3rd edn., *ut supra.*
WRIGHT, J. H. [Am.] Herondas—*in* Harvard Studies in Classical Philology, vol. iv., *ut* K § 173 [mainly palæographical].

Hesiod [B.C. ?8th cent.].

LEO, Friedr. Hesiodea [school-programme] 50*pf.* r 8° Dieterich, *Göttgn.* 94
PAULSON, J. Index Hesiodeus 3*m.* 50 8° Möller, *Lund*
" " Studia Hesiodea, pt. i. : De re metrica 4*m.* 8° " "
SCHMIDT, Hubert Observationes Archæologicæ in Carmina Hesiodea [diss. inaug.] 8° *Halle* 91

Homer [B.C. ?10th cent.].

Batrachomyomachiæ homer. archetypon ad fid. codd. antiq. Arth. Ludwich restit. [sch.-prg.] 20 *pf.* 4° Schubert, *Königsbg.* 94
Hymni : Hymni Homerici ; w. appar. crit. and Latin notes A. Baumeister
o.p. [*scarce* ; pb. 7*m.* 50, *w.* 30*m.*] 8° Teubner, *Lpz.* 60
" " codicibus duo collatis, rec. Alf. Goodwin ; 4 photogr. tables s f° 21/- *nt.* Clar. Press; $7.50 *nt.* Macmillan, *N.Y.* 93
Hymnus in Mercurium : rec. Arth. Ludwich 2*m.* 4° Koch, *Königsberg* 90

K § 190

Ilias : ed. Arth. Platt, *sub tit.* The Cambridge Homer : Iliad c 8° 4/6 Camb. Press / $1.25 *nt.* Macmillan, *N.Y.* 94

A good text, ed. in acc. w. mod. criticism; w. Introd. and short *appar. crit.* at foot of page. No notes.

ed. Paul Cauer : Ed. Major i.–xii. 3*m.*, xiii.–xxiv. 3*m.* 50 ; Ed. Minor, 2 pts., ea. 1*m.* 50 8° Tempsky, *Prague* 90 ; 91

bk. iii. : w. English notes M. T. Tatham [w. Introd. and short Homer. gram.] f 8° 1/6 Clar. Press / 40*c. nt.* Macmillan, *N.Y.* 92

bk. iv.–vi. : „ „ „ Prf. Thos. D. Seymour [Am.] [Coll. Ser. of Gk. Auth.] 12° $1.50 Ginn, *Boston* / 6/- Arnold 91

Based on the AMEIS-HENTZE edn. [*ut* B.B. K § 190].

bk. vi. : w. Engl. Notes Walt. Leaf + M. A. Bayfield ; Intro. & vocab. [Macm. Elem. Class.] 1/6 (40*c.*) pott 8° Macmillan 93

w. English notes G. M. Edwards ; Introd. [Pitt Press Series] f 8° 2/- Camb. Press / 50*c. nt.* Macmillan, *N.Y.* 92

„ „ „ vocab. and tr. B. J. Hayes [Univ. Corr. Coll. Tut. Ser.] 2/6 c 8° Clive 92

bk. ix. : „ „ „ Jno. Hy. Platt + Walt. Leaf [Macm. Elem. Classics] 2/- (60*c.*) pott 8° Macmillan 94

Repr. fr. *The Story of Achilles* [*ut* B.B. K § 190], wh. incl. the 12 bks. of the *Iliad* in wh. the tale of ACHILLES may be read as a whole.

bk. xxi. ; xxii. ; xxiii. : w. English notes G. M. Edwards ; Introd. [Pitt Press Series] f 8° ea. 2/- Camb. Press / ea. 50*c. nt.* Macmillan, *N.Y.* 90 ; 91 ; 91

bk. xxiv. : w. Engl. notes Walt. Leaf + A. M. Bayfield ; Introd. & vocab. [Macm. Elem. Classics] 1/6 (40*c.*) pott 8° Macmillan 94

Odysseia : ed. Arth. Platt, *sub tit.* The Cambridge Homer : Odyssey c 8° 4/6 Camb. Press / $1.25 *nt.* Macmillan, *N.Y.* 92

A good text, ed. in acc. w. mod. criticism, w. Introd. (21 pp.), a short *crit. appar.* at ft. of page. No notes.

rec. Arth. Ludwich ; w. selected var. rgs., vol. ii. 8*m.* 8° Teubner, *Lps.* 91

„ „ „ Editio Minor, 2 pts. ea. 75*pf.* 8° „ „ 89 ; 91

w. Latin notes J. La Roche, 2 vols. [for school-use] ea. 1*m.* 8° Tempsky, *Prague* 90 ; 92

bk. i.–iv. : w. English notes Prf. B. Perrin [Am.] [Coll. Ser. of Gk. Auth.] 12° $1.25 Ginn, *Boston* / 6/- Arnold 89

Based on the AMEIS-HENTZE edn. [*ut* B.B. K § 190].

bk. i.–vi. : w. English notes R. D. Heef [Am.] [prob. the best Amer. edn.] 12° Allyn, *Boston*

* bk. vii.–xii. : „ „ „ Rev. W. W. Merry ; Introd. and table of Homeric forms f 8° 3/- Clar. Press / 80*c. nt.* Macmillan, *N.Y.* [71] 91

Adapted (w. only slight alterns.) fr. the well-known edn. of bks. i.–xii. [*ut* B.B. K § 190]. Bks. i.–ii. separ. ea. 1/6 (40*c. nt.*) ; iii.–v. not pub. separ. ; vi.–vii. 1/6 (40*c. nt.*) '91.

Translations.

Hymns : tr. Jno. Edgar, *sub tit.* Homeric Hymns ; w. Introd. essay [prose] 3/6 c 8° Thin, *Edinb.* 91

A faithful and scholarly tr. Introd. states nature of the poems, and questns. raised in conn. w. them.

Hymns and Batrachomyomachia : tr. Thos. Parnell + Geo. Chapman + P. B. Shelley + Wm. Congreve $1.50 12° Denham, *N. Y.* 72

With Introductions by Hy. Nelson COLERIDGE and tr. of the *Life* attrib. to *Herodotus*. No English edn. in print.

Iliad : tr. Geo. Chapman [1596–1611 ; *ut* B.B. K § 190] : new ed. *s.t.* Iliads of Homer, 3 v. ; ill. [Knickerb. Nuggets ; verse] $3.75 (7/6) 32° Putnam 93

The size of the vols. is enlarged to suit CHAPMAN'S long lines : his notes, Epist. Dedic., dedic. sonnets and verses to the reader are omitted. Flaxman's ill. added.

tr. Wm. Cowper [1791]

tr. Sir J. W. F. Herschell [English hexameters] *o.p.* [*pb.* 18/- ; *w.* 7/6] 8° Macmillan 66

tr. C. Merivale, 2 vols. [rhymed verse] *o.p.* 8° Strahan [69] 78

tr. Prf. F. W. Newman [unrhymed English metre] *o.p.* [*pb.* 10/6 ; *w* 5/-] r 8° Trübner [56] 71

tr. Jno. Purves, [posthum.] ed. Evelyn Abbott ; w. Introd. [prose] 18/- *nt.* 8° Percival (Riv. & Perc.) 91

On the whole a good piece of wk., but unnecessary with LANG + LEAF + MYERS' tr. [*ut* B.B. K § 190] available.

Odyssey : tr. Wm. Cowper, w. commentary ; 2 vols. *o.p.* [*pb.* 15/- ; *w.* 7/6] c 8° Harvey [1791] 43

tr. Prf. G. Herb. Palmer [Am.] [prose] 12° $1 Houghton, *Boston* / 8/- *nt.* Gay & Bird 91

Aids.

CLERKE, [Miss] Agnes M. Familiar Studies in Homer 7/6 ($1.75) c 8° Longman 92

Popularizes the results of recent research, pleasantly discussing Homeric *Realien* (1) Homer as a Poet, (2) Homeric Astron., (3) The Dog in Homer, (4) Horses, (5) Zoology, (6) Trees and Flowers, (7) Meals, (8) Magic Herbs, (9) Metals, (10) Metallurgy, (11) Amber, Ivory and Ultramarine.

GLADSTONE, Wm. Ewart Landmarks of Homeric Study 3/6 (75*c.*) c 8° Macmillan 90

A very misapprop. title : it shd. have been "High-water Marks of Hom. Study Fifty yrs. ago." The bk. ignores modern criticism, regarding both *Iliad* and *Odyss.* as great original wks. by the same writer, free fr. later interpolations. It is popularly written, and *pro tanto* more misleading. Conts. also essay on pts. of contact betw. Assyr. tablets and Homeric text.

GOEBEL, Ed. Homerische Blätter, pt. i. 80*pf.* ; ii. [lexicographical] 80*pf.* [Fulda School-programmes] 4° Schöningh, *Paderb.* 91 ; 93

KLÖTZER, R. F. J. Die griechische Erziehung in Homer's Ilias und Odyssee—*ut* D § 157.

LA ROCHE, J. Homerische Untersuchungen, pt. i. 6*m.* ; ii. 5*m.* 8° Teubner, *Lps.* 91 ; 93

LUDWICH, Alf. Homerica, i.–v. 93

PETERS, Wilh. Zur Geschichte d. Wolf'schen Prolegomena zu Homer [school progr.] 4° *Frankfort* 90

An interesting contrib. to hist. of WOLF'S *Prolegg.* [*ut* B.B. K § 190], based on unpub. letters fr. WOLF to Karl Aug. BÖTTIGER.

SCHWARTZ, W. Nachklänge prähistorischen Volksglaubens in Homer 1*m.* 60 8° Seehagen, *Berlin* 94

Hymns.

HIGNARD, H. Les Hymnes Homériques 4*fr.* 8° Maisonneuve, *Paris* 64

Iliad.

FORCHHAMMER, P. W. Homer : s. Sprache, Kampfplätze s. Heroen in d. Troas ; map 3*m.* 4° Lipsius, *Kiel* 94

GRIMM, Herm. Ilias : erster bis neunter Gesang 6*m.* 8° Hertz, *Berlin* 90

Criticizes the *Iliad* fr. a purely liter. and æsthet. stdpt., seeing in it the carefully-planned wk. of a single poet : w. full anal. of first 9 bks.

*LEAF, Dr. Walt. A Companion to the Iliad for English Readers 7/6 ($1.62) c 8° Macmillan 92

An imprt. contrib. to Homeric liter., and (tho' designed for studs. who can read Homer in a tr. only) of great value for advanced studts. also. Consists of an Introd. (dealing w. the Hom. Quest.—the decisn. on wh. the author contends must be based on "the broad grounds of the constrn. and motives of the poem" and not on merely linguist. considns.) and copious fascinating literary Notes, referring not to the text but to the tr. of wh. Dr. LEAF is co-author [*ut* B.B. K § 190]—to wh. bk. the present is intended to serve as a "Companion."

Odyssey.

CZYCZKIEWICZ, Andr. Betrachtungen über Homer's Odyssee, 2 pts. ea. 1*m.* 8° West, *Brody* 93 ; 93

LA ROCHE, J. Commentar zur Homer's Odyssee, 4 pts. [*also sep.* 60*pf.* *to* 1*m.*] 2*m.* 10 s 8° Tempsky, *Prague* 91–92

PORPHYRIO Quæst. homer. ad. Odyss. pertin. Reliquiæ, ed. Herm. Schrader 10*m.* 8° Teubner, *Lps.* 90

Language. Textual Criticism. Metrics. Style.

ALTON, J. Ueber die Negation des Infinitivs bei Homer [school-programme] 8° *Krumau* 92

HENTZE, C. Die Parataxis bei Homer, pt. i. 1*m.* 20 ; ii. 80*pf.* ; iii. 80*pf.* [school-progr.] 4° Vandenhoeck, *Gött.* 88 ; 89 ; 91

HYLAN, F. Ueb. d. passive Bedeutg. medialer Aorist- u. Futurformen d. Homer [sch.-prg.] 8° *Meseritsch* 91

v. JAN, F. De Callimacho Homeri interprete 2*m.* 8° Teubner, *Lps.* 93

NAUMANN, Max Eustathios als kritische Quelle fur d. Iliastext [*extr. fr.* Jahrb. Class. Phil.] 5*m.* 8° „ „ 93

SCHNEIDER, Geo. Beiträge zur homerischen Wortforschung u. Textkritik [progr.] 1m. 8° Rother, *Görlitz* 93

SEYMOUR, Prf. Thos. D. [Am.] Introduction to the Language and Verse of Homer [Coll. Ser. of Gk. Auth.] 12° 6s. Ginn, *Boston* 4/6 Arnold 85

" " On Homeric Cæsura and Close of Verse as rel. to express. of Thought—*in* Harv. Studs., v. iii., *ut* K § 173.

SKERLO, H. Einiges über den Gebrauch von ἀνά bei Homer [school-programme] 4° *Graudenz* 90

Concordance.

GEHRING, Aug. Index Homericus 16m. r 8° Teubner, *Lps.* 91

Dictionary.

AUTENRIETH, Dr. Geo. A Homeric Dictionary, tr. Rob. P. Keep, revised Prf. Is. Flag; [Am.]; maps and ill. $1.10 12° Harper, *N.Y.* [76] 91

A revision of the bk. in 𝔅.𝔖. K § 190, wh. however, bg. abridged, it does not entirely supplant. This is the better bk. for the average student, the old one for the teacher. The 7th Germ. edn. appeared 3m. 8° Teubner, *Lps.* '89.

CAPELLE, Dr. Carl Vollständiges Wörterbuch üb. d. Gedichte d. Homeros 4m.80 8° Hahn, *Lps.* [78] 89

MEHLER, E. Woordenboek op de Gedichten van Homerus 4*fl.*90 8° van Druten, *Sneek* 92

Grammar.

THOMPSON, F. E. Homeric Grammar for Upper Forms of Schools 2/6 c 8° Rivington (Longman) 90

Manuscripts. Scholia.

LUDWICH, Arth. Scholia in Homeri Odysseam, 4 pts. ea. 20*pf.* 4° Schubert, *Königsbg.* 88

MAHAFFY, Prf. J. P. [ed.] —*in his* The Flinders Petrie Papyri, *ut* K § 179.

Incl. an early fragmt. of the *Iliad*, bk. xi., contg. 5 hitherto unknown lines.

NICHOLE, Jules [ed.] Les Scholies Genevoises de l'Iliade, 2 vols ; 2 facss. 25*fr.* r 8° Georg, *Basle* 91

An exact reprodn. of the MS. in the Geneva Publ. Libr., minutely ed., w. careful collata. of text, and hist. and geneal. of the MS., wh. conts an enormous mass of Byzantine lucubrations. Its main value, however, is for the scholia on the 21st bk., wh. are fr. an entirely differ. source, compiled fr. some unknown source of Alexandrian learning akin to that wh. formed the basis of the famous Venetian scholia: these quote the *ipsissima verba* of their authorities, and add consid. to our knowl. of Alexandrian criticism, and introduce us to several authors and bks. on HOMER hitherto unknown.

" " [ed.] *Paris* 94

An edn. of the texts of the papyrus fragmts. of Homer bought in Egypt for the Geneva Publ. Libr., one of wh. is of great interest, as it conts. a text varying substantially fr. that hitherto known: *inter alia* in *Iliad* xi. 788-xii. 9 thirteen addl. lines are introduced.

POLAK, H. J. Ad Odysseam ejusque Scholiastas Curæ secundæ 2*fl.* 8° Brill, *Leyden* 80

SCHIMBERG, Adolf Die handschriftl. Ueberlieferung d. Scholia Vulgata gen. Didymi 3m. 8° Dieterich, *Göttingen* 93

Partly repr. fr. *Philologus*. A 3rd Part appeared as a School-Programme. 8° *Ratibor* '92.

Origin of the Homeric Poems—*v. also* GRIMM, and *LEAF, *ut supra*.

BUTLER, Saml. On the Trepanese Origin of the Odyssey [ingenious speculations] 6*d.* 8° Metcalfe, *Cambr.* 93

ERHARDT, Louis Die Entstehung der homerischen Gedichte 12m. 8° Duncker, *Lps.* 93

GARDNER, Prf. Percy —*in his* New Chapters in Greek History, *ut* G § 5.

Assigns the latest pts. of *Iliad* to 8 cent., the *Odyss.* to 8 and 7 cent., admitting that both incorporate legends and even ballads of a much earlier period. The whole of the first 4 chaps. are of importance here.

KLUGE, Herm. Zur Entstehungsgeschichte der Ilias 4m.50 8° *Schulze, Cöthen* 88

LANG, Andr. Homer and the Epic 9/- *nt.* ($2.50) c 8° Longman 93

Standpoint strictly conservative: opposes KIRCHHOFF'S views reg. compos. of *Odyss.*, and deals at length w. WOLF'S theory, concludg. w. a compara. of other epical poems, such as *Song of Roland*, *Kalevala*. It is the most thorough and able defence of the literary unity of HOMER since MURE'S in his *Hist. of Gk. Liter.* [*ut* 𝔅.𝔖. K § 167].

NEWMAN, Prf. F. W. The Authorship of the Odyssey—*in his* Miscellanies, vol. v. : Chiefly Academic, *ut* K § 83.

A forcible argument on the side of the "Chorizontes."

ROTHE, Dr. C. Die Bedeutung der Widersprüche für die homerische Frage [schl.-progr.] 1m.20 4° *Berlin* (Fock, *Lps.*) 94

SELLENSTEDT, H. Striden om Homer : försök till framställing. a. d. hom. frågan 2*kr.*75 8° Wallberg, *Norrköping* 93

WEISSENBORN, Edm. Achilleis und Ilias [in fav. of unity of Hom. poems ; sch.-prg.] 8° *Mühlhausen* 90

Topography. Archæology.

ENGELMANN, Dr. R. [ed.] Pictorial Atlas to the *Iliad* and *Odyssey*, ed. Prf. W. C. F. Anderson 4° 10/6 Grevel $3 Westermann, *N.Y.* 92

Conts. 225 illns. of the poems, almost equally divided betw. the two. The ill., derived fr. all sources, Gk., Oriental and Roman, incl. designs actually illustrative of the poems, cognate designs fr. other sources and some representing legends to wh. HOMER refers. The text supplies a useful comment on their characteristics. Every school library should possess a copy. Germ. edn, costs 2m. ea. vol. (in 1 vol. 3m.60, *bud.* 4m.) 4° Litter.-Jahresber. *Lps.* '89 ; '89.

JOSEPH, D. Die Paläste d. homer. Epos m. Rücks. a. Schliemann's Ausgrabungen 1m.40 8° Siemens, *Berlin* 93

OHNEFALSCH-RICHTER, Dr. Max. Kypros, the Bible and Homer [tr.]—*ut* G § 8.

SORTAIS, Gaston Ilios et Iliade ; map [pp. xv., 418] 5*fr.* 8° Bouillon, *Paris* 94

Ruines d'Ilios ; Formatn. de l'Iliade ; Ess. d. Restaur. de l'Iliade primitive ; l'Olympe et l'Art homér.

Meleager [B.C. *fl.* 60].

Fifty Poems : ed. Walter Headlam ; w. English tr. [text and trs. *en regard*] 7/6 ($2.50) f 8° Macmillan 90

Exhibits the gems of the Greek *Anthology* in a very delightful form, the verse trs. however being accurate and scholarly rather than poetical.

Moschus [B.C. *fl.* 150]—*v.* Bion, *supra*.

Oracles.

Alexandre, C. [ed.] Χρησμοὶ Σιβυλλιακοί 9*fr.* 8° Didot, *Paris* [41–56] 69

Friedlieb, Dr. J. H. [ed. & tr.] Die Sibyllinischen Weissagungen [w. Germ. tr. & notes] 7m. ; *red. to* 4m. 8° Weigel, *Lps.* 52

Hendess, Rich. [ed.] Oracula Græca quæ apud Script. Græc. et Roman. extant 2m.40 8° Lippert, *Halle* 77

*Rzach, A. [ed.] Oracula Sibyllina 12m. 8° Tempsky, *Prague* 91

Translations.

Friedlieb, Dr. J. H. [tr.]—*in his edn. of the text, ut supra*.

Terry, Milton S. [Am. ; tr.] The Sibylline Oracles : transl. [blank verse] $1.50 c 8° Hunt & Eaton, *N.Y.* 90

Aids.

BADT, Benno W. Ursprung, Inhalt u. Text d. 4 Buches d. Sibyllischen Orakel : eine Studie [schl.-progr.] 1m. 4° Hepner, *Breslau* 78

BURESCH, K. Klaros : Untersuchungen z. Orakelwesen d. späteren Alterthums 3m.60 8° Teubner, *Lps.* 89

DECHENT, H. Ueber das erste, zweite u. elfte Buch der Sibyllischen Weissagungen [diss. inaug.] 2m. 8° Völcker, *Frankft.* 73

DELAUNAY, Ferd. Moines et Sibylles dans l'Antiquité Judéo-grecque 2*fr.* 8° ; 3*fr.*50 12° Didier, *Paris* 74

DIELS, H. Sibyllinische Blätter Reimer, *Berlin* 91

Publishes text of the 2 hermaphrodite oracles as given by PHLEGON of Tralles, and endeavours to show that they are real Sibyll. verses, once kept in the Capitol and consulted by the *decemviri*, tho' not deliv. by a Sibyl : compos. about end 3 cent. by a Roman.

DU PREL, Carl —*in his* Die Mystik der alten Griechen 3m. 8° Günther, *Lps.* 88

Tempelschlaf, Orakel, Mysterien, Dämon des Sokrates.

FEHR, Emil Studia in Oracula Sibyllina [dissert.] 2m.40 8° Akad. Buchhdg., *Upsala* 93

*RZACH, A. Kritische Studie zu den Sibyllischen Orakeln 6m.80 8° Freytag, *Lps.* 90

" " Metrische Studien z. d. Sibyllischen Orakeln [*extr. fr.* Sitzb. Wien. Ak.] 1m.60 8° " " 92

VERNES, Maur. Histoire des Idées Messianiques dep. Alexandre jusqu' à Hadrien 5*fr.* 8° Sandoz, *Paris* 74

K § 191

Orpheus.

Argonautica: trad. Enrico Ottino [in Italian; w. prolog. and notes] 8° *Turin* 74
übers. Karl Seidenadel [German; in orig. metre; schl.-progr.] 8° *Bruchsal* 73

Lithika [epic poem on magic powers of precious stones].
Translation: übers. Karl Seidenadel [German; in orig. metre; schl.-progr.] 4° *Bruchsal* 76

Orphica: Editio Tauchnitiana 90 *pf.* 16° Holtze, *Lps.* [ ] 76

Aids.
DIETERICH, Albrecht — De Hymnis Orphicis capita quinque 1*m.* 20 8° Elwert, *Marburg* 91
GERHARD, Ed. — Ueber Orpheus und die Orphiker [*extr. fr.* Abhandl. Akad. Wiss. Berl.] 2*m.* 80 4° Dümmler, *Berl.* 61
KERN, Otto — De Orphei, Epimenidis, Pherecydis Theogoniis Quaestiones criticae 3*m.* 8° Nicolai, *Berlin* 88
LOBECK, Chr. A. — *in his* Aglaophamos: sive de theol. myst. Graec., *ut* B.B. B § 12.
SCHUSTER, Paul R. — De Veteris Orphicae theogoniae indole atque origine [diss. inaug.] 1*m.* 80 8° *Leipzig* 69
SUSEMIHL, F. — De Theogoniae Orphicae forma antiquissima dissertatio 1*m.* 60 4° *Greifswald* 90

Pindar [B.C. *c.* 522–442].

Odes: ed. w. English notes, Introds. and partial trs. J. B. Bury, 2 vols. [Classical Lib.] 22/6 ($5.25) 8° Macmillan 91; 92

Isthmian Odes, 10/6 ($2.25) '92; *Nemean Odes*, 12/- ($4) '91. A very valuable edn. w. full and minute comm. and criticism, clear explans. of ea. Ode beneath the text, w. anal. of contents and particulars of the man and the occasion, as well as vigorous literal tr. of all difficult passages. A prominent feature of the bk is the author's "theory of verbal responsions," very ingeniously if not very convincingly detected or unravelled. Several Appendices, *e.g.* (in *Nemean Odes*) on the orig. of the Gt. Games. Introd. to *Isth. Odes*, pp. xvi.–xxxiii. is an excell. sketch of Aegina in her histor., social and artistic aspects, a very useful piece of wk.

Translation: tr. F. D. Morice, *sub tit.* The Olympian and Pythian Odes of Pindar, 5/- c. 8° Percival (Riv. & Perc.) 93

Aids.
DRACHMANN, A. B. — Moderne Pindarfortolkning: Kritiske og positive Bidrag 5*kr.* 8° Gad, *Copenhagen* 91
GRAF, Ernst — Pindars Logaoedische Strophen 1*m.* 8° Elwert, *Marburg* 92
REINHOLD, Dr. Hugo — Griechische Oertlichkiten bei Pindaros 1*m.* 20 4° *Quedlinb.* (Fock, *Lps.*) 94
SCHMIDT, Ernst — De Pindari Carmine Nemeorum tertio [school-programme] 4° *Seehausen* 91
SCHWICKERT, Joh. Jos. — Kritisch-exeget. Untersuchungen z. d. zten. Olymp. Siegesgesang Pindars 1*m.* 4° Lintz, *Trèves* 92

Scholia.
ABEL, Eug. [ed.] — Scholia in Pindari Epinicia, pt. iii.: Scholia Recentia, vol. i. [*Olymp. Pyth.*] 15*m.* 8° *Budapest* (Calvary, *Berl.*) 90

Sappho [B.C. *c.* 630–570].

Translation: tr. Jas. S. Easby-Smith [Am.] *sub tit.* The Songs of Sappho $1 12° Stormont, *Washington* 91

Aid.
GERSTENHAUER, Arth. — De Alcaei et Sapphonis Copia Vocabulorum—*ut supra*, *s.n.* Alcaeus.

Sext(i)us Pythagoreus.

Sententiae: rec. Ant. Elter; cum versione Rufini, 2 pts. [school-programmes] 4° *Bonn* 91; 92
rec. Joh. Gildemeister [w. Latin and Syriac recensions] 4*m.* 8° Marcus, *Bonn* 73

OTT, Meinrad — Charakter u. Ursprung d. Sprüche d. Philosoph. Sextius 2*m.* 4° *Rottweil* 61
" " — Die syrischen "Auserles. Sprüche des Herm. Xistus, Bischofs v. Rom," 2 pts. 2*m.* 50 4° " 62; 63

Not a Xistus writing, but a re-edited one of Sextius.

Sophron [B.C. 5th cent.].

Mimorum Reliquiae: ed. Ludw. Botzon [w. Latin notes] [schl.-prog.] 1*m.* 4° Hempel, *Marienbg.* 67

Theocritus [B.C. *c.* 325 *c.* 267].

Translation: tr. Jas. Hy. Hallard [v. fairly good; Engl. verse, varying metres] 6/6 sq. 8° Longman 94

Aids.
PATON, W. R. — *Appendix entitled* Theocritus: was he a Coan?—*in* his & E. L. Hicks' Inscripp. of Cos, *ut* K § 184.
VAHLEN, Joh. — De Versibus nonnullis Theocriteis Disputatio [Index Lectt.] 4° *Berlin* 91
TRAUT, Hugo — Quaestiones Theocriteae, 3 pts. [school-programmes] 4° *Krotoschin* –90
WINTZELL, Cnut — Studia Theocritea [Comm. Acad.] 2*kr.* 50 8° Gleerup, *Lund* 89

Theognis [B.C. *c.* 540–*c.* 444 (?)].

Aids.
v. GRYSO, Em. — Studia Theognidea [dissert. inaug.] 8° *Strassburg* 92
LA ROCHE, J. — Studien zu Theognis [school-programme] 8° *Linz* 91
LUCAS, Joh. — Studia Theognidea 2*m.* 8° Heinrich, *Berlin* 93
SCHÄFER, M. — De Iteratis apud Theognidem Distichis 1*m.* 8° Mayer & Müller, *Berl.* 92

101. GREEK DRAMATISTS.

Collectively.

Comicorum Graec. Fragmenta: ed. Dr. F. A. Paley; w. Engl. trs. *en regard* [Dilettante Lib.] f. 8° 2/6 Sonnenschein; 90c. Macmillan, *N.Y.* [88] 92
BLAYDES, F. H. M. — Adversaria in Comicorum Graec. Fragmenta, pt. i sec. edit. Meinekianam (*ut* B.B. K § 151) 5*m.* 8° Waisenhaus, *Halle* 90

Tragicorum Graec. Fragmenta: ed. Aug. Nauck [*ut* B.B. K § 191]: new edn. [1022 pp.] 26*m.* 8° Teubner, *Lps.* [56] 89
BLAYDES, F. H. M. — Adversaria in Tragicorum Graecorum Fragmenta 8° Waisenhaus, *Halle* 94
NAUCK, Aug. — Tragicae Dictionis Index spectans ad Trag. Graec. Fragm. 12*m.* 25 8° Eggers, *St. Petersb.* (Haessel, *Lps.*) 92
v. WILAMOWITZ-MOELLENDORFF, Ulr. — De Tragicorum Graecorum Fragmentis Comment. 55*pf.* 8° Dieterich, *Göttingen* 93

Translations.

Pollard, Alf. W. [ed.] Odes from the Greek Dramatists: transl. in lyric metres c 8° 7/6 Stott; $1.75 McClurg, *Chicago* 90

An attractive colln. of some of the best wk. of Engl. trs. of former and present times.

Smith, Prf. Goldwin [tr.] Specimens of Greek Tragedy: transl., 2 vols. [verse] 10/- (ea. $1.25) gl 8° Macmillan 93

Readable verse trs. of favourite passages (choruses avoided) strung together by brief prose outlines, thus giving the purely English reader something like an equivalent of the originals. A short Introd. deals w. some leading characteristics of the Greek drama, and of ÆSCHYL., SOPH. [=vol. i.] and EURIP. [=vol. ii.] fr. whom the selns. are made.

Æschylus [B.C. 525–456].

Fabulæ: *ed. N. Wecklein, cum lectt. et scholl. cod. Medicei et in Agamem. cod. Florent. ab Hieron. Vitelli denuo collatis, vols. i.–ii. auctaria 8m.40 8° Calvary, *Berlin* 93

Vol. i. *Fragmenta*; ii. *Appendix Propagata*.

ed. w. Greek notes N. Wecklein + Eug. Zomarides, *s.t.* *Αἰσχύλου Δράματα Σωζόμενα*, vol. i.

This vol. conts. the *Persae* and *Septem contra Thebas*, w. Prologue [by WECKLEIN], general Introd., spec. Introd. to each play, copious footnotes, and crit. indices at end—all in Greek. The intention is to give to Gk.-reading studts. in Constant., Athens, etc., the results of recent Germ. learning. Beautifully prtd. by Bär and Hermann, of Lpz.

Choephori: ed. Dr. A. W. Verrall; w. Introd., comm. & tr. [Class. Lib.] 12/- ($2.75 *net.*) 8° Macmillan 93

A learned and suggestive edn., rich in conjectural emendation—and occas. also in conjectural interpretation; w. a long Introd., interesting and persuasive comm., and Appendices. The Edr. is seen at his best in this play, where so many obscurities and difficulties exist, wh. can be dealt w. only by conjecture.

Persae: ed. Rev. T. S. Ramsbotham [Scenes fr. Greek Plays] 1/6 f 8° Longman 94

Prometheus Vinctus: w. Engl. notes & Introd. F. G. Plaistowe + W. F. Masom [Univ. Corr. Coll. Tut. Ser.] 3/6 c 8° Clive 92

" " " N. Wecklein [*ut* 𝔅.𝔅. K § 191], tr. Prf. F. D. Allen [Am.] [Coll. Ser. Gk. Auth.] 12° $1.50 Ginn, *Boston* / 7/6 Arnold 91

Septem contra Thebas: w. English notes Arth. Sidgwick f 8° Clar. Press / Macmillan, *N.Y.* *in prep.*

Translations.

Works: tr. Prf. Lewis Campbell, *s.t.* The Seven Plays of Æschylus; w. Introd. & brief notes [verse] 7/6 c 8° Paul 91

Choephori: tr. Dr. A. W. Verrall—*in his edn. of the text, ut supra.*

Eumenides: tr. F. G. Plaistowe [Univ. Corresp. Coll. Tutor. Series] 2/6 c 8° Clive 94

Oresteia [= Agam., Coeph., Eumen.]: tr. Prf. Lewis Campbell; w. Introd. [prose; Class. Trans.] 5/- c 8° Methuen 93

By no means so good or so readable a tr. as his verse tr., *ut supra.*

Agam., Choeph., Eumen. tr. J. Dunning Cooper [verse] 6/- c 8° Simpkin 90

Prometheus Bound: tr. Hy. Howard Molyneux, [5th] Earl of Carnarvon [verse] 6/- c 8° Murray 93

Posthumously publ., and had not received his final revision; but as pub. not so good as his tr. of the *Agam.* [*ut* 𝔅.𝔅. K § 191].

Aids.

BISHOP, Chas. Edw. De Adiectivum verbalium -τος Terminatione insignium usu Æschyleo [diss. inaug.] 8° *Leipzig* 89

HAUSLER, Rich. De Proprietate quadam Elocutionis Æschyleae [diss. inaug.] 8° *Berlin* 89

HEADLAM, Walt. On Editing Æschylus: a criticism 6/- 8° Nutt 91

A diatribe agst. Dr. A. W. VERRALL for his edns. of the *Agamemnon* and the *Seven against Thebes.* Replied to by VERRALL *On Editing Æschylus: a reply* 1/- net (33 pp.) 8° Macmillan '92. *Litterae inhumaniores!*

MUNK, Dr. Edw. Æschylus—*in his* Student's Greek Tragedians, ed. Dr. A. W. Verrall, *ut* 𝔅.𝔅. K § 188.

A useful book, well adapted to the beginner in ÆSCHYLUS.

RICHTER, P. Zur Dramaturgie des Æschylus 6m.50 8° Teubner, *Lpz.* 92

ULLMANN, C. Theod. Proprietates Sermonis Æschylei [school-programme] 4° *Donaueschingen* 92

ZAKKA, A. Κριτικαὶ καὶ ἑρμηνευτικαὶ παρατηρήσεις εἰς Αἰσχύλον 3m. 8° 91

Oresteia.

FINSLER, Geo. Die Orestie des Aischylos 2m. 4° Schmid, *Berne* 89

Persae.

GRAVENHORST, H. Ueber d. Perser d. Æschylos: Beitrag z. Verstandn. u. Würdigung d. Trag. 6 pf. 8° Fock, *Lpz.* 91

STAVRIDES, Jean Quelques Remarques critiques sur les Perses d'Eschyle 2fr. 8° Leroux, *Paris* 92

Vespae.

EHRHARDT, Gust. Ueber Interpolationen in Aristophanes Wespen [school-progr.] 4° *Rossleben* 90

Scholia.

DÄHNHARDT, Osc. [ed.] Scholia in Æschyli Persas [w. crit. appar.] 3m.60 8° Teubner, *Lpz.* 94

A supplemt. from other MSS. of the Vitelli colln. [in ed. WECKLEIN] of the Codex Mendiceus.

Textual Criticism.

NEWMAN, Prf. F. W. Comments on the Text of Æschylus and Euripides 6/- 8° Paul 90

A supplement to his *Comments on the Text of Æschylus* (*ut* 𝔅.𝔅. K § 191). Ingenious, but not very convincing.

Aristophanes [B.C. 444–388].

Equites: w. English notes and Introd. R. A. Neil 8° Camb. Press / Macmillan, *N.Y.* *in prep.*

w. Latin notes (crit. & exeg.) Fred. H. M. Blaydes; & scholia [= Comoed. pt. x.] 9m. 8° Waisenhaus, *Halle* 92

Nubes: w. Latin notes (crit. & exeg.) Fred. H. M. Blaydes; & scholia [= Comoed. pt. ix.] 10m. 8° " " 90

Ranæ: w. Latin notes (crit. & exeg.) Fred. H. M. Blaydes; & scholia [= Comoed. pt. viii.] 10m. 8° " " 88

Vespae: w. English notes C. E. Graves [Pitt Press Ser.] f 8° 3/6 Camb. Press / Macmillan, *N.Y.* 94

" " " and Introd. Dr. W. W. Merry [Clar. Press Ser.] f 8° 3/6 Clar. Press / $1 Macmillan, *N.Y.* 93

" Latin " (crit. & exeg.) Fred. H. M. Blaydes; & scholia [Comoed. pt. xi.] 9m. 8° Waisenhausen, *Halle* 93

" " " and prolegg. J. van Leeuwen 5m. 8° Brill, *Leyden* 93

Translation.

Wasps: tr. F. G. Plaistowe [Univ. Corr. Coll. Tut. Ser.] 2/6 c 8° Clive 93

Aids.

GRÖBLE, Joh. Nep. Die ältesten Hypothesis zu Aristophanes [school-progr.] 8° *Dillingen* 90

ILTZ, Joh. De Vi et Usu Praeposit. ἐπί, μετά, παρά, περί, πρός, ὑπό ap. Aristoph. [diss.] 8° *Halle* 90

MURRAY, A. T. On Parody and Paratragoedia in Aristophanes [in English] 1m 50 8° Mayer & Müller, *Berl.* 91

SCHENK, Rich. Observationes criticae in fabulas Aristophaneas [schl.-progr.] 1m. 4° Fock, *Lpz.* 91

SOBOLEWSKI, Sergius De Praepositionum usu Aristophaneo 4m. 8° Lang, *Moscow* 90

" " Syntaxis Aristoph. capita duo: De sententiarum condic., tempor., relat. formis et usu 8° Lang, *Moscow* 91

UCKERMANN, Wilh. Ueber den Artikel bei Eigennamen in Aristophanes [progr.] 1m. 4° Gaertner, *Berlin* 92

ZURETTI, C. O. Analecta Aristophanea 5l. 8° Loescher, *Turin* 92

Onomasticon.

HOLDEN, Dr. Hub. A. Onomasticon = vol. ii. *of his edn.* of Aristophanes, *ut* 𝔅.𝔅. K § 191.

Conts. an elaborate account, with full refs., of all persons and places mentioned in ARISTOPHANES.

K § 191

Scholia.

MEINERS, Wilh. Quaestiones ad Scholia Aristophanea historica pertinentes [diss.] 8° *Halle* 90

RUTHERFORD, Dr. W. G. [ed. & tr.] Scholia Aristophanica [comments and adscripts preserved in *Codex Ravennas*; w. trs.] 8° Macmillan *in prep.*

STEIN, Gust. [ed.] Scholia in Aristophanis Lysistratam 2*m*.50 8° Dieterich, *Göttingen* 91

ZACHER, Konr. Die HSS. u. Classen d. Aristophanes-Scholien: Mittheiln. u. Untersuchn. 6*m*. 8° Teubner, *Lps.* 88

ZURETTI, C. O. [ed.] Scolii al Pluto ed alle Rane d'Aristophane [Venet. and Cremona codd.] 4*l*. 8° Loescher, *Turin* 90

Pax.

HELMBOLD, Herm. Aristophanis Pax superstes utrum prior sit an retractata [diss.] 1*m*.60 8° Neuenhahn, *Jena* 90

Thesmophoriazusae.

LANGE, Wilh. Quæstiones in Aristophanis Thesmophoriazusas [dissert. inaug.] 1*m*.20 8° Dieterich, *Göttingen* 91

Euripides [B.C. 480–405].

Tragœdiæ: ed. crit. Ad. Kirchoff, 3 vols. 4*m*.80 8° Weidmann, *Berl.* [55] 67–68

Alcestis: w. Engl. notes & introd. Dr. Mortimer L. Earle [Am.] [Class. Ser.; based on Prinz's ed.] 3/6 f 8° Macmillan 94

" " " and vocab. M. A. Bayfield [Elementary Classics] 1/6 (40c.) 18° " 90

" " " and Introd. C. H. Keene 8° 10/6 Deighton, *Camb.*; $1.50 Macmillan, *N.Y.* 93

" French notes and Introd. H. Weil 2*fr*.50 8° Hachette, *Paris* 91

Antiope: —*v. infra, sub nom.* Mahaffy.

Bacchæ: w. English notes and Introd. A. H. Cruickshank f 8° 3/6 Clar. Press; $1 *nt.* Macmillan, *N.Y.* 92

" " " " & revis. text Prf. Rob. Y. Tyrrell [Class. Ser.] 3/6 (90c.) f 8° Macmillan 92

A fresh and more mature edn. of the play than that formerly ed. by him in 1871 (*ut* B.B. K § 191), w. an excellent essay on the æsthetic and dramatic sides of the play, its relig. and moral import. Incl. a repr. of Walt. PATER'S fine study, and a fine tr. of the Choral Odes by Geo. WILKINS.

Cyclops: w. English notes and Introd. Rev. W. E. Long f 8° 2/6 Clar. Press; 60c. *nt.* Macmillan, *N.Y.* 91

Electra: " " " " Chas. Haines Keene; front. 8° 10/6 Bell; $3.50 *nt.* Macmillan, *N.Y.* 93

An elaborate edn., w. exhaustive crit. appar., incl. a collation of the Florentine Laurentian MS. (WEIL'S L).

Hecuba: rec. Rud. Prinz 1*m*.60 8° Teubner, *Lps.* 83

w. English notes and Introd. W. S. Hadley [Pitt Press Series] f 8° 2/6 Camb. Press; 60c. *nt.* Macmillan, *N.Y.* 94

" " " Jno. Bond + A. S. Walpole [Elemt. Classics] 1/6 (40c.) 18° Macmillan 82

Heraclidæ: " " " and Introd. C. S. Jerram f 8° 3/- Clar. Press; 75c. *nt.* Macmillan, *N.Y.* 88

Hippolutos: w. Germ. tr. Ulr. v. Wilamowitz-Moellendorf 8*m*. 8° Weidmann, *Berlin* 91

Ion: *w. English notes and Introd. Dr. A. W. Verrall; and [verse] tr. 8° 7/6 Camb. Press; $2.00 *nt.* Macmillan, *N.Y.* 90

" " " C. S. Jerram f 8° Clar. Press; Macmillan, *N.Y.* *in prep.*

" " " J. Thompson + A. F. Burnet [Univ. Corr. Coll. Tut. Ser.] 3/6 c 8° Clive 91

Iphigenia in Aulide: *w. Engl. notes & Introd. E. B. England; & crit. appar. [Classical Lib.] 7/6 ($1.75) 8° Macmillan 91

An excellent edn., sober and learned, w. useful comm., and exhaustive crit. appar. embodying his collatn. of P (Palat. MS. no. 287 of Vatic. Lib.)—a valuable contribn. to palæography. Introd. furnishes a complete acc. of discussns. and discovs. of last 130 yrs. (incl. his own) as to authenticity of *Iph. in Aulide*.

Iphigenia in Tauris: w. English notes Prf. I. Flagg [Am.] [Coll. Ser. of Gk. Auth.] 12° $1.50 Ginn, *Boston*; 6/- Arnold 89

" German " Siegfr. Merkler 1*m*.20 8° F. A. Perthes, *Gotha* 92

Medea: w. Engl. notes M. A. Bayfield; vocab. & appendices [Elem. Classics] 1/6 (40c.) 18° Macmillan 92

Translations.

Plays: tr. Edw. P. Coleridge, *sub tit.* The Plays of Euripides, 2 vols. [prose] c 8° ea. 6/- Bell; ea. $1.50 Macmillan, *N.Y.* 91; 91

Vol. i.: *Rhesus, Medea, Hippolytus, Alcestis, Heraclidæ, Supplices, Troades, Ion, Helena*; vol. ii.: *Andromache, Electra, Bacchae, Hecuba, Hercules Furens, Phœnissae, Orestes, Iphig. in Tauris, Iph. in Aulide, Cyclops*. An accurate and careful prose tr. based on PALEY'S text.

tr. Arth. S. Way, *sub tit.* Euripides in Engl. Verse, pts. i.–iii. ea 1/6 (50c. *nt.*) c 8° Macmillan 94

Alcestis; *Hecuba*; *Medea*. Scholarly verse trs. by the tr. of HOMER (*ut* B.B. K § 190).

Hippolytus: tr. H. B. L., *sub tit.* The Hippolutos of Euripides; w. notes [in orig. metres] 3/- 8° Williams 94

übers. U. v. Wilamowitz-Moellendorf—*in his edn. of the text, ut supra.*

Ion: tr. H. B. L.; w. notes [original English metres] 4/6 4° Williams 89

" Dr. A. W. Verrall—*in his edn. of the text, ut supra.*

Aids.

v. HOLZINGER, Carl R. Exegetische und Kritische Bemerkungen z. Eurip. Alkestis [*extr. fr.* Sitzb. Wien Akad.] 1*m*. 8° Tempsky, *Vienna* 92

MUNK, Dr. Ed. Euripides—*in his* Student's Greek Tragedians, ed. Dr. A. W. Verrall, *ut* K § 188.

A useful book, well adapted to the beginner in Euripides.

NEUMANN, Jul. Menelaos und Helena in d. Dramen d. Euripides [schl.-progr.] 4° *Zittau* 93

NEWMAN, Prf. F. W. Comments on the Text of Æschylus and Euripides—*ut supra, s.n.* Æschylus.

NINDEL, Otto Kritische Bemerkungen zu Euripides (Alcestis) [school-progr.] 4° *Bernburg* 93

PARMENTIER, L. Euripide et Anaxore 3*fr*. 8° Bouillon, *Paris* 93

RADERMACHER, Ludw. Observationes in Euripidem Miscellae [diss. inaug.] 8° *Bonn* 91

ROLFE, Prf. J. C. [Am.] The Tragedy Rhesus—*in* Harvard Studies in Class. Philol.—*ut* K § 173.

Orig. [1885] written in Lat. for degree of Ph. D. at Cornell Univ. Also repr. as a pamphlet, Ginn, *Bost.* '93. Concludes that the *Rhesus* is not the wk. of EURIP., but was written by an Athenian betw. end of Pelop. War and time of DEMOSTH., who attempted to write a play of the old schl., taking EURIP. as his model.

VAHLEN, Joh. De Euripidis Hercule quem furentem dicere solebant [Ind. Lectt.] 4° *Berlin* 93

ZANCHI, V. L'Ecuba e le Trojane di Euripide 3*m*. 8° Konegen, *Vienna* 93

Language. Metre. Scholia.

BALLY, Chas. De Euripidis Tragoed. Partibus lyricis Quæstiunculae [diss. inaug.] 8° *Berlin* 80

EVSERT, Leop. Rhesus im Lichte des euripideischen Sprachgebrauches [schl.-progr.] 8° *Leipa* 91

GRIGORAKIS, Geo. Σύγκρισις τῶν Σχολίων τῶν Φοινισσῶν πρὸς τὸ τούτων κείμενον [diss.] 8° *Jena* 90

GROEPPEL, A. De Euripidis versibus logaoedicis 1*m*.50 4° Fock, *Lps.* 90

JOHNSON, F. De Conjunct. et Optat. usu Eurip. in enuntiatis finalibus et condicionalibus 2*m*. 8° Heinrich, *Berl* 93

MAHAFFY, Prf. Jno. [ed.] —*in his edn. of* The Flinders Petrie Papyri, *ut* K § 170.

Vol. i. conts. a revised text of the fragmts. of the lost *Antiope* (prev. pb. separ.), the most important of the classical texts discov. by Mr. PETRIE.

PAPADIMITRIU, Synodis — Kritische Beiträge zu d. Scholien des Euripides [Erlangen diss. inaug.] 8° *Constantinople* 88
REITER, Siegfr. — Drei- u. vierzeitige Längen b. Euripides [*extr. fr.* Sitzb. Wien. Akad.] 1m.60 r 8° Tempsky, *Vienna* 93
SCHWARTZ, Elimar — De numerorum usu Euripideo capita selecta, pt. i.–ii. ea. 1m.20 8° Lipsius, *Kiel* 91 ; 92
„ „ [ed.] — Scholia in Euripidem collegit, recensuit et edidit, vol. ii. 9m. 8° G. Reimer, *Berlin* 91

Menander [B.C. 342–291].

GUIZOT, Guill. — Ménandre : étude historique et littéraire s. l. coméd. et l. soc. grec. *o.p.* [*pb.* 3*fr.*50] s 8° Didier, *Paris* [55] 55
LÜBKE, Herm. — Menander und seine Kunst [programme] 1m. 4° Gaertner, *Berlin* 92
STERNBACH, Leo — Curae Menandreae 2m. 8° Poln. Verlags-Gesell., *Cracow* 92

Sophocles [B.C. *c.* 495–405].

Tragoediae : w. Latin notes Ed. Wunder [*ut* B.B. K § 191]: new ed. by N. Wecklein *in pts.* ea. 1m.50 to 1m.80 r 8° Teubner, *Lpz.* [31–37] 86 *in prg.*
*w. English notes and comm. Prf. R. C. Jebb ; and [prose] tr. 8° ea. 12/6 Camb. Press / ea. $3.25 *nt.* Macmillan, *N.Y.* 92 ; 94

New vols. :—v. *Trachiniae* ; vi. *Electra*. A monumental and incomparable edn.—learned, lucid and exhaustive : probably the most perfect English edn. of a Gk. classical writer wh. has yet appeared. Vol. vii. will be *Ajax*.

Ajax : w. English notes and append. Milt. W. Humphreys [Am.] $1.50 12° Harper, *N.Y.* 91
„ German notes Friedr. Schubert ; 6 ill. 60*pf.* 8° Tempsky, *Vienna* [83] 92
Antigone : „ English notes & Introd. A. H. Allcroft + B. J. Hayes 2/6; w. vocab. & tr. 4/6 c 8° Clive 90
w. German notes Friedr. Schubert ; 6 ill. 60*pf.* 8° Tempsky, *Vienna* [84] 92
Philoctetes: w. English notes and Introd. Fk. Pierrepont Graves [Am.] $1 sq 16° Leach, *Boston* 93
Introd. is on source of plot, w. acc. of characters, *etc.* Also a "Metrical Introd." Copious notes.

Translations.

Tragedies : tr. Edw. P. Coleridge, *subtit.* The Plays of Sophocles ; w. notes [Bohn's Lib.] c 8° 5/- Bell / $1.50 *nt.* Macmillan, *N.Y.* 93
An accurate and careful literal prose tr., based on JEBB'S text ; rather better than his tr. of EURIPIDES, *ut supra*. Replaces the former tr. of SOPHOCLES in Bohn's "Classical Library," wh. is a thoroughly bad one.

Antigone : tr. A. H. Allcroft + B. J. Hayes—*in their edn. of the text, ut supra* [not sold separ.].
Electra : *tr. Prf. R. C. Jebb—*in his edn. of the text, ut supra* [prose].
Œdipus Coloneus : tr. Arth. C. Auchmuty [verse ; moderately good] 2/- c 8° Andrews, *Hull* 94
Trachiniæ : *tr. Prf. R. C. Jebb—*in his edn. of the text, ut supra* [prose].

Aids.
BECKER, J. — Die Ueberarbeitung d. ursprünglichen Œdipus von Sophokles 1m.50 8° Fock, *Lpz.* 91
BÜCHNER, Dr. Wilh. — Ueber den Aias des Sophokles [school programme] 1m.20 4° *Offenbach* (Fock, *Lpz.*) 94
BUTCHER, Prf. S. H. — Sophocles—*in his* Some Aspects of the Gk. Genius, *ut* K § 187.
HOLUB, Joh. — Doppelsinn in drei Scenen der Elektra der Sophokles 1m. 8° Neugebauer, *Prague* 89
„ „ — Noch 30 doppelsinnige Stellen in der Elektra des Sophokles 40*pf.* 8° „ „ 90
KRAH, Alf. — De Infinitivo sophocleo [dissert. inaug.] 8° *Halle* 88
MAURER, Theod. — Die Cantica der Antigone kritisch-exegetisch revidiert [school-progr.] 4° *Worms* 92
MEIFERT, Carl — De Sophoclis Codicibus [dissert. inaug.] 8° *Halle* 91
MUNK, Dr. Ed. — Sophocles—*in his* Student's Greek Tragedians, ed. Dr. A. W. Verrall—*ut* K § 188.
NEUMANN, Walth. — Die Entwickelung d. Philoktet-Mythus [esp. by Sophocles : schl.-progr.] 4° *Coburg* 93
PÄHLER, K. — Kritische u. erklärende Bemerkungen zu Sophokles Aias [schl.-progr.] 4° *Wiesbaden* 92
PAPAGEORGIUS, Pet. N. [ed.] — Scholia in Sophoclis Tragoedias vetera e Cod. Laurentiano 4m.80 8° Teubner, *Lpz.* 88
PLÜSS, T. — Sophokles' Elektra : eine Auslegung ; pl. 3m. 8° „ „ 91
SCHWARZ, Ant. — Beiträge zur Kritik und Erklärung des Sophokles [schl.-progr.] 8° *Horn* 91
SPROTTE, Jos. — Die Syntax d. Infinitivs b. Sophokles, 2 pts. [schl.-programmes] 4° *Glatz* (Fock, *Lpz.*) 90 ; 91
TECTZ, F. — Die Kolometrie in den Cantica der Antigone des Sophokles 1m.20 8° Mocker, *Bremerhaven* 93
WELZHOFER, Heinr. — Sophokles' Antigone : Beitrag z. Gesch. *etc.* d. antik. Dramas 1m. 8° Seehagen, *Berlin* 91

192. GREEK HISTORIANS AND GEOGRAPHERS.

Collectively.

SCHMIDT, B. — Korkyraeische Studien 2m.40 8° Teubner, *Lpz.* 90
Topography of Corcyra (Corfu) in reference to THUCYDIDES, XENOPHON and DIODORUS
WEHMANN, M. — De ὥστε particulae usu Herodoteo, Thucyd., Xenophonteo 1m.50 8° Trübner, *Strassburg* 91

Appian [A.D. mid. 2nd cent.].

LÖSCH, Karl — Sprachliche und erläuternde Bemerkungen zu Appian [school-progr.] 8° *Nuremberg* 92

Aristotle [B.C. 384–322]—*v.* K § 194.

Arrian [A.D. 1st. cent.].

Translation.

Anabasis Alexandri *and* Indica : tr. Dr. E. J. Chinnock ; w. Introd., notes and maps [Bohn's Lib.] c 8° 5/- Bell / $1.50 *nt.* Macmillan, *N.Y.* 93
The commentary is full, rendering the bk. almost a complete history of the Great ALEXANDER.

Dio Cassius [A.D. 155—*post* 229].

Historia Romana : cur. L. Dindorf, rec. Joh. Melber, vol. i. 4m.50 ; ii. 3m.60 8° Teubner, *Lpz.* 90 ; 94
MAISEL, H. — Beiträge zur Würdigung der HSS. des Cassius Dio 1m.50 4° Fock, *Lpz.* 94

Diodorus Siculus [B.C. 1st cent.].

Bibliotheca Historica: ex rec. Imm. Bekker, et Lud. Dindorf, ed. Friedr. Vogel, vol. i. 3m.60; ii. 3m.60; iii. 4m. 8° Teubner, *Lpz.* 88 ; 90 ; 93

Aids —*v. also supra, sub voc.* Generally (SCHMIDT).
SCHÖNLE, Ferd. L. — Diodorstudien [dissert.] 1m.50 8° Speyer, *Berlin* 91
WACHSMUTH, Curt — Ueber d. Geschichtswerk d. Diodorus, 2 pts. [programmes] 4° Dr. v. Edelmann, *Lpz.* 92

K § 192

Diogenes Laertius [A.D. *fl.* 150]—*for text and tr. v.* B.B. C § 3.

De Vitis Dogmatibus et Apothegm. Clarorum Philosophorum : ed. Prf. Ingram Bywater *in prep.*
VOLKMANN, Walther — Untersuchungen zu Diogenes Laertius 1m.20 8° Guercke, *Jauer* 91

Dionysius Halicarnassensis [B.C. *c.* 78(54–)–*c.* 8].

Antiquitatum Romanarum quae supersunt, rec. C. Jacoby, vols. ii.–iii. ea. 3*m.* 8° Teubner, *Lpz.* 88; 91
AMMON, Geo. — De Dionysii Halicarnass. librorum rhetoricorum Fontibus [diss. inaug.] 1*m.*80 8° Lindauer, *Munich* 89
GOETZELER, Ludw. — Animadversiones in Dionysii Halicarnassensis Antiquitates Romanas, pt. i. 2*m.*; ii. 2*m.*40 8° Ackermann, *Munich* 93: 94
NORDSTRÖM, Väinö — Institutorum Romanorum Vocabula apud Dionysium Halicarnassensem 1*m.*60 8° *Helsingfors* (Weber, *Ber.*) 90

Hanno Carthaginiensis [date uncertain].

Periplus (ZOSIMUS) : rec. Karl Müller—*in* Geographi Minores, vol. i., *ut* B.B. K § 192.
FISCHER, C. Th. — De Hannonis Carthag. Periplo [= Unters. a. d. Geb. d. alt. Länderkunde, v. i.] 3*m.* 8° Teubner, *Lpz.* 93

Herodianus [A.D. 170–240].

Opera Historica : ed. J. A. C. Buchon [w. Polybius and Zosimus] 7*fr.*50 8° Herluison, *Orleans* 75
KRAUSE, Karl — Gebrauch d. Präpositionen bei Herodian, pt. i. [σύν u. μετά c. genit.] [sch.-progr.] 8° *Strehlen* 93
SCHMIDT, Phil. — Die Syntax des Historikers Herodian, 2 pts. [school-progr.] 4° *Gütersloh* 91 : 93

Herodotus [B.C. 490(–80)–*c.* 424].

Historiae : bk. iii. : w. English notes and Introd. G. C. Macaulay [Classical Series] 2/6 (60*c.*) f 8° Macmillan 91
bk. v.–vi. [Terpsichore and Erato] : with English notes and Intro. Dr. Evelyn Abbott ; maps 8° 10/6 Clar. Press / $2.75 *nt.* Macmillan, *N.Y.* 93
The text of STEIN [*ut* B.B. K § 192], w. full and instructive notes, giving the latest historical results. Appendices on Cleomenes, on the Alcmaeonidae, on the Tyrants, on hero-worship, *etc.*
bk. vi. : w. Engl. notes and Introd. Prf. J. Strachan ; maps and ill. [Classical Sers.] 3/6 ($1) f 8° Macmillan 91
Forms a good introd. to study of HERODOTUS, for wh. bk. vi. is spec. suited ; and conts. a good acc. of dialect of HERODOTUS. 2 Appendices.
w. Engl. notes and Introd. W. F. Masom + C. Fearnside [Univ. Corr. Coll. Ser.] 3/6 c 8° Clive 90
,, vii. : ,, ,, Agnata F. [= Mrs. Montagu] Butler 3/6 (50*c.*) f 8° Macmillan 91
,, viii. ,, ,, and Introd. E. S. Shuckburgh [Pitt Press Series] f 8° 4/- Camb. Press / $1.10 *nt.* Macmillan, *N.Y.* 93
,, ,, [Artemisium and Salamis] : w. Engl. notes and Introd. E. S. Shuckburgh [Pitt Press Series] f 8° 2/6 Camb. Press / 60*c. nt.* Macmillan, *N.Y.* 93
,, ,, ,, ,, ,, ,, J. Thompson + R. M. Thomas [Univ. Corr. Coll. Tut. Ser.] 5/6 c 8° Clive 93
,, ix. 1–89 [Platæa] : w. Engl. notes and Introd. E. S. Shuckburgh [Pitt Press Series] f 8° 2/6 Camb. Press / 60*c. nt.* Macmillan, *N.Y.* 93
,, ,, ,, ,, ,, E. S. Shuckburgh [Pitt Press Series] f 8° 4/- Camb. Press / $1.10 *nt.* Macmillan, *N.Y.* 93

Translations.

Histories : tr. Hy. Carey ; w. geogr. and gen. index [fr. text of Baehr ; Lubbock's 100 Best Bks.] c 8° 3/6 Routledge [ ] 92 / $1.50 Harper, *N.Y.* [ ]
Euterpe : Englished by R. R. [1584], ed. Andr. Lang [Bibliothèque de Carabas] 10/- *nt.* 8° Nutt 88

Aids. —*v. also supra, sub voc.* Generally (WEHMANN).

ADAM, Rud. — De Herodoti Ratione Historica Quaestiones selectae [on Salamis and Plataea] [diss.] 8° Heinrich, *Berlin* 90
AMBHEIN, Wilh. — De abundanti Genere dicendi Herod. et Thucyd. Quaestt. select. [diss.] 8° *Marburg* 93
FÖRSTEMANN, Albr. W. — De Vocabulis quae videntur esse apud Herod. poeticis 1*m.*20 8° Creutz, *Magdeburg* 92
FRIES, K. — Quaestiones Herodoteae 1*m.*20 8° Heinrich, *Berlin* 93
HAUVETTE, Amédée — Hérodote : historien des guerres médiques 10*fr.* 8° Hachette, *Paris* 94
A useful summary and criticism of recent Germ. and French Herodotean investigation and speculation, however minute (of English the author seems to be almost entirely ignorant). Its general result is liberal-conservative ; its key-note scholarly commonsense.
KLEBER, Paul — De Genere Dicendi Herodoteo Quaestiones selectae [diss. inaug.] 4° *Erlangen* 90
MACLAREN, Jno. W. H. — Studia Herodotea [Rostock dissert. inaug.] 8° *Oxford* 88
RODEMEYER, Karl Theod. — Das Praesens Historicum bei Herodot u Thukydides [diss. inaug.] 1*m.*60 8° *Basle* (Fock, *Lpz.*) 89
SCHUBERT, Rud. — Herodots Darstellung der Cyrussage 2*m.*40 8° Koebner, *Breslau* 90
STOURAC, Frz. — Ueber den Gebrauch d. Genitivus bei Herodot [schl.-progr.] 8° *Olmütz* 84

Pausanias [A.D. 2nd cent.].

Descriptio Arcis Athenarum : rec. Otto Jahn [1860], ed. Ad. Michaelis ; 2 pl. 1*m.*80 8° Marcus, *Bonn* 80

Translation.

Attica : tr. Marg. de Verrall, *sub tit.* Monuments and Mythology of Ancient Athens—*ut* B § 12.
With an introd. essay and sort of archæolog. commentary, elucidating the mythol. of Athens, by [Miss] Jane C. HARRISON.

Aids.

EBELING, Herm. L. [Am.] — Study in the Sources of Messeniaca of Pausanias [diss.] 8° Johns Hopk. Univ., *Baltim.* 93
GURLITT, Wilh. — Ueber Pausanias : Untersuchungen 10*m.* 8° Leuschner, *Graz* 90
HEBERDEY, Rud. — Die Reisen d. Pausanias in Griechenld. [Abhgn. d. Arch.-Epig. Sem. Wien] 10*m.* r 8° Tempsky, *Vienna* 94
IMHOOF-BLUMER + GARDNER, F./Prf. P. Numismatic Commentary on Pausanias, 3 pts.—*ut* G § 20.
IMMERWAHR, W. — Die Lakonika des Pausanias auf ihre Quellen untersucht 3*m.* 8° Mayer & Müller, *Berl.* 89
KALKMANN, A. — Pausanias der Perieget : Unters. üb. s. Schriftstellerei u. Quellen 8*m.* 8° Reimer, *Berlin* 86
KRITZ, Ed. — De Praepositionis ὑπέρ apud Pausaniam Usu locali [diss. inaug.] 8° *Freiburg i.-B.* 91
RUGER, Ant. — Die Präpositionen bei Pausanias : Beitrag zur histor. Syntax [diss. inaug.] 8° *Bamberg* 89

Plutarch [A.D. *c.* 50–*c.* 120].

Vitae :
Brutus : w. German notes R. Paukstadt 1*m.*30 8° F. A. Perthes, *Gotha* 93
Demosthenes : *w. English notes and Introd. Dr. Hub. A. Holden [Pitt Press Series] f 8° 4/6 Camb. Press / $1.25 *nt.* Macmillan, *N.Y.* 93
An excellent edn. ; w. introd. giving a good succinct sketch of DEMOSTHENES' life, and *index graecitatis.*
Gracchi : w. English notes and Introd. G. E. Underhill ; indices c 8° 4/6 Clar. Press / $1.25 *nt.* Macmillan, *N.Y.* 92
Pericles : ,, ,, ,, Dr. Hub. A. Holden [Classical Series] 4/- f 8° Macmillan 94
Themistocles : w. English notes Dr. Hub. A. Holden [*ut* B.B. K § 892] : new ed. (rewritten) [Classical Ser.] 3/6 (90*c.*) f 8° Macmillan [81] 92

Translation: Romane Questions: tr. Philemon Holland [1603], ed. Fk. B. Jevons—*ut* B § 14.

Aids.

PRASSE, Ant. De Plutarchi quae feruntur Vitis decem Oratorum [diss. inaug.] 8° *Marburg* 91
SCHWARTZ, Wold. Quibus Fontibus Plutarchus in Vita L. Aemilii Paulli usus sit [diss.] 8° *Leipzig* 91
WACHENDORF, Hugo Observationes criticae in nonnullos locos Plutarchi [schl.-prog.] 4° *Düsseldorf* 90

Polybius [B.C. *c.* 204–122].

Historiae: rec. Friedr. Hultsch; w. crit. app. [*ut* B.B. K § 192]: new ed., vol. i. 4*m.* 50; ii. 6*m.* 8° Weidm., *Berl.* [67] 88; [71] 92
" ed. Theod. Büttner-Wobst, vols. i.–iii. ea. 3*m.* 60 8° Teubner, *Lps.* 82; 89; 93
BRIEF, Siegm. Die Conjunctionen bei Polybius [school-programme] 8° *Vienna* 91
HULTSCH, Friedr. Die erzählenden Zeitformen b. Polybios, i. 7*m.*; ii. 3*m.* 60; iii. 3*m.* 60 [*extr. fr.* Abh. Sächs. Ak.] r 8° Hirzel, *Lps.* 91; 92; 93

Ptolemy [B.C. 366–283].

BOLL Studien über Ptolemaeus Teubner, *Lps.* *in prep.*

Strabo [B.C. 66–21(–25)].

Selections: w. Engl. notes and Introd. Rev. H. F. Tozer; maps and plans 8° 12/- Clar. Press / $3 *net.* Macmillan, *N.Y.* 93

An instructive series of passages, sel. by one who is himself an experienced traveller in classic lands; w. good Introd. on STRABO'S life and wks.

DUBOIS, Marcel Examen de la Géographie de Strabon 12*fr.* 8° Colin, *Paris* 91
KUNZE, Rich. Symbolae Strabonianae [dissert. inaug.] 8° *Leipzig* 92

A critical examination of STRABO'S methods and sources.

MEYER, Paul Straboniana [school-programme] 1*m.* 4° Gensel, *Grimma* 90
MILLER, Ant. Die Alexandergeschichte nach Strabo, 2 pts. 4*m.* 4° Stahel, *Würzburg* 90; 92
SERBIN, A. Bemerkungen Strabo's üb. d. Vulkanismus u. vulkan. Gebiete [schl.-progr.] 1*m.* 20 8° *Berlin* (Fock, *Lps.*) 93
STEMPLINGER, E. Strabons litterhistorische Notizen 2*m.* 8° Ackermann, *Munich* 93

Thucydides [B.C. 471–*c.* 395].

Historiae: bk. i.: w. English notes W. H. Forbes f 8° Clar. Press / Macmillan, *N.Y.* *in prep.*
" " " Prf. C. D. Morris [Am.] [Coll. Ser. of Gk.; based on Classen] sq 8° $1.75 Ginn, *Boston* / 7/6 Arnold 87
" German " J Sitzler 2*m.* 10 8° F. A. Perthes, *Gotha* 91
*" " " Franz Müller, 2*m.* 40; School Edn. 1*m.* 8° Schöningh, *Paderborn* 93; 93
bk. ii: " English " and Introd. E. C. Marchant [Classical Sers.] [good] 3/6 (90*c.*) f 8° Macmillan 91
w. German " J. Sitzler 1*m.* 80 8° F. A. Perthes, *Gotha* 92
" ii.–iii. [Fall of Plataea; Plague at Athens]: w. Engl. notes W. T. Sutthery + A. S. Graves [Elem. Classics] 1/6 (40*c.*) f 8° Macmillan 94
[Siege of Plataea]: with English notes Jno. M. Ling 1/6 f 8° Rivington & Perc. 93
" iv.: w. English notes C. E. Graves [Classical Series] [good] 3/6 (90*c.*) 8° Macmillan
" v.: " " " Prf. Har. N. Fowler [Am.] [Coll. Ser. of Gk. Auth.] sq 8° $1.50 Ginn, *Boston* / 6/- Arnold 88
" " " and Introd. C. E. Graves [Classical Series] [good] 3/6 (90*c.*) f 8° Macmillan 91
" vi.–viii.: rec. Dr. Carl Hude; w. very full crit. appar. 5/- 8° Gyldendahl, *Copenh.* 92

An accurate and judicious text of the last 3 Bks., based on a personal collatn. of the 7 princ. MSS. *etc.*

" vi. w. German notes J. Sitzler 1*m.* 20 8° F. A. Perthes, *Gotha* 88
" " " Franz Müller, 1*m.* 80; School Edn. 1*m.* 8° Schöningh, *Paderborn* 88; 88
" vii.: *w. English notes, revised text and Introd. Dr. Hub. A. Holden; maps f 8° 5/- Camb. Press / $1.50 *net.* Macmillan, *N.Y.* 91

A compreh. and lucid edn. of THUCYDIDES' masterpiece: prob. as elaborate an edn. of a single bk. as exists in the Engl. lang. Pitt Press Series. Also in 2 pts.: i. *Introd. and Text*: ii. *Notes and Indexes.*

w. English notes and Introd. E. C. Marchant [Classical Series] 3/6 ($1.10) f 8° Macmillan 93
" " " " J. F. Stout + F. G. Plaistowe [Univ. Corr. Coll. Tut. Ser.] 4/6 8° Clive 91
" German notes J. Sitzler 1*m.* 80 8° F. A. Perthes, *Gotha* 89
" " " Franz Müller, 1*m.* 80; School Edn. 1*m.* 8° Schöningh, *Paderborn* 89; 89
" viii: " " " " Prf. H. C. Goodhart [Class. Lib.] 9/- ($1.90) *net.* f 8° Macmillan 93
" " " " and comm. Prf. T. G. Tucker [Austral.] [Class Ser.] 3/6 ($1) c 8° " 92

Both the above edns. of bk. viii. are good edns. The notes of the former deal fully w. both textual and historical points, of the latter mainly with linguistic. Both strenuously maintain the genuineness of this often-despised bk.

Aids. —*v. also supra, sub voc.* Generally (SCHMIDT, WEHMANN).

BUDINGER, Max Poesie u. Urkunde b. Thukydides, pt. i. 2*m.* 60; ii. 4*m.* 20 [*extr. fr.* Denkschr. Wien. Akad.] r 4° Tempsky, *Vienna* 90; 91
HERBST, Ludw. Zu Thukydides: Erklärungen u. Wiederherstlgn.: bks. i.–iv. 2*m.* 80; v.–viii. 3*m.* 60 8° Teubner, *Lps.* 92; 93
LANGE, Edm. Thukydides und sein Geschichtswerk: 3 pl. [Gymnasial Bibliothek] 1*m.* 8° Bertelsmann, *Gütersloh* 93
SCHRADER, H. De archaeologiae Thucydideae apud veteres scriptores auctoritate 1*m.* 60 8° Herold, *Hamburg* 91

Language.

DIENER, Oswald De Sermone Thuc. quatenus cum Herod. congruens differat a scriptt. attic 1*m.* 20 8° Gräfe, *Lps.* 89
EISMANN, Paul De Participii Temporum usu Thucydideo [schl.-progr.] 8° *Inowraslaw* 90
KOHN, Max De Usu Adjectiv. et Particip. pro Substantivis, item Substantivorum Verbalium ap. Thuc. 1*m.* 8° Mayer & Müller, *Berl.* 91
REINHARDT, Reinhold De infinitivi cum articulo conjuncti usu Thucydideo [schl.-progr.] 1*m.* 4° *Oldenbg.* (Fock, *Lps.*) 91

Timaeus [B.C. 352–256].

Aid.

GEFFCKEN, Joh. Timaios Geographie des Westens; 2 pl. [= Philolog. Untersuchungen, pt. xiii.] 7*m.* 8° Weidmann, *Berlin* 92

K § 193

Xenophon [B.C. *c.* 431–*c.* 355].

Agesilaus : w. German notes Otto Güthling 1*m*.50 8° Teubner, *Lpz.* 88
Anabasis : rec. Dr. Friedr. Gust. Sorof, vol. i.: Text " " *in prep.*
" w. English notes and vocab. M. J. F. Brackenbury ; map 2/- Percival (Riv. & Perc.) 92
bk. i.: " " " and Introd. A. H. Allcroft + F. L. D. Richardson [Univ. Corr. Coll. Tut. Ser.] 1/6 ; w. Tr. 3/- c 8° Clive 92 ; 92
" i.–ii.: " " " " Alf. Pretor ; map [Pitt Press Series] f 8° 2/- Camb. Press / $1.10 *nt.* Macmillan, *N.Y.* 93
" i.–iv.: " " " " Irving J. Manatt [Am.] 12° $1 Ginn, *Boston* / 5/- Arnold 88
" " " German " " Dr. Friedr. Gust. Sorof ; map and ill. 1*m*.20 8° Teubner, *Lps.* 93
" iii.–iv. " English " " Dr. J. Marshall [Clar. Press Series] f 8° 3/- Clar. Press / 75*c. nt.* Macmillan, *N.Y.* 92
" iv.: " " " " Rev. E. D. Stone; vocab. [Element. Classics] 1/6 (40*c.*) 18° Macmillan 90
" vi.: " " " " Rev. G. H. Nall ; vocab. and map [Element. Classics] 1/6 (40*c.*) 18° Macmillan 93
Cyropædia : textum const. C. G. Cobet, ed. C. C. Mauve 2*m*.15 8° Brill, *Leyden* 93
bks. vi.–viii.: w. English notes and index Dr. Hub. A. Holden [Pitt Press Series] f 8° 5/- Camb. Press / $1.10 *nt.* Macmillan, *N.Y.* 90
Tales fr. Cyropædia : w. English notes Chas. Haines Keene ; vocab. [Element. Classics] 1/6 (40*c.*) 18° Macmillan 93
Hellenica :
bks. i.; ii.: w. English notes and analysis Rev. L. D. Dowdall [Camb. Texts w. notes] f 8° ea. 2/- Bell / ea. 40*c.* Macmillan, *N.Y.* 91
" iii.: " " " and Introd. A. H. Allcroft + F. L. D. Richardson [Univ. Corr. Coll. Tut. Ser.] 3/6 c 8° Clive 93
" iv.: " " " A. Waugh Young [Univ. Corr. Coll. Tut. Ser.] 3/6 c 8° " 94
" v.–vii.: " " " Prf. Chas. E. Bennett [Am.] [bas. on Büchsenschütz] [Coll. Ser. of Gk. Auth.] sq 8° $1.50 Ginn, *Boston* / 6/- Arnold 92
Memorabilia : w. English notes and Introd. Dr. J. Marshall f 8° 4/6 Clar. Press / $1.10 *nt.* Macmillan, *N.Y.* 90
Selections : Anab. and Hell. in Auswahl, w. Germ. notes Friedr. Gust. Sorof, pt. i. [Anab. 1–4] 1*m*.20; ii. [5–7 and Hell.] 2*m*. 8° Teubner, *Lps.* 93 ; 94
Translations: *Works: tr. H. G. Dakyns; w. Introds. & notes, vols. ii.–iii.; maps & plans ea. 10/6 ($2.50) 8° Macmillan 92 ; 94

An accurate, careful, and enthusiastic tr. of the whole wks., w. very full and useful annotatns., Introds., and analyses. Vol. ii. incl. *Hellenica iii.–vii.* [w. a good estimate of X.'s posn. am. the historns. of Athens] and the rest of the wks. bearing on history proper, *viz.*, the two Polities—the "Athenian" and the "Laconian"—the *Agesilaus*, and the tract on the *Revenues* or *Ways and Means*; vol. iii. the *Memorab.* and *Apology*, the *Economist*, the *Symposium*, *Hiero*, *Cynegeticus*, Περὶ ἱππικῆς, and *Hipparchicus*.

Anabasis : tr. Frances Younghusband, *sub tit.* Retreat of the Ten Thousand. *ut* F § 10.
bk. i.: tr. A. H. Allcroft + F. L. D. Richardson—*in their edn of the text, ut supra.*
Art of Horsemanship : tr. Dr. Morris H. Morgan [Am.]—*ut* I § 152.
Hellenica, bks. iii.–iv.: tr. A. H. Allcroft + A. Waugh Young [Univ. Corr. Coll. Tut. Ser.] 2/6 c 8° Clive 94
Memorabilia : tr. Edw. Levien, *sub tit.* Memoirs of Socrates [Bayard Series] 2/6 16° Low [72] 92

Aids.
Generally —*v. also supra, sub voc.* Collectively (SCHMIDT, WEHMANN).
HARTMAN, Dr. J. J. Analecta Xenophontea Nova 10/6 8° *Leyden* 89
LÖNEBERG, Heinr. De Xenoph. Aetate quid ex Anab. statui possit Commentatio [diss. inaug.] 8° *Munich* 92
RICHTER, Ernst Xenophon-Studien [*extr. fr.* Jahrb. f. Class. Philol.] 2*m*.40 8° Teubner, *Lps.* 92
SIMON, Joh. Alph. Xenophon-Studien, pts. i.–iv. [school-progrs.] 4*m*.80 4° Fock, *Lps.* 87–89
Anabasis.
HOLLAENDER, L. Kunaxa : historisch-krit. Beiträge z. Erklärung v. Xenophons Anabasis [schl.-prg.] 1*m*.20 8° Fock, *Lps.* 93
SICKINGER, A. Beitrag z. Verständniss d. Xenophont. Anab. u. d. altgriech. Taktik [progr.] 80*pf.* 4° *Bruchsal* (Fock, *Lps.*) 93
Memorabilia.
BIRT, Theod. De Xenophontis Commentariorum Socraticorum Compositione 1*m*. 4° Elwert, *Marburg* 93
JOEL, Karl Der echte und der xenophontische Sokrates, vol. i. [in 2 vols.] 14*m*. 8° Gaertner, *Berlin* 93
LINCKE, K. De Xenophontis Libris Socraticis 1*m*. 4° Frommann, *Jena* 90
Language. Manuscripts.
BUCHWALD, F. Ueber d. Sprachgebrauch Xenophons in d. Hellenika [schl.-progr.] 4° *Görlitz* 92
EICHLER, G. Die Redebilder in den Schriften Xenophons [school-programme] 1*m*.20 Fock, *Lps.* 94
JOOST, Art. Was ergiebt sich aus d. Sprachgebrauch Xenophon's in d. Anab. f. d. Behdg. d. Syntax 8*m*. Weidmann, *Berlin* 92
JORIO, G. [ed.] Codici Ignorati nelle Biblioteche di Napoli, pt. i. 3*m*.50 8° Harrassowitz, *Lps.* 92

This pt. conts. Ξενοφῶντος τὰ παραλειπόμενα.

LEHNER, Fr. X. Der Infinitiv bei Xenophon [school-programme] 8° *Freistadt* 91
TETZNER, R. Der Gebrauch des Infinitivs in Xenophons Anabasis [schl.-progr.] 8° *Doberan* 91
Dictionaries.
DE BOER, C. Z. Woordenboek op Xenophons Anabasis 2*fl*.50 8° Campagne, *Tiel* 93
HANSEN, Reiner Wörterbuch zu Xenophons Anabasis und Hellenika 1*m*.60 8° F. A. Perthes, *Gotha* 89
MEHLER, E. Woordenboek op de Anabasis van Xenophon 2*fl*.25 8° van der Post, *Utrecht* 94
STRACK, Herm. L. Vollständiges Wörterbuch zu Xenophons Kyropädie 2*m*.25 8° Hahn, *Lps.* [81] 92
WHITE + MORGAN, J. W. M. H. [Ams.] Illustrated Dictionary to Xenophon's Anabasis 12° $1.25 Ginn, *Boston* / 6/- Arnold 93

193. GREEK ORATORS.

Æschines [B.C. 389–314].

In Ctesiphontem : w. Eng. notes & indices, Rev. T. Gwatkin + E. S. Shuckburgh [Class. Ser.] 5/- ($1.10) f 8° Macmillan 90
" " " Prf. Rufus B. Richardson [Am.]; w. proleg. [based on Weidner] [Coll. Ser. Gk. Auth.] 12° $1.50 Ginn, *Boston* / 6/- Arnold 89

Antiphon [B.C. 480–411].

HAUSEN, Friedr. De Antiphontis Tetralogiis [programme] 1*m*. 4° Gaertner, *Berlin* 92

Choricius Gazæus.
Orationes : rec. Foerster 8° Teubner, *Lpz.* 94

Demosthenes [B.C. 384–322].
Orationes : rec. Wilh. Dindorf, cur. Friedr. Blass, vol. ii.–iii. ea. 2*m*.40 ; Ed. Minor, ea. 1*m*.50 8° Teubner, *Lpz.* [50–51] 88 ; 89
De Corona : w. German notes, C. Rehdantz + F. Blass 2*m*.10 8° Teubner, *Lpz.* 90
„ French „ E. Sommer 3*fr*.50 12° Hachette, *Paris* 91
„ Latin „ J. H. Lipsius 1*m*.60 8° Teubner, *Lpz.* 87
Pro Megalopolit. Libertate : w. German notes and tr. W. Fox 4*m*.50 ; School Edn. 50*pf*. 8° Herder, *Freiburg* 90 ; 90
Selections : w. German notes Ant. Westermann, *sub tit.* Ausgewählte Reden, vol. i. 2*m*.25 8° Weidmann, *Berl.* 91

Translations.
Adversus Leptinem : tr. F. E. A. Hayes [Univ. Corr. Coll. Tut. Series] 2/6 c 8° Clive 93
De Corona : tr. Ld. Brougham, *sub tit.* Oration upon the Crown ; w. notes [Lubbock's 100 Best Bks.] 2/6 ($1) c 8° Routledge [40] 93
Pro Megalopolit. : libera. W. Fox—*in his edn. of the text, ut supra.*

Aids.
Harry, J. E. [Am.] A Rhetorical Study of the Leptinean Orations [thesis] 8° Johns Hopk. Univ., *Baltimore* 91
Rabe, Alb. Die Redaktion der demosthenischen Kranzrede 1*m*.20 8° Dieterich, *Göttingen* 92
Schwartz, Prf. E. Demosthenes erste Philippika [*extr. fr.* Festschrift f. Mommsen, *ut* K § 168] 1*m*.50 8° Elwert, *Marburg* 94
Wichmann, Carl De Numeris quos adhibuit Demosth. in Orat. Philipp. I. [diss.] 8° *Kiel* 92

Index.
*Preuss, Siegm. Index Demosthenicus 10*m*. 8° Teubner, *Lpz.* 92

Palæography. Manuscript.
Burger, Friedr. Stichometrische Untersuchungen z. Demosthenes u. Herodot [schl.-progr.] 8° *Munich* 92
A contribution to the history of ancient book-production.
Omont, Henri [ed.] Demosth. Codex Σ : facs. du MS. grec 2934 d. l. Bibl. Nat., 2 vols. 600*fr*. f° Leroux, *Paris* 93
A fine heliographic reproduction, on 1,100 plates, of the 10th century codex ; w. 42 pp. of text.

Hermagoras [B.C. 2nd cent.].
Thiele, Geo. Hermagoras : ein Beitrag z. Geschichte d. Rhetorik 6*m*. 8° Trübner, *Strassbg.* 93

Hyperides [B.C. 390–322].
Oration agst. Athenogenes : publ. p. Eug. Revillout ; w. 15 facs. pl. [Corpus Papyrorum Aegypti] 40*fr*. 4° Leroux, *Paris* 92
A new oration discov. in 1888 by edr., who has already pub. a full descr. of it, w. substantially the whole text, in *Revue Egyptologique.*
„ „ *and* Philippides : w. Latin notes [crit.] F. G. Kenyon ; w. Engl. tr. c 8° 5/- *nt.* Bell / $1.60 Macmillan, *N.Y.* 93
A revised text of the two recently discov. speeches, w. palæogr. and histor. Introd. and Engl. tr. *en regard.* Facs. of several pp. of the second oration are contained in *Class. Texts fr. the Brit. Mus.* [*ut* K § 179, *s.n.* Kenyon].

Isocrates [B.C. 436–338].
Panegyrikos : w. German notes Bruno Keil 75*pf*. 8° Freytag, *Lpz.* 90
Translation : Orations : tr. J. H. Freese, w. Introds. and notes, vol. i. [Bohn's Lib.] c 8° 5/- Bell / Macmillan, *N.Y.* 94

Aids.
Höss, Wilh. De Ubertate et Abundantia Sermonis Isocratei [schl.-progr.] 8° *Pforzheim* 92
Koch, Max Der Gebrauch der Präpositionen bei Isokrates, pt. i. [school-programme] 1*m*. 4° Gaertner, *Berlin* 89
Reuss, Prf. Friedr. Isokrates Panegyrikus und der kyprische Krieg [school-programme] 80*pf*. 4° Fock, *Lpz.* 94

Lysias [B.C. *c.* 445–362].
Selections : w. English notes W. A. Stevens [Am.] $1.50 12° Griggs, *Chicago* [76] 78
„ „ „ G. P. Bristol [Am.] [10 orations] $1 16° Allyn, *Boston* 92
Devries, Wm. Levering [Am.] Ethopoiia : rhetor. study of types of char. in Lysias [diss.] 8° Johns Hopk. Univ., *Baltimore* 93
Erdmann, Mart. Lysiaca [school-programme] 4° *Strassburg* 91
Pabst, Otto Rud. De Orat. ὑπὲρ τοῦ στρατιώτου causa, authentia, integritate 8° *Leipzig* 91

194. GREEK PHILOSOPHERS.

Antoninus, M. Aurelius [A.D. 121–180]—*erroneously ref. in* C § 11 *to here : no new text is issued.*

Aristotle [B.C. 384–322].
Athenaion Politeia :
Blass, Friedr. [ed.] Aristotelis Πολιτεία Ἀθηναίων 1*m*.50 8° Teubner, *Lpz.* 92
British Museum : Facsimile of the Athenaion Politeia of Aristotle [by autotype process] 42/- 4° British Museum 91
The *Editio Princeps.* The MS. consists of four rolls of papyrus : longest 7 ft., shortest 3 ft. It is no. cxxxi. in Brit. Mus. papyri. To Mr. Kenyon is due the largest share in its discovery, wh. is without a parallel for importance since the memorable discov. in 16th cent. of 5 bks. of Tacitus' *Annals* in the libr. of a Germ. monastery.
„ „ Text of the Athenaion Politeia of Aristotle—*v.* Kenyon, *infra.*
Ferrini, C. [ed.] Aristotelis Ἀθηναίων Πολιτεία [w. Latin tr. and a few notes in Italian] 3*l*.50 16° Hoepli, *Milan* 91
An excellent text : based on those of Kenyon, Herwerden and Blass, incorporating some of the best readings of each.
van Herwerden + van Leeuwen, H.; J. [eds.] Aristotelis De Republica Atheniensium [after Kenyon] 6/- 8° Sijthoff, *Leyden* 91
Kaibel + v. Wilamowitz-Moellendorf, G.; U. [eds.] Aristotelis Πολιτεία Ἀθηναίων 1*m*.80 8° Weidmann, *Berlin* 91
Kenyon, F. G. [ed.] Aristotle's Athenaion Politeia ; w. notes and Introd. 8° 10/6 Brit. Mus. / $3.50 Macmillan, *N.Y.* [91] 92
*Sandys, Dr. Jno. Edwin [ed.] Aristotle's Constitution of Athens ; w. notes etc. ; front. [Class. Lib.] 15/- ($3.75 *nt.*) 8° Macmillan 92
The latest, most elaborate and most competent edn. so far published, w. revised text, Introd. (on authorship, abstr. of contents and review of liter. of subj. [8 edns., 14 trs. and 135 articles]), crit. and explan. notes, testimonia [evid. fr. Gk. lexicographers, scholiasts, *etc.*] indices. The edr. spec. brings out the importance of the treatise for the constit. hist. and for the legal antiqs. of Athens.

K § 194

Ethica Nicomachea: rec. Prf. Ingram Bywater [also 10/6, 4°] 8° 4/- Clar. Press; $1.50 nt. Macmillan, N.Y. 90

A new and exceedingly accurate and sound text of the *Ethics*; very conservative, but with good emendations, mostly small. A brief *Adnotatio Critica* at foot of each page records the more import. variants of Kb (the Laurentian MS., on wh. this edn. is based), as well as the rgs. taken by BEKKER fr. the inferior class of MSS. *Index Verborum* (40 pp.) conts. 6,000 references.

" " ed. Prf. Ingram Bywater [Clar. Press Ser.] f 8° 3/6 Clar. Press; 90c. nt. Macmillan, N.Y. 94

Physica, bk. vii.: ed. R. Shute; w. Introd. [Anecdota Oxon.] s 4° 2/- Clar. Press; 50c. nt. Macmillan, N.Y.

Poetica: rec. Prf. Ingram Bywater

Politica: w. English notes and Introd. W. L. Newman—erroneously referred to as here: *v.* **B.B.** K § 194.

Translations —*v. also* C § 9.

Oeuvres: trad. J. Barthélemy Saint-Hilaire many vols.; at var. prices 8° var. pubs., *Paris* 39–70

" " " Table Alphab. des Matières, 2 vols. ea. 15*fr.* 8° Alcan, *Paris* 92

Athenaion Politeia:

Dymes, Thos. J. [tr.] Aristotle's Constitution of Athens 2/6 c 8° Seeley 91

Erdmann, Mart. [tr.] Der Athenerstaat: eine aristotel. Schrift, übersetzt 1*m*.60 8° Neumann, *Lpz.* 92

Ferrini, C. [tr.] —*in his edn. of the text, ut supra* [Italian tr.].

Haussoullier, B. [tr.] Constitution d'Athènes [Bibl. Ecole Htes. Etudes] 8° Bouillon, *Paris* 91

Kaibel + Kiessling, Geo. Adf. [trs.] Aristoteles Schrift vom Staatswesen der Athener: verdeutscht 2*m.* s 8° Trübner, *Strassburg* [91] 91

*Kenyon, F. G. [tr.] Aristotle on the Athenian Constitution: transl.; w. Introd., notes and facs. p 8° 4/6 Bell; $1.10 Macmillan, N.Y. 91

L.P. (1891) 10/- *nt.* The Introd., commentary and notes define the bearing of the new inform. on previously received notions of the hist. and polity of Athens. Regards the treatise as bg. "at least the outcome of ARISTOTLE'S inspiration and direction." Index.

Poste, E. [tr.] Aristotle on the Constitution of Athens: transl. & [slightly] annotated 3/6 ($1) c 8° Macmillan [91] 92

The 2nd edn. (1892) has a new Preface, in defence of Aristot. authorship of the treatise, explans. of techn. terms, and an outline of legal procedure in Athens.

*Reinach, Théod. [tr.] La République Athénienne d'Aristote 1*fr.*50 8° Hachette, *Paris* 91

The clearest, most accurate and cheapest tr., incl. an attempt at reconstrn. of text, and a brief but pregnant Introd. Claims the wk. as ARISTOTLE'S; but admits interpolation of much alien matter.

Saint-Hilaire, J. Barthélemy [tr.]—*in his* Problèmes d'Aristot., *ut infra.*

Metaphysica: übers. Herm. Bonitz, hrsg. Ed. Wellmann [posthum. edited] 6*m.* 8° G. Reimer, *Berlin* 90

Politica: übers. Garves, hrsg. Mor. Brasch; w. Germ. Introd. and notes 3*m.* 8° Pfeffer, *Halle* 93

Aids.

HUIT, Chas. La Vie et l'Oeuvre de Platon, 2 vols. 8° Thorin, *Paris* 93

NORDSTRÖM, V. Quaestiones Aristotelicae, · pt. i. ; ii. 1*m*.20 8° *Helsingfors* (Weber, *Berl.*) 92; 93

ROLFES, Eug. Die aristot. Auffassung v. Verhältn. Gottes z. Welt u. Menschen 3*m.* 8° Mayer & Müller, *Berl.* 92

SAINT-HILAIRE, J. Barthélemy Les Problèmes d'Aristote (Fch. tr., w. running comm.) 20*fr.* 8° Hachette, *Paris* 91

SCHVARCZ, Julius Kritik der Staatsformen des Aristoteles 3*m*.60 r 8° Bacmeister, *Eisenach* [ ] 90

SUSEMIHL, Prf. Frz. Quaestionum Aristotelearum crit. et exeget. pars i. 1*m*.50 4° *Greifswald* (Calvary, *Berl.*) 92

Athenaion Politeia.

BAUER, Adf. Literarische und historische Forschungen zu Aristoteles 'Αθηναίων Πολιτεία [favours Aristot. authorship] 3*m.* 8° Beck, *Munich* 91

CASSEL, Paulus Vom neuen Aristoteles und seiner Tendenz 80*pf.* 8° Bibl. Bureau, *Berlin* 91

CAUER, Friedr. Hat Aristoteles die Schrift vom Staate der Athener geschrieben? 1*m.* 8° Göschen, *Stuttgart* 91

Strongly opposed to the view that the wk. is ARISTOTLE'S; but believes it is that cited in antiquity as his. Clever and suggestive.

DROYSEN, Hans Zu Aristoteles' 'Αθηναίων Πολιτεία [school-programme] 1*m.* 4° Gaertner, *Berlin* 91

ERDMANN, M. Der Athenerstaat: eine aristotelische Schrift 1*m*.60 8° Neumann, *Lpz.* 92

GOMPERZ, Theod. Die Schrift vom Staatswesen der Athener u. ihr neuester Beurtheiler 1*m*.20 8° Hölder, *Vienna* 91

GRUNZEL, J. Aristoteles und die 'Αθηναίων Πολιτεία 1*m.* 8° Friedrich, *Lpz.* 91

HELLER, Mart. Quibus Auctt. Arist. in Repub. Athen. conscribenda et qua ratione usus sit 1*m*.50 8° Mayer & Müller, *Berl.* 93

KAIBEL, G. Stil und Text der Πολιτεία 'Αθηναίων des Aristoteles 8*m.* 8° Weidmann, *Berlin* 93

A valuable discussn. of the language and style; w. a commentary on the text: learned and fresh, and very polemical.

KEIL, Bruno Die Solonische Verfassung in Aristoteles' Verfassungsgeschichte Athens 6*m.* 8° Gaertner, *Berlin* 92

MEYER, Peter Des Aristoteles Politik und die 'Αθηναίων Πολιτεία 1*m*.20 8° Cohen, *Bonn* 91

RÜHL, Frz. Der Staat d. Athener u. sein Ende [*extr. fr.* Jahrb. Class. Philol.] 1*m*.20 8° Teubner, *Lpz.* 91

SCHVARCZ, Julius Aristoteles und die Schrift vom Staate der Athener 1*m.* 8° 91

Regards DEMETRIUS OF PHALERUM as the author.

v. WILAMOWITZ-MOELLENDORF, Ulr. Aristoteles und Athen 20*m.* 8° Weidmann, *Berlin* 93

An attempt to see how the problems of Athen. constit. hist. look when consid. afresh fr. the stdpt. of the *Athen. Polit.*

Ethics: Nicomachean —*v. also* C § 9 (STEWART).

BYWATER, Prf. Ingram Contribs. to Textual Criticism of Aristotle's Nicomachean Ethics 2/6 8° Clar. Press 92

Affords reasons wh. led author to diverge in his edn. of the *Ethics*, *ut sup.*, in so many passages fr. the received text. Confirms the conviction of the soundness of the edn. itself. He (in common w. many recent scholars) assigns the first place in importance among the MSS. of the *Ethics* to the Laurentian MS. (Kb).

Metaphysics.

BULLINGER, A. Aristoteles Metaphysik in Bezug a. Entstehg., Text u. Gedanken 4*m.* 8° Ackermann, *Munich* 92

With an Introd. on ARISTOTLE'S theory of the will, and an epilogue on Pantheism and Christendom.

Poetics —*v.* C § 9 (BUTCHER, PRICKARD).

ADAM, Dr. Ludw. Die Aristot. Theorie v. Epos n. ihre. Entwickel. b. Griechen u. Römern 3*m.* 8° Limbarth, *Wiesbaden* 89

BUTCHER, Prf. S. H. —*has in prep. a treat. on the* Poetics, *to incorpor. his essay incl. in 1st ed. of his* Some Aspects [*ut* K § 187].

OMONT, Henri [ed.] La Poëtique d'Aristote: MS. 1741 d. Fonds Grec d. l. Bibl. Nat. 17*fr.* s 4° Leroux, *Paris*

Education —*v.* D § 160 (DAVIDSON).

Language. Style.

HAUFORS, Edvin De Praepositionum in Aristotelis Politicis et in Ath. Polit. usu [diss.] 8° *Helsingfors* (2*m.* Mayer & M., *Berl.*) 91

Dictionary.

KAPPES, Matthias Aristoteles-Lexicon 1*m*.50 8° Schöningh, *Paderborn* 94

An explanation of the *termini technici* of ARISTOTLE.

Textual Criticism. Gk. and Oriental Translations and Commentaries.

Commentaria in Aristotelem Graeca: ed. consilio Acad. Litt. Reg. Boruss. 4° G. Reimer, *Berlin* 91–93

i. ALEXANDER APHROD. *In Arist. Metaphys. Comm.*, ed. Mich. HAYDUCK, 22*m.* '91; ii. (2) ALEX. APHROD. *In Arist. Topicorum libros Octo Comm.*, ed. Max WALLIES, 16*m.* '91; iv. (3) AMMONIUS *in Porphyrii Isagogen*, ed. Ad. BUSSE, 7*m.* '91; xx. EUSTRATIUS and MICHAELIS *et anon. comm. in Eth. Nic.*, ed. Gust. HEYLBUT, 24*m.* '92.

CONYBEARE, Fred. C. [ed.] Collation w. the Ancient Armenian Versions of Gk. Text of Aristotle's Categories [Anecdota Oxon.] s 4° 12/- Clar. Press; Macmillan, N.Y. 92

De Interpretatione, De Mundo, De Virtutibus et Vitiis, and PORPHYRY'S *Introduction*.

HOFFMAN, I. G. E. De Hermeneuticis apud Syros Aristotelicis, syriace, arabice, graec. et lat.; w. glossary 12m. r 8° Hinrichs, *Lps.* 69

MARGOLIOUTH, Prf. D. S. [ed.] Aristotle's Rhetoric: Arabic tr.: w. notes on the Gk. text *in prep.*

Edited from the unique MS. in the Bibl. Nat., Paris.

" " " [ed.] Aristotle's De Pomo: Persian tr. of Arabic text fr. Bodl. MS.; w. Engl. tr.—*in* Jl. Roy. Asiatic Soc. 92

One of the many wks. attrib. to ARISTOTLE. It conts. a philosophical dialogue betw. him and other Greek sages. The Arab. text is not at present known; the Hebr. tr. by ABRAHAM BEN HASDAI, wh. has been prin. several times and tr. into Latin by J. LOSIUS [1706], is a paraphrase rather than a tr.

STEWART, J. A. The English MSS. of the Nicomach. Ethics [Anecdota Oxon.] s 4° 3/6 Clar. Press / 90c. n/. Macmillan, *N.Y.*

Supplementum Aristotelicum, ed. consilio Academiae Litterarum Regiae Borussicae, vol. ii. (2) 13m.; iii. (1) 5m. 8° G. Reimer, *Berlin* 92; 93

& (2) ALEXAND. APHRODISIENSIS *Scripta Minora* (ed. Ivo BRUNS); iii. (1) *Anonymi Londoniensis ex Aristotelis iatricis Menoniis et aliis Medicis Eclogae* (ed. Herm. DIELS).

Philosophy —*v. also* O § 9.

BULLINGER, Ant. Aristoteles Metaphysik in Bezug auf Entstehungsweise 4m. 8° 9–

CALDI, G. Metodologia generale della Interpretazione Scientifica, vol. i.; La Logica di Aristotele 10*l.* 8° Loescher, *Turin* 92

LÖWENTHAL, A. Pseudo-Aristoteles über die Seele 3m. 8° Mayer & Müller, *Berlin* 91

A psychological treatise of the 11th cent., w. discussn. of its relation to AVICEBRON.

ROLFES, Dr. Eug. Die aristotelische Auffassung vom Verhältnisse Gottes zur Welt u. zum Menschen 3m. 8° Mayer & Müller, *Berlin* 92

Acc. to author's views and such evidence as he produces, ARISTOTLE bears witness to the existce. of a personal god, the creator of all things, and the eternal object of man, whose very soul is of divine origin, and over whom the god exercises providence.

Cleanthes [B.C. 3rd cent.]—*v. infra, sub voc.* Zeno.

Democritus [B.C. *c.* 460–*c.* 357].

Fragmenta: coll. rec. vertit explic. F. W. A. Mullach 6m. 8° Besser, *Berlin* 43

Also in the *Philosophorum Graecorum Fragmenta*, ed. MULLACH, vol. i. [1860]—*ut* B.B. K § 194.

rec. Paul Natorp—*in his* Die Ethika des Demokritos, *ut infra*.

Aids.

LIARD, Louis De Democrito Philosopho [thesis] 2/fr. 8° Ladrange, *Paris* 73

LORTZING, F. Ueber die ethischen Fragmente Demokrits [school-programme] 4° *Berlin* 73

NATORP, Paul Die Ethika des Demokritos: Text und Untersuchungen 3m. 8° Elwert, *Marburg* 93

Epictetus [A.D. 1st–2nd cent.].

Dissertationes ab Arriano Digestae: rec. H. Schenkl [fr. Bodleian MS.] 10m. 8° Teubner, *Lps.* 94

Sententiae Epicteti et Moschionis: ed. Ant. Elter [15 pp.] 4° *Bonn* 92

Aids.

ASMUS, Rud. Quaestiones Epicteteae 1m.50 8° Mohr, *Freiburg-i.-Br.* 88

SCHENKL, Heinr. Die Epictetischen Fragmente: eine Untersuchung [reprint] 1m.60 r 8° Tempsky, *Vienna* 88

Epicurus [B.C. 342–268].

THOMAS, P.-M. Félix De Epicuri Canonica [thesis] 3/fr.50 8° Alcan, *Paris* 89

Heraclitus [B.C. *c.* 535–*c.* 475].

WARMBIER, E. Studia Heraclitea 1m. 8° Mayer & Müller, *Berlin* 92

Iamblichus (Chalcidensis) [A.D. 2nd cent.].

De Mysteriis: rec. Gust. Parthey 10m.50 8° Nicolai, *Berlin* 57

For tr. (as well as for tr. of his *De Vita Pythagorica*), v. B.B. C § 15. For his mathem. wks., v. K § 196.

Longinus, Cassius [A.D. 213–273].

De Sublimitate: ed. Otto Jahn [for tr. *v.* C § 15] 1m.60 8° Marcus, *Bonn* 67

Metrodorus [B.C. 330–277; Epicurean].

Fragmenta: coll. A. Körte, scriptoris incerti Epicur. comment. moralem subjecit 2m.40 8° Teubner, *Lps.* 90

Aid.

DÜNING, Herm. H. A. De Metrodori Vita et Scriptis [w. Fragmenta added] 1m.20 8° Teubner, *Lps.* 70

Plato [B.C. 428–348].

Opera: w. Latin notes and prolegg. Dr. Mart. Wohlrab ea. 90pf. to 3m.60 8° Teubner, *Lps.*, 77 *sqq.*, *in prg.*

Apologia *and* Crito w. English notes Prf. L. Dyer [Am.] [Coll. Ser. of Gk. Auth.] sq 8° $1.50 Ginn, *Boston* / 6/- Arnold 85

Crito: " " " and Introd. St. George Stock [Clar. Press Series] f 8° 2/- Clar. Press / 50c. Macmillan, *N.Y.* [87] 91

Euthyphro: w. German notes A. Theod. Christ 40pf. s 8° Freytag, *Lps.* 90

Gorgias: w. English notes and Introd. Gonzalez Lodge [Am.] sq 8° $1.75 Ginn, *Boston* / 7/6 Arnold 91

Based on DEUSCHLE+CRON'S text (*ut* B.B. K § 194), w. careful notes and good Introd. on histor. beginnings of rhetoric and on the life and activity of Gorgias, in wh. the results of the wk. of BLASS and of VOLKMANN are excellently summarized.

w. English notes A. Th. Christ; front. 1m. s 8° Freytag, *Lps.* 90

Protagoras: " " " and Introd. Jas. Adam+A. M. Adam [good schl.-edn. Pitt Press Series] f 8° 4/6 Camb. Press / $1.25 n/. Macmillan, *N.Y.* 93

" " " Herm. Sauppe, tr. J. A. Towle [Am.] [Coll. Ser. of Gk. Auth.] 12° 95c. Ginn, *Boston* / 6/- Arnold 89

" " " and Introd. B. T. Turner [good school-edn.] 6/- c 8° Percival (Riv. and Perc.) 91

Respublica: " " " Prfs. B. Jowett+Lewis Campbell; w. prolegomena Clar. Press / Macmillan, *N.Y.* *in prep.*

Translations —*v.* C § 8.

Aids.

ADAM, Jas. The Nuptial Number—*v.* C § 8.
BARON, Chas. De Platonis dicendi genere [thesis] 8° Picard, *Paris* 91
GRÜNWALD, Eug. Sprichwörter u. sprichwörtliche Redensarten b. Plato [schl.-progr.] 4° *Berlin* 93
HORN, Ferd. Platonstudien 6*m.* 8° Tempsky, *Vienna* 93
JOHNSON, [Am.: ed.] Bibliotheca Platonica: a series of papers [of small value] 8° *Osceola, U.S.A.*
LINA, Theod. De Praepositionum usu platonico Quaestiones selectae [diss. inaug.] 1*m.*50 8° Elwert, *Marburg* 89
*PATER, Walt. Plato and Platonism—*v.* C § 8.
RITTER, Const. Untersuchungen über Plato [authenticity and chronology] 2*m* 50 8° Kohlhammer, *Stuttgt.* 88
SCHMITT, Fr. Die Verschiedenheit d. Ideenlehre in Platos Republ. u. Philebus [diss. inaug.] 8° *Giessen* 91
THEON SMYRNAEUS Expositio Rerum Mathemat. ad legendum Plat. utilium, rec. Ed. Hiller 3*m.* 8° Teubner, *Lps.* 78
" " Exposition des Connaissances Mathémat. utile p. l. lect. de Platon, trad. J. Dupuis 7*fr.*50 8° Hachette, *Paris* 92

Gorgias.
KOCH, Konr. Platos Gorgias als Schullektüre [school-programme] 4° *Brunswick* 92
NEWHALL, Barker [Am.] The Dramatic and Mimetic Feature of the Gorgias of Plato [diss.] 8° Johns Hopk. Univ., *Baltimore* 91

Kratylus.
KIRSCHNER, Hans Die verschied. Auffassungen d. plat. Dial. Kratylus, pt. i. Sprachphilos. vor Plato [progr.] 4° *Brieg* 92
SCHÄUBLIN, Friedr. Ueber den platonischen Dialog Kratylos [dissert.] 1*m.*80 8° Reich, *Basle* 91

Parmenides.
DAMASCIUS SUCCESSOR Dubitationes et Solutiones de Primis Principiis in Plat. Parmen., ed. C. Ae. Ruelle 25*fr.* 8° Klincksieck, *Paris* 91

Phaedo.
BAUMANN, Joh. Kritische u. exeget. Bemerkungen zu Platos Phaedo [schl-progr.] 80*pf.* 8° *Augsbg.* (Fock, *Lps.*) 89

Protagoras.
HEIDHUES, Bernh. Das Gedicht des Simonides in Platons Protagoras [schl.-progr.] 4° *Cologne* 90

Theaetetus.
RICK, Hubert Neue Untersuchungen über den platonischen Theätet [schl.-progr.] 4° (Fock, *Lps.*) 91

Philosophy Generally —*v. also* C § 8.
FOUILLÉE, Alf. La Philosophie de Platon, 4 vols. ea. 3*fr.*50 18° Hachette, *Paris* [69] 88-89
HAMMOND, W. A. Notion of Virtue in the Dialogues of Plato—*in* Harvard Studies, vol. iii., *v.* K § 173.
HILLE, Hugo Ueber die platonische Lehre vom Eros [programme] 4° *Liegnitz* 92
LUKAS, Fr. Die Methode der Eintheilung bei Platon 6*m.*80 8° Pfeffer, *Halle* 88
LUTOSLAWSKI, Prf. W. O Logice Platona, vols. i.-ii. 8° *Warsaw* 91; 92

In Polish. Will occupy 3 vols. Analyses the differ. opinions on Plato's Logic fr. 15 cent. to pres. day, studies its developmt. in each dialogue separately, and then gives a systemat. exposition of it as a whole. A German tr. is to appear.

THIEMANN, Karl Die platonische Eschatologie in ihrer genetischen Entwickelung [programme] 1*m.* 4° Gaertner, *Berlin* 92

Textual Criticism: Laches, Phaedo.
MAHAFFY, Prf. J. P. [ed.] —*in his* Petrie Flinders Papyri, *v.* K § 179.

Plutarch [A.D. *c.* 50–*c.* 120].

Dialogi Tres: *rec. Wm. R. Paton [w. a learned acc. of the MSS.] 5*m.* 8° Weidmann, *Berl.* 93
Moralia: rec. Greg. N. Bernardakis, vols. iii.-v. [last but one] ea. 3*m.* s 8° Teubner, *Lps.*, 91; 92; 93

An edn. wh. has been attacked w. much acrimony by German scholars.

Aids.

DASARITIS, Elias Die Psychologie und Pädagogik des Plutarch—*v.* D § 160.
GIESEN, Carl De Plutarchi contra Stoicos Disputationibus [diss. inaug.] 8° *Münster* 89
LASSEL, Eug. De Fortunae in Plutarchi Operibus Notione [diss. inaug.] 8° *Marburg* 91
MEYER, Wolfg. De Codice Plutarcheo Seitenstettensi ejusque asseclis [diss. inaug.] 8° *Leipzig* 91
MICHAELIS, Karl Th. De Plutarchi Codice manuscripto Matritensi [programme] 1*m.* 4° Gaertner, *Berlin* 93
SCHLEMM, Aug. De Fontibus Plutarchi Comment. de Audiendis Poetis et de Fortuna [dissert.] 2*m.* 8° Dieterich, *Göttingen* 94
VOGEL, Carl Quaestiones Plutarcheae [Marburg diss. inaug.] 1*m.*20 8° Fock, *Lps.* 89
WESTERWICK, Osc. De Plutarchi Studiis Hesiodeis [dissert. inaug.] 1*m.*20 8° *Münster* (Köber, *Minden*) 94

Pyrrhon [B.C. *c.* 365–275].

SEPP, Simon Pyrrhoneische Studien [dissert.; 149 pp.] 2*m.*50 8° Fellerer, *Freising* 93

Papers on pyrrhon. scepticism, the first bg. on Cornelius CELSUS as a sceptic.

WADDINGTON, Chas. Pyrrhon et le Pyrrhonisme: mém. p. serv. à l'hist. d. scepticisme 8° Picard, *Paris* 77

Theophrastus [B.C. 371–287].

JOACHIM, Herm. De Theophrasti libris Περὶ ζῴων [dissert.] 1*m.*50 8° *Bonn* (Fock, *Lps.*) 92
RABE, Hugo De Theophrasti libris Περὶ λέξεως [dissert.] 1*m.*50 8° " " " 90

Xenocrates [B.C. 396–314].

*Fragmenta: rec. Rich. Heinze [w. crit. exposn. of his philosophy] 5*m.*60 8° Teubner, *Lps.* 92

Zeno Citiensis [B.C. *c.* 4th–3rd cent.].

*Fragments of Zeno and Cleanthes: ed. A. C. Pearson; w. intro. and notes [Hare Prize Essay, 1889] c 8° 10/- Camb. Press / $2.40 *n.* Macmillan, *N.Y.* 91

An excellent and workmanlike book—*v.* note appended to it in C § 22: Stoics.

TROOST, Karl Zenonis Citiensis de rebus physic. doctrinae fundamentum, pt. i. [diss.] 1*m.* 8° Köhler, *Breslau* 91

195. GREEK WRITERS ON GRAMMAR, METRICS, MUSIC AND RHETORIC.

Grammarians.

Collectively.

Grammatici Graeci: rec. Rich. Schneider r 8° Teubner, *Lps.*, 78–94

i. APOLLONIUS DYSKOLUS, *Scripta Minora* (Rich. SCHNEIDER + Gust. UHLIG) 10*m.* 78. iv. (2 pts.) THEODOSIUS ALEX., *Canones*; GEORGIUS CHOEROBOSCUS, *Scholia*; SOPHRONIUS, *Excerpta* (Alf. HILGARD), pt. i. 14*m.* '89, ii. 20*m.* '94.

DIONYSIUS HALICARNASS.; and PAUSANIAS GRAMMATICUS [Atticists who *fl.* end 1st. cent. A.D.].
Fragmenta: coll. Ern. Schwabe 12*m.* 8° Dyk, *Lps.* 90
Reliquiae: ed. C. Theod. Ph. Schwartz 5/- 8° Kemink, *Utrecht* 77
RINDFLEISCH, Walter De Aelii Dionysii et Pausaniae lexicis rhetoricis [diss. inaug.] 1*m.*25 8° Schuberth, *Ratisbon* 66

HIEROCLES [Grammaticus].

Synecdemus : rec. A. Burckhardt 1*m*.20 . 8° Teubner, *Lps.* 93

LESBONAX [A.D. 1st cent.].

MÜLLER, Rud. De Lesbonacte Grammatico [dissert. inaug.] 8° *Greifswald* 91

PAUSANIAS GRAMMATICUS—*v.* Halicarnass. Dionysius, *supra.*

Writers on Music and Metre.

ARISTOXENUS [B.C. 4th cent.] : * Melik u. Rhythmik, hrsg. F. Sadan, vol. ii. [Bericht, w. orig. text and prolegg. by R. Westphal] 20*m*. 8° Abel, *Lps.* 93

Writers on Rhetoric.

CORNUTUS, L. Annaeus [A.D. 20–*c*. 68] Artis Rhetoricae Epitome, ed. w. Latin comm. Joh. Graeven 4*m*. 8° Weidmann, *Berl.* 91

CORNUTUS was a Roman stoic, who wrote in both the Greek and Latin languages.

GRAEVEN, J. Prolegomenorum in Corn. Artis Rhet. Epitomen pars prior [diss.] 8° *Göttingen* 91

196. GREEK WRITERS ON PHYSICAL SCIENCE (INCL. MATHEMATICS AND MEDICINE).

Alchemists.

Collection des Anciens Alchimistes Grecs, ed. M. Berthelot + C. E. Ruelle, 4 vols.; w. French trs. and notes 80*fr*. 4° Steinheil, *Paris* 88

Vol. I. DEMOCRITUS, SYNESIUS, OLYMPIODORUS; vol. ii. ZOSIMUS. Only 150 for sale.

Mathematicians. Astronomers.

APOLLONIUS PERGAEUS [B.C. 1st cent.] Opera : rec. I. L. Heiberg, 2 vols. ea. 4*m*.50 s 8° Teubner, *Lps.* 90; 93

Includes all his wks. that remain, w. the ancient commentaries and a Latin tr.

Translation.

Sieben Bücher üb. Kegelschnitte [w. 8th bk. discov. by Halley], übers. H. Balsam ; 31 lithog. pl. in 4° 10*m*. r 8° Reimer, *Berl.* 63

SCHÖMANN, G. Apollonius von Perga [school-programme] 4° *Treptow* 78

STOLL Neue Beiträge zum Problem des Apollonius, 2 pts. [school-programme] 4° *Bensheim* 74

ARATUS [B.C. 3rd cent.] Phaenomena : rec. Ernst Maass ; w. Latin notes, prolegg. and index 5*m*. 8° Weidmann, *Berl.* 93

,, rec. C. Manutius ; w. Germ. notes [*incl. also* Eudoxus' Phaenomena] 4*m*. 8° Teubner, *Lps.* 94

MAASS, Ernst Aratea [= Philolog. Untersuchungen, pt. xii.] 16*m*. 8° Weidmann, *Berlin* 92

CLEOMEDES [A.D. 2nd cent.] De motu circulari corporum caelestium : ed. H. Ziegler ; w. Latin tr. 2*m*.70 8° Teubner, *Lps.* 91

DIOPHANTUS ALEXANDRINUS [B.C. *fl.* 360] Opera Omnia, ed. Paul Tannery; w. Latin notes, vol. i. 5*m*. 8° ,, ,, 93

Vol. i. conts. his *Arithmetica* and all his other extant wks. ; vol. ii. will cont. the Greek commentaries.

EUCLID [B.C. *fl.* 300] Omnia Opera : rec. J. L. Heiberg + H. Menge, vol. v. [last] [for vols. i.–iv. *v.* 𝔅.𝔇. H § 8] 7*m*.50 8° Teubner, *Lps.* 88

BESTHORN + HEIBERG, R. O. / J. L. [eds.] Codex Leidensis 399(1), pt. i., facs. 1 4*kr*. 8° Gyldendal, *Copenh.* 93

Euclidis Elementa ex interpret. Al-Hadschaschadschii cum comm. Al-Narizii. Arabic and Latin ; w. notes.

KLUGE, Gust. De Euclidis Elementorum libris qui feruntur xiv et xv ; pl. [diss. inaug.] 8° Fock, *Lps.* 91

EUDOXUS [B.C. 406–360] Phaenomena, ed. C. Manitius—*v.* Aratus, *supra.*

IAMBLICHUS [A.D. 2nd cent.] De Communi Mathem. Scientia, ed. Nic. Festa [*fr.* Florent. MS.] 1*m*.80 8° Teubner, *Lps.* 91

In Nicomachi Arithmet. Introductionem liber, ed. H. Pistelli [*fr.* Flor. MS.] 2*m*.40 8° ,, ,, 94

PHILO BYZANTINUS [B.C. 2nd cent.] Mechanicae Syntaxis lib. iv. et v., rec. Rich. Schoene 2*m*. 8° G. Reimer, *Berlin* 93

Medical Writers.

Collectively.

Medicorum Graecorum Opera : ed. C. G. Kühn, 26 vols. [w. Latin trs.] *o.p.* [*w.* £6] 8° *Leipzig* 21–33

ARETAEUS ; DIOSCORIDES, 2 vols. ; GALEN, 20 vols. ; HIPPOCRATES.

COSTOMIRIS, G. A. Etudes sur les Ecrits inédits des anciens Médécins Grecs 5*fr*. 8° Klincksieck, *Paris* 91

Individually.

GALEN, Claudius [A.D. 131–200] Scripta minora, rec. J. Marquardt + I. Mueller + Geo. Helmreich —*ut* H° § 3.

,, ,, Protreptici quae supersunt, rec. G. Kaibel 2*m*. 8° Weidmann, *Berlin* 94

HIPPOCRATES [B.C. *c.* 460–*c.* 377].

Erotianus [A.D. 1st. cent.]

ILBERG, Joh. Das Hippokrates-Glossar d. Erot. u. s. urspr. Gestalt [*extr. fr.* Abh. Sächs. Ak.] 2*m*. r 8° Hirzel, *Lps.* 93

HEIBERG, J. L. Aphorismer om Hippocrates [Studier fra Sprog- og Oldtidsforsk.] 60 *øre* 8° Klein, *Copenhagen* 92

NICANDER [A.D. 2nd cent ; medical poet]

ABEL + VÁRI, Eug. / Rud. [eds.] Scholia Vetera in Nicandri Alexipharmaca e Codice Goettingensi 8° *Budapesth* (3*m*.50. Calvary, *Berl.*) 91

Physiognomers : *Collectively.*

*Scriptores Physiognomici Graeci et Latini, rec. Rich. Foerster, 2 vols. 14*m*. 8° Teubner, *Lps.* 93 ; 93

Vol. i. *Physiognomica Pseudo-aristotelis* [Gk. and Lat.], ADAMANTIUS [w. Gk. epitome], POLEMO [Arabic and Lat.], 8*m*. ; *Physiognomica anon.*, *Pseudopolemonis, Rasis, Secreti Secretorum latine, Anon. graeca, Fragmenta, Index,* 6*m*. A model of erudition and careful editing.

198. GREEK MISCELLANEOUS PROSE WRITERS.

ATHENAEUS NAUCRATIT. [A.D. 170-230].
RUDOLPH, F. Die Quelle und die Schriftstellerei des Athanaios 1m. 20 8° Dieterich, *Göttingen* 91
LUCIAN [A.D. *c.* 120-*c.* 200].
Opera: rec. Jul. Sommerbrodt, vol. ii., pt. 1 6m. s 8° Weidmann, *Berl.* 93
Menippus and Timon: w. English notes and Introd. E. C. Mackie [Pitt Press Series] *f* 8° 3/6 Camb. Press; 90c. *nt.* Macmillan, *N.Y.* 92
Περὶ τῆς Περεγρίνου τελευτῆς: rec. Lion. Levi 1m. 80 s 8° Weidmann, *Berl.* 92
True History: text. w. tr. Fcs. Hickes [*en regard*] and Introd. Chas. Whibley; ill. Aubrey Beardsley [vell. ppr. 63/-] 42/- *nt.* 4° Lawrence & Bullen 94
BIELER, Joh. Ueber die Echtheit des Lucianischen Dialogs Cynicus [school-programme] 1m. 4° *Hildesheim* (Fock. *Lps.*) 90
" " Ueber die Echtheit der Lucianischen Schrift De Saltatione 80*pf.* 8° Fock, *Lps.* 94
KRETZ, C. De Luciani Dialogo Toxarida [school-programme] 4° *Offenburg* 91
VOGT, Paul De Luciani Libellorum pristine Ordine Quaestiones, pt. i.; 5 pl. 1m. 50 8° Hühn, *Cassel* 89

Anecdota Græca —*v. also* K § 173 *sub tit.* Anecdota Oxoniensia.

Anecdota Varia Graeca et Latina, ed. Rud. Schoell + Wilh. Studemund, vols. i-ii. ea. 10m. r 8° Weidmann, *Berl.* 86; 86
i. *Anecd. Varia Graeca Musica, Metrica, Grammatica* (STUDEMUND); ii. PROCLI *Comment. in Rempubl. Platonis partes inedita* (SCHOELL).

Mythographers.

APOLLODORUS ATHENIENSIS [B.C. 2nd cent.] Bibliotheca, rec. Imman. Bekker 1m. 8° Teubner, *Lps.* 54
" " rec. Rud. Hercher 2m. 40 8° Weidmann, *Berlin* 74
" " rec. Dr. R. Wagner; 1 pl. [Mythographi Graeci, vol. i.] 3m. 60 8° Teubner, *Lps.* 94
Includes also PEDIASMUS, *Libellus de XII. Herculis Laboribus.*
" " Fragmenta Sabbaltica, ed. A. P. Kerameus *Bonn* 91
Some fragments of APOLLODORUS found at Jerusalem: continue the text even further than the Vatican epitome, *ut inf.* Repr. fr. *Rheinisches Museum.*
" " Epitoma Vaticana ex Apollodori Bibliotheca, rec. R. Wagner 6m. 8° Hirzel, *Lps.* 91
Edn. of a 14 cent. MS. discov. at Vatican by Dr. Wagner: an abridgement of the *Bibliotheca*, *sub tit. Fabulae Periinae et quaedam grammaticalia ex Eustathio eius principio et fine.* With a few notes, and half a vol. of *Curae Mythographae* (essays on the shapes of the legends) and 2 indices.
FUNK, Herm. De Apollodoro Atheniensi [diss. inaug.; 61 pp.] 8° *Berlin* 69
HÄNICHE, O. E. Quaestiones Apollodoreae duo [diss. inaug.; 30 pp.] 8° *Halle* 75
ROBERT, C. De Apollodori Bibliotheca [diss. inaug.; 91 pp.] 8° *Berlin* 73

XXVI. Latin Philology and Literature.

199. LATIN GRAMMAR (*a*): GENERALLY. INTRODUCTION. HISTORY OF LANGUAGE.

Introduction.

WEISE, Prf. F. Oskar Characteristik der lateinischen Sprache 2m. 40 8° Teubner, *Leipzig* 91
An ingenious and very readable sketch of Latin in its various phases and aspects.

Grammar.

Historische Grammatik d. latein. Sprache, vol. i. pt. 1. [Einleitg. u. Lautlehre, by F. Stolz] 7m. 8° Teubner, *Lps.* 94
The wk. is to be ed. by H. BLASS, G. LANDGRAF, J. H. SCHMALZ, F. STOLZ, J. THÜSSING, C. WAGENER and A. WEINHOLD.
ROBY + WILKINS, H. J. / Prf. A. S. An Elementary Latin Grammar 2/6 (60 *c.*) c 8° Macmillan 92
ROBY'S *Gram. of Lat. Lang.*, 2 vols. [*ut* B.B. K § 199] was reduced to 1 vol. *sub tit. Short Lat. Gram.* [*ut ib.*], and is here further reduced—on the whole to its detriment as a school-bk.
SKUTSCH, Frz. Forschungen zur latein. Gramm. u. Metrik, vol. i. [*ut* K § 215] 4m. 40 8° Teubner, *Lps.* 91

History of the Language.

KELLER, Otto Zur lateinischen Sprachgeschichte, pt. i.: Latein. Etymologien 5m. 8° Teubner, *Lps.* 92
LINDSAY, W. M. The Latin Language: histor. acc. of Lat. sounds, stems and flexions Clar. Press *in prep.*
SKUTSCH, F. Forschungen zur lateinischen Grammatik u. Metrik, vol. i. 4m. 40 8° Teubner, *Lps.* 92

Semasiology.

HEERDEGEN, Friedr. —*in his ed. of* vol. ii. of Reisig's Vorlesgn. üb. lat. Sprachw., *ut* B.B. K § 199.
*HEY, Osk. Semasiologische Studien [*extr. fr.* Jahrbb. Class. Phil.] 3m. 20 8° Teubner, *Lps.* 91
A valuable contribn. to this new science. In two pts., (1) theoretical, (2) historical.
HÖLZER, V. Beiträge zur Theorie d. latein. Semasiologie *ut* B.B. K § 216, *s.v.* Nepos.
Of some interest fr. a practical pedagogic point-of-view; but no great contribn. to science.
RÖNSCH, Herm. Semasiologische Beiträge z. latein. Wörterbuch—*ut* K § 205.

200-201. LATIN GRAMMAR (*b*): ACCIDENCE; (*c*) SYNTAX.

Generally: *Syntax.*

*DRÄGER, A. Historische Syntax der lateinischen Sprache, 2 vols.—*ut* B.B. K § 201.
Sjöstrand, Nils In Syntaxin Draegerianam Notationes nonnullae 1m. 8° Möller, *Lund* 92
MENGE, Dr. Herm. Repetitorium der latein. Syntax u. Stilistik 7m. 8° Zwissler, *Wolfenb.* [2nd ed. 74] 90

Adjective.

ALBRECHT, Ern. De Adiectivi Attrib. in Ling. Lat. Collocatione Specimen [diss. inaug.] 2m. 8° *Marburg* (Fock), *Lps.* 90

Adverbs.

LUTZ, L. Die Casus-Adverbien bei den attischen Rednern 1m.20 8° Fock, *Lpz.* 91

Conditional Sentences—*v.* K § 176 (R. Horton SMITH).

Conjunctions.

HALE, Prf. W. G. [Am.] The 'Cum' Constructions: their history and functions—*ut* B.B. K § 201.
" " The same, tr. A. Neitzert, w. Pref. Prf. B. Delbrück 6m. 8° Teubner, *Lpz.* 91
Hoffmann, Eman. Das Modus-Gesetz im Lat. Zeitsatze [reply to Hale] 1m. 8° Gerold, *Vienna* 91

Negation.

VICOL, F. L. Die Negation im Lateinischen [school-programme] 8° *Suczawa* 93

Noun.

BELL, Andr. De Locativi in prisca Latinitate vi et usu [diss. inaug.] 1m.50 8° Preuss, *Breslau* 89
CLAIRIN, P. Du Génitif Latin et de la Preposition *De*: Etude d. syntaxe histor. 7/fr.50 8° Bouillon, *Paris* 80
ZIELER, Gust. Beiträge zur Geschichte d. Lat. Ablativus [diss. inaug.] 8° *Bonn* 92

Particles.

MAYEN, Geo. De Particulis Quod, Quia, Quoniam, Quomodo, Ut, Pro, Acc. c. Infin. post verba sentiendi pos. 2m. 8° Lipsius, *Kiel* 89
MERTEN, Wilh. De Particularum Copulativ. ap. veter. roman. Scriptores Usu [diss.] 8° *Marburg* 93
SEILER, Joh. De Particulis Copulativis Quaest. Gram. et Metrica: [diss.] 8° *Halle* 91
WHARTON, E. R. Quelques *a* Latins [repr. fr. Mémoires d. l. Soc. d. Linguistique, vol. vii.; 10 pp.] 8° Author, Jesus Coll., Oxon 91

Deals w. certain classes of cases where *a* is found where *e* or *o* would be expected, usually expl. by *Ablaut*, his theory being that it is due to the influence of a tonic accent.

Prepositions.

GRÄBER, Rud. De Praepositionum latinarum Collocatione [diss. inaug.] 8° *Marburg* 92

Verb.

BLASE, Dr. H. Geschichte des Plusquamperfects im Lateinischen 3m. 8° Ricker, *Giessen* 94
" " De mod. temporumque in enunt. condic. lat. permutatione quaestt. selectae [diss.] 1m.50 8° Fock, *Lpz.* 85
ENGELHARDT, Max Die Stammzeiten der lateinischen Konjugation 1m.20 8° Weidmann, *Berlin* 92
JOB, L. Le Présent et ses Dérivés dans la Conjugaison latine 10/fr. 8° Bouillon, *Paris* 94
LATTMANN, Dr. J. Selbständiger u. bezogener Gebrauch d. Tempora im Lateinischen 4m. 8° Vandenhoeck, *Gött.* 90
SJÖSTRAND, Nils De Vi et Usu Supini Secundi Latinorum 1m.10 8° Möller, *Lund* 91
WEIHENMAJER Zur Geschichte d. absoluten Partizips im Latein. [schl.-progr.] 4° *Reutlingen* 91
WEISWEILER, Jos. Der finale Genitivus Gerundii [school-progr.] 4° *Cologne* 90
WENTZEL, H. De Infinitivo apud Justinum Usu 1m.20 8° Weidmann, *Berlin* 93

202. LATIN GRAMMAR (*d*): PHONOLOGY.

CONSOLI, Santi Fonologia Latina: secondo il metodo scientifico [pp. 205] 16° Hoepli, *Milan* [ ] 92
SOLMSEN, F. Studien zur lateinischen Lautgeschichte 3m.50 8° Trübner, *Strassburg* 94
STOLZ, F. Einleitung u. Lautlehre d. lat. Spr. = vol. i. pt. of Histor. Grammatik—*ut* K § 199.

203. LATIN GRAMMAR (*e*): PALÆOGRAPHY, MSS. AND TEXTUAL CRITICISM.

Generally.

CHATELAIN, E. [ed.] La Paléographie des Classiques Latins, pt. i. 105/fr. f° *Paris* 93
MARTIN, Chas. Trice The Record Interpreter 12/6 8° Reeves & Turner 92

A colln. of abbrevns., Lat. words, and names used in Engl. histor. MSS. and records, the first half of bk. bg. devoted to a very useful list of abbrev. forms of Lat. and French wds. found in records, followed by list of Lat. forms of Engl. Place-names (less satisfactory) and by list of Lat. forms of Engl. Surnames (not satisfactory).

MIDDLETON, Prf. J. H. —*in his* Illuminated MSS. in Class. and Mediæval Times, *ut* I § 111.
PAOLI, Ces. Grundr. z. Vorlesn. üb. lat. Paläogr. u. Urkundenlehre, pt. i. [Paläogr.]; übers. 2m. 8° Wagner, *Innsbruck* [85] 89
" " Le Abbreviature nella Paleogr. Lat. del Medio Evo [pp. 41] 8° Le Monnier, *Florence* 91
" " Die Abkürzungen in d. lat. Schrift d. Mittelalt., übers. Karl Lohmeyer 1m.20 8° Wagner, *Innsbruck* 92
PROU, Maur. [ed.] Recueil de Facss d'Ecritures du 12 au 17 siècle [Lat. & Fch. MSS. only; w. trscpns.] 6/fr. 8° Picard, *Paris* 91
THOMPSON, Edw. Maunde Handbook of Greek and Roman Palæography—*ut* K § 179.
VOLTA ZANINO Delle Abbreviature nella Paleografia Latina: studio; 16 ill. 7l. 8° Paganini, *Milan* 92

Manuscripts.

Berlin, Königl. Bibl.: Verzeichniss d. latein. HSS., by Val. Rose—*ut* K § 4.
Paris: Catalogus Codd. Hagiograph. Lat. antiq. sæc. xvi. in Bib. Nat., vol. i. ?; ii. ?; iii. 15/fr. 8° Schepens, *Brussels* ?; ?; 93
" MSS. Latins et Frc. ajoutés à la Bibl. Nat. 1875–1891; ed. Léop. Delisle—*ut* K § 4.
Haureau, B. [ed.] Notices et Extraits d. quelq. MSS. Latins d. l. Bib. Nat., 6 vols. ea. 8/fr. 8° Klincksieck, *Paris* 91–93
" La Catulle de Saint-Germain des Prés, ed. Em. Chatelaine—*ut* K § 214.

204. LATIN GRAMMAR (*f*): ORTHOGRAPHY AND PRONUNCIATION.

Orthography.

ECKINGER, T. Die Orthographie lateinischer Wörter in griech. Inschriften [diss.] 2m.50 8° *Munich* (Fock, *Lpz.*) 92
OBERDICK, Joh. Studien zur lateinischen Orthographie [schl.-progr.] 4° *Breslau* 91

Pronunciation.

HICKETIER, Fritz Zur Betonung des Lateinischen auf d. Schule [schl.-progr.] 4° *Cüstrin* 92
KARSTEN, H. T. De Uitspraak van het Latijn 1/f.90 8° Delsman, *Amsterd.* 93
LORD, Prf. Fcs. E. [Am.] The Roman Pronunciation of Latin: why...and how we use it 12° Ginn, *Boston* / Arnold
RAMORINO, Fel. La Pronunzia popol. dei Versi quantit. latini [70 pp.] 4° Clausen, *Turin* 93

205. LATIN GRAMMAR (*g*): ETYMOLOGY.

Lexicography.

Commentationes Woelfflinianae—*ut* K § 168.

DRÄGER, A. Zur Lexicographie der lateinischen Sprache [schl.-progr.] 8° *Aurich* 90

KELLER, Otto Lateinische Etymologien = Zur latein. Sprachgesch., pt. i.—*ut* K § 199.

RÖNSCH, Herm. Semasiologische Beiträge z. lat. Wörterbuch, 3 pts. 8*m*.40 8° Fues, *Lps*. 87; 88; 89
i. *Substantiva*, 2*m*. 40; ii. *Adjectiva u. Pronom., Adverbia u. Adverbialia*, 3*m*.; iii. *Verba*, 3*m*.

STOWASSER, Dr. J. M. Dunkle Wörter, 1*m*.; Zweite Reihe, Dritte Reihe, ea. 60 *pf*. 8° Tempsky, *Prague* 90; 91; 92
The 1st series is a 32 pp. pamphlet, discussing w. learning and impartiality some 90 wds. whose derivns. or forms are doubtful. The third deals w. the verb *lare*.

ZIMMERMANN, Aug. Etymologische Versuche, pts. i.–ii. [school-programmes] 4° *Celle* 91; 92

Glosses.

Corpus Glossariorum Latinorum rec. Gust. Loewe + Geo. Goetz, vols. iii.–v. 62*m*. r 8° Teubner, *Lps*. 89–94 *in prg.*
iii. *Hermeneumata Pseudodositheana*, rec. G. GOETZ, 20*m*. '92; iv. *Glossæ Codd. Vatic.* 3,321, *Sangallensis* 912, *Lugd.* 67 F., rec. G. GOETZ, 20*m*. '89; v. PLACIDUS, *Liber Glossarum Glossæ in Reliquiæ*, rec. G. GOETZ, 27*m*. '94.

Goetz, Geo. Der Liber Glossarum; 1 facs. [*extr. fr.* Abhandl. Königl. Säch. Ges. Lpz.] 3*m*. r 8° Hirzel, *Lps*. 91

Dictionaries.

CASSELL & Co. [pubs.] New Latin Dictionary, revised J. R. V. Marchant + Jos. F. Charles 3/6 8° Cassell [87] 93
Latin-English and English-Latin. A very cheap bk.; and passably good for ordinary purposes.

*FACCIOLATI + FORCELLINI + FURLANETTO, $\frac{\text{L.i.Aeg.}}{\text{J.}}$ Lexicon totius Latinitatis [*ut* B.B. K § 205]: cur. Fr. Corradini, vols. i.–iv. (4) r 4° Seminarium, *Padua* [1771]?–92 *in prg.*
A mine of lexicographical wealth.

HERTZ, Prf. Martin [ed.]
A new Lat. dict. under his edrship., to be pub. at expense of Prussian govt., is said to be in prep. The wk. is estimated to occupy ab. 18 yrs. and the cost to amt. to bet. 900,000 and 1,000,000 marks.

*LEWIS, Dr. Charlton T. [Am.] Elementary Latin Dictionary 8q12° $\frac{\text{7/6 Clar. Press}}{\text{\$2 Harper, N.Y.}}$ 91
By the author of the *Latin Dict. for Schools* and co-author, w. Dr. C. SHORT, of the *Latin Dict.* [*ut* B.B. K § 205]. An excellent school bk.

STOWASSER, J. M. Lateinisch-deutsches Schulwörterbuch 8*m*.40 r 8° Tempsky, *Prague* 93

Folk Etymology.

KELLER, Otto Lateinische Volksetymologie und Verwandtes 10*m*. 8° Teubner, *Lps*. 91

Forms of Words.

GEORGES, K. E. Lexicon der lateinischen Wortformen, pt. v. [last] 3*m*.; compl. 11*m*. 8° Hahn, *Lps*. 90

Hybrid Words.

WITKOWSKI, Stanisl. De Vocibus hybridis apud antiq. Poetas romanos 1*m*.20 8° Poln. Verlagsges., *Cracow* 93

Loan Words, etc.

MUSS-ARNOLT, Rev. W. On Semitic Words in Greek and Latin—*ut* K § 181.

SAALFELD, G. A. De Bibliorum Sacrorum Vulgatæ Editionis Græcitate—*ut* A § 22.

Names: Personal.

BRAASCH, Karl. Lateinische Personennamen: nach ihrer Bedeutg. zusammengestellt [progr.] 4° *Zeitz* 92

206. LATIN GRAMMAR (*h*): STYLE.

MENGE, Herm. Repetitorium d. latein. Grammatik u. Stilistik—*ut* K § 201.

Alliteration.

LAHMEYER, Ludw. Studien z. lat. Gram., pt. i. [Allit. in Cic. Pompeiana] [schl.-prg.] 4° *Rosslében* 91

Chiasmus.

STEELE, R. B. [Am.] Chiasmus in Sallust, Cæsar, Tacitus, Justinus [diss.] 8° *Northfield, Minn.* 91

207. LATIN GRAMMAR (*i*): PROSODY, METRICS.

BAINVEL, J. V. Métrique Latine [196 pp.] 18° Poussielgue, *Paris* 93

BOISSIÈRE, G. Notions de Prosodie et Métrique Latines [184 pp.] 18° Delagrave, *Paris* 93

DINGELDEIN, Otto Der Reim bei den Griechen und Römern—*ut* K § 183.

GOTTSCHALK, Frz. Senarius qui vocatur Terent. compar. c. trimetro Græc. [sch.-pr.] 4°

JUSATZ, Carl Hugo De Irrationalitate Studia rhythmica [Leipz. Studien, vol. xiv.] 8° Hirzel, *Lps*. 93

KALKNER, Friedr. Symbolæ ad Historiam Versuum Logaoedicorum 1*m*.20 8° Elwert, *Marburg* 92

KUHN, Friedr. Symbolæ ad Doctrinæ περὶ διχρόνων Historiam pertinentes [diss.] 8° Koebner, *Breslau* 92

LEJARD, J. Nouveau Traité de Prosodie Latine 18° Poussielgue, *Paris* [ ] 92

MEYER, W. Anfang u. Ursprung d. latein. u. griech. rhythmischen Dichtung—*ut* K § 183.

RONCA, Umb. Metrica e Ritmica latina nel Medio Evo, pt. i. 5/. 8° Loescher, *Rome* 90
SCHEFFLER, Lud. De Perfecti in "vi" exeuntis formis ap. Poet. Lat. dactyl. occurr. 8° *Marburg* 90
SKUTSCH, Frz. Forschungen zur lateinischen Grammatik u. Metrik—*ut* K § 199.
TURNER, B. D. Advanced Manual of Latin Prose Composition 5/- c 8° Rivington 93
VERNIER, Léon Etude sur la Versification populaire d. Romains à l'époque class. [68 pp.] 8° Dodivers, *Besançon* 90
ZANDER, Carl M. De Lege Uersificationis lat. summa et antiquiss. 80pf. 4° Möller, *Lund* 92
" " Treatise on Metre—*in his* Versus Italici Antiqui, *ut* K § 214.

Gradus.

AINGER + WINTLE, A. C. + B. C. English-Latin Gradus or Verse Dictionary 9/- c 8° Murray 90
NOËL + de PARNAJON, F. + F. Gradus ad Parnassum [*on plan of* Magn. Dict. Poet. *of* P. Vanière] 8/fr. 8° Hachette, *Paris* [73] 93
PESSONNEAUX, Em. Gradus ad Parnassum : dictionnaire prosodique [672 double-col. pp.] 6/fr. 8° Delalain, *Paris* [67] 91

Sapphic Verse.

SKOBIELSKI, Joh. Der Sapphische Vers bei d. Lateinischen Dichtern [schl.-progr.] 8° *Czernowitz* 89

Saturnian Verse.

REICHARDT, Alex. D. saturnische Vers in d. röm. Kunstdichtung [*extr. fr.* Jahrb. f. Class. Phil.] 1m.20 8° Teubner, *Lps.* 92

Synonyms.

v. KOBILINSKI, Geo. Die gebräuchlichsten lat. Synonyma zusammengestellt [schl.-prg.] 8° *Königsberg* 91

208. LATIN EPIGRAPHY.

Bibliography.

Année Epigraphique : ed. Prf. René Cagnat, v. i.–vii. [Roman only; v. i.–vii. for 25/fr.] ea. 5/fr. s 8° Leroux, *Paris* 89–94 *in prg.*

Collection.

*Corpus Inscriptionum Latinarum [Berlin. Acad. pubn.] f° G. Reimer, *Berl.* 91–93 *in prg.*

New Volumes and New Edns. :
Vol. I., pt. i. : *Inscr. Lat. Antiquiss. ad C. Cæsaris Mortem* W. HENZEN + Ch. HUELSEN + Th. MOMMSEN, 52m. [63] 93
ii. *Hispan. Latin.* Suppl. i. .... Em. HÜBNER 54m. 92
" *Hispan. Latin.* Suppl. iii. A. de DOMASZEWSKI + HIRSCHFELD + Th. MOMMSEN, 32m. 93
iii. *Asia, Prov. Eur. Græc., Illyr.*, Suppl. ii.–iii. Th. MOMMSEN. 29m. : 32m., 91 ; 93
viii. *Africa*, Suppl. i. .... GUST. WILMANNS, 52m. 91
" " " ii. *Inscr. Provinc. Numid. Lat.* R. CAGNAT + J. SCHMIDT, 22m. 94
xv. (i.) *Urbs Roma Latina* .... H. DRESSEL, 55m. 91

Ephemeris Epigraphica [Supplemt. to above] vii. 18m. ; viii. (1) 7m., (2) 6m., (3), (4) 5m. r 8° Reimer, *Berl.* 92; 91–92 *in prg.*
Mommsen, Theod. [ed.] Der Maximaltarif des Diocletian [*extr. fr.* Corp. Inscr. Lat., iii. Suppl.] 14m. r 4° G. Reimer, *Berlin* 93
PAIS, Ettore [ed.] Corporis Inscripp. Latin. Supplementa Italica, pt. i. [305 pp.] 4° Acad. dei Lincei, *Rome* 88
This Pt. conts. supplem. inscripp. to *Corp. Inscr. Lat.* (*ut sup.*), vol. v. : Gallia Cisalpina. *Atti della r. Accad. dei Lincei.*
WALTZING, J.-P. Le Recueil Gén. d. Inscr. Lat. [= Corp. Ins. Lat.] et l'Epigr. lat. depuis 50 ans 5/fr. 8° Peeters, *Louvain* 91
DESSAU, Herm. [ed.] Inscriptiones Latinæ, vol. i. 16m. r 8° Weidmann, *Berlin* 92
ESPÉRANDIEU, Em. [ed.] Inscriptions Antiques au Musée de Périgueux ; 123 pl. and 8 pp. text 8° Thorin, *Paris* 93
Publicns. de la Soc. Histor. et Archéolog. du Périgord.

Monumenti Inediti, pubbl. dall' Inst. di Corresp. Arch. : Supplemento 40m. 4° G. Reimer, *Berlin* 91
DE RUGGIERO, Prf. Ett. [ed.] Sylloge Epigraphica orbis Romani, vols. i.; ii. ed. D. Vaglieri ea. 1/.50 8° Loescher, *Roma* 92–93 *in prg.*
To occupy 4 vols., devoted to (i.) The City of Rome, (ii.) Rest of Italy, (iii.) Eastern Provinces, (iv.) Western Provinces. An extensive *corpus* of such Gk. and Lat. inscr. as throw any light on Rom. Antiqs., mere fragments and epitaphs bg. excluded. Appearing in fortnightly parts at 1/.50 or 1/.75c. acc. as one vol. or two are subscr. for. Each Gk. inscr. is accomp. by Lat. tr. and brief notes are occas. given (in Latin). The several vols. are edited by various hands.
" " Dizionario Epigrafico di Antichità Romane, pts. 1–30 [to Auctor] ea. 1/.50 8° Pasqualucci, *Rome* 87–93 *in prg.*
RUSHWORTH, G. McN. [ed.] Latin Historical Inscriptions 8° 10/- *n.* Clar. Press / Macmillan, *N.Y.* 93
A very useful colln. of 200 inscripp. B.C. 50–A.D. 99, illustrg. hist. of early Rom. Empire, *i.e.*, the period about wh. the ordinary Oxford student is most in need of assistance : arrgd. on plan of (but less epigraphical and more historical than) E. L. HICKS' *Man. of Gk. Histor. Inscripp.* [*ut* K § 184]. A consid. number of coin-legends are incl.

Magazines —v. K § 173.

Etruscan.

PAULI, Carl. [ed.] Corpus Inscriptionum Etruscarum, pt. i. 10m. f° Barth, *Lps.* 93

Euxine.

LATYSCHEW, B. [ed.] Inscripp. antiq. Oræ Septentr. Ponti Euxini græc. et. lat., vol. ii.—*ut* K § 184.

Iberian.

HÜBNER, Emil [ed.] Monumenta Linguæ Ibericæ ; map and ill. 48m. r 4° G. Reimer, *Berlin* 93

Umbrian.

Eugubine Tables.

Tabulæ Iguvinæ in usum academicum ed. Aloys. Ceci 1/.50 8° Loescher, *Turin* 92

France. Africa.

BLADÉ, Jean Frç. [ed.] Epigraphie Antique de la Gascogne 7*fr.*50 8° Chollet, *Bordeaux* 85
LE BLANT, Edm. [ed.] L'Epigraphie Chrétienne en Gaule et dans l'Afrique rom. ; 144 pl. 4*fr.* r 8° Leroux, *Paris* 90
" " [ed.] Nouveau Recueil d. Inscripp. Chrét. d. l. Gaule antér. au 8 siéc. 4° Hachette, " 92

Bordeaux.

JULLIAN, Cam. [ed.] Inscriptions Romaines de Bordeaux, 2 vols. ; pl. 60*fr.* 4° Gounouilhou, *Bordeaux* 87 ; 90

Great Britain —*v.* G § 1°.

Germany.

Rhine.

KRAUS, F. X. [ed.] Die christlichen Inschriften der Rheinlande, pt. i. 30*m.*; ii. (1) 20*m.*, (2) 30*m.*; pl. and ill. 4° Mohr, *Freiburg* 90 ; 91 ; 94
Pt. i. conts. the Old-Christian inscriptions *fr.* commencemt. of Xtn. era to middle 8 cent.; ii. to middle 13 cent.

Italy.

DE ROSSI, J. Bapt. [ed.] Inscriptiones Christianæ Urbis Romæ vii. sæc. antiquiores, v. ii. pt. 1 ; 6 pl. 80*l.* f° Cuggiani, *Roma* 88

Norway.

Norges Indskrifter : De ældre Runor, pt. i., ed. Sophus Bugge—*ut* K § 235.

Pyrenees.

SACAZE, Julien [ed.] Inscriptions Antiques des Pyrénées : avant-propos p. Alb. Lebègue ; 350 ill. 8° Deladoure, *Toulouse* 93

209. ANCIENT DIALECTS OF ITALY.

Collectively.

JOB, Leo De Grammaticis Vocabulis apud Latinos [pp. 185 ; thesis] 8° Bouillon, *Paris* 93
ZANARDELLI, T. L'Etrusque, l'Ombrien et l'Osque 2*fr.* 8° " " 91
In some of their relations to Italian. Almost worthless. Extr. fr. *Bull. d. l. Soc. d'Anthrop. d. Bruxelles.*

Early Latin.

MERRY, Dr. W. W. [ed.] Selected Fragments of Roman Poetry—*ut* K § 214.
STUDEMUND, Wilh. [ed.] Studia in Priscos Scriptores Latinos, vol. ii. 9*m.* 8° Weidmann, *Berl.* 91
Posthumously edited by his pupils, partic. Prf. Osk. Seyffert. Chiefly Plautine, *v.* K § 215, *s.v.* Plautus, with other less-important papers by Joh. SCHROEDER, Ed. KELLERHOF, Peter SCHERER, and on the *Cistellaria* by STUDEMUND.

Inscriptions —*v.* K § 208.

African-Latin.

BLASE, H. Geschichte des Irrealis im Lateinischen 2*m.* 8° Deichert, *Erlangen* 88

Etruscan.

BORROMEI, Ad. Grammatica etrusca [*extr. fr.* Giornale Lingustico] 8° *Genoa* 87
BRINTON, Prf. Dan. G. [Am.] Ethnologic Affinities of the Ancient Etruscans 8° *Philadelphia* 89
" " On Etruscan and Lybian Names [*v.* K § 103] 8° " 90
DEECKE, Wilh. Die Falisker : geschichtl.-sprachl. Untersuchg. ; map and 4 pl. 9*m.* 8° Trübner, *Strassbg.* 88
MORATTI, Car. Studi sulle antiche Lingue italiche *Florence* 87
PAULI, Dr. Carl Altitalische Forschungen, vols. ii. (2 pts.) 18*m.* ; iii., 9 pl., 40*m.* 8° Barth, *Lpz.* 86–94 ; 91
Vol. ii. *Eine vorgriech. Inschr. v. Lemnos*, pt 1, 4*m.* '86 ; 2. 14*m.* '94 ; vol. iii. : *Die Veneter u. ihre Schriftdenkmäler* (proves that the so-called N.-Etruscan inscripp. (some 330 in no.) obt. fr. cemeteries at Este, Padua, Vicenza, *etc.*, are not Etruscan, but Aryan, some Celtic, some Gaulish but the majority in a hitherto unknown lang., wh. he calls Venetic and wh. he regards as the prototype of mod. Albanian).

Oscan. Umbrian.

BRONISCH, Ghelf. Die oskischen *i*- und *e*- Vocale 6*m.* c 8° Harrassowitz, *Lpz.* 92
*BUCK, Carl D. [Am.] Der Vocalismus der oskischen Sprache 7*m.*50 8° Köhler, *Lpz.* 92
The first connected attempt since BRUPPACHER [1869; *ut* B.B. K § 209; now necessarily antiquated] to reduce to order the sound-laws of the Oscan dialect. By an American, tho' dated from Lpz., a pupil of Brugmann. This vol. treats of the vowel-laws; another dealing w. the consonant-laws will no doubt follow.
v. PLANTA, R. Grammatik der oskisch-umbrischen Dialekte, vol. i. 15*m.* 8° Trübner, *Strassbg.* 92
This vol. conts. an introductory section, and deals w. phonology. A second will complete the wk.

210. POST-CLASSICAL AND VULGAR LATIN PHILOLOGY AND LITERATURE.

Philology.

GORRA, Eg. Lingue neolatine [pp. 147] 16° Hoepli, *Milan* 93

Etymology : Proper Names.

FISCH, Rich. Die lat. Nomina Personalia auf *-o, -onis* : Beitr. z. Kenntn. d. Vulg.-Lat. 5*m.* 8° Gaertner, *Berlin* 90

Metrics.

SCHREIBER, Dr. J. Vaganten-Strophe d. mittellat. Dichtg. [in rel. to Mid.-High Germ.] 5*m.* 8° Schlesier, *Strassbg.* 94

Preposition.

BOURCIEZ, Ed. De Præpositione *ad* casuali in Latinit. Aevi Meroving. [thesis] 4*fr.* 8° Klincksieck, *Paris* 86

Church Latin.

CONDER, René F. R. Primer of Church Latin 2/- c 8° Burns & Oates 93

Relation of Latin to the Romance Languages.

COHN, Geo. Die Suffixwandlungen im Vulgärlateinischen und im vorlitterar. Französisch 8*m.* 8° Niemeyer, *Halle* 90
From their traces in modern French.

GAUL, K. W. Romanische Elemente i. d. Latein der Lex Salica [dissert.] 8° Fock, *Lpz.* 86

Vulgate [Latin version of Bible, A.D. 385].

MILROY, Wm. McC. [Am.] The Participle in the Vulgate [dissert.] 8° Johns Hopk. Univ., *Baltimore* 92

SAALFELD, G. A. De Bibliorum Sacrorum Uulgatæ Editionis Græcitate—*ut* A § 22.

Literature.

History.

DE GREGORIO, G. Per la Storia comparata delle Litterature Neo-latine 4*fr.* 8° Bouillon, *Paris* 93

Writers —*v. also* K §§ 214-223, *passim.*

Songs.

SCHMELLER, J. A. [ed.] Carmina Burana: latein. u. deut. Lieder u. Gedichte 8*m.* 8° Koebner, *Breslau* [ ]83
Edited from a 13th century MS. at Munich.

211. HISTORY OF LATIN LITERATURE (*a*): GENERALLY.

Bibliography —*in* Schanz *and in* Teuffel, *ut infra.*

General History.

GOUMY, Ed. Les Latins 3*fr.* 50 16° Hachette, *Paris* 93
PLAUTUS and TERENCE; CICERO; LUCRETIUS; CATULLUS; CÆSAR; SALLUST; VERGIL; HORACE.

MACKAIL, J. W. Latin Literature [University Extension Ser.] p 8° Murray / Scribner, *N.Y.* *in prep.*

*SCHANZ, Prf. Mart. Gesch. d. römischen Litter. bis z. Justinian; pt. ii. [Müller's *Hdb. Klass. Alterth.*] 8*m.* r 8° Beck, *Munich* 92
As learned as TEUFFEL'S wk., and much more interesting.

TEUFFEL, Prf. W. S. History of Roman Literature, tr. Prf. G. C. W. Warr, 2 vols. m 8° ea. 15/- Bell / ea. $4 Macmillan, *N.Y.* 91; 94
A much better tr. than the prev. one by Dr. W. WAGNER [1873, *ut* B.B. K § 211] incorpor. the addns. of Dr. Ludw. SCHWABE'S 5th edn. of the orig. [2 pts., ea. 7*m.*, 8° Teubner, *Lpz.* '91] and bringing the bibliogr. down to date. For the no. of authors included, for biogr. and bibliogr. details and for accuracy of references it has no rival; tho' it is weak in criticism, occas. unfair [*e.g.* in case of MARTIAL, in vol. ii.], and always rather scanty. Vol. i. *The Republican Period*; ii. *The Imperial Period.*

ZÖLLER, Max. Grundriss d. Gesch. d. röm. Litt. [Samml. v. Kompendien] 3*m.* 60 8° Schöningh, *Münster* 90

Early Christian —*v. also* A § 119.

TEUFFEL, Prf. W. S. —*in his* History of Roman Literature, *ut supra.*

212. HISTORY OF LATIN LITERATURE (*b*): SPECIAL DEPARTMENTS (*a*): POETRY AND DRAMA.

Generally.

BLÜMNER, Hugo Die Farbenbezeichnungen b. d. römischen Dichtern [= Berl. Stud. xiii. (3)] 7*m.* 50 8° Calvary, *Berlin* 92

*RIBBECK, Prf. Otto Geschichte der römischen Dichtung, vol. iii. [Imperial period] 9*m.* 8° Cotta, *Stuttgart* 92
An excellent wk., essentially popular, by a first-rate authority. Closes w. NAMATIANUS, and thus excludes the Christian Latin poets.

" " Histoire de la Poésie latine, trad. Prfs. E. Droz + Alb. Kontz, vol. i. 7*fr.* 50 8° Leroux, *Paris* 90

Early Christian —*v. also* A § 119.

MANITIUS, M. Geschichte der christlich-lateinischen Poesie [to middle 8 cent.] 12*m.* 8° Cotta, *Stuttg.* 91

Lyrical Poetry.

Elegiac Poetry.

SCHULZE, Karl Paul Beiträge zur Erklärung d. römischen Elegiker [programme] 1*m.* 4° Gaertner, *Berlin* 93

*SELLAR, Prf. W. Y. Roman Poets of Augustan Age: Horace and the Elegiac Poets—*ut* K § 224, *sub nomm.* Horace, Ovid.

Popular Poetry.

MÜLLER, Luc. Ueber die Volksdichtung der Römer [Samml. gemeinverst. Vortr.] 60*pf.* 8° Verlags-Anst., *Hambg.* 91

Satirical Poetry.

BARILLARI, Mich. Studi su la Satira Latina 2/.50 16° Epoca Saya, *Messina* 91

Drama.

SCHÖNE, A. Das historische Nationaldrama d. Römer: die Fabula Praetexta 1*m.* 8° Univ. Buchhg., *Kiel* 93

213. HISTORY OF LATIN LITERATURE (ε): SPECIAL DEPARTMENTS (β): PROSE.

Grammarians.

JEEP, Ludw. Geschichte der Lehre v. d. Redetheilen bei d. latein. Grammatikern 8m. 8° Teubner, *Lps.* 93

Historians.

Tractatus de diversis Historiis Romanorum et quibusdam aliis 1m.60 8° Junge, *Erlangen* 93

Erlangener Beiträge, pt. xiv., ed. fr. a MS. of Bologna, 1326 A.D. (now in Wolfenbüttel) by Solomon HERZSTEIN.

Medical Writers —*v. also* B.B. K § 189.

BRUNNER, C. Die Spuren der römischen Aerzte auf d. Boden der Schweiz 4m. 8° Müller, *Zürich* 93

DUPOUY, E. Médicine et Moeurs de l'anc. Rome d'après l. poètes latins 3fr.50 8° Baillière, *Paris* 91

Orators.

CUCHEVAL, Prf. Histoire de l'Eloquence lat. jusqu'à Cicéron 16° Hachette, *Paris*

" " Histoire de l'Eloquence lat. dep. Cic. jusqu'à avènemt. d' Hadrien, 2 v. 7fr. 16° " " 93

" " Sur Cicéron et sur l'Eloquence de son temps " " *in prp.*

Proverbs: Collections.

HENDERSON, A. [ed. & tr.] Latin Proverbs and Quotations [w. trs. and parallel passages, and Engl. index] 16/-; *red. to* 10/6 8° Low [69] 70

*OTTO, Dr. A. [ed.] Die Sprichwörter und sprichwörtlichen Redensarten der Römer 10m. 8° Teubner, *Lpz.* 90

Szelinski, Vict. Nachträge u. Ergänzungen zu Otto's "Sprichw. d. Röm." [diss.] 8° *Jena* 93

Aid.

Wyss, Wilh. Die Sprichwörter bei den römischen Komikern 2m. 8° Schulthess, *Zürich* 89

214. LATIN POETS.

Collectively.

*POSTGATE, Prf. Jno. [ed.] Corpus Poetarum Latinorum, pt. i. p 4° 9/- *net*, Bell; $2.75 *net*, Macmillan, *N.Y.* 93

Pt. i. conts. ENNIUS (ed. Lucian MÜLLER), LUCRET. (Ed. after MUNRO), CATULL. (EDK.), VERGIL (Prf. Hy. NETTLESHIP), HORACE (Jas. GOW), TIBULL. (Eduard HILLER), forming the 1st instalmt. (out of four ? vols.) of a new ed. of the *Corpus* formerly ed. W. S. WALKER [*ut* B.B. K § 214]. The texts are thoroughly revised, and something approaching a compl. *appar. criticus* is added. A valuable colln. in 1 bk. of the wks. of the various Lat. poets. Part ii. will complete the Augustan period.

Anthology.

Anthologia Latina: rec. F. Bücheler + A. Riese, Pars i., fasc. 1 4m. 8° Teubner, *Lps.* 94 *in prg.*

Fragments of Early Poetry.

MERRY, Dr. W. W. [ed.] Selected Fragments of Roman Poetry; w. intro. and notes c 8° 6/6 Clar. Press; $1.75 net, Macmillan, *N.Y.* 91

Selns. fr. the earliest times of the Republic, commenc. w. the *Carmen Saliare* and the *Carmen Fratrum Arvalium* to the Augustan Age (PLAUTUS and TERENCE excluded; ENNIUS and LUCILIUS well represented). A very handy bk. of reference.

WORDSWORTH, J. [ed.] Fragments and Specimens of Early Latin—*ut* B.B. K § 209.

Italic.

ZANDER, Carl M. [ed.] Versus Italici Antiqui [w. treatise on metre] 5m. 8° Möller, *Lund* 90

Mediæval.

Monumenta Germaniae Historica: Poetae Latini Medii Aevi, vol. i. (2 pts.) 17m.; ii. (2 pts.) 19m.; iii. (1) 8m., iii. (2) fasc. 1, 10m. 4° Weidmann, *Berl.* 80–1; 84; 86; 92

Vol. i.-ii. ed. Ern. DÜMMLER, vol. iii. ed. Ludw. TRAUBE.

Concordance.

BENECKE, E. F. Index Poetarum Latinorum [lyric poets only] 4/6 c 8° Methuen 94

Translations.

SMITH, Prf. Goldwin [tr.] Bay Leaves; a collection of translations fr. the Latin poets 5/- ($1.25) c 8° Macmillan 93

Sound and readable trs.; sometimes very happy.

Fables —*v. infra, sub nom.* Avianus, *and* B § 3 (*HERVIEUX).

Lyrical.

Elegiac.

BIESE, Alf. [ed.] Römische Elegiker [Catull., Tibull., Propert., Ovid; for schl.-use] 75pf. c 8° Freytag, *Lps.* 90

PETERS, Karl [ed.] Anthologie aus dem römischen Elegikern, pts. i.–ii. [spec. Ovid.] ea. 1m.50 8° F. A. Perthes, *Gotha* 91; 92

SCHULZE, K. P. [ed.] Römische Elegiker [Catull., Tibull., Propert., Ovid] 2m.40 8° Weidmann, *Berl.* [79] 90

Ausonius, Dec. Magnus [A.D. 310–390].

Mosella: ed. crit. H. de La Ville de Mirmont; w. French Intro. and tr. 8° Gounouilhou, *Bordeaux* 90

An elabor. edn., of chief value for its extensive introd. on MSS. and edns. of the poems; w. facs. of title-pp. of rare edn. and map of the Moselle.

" w. German notes C. Hosius 1m.40 8° Elwert, *Marburg* 94

Avianus Flavius [A.D. 4th cent.].

*HERVIEUX, Léop. — Les Fabulistes Latins, vol. iii.: Avianus et ses Anc. Imitateurs—*ut* B § 3.

Bk. i. conts. a learned discussn. on name and age of the fabulist, and account of the numerous MSS., edns., and trs.; Bk. ii. descr. the prose and verse paraphrases or abridgmts. exec. in Mid. Ages, w. full account of the MSS. (mostly discov. by the author), followed by text of *Fables* as given in 10 cent. MS. of Trèves, Gk. Text of the fables of BABRIUS wh. Avianus has tult., the passages of VERGIL copied by AVIANUS, a prose version, a leonine verse tr. by a Piedmont poet, another fr. an Austrian codex, and other verses, paraphrases, and moralizations on the fables.

Calpurnius Siculus, Titus [A.D. 1st cent.].

Eclogues: ed. C. H. Keene; w. Intro. and notes [incl. also M. Aurel. Olympius Nemesianus] c 8° 6/- Bell / $1.40 Macmillan, *N.Y.* 87

" ed. Edw. J. L. Scott; w. English tr. [verse tr.] f 8° 3/6 Bell / Macmillan, *N.Y.* 91

The only English tr. wh. has ever appeared, either in prose or verse, of an author whose poems are of some archæological interest, and who was, perhaps, not more of a borrower and imitator than STATIUS, VALERIUS FLACCUS, SILIUS, CLAUDIANUS, or almost any other Latin verse-writer of note after time of LUCAN.

Catullus, Caius (or Q.) Valerius [B.C. 87–54].

Opera: rec. Prf. J. P. Postgate—*in his* Corpus Poetarum Latinorum, *ut supra.*

ed. S. G. Owen, w. notes (textual); ill. J. R. Weguelin s 4° [illegible] *nt.* Lawrence and Bullen / $5 *nt.* Macmillan, *N.Y.* 92

Also 120 on Jap. vell., w. an addl. ill., 31/6 *nt.* A good text, w. fine illus. The *Pervigilium Veneris*, which, tho' much later than CATULLUS, has much of his spirit, is added. Uniform w. A. H. BULLEN'S ed. of ANACREON, *ut* K § 190, but without a tr.

Photograph. facs. of the Venetian MS., ed. Constantino Nigra *priv. prin.* 93

The MS. is in the Library of St. Mark, Venice (cod. Lat. lxxx., classis xii.). A beautiful facs.; only 30 copies printed.

Tr. of Callimachus' Coma: ed. Constantino Nigra, *sub tit.* La Chioma di Berenice col testo latino di Catullo riscontrato sui codici Hoepli, *Milan* 91

With *appar. crit.*, Ital. tr. and comm. (about 57 other Ital. trs. of the poem have appeared since 1742, incl. that by Ugo FOSCOLO (1803), who added a long comm. wh. is still of value). The *Coma Berenices* of CALLIMACHUS is an artificial elegy, scarcely worthy of tr. by the most sincere of Latin poets, whose tr., moreover, is somewhat crude. 5 Appendices: (1) discussn. of vv. 51–58, (2) rel. of CATULLUS' poem to its Gk. original, (3) other Ital. trs. of the Coma, (4) FOSCOLO'S verse, (5) MSS. of CATULLUS (espec. later Italian).

w. Engl. notes and Introd. Prf. Elmer T. Merrill [Am.] [Coll. Ser. of Lat. Auth.] sq 8° $1.50 Ginn, *Boston* / 4/6 Arnold 93

A very satisfactory text, w. judicious foot-notes and valuable but rather prolix Introduction.

Translations.

Carmina: tr. Sir Rich. F. Burton + Leon. C. Smithers; port. 63/- 8° Nichols 94

L.P. (50) £6 6s. The metrical part by BURTON, the prose, w. Introd. and notes, by SMITHERS.

Attis: tr. Grant Allen [verse] [Bibliothèque de Carabas] *subscr.* 7/6 p 8° Nutt 92

Only 350 prtn., and 60 *L.P.* A fairly good tr. of the poem wh. author pronounces "the greatest poem in the Latin lang.," w. interesting disserts. on (1) the myth of Attis, (2) orig. of Tree-Worship (upholding the theory of relig. origins expounded by J. G. FRAZER in his *Golden Bough* (*ut* A § 9)), (3) on the Galliambic metre.

Aids.

BIRT, Theod. — De Catulli ad Mallium Epistula [progr.] 1*m.* 4° Elwert, *Marburg* 90

" " — Commentarioli Catulliani Supplementum 4° " " 90

" " — De Amorum in arte antiq. Simulacris, *etc.*: 10 pl. [= Commentariolus Catull. iii.] 1*m.*80 4° " " 92

CLÉDAT, Prf. M. L. [ed.] — Catulle: facs. d. MS. de St. Germain-des-Prés [Bibl. Nat. 14137]; w. Introd. [Coll. d. Réprod. d. MSS.] 15 *fr.* 8° Leroux, *Paris* 90

FRESE, Frz. — C. Val. Catullus: eine biograph. Skizze, *etc.* [w. some trs.] [schl.-progr.] 1*m.* 4° *Salzwedel* (Fock, *Lps.*) 90

LAFAYE, Geo. — Catulle et ses Modèles 8° Hachette, *Paris* 94

LEMERCIER, A. P. — Études sur les Sources du Poème laiv. de Catulle [55 pp.] 8° Delesques, *Caen* 93

MORGENSTERN, Otto — Curae Catullianae [programme] 1*m.* 8° Author, *Gross-Lichterfeld* 94

SCHRÖDER, Ferd. — Catulliana [school-programme] 4° *Cleve* 91

SMITH, Clem. Lawr. [Am.] — Catullus and the Phaselus of his 4th Poem—*in* Harvard Studies, vol. iii., *ut* K § 173.

ZAPPATA, Alex. — De Q. Valerii Catulli Vita et Carminibus [59 pp.] 8° Rocchetti, *Urbino* 90

Claudianus, Claudius [A.D. middle and end 4th cent.].

Carmina: rec. Theod. Birt [Monum. German. Auctt. Antiquiss.] 30*m.* 4° Weidmann, *Berl.* 92

An Appendix contains the spurious and the doubtful pieces.

rec. Jul. Koch 3*m.*60 8° Teubner, *Lps.* 93

MÜLLNER, Carl — De Imaginibus Similitudinibusque quae in Claud. Carminibus inveniuntur—*in* Diss. Phil. Vindob., vol. iv.—*ut* K § 173.

Ennius, Q. [B.C. 239–170].

Opera: rec. Lucian Müller—*in* Postgate's [ed.] Corpus Poet. Latin., *ut supra.*

Selecta: " Dr. W. W. Merry—*in his* Selected Fragments of Roman Poetry, *ut supra.*

REICHARDT, Alex. — De Q. Ennii Annalibus [dissert. inaug.] 8° *Halle* 89

VAHLEN, Joh. — Quaestiones Ennianae [Index Lectionum] 4° *Berlin* 88

" " — De Versibus nonnullis Ennianis Disputatio [Index Lectionum] 4° " 90

Horatius Flaccus, Q. [B.C. 65–B.C. 8].

Opera: rec. Dr. Jas. Gow—*in* Prf. J. P. Postgate's [ed.] Corpus Poet. Latin., *ut supra.*

" O. Keller + J. Haeussner 1*m.*25 8° Tempsky, *Prague* [ ]92

w. English comment. E. C. Wickham, 2 vols. [*ut* B.B. K § 214] 8° ea. 12/- Clar. Press / ea. $3 *nt.* Macmillan, *N.Y.* [74] 77; 91

Vol. i.: *Odes, Epodes, Carmen Seculare*; vol. ii.: *Satires, Epistles, De Arte Poetica*; w. map. A scholarly edn., w. adequate comm. Text somewhat conservative (based mainly on the MS. known as *vetus Blandinianus*): no variants given. The 2nd vol. not so satisfactory as the 1st; Prf. A. PALMER'S ed. of the *Satires* [*ut* B.B. K § 214] and Prf. A. S. WILKINS' of the *Epistolae* [*ut ib.*] remain the best Engl. edns.

Carmina: relegit et appar. crit. selecto instrux. Mart. Hertz 2*m.*40 8° Weidmann, *Berl.* 92

recogn. Hector Stampini; w. crit. notes in Latin 4*l.* 8° *Bologna* 93

bk. i.: w. English notes E. C. Wickham [Clar. Press Series] f 8° 2/- Clar. Press / 50c. *nt.* Macmillan, *N.Y.* 92

" iii.: " " " A. H. Allcroft + B. J. Hayes [Univ. Corr. Coll. Tut. Ser.] 3/- c 8° Clive 92

" Latin " W. Dillenburger—*ut* B.B. K § 214.

PÖPPELMANN, Ludw. — Bemerkungen zu Dillenburger's Horazausgabe, 3 pts. [schl.-prog.] 4° *Trèves* 90–92

Epistolae: w. Engl. notes F. G. Plaistowe + F. P. Shipham [Univ. Corr. Coll. Tut. Ser.] 5/6 c 8° Clive 93

Satirae: w. English notes and Introd. Prf. Ashmore [Am.] Amer. Bk. Co., *N.Y.*, *in prep.*

" " " " F. G. Plaistowe + F. Burnet [Univ. Corr. Coll. Tut. Ser.] 4/6 c 8° Clive 91

" et Epistolae: *w. German notes Lucian Mueller, pt. i. [Satires]; ii. [Epistles] ca. 8*m.* 8° Tempsky, *Prague* 91: 93

" English " J. B. Greenough [Am.] 12° $1.35 Ginn, *Boston* / 4/6 Arnold 88

K § 214

Translations.

Works: tr. Rev. J. C. Elgood [not very good] 4/6 c 8° Sonnenschein [86] 93
Odes: tr. J. Osborne Sargent [Am.]; w. Introd. Oliver Wendell Holmes [Am.] $1.50 12° *Boston* 93
,, and Carmen Sæculare: tr. Wm. Ewart Gladstone [verse] c 8° Murray *in prep.*
,, and ,, ,, tr. T. A. Walker [verse] [poor] 3/6 c 8° Stock 93
,, and Epodes: tr. Jno. B. Hague [Am.]; w. Introd., notes, and text [verse] Putnam 92

A slovenly, though occasionally neat, tr.: the text is of no value; its orthography that of 30 yrs. ago.

,, and ,, *tr. Sir Stephen De Vere; w. pref. and notes i 16° 7/6 *n.* Bell / $3 Macmillan, *N.Y.* [85] 93

75 on Jap. vell. 21/- *nt.* A very pleas. and poet. tr. as a whole. This 3rd edn. conts. 87 trs.: 1st (1885) contd. ten, and (1886) thirty, out of HORACE'S 103 Odes and 17 Epodes.

Epistles: tr. W. F. Masom [Univ. Corr. Coll. Tut. Ser.] 1/6 c 8° Clive 93
übers. Bacmeister + Keller [in orig. metre] 2*m.*40 8° Teubner, *Lps.* 91
Satires, bk. i.: tr. E. R. Wharton 2/- c 8° Parker, *Oxon.* 93

An endeavour to tr. every distinctive word in same way wherever it occurs, and to avoid trg. any two Lat. wds. in diff. places by same Engl. word.

Aids.
ARNOLD, Theod. Die griechischen Studien d. Horaz, hrsg. Wilh. Fries 2*m.* 8° Waisenhaus, *Halle* [53–56] 91
BOISSIER, Gaston Nouvelles Promenades archéol.: Horace et Virgile: 2 maps 3/*fr.*50 s 8° Hachette, *Paris* 86
FRIEDRICH, G. Q. Horatius Flaccus: philologische Untersuchungen 6*m.* 8° Teubner, *Lps.* 94
GEMOLL, Wilh Die Realien bei Horaz, pt. i. 1*m.*80, ii. 2*m.*40, iii. 3*m.*60 8° Gaertner, *Berl.* 91; 92; 93
NETTLESHIP, Prf. Hy. —*in his* Lectures and Essays on Subjects conn. w. Latin Liter., *ut* B.B. K § 211.
SAINTE-BEUVE, C. A.
*SELLAR, Prf. W. Y. Roman Poets of Augustan Age: Horace and Elegiac Poets 8° 14/- Clar. Press / $3.50 *nt.* Macmillan, *N.Y.* 92

Posthum. ed. W. P. KER, w. port., and a memr. by Andr. LANG (his nephew). Every side of HORACE'S wk. is thoroughly treated w. the loving-care of a classical critic of the first order, of ripe scholarship and fine literary taste.

Odes.
CAUER, Paul Wort- u. Gedankenspiele in den Oden d. Horaz 1*m.*60 8° Lipsius, *Kiel* 92
GEBHARD, F. Gedankengang Horazischer Oden in dispositioneller Uebersicht 1*m.*50 8° Lindauer, *Munich* 91

Epistles.
JERSSEN, Karl Bemerkungen zu Horazens Epistel an die Pisonen, 2 pts. [schl.-progr.] 4° Werden 91; 92
MÜLLER, Lucian De Horatii Epistularum ii., 1, 50–62 Disputatio [Acta Minist. Publ. Ross.] 1*m.*20 8° Calvary, *Berlin* 90

Satires.
DITTMAR, Herm. Horati libri ii. satiram 6 interpretatus est [school-programme] 8° *Magdeburg* 92

Horace in the Middle Ages.
MANITIUS, M. Analekten zur Geschichte d. Horaz im Mittelalter [down to A.D. 1300] 2*m.*80 8° Dieterich, *Göttingen* 93

Life.
HARTMAN, J. De Horatio Poeta 2*fl.*90 8° van Doesburgh, *Leyden* 91
KÖHNE, K. Selbstbiographie des Q. Horatius Flaccus 2*m.* 4° Benziger, *Einsiedeln* 91
RAPOLLA, D. Vita di Quinto Orazio Flacco con ragguagli novissimi 5*l.* 8° Detken, *Naples* 92
SEMISCH, Frz. Leben und Dichten des Horaz, pt. i. [school-progr.] 4° *Friedeberg* 93

Scholia. Text. Language.
HAGBY, Alf. [Am.] Adverbs in Horace and Juvenal [dissert.] 8° Johns Hopk. Univ., *Baltimore* 91
CAMPAUX, Ant. Histoire du Texte d'Horace [pp. 108] 8° Berger-Levrault, *Nancy* 91
HOLDER + KELLER, Alf. / Otto (eds.) Scholia Antiqua in Horatium Flaccum 20*m.* 8° Wagner, *Innsbruck* 94
LEWICKI, Pet. De Natura Infinitivi atque Usu apud Horatium, pt. [progr.] 8° *Lemberg* 91

Scholia.
PORPHYRIO, Pomponius Commentarii in Q. Horat. Flacc., rec. Wilh. Meyer 4*m.*20 8° Teubner, *Lps.* 74
PAULY, Friedr. Neue Beiträge z. Kritik d. Porphyrion 1*m.*75 8° Dominicus, *Prague* 58; 77
PETSCHENIG, Mich. —*in his* Zur Kritik d. Hor.-scholiasten, and Zu d. Scholiasten d. Hor. [progr.[ea. 1*m.* *Klagenft.* 72: *Graz* 73
WESSNER, Paul Quaestiones Porphyrioneae [dissert. inaug.] 8° *Leipzig* 93
Scholia Acronis et Porphyrionis, rec. Ferd. Hauthal, pt. i. 9*m.*; ii. 12*m.* 8° Springer, *Berlin* 64–66
Scholia Horatiana quae feruntur Acronis et Porphyrionis, ed. Fr. Pauly [after G. Fabricius (*Basle* 1555)], 2 vols. 12*m.* Bellmann, *Prague* [58–59] 61

Juvenalis, Dec. Junius [A.D. *c.* 47–*c.* 127].

Satiræ: *cum schol. vet. rec. Otto Jahn *o.p.* [*scarce*; *pb.* 6*m.*75, *w.* 30*m.*] 8° G. Reimer, *Berlin* 51
bks. viii., x., xiii.: w. English notes A. H. Allcroft [Univ. Corr. Coll. Tut. Ser.] 3/6 c 8° Clive 91
Decimus Junius, two satires: w. English notes Fcs. Pp. Nash [Am.] 12° $1.25 Houghton, *Boston* / 5/- *nt.* Gay & Bird 92

Translations.

Satires: *Thirteen Satires of Juvenal, tr. Dr. Alex. Leeper [Austral.[[prose] 3/6 (90*c.*) c 8° Macmillan [82] 92

A vigorous prose tr., less literal but more literary than that of J. D. LEWIS [*ut* B.B. K § 214]. The name of Prf. A. H. STRONG, at that time Prof. of Classics in Melb. Univ., appeared on title-page of the first three edns. as co-translator.

,, i.–viii.: tr. A. H. Allcroft [Univ. Corr. Coll. Tut. Ser.] 2/6 c 8° Clive 94
,, viii., x.–xiii.: tr. A. H. Allcroft + A. F. Barnet [Univ. Corr. Coll. Tut. Ser.] 2/- c 8° ,, 91

Aids.
BAGBY, Alf. [Am.] Adverbs in Horace and Juvenal—*ut supra*, *s.v.* Horace.
HOFMANN, M. J. Kritische u. exeget. Bemerkungen zu den Satiren Juvenals [schl.-progr.] 8° *Munich* 90
HÖHLER, Wilh. [ed.] Scholia Juvenaliana Inedita, pt. i. 1*m.*; ii. 1*m.*50 4° *Ettenheim* (Fock, *Lps.*) 89; 90
KJÆR, Lud. O. De Sermone D. Jun. Juvenalis 6/- 8° Host, *Copenhagen* 75
STREIFINGER, Jos. Der Styl des Satirikers Juvenalis [school-programme] 8° *Ratisbon* 92
SYDOW, Hugo De Juvenalis Arte Compositionis [dissert. inaug.] 8° *Halle* 90

Lucanus, M. Annæus [A.D. 39–65].

De Bello Ciuili libri x. (Pharsalia): *rec. Carol. Hosius 3*m.*60 8° Teubner, *Lps.* 92

An excellent edn., based on a thoroughly critical exam. of the MSS.

FRITSCHE, Rob. Quæstiones Lucaneæ [dissert.] 1*m.* 8° *Gotha* 92
GREGORIUS, Alph. De M. Annæi Lucani Pharsaliæ tropis, pt. i. [dissert.] 1*m.*50 8° Fock, *Lps.* 93
MILLARD, Jos. E. Lucani Sententia de Deis et Fato [dissert.] 8° Reyers, *Utrecht* 91

Lucilius, G. [B.C. *c.* 180–103].

Opera: rec. Prf. J. P. Postgate—*in his* Corpus Poetarum Latinorum, *ut supra.*
Selecta: rec. Dr. W. W. Merry—*in his* Selected Fragments of Roman Poetry, *ut supra.*

Lucretius Carus, Titus [B.C. *c.* 98–55].

De Rerum Natura: ed. A. Brieger 1*m*.80 8° Teubner, *Lps.* 94
bk. v.: w. English notes, Introd. and tr. J. D. Duff c 8° 2/- Camb. Press; 50c. *net.* Macmillan, *N.Y.* 90

Feustell, Heinr. De Comparationibus Lucretianis [dissert. inaug.] 8° *Halle* 93
Frerichs, Heinr. Quaestiones Lucretianae [school-programme] 4° *Oldenburg* 92
Meissner, Joh. Quaest. ad Usum Casuum el. q. Lucretianum pertinentes [dissert. inaug.] 8° *Halle* 91
Morselli, Em. Il Pessimismo di Tito Lucrezio Caro 1*l.* 8° Clausen, *Turin* 92
v. Raumer, Siegm. Die Metapher bei Lucrez 1*m*.50 8° Blaesing, *Erlangen* 93
Siemering, Fr. Die Behandlung der Mythen u. d. Götterglaubens b. Lucrez [schl.-progr.] 1*m.* 4° *Tilsit* (Fock, *Lps.*) 91
" " Quaestionum Lucretianarum partic. i. et ii. [dissert. inaug.] 8°

Manilius, M. [A.D. 1st cent.].

Astronomicon rec. Richard Bentley *o.p.* *London* 1739
An early work of Bentley, ed. by his nephew three years before the death of his uncle.
rec. Friedr. Jacob, w. notes; 4 pl. 2*m.* 8° G. Reimer, *Berlin* 49
The best text for general purposes, though curiously inaccurate in its critical apparatus.

Aids.
Bechert, Melvin De M. Manilio astronomicorum poeta [schl.-progr.] 1*m*.20 4° Hinrichs, *Lps.* 91
De M. Manilii emendandi ratione—*in* Leipziger Studien, vol. i. 78
Regards the Gembloux MS. (10 cent.) as the best.
*Ellis, Prf. Robinson Noctes Manilianae: sive dissertationes in Astron. Manilii c 8° 6/- Clar. Press; $1.90 *net.* Macmillan, *N.Y.* 91
Written in form of Latin notes on detached passages of Manilius, to wh. are appended an Engl. dissert. on name of Manilius and a few remarks on the *Aratea* of Germanicus. Regards the Gembloux MS. and Voss[a] as essential to the crit. of Manilius.
Lanson, G. De Manilio Poeta eiusque ingenio [thesis] 3*fr.* 8° Hachette, *Paris* 87
Tappertz, Ed. De Coniunctionum usu apud Manilium Quaestt. [diss. inaug.] 8° *Münster* 92
Thomas, P. Lucubrationes Manilianae [Recueil d. Travaux; Univ. d. Gand] 2*fr.* 8° Clemm, *Gand* 88
Cont. an accurate collation of the Gembloux MS. a valuable supplement to Jacob's edn. Manilius, tho' one of the most important poets of the Roman Stoicism, and tho' he attracted the attention of two of the greatest scholars of all time, Scaliger and Bentley (not to mention Huet), is very little read now.

Martial, M. Valerius [A.D. 40(–43)–*c.* 102].

Renn, Em. Die griechischen Eigennamen bei Martial [school-programme] 1*m*.20 8° *Landshut* 89
Söding, Heinr. De Infinitivi apud Martialem Usurpatione [diss. inaug.] 8° *Marburg* 91
Spiegel, Gebh. Zur Charakteristik d. Epigrammatikers M. Val. Martialis [schl.-progr.] 8° *Halle* 91

Maximianus (Etruscus) [A.D. 6th cent.].

Elegiæ: rec. et emend. M. Petschenig [= Berl. Studien, vol. xi. (37 pp.)] 1*m*.50 8° Calvary, *Berlin* 90
Based on the Eton MS. (the best there is), w. brief appar. criticus, notes on the text, and full index of words, usages and constructions.

Nemesianus, M. Aur. Olympius—*v.* Capurnius, *supra.*

Ovidius Naso, P. [B.C. 43–A.D. 17].

Epistola Sapphus ad Phaonem: ed. S. G. de Vries; w. crit. appar. and Latin comm. 4*m*.50 8° Calvary, *Berlin* 88
Fasti, bks. iii.–iv.: w. Engl. notes & Introd. T. M. Neatby + F. G. Plaistowe [Univ. Corr. Coll. Tut. Ser.] 3/6 c 8° Clive 92
Metamorphoses: rec. Fickelscherer Teubner, *Lps. in prep.*
bks. i.–iii.: ed. Prf. Robinson Ellis, fr. Harleian MS. 2610 [Anecdota Oxon.] s 4° 4/- Clar. Press; $1 *net.* Macmillan, *N.Y.*
bk. i.: w. English notes and var. rgs. Rev. Launcelot D. Dowdall f 8° 1/6 Camb. Press; 50c. *net.* Macmillan, *N.Y.* 92
Tristia, bk. i.: " " " A. H. Allcroft + E. P. Shipham [Univ. Corr. Coll. Tut. Ser.] 3/- c 8° Clive 93
bk. iii.: " " " A. H. Allcroft + F. G. Plaistowe [Univ. Corr. Coll. Tut. Ser.] 3/- c 8° " 93
Selections: " " " and vocab. J. F. Brackenbury 2/- *nt.* f 8° Percival (Riv. & Perc.) 93
" " " " Fcs. W. Kelsey [Am.] $1.25 12° Allyn, *Boston* 90

Aids.
Duplessis, Georges Essai Bibliographique sur l. différ. Edns. d'Ovide ornées au 15 et 16 siècles 4*fr.* 8° Techener, *Paris* 89
Descr. of 164 ill. edns. of *Ovid* fr. 1484 to 1599, printed at Bruges, Strassburg, Paris, Lyons, Venice, Antwerp, Basle, etc.
Jezienski, And. St. De universis Ovidii epp. Heroid. et de Sapph. ad Phaon. ep. [progr.] 3*m.* 8° *Tarnopol* (Fock, *Lps.*) 86
Löwe, Ueber d. Präpositionen *a*, *de*, *ex* bei Ovid [school-programme] 8° *Strehlen* 89
Magnus, Hugo Studien zur Ueberlieferung u. Kritik d. Metam. Ovids, pts. i.–iv. ea. 1*m.* 4° Gaertner, *Berlin* 87–93
*Sellar, Prf. W. Y. —*in his* Roman Poets of Augustan Age: Horace and Elegiac Poets, *ut supra*, *s.n.* Horace.
Should be supplem. by author's art. *Ovid* in *Encyclo. Brit.* (ed. 9), unfortunately not incl. in this posth. bk. wh. was incomplete as regards Ovid at author's death.

Archæology.
Engelmann, R. [ed.] Bilderatlas zu Ovids Metamorphosen: 26 pl., w. descr. text 2*m*.60; *bnd.* 3*m*.20 obl Verlag d. Litt. Jahresb., *Lps.* 90

Language.
Guttmann, Karl Sogenanntes Instrumentales *ab* bei Ovid [school-programme] 4° *Dortmund* 90
Hilberg, I. Die Gesetze der Wortstellung im Pentameter d. Ovid 28*m.* 8° Teubner, *Lps.* 94
Linse, E. De P. Ovidio Nasone Vocabulorum inventore [school-programme] 1*m*.50 8° Fock, *Lps.* 91

Dictionary.
Peters, Dr. Karl [ed.] Schulwörterbuch zu Ovids sämmtlichen Dichtungen 2*m*.50 8° F. A. Perthes, *Gotha* 94

Textual Criticism.
Grau, Rud. De Ovidii Metamorphoseon codice Amploniano priore [dissert.] 2*m.* 8° Peter, *Halle* 92

Persius Flaccus, Aulus [A.D. 34–62].

Satirae: *cum schol. antiq. ed. Otto Jahn *o.p.* [*scarce*; *pb.* 9*m.*, *w.* 25*m.*] 8° Breitkopf, *Lps.* 43
Sobr, Jos. Die Sprache der Satirikers Persius [school-programme] 8° *Laibach* 90

K § 214

Petronius Arbiter, (T ?) [A.D. ?–66].

Satiræ :

Cena Trimalchionis : *w. German notes and tr. Prf. Ludw. Friedländer 5*m.* 8° Hirzel, *Lps.* 91

An excellent edn., w. minute comm., repres. the latest crit., and introductory sketch of the condn., life, and manners of the Ital. towns under the Empire, partic. in 1st cent. A.D., on wh. subj. FRIEDLÄNDER (author of the well-known *Sittengeschichte Roms*, 3 vols. 36*m.* 8° Hirzel, *Lps.* ('71–'74) '88–'90, and edr. of MARTIAL) has very wide knowl. The tr. is spirited and idiomatic.

Aids.

BECK, Chas. [Am.] — The Age of Petronius Arbiter [important] 4° Cambridge, *Mass.* 56
" " — The Manuscripts of the Satyricon of Petronius Arbiter descr. and collated 4° " " 63
Extracts from the *Memoirs of the Amer. Acad. of Arts and Sciences.*

CESAREO — De Petronii Sermone 8° *Rome* 87
Freely quoted from by FRIEDLÄNDER in the notes to his edn. of text of *Cena Trimalch.*, *ut sup.*

COLLIGNON, A. — Etude sur Pétrone : crit. littéraire, l'imitation et la parode d. l. Satiricon 6*fr.* 8° Hachette, *Paris* 92
Its main purpose is to show what resemblance the wk. of PETRONIUS, espec. his poems, offers to other earlier or contemp. writers—a large space bg. devoted to the longest poem—that on the Civil War.

HALEY [Am.] — Quæstiones Petronianæ—*in* Harvard Studies in Class. Philol., vol. ii. [*ut* K § 173].
Among the most important contribs. to the study of PETRONIUS.

Phædrus [B.C. 1st cent.—A.D. 1st cent.].

Fabulæ : éd. paléograph. p. Ulysse Robert 10*fr.* 8° Hachette, *Paris* 94

Based on the unique 9th cent. MS. discov. at Rheims by Pierre PITHOU and printed in 1596, now in possessn. of Marq. de ROSANBO. The only other crit. edn. is that of BERGER DE XIVREY, 1830, wh. is apparently full of blunders.

ELLIS, Prf. Robinson — The Fables of Phædrus (inaug. lecture) 1/- *nt.* 8° Clar. Press 94
*HERVIEUX, Léop. — Les Fabulistes Latins, vols. i.–ii. : Phædrus et ses Anciens Imitateurs—*ut* B § 3.

Propertius, Sextus Aurelius [B.C. *c.* 50–? 17].

BONAFOUS, Raim. — De Sex. Propertii Amoribus et Poesi [110 pp.] 8° *Paris* 94
Seven readable papers on the life and poems of PROPERTIUS, largely indebted to PLESSY'S excellent bk., *ut infra.*

HETZEL, J. — Beiträge zur Erklärung des Propertius [programme] 8° *Dillenburg* 90
*PLESSIS, Fréd. — Etude critique sur Properce [an excellent *étude*] 7*fr.*50 8° Hachette, *Paris* 86
SCHNEIDER, Wilh. — De Propertio Sermonis Novatore et Amplificatore, 2 pts. [diss. inaug.] 8° Schultz, *Strassburg* 88
SPANDAU, Ad. — De Sermone Propertiano Specimen primum [diss. inaug.] 8° *Leipzig* 83
SPINDLER, Herm. — Syntaxeos Propertianæ Capita duo [tenses and moods of verbs] [diss. inaug.] 8° *Marburg* 88

Prudentius Clemens, Aurelius [A.D. 348–*c.* 410].

PUECH, Aimé — Prudence : études sur la poésie latine chrétienne du 4 siècle 5*fr.* 8° Hachette, *Paris* 88
SCHMITZ, Matthias — Die Gedichte des Prudentius u. ihre Entstehungszeit [schl.-progr.] 1*m.* 4° *Aix-la-Chap.* (Fock, *Lps.*) 89
SIXT, G. — Die lyrischen Gedichte d. Aurelius Prudentius Clemens [schl.-progr.] 4° *Stuttgart* 89
ZANIOL, Aug. — Aurelio Prudenzano Clemente, poeta cristiano : lettura [38 pp.] 1*l.* 8° Typ. Emiliana, *Venice* [ ] 90

Silius Italicus, C. [A.D. 25–102].

Punica : ed. Ludw. Bauer, vol. i. [lib. 1–10]; ii. [lib. 11–17] ea. 2*m.*40 s 8° Teubner, *Lps.* 90; 92

Aids.

ALTENBURG, Ed. — Observv. in Italici Iliadis lat. et Sil. Ital. Punic. dictionem 8° *Marburg* 90
BAUER, Ludw. — Handschriftl. u. Kritisch-exeget. Erörterungen z. d. Punica d. Silius Italicus 8° *Augsbg.* (Fock, *Lps.*) 93
BLASS, Herm. — Die Textesquellen des Silius Italicus [*repr. fr.* Jahrbb. f. Class. Philol.] 2*m.*40 8° Teubner, *Lps.* 75
HEYNACHER, Max — Stellung d. Silius Italicus unter d. Quellen zum zweiten punischen Kriege [schl.-progr.] 2*m.* 4° *Nordhausen* 77
HILFF, Frz. — Observationes criticæ et exegeticæ ad Sil. Ital. Punic. i., 5–10 [diss. inaug.] 8° *Münster* 93
OCCIONI, Onor. — Caio Silio Italico e il suo poema : studi 4*l.* 16° Le Monnier, *Flor.* (68) 71
SCHÄFER, Jos. — Quæstiones criticæ et exegeticæ ad Sil. Ital. Punic., i. 1–4 [diss. inaug.] 8° *Münster* 93
WEZEL, Ernest — De C. Silii Italici cum fontibus tum exemplis [dissert. inaug. ; 105 pp.] 1*m.*50 8° Koch, *Lps.* 73

Statius, P. Papinius [A.D. *c.* 45–*c.* 96].

(Silv. iii. (3)) : Statius' Trostgedicht an d. Claudius Etruscus, hrsg. O. Lottich ; w. Germ. notes [progr.] 2*m.*50 4° Herold, *Hamburg* 93

Translation.

Thebais : übers. A. Imhof, *sub tit.* Das Lied von Theben ; w. notes, 2 pts. 5*m.*50 8° Schröter, *Ilmenau* 85 ; 89

ADRIAN, Gerh. — Quaestiones Statianae [dissert. inaug.] 8° *Würzburg* 93
CLARETIE, Leo — De P. Papinii Statii Silvis [86 pp. ; thesis] 8° *Lutetiae* (=*Paris*) 91
HELM, R. — De P. Papinii Statii Thebaide i. 3*m.* 60 8° Mayer & Müller, *Berl.* 92
LEO, Friedr. — De Stati Silvis Commentatio [Index Scholarum] 4° *Göttingen* 92
LUNDSTRÖM, Wilh. — Quaestiones Papinianae [Comm. Acad.] 2/- 8° Lundequist, *Upsala* 93
MÜLLER, H. — Studia Statiana 1*m.* 20 8° Heinrich, *Berlin* 94
POLSTER, Ludw. — Quaestionum Statianarum partic. i.–iv. [school-programmes] 4° *Inowrazlaw* 78–90

Tibullus, Albius [B.C. *c.* 55–19 (18)].

Opera : rec. Eduard Hiller—*in* Prf. J. P. Postgate's [ed.] Corpus Poet. Latin., *ut supra.*

BELLING, H. — Kritische prolegomena zu Tibull 3*m.* 8° Weidmann, *Berlin* 93
ULLRICH, Rich. — De Lib. Sec. Tib. statu integro et compositione [*extr. fr.* Jahrb. Cl. Phil.] 2*m.*40 8° Teubner, *Lps.* 90

Valerius Flaccus, C. [A.D. ?—before 90].

Argonautica : übers. Mor. Gürsching, *s. t.* Argonautenfahrt : Uebersetzungsproben [progr.] 8° *Ansbach* 90

GRUENBERG, Arth. — De Valerio Flacco Imitatore 2*m.*40 8° Heinrich, *Berlin* 93
KOESTERS, H. — Quaestiones Metricae et Prosodiacae ad Valer. Flaccum pertinentes [dissert.] 2*m.* 8° *Münster* (Fock, *Lps.*) 94
MOLTZER, M. N. J. — De Apollonii Rhodii et Valerii Flacci Argonauticis [dissertatio] 8° Breijer, *Utrecht* 91
SUMMERS, Walt. C. — A Study of the Argonautica of Valerius Flaccus 2/6 8° Deighton, *Camb.* 94

Varro, M. Terentius (Reatinus) [B.C. 116–27].

HOLZER, Ern. — Varroniana [school-programme] 4° *Ulm* 90
NORDEN, E. — In Varronis Saturas Menippeas Observationes selectae [*extr. fr.* Jahrbb. Cl. Phil.] 2*m.* 40 s 8° Teubner, *Lps.* 92
SANTER, Ern. — Quaestiones Varronianae ; 1 pl. [dissert. inaug.] 2*m.* 8° Heinrich, *Berlin* 92

Vergilius Maro, P. [B.C. 70–19].

Opera : rec. Prf. Hy. Nettleship—*in* Prf. J. P. Postgate's [ed.] Corpus Poet. Latin., *ut supra*.

w. English notes and Introd. T. L. Papillon + E. A. Haigh, 2 vols. c 8° 12/- Clar. Press / $2.75 *net* Macmillan, *N.Y.* 92

Æneid, bks. i.–iii., iv.–vi., vii.–ix., x.–xii., 4 pts. ea. pt. 3/- (75c. *net*) '90–'91 : *Bucolics* and *Georgics* (90c. *net*) 3/6, '91.

w. English notes and Introd. Arth. Sidgwick, 2 vols. c 8° 8/- Camb. Press / $2.25 *net* Macmillan, *N.Y.* 90 ; 90

i. *Text* and *Introd.* 3/6 ; ii. *Notes* 4/6. A compendious and convenient edn. for schl.-use or private reading.

Æneis : bks. i.–vi. *w. English notes T. E. Page [Classical Series] 6/- f 8° Macmillan 94

A very good schl. edn., the chief feature of which is its copious notes based on the poem and its various commentators and critics. Introd. conts. a biogr. and crit. sketch of the poet.

bk. i. : w. English notes T. E. Page, w. vocab. [Elementary Classics] 1/6 (40c.) 18° Macmillan 93

,, iii. : ,, ,, ,, ,, w. vocab. [Elementary Classics] 1/6 (40c.) 18° ,, 90

,, ,, ,, ,, ,, A. H. Allcroft + W. F. Masom, 1/6 ; w. vocab. & tr. 3/- [Univ. Corr. Coll. Tut. Ser.] c 8° Clive 93

,, iv. ,, ,, ,, H. M. Stephenson [Elementary Classics] 1/6 (40c.) 18° Macmillan 88

,, v. : ,, ,, ,, A. H. Allcroft + W. F. Masom [Univ. Corr. Coll. Tut. Ser.] 3/- c 8° Clive 94

,, vi. : ,, ,, ,, A. H. Allcroft + B. J. Hayes [Univ. Corr. Coll. Tut. Ser.] 1/6 c 8° ,, 92

,, vii. : ,, ,, ,, and Introd. A. H. Allcroft + T. M. Neatly [Univ. Corr. Coll. Tut. Ser.] 3/- c 8° Clive 92

,, ,, ,, ,, ,, and vocab. W. C. Collar [Am.] 16° 90c. Ginn, *Boston* / 2/- Arnold 93

,, viii. : ,, ,, ,, J. Tetlaw [Am.] 16° 90c. Ginn, *Boston* / 2/- Arnold 93

,, ,, [Evander and Shield of Achilles] w. Engl. notes Arth. Calvert [Elementary Class.] 1/6 (40c.) 8° Macmillan 90

,, x. ,, ,, ,, S. G. Owen [Elementary Classics] 1/6 (40c.) 18° ,, 90

Bucolica : ,, ,, ,, T. E. Page ; vocab. [Elementary Classics] 1/6 (40c.) 18° ,, 91

,, and Georgics ,, ,, ,, and Introd. T. L. Papillon + A. E. Haigh [Clar. Press Series] f 8° 3/6 Clar. Press / 90c. *net* Macmillan *N.Y.* 91

Culex rec. Prf. F. Leo ; w. Latin Commentary 3*m.* 8° Weidmann, *Berl.* 91

A reconstruction of the text, based on the Bembine MS. (the earliest known : ? 9th cent.—in Vatican Lib.).

Georgica :

bk. i. : w. English notes and Introd. T. E. Page [good Introd. ; Element Class.] 1/6 (40c.) 18° Macmillan 90

,, i.–ii. ; iii.–iv. : ,, ,, ,, ,, C. S. Jerram f 8° ea. 2/6 Clar. Press / ea. 60c. *net* Macmillan, *N.Y.* 92 ; 92

,, vii. : ,, ,, ,, Wm. C. Collar [Am.] ; ill. 16° 90c. Ginn, *Boston* / 2/- Arnold 93

Translations.

Works : tr. Dr. A. Hamilton Bryce ; w. notes & Introds. ; port. [literal prose] [Bohn's Lib.] c 8° 3/6 Bell / Macmillan, *N.Y.* 94

Aeneid : tr. Wm. Caxton [1590], ed. M. T. Culley 8° Early Eng. Text Soc., *in prep.*

bk. i.–vi. : tr. Jas. Rhoades [blank verse] 5/- ($1.75) c 8° Longman 93

A readable and faithful tr. of the first half of the *Æneid* into the natural Engl. metre for epic, by the tr. of the *Georgics* (*vid.* B.B. K § 214).

Aids.

EHRLICH, Frz. Mittelitalien, Land u. Leute, in d. Æneide Vergils [schl.-progr.] 8° *Eichstädt* 92

GALBO, Joakim De Personarum in Virg. Æneide Natura et Moribus 3*l.*50 8° Clausen, *Panormi* 91

MONTANO d' Ivedria Torniamo a Virgilio : note e saggio di interpretazione 4*l.*50 8° Roux, *Turin* 92

NETTLESHIP, Prf. Hy. —*in* his Lectures and Essays on subjects conn. w. Latin Literature, *ut* B.B. K § 211.

SERVIUS, Maurus Honoratus Commentarii in Vergilium—*ut* B.B. K § 214.

Mustard, Prof. Wilf. P. [Am.] The Etymols. in the Servian Comm. to Vergil [*repr. fr.* Colorado Coll. Studs.] 8° Univ. of Colorado 92

THOMSON, J. A. De Comparationibus Vergilianis 1*m.* 30 8° Möller, *Lund* 93

Æneid.

FÖRSTEMANN, Albr. Zur Geschichte des Æneasmythus 2*m.* 80 8° Creutz, *Magdeburg* 94

GEORG, Heinr. Die antike Aeneis Kritik aus den Scholien u. anderen Quellen dargestellt 10*m.* 8° Kohlhammer, *Stuttgt.* 91

KUNZ, F. Realien in Vergils Æneis, pt. i. [Kriegswesen u. Privatleben] 1*m.* 8° Fock, *Lps.* 94

Bucolics.

SONNTAG, M. Vergil als bukolischer Dichter 5*m.* 8° Teubner, *Lps* 91

Culex and *Ciris.*

GANZENMÜLLER, Dr. Carl Beiträge zur Ciris [*extr. fr.* Jahrbb. f. Class. Philol.] 3*m.*20 8° Teubner. *Lps.* 94

LEDERER, Siegfr. Ist Virgil der Verfasser von *Culex* and *Ciris*? 1*m.* 8° Fock, *Lps.* 90

RÖHRICH, Max De Culicis potissimis Codicibus recte æstimandis [diss. inaug.] 1*m.*50 8° Henrich, *Berlin* 91

Georgics.

PULVERMACHER, N. De *Georgicis* a Vergilio retractatis [diss.] 1*m.* 8° Heinrich, *Berlin* 90

Metrics. Style.

MOORE, Jno. Leverett [Am.] Servius on the Tropes and Figures of Vergil [thesis] 8° Johns Hopk. Univ., *Baltimore* 92

RÖNSTRÖM, Th. O. Joh. Metri Vergiliani Recensio 1*m.* 20 8° Möller, *Lund* 93

Vergil in the Middle Ages—*v.* B § 3, *s.v.* Vergil (STECHER).

215. LATIN DRAMATISTS.

Plautus, T. Maccius [B.C. 254–184].

Comoediae : * rec. Friedr. Ritschl, cur. Geo. Goetz + G. Loewe + Friedr. Schoell 8° Teubner, *Lps.* 83–93

New vols. : *Casina* .... SCHOELL, 5*m.*60, 90 | *Miles Gloriosus* .... 6*m.* RITSCHL-GOETZ, 90
Cistellaria .... SCHOELL, 5*m.*60, 94 | *Mostellaria* .... RITSCHL-SCHOELL, 6*m.* 93
Menaechmi .... RITSCHL-SCHOELL, 5*m.*60, 89 | *Persa* .... SCHOELL, 5*m.*60, 90

,, ex rec. Geo. Goetz + Friedr. Schoell, pts. i.–ii. 2*m.*70 8° Teubner, *Lps.* 93 ; 93

i. *Amphyt.*, *Asin.*, *Aulul* [w. Latin life of PLAUTUS] 1*m.*50 ; ii. *Bacch.*, *Capt.*, *Casina*, 1*m.*20.

An admirable small edn. The brief and excellent crit. appar. conts. only the essential variants : text represents the best scientific criticism (conservative) of pres. day, consid. improved on that of the large edn.

Asinaria : w. English notes Rev. J. H. Gray [Pitt Press Series]; fr. Goetz + Schoell's text f 8° 3/6 Camb. Press / 90c. *nt.* Macmillan, *N.Y.* 94
Captivi : w. English notes and Introd. J. H. Freese 1/6 f 8° Methuen 94
Intended for lower Forms, and omits about a third of the play—for no obvious reason, as the play is short and exceptionably unobjectionable.
" w. English notes and Introd. A. R. S. Hallidie [Classical Series] 3/6 (90c.) f 8° Macmillan 91
Epidicus : " " " " Rev. J. H. Gray [Goetz's text] [Pitt Press Series] f 8° 3/- Camb. Press / 80c. *nt.* Macmillan *N.Y.* 93
Pseudolus : " " " " E. P. Morris [Am.] $1.20 12° Allyn, *Boston* 91
Rudens *ed. crit. Prf. Edw. A. Sonnenschein; w. critical and explan. notes 8° 8/6 Clar. Press / $2.25 *nt.* Macmillan, *N.Y.* 91
An important and erudite work, a solid contribution to Plautine scholarship. The only edn. of the Rudens w. English notes, and since BENOIST'S edn. (1864) the only annot. edn. in any language.
Stichus : w. English notes and Introd. Dr. C. G. M. Fennell [Pitt Press Series] f 8° 2/6 Camb Press / 60c. *nt.* Macmillan *N.Y.* 93
An unsatisfactory edn. based on RITSCHL'S text (why not on the edn. of Goetz, 1883?)

Translations.

Comedies : tr. Edw. H. Sugden, vol. i. [in orig. metres] c 8° 6/- Sonnenschein / $1.75 Macmillan, *N.Y.* 93
A successful attempt to perform a difficult and delicate task. This vol. conts. *Amphitruo, Asinaria, Aulularia, Bacchides* and *Captivi.*

Aids.
NIEMEYER, Max Plautinische Studien [school-programme] 4° *Potsdam* 90
*STUDEMUND, Wilh. [ed.] Studia in Priscos Scriptores Latinos—*ut* K § 209.

Bibliography.
*SEYFFERT, Prf. Oscar Jahresber. üb. Plautus: 1886–89 [*extr. fr.* Jahresb. üb. Forts. Kl. Alterth. vol. xviii.] 8° Calvary, *Berlin* 91
An admirable summary of the Plautine literature of the period included. To be continued.

Amphitruo.
SIEWERT, Dr. Paul Plautus in Amphitr. fabula quomodo exemplar graec. transtulerit 2m. 8° Fock, *Lpz.* 94
Bacchides.
HAAR, Jos. De *Bacchidibus* Plautinis Quaestiones 1m. 8° Theissing, *Münster* 91
Miles Gloriosus.
GÖTZ, Geo. Emendationes Militis Gloriosi Plautinae 50*pf.* 4° Neuenhahn, *Jena* 90
Poenulus.
SOLTAU, Friedr. Zur Erklärg. d. in Punischer Sprache gehalt. Reden des Hanno [Berl. Stud.] 1m.20 8° Calvary, *Berlin* 89

Chronology of the Plays.
HÜFFNER, Friedr. De Plauti Comoediarum exempl. atticis quaestt. maxime chronolog. [diss.] 1m.50 8° Dieterich, *Göttgn.* 94

Language. Grammar. Metre.
FERGER, Wilh. De Vocativi Usu Plautino Terentianoque [dissert. inaug.] 8° Heitz, *Strassbg.* 89
LUCHS, Aug. Quaestiones Metricae [chiefly Plautine]—*in* Studemund's Studien, vol. i. pt. i., *ut* B.B. K § 209.
SKUTSCH, Frz. Forschung. z. lat. Gram. u. Metrik, vol. i.: Plautinisches u. Romanisches—*ut* K § 119.
Adjectives.
GIMM, Jul. De Adiectivis Plautinis [school-programme] 4° *Altkirch* 92
Adverbs.
GEHLHARDT, Paul De Adverbiis ad Notionem augendam a Plauto usurpatis [diss. inaug.] 8° *Halle* 92
Genitive.
BLOMQVIST, A. W. De Genetivi apud Plautum Usu [dissert.] 8° *Helsingfors* 92
Particles.
*RICHTER, Paul De usu Particularum exclamativ. [chiefly Plautine; Important]—*in* Studemund's Studien, vol. i. pt. 2, *ut* B.B. K § 209.
Pronouns.
BACH, Jos. De usu Pronominum Demonstrativorum—*in* Studemund's Studien, vol. ii., *ut supra.*
LUCHS, Aug. Genetivbildung der Pronomina [chiefly Plautine]—*in* Studemund's Studien, vol. i. pt. 2, *ut* B.B. K § 209.
Syntax.
*BECKER, Ed. De Syntaxi Interrogationum [chiefly Plautine]—*in* Studemund's Studien, vol. i. pt. 1, *ut* B.B. K § 209.

Prologues.
TRAUTWEIN, Paul De Prologorum Plautinorum indole atque natura 1m.20 8° Heinrich, *Berlin* 90

Textual Criticism.
SONNENSCHEIN, Prf. Edw. A. The Scientific Emendation of Classical Texts—*in* Transns. of Amer. Philol. Assoc. (1891) [*ut* B.B. K § 95].
An attempt to lay down certain canons of textual crit., and to ill. them fr. the example of PLAUTUS, where questns. of metre and prosody are almost more important than those of MSS.

Seneca, Lucius Annaeus [B.C. *c.* 5–A.D. 65].

MELZER, P. De Hercule Oetaeo Annaeana [schl.-progr.] 4° *Chemnitz* 90
PAIS, Alf. Il Teatro di L. Annaeo Seneca illustrato 3/. 8° Loescher, *Turin* 90
PREISING, Aug. De L. Ann. Senecae poetae tragici casuum Usu, Ratione potissimum habita Vergilii, Ovidii, Lucani [diss. inaug.] 8° *Münster* 91

Terentius Afer, P. [B.C. *c.* 185–159].

Adelphi : with English notes and Introd. Prf. Sid. G. Ashmore [Am.] $1 *nt.* (3/6) f 8° Macmillan 93
A good and careful edn., w. introd. on hist. of later comedy, plays of TERENCE and their metres and prosody.

Translation.

Phormio : tr. F. G. Plaistowe [Univ. Corr. Coll. Tut. Series] 2/6 c 8° Clive 93

Aids.
BAUMANN, Ed. Quaestt. Terent. liber prior [De Verb. Substantivi Usu] [schl.-prog.] 4° *Mannheim* 90
DONATUS Commentum in Terentium
Sabbadini, Prf. Remigio Il Commento di Donato a Terenzio 8° *Florence* 93
An interesting account of orig. and nature of DONATUS'S *Commentary*, its discov. (or rather resurrectn.) in early pt. of 15 cent., the MSS. [earliest (in Paris) 11 cent.], a list of edns. and a hist. of the controversy it has aroused since pubn. of SCHOPEN'S 2 dissertn. in 1821 and 1825 [Reinhold, Klotz, Königshoff (1840), Richter ('34), Umpfenbach ('67), Usener ('68), Dziatzko, Helfferscheid, Becker, Hahn, Teuber, Leo, Gerstenberg, Weinberger, etc.], and—most import. of all—specimens of a new revisn. of the text, based largely on new collatns.

FABIA, Philippe Les Prologues de Térence [thesis; 322 pp.] 6/*fr.* 8° Thorin, *Paris* 88
HERRMANOWSKI, Ern. Quaestiones Terentianae Selectae [diss. inaug.] 8° *Halle* 92
KARSTEN, H. T. Terentiani Prologi quot qualesque fuerint, *etc.* [*extr. fr.* Mnemosyne] 1m.25 8° Brille, *Leyden* 94
LALIN, Dr. Esias De Particularum comparativarum Usu apud Terentium 1m.60 8° Simmel, *Lpz.* 94
NENCINI, Flaminus De Terentio ejusque Fontibus 4m.30 Loescher, *Turin* 91
RÖTTER, Ed. De Heautontimorumeno Terentiana [school-programme] 8° *Bayreuth* 92
SCHLEE, F. [ed.] Scholia Terentiana 2m. 8° Teubner, *Lpz.* 93
SLAUGHTER, Moses S. [Am.] The Substantives of Terence [thesis] 8° Johns Hopk. Univ., *Baltimore* 91
SMITH, Kirby W. [Am.] Archaisms of Terence ment. in Comm. of Donatus [thesis] 8° " " 90
STANGE, Ern. De Archaismis Terentianis [school-programme] 8° *Wehlau* 90

216. LATIN HISTORIANS AND GEOGRAPHERS.

Collectively.

FRICK, Carl [ed.] Chronica Minora, vol. i. [w. textual emendns.] 6*m.*80 8° Teubner, *Lps.* 93

Ammianus Marcellinus [A.D. 330–*c.* 400].

GIMAZANE, Jean Ammien Marcellin : sa vie et son œuvre [Bordeaux diss.: 432 pp.] 8° *priv. prin., Toulouse* 89
LIESENBERG, Friedr. Die Sprache d. Ammianus Marcellinus, 2 pts. [schl.-progrs.] 4° *Blankenburg* 90
NAUMANN, Fr. De Verborum cum Praepositionibus Compositorum Usu Aram. Marcell. [schl.-progr.] 2*m.* 8° *Halle* 92
REICHE, Friedr. Chronologie d. letzten 6 Bücher d. Amm. Marcell. [diss. inaug.] 80*pf.* 8° Dabis, *Jena* 89
WITTE, Ern. Ammianvs Marcellinvs qvid ivdicaverit de Rebvs divinis [diss.-inaug.] 8° *Jena* 91

Cæsar, G. Julius [B.C. 102 (*or* 100)–44].

ex rec. Bern. Kübler, vols. i.–ii. [Bell. Gall.]: Ed. Major, 1*m.*20, 90*pf.*; Ed. Min. 75*pf.*, 60*pf.* 8° Teubner, *Lps.* 93; 94

De Bello Civili :
bk. i.: w. English notes and vocab. Malcolm Montgomery [Elem. Class.] 1/6 (40*c.*) 18° Macmillan 91
,, iii.: ,, ,, ,, A. G. Peskett [Pitt Press Ser.] f 8° Camb. Press / Macmillan, *N.Y.* *in prep.*
Selection : ,, ,, ,, and vocab. C. H. Keene, *sub tit.* Tales of the Civil War [Elem. Class.] 1/6 (40*c.*) 18° Macmillan 94

De Bello Gallico : ed. W. R. Harper + H. C. Tolman [Ams.] $1.20 12° Amer. Bk. Co., *N. Y.* 91
bk. i.: w. English notes A. G. Peskett; map [Pitt Press Series] f 8° 3/- Camb. Press / 90*c. nt.* Macmillan, *N.Y.* 90
,, ,, ,, A. H. Allcroft + F. G. Paistowe [Univ. Corr. Coll. Tut. Ser.] 3/- c 8° Clive 93
,, ii.: ,, ,, ,, and Introd. J. Brown 1/6 f 8° Blackie 93
,, ,, iii., iv., vi.: ,, ,, ,, ,, vocabs. M. J. F. Brackenbury ea. 1/6 f 8° Percival (Riv. & Perc.) 91–92
,, vi.–viii.: ,, ,, ,, Chas. E. Moberly f 8° 3/6 Clar. Press / $1 *nt.* Macmillan, *N.Y.* 90
,, viii.: rec. Heinr. Meusel; w. *appar. crit.*; map 3*m.* 8° Weber, *Berlin* 94
w. German notes Heinr. Meusel; map [school-edn.] 1*m.*25 s 8° ,, ,, 94
With an Appendix, *Das römische Kriegswesen zu Caesar's Zeit*, by H. SCHNEIDER.

Translation.

De Bello Gallico : tr. A. A. J. Nesbitt + F. G. Plaistowe [Univ. Corr. Coll. Tut. Ser.] 1/- c 8° Clive 93

Aids.
WAITE + WHITE, Geo. W. [Am.] / Geo. H. [Am.] A Straight Road to Cæsar [preliminary drill for Cæsar] sq 12° $1.25 Ginn, *Boston* / 6/- Arnold 92

Archæology.
OEHLER, Raim. [ed.] Bilder-Atlas zu Caesar's Büchern de Bello Gallico: 7 maps and *c.* 100 ill. 2*m.*85 r 4° Schmidt & Günther, *Lps.* 90

Language.
ELIAS, Sam. Vor- u. Gleichzeitigkeit bei Caesar, pt. i. [Beding.- u. Folgesätze] [progr.] 1*m.* 4° Gaertner, *Berlin* 93
PLOCHMANN, Friedr. Cæsars Sprachgebrauch in Bezug auf d. Syntax d. Casus [progr.] 8° *Schweinfurt* 91

Dictionaries.
GARIZIO, Eus. Vocabolario dei Commentari di Cesare [Bell. Gall., Bell. Civ.] 1*l.*60 8° Paravia, *Turin* 94
MENGE + PREUSS, R. / S. Lexicon Caesarianum [*ut* B.B. K § 216]; complete in 11 pts. 18*m.* r 8° Teubner, *Lps.* 85–90
MEUSEL, H. Lexicon Caesarianum, pts. 1–8 = vol. i. 19*m.*20; pts. 9–19 [end] 26*m.*40 2 vols. 45*m.* r 8° Weber, *Berlin* 87; 93
MÜLLER, Dr. Hans Vokabularium zu Cäsar's Commentarii de Bello Gallico 75*pf.* 8° Meyer, *Hanover* 94
SIHLER, E. G. [Am.] Complete Lexicon of the Latinity of Cæsar's Gallic War $1.60 8° Ginn, *Boston* 91
Names, Celtic, used by Cæsar—v. K § 280 (d'ARBOIS DE JUBAINVILLE).

Textual Criticism.
MEUSEL, H. Coniecturae Caesarianae [*repr. fr. his* Lex. Cæs., *ut supra*] 4*m.* r 8° Weber, *Berlin* 93

War in Africa.
MÜLLER, Wern. De Caesaris quod fertur Belli Afric. Recensione [dissert. inaug.] 8° *Rostock* 93

War with Ariovistus.
STOFFEL, Col. Guerre de César et d'Arioviste, et Premières Opérations de César en l'an 702; 2 maps 30*fr.* 4° Bouillon, *Paris* 91

Curtius Rufus, Q. [A.D. 1st cent.].

Historiae Alexandri Magni: ed. Max. C. P. Schmidt 1*m.* 8° Tempsky, *Prague* 86
Selections : w. English notes, vocab. and exx. F. Coverley Smith [Elem. Class.] 1/6 (40*c.*) pott 8° Macmillan 94
DOSSON, S. Étude sur Quinte Curce: sa vie et son œuvre [a good *étude*] 9*fr.* 8° Hachette, *Paris* 86
RAUCH Gerundium und Gerundivum bei Curtius 1*m.* 4° v. Eye, *Meiningen* 89

Ennius, Q. [B.C. 239–170]—*v.* K § 214.

Eutropius, Flavius [A.D. 4th cent.].

Historiae Romanae : rec. Aug. Luchs, vol. iv. [lib. xxvi.–xxx.] 3*m.* 8° Weidmann, *Berlin* 89
bks. i.–ii. with English notes and vocab. W. Caldecott 1/6 (50*c.*) 18° Longman 93
,, i.–vi. ,, ,, ,, A. R. S. Hallidie; maps 2/- f 8° Percival (Riv. & Perc.) 92

Florus, Iulius [A.D. 117–138].

BECK, J. W. Observationes Criticae et Palaeogr. ad Flor. Epitom. de T. Livio 3*m.*20 4° *Groningen* (Calvary, *Berl.*) 91
SCHMIDINGER, Dr. Frz. Untersuchungen über Florus [*extr. fr.* Jahrbb. f. Class. Philol.] 1*m.*20 8° Teubner, *Lps.* 94
SORN, Jos. Der Sprachgebrauch des Historikers Eutropius 1*m.*20 8° Fischer, *Laibach* [88–89] 93

K § 216

Livius Patavinus, Titus [B.C. 59–A.D. 17].

Ab Urbe Condita libri: rec. Ant. Zingerle, in pts. ea. 1*m*.20 8° Tempsky, *Prague* 89–94 *in prg.*
w. German notes Mor. Müller + Frz. Luterbacher + E. Wölfflin + F. Friedersdorff 8° Teubner, *Lps.* 75–93
Lib. i.–ii. (by MÜLLER) ea. 1*m*.50; iii.–x., xix. (LUTERBACHER) ea. 1*m*.20; xxi.–xxii. (WÖLFFLIN) ea. 1*m*.20; viii. (WÖLFFLIN + LUTERBACHER) 1*m*.20; xxiv.–xxv. (MÜLLER) 1*m*., 1*m*.20; xxvi.–xxviii. (FRIEDERSDORFF) ea. 1*m*.20; xxix.–xxx. (LUTERBACHER) ea. 1*m*.20.

Livius Commentar f. d. Schulgebr., v. Carl Haupt, bks. i.–vii., xxii. ea. 80*pf.*, xxi. 2*m*. 8° Teubner, *Lps.* 91–94 *in prg.*

bk. i.: w. English notes A. H. Allcroft + W. F. Masom [Univ. Corr. Coll. Tut. Ser.] 2/6 c 8° Clive [90] 93
„ German „ Max Heynacher 1*m*. 8° F. A. Perthes, *Gotha* 85
„ i., xxi., xxii.: „ English „ J. Howell Westcott [Am.] $1.25 12° Allyn, *Boston* 91
„ i.–ii.: „ „ „ & Introd. Prf. J. B. Greenough [Am.] [Coll. Ser. of Lat. Authrs.] sq 8° $1.35 Ginn, *Boston* / 6/- Arnold 91
„ i.–ii.; iii.; iv.: „ „ „ J. Prendeville [*ut* B.B. K § 216], ed. J. H. Freese 12° ea. 1/6 Bell / ea. 40c. Macmillan, *N.Y.* [78] 92–93
„ ii.: „ German „ Theod. Klett 1*m*. 8° F. A. Perthes, *Gotha* 83
„ iii.: „ English „ W. F. Masom, 3/-; w. vocab. and tr. 3/6 c 8° Clive 94
„ iv.: „ „ „ Rev. H. M. Stephenson [Pitt Press Series] f 8° 2/6 Camb. Press / 65c. *nt.* Macmillan, *N.Y.* 90
„ v.: „ „ „ and Introd. L. Whibley; map [Pitt Press Series] f 8° 2/6 Camb. Press / 70c. *nt.* Macmillan, *N.Y.* 90
„ „ „ W. M. Masom + A. H. Allcroft [Univ. Corr. Coll. Tut. Ser.] 2/6 c 8° Clive 93
„ „ „ M. Alford [Elementary Classics] 1/6 (40c.) 18° Macmillan 92
„ vi.: „ „ „ and Introd. H. M. Stephenson [Pitt Press Series] f 8° 2/6 Camb. Press / 70c. *nt.* Macmillan, *N.Y.* 92
„ viii. „ German „ Ern. Ziegeler 1*m*. 8° F. A. Perthes, *Gotha* 89
„ ix.: „ English „ and Introd. H. M. Stephenson [Pitt Press Series] f 8° 2/6 Camb. Press / 60c. *nt.* Macmillan, *N.Y.* 92
„ German „ Ern. Ziegeler 1*m*.10 8° F. A. Perthes, *Gotha* 92
„ xxi.: „ English „ J. E. Melhuish [Elementary Classics] 1/6 (40c.) 18° Macmillan 90
„ „ „ and Introd. A. H. Allcroft + W. F. Masom, 2/6; w. tr. 4/6 c 8° Clive [92] 94
„ German notes Frz. Luterbacher 1*m*.20 8° F. A. Perthes, *Gotha* [82]
„ xxi.–xxii.: „ English „ and Introds. Prfs. J. B. Greenough + Tracy Peck [Ams.] [Coll. Ser. of Lat. Auths.] sq 8° $1.35 Ginn, *Boston* / 6/6 Arnold 93
„ xxii.: „ „ „ „ „ L. Dowdall; map c 8° 3/6 Bell / Macmillan, *N.Y.* 88
„ German notes Glob. Engelhaaf 1*m*.20 8° F. A. Perthes, *Gotha* 84
„ „ „ Frz. Luterbacher 1*m*.10 8° „ „ 83
„ xxvii.: „ English „ and Introd. H. M. Stephenson [Pitt Press Series] f 8° 2/6 Camb. Press / 60c. *nt.* Macmillan, *N.Y.* 90

Selections: „ „ „ J. C. Nicol + Rev. J. Hunter Smith, *sub tit.* Livy Lessons [Parallel Gram. Ser.: Readers] 1/6 16° Sonnenschein 91

Translations —*ut sup.*: bk. iii. (MASOM); xxi. (ALLCROFT + MASOM).

Aids.
COCCHIA, E. Tito Livio e Polibio: innanzi alla critica storica 1*l*.50 8° Loescher, *Turin* 91
FÜGNER, Frz. Livius xxi.–xxiii. m. Verweisungen a. Cäsars Bell. Gallicum 3*m*.50 8° Weidmann, *Berlin* 88
KÖBERLIN, Alf. De Participiorum Usu Liviano Capita selecta [dissert. inaug.] 8° *Erlangen* 88
GUSTAFSSON, F. De Livii libro xxi. emendando 1*m*.20 4° *Helsingfors* 90
HAUPT, Carl Livius-Kommentar für den Schulgebrauch, bks. i.–vii. ea. 80*pf.*; xxi. 2*m*.; xxii. 80*pf.* 8° Teubner, *Lps.* 91–94 *in prg.*
HESSELBARTH, Herm. Historisch-kritische Untersuchungen z. 3ten. Dekade d. Livius; map 10*m*. 8° Waisenhaus, *Halle* 89
HERAEUS, Wilh. Vindiciae Livianae, 2 pts. [school-programmes] 4° *Offenbach* 89–91
LE BAS, Ph. Commentaire sur Tite-Live *o.p.* 8° *Paris* 40
SCHMIDT, Ad. M. A. Beiträge zur Livianischen Lexikographie, pts. i.–iii. 8° *Waidhofen* 88, 92
„ „ Schul-Commentar zu T. Livii Ab Urbe Condita libros i., ii., xxi., xxii. 1*m*.25 8° Tempsky, *Vienna* 94
VAHLEN, Joh. Observationes Sermonis Liviani [Index Lectt.] 4° *Berlin* 90
ZINGERLE, Ant. Zur vierten Decade des Livius [*extr. fr.* Sitzb. Wien. Akad.] 70*pf.* r 8° Tempsky, *Vienna* 93

Dictionary.
*FÜGNER, Frz. [ed.] Lexicon Livianum, facs. ii.–vi. ea. 2*m*.40 8° Teubner, *Lps.* 91–94 *in prg.*

Sources.
JUMPERTZ, M. Der Römisch-Karthagische Krieg in Spanien [doctor-dissert.] 1*m*. 8° Weber, *Berlin* 92
Maintains (w. SOLTAU, in *Hermes* xxvi.) that LIVY used POLYBIUS only indirectly thro' some intermediate author. It also clears up the faulty chronology of LIVY for the Spanish events of B.C. 211–206.
v. STERN, Prf. E. Das Hannibalische Truppenverzeichniss bei Livius Calvary, *Berlin* 92
On the question of what authority or authorities LIVY had in writing his third Decade, maintaining that he took his list of troops directly fr. POLYBIUS.

Lucanus, M. Annæus [A.D. 39–65]—*v.* K § 214: Latin Poets.

Nepos, Cornelius [B.C. 94–24].

Opera: Cornelii Nepotis quae extant: edizione crit.-esegetia G. Cortese 6*l*. 8° Loescher, *Turin* 91
Selecta: w. English notes H. N. Kingdon 2/- *nt.* f 8° Percival (Riv. & Perc.) 93

Aids.
PRETSCH, Bernh. Zur Stilistik d. Cornelius Nepos [school-progr.] 8° *Spandau* 90
CONTESSA, Giac. Vocabolario per le Vite di Cornelio Nepote 2*l*. 8° Loescher, *Turin* 92
SCHÄFER, Em. Nepos-Vokabular, ed. Ortmann, pts. i.–iii. ea. 40*pf.* 8° Teubner, *Lps.* [85–86] 89–93
SCHMIDT, Joh. Commentar zu den Lebensbeschreibungen d. Cornelius Nepos 90*pf.* 8° Tempsky, *Vienna* 90
WEIDNER, A. Schulwörterbuch zu Cornelius Nepos; ill. 1*m*.40 8° „ „ 87

Pollio, C. Asinius [B.C. 75–B.C. 4].

[Bellum Alex. 48–64]: ed. Gust. Landgraf, *s.v.* Pollio's Bericht üb. d. Span. Unruhen d. J. 48 v. Chr. 1*m*. 8° Deichert, *Lps.* 90
Edited from the Ashburnham MS.
SCHMALZ, J. H. Ueber den Sprachgebrauch d. Asinius Pollio 1*m*.40 8° Beck, *Munich* [82] 90

Porcius Licinus.

BÜTTNER, Rich. Porcius Licinus u. der litterarische Kreis d. Q. Lutatius Catullus 5*m*. 8° Teubner, *Lps.* 93

Sallustius Crispus, G. [B.C. 86–35].

Opera : ed. Aug. Scheindler 1m. 8° Tempsky, *Prague* 83
Catil. et Jug. Orr. et Epistt. ex histor. Libris deperd., rec. J. C. Orelli 8° Meyer, *Zürich* 40
With the Catiline Orat. of CICERO and the epitomes on books of LIVY.

Historiarum Reliquiae : rec. Bert. Maurenbrecher: ed. crit., fasc. i. [Prolegg.] 2m.; ii. [Fragmenta] 8m. 8° Teubner, *Lpz.* 91; 93
w. German notes Theod. Opitz, pt. i.: Bellum Catilinarium 60pf. 8° " " 94
Bellum Jugurthinum : rec. Rob Novák 72pf. 8° Storch, *Prague* 88
Conjuratio Catilinæ : w. English notes and Introd. T. M. Neatby + B. J. Haynes [Univ. Corr. Coll. Tut. Ser.] 4/- c 8° Clive 93
" German " Theod. Opitz 60pf. 8° Teubner, *Lpz.* 94
" French " and Introd. F. Antoine + R. Lallier 6fr. 8° Hachette, *Paris* 88

Translation.

Catiline Conspiracy : tr. T. M. Neatby + B. J. Haynes [Univ. Corr. Coll. Tut. Ser.] 1/- c 8° Clive 93
übers. A. Mogk [school-programme] 1m.20 4° *Tilsit* 72

Aids.

BELLEZZA, Paolo — Dei Fonti e dell' Autorità storica di Sallustio [dissert.] 2l.50 16° Co-oper. Edit., Ital., *Milan* 91
GERSTENBERG, Carl — Ueber die Reden bei Sallust [school-programme] 1m. 4° Gaertner, *Berlin* 92
" " — Ist Sallust ein Partei-Schriftsteller? [school-programme] 1m. 4° " " 93
HAMANN, K. [ed.] — Bruchstücke e. Sallust-Handschrift in d. Dombibliothek zu Trier [progr.] 1m. 4° Herold, *Hamburg* 93
JURGES, Paul — De Sallustii Historiarum Reliquiis Capita Selecta [diss.] 2m. 8° Dieterich, *Göttingen* 93
KUNZE, Alf. — Sallustiana, pt. i. : ii. 2m. 8° Simmel, *Lpz.* 92; 93
ii. *Der Gebrauch v. "fore," "futurum esse," "foret," "forent," "essem" u. seine Formen.*
MAURENBRECHER, Bert. — Quaestionum Sallustianarum capita tria [diss. inaug.] 8° *Leipzig* 91
MOLLWEIDE, Rich. — Ueber die Glossen zu Sallust 1m.20 4° Trübner, *Strassburg* 88
MÜLLER, G. — Die Phraseologie des Sallust, 2 pts. [school-programmes] 4° *Cöthen* 88; 90
RAMBEAU, Theod. — Charakteristik der histor. Darstellung des Sallustius, 2 pts. [school-programmes] 4° *Burg* 79; 99

Dictionary.

NATTA, Fil. — Vocabolario Sallustiano 2l. 8° Loescher, *Turin* 94

Silius Italicus, C. [A.D. 25–102]—*v.* K § 214: Latin Poets.

Suetonius, C. Tranquillus [A.D. *c.* 75–*c.* 150].

Opera : c. I. Casauboni comm. ed. Fr. Aug. Wolf, 4 vols. *o.p.* [*pb.* 18m.] 8° Fritsch, *Lpz.* 02
Duodecim Caesares et Minora Opera, ed. Carl Bened. Hase, w. var. rgs.; 2 vols. *o.p.* [*pb.* 15fr.] 8° Lemaire, *Paris* 28
De Vita Augusti w. English notes and Introd. E. S. Shuckburgh [Pitt Press Series] f 8° Camb. Press Macmillan, N.Y. *in prep.*
De Vita Cæsarum : w. English notes and Introd. Prf. H. T. Peck [Am.] *New York* 93
A useful and fairly successful schl. edn. of an over-neglected author.

Aid.

SCHMIDT, W. — De Romanorum imprimis Suetonii arte biographica [diss.] 1m. 8° 91

Tacitus, (C.?) Cornelius [A.D. 54–*post* 117].

Agricola and Germania : w. English notes Rev. H. M. Stephenson [Pitt Press Ser.] f 8° 3/- Camb. Press / 75c. *nt.* Macmillan, *N.Y.* 94
Annales : *" " " Hy. Furneaux, vol. ii.; map [bks. xi.–xvi., compl. the wk.] 8° 20/- Clar. Press / $5 *nt.* Macmillan, *N.Y.* 91
Based on the text of HALM, with a business-like and excell. commentary and a very useful historical Introduction.
w. English notes Introd. Hy. Furneaux c 8° 6/- Clar. Press / Macmillan, *N.Y.* 94
bk. i. : w. Engl. notes & Introd. W. F. Masom + C. S. Fearenside; vocab. [Univ. Corr. Coll. Tut. Ser.] 4/- c 8° Clive 90
" i.–vi. : w. Engl. notes & Intro. Prf. W. F. Allen [Am.] [bas. on Dräger's ed. *ut* 𝔅.𝔅. K § 216] 12° $1.65 Ginn, *Boston* / 7/6 Arnold 90
Dialogus de Oratoribus : *revis. text Prc. W. Peterson; w. Introd. essays and notes 8° 10/6 Clar. Press / $2.90 *nt.* Macmillan, *N.Y.* 93
The first really scholarly Engl. edn. of the bk., which ever since its recovery fr. oblivion in middle 15 cent. has excited much interest on the Continent. The Introd. Essays are elabor. and full of interest, discussing the problems raised by the treatise incl. that of authorship (inclining in favour of TACITUS).
revis. text Prf. Alf. Gudeman [Am.]; w. prolegg., crit. and exeg. comm. [Coll. Ser. Lat. Auth.] sq 8° $3 Ginn, *Boston* / 12/- Arnold 94
A good edn., the Prolegg. dealing at length w. the "Dialogus Controversy," and the Introd. discussing style, syntax, sources, MSS., *etc.* Good Bibliogr. appended.
w. English notes Prf. Chas. Edwin Bennett [Am.] sq 8° 80c. Ginn, *Boston* / 3/6 Arnold 94
w. German notes Ed. Wolff 1m.20 8° F. A. Perthes, *Gotha* 90
" French " Henri Goelzer [a good bk.] 4fr. 8° Hachette, *Paris* 87
Germania : " English " and Introd. Hy. Furneaux; map 8° 6/6 Clar. Press / Macmillan, *N.Y.* 94
Historiæ : " " " Rev. W. A. Spooner; w. intro., anal. prefixed to ea. bk., and index [Class. Lib.] 16/- ($3.50) 8° Macmillan 91
The Introd. consists of 7 essays, dealing w. such questions as the MSS., earlier edns. of text, materials used by Tac., cond. of provinces, *etc.* A solid and scholarly piece of wk. Text followed is that of ORELLI, ed. MEISTER [*ut* 𝔅.𝔅. K § 216]. Copious index.
w. German notes Ed. Wolff, pt. ii. [= bks. iii.–v.] 2m.25 8° Weidmann, *Berlin* 88
bk. i. : " English " and Introd. F. G. Plaistowe + H. J. Maidment [Univ. Corr. Coll. Tut. Ser.] 3/6 c 8° Clive 93
" i.–ii. : " French " Henri Goelzer; and Life of Tacitus and Index 1fr.80 16° Hachette, *Paris* 86

K § 217

Translation —*v. also* F § 12.

Histories: tr. Alb. Wm. Quill, v. i. [= Introd. & bks. i.–ii.]; w. notes [to occupy 2 v.] 7/6 8° Murray 92

A characteristic version, prob. as good a one as can be made, but if any class. author ever be really tr., it will be some second-rate writer with a neutral, colourless style (*e.g.* Pausanias). The annotations, however, are of real scholarly value, and based on the latest critical research.

Aids.

BAIER, Chrn. Tacitus und Plutarch [school-programme] 4° *Frankfort* 93

HOCHART, Polydore De l'Authenticité des Annales et d. Histoires de Tacite 8*fr.* 8° Thorin, *Paris* 90

With photograph. reprodns. of 5 pp. of Florentine MSS., and of 68 letters of POGGIO BRACCIOLINI.

RÖSCH, W. Der Geschichtschreiber Cornelius Tacitus [Samml. gemeinverst. Vorträge] 80*pf.* 8° Verlags-Anst., *Hamby.* 91

Annals.

EICHLER, H. Variationen zu Tacitus' Annalen, pt. i. [=bk. 1] 1*m.*; ii. [=bk. 2] 1*m.*20 8° Weidmann, *Berl.* 93; 94

ZOECHBAUER, F. Studien zur den Annalen des Tacitus [dissert.] 2*m.* 8° *Vienna* (Fock, *Lpz.*) 93

Germany.

MANINA, G. Romania e Germania ovvero il Mondo german. sec. l. relaz. di Tacito 6*m.* 8° Schimpff, *Trieste* 92

RIESE, Alex. —*in his* Das rheinische Germanien in der antiken Litteratur 14*m.* 8° Teubner, *Lpz.* 92

WEINBERGER, Ignaz Die Frage nach Entstehung u. Tendenz d. Taciteischen Germania, 2 pts. [progr.] 8° *Olmütz* 90; 91

De Oratoribus.

BUCHHOLZ, Heinr. Verbesserungsvorschläge z. Dialogus de Oratoribus d. Tacitus [progr.] 8° *Hof* 91

LEVIGHI, Leon. Disposizione e Critica del Dialogus de Oratoribus [schl.-progr.] 8° *Trieste* 90

SCHEUER, Friedr. De Tacitei de Oratoribus dialogi codicum nexu et fide [diss.] 2*m.* 8° Koebner, *Breslau* 91

Appended is a Collation of the Viennese codex DCCXI.

Language. Manuscripts.

ANDRESEN, Geo. De Codicibus Mediceis Annalium Taciti 1*m.* 4° Gaertner, *Berlin* 92

CONSTANS, Léop. Étude sur la Langue de Tacite [pp. 158] 18° Delagrave, *Paris* 93

CYCZKICWICZ, Andreas De Tacitei Sermonis Proprietatibus, pt. i. 1*m.*; ii. 1*m.* [schl.-progr.] 8° West, *Brody* 90; 91

GERICKE, T. De abundanti dicendi genere Taciteo [diss.-inaug.] 8° *Berlin* 82

LICHOTINSKI, Serg. The Use of the Participle in Tacitus, pt. i. [in Russian] 8° *Kiev* 91

WÜNSCH, Rich. De Taciti Germaniae Codicibus germanis [dissert. inaug.] 8° *Marburg* 93

Dictionary.

*GERBER + GREEF, A. A. Lexicon Taciteum, pts. ix.–xi. ea. 3*m.*60 r 8° Teubner, *Lpz.* 91; 92; 93 *in prg.*

Sources.

FABIA, Ph. Les Sources de Tacites dans les Histoires et les Annales 12*fr.* 8° Colin, Paris 93

An elabor. discussn.—the first in French—of the vexed questn. of TACITUS' sources.

LÜCKENBACH, A. De Germaniæ quæ vocatur Taciteæ Fontibus (dissert.) 1*m.*20 8° *Marburg* (Fock, *Lpz.*) 91

Valerius Maximus [A.D. 1st cent.].

HERAEUS, Wilh. Spicilegium Crit. in Val. Maxim. eiusque Epitomatoribus [*extr. fr.* Jahrb. Cl. Phil.] 1*m.*60 8° Teubner, *Lpz.* 93

Velleius Paterculus, M. [B.C. *c.* 19–A.D. *c.* 30].

Opera Omnia rec. C. B. Hase, 2 vols. in 3; pl. *o.p.* 8° Lemaire, *Paris* 22–23

rec. Prf. Fr. Kritz; w. index *o.p.* 8° Wöller, *Lpz.* [40] 48

rec. N. E. Lemaire *o.p.* 8° Lemaire, *Paris* 22

Historia Romana, bk. ii., ch. 40–131: w. English notes and Introd. Fk. E. Rockwood [Am.] $1 16° Leach, *Boston* 93

Aids.

BURMEISTER, Friedr. De Fontibus Vellei Paterculi [Berl. Stud. f. Class. Philol.] 2*m.*50 8° Calvary, *Berlin* 94

HELBING, Fritz Velleius Paterculus: Beitrag z. Kritik u. Histor. Roman [diss. inaug.] 8° *Rostock* 88

KÜMMEL, Joh. De Fontibus eorum quæ Vell. Pat. Libri i. capp. 1–8 tradit [diss. inaug.] 8° *Halle* 92

THOMAS, E. De Velleiani Voluminis Condicione aliquot Capita 1*m.*80 8° Gaertner, *Berlin* 93

217. LATIN ORATORS.

Fragments.

Reliquiæ Oratorum Romanorum, rec. Jac. Cortese 3*l.* 8° Bona, *Turin* 92

Cassius Severus [B.C. 1st cent.–A.D. 1st cent.].

Opera: rec. Heinr. Meyer—*in* Oratorum Roman. cxxv. Fragmenta 9*m.* 8° Orell, *Zürich* [22] 42

ROBERT, Pierre De Cassii Severi Eloquentia [thesis] 3*fr.* 8° Hachette, *Paris* 99

Cicero, M. Tullius [B.C. 106–43].

Opera Omnia: rec. C. F. W. Mueller: Pars I.: Opera Rhetorica, rec. W. Friedrich—*v.* K § 220.

Epistolæ: „ Ludw. Mendelssohn 12*m.* 8° Teubner, *Lpz.* 93

A valuable text; w. chronolog. tables by Em. KOERNER + O. E. SCHMIDT.

*w. Engl. notes & prolegg. Prf. Rob. Y. Tyrrell + Louis C. Purser, vol. iv. [Dubl. Univ. Pr. Ser.] 15/- 8° Longman 94

A contin. of a very scholarly work: revised text, comm. and introd. essays.

Selectae: *Cicero in his Letters, ed. w. Engl. notes and Introd. Prf. Rob. Y. Tyrrell [Classical Series] 4/6 ($1.10) f 8° Macmillan 91

An excellent seln. fr. the *Letters* on a new plan, shewing CICERO in the character of a private gentleman, in his everyday life, amusements, pleasures, domestic worries, ailments, studies, views on social surroundings, *etc.*

w. German notes Friedr. Aly 1*m.*60 8° Gaertner, *Berlin* 92

Ad Atticum: rec. et emend. C. A. Lehmann 6*m.* 8° Weidmann, *Berlin* 92

w. Engl. notes & Introd. J. H. Haydon; w. tr. [Univ. Corr. Coll. Tut. Ser.] 3/6 c 8° Clive 93

bk. iv.: „ „ „ and Introd. Prf. J. Brown [School Authors] 1/6 i 16° Sonnenschein 94

Orationes :

Cæsarianæ : w. English notes and Introd. Rev. W. Yorke Fausset f 8° 2/6 Clar. Press / doc. nt. Macmillan, *N.Y.* 93

A good edn. of the Cæsarian speeches (*Pro Marcello, Pro Ligario, Pro Rege Deiotaro*); well suited for upper-form boys.

In C. Verrem II., lib. iv. [De Signis] : w. Italian notes Ett. Stampini 1*l.*20 16° Paravia, *Turin* 93

lib. v. [De Suppliciis] : w. English notes and Introd. W. C. Laming 3/6 c 8° Rivington & Perc. 93

Pro Archia : w. Engl. notes & Introd. A. H. Allcroft + F. G. Plaistowe [Un. Corr. Coll. Tut. Ser.] 3/- c 8° Clive 92

Pro Lege Manilia : w. English notes and anal. Rev. J. Hunter Smith [School Authors] 1/6 i 16° Sonnenschein 92

Pro Milone : " " " and Introd. F. H. Colson [Classical Series] 2/6 (60c. nt.) f 8° Macmillan 93

" " " " Rev. W. Yorke Fausset [School Authors] 1/6 i 16° Sonnenschein 93

" " " " A. B. Poynton f 8° 2/6 Clar. Press / doc. nt. Macmillan, *N.Y.* 92

" " " " Jas. Smith Reid f 8° 2/6 Camb. Press / doc. nt. Macmillan, *N.Y.* 94

Above 4 are all excellent edns. of a speech wh. is as good for schl. purposes as any one of CICERO'S.

Pro Murena : w. English notes J. H. Freese [Classical Series] 2/6 (60c.) f 8° Macmillan 94

" German " Jul. Strenge 75*pf.* 8° F. A. Perthes, *Gotha* 92

Pro S. Roscio Amerino w. German notes G. Landraf 1*m.* 8° " " 92

Translations.

Ad Atticum : tr. J. H. Haydon—*in his edn. of the text, ut supra* [separ. 2/6].

Pro S. Roscio Amerino : tr. F. G. Plaistowe [Univ. Corr. Coll. Tut. Ser.] 2/6 c 8° Clive 94

Aids.

ALY, Friedr. Cicero : sein Leben und seine Schriften ; port. 3*m.*60 8° Gaertner, *Berlin* 91

CUCHEVAL, Prf. —*v* K § 213.

DETTWEILER, P. Untersuchungen üb. d. didakt. Werth Ciceron. Schulschriften, 2 pts. 3*m.* 8° Waisenhaus, *Halle* 91 ; 92

DRUERLING, A. Cicero als Schul-Schriftsteller [*extr. fr.* Blätt. f. bayer. Gymn. Schulwesen] 1*m.* 8° Lindauer, *Munich* 93

HARTMAN, J. J. De M. Tullio Cicerone : allocutio ad studiosos 1*fr.* 8° Doesburgh, *Leyden* 94

PLASBERG, Otto De M. Tull. Ciceronis Hortensio Dialogo [dissert.] 1*m.*80 8° Fock, *Lps.* 92

RIGAL, Eug. M. T. Cicero quatenus Artium optimarum Amator exstiterit [thesis] 3*fr.* 8° Hachette, *Paris* 90

SCHMIDT, Friedr. Zur Kritik u. Erklärung d. Briefe Ciceros an Atticus [schl.-progr.] 8° *Würzburg* 79

" Otto Ed. Der Briefwechsel des M. Tullius Cicero 12*m.* 8° Teubner, *Lps.* 93

From his proconsulate in Cilicia to the death of CÆSAR ; w. repr. of 12 and 13 bk. of the letters to ATTICUS.

STRACHAN-DAVIDSON, J. L. Cicero and the Fall of the Roman Republic—*v* F § 12 [*pub. in Aug.* '94].

WEISSENFELS, O. Cicero als Schulschriftsteller 4*m.* 8° Teubner, *Lps.* 92

Language, Grammar, Textual Criticism.

CLARK, Alb. C. [ed.] Collations from the Harleian MS. of Cicero, 2,682 ; w. facs. [Anecd. Oxon.] s 4° 7/6 Clar. Press / Macmillan, *N.Y.* 91

MS. discovered in Brit. Mus., where it has lain for the last century and three-quarters, having prev. been in the Cathedral Lib. at Cologne, where it was consulted by MODIUS and GULIELMIUS, being none other than the "Coloniensis," the loss of wh. MADVIG deplored. GRAEVIUS borrowed fr. it, and on his d. it was purchased by HARLEY, Lord OXFORD, fr. whom it passed, w. other MSS., to Brit. Mus. It is designated H, and is of considerable value for purposes of textual criticism. Well ed. w. hist. of the MS., est. of its crit. value, and essay on its age and form by E. Maunde THOMPSON.

DEITER, H. Vergleichung d. Amsterd. Cod. 80 z. Cic. de Finibus u. Academica posteriora [schl.-pr.] 4° *Aurich* 92

HILDEBRANDT, P. De Scholiis Ciceronis Bobiensibus 1*m.*60 8° Mayer & Müller, *Berlin* 94

KÖHLER, Albr. Ueber d. Sprache der Briefe d. P. Corn. Lentulus Spinther (=Ep. ad Fam. xii., 14, 15) 1*m.* 8° Ballhorn, *Nuremberg* 90

KORNITZER, Alois Textkritische Bemerkungen zu Ciceros Reden [schl.-progr.] 8° *Nikolsburg* 91

LEHMANN, C. A. De Ciceronis Ad Attic. Epistulis recensendis et emendandis 6*m.* 8° Weidmann, *Berlin* 92

LEIGHTON, R. F. [Am.] The Medicean MSS. of Cicero's Letters—*in* Transns. Amer. Philol. Assoc. xxi., pp. 59–87.

LINDERBAUER, Benno De Verborum Mutuatorum et Peregrin. ap. Cic. Usu et Compensat., 2 pts. [progr.] 4° *Metten* (Fock, *Lps.*) 92 : 93

SCHENK, R. De Dativi possessivi usu Ciceroniano, pt. i. [dissert.] 2*m.*50 8° Herold, *Hamburg* 92

SCHILLING, Bern. De Scholiis Bobiensibus [school-programme] 4° *Dresden* 92

SPANOGHE, Em. Emendationes Tullianæ : miscella 1*m.*70 8° Brill, *Leyden* 80

ZIMMERMANN, Em. De epistulari temporum usu Ciceroniano quæstiones grammaticae, 4 pts. 3*m.*60 4° Fock, *Lps.* 86 ; 87 : 90 : 91

Dictionary.

*MERGUET, H. Lexikon zu den Schriften Cicero's, Theil ii. : Philosoph. Schriften—*v* K § 218.

Asconius Pedianus Oratt. Cic. quinque enarratio rec. Kiessling + Schoell 3*m.*60 8° Weidmann, *Berlin*

Quintilianus, M. Fabius [A.D. *c.* 35–97 (to 100)]—*v.* K § 220.

Symmachus, Q. Aurelius [A.D. latter pt. 4th cent.].

Relationes : rec. Wilh. Meyer 1*m.*60 8° Teubner, *Lps.* 72

Havet, Louis La Prose Métrique d. Symmache et l. origines métr. d. Cursus [Bibl. Ec. Ht. Etud.] 8° Bouillon, *Paris* 92

218. LATIN PHILOSOPHERS.

"Cato Dionysius Philosophus" [unknown author and age].

Disticha de Moribus ad Filium : rec. Ferd. Hauthal 3*m.* 8° Calvary, *Berlin* 69

BISCHOFF, Erich Prolegomena zu Dionysius Cato ; pt. i. [dissert. inaug.] 8° *Jena* 90

ZARNCKE, Friedr. Der deutsche Cato 4*m.* r 8° G. Wiegand, *Lps.* 52

A hist. of the Germ. trs. of the distichs known under the name of CATO wh. had an enormous vogue during the Mid. Ages, when they were supplanted by Seb. BRANDT'S tr. (end of 15 cent.).

Cicero, M. Tullius [B.C. 106–43].

De Amicitia (*sive* Laelius) : w. English notes and Introd. St. George Stock, pt. i. [Introd. and text] [Clar. Press Ser.] f 8° 3/- Clar Press / doc. Macmillan, *N.Y.* 93

De Senectute (*sive* Cato Major) : w. English notes and Introd. Leon Huxley [Clar. Press Ser.] f 8° 2/- Clar. Press / doc. nt. Macmillan, *N.Y.* 87

w. Engl. notes & Introd. A. H. Allcroft + W. F. Masom [Univ. Corr. Coll. Tut. Ser.] 3/- c 8° Clive 92

w. German notes Alois Kornitzer [school-edn.] 60*pf.* 12° Gerold, *Vienna* [ ] 93

Tusculanae Disputationes : w. Italian notes and tr. [literal] 3*l.* 8° Tedeschi, *Verona* 91

K §§ 219-220

Translations —*v.* C § 14: Eclectics.

Aids —*v.* K § 217, *s. nom.* Cicero.

Dictionary.

*MERGUET, H. Lexikon zu d. Schriften Cicero's: Theil ii.: Philosophische Schriften, vol. 2 [last] 43*m.* r 8° Fischer, *Jena* 92

Lucretius Carus, Titus [B.C. *c.* 98–55]—*v.* K § 214: Latin Poets.

Nigidius Figulus, P. [B.C. *c.* 98–45].

Reliquiae: rec. Ant. Swoboda; w. Latin notes 6*m.* 8° Tempsky, *Vienna* 89

Aids.

FREY, Jos. Quaestiones Nigidianae [schl.-progr.] 4° *Rössel* 67
KLEIN, Jos. Quaestiones Nigidianae [diss. inaug.] 8° *Bonn* 61
SWOBODA, Ant. Quaestiones Nigidianae [diss.; *also in* Dissert. Philol. Vindob. ii., *ut* K § 273] 2*m*.50 8° *Vienna* 90

Seneca, Lucius Annaeus [B.C. *c.* 5–A.D. 65].

CUNLIFFE, Dr. Jno. W. The Influence of Seneca on the Elizabethan Tragedy—*ut* K § 25.
GERCKE Seneca Studien Teubner, *Lps.*, *in prep.*
HILGENFELD, Heinr. Senecae Epist. morales quo ordine et quo temp. sint scriptae, coll., edit. 2*m.* 8° „ „ 90
MÜCK, Herm. Observationes crit. gramm. in L. Ann. Sen. Scripta philos. [diss. inaug.] 8° *Marburg* 90
MÜLLER, Joh. Kritische Studien zu den Naturales Quaestiones Seneca's [*extr. fr.* Sitzber. d. Wien. Akad.] 80*pf.* r 8° Tempsky, *Vienna* 94
REINECKE, Geo. De Coniunctionum Usu apud Senecam philosophum [diss. inaug.] 8° *Münster* 89
RIEGER, Herm. Observationes Annaeanae [dissert. inaug.] 8° *Freiburg* 89
SCHULTESS, F. Annaeana Studia 2*m*.50 4° Herold, *Hamburg* 88
WALDÄSTEL, Otto De Enuntiatorum temporalium Structura ap. L. Ann. Senec. [diss.] 8° *Halle* 88

219. LATIN WRITERS ON GRAMMAR.

Caper, Flavius [A.D. 2nd cent.] rec. H. Keil—*in* Grammatici Latini, vol. vii. (1) *ut* 𝔅.𝔅. K § 219.

KEIL, Gottfr. De Flavio Capro Grammatico Quaestionum capita duo [diss. inaug.] 8° *Halle* 89

Festus, Sextus, Pompeius [A.D. 2nd cent.].

*De Verb. Sign, c. Pauli Epitom., emend. et annot. C. O. Müller 4° Simmel, *Lps.* [39] 80
Codex Festi Farnesianus xlii. Tabulis [phototyp.] expressus, ed. Em. Thewrewk de Ponor 42*m.* f° *Budapest* (Calvary, *Berl.*) 93

Nonius Marcellus [A.D. beg. 4th cent.].

Compendiosa Doctrina w. Latin notes Lucian Müller, pt. i. 20*m.*; ii. 12*m.* r 8° Teubner, *Lps.* 88; 89
GOETZ, Geo. Meletemata Festina; Nova Meletemata Festina [ea. 8 pp.] ea. 50*pf.* 4° Neuenhahn, *Jena* 85; 87
MEYLAN, Henri [ed.] Non. Marcellus: collatn. d. plusieurs MSS. [Bibl. d. l'Ec. d. Ht. Etud.] 5*fr.* 8° Bouillon, *Paris* 87
STOWASSER, J. M. Noniana [schl.-progr.] 84

Appended is a notice on the principal MSS. of NONIUS, bks. i., ii., and iii. by L. HAVET.

Probus, M. Valerius [A.D. 1st cent.].

ULLMANN, Karl Die Appendix Probi [diss. inaug. Bonnae] 8° *Erlangen* 91

Vergilius Maro (Grammaticus).

Opera: ed. J. Huemer 8° *Leipzig* 86
STANGL, Theod. Virgiliana: die gramm. Schriften d. Galliers Virg. Mar. . . . text-Krit. untersucht 3*m.* 8° *Munich* (Fock, *Lps.*) 91

220. LATIN WRITERS ON ORATORY.

Cicero, M. Tullius [B.C. 106–43].

Opera Rhetorica: rec. Wilh. Friedrich, vol. i. 1*m*.35; ii. 2*m*.10 8° Teubner, *Lps.* 84; 91

Forms *Pars Prima* of the *Opera Omnia* rec. C. F. W. MUELLER.

Brutus (*sive* De Claris Oratoribus): rec. Theod. Stangl 80*pf.* 8° Freytag, *Lps.* 86
w. French tr. and Introd. Jules Martha 6*fr.* 8° Hachette, *Paris* 92
De Oratore: * w. English notes and Introd. Prf. A. S. Wilkins [*ut* 𝔅.𝔅. K § 214]: Book iii. 8° 6/- Clar. Press / $1.25 *n.* Macmillan, *N.Y.* 92

Bk. i. 7/6 ($1.90 *n.*) [’79] ’88; ii. 5/- ($1.25 *n.*) [’81] ’90—*ut* 𝔅.𝔅. K § 220: complete in 1 vol. 18/- ($4.50 *n.*). A careful and learned edn., into wh. 15 yrs'. labour of love have been put, w. a revised text, notes on syntax, history, antiqs. and technics of rhetoric, index, and facs. of Codex Harleianus.

Orator ad Brutum: rec. Theod. Stangl 60*pf.* 8° Freytag, *Lps.* 85
Rhetorica [Ad Herennium]: rec. Friedr. Marx 14*m.* 8° Teubner, *Lps.* 94

Translation.

De Oratore, bk. i.: tr. E. N. P. Moor [Classical Translations] 3/6 c 8° Methuen 93

An excellent tr. into "natural English": idiomatic and graceful.

Aids.

HEINICKE, Wilh. De Ciceronis Doctrina quae pertin. ad. mater. art. rhetoricae et ad inv. 1*m*.20 8° *Königsberg* 91
MERCHANT, Frz. Joh. De Ciceronis Partitionibus oratoriis Commentatio [diss. inaug.] 1*m*.50 8° Heinrich, *Berlin* 90

Cornificius [B.C. 1st cent.].

RADTKE, Joh. Observationes Criticae in Cornifici libros de arte rhetor. [diss.] 1*m.* 8° *Königsbg.* (Koch, *Lps.*) 92
THIELE, Geo. Quaestiones de Cornifici et Ciceronis Artibus Rhetoricis [diss. inaug.] 1*m*.50 *Greifswald* (Fock, *Lps.*) 89

Cornutus, L. Ann. [A.D. mid. 1st cent.; Roman Stoic, who wrote in Greek]—*v.* K § 195.

Quintilianus, M. Fabius [A.D. c. 35-97].

De Institutione Oratoria, bk. x.: *w. English comm. and crit. appends. Prc. W. Peterson 8° 12/6 Clar. Press / $3.25 *nt.* Macmillan, *N.Y.* 91

The revision of text is based on collatn. of several important codices. The Introd. essays are on Q.'s life and work, his literary crit., style and language, and on the MSS. The whole of the *Institutio*, similarly treated, is promised by Dr. FASKNETT. Facs. of Harl. MS. is added.

lib. x.: w. English Introd. Prc. W. Peterson: School Edn. [Clar. Press Ser.] f 8° 3/- Clar. Press / $1 *nt.* Macmillan, *N.Y.* 92

lib. i.: *ed. Chas. Fierville; w. French Introd. 10*fr.* 8° Didot, *Paris* 90

A very important recension of bk. i., w. elabor. Introd. giving an exhaustive classifn. of the MSS. and a hist. of the text. Prf. PETERSON'S investign. into the Engl. MSS. usefully supplements this.

BECHER, Ferd. Zum toten. Buche des Quintilian [school programme] 1*m*.20 4° *Aurich* (Fock, *Lpz.*) 91
FLEITER, G. De minoribus quae sub nomine Quintiliani feruntur declamationibus [dissert.] 1*m*.20 8° Fock, *Leipzig* 90
HAMMER, C. Beiträge z. d. 19 grösseren v. quintilianischen Deklamationen [progr.] 8° *Munich* (Fock, *Lpz.*) 93
HIRT, Paul Ueber die Substantivierung des Adjektivums bei Quintilian [schl.-progr.] 1*m*. 4° Gaertner, *Berlin* 90

Tacitus, Cornelius [A.D. c. 54-c. 117] Dialogus de Oratoribus—v. K § 216.

221. LATIN WRITERS ON AGRICULTURE.

Cato, M. Porcius, Censorius [B.C. 234-149].

De Agri Cultura: ex rec. Heinr. Keil [*ut* B.B. K § 221], w. Latin notes; vol. i. 8*m*.; ii. (1) 6*m*.; ii. (2) 8*m*. 8° Teubner, *Lps.* 91; 94; 9?

Vol. i. incl. text, together w. VARRO'S *Rerum Rusticarum libri tres*. ii. (1): *Comment. in Catonis De Agri Cultura*; ii. (2) *Comm. in Varronis Rer. Rust. libr. tr.*

Varro, M. Terentius (Reatinus) [B.C. 116-27].

Rerum Rustic. libri iii.: rec. Heinr. Keil; w. Latin notes—*ut supra, sub nom.* Cato
rec. Heinr. Keil 1*m*.50 8° Teubner, *Lps.* 89

222. LATIN WRITERS ON PHYSICAL SCIENCE AND MEDICINE.

Astronomy.

HYGINUS, C. Iul. [B.C. 1st cent.-A.D. 1st cent.] Astronomica, rec. Bernh. Bunte 4*m*.; *red. to* 2*m*. 8° Weigel, *Lps.* 75
Fabulae, rec. Bern. Bunte 3*m*.30 8° Dyk, *Lps.* 57
DIETZE, Joh. Quaestiones Hyginianae [dissert. inaug.] 1*m*.50 8° *Kiel* (Lorenzen, *Altona*) 90
LANGE, Carl De Nexu inter Hygini Opera mythol. et Fabul. [diss. inaug.] 1*m*.20 8° Kunze, *Bonn* 65
MANILIUS, M. [A.D. 1st cent.] Astronomicon—*ut* K § 214: Latin Poets.

Natural History.

PLINIUS SECUNDUS [A.D. 23-79] Historia Naturalis, ed. Lud. Jan + Carl Mayhoff, vol. iii. [bks. 16-22] 4*m*. 8° Teubner, *Lps.* 92
BECK, J. W. Studiana Gelliana et Pliniana—*ut* K § 224.
CUNTZ, Otto Agrippa u. Augustus als Quellenschriftsteller d. Plin.; 2 col. maps [*extr. f.* Jahrb. Cl. Phil.] 2*m*. 8° Teubner, *Lps.* 90
STADLER, Herm. Die Quellen des Plinius im 19 Buche der Nat. Hist. [progr.] 8° *Munich* 91
THÜSSING, Jos. De Temporum et Modorum in enunt. pendentibus ap. Plin. Sec. Usu, 2 pts. 2*m*.10 8° Dominicus, *Prague* 89; 90

Physiognomists: *Collectively.*

Physiognomici Scriptores Graeci et Latini: rec. R. Foerster—*ut* K § 196.

Medical Writers.

MARCELLUS EMPIRICUS [A.D. 5th cent.] De Medicamentis liber, rec. G. Helmreich 3*m*.60 8° Teubner, *Lps.* 89
HEIM, R. De Rebus Magicis Marcelli med. 1*m*. 8° 91
PRISCIANUS THEODORUS [A.D. 5th cent.] Euporiston, cum Physicorum Fragmento, ed. V. Rose 5*m*. 8° 94

Veterinary Writers.

PELAGONIUS Artis Veterinariae quae extant, rec. . . . Max Ihm 2*m*.40 8° Teubner, *Lps.* 92

223. LATIN WRITERS ON MILITARY SCIENCE AND ON ARCHITECTURE.

Frontinus, Sextus Iulius [A.D. c. 40-103 (or 4)].

FRITZE, Ern. De Iuli Frontini Strategematon libro iv. [diss. inaug.] 8° *Halle* 88
KORTZ, Fred. Quaestiones grammaticae de Frontini Operibus institutae [diss. inaug.] 8° Iserlohn, *Münster* 93

Vitruvius Pollio, M. [B.C. 1st cent.].

De Architectura libri x.: ad antiquiss. codd. ed. Val. Rose + H. Müller-Strubing 7*m*. 16° Teubner, *Lps.* 67
ed. C. Lorentzen, w. German tr.; vol. i., pt. i. 4*m*. 8° " " 55
CAPPS, Edw. [Am.] Vitruvius and the Greek Stage—*in* Chicago Univ. Studies in Class. Phil., vol. i. *ut* K § 173.
HULTSCH, Fr. Die Bruchzeichen bei Vitruvius 8° 76

K § 224. LATIN MISCELLANEOUS WRITERS.

Apuleius Madaurensis, L. [A.D. c. 130-?]—*v.* K § 45 *and* B.B. K § 45.

BECKER, Heinr. Studia Apuleiana 3*m*. 8° Weidmann, *Berlin* 79
BEYTE, F. Quaestiones Apuleianae [diss.] 1*m*.50 8° Fock, *Lps.* ?8
BURSIAN, K. Beiträge zur Kritik der Metamorphosen des Apuleius 8?
PIECHOTTA, Joh. Curae Apuleianae [diss. inaug.] 1*m*. 8° Koebner, *Breslau* 82

K § 225

Gellius, Aulus [A.D. c. 130–c. 170].

BECK, J. W. Studia Gelliana et Pliniana 1m.60 8° Teubner, *Lpz.* 92
HERTZ, W. Supplementum Apparatus Gelliani [*extr. fr.* Jahrbb. f. Class. Philol.] 1m.40 8° „ „ 94
NEUBAUER, Rich. De Coniunctionum causalium apud Gellium Usu (diss. inaug.) 1m. 8° *Magdebg.* (Fock, *Lpz.*) 90

Macrobius, Aurel., Ambrosius, Theodosius [A.D. 5th cent.].

Opera: iterum rec. F. Eyssenhardt [*ut* B.B. K § 224]: 2nd Edn. 6m. 8° Teubner, *Lpz.* [68] 93

Plinius Cæcilius Secundus (Minor) [A.D. 62–c. 114].

Epistolae Selectae: w. German notes Dr. Ant. Kreuser; pl. of Roman villa 1m.50 8° Teubner, *Lpz.* 94
VAN VRIES, S. G. Exercitationes Palæographicæ 1fl.20 8° Brill, *Leyden* 90
Consists of *Commentatiuncula de C. Plin. Cæc. Sec. Epistularum Fragmento Vossiano notis tironianis descripto.*

Tiro, M. Tullius [B.C. 1st cent.].

Commentarii Notarum Tironianarum, ed. Wilh. Schmitz; w. Lat. prolegg. and crit. notes; 132 pl. 40m. f° Teubner, *Lpz.* 94
SCHMITZ has also pub. numerous papers on the Tironian controversy in *Rhein. Mus.*, *Jahrbb. f. Class. Philol.*, etc.

XXVII. Teutonic Philology.

225. GENERALLY.

Bibliography.

*PAUL, Prf. H. [ed.] —*in his* Grundriss d. german. Philologie, *ut infra.*

Linguistic Ethnology.

GUMMERE, Prf. Fcs. B. [Am.] Germanic Origin of the English People—*ut* F § 5.
NABERT, Prf. H. Das deutsche Sprachgebiet in Europa u. die deutsche Sprache 2m. 8° Strecker, *Stuttgt.* 93
PENKA, K. Die Heimat der Germanen 2m. 8° Hiersemann, *Lpz.* 93
THIS, Constant Die deut.-frz. Sprachgrenze in Lothringen, pt. i. [Beitr. z. Kunde v. Elsass] 1m.50 8° Heitz, *Strassburg* 87
ZIMMERLI, J. Die deut.-frz. Sprachgrenze in d. Schweiz, pt. i. [Jura]; map & 16 tables 3fr.50 8° Genf, *Basle* 91

Map.

NABERT, Prf. H. Map of Distribn. of Germans in Eur., [posth.] ed. Dr. R. Böckh, sects. i.–ii. Flemming, *Glogau* 91 *in prg.*
A laborious and painstaking wk., on a vast scale, giving at a glance a clear view of the distrib. of races and langs. in Europe.

History and Biography of the Study.

Biography.

BARTSCH, Karl [1832–1888]—*in* Briefwechsel zwisch. J. v. Lassberg u. L. Uhland, *ut infra.*
GRIMM, Jak. [1785–1863] *and* Wilhelm [Karl] [1786–1859].
Briefe d. Jak. Grimm an Hendrik Willem Tydemann, hrsg. Alex. Reifferscheid 3m.60 Henninger, *Heilbr.* (Tbnr. *Stuttg.*) 83
„ d. Jak. u. Wilh. Grimm and Geo. Friedr. Benecke, hrsg. Wilh. Müller [1808–1829] 4m. 8° Vandenhoeck, *Göttgn.* 89
Briefwechsel d. Gebrüder Grimm mit nordischen Gelehrten, hrsg. Ern. Schmidt 8m. 8° Dümmler, *Berlin* 85
„ zwisch. Jak. u. Wilh. Grimm aus d. Jugendzeit, hrsg. Herm. Grimm + G. Hinrichs 10m. 8° Böhlau, *Weimar* 81
„ zwisch. Jak. Grimm u. Friedr. Dav. Graeter, hrsg. Herm. Fischer [1810–13] 1m.60 8° Henninger, *Heilbr.* (Tbnr. *Stuttg.*) 77
„ zwisch. Jak. u. Wilh. Grimm, Dahlmann u. Gervinus, hrsg. Ed. Ippel, 2 vols. 10m. 8° Dümmler, *Berlin* 85; 86
„ v. Jak. Grimm. u. Hoffm. v. Fallersleben m. Hend. v. Wyn, hrsg. K. T. Gaedertz 1m.80 8° Müller, *Bremen* 88
„ Friedr. Lückes mit den Brüdern Grimm, hrsg. F. Sander 5m. 8° Manz, *Hanover* 91
Grimm, Herm. The Brothers Grimm—*in his* Literature, *ut* B.B. K § 23.
Scherer, Wilh. Jacob Grimm 5m. 8° Weidmann, *Berlin* [65] 84
HAUPT, Moriz [1808–1874].
Belger, Chrn. Moritz Haupt als academischer Lehrer 8m. 8° Weber, *Berlin* 79
With HAUPT'S observns. on Gk., Lat. and Germ. authors, and a biograph. Introduction.
Kirchhoff, A. Gedächtnisrede auf Moriz Haupt [*extr. fr.* Abhgn. Berl. Akad.] 80pf. 4° Dümmler, *Berlin* 75
HOFFMANN v. FALLERSLEBEN, A. Heinr. [1798–1874] Mein Leben [abgd.], hrsg. Dr. H. Gerstenberg, 2 pts. 7m. 8° Fontane, *Berlin* [68–70] 94
Wagner, J. M. Hoffmann von Fallersleben, 2m.; Nachtrag 1m. [bibliographical] 8° Gerold, *Vienna* 69; 70
LACHMANN, Karl [1793–1851].
Hertz, Mart. Karl Lachmann: eine Biographie 6m. 8° Hertz, *Berlin* 51
UHLAND, Joh. Ludw. [1787–1862] Briefwechsel zwisch. J. v. Lassberg u. L. Uhland, hrsg. Frz. Pfeiffer 12m. 8° Braumüller, *Vienna* 70
Fischer, H. Ludwig Uhland: eine Studie 3m. 8° Cotta, *Stuttgart* 87
Leben, zusammengestellt v. seiner Witwe 3m.60 8° „ „ 74
WACKERNAGEL, Wilh. [1806–1869].
Wackernagel, Rud. Wilhelm Wackernagel; Jugendjahre: 1806–1833; 2 ports. 4m. 8° Detloff, *Basle* 85

Philology. Grammar. History of the Teutonic Languages.

*HENRY, Prf. Vict. Comparative Grammar of English and German c 8° 7/6 Sonnenschein / Macmillan, *N.Y.* 94
The Engl. edn. is tr. and ed. fr. the Fch. by the Author himself [7fr.50 8° Hachette, *Paris* '93]. An able and interesting bk. on the relation in phonology and grammar betw. Engl. and Germ., and their common rel. to Gk. and Latin: forming an excellent Introd. to the compar. philol. of the Indogermanic langs.
MEYER, R. Einführung in das ältere Neuhochdeutsche 1m.60 8° Reisland, *Lpz.* 94
Intended to serve as an Introduction to Germanic Philology in general.

*PAUL, Prf. Herm. [ed.] Grundriss d. german. Philologie : now complete, 2 vols. 42m. r 8° Trübner, *Strassbg.* 91 ; 93

New Parts since pubn. of B.B. Vol. I., Lfg. 4 sm., 5 4m. '91, 6 sm. '92 ; II. pt. i. 16m., II. pt. ii. 8m. '93.

The most compreh., scientific and accur. wk. hitherto pub. on Germanic philology (in its widest sense), many of the monographs being of exceptional importance.

Abschn. I. *Begriff u. Aufgabe* .... PAUL
II. *Geschichte* .... PAUL
III. *Methodenlehre* .... PAUL
IV. *Schriftkunde.*
Runen [*ut* K § 235] .... Ed. SIEVERS.
Latein. Schrift .... W. ARNDT
V. *Sprachgeschichte.*
Phonetik .... SIEVERS
Vorgesch. d. altgerm. Dial. .... Friedr. KLUGE
Gesch. d. gotisch. Spr. [*ut* K § 226] .... SIEVERS
" *nordisch Spr.* [*ut* K § 233] .... Ad. NOREEN
" *deut. Spr.* [*ut* K § 230] .... Otto BEHAGHEL
" *niederl. Spr.* [*ut* K § 232] .... Jan te WINKEL
" *friesisch. Spr.* [*ut* K § 227] .... Theod. SIEBS
" *englisch. Spr.* [*ut* K § 236] .... Friedr. KLUGE
With contribs. by D. Behrens and E. Einenkel.
VI. *Mythologie* [*ut* B § 19*] .... E. MOGK
VII. *Heldensage* [*ut* B § 19*] .... B. SYMONS
VIII. *Literaturgeschichte.*
Gotische Liter. [*ut* K § 225] .... SIEVERS
Nordische Liter. [*ut* K § 234] .... MOGK ; Hk. SCHÜCK
Deutsche Liter. : Althochd. .... Rud. KÖGEL
" *Mittelhochd.* .... Friedr. VOGT
Deutsche Liter. : Mittelniederd. .... HERM. JELLINGHAUS
Niederländ Liter. .... TE WINKEL
Friesische Liter. .... SIEBS
Englische : Altengl. [*ut* K § 245] .... Bern. TEN BRINK
" *Mittelengl.* [*ut* K § 245] .... Al. BRANDL
Anhang : *Volkspoesie.*
Skandinavische [*ut* B § 20] .... J. A. LUNDELL
Deut. u. niederländ. [*ut* B § 24] .... John MEIER
Englische [*ut* B § 23] .... BRANDL
IX. *Metrik.*
Altgermanische .... SIEVERS
Deutsche [*ut* K § 230] .... PAUL
Englische [*ut* K § 240] .... Karl LUICK ; J. SCHIPPER
X. *Wirtschaft* .... K. Th. v. INAMA-STERNEGG
XI. *Recht* .... Karl v. AMIRA
XII. *Kriegswesen* .... Alwin SCHULTZ
XIII. *Sitte.*
Skandinav. .... Kr. KALUND
Deut.-engl. .... SCHULTZ
XIV. *Kunst.*
Bildende Kunst .... SCHULTZ
Musik .... Rochus v. LILIENCRON
Index of Names, Subj. and Words .... W. LIST

STREITBERG, Wilh. Zur germanischen Sprachgeschichte 2m.50 8° Trübner, *Strassbg.* 92
WILMANNS, Prf. W. Deutsche Grammatik [Gothic, Old-, Middle- and Mod.-High Germ.]—*ut* K § 230.

Collected Essays.

HILDEBRAND, Rud. Aufsätze u. Vorträge zur deutschen Philologie u. deut. Unterricht 8m. 8° Teubner, *Lps.* 90
Forschungen z. deutsch. Philologie : Festgabe für Rud. Hildebrand 7m.50 8° Veit, *Lps.* 94
KÖCHLY, Herm. Opuscula Philologica, vol. ii. [Deutsche Aufsätze] ; 1 pl. 10m.80 8° Teubner, *Lps.* 82
LACHMANN, Karl Kleinere Schriften zur deutschen Philol., hrsg. Karl Müllenhoff 9m. 8° G. Reimer, *Berlin* 76
[V. MAURER, Konr.] Germanistische Abhandlungen z. LXX. Geburtstag v. K. v. M. 16m. 8° Dieterich, *Göttgn.* 93

By Osc. BRENNER, Fel. DAHN, Carl GAREIS, Wolfg. GOLTHER, Valtyr GUDMUNDSSON, Ebbe HERTZBERG, Finnur JÓNSSON, Karl LEHMANN, Ern. MEYER, Bj. M. OLSEN, Axel PETERSEN, V. A. SECHER, Pp. ZORN.

MAY, M. Beiträge zur Stammkunde d. deutschen Sprache 8m. 8° Biedermann, *Lps.* 93
SCHERER, Wilh. Kleine Schriften, hrsg. K. Burdach + E. Schmidt, 2 vols. 23m. 8° Weidmann, *Berlin* 93

i. *Kleine Sch. z. altdeutsch. Philol.* (BURDACH), 15m. ; ii. *Kl. Schr. z. neueren Litter., Kunst, etc.* (SCHMIDT), 8m.

WACKERNAGEL, Wilh. Kleinere Schriften, 3 vols. ea. 8m. 8° Hirzel, *Lps.* 72–74

i. *Deut. Alterthumskunde u. Kunstgesch.* ; *Deutsch. Litteraturgesch.* ; *Abhgn. z. Sprachkunde.*

Series, and Permanent Serials.

Acta Germanica : Organ f. deut. Philol., hrsg. R. Henning + J. Hoffory, v. i.–ii. ea. v. [= 4 pts.] 12m. r 8° Mayer & Müller, *Berl.* 89–90
Beiträge, Berliner, zur Germ. u. Rom. Philol., hrsg. Dr. Em. Ebering : Germ. Abthg., nos. i.–v. 10m.40 8° Vogt, *Berlin* 94 *in prg.*

i. *Gesch. d. Knittelverses v. 17 Jahrh. bis Goethe* Otto FLOHR, 2m.40
ii. *Zach. Werner, Mystik u. Romantik* .... Fel. POPPENBERG, 1m.80
iii. *Aelteste deut. Ueberstg. Molière* .... Arth. FLOSSER, 1m.80
iv. *Temporalconjunctionen* [*ut* K § 230] .... Ewald FREY, 2m.
v. *Tannhäuser : Inhalt u. Form.* .... Joh. SIEBERT, 2m.40
For ROMANISCHE ABTHEILUNG—*v.* K § 256.

" Erlanger, zur Englischen Philologie—*v.* K § 236.
" Münchener, zur Roman. u. Englischen Philologie—*v.* K § 256.
" Wiener, zur Deutschen u. Englischen Philologie—*v.* K § 236.

Grammatiken, Samml. kurzer, german. Dialekte : hrsg. Wilh. Braune *v.p.* 8° Niemeyer, *Halle* [80–92] 86–92

BRAUNE, Wilh. *Althochd. Gramm.* [*ut* B.B. K § 228] .. 5m.20 [86] 91
" *Gotische Gramm.* [*ut* B.B. K § 226] .... 2m.40 [80] 87
KLUGE, Dr. Friedr. *Nomin. Stammbild. d. altgerm. Dial.* [*ut* B.B. K § 225] 2m.60 86
NOREEN, Adf. *Altisländ. u. altnorw. Gramm.* [*ut* K § 233] 6m. [84] 92
PAUL, Prf. Herm. *Mittelhochdeutsche Grammatik* [*ut* B.B. K § 229] 2m.60 [81] 89
SIEVERS, Prf. Ed. *Altgerman. Metrik* [*ut infra*] 5m. 92
" *Angelsächs. Gramm.* [*ut* B.B. K § 242] ...... 4m.20 [82] 86

" Samml. kurzer, deutscher Mundarten—*ut* K § 231.

Lehrbücher der germanischen Philologie 8° Mayer & Müller, *Berl.* 91 *in prg.*

Vol. i. *Germanische Mythologie* [*ut* B § 24] ...... Elard Hugo MEYER, 5m. 91

Neueren Sprachen, Die : Ztschr. f. neuspr. Unterricht, hrsg. Prf. Wilh. Vietor, vols. i.–ii. [ea. 10 pts.] ea. vol. 12m. 8° Elwert, *Marbg.* 93 ; 94 *in prg.*

PAUL + BRAUNE, Prf. Herm. / W. [eds.] Beiträge zur Geschichte d. deutsch. Sprache u. Litter., vol. xvi. ea. vol. [= 3 pts.] 15m. 8° Niemeyer, *Halle* 90 *in prg.*

Quellen u. Forschungen z. Sprach.- u. Culturgesch. d. germ. Völker, pts. i.–cxx. *v.p.* 8° Trübner, *Strassbg.* 74–92 *in prg.*
Schriften zur german. Philologie, hrsg. Prf. Max Roediger, pts. i.–vii. 8° Weidmann, *Berl.* 88–94 *in prg.*

i. *Karolingische Dichtungen* .... L. TRAUBE, 4m. 88
ii. *Satzbau d. Althd. Isidor* .... M. RANNOW, 4m. 88
iii. *Untersuchgn. z. Psalmen Notkers* .... J. KELLE, 7m. 89
iv.–v. *Deut. Schr. d.* Albr. v. Eyb. .... ed. Herm. MAX, 13m. 90
vii. *Ueber german. Versbau* [*ut infra*] .... Andr. HEUSLER, 6m. 94

Studien, Neuphilologische : hrsg. Gust. Körting, pt. vi. [Friedwagner's Spr. v. Huon de Bord. (*ut* K § 277)] 2m.40 8° Schöningh, *Paderb.* 91

Accidence.

Comparatives.

STREITBERG, W. Die germanischen Comparative auf -ōz- 3m. 8° Friesenhahn, *Freibg.* 91

Inflection.

JELLINEK, Max Herm. Beiträge zur Erklärung der germanischen Flexion 2m.80 8° Speyer, *Berlin* 91

Syntax.

Prepositions.

MOUREK, Prf. V. E. Ukazky ze Syntaxe Gotských Predlozek [Syntax of Gothic prepositions] 8° *Prague* 89

Extr. fr *Sitz.-Ber.* of Bohem. Soc. of Arts: a good study, tracing ea. prepos. in the remains of the Gothic language wh. have come down to us, w. frequent references to the orig. Greek.

Verb.

LORENTZ, Dr. Friedr. Das schwache Präterit d. German. u. verw. Bdgn. d. Schwesterspr. 2*m.* 8° Koehler, *Lps.* 94

OTTMANN, Rich. Eduard Reduplic. Präterita i. d. german. Sprachen [schl.-progr.] 1*m.* 4° Fock, *Lps.* 90

Etymology.

ATZLER, Fel. *Qu* i. d. german. Sprachen u. s. Wechsel mit *p* [progr.] 4° *Barmen* 90

Dictionaries —*v. also* K § 230.

*GRIMM, Jak. + Wilh. Deutsches Wörterbuch r 8° Hirzel, *Lps.* 54–94 *in prg.*

Vol. I. 16*m.* '54; II. 15*m.* '60; III. 16*m.* '62; IV. i. (1) 20*m.* '78; IV. ii. 27*m.* '77; V. 25*m.* 73; VI. 30*m.* '85; VII. 25*m.* '89; VIII. 28*m.* '94; IV. i. (2) IX. *in prg.*; XI. *in prg.* [*v.* S.S. K § 225].

Metrics. Poetics.

FUHR, Karl Die Metrik d. westgerman. Alliterationsverses [Otfried, Nibel., *etc.*] 3*m.*60 8° Elwert, *Marburg* 92

HEUSLER, Andreas Ueber die german. Versbau [Schr. z. germ. Phil., vii.] 6*m.* 8° Weidmann, *Berl.* 94

MEYER, Rich. M. Die altgermanische Poesie, nach ihr. formelhaft. Elementen 10*m.* 8° Hertz, *Berlin* 89

*SIEVERS, Prf. Ed. Altgermanische Metrik [Samml. kurz. Gramm. germ. Dial.] 5*m.* 8° Niemeyer, *Halle* 92

Studien z. german. Alliterationsvers, hrsg. Prf. Max Kaluza, pt. i.–ii. [Altenglisch]—*ut* K § 242; *s.v.* Metrics.

Phonology.

HOLZ, Geo. Urgermanisches geschlossenes *ē* und Verwandtes 1*m.*50 8° Fock, *Lps.* 90

NOREEN, Adl. Abriss d. urgerm. Lautlehre m. Rücksicht a. d. nord. Spra. 5*m.* 8° Trübner, *Strassbg.* 94

226. GOTHIC PHILOLOGY.

Grammar.

BORRMANN, Joh. Ruhe u. Richtung in d. gotisch. Verbalbegriffen [diss. inaug.] 8° *Halle* 92

WREDE, Ferd. Specimen einer ostgot. Gram. [Hab.-Schr.; *repr. fr.* Quellen u. Forsch.] 8° *Marburg* 90

WRIGHT, Prf. Jos. A Primer of the Gothic Language, w. grammar, notes and glossary f 8° 4/6 Clar. Press / $1.25 *nt.* Macmillan, *N.Y.* 92

East-Gothic.

WREDE, Ferd. Ueber die Sprache der Ostgoten in Italien [Quellen u. Forschn.] 4*m.* 8° Trübner, *Strassbg.* 91

Syntax.

MOUREK, V. E. Einfluss d. Hauptsatzes a. d. Modus d. Nebensatzes i. Got. [*extr.*] 60*pf.* 8° Rivnác, *Prague* 93

Pronoun.

FRIEDRICHS, Ern. Die Stellung d. Pronomen personale in Gotischen [Lpz. diss. inaug.] 8° *Jena* 93

History of the Language.

SIEVERS, Prf. Ed. Geschichte der gotischen Sprache—*in* Paul's Grundriss, *ut* K § 225.

Etymology.

GALLÉE, Prf. Joh. Hen. Gustiska; lijst van gotische woorden, 2 pts. 8° *Haarlem* 80; *Utrecht* 82

i. *Wörgeslacht of buiging naar analogie v. and. Got. woorden, of van het Oud-Germaan. wordt opgegeven*; ii. *De adjectiva in het Got. en hunne suffixen.*

Dictionary.

PRIESE, Osk. Deutsch-gotisches Wörterbuch [w. specs. of provbs., *etc.*] 1*m.*80 8° Voigtländer, *Lps.* 90

Literature.

History.

SIEVERS, Prf. Ed. Gotische Literaturgeschichte—*in* Paul's Grundriss, *ut* K § 225.

Specimens.

ULFILAS, Bp. [A.D. 311–383].

Balg, G. H. [Am.; ed.] Ulfilas: w. other remains of Gothic lang.; w. intro., synt. and gloss. $2.75 4° Westermann, *N.Y.* 91

227. FRISIAN PHILOLOGY AND LITERATURE.

History of the Language.

SIEBS, Theod. Geschichte der friesischen Sprache—*in* Paul's Grundriss, *ut* K § 225.

Lexicography.

HETTEMA, Dr. F. Buitenrust Bijdragen tot het Oud-friesch Woordenboek 1*fl.*50 8° Brill, *Leyden* 88

Dictionary.

DYKSTRA + HETTEMA, Waling / Dr. F. B. Friesch Wdb., met eene Lyst v. Friesch. Eigennamen 10*fl.* 8° Meyer & Schaafsma, *Leeuwarden*, *in prep.*

Likely to be of great importance. An elabor. prospectus, w. specimens, has been pubd.

Chrestomathies.

HETTEMA, Dr. F. Buitenrust [ed.] Bloemlezing uit Oud-, Middel- en Nieuw Friesch, 3 pts. ea. 1*fl.*50 8° Brill, *Leyden* 90; 87; 88

i. *Oud-friesch*, '90; ii. *Middelfriesch*, '87; iii. *Nieuwefriesch*, '88. Contains a glossary.

RIEGER, Max [ed.] —*in his* Alt- u. angelsächsisches Lesebuch, *ut* K § 238.

228. GERMAN PHILOLOGY (*a*): OLD-HIGH AND OLD-LOW GERMAN.

Old-High German.

Grammar.

BRAUNE, Wilh. Abriss der althochdeutschen Grammatik 1*m*.20 8° Niemeyer, *Halle* 91

An excellent little book; w. Middle-High Germ., Old-Saxon and Gothic paradigms.

ZIMMER, Hans Repetitorium u. Examinatorium üb. d. althd. Grammatik 2*m*.40 8° Rossberg, *Lps.* 91

Manuscripts —*v.* K § 4, *s.v.* Germany (Heidelberg; by Karl BARSTCH).

Phonology.

GARKE, Herm. Prothese u. Aphaerese d. H. im Althd. [Quell. u. Forsch.] 3*m*. 8° Trübner, *Strassb.* 92

WILKENS, Friedr. Zum hochalemann. Konsonantismus d. althochd. Zeit 3*m*. 8° Fock, *Lps.* 91

Based on the German Proper Names in the Saint Gallen records to A.D. 805

Metrics.

PRALLE, Geo. Die Frauenstrophen im ältesten deut. Minnesang [diss. inaug.] 8° *Halle* 92

WILMANNS, Prf. W. Der altdeutsche Reimvers [Beitr. z. altd. Lit., pt. iii.] 4*m*. 8° Weber, *Bonn* 87

Old-Low German (incl. Old-Saxon).

Grammar.

BEHAGHEL + GALLÉE, Prf. O. / Prf. J. H. Altsächsische Grammatik, pt. i. 2*m*. 8° Niemeyer, *Halle* 91

This pt. conns. the *Laut- u. Flexionslehre* (by GALLÉE). A second pt. is to complete the book.

SCHLÜTER, W. Untersuchungen z. Gesch. d. altsächs. Sprache, pt. i. 6*m*. 8° Peppmüller, *Göttgn.* 92

This pt. deals w. the Weak Declension in lang. of the *Heliand* and the minor Old-Saxon texts.

Prepositions.

REIMANN, P. Die altniederdeutschen Präpositionen [schl.-progr] 1*m*. *Danzig* (Fock, *Lps.*) 91

Chrestomathy.

RIEGER, Max [ed.] Alt- u. angelsächsisches Lesebuch [w. good vocabulary] 8*m*. 8° Ricker, *Giessen* 61

Contains also some Old Frisian pieces.

Bibliography.

ECKART, Rud. Niedersächs. Sprachdenkmäler in übersichtl. Darstellg. [w. refs. to sources] 3*m*. 8° Zickfeldt, *Oesterwieck* 93

Collected Essays.

SCHERER, Wilh. Kleine Schriften zur altdeutschen Philologie—*ut* K § 225.

WILMANNS, Prf. W. Beiträge z. Gesch. d. älteren deutsch. Literatur, pts. i.–iv. 8*m*.50 8° Weber, *Bonn* 85–88

i. *Der sogenannt. Heinr. v. Melk*, 1*m*.50 '85; ii. *Ueb. das Anno-Lied*, 3*m*. '86; iii. *D. altdeut. Reimvers* (*ut supra*) 4*m*. '87; iv. *Untersuchgn. z. mhd. Metrik* (*ut* K § 229) 4*m*. '88.

Texts.

Collections.

*GALLÉE, Prf. Joh. Hen. [ed.] Old Saxon Texts, pts. i.–iv. f° Brill, *Leyden* 91–94 *in prg.*

A crit. edn. of all extant documts. in the Low-Germ. dial. known as Old-Saxon, incl. a new edn. of the *Heliand* (taking account of the 3rd fragmentary MS. discov. by Prf. H. LAMBEL. A phototype facs. of ea. MS. is given, preceded by crit. and palæograph. inform. and a general introd. essay. Two edns., in Germ. & Engl., are issued.

HEYNE, Moritz [ed.] Kleinere altniederdeut. Denkmäler; w. gloss. [Bibl. ältest. d. Lit.-Denk.] 4*m*. 8° Schöningh, *Paderb.* [67] 78

Individually.

Bible: Bruchstück d. altsächs. Bibeldichtung aus d. Bibl. Palatina, hrsg. K. Zangemeister + W. Braune 3*m*. 8° Koester, *Heidelbg.* 94

Also in the *Heidelberger Jahrbb.*, iv. 2 [5*m*.], where the *whole* text is facsimiled. An important find, contg. the Old-Saxon original, wh. SIEVERS in 1875 suspected to be pt. of the Ang.-Saxon *Genesis*, and a fragmt. of the *Heliand* (1297-1358).

Heliand.

(An Old-Sax. poem on Gospel hist., having import. relns. to CÆDMON and in a less degree to CYNEWULF; comp. c. 830)

BEHRINGER, E. Zur Würdigung des Heliand 2*m*.40 8° Krebs, *Aschaffenbg.* 91

HEULER, A. Geschichte der Heliandforschung [Rostock diss. inaug.] 1*m*.50 8° Hedeler, *Lps.* 91

From its first discovery to J. A. SCHMELLER'S edn. (4° Cotta, *Stuttgt.*, 1830).

LANGENFUSCH, Emil Das germanische Recht im Heliand [Unters. z. Staatsgesch.] 2*m*.50 8° Koebner, *Breslau* 9-

WUSTMANN, R. Verba Perfektiva, namentlich im Heliand 2*m*. 8° Grunow, *Lps.* 94

Old West Saxon [the lang. of ALFRED]—*v.* K § 242.

Middle-Low German—*v.* K § 231, *sub voc.* Platt-Deutsch.

229. GERMAN PHILOLOGY (*b*): MIDDLE-HIGH GERMAN.

Grammar.

BACHMANN, Alb. Mittelhochdeutsche Grammatik [*repr. fr. his* MHD. Leseb., *ut inf.*] 60*pf.* 8° Höhr, *Zürich* 92

BRENNER, Osc. Mittelhochdeutsche Grammatik [*repr. fr.* Englmann's MHD. Leseb., *ut* B.B. K § 229] 60*pf.* 8° Lindauer, *Munich* [63] 90

History of the Language.

FISCHER, Herm. Zur Geschichte des Mittelhochdeutschen; 1 map 2*m.* 4° Fues, *Tübingen* 89

Article.

KUNZ, Frz. Der Artikel im Mittelhochdeutschen [school-programme] 8° *Teschen* 91

Metrics.

FREERICKS, Herm. Der Kehrreim in der mittelhochdeutschen Dichtung [school-programme] 1*m.* 4° Fock, *Lpz.* 90

MÜLDER, D. Albrecht v. Johannsdorf: Beitr. z. mittelhochd. Metrik 1*m.*20 8° " " 94

SCHREIBER, Dr. J. Vaganten-Strophe d. mittellatein. Dichtg. u. d. Verh. ders. z. mhd. Strophenformen—*ut* K § 210.

WILMANNS, Prf. W. Untersuchgn. zur mhd. Metrik [Beitr. z. älter. deut. Lit.] 4*m.* 8° Weber, *Bonn* 88

(1) *Daktyl. Rhythmus i. Minnesang*; (2) *Die Kürenbergus wise*; (3) *Gebrauch d. Wörter m. kurz. Stammsilbe b. d. Minnesgr.*

Chrestomathy.

BACHMANN, Alb. [ed.] Mittelhochdeutsches Lesebuch [w. short grammar] 4*m.* 8° Höhr, *Zürich* 92

230. GERMAN PHILOLOGY (*c*): MODERN-HIGH GERMAN.

Collected Essays.

HILDEBRAND, Rud. Gesammelte Aufsätze u. Vorträge zur deut. Philol. u. Unterricht 8*m.* 8° Teubner, *Lpz.* 90

History of the Language. Grammar.

*BEHAGHEL, Prf. Otto Short Historical Gram. of the German Language, tr. Dr. Emil Trechmann 4/6 ($1) gl 8° Macmillan 91

A tr. of his *Die Deutsche Sprache*, *ut* B.B. K § 225. A sound popular exposition of mod. philological research. In this tr. the examples are substituted by English ones, and the matter has otherwise been here and there adapted to Engl. requirements. Good index.

" " " Geschichte der deutschen Sprache—*in* Paul's Grundriss, *ut* K § 225.

BRANDSTETTER, R. Die Reception d. nhd. Schriftsprache in Luzern: 1600–1830 2*m.* 8° Benziger, *Einsiedeln* 92

ENGELIEN, Aug. Grammatik der neuhochdeutschen Sprache 7*m.*50 8° Schulze, *Berlin* [67] 92

*HENRY, Prf. Vict. Comparative Grammar of English and German—*ut* K § 225.

WILMANNS, Prf. W. Deutsche Grammatik, Abtheilg. i. [Lautlehre], 4 pts. 6*m.*50 8° Trübner, *Strassbg.* 93

Gothic, Old-, Middle- and Modern-High German.

Change of Gender.

BLUMER, J. Zum Geschlechtswandel d. Lehn- u. Fremdwörter im Hochd., 2 pts. ea. 1*m.*50 r 8° *Leitmeritz* (Fock, *Lpz.*) 90; 91

MICHELS, Vict. Zum Wechsel d. Nominalgeschlechts im Deutschen, pt. i. 1*m.*50 8° Trübner, *Strassbg.* 89

Early Grammars.

Grammatiken, Aeltere deutsche, in Neudrucken, hrsg. John Meier, vol. ii. 6*m.* 8° Trübner, *Strassburg* 94 *in prg.*

i. [to appear later]; ii. J. CLAJUS, *Deutsche Grammatik* [1578], w. variants of other edns., ed. F. WEIDLING, 6*m.* '94

Conjunctions.

FREY, Ewald D. Temporalconjn. i. d. Uebergangszt. v. mhd. z. nhd. [Berl. Beitr.] 2*m.* 8° Vogt, *Berlin* 94

Noun.

BOJUNGA, K. Die Entwickelung der neuhochdeutschen Substantivflexion [diss. inaug.] 3*m.* 8° Gräfe, *Lpz.* 90

Change of Gender.

MICHELS, Vict. Zum Wechsel des Nominalgeschlechts im Deutschen; pt. i. 1*m.*50 8° Trübner, *Strassbg.* 90

Numerals.

RUMPELT, H. B. The German Numerals: historically treated, ed. Karl Lentzner 5/- r 8° Truslove 94

Syntax.

WUNDERICH, Herm. Der deutsche Satzbau 4*m.* 8° Cotta, *Stuttgart* 92

Etymology.

DUDEN, Konr. Etymologie d. neuhochd. Sprache [w. etym. glossary] 3*m.*60 8° Beck, *Munich* 93

Forms the 3rd edn. of Bauer-Frommann's *Etymologie*.

Dictionaries.

DUDEN, Konr. Orthographisches Wörterbuch d. deutschen Sprache 1*m.*50 8° Bibl. Instit., *Lpz.* [80] 93

FAULMANN, Prf. Karl Etymologisches Wörterbuch d. deutschen Sprache 12*m.* 8° Karras, *Halle* 93

FLÜGEL, Dr. J. G. Engl.-Germ. [pp. 1,872] and Germ.-Engl. [pp. 940] Dicty., ed. Dr. Felix Flügel, 3 vols. r 8° Westermann, *Brunswick* / 45/- Asher; $16.50 Westermann, *N.Y.* 91; 92

Engl.-Germ., 2 vols. 30/-; Germ.-Engl., 1 vol. 15/-. A v. great improvt. on the 2 prev. edns. (2nd and 3rd) by Dr. MEISSNER (*not* the author of *Phil. of Fch. Lang.*), wh. was no great improvt. on the first edn. (1830), of wh. the Germ.-Engl. pt. was by FLÜGEL; Engl.-Germ. pt. (much inferior) by Dr. SPORSCHIL. Present is 4th edn., and both pts. have been cpltly. revised by Dr. Felix FLÜGEL, son of author. The Engl.-Germ. pt. is a v. excellent piece of work, nearly every word in standard English liter. bg. found in each of its senses, often w. admirable histor. explans., almost entitling it to rank as a lexicograph. authority. Bibliogr. occupying 27 pp. Germ.-Engl. pt. much less satisfactory; only "about 30 writers" being quoted, but as good as other bilingual dicts. Of special value for Germans; less for English.

GRIMM, Jak. + Wilh. Deutsches Wörterbuch—*ut* K § 225.

HEYNE, Moritz Deutsches Wörterbuch, vol. ii., pts. i.–iii., pt. i. ea. 5*m.* r 8° Hirzel, *Lps.* 91–94 *in prg.*

A good bk., intended however primarily for the use of Germans.

HILPERT, Dr. J. L. Dictionary of the English and German and Germ. and Engl. Languages, 4 vols. *o.p.* [*pb.* 54*m.*; *w.* 60/-] r 4° Braun, *Carlsruhe* 28–46

Though old, still a very useful dicty., not much inferior to LUCAS [*ut* B.S. K § 230]. An edn. on superior paper ("Schreibpapier") was printed, pb. 69*m.* [*w.* 84/-].

*KLUGE, Prf. Friedr. Etymologisches Wörterbuch der deutschen Sprache 10*m.* ½ 8° Tbnr., *Strassb.* [82–83] 93

" " Etymological Dictionary of the German Language, tr. Jno. Frcs. Davis 8° 18/- Bell; $3 Macmillan, *N.Y.* 91

The original Germ. (5th edn.) is vastly preferable to this inadequate and (in places) incorrect tr., wh. moreover was made fr. the edn. of 1889. On JANNSEN'S Index to 1st (not to 2nd) Germ. edn. *v. Mod. Lang. Notes*, v. 408, vi. 210.

MUSS-ARNOLT, W. Semitic and other Glosses to Kluge's Etymol. Wörterbuch—*in* Mod. Lang. Notes, v., vi.

*MURET, Prf. Ed. [ed.] Encyclopædic Engl.-Germ. [20 pts.] and Germ.-Engl. Dictionary [16 pts.] [36 pts. in all] r 8° ea. 1*m.*50 Langenscheidt, *Berlin*; ea. 1/6 Grevel; 50c. Int. News Co., *N.Y.* 91–94 *in prg.*

Names.

Family-Names.

KEIPER, Phil. Französische Familiennamen in der Pfalz 1*m* 8° Gotthold, *Kaiserlautern* [91] 91

TOBLER-MEYER, Wilh. Deutsche Familiennamen n. ihr. Entstehg. u. Bedeutg. 4*m.* 8° Müller, *Zürich* 94

Refers mainly to family-names of Zürich and Eastern Switzerland.

Place Names.

BESLER, M. Die Ortsnamen d. lothring. Kreises Forbach, 2 pts. [schl.-progrs.] 4° *Forbach* 90; 91

EGLI, Dr. J. J. Der Völkergeist in den geograph. Namen [*repr. fr.* Das Ausland] 2*m.* 8° Brandstetter, *Lps.* 93

GRADL, Heinr. Die Ortsnamen am Fichtelgebirge u. Vorlanden, pt. i. 3*m.*; ii. [Slavonic] 1*m.*40 8° Kobrtsch, *Eger* 92; 93

JACOB, Dr. G. Die Ortsnamen des Herzogthums Meiningen 4*m.* 8° Kesselring, *Hildburghausen* 94

RIEMANN Die Ortsnamen des Herzogtums Coburg [school programme] 4° *Coburg* 91

WOLFF, J. Deutsche Dorf- u. Stadtnamen in Siebenbürgen [school-programme] 4° *Mühlbach* 91

v. ZAHN, Jos. Ortsnamenbuch der Steiermark im Mittelalter 40*m.* r 8° Hölder, *Vienna* 93

Technical Terms —*v.* K § 276.

Metrics. Poetics.

BOHM, Herm. Zur deutschen Metrik [school-progr.] 1*m.* 4° Gaertner, *Berlin* 90

BÜCKMANN, Ludw. Der Vers v. 7 Hebungen im deut. Strophenbau [progr.] 1*m.* 4° *Lüneberg* (Fock, *Lps.*) 93

ERBE, Karl Leichtfassl. Regeln f. d. Aussprache d. Deutschen 1*m.*50 8° Neff, *Stuttgart* 93

GOLDBECK-LÖWE, Ad. Zur Gesch. d. freien Verse in d. deutsch. Dichtg. [Klopst. to Goethe; diss.] 2*m.* 8° Buchholz, *Munich* 91

HEINZE + GÖTTE, Paul / Rud. Deutsche Poetik: Wesen u. Formen der Dichtkunst 5*m.* 8° Heinze, *Dresden* 91

MINOR, J. Neuhochdeutsche Metrik; ein Handbuch 10*m.* 8° Trübner, *Strassburg* 93

PAUL, Prf. Herm. Deutsche Metrik—*in his* Grundriss, *ut* K § 225.

SANDERS, Dan. Abriss d. deutschen Silbenmessung u. Verskunst 2*m.*50 8° Langenscheidt, *Berl.* [81] 91

Orthoepy and Orthography. Pronunciation.

ANDRESEN, Karl Gust. Sprachgebrauch u. Sprachrichtigkeit im Deutschen 6*m.* 8° Reisland, *Lps.* [80] 92

A new edn. of the bk. in B.S. K § 230—the best on the subject.

BÜCHLER, W. Orthographie-Reform in der deut. Schweiz: Offiz. Protokoll 24 Aug. '92 1*fr.*20 8° Michel, *Berne* 92

HEINTZE, Alb. Gut Deutsch [pop. bk. on common errors of speech] 2*m.*50 8° Regenhardt, *Berlin* 93

MATTHIAS, Theod. Sprachleben u. Sprachschäden [on common difficulties of Germ. lang.] 5*m.*50 8° Richter, *Lps.* 92

VIETOR, Prf. Wilh. Aussprache d. Schriftdeutschen; 1 pl. 1*m.*60 8° Reisland, *Lps.* [85] 90

With the *Wörterverzeichn. f. d. deut. Rechtschreibg. z. Gebrauch i. d. preus. Schulen* in phonetic transcription.

" " Wie ist d. Aussprache des Deutschen zu lehren? [a lecture] 50*pf.* 8° Elwert, *Marburg* 93

WUSTMANN, Gust. Allerhand Sprachdummheiten 2*m.* 8° Grunow, *Lps.* 91

Phonology.

BREMER, D. Deutsche Phonetik [Samml. kurz. Gramm. deut. M'arten] 5*m.* 8° Breitkopf, *Lps.* 93

GRANDGENT, C. H. [Am.] German and English Sounds; w. diagrs. of vocal organs 12° 55c. Ginn, *Boston*; 2/6 Arnold 92

HEMPL, Prf. Geo. [Am.] German Orthography and Phonology, 2 pts. 12° Ginn, *Boston* 93

Pt. i. is a system. treatmt. of Germ. spelling, punctuatn., pronuncn. and stress; ii. is a word-list of the words in the Pruss., Bavar. and Wurtembg. spelling-bks. and many others in official spelling and in phonetic transcriptn.

HOFFMANN, Ed. Stärke, Höhe, Länge: Physiol. d. Akzentuatn. [esp. German] 1*m.*50 8° Trübner, *Strassbg.* 91

WILMANNS, Prf. W. Deutsche Grammatik, Abtheilg. i.: Lautlehre—*ut supra*.

Style.

HÖRTNAGEL, Joh. Versuch e. syst. Darstellg. d. Gesetze d. deut. Stiles [progr.] 8° *Vienna* 92

TUMLIRZ, Karl Die Lehre v. den Tropen u. Figuren, nebst kurzgef. Metrik 1*m.*60 8° Dominicus, *Prague* [81] 92

231. GERMAN PHILOLOGY (*d*): DIALECTS.

Generally.

HERTEL Ueber den Werth mundartlicher Untersuchungen [schl.-progr.] 4° *Greiz* 92

Bibliography.

MENTZ, Ferd. Bibliographie d. deutsch. Mundartenforschung [Samml. Gram. deut. M'darten] 5*m.* 8° Breitkopf, *Lps.* 93

A good bibliography, covering the period fr. beginning of 18th cent. to end of 1889.

K § 231

Series.

Grammatiken, Samml. kurzer, deutscher Mundarten, hrsg. Otto Bremer, vols. i.–ii. ea. 5*m.* 8° Breitkopf, *Lps.* 93; 93

i. *Deutsche Phonetik* [*ut* K § 230] .... D. BREMER | ii. *Bibliogr. d. deut. Mundartenforschg.* [*ut supra*] ...... F. MENTZ.

Specimens.

FIRMENICH-RICHARTZ, J. M. [ed.] Germanien's Völkerstimmen, 4 vols. *o.p.* [*pb.* 45*m.*; *w.* 35/–] 4° Schlesinger, *Berlin* 43–68

The best and most comprehensive work on Germ. dialects, consisting of a coll. of dialect poems, tales, songs, etc. An Appendix conts. the Germ. dialects of Belgium, England and Scandinavia.

Aachen (Aix-la-Chapelle).

JARDON, Arn. Grammatik der Achener Mundart, pt. i. 1*m.*50 8° Cremer, *Aix-l.-Chap.* 91

Alsace.

HÄNDCKE, Dr. Erwin Mundartl. Elemente i. d. elsäss. Urkunden [Alsat. Stud., v.] 1*m.*50 8° Trübner, *Strassb.* 94

KAHL, Wilh. Mundart und Schriftsprache im Elsass 1*m.*50 8° Fuchs, *Zabern* 93

LIENHART, Hans Laut- u. Flexionslehre d. Mundarten d. mittler. Zornthales [Alsat. Stud., i.] 2*m.* 8° Trübner, *Strassb.* 91

MENGES, Heinr. Volksmundart u. Volksschule im Elsass 2*m.* 8° Boltze, *Gebweiler* 93

SÜTTERLIN, Ad. Laut- u. Flexionslehre d. Strassb. Mundart [Alsat. Studien, ii.] 2*m.*50 8° ,, ,, 91

Bavaria.

BRENNER + HARTMANN, O. A. [eds.] Beiträge z. deut. Sprach- u. Volkskunde Bayerns Mundarten, vol. i. (3 pts.), ii. (1) ea. 4*m.* 8° Kaiser, *Munich* 91–93 *in prg.*

BRENNER, Osk. Mundarten und Schriftsprache in Bayern; map and ill. [Bayer. Bibl.] 1*m.*60 8° Buchner, *Bamberg* 90

Hesse.

SALZMANN, J. Die Herzfelder Mundart 2*m.*50 8° Ehrhardt, *Marburg* 89

VILMAR + V. PFISTER, A. F. C. Herm. Idiotikon von Hessen [*ut* B.B. K § 231]: 2nd Suppl. by H. v. Pfister 1*m.*20 8° Elwert, *Marburg* 94

Lithuanian. Lettish-Old-Prussian—*v.* K § 284: Slavonic.

Livonia.

V. GUTZEIT, W. Wörterschatz der Sprache Livlands, pt. i. (5), pt. ii. (5), iii. (3), iv. (2) & Suppls. 3*m.*80 8° Kimmel, *Riga* 89–93

Lorraine. Luxemburg—*for* French Dialect *v.* K § 275.

FOLLMANN, M. F. Mundart d. Deutsch-Lothringer u. Luxemburger, 2 pts. [sch. prgs.] 4° *Metz* 86; 90

Mayence.

REIS, Hans Beiträge zur Syntax der Mainzer-Mundart [diss.] 1*m.*50 8° Ricker, *Giessen* 92

Mühlheim.

MAURMANN, Em. Grammatik d. Mundart v. Mühlheim a. d. Ruhr 8° *Leipzig* 90

Platt-Deutsch.

KNOOP, Otto Plattdeutsches aus Hinterpommern, pts. i.–iii. ea. 1*m.* 4° *Rogasen* (Fock, *Lps.*) 90–92

LEITHÄUSER, J. Gallicismen in niederrheinischen Mundarten, pts. i.–ii. [progrs.] ea. 1*m.* 4° ,, ,, 91; 94

Middle Low-German.

LÜBBEN, Dr. A. Mittelniederdeutsche Grammatik [w. chrestomathy and glossary] 6*m.* 8° Weigel, *Lps.* 82

Serials.

Blätter f. Pommersche Volkskunde: hrsg. O. Knoop + A. Haas [monthly; folklore only] *ann.* 4*m.* 8° Burmeister, *Stettin* 92 *sqq. in prg.*

Denkmäler, Niederdeutsche: hrsg. v. Verein f. Niederdeut. Sprachforschung, vols. i.–v. 3*m.* 8° Soltau, *Norden* 76–92 *in prg.*

i. KOPPMANN, Karl *Das Seebuch* .... A. BREUSING, 4*m.* 76 | iv. *Valentin u. Namelos* .... W. SEELMANN, 5*m.* 84
ii. GERHARD V. MINDEN .... W. SEELMANN, 6*m.* 78 | v. *Redentiner Osterspiel* .... Carl SCHRÖDER, 3*m.* 92
iii. (1) *Flos unde Blankflos*, pt. i. ...... Steph. WAETZOLDT, 1*m.*60 80

Forschungen des Vereins für niederdeutsche Sprachforschung, vols. i.–vi. 8° Soltau, *Norden* 86–92 *in prg.*

i. *Die Soester Mundart* .... Ferd. HOLTHAUSEN, 3*m.* 86 | iv. .... *not yet publ.* 86–92 *in prg.*
ii. *Volksmärch. a. Pommern u. Rügen*, pt. i. .. Ulr. JAHN, 7*m.*50 91 | v. *Niederländ. Volksmundarten* ...... Herm. JELLINGHAUS, 4*m.* 92
vi. *Niederdeutsche Alliterationen* .... Prf. D. K. SEITZ, 3*m.* 92

Jahrbuch des Vereins für niederdeutsche Sprachforschung, vol. xv.–xviii. ea. 4*m.* 8° Soltau, *Norden* 91–94 *in prg.*

Riddles.

ECKART, Rud. Die allgemeine Sammlung niederdeutscher Rätsel 1*m.*50 8° Weigel, *Lps.* 94

Slang.

GENTHE, Arn. Deutsches Slang [coll. of phrases and expressns.] 1*m.*20 16° Trübner, *Strassbg.* 92

Swabian.

BOHNENBERGER, Karl Geschichte der schwäbischen Mundart im 15 Jahrh., pt. i. 4*m.* 8° Lauppe, *Tübingen* 92

BOPP, Karl Volkalismus d. Schwäbischen in d. Mundart von Münsingen 2*m.* 8° Trübner, *Strassbg.* 90

WAGNER Gegenwärt. Lautbestand d. Schwäb. in Mundt. v. Reutlingen, pt. i. 2*m.*; ii. 2*m.*50 4° *Reutlgn.* (Fock, *Lps.*) 89; 91

Switzerland.

Generally.

*STAUB + TOBLER, F. + L. [eds.] Schweizerisches Idiotikon, pts. xvii.–xxv. [a dictionary] ea. 2*m.* 4° Huber, *Frauenfd.* 90–93 *in prg.*

Basle.

HOFFMANN, Ed. Der mundartliche Vokalismus v. Basel-Stadt 2*m.* 8° Geering, *Basle* 90

Lucerne.

BRANDSTETTER, Renw. Prolegomena zu einer urkundlichen Geschichte d. Luzerner Mundart 2*m.* 8° Benziger, *Einsiedeln* 90

Tyrol.

SCHNELLER, Chr. Tirolische Namenforschung 8*m.* 8° Wagner, *Innsbruck* 90

" " Beiträge zur Ortsnamenkunde Tirols, pt. i. 2*m.* 8° Leo Gesellsch., *Innsbruck* 93 *in prg.*

Specimens.

WINDER, E. [ed.] Die Vorarlberger Dialectdichtung 2*m.*40 8° Wagner, *Innsbruck* 90

Westphalia.

TIBUS, A. Beiträge zur Namenkunde westfälischer Orte 2*m.*40 8° Münster, *Regensburg* 90

232. DUTCH AND FLEMISH PHILOLOGY.

History of the Language.

TE WINKEL, Jan Geschichte der niederländischen Sprache—*in* Paul's Grundriss, *ut* K § 225.

Grammar.

BRILL, W. G. Nederlandsche Spraakleer, 3 pts. [standard] 9*fl.*95 8° Brill, *Leyden* [43] 71; [52] 81; [66] 80

i. *Klankleer, Woordvorming, etc.* 3*fl.*60; *Leer van d. Volzin* (Syntax) 3*fl.*60; iii. *Stijlleer, Rhetorica, etc.* 2*fl.*75.

COSIJN, Prf. P. J. Nederlandsche Spraakkunst, pt. i. [Etymology], ii. [Syntax], ed. Jan te Winkel 8° *Haarlem* [67] 86; [69] 88

DUIJSER + DE VRIES, $\frac{\text{L. [-P.}}{\text{L.}}$ De Studie van het Nederlandsch [lang., style, liter.] 1*fl.*90 8° Wolters, *Groningen* 93

DE GROOT, D. Nederlandsche Spraakleer 8° *Amsterdam* [63] 82

VAN HELTEN, Prf. W. L. Nederlandsche Spraakkunst, 2 pts. 3*fl.*75 8° Wolters, *Groningen*

" " Kleine Nederlandsche Spraakkunst 8° Wolters, *Groningen* [77–78] 85

KERN, H. Handleiding tot het Onderwijs der Nederl. Taal 8° *Amsterdam* [59–60] 83

TERWEIJ, T. Nederlandsche Spraakkunst 1*fl.*25 8° Wolters, *Groningen* [76] 89

" " Beginselen d. nederl. Spraakk., 1*fl.*; Korte nederl. Spraak. 60*c.* 8° " "

VERCOULLIE, Prf. J. Schets eener Histor. Gram. der Nederl. Taal 2*fl.*50 8° *Ghent* 92

" " Nederlandsche Spraakkunst voor de Athenaeen, *etc.* 1*fl.*50 8° " 94

Etymology : *Dictionary.*

*ten BRUGGENCATE, K. Engelsch Woordenboek, pt. i. [Engelsch-Nederl.] 8° *Groningen* 95

Pt. ii. (Nederl.-Engelsch) to appear shortly. A good bk., contg. however some slang expressns. not so indicated.

FRANCK, Prf. Joh. Etymologisch Woordenboek d. nederlandsche Taal [pp. 1238] 9*fl.* r 8° Nijhoff, *The Hague* 92

VERCOULLIE, Prf. J. Beknopt etymol. Woordenb. d. nederlandsche Taal [pp. 320] 1*fl.*90 8° " " 90

DE VRIES, M. [ed.] Woordenboek d. nederlandsche Taal, pt. ii. (13)–iii. (1) ea. 87½*c.* r 8° Nijhoff, *The Hague* 91; 92 *in prg.*

Early Dictionaries.

KILIAEN, Corn. [*d.* 1607] Synonymia Latino-Teutonica (ex etymol. C. Kiliani deprompta), pt. i. 5*fl.* 8° Nijhoff, *The Hague* [1599] 89

A Latin-Dutch dict.; ed. Em. SPANOGHE. Pub. for Maatschappij d. Antwerpsche Bibliophilen.
The best edn. of KILIAEN'S dict. itself (first pb. *Antwerp.* 1583) is that ed. HASSELT, 2 vols., Roelandom De Meyere, *Trajecti Batav.* 1777

KLUYVER, A. Proeve eener Critiek op het Woordenbk. van Kiliaan Nijhoff, *The Hague* 84

The other great early dicts. are

PLANTIN, Thesaurus Theutonicae Linguae Schat. d. Nederduyt. Spraken Plantin, *Antwerp* 1573

van der SCHUEREN, Gerh. Teuthonista of Duytschlender, uitgeg. C. Boonzajer + J. A. Clignett Herdingh, *Leyden* [1477] 04

The only modern edition.

Phrases, Idioms, *etc.*

DELINOTTE + NOLEN, $\frac{\text{L. P.}}{\text{Fh.}}$ Dict. des Idiotismes, Néerlandismes, Gallicismes, etc. [Dutch-Fch.] 2*fr.*50 16° Hoste, *Ghent* 91

Chrestomathy.

PENON, G. [ed.] Nederlandsche Dicht- en Prozawerken 2*fl.*90 s 8° Wolters, *Groningen* 93

A companion volume to JONCKBLOET'S *Geschiedenis*, *ut infra*.

Synonyms.

BRUINING, G. De Nederduitsche Synoniemen [standard] *o.p.* *Rotterdam* 20

Dialects.

LEOPOLD, $\frac{\text{Joh. A.}}{\text{L. [eds.]}}$ Van de Schelde tot de Weichsel: Nederl. dialecten in dicht en ondicht, 3 pts. 17*fl.*50 8° Wolters, *Groningen*

West Flemish.

Etymology : Dictionary.

DE BO, L. L. Westvlaamsch Idioticon [*ut* B.B. K § 232]; new edn.; ed. Jos. Samyn 11*fr.* 8° Siffer, *Ghent* [70–73] 91

K § 233

Middle Dutch.

Grammar.

VAN HELTEN, Prf. W. L. Middelnederlandsche Spraakkunst 7*fl.* 50 8° Wolters, *Groningen*
" " Vondel's Taal [on the language of Vondel] 3*fl.* 75 8° " "
STOETT, F. A. Beknopte middelnederl. Spraakkunst, 2 pts.; pt. i. [Synt.] 1*fl.* 90; ii. [Etym.] 1*fl.* 50 8° Nijhoff, *The Hague* 89; 90

Etymology.

Dictionary.

VERWIJS + VERDAM, E. J. Middelnederlandsch Woordenboek, in pts. ea. 1*fl.* m 8° Nijhoff, *The Hague* 82–94 *in prg.*

Metrics.

VAN HELTEN, Prf. W. L. Middelnederlandsche Versbouw 1*fl.* 90 8° Wolters, *Groningen*

History of Literature.

JONCKBLOET, W. J. A. Geschiedenis d. nederlandsche Letterkunde, pt. iii.–vi. ea. 2*fl.* 90 s 8° Wolters, *Groningen* [ ] 87–92
" " Beknopte Geschiedenis d. Nederl. Letterkunde, ed. Dr. G. Penon 2*fl.* 50 " " [ ]
PENON, Dr. G. Bijdragen Geschiedenis der Nederlandsche Letterkunde 5*fl.* 70 8° " " [ ]
" " [ed.] Nederlandsche Dicht- en Prozawerken, 6 pts. ea. 2*fl.* 90 8° " " [ ]

A chrestomathy to illustrate JONCKBLOET'S Nederl. *Letterkunde*, *ut supra*.

Mediæval.

TE WINKEL, J. Geschiedenis d. nederland. Letterkunde i. d. Middeleeuwen 8° *Groningen* 88

Nineteenth Century.

TEN BRINK, Jan Geschiedenis d. nederlandsche Letteren i. d. 19 eeuw, 16 pts. ea. 80*c.* 8° Vuylsteke, *Ghent* 87 *sqq.*

Biographies and bibliographies: 1830–1880.

Texts: Collections of.

Bibliotheek van Middelnederl. Letterkunde, ed. H. E. Moltzer + Dr. Jan te Winkel, pts. i.–xlix. ea. 1*fl.* to 1*fl.* 50 8° Wolters, *Groningen* 68–93 *in prg.*

A good series of Middle-Dutch texts, ed. by various Dutch scholars.

" van Nederlandsche Letterkunde, ed. T. Terweij, pts. i.–vi. ea. 50*c.* 8° Wolters, *Groningen*, *in prg.*

233. SCANDINAVIAN (*a*): ICELANDIC, AND OLD AND MIDDLE NORSE PHILOLOGY.

Grammar.

*NOREEN, Adf. Altisländ. u. altnorweg. Grammatik [Samml. kurz. Gramm.] 6*m.* 8° Niemeyer, *Halle* [84] 92

A second and entirely rewritten edn. of his *Altnordische Grammatik*, *ut* B.B. K § 72.

SPECHT, Friedr. Ein Beitrag zur nord. Grammatik [*extr. fr.* Acta Germanica] 1*m.* 80 8° Mayer & Müller, *Berl.* 91

Middle-Norse.

LÅLES, Peder Ordspråk och en Motsvarande svensk samling, ed. A. Kock + C. af Petersens, 2 vols. 18*kr.* 8° *Lund* 89–92

i. Texts, 2 pts. 7*kr.*; ii. Commentary, 11*kr.*

Verb.

SPECHT, Friedr. Das Verbum reflexivum u. d. Superlative im Westnordischen [diss.] 8° *Berlin* 91

History of the Language.

KAHLE, Bernh. Die altnordische Sprache im Dienste d. Christentums [Acta German. i. 4] 4*m.* r 8° Mayer & Müller, *Berl.* 90
NOREEN, Adf. Geschichte der nordischen Sprache—*in* Paul's Grundriss, *ut* K § 233.

Etymology.

LARSSON, L. [ed.] Ordförrådet i de äldsta isländska Handskrifterna. 20*kr.* r 8° Lindstedt, *Lund* 91

A glossary of the oldest Icelandic MSS., lexicograph. and grammatically arranged.

THORKELSSON, Jón Supplement till islandske Ordböger, ser. i.–iii. (5) [to Heild] 8° *Reykjavik* ?–92 *in prg.*

Metrics.

KAHLE, Bernh. Die Sprache d. Skalden auf Grund der Binnen u. Endreime verbunden mit einem Reimarium 7*m.* 8° Trübner, *Strassbg.* 92

Phonology.

NOREEN, Adf. —*in his* Abriss der urgermanischen Lautlehre, *ut* K § 225.
REUTER, J. N. Die altnord. Nominalcomposita ihr. Betong. nach untersucht, pt. i. [diss.] 8° *Helsingfors* 91

Manuscripts.

Magnusson, Arne, MSS.: Katalog over d. arnamagnæanske HSS., vols. i.–ii. (1) Gyldendal, *Copenh.* 89; 93 *in prg.*

A good catal., ea. title w. brief intrody. descrn. and a note (mostly in Icel., some in Latin) of the unique colln. of Icel. MSS. bequeathed by MAGNUSSON in 1730 to Univ. of Copenh.

Magazines and Permanent Serials—*v.* K § 235.

234. SCANDINAVIAN (*b*): ICELANDIC AND OLD-NORSE LITERATURE.

History of the Literature.

JÓNSSON, F. Den oldnorske og oldislandske Litteraturs Historie, vol. i. 10*kr.* 8° Gad, *Copenhagen* 94

MOGK, Dr. E. Norwegisch-isländische Literatur—*in* Paul's Grundriss, *ut* K § 225.

Collections.

Altnordische Saga-Bibliothek: hrsg. Gust. Cederschiöld + Hugo Gering + Eug. Mogk, pts. i.-ii. 5*m.* 20 8° Niemeyer, *Halle* 92 *in prg.*

i. *Arí's Isländerbuch* [*ut infra*]......ed. Wolfg. GOLTHER, 1*m.*60 92 | ii. *Orvar-Odds Saga* [*ut infra*] ....ed. R. C. BOER, 3*m.*60 92

,, Textbibliothek: hrsg. E. Mogk, vols. i.-ii. 4*m.*60 8° Niemeyer, *Halle* 86-87

i. *Gunnlaugssaga* [*ut infra*]....................E. MOGK, 1*m.*60 86 | ii. *Eddalieder* [*ut infra*] ....Finnur JÓNSSON, 3*m.* 87

Saga Library: tr. Wm. Morris + Eiríkr Magnússon [*L. P.* (125) 31/6 *nt.*] ea. 7/6 *nt.* c 8° Quaritch 90-93 *in prg.*

i. *Howard the Halt, The Banded Men, Hen Thorir* .... 90 | iii.-iv. *Heimskringla Saga*, vols. i.-ii.; map [*ut infra*].......93, 94
ii. *Eyrbiggja Saga* [*ut infra*]...........................(5/- *nt.*) 92 |

A delightful series, to be recommended to all lovers of good literature.

Faroese.

HAMMERSHAIMB, V. U. [ed.] Foesk Anthologi [w. literary and grammat. Introd.] 21*kr.*50 8° Möller, *Copenhagen* 89-91

Individual Sagas.

ARÉS Isländerbuch, ed. Wolfg. Golther [Altnord. Saga-Bibl.] 1*m.*60 8° Niemeyer, *Halle* 92
Bjarnar Saga Hétdoelakappa: hrsg. R. C. Boer 4*m.* 8° ,, ,, 93
Bósa Saga in zwei Fassungen: hrsg. Otto L. Jiriczek [w. specs. of the Bósa-Rimur] 7*m.* 8° Trübner, *Strassbg.* 93
Edda Saemundar [the elder (verse) Edda]: Codex Regius af d. ældre Edda 25*kr.* 4° Gyldendal, *Copenhagen* 92

A photographic, diplomatic facs., ed. Ludv. F. A. WIMMER + Finnur JÓNSSON, of the *Codex Regius* (45 ll.), one of the most precious treasures of the Royal Lib. of Copenh., first brought to light by the famous historian and scholar Thormod TORFAEUS, who in 1662 (when Icel. lang. and liter. were beginning to attract some interest) was sent by FREDERICK III. of Denmk. on a voyage of discov. to Iceland to collect old Norse MSS. and other relics.

Edda-Lieder: hrsg. Finnur Jónsson [Altnord. Textbibl.] 3*m.* 8° Niemeyer, *Halle* 87

Translations.

Anderson, Prf. Rasm. B. [tr.] The Elder Edda: translated *in prep.*
Ebering, H. [tr.] Die Lieder der sogenannten älteren Edda: übers. u. erläut. 4*m.* 8° Bibl. Inst., *Lpz.* 93
Egils Skallagrímssonar Saga [10 cent.] ed. Valdimar Asmundarson 1*kr.*25 8° *Reykjavik* 92
,, ,, ,, tr. Rev. W. C. Green [prose] 6/- c 8° Stock 93
,, ,, ,, nach d. altisländ. Ferd. Khull 3*m.* 8° Graesser, *Vienna* 87

An Icelandic family-history of the 9th and 10th centuries.

Eiriks Saga: ed. G. Storm [*w. extr. fr.* Olafs Saga] 2*kr.*50 8° Gyldendal, *Copenhagen* 91
Eyrbyggja Saga tr. Wm. Morris + Eiríkr Magnússon, *sub tit.* story of the Ere-Dwellers [Saga Lib.] 5/- *nt.* c 8° Quaritch 92

Incl. also a tr. of the *Heidarvíga Saga*, *sub tit.* *Story of the Heath Slayings* (a fragment).

Fornaldarsögur: Zwei Fornaldarsögur hrsg. Ferd. Detter [after Cod. Holm.] 4*m.* r 8° Niemeyer, *Halle* 91
Gunnlaugssaga Ormstungu ed. E. Mogk; w. Germ. Introd. and gloss. [Altnord. Text-Bibl.] 1*m.*60 8° ,, ,, 86
Heilagra Manna Sögur
Arnamagnäanische Fragmenta: hrsg. G. Morgenstern [suppl. to Heilagra Manna Sögur] 3*m.* 8° *Copenh.* (Gräfe, *Lps.*) 93
Heimskringla: ed. Finnur Jónsson, pt. i. [*v. also* Ynglinga-Saga, *infra*] 5*kr.* 8° Gyldendal, *Copenhagen* 93
,, tr. Wm. Morris + Eiríkr Magnússon, vol. i.-ii. [Saga Library] ea. 7/6 *nt.* c 8° Quaritch 93; 94
Huldar Saga: hrsg. Konrad Maurer 3*m.* 8° Franz, *Munich* 94
Heiðarvíga Saga: —*v.* Eyrbyggja Saga, *supra.*
Hrafnkell Freysgodi Saga [10 cent.]: H. Lenk 2*m.*80 8° Konegen, *Vienna* 94
Landnáma Bóc ["Bk. of the Taking of the Land"]: tr. Rev. Thos. Ellwood 3/- 8° Wilson, *Kendal* 94
Ludbroc, Death Song of: transl., w. notes [printed in red and black in red borders] [*w.* 5/-] c 8° *priv. prin.*, *Edin.* 87
Nordurlandasaga: ed. Páll Melsted 8° *Reykjavik* 91
Orvar-Odds Saga: hrsg. R. C. Boer [Altnord. Saga-Bibl.] 3*m.*60 8° Niemeyer, *Halle* 92
Volsungasaga: hrsg. W. Ranisch; w. Germ. intro. & gloss [ed. after Bugge's text] 3*m.*60 8° Mayer & Müller, *Berl.* 91
Ynglinga Saga: saertryk af Heimskringla, ed. Finnur Jónsson 1*kr.*50 8° Gyldendal, *Copenhagen* 93

235. SCANDINAVIAN (*c*): SWEDISH AND DANO-NORWEGIAN.

Dano-Norwegian.

Grammar.

SARGENT, J. Y. Grammar of the Dano-Norwegian Language c 8° 3/6 Clar. Press / $1.90 *nt.* Macmillan, *N.Y.* 92

Etymology.

HELLQUIST, Elof Bidrag till läran om d. nordiska Nominalbildningen [pp. 94] 8° Akad. Abhandl., *Upsala* 90

Etymology: Dictionaries.

BRYNILDSEN, J. Norsk-engelsk Ordbog [1331] pp. 6*kr.*85 8° Malling, *Christiania* 92
FRITZNER, J. Ordbog over d. gamle norske Sprog, pts. i.-xviii. ea. 1*kr.*50 8° Norsk. Forlag, *Christiania* ?-90 *in prg.*
JESSEN, E. Dansk Etymologisk Ordbog, pt. i. [A-O], ii. [O-Ö] ea. 1*kr.*50 8° Gyldendal, *Copenhagen* 92; 93

Early Danish.

KALKAR, O. Ordbog til det ældre danske Sprog [1300-1700], pts. i.-xxi. ea. 3*kr. or* 2*kr.*50 8° Klein, *Copenh.* 94 *in prg.*

Jutland Dialects.

FEILBERG, Rev. H. F. Bidrag til en Ordbog over Jyske Almuesmaal, vol. i. [A-H] Thiele, *Copenhagen* 94

Based on the matls. of late Prf. K. LYNGBY; w. much reference to folklore, customs etc. of Teut., Latin and Slav. peoples.

Epigraphy. Runes.

BUGGE, Dr. Sophus — Om Runeindskrifterne paa Rök-stenen i Oestergötld. *etc.*; 5 pl. *Stockholm* 88

Norges Indskrifter: De ældre Runer, pts. i.-ii., ed. Dr. Sophus Bugge; pl. ea. 2*kr.*40 4° Brøgger, *Christiania* 92; 93 *in prg.*

Forms the first 2 Pts. of an important new archæolog. series, pub. by Det Norske Historiske Kilde-skriftfond: to be issued in 3 sections, 1 and 2 dealing w. Norway's earlier and later runes respectively (ed. BUGGE), 3 w. the Latin inscripp. of Norway (ed. Dr. Ingvald UNDSET).

SIEVERS, Prf. Ed. — Runen u. Runeninschriften—*in* Paul's Grundriss, *ut* K § 225.

STEPHENS, Geo. — The Runes: whence came they? 6/- 4° Williams 94

A classif. descr. catal. of the more import. runic inscripp., w. object of showing, in opposn. to Prf. WIMMER and his schl., that runic wrtg. could not have been evolved out of the Roman alphab. in Gaul and transmitted to the Scandinavians by the Germans; but that it was prob. derived fr. an early form of the Gk. alphab. obtd. fr. traders who penetrated to the North fr. the Gk. colonies on the Euxine.

Magazines.

Arkiv för Nordisk Filologi: redgiv Axel Koch + [*later*] Prf. Gust. Storm, vols. i.-vii. *Christiania* 83-90 *in prg.*

Nordisk Tidskrift för Filologie og Paedagogik: ed. Dr. Hude *Copenhagen* 74 *sqq.*, *in prg.*

A new series of the *Tidskrift för Filologi og Paedagogik*, *Copenhagen* '60-'73.

Skandinavisches Archiv: hrsg. Ed. Theod. Walter, v. i.-iii. [philology, philos. & history] *p. vol.* 15/- 8° Möller, *Lund* 91-93 *in prg.*

Swedish.

Etymology: Dictionaries.

HOPPE, Otto. — Schwedisch-deutsches Wörterbuch 8*m.* 8° Friedländer, *Berlin* 93

*TAMM, Fredr. — Etymologisk Svensk Ordbok, pt. [A-BÄRGA] [to occupy 10 pts.] r 8° *Stockholm* 90 *in prg.*

WIDMARK, P. F. — Tysk-Svensk [Germ.-Swed.] Ordbok [1582 two-col. pp.] 18/- 8° Linnström, *Stockh.* 90

236. ENGLISH PHILOLOGY (*a*): GENERALLY. HISTORY OF THE LANGUAGE.

Bibliography. "Encyclopædia."

*STORM, Prf. Joh. — Englische Philologie [*ut* B.B. K § 236]; 2nd edn., v. i., pt. i. [Phonet. & Pronunc.] 9*m.* 8° Reisland, *Lps.* [81] 92

Programmes, Dissertations and Habilitationschriften.

VARNHAGEN, Herm. — System. Verzeichniss d. Programmabhandl., *etc.*, hrsg. Joh. Martin—*ut* K § 92 [mainly German pubns.].

Introduction.

BÜLBRING, Dr. Karl D. — Wege und Ziele d. englischen Philologie: eine Rede 65*c.* 8° Wolters, *Groningen* 93

History of the Language.

CHAMPNEYS, A. C. — History of English: sketch of orig. and progr. of Eng. lang.; maps c 8° 7/6 Percival / $1.25 Macmillan, *N.Y.* 93

An amateur's attempt to write a "popular" handbk. of the subj. Its best feature is its copious citation of well-chosen illustr. examples.

EMERSON, Prf. Oliver F. [Am.] History of the English Language (6/- *nt.*) c 8° Macmillan 94

GASNER, Ernst — Beiträge z. Entwickelungsgang d. neuengl. Schriftsprache [Nuremb. diss.] 2*m.*80 8° Vandenhoeck, *Göttgn.* 91

On the basis of the Middle-English Bible translations.

*JESPERSEN, Prf. Otto — Progress in Language, w. spec. reference to English 7/6 Sonnenschein / Macmillan, *N.Y.* 94

A brilliant and original bk., expanded fr. author's *Studier over Engelske Kasus* [Klein, *Copenh.* '91], intended to establish that the change fr. the synthetic to the analytic type of lang. ought not to be regarded as "decay," but as progress—in Spencerian phrase as "evolution" not "dissolution." Full of acute reasoning and new observations: an important contribution to the history of the contemporary evolution of grammar.

KLUGE, Prf. Friedr. — Geschichte der englischen Sprache—*in* Paul's Grundriss, *ut* K § 225.

LOW, W. H. — The English Language: its orig. & structure [Univ. Corr. Coll. Tut. Ser.] 3/6 c 8° Clive [92] 93

RAMSEY, S. [Am.] — The English Language and English Grammar: an histor. study $3 (15/-) 8° Putnam, *N.Y.* 92

Comparative.

*HENRY, Prf. Vict. — Comparative Grammar of English and German—*ut* K § 225.

Change of Gender.

KÖRNER, Karl — Beiträge zur Geschichte d. Geschlectswandel d. engl. Substantiva [diss.] 1*m.* 8° *Greifswald* 89

Syntax.

KELLNER, Leon — Historical Outlines of English Syntax 6/- ($1.40) 8° Macmillan 92

A comp. vol. to Dr. Rich. MORRIS' *Histor. Lessons in Engl. Accid.* [*ut* B.B. K § 237]. A sound book, but not altogether well arranged.

WESTERN, Aug. — De Engelske Bisætninger: en historisk-syntaktisk studie 8° Cappelen, *Christiania* 93

Grammar of Individual Writers.

Anglo-Saxon —*v.* K §§ 248-253 *passim.*

Old and Middle English—*v.* K § 244; *and* K §§ 254-255 *passim.*

Modern English.

JONSON, Ben. [1574-1637].

Ljungren, Carl Aug. — Poetical Gender of Substantives in Ben Jonson [acad. diss.] 4° *Lund* 92

LANGLAND, Wm. [14 cent.].

KLAPPROTT, Ludw. — Das End-e in Langland's Buch. v. Peter d. Pflüger, Text B. [diss.] 1*m.* 4° Vandenhoeck, *Göttgn.* 90

WANDSCHNEIDER, W. — Zur Syntax d. Verbs in Langley [*sic*] [diss.] 1*m.*20 8° Fock, *Lps.* 87

LYLY, Jno. [1553-1601] —*v. also* K § 24, *s.v.* Sixteenth Cent., *sub nom.* Lyly (CHILD).

Landmann, Dr. —*in his* Der Euphuismus: sein Wesen, seine Quelle, Geschichte, *etc.* [diss.] 8° *Giessen* 81

Attributes all the peculiarities of LYLY'S language to influence of Antonio de GUEVARA, a Spanish writer of *El Libro Aureo Marco Aurelio*, based on the *Meditations* of MARCUS AURELIUS. Abstracted in *Trans. Philol. Soc.* *Cf.* also the Introd. to his edn. of *Euphues* [in *Engl. Spr.- u. Litter.-Denkm.*, 2m. to 8° Henninger, *Heilbronn* (Trübner, *Strassb.*) '77].

Magazines and Permanent Serials.

Beiträge, Berliner, zur German. u. Roman. Philologie—*v.* K § 225, § 256.

„ zur englischen Philologie, hrsg. Herm. Varnhagen, pts. i.-xv. [*ut* B.B. K § 236] 8° Junge, *Erlangen* 89–93 *in prg.*

i. *Desput. betw. Bodi and Soule* [*ut* K § 249] .. W. LINOW 3m.60 89
ii. *How the Wyse Man taught hys Sone* ...... R. FISCHER, 1m.20 89
iii. *Trentalle Sancti Gregorii* [*ut* K § 255] .. A. KAUFMANN, 1m.20 89
iv. *Fehlen d. Auftakts in Chaucer* [*ut* K § 237] M. FREUDENBERGER, 1m.60 89
v. *Historia Septem Sapientum* [*ut* B § 3] ...... G. BUCHNER, 2m.89
vi. *Reden d. Seele a.d. Leichnam* [*ut* K § 249] .. R. BUCHHOLZ, 1m.80 90
vii. *Gesta Romanorum* [*ut* B § 3] .... Wilh. DICK, 6m. 90
viii. *D. Sprichwort C. Chaucer* [*ut* K § 237] .. W. HÄCKEL, 1m.80 90
ix. *Quellen v. Morris' "Earthly Parad."* ...... J. RIEGEL, 1m.60 91
x. ARMENO, Christof. [tr.] *Peregrin. d. s. Giovani* [*ut* K § 134] .. H. GASSNER, 2m.50 91
xi. BYRON'S *Werner* [drama] *u. s. Quelle* .. Karl STÖHSEL, 1m.80 91
xii. *Peri Didaxeon* [*ut* K § 255] .... M. LÖWENECK, *in prep.*
xiii. BOCCACCIO'S *Novelle v. Falken u.i. Verbreitg.* R. ANSCHÜTZ, 2m. 91
xiv. *Tractatus de Diversis Hist. Roman.* [1326] S. HERZSTEIN, 1m.60 93
xv. CHETTLE, H. *etc. Patient Grissil* [*ut* K § 80] .. G. HÜBSCH, 2m.60 93
xvi. MUNDAY, Ant. *Downfall of Rob., E. of Huntingdon* [1601] E. E. MATTHEWS, *in prep.*

Parts i.-ix. were orig. pub. by Deichert, of Erlangen; but all are now pub. by Junge.

„ Münchener, zur romanischen u. engl. Philologie—*ut* K § 256.

„ Wiener, zur deutsch. u. engl. Philol.: hrsg. R. Heinzel + J. Minor + J. Schipper, pts. i.-iii. 12m. 8° Braumüller, *Vienna* 86–88

i. *Sir Thos. Wyatt u. s. Stellung* [*ut* B.B. K § 240] Rud. ALSCHER, 4m. 86
ii. *D. ältest. Passionspiele in Tirol* ...... J. E. WACKERNELL, 5m. 87
iii. *John Heywood als Dramatiker* .... W. SWOBODA, 3m. 88

Collected Essays.

Studies and Notes in Philology and Literature, vols. i.–ii. [Harvard Univ. Studies] 8° ea. $1 Ginn, *Boston* / ea. 5/- Arnold 92; 94

Vol. i.: *Authorship of Engl. Romaunt of Rose* (G. L. KITTREDGE [Am.]); *Orig. of Engl. Names of Letters of Alphab.* (E. S. SHELDON [Am.]); *Lob Sounday* (J. M. MANLEY [Am.]); *Hy. Scogan* (KITTREDGE); *Etymol. Notes* (SHELDON).

237. ENGLISH PHILOLOGY (*b*): GRAMMAR: GENERALLY. PHONOLOGY. ORTHOGRAPHY.

Grammar Generally.

STOFFEL, C. Studies in English, written and spoken; ser. i. [*repr. fr.* Taalstudie] 8° 4fl.50 Thieme, *Zutphen* / 7/6 Luzac 94

A good series of studies, incl. one on slang [*ut* K § 241].

Bibliography.

BROWN, Goold [Am.; 1791–1857]—*in his* Grammar of English Grammars [1,070 pp.] *o.p.* [*pb.* $6.25] i 8° Wood, *N. Y.* [50–51] 57

Prefixed is a valuable Digested Catalogue of English Grammars and Grammarians, *etc.*

Text-books.

GOW, Dr. Jas. Method of English for Secondary Schools, pt. i. Grammar 2/- (60c.) f 8° Macmillan 92

An excellent bk.; very suggestive and readable; but more suited for teachers' than pupils' use. Good in illus., *e.g.* as representing the differ. sounds of *ough*. "A rough-coated, dough-faced ploughman, strode, coughing and hiccoughing, thoughtfully through Scarborough."

*SWEET, Dr. Hy. A New English Grammar, pt. i. [Introd., Phonology, Accidence] c 8° 10/6 Clar. Press / $2.60 *nt.* Macmillan, *N.Y.* 92

An excellent scientific Engl. grammar, chfly. historical but at the same time logical, founded on an indepen. critical survey of the latest results of linguistic investign. of the subjects. Spec. attention paid to definitions of pts. of speech, to principles of linguistic developmt., to the chronol. and dialectology of English and to phonology. Psychology, however, rather amateurish.

„ „ A Short Historical English Grammar f 8° 4/6 Clar. Press / $1.25 *nt.* Macmillan, *N.Y.* 92

„ „ A Primer of Historical English Grammar f 8° 2/- Clar. Press / 60c. *nt.* Macmillan, *N.Y.* 93

A futile attempt to compress into 110 small pp. a satisfactory primer of Eng. hist.-gram., incl. phonetics.

WEST, A. S. The Elements of English Grammar [Pitt Press Series] f 8° 2/6 Camb. Press / 60c. *nt.* Macmillan, *N.Y.* 94

Phonology.

BÜLBRING, Karl D. Gesch. d. Ablaute d. stark. Zeitwort. d. Sudengl. [Qu. u. Forsch.] 3m.50 8° Trübner, *Strassbg.* 89
CLARKE, Jno. Manual of Linguistics: general and English phonology—*ut* K § 98.
KÖLLMANN, Aug. Die englischen a-Laute: kurz. Uebersicht ihrer Entwickelung [diss.] 1m. 8° *Marburg* (Fock, *Lpz.*) 89
TECHMER, F. Beiträge z. Gesch. d. frz. u. engl. Phonetik u. Phonographie, pt. i. 6m. 8° Kerler, *Ulm* 91

Hawes, Steph.

FUHR, Karl Lautuntersuchungen zu Hawes Gedicht The Pastime of Pleasure [diss.] 8° *Marburg* 91

Dialects —*v.* K § 241 (BÜLBRING, SKEAT).

Old-English —*v.* K § 244 (MAYHEW).

Orthoepy. Orthography. Pronunciation.

GIETMANN, G. Die Aussprache des Englischen in systemat. Vollständigkeit 1m.50 8° Herder, *Freiburg* 91
HART, Orthographie, ed. Prf. Otto Jespersen E. Eng. Text Soc. (Paul), *in prep.*
LÖWISCH, Max Zur englischen Aussprache v. 1650–1750 [fr. early Eng. grammars; diss.] 8° Kay, *Kassel* 89
MEAD, Theod. H. [Am.] Our Mother Tongue [Portia Ser.; popular bk. on orthoepy] $1.50 12° Dodd & Mead, *N. Y.* 90
MOON, G. Washgtn. Learned Men's English: the grammarians 3/6 c 8° Routledge 91

Repr. of his *The Revisers' English* [*ut* B.B. A § 18] and *Ecclesiastical English* [*ut* B.B. K § 238], a ser. of criticisms on the English of the Revis. Vern. of Bible.

238. ENGLISH PHILOLOGY (c): ETYMOLOGY.

Principles.

SKEAT, Prf. Walt. W. Principles of English Etymology, Ser. ii.: The Foreign Element c 8° 10/6 Clar. Press / $2.60 n/. Macmillan, N.Y. 91

In this vol. the Anglo-French element is incl., the Celtic and Teuton. words (borrowed directly) and Scand. words, tog. w. Gk. and Lat. words borrowed thro' Ang.-Sax. having been dealt w. in the First Series [ut B.B. K § 238].

" " A Primer of English Etymology f 8° 1/6 Clar. Press / 30c. n/. Macmillan, N.Y. 92

A brief sketch of the more important principles; limited to the Native Elements.

Compounding of Words—v. K § 240 (Teall).

Dictionaries.

CASSELL & Co. [pubs.] Cassell's English Dictionary [1,100 pp.] 3/6 8° Cassell [91] 92

Based on *The Encyclopædic Dictionary* [ut B.B. K § 238]; gives definitions of about 100,000 words and phrases, spec. complete for the lang. as spoken and written to-day. Appendix has short hist. of the lang. and specs. of its liter. at various periods. A sound and compact work, judiciously printed as regards choice of types and symbols.

Century Dictionary: an encyclo. lexicon of Engl. lang. [ut B.B. K § 238]: now cpl. in 6 vols. i 8° ea. $15 shp., Cent. Co., N.Y. / ea. 42/- d. Unwin 89–91

An elaborate and showy illustr. work, wh. has been lavishly produced, but is not very good fr. a scholarly pt.-of-view. Intended to rival MURRAY [ut inf.], but may be said to occupy an intermediate place betw. his and OGILVIE'S dicts. [ut B.B. K § 238].

FENNELL, Dr. C. A. M. National Dictionary of English Language and Literature, 3 vols. *in prep.*

To incl. all words and phrase-words found in Engl. liter. betw. A.D. 1360 and pres. day, based on indexes of selected authors, incl. Chaucer, Caxton, Elyot, North, Phil. Holland, Bacon, Pope, Johnson, Burke, Thackeray, Macaulay, and Ruskin, w. quotns. fr. hundreds of other authors, dates of authorship, and exact references.

HOPPE, A. English-deutsches Supplementlexikon, vol. ii., pt. i. 4*m.* r 8° Langenscheidt, *Berlin* [71] 93

*MURRAY + BRADLEY, Dr. J. A. H. / Hy. [eds.] New Engl. Dict. on Histor. Prinpls. [ut B.B. K § 238]: in *pts.* i 4° ea. 12/6 Clar. Press / ea. $3.25 n/. Macmillan, N.Y. 84–94 *in prg.*

Vol. i. [A–B] 52/6 ($13 n/.); ii. [C] 52/6 ($13 n/.)—both ed. MURRAY; iii. [D (MURRAY; some ph. yet) to E (BRADLEY, in 2 pts., 12/6, 5/-)]; iv. F, G, H. (BRADLEY) *in prep.* An extremely important national wk., a series of learned monographs as much as a dict. Orig. based on materials coll. by the Philolog. Soc.

Royal English Dictionary and Word Treasury: ed. Thos. T. Maclagan [714 pp.] 2/6 p 8° Nelson 94

Standard Dictionary: ed. Dr. Is. K. Funk, *etc.* [Ams.] vol. i. [A–L]; ill. and pl. [1,079 pp.] *subscr.* *for* 2 *v.* $15, in 1 v. $12 r 4° Funk & Wagnalls, *N.Y.* 93

Not so elabor. as the *Century Dictionary*, yet contg. more words. [The numbers are about as follows: JOHNSON [1755] 45,000, WORCESTER 105,000, WEBSTER 125,000, *Century Dict.* 225,000, *Standard Dict.* 301,000.] One of its distinguishing characteristics is the introdn. of the phonetic element, and another is its numerous (fairly good) illns. The illustr. quotns. are largely fresh, but mostly modern.

*WEBSTER, Noah [Am.] Internat. Dict. of the Engl. Lang., ed. Prf. Noah Porter [Am.] [2,118 pp.] 31/6 4° Bell [28] 91

Orig. pub. in 1828, revisions were made in 1847, 1864, 1880, and 1891, the last having been 10 years in hand (stated to have cost over £60,000). In addn. to the dict. of words, w. pronunc., etymol., and var. meanings, ill. by quotations and woodcuts, there are several appendices, *viz.*, a Gazetteer, vocabs. of Scripture, Gk., Lat., and Engl. Proper Names, a dict. of noted names in fiction, brief hist. of Eng. lang., dict. of foreign quots., etc.; biogr. dict. of 10,000 names, *etc.*

Criticism.

WILLIAMS, R. O. [Am.] Our Dictionaries: and other English language topics $1.25 12° Holt, *N.Y.* 90

Early Dictionary.

Catholicon Anglicum [1483]: ed. Sid. J. Herrtage 10/- s 4° Camden Society 82

An English-Latin word-bk. dated 1483, of consid. philolog. interest. Previously issued by Early Engl. Text Soc. 8° 1881.

Folk-Etymology.

SCHRÖDER, Geo. Ueb. d. Einfluss d. Volksetym. auf d. Lond. Slang-Dialekt—*ut* K § 241.

Foreign Elements.

Generally.

SKEAT, Prf. Walt. W. —*in his* Principles of English Etymology, *ut supra.*

Dictionary.

Stanford Dictionary of Anglicised Words and Phrases, ed. Dr. C. A. M. Fennell 4° 31/6 Camb. Press / Macmillan, *N.Y.* 92

A useful and interesting contrib. to Engl. lexicography; but its scope is much too wide, and illns. w. dates and refs. are frequently wanting. "Anglicised" is taken to mean (a) borrowed and wholly or partly naturalized, (b) used in Engl. liter. without naturalizn., (c) familiarized by frequent quotn. The wk. thus incl. 12,798 articles (treating of 10,997 words, 1,813 phrases, and 278 quotns., w. 2,708 cross-refs.). Mr. J. F. STANFORD, who had himself coll. a good suln. of materl., in 1880 left £5,000 for its compln. and pubn., and the scheme for its constructn. was drawn up by Prfs. MAYOR, SKEAT, BENSLY, Aldis WRIGHT and POSTGATE.

Dutch.

LOGEMAN, Prf. Henri [of Ghent].

Has *in prep.* a study on the Dutch element in the Engl. lang., wh. is likely to be of exceptional value. His studies on the liter. relns. of Holland and Engl. in 15 cent. [cf. K § 80 (*Elckerlijk*) and 88 § 7 (*Reynaert*)] have paved the way for the wk.

French.

Dryden, Jno. [1631–1701].

BELJAME, Prf. Alex. Quæ a Gallicis verb. in Angl. ling. Dryden introduxerit 8° *Paris*

An interesting essay; but attribs. many words to DRYDEN'S introdn. wh. were used much earlier.

Greek.

CAPELLER, Gust. Die wichtigst. a. d. Griech. gebild. Wörter d. frz. u. engl. Spr.—*ut* K § 270.

Names.

WAGNER, Leop. Names and their Meaning: a bk. for the curious c 8° 7/6 Unwin [92] 93 / $1.75 Putnam, *N.Y.* 92

" " More about Names [supplement to above] c 8° 7/6 Unwin / $1.75 Whittaker, *N.Y.* 93

Two utterly worthless prodns., reproducing all the traditional blunders and sowing a crop of fresh ones, *e.g.* Arithmetic deriv. fr. *Arithmos* and *Techne*, the skylark is so called fr. its habit of "larking," Torres Strait fr. "the Latin *toridus* (*sic*), signifying parched," and so forth.

Bird-Names; Plant-Names—*v.* K § 241.

Place-Names.

Latin Forms of Place-names [and Sur-names].

MARTIN, Chas. Trice —*his* Record Interpreter [*ut* K § 203] *conts. a gloss. of them.*

France.

WESTPHAL, Joh. Englische Ortsnamen in Altfranzösischen [diss. inaug.] 8° *Strassburg* 91

Lincolnshire.

STREATFIELD, Rev. G. S. —*in his* Lincolnshire and the Danes, *ut* B.B. F § 18 [w. a 63-pp. gloss. of the dialect].

Oxford.

DOBLE, C. E. Place Names in the Diocese of Oxford [*in prep.*]—*ut* D § 157.

Surnames —*v.* G § 24.

Obsolete Words.

Bible English.

MAYHEW, Rev. A. L. Glossary of Bible Words 1/6 r 8° Eyre & Spottiswoode 90

With illustrative passages, sel. mainly fr. the earlier Engl. versions of the Bible, w. the purpose of indicating the source of the Biblical expressions found in the Authorised Version [1611].

Quotations —*v.* K § 2.

Technical Terms —*v.* I § 1, *and* K § 276.

240. ENGLISH PHILOLOGY (*c*): METRICS. PHRASES. PROSODY. STYLE.

Metrics —*v. also* K § 62.

LAWRENCE, Dr. Jno. A History of English Metre *in prep.*

QUICK, Karl Geschichte d. heimischen [Engl.] Metra—*in* Paul's Grundriss, *ut* K § 225.

SCHIPPER, J. Fremde [Engl.] Metra—*in* Paul's Grundriss, *ut* K § 255.

Chaucer, Geoff. [1328–1400]—*v.* K § 237 (CHILD).

Gower, Jno. [*c.* 1330–1408].

HAFER, Paul Alliteration bei Gower [dissert. inaug.] 8° *Leipzig* 90

Peele, Geo. [1558(?)–1598(?)].

PENNER, Em. Metrische Untersuchungen zu George Peele [dissert. inaug.] 8° *Halle* 90

Principles and History of Style.

EARLE, Prf. Jno. English Prose: its elements, history, and usage 8° 16/- Smith & Elder; $3.50 Putnam, *N.Y.* 90

The Bible.

COOK, Prf. Alb. S. [Am.; ed.] The Bible and English Prose Style 12° $1. Heath, *Boston*; 1/6 Isbister 92

Brings together pieces of Scripture (wh. RUSKIN calls "the one essential part" of all his educn.), to wh. are prefixed comments by critics and scholars, showing the influence of the Bible on Engl. style.

Psalter of 1539.

EARLE, Prf. Jno. [ed.] The Psalter of 1539: a landmark of English literature 16/- sq 8° Murray 94

A handsome edn. of the text, in Black-Letter, w. Introd. and notes. The *Psalter* first appeared in 1535, tho' no hint to that effect is given.

Specimens of Style —*v.* K § 19.

Compounding of Words and Phrases.

TEALL, F. Hor. [Am.] English Compound Words and Phrases $2.50 8° Funk & Wagnalls, *N.Y.* [91] 92

Its main feature is a list of *c.* 40,000 compound words, w. explans. and an Introd. explaining when and why the joining and separn. of words is preferable. The word-lists were orig. prepared for the *Standard Dict.* [*ut* K § 238].

Phrases. Idioms.

BOENSEL, O. English Idioms: sel. list of everyday words and phrases [schl.-progr.] 2*m.*50 4° 94

DIXON, Prf. Jas. Main [ed.] Dictionary of Idiomatic English Phrases 3/6 ($1.50) c 8° Nelson 91

By Prf. of Engl. in Univ. of Japan, and intended mainly for foreigners. In alphab. order under principal words, each phrase indicated by a symbol showing that it is used "in serious composition," "in polite conversn.," "in familiar conversn.," or that it is "vulgar."

REGEL + SCHULER, Em., J. G. C. Einführung in das heutige Englisch 4*m.*80 8° Teubner, *Lps.* 89

Synonyms.

SOULE, Rich. [Am.] Dict. of Engl. Synonyms and Parallel Exprns. [1871], ed. Dr. Geo. H. Hewitson [Am.] 8° $2.25 Lippincott, *Phila.*; 7/6 Warne 92

241. ENGLISH DIALECTS.

Collectively.

AXON, W. E. A. [ed.] Eng. Dialects in the 18th Cent.; w. Introd. [*compiled fr.* Bailey's *Dict.*] 9/- 8° Eng. Dialect Soc. (Frowde) 83

HALLAM, T. Four Dialect Words [*clem, lake, nesh, oss*] 4/- 8° ,, ,, 85

Phonology.

BÜLBRING, Dr. Karl B. "Ablaut" in the Mod. Dialects of S. of Eng., tr. A. W. Badham 3/- 8° Engl. Dial. Soc. (Frowde) 91

A sound treatise on the strong verbs in the modern dialects.

SKEAT, Miss Anglo-French Vowel Sounds: word-list ill. corresp. w. mod. Engl. 4/- 8° Engl. Dial. Soc. (Frowde) 84

K § 241

Bird-Names.

SHADWELL, [Miss] Ellen Dictionary of English Bird-Names 8° Engl. Dial. Soc. (Frowde) *in prep.*

Plant-Names.

BRITTEN + HOLLAND, J. R. Supplement *to their* Dict. of Engl. Plant-Names [*ut* B.B. K § 241] 8° Engl. Dial. Soc. (Frowde) *in prep.*

HOOPS, Joh. Ueber die altenglischen Pflanzennamen [diss. inaug.] 8° *Freiburg-in-B.* 90

Slang and Cant.

FARMER, Jno. S. [ed.] Slang and its Analogues: past and present. 5 vols. f 4° *subscr.* £3 3s. Nutt / *subscr.* $45 Scribner, *N.Y.* 90 *sqq.*, *in prg.*

Vol. i. [A-B] '90; vol. ii. [C to Fizzle] '91 (w. assistance of W. E. HENLEY).

SCHRÖDER, Geo. Ueb. d. Einfluss d. Volksetym. auf d. Lond. Slang-Dialekt [diss.] 8° *Rostock* 93

STOFFEL, C. —*in his* Studies in English, written and spoken; ser. i., *ut* K § 237.

Pp. 170-317 consist of *Annot. Specs. of "'Arryese"*: an excellent paper on the letters in verse contrib. to *Punch* by "'ARRY" from 1883 to 1889, illustratg. the vocab., spelling, and gram. fr. an immensely wide number of sources, incl., in some instances, Dutch sources.

America —*v. infra, sub voc.* Americanisms.

Winchester College.

WRENCH, R. G. K. [ed.] Winchester Word Book: a collection of past and present notions—*ut* D § 157, *s.v.* Great Britain.

NON-EUROPEAN ENGLISH DIALECTS.

Africa: *Negro-English.*

GRADE, P. Das Negerenglisch an d. Westküste v. Afrika [*extr. fr.* Anglia] 1*m.* 8° Plahn, *Halle* 93

Americanisms.

MATTHEWS, Jas. Brander [Am.] Americanisms and Briticisms: w. essays on other isms $1 16° Harper, *N.Y.* 92

NORTON, Chas. L. [Am.] Political Americanisms—*ut* D § 146.

Slang.

MAITLAND, J. [Am.] American Slang Dictionary *subscr.* $5 8° Kittredge, *Chicago* 91

Dialects.

American Dialect Soc.: Dialect Notes, pts. i.–iv. 8° Amer. Dialect Soc. –92 *in prg.*

Colonial and Anglo-Indian.

LENTZNER, Dr. Karl Colonial English 7/6 r 8° Paul 91

A glossary of Australian, Anglo-Indian, Pidgin-English, West Indian and South African words.

Australia.

LENTZNER, Dr. Karl Dict. of Slang-English of Australia 8*m.* r 8° Karras, *Halle* 92

An instance of Germ. plagiarism—a rare occurrence, at any rate in literary matters. The book consists largely of extrs. fr. FARMER'S bk. [*ut sup.*] and fr. BARRÈRE + LELAND'S [*ut* B.B. K § 241].

India.

WRIGHT, Arn. Baboo' English as 'tis Writ [curiosities of Ind. journalism] 1/- s 4° Unwin [91] 91

ENGLISH DIALECTS ACCORDING TO COUNTIES.

Vide also E § 17: English Topography, *passim.*

Cornwall.

*JAGO, Fred. W. P. Glossary of the Cornish Dialect 30/- 4° *Truro* (Simpkin) 86

With good chap. on decline of Anc. Cornish, and a long list of "Words in Corn. lang. compared w. several found in the writings of Chaucer."

Derbyshire.

KIRKLAND, Walt. Glossary of Archaic and Provincial Words and Phrases used in Co. of Derby 8° Murray, *Derby*, *in prep.*

Only 500 to be printed and 50 in *L.P.*

Devonshire.

CHOPE, R. Pearse The Dialect of Hartland, Devonshire 7/6 8° Engl. Dial. Soc. (Frowde) 91

With glossary, and chaps. on grammar, pronunciation and folklore.

HEWETT, [Mrs.] Sarah The Peasant Speech of Devon 5/- c 8° Stock [92] 92

The bulk of the bk. consists of a gloss. and specs. of phraseol., rhymes, provbs. and stories, arrgd. alphab. under chief words.

Gloucestershire.

ROBERTSON, J. Drummond Gloss. of Dialect & Archaic Wds. of Gloucester, ed. Lord Moreton 10/- 8° Eng. Dial. Soc. (Frowde) 90

An Appendix contg. an interesting acc. of the dialect in beg. of 17 cent. fr. MSS. of John SMYTH, author of the well-known *Description of the Hundred of Berkeley* [still in MS.; v. WOOD'S Athen. Oxon. iii. 1030].

Lancashire.

Specimens.

"BOBBIN, Tim" [=Jno. COLLIER] Complete Works, ed. Lt.-Col. Fishwick 27/6 4° Clegg, *Oldham* (Stock) 93

Only 250 ptd., and *L.P.* (50) 42/-, and Whatman-ppr. edn. (20) 63/-. Conts. reprodns. of the orig. pl. (some by Geo. CRUIKSHANK), and a new Life of "TIM BOBBIN" by FISHWICK.

BRIERLEY, Ben — ea. 3/6 c 8° *Simpkin*

Ab-O' Th' Yate Yankeeland 87
Two trips to America.
Cotters of Mossburn .... [71] 87
Daisy-Nook Sketches .... [67] 82
Out of Work, etc. 87
Tales of Lancs. Life, 3 series .... [62–86] 84–87
And many others.

LAYCOCK, Saml. Warblins fro' an Owd Songster; w. Introd. sketch 7/6 8° Clegg, *Oldham* (Simpkin) 93
By the popular vernacular poet of Lancs., who since the Cotton Famine has been recognized as the lyrical spokesman of the people. Vigorous and racy.

WAUGH, Edwin [1817–1886] Works, ed Geo. Milner, 8 vols.; port. and fronts.; w. memoir ea. 3/6 c 8° J. Heywood [*v.y.*] 92–93

i.–ii. **Lancashire Sketches* [his *chef-d'œuvre*] .... [55] 92
iii. *Besom Ben Stories* .... [65, *etc.*] 92
iv. *Chimney Corner Stories* .... [79] 92
v.–vi. *Tufts of Heather* .... [64] 93
vii. *Rambles in the Lake Country* .... [62] 93
viii. *Poems and Songs* .... [59] 93

Lincolnshire.

STREATFEILD, Rev. G. S. —*his* Lincolnshire and the Danes [*ut* 𝔅.𝔅. E § 17] *conts. a 63-pp. gloss. of the dialect.*

Norfolk.

RYE, Walt. Norfolk and Suffolk Words 8° Eng. Dialect Soc. (Frowde) *in prep.*

Northern Dialects.

English Miscellanies ill. the Hist. and Lang. of the Northern Counties 6/- 8° Surtees Soc. (Whittaker) 91

Northumberland.

HESLOP, Rich. Oliv. Northumberland Words: a glossary, vol. i. 12/6; ii. (1) 10/6 [N'humberld. and Tyneside] 8° Engl. Dial. Soc. (Frowde) 92; 93

Rutland.

WORDSWORTH, Rev. Christoph. Rutland Words [a glossary] 4/6 8° Engl. Dial. Soc. (Frowde) 91
Of small value: only 40 pp., and even of the words incl. many are not dialectical at all.

Suffolk

—*v.* NORFOLK, *supra.*

Surrey.

GOWER, Granv. Leveson Glossary of Surrey Words 4/6 8° Engl. Dial. Soc. (Frowde) 94

Wiltshire.

DARTNELL + GODDARD, Geo. E. / Rev. E. H. Wiltshire Words 15/- 8° Engl. Dial. Soc. (Frowde) 94

Worcestershire.

SALISBURY, Jesse Glossary of Words and Phrases of South-East Worcestershire 4/6 8° Salisbury, Fleet St. London 93

Yorkshire.

Idle and *Windhill.*

WRIGHT, Dr. Jos. Grammar of Dialect of Windhill [w. specs. phonet. rendered & gloss. index] 12/6 8° Eng. Dial. Soc. (Frowde) 92

Sheffield.

ADDY, Sid. O. Supplement to his Glossary of Words used in neighbourhd. of Sheffield [*ut* 𝔅.𝔅. K § 241] 5/- 8° Eng. Dial. Soc. (Frowde) 91

Specimens.

MORRIS, Rev. M. C. F. [ed.] Yorkshire Folk-Talk [a good coll.; N. and E. Ridings] 7/6 *nt.* c 8° Frowde 92
"Truly," said the Knight, "these northern men's names and titles smack of their origin—they sound like a north-west wind, rambling and roaring among the heather and rocks"—SCOTT'S *Wanderer*.

Scottish.

Alexander the Great [Buik of the Most Noble and Vailyeand Conqueror Alexander].
HERMANN, Alb. Untersuchgn. üb. d. schott. Alexanderbuch 1m.60 8° Vogt, *Berlin* 94

Sir Eger, Sir Grime and Sir Gray-Steel—*ut* K § 254.

Series.

Scottish History Soc. *Publications*—*ut* F § 35.
Scottish Text Soc. *Publications* 8° Scott. Text Soc., *Edin.* 83–94 *in prg.*

Alliterative Poems .... ed. AMOURS
incl. 4 versns. of *Susanna* in parall. cols.
BARBOUR, Bp. J. *The Bruce* [*ut* K § 254] .. Prf. W. W. SKEAT 93–94
BELLENDEN *Tr. of First Five Bks. of Livy* ...... OGILVIE FORBES
BONNET *L'Arbre des Batailles* [tr. fr. his Fch.] J. H. STEVENSON, *i.p.*
BUCHANAN *Scottish Writings* .... P. Hume BROWN
Buke of ye Chesse
A Scots versn. of the well-known wk.
DUNBAR *Poems*, 5 pts. [*ut* K § 68] .... Dr. Jno. SMALL 91–94
GAU, Jno. *Richt Way to Kgdom. of Hevine* .. Prf. A. F. MITCHELL
Gude and Godlie Ballads .... Prf. A. F. MITCHELL
HENRY THE MINSTREL *Schir Wm. Wallace*, 3 pts. ...... Jas. MOIR
HENRYSON, Rob. *Poems* .... Prf. W. MINTO, *i.p.*
HOLLAND *Buke of the Howlat* [*ut* K § 254] .... AMOURS
HUME, Rev. Alex. *Hymns or Sacr. Songs* .... Dr. Walt. GREGOR, *i.p.*
King's Quhair, The .... Prf. W. W. SKEAT
Legends of Saints [14 cent.], pts. i.–iii. .. Dr. W. M. METCALFE ?–93
LESLEY, Bp. *Historie of Scotld.*, 3 pts. .... Fr. CODY
Minor Poets of Time of James iii., pts. i.–ii. .. Gregory SMITH ?; 93
MONTGOMERIE, Alex. *Poems*, 3 pts. .... Dr. Jas. CRANSTOUN
MURE OF ROWALLAN *Works* .... Wm. TOUGH, *i.p.*
ROLLAND *Court of Venus* .... Dr. Walt. GREGOR
,, *Seven Sages* .... Dr. VARNHAGEN
Satirical Poems of Time of Reformn., 2 pts. .. Dr. Jas. CRANSTOUN ?; *i.p.*
SCOTT, Alex. *Poems* .... Dr. Jas. CRANSTOUN, *i.p.*
"The Anacreon of Scotland."
Tristrem, Sir .... G. P. MCNEIL
Trojan War Fragments .... Moore SMITH
A work at one time attrib. to Barbour.
WINZET, Ninian *Certain Tractates*, 2 pts. .... K. HEWISON
Carefully collated texts fr. the MSS. and early edns., w. Introds., notes, glossaries and appendices.

Shetland.

BURGESS, J. J. H. Rasmie's Büddie: poems in the Shetlandic [w. glossary] 2/6 c 8° Gardner, *Paisley* 92

242. ANGLO-SAXON PHILOLOGY.

Grammar · Introduction.

CARPENTER, Prf. Steph. H. [Am.] Introduction to the Study of Anglo-Saxon [elem. gram., selns., vocab. 212 pp.] 12° Heath, *Boston* 3/6 Arnold 9-

COOK, Prf. Alb. S. [Am.] First Book in Old English 12° $1.60 Ginn, *Boston* 4/6 Arnold 94
Selns. fr. *Apollonius*, *Andreas*, A.-S. tr. of BEDE'S *History*, BOETHIUS, *Beowulf* and *Judith*; w gram., notes and good vocab.

WYATT, A. J. Notabilia of Anglo-Saxon Grammar 1/6 c 8° Clive 92

Old-West Saxon.

COSIJN, P. J. Kurzgefasste altwestsächs. Grammatik pts. i.–ii. [Lautlehre, Flexionsl.] 1*m*.50 8° Brill, *Leyden* 93
An entirely different bk. fr. the fragmt. pb. in 1880 [*ut* B.B. K § 242, there erroneously dated 1881].

Noun.

MAACK, Rich. Flexion des engl. Substantivs v. 1100 bis etwa 1250 1*m*.50 Meissner, *Hamburg* 88

Participle.

CALLAWAY, Morgan [Am.] The Absolute Participle in Anglo-Saxon [dissert.] 8° Johns Hopk. Univ., *Baltimore* 89

Prefixes.

HARRISON, Thos. [Am.] The Separable Prefixes in Anglo-Saxon [dissert.] 8° Johns Hopk. Univ., *Baltimore* 92

Etymology.

STORCH, Theod. Angelsächsische Nominalcomposita [a good piece of wk.] 1*m*.50 8° Trübner, *Strassbg.* 86

Dictionaries.

BOSWORTH, Dr. Jos. Anglo-Saxon Dict., ed. Prf. T. N. Toller, pt. iv., sect. 1 [to Swi] 4° 8/6 Clar. Press $2 n/. Macmillan, *N.Y.* 92

HALL, Dr. J. R. Clark Concise Anglo-Saxon Dictionary for the Use of Students 4° 15/- Sonnenschein Macmillan, *N.Y.* 94
A useful student's dict., mainly based on the glossaries accompanying A.-S. texts, Readers, *etc.*, wh. have appeared in Engl., Amer. and Germ. during the past 10 or 15 yrs.

TOLLER, Prf. T. N. —*v.* Bosworth, *supra.*

Glosses.

BEDE, Ven. [672–735] Liber Scintillarum, ed. Ern. Rhodes 12/- 8° Early Eng. Text Soc. (Paul) 89
Interlinear Anglo-Saxon glosses and original Latin text.

NAPIER, Prf. A. [ed.] The Aldhelm Glosses [Anecdota Oxon.] s 4° Clar. Press Macmillan, *N.Y.* *in prep.*
Lists of rare words fr. all the known Aldhelm MSS. in Engld. (so in number) wh. cont. Saxon glosses (17 in number).

Northumbrian Gloss to Gospels in the Lindisfarne Gospels.
• COOK, Prf. A. S. [Am.] Glossary of the Old Northumbrian Lindisfarne Gospels or Durham Bk. 10*m*. 8° Niemeyer, *Halle* 94
LEA, [Miss] Eliz. M. Phonology and Grammar of Northumbr. Gloss to Mark—*in* Anglia, 1893 (2 pts.).
An admirable monograph, extending to some 150 pp.

Rule of St. Benedict: Ang.-Sax. & Lat. Rule of St. Benet, ed. Prf. H. Logeman; w. interlin. glosses 12/- 8° Early Eng. Text Soc. (Paul) 88

Rushworth Gloss to Matthew.
BROWN, Edw. Miles Die Sprache d. Rushworth Glossen z. Matthias u. d. mercische Dialekt, pt. i. [diss.] 1*m*.60 8° Vandenhoeck, *Gttgn.* 91
OTTEN, Geo. The Language of the Rushworth Gloss. to Gosp. of S. Matth., pts. i.–ii. (Nordhausen schl. progrs.) ea. 1*m*. 4° Fock, *Lpz.* 90; 91

Palæography.

SKEAT, Prf. W. W. [ed.] Twelve Facs. of Old English MSS.; w. transcriptions and Introd. 4° 7/6 Clar. Press Macmillan, *N.Y.* 92
An admir. series of facs., w. good Introd., giving a summary of Engl. paleogr. down to 15 cent. Contents purely literary, incl. *Pastoral Care* (Hatton MS.), so-called CÆDMON'S *Exod.*, *Peterb. Chron.*, *Ormulum*, *Kentish Serms.* (Laud MS., early 13 cent.), *Moral Ode* (Jesus Coll. MS.), *Havelok*, WICLIF'S Bible (Douce MS.), *Piers Plowman* (Laud MS., wh. SKEAT believes to be LANGLAND'S autograph), *Legend of Good Women* (Fairfax MS.), *Wars of Alex.* (Ashmole MS.), CHAUCER'S *Roamounde* (late 15 cent.): all but one fr. MSS. in Bodl. Lib.

Codex Vercellensis: Photographic Reprodn. of, pb. Prf. Rich. P. Wülker—*ut* K § 246.

Chrestomathy.

*BRIGHT, Prf. Jas. W. [Am.; ed.] An Anglo-Saxon Reader; w. Introd., notes and gloss. c 8° $1.75 Holt, *N.Y.* 6/6 Sonnenschein 92
More interesting and varied selns. than those in SWEET [*ut* B.B. K § 242], many based on fresh collams. of the MSS. The Introd. furnishes an outline of SIEVERS' discoveries in A.-S. metre. Copious glossary.

*GREIN, Chr. W. M. [ed.] Bibliothek d. A.-S. Poesie, hrsg. Prf. Rich. P. Wülker, vol. ii., pt. 1, 8*m*.; pt. 2, 18*m*. r 8° Wigand, *Lpz.* 88; 94
This second vol. conts. *Die Vercelier Handsch.*, *die HS. d. Camb. Corp. Chr. Coll. CCI*, *die Gedichte d. sogen. Cædmonhandsch.*, *Judith*, *der Hymnus Cædmons*, *Heiligenkalender*, *nebst kleineren geistl. Dichtungen.*

• „ „ „ [ed.] Bibliothek d. A.-S. Prosa, hrsg. Prf. Rich. P. Wülker, vol. ii.(2)–iii. 16*m*. r 8° Wigand, *Lpz.* 88; 89
ii. (2) *A.-S. Prosabearb. d. Bened.-regel.* [*ut* K § 232] A. SCHRÖER, 6*m*.'88; iii. *A.-S. Homilien u. Heiligenleben* [*ut* K § 232] P. ASSMANN, 10*m*.'89

Metrics. Phonology.

BOWEN, Edw. W. [Am.] The *ē* Vowel in Accented Syllables fr. A.-S. to Mod. Engl. [78 pp.; diss.] 8° Murphy, *Baltimore* 93
KALUZA, Prf. Max Der altengl. Vers, pts. i.–ii. [Stud. z. germ. Alliterationsvers] ea. 2*m*.40 8° Felber, *Berl.* 93; 94
Pt. i.: *Kritik der bisherigen Theorien*; ii.: *Metrik des Béowulf* [*ut* K § 247].

*SIEVERS, Prf. Ed. —*in his* Altgermanische Metrik, *ut* K § 225 [*and in* Paul's Grundriss, *ut ib.*].

Epigraphy.

LOGEMAN, Prf. Henri — L'Inscription A.-S. du Reliquaire d. l. Vraie Croix du Trésor de l'Eglise de SS. Michel et Gudule à Bruxelles; 2 pl. — 2fr.50 8° Engelcke, *Ghent* 91

The inscr. is of interest as cont. phrases clearly suggested by a recolln. of *The Vision of the Rood*, preserved in *Codex Vercell.* [*ut* K § 248] and in the rimes of Ruthwell Cross [*v.* 𝔅.𝔅. K § 225]. Author is inclined to refer the relic to c. yr. 1100.

244. OLD [A.D. 1250-1350] AND MIDDLE [1350-1500] ENGLISH PHILOLOGY.

Grammar.

Introduction.

COOK, Prf. Alb. S. [Am.] First Book in Old English—*v.* K § 242.

Grammar of Individual Writers—v. also K §§ 24, *and* 254-255 *passim.*

CAXTON, Wm. [1412-1491].
Logeman, Prf. Henri — *—in the Introd. to his+* J. W. Muller's Raynaert de Vos, *ut* B § 7.
Römstedt, Herm. — Die englische Schriftsprache bei Caxton — 2m.50 4° Vandenhoeck, *Göttgn.* 91

CHAUCER, Geoffrey [1328-1400]—*v. also* K § 24.
Child, Prf. F. J. [Am.] — On Chaucer's Grammar and Metre
Freudenberger, M. — Das Fehlen d. Auftakts in Chaucer's heroisch. Verse — [Erlanger Beiträge] 1m.60 8° Junge, *Erlangen* 89
Gräf, A. — Das Futurum u. d. Entwickg. v. *schal.* u. *wil* b. Chaucer — [diss.] 1m.20 8° Fock, *Lpz.* 93
Häckel, W. — Das Sprichwort bei Chaucer — [Erlanger Beiträge] 1m.80 8° Junge, *Erlangen* 90
Hagedorn, Wilh. — Ueber d. Sprache einiger nördlicher Chaucerschüler — [dissert] 80pf. 8° Vandenhoeck, *Göttgn.* 93
Hempl, Prf. Geo. [Am.] — Chaucer's Pronunciation and the Spelling of the Ellesmere MS. — s 8° Heath, *Boston* / 2/- Isbister 94
Petzold, Ern. — Ueb. Alliteration in d. Werken Chaucers, m. Ausschl. d. Cant. Tales — [diss.] 8° *Marburg* 89

English Gilds [A.D. 1389].
Schultz, E. — Die Sprache der *English Gilds* — 1m.20 8° Dabis, *Rudolstadt* 91

MALORY, Sir Thos. [*b.* (?) 1430] Morte d'Arthur—*ut* K § 46.
Baldwin, C. S. [Am.] — The Inflections and Syntax of Sir Thos. Malory — [enlarged dissert.] 12° $1.60 Ginn, *Boston* / 6/6 Arnold 94

A minute and elabor. exam. and tabuln. of the inflectns. in elucidn. of the syntax.

TOTTEL, Rich. [16th cent.] Miscellany.
Hölper, Franz — Die englische Schriftspr. in Tottel's Misc., u. Ausg. v. Brooke's Rom. and Jul. [diss.] 1m.50 8° *Strassbg.* (Fock, *Lpz.*) 94

WICLIF, Jno. [1324-1384].
Grimm, Friedr. — Syntact. Gebrauch d. Präpos. b. Wycliffe u. Jno. Purvey [tr. of Gosps.] — [diss.] 8° *Marburg* 91

Syntax.

Participle.

Ross, Dr. Chas. Hunter [Am.] Absolute Participle in Mid. & Mod. Engl. [*extr. fr.* pbs. of Mod. Lang. Ass.; diss.] 93

Etymology: *Dictionary.*

*MÄTZNER, E. [ed.] — Altenglische Sprachproben, vol. ii. [Dictionary]—*ut infra, s.v.* Chrestomathies.
*STRATMANN, Fcs. H. — Middle-English Dictionary, ed. Henry Bradley — [12-15 cent.] 4° 31/6 Clar. Press / $8 nt. Macmillan, *N.Y.* [64-67] 90

Mr. BRADLEY'S new edn. of this book (hitherto pub. sub tit. *Old Engl. Dict.*, *ut* 𝔅.𝔅. K § 244) is practically a new (and very important) work, cont. nearly twice as much matter (tho' of little greater bulk) than the 3rd edn., the addns. bg. largely of Romanic and Latin origin. With a list of works consulted (390 in all), forming a v. useful bibl.; date of ea. MS. original, and locality (where necessary) are added.

Metrics.

CROW, Chas. Langley — Zur Gesch. d. kurz. Reimpaars im Mittelenglisch — [diss.] 1m.40 8° Vandenhoeck, *Göttgn.* 92

The Harrowing of Hell, Cursor Mundi, CHAUCER'S *House of Fame.*

SIEVERS, Prf. Ed. — Altgermanische Metrik—*ut* K § 225.

Phonology.

HEMPL, Prf. Geo [Am.] — Old English Phonology — [44 pp.] s 8° Heath, *Boston* / Isbister 93

The 1st. Pt. of the author's forthcoming *Old English Grammar and Reader.*

*MAYHEW, A. L. — Synopsis of Old English Phonology — f 8° 8/6 Clar. Press / $2.25 nt. Macmillan, *N.Y.* 91

A systematic acc. (1) of O.-E. vowels and consonants and their correspondence to cognate languages, and (2) of the correspondence of O.-E. sounds with Mod. Engl. pronunciation and spelling, consisting princ. of classified lists of words, exemplifying the etymol. relation betw. the sounds of Old-Engl. and those of the cognate langs. and Mod.-English.

Chrestomathies.

*MACLEAN, Prf. Geo. E. [Am.; tr.] Old & Middle English Reader; w. Introd., notes & gloss. $2 *nt.* (8/- *nt.*) c 8° Macmillan 93

Based on Prf. ZUPITZA'S *Alt- u. mittelenglisches Uebungsbuch*, *ut* 𝔅.𝔅. K § 244. Conts. 34 extrs. in O.-E. and 36 in M.-E., incl. a chap. of WICLIF'S *N.T.*, giving a fairly repres. view of liter. style and of dialect in O. and M.-E., w. an excellent glossary, full of etymol. informn. condensed by ingenious typograph. arrangements.

*MÄTZNER, E. [ed.] — Altenglische Sprachproben, vol. ii. [Dictionary], pt. 11 — 8m. r 8° Weidmann, *Berl.* 91 *in prg.*
*ZUPITZA, Prf. Julius [ed.] Old and Middle English Reader—*v.* Maclean, *supra.*

Series of Texts.

Altenglische Bibliothek: hrsg. Prf. Eug. Kölbing, vols. iv.-v. — 24m. 8° Reisland, *Lpz.* 90; 90

iv. *Arthour and Merlin* [*ut* K § 46] .... Prf. Eug. KÖLBING, 14m. 90 | v. *Li Beaus Desconus* .... MAX KALUZA, 10m. 90

Old English Library: ed. Dr. Carl Horstman, vol. i. — 8° ea. 10/6 Sonnenschein / Macmillan, *N.Y.* 94 *in prg.*

Vol. i. *Prose Treatises of Rich. Hampole*, ed. Dr. Carl HORSTMAN. To be followed by *The Festial* (the most import. O.-E. Sermon-book for the whole year); *Early English Prose*, 2 vols. (prose-tracts of 12-14 cents., in their orig. dialects); *The Great South-English Legendary* (in verse, in Glouce. dial., c. 1250); *Old-English Lyrics*; *Legenda Angliae*, and others.

245. ANGLO-SAXON AND OLD AND MIDDLE-ENGLISH LITERATURE: (a): HISTORY.

BRANDL, Alois — Mittelenglische Literaturgeschichte—*in* Paul's Grundriss, *ut* K § 225.

*BROOKE, Rev. A. Stopford — History of Early English Liter. : from its beginnings to access. of Alfred, 2 vols. 20/- *nt.* 8° (1 vol. $2.50) 12° Macmillan 92

The first serious attempt by a British (accurately Irish) writer to describe at length and appreciate from the pt.-of-view of an æsthetic critic and literary historian the remaining *corpus* of A.-S. poetry. Popular yet scholarly, stimulating and charmingly written; w. many excellent trs. of characteristic passages. Further vols., event. covering the whole field of Brit. poetry, are to follow.

*TEN BRINK, Prf. Bernh. — Geschichte der englischen Litteratur, vol. ii. pt. 2 [to access. of Elizab.], hrs. Alois Brandl 6*m*.50'; ii. cpl. 13*m*. 8° Trübner, *Strassb.* 93

* „ „ — History of English Literature, tr. Dr. W. Clarke Robinson [Am.], vol. ii. c 8° $1 Holt, *N.Y.* / 3/6 Bell [Bohn's Lib.] 93

This vol. is tr. of orig. vol. ii., pt. 1—*ut* B.B. K § 245, and incl. WICLIF, CHAUCER, Earliest Drama, Renaissance (mainly CHAUCER). An excellent wk. characterised by a richness of detail and a depth of insight quite uncommon in literary histories. The d. of author in Jan., 1892, will prevent the completion of the wk. by him.

„ „ — Altenglische Literaturgeschichte—*in* Paul's Grundriss, *ut* K § 225.

Poetry.

DEERING, Waller — The Anglo-Saxon Poets on the Judgment Day 2*m*. 8° Niemeyer, *Halle* 90

246. ANGLO-SAXON LITERATURE (b): COLLECTIONS.

Codex Exoniensis [*ut* B.B. K § 246] new edn., ed. Israel Gollancz, w. Introd., tr. & notes, pt. i. 8° Early Eng. Text Soc. (Paul) 95 *in prep.*

The *Cod. Exon.* is an anthology of A.-S. poetry cont. in a MS. wh. was presented to Exeter Cathed. by LEOFRIC, 1st Bp. of Exeter [1050-1071], still in possession there. This First Pt. conts. all the longer poems, incl. CYNEWULF'S *Christ, St. Guthlac, Phœnix*, and *St. Juliana* : texts w. trs. *en regard* (introds., notes and indices to follow). For his edn. of *Christ* v. K § 248. For *Riddles* (part of *Codex Exon.*) v. K § 250.

Codex Vercellensis : — hrsg. Prf. Rich. P. Wülker—*ut* K § 242, *sub voc.* Chrestomathies (GREIN).

„ „ — Photographic Reprodn. of, pb. Prf. Rich. P. Wülker 20*m*. Veit, *Lpz.* *in prep.*

To comprise the whole 86 leaves, half the size of the originals. Besides some *Homilies* the *Vercelli Book* (the only A.-S. MS. of importance not in English possession) conts. CYNEWULF'S two long poems *Andreas* and *Elene*.

247. ANGLO-SAXON LITERATURE (c): POPULAR EPICS.

Béowulf [8 cent.] — ed. A. J. Wyatt c 8° 8/6 Camb. Press / Macmillan, *N.Y.* 94

A handy edn. for Engl. students—the best available; w. textual footnotes, index of proper names and good glossary (no etymols., but mod. Engl. forms given).

Translations.

EARLE, Prf. Jno. [tr.] — The Deeds of Béowulf : an English epic : tr. ; w. Introd. and notes c 8° 8/6 Clar. Press / $2.10 *nt.* Macmillan, *N.Y.* 92

A readable prose tr., w. Introd. giving account of liter. hist. of the poem since the first mention of it by WANLEY in 1705 and of the various subsequent theories of its origin. His own theory is that it was written at the Court of OFFA of Mercia by HYGEBERHT, Abp. of Lichfd., for purpose of affording instructn. in princely virtues to OFFA'S son, ECGFERTH (!).

HALL, Prf. Jas. Leslie [Am.; tr.] Béowulf : an Anglo-Saxon epic poem : transl. 8° $1 Heath, *Boston* / 5/- Isbister 92

A close and accurate verse tr. fr. the HEYNE-SOCIN text (*ut* B.B. K § 247): but at best only rhythmical prose.

HOFFMANN, P. [tr.] — Béowulf : ältestes deutsches Heldengedicht : übers. 3*m*. 8° Liebisch, *Zullichau* 93

MORRIS + WYATT, Wm. / A. J. — Béowulf : translated *in prep.*

Allit.

KALUZA, Prf. Max — Die Metrik des Beowulfliedes = Studien z. germ. Alliterationsvers, ii.—*ut* K § 242.

SONNEFELD, Gottfr. — Stilistisches u. Wortschatz im Beówulf [dissert.] 1*m*.60 8° *Würzburg* (Fock, *Lpz.*) 94

Waldere's Lay, King [9 cent.] : A.-S. text, *in* Learned's Saga of Walther of Aquitaine—*ut infra.*

LEARNED, Dr. Marion D. [Am.] The Saga of Walther of Aquitaine Mod.-Langs. Assoc. of Amer. 92

(1) Critical texts of all the versns. of the saga, or fragmts. of it, preserved—A.-S., Lat., Middle Old-Germ., O.-Norse, Polish; (2) tabular conspectus of contents; (3) discrimn. of histor. fr. legendary elements; (4) determn. of orig. form and accretns.; (5) vindicn. of WALTHER as an histor. personage; (6) bibliogr. and index.

248. ANGLO-SAXON LITERATURE (d): CHRISTIAN EPICS.

Caedmon [*d.* 680].

Exodus.

GROTH, E. — Composition und Alter der altenglischen [= Anglo-Sax.] Exodus 1*m*.20 8° Mayer & Müller, *Berl.* 83

Judith : — tr. in Prf. Hy. Morley's English Writers, vol. ii.—*ut* B.B. K § 18.

FOSTER, T. Gregory — Judith : studies in metre, lang. and style [Quellen u. Forsch.] 3*m*. 8° Trübner, *Strassburg* 92

KLUGE, Friedr. — —*in his* Zur Gesch. d. Reimes im Altgermanischen, *in* Paul + Braune's Beiträge, ix., 444-49 [*ut* B.B. K § 225].

LUICK, Karl — Ueber d. Versbau des Gedichtes Judith, *in* Paul + Braune's Beiträge xi., 470-92.

MÜLLER, Aug. — Der syntaktische Gebrauch d. Verbums in Judith [dissert. inaug.] 8° *Leipzig* 92

NEUMANN, Max — Ueber das altenglische Gedicht von Judith [dissert. inaug.] 8° *Kiel* 92

SIEVERS, Prf. Ed. — —*in his* Der Schwellvers, *in* Paul + Braune's Beiträge, xii. 454-82.

Cynewulf [8 cent.].

Andreas : — —*v.* K § 246, *sub tit.* Codex Vercellensis.

BAUER, Herm. — Ueb. d. Spr. u. Mundart d. Andreas, Guthlac, Phönix, *etc.* [diss.] 8° *Marburg* 92

HINZE, Wilh. — Zum altenglischen Gedicht Andreas, pt. i. [schl.-progr.] 1*m*. 4° Gaertner, *Berlin* 90

REUSSNER, H. Adf. — Untersuchungen üb. d. Syntax in d. Andreas [Leipzig diss. inaug.] 8° *Halle* 89

Christ: ed. Israel Gollancz, w. tr.; col. front. of an A.-S. MS. [Pre-Tudor Lib.] *subscr.* 10/6 8° Nutt 92

Text based on a collatn. of Exeter MS. Contains a glossary and excursus on the CYNEWULF runes. Blank verse tr., verse by verse *en regard*; w. scholarly excursus, notes and Appendices. This is the 1st time the text has been printed by itself. GOLLANCZ is re-editing the whole of the *Cod. Exon.* for E. E. T. Soc. [*ut* K § 246], and his final treatment of text of *Christ* (wh. is pt. of *Cod. Exon.*) will be found there. Only 500 printed; and 60 on Jap. ppr. *Subscr.* 25/-.

Hertel, Bruno — Der syntakt. Gebrauch d. Verbums in d. angelsächs Crist — [diss. inaug.] 8° *Leipzig* 91

Rose, A. — Darstellung der Syntax in Cynewulfs Crist — 1m.50 8° Fock, *Leipzig* 90

Elene: —*v.* K § 246, *sub tit.* Codex Vercellensis.

Phoenix: ed. Israel Gollancz, w. [blank verse] tr.—*in his edn. of* Codex Exon., *ut* K § 246.

Planer, J. — Unters. üb. d. syntakt. Gebrauch d. Verbums im Phoenix — [diss.] 1m.20 8° Gräse, *Lps.* 91

St. Guthlac: ed. Israel Gollancz, w. [blank verse] tr.—*in his edn. of* Codex Exon., *ut* K § 246.

Furkert, Max — Syntakt. Gebrauch d. Verbums i. d. a.-s. Gedichte v. heil. Guthlac — [diss.] 8° *Leipzig* 89

St. Juliana: ed. Israel Gollancz, w. [blank verse] tr.—*in his edn. of* Codex Exon., *ut* K § 246.

249. ANGLO-SAXON LITERATURE (*e*): DIDACTIC POETRY.

Codex Exoniensis —*ut* K § 246.

Codex Vercellensis —*ut* K § 246.

250. ANGLO-SAXON LITERATURE (*f*): LYRICAL POETRY.

A. Religious.

Psalms: ed. Prf. Henri Logeman — Early Engl. Text Soc., *in prep.*

To form a parallel edn. of all the interlinear A.-S. psalms that have come down to us, incl. those ptd. in SWEET'S Vespasian MS., as well as those wh. have never yet been repr. The Paris Psalter, ed. B. THORPE in 1835 [*ut* B.B. K § 250] and collated HAUSKNECHT will prob. be incl.; and Romance and Gallic versns. (of the Lat. texts) will be added in one column.

Psalter ("Kentish").

Zeuner, R. — Wortschatz d. sogenannten Kentischen Psalter, pt. i. — [school-progr.] 1m. 4° Nusel, *Gera* 91

B. Secular.

Codex Exoniensis [*ut* K § 246].

Riddles.

Herzfeld, Geo. — Die Räthsel des Exeterbuches und ihr Verfasser — [Acta German. ii. (1)] 2m. 8° Mayer & Müller, *Berlin* 90

Müller, Hugo — Ueber d. angelsächs. Versus Gnomici — [dissert. inaug.] 8° *Jena* 93

251. ANGLO-SAXON LITERATURE (*g*): PRINCIPAL PROSE WORKS.

Aelfric, Abbot [955(?)-1020(-25)].

Homilies:

Förster, Max — Ueber d. Quellen v. Aelfrics Homiliae Catholicae, pt. i. (Legenden) — [dissert. inaug.] 8° *Berlin* 92

A Second Part appeared in *Anglia*.

Schwerdtfeger, Gust. — Das schwache Verbum in Aelfric's Homilien — [dissert. inaug.] 8° *Marburg* 93

Glossary.

Wyatt + Johnson, A. J. / H. R. [eds.] Glossary to Aelfric's Homilies [Univ. Corr. Coll. Tutorial Ser.] 2/6 f 8° Clive 91

Braunschweiger, Meyer — Die Flexion des Verbums in Alfrics Grammatik — [dissert. inaug.] 8° *Marburg* 90

Brühl, Carl — Die Flexion des Verbums in Aelfrics Heptateuch u. Buch Hiob — [dissert. inaug.] 8° " 91

Ott, J. H. — Ueb. d. Quellen d. Heiligenleben in Aelfrics Lives of Saints, pt. i. — [dissert. inaug.] 8° *Halle* 92

Alfred the Great [849(?)-901].

Bede, Ven. — Ecclesiastical History, tr. King Alfred, ed. Dr. Thos. Miller, pt. i., 18/-; ii. 15/- [*v. also* A § 62] 8° E. Eng. Text Soc. (Paul) 90; 91

Pt. i. conts. the Lat. vers. w. KG. ALFRED'S tr. in parallel cols., and mod. Eng. versn. at foot; pt. ii. the full crit. apparatus, glossary and conspectus of dialectical peculiarities of all the MSS. The wk. is, however, now supposed not to be ALFRED'S.

Laws: The Legal Code of Alfred the Great, ed. Prf. Milton H. Turk [Am.]—*ut* D § 5 [the price is $1].

Stearns, J. M. [Am.; tr.] Germs and Developmts. of Laws of England: tr., w. notes $2 *nt.* 12° Banks, *N. Y.* 90

Embraces the A.-S. laws extant fr. 6th cent. to A.D. 1066 as tr. into Engl. under the Roy. Commissn. of William iv., w. the introd. of the Common Law by Norman Judges after the Conquest and its earliest proferts in Magna Carta.

Orosius: Extracts from, ed. Dr. Hy. Sweet [74 pp.] f 8° 2/- Clar. Press / 90 *c.* *nt.* Macmillan, *N. Y.* [86] 93

Girschner, Ludw. — Die charakt. Unterschiede d. einzelnen Schreiber i. Hatton MS. d. Cura Past. — 8° *Greifswd.* 87

Hanstrick, Aug. — Untersuchung üb d. Präpositionen bei Alfred d. Grossen — [dissert. inaug.] 8° *Kiel* 90

Philipsen, Hy. — Wesen u. Gebrauch d. bestimmt. Artikels i. Alfred — [diss.] 8° *Greifswald* 87

Wülfing, J. E. — Die Syntax in den Werken Alfreds des Grossen, vol. i. — 8m. 8° Hanstein, *Bonn* 94

Anglo-Saxon Chronicle—*v.* F § 18.

252. ANGLO-SAXON LITERATURE (*h*): MINOR PROSE WORKS.

Gospels.

Gospel of St. Luke in Anglo-Saxon, ed. [fr. the MSS.] Prf. Jas. W. Bright [Am.]—*ut* A § 17.

Gospel of St. Mark: tr. [literal] Rev. H. C. Leonard, *s.t.* Good News after Marcus' Telling 1/- c 8° J. Clarke [94] 94

Glosses —*v.* K § 242, *sub voc.* Glosses.

Gregory's Dialogues : tr. Werfrid ed. Prf. Zupitza.

Dialogues of St Gregory the Great: an old English version, ed. Rev. H. J. Coleridge [S.-J.] 6/- c 8° Manresa Press (Burns & Oates) 72

Homilies. Lives of Saints.

ASSMANN, P. [ed.] Angelsächs. Homilien u. Heiligenleben [= Grein's Bibl. A.-S. Prosa, iii.] 10m. r 8° Wigand, *Lps.* 89

Codex Vercellensis —*v.* K § 246.

Laws —*v. also* D § 5.

LIEBERMANN, Dr. F. Ueber d. Leges Anglorum saec. xiii. ineunte Lond. collectae 3m. 8° Niemeyer, *Halle* 94

Appeared too late for insertion in D § 5, *q.v.* for the whole subject.

Rule of St. Benedict : *for* A.-S. and Lat. glosses *v.* K § 242; *for* Mid.-Engl, (Whiteney) versn. *v.* K § 255.

Schröer, Arn. [ed.] Die A.-S. Prosabearbeitgn. d. Benediktinerregel—*in* Grein's [ed.] Bibl. A.-S. Prosa, ii., *ut* K § 242.

253. LATER ANGLO-SAXON LITERATURE.

Historical.

LAYAMON [13 cent.] Brut—*ut* B.B. K § 253.

KOLBE, Max Schild, Helm u. Panzer z. Zeit Layamons: verglichen m. Wace [diss.] 8° *Trebnitz* 93

Religious.

Genesis : [Old-Sax. versn.] hrsg. K. Zangemeister + W. Braune—*ut* K § 228.

RAU, Max Germanische Altertümer in d. angelsächs. Genesis [dissert. inaug.] 8° *Trebnitz* 89

254. OLD [1250-1350] AND MIDDLE [1350-1500] ENGLISH LITERATURE (*a*): POETRY.

Didactic and Religious.

Childhood of Jesus [14 cent.].

LANDSHOFF, Herm. Kindheit Jesu, pt. i.: Verhaltniss der Handschriften [dissert. inaug.] 8° *Berlin* 89

Cursor Mundi [*c.* 1320] : ed. Dr. Rich. Morris, pts. vi.–vii. [Introduction and Notes] 8° Early Eng. Text Soc. (Paul) 92; 93

Pt. vi.—Preface and Notes, w. Glossary, by Max KALUZA; vii. [last] has a long essay on the sources by HAENISCH, and another on the MSS., their dialects, etc., by Dr. H. HUPE. Pt. i. was pub. as long ago as 1874 [*ut* B.B. K § 254].

Disputisoun bitwen the Bodi and the Soule : hrsg. Wilh. Linow [Erlanger Beitr.] 3m.60 8° Junge, *Erlangen* 89

With the Old-Fch. version, ed. Herm. VARNHAGEN.

" " hrsg. Rich. Buchholz; w. Introd. and tr. [fr. Worc. and Oxon. MSS.; Erlang. Beitr.] 1m.80 8° Junge, *Erlangen* 90

KUNZE, Otto The Desputisoun bitwen the Bodi and the Soule: textkritischer Versuch 2m.40 8° Mayer & Müller, *Berl.* 92

HOLLAND The Buke of the Howlat, ed. Amours 8° Scottish Text Soc., *Edin.*

" " ed. Arth. Diebler, fr. Bannatyne MS. 3m. 4° Reisland, *Lps.* 93

Previously pub. by Bannatyne Club, and repr. and ed. Dav. DONALDSON, 4° *Paisley,* '82 [w. 10/6].

GUTMANN, Jos. Untersuchgn. üb. d. mittelengl. Gedicht Buke of the Howlat [dissert. inaug.] 8° *Halle* 90

Pearl [14 cent.] : ed. Israel Gollancz; w. rhythmical tr., Intro., a few notes & glossary 14/- *nt.* sq 8° Nutt 91

An excellent edn. of a remarkable and beautiful poem—a father's lament for a lost child, with wh. is combined a vision, Apocalyptic in source: a kind of mediæval *In Memoriam.* Authorship unknown, but to the same writer are ascribed *Sir Gawain and the Green Knight, Cleanness* and *Patience.* The text and lineal tr. are *en regard*; and Mr. Holman HUNT supplies a frontispiece. Prev. ed. Dr. Rich. MORRIS in Early Engl. Text Soc. pbs. in its *Early English Alliterative Poems,* 16/- 8° ['64] '69. [Prf. HORSTMAN (1891) claims *Pearl* for Ralf STRODE, "the philosophical Strode," referred to by Chaucer in the *Troilus,* w. wh. view GOLLANCZ coincides].

Tale of an Incestuous Daughter.

THUM, Otto Untersuchgn. üb. d. mittelengl. Tale of an Incestuous Daughter [dissert. inaug.] 8° *Berlin* 92

Vernon MS. : Minor Poems of the Vernon MS., pt. i., ed. Dr. C. Horstmann 20/- 8° Early Engl. Text Soc. (Paul) 92

Pt. ii. to be edited by Dr. J. KAIL.

Historical Poems, Chronicles and Romances.

BARBOUR, Bp. J. [1316-96] The Bruce [1375-77], ed. Prf. W. W. Skeat, 3 pts.; w. elab. Introd. 8° Scot. Text Soc. 93-94

RITSON, Jos. [ed.] Ancient English Metrical Romances—*ut* B.B. K § 47.

STERNBERG, Rud. Ueb. e. versif. metr. Chronik [Ritson, ii., pp. 270 *sqq.*] [Breslau diss. inaug.] *Darmstadt* 92

ROBERT OF BRUNNE [Rob. MANNING; 13-14 cent.].

PREUSSNER, Osk. Rob. Manning's Uebersetzg. v. Lantoft's Chronicle [diss.] 1m. 8° Koehler, *Breslau* 91

THUMMIG, Max Ueb. d. Uebers. d. Reimchronik Langtofts durch Rob. Manning [diss.] 8° *Leipzig* 91

ROBERT OF GLOUCESTER [? 13 cent.].

PABST, Felix Sprache d. mittelengl. Reimchronik d. Rob. v. Glouca., pt. i. [Phonol.] 8° Mayer & Müller, *Berl.* 89

STROHMEYER, Hans Der Stil der mittelenglischen Reimchronik Roberts von Gloucester [diss.] 2m. 8° Heinrich, *Berlin* 91

Sir Eger, Sir Grime and Sir Gray-Steel.

REICHEL, Geo. Stud. z. d. schott. Romanze Hist. of Sir Eger, Sir Grime and Sir Gray-Steel, 4 pts. [*extr. fr.* Engl. Stud.] 8° *Darmstadt* 93

Wars of Alexander.

HENNEMANN, Jno. Bell Untersuchungen üb. d. mittelengl. Gedicht "Wars of Alex. [diss. inaug.] 8° *Berlin* 89

Homilies (Metrical). Religious Poetry.

Canticum de Creatione.

BACHMANN, Friedr. Die beiden metrisch. Versionen d. mittelengl. Cant. de Creat. [progr.] 2m.60 4° *Hamburg* 92

Holy Rood-tree, Hist. of [12 cent.] ed. Prf. Arth. S. Napier; w. tr., preface and notes 8° Early Eng. Text Soc. (Paul) 93

The 1st. instalmt. of a coll. of hitherto unpub. O.-E. Homilies. The MS. fr. wh. the *Holy Rood-tree* is prin. is of latter hf. 12 cent., and conts. some 80 Engl. homilies, of wh. 13 are still unpub. and will be incl. in the next vol. Appended are *Notes on Orthogr. of the Ormulum,* and *A Mid.-Engl. Compassio Mariae* in hexam., a unique spec. of Chesh. dialect of 13 cent., in metre of *Stabat Mater*.

Lais.

Havelock the Dane.

WITTENBRINCK, G. Zur Kritik u. Rhythmik d. alteng. Lais v. Havel. d. Dänen [sch.-progr.] 8° *Burgsteinfurt* 92

WOHLFEIL, Paul The Lay of Havelock the Dane [dissert. inaug.] 8° *Leipzig* 90

255. OLD [1250-1350] AND MIDDLE [1350-1500] ENGLISH LITERATURE (*b*): PROSE.

Agriculture.

WALTER OF HENLEY [13 cent.] Husbandry [and 3 other 13 cent. treatises on agriculture]—*ut* D § 119.

Interesting here, as bg. written in an Anglicised Norman-Fch. dialect rarely found beyond the limits of the Statute-Book.

Devotional Books.

CHAUCER, Geoff. [1328–1400] Boece, fr. Camb. MS.; also ed. Dr. R. Morris [*repr. fr.* E. E. T. S. '68] 8° Chaucer Soc. 86; 86

A tr. of BOETHIUS' *De Consolatione Philosophiæ*: prose. (It is curious that CHAUCER was not tempted by the interspersed *metra* of the original to employ verse as his medium for tr.).

À KEMPIS, Thos. [*c.* 1380–1471] Two Translations [15 cent.] of The Imitation of Christ, ed. Dr. J. K. Ingram—*ut* A § 116.

WIECK, Dr. [ed.] Stories for Sermons [fr. MS. in British Museum] 8° Early Engl. Text Soc. (Paul) *in prep.*

Tr. in 1st half of 15 cent. fr. Latin *Alphabetum Narrationum*, a set of tales of shocking disasters to sinners of divers kinds, regularly used for spicing sermons.

Fiction.

Salomon and Marcolphus, Dyalogus betwixt [*c.* 1492]: ed. E. Gordon Duff [350 prin.] 10/6 *nt.* s 4° Nutt 92

A neat facs. of the unique copy in Bodl. Lib. of edn. printed [*Antwp.*, *c.* 1490] by Gerard LEEU, one of the most import. printers of the Low Cties., who exercised his craft at Gouda [1477–84] and later at Antwp. [1484–93], extending his operations to supplying bks. for the Engl. market dur. 1492–93, *i.e.* immed. after CAXTON'S death, when the Engl. press seems to have lost nearly all its vitality (*e.g.*, *Hist. of Jason*, *Hist. of Knight Paris and the Fair Vienne*, *Chronicles of Engld.*). The bk. itself in its Latin (prob. the original) version, was one of the most popular stories of the Mid. Ages, and is the only one of wh. an Engl. tr. was made (or, at least, is extant). A second Engl. tr. (fr. French) was pub. by PYNSON 35 yrs. later, and DUFF mentions 4 vernac. German, as well as 23 Latin, editions.

Legends and Lives of the Saints.

The Great Collections.

(F) Legenda Aurea, tr. W. Caxton [prose; (1484) 1487], ed. Fred. S. Ellis + Wm. Morris, 3 v. 126/– [w. £10 10*s.*] 4° Kelmsc. Pr. (Qu'itch) 92

With glossary, bibliogr., memoranda and index. Only 500 printed, w. front. by W. Burne JONES. Ed. fr. 1484 edn. (in Univ. Lib. Camb.). The *Legenda Aurea* was compiled in 13 cent. by JACOB de VORAGINE, Abp. of Genoa; early in 14 cent. it was tr. into Fch. by JEAN BELET, whose vers. was worked over again by JEAN DE VIGNAY, w. addn. of 44 legends: the latter vers. was used in making an English *Lives of the Saints* *c.* 1438, and out of these books CAXTON made his. Of the 1st. ed. only 30 copies are known to exist. This is a delightful repr. on handmade paper, w. beautiful capitals designed by Morris and engr. by H. H. Hooper, one of the choicest productions of the modern press which will hand down the name of Mr. Morris' Kelmscott Press to future generations.

Individually.

Baarlam, St. Two 15 cent. Engl. Lives of, ed. Joseph Jacobs [Bibl. de Carabas] *subscr.* 7/6 c 8° Nutt 93

With dissrts. on the influence of Buddhist legend on western mediæval literature. Only 550 printed, and 60 on L.P. (50 of wh. for sale).

CAPGRAVE, J. [1393–1464] Life of St. Katharine, ed. Dr. C. Horstmann 20/– 8° Early Engl. Text Soc. (Paul) 93

With a discussion of CHAUCER'S *gh* and SHAKSPERE'S long *i*, by Dr. F. J. FURNIVALL.

CUTHBERT, St., Life of [*c.* 1450]: ed. Rev. J. T. Fowler [in verse] 15/– 8° Surtees Soc. (Whittaker) 91

A careful edn. fr. the MS. in libr. at Castle Howard. The wk. is of no histor. value, bg. a tr. of var. bks. already pub.; but it is an interesting specimen of 15-cent. Northern English.

Gregory, St.: Trentalle Sancti Gregorii, eine mittelengl. Legende, hrsg. A. Kaufmann [2 texts; Erlang. Beitr.] 1*m.*20 8° Junge, *Erlangen* 89

TUNDALE [12 cent.] Visions of [*ante* 1451]: hrsg. Albr. Wagner 4*m.* 8° Niemeyer, *Halle* 93

A careful edn., based on 4 MSS. (Brit. Mus., Edinb., Cotton, Bodl.); w. Introd., var. rgs., and notes.

Visio Tnugdali ed. Albr. Wagner 5*m.* 8° Deichert, *Erlangen* 82

A learned edn. of the Latin and Old-German texts.

MUSSAFIA, Adf. Sulla Visione di Tundalo (*extr. fr.* Sitzber. Wien. Akad.) 75*kr.* r 8° Tempsky, *Vienna* 71

Manners

—*v.* I § 139 (FURNIVALL).

Medicine. Surgery.

LANFRANC Science of Chirurgie: Engl. version [*c.* 1400], ed. Dr. R. v. Fleischacker 8° E. Eng. Text Soc. (Paul) *in prep.*

Peri Didaxeon: hrsg. M. Löweneck [Erlanger Beiträge] 8° Junge, *Erlangen*, *in prep.*

A coll. of medical receipts in English language, fr. 12-cent. MS.

Miracle-Mysteries and Plays—*v.* K § 82.

Poetry

—*v. also* K § 68 (where this shd. have been inserted).

HOCCLEVE, Thos. [*c.* 1370–*c.* 1454] Minor Poems, ed. Dr. F. J. Furnivall; v. i. [fr. Phillipps and Durham MSS.] 15/– 8° E. Eng. Text Soc. (Paul) 92

Psalter.

Eadwine Canterbury Psalter, ed. F. Harsley, pt. i. [fr. Trin. Camb. MS.; *c.* 1150] 12/– Early Eng. Text Soc. (Paul) 89

Earliest English Prose Psalter, The: ed. Dr. Karl D. Buelbring, pt. i. 15/– " " " 91

Romances

—*v. also* K §§ 46–48 (where these shd. have been inserted).

Eneydos: tr. Wm. Caxton [1490], ed. M. T. Culley + Dr. F. J. Furnivall [w. collation of Fch. orig.] 13/– 8° E. Eng. Text Soc. (Paul) 90

Tr. fr. the French prose *Livre des Eneydes* (*Lyons* 1483). For CAXTON'S other trs. *v.* General Index.

Florence of Rome, le Bone: hrsg. Prf. Wilh. Vietor, pt. i. [fr. MS. at Univ. Lib., Camb.] 2*m.*40 8° Elwert, *Marburg* 93

Li Beaus Desconus: hrsg. Max Kaluza [crit. edn. fr. 6 MSS.] [Altengl. Bibl.] 10*m.* 8° Reisland, *Lpz.* 90

Rule of St. Benedict: Whiteney version (early Mid.-Engl.).

SCHRÖER, Arn. (ed.) Regula S. Benedicti: Lat. and Engl., w. Introd., notes and gloss. (Whiteney versn.) 5*m.* 8° Niemeyer, *Halle* 88

Travel.

MAUNDEVILLE, Sir J. [1300 (?)–1371 (–2)].

VOGELS, Joh. Handschriftliche Untersuchgn üb. d. engl. Version Mandevilles [schl.-progr.] 4° *Crefeld* 91

XXVIII. Romance Philology and Literature.

256. ROMANCE PHILOLOGY: GENERALLY.

Bibliography.

School-Programmes, Dissertations and Habilitationsschriften.

VARNHAGEN, Herm. System. Verzeichniss d. Programmabhandlungen, Dissertationen u. Habilitationsschriften a. d. Gebiete d. roman. u. engl. Philol., hrsg. Joh. Martin 4*m.* 8° Koch, *Lps.* [77] 93

Pp. 1-33 occupied w. General Philology, pp. 35-163 w. Romance, pp. 164-200 w. English, pp. 200-260 w. educat. liter. [*ut* D § 155]. German pubns. only.

Introduction. "Encyclopædia."

*GRÖBER, Prf. Gust. [ed.] Grundriss der romanischen Philologie [*ut* B.B. K § 256], 2 vols. r 8° Trübner, *Strassb.* 88; 93 *in prg.*

A very compreh. and import. wk., the Romance counterpart of PAUL'S *Grundriss d. German. Philol.* [*ut* K § 225]. Vol. I., 13 maps and 4 pl. 14*m.*; vol. II. (i.) 1. 4*m.*, 2. 2*m.*80; (ii.) 1. 2*m.*, 2. 2*m.*

(I.) Teil i. *Gesch. d. rom. Philol.* .... G. GRÖBER
Aufgabe u. Gliederung .... GRÖBER
" ii. *Quellen: Schriftliche* .... W. SCHUM
" *Mündliche* .... GRÖBER
Methodik u. Aufgaben .... GRÖBER + A. TOBLER
" iii. *Roman. Sprachwissenschaft:*
(A) *Vor-rom. Volkssprachen.*
Kelt. (WINDISCH), *Bask. u. Iber.* (G. GERLAND), *Ital.* (W. DEECKE), *Lat.* (W. MEYER), *Romanen u. Germanen* (F. KLUGE), *Arab. Spr. in rom. Ländern* (Chr. SEYBOLD), *Nicht-lat. Elem. i. Rumän.* (M. GASTER).
(B) *Die romanischen Sprachen.*
Einteilg. u. Gesch. (GRÖBER), *Rumän.* (H. TIKTIN), *Rätorom.* (TH. GARTNER), *Italien.* (F. d'OVIDIO + W. MEYER), *Frz. u. Provenz.* (H. SUCHIER), *Catal.* (A. MOREL-FATIO), *Span.* (Gottf. BAIST), *Portug.* (J. CORNU), *Latein. Elem. im Alban.* (G. MEYER).
(II.) i. *Roman. Verslehre* .... E. STENGEL
Literaturgesch. d. rom. Völker:
Latein. (GRÖBER), *Provenc.* (A. STIMMING), *Catal.* (MOREL-FATIO), *Portug.* (C. MICHAËLIS DE VASCONCELLOS + Theoph. BRAGA), *Span.* (BAIST). In prep. are *Ital.* (T. CASINI), *Rumän.* (GASTER), *Rätorom.* (C. DE CURTIUS).
(II.) ii. *Gesch. d. rom. Völker* (H. BRESSLAU + M. PHILIPPSON), *Culturgesch.* (A. SCHULTZ), *Kunstgesch.: Musik* (G. JAKOBSTHAL), *Bild. Künste* (not annod. yet); *Die Wissenschaften i. d. rom. Ländern* (W. WINDELBAND).

STORM, Joh. —*article* Romance Languages, *in* Encyclo. Brit., 9th edn., vol. xx., *ut* B.B. K § 1.

History of the Romance Languages.

ISOLA, Prf. Hippolyt. Storia delle Lingue e Letterature Romanze, pt. iii. fasc. 1 8° *Bologna* 91 *in prg.*

The first two pts. are incl. in the 3rd vol. of the *Storie Nerbonesi*, pub. in the *Collezione d'Opere Inedite e Rare* [*ut* B.B. K § 257]. Will deal w. all the Romance langs. and literatures.

RYDBERG, Gust. Le Développement de *facere* dans les Langues romanes 10*fr.* 8° Welter, *Paris* 93

Relation of Romance to Latin.

v. REINHARDSTÖTTNER, Dr. Carl—*in his* Grammatik d. portug. Sprache [based on Lat. and Rom. research], *ut* B.B. K § 262.
SKUTSCH, F. Forschungen zur latein. Gramm. u. Metrik, vol. i.—*ut* K § 215, *s.v.* Plautus.

Grammar.

*MEYER-LÜBKE, Wilh. Grammatik d. roman. Sprachen, vol. i. [Phonol.] 16*m.*, ii. [Accid.] pt. 1 11*m.*, 2, 8*m.* 8° Reisland, *Lps.* 89; 93; 94
" " " trad. Eug. Rabiet, *s.t.* Gramm. d. Langues romanes, vol. i. [Phon.], pt. 1 [Vowels], 2 [Conson.] *together* 20*fr.* r 8° Welter, *Paris* 89; 90

Adjectives.

NYROP, K. Adjecktivernes kønsbøjning in de romanska Sprog 8° *Copenhagen* 86

Prefixes.

BUCHEGGER, Herm. Ueber d. Präfixe in d. roman. Sprachen [diss. inaug.] 8° Bühl, *Heidelbg.* 90

Verb.

VISING, Joh. Die realen Tempora d. Vergangenht. i. Frz. u. übrig. rom. Sprachen, pt. i. 7*m.*40 8° Henninger, *Heilbr.* (Tbnr., *Strsb.*) 88

Latin, Portuguese, Spanish, Italian. Forms pt. 3 of vol. vi. of *Französische Studien*.

Etymology: *Dictionary.*

DIEZ, F. Etymologisches Wörterbuch d. romanischen Sprachen—*ut* B.B. K § 256.
Jarník, Joh. Urb. Neuer vollst. Index zu Diez' Etym. Wörterb. [*for former* Index *v.* B.B. K § 256] 8*m.* 8° Henninger, *Heilbr.* (Tbnr., *Strassb.*) 89
KÖRTING, Gust. Lateinisch-Romanisches Wörterbuch, 2 vols. [now complete] 22*m.* r 8° Schöningh, *Paderborn* 91

Place-Names.

GÖTZINGER, Wilh. Die romanischen Ortsnamen d. Kantons St. Gallen 2*m.*40 8° Huber, *St. Gallen* 91
v. GRIENBERGER, Theod. Ueber romanische Ortsnamen in Salzburg 80*pf.* 12° Dieter, *Salzburg* 86

Metrics.

BECKER, Pp. Aug. Ueber den Ursprung der romanischen Versmaase [Habil.-Schr.] 1*m.*20 8° Trübner, *Strassbg.* 90
HENRY, Prf. Vict. Contrib. à l'Étude des Origines du Décasyllable roman [clear] 8° *Paris* 86
MASING, Woldem. Ueber Ursprung und Verbreitung des Reims [dissert.] 8° *Dorpat* 66
SKUTSCH, F. Forschungen zur latein. Grammatik und Metrik—*ut* K § 215, *s.v.* Plautus.
STENGEL, E. Romanische Verslehre—*in* Gröber's Grundriss, *ut supra*.

Phonology —*vide supra, sub voc.* Grammar (MEYER-LÜDKE, vol. i.).

History and Biography of the Study.

SĂINEANŬ, Lazăr — Istoria filologicĭ române: studiĭ critice — 4/- 8° Socecŭ, *Bucharest* 92

Sixteenth Century.

PASQUIER, Etienne [1529–1615].
Scharschmidt, Em. — Estienne Pasquiers Thätigkeit a. d. Gebiete d. frz. Sprachgesch. [prg.] — 1*m.* 4° *Bautzen* 92

Nineteenth Century.

DARMESTETER, Prf. Arsène [1846–1888].
Darmesteter, Prf. James—*biograph. essay pref. to his* Arsène Darmesteter: reliques scientifiques, *ut* K § 94.
DIEZ, Friedr. [1794–1876].
Breymann, Prf. Herm. — Friedrich Diez: sein Leben und Wirken: Festrede — 90*pf.* 8° Deichert, *Lpz.* 94
Ritter, E. — Le Centénaire de Diez — 2*m.* 8° Georg, *Basle* 94

Collected Essays.

DARMESTETER, Prf. Arsène — Reliques Scientifiques, ed. Prf. James Darmesteter [brother]—*ut* K § 94.
DIEZ, Friedr. — Diez-Reliquien, a. Anlass d. 100. Geburtstages, hrsg. Edm. Stengel [Ausg. u. Abhgn.] 1*m.*20 8° Elwert, *Marburg* 94
Etudes Romanes dédiées à Gaston Paris [29 Dec. '90] par ses Elèves franç., *etc.* — 20*fr.* 8° Bouillon, *Paris* 91
Münster Univ. — Dissertationes [mostly on Romance and English subjects] 8° *Münster*
WOLF, Ferd. — Kleinere Schriften, zusammengest. Edm. Stengel; port. [Ausgaben u. Abhgn.] 9*m.* 8° Elwert, *Marburg* 90

History of Literature in Switzerland.

ROSSEL, Virgile — Histoire littéraire de la Suisse romande, 2 vols. — 15*fr.* 8° Georg, *Geneva* 89; 91
From the earliest to the present times. Crowned by the *Académie Française.*

Magazines and Serials—*v. also* B.B. K § 256.

Annales du Midi: ed. A. Thomas — *Toulouse* 89 *in prg.*
Beiträge, Berliner, zur German. u. Roman. Philologie, hrsg. Dr. Em. Ebering: Roman. Abthg., no. i. 3*m.*60 8° Vogt, *Berlin* 94 *in prg.*
i. *Guiraut v. Bornelh, d. Meister d. Trobadors*, hrsg. A. KOLSEN, 3*m.*60 [*ut* K § 257]. For German Abtheilung *v.* K § 205.
" Münchener, zur romanischen u. englischen Philologie: hrsg. Prf. H. Breymann, pts. i.–iii. 8*m.*70 8° Deichert, *Lpz.* 90–92 *in prg.*
i. *Quellen d. 5 ersten Chester-Plays* [*ut* K § 82].. Heinr. UNGEMACH, 4*m.*50 90
ii. *Quellen, Vorbilder etc. a. Shelley* .. Rich. ACKERMANN, 1*m.*50 90
iii. *Figürl. Gebrauch d. Zahlen im Altfrz.* A. RAUSCHMAIER, 2*m.*70 92
v. *Sprache d. Philippe d. Beaumanoir* [*ut* K § 277].. A. G. ALBERT, 1*m.*50 93
vi. *Scarron's Jodelet u. s. span. Quelle* .... R. PETERS, 2*m.* 93
vii. *John Lyly and Euphuism* [*ut* K § 24] Clar. G. CHILD (Am.) 2*m.*40 94
*Jahresbericht, Krit., üb. d. Fortschritte d. roman. Philologie: hrsg. K. Vollmöller + R. Otto *ann.* [6 pts.] 16*m.* 1 8° Oldenburg, *Münich* 91 *sqq.*, *in prg.*
Revue de l'Enseignement des Langues Vivantes—*ut* K § 225.
Rivista di Filologia Romanza: ed. L. Manzoni + E. Monaci + E. Stengel, 8 pts. [= 2 vols.] 8° *Rome* 72–76 *not cont.*
Contin. as *Giornale di Filol. Rom.* 1878–83 [*ut* B.B. K § 256], and then as *Giornale storico della Letteratura ital.* [*ut* K § 257].

Series of Texts.

Ausgaben u. Abhandlungen a. d. Gebiete d. roman. Philol., hrsg. E. Stengel, pts. lxxx.–xci. *v.p.* 8° Elwert, *Marburg* 88–94 *in prg.*
New Vols.:—
lxxx. WAHLE, H. *Die Pharsale d. Nic. v. Verona* 3*m.* 88
lxxxi. BOUNIN, G. *La Soltane* [tragedy, 1641] .... STENGEL + J. VENEMA, 1*m.*80 88
lxxxii. DREYLING, G. *Verbleing. in Karlsepos* [*ut* K § 277] .. 4*m.* 88
lxxxiii. HUON DE BORDEAUX *Drei Fortsetzn.* [*ut* K § 277].. 4*m.*50 89
lxxxiv. GALIENS *Li Restorés* .... STENGEL, 14*m.* 90
lxxxv. MONTCHRESTIENS *Sophonisbe* .... Ludw. FRIES, 4*m.*40 89
lxxxvi. STICHEL, K. *Altprov. Verbum* [*ut* K § 265] 2*m.*40 90
lxxxvii. WOLF, F. *Kleiner Schriften* [*ut* K § 236].. STENGEL, 9*m.* 90
lxxxviii. WITTHÖFT, F. *Sirventes Joglaresc* 2*m.*40 90
Ein Blick auf d. altfrz. Spielmannsleben.
lxxxix. MEYER, Fritz *Die Stände, etc.* [*ut* K 277] 3*m.*50 91
xc. SCHÄFER, Herm. *HSS. d. Huon d. Bord.* [*ut* K § 277].. 2*m.*80 91
xci. STENGEL, Edm. [ed.] *Diez-Reliquien* [*ut supra*] 1*m.*20 94
Neueren Sprachen, Die: —*ut* K § 225.
Romanische Bibliothek: hrs. Prf. Wendelin Foerster — 8° Niemeyer, *Halle* 89–93 *in prg.*
i. CHRESTIEN D. TROIES, *Cligés* [*ut* K § 277].. W. FOERSTER, 4*m.* 89
ii. *D. beiden Bücher d. Makkabäer* [13 cent.].. Ew. GÖRLICH, 4*m.* 89
iii. *Altprovenz. Marienklage* [*ut* K § 267] .. W. MUSHACKE, 2*m.* 90
iv. *Wistasse le Moine* [*ut* K § 277] .... W. FOERSTER + Joh. TROST, 3*m.* 91
v. CHRESTIAN V. TROYES, *Yvain* [*ut* K § 277] W. FOERSTER, 4*m.* 91
vi. *Adamsspiel* [*ut* K § 275] .... Karl GRASS, 4*m.* 91
vii. WALTER V. ARRAS *Ille u. Galeron* [*ut* K § 277] .. W. FOERSTER, 7*m.*60 91
viii. BERTRAND V. BORN *Oeuvres* [*ut* K § 267] Alb. STIMMING, 4*m.* 92
ix. *Don Baltasar de Carvajal* [17 cent. comedy].... Ant. RESTORI, 2*m.*80 93
x. *Altbergamaskische Sprachdenkmäler* [9–15 cent.].. J. E. LORCK, 5*m.* 93
Société pour l'Etude des Langues Romanes: *Publications* — 8° *Montpellier* (Maisonneuve, *Paris*) 76–88 *in prg.*
i. MILÁ Y FONTANALS [ed.] *Poètes Catalanes* [*ut* B.B. K § 264] 3*fr.*50 76
ii. LESPY, V. *Proverbes d. Pays Béarn* [*ut* B.B. B § 16] 5*fr.* 76
iii. NOULET, J. B. [ed.] *Ordenansas et Coustum. del Libre Blanc* 7*fr.* 78
iv. DONIOL, Hi. *Patois de la Basse Auvergne* [*ut* B.B. K § 266] 6*fr.* 77
v. AZAIS, G. *Idiomes d. Midi d. Frce.*, 3 v. [*ut* B.B. K § 266] 48*fr.* 77–81
vi. NOULET, J. B. [ed.] *Las Nonpareilhas Receptas* 6*fr.* 80
vii. TURPIN [8 cent.] *Karol. Magn. et Rothol.*, ed. Castets [*ut* B.B. K § 277] 4*fr.* 80
viii. THÉNARD [ed.] *Mém. d'un Bourgeois d. Marseille* 5*fr.* 81
ix. DURANTE *Il Fiore*, ed. Fréd. Castets 9*fr.* 81
A 13th cent. Ital. poem, in 232 sonnets, in imit. of *Roman d. l. Rose.*
x. MISTRAL, Fr. [19 cent.] *Mireio*, trad. en prose Dauph. Rivière 6*fr.* [*ut* K § 267] 81
xi. CONSTANS, L. *Le Livre de l'Epervier* 10*fr.* 82
xii. AZAIS, J. *Verses Beziéirencs* 5*fr.*50 82
xiii. NOULET + CHABANEAU [eds.] *Deux MSS. Prov.* [*ut* K § 267] 15*fr.* 88
xiv. RENAUT [12 cent.] *Roman de Galerent* [*ut* K § 277] 12*fr.* 88

257. MODERN ITALIAN PHILOLOGY (a): GRAMMAR, ETC.

Generally.

D'OVIDIO + MEYER, Pr. W. — Die italien. Sprache u. ihre Mundarten—*in* Gröber's Grundriss, *ut* K § 256.

History of the Language.

SENES, G. — Evoluzione del Linguaggio, Origine della Ling. ital., *etc.* — 8° *Rome* 87
TORQUATI, Girol. — Origine della Lingua italiana — 8° ,, 86

Grammar.

COMPAGNONI, S. — Grammatica scientifica ossia l. Teorica d. ling. ital. — 2l.50 8° Trevisini, *Milan* 93
DANTE, Alighieri [1265–1321] De Vulgari Eloquio: photograph. facs. — 7fr. 8° Magnien, *Grenoble* 92
A facs. of the MS. in Grenoble Pub. Libr., fr. wh. the *editio princeps* was prin. by CORBINELLI in 1577.
" " — De Vulgari Eloquentiá, tr. A. G. Ferrers Howell; w. notes — 3/6 c 8° Paul 90
FORNACIARI, R. — Grammatica Storica della Lingua italiana, pt. i. [all pub.] 8° *Turin* 72

Inflection.

BOSSOLA, Amilc. — La Flessione verbale nella Lingua ital. [comparative] 2l. 8° Paravia, *Turin* 89

Nouns.

BARMEYER, E. — Die Nominalcomposition im Italienischen [school-programme] 8° *Lüneberg* 86

Pronouns.

MENGER, L. E. — Histor. Developmt. of Possessive Pronouns in Italian [Mod. Lang. Assoc., viii. 2] 8° *Baltimore* 93

Syntax.

DAVID, Rud. — Ueber die Syntax des Italienischen im Trecento [dissert.] 8° *Strassburg* 86

Negation.

ZATELLI, D. — De l'Emploi de la Négation en frç. et en ital.—*ut* K § 269.

Verbs: Participles.

SCHÜRMANN, Joh. — Entstehg. u. Verbreitg. d. sogen. "Verkürzt. Partic." im Ital. [dissert.] 8° *Strassburg* 91

Etymology.

SACERDOTE, Gust. — Has a crit. edn. of the 900 Ital. word. given by NATHAN BEN YEHIEL (11 cent.) in his *Aruch* [*ut* A § 12] in prep.

Dictionaries.

*Academia della Crusca — Vocabolario novo della Lingua italiana, vols. vi.–vii. (3 pts.) — r 8° Cellini, *Florence* 90–93 *in prg.*
FANFANI, P. — Nuovissimo Vocabolario della Lingua italiana — 8° *Milan* [ ] 86
JÄSCHKE, Rich. — English-Italian Conversation Dictionary [useful for travellers] 2/6 16° Nutt 94
*PETRÒCCHI, P. — Nòvo Dizionàrio universale d. Lingua ital., pts. xvi.–xli. [last] ea. 1l. 8° Treves, *Milan* 87–90
Includes also, in a separate section, Old-Italian.

Names.

MANNUCCI, Vicenzio — Teorica dei nomi della lingua italiana — *Florence* 58

Metrics.

DA CAMINO, Vit. — La Metrica comparata latina-italiana e le odi Barb. d. Carducci — 6l. 8° Paravia, *Turin* 91
FERRARI, Dem. — La Storia del Sonetto ital. — *Modena* 87
FRACCAROLI, Gius. — D'una Teoria razionale di Metrica italiana — *Turin* 86
GUARNERIO, Pier En. — Manuale di Versificazione italiana — 2l.50 16° Vallardi, *Milan* 93
MIGNINI, Girol. — Saggio di Gram. stor. ital., pt. i. I Versi ital. in Metr. lat. — *Perugia* 86
MURARI, Rocco — Ritmica e Metrica razionale italiana — 16° Hoepli, *Milan* 91
SOLERTI, Ang. — Manuale di Metrica classica ital. ad. accento Ritmico — *Turin* 86

Orthography. Pronunciation.

CAIVANO, Em. — Ortografia italiana — 3l. 16° Artero, *Rome* 89
GELMETTI, L. — Riforma ortogr. contre nuovi Segni alfab. p. l. buona Pron. ital. — *Milan* 86
ZANARDELLI, Prf. Tito — Traité comparé de Prononciation italienne — 4fr. 8° Mayolez, *Brussels* 87

Palæography: *Serial.*

Archivio Palæografico Italiano: vol. i., pts. 1–6 — Hoepli, *Milan, in prg.*

Phonology.

STOPPATO, Lor. — Fonologia Italiana [elementary] 12° *Milan* 86
WALTER, E. L. — Rhotacism in the Old Ital. Langs. and the Exceptions [diss.] 8° Fock, *Lps.* 77

Style: *Synonyms.*

ORLANDO, Gen. — Piccolo Dizionario dei Sinonimi italiani — 2l.50 16° Paravia, *Turin* 92
ZECCHINI, S. B. — Dizionario delle Frasi sinonime della Ling. ital. — 5l. 16° Unione Typ.-Ed., *Turin* 91

Chrestomathies.

BÜHLER + MEYER, G. W. [eds.] Italienische Chrestomathie, 2 vols. [chiefly modern specimens] ea. 2m.40 8° Schulthess, *Zürich* 87

*D'ANCONA + BACCI, A. O. [eds.] Manuale della letteratura italiana, 4 vols. *Florence* [92] 93 *in prg.*

A most admirable book.

MONACI, Ern. [ed.] Crestomazia ital. dei primi secoli, pt. i. 5/. 8° Lapi, *Castello* 89

ULRICH, J. [ed.] Altitalienisches Lesebuch des xiii. Jahrhunderts 2m.80 8° Niemeyer, *Halle* 86

Magazines.

Giornale storico della Letteratura italiana 83 *sqq., in prg.*

A continuation of the *Giornali di Filol. Rom.* [1873-83; *ut* K § 256], itself a contin. of the *Rivista di Filol. Rom.* [1872-76; *ut ib.*]

L'Alighieri [devoted to study of Dante] *in prg.*

Propugnatore, Il *in prg.*

Rivista critica della Letteratura italiana *in prg.*

Series.

Bibliotechnica Grassoccia, Capricci e Curiosità litter. ined., racc. F. Orlando + E. Baccini, 2 vols. 8° *Florence* 86

Bibliothek, Italienische: hrsg. J. Ulrich; w. Introd. and notes, vols. i.-ii. 6m.80 8° Renger, *Lpz.* 90; 91 *in prg.*

Vol. i. *Aeltere Novellen*, 2m.80; ii. *Ausgew. Novellen* SACCHETTIS, GIOVANNIS u. SERCAMBIS, 4m. To comprise 10 vols., forming a companion to A. GASPARY'S *Geschichte d. ital. Litter.*, 2 vols. 21m. 8° Oppenheim, *Berlin* (now Trübner, *Strassb.*) '85, '88; [Ital. tr. by N. ZINGARELLI, 2 vols., 8° *Turin* '87, '89]

JARRO, [ed.] Teatro ital. antico: commedie rivedute e corr. sugli ant. Testi, vol. i. 8° *Florence* 88

Conts. (1) Card. B. DOVIZZI DI BIBBIENA, *La Calandria*; (2) Nicc. MACHIAVELLI, *La Mandragola e la Clizia*; (3) LORENZO DE' MEDICI, *L'Aridosia*; (4) Pietro ARETINO, *Lo Ipocrito*.

Opere nova nella quale si contengono bellissime Historie, Contrasti, Lamenti e Frottole *etc.*, edd. S. Morpugo + A. Rödiger + A. Zenatti 8° *Florence* 86

Sammlung Ital. Neudrucke: vol. i. Strambotti d. Frcso. Pulci, ed. A. Zenatti 8° ,, 87

258. MODERN ITALIAN PHILOLOGY (b): DIALECTS.

Generally: *Magazine.*

Archivio Glottologico Italiano, ed. Prf. G. J. Ascoli [*ut* B.B. K § 258]: Series of Supplements, pt. i. 8° Loescher, *Turin* 92 *in prg.*

Abruzzi

—*for* Folklore *v.* B § 17.

Bergamo.

ZERBINI, Elia Note storiche sul Dialetto bergamasco 8° *Bergamo* 86

Calabria.

SCERBO Sul Dialetto calabro 8° *Florence* 86

Lombardy.

Specimen of Literature.

Margarethen-Legende, Eine altlombardische: hrsg. B. Wiese 4m.50 8° Niemeyer, *Halle* 90

Mantua.

ARRIVABENE, Ferd. Vocabolario italiano-mantovano [110 pp.] 8° Manuzio, *Mantova* 92

,, ,, Vocabolario mantovano-italiano [902 pp.] 8° ,, ,, ?-92

Modena.

GALVANI, G. Saggio di un Glossario modenese c 8° *Modena* 68

MARANESI, Enn. Vocabolario modenese-italiano, pts. i.-cvi. ea. 10c. 4° Soliani, *Modena* 92-94 *in prg.*

Monferrino.

FERRARO, Gius. Glossario Monferrino 2/.50 8° Loescher, *Turin* [ ] 89

Parma.

PARISET, Car. Vocabolario parmigiano italiano, 18 pts. ea. 50c. 16° Ferrari, *Parma* ?-92

Piedmont

—*for* Folklore *v.* B § 17.

GAVUZZI, Gius. Vocabolario Piemontese-Italiano 5/. 16° Roux, *Turin* 91

Riviera

—*for* Folklore *v.* B § 17.

Sardinia

—*for* Folklore *v.* B § 17.

MARCIALIS, Efisio Piccolo Vocabolario sardo-italiano [pp. 43] 8° Dessì, *Cagliari* 92

ROLLA, Pietro Alcune Etimologie dei Dialetti sardi [pp 80] 8° Tip. Commerc. *Cagliari* 93

ROMANI, Dr. Fed. Sardismi [on errors of orthogr., of vocabs., gram., *etc.*] *Sassari* 86

Dettori, Giac. I Sardismi del Dott. F. Romani ,, 86

Sicily.

BEHRING, W. — Sicilianische Untersuchungen, pt. i. [school-programme] 8° Fock, *Lpz.* 82

DE GREGORIA, Giac. — Appunti di Fonologia Siciliana, pt. i. [Suoni voc., spir. e nasali] *Palermo* 86

SCHNEEGANS, Heinr. — Laute u. Lautentwickelung des sicilianischen Dialectes [good] 4*m.* 8° Trübner, *Strassbg.* 88

Specimen of Literature.

Libro dei Vizii e delle Vertù [14 cent.]: ed. G. de Gregorio [hitherto inedited] 8*fr.* 8° Bouillon, *Paris* 93

Trieste.

KOSORITZ, Ern. — Dizionario Vocabolario del Dialetto triestino e d. ling. ital., 12 pts. 8° Kosovitz, *Trieste* 89

MAINATI — Avanzi dell' antico Dialetto triestine, ed. Em. Schatzmayr; w. Ital. tr. 2*l.*50 8° Balestra, *Trieste* [28] 91

Tuscany: *Specimen of Literature—for* Folklore *v.* B § 17.

GOLDSTAUB + WENDRINER, Max. Rich. [eds.] E Tosco-venezianischer Bestiarius—*ut* B.B. § 7.

Venice.

BOERIO, Gius. — Dizionario del Dialetto veneziano—*ut* B.B. K § 258.

Ninni, A. P. — Giunte e Correzioni al Dizion. d. Dial. ven. [di Boerio], 3 ser. 16° Longhi, *Venice* 89; 90; 90

CHIARELLI, Bonav. — Vocabolario del Dialetto veneto, pt. i. [chfly. Treviso] ea. 30*c.* 8° Tip. Lit. Sociale, *Treviso* 92 *in prg.*

LUZZATTO, Leo — I Dialetti moderni delle Città di Venezia e Padova, pt. i. 8° Tip. Co-op., *Padua* 92

Treviso.

NINNI, A. P. — Materiali p. un Vocab. della Ling. rusticana d. Treviso, 3 ser. 16° Longhi, *Venice* 91; 91; 92

„ I. — Appendice ai Materiali p. un Voc. d. Ling. rust. d. Treviso [pp. 114] 16° „ „ 93

259. ROUMANIAN (WALLACHIAN) PHILOLOGY AND LITERATURE.

Linguistic Ethnography.

BERGNER, Rud. — Rümanien: eine Darstellung des Landes und der Leute; map and 26 ill. 10*m.* 8° Kern, *Breslau* 87

DE ROSNY, L. — Les Populations Danubiennes; w. f° atlas of pl., *etc.* 150*fr.* 4° Maisonneuve, *Paris* 82-83
A handsome wk. on the ethnology, geography, social economy and literature of the Eastern Roumanians.

„ „ — Les Romains d' Orient: aperçu de l'ethnographie d. l. Roumanie; 12 ill. 5*fr.*50 18° Maisonneuve, *Paris* 85

WEIGAND, Dr. Gust. — Vlacho-Meglen: eine ethnograph.-philologische Untersuchung; 4 pl. 3*m.*60 8° Barth, *Lpz.* 92
Descrn. of visit to a small colony of Wallachs living in district of Mt. Pindus (south of Danube). Their lang. is treated by F. MIKLOSICH (in his *Beiträge z. Lautlehre d. rumän. Dialekte, ut* B.B. K § 259). Conts. a good deal of matter of philolog. interest, w. specs. of folklore, *etc.*

„ „ — Die Aromunen: eine ethnograph.-philolog. Untersuchung, vol. i.? ii. 8*m.* 8° Barth, *Lpz.* ?; 94

„ „ — *his* Olympo Walachen, *ut inf., conts. a valuable Intro. on the land and the people.*

History of the Study.

MANGIUCA, Sim. — Daco-romanische Sprach. u. Geschichtsforschung, pt. i. 3*m.* 8° *Oravicza* (Köhler, *Lps.*) 90

Philology. Grammar.

CIONCA, L. — Praktische Grammatik d. romän. Sprache [school.-bk] 2*m.* 8° Socecu, *Bucharest* [80] 92

CRASAN, Flor. — Notiunti de gram. aplicate la limba româneseă 8° *Bucharest* 82

LOVERA, Prf. Romeo — Grammatica della Lingua rumena [w. vocab. of spoken lang.] 1*l.*50 16° Hoepli, *Milan* 92

NĂADRDJE, Ivan — Gramatica limbei române 8° *Jassy* 84

TITKIN, H. — Gramatica rumînă pentru învă, tămintul secundar, pt. i. [Etymology] 2.80*l.* 8° Saraga, *Jassy* 92

„ „ — Die romanische Sprache—*in* Gröber's Grundriss, *ut* K § 256.

VIDAL, F. — Etude sur les Analogies linguist. du Roumain et du Provençal 8° *Aix-les-Chapelles* 85

WEIGAND, Gust. — Die Sprache der Olympo-Walachen [*v. supra*] 3*m.* 8° Barth, *Lps.* 88

Accidence.

GRUBER, E. — Studiu asupra genului elementelor latine in romănește 8° *Jassy* 84

Verbs.

BARCIANU, A. Drocu- — Teoria verbului, pt. i.; pt. ii. by Fratii Bescherelle 8° *Bucharest* 82; 83

BUMBACU, B. — Die Conjugation im Román. i. ihr. Verhältn. z. Latein. [progr.] 8° *Czernowitz* 84

Etymology: *Dictionaries.*

ALEXI, Theod. — Rumänisch-deutsches Wörterbuch 3*m.* 8° 94

ANTONESCOU, G. M. — Dictionnaire Frçs.-roumain et roumain-frç., 2 vols. 12° *Bucharest* (16*fr.* Maisonneuve, *Paris*) 84

SAINEANU, Lazar — Dictionar Romăno-German. [pp. xii., 429] 4*m.*80 8° Socecu, *Bucharest* 89

„ „ — Dictionar German.-Romăno [pp. xvi., 502] 4*m.*80 8° „ „ 90

Foreign Elements: Turkish.

GASTER, M. — Nicht-latein. Elemente im Rumänischen—*in* Gröber's Grundriss, *ut* K § 256.

HASDEU, B. Petriceicu — Sur les Eléments turcs dans la Langue roumaine 8° *Bucharest* 86

MIKLOSISCH, F. — *in his* Türk. Elemente i. d. südost- u. osteurop. Sprachen [Gk., Alban., Rouman., *etc.*].
Forms a *Nachtrag* to the *Denkschriften d. Wiener Akad.*

Chrestomathies.

*GASTER, Dr. M. [ed.] Chrestomathie Roumaine, 2 vols. 18*m.* 8° Brockhaus, *Lpz.* 91

An important wk., contg. extrs. fr. 300 Roum. wks. and nearly 100 MSS. and docums., incl. also the dialects of the Roumaniars in Moldavia and Wallachia, in Maced. and Istria, w. numerous specs. of folk-liter., tales, legends, songs, jests, *etc.*, fr. all provinces. Vol. i. conts. Introd. (w. Fch. tr. of it) giving a good outline of hist. of the liter., a Gram. of the lang., and Texts 1550–1710; vol. ii. Texts 1710–1830, a Dialectology and compreh. Roum. Fch. gloss. Dedicated to the King of Roumania.

STANLEY, H. [ed.] Rouman Anthology [anc. and mod. Texts and Engl. trs.] *o.p.* [*w.* 15/–] 8° Austin, *Hertfd.* 56

Metrics. Style.

RUDOW, C. Fr. W. Verslehre u. Stil d. rumänischen Volkslieder [diss.; of small value] 1*m.* 8° Fock, *Lpz.* 86

TEMPEA, J. Stilistica limbei române 8° *Hermanstadt* 76

Semasiology.

SAINEANU, Lazar Incerare asupra semasiologiei limbei române 8° *Bucharest* 87

Serial.

Arhiva Societatii Stiintifice si Literare din Jasi [Record of Scient. and Lit. Soc. of Jassy] 8° *Jassy* 89–94 *in prg.*

Dialects.

PETRESCU VANGHELIU Mostre de Dialectul Macedo-Roman, pts. i.–ii. 8° *Bucharest* ? ; 82

History of Literature.

Codicele române anotate: ed. and anot. A. Stern *Bucharest* [ ] 90 *in prg.*

GASTER, M. Die rumänische Litteratur—*in* Gröber's Grundriss, *ut* K § 256.

LUPUL-ANTONESCUL, A. Veacula xvi. limba şi lit. Romànistorŭ 8° *Bucharest* 90

NĂDEDJE, Ivan Istorica limbeĭ si literatureĭ romane *Jassy* 86

PHILIPPIDE, A. Introducere in istoria limbeĭ şi literatureĭ Romîne " " 88

RUDOW, C. Fr. W. Geschichte d. rumän. Schrifttums, hrsg. J. Negruzzi + G. Bogdan 4*m.* 8° Rudow, *Wernigerode* [ ] 92

Specimens of Literature—*for* Folklore *v.* B § 18.

Bible: Codicele Veronet. cu un Vocab., ed. Gr. Cretu + G. Sbiera 8° *Bucharest* 86

Hiob: ein oberengadin. Drama aus d. 17ten Jahrh., hrsg. E. A. Kofmel [w. Introd. and gloss.] 2*m.* 8° *Solothurn* 89

Physiologus, Il rumeno edito e illustr. da M. Gaster—*in* Archiv. Glott., vol. x. [*ut* B.B. K § 258].

Psaltirea in Versuri intocmita de Dosofteiu Mitrop. Moldav. 1671–86, ed. J. Bianu 8° *Bucharest* 87

URECHI, Grégoire Chronique de Moldavie, ed. Em. Picot, 5 pts. [École Langs. Or. Viv.] 25*fr.* 8° Leroux, *Paris* 78

A history of Moldavia from middle of 14th cent. to 1534, in Slavonic characters, w. French tr..

260. RHÆTO-ROMANIAN PHILOLOGY AND LITERATURE.

Generally.

GARTNER, Th. Die räteromanischen Mundarten—*in* Gröber's Grundriss, *ut* K § 256.

Societad Rhaeto-Romanscha: Annales *ann. c.* 7/– 8° Rich, *Chur* 86 *sqq.*, *in prg.*

Grammar.

MUOTH, G. C. Grammatica romontscha-tudesga 2/6 8° Rich, *Chur* 90

History of the Language.

MORF, H. Die sprachlichen Einheitsbestrebgn. in d. rät. Schweiz 80*pf.* 8° Wyss, *Berne* 87

SAINEANU, Lazăr Incercare asupră semasiologieĭ Limbei române 8° Akad. Druck., *Bucharest* 87

Etymology.

Dictionary: Engadin.

PALLIOPPI, Zacc. + Em. Dizionari des Idioms Romauntschs d'Engadin' ota e bassa, pts. i.–iii. ea. 5*m.* 8° *Samedan* (Geering, *Basle*) 93 ; 94 ; 94 *in prg.*

The MS. was commenced by late J. PALLIOPPI, father of the present authors, who have been assisted by many Romansch students. The wk. is bg. pub. at expense of Dept. of Interior of Council of Swiss Confedn.

Names.

SCHNELLER, Chrn. Tirolische Namenforschungen; map [personal and place-names] 8*m.* 8° Wagner, *Innsbruck* 90

STEUB, Ludw. Zur Namen- und Landeskunde der deutschen Alpen 2*m.*80 8° Beck, *Nördlingen* 85

UMLAUFT, Friedr. Geographisches Namenbuch von Oesterreich-Ungarn 4*m.* 8° Hölder, *Vienna* 86

Chrestomathy.

DECURTINS, C. [ed.] Rätoromanische Chrestomathie, vol. i., pt. 2 [Eighteenth Century] 9*m.* 8° Junge, *Erlangen* 94

History of Literature.

DECURTINS, C. Die rätoromanische Litteratur—*in* Gröber's Grundriss, *ut* K § 256.

Specimens of Literature.

CARATSCH, S. [ed.] Poesias umoristicas e populares in Romauntsch d'Engadin' ota *Turin* [ ] 81

Susanna [Upper-Engad. drama; 16 cent.]: hrsg. Jak. Ulrich; w. notes, gramm. and gloss. 3*m.* 8° Huber, *Frauenfeld* 87

WIEZEL, Gioerin Veltlinerkrieg, hrsg. Dr. Gottfr. Hartmann [ed. fr. 2 MSS.] 1*m.*50 8° Trübner, *Strassburg* 87

Proverbs —*v.* B § 4 (BÜHLER).

231. SPANISH PHILOLOGY.

Bibliography.

DE LA VIÑAZA, Conde — Biblioteca histórica de la filologia castellana [pp. xxxv., 1112] 19.50*pes.* 4° Murillo, *Madrid* 93

Manuscripts.

Bibl. Natl., Paris: Catalogues des Manuscrits espagnols et portug., 2 pts. [by Alf. Morel-Fatio] 4° Didot, *Paris* 81; 92
British Museum: Catalogue of the Spanish MSS., vol. iv. [by Pascual de Gayangos] 12/- 8° British Museum 93

General Philology.

BAIST, G. — Die spanische Sprache—*in* Gröber's Grundriss, *ut* K § 256.

History of the Language.

HEFFERICH + DE CLERMONT Aperçu de l'hist. d. Langues néo-latines en Espagne *o.p.* 8° *Madrid* 57

Grammar.

BÉASE — Gramátiqa de la Aqademia Española 8° *Madrid* 80
BELLO, Andr. — Gramática de la lengua Castellana, ed. R. J. Cuervo 8° Roger, *Paris* [8-] 91
CLARKE, H. Butler — Spanish Grammar: Accidence and Syntax [Parallel Grammar Ser.] 16° 4/6 Sonnenschein / $1.25 Macmillan, *N.Y.* 93
DÍAZ-RUBIÓ Y CARMENA, M.M. Primera Gramática española, 2 vols. 16*pes.* 4° Bailly-Ballière, *Madrid* [ ] 87
" " Complemento al Estudio de la Gramática española 9*pes.* 4° Saenz de Jubera, *Madrid* 92
HOVERMANN, F. — Grammatik der spanischen Sprache [w. Reader] 4*m.*50 8° Heinsius, *Bremen* 86
RIVODÓ, Baldomero — Entretenimientos gramaticales, vols. i.-vi. 8° Garnier, *Paris* 90-93

A colln. of essays on various points of Castilian idiom.

YBARRA, Prf. Alejandro — Practical Method for Learning Spanish 12° $1.00 Heath, *Boston* / 6/- Isbister [84] 9-

Accidence.

KELLER, A. — Historische Formenlehre der spanischen Sprache 2*m.* 8° Keller, *Murrhardt* 94

Verb.

BELLO, Andr. — Análisis ideológ. d. l. Tiempos d. l. Conjug. castellana 8° *Madrid* 83

Etymology: *Dictionaries.*

Accademia Española: Diccionario de la Lengua castellana—*ut* B.B. K § 261.
DE VALBUENA, Ant. — Fe de Erratas del Nuevo Diccionario de la Academia, vols. i.-iii. ea. 3.50*pes.* 8° Cruzado, *Madrid* 91

A bitter criticism of the members of the Span. Academy and their Dictionary.

Diccionario Novísimo de la Lengua castellana [pp. 1455; 3 cols.] 4° Garnier, *Paris* 90
Juarraes Bombasnn, Lucia — Novela histórica ó historia novelexica [criticism of Acad. dict.] 8° *Madrid* 86
DE OCHOA, Carlos [ed.] — Diccionario Novísimo de la Lengua castellana [1734 pp.] 4° Bouret, " 92
RIVODÓ, Baldomero — Voces nuevas en l. Leng. castell.: glosario d. voces, frases, *etc.* 8° Garnier, " [ ] 89
SIMONET, F. X. — Glosario de Voces Ibéricas y Lat. us. entre l. Mozarabes 8° *Madrid* 89
VÉLEZ DE ARAGÓN — Diccionario general de la Lengua castell. [w. the new orthogr.] " 88
VERA Y GONZÁLEZ — Diccion. enciclopédico d. l. Leng. castell. [" "] " 88
Technical Terms —*v.* I § 1 (de LEON).

Foreign Elements.

GOLDSCHMIDT, Mor. — Zur Kritik d. altgerman. Elemente im Span. [diss. inaug.; good] 8° *Lingen* 87

Phrases, Popular Speech, etc.

CABALLERO Y RUBIO, Ram. Dicc. de Modismos, Voces pop. y Frases, vol. i. (1-2) ea. 75*pes.* 4° Herrero, *Madrid* 90-91 *in prg.*
RATO DE ARGÜELLES, Apol. Vocabulario de las Palabras y Frases Bables antig. 4.50*pes.* 4° Suarez, *Madrid* 91

Orthoepy.

ORTUZAR, Cam. — Diccion. Manual d. Locuciones viciosas y d. Correcciones [pp. 320] 16° Sales, *S. Benigno Canavese* 93

Phonology. Accentuation.

BAIST, G. — Die arab. Hauchlaute u. Gutturalen im Spanishen [Habil.-Schr.] 8° *Erlangen* 89
BENOT, Eduard — Examen crítico de la Acentuación castellana 4.50*pes.* 4° Hernando, *Madrid* 88

Orthography.

AGIUS, J. Jimeno — La Reforma de la Ortografia Qastellana [84 pp.] 12° Enriquez, *Paris* [92] 92

A reprint of two articles fr. "*La Rebista Qontemporanea*" (*Madrid*) 1891.

ESGRICHE I MIEG — Reforma de la Ortografia Qastellana 12° *Bilbao* [ ] 90
QABEZON, Qárlos — Notas sobre la Reforma Ortográfiqa [67 pp.] 12° Impr. Barselona, *Santiago* 92

Palæography.

MUÑOZ Y RIVERO, Jesús Paleografía popular : arte de leer l. docums. antig. castell. *Madrid* 87
,, ,, [ed.] Chrestomathia Palaeographica Scripturae Hispan. Veteris Specimina, pt. i. : Scriptura Chartarum 5.50*pes.* 8° Hernando, *Madrid* 90
,, ,, Idioma y escistura de Espana *Madrid* 88
* ,, ,, Manual de paleografía española d. l. siglos xii. al xvii. ; 179 ill. ,, 81
,, ,, Nociones de las caracteres que distinguen los docums. anter. al siglo xviii. de las que son falso ó sospechosos ,, 81

Hispano-Gothic (Visigothic).

*EWALD + LOEWE, Paul/Gust. [eds.] Exempla Scripturae Visigothicae ; 40 tabb. 50*m.* f° Köster, *Heidelberg* 83
MUÑOZ Y RIVERO, Jesús Paleografía Visigoda : método para aprender á leer los códices y docs. españ. de las siglos v. al xii. *Madrid* 81

Chrestomathies.

CLARKE, H. Butler [ed.] First Spanish Reader and Writer [Parallel Grammar Ser.] 16° Sonnenschein; Macmillan, N.Y. 93
MENÉNDEZ Y PELAYO, Marc. [ed.] Antología d. Poetas líricos castellanos, vols. i.–v. ea. 3.50*pes.* 8° Hernando, *Madrid* ?–94
MICHAËLIS, C. [*afterw.* Mme. Vasconcellos ; ed.] Antologia Española [Colec. d. l. Autor. Españ.] 3*m.*50 s 8° Brockhaus, *Lps.* 75
RESTORI, Ant. [ed.] Antologia Spagnuola : le gesta del Cid, racc. e ordinate 6.50*pes.* 8° Hoepli, *Milan* 90

Old Spanish.

KELLER, Adf. [ed.] Altspanisches Lesebuch [w. grammar and glossary] 4*m.*50 8° Brockhaus, *Lps.* 90

Dialogues.

TOBRÁ Y FORNÉS, Prf. Ed. New Spanish-English Dialogues for Travellers and Students 2/- 12° Hachette 93

Dialects.

Aljamia [Spanish in Arabic characters].

DUIMOVICH, A. M. Poetas arábigo-almerienses : estudio histórico 8° *Almeria* 84
GIL + RIBERA + SÁNCHEZ [eds.] Colleción de Textos Aljamiados 8° *Zaragoza* 88

Aragon.

URIEL, Mig. Gomez Biblioteca antig. y nueva d. Escritores arag. de Latassa, 3 vols. 8° *Madrid* ?–86

Asturian.

CANELLA SECADES, Fermín. Estudias asturianos : cartafueyos d'Asturies *Oviedo* 86
Historical and typographical studies.
CAVEDA, José Poésias selectos en dial. astur. anot. y aum. F. Canella Secades *Oviedo* 87

Gallego.

BESADA, Aug. G. Historia crítica d. l. Liter. gallega : Edad antigua, v. i., pts. 1–2 [Bibl. Gallega viii., xi.] 8° *Corunna* 86 ; 87
DE LA IGLESIA, Ant. El Dialecto gallego : su antigüedad y su vida, 2 vols. [Bibl. Gallega iv., v.] 8° ,, 86

Old Castilian and Old Spanish.

DE MUGICA, Pedro Gramática del Castellano antiguo, pt. i. [Phonetics] 2*m.* 8° Heinrich, *Berl.* 91

Specimen.

El Misterio de los Reyes Magos : Abdruck der HS., hrsg. G. Baist 1*m.* 8° Deichert, *Lps.* 87
Hartmann, K. A. M. El Misterio de los Reyes Magos [Bautzen dissert. ; incl. also the text] 8° *Leipzig* 75
The oldest piece of Span. liter.—perhaps the earliest mystery-play in any language.

Spanish American : Dictionary.

LENTZNER, Dr. C. [ed.] Tesoro de Voces y Provincialismos Hispano-Americanos, v. i., pt. 1 [*ut inf.*] 3*m.* r 8° Karras, *Halle* 92

Chrestomathies. Anthologies.

MENÉNDEZ Y PELAYO, M. [ed.] Antología de Poetas hispano-americ., vols. i.–iii. ea. 11*pes.* 4° Murillo, *Madrid* 93 ; 93 ; 94
Vol. i. Mexico and Central America ; ii. Cuba, San Domingo, Porto Rico, Venezuela ; iii. Columbia, Ecuador, Peru, Bolivia.

Brazil.

Musa das Escolas : colleção d. poes. brazil. e portug. do sec. xix. 18° Mellier, *Paris* 91

Costa-Rica.

FERNÁNDEZ FERRAZ, Juan Nahuatlismos de Costa-Rica : ensayo lexicográfico 10.50*pes.* 4° Tip. Nac., *San José d. Costa-Rica* 92
GAGIN, C. Diccionario de Barbarismos y Provincialismos de Costa-Rica 14*pes.* 8° Suárez, *Madrid* 93

Peru.

DE ARONA, Juan Diccionario de Peruanismos 40/- 8° *Buenos Ayres* 84

River-Plate.

GRANADA, D. Diccionario Rioplatense, pt. i. [A–C] = pt. i. *of* Lentzner's Tesoro, *ut supra.*
Includes a tr. of a valuable essay, contrib. to *Mémoire* of Société de Linguistique of Paris by MASPÉRO, on the deviatns. of inhabitants of Buenos Ayres and Montevideo fr. pronunca. of the mother country.

Valencian.

ESCRIG Y MARTÍNEZ Diccionario Valenciano-Castellano [51] 87 *in prg.*
Issued by a syndicate of literary men under Constantin LLOMBART'S direction.

262. PORTUGUESE PHILOLOGY.

General Philology.

CORNU, J. Die portugesische Sprache—*in* Gröber's Grundriss, *ut* K § 256.

Manuscripts —*v.* K § 261.

Grammar.

GRAUERT, E. F. New Method for Learning the Portuguese Language [of small value] 5/– c 8° Hirschfeld 92

Verb.

OTTO, Rich. Der portugiesische Infinitiv bei Camões [*repr. fr.* Roman. Forsch.] 8° *Erlangen* 88

Etymology : *Dictionary.*

MICHAELIS, Dr. H. New Dictionary of Portuguese and English, 2 vols. [both parts.] 8° ea. 13*m*.50 *ppr.* Brockhaus, *Lpz.* / ea. 15/- *cl.* Simpkin 93

More compl. than VIEIRA (*ut* B.B. K § 260) and LACERDA (*ut ib.*), incl. many more technical terms; and therefore better for use of commercial men.

Dialects.

Beria.

LEITE DE VASCONCELLOS, J. Dialectos beirões 8° *Oporto* 84

Creolese.

SCHUCHHARDT, Prf. Hugo Kreolische Studien, pt. ix. [Malaioportug. v. Batavia u. Tugu] 4*m*.50 8° Tempsky, *Vienna* 91

Galician-Portuguese : Specimen of Literature.

EL SABIO, Alfonso Cantigas de Santa Maria, ed. Marqués de Valmar [*formerly* Leop. de Cueto], 2 vols. 4° *Madrid* 89

The best example of the Galician-Portuguese dialect.

Raiana.

LEITE DE VASCONCELLOS, J. Lingoas Raianas de Tras-os-Montes 8° *Oporto* 86

Serial.

Revista Lusitana : archiv. d. l. estud. philol. e ethnol., ed. J. Leite de Vasconcellos 87 *sqq.*, *in prg.*

Chrestomathy.

Parnaso Lusitano : poesias sel. d. auct. portug. antig. e modern., 6 vols. *o.p.* 16° *Paris* 26–34

History of Literature.

LOISEAU, Arth. Hist. de la Littér. Portugaise depuis ses Origines 4*fr.* 12° Thorin, *Paris* 86

Collections. Folklore, etc.

BRAGA, T., *etc.* [eds.] Fontes tradicionaes da litter. Portugueza, 13 vols. *o.p.* 8° *Oporto* 67

i. *Cancioneiro popular*
ii.–iii. *Cantos popul. do Brasil* ... coll. S. ROMERO, 2 v.
iv. *Cantos popul. do Archipel. açoriano*
v. *Contos popul. do Brasil* ... coll. S. ROMERO
vi.–vii. *Contos tradicionaes do povo portug.*, 2 vols.
viii. *Floresta de varias romances com forma liter. d. sec. 16 a 17*
ix. *Hist. da poesia popular portug.*
x.–xi. *O povo portug. nas seus costum., crenç. e trad.*, 2 v.
xii. *Romanceiro do Archipel. da Madeira*
xiii. *Romanceiro geral*

The vols. are no longer sold separ.

,, ,, [ed.] Cancioneiro portuguez da Vaticana 25/– r 8° *Lisbon* 78

COROLEU, Jos. [ed.] Documents HistóricHs Catalans del siglo xiv. 5.50*pes.* 4° *La Renaixensa, Barcelona* 89

Anuari de la Associació d'Excursions Catalana *Any* 81 *sqq.*

Papers and communications on Catalan history, archæology, folklore, *etc.*

DE BELL-LLOCH, M. [ed.] Llegendas Catalanas—*ut* B.B. B § 18.

Biblioteca Popular de la Associació d'Excursions Catalana, vols. i.–iii. *Barcelona* 84 ; 85 ; 86

i. *Lo Llamp y'ils temporals* ... D. CELS GOMIS
ii. *Cuentos populars catal.* ... Dr. D. Fr'co. d. S. MASPONS Y LABROS
iii. *Ethnologia de Blánes* ... D. Jos. CORTILS Y VIETA

Biblioteca dels Escons de Catalunya : ed. J. Colell, vols. i.–iii. *Vich* 80–81

i. *Cansons de Montserrat* ... Jacinto VERDAGUER
ii. *Llegenda de Montserrat* ... Jacinto VERDAGUER
iii. *Faules y Simils* ... J. COLELL

CARETA Y VIDAL, A. [ed.] Qüentos, Escenas de Costumes, Trads., Novelas, *etc.* *Barcelona* 78

Folklore Catalá vols. i.–iv. ,, ?–87

MASPONS Y LABRÓS, F. [ed.] Jochs de la Infancia ,, 74

,, ,, [ed.] Lo Rondallayre : cuentos populars catalans, 3 pts. 12° ,, ?–75

PELAY-BRIZ, Franc. [ed.] Cansons de la Terra, 5 vols.—*ut* B.B. B § 18.

,, ,, [ed.] Endevinallas pop. catalanas [w. Fch., Lith., Ital. and other variants] 8° *Barcelona* 74

UBACH Y VINYETA, Fr. [ed.] Romancer catalá histor., tradicion., y de costums ,, 77

Translations.

FASTENRATH, Joh. [tr.] Catalanische Troubadoure der Gegenwart : verdeutscht 8*m.* 8° Reissner, *Lpz.* 90

With a bibliography of Catalanian literature.

263. CATALANIAN PHILOLOGY.

General Philology.

MOREL-FATIO, A. Die catalanische Sprache—*in* Gröber's Grundriss, *ut* K § 256.

Grammar.

FALERA, Pomp. Ensayo de Gramática de Catalán moderno 3.50*pes.* 8° Massó y Casas, *Barcelona* 91
SALA, Bartomeu Gramática Catalana [pp. 84] 8° Aymerich, *San Martí* 89

Article.

MOREL-FATIO, A. Note sur l'Article *ipse* dans l. Dialectes catal.—*in* Mélanges Renier, *ut* K § 94.

Etymology: *Dictionaries.*

ESCRIG Y MARTÍNEZ, José [ed.] Diccionario Valenciano-Castell.: 3rd edn., pts. xix-xxvii, ea. 1.25*pes.* 4° Aguilar, *Valencia* [ ]-92 *in prg.*
MARCET CARBONELL, Mig. Vocabulario de Catalanismos 2.50*pes.* 8° Altés, *Barcelona* 87

Phonology.

OLLERICH, Carl Ueb. d. Vertretg. dentaler Consonanz durch *u* in Catal. [diss.] 8° *Bonn* 87

264. CATALANIAN LITERATURE.

History of Literature. Bibliography.

DENK, Dr. V. N. Otto Einführung in d. Gesch. d. altcatalan. Literatur 9*m.* 1 8° Poessl, *Munich* 93
Fr. earliest times to 18 cent. With specimens of the literature, bibliography, critical notes and a glossary.
FASTENRATH, Joh. —*in his* Catalanische Troubadoure der Gegenwart: verdeutscht, *ut infra.*
MILÁ Y FONTANALS, Man. Estudios sobre Hist., Leng. y Liter. d. Cataluña [= Obras, v. iii.] 9.50*pes.* 8° Impr. Barcelonesa 90
MOREL-FATIO, A. Die catalanische Litteratur—*in* Gröber's Grundriss, *ut* K § 256.
TODA, Ed. La Poesía catalana á Sardenya 2*pes.* Est. de Giró, *Barcelona* 88

Nineteenth Century.

DE MOLINS, Ant. Dicc. biogr. y bibliogr. de Escrit. y Artistas catal. d. 19 sigl., pts. xi.-xxxv. ea. 1.25*pes.* 4° *Barcelona* 91-94 *in prg.*

Drama.

*UBACH Y VINYETA, Francesch. Teatre Catalá: apuntaciones histór.-críticas 8° *Barcelona* 76

Individual Writers.

JAHUDA BONSENVOR [JAYME; 13-14 cent.] Libre de Paraules e Dits de Savis e Filosofs, ed. Gabriel Llabrés y Quintana [Proverbes de Salomo; Libre de Cato] 3.50*pes.* 8° Murillo, *Madrid* 89
METGE, Bernat [*d.* 1410(?)] Le Songe: ed. J. M. Guardia; w. Fch. Introd., notes and tr. 6*fr.* 16° Lemerre, *Paris* 89
A good edn. of the *Somni*, w. the first Fch. tr. yet made of it.
RUBIÓ Y ORS, Joaq. [1818-?] Lo Gayté del Llobregat; poésias: ed. Poliglota by Menendez y Pelayo 2 vols., ea. 7.50*pes.* 8° Jepús, *Barcelona* [41] 89
VERDAGUER, Jacinto La Atlántida: poem que obtingué 'l premi de la Diputació Provincial de Barcelona en las Jochs Florals de 1877 8° Jepús, *Barcelona* 78
" " " Catalan text, w. Fch. tr. Alb. Savine 4*fr.* 16° *Paris* 83
" " " Castil. tr. by J. M. de Despujol y de Dusay 8° *Barcelona* 78
" " " " " J. Diaz Carmona 8° *Madrid* 78
" " " French tr. by Justin Pépratx 3*fr.*50 16° Hachette, *Paris* [84] 87
" " " Provençal tr. by Jan Monne 8° *Montpelier* 88

265. PROVENÇAL (LANGUE D'OC) PHILOLOGY.

History of the Language. Historical Grammar.

GOTTSCHALK, A. Ueber die Sprache v. Provins im 13ten. Jahrhundert 1*m.*50 8° Hühn, *Cassel* 93
KOSCHWITZ, E. Grammaire historique de la Langue des Félibres 4*m.* 8° Abel, *Greifswald* 94
SUCHIER, H. Die frz. u. provenz. Spr. u. ihre Mundarten [w. 12 maps]—*in* Gröber's Grundriss, *ut* K § 256.
" " Le Français et le Provençal, trad. P. Monet [pp. xii., 224] 8° Bouillon, *Paris* 91
VIDAL, F. Étude sur les Analogies linguist. du Roumain et du Provençal—*ut* K § 259.

Adverb.

GENTSCH, Ed. Ueb. d. Formen d. Adverb. d. Gegenwart im Altprov. [dissert. inaug.] 8° *Marburg* 92

Inclination.

HENGESBACH, Jos. Beitrag z. Lehre v. d. Inclination im Provenzal. [Ausg. u. Abhgn.] 2*m.* 8° Elwert, *Marburg* 85

Negation.

KALEPKY, Theod. Von der Negation im Provenzalischen [schl.-progr.] 1*m.* 4° Gaertner, *Berlin* 91

K § 266

Prepositions.

KÖCHER, Edm. Beitrag zum Gebrauch d. Präposit. *de* im Provenzal. [dissert. inaug.] 1*m*.20 8° *Marburg* 88

Verb.

SCHMIDT, Otto Ueb. d. Endungen d. Präsens im Altprovenzalischen [dissert. inaug.] 8° Leske, *Darmstadt* 87

Etymology.

STICHEL, Karl Beiträge zur Lexicographie d. altprov. Verbums [Ausg. u. Abhdgn.] 2*m*.40 8° Elwert, *Marburg* 90

Dictionaries.

LEVY, Prf. Emil Provenzalisches Supplement-Wörterbuch, pts. i.-vi. ea. 4*m*. 8° Reisland, *Lpz.* 92-94 *in prg.*
To occupy 10 pts., supplying correctns. and additns. to RAYNOUARD'S *Lexique Roman.*

PIAT, L. Dictionnaire Frç.-Occitanien, vol. i. [A-H] [in 2 vols.] *compl. wk.* 24*fr.* 8° Hamelin, *Montpelier* 93
Gives the equivalents of Fch. words in all the Modern Langue d'Oc dialects [*ut* B.B. K § 265].

RAYNOUARD, F. J. M. Lexique Roman—*ut* B.B. K § 265.
Sternbeck, H. Unrichtige Wortaufstellgen. u. Wortdeutgn. in Raynouard [diss.] 2*m*. 8° Mayer & Müller, *Berl.* 87

Foreign Elements.

*MACKEL, Dr. Em. Die german. Elemente i. d. frz. u. provenz. Spr.—*ut* K § 270 [an excellent wk.]

Phonology.

WIECHMANN, E. Prov. geschlossenes *E* n. d. Grammatiken, Dichter u. neuprov. Mundarten 1*m*.60 8° Fock, *Lpz.* 91

Metrics.

OREANS, Karl Die *E*-Reime im Altprovenzalischen [*extr. fr.* Herrig's Archiv.] 8° *Brunswick* 83
PFUHL, Heinr. Untersuchgn. üb. d. Rondeaux u. Virelais [chfly. 14-15 cents.] [diss.] 8° *Königsberg* 87
PLEINES, Aug. Hiat und Elision im Altprovenzalischen [Ausg. u. Abhandgn.] 2*m*. 8° Elwert, *Marburg* 86

Serial.

Le Félibrige Latin : revue mensuelle, ed. M. Rogue Ferrier *Montpelier* 90 *in prg.*

238. PROVENÇAL DIALECTS (WITH SOME SPECIMENS OF LITERATURE).

Agenais : *Folk-tales* —*v.* B.B. B § 16.

Ariège.

DUCLAS, H. Histoire des Ariégeois, vol. i.: Les Poètes de l'Ariège 8° *Paris* 86

Dauphiné.

MONTEIR, Abbé L. Bibliographie des Dialectes dauphinois 1*fr*.50 8° *Valence* (Maisonneuve, *Paris*) 85
Appended are texts of *Charte de Die* [11 cent.], *Inscrs. Murales à Die, Noëls d. Taulignan* [17 cent.], *Formules d. Conjuratns. et Recettes médic.* [16 cent.].
" " [ed.] Un Brounché de Nouvèus e quauqueis Vers per Chalendas 2*fr*.50 8° *Montélimar* (Maisonneuve, *Paris*) 79
A collection of Christmas carols in the Dauphiné patois.

Gascon.

Influence on French Language.

LANUSSE, Max Influence du dial. gasc. sur la lang. frç. [15-16 cent.] 7*fr*.50 8° Maisonneuve, *Paris* 93

Specimens of Literature—for Folklore *v.* B § 16.

DARDY, Léop. [ed.] Anthologie pop. de l'Albret, i. Poésies gasconnes ; ii. Contes pop. 16° Michel, *Agen* 91 ; 91
TROSS, A. [ed.] Poésies Gasconnes, 2 vols. 60*fr*. ; *red. to* 10*fr*. 8° Welter, *Paris* 67 ; 69

Languedoc : *Specimens of Literature.*

LAURÈS, J. [ed.] Lou Campestre [Langued. poems ; w. a glossary] 3*fr*. 12° *Montpelier* (Maisonneuve, *Paris*) 78
ROQUEFERRIER, Alph. [ed.] Quatre Contes languedoc. recueillies à Gignac [Herault] 2*fr*.50 8° " " 78

Limousin : *Place-names.*

ARBELLOT, Abbé Frçois. Originè des Noms de Lieu en Limousin et Provs. limous. 2*fr*. 8° Haton, *Paris* 87

Lyons.

"NIZIER DU PUITSPELU" [Clair TISSEUR] Dict. étymolog. du Patois Lyonnais, pts. iii.-v. [last] ea. 5*fr*. ; cpl. 25*fr*. 8° Georg, *Lyons* 89 90
VILLEFRANCHE, J. M. Essai de Grammaire du Patois lyonnais [pp. xxi., 312] 8° Villefranche, *Bourg* 91

Specimens of Literature.

"NIZIER DE PUITSPELU" [Clair TISSEUR; ed.] Fragments en Patois du Lyonnais, pt. i. 8° Georg, *Lyons* 86
" " [tr.] Un Noël satirique en Patois lyonn. : trad. et annot. 6*fr*. 8° Stork, *Lyons* [82] 87

Piedmont.

BARTH, Andr. Laut- u. Formenlehre des Waldensichen [Bonn dissert. inaug.] 8° *Erlangen* 90

Provence —*for* Folklore *v.* B § 16.

Savoy.

DURET, Vict. Grammaire Savoyarde, publ. par Ed. Koschwitz [w. biogr. of author] 3*fr*.75 8° Burkhardt, *Geneva* 94

267. PROVENÇAL LITERATURE.

Manuscripts.

DE LOLLIS — Il Canzoniere prov. O (Cod. Vatic. 3208) — 8° *Rome* 86

History. Treatises. Troubadours.

BASCLE DE LAGREZE, Gust. — La Société et les Mœurs en Béarn — 5*fr.* 12° Cazaux, *Pau* 86

CHABANEAU, Prf. Cam. — La Langue et la Littérature de Limousin [extr.; pp. 58] 8° Maisonneuve, *Paris* 92

COLL Y VEHI, José — La Sátira provenzal — 8° *Madrid* 61

COURT, J. Félix — Les Troubadours dé l'escolo toulousèno, vol. i. — 18° *Le Gril* Office, *Toulouse* 91

Biographies, in Languedocian.

CRAIG, J. Duncan — Miejour: Provençal Legend, Life, and Literature, in land of Felibre 6/- c 8° Nisbet 77

In 1854 the little band of Prov. poets who gathered rd. ROUMANILLE—MISTRAL, AUBANEL, MATTHIEUX, and others—formed themselves into the organizatn. of the Félibrige. This bk. deals with them and their wks. fairly well.

DUCÉRÉ, Ed. — Etudes sur la Vie privée bayonnaise au 16e. Siècle 3*fr.*50 8° *Pau* (Lechevalier, *Paris*) 86

„ „ — La Bourgeoisie bayonnaise sous l'ancien Régime [*extr. fr.* Bull. Soc. Scien. d. Pau] 3*fr.* 8° Garet, *Pau* 89

JANVIER, Thos. [Am.] — An Embassy to Provence; port. [of Mistral] 12° $1.25 *Century* Co., *N.Y.* / 4/6 Unwin 93

Describes a visit by an Amer. and his wife to some Provençal poets, ROUMANILLE, MATTHIEUX, WYSE, AUBANEL, GRAS, and MISTRAL. Of small value.

KNOBLOCH, Heinr. — Die Streitgedichte im Provenz. u. Altfranz. [dissert.] 1*m.* 8° Köhler, *Breslau* 86

MEYER, Paul — Le Salut d'Amour d. les Littér. prov. et frç. [Bibl. Ec. Chartes] 2*fr.* 8° Franck, *Paris* 67

V. NAPOLSKI, St. — Beitr. z. Charakt. mittelalt. Lebens a. d. Höfen Südfrankr. [diss.] 8° *Marburg* 85

PERK, M. A. — De Troubadours — 8° *Amsterdam* 87

RESTORI, A. — Letteratura Provenzale [excellent little handbk.] s 8° *Milan* 91

ROQUE-FERRIER, A. — Mélanges de Critique littér. et de Philol.: le Midi d. l. Frce., ses poètes et ses lettres de 1874 à 1890 12*fr.*50 8° Calas, *Montpelier* 92

ROWBOTHAM, J. F. — Troubadours and Courts of Love; ill. and 2 maps [Social England Ser.] c 8° Sonnenschein / Macmillan, *N.Y.* 95

SELBACH, Ludw. — Das Streitgedicht in d. altprov. Lyrik [Ausg. u. Abhandl.] 3*m.*20 8° Elwert, *Marburg* 86

SETTEGAST, Friedr. — Die Ehre in den Liedern d. Troubadours 1*m.*35 8° Veit, *Lps.* 87

STIMMING, A. — Die provenzalische Litteratur—*in* Gröber's Grundriss—*ut* K § 256.

STÖSSEL, Chr. — Bilder u. Vergleiche d. altprovenz. Lyrik [dissert. inaug.] 8° *Marburg* 85

ZENKER, Rud. — Die provenzalische Tenzone 2*m.* 8° Vogel, *Lps.* 88

Crusades in Old-Provençal Literature.

SCHINDLER, Herm. — Die Kreuzzüge in d. altprov. u. mittelhochdeutscher Lyrik 1*m.* 4° Fock, *Lps.* 91

Poetesses.

SCHULTZ, Osc. — Die provenzalischen Dichterinnen [biogs., w. texts and notes; progr.] 1*m.*20 4° *Altenburg* 88

Collections.

Bibliothèque Méridionale: pub. s. l. auspices d. l. Faculté d. Lettres de Toulouse, vols. i.-iii. 15*fr.* 8° Privat, *Toulouse* 88-93 *in prg.*

i. BERTRAN DE BORN *Poésies* (*ut inf.*) ...... ed. A. THOMAS 4*fr.* 88 | iii. *Mystères Provenç.* (*ut inf.*) ...... ed. JEANROY + TEULIÉ 7*fr.* 93
ii. GUILLÉN DE CASTRO *Mocedades del Cid*, pt. i. E. MÉRIMÉE 4*fr.* 90 |

Poetry.

APPEL, Carl [ed.] — Provenzalische Inedita [fr. Paris MSS.] [Altfrz. Bibl.] 5*m.* 8° Reisland, *Lps.* 90

ARBAUD, D. [ed.] — Chants Populaires

CHABANEAU, Prf. Cam. [ed.] Poésies inédites des Troubads. d. Périgord [*extr. fr.* Rev. Langs. Rom.] 3*fr.*50 8° Maisonneuve, *Paris* 85

DEMATTIO, T. [ed.] — Raccolta di Poesie e Prose provenzali [w. Ital. vocab. and gram.] 2*m* 60 8° Wagner, *Innsbruck* 86

FOURÈS, Aug. [ed.] — Les Cants del Souleih: poésies languedociennes 5*fr.*50 8° Savine, *Paris* 91

GRAS, Fél. [ed.] — Romancero provençal 4*fr.* 18° Roumanille, *Avignon* 87

LEVY, Emile [ed.] — Poésies relig. frçses. et prov. d. MS. extrav. 268 d. l. Bibl. d. Wolfenbüttel 6*fr.* 8° Maisonneuve, *Paris* 87

Extract from *La Revue des Langues Romanes.*

NOULET + CHABANEAU, J. B.–C. [eds.] Deux MSS. provençaux du 14e. siècle 15*fr.* 8° *Montpelier* (Maisonneuve, *Paris*) 88

Con's. poems by RAIMON DE CORNET, PEIRE DE LADILS and other poets of Toulouse schl. One of the pubs. of *Soc. p. l'Etude d. Langs. Rom.*

Gascon, Languedocien, Lyonnais—*v.* K § 266.

Folktales, Proverbs —*v. also* B § 3, B § 4 and B.B. B § 3.

Bvgada Prouençalo vonte cadvn l'y a pannuchon enliassado de Proverbis, Sentencis, Similitudos et Mouts pour rire *Aix* [17 cent.] 59

CNYRIM, Eug. [ed.] — Sprichwörter *etc.* b. d. provenz. Lyrikern [Ausg. u. Abhgn.] 2*m.* 8° Elwert, *Marburg* 87

DE LA TOUR KEYRIÉ, A. M. [ed.] Recueil d. Proverbes, Maximes, Sentences et Dictons prov. 3*fr.* 8° Makaire, *Aix* 82

PERETZ, B. [ed.] — Altprov. Sprichwörter; mit Hinblick a. d. mhd. Freidank—*in* Rom. Forschgn., vol. iii., *ut* B.B. K § 256.

Mysteries.

JEANROY + TEULIÉ, A.–H. [eds.] Mystères provençaux d. 15 siècle; w. Introd. and glossary [Bibl. Mèrid.] 7*fr.* 8° Privat, *Toulouse* 93

Individual Writers, Texts and Aids.

Apôtres, Les Sorts des [13 cent.]: ed. Prf. Cam. Chabaneau; w. Lat. orig. [*extr. fr.* Rev. Langs. Rom.] 2*fr.*50 8° Maisonneuve, *Paris* 81

BERTRAN DE BORN [*fl.* 1180-95] Œuvres, hrsg. Alb. Stimming [Roman. Bibl.] 4*m.* 8° Niemeyer, *Halle* 92

„ „ — Poésies complètes, ed. Ant. Thomas [Bibl. Méridionale, vol. i.] 4*fr.* 8° Privat, *Toulouse* 88

STEINMÜLLER, Geo. — Ueb. Bildung u. Gebrauch d. Tempora u. Modi b. Bertran [diss.] 8° *Würzburg* 87

K § 267

Bibl. National, Paris : Manuscripts : Acq. Nouv. Frç., No. 4138.
WESEMANN, Otto — Ueber die Sprache der altprovenz. HS. 4138 in Bibl. Nat. [dissert. inaug.] 8° *Halle* 91

BLACASSETZ.
KLEIN, Otto — Der Troubadour Blacassetz [school-programme] 8° *Wiesbaden* 86

Chanson Lemouzina, La (L'Epopée Limousine) : ed. Jos. Roux ; w. Fch. tr. and notes 5*fr.* 8° Picard, *Paris* 89

Comput en Vers Provençaux : ed. Prf. Cam. Chabaneau ; w. Fch. tr. and notes [*extr. fr.* Rev. Langs. Rom.] 2*fr.*50 8° Maisonneuve, *Paris* 81

Delphine Mysteries [Provençal].
ISELLOH, Hugo — Darstellung d. Mundart d. delphinatischen Mysterien [diss.] 8° *Bonn* 91

Flamenca, Roman de — *v.* B.B. K § 267.
SIEBERT, G. — Sprachliche Untersuchung d. Reime des prov. Romans Flamenca [diss.] *Marburg* 86

GIRARD PATEG.
TOBLER, Adolf — Das Spruchgedicht des Girard Pateg [*extr. fr.* Abhgn. Berl. Akad.] 5*m.* r 4° G. Reimer, *Berlin* 86

GIRART DE ROSSILLO [9 cent.].
MÜLLER, Konr. — Die Assonanzen im Girart von Rossillon [= Franzős. Studien, iii. 5] 2*m.*40 8° Henninger, *Heilbronn* 8–
STIMMING, Alb. — Ueber Girart v. Rossillon ; Beitr. z. Entwickelungsgesch. d. Volksepen 10*m.* 8° Niemeyer, *Halle* 88

GIRAUT DE CALANSO.
DAMMANN, Osc. — Die allegorische Canzone de Giraut de Calanso, pt. i. 2*m.* 8° Koebner, *Breslau* 91
On the *A leis cui am de cór et de saber*, and their interpretation.

GOUDELIN, Pierre — Œuvres, ed. J. B. Noulet, w. biogr. and bibliogr. ; port. 2*fr.* 8° Privat, *Toulouse* 88

Guerre des Camisards [1692–1709] : Fragment, ed. Marius Tallon ; w. Fch. Introd. and notes 3*fr.* 8° Impr. d. *Patriote*, Privas 87

GUIRALDENC, Louis Diog. [19 cent.] Poésies languedociennes, ed. A. Roque-Ferrier 8° Hamelin, *Montpelier* 89

GUIRAUT DE BORNELH : hrsg. A. Kolsen [Berl. Beiträge z. Germ. u. Rom. Phil.] 3*m.*60 8° Vogt, *Berlin* 94
Incl. three hitherto unknown poems, attributed to him.

Istoria Petri et Pauli — *v. infra, sub tit.* Mystère de SS. Petri et Pauli.

JASMIN, Jacques [1798–1864] Œuvres, ed. Boyer d'Agen : Gascon text w. Fch. [prose] tr. *en regard*, and gloss., 4 v. 8° Bellier, *Bordeaux* 91
SMILES, Dr. Saml. — Jasmin : Barber, Poet, Philanthropist — *v.* K § 35.

Leys d'Amors.
Chabaneau, Prf. Cam. [ed.] Origine et Etablissemt. de l'Acad. d. Jeux Floraux 8° *Toulouse* 85

Litanies en Vers Provençaux : ed. Prf. Cam. Chabaneau ; w. Fch. Introd. and notes 3*fr.*50 8° Maisonneuve, *Paris* 86

Marie Madeleine, Ste.
Chabaneau, Prf. Cam. [ed.] Ste. Marie Madel. d. l. Littér. provençale [*extr. fr.* Rev. Lang. Rom.] 12*fr.* 8° Maisonneuve, *Paris* 87
A colln. of Provençal texts in prose and verse relating to the Saint ; w. Introds. and notes.

Marienklage, Altprovenz. [12 cent.] : hrsg. W. Mushacke [Roman. Bibl.] 3*m.* 8° Niemeyer, *Halle* 90

Merlin, Roman de : Fragments d'une Trad. prov., ed. Cam. Chabaneau [*extr. fr.* Rev. Langs. Rom.] 1*fr.*50 8° Maisonneuve, *Paris* 83

MISTRAL, Fréd. [19 cent.] Calendal [1867] : text and Fch. tr. 6*fr.* s 12° Lemerre, *Paris* 87
" " Nerto : provençalische Erzählung, übers. Aug. Bertuch 3*m.* 8° Trübner, *Strassbg.* 91
" " Mirèio, übers. Aug. Bertuch [w. Germ. Introd. Ed. Boehmer] 5*m.* 8° " " 93
" " trad. en prose Dauph. Rivière [Soc. p. Etude de Langs. Rom.] 6*fr.* 8° *Montpelier* (Maisonn., *Paris*) 81
CROMBIE, W. — Mistral — *in his* Poets and Peoples of Foreign Lands, *v.* K § 17.

Mystère de Saint Anthoni de Viennès : ed. Abbé Paul Guillaume [ed. fr. MS. of 1506] 10*fr.* 8° *Gap* (Maisonneuve, *Paris*) 84
" " Saint Eustache ed. Abbé Paul Guillaume ; w. Fch. tr. [played in 1504] 7*fr.*50 8° Hamelin, *Montpelier* [80] 91
" " SS. Petri et Pauli : ed. Abbé Paul Guillaume [ed. fr. 15 cent. MS.] 7*fr.*50 8° *Gap* (Maisonneuve, *Paris*) 87
" des Trois Doms [repres. at Romans 1509] : ed. P. E. Giraud + U. Chevalier ; w. Introd. [pp. cxlviii., 928] 25*fr.* 8° Brun, *Lyons* 87

Nouveau Testament [13 cent.] : photolith. facs. fr. Lyons MS., by Prf. Léon Clédat 30*fr.* 8° Leroux, *Paris* 90
Forms vol. iv. of the *Bibl. de la Faculté des Lettres de Lyon.*
Rituel du Nouv. Test. Provençal de Lyon : Facs., by Prf. Léon Clédat [Coll. d. Réprod. d. MSS.] 3*fr.* 8° Leroux, *Paris* 90

Nobla Leyczon : ed. Prf. Ed. Montet ; w. Fch. tr. and Mod.-Vaudois trs. 12*fr.* 8° Georg, *Geneva* 88
From the Cambridge MS., with the variants fr. those of Geneva and Dublin.

PAULET DE MARSEILLES.
LÉVY, Emile — Le Troubadour Paulet de Marseilles [31 pp.] 2*fr.* 8° Maisonneuve, *Paris* 92

PEIRE CARDENAL.
MAUS, F. W. — Peire Cardenal's Strophenbau [*v.* B.B. K § 267].
The list of Provençal rhythms contd. in this bk. is corrected and slightly enlarged in L. SELBACH'S *Das Streitgedicht*, *v.* K § 267.

PEIRE LADILS — Poésies — *v.* Noulet + Chabaneau [eds.], *supra.*

PEIRE VIDAL.
SCHOPF, S. — Beiträge z. Biogr. u. Chronol. d. Lieder d. Peire Vidal 1*m.*20 8° Koebner, *Breslau* 87

PHILIPPE — Les Merveilles d'Irlande : Provençal text, ed. J. Ulrich 2*m.* 8° Renger, *Lpz.* 92

Psaumes de la Pénitence [verse] : ed. Prf. Cam. Chabaneau [*extr. fr.* Rev. Langs. Rom.] 2*fr.*50 8° Maisonneuve, *Paris* 81
" " Paraphrase en Vers gasçons, ed. same 2*fr.* 8° " " 86

RAIMBAUT DE VAQUEIRAS [1180–1207] Briefe an Bonifaz I., Markgrafen v. Monferrat, ed. Osc. Schultz 4*m.* 8° Niemeyer, *Halle* 93

RAIMON DE CORNET — Poésies — *v.* Noulet + Chabaneau [eds.], *supra.*

RAIMON FERAUT.
KLEY, Friedr. — Die Reime d. Vida St. Honorat : sprachl. Untersuchg. [dissert. inaug.] 8° *Marburg* 87

RENAUD *and* GEOFFROY DE PONS.
CHABANEAU, Cam. — Les Troubadours Renaud et Geoff. de Pons [*extr. fr.* Courier d. l'Ouest] 2*fr.*50 8° Maisonneuve, *Paris* 81

Rituel Provençal : MS. 36 d. l. Bibl. Munic. de Lyons, ed. Prf. Léon Clédat 3*fr.* 8° Leroux, *Paris* 90

SERVERI DE GERONA : Vier bisher ungedruckte Pastoralen, hrs. Max Kleinert [diss.] 8° *Halle* 90

SORDELLO — Poesies Ined., ed. Pio Gius. Palazzi [*extr. fr.* Atti d. Inst. Venet.] *Venice* 87

THIBAUT IV. DE CHAMPAGNE.
DAVIDS, Friedr. — Ueber Form und Sprache d. Gedichte Thibaut iv. von Champagne [diss.] 8° *Leipzig* 86

268. FRENCH PHILOLOGY (a): BIBLIOGRAPHY. HISTORY OF THE LANGUAGE.

Bibliography. "Encyclopædia."

KÖRTING, Gust. Encyclopädie u. Methodologie d. französ. Philologie 6m. 8° 94

Linguistic Ethnology—v. also K § 225.

CLAUS Die geographische Verbreitung d. frz. Sprache [pp. 21] 8° Fues, *Tübingen* 90

General Philology.

SUCHIER, H. Die frz. u. provenz. Spr. u. ihre Mundarten [w. 12 maps]—*in* Gröber's Grundriss, *ut* K § 256.

Collected Essays.

GEIJER, P. A. Studier: Fransk Linguistik 8° *Upsala* 87

Series.

Französische Studien: hrsg. Gust. Körting + E. Koschwitz: Neue Folge, vol. i. 6m. 8° Gronau, *Berlin* 93

BEHRENS, D. *Bibliogr. des Patois Gallo-Romans*, trad. Eug. RABIET [*ut* K § 276], 6m. '93.

History of the Language.

EBELING, W. Examen d. différ. hypothèses . . . [sur] . . . l'Orig. et l. Formn. d. l. L. Fr. Fock, *Lpz.* 78

ESPAGNOLLE, Abbé J. L'Origine du Français, 3 vols. [of no value: derives Fch. fr. Gk.!] 30/r. 8° Delagrave, *Paris* 86; 91

ETIENNE, E. La Langue Frç. depuis l'Origines jusqu'à fin d. 11 siècle, vol. i. 10/r. 8° Bouillon, *Paris* 90

Vol. i. comprises Phonology, Declension, and Conjugation.

PETIT DE JULLEVILLE, L. Notions générales d. les Origines et s. l'Hist. d. l. lang. frç. 2/r.50 12° Delalain, *Paris* [83] 90

Hellenism.

TOUGARD, Abbé Alb. L'Hellénisme dans les Ecrivains du moyen age [7–12 cents.] 3/r. 8° Lecoffre, *Paris* 86

Historical Grammar —v. K § 269.

Modern French [17 cent. to present time].

Verb.

KRAFT, Pp. Konjugationswechsel im Neufrz. von 1500 bis 1800 u. Zeugn. v. Grammatikern 2m.50 8° Herold, *Hamburg* 91

Hôtel de Rambouillet and the Précieux.

DE BRÉMOND D'ARS, V'cte. Guy Le Père de Mme. de Rambouillet [Jean d. Vivonne] 7/r.50 8° Plon, *Paris* 84

de Balzac, Honoré [1799–1850].

LEESI, Wilh. Syntaktische Studien über Balzac [dissert. inaug.] 2m. 8° Gräfe, *Königsberg* 89

Corneille, Pierre [1606–1684].

UHLEMANN, Em. Grammatische Eigentümlichkeiten in Corneille's Prosaschriften [schl.-progr.] 4° *Ilfeld* 91

Molière, J. P. Bapt. [1622–1673].

HERG, Otto Die Syntax des Verbums bei Molière [dissert. inaug.] 8° *Kiel* 86

BLONDEAU, Nic. [17 cent.] Dictionnaire érotique latin-français, ed. Fçois. Noël; w. notes and Introd. 60/r. 8° Liseux, *Paris* 86

GALLERT Ueber den Gebrauch des Infinitivs bei Molière [dissert. inaug.] 8° *Halle* 86

KAYSER, Herm. Zur Syntax Molières [dissert. inaug.] 1m.20 8° Lipsius, *Kiel* 85

LIVET, Chas. L. Dictionnaire de la Langue de Molière 30/r. 8° Welter, *Paris* 94

The language of MOLIÈRE compared with that of his contemporaries.

MEYER, D. Vergleich und Metapher in d. Lustspielen Molières [diss.] 8° *Marburg* 85

269. FRENCH PHILOLOGY (b): GRAMMAR, ORTHOGR., PALÆOGR., PHONOLOGY, ETC.

Grammar.

TOBLER, A. Vermischte Beiträge zur frz. Grammatik, Reihe ii. 5m.60 8° Hirzel, *Lps.* 94

Historical Grammar. History of the Language.

DARMESTETER, Prf. Arsène Cours de Gram. histor. d. l. lang. frç., pt. i. [Phonology] 2/r. 8° Delagrave, *Paris* 92

KOSCHWITZ, Ed. Grammatik der neufrz. Schriftsprache (16–19 Jahrh.), pt. i. [Phonology] 5m. 8° Franck, *Oppeln* 89

Change of Gender.

SACHS, H. Geschlechtswandel im Frz.: Versuch d. Erklärg. d. G. l. Ursprungl. Neutra [diss.] 8° *Göttingen* 86

Change of Meaning.

FRANZ, Gerh. Ueb. d. Bedeutungswandel latein. Wörter im Frz. [schl.-progr.] 4° *Dresden* 90

JÖRSS, Paul Ueb. d. Genuswechsel latein. Mask. u. Femin. in Frz. [progr.] 1m.20 4° Fock, *Lps.* 92

Accidence.

KÖRTING, Dr. Gust. Formenlehre d. frz. Sprache, vol. i. [historical devel. of verb] 8m. 8° Schöningh, *Paderborn* 93

Adjective.

DÜHR Zur Theorie der Stellung d. frz. Adjektivs [school-progr.] 4° *Stendal* 90

HENDRYCH, Prf. Just. Die Stellung des französischen Adjectivs [school-progr.] 2m. 4° *Görz* (Fock, *Lps.*) 94

PLATHE, P. Entwickelgsgesch. d. einformigen Adjective im Frz. [11–16 cents.] *Greifswald* 86

Adverb.

BASTIN, J. Etude sur les principaux adverbes [français] 3/r. 8° Bouillon, *Paris* 91

Article.

HÜBNER, Hans Syntakt. Studien üb. d. bestimmt. Art. b. Eigennamen i. Alt- u. Neufrz. [diss.] 3m. 8° *Kiel* (Fock, *Lps.*) 92

K § 269

Conjunction.

SCHNELLBÄCHER, K. — Ueb. d. synt. Gebrauch d. Conjunctivs in d. Chansons de Geste [diss.] 8° *Giessen* 91

Noun.

KOHLSCHEIN — Formation du Pluriel d. Substfs. frç. anc. et moderne [schl.-progr.] 4° *Schalke* 86

Prepositions.

BARTHE, A. — Ueber d. Präpositionen *par* u. *pur* in einigen anglonorm. Denkmälern—*ut* K § 275.

Pronoun.

BADKE, Otto — Beiträge zur Lehre v. d. frz. Fürwörtern [school-programme] 4° *Stralsund* 91

HILMER, H. — Etudes sur le Pronom Personnel français 8° Fock, *Lps.* 73

MARGOT, A. — Ueb. d. Durchbruch d. "Extrinsèque" i. d. Pronom. d. frz. Spr. [progr.] 8° ,, ,, 80

NEUMANN, Wilh. — Zur Syntax d. Relativpronomens im Französischen [dissert. inaug.] 8° *Frerau* 90

ZILCH, Geo. — Gebrauch d. frz. Pronomens i. 2 Hälfte d. 16 Jahrh. [diss.] 8° *Giessen* 91

Based mainly on the writings of Estienne PASQUIER.

Suffixes.

GELOSI, Jean — Les Suffixes frç.: dérivatn. et analogie avec l'italien 1*l.*20 8° Trèves, *Rome* 89

NATHAN, Nath. — Das latein. Suffix *-alis* im Französischen [Strassburg dissert. inaug.] 8° Otto, *Darmstadt* 86

Syntax.

HAASE, A. — Französische Syntax des 17ten. Jahrhunderts 7*m.* 8° Franck, *Oppeln* 88

Negation.

ZATELLI, D. — De l'Emploi de la Négation en frç. et en italien 8° Fock, *Lps.* 85

Verb.

HAHN, Gust. — Das französische Zeitwort in tabellarischer Uebersicht [pp. iv., 77] 1*m.*20 4° Teubner, *Lps.* 90

KRAFT, Pp. — Konjugationswechsel im Neufrz. v. 1500–1800 [diss.] 4° *Marburg* 92

MARCOU, Ppe. — Der historische Infinitiv im Französischen [dissert. inaug.] 80*pf.* 8° Mayer & Müller, *Berl.* 88

RISOP, A. — Studien zur Geschichte der frz. Konjugation auf *-ir* 2*m.*80 8° Niemeyer, *Halle* 91

THEROULDE, St. Hub. — Traité raisonné de la Conjugaison française 3*fr.*50 8° Leblanc, *Dieppe* 91

DE VERE, Schèle — The French Verb: a new clear and easy method for its study $1.25 12° Jenkins, *N.Y.* 91

WILLIAMS, A. [Am.] — The Syntax of the Subjunctive Mood in French 12° *Boston* 85

Orthography. Pronunciation.

BLOCH, Gilb. — Reform der französischen Orthographie 3*m.*20 8° Sauerländer, *Aarau* 94

With reference to Prf. HAVET'S petition to the *Académie Française*.

BRÉAL, Mich. — La Réforme de l'Orthographie française [*extr. fr.* Rev. d. Deux Mondes] 1*fr.* 16° Hachette, *Paris* 90

Changements orthograph. introduits d. l. Dict. de l'Acad. Frç. (ed. 1877) 1*fr.* 8° Larousse, *Paris* [ ] 91

CLÉDAT, Prf. Léon — L'Orthographie française [a lecture] 1*fr.* 8° Plan, *Lyons* 90

Dictionnaire des Mots réformés par la Soc. Philologique Française 1*fr.* 8° Delagrave, *Paris* 91

DURAND, Aug. — Nouvelle Orthographie française, proposée: Partie pratique 2*fr.* 18° Author, *Paris* 91

HANE, G. — Sur le Rôle de l'Accent latin dans la Formn. d. l. Lang. frç. [progr.] Fock, *Lps.* 80

HAVET, Louis — La Simplification de l'Orthographie 1*fr.* 18° Hachette, *Paris* 90

JACOBY, J. — L'Action de l'Accent latin sur la Formn. d. l. Lang. frç. Fock, *Lps.* 73

KOSCHWITZ, E. — Zur Aussprache d. Frz. in Genf u. Frankreich [*extr. fr.* Zts. f. frz. Spr.] 3*m.* 8° Gronow, *Berlin* 92

LESAINT, M. A. — Traité complet de la Prononciation frç. d. l. 2 moitié d. 19 siéc. 8*m.* 8° Gesenius, *Halle* [ ] 90

QUIEHL, Karl — Französische Aussprache und Sprachfertigkeit [schl.-bk.] 2*m.*70 8° Elwert, *Marburg* [89] 93

REININGER, G. — Système de l'Accentn. frç. et s. Applicn. à Racine [progr.; interesting] *Prague* 86

SALZMANN, J. — Ueber die Aussprache der frz. Laute [school-progr.] Fock, *Lps.* 84

TALBERT, F. — De la Prononciation en France au 16e. Siècle *Paris* 87

Deals also with Ch. THUROT'S *Prononc. frçse. depuis l. 16e. Siècle, pt. i.: Voyelles* [*ut* 𝔅.𝔅. K § 269].

Manuscripts.

France, Bibl. Natl.: Manuscrits Français, vols. i.–iii. ea. 25*fr.* 4° Didot, *Paris* 68; 74; 81

" " Manuscrits Latins et Français: 1875–1891. By Léop. Delisle, *and* Notices et Extraits—*ut* K § 4.

Great Britain: Documents Manuscripts de l'anc. litt. franç. dans les bibl. de Gr.-Bret. By Paul Meyer, pt. i. 6*fr.* 8° *Paris* 71

This pt. deals with MSS. at the British Museum, Durham, Edinburgh, Glasgow and Bodleian Libs.

Palæography

—*v. also* K § 99 (espec. GIRY).

PROU, Maurice [ed.] — Recueil de Facss. d'Ecritures du 12 au 17 siècle [Lat. and French], *ut* K § 203.

Phonology. Accentuation.

GEIJER, P. A. — Om Ljuden *y* och *ö* in Frsk.; Accessoriska Ljud i Frsk. Ord—*in his* Studier, *ut* K § 268.

GUTHEIM, Ferd. — Ueber Konsonanten-Assimilation im Französischen 3*m.* 8° Siebert, *Heidelbg.* 91

HOSSNER, Max — Zur Gesch. d. unbetonten Vocale im Altfrz. u. Neufrz. [diss.] 8° *Freiburg* 86

HUMBERT, C. — Nochmals das *e muet* u. d. Vortrag frz. Verse [progr.] 60*pf.* 8° Vandenhoeck, *Göttgn.* 90

MARCHOT, P. — Solutions d. quelq. difficultés d. l. phonétique frç. 3*fr.*50 8° Bouillon, *Paris* 93

SCHWAN + PRINGSHEIM, Ed. E. — Der frz. Accent: eine phonet. Untersuchg. [*extr. fr.* Archiv. f. neu. Spr.] 2*m.* 8° Reisland, *Lps.* 90

STORK, Max Aug. — Ueb. frz. *r* im Auslaute n. d. Grammatikerzeug. d. 16 Jahrh. [diss.] 8° *Heidelbg.* 91

TECHMER, F. — Beiträge z. Geschichte der frz. u. engl. Phonetik u. Phonographie—*ut* K § 237.

270. FRENCH PHILOLOGY (c): ETYMOLOGY.

Lexicography.

DARMESTETER, Prf. Arsène [ed.] Crit. edn. of the 2,500 Fch. words in Comms. of Rashi (Solomon of Troyes, *d.* 1105) *in prep.*
DELACROIX, Prf. Modeste Les Racines et la Signification des mots frçs. 2/*fr.*75 12° Fouraut, *Paris* [74] 86
Elementary lessons on etymology and synonyms.

HÉRICHER, L. Les Etymologies difficiles [those wh. Littré declar. unknown] 6/*fr.* 8° *Avranches* (Maisonneuve, *Paris*) 86
PAVOT, T. Etymologies Dites Inconnues: solutions de problèmes 7/*fr.*50 8° Leroux, *Paris* 91

Dictionaries.

Académie Française Dictionnaire historique de la Langue frç. [*ut* B.B. K § 270]: new edn., vols. i.–iv. ea. 18/*fr.* 4° Didot, *Paris* [1694] 86–93 *in prg.*
Continued in parts at 4/*fr.*50 each, four parts making a volume.

Stoffels, A. Le Dict. de l'Acad. Frç.: s. hist., mérites, défaults [progr.] Fock, *Lps.* 83
Acc. to M. GRÉARD, who recently made some important proposals to the Acad. on spelling-reforms, a Fch. dict. shd. contain some 32,000 words. In the time of FÉNELON the lang. numbered 16,000–18,000 wds., and in 1740 it was computed to have *c.* 20,000. The best Dict. prior to that of the Acad. was that by Randle COTGRAVE [1° *Lond.* 1611, repr. 1632, 1650; ed. Jas. Howell 1673].

BESCHERELLE, L. N. Nouveau Dictionnaire national, 4 vols. [entirely revised edn.] 90/*fr.* 4° Garnier, *Paris* [43–46] 86–87
Published in 180 *livraisons* at 50*c.* each.

LITTRÉ, Em. Dictionnaire de la Langue Française [*ut* B.B. K § 270]: Supplément 12/*fr.* 4° Hachette, *Paris* 92
Technical terms of art, science, agriculture, etc., neologisms, and errata: w. an etymol. dict. of Fch. words of Oriental orig. by Marc. DEVIC.

SACHS + VILLATTE, Prf. Karl / Prf. Césaire Französisch-deutsches Supplement-Lexikon 10*m.* r 8° Langenscheidt, *Berlin* 94
A supplement to their *Encyclop. Wörterbuch* [*ut* B.B. K § 270], and to other French-Germ. dicts.

TARVER, Jno. C. Royal Phraseological Engl.-Fch. & Fch.-Engl. Dictionary, 2 vols. *o.p.* [*pb.* 50/–] r 8° [45; 50] 58; 62
Technical Terms —*v.* K § 276.

Folk-Etymology.

ROLL, Otto Einfluss d. Volksetymol. a. d. neufrz. Schriftspr. [dissert. inaug.] 1*m.* 8° Lipsius, *Kiel* 88

Foreign Elements.

CAPELLER, Gust. Die wichtigst. a. d. Griech. gebild. Wörter d. frz. u. engl. Spr., pts. i.–iv. [progrs.] 4° *Gumbinnen* 90–92
A colln. of the most important Fch. and Engl. *mots savants* derived fr. Greek.

LAMMENS, H. Remarques sur les Mots frç. derivés de l'Arabe 10/*fr.* s 8° *Beyrouth* 90
An attempt to trace some 800 Fch. words to an Arab. source: a good study on the lines of DOZY + ENGELMANN [*ut* B.B. K § 261], DEVIC [*ut* B.B. K § 270] and de EGUILAZ.

*MACKEL, Dr. Emil Die german. Elemente in d. frz. u. provenz. Spr.—*in* Frz. Studien, vi. (1), *ut* B.B. K § 268.
An excellent piece of work.

SÜPFLE, Theod. Gesch. d. deut. Cultureinflusses auf Frankreich, vol. i. [to Klopstock] 7*m.* 8° Thienemann, *Gotha* 86

Glosses.

Catholicon de Lille: ed. A. Scheler [a Latin-French glossary] 8° *Brussels* 85

Names: *Place-Names.*

HÄDICKE, H. Ueber einige Ländernamen im Französischen [schl.-progr.] 4° *Pforta* 94
HÖLSCHER, Mat. Die mit d. Suffix *-acum*, *-iacum*, gebild. frz. Ortsnamen [diss.] 8° *Strassburg* 91
WILLIAMS, C. A. Die französischen Ortsnamen keltischer Abkunft 2*m.* 8° Heitz, *Strassburg* 91

Rare Words.

ALBRECHT, Aug. Vocabulaire systémat. frç. et allem. d. Mots rares et importants 2*m.*25 8° Strauch, *Lps.* 85

Slang; Technical Terms—*v.* K § 276.

272. FRENCH PHILOLOGY (e): METRICS. STYLE.

Metrics.

D'EICHTHAL, Eug. Du Rythme dans la Versification française [61 pp.] 18° Lemerre, *Paris* 92
SONNENBURG, Rud. Wie sind die frz. Verse zulesen? [a good little bk.; 26 pp.] 80*pf.* 8° Springer, *Berlin* 85
SOURIAU, Maur. L'Evolution du Vers français au 17e. Siècle 10/*fr.* 8° Hachette, *Paris* 93

Magazine.

Revue de Metrique et de Versification, vol. i., no. i. 1/*fr.*50 8° Cerf, *Paris* 94 *in prg.*

Prosody. Composition.

MEISSNER, A. L. Introduction to French Prose Composition [school-book] 3/6 c 8° Percival (Riv. & Perc.) 93
SCHERFFIG, Dr. Rich. Französischer Antibarbarus 3*m.*50 8° Pahl, *Zittau* 94

Rhyming Dictionary.

MORANDINI D'ECCATAGE, F. Grand Dictionnaire des Rimes françaises 10/*fr.* r 8° Ghio, *Paris* 86

K § 273

Style.

Similes.

BAUDISCH, Jul. — Ueber Vergleiche im Neufranzösischen [useful] [school-programme] *Marburg* 87

Synonyms.

*LAFAYE, Prf. Benj. — Dictionnaire des Synonymes d. l. Langue frç. [*ut* B.B. K § 270]: new (6th) edn. 23*fr.* 8° Hachette, *Paris* [58] 93
The standard work, w. an Introd. on the theory of synonyms.

MARTENS, Friedr. — Geschichte der frz. Synonymik, pt. i. [Die Anfänge] [dissert. inaug.] 8° *Stralsund* 87

WALDMANN, Mich. — Die wichtigsten französ. Synonyma [school-bk.; progr.] 8° *Regensburg* 91

273. OLD FRENCH [A.D. 842-14TH CENT.] PHILOLOGY [LANGUE D'OIL].

Grammar.

SCHWAN, Ed. — Grammatik des Altfranzösischen [*ut* B.B. K § 273]: new edn. 4*m*.80 8° Reisland, *Lpz.* [88] 92
A second edn. of the most convenient and prob. best compendium of O.-F. phonology and accidence: confined strictly to Central French, other dialects being seldom referred to.

SUCHIER, Herm. — Altfranzösische Grammatik, pt. i. [Die Schriftsprache], fasc. 1 2*m*. 8° Niemeyer, *Halle* 93

Adjective.

CRON, Jos. — Die Stellung d. attribut. Adjektivs im Altfrz. [schl.-progr.] 4° *Strassburg* 92

Negatives.

MEDER, Frz. — *Pas, mie, point* im Altfranzösischen [dissert. inaug.] 8° *Marburg* 91

Pronouns.

DITTMER, Wilh. — Die Pronomina possessiva im Altfranzösischen [dissert. inaug.] 8° *Greifswald* 88

Relative Sentences.

STROHMEYER, Fritz — Ueb. verschiedene Functionen d. altfrz. Relativsatzes [dissert.] 1*m*.20 8° Heinrich, *Berlin* 92

Syntax.

HÖFER, Joh. — Ueber d. Gebrauch d. Apposition im Altfranzösischen [dissert. inaug.] 8° *Halle* 91

KLATT, L. — Zur Syntax des Altfranzösischen [schl-progr.] Fock, *Lpz.* 78

ROSENBAUR, Friedr. — Zur Lehre v. d. Unterordnung d. Sätze im Altfrz. [diss.] 8° *Strassburg* 86

Verb.

BEHRENS, Alb. — Endung d. zweit. Pers. Pluralis d. Altfrz. Verbums [dissert. inaug.] 1*m*.20 8° *Greifswald* 90

BURGATZCKY, Dr. Otto — Das Imperfect u. Plusquamperfectum d. Futurs im Altfrz. 8° ,, 86

BUSSE, Gust. — Der Conjunctiv im altfrz. Volksepos 2*m* 8° Lipsius, *Kiel* 86

CZISCHKE, Ludw. — Perfektbildg. d. stark. Verba d. *si*-Klasse i. Frz. (11-16 siéc.) [diss.] 8° *Greifswald* 88

ENGLÄNDER, Dav. — Der Imperativ im Altfranzösischen [dissert. inaug.] 1*m*. 8° Preuss, *Breslau* 89

HOFMANN, Fritz — *Avoir* u. *estre* i. d. umschreib. Zeiten d. altfrz. intrans. Ztwt. [diss.] 1*m*.20 8° Mayer & Müller, *Berl.* 90

LORENTZ, Alb. — Die 1 Pers. Pluralis des Verbums im Altfrz. [dissert. inaug.] 8° *Heidelberg* 86

MÄTSCHKE, Osc. — Die Nebensätze d. Zeit im Altfranzösischen [dissert. inaug.] 8° *Kiel* 87

WEHLITZ, Herm. — Congruenz d. Partic. Präterit. in activer Verbalconstr. [13-15 cents.] [diss.] 8° *Greifswald* 87

Etymology: *Dictionaries.*

BOS, A. — Glossaire de la Langue d'Oil [11-14 cents.] 16*fr.* m 8° Maisonneuve, *Paris* 91

GODEFROY, Fréd. — Dictionnaire de l'ancienne Langue frç., pts. 61-75 [9-15 cent., to occupy 10 v.] ea. pt. 5*fr.* 4° Bouillon, *Paris* 90-93 *in prg.*

,, ,, — Réponse à quelq. Attaques contre Le Dict. d. l'Anc. Lang. [*repr. fr.* vol. vi.] 8° ,, ,, 90

TOYNBEE, Paget J. — Concise Dictionary of Old French Clar. Press Macmillan, *N.Y.* *in prep.*

Chrestomathies.

AUBERTIN, Chas. [ed.] — Choix de Textes de l'Anc. Français [10-16 cents.] 2*fr.* 12° Belin, *Paris* [83] 92

DEVILLARD, Ev. [ed.] — Chrestomathie de l'Ancien Français; w. tr. and glossary [9-15 cents.] 3*fr*.50 12° Klincksieck, *Paris* 87

MEYER, Prf. Paul [ed.] — Recueil d'anciens Textes Bas-Lat., Provenç. et Frç. [*ut* B.B. K § 273].
The Third Pt. is not yet pub. A Fourth is to comprise a Comparative Grammar of Old-Fch. and Provençal.

TOYNBEE, Paget [ed.] — Specimens of Old French; w. Introd., notes and glossary c 8° 16/- Clar. Press; $4 net Macmillan, *N.Y.* 92
A good sels. fr. interesting pieces (*Lancelot du Lac, Renart*, JOINVILLE, *Pèlerinage de Charlemagne, Merlin, etc.*), mostly fr. *textes critiques*; w. a brief grammar (assuming a knowledge of Latin) and extensive glossary.

Manuscripts

—*v.* K § 277.

Metrics.

GALINO, Tit. — Musique et Versification frç. au Moyen Age [dissert. inaug.] 8° *Leipzig* 91

DE LA GRASSERIE, Raoul — De la Strophé et du Poème dans l. versif. frçse. [spec. O.-Fch.] 8° Leroux, *Paris* 94

NAETEBUS, Gotth. — Die nichtlyrischen Strophenformen des Altfranzösischen 5*m*. 8° Hirzel, *Lpz.* 91

ORTH, Ferd. — Ueber Reim u. Strophenbau in d. altfrz. Lyrik 1*m*.50 8° Hühn, *Kassel* 82

STRAMWITZ, Ed. — Ueber Strophen- u. Vers-Enjambement in Altfrz. [dissert.] 8° *Greifswald* 86

TRÄGER, Ern. — Geschichte d. Alexandriners, pt. i. [Frz. Alex. bis Ronsard] [dissert. inaug.] 8° *Leipzig* 89

Cæsura.

OTTEN, S. — Ueber die Cäsur im Altfranzösischen [dissert. inaug.] 8° *Greifswald* 84

Phonology.

BEETZ, Karl — *C* und *ch* vor latein. *a* in altfrz. Texten [dissert. inaug.] 8° *Strassburg* 87
HAASE, H. — Verhalten d. pikard. u. wallon. Denkmäler d. MA. [*e* u. *i* vor gedeck. *n*] [diss.] *Halle* 86
KARSTEN, G. — Zur Geschichte der altfrz. Consonantenverbindungen Fock, *Lpz.* 84
MATZKE, J. E. — Dialekt. Eigentümlichkeiten i. d. Entwick. d. mouilliert. *l* im Altfrz.—*in* Mod. Lang. Notes, v. 2 [1890].
WALDNER, Eug. — Die Quellen d. parasitischen *i* im Altfrz. [diss.] 87
WEIGELT, R. — Franz. *oi* aus *ei* auf Grund latein. Urkunden d. 12 Jahrh. [diss.] *Halle* 85

Style.

GÜNTHER, Herm. — Ueb. d. Ausdruckungsweise d. altfrz. Kunstromans *Halle* 86
LOTZ, Ern. — Auslassung, Wiederholung u. Stellvertretg. im altfrz. [Marbg. dissert.] 75*pf.* 8° Pohle, *Jena* 85
RAUSCHMAIER, A. — Ueber d. figürlichen Gebrauch einiger Zahlen im Altfrz. [diss.] 8° *Leipzig* 92
ROSENBAUER, Friedr. — Zur Lehre von der Unterordnung d. Sätze im Altfrz. [diss.] 8° *Strassburg* 86
SCHLIEBITZ, V. — Die Person der Anrede in der frz. Sprache [Breslau diss.] 1*m.* 8° Köhler, *Lpz.* 87

274. MIDDLE-FRENCH [16TH TO BEGINNING 17TH CENT.] PHILOLOGY.

Grammar.

MEIGRET, Louis — Le Tretté de la Grammaire françoeze [1550], hrsg. Wend. Foerster [Samml. frz. Neudr.] 3*m.*80 8° Henninger, *Heilbr.* (Tbn., *Strsb.*) 88

Article.

ZANDER, Em. — L'Emploi de l'article dans le Frç. du 16 siècle [diss.] 4° *Lund* 92
On use of article in 16 cent. compared w. that in other centuries.

Syntax.

*BENOIST, Ant. — De la Syntaxe française entre Palsgrave et Vaugelas 6*fr.* 8° Thorin, *Paris* 76
John PALSGRAVE, an Englishman and teacher to Princess (afterw. Queen) Mary, was the first author of a regular French Grammar: *Lesclarissement de la Langue Françoyse, suivi An Introductorie for to Lerne to Rede, to Pronounce and to Speke French trewly*, 1530 [ed. w. intro. F. GÉNIN (1st time in Frce.) 1100 pp.] w. 34 4° (Docum. inéd. sur l'Hist. d. Frce.) Imprim. Nat., *Paris* 52]. VAUGELAS was a Frenchman (1585–1650).

Metrics : *Cæsura.*

HEUME, Wilh. — Die Cäsur im Mittelfranzösischen [dissert. inaug.] 8° *Greifswald* 86

Style : *Metaphors.*

DEGENHARDT, E. — Die Metapher bei d. Vorläufern Molières [1612–1654] *Marburg* 86

Chrestomathies.

GODEFROY, Fréd. [ed.] — Morceaux choisis des Prosateurs et Poètes frçs. [17–19 cents.] 12° Gaume, *Paris* [68–69] 77
MARCOU, Prf. F. L. [ed.] — Morceaux choisis d. Classiques frç. [16–19 cents.] 4*fr.* 12° Garnier, *Paris* 82
,, ,, [ed.] — The same: Poètes 4*fr.* 12° ,, ,, 82

275. FRENCH DIALECTS (*a*): ANCIENT: WITH SPECIMENS OF LITERATURE.

Eastern Dialects.

Burgundian.

GÖRLICH, Ewald — Der burgundische Dialekt im 13 u. 14 Jahrh. [Frz. Studien] 5*m.* 8° Henninger, *Heilbr.* (Trbnr., *Strsb.*) 89

Lorraine —*for* Germ. Dialect. *v.* K § 231.

KESSELRING, Max — Die betonten Vocale im Altlothringischen [dissert. inaug.] 8° *Halle* 90
PLÖGER, Ern. — Die Partikeln in Altlothringischen [dissert. inaug.] 1*m.*50 8° ,, (Fock, *Lpz.*) 90
WIEPRECHT, Joh. — D. latein. Homilien d. Haimo v. Halberstadt als Quelle d. altloth. Haimo Uebersg. [diss.] 8° *Halle* 90

Western Dialects.

Anglo-Norman.

BUSCH, Ern. — Laut- u. Formenlehre d. anglonormann. Sprache d. 14 Jahrh. [diss.] 1*m.* 8° *Greifswald* (Fock, *Lpz.* 87

Prepositions.

BARTHE, Alf. — Ueb. d. Präposita. *par* u. *pur* in anglonorm. Denkmälern [diss.] 1*m.*20 8° Lipsius, *Kiel* 87

Etymology: Dictionary.

MOISY, Henri — Glossaire comparatif anglo-normand, 2 vols. 12*fr.* 8° Delesques, *Caen* 92; 93

Metrics.

GNERLICH, Rob. — Bemerkungen über d. Versbau der Anglonormannen [dissert. inaug.] 8° *Breslau* 89

Literature.

Adam [12 cent. mystery]: hrsg. Karl Grass [Romanische Bibliothek] 4*m.* 8° Niemeyer, *Halle* 91
One of the most anc. of all mystery-plays: v. an interesting crit. of it by Ad. EBERT in *Gött. Gelehrt. Anzeigen*, 14 Feb., 1896.
GRASS, Karl — Ueb. Versmass u. Reim d. Adamsspieles [dissert. inaug.] 8° *Bonn* 91

K § 276

ADGAR Légendes de Marie—*ut* K § 277, *s.v.* Didactic Poetry (*d.*) : Lives of the Saints.
BENOÎT DE STE. MORE Eneas ; Roman de Troie—*ut* K § 277, *s.v.* Classical Romances.
BEROT, Purgatoire de St. Patrice, ed. Paul Meyer *in prep.*
CHARDRY [13 cent.] Josaphat, Set Dormanz, *etc*—*ut* K § 277, *s.v.* Didactic Poetry (*d*) : Lives of the Saints.
GAYMAR, Geoff. [12 cent.] Lestorie des Engles, ed. and tr. Sir Thos. Duffus Hardy + Chas. Trice Martin—*ut* F § 19.
The chief interest of the work is linguistic, rather than historical.
KUPFERSCHMIDT, M. Die Havelocksage bei Gaimar u. i. Verhältn. z. Lai d'Havelok 8° Fock, *Lpz.* 80
GROSSETETE, Rob. [12-13 cent.] Carmina Anglo-Normannica, Chasteau d'Amour, *etc.*, ed. M. Cooke [*w.* 9/-] 8° Caxton Soc. 52
HAASE, Friedr. Karl Die altengl. Bearbeitungen v. Chast. d'Am. vergl. m. d. Quelle [diss.] 8° *Halle* 89
Guillaume d'Angleterre.
MÜLLER, R. Untersuchung üb. d. Verfasser d. altfrz. Dichtung Wilhelm v. England 2m. 8° Röhrscheidt, *Bonn* 91
Guillaume le Maréchal, Conte de Strigull et de Pembroke [13 cent.] : ed. Paul Meyer, vol. i. 8° Soc. de l'Hist. d. Fce., *Paris* 92
An Anglo-Norm. poem discov. by MEYER among the MSS. of late Sir Thos. PHILLIPPS, of Cheltenham, describing the life and advents. of William the Marshall, Earl of Pembroke, Regent of Engld. 1216 till his d. in 1219, opening w. siege of Winch. by Empress MATILDA [1141], and thus embracing rns. of 4 Engl. kings and pt. of that of Hy. iii. Vol. ii. to cont. glossary ; vol. iii. Introd., abgd. tr. and notes. [Too late for insertion also in F §§ 19, 20].
GUILLAUME DE ST. PAIX [12 cent.] Roman du Mont-St.-Michel, ed. Fresque. Michel 8° *Caen* 56
HUBER, Karl Die Sprache des Roman du Mont-St.-Michel [Strassb. dissert.] 8° *Braunschweig* 86
REDLICH, Paul Einleitg. z. e. neuen Abdruck d. Roman d. Mt.-St.-Mich. [dissert. inaug.] 8° *Marburg* 86
Havelock, Lay of : ed. and tr. Sir Thos. Duffus Hardy + Chas. Trice Martin—*in their ed. of* Gaymar, *ut supra.*
Horn.
METTLICH, Jos. Bemerkungen z. d. Lied vom wackern Ritter Horn [schl.-progr.] 4° *Münster* 90
Laurent, Vie de St. [12 cent.] : ed. Prf. Werner Söderhjelm 4*fr.*40 4° Bouillon, *Paris* 88
An Anglo-Norman poem of 12 cent., here pubd. for the first time, fr. the unique Paris MS.
LIEBERMANN, Dr. F. [ed.] Ungedruckte anglo-normannische Geschichtsquellen—*ut* D § 5.
MARGUERITE, St., Vie de : Anglo-Norman Version [13 cent.], ed. Fred. Spencer [dissert. inaug.] 8° *Leipzig* 89
Ed. (for 1st time) for unique MS. in Univ. Lib., Cambr., w. Introd., notes, and short acc. of develop. of the legend.
MARIE OF FRANCE [13 cent.]—*ut* K § 277, *s.v.* Didactic Poetry (*b*) : Lais.
PHILIPPE DE THAÜN [12 cent.] Li Compoz [a verse astronomy, w. calendar].
FENGE, Ludw. Sprachliche Untersuchung der Reime des Computus [Ausg. u. Abhdgn.] 2m. 8° Elwert, *Marburg* 86
Song of Dermot & the Earl : ed. Goddard Hy. Orpen, w. Engl. tr., Introd., notes & glossary; map & 1 facs. f 8° Clar. Press / Macmillan, *N.Y.* 92
A scholarly edn. fr. MS. among the Carew Papers at Lambeth. In Fch. rhymes of 13 cent., relating the story of Strongbow's invasion of Ireland, based on contemp. Irish information. Previously available only in an inaccurate abstract by Sir Geo. CAREW [1617] and in a transcript of the Fch. text pub. by Pickering in 1837.
WACE, Rob. [1120–1174].
BAIST, G. Roman der Rou III., 3079–3099—*in* Romanische Forschungen, vol. iii., *ut* B.B. K § 256.
KELLER, W. L. Maistre Wace : eine stilistische Untersuchg. [Rou *and* Brut] [Zürich diss.] 8° *St. Gallen* 86
LORENZ, F. W. Stil in Maistre Waces Roman de Rou [dissert.] 8° Fock, *Lpz.* 86
POHL, Theod. Untersuchung d. Reime in Wace's Rom. de Rou et Ducs de Normandie—*in* Roman. Forschgn., vol. ii., *ut* B.B. K § 256.
ZETSCHE, Æm. Wm. Ueb. d. ersten Thl. d. Bearbg. d. Rom. de Brut durch Rob. Mannyng of Brunne [diss.] 1m.20 8° Fock, *Lpz.* 87
WALTER OF HENLEY [13 cent.] Husbandry [and 3 other 13 cent. treats. on Agriculture]—*ut* D § 119.
WILLIAM i. Laws—*ut* D § 5.
HEIM, H. Ueber d. Aechtht. d. frz. Textes d. Gesetze Wilh. d. Eroberers 8° Fock, *Lpz.* 82
HILDEBRAND, F. Ueber d. Sprachelement in Liber Censualis [Exchequer and Domesday Bk.] 8° " " 84

Franco-Norman (MAINE, BRITTANY, PERCHE, POITOU, ANJOU).

ETIENNE, E. De Diminutivis, Intentivis, Collectivis in Frco.-Gall. sermone nominibus 4*fr.* 8° Vieweg (Bouillon, *Paris*) 83

Phonology.

SCHULZE, Andr. Der Konsonantismus des Francischen im 13ten. Jahrh. [dissert. inaug.] 8° *Halle* 90

Literature.

Bibliotheca Normannica: Denkmäler normann. Litter. u. Sprache, hrsg. H. Suchier, vol. iv.–v. 20*m.* 8° Niemeyer, *Halle* 90–91 *in prg.*
iv. BENOIT D. STE. MORE *Eneas* [*ut* K § 277] SALVERDA DE GRAVE 14*m.* 91 | v. *Le Clef d'Amors* [*ut* K § 277] .... A. DOUTREPONT, 6*m.* 90
GASTÉ, Armand [ed.] Chansons Normandes du Siècle *o.p.* [*pb.* 6*fr.*] c 8° Le Gost-Clérisse, *Caen* 66
Pub. for 1st time fr. the MSS. of Bayeux and Vire. With a learned Introduction and notes. Only 200 printed.

Individual Writers.

BLONDEL, Rob. [15 cent.] Œuvres, ed. A. Héron ; w. Introd., notes, var. rgs. and gloss., vol. i. 8° Lestringant, *Rouen* 91
" " De Reductione Normanniae—*ut* B.B. F § 21, *s.v.* Stevenson [ed.]
GUILLAUME LE CLERC [13 cent.] Bestiaire divin, hrsg. Max F. Mann [Französische Studien] 3*m.*60 8° Henninger, *Heilbr.* (Trübn., *Strassb.*) 88
Includes also the *Bestiarius Reg. C. xii.* of the British Museum.
" " Bestiare, hrsg. Rob. Reinsch—*ut* B § 7.
SEEGER, H. Ueber d. Sprache d. Guillaume le Clerc de Normandie [diss.] 8° *Halle* 81
1 STEFAN, Alois Laut- u. Formenbestand in Guill. li Cler's Roman "Fergus" [diss.] 1*m.* 8° Kleinmayr, *Klagenfurt* 93
Picardian —*v.* K. § 277, *s.vv.* Didactic (*d.*) [Alexis, St., Vie de] ; Rom. d' Avent. [RAOUL DE HOUDENC] ; Prose : Fiction [Aucassin et Nicolete]

278. FRENCH DIALECTS (*b*): MODERN (INCL. SLANG).

Collectively.

BEHRENS, Dietr. Bibliographie des Patois gallo-romans, trad. Eug. Rabiet [Frz. Stud. 6*m.*] 8° Gronau, *Berlin* [ ] 93

Serial.

Revue des Patois et des anc. Dialectes romans d. l. Fce., ed. Prf. Léon Clédat, vols. i.–ii. ea. 15*fr.* 8° Bouillon, *Paris* 87 ; 88
From 1889 continued *sub tit.* Revue de Philologie Frçse. et Provençale (quarterly) *ann.* 15*fr.* 8° *ib.* '89–'94 *in prg.*

K § 276

Bas Valais [South of the Rhine].

GILLIÉRON, Jules — Patois de la Commune d. Vionnaz; map [Bibl. Ecole Htes. Etudes] 7/fr.50 8° Vieweg (Bouillon) *Paris* 80
" " [ed.] — Petit Atlas phonétique du Valais roman 6/fr. 8° Champion, *Paris* 81

Béarnais.

LESPY + RAYMOND, V. F. — Glossaire Béarnais ancien et moderne, 2 vols. 8° Hamelin, *Montpellier* 87; 87

Beaune.

BIGARNE, Ch. — Patois et Locutions du Pays de Beaune: contes, légendes, *etc.* [200 prin.] 8° Batault, *Beaune* 91

Blaisois.

THIBAULT, Andr. — Glossaire du Pays Blaisois [pp. xxv., 363] 8° Herluison, *Orleans* 92

Breton —*v.* K § 282.

Cachy.

LOGIE, T. — Phonology of the Patois of Cachy, Somme [*repr. fr.* Mod. Lang. Notes] 8° *Baltimore* 92

Charante.

ROUSSELOT, P. J. — Modificns. phonét. du Lang. étud. dans le Pat. d. Cellefrouin [382 pp.] 8° Welter, *Paris* 91

Clairvaux.

BAUDOUIN, Alph. — Glossaire du Patois de la Forêt de Clairvaux 15/fr. 8° *Troyes* 86

Dauphiné.

DEVAUX, Abbé A. — De l'Etude des Patois du Haut-Dauphiné *Grenoble* 90–92
In the Bulletin de l'Acad. Delphinale, ser. IV., vols. iii. and v
" " — Essai sur la Langue vulgaire d. Dauphiné au moyen-âge *Paris* 92

Démuin.

LEDIEU, A. — Petit Glossaire du Patois de Démuin 5/fr. 8° Bouillon, *Paris* 93

Dijon —*for* Folklore *v.* B § 16.

CUNISSET-CARNOT — Vocables dijonnais 3/fr. 32° Kolb, *Paris* 89

Doubs, Haute-Saône and Jura—*for* Folklore *v.* B § 16.

Flanders (French Dialect).

CARNEL, D. — Le Dialect flamand de France 2/fr.50 8° Bouillon, *Paris* 91

Franco-Gallia.

GILLIÉRON, Jules [ed.] — Mélanges Gallo-Romanes 8° *Paris* 86

Serial.

Revue des Patois Gallo-romans, ed. J. Gilliéron + Rousselot [*quarterly*] *ann.* 12/fr. 8° Champion, *Paris* 87–94 *in prg.*

Gascon —*v.* K § 266: Provençal Dialects.

Guyenne —*for* Folklore *v.* B § 16.

Ille-et-Vilaine.

ORAIN, Adphe. — Glossaire patois du Département d'Ille-et-Vilaine [w. some pop. songs] 10/fr. 8° Maisonneuve, *Paris* 86

Lauraguais —*for* Folklore *v.* B § 16.

Lorraine —*v.* K § 231; Old-Lorraine, *v.* K § 275.

Meuse.

LABOURASSE, H. — Glossaire abrégé du Patois de la Meuse 10/fr. 8° *Nancy* 87

Normandy —*for* Folklore *v.* B § 16.

FLEURY, Prf. Jean — Essai sur le Patois Normand de la Hague 10/fr. 8° Maisonneuve, *Paris* 89
MOISSY, Henri — Glossaire comp. Anglo-Normand *Caen* 89 *in prg.*
To contain 5000 words now banished fr. Fch. lang. and common to Norm. dialect and English.

Anthology.

FERRAND, Dav. [ed.] — La Muse Normande; w. Introd., notes and gloss. A. Héron, vol. i. 25/fr. s 4° Cagniard, *Rouen* 91
Edited from original *livrets* 1625–1653 and the General Inventory of 1655.

Parisianisms —*v.* Slang, *infra.*

Picardy.

JOUANCOUX + DEVAUCHELLE, I. B. / J. — Etudes p. serv. à un Gloss. étymol. d. patois picard, pts. i. 9/fr.; ii. 7/fr. 4° Jeunet, *Amiens* 80; 91

Poitou —*for* Folklore *v.* B § 16.

K § 276

Switzerland.

ODIN, Alf. — Phonologie des Patois du Canton de Vaud [Leipzig dissert.] 4*m.* 8° Niemeyer, *Halle* 86
" " — Etude sur le Verbe dans le Patois de Blonay [Habil.-Schrift] 1*m.*20 8° " " 87

Vellavien.

DE MONTFLEURY, Bar. de Vinols — Vocab. Patois Vellavien-Frç. et Frç.-Patois Vellavien *Le Puy* 91
Repr. fr. the *Annales d. l. Soc. d'Agriculture*, vol. xxxiv., *Le Puy-en-Velay*, '91.

Vendôme.

MARTELLIÈRE, Paul — Glossaire du Vendômois [pp. xiii. 374] 8° Herluison, *Orleans* 93

Verduno-Chalonnais [SAÔNE and LOIRE].

FERTIAULT, F. — Dictionnaire du Langage populaire Verduno-Chalonnais, pt. i. 2/*fr.*50 8° Bouillon, *Paris* 91 *in prg.*

Walloon.

BOCLINVILLE, Clem., *etc.* — Mélanges Wallons [*by* Bovy, Doutrepont, Gittée, Simon, etc.] 4/*fr.* 8° Vaillant-Carmanne, *Liège* 92
DEFRECHEUX, Jos. — Vocabulaire d. Noms wallons d'Animaux; ill. [w. Lat., Fch. & Flem. equivalents] 3/*fr.*50 8° Vaillant-Carmanne, *Liège* [91] 93
DELAITE, Julien — Essai de Gram. Wallonne [verb] 2/*fr.*; Le Wallon est-il une langue? 50*c.* 8° " " 93; 93
" " — Glossaire des Jeux wallons de Liège, 1/*fr.*; Liège la Wallonne, 1/*fr.* 8° " " 89; 93
MARCHOT, P. — Phonologie détaillée d'un Patois Wallon 3/*fr.* 18° Bouillon, *Paris* 92
WILMOTTE, Maur. — Etudes de Dialectologie Wallonne 5/*fr.* 8° " " 90
" " — Le Wallon: hist. et littér. des origs. à l. fin. d. 18 siècle 1/*fr.*25 16° Rozez, *Brussels* 93
ZÉLIQZON, Léo — Aus der Wallonie [schl.-programme] 2*m.* 4° Scriba, *Metz* 93

Chrestomathy.

Anthologie des Poètes Wallons, *etc.*, ed. Ch. + Jos. Defrecheux + Ch. Gothier, pts. i.–xvi. 8° Gothier, *Liège* ?–93 *in prg.*

Folklore —*v.* B § 16. *Proverbs*—*v.* B § 4 (DEJARDIN).

Slang (Argot).

DELVAU, A. — Dictionnaire de la Langue verte [*ut* B.B. K § 276]: new edn. 15/*fr.* 16° Marpon, *Paris* [65] 89
LARCHEY, Lorédan — Nouv. Supplémt. du Dict. d'Argot [*ut* B.B. K § 276] 3/*fr.*50 18° Dentu, " 89
LA RUE, Jean — La Langue verte [pp. 186] 1/*fr.* 8° Arnold, " 94
RIGAUD, Lucien — Dict. d. Lieux communs d. l. Conversn., Théâtre, Journal, *etc.* 6/*fr.* 8° Ollendorff, *Paris* 81
SCHWOB, Marcel — Jargon des Coquillards—*ut* K § 278.
" " + GUIEYSSE, G. — Étude sur l'Argot franç.—*ut* K § 278.

Neologisms. "Fin-de-Siècle" Words.

RIGAUD, Lucien — Dictionnaire de l'Argot moderne 6/*fr.* 12° Ollendorff, *Paris* 81
VIRMAÎTRE, Chas. — Dictionnaire d'Argot fin-de-siècle 6/*fr.* 18° Charles, *Paris* 94
The author states that he has studied these expressions *sur le vif*—in the prison, the workshop, the slum and the *bouge*.

Parisianisms.

HAMDORF, A. — Ueber die Bestandtheile des Pariser Argots [Greifswald dissert.] 8° *Berlin* 86
KOSCHWITZ, E. — Les Parlers Parisiens: anthologie phonétique 4/*fr.*50 8° Welter, *Paris* 93
RIGAUD, Lucien — Dictionnaire du Jargon Parisien [ancient and modern] 5/*fr.* 32° Ollendorff, *Paris* 78
TIMMERMANS, Adr. — L'Argot Parisien: étude d'étymologie comparée 6/*fr.* 8° Klincksieck, " 92

Provincialisms.

BUIER, Arth. — Anglicismes et Canadianismes 12° *Quebec* 88

Technical Terms. Generally—*v. also* B.B. I § 1.

FLETCHER, J. J. — Pocket Glossary of Technical Terms: Engl.-Fch. and Fch.-Engl. 1/6 64m° Lockwood [87] 93
LITTRÉ, Em. — Supplement—*to his* Dictionn. de la Langue Frçse., *ut* K § 270.

Commercial. Export Trade.

MELZER, A. L. — Deutsch-engl.-frz. Lexikon d. Ausfuhrindustrie u. d. Handels [fairly good] 8*m.* 8° Föllen, *Berlin* 85
ODERMANN + CÔTE, Elie — Deutsch-frz. Hauswörterbuch d. Spr. d. Handels u. Volkswirthschaft 8*m.* 8° Haessel, *Lpz.* 83

Military.

L'Argot de Saint-Cyr 12° *Paris* 93
MERLIN, Léon — La Langue verte du Troupier 2/*fr.* 12° Charles-Lavauzelle, *Paris* 80

Mining.

GÖTZSCHMANN, M. F. — Sammlg. bergmännischer Ausdrücke [w. Engl. and Fch. synons. and indexes] 8° *Freiberg* [ ] 81
KÖHLEN, G. — W'buch d. bei Bergbau angewend. techn. Ausdrücke [Fch., Engl., Germ.] 2*m.*80 12° *Clausthal* 85

Musical.

GOUGET, E. — L'Argot Musical 5/*fr.* 8° Fischbacher, *Paris* 92

Pharmaceutical.

MÖLLER, Geo. Herm. — Dictionnaire internat. medico-pharmac. [Fch., Engl., Germ.] 4*m.* 8° Grubert, *Munich* 79

Printing.

BOUTMY, Eug. Dictionnaire de la Langue verte typographique 3/fr. 18° Liseux, *Paris* 78
" " Dictionnaire de l'Argot des Typographes 2/fr. 12° Marpon, " 83

Railway.

HIRCHE, Paul System. Samml. d. Fachausdr. d. Eisenb'wesens: Germ.-Fch. 3m.; Fch.-Germ. 6m. 16° Steinitz 82; Heymann, *Berl.* [82] 86

Telegraph and Postal.

v. MACK, T. Technisches Wörterbuch für Telegraphie und Post [Germ.-Fch. and Fch.-Germ.] *Berlin* 84

277. OLD-FRENCH LITERATURE.

Manuscripts.

Paris, Bibl. Natl.: Inventaire génér. et méth. d. MSS. frç., 2 vols. [by Léop. Delisle] ea. 7/fr.50 8° Champion, *Paris* 76; 78
" " MSS. Latins et Français ajoutés pendant 1875–1891 [by the same]—*ut* K § 4.
" " Notices et Extraits des MSS.—*ut* K § 4.
" " Les MSS. françois de la Bibl. du Roi, 7 vols. [by Paulin Paris] *Paris* 36–48
SCHWAN, Ed. Die altfranzösischen Liederhandschriften 8m. 8° Weidmann, *Berlin* 85
A study of the relations, origin and determinatn. of the O.-F. *chanson* MSS.

History of Literature: Generally. Poetry—*v. also* K §§ 33–35.

AUBERTIN, Chas. Histoire de la Langue et d. l. Littér. frç. au Moyen Age, 2 vols.—*ut* B.B. K § 268.
DE BEAUREPAIRE Etudes sur la Poésie populaire en Normandie [good] *o.p.* [*pb.* 6/fr.] 8° Tostain, *Avranches* 56
FREYMOND, E. Jongleurs und Menestrels *Halle* 83
GAUTIER, Léon Histoire de la Poésie Liturgique au Moyen Age, vol. i. [Tropes] 10/fr. 8° Picard, *Paris* 87
" " La Poésie Religieuse dans l. Cloîtres d. 9–11 siècles 2/fr.50 r 8° " " 87
*Histoire Littéraire de la France, par les religieux Bénédictins de la Congreg. d. Saint Maur, contin. p. des Membres de l'Institut, vols. i.–xxx. ea. 21/fr. 4° Impr. Nat. (Klincksieck), *Paris* 1733–1888 *in prg.*
Of great importance. Vol. xxx. continues the wk. into the 14 cent.
JEANROY, Alf. Les Origines de la Poésie lyrique en France au Moyen Age [*ut* B § 16] 10/fr. 8° Hachette, *Paris* 89
" " De Nostratibus medii aevi poetis qui primum lyrica Aquitania Carmina imitati sunt [both excellent bks.] 3/fr. 8° " " 89
KURTH, Godefr. Histoire poétique des Mérovingiens [a good book] 10/fr. 8° Picard, *Paris* 93
LECOY DE LA MARCHE, Alb. Le Troisième Siècle: Littéraire et Scientifique 4/fr.; Artistique 5/fr. 8° Desclée, *Lille* 87; 89
LÉNIENT, C. La Poésie patriotique en France au Moyen Age 3/fr.50 18° Hachette, *Paris* 91
*PARIS, Prf. Gaston Manuel de l'Anc. Frç.: la littérature frç. au Moyen Age [11–14 cent.] 2/fr.50 12° " " [88] 90
* " " La Poésie du Moyen Age: leçons et lectures 3/fr.50 18° " " [85] 87
An admirable little reference-book; w. short bibliog. *et sub.* WARREN'S *Primer of Fch. Lit.* [*ut* K § 33] is the English [Amer.] counterpt. of it, and is largely based upon it.
" " Origines d. l. Poésie lyrique en France [*extr. fr.* Jl. d. Savants] 3/fr. 4° Bouillon, *Paris* 92
SCHRÖDER, Rich. Glaube u. Aberglaube in d. altfrz. Dichtungen [diss.] 8° Schlüter, *Hanover* 86
WECKERLIN, Jean Bapt. La Chanson Populaire 5/fr. 8° Didot, *Paris* 86
" " L'ancienne Chanson populaire en France [16–17 cents.] 5/fr. 12° Garnier, *Paris* 87

Arthurian Romances —*v. also* Chansons de Geste, *infra*.

BORMANN, Ern. Die Jagd i. d. altfrz. Artus- u. Abenteuer Romanen [diss.] 8° *Marburg* 87
HEINZEL, R. Ueber die französischen Gralromane 10m. 8° Freytag, *Lps.* 91
KITZE, Adf. Das Ross in d. altfrz. Artus- u. Abenteuer-Romanen [Ausg. u. Abhgn.] 1m.20 8° Elwert, *Marburg* 88
LÖSETH, E. Le Roman en prose de Tristan, le roman de Palamède et la Compilation de Rusticien de Pise [crit. anal. fr. Paris MSS.; pp. 547; Bibl. Ec. Htes. Et.] 18/fr. 8° Bouillon, *Paris* 91
MENTZ, Rich. Die Träume i. d. altfrz. Karls- u. Artus-Epen [Ausg. u. Abhgn.] 2m.80 8° Elwert, *Marburg* 88
MEYER, Fritz Die Stände, ihr Leben u. Treiben n. d. altfrz. Artus- u. Abent.-Romanen—*ut infra*.
MÜLLER, Otto Die täglich. Lebensgewohnheiten i. d. altfrz. Artusromanen [diss.] 1m.20 8° *Marburg* 89
PARIS, Prf. Gaston Les Romans en Vers du Cycle d. l. Table Ronde 4° Impr. Nat., *Paris* 87
Extr. fr. *Histoire littér. de la France*, vol. xxx.: pp. 274.

Chansons de Geste —*v. also* Arthurian Romances, *supra*.

ALTONA, Joh. Gebete u. Anrufungen in d. altfrz. Chansons de Geste [Ausg. u. Abhgn.] 1m. 8° Elwert, *Marburg* 83
BANGERT, Friedr. Die Tiere im altfrz. Epos [Ausg. u. Abhandgn.] 6m. 8° " " 85
DETERMANN, J. W. Epische Verwandschaften im altfrz. Volksepos [diss.] 8° *Göttingen* 88
DREYLING, G. D. Ausdrucksweise d. übertrieb. Verkleinerg. i. altfrz. Karlsepos [Ausg. u. Abhgn.] 4m. 8° Elwert, *Marburg* 88
EBERT, Em. Die Sprichwörter der altfrz. Karlsepen [Ausg. u. Abhandgn.] 1m.50 8° " " 84
EULER, Aug. Das Königthum im altfrz. Karl-Epos [Ausg. u. Abhgn.] 1m.60 8° " " 86
FISCHER, Wilh. Der Bote im altfranzösischen Epos [dissert. inaug.] 8° *Marburg* 87
*GAUTIER, Prf. Léon Les Epopées françaises, vol. ii. [for vols. i., iii.–iv. *v.* B.B. K § 277] 20/fr. 8° Welter, *Paris* [67] 94
An admirable and exhaustive study of the origins and history of the Fch. heroic epic, "the product of the fusion of the Germanic spirit, in a Romance form, with the new Christian civilization of France" (Gaston PARIS).
" " —*in his* La Chevallerie; 25 pl. and 150 ill. [crowned by Acad. Frçe.] 40/fr. 4° Palmé, *Paris* 84
GRABEIN, Paul Die altfrz. Gedichte üb. d. verschied. Stände d. Gesellsch. [diss.] 8° *Halle* 93
HASE, Berth. Ueb. d. Gesandten in d. altfrz. Chansons de Geste [diss.] 8° " 91
D'HÉRICAULT, Chas. Essai sur l'Orig. d. l'Epopée frç. et s. Hist. au Moy. Age 3/fr. 8° Vieweg (Bouillon), *Paris* 60

K § 277

HUSSE, Otto — Die schmückenden Beiwörter u. Beisätze i. d. Chans. d. Geste [diss.] 8° *Halle* 87
KADLER, Alf. — Sprichwörter u. Sentenzen d. altfrz. Artus-u. Abenteurromane [Ausg. u. Abgn.] 2*m*.40 8° Elwert, *Marburg* 86
KEUTEL, Gottfr. — Die Anrufung d. höheren Wesen i. d. altfrz. Ritterromanen [Ausg. u. Abgn.] 1*m*.20 8° „ „ 86
KRABBES, Theod. — Die Frau im altfrz. Karls-Epos [Ausg. u. Abhdgn.] 2*m*. 8° „ „ 84
MEYER, Fritz — Die Stände, ihr Leben u. Treiben n. d. altfrz. Artus- u. Abenteuerromanen [Ausg. u. Abgn.] 3*m*.50 8° „ „ 91
„ Paul — Recherches sur l'Epopée française 3*fr*. 8° Franck, *Paris* 67

A crit. exam. of Gaston PARIS' *Hist. poétique d. Charlem.* [*ut* B.B. K § 277] and of L. GAUTIER'S *Epopées frçses.* [*ut* *ib*.] Extr. fr. *Bibl. d. l'Ecole d. Chartes*.

NYROP, C. — Den oldfranske Heltedigning [w. good bibliogr.] 8° *Copenhagen* (10*fr*. Bouillon, *Paris*) 83
„ „ — Ital. tr. by Egidio Gorra, *sub tit.* Storia de l'Epopea francese nel med. evo 8° *Florence* 86
OSTERHAGE, Geo. — Ueb. einiger Chansons d. Geste d. Lohengrin Kreises [sch.-prg.] 1*m*. 4° Gaertner, *Berlin* 88
PARIS, Paulin — Les Chansons de Geste : poèmes d. 12e. Siècle [an address] 2*fr*. 8° Techener, *Paris*
PFUHL, Heinr. — Untersuchgn. üb. d. Rondeaux u. Virelais spec. d. 14 u. 15 Jahrh. [diss.] 8° Hartung, *Regensbg.* 87
RUST, Ern. — Die Erziehung d. Ritters in d. altfrz. Epik [dissert. inaug.] 8° *Berlin* 88
SCHIRLING, Vict. — Die Verteidigungswaffen im altfrz. Epos [dissert. inaug.] 8° *Marburg* 87
STERNBERG, Aron — Die Angriffswaffen im altfrz. Epos [Ausg. u. Abhgn.] 1*m*.20 8° Elwert, *Marburg* 86
TREBE, Joh. Heinr. — Les Trouvères et leurs Exhortations aux Croisades 1*m*. 4° Hinrichs, *Lpz.* 86
TREIS, Karl — Die Formalität d. Ritterschlags in d. altfrz. Epik [dissert. inaug.] 1*m*.80 8° *Marburg* (Fock, *Lpz.*) 87
VOIGT, Osk. — Ideal d. Schönht. u. Hässlichkt. i. d. altfrz. Chan. d. Geste [diss.] 8° „ 91
VORETZSCH, Prf. Carl — Die französische Heldensage [Akad. Antrittsvorlesg., Tübgn.] 80*pf*. 8° Winter, *Heidelbg.* 94
WINTER, Max — Kleidung u. Putz d. Frau n. d. altfrz. Chans. d. Geste [Ausg. u. Abhgn.] 1*m*.60 8° Elwert, *Marburg* 86
ZELLER, Paul — Die täglichen Lebensgewohnheiten i. altfrz. Karlsepos [Ausg. u. Abgn.] 1*m*.80 8° „ „ 85

Drama.

CALLENBERG, C. — Das geistliche Schauspiel des Mittelalters in Frankreich 8° Fock, *Lpz.* 76
FOURNEL, Vict. — —*in his* Le Vieux Paris : fêtes, jeux et spectacles ; ill. 15*fr*. 8° Mame, *Tours* 87
[LACROIX, Paul] — L'Ancienne France : Le Théâtre ; [after Lacroix's wks. on Mid. Ages] 4*fr*. 8° Didot, *Paris* 87
MÜLLER, Ludw. — Das Rondel in d. frz. Mirakelsp. u. Myst. d. 15 u. 16 Jahrh. [Ausg. u. Abgn.] 1*m*.60 8° Elwert, *Marburg* 84
NEUKOMM, Edm. — —*in his* Fêtes et Spectacles du Vieux Paris 3*fr*. 12° Dentu, *Paris* 86
PETIT DE JULLEVILLE, Prf. Louis — Histoire du Théâtre en France : Les Mystères, 2 vols. 15*fr*. 8° Hachette, *Paris* 89

A good book with a very full Bibliography.

The other vols. of the series are—
Les Comédiens au Moy. Age ....3*fr*.50 12° Cerf, *Paris* 85
La Comédie et les Mœurs a. Moy. Age ....3*fr*.50 12° „ „ 86
Répertoire d. Théât. comique a. Moy. Age 10*fr*. 8° Hachette, *Paris* 86
Hist. d. l. Litt. dramatique ....3*fr*.50 12° Colin, „ 89

RIGAL, Prf. Eug. — Hôtel d. Bourgogne et Marais : hist. d. Théâtres d. Paris d. 1548 à 1635 [a learned essay] 1*fr*. 18° *Aix* (Dupret, *Paris*) 87
„ „ — Alex. Hardy et le Théât. frç. à la fin d. 16e. et comm. d. 17e. Siéc. [crowned by Acad.] 15*fr*. 8° Hachette, *Paris* 90
STODDARD, Fcs. H. [Am.]—*in his* References for Students of Miracle Plays and Mysteries—*ut* B.B. K § 82.
VIALIS, [ed.] — Documts. rel. aux Représentns. théâtr. en Dauphiné d. 1484 à 1635 8° *Montbéliard* 87
WANDELT, Osw. — Sprichwörter u. Sentenzen d. altfrz. Dramas [1100–1400 ; dissert. inaug.] 8° *Marburg* 87
WIECK, Heinr. — Die Teufel auf. d. mittelalt. Mysterienbühne Frankreichs [diss.] 8° Fock, *Lpz.* 87

Fabliaux.

BÉDIER, Jos. — Les Fabliaux—*ut* B § 1.
PARIS, Gaston — Contes Orientaux dans la littér. frç. d. Moy.-Age—*ut* B.B. K § 277, *s.v.* Fiction.
PITZ, Oskar — Beiträge zur Kenntniss d. altfrz. Fableaux, pts. i.–ii. ea. 1*m*. 4° Fock, *Lpz.* 89 ; 89

Historians.

PARIS, Paulin — Les Historiens des Croisades [an address ; 100 printed] 2*fr*.50 8° Techener, *Paris*

Law.

History.

VIOLLET, Paul — Précis de l'Histoire du Droit français 10*fr*. 8° Larose, *Paris* 84

Pulpit Oratory.

BOURGAIN — La Chaire française au 12e. Siècle 7*fr*.50 8° Palmé, *Paris* 79
LECOY DE LA MARCHE, A. — La Chaire frç. au Moyen Age 8*fr*. 8° Laurens, *Paris* [68] 86

A valuable wk., dealing principally w. 13 cent. and based on MS. authorities. Crowned by *Acad. Frçse.*

General Collections of Texts.

Altfranzösische Bibliothek : hrsg. Wendelin Foerster, vols. xii.–xiv. 8° Reisland, *Lpz.* 90–91 *in prg.*

xii. ROBERT DE BLOIS *Floris et Liriope* [*ut* K § 277] Wolfr. v. ZINGERLE, 2*m*.50 91
xiii. *Provensal. Inedita* [*ut* K § 267] ....Carl APPEL, 5*m*. 90
xiv. GUILL. LE CLERC *Bestiaire* [*ut* K § 275]..Rob. REINSCH, 6*m*. 90

Bibliothèque de l'Ecole des Chartes [largely mediæval] 8° *Paris* 31 *sqq.*, *in prg.*
„ de l'Ecole des Hautes Etudes—*ut* K § 95 [conts. some French vols.].
„ Française du Moyen Age : ed. Paul Meyer + Gaston Paris, vols. iii.–vii. ea. vol. 9*fr*. 8° Bouillon, *Paris* 85–90 *in prg.*

New Vols. iii. *Psautier de Metz* [14 cent.] vol. i. Frc. BONNARDOT 85
A second vol. to cont. Introd., gram. and gloss.
iv.–v. MEYER, Paul *Alex. le Grd. dans la Litt. frç.*, 2 v. [*ut infra*] 86
vi.–vii. GAUTIER D'ARRAS, *Oeuvres*, 2 v. [*ut inf.*] ....E. LÖSETH 90

Société des Anciens Textes: 8° Soc. d. Anc. Textes (Didot), *Paris* 75–93 *in prg.*

Aiol [*ut* B.B. K § 277] Jacq. Normand + Gast. Raynaud 12*fr.* (24*fr.*) 78
d'Auvergne, *Amant rendu Cordelier à l'Observance d'Amours* [*ut* B.B. K § 278] .... A. de Montaiglon, 10*fr.* (20*fr.*) 81
Aymeri de Narbonne 2 v. [*ut* B.B. K § 277] M. L. Demaison, 20*fr.* (40*fr.*) 87
Beroul, *Tristan* [*ut* K § 277] ...... W. Meyer + E. Muret, *in prep.*
Bozon, Nic. *Contes Moralisés* [*ut* B § 3] Lucy T. Smith + Paul Meyer 15*fr.* (30*fr.*) 89
Brun de la Montaigne [*ut* B.B. K § 277] Paul Meyer 5*fr.* (10*fr.*) 76
Chansonnier frç. d. St. Germain des Prés, v. i. [*ut* K § 277] P. Meyer + G. Raynaud, 40*fr.* 92
Chansons frç. d. 15 Siècle [*ut* B.B. K § 278] Gast. Paris + Aug. Gevaert, 18*fr.*75 (37*fr.*50) 75
Christine de Pisan, *Oeuvres Poëtiques*, v. i.–ii. [*ut* K § 277] M. Roy, 20*fr.* (40*fr.*) 87 ; 91
Chronique du Mt. St. Michel, vols. i.–ii. [*ut* K § 277] Siméon Luce, 24*fr.* (48*fr.*) 79 ; 86
Couronnemt. d. Louis [*ut* K § 277] .... E. Langlois, 15*fr.* (30*fr.*) 88
Daurel et Beton [*ut* B B. K § 267] .... P. Meyer, 8*fr.* (16*fr.*)
Débat d. Hérauts d'Armes d. Frç. et d. Angleterre .. 10*fr.* (20*fr.*) 77
Deschamps, Eust. *Oeuvres*, vols. i.–viii. [*ut* K § 277] Marq. d. Queux d. St. Hilaire + G. Raynaud, 96*fr.* (144*fr.*) 80–93
Élie d. St.-Gille [*ut* B.B. K § 277] G. Raynaud + Eug. Kölbing, 8*fr.* (16*fr.*) 79
Evangile d. Nicodème .... G. Paris + Alph. Bos, 8*fr.* (16*fr.*)
Guillaume de Berneville, *Vie d. St.-Gilles* [*ut* K § 277] G. Paris + A. Bos, 10*fr.* (20*fr.*) 81
Guillaume de Palerne [*ut* B.B. K § 277] .. H. Michelant, 10*fr.* (20*fr.*) 76
de Margival, Nic. *Panthère d'Amours* [*ut* K § 277] H. A. Todd, 6*fr.* (12*fr.*) 82
Merlin, 2 vols. [*ut* K § 277] .. G. Paris + J. Ulrich, 20*fr.* (40*fr.*) 86
Miracles d. Nostre Dame, 8 v. [*ut* K § 277] G. Paris + Ul. Robert, i.–vii. ea. 10*fr.* (20*fr.*) ; viii. 15*fr.* (30*fr.*) 76–93
Mistère d. St. Bern. d. Menthon [*ut* K § 277] A. Lecoy de la Marche, 8*fr.* (16*fr.*) 89
Mistère d. Vieil Testament, v. i.–vi. [*ut* K § 277] Bar. Jas. de Rothschild, 60*fr.* (120*fr.*) 79–91
Morte Aymeri d. Narbonne [*ut* K § 277] Courage du Parc, 10*fr.* (20*fr.*) 84
Philippe d. Navarre, *Quatre Ages de l'Homme* [*ut* K § 277] de Fréville, 7*fr.* (14*fr.*) 88
Philippe de Remi, *Oeuvres Poëtiques* v. i.–ii. [*ut* B.B. K § 277] H. Suchier, 50*fr.* (100*fr.*) 81 ; 84
Plus Anciens Monumts., Les [*ut* B.B. K § 277] G. Paris [f°] 30*fr.* 75
Raoul de Cambrai [*ut* K § 277] P. Meyer + A. Longnon, 15*fr.* (30*fr.*) 82
Rondeaux etc. d. 15 Siècle [*ut* K § 278] G. Raynaud, 8*fr.* (16*fr.*) 89
Saint Voyage d. Jhérusalem du Seign. d'Anglure [*ut* B.B. K § 277] F. Bonnardot + A. Longnon, 10*fr.* (20*fr.*) 78
Sept Sages d. Rome [*ut* B.B. K § 277] ...... G. Paris, 8*fr.* (16*fr.*) 76
Thèbes, Roman de, 2 vols. [*ut* K § 277] L. Constans, 30*fr.* (60*fr.*) 90
Thos. de Cantorbéry, Vie de St. [*ut* K § 277] P. Meyer, 10*fr.* (20*fr.*) 85

The prices in brackets are for eds. on Whatman ppr.

Chrestomathies —*v.* K § 273.

Chansons de Geste.

Collections.

Chansons d. Gestes et Romans des Douze Pairs de France, 12 vols. *o.p.* [*w.* £6 6/-] 8° Techener, *Paris* 36–48

Romans de Parise la Duchesse .... ed. G. F. Martonne
Bodel, Jean *Chanson des Saxons*, 2 v. .... Fesq. Michel
Raoul de Cambrai and Bernier *Romans* .... Ed. Le Glay
Raimbert de Paris *Chevalier Ogier de Danemk.*, 2 v. [G. Barrois]
Richard le Pèlerin *Chanson d'Antioche*, 2 v. ...... Paulin Paris
Romancero Français .... „ „
Romans d. Berte au Grans Piés .... „ „
Jean de Flagy *Garin de Loherain*, 2 v. .... „ „

Individual Texts.

Adenès li Rois [13 cent.].
Essert, Otto — Bueves de Commarchis [school-programme] 4° *Königsberg* 90
Aie d'Avignon —*ut* B.B. K § 277.
Oesten, Rud. — Die Verfasser d. altfrz. Aye d'Avignon [Ausg. u. Abhgn.] 1*m.*20 8° Elwert, *Marburg* 85
Aliscans [12 cent.]: hrsg. G. Rolin, mit Berücksichtigung Wolframs v. Eschenbach Willehalm 10*m.* 8° 94
Amis et Amiles: tr. Wm. Morris, *sub voc.* The Story of Amis and Amile 7/6 *nt.* 8° Kelmscott Press 94
Only 475 offered for sale; and 15 on vellum at 30/- *nt.*
Bock, Mor. — Ueber den Gebrauch der Pronomina in Amis et Amiles [school-progr.] 8° *Linz* 89
Mager, A. — Grammatik u. Wortstellung d. Amis et Amiles *Berlin* 86
Schwieger, P. — Die Sage von Amis uud Amiles in Frankreich u. Deutschland [school-progr.] Fock, *Lpz.* 85
Anseïs de Mes [13 cent.].
Hoepf, C. — Anseïs de Mes: chanson de geste [school-progr.] Fock, *Lpz.* 85
Chanson d'Antioche [Crusade series]: ed. Prf. Paulin Paris, 2 vols. 16*fr.* s 8° Techener, *Paris* 48
Paris, Paulin — Nouvelle Étude sur la Chanson d'Antioche 3*fr.*50 8° Techener, *Paris*
Chanson de Roland [attrib. to Théroulde, or Turold, troubad. of 11 cent.].
ed. Prf. Léon Clédat; w. Fch. Introd. and glossary 1*fr.*80 12° Garnier, *Paris* [85] 86
Translation: trad. archaïque et rhythmique Prf. Léon Clédat; w. notes [*extr. fr.* Bibl. Facult. Lettr. Lyon] 5*fr.* 8° Leroux, *Paris* 87
„ Amédée Jubert [verse] 3*fr.*50 12° Libr. d. Biblioph., *Paris* 86
Bibliography.
Eicke, Theod. — Zur neueren Literaturgeschichte d. Rolandsage in Deutschld. u. Frankreich 2*m.* 8° Fock, *Lpz.* 91
Generally.
Brunetière, Ferd. — Chans. d. Rol.—*in his* Études crit. sur l'hist. de la littér. frçse., ser. i. 3*fr.*50 12° Hachette, *Paris* 80
Dreyling, Gust. — Ausdrucksweise d. übertriebenen Verkleinerg. i. Ch. d. R. [Ausg. u. Abhgn.] 4*m.* 8° Elwert, *Marburg* 89
Fassbender, Ludw. — Die frz. Roland-HSS. i. ihr. Verhält. z. einand. u. z. Karlamagnussaga [a good diss.] 8° *Cologne* 87
Gasté, Prf. Armand — La mort de Roland: trad. en Lat., et notes [on verses 2164 to 2396] 8° *Paris* 87
Göhling, V. — Satzverbindung im altfranzösischen Rolandsliede [school-programme] 8° *Brandenburg* 86
Golther, Wolfg. — Das Rolandslied d. Pfaffen Konrad [12 cent.]: Verhältn. z. frz. Chans. d. Rol. [a good diss.] 4*m.* 8° Kaiser, *Munich* 86
Hagberg, Theod. — Rolandssagan till sin historiska Kærna och poetiska Omklædning 8° *Upsala* 84
Höfft, Carl Th. — France, Franceis und Franc im Rolandliede 2*m.* 8° Trübner, *Strassbg.* 91
Sauerland, E. — Ganelon und sein Geschlecht [Ausg. u. Abhandgn.] 1*m.*60 8° Elwert, *Marburg* 86
Scholle, Fra. — Stammbaum d. altfrz. u. altnord. Ueberliefgn. d. Rolandsliedes u. d. Oxfd. HS. [prog.] 1*m.* 4° Gaertner, *Berlin* 89
Schürer, Heinr. — Die Sprache der HS. P. des Rolandsliedes [school-programme] 4° *Komotau* 87
Sudre, F. — Les Sources du Roman de Renart 8° *Paris* 93
Wichmann, Clem. — Abhängigkeitsverhältn. d. altengl. Roland zur altfrz. Dichtg. [diss.] 8° *Essen* 89
Clarisse et Florent —*v. infra, sub voc.* Huon de Bordeaux.
Couronnement de Louis: ed. E. Langlois 15*fr.* 8° Soc. d. Anc. Textes (Didot) *Paris* 88
Durmars li Galois.
v. Kirchrath, Leonh. — Li Romans de Durmars le Gallois [Ausg. u. Abhandlgn.] 2*m.* 8° Elwert, *Marburg* 84
On its relations to *Meraugis de Portlesguez* and the wks. of Crestien de Troies. *V.* also *Garin de Monglane* (Störikol), *infra.*
Enfances Vivien, Les: ed. Prf. Carl Wahlund + Hugo v. Fellitzen, pt. i. [fr. Paris, Boulogne, Lond. and Milan MSS.] 4° *Upsala* (6*fr.* Bouillon, *Paris*) 86

K § 277

Esclarmonde : ed. Max Schweigel—*ut infra, sub tit.* Huon d. Bordeaux.
MALHERBE, Charl. Notice sur Esclaremond 2fr. 18° Fischbacher, *Paris* 90
Fierabras :
REICHEL, C. Die mittelengl. Romanze Sir Fyrumbras [and its rel. to O.-F. and Provenç. Fierabras]—*ut* K § 48.
Floovant : ed. H. Michelant + F. Guessard—*in their* Anciens Poètes [1858; *ut* B.B. K § 277, *s.v.* Early Poetry].
BANGERT, F. Beitrag zur Geschichte der Fl. sage *o.p.* 8° Henninger, *Heilbronn* 79
DARMESTETER, Prf. Arsène De Floovante vetustiore Gall. poemate et de Merov. Cyclo 5fr.; *red. to* 3fr. 8° Vieweg (Bouillon), *Paris* 77
Added is a Slavonic vers. of the romance, here first ed. fr. Paris MS., *Il Libro di Fioravante.*

Garin de Monglane.
RUDOLPH, Karl Verhältn. d. beid. Fassgn. i. welch. d. Chanson G. d. M. überlief. ist [diss.] 8° *Marburg* 90
STÖRIKO, Adf. Verhältn. d. Romane Durmart u. Garin de Monglane [Ausg. u. Abhgn.] 1m.60 8° Elwert, *Marburg* 88
GIRARD D'AMIENS [13–14 cent.] : Roman von Escanor, hrsg. H. Michelant [Bibl. d. Litter. Verein in Stuttg.] 8° (Fues, *Tübingen*) 87
GIRART DE VIANE [Vienna]—*ut* B.B. K § 277.
HARTMANN, Karl Ueber d. Eingangsepisoden d. Cheltenh. Version d. Gir. d. Viane [dissert. inaug.] 8° *Marburg* 89
KUNZE, A. Das Formelhafte in Girart d. Viane verglichen m. d. Rolandsliede [diss.] 8° *Halle* 86
Gui de Bourgogne : ed. Frçois. Guessard + H. Michelant 5fr. 8° Franck, *Paris* 58
Vol. i. of GUESSARD'S *Anciens Poëtes d. Frce.* [*ut* B.B. K § 277, *s.v.* Early Poetry]. Ed. (for 1st time) fr. Tours and London MSS.
FREUND La Chanson de Gui d. Bourg. et s. Rapports avec Ch. d. Rol. et Turpin [progr.] 8° Fock, *Lpz.* 85
MAUSS, Frz. Charakteristik der in d. Gui de Bourgogne auftretenden Personen [diss.] 1m.60 8° *Münster* 83
Guillaume d'Orange :
SALTZMANN, Hugo Der histor.-myth. Hintergrund u. d. Syst. d. Sage i. Cyklus d. Gu. d'Or. *etc.* [progr.] 1m. 4° *Königsberg* 90
Huon de Bordeaux :
BACHT, H. Sprachliche Untersuchungen über Huon de Bordeaux Fock, *Lpz.* 84
FRIEDWAGNER, Math. Ueb. d. Spr. d. altfrz. Huon de Bordeaux [Neuphil. Stud.] 2m.40 8° Schöningh, *Paderborn* 91
SCHÄFER, Herm. Ueb. d. Pariser HSS. 1451 u. 22555 d. Huon de Bordeaux-Sage [diss.] 8° *Marburg* 91
Appears also in pt. cxi. of the *Ausgaben und Abhandlungen, ut* K § [illegible].
SCHWEIGEL, Max [ed.] Esclarmonde, Clarisse et Florent, Yde et Olive [Ausg. u. Abhandlgn.] 4m.50 8° Elwert, *Marburg* 89
Texts of 3 continuations of *Huon de Bordeaux*, here first ed. fr. the unique Turin MS.
JEAN DE FLAGY [12 cent.] Garin le Loherain : trad. Prf. Paulin Paris [*for his ed. of text v.* B.B. K § 277] 3fr. 12° Techener, *Paris* 62
BÜCHNER, Dr. Geo. Das altfrz. Lothringer-Epos : Inhalt, Form u. Entstehung [Giessen diss.] 1m.50 8° Thomas, *Lpz.* 87
In support of STEINTHAL'S theory as to the origin of the national-epos.
FRIST, Alt. Die Geste d. Loherains i. d. Prosabearbeitg. d. Arsenal-HS. [Ausg. u. Abhgn.] 1m.20 8° Elwert, *Marburg* 84
HEUSER, E. W. Ueb. d. Theile in welche d. Lothr. Geste sich zerlegen lässt 8° Fock, *Lpz* 84
KRÜGER, Carl Stellung d. HS. J. in der Ueberlieferg. d. Geste d. Loherains [Ausg. u. Abhgn.] 2m.80 8° Elwert, *Marburg* 86
W. 2 Appends. (1) on *Chans. d. Loh.* as source of *Chev. Ogier*, by Em. HEUSER ; (2) text of Lorraine fragmt., ed. HEUSER.
MARSEILLE, H. Ueber die Handschriftgruppe E, M, P, X. der Geste des Loherains 8° Fock, *Lpz.* 84
PARIS, Prf. Paulin Étude sur les Chans. d. Geste et s. le Garin de Loherain 1fr.50 8° Douniol, *Paris* 63
Vengeance Fromondin [contin. of GIRBERS DE MES (Metz)].
RUDOLPH, Alf. Ueber die Vengeance Fromondin [Ausg. u. Abhgn.] 1m.20 8° Elwert, *Marburg* 85
Maugis d'Aigremont : ed F. Castets 10fr. 8° *Paris* 93
Morte Aymeri de Narbonne : ed. Couraye du Parc 10fr. 8° Soc. d. Anc. Textes (Didot), *Paris* 84
Pseudo-Philomena
SCHNEEGANS, C. Die Quellen d. sogenannten Pseudo-Philomena u. d. Officiums v. Gerona zu Ehren Karls d. Grossen : als Beitrag z. Gesch. d. altfrz. Epos 2m.50 8° Heitz, *Strassbg.* 91
Raoul de Cambrai : ed. Paul Meyer + A. Longnon 15fr. 8° Soc. d. Anc. Textes (Didot), *Paris* 82
GÖRKE, Rich. Die Sprache d. Raoul de Cambrai : eine Lautuntersuchung [dissert. inaug.] 1m.20 8° Lipsius, *Kiel* 87
Renaus de Montauban.
ZWICK, R. Ueber die Sprache des Renaut von Montauban [diss.] 8° Fock, *Lpz.* 84
Richars li Biaus : hrsg. Prf. Wendelin Foerster 6m. 8° Hölder, *Vienna* 74
Here ed. for first time, tho' *Analyse et Fragments* were ed. C. C. CASATI, 1868.

Yde et Olive : —*v. supra, sub tit.* Huon de Bordeaux.

Arthurian Romances [and their Sources].

BÉROUL [12 cent.] Tristan, ed. W. Meyer + E. Muret 8° Soc. d. Anc. Textes (Didot), *Paris, in prep.*
LÖSETH, E. Tristanromanens gammel-franske Prosahaandskr. Pariser Nat. Bibl. 2kr. 8° Cammermeyer, *Christiania* 88
LUTASLAWSKI, Wincenty Les Folies de Tristan [*extr. fr.* Romania] 8° *Paris* 87
WARNECKE, Herm. Metrische u. sprachl. Abhdg. üb. d. dem. Berol zugeschr. Tristan-Fragmt. 1m.50 8° Deichert, *Erlangen* 88
CRESTIEN DE TROIES.
Cliges : hrsg. Prf. Wendelin Foerster ; w. Germ. Introd. and glossary [Roman Bibl.] 4m. 8° Niemeyer, *Halle* 89
Yvain [Chevalier au Lyon] : hrsg. Prf. Wend. Foerster ; w. Germ. Introd. and glossary [Roman Bibl.] 4m. 8° „ „ 91
ELLINGER, Joh. Syntax der Pronomina bei Crestien de Troies [schl.-progr.] 1m. 8° Fock, *Lpz.* 86
EMECKE, Heinr. Chrestien v. Troyes als Persönlichkeit u. als Dichter [diss. inaug.] 8° *Würzburg* 92
NASTASI, Prf. Jean Monographie sur Cligés de Chrestien de Troyes [progr.] 80*pf.* 8° Fink, *Linz* 93
" " Die Lehre d. Nebensätze im Cligés de Chrestien de Troyes [progr.] 1m. 8° " " 94
OTHMER, Karl Das Verhältniss v. Chr. v. Troyes Erec et Enide z. d. Mabinogion [diss.] 2m. 8° *Cologne* 89
ROITZSCH, Max Das Particip bei Crestien de Troies [diss.] 1m.60 8° Fock, *Lpz.* 86
SCHWIEDER, Adph. Le Discours indirect dans Chrestien de Troyes [school-progr.] 1m. 4° Gaertner, *Berlin* 90
STEINBACH, Dr. Paul Einfluss d. Crestien de Troies auf. d. englische Literatur [*on* Chev. au Lyon] [diss.] 1m.80 8° Fock, *Lpz.* 86
SVENONIUS, T. L. Om Bruket af Subjonctif hos Chrestien de Troies 8° " " 80
WAITZ, H. Die Fortsetzungen v. Crestien's *Perceval le Gallois* nach d. Pariser Handschriften [diss.] 2m. 8° Trübner, *Strassbg.* 90
FROISSART, Jean [1337–1409] Meliador, ed. Mme. James Darmesteter Soc. d. Anc. Textes Frç., *Paris, in prep.*
A once-famous romance, prob. the last of the Round Table series, recently rediscovered by LOGNON in Bibl. Nat. classed under the erroneous title *Roman de Camel et de Hermondine.* Besides some 30,000 lines, it conts. all the lyrics of WENCESLAS DE BRABANT.
Merlin [13 cent.] : *ed. Prf. Gaston Paris + Jacob Ulrich, 2 vols. 20fr. 8° Soc. d. Anc. Textes (Didot), *Paris* 86
With the prose version by ROBERT DE BORON, ed. fr. the Huth MS.
Vers de la Mort, Li [13 cent.] : ed. C. A. Windahl ; w. Fch. Introd., notes and gloss. 3kr. 8° Gleerup, *Lund* 87

Classical and Oriental.

Alexandre.

MEYER, Paul — Alexandre le Grand dans l. Littér. frç. d. Moy. Age, 2 vols. [Bibl. Frç. d. Moy. Age] 18/fr. 12° Bouillon, *Paris* 86

Vol. i. conts. (1) the fragmt. of ALBÉRIC DE BESANÇON, (2) the metr. versn. fr. MSS. at Paris and Venice, (3) the *Enfances d'Alexandre* (MS. 789 in Bibl. Nat.), (4) extrs. fr. the *Alexander* of THOMAS OF KENT; vol. ii. the History of the Legend.

ALEXANDRE DU PONT [13 cent.] Roman de Mahomet, hrsg. B. Ziolecki — *Oppeln* 86

Previously edited by REINAUD+Fr. MICHEL, 8° *Paris* '31.

PETERS, Rich. — Der Roman de Mahomet: eine sprachliche Untersuchung [diss.] 1m. 8° Dieterich, *Göttingen* 85

BENOIT DE STE [... 54–89] Eneas, ed. Salverda de Grave [Bibl. Normann.] 14m. 8° Niemeyer, *Halle* 91

" " [Ro]man de Troie—*vd* B.B. K § 277.

COLLILIEUX, Fr — [Ét]ude sur Dictys de Crète et Darès de Phrygie 2/fr.50 8° Drevet, *Grenoble* 87

" " — *in his* Deux Éditeurs de Virgile 8° " " 87

CORRA, E. — *in his* Testi inediti di Storia Trojana 8° *Turin* 87

The Introduction deals with the history of the Troy cycle. For Jac. van MAERLANT'S *Istory van Troje*, v. B § 3.

JACOBS, Carl — Ein Fragment d. Roman d. Troie v. Benoit de Ste. More z. Bordeaux [schl.-progr.] 4° *Hamburg* 91

" " — Zur Kritik u. Sprache des zu Bordeaux befindl. Fragm. d. Rom. d. Troie [schl.-progr.] 4° " 90

JEHAN DE TUIM [13 cent.] Roman de Jules César.

GRAF, A. — *in his* Roma nella Memoria e n. Immaginazioni d. Medio Evo 8° *Rome* 82–83

Sept Sages, Li Romans des—*vd* B.B. K § 277; *v. also* B § 3.

EHRET, Ph. — D. Verfasser d. versific. Romans d. Sept Sages u. Herbers, d. Verfass. d. altfrz. Dolopathos [diss.] 8° *Heidelberg* 86

PARIS, Paulin — Études sur les différ. Textes [printed and MS.] des Rom. d. Sept Sages, pt. i.—*vd* B § 3.

Thebes, Roman de [12 cent.]: ed. Léop. Constans, 2 vols. 30/fr. 8° Soc. d. Anc. Textes (Didot), *Paris* 90

Fabliaux, Contes, etc.

Collection.

JUBINAL, M. L. A. [ed.] Nouv. Recueil de Contes, Dits, Fabliaux *etc.* d. xiii.–xv. siècl., 2 vols. *o.p.* [*pb.* 16/*fr.*] 8° Challamel, *Paris* 39; 42

Individual Texts.

Auberee [O.-F. fable]: hrsg. Geo. Ebeling, pt. i. [Einleitung] 8° Niemeyer, *Halle* 91

Renart, Roman de [13 cent.]: *ed. Ern. Martin, vol. iii. [Variants] [an excellent critical edn.] 12m. 8° Trübner, *Strassbg.* 87

Aids: —*for other* Treatises, *v. sup.*, *s. v.* Fabliaux, B § 7: *for* Engl. trs. *v.* B § 7, K § 47.

BÜTTNER, Dr. Herm. — Studien zu dem Roman de Renart und dem Reinhart Fuchs, 2 pts. 7m.50 8° Trübner, *Strassb.* 91; 91

i. *D. Ueberlieferung d. R. de R. u. d. HS. O.* 5m.; ii. *Reinhart Fuchs u. seine Quelle* 2m.50.

LANGE — Les Rapports du Roman de Reynart au Poème allemand d. Henri le Gleissner [progr.] 8° *Neumark* 86

*MARTIN, Ern. — Observations sur le Roman de Renart 3m.50 8° Trübner, *Strassbg.* 87

Supplemt. to his edn., *ut supra*. Conts. an Index of Proper Names.

Early Poetry.

Collections.

BRAKELMANN, Jules [ed.] Les plus anciens Chansonniers frç. d'apr. l. MSS.; pt. i. [12 cent.] 5/fr. 8° Bouillon, *Paris* 91

Gautier d'ESPINAL, Crestien de TROYES, Mesire Morrisses de CREON, Mesire HUES D'OISY, Mesire QUENES DE BETHUNE, RENALS, li Chastelains de COUCI, BLONDELS DE NESLE, Li Roi RICHARDS d'Engleterre.

GROSSETESTE, Rob. [12–13 cent.] Carmina *etc.*—*v.* K § 275, *s.v.* Anglo-Norman.

MEYER+RAYNAUD, Paul G. [eds.] Le Chansonnier frç. de St.-Germain-des-Pres [Bibl. Nat. 20050], vol. i. 40/fr. 8° Soc. d. Anc. Textes, *Paris* 92

Translations.

HERTZ, Wilh. [tr.] Spielmannsbuch: Novellen in Versen a. d. 12 u. 13 Jahrh. 6m. 8° Kröner, *Stuttgt.* 86

Individual Writers.

CHÂTELAIN (RAOUL) DE COUCY [13 cent.] Lieder d. Castellans v. Coucy, hrsg. Fritz Fath [a good ed. fr. the MSS.] 1m.80 8° Weiss, *Heidelberg* 83

DAVIDS, F. — Strophen- u. Versbau d. Lieder d. Kastellans v. Coucy [schl.-progr.] 4° *Hamburg* 87

RUTEBOEUF [*c.* 1230–*c.* 1285].

CLÉDAT, Prf. Léon — Rutebeuf [Coll. d. Ecrivains Frç.] 18° Hachette, *Paris* 91

JORDAN, Ludw. — Metrik und Sprache Rutebeufs [dissert. inaug.] 1m.60 8° *Wolfenbuttel* (Vandenhoeck, *Gött.*) 89

SCHUMACHER, Ern. — Zur Syntax Rusteboeufs [dissert. inaug.] 1m.60 8° Lipsius, *Kiel* 86

TJADEN, P. — Untersuchung über die Poetik Rutteboeufs [dissert. inaug.] 8° *Marburg* 85

Chronicles in Verse.

Chronique du Mont-St. Michel [1343–1468], ed. Siméon Luce, vols. i.–ii. ea. 12/fr. 8° Soc. d. Anc. Textes (Didot), *Paris* 79; 86

WACE, Rob. [1120–74] —*vd* K § 275, *s.v.* Anglo-Norman.

Didactic Poetry (*a*): *Dits.*

DE CONDÉ, Jean [*and* BAUDOUIN].

KRAUSE, Arn. — Bemerkungen zu den Gedichten d. Baudouin u. d. Jean de Condé [progr.] 1m. 4° Gaertner, *Berlin* 90

Didactic Poetry (*b*): *Lais* [narrative poems].

MARIE OF FRANCE [13 cent.]—*vd* B.B. K § 277.

BÉDIER, J. — Les Lais de Marie de France—*in* Revue des Deux Mondes, Oct. 1891 2/fr.50 8° *Paris* 91

KOLLS, Ant. — Zur Lanvalsage: eine Quellenuntersuchung *Berlin* 86

Conts. a comparison of the *Lai* of MARY OF FRANCE with the *Lai de Graelent.*

Didactic Poetry (*c*): *Miscellaneous.*

JEAN PRIORAT [of Besançon; 13 cent.]: ed. U. Robert+W. Foerster *in prep.*

A tr. in verse of 8 syllables of the prose tr. by JEAN DE MEUN of VEGETIUS' *De Re Militari.*

WENDELBORN, Fritz — Sprachliche Untersuchung der Reime d. Végéce [dissert.] 8° *Bonn* 87

K § 277

Ordene de Chevalerie [13 cent.]: w. Engl. tr. Wm. Morris—*in* Caxton's [tr.] Order of Chivalry, *ut* F § 14.
Describes, in verse, the ceremonies of the *adoubement*, and draws a picture of the ideal knight.

GAUTIER DE METZ [13 cent.] Image du Monde—*ut* B.B. K § 277.
FANT, Carl — L'Image du Monde étudié dans s. diverses Rédactions frç. [Paris and Stockh. MSS.] 8° *Upsala* 86
HUON DE MÉRI [13 cent.] Tournoiement d'Antéchrist.
GREBEL, M. — Le Tornoiment Antéchrist in seiner literarhistorischen Bedeutung 8° Fock, *Lpz.* 83
WIMMER, Geo. — Prolegomena zu einer kritischen Bearbeitung von Li Tornoiemenz Antéchrist [diss.] 8° *Marburg* 86
LE FÈVRE, Jehan [14 cent.] Lamentations de Matheolus et Livre de Leesce: ed. crit. A. G. van Hamel, vol. i. 10*fr.* 8° Bouillon, *Paris* 93
This vol. conts. the French and (original) Latin texts of the *Lamentations*, fr. the unique MS. at Utrecht. Introd. and a gloss. to follow. *Bibl. de l'Écol. Htes. Études.*
Song of Dermot: —*ut* K § 275, *s.v.* Anglo-Norman.

Didactic (d): Lives and Legends of the Saints.

Alexis, St. [12 cent.] Vie de—*in* Les Plus Anciens Monuments, *ut* B.B. K § 277 (p. 991).
AMIAUD, Arth. —*in his* La Légende Syriaque de St. Alexis—*ut* K § 112.
JORET, Ch. — La Légende de St. Alexis en Allemagne 2*fr.*50: *red. to* 1*fr.*50 8° Vieweg (Bouillon), *Paris* 81
KÖTTING, Geo. — Studien über altfrz. Bearbeitungen d. Alexiuslegende [programme] 4° *Treves* 90
Barlaam et Josaphat —*v. also* B § 3 (KUHN).
CHARDRY [Engl. trouvère; 13 cent.] Josaphat, Set Dormanz *etc.*, ed. J. Koch—*ut* B.B. K § 277.
ZOTENBERG, H. — Notice sur le Livre de B. et J. [w. extrs. fr. Gk., Arab. and Ethiop. versns.] *Paris* 86
GUI DE CAMBRAI [13 cent.] Barlaam u. Josaphat, hrsg. Herm. Zotenberg + Paul Meyer *o.p.* 12° *Stuttgart* 64
" " Fragmts. d'une Tradn. frç. de Barlaam et Josaph. ed. Prf. Paul Meyer 2*fr.* 8° Impr. Nat., *Paris* 66
Fragments of a French tr. made under the Gk. text at beginning of 13 cent. *Bibl. de l'École d. Chartes.*
BRAUNHOLTZ, E. — Die erste nicht-christliche Parabel d. Barl. u. Josaph. 3*m.* 8° Niemeyer, *Halle* 84
KRULL, Alb. — Gui de Cambrai: eine sprachliche Untersuchung [diss.] 1*m.*20 8° Vandenhoeck, *Göttingen* 87
Catherine, Ste.
TENDERING, F. — Das poitevinische Katherinenleben u. d. übrigen südwestlich. Denkmäler [diss.] 8° *Bonn* 85
Eloi, St. [13 cent.] Miracles de St. Eloi, ed. Achille Peigné-Delacourt *o.p.* 8° *Paris* 59
WIRTZ, Em. — Lautliche Untersuchung der Miracles d. St. Eloi [Ausg. u. Abhgn.] 2*m.*50 8° Elwert, *Marburg* 85
Eulalie, St. —*in* Les Plus Anciens Monuments, *ut* B.B. K § 277 (p. 991).
Gilles, St.
GUILLAUME DE BERNEVILLE [12 cent.] Vie de St. Gilles, ed. Prf. Gaston Paris + Alphonse Bos 10*fr.* 8° Soc. d. Anc. Textes (Didot), *Paris* 81
Gregoire, St. [12 cent.] Légende de S. Grégoire: red. d. 14 siècle, ed. Carl Fant [fr. MS. in Bibl. Nat.] 8° *Upsala* 87
KUCHENBÄCKER, Karl — Ueber die Sprache des altfrz. Gregors [diss.] 8° *Halle* 86
NEUSSEL, Otto — Ueb. d. altfrz., mhd. u. mittelengl. Bearbeitgn. d. Sage v. Gregorius [diss.] 8° " 86
RÜHLEMANN, O. — Ueber die Quellen eines altfrz. Lebens Gregorius des Grossen 8° Fock, *Lpz.* 85
Jean le Paulu, St.
D'ANCONA, A. —*in his* La Leggenda di Sant' Albano 8° *Bologna* 65
Julienne, St. Vie de St. Julienne, ed. H. v. Feilitzen—*in* Li Ver del Juise 8° *Upsala* 83
Laurent, St. [12 cent.] Vie de St. Laurent, ed. Prf. Werner Söderhjelm—*v.* K § 275, *s.v.* Anglo-Norman.
Marguerite, St. Vie de: Anglo-Norman version [13 cent.]—*v.* K § 275, *s.v.* Anglo-Norman.
Marie, La Vierge —*for* Miracle Plays on the Virgin *v. infra*, *s.v.* Early Drama.
ADGAR Légendes de Marie—*ut* B.B. K § 277.
NEUHAUS, Carl — Die Latein. Vorlagen zu d. altfrz. Adgarschen Marienlegenden, 3 pts. 2*m.* 8° Henninger, *Heilbronn* (Thor., *Strasb.*) 86–87
GAUTIER DE COINSY [12–13 cent.] Miracles de la Ste. Vierge, ed. Abbé Poquet *o.p.* [*pb.* 50*fr.*; 167 prin.] 4° Didron, *Paris* 57
MUSSAFIA, A. — Ueber den von Gautier de Coincy benutzten Quellen 3*m.*10 94
Marienlob: ein altfrz., aus e. Pariser HS. [13 cent.], ed. Hugo Andresen 1*m.*20 8° Niemeyer, *Halle* 91
MUSSAFIA, Adf. —*in his* Studien zu den mittelalterl. Marienlegenden, pts. i.–iv. [*extr. fr.* Sitz. Wien. Ak.] 5*m.*30 r 8° Tempsky, *Vienna* 87; 90; 89; 91
WECHSSLER, F. — Die romanischen Marienklagen 2*m.*40 8° Niemeyer, *Halle* 93
Patrice, St.:
BEROT Purgatoire de St. Patrice, ed. Paul Meyer—*v.* K § 275, *s.v.* Anglo-Norman.
Thomas le Martyr [12 cent.] Fragmts. d'une Vie de St. Thomas, ed. Paul Meyer 10*fr.* 8° Soc. d. Anc. Textes (Didot), *Paris* 85
ETIENNE, Prf. Eug. — La Vie de St. Thomas p. Garnier de Pont-Ste-Maxence: étude histor., littér. et philol. 6*fr.* 8° Bouillon, *Paris* 83
Tundal —*v.* K § 254, *s.v.* Lives of the Saints, *sub tit.* Tundale.

Didactic Poetry (e): Religious and Devotional.

GILLEBERT DE CAMBRAI [13 cent.] Lucidaire
EBERHARDT, P. — Der Lucidaire Gilleberts de Cambray 8° Fock, *Lpz.* 84
SCHLADEBACH, H. — Das Elucidarium d. Honorius Augustodunensis u. d. frz. metr. Lucid. v. Gill. d. C. 1*m.*20 8° " " 84
Romans de Carité, Li, et Miserere du Re(n)clus de Moiliens [=? BARTHELEMI; 12 cent.]: ed. crit. Prf. A. G. van Hamel, 2 vols.; w. Fch. Introd., notes, gloss. and list of rhymes [Bibl. d. l'École d. Htes. Etudes] 20*fr.* 8° Vieweg (Bouillon), *Paris* 85

Didactic Poetry (f): Bestiaries [Beast-Epics]—v. also B § 7.

DE FOURNIVAL, Rich. [13 cent.] Bestiaire d'Amour: ed. C. Hippeau; 48 ill. 8*fr.* 8° Aubry, *Paris* 60
GUILLAUME LE CLERC [13 cent.] Bestiaire divin—*ut* K § 275, *s.v.* Franco-Norman.
Renart —*v. supra*, *s.v.* Fabliaux.

Allegorical Poetry. "Art of Love."

Clef d'Amors [*c.* 1300]: ed. A. Doutrepont [Bibliotheca Normannica] 6*m.* 8° Niemeyer, *Halle* 90
ed. Edwin Tross; w. Fch. Introd. Michelant [222 printed] 12*fr.* 8° Tross, *Paris* 66
ELIE, MAISTRE [13 cent.] Ueberarbtg. v. Ovid's Ars Amatoria, hrsg. H. Kühne + E. Stengel [Ausg. u. Abhdgn.] 3*m.*60 8° Elwert, *Marburg* 86
Includes also translations of the *Disticha Catonis.*
HUON DE MÉRI [13 cent.] Li Tornoiemenz Antecrit, hrsg. Geo. Wimmer [Ausg. u. Abhdgn.] 4*m.*40 8° Elwert, *Marburg* 88
A combat in Paradise betw. Christ at the head of the Virtues and Antechrist leading the Vices. Ed. fr. Paris, Lond. and Oxfd. MSS.

NICOLE DE MARGIVAL [13 cent.] Dit de la Panthere d'Amours, ed. Hy. Todd 6/*fr.* 8° Soc.d.Anc.Textes (Didot) *Paris* 83

Roman de la Rose [attrib. to GUILLAUME DE LORRIS; 13 cent.] ed. Dr. M. Kaluza —*in his* ed. of Chaucer's Romaunt of Rose, *ut* K § 68.

DOINEL, Jules — Gui Fabi et Guillaume Rebrachien — 8° Herluison, *Orléans* 87

" " — Note addit. à Guy Fabi [*extr. fr.* Annales d. l. Soc. d. Gâtinais; pp. 6] 8° " " 90

FABI, Guy — Guillaume le Doyen, auteur de la Roman d. Rose [" "] 8° " "

LANGLOIS, E. — Origines et Sources du Roman de la Rose 5/*fr.* 8° Thorin, *Paris* 91

Venus la Deesse d'Amor [13 cent.]: hrsg. Prf. Wendelin Foerster—*ut* B.B. K § 277, *s.v.* Allegor. Poetry.

Romans d'Adventures.

Châtelaine de Vergi [13 cent.]: ed. Gaston Raynaud *in prep.*

"Ce joli et touchant petit poème mérite une mention toute spéciale."—Gaston PARIS.

Flore et Blanchefleur: tr. Wm. Morris, *sub tit.* Story of King Florus 12/6 *nt.* 16° Kelmscott Press 93

CRESCINI, Vinc. — Il Cantare di Fiorio e Biancifiore: ill. [Scelta di Curios.] 16*l.*25 8° *Bologna* 89

HERZOG, Hans — Die beiden Sagenkreise v. Flore u. Blanscheflur (diss.) 1*m.*50 8° *Vienna* (Fock, *Lpz.*) 84

GALÏENS LI RESTORÉS: Schlusstheil d. Cheltenh. Guerin de Monglane, hrs. E. Stengel [Ausg. u. Abh.] 14*m.* 8° Elwert, *Marburg* 90

With a prelimin. article by K. PFEIL: *Ueb. d. gegenseit. Verhältn. d. erhaltenen Galïen-Fassungen.*

GAUTIER D'ARRAS [12 cent.] Oeuvres, ed. E. Löseth, 2 vols. [Bibl. Frç. d. Moy. Age] 18*fr.* 8° Bouillon, *Paris* 90; 90

i. *Eracle*; ii. *Ille et Galeron.*

Ille et Galeron, hrsg. Wend. Foerster [fr. uniq. Paris MS.; Roman Bibl.] 7*m.*60 8° Niemeyer, *Halle* 91

GERBERT DE MONTREUIL [13 cent.] Roman de la Violette: ou de Gérard de Nevers—*ut* B.B. K § 277.

ROCHS, A. — Ueber den Veilchen-Roman u. d. Wanderung d. Euriaut-Sage 8° Fock, *Lpz.* 82

GUILLAUME DE ST. PAIX [12 cent.] Roman du Mont-St. Michel—*v.* K § 275, *s.v.* Anglo-Norman.

GUILLAUME, LE CLERC —*v.* K § 275, *s.v.* Franco-Norman.

Havelock, Lay of: —*v.* K § 275, *s.v.* Anglo-Norman.

HUE DE ROTELUNDE [12 cent.] Ipomedon, ed. Eug. Kölbing + E. Koschwitz 6*m.* 8° Koebner, *Breslau* 89

Pub. as an Appendix to KÖLBING'S edn. of the 3 Middle-Engl. versions [*ut* B.B. K § 47].

MUSSAFIA, Adf. — Sulla Critica del Testo del Romanzo in Francese antico Ipomedon [*extr. fr.* Sitz. Wien. Ak.] 1*m.*50 *r* 8° Tempsky, *Vienna* 90

Partonopéus de Blois.

v. LOOK, H. — Der Partenopier Konrads v. Würzburg u. d. Partenopeus de Blois Fock, *Lpz.* 81

PFEIFFER, Ernst — Ueb. d. HSS. d. altfrz. Partenopeus de Blois [Ausg. u. Abhgn.] 1*m.*60 8° Elwert, *Marburg* 85

RAIMBERT DE PARIS — Ogier le Danois: ed. F. Barrois, 2 vols. *o.p.* [*pb.* 16/*fr.*] 12° Techner, *Paris* 42

FIEBIGER, E. — Ueber die Sprache d. Chevalier Ogier d. Dänen [dissert.] 8° *Halle* 81

MATTHES, J. C. — De nederlandsche Ogier 8° *Groningen* 76

VORETZSCH, Carl — Ueb. d. Sage v. Ogier d. Dänen: Beitr. z. Entwkg. d. altfrz. Epos 3*m.* 8° Niemeyer, *Halle* 91

RAOUL DE HOUDENC [13 cent.].

ABBEHUSEN, Carl — Zur Syntax Raoul's de Houdenc [Ausg. u. Abhgn.] 2*m.*40 8° Elwert, *Marburg* 88

BÖRNER, Otto — Raoul de Houdenc: eine stilistische Untersuchung [dissert. inaug.] 2*m.*40 8° Fock, *Lpz.* 84

Seeks to show his identity with the author of *Messire Gauvain* (advents. of GAWAIN, nephew of Kg. Arthur).

RENAUS DE BEAUJEAU

MENNUNG, A. — Der Bel Inconnu in s. Verhältn. z. Lybeaus Disconus, Carduino u. Wigalois (diss.) 1*m.*50 8° *Halle* (Fock, *Lpz.*) 90

RENAUT, Jean [12 cent.] Le Roman de Galerent, comte de Bretagne, ed. Anat. Boucherie [Soc. d. Etud. d. Langs. Rom.] 12/*fr.* 8° *Montpellier* (Maisonneuve, *Paris*) 88

Edited for the first time fr. a unique MS. in the Bibl. Nationale de Paris.

ROBERT DE BLOIS [13 cent.] Sämmtliche Werke, hrsg. Jac. Ulrich, vols. i.–ii. ea. 3*m.* 8° Mayer & Müller, *Berl.* 89; 91

ii. *Floris et Liriopé; Chansons d'Amors, Lyrical Poems.*

" " Floris et Liriopé, hrsg. Wolfr. v. Zingerle [now 1st ed.; Altfrz. Bibl.] 2*m.*50 8° Reisland, *Lpz.* 91

Wistasse le Moine [13 cent.]: hrsg. Wend. Foerster + Joh. Trost [fr. uniq. Paris MS.; Roman. Bibl.] 3*m.* 8° Niemeyer, *Halle* 91

Later Poetry.

CHARLES D' ORLÉANS [1391–1465; father of Louis xii.].

KUHL, Ferd. — Die Allegorie bei Charles d'Orléans (diss. inaug.) 8° *Marburg* 86

CHARTIER, Alain [1390(?)–1458] Curial: Caxton's tr., ed. Dr. F. J. Furnivall + Prf. Paul Meyer 5/- 8° E. Eng. Text Soc. (Paul) 88

EDER, Hugo — Syntaktische Studien zu Alain Chartiers Prosa 3*m.*50 8° Hertz, *Würzburg* 89

REQUIN — Jean d. Fontay et le Tombeau d'Alan Chartier [*extr.*; 10 pp.] 8° Leroux, *Paris* 92

CHRISTINE DE PISAN [1363–1420] Oeuvres poétiques, ed. Maur. Roy, vols. i.–ii. ea. 10/*fr.* 8° Soc.d.Anc.Textes (Didot) *Paris* 87; 91

" " Livre du Chemin de long Estudes, hrsg. R. Püschel [w. glossary] 8° Hettler, *Berlin* [81] 87

KOCH, Dr. Friedr. — Leben und Werke der Christine de Pisan 2*m.* 8° Koch, *Goslar* 85

MÜLLER, E. — Zur Syntax der Christine de Pisan 8° Koch, *Lpz.* 86

DESCHAMPS, Eustache [1328–1415] Oeuvres Complètes, ed. Marq. d. Queux d. St. Hilaire + G. Raynaud, vols. iii.–viii. ea. 12/*fr.* 8° Soc.d.Anc.Textes (Didot) *Paris* 84–93

Early Drama.

Mysteries and Miracle Plays.

Adam [12 cent.] —*v.* K § 275, *s.v.* Anglo-Norman.

Miracles de Nostre Dame par Personnages: ed. Gaston Paris + Ulysse Robert, vol. viii. [gloss. *etc.*] 15/*fr.* 8° Soc. d. Anc. Textes (Didot) *Paris* 93

" " coll. by Jean Mielot: facs. edn. F. Warner; w. Introd. and notes [fr. Douce MS.] *priv. prin.*, *Westminster* 85

BUSCH, Rich. — Die Betheuerungs- u. Beschwörungsformeln i. d. M. d. N.D. [Marburg, dissert.] *Darmstadt* 86

DELISLE, Léop. — Les Miracles de Nostre Dame: rédaction en prose d. Miélot [*extract*] 8° *Paris* 86

DUNKER, Karl — Zu Jehan le Marchant [dissert.] *Göttingen* 88

FÖLSTER, Herm. — Sprachliche Reim-Untersuchgn. d. Miracles d. Notre Dame [Ausg. u. Abhdgn.] 1*m.*60 8° Elwert, *Marburg* 86

JENSEN, Hans C. — D. Miracles d. Nostre Dame [w. ref. to Gautier de Coincy] [diss. inaug.] 8° *Bonn* 90

MEYER, Paul — Notice sur un MS. d. Orléans cont. d'anc. Miracles de la Vierge en vers 4° Klincksieck, *Paris* 93

NAPP, Ludw. — Untersuchn. üb. d. sprachl. Eigentümlichktn. d. Mir. d. N.D. (diss.) 2*m.* 8° Bergmann, *Wiesbaden* 88

Miracles d. l. bienheureuse Vièrge Marie [13 cent.]: ed. Ch. Bouchet; w. Fch. tr. and notes [fr. MS. in Bibl. d. Vendôme] 4/*fr.* 8° Herluison, *Orleans* 88

Mistère de Saint Bernard de Merthon: ed. Lecoy de la Marche 8/*r.* 8° Soc.d.Anc.Textes (Didot), *Paris* 89

K § 277

Mistère du Viel Testament : ed. Bar. J. de Rothschild, w. Introd., notes and gloss., vol. iv.-vi. ea. 10*fr.* 8° Soc. d. Anc. Textes (Didot), *Paris* 84; 87; 91

Mystère de la Passion : ed. J. M. Richard [fr. MS. at Arras libr.] 10*fr.* 8° Picard, *Paris* 94

Secular Drama.

Pathelin, Farce de [mid. 15 cent.]—*ut* B.B. K § 277.
SCHÄFFER, L. La Farce du Maistre Pathelin : grammat. Abhdg. [schl.-progr.] 8° Fock, *Lpz.* 77

Prose.

Agriculture.

WALTER OF HENLEY [13 cent.] Husbandry—*v.* D § 119.

Bible Translations.

BERGER, Saml. La Bible française au Moyen Age 10*fr.* 8° Champion, *Paris* 84
On the earliest Old-French *prose* translations.
BONNARD, Jean Les Traductns. d. l. Bible en vers frç. au Moyen Age 5*fr.* 8° Champion, *Paris* 84

Kings, Books of.
Quatre Livres des Rois [12 cent.] : ed. Leroux de Lincy [Coll. de Documts.] 12*fr.* 4° Didot, *Paris* 42
BARTELS, W. Die Wortstellung in den Quatre Livres des Rois [dissert.] 8° *Erlangen* 86
LANGSTROFF, C. Die Verbalflexion der Quatre Livres des Rois [dissert.] 8° Fock, *Lpz.* 84
MERWART, K. Grammatische Untersuchung über d. Quatre Livres des Rois [schl.-progr.] 8° *Marburg* 81
SCHLÖSSER, Paul Die Lautverhältnisse der Quatre Livres des Rois [diss.] 8° *Bonn* 86

Chronicles. Historians.

Collection.

Recueil des Historiens des Gaules et d. l. Fce., p. Dom Bouquet et d'autres Bénédictins, contin. p. des Membres de l'Institut, vols. i.-xxvi. [ed. Léop. Delisle] ea. 50*fr.* f° Impr. Nat. (Klincksieck), *Paris* [1738 *sqq.*] 69–85 *in prg.*

Individual Texts:

FROISSART, Jean [1337–1409].
DARMESTETER, Mme. M. Froissart [popular] 2*fr.* 8° Hachette, *Paris* 94
PARIS, Paulin Nouvelles Recherches sur la Vie de Froissart 2*fr.* 8° Techener, *Paris*
Kervyn de Lettenhove Lettre à l'Occas. d. Nouv. Recherch. de M. Paulin Paris 2*fr.* 8° " "
Added are *Observations* by PARIS in counter-reply.
" " Réponse aux Observations de M. Paulin Paris [w. final reply by Paris] 2*fr.* 8° Techener, *Paris*

GAYMAR, Geoff. [12 cent.] Lestorie des Engles—*v.* K § 275, *s.v.* Anglo-Norman.
Guillaume le Maréchal [13 cent.]—*v.* K § 275, *s.v.* Anglo-Norman.
Récits d'un Ménéstrel de Reims [1260] : ed. Natalis de Wailly [Soc. Hist. d. Fce.] 9*fr.* 8° Renouard, *Paris* 77
DE VILLEHARDOUIN, Geoff. [1160–1213] Conquête de Constantinople, ed. D. Grand *in prep.*
LUCAS Gottfried von Villehardouin [school-programme] 8° Fock, *Lpz.* 60
RÖSCHEN Der syntaktische Gebrauch der Negation bei Villehardouin 8° " " 84

Cookery.

Ménagier de Paris : ed. Bar. Jérôme Pichon 8° Soc. d. Bibliophiles, *Paris*
TIREL, Guill. [="TAILLEVENT"; 1326–95] Le Viandier, ed. Bar. Jerome Pichon + Geo. Vicaire 30*fr.* Suppl. 5*fr.* 8° Techener, *Paris* 91; 92
TIREL was *chef* to CHARLES vi., and this edn. of his wk. is ed. fr. MSS. in Bibl. Nat. and Vatican, w. var. rgs. fr. others, Introd. and notes.

Dits : Collections.

BORDIER, Henri L. [ed.] Les Eglises et Monastères de Paris *o.p.* [*pb.* 5*fr.*] s 8° Aubry, *Paris* 56
A colln. of pieces, in prose and verse, of 9th, 13th, and 14th centuries.
FRANKLIN, Alf. Les Cris de Paris au Moyen Age 3*fr.* 50 12° Plon, *Paris* 87
Forms part of vol. i. of his *La Vie privée d'autrefois* [9 vols., ea. 3*fr.* 50 '87–'90].

Exempla. Moral Tales. Homilies, Sermons, etc.

BERNARD, St. [*d.* 1153] Sermons trad. [fr. Latin] Morice de Sulli [*d.* 1195].
LESER, Eug. Fehler u. Lücken in d. Li Sermon St.-Bern. benannt. Predigtsammlg. [diss.] 2m. 8° *Sondershausen* (Weber, *Berl.*) 87
PARIS + BOS, Gaston Alph. —*in their* La Vie de Saint Gilles, *ut supra.*
BOZON, Nicole Contes Moralisés, ed. Lucy Toulmin Smith + Paul Meyer—*ut* B § 3.
Durham, Cathed. Lib. : Notice s. un Recueil d'Exempla d. MS. B. iv. 19. By Paul Meyer 2*fr.* 8° Klincksieck, *Paris* 92
JACQUES DE VITRI Exempla, ed. Prf. T. F. Crane [Am.] [*fr. his* Sermones Vulgares]—*ut* B § 3.
Judenknabe, Der : hrsg. Eug. Wolter [Bibl. Normannica] 4*m.* 8° Niemeyer, *Halle* 79
Five Greek, fourteen Latin and eight French texts.

Fiction : Collection.

JUBINAL, M. L. A. [ed.] Nouv. Recueil de Contes, Dits, Fabliaux, *etc.*, 2 vols. [13–15 cents.]—*ut supra*, *s.v.* Fabliaux.

Individual Texts.

Aucassin et Nicolete [13 cent.].
WAGNER Auc. et Nic. comme Imitation d. Floire et Blanchefleur et comme Modèle d. Treue um Treue [progr.] Fock, *Lpz.* 83

Lapidaries [treatises on Precious Stones].

Panniers, Léop. [ed.] Les Lapidaires frçs. du Moyen Age [12–14 cents.] 10*fr.* 8° Bouillon, *Paris* 81
With Introd. by Prf. Gaston PARIS, and a glossary. Forms pt. lii. of *Bibl. de l'Ecole d. Htes. Etudes.*
JOHANNSSON, Alf. Språklig Undersökning af le Lapidaire de Cambridge 8° *Upsala* 86
MANN, Max Friedr. Eine altfrz. Prosaversion d. Lapidarius M.'s—*in* Roman. Forschgn., vol. ii., *ut* B.B. K § 256.

Law.

Assises de Jérusalem : ed. Comte Arth. Aug. Beugnot, 2 vols. [Historiens d. Croisades] 72*fr.* f° Imprim. Royale, *Paris* 41; 43
Etablissements de Saint Louis : ed. Paul Viollet; w. Introd. and notes, vols. i.–iv. 36*fr.*; v. 9*fr.* [Soc. de l'Hist. d. Fce.] 8° Loones, *Paris* 81–86; 87
VIOLLET, Paul Les Sources des Etablissements de Saint Louis 2*fr.*50 8° Champion, *Paris* 77
LIEBERMANN, Dr. F. [ed.] Ungedruckte anglo-normannische Geschichtsquellen—*ut* D § 5.
PHILIPPE DE BEAUMANOIR [*d.* 1296] Le Coutumier de Beauvoisis, ed. Comte Arth. Aug. Beugnot, 2 vols. *o.p.* [*pb.* 18*fr.*] 8° Renouard, *Paris* 42
ALBERT, A. C. Die Sprache Philippes de Beaumanoir in seinen poetischen Werken [Münch. Beitr.] 1*m.*50 8° Deichert, *Lps.* 93
PIERRE DE FONTAINE [13 cent.] Le Conseil, ed. A. J. Marnier [Bibl. de Troyes] *o.p.* [*pb.* 9*fr.*] 8° Joubert, *Paris* 46

Manners. Morals.

ESTIENNE DE FOUGIÈRES Livre des Manières, hrsg. Jos. Kremer; w. gramm. and vocab. [Ausg. u. Abhgn.] 4*m.* 8° Elwert, *Marburg* 87
PHILIPPE DE NAVARRE [*d.* 1270] Quatre Ages de l'Homme, ed. Marcel de Fréville 7*fr.* 8° Soc. d. Anc. Textes (Didot), *Paris* 88

Medicine and Surgery.

DE CHAVLIAC, GVY Grande Chirvrgie, ed. E. Nicaise [comp. 1363; in Lat. and Fch.]—*ut* H* § 3.

Philology.

HUON LE ROI La Senefiance de l' a b c—*in* Jubinal's [ed.] Contes, Dits et Fabliaux, *ut sup.*
Orthographia Gallica : ed. G. Stürzinger—*ut* B.B. K § 269.

Glossaries.

DIEZ, Friedr. [ed.] Anciens Glossaires romans, trad. A. Bauer [Bibl. Ec. Prat.] 4*fr.*75 8° Bouillon, *Paris* 70
A tr. of his *Altromanische Glossare* [*ut* B.B. K § 271], forming vol. v. of the *Bibl. de l'Ecole d. Hts. Etudes.*
PARIS + MEYER, Prf. Gaston + Paul [eds.] Corpus Gloss. Lat.-Fr. Medii Aevi *in prep.*

Political.

Complainte de Jérusalem [*c.* 1214]: hrsg. E. Stengel—*in* Codex Manuscriptus Digby 86 3*m.* 8° Waisenhaus, *Halle* 71
A satirical piece.
Dit de la Rébellion d'Angleterre [early 14 cent.]—*in* Jubinal's [ed.] Contes, Dits, Fabliaux, *ut sup.*

Travels.

Itinéraires de Jérusalem rédigés en frc.: ed. Hy. Michelant + Gast. Raynaud, vol. i. [Soc. de l'Orient Latin] 12*fr.* 8° *Geneva* 82
Contains the 13th cent. (prose) *Description de Jérusalem.*

278. MIDDLE-FRENCH [15 TO BEG. 17 CENT.] LITERATURE.

History of Literature : Generally.

COIGNET, Mme. Clarisse [*née* GAUTHIER] Portraits et Récits du seizième Siècle [good popular bk.] 8° *Paris* 85
GÉRUSEZ, Prf. Eug. Etudes littéraires s. l. Auteurs frçs. du 17e. et 18e. Siècle 2*fr.*50 12° Delalain, *Paris* [49] 87
GODEFROY, Fréd. Histoire de la Littér. frçe. [10 vols.]: vol. i.: Au 16e. Siècle 10 vols. 65*fr.* 8° Gaume, *Paris* [59] 78
HANOTAUX, Gabr. Etudes historiques sur le 16e. et le 17e. Siècle en France 3*fr.*50 12° Hachette, *Paris* 86
Influ. espagn. en Fce. à propos de Brantome, Œuvres inéd. de St. Simon, Idées polit. de St. Simon, etc.
MERLET, Prf. Gust. Etudes littéraires sur les Classiques frçs., 2 vols. 8*fr.* 16°; 10*fr.* 8° Hachette, *Paris* [75] 86; [82] 87
i. CORNEILLE, RACINE, MOLIÈRE; ii. *Chans. d. Roland,* JOINVILLE, MONTAIGNE, PASCAL, LA FONTAINE, BOILEAU, MONTESQUIEU, LA BRUYÈRE, BOSSUET, FÉNELON, VOLTAIRE, BUFFON.
RHODE Etudes sur la Littér. frç., pt. i.: Le 17e. Siècle [progr.] Fock, *Lps.* 79
STIERNET, J. B. La Littérature frç. au 17e. Siècle : essais et notices 8° *Brussels* 87

Council of Trent : Influence of.

DEJOB, Prf. Chas. De l'Influ. du Conc. d. Tr. s. l. Litt. et Beaux-Arts 5*fr.*50 8° Thorin, *Paris* 84

Almanacks.

CHAMPIER, Vict. Les anciens Almanachs illustrés : histoire du calendrier; 50 pl. 75*fr.* f° Frinzine, *Paris* 85

Criticism.

CARTON, Henri —*in his* Histoire de la Critique littéraire en France 2*fr.* 12° Dupret, *Paris* 86

Drama, Mysteries, and Miracle Plays—v. also K § 277.

KINNE, Carl Formulas in Lang. of Fch. Poet-dramatists of 17 Cent. [Strassb. diss. inaug.] 8° *Boston* 91

Fiction.

KÖRTING, Heinr. Geschichte des französischen Romans im 17ten. Jahrhundert, 2 vols. 16*m.* 8° Franck, *Oppeln* 85; 86
[LACROIX, Paul] "BIBLIOPHILE JACOB" Paris ridicule et burlesque au 17e. Siècle [Bibl. Gauloise] 5*fr.* 16° Delahays, *Paris* [ ] 59
Claude LE PETIT, BERTHOD, SCARRON, Frçois. COLLETET, BOILEAU, etc.

L'Esprit Gaulois.

DROZ, Theod. L'Esprit Gaulois dans la Littérature française 80*pf.* 8° Meyer and Zeller, *Zürich* 85

Law.

DELACHENAL, Roland —*in his* Histoire des Avocats au Parlement de Paris 8*fr.* 8° *Paris* 85
Fourteenth to seventeenth cents.: important for certain literary-historical parties.

K § 278

Morals.

DESJARDINS, Prf. Alb. — Les Sentiments moraux au 16e. Siècle — 7*fr*.50 8° Pedone-Lauriel, *Paris* 86

Oratory: Pulpit.

JACQUINET, P. — Les Prédicateurs du 17e. Siècle avant Bossuet — 7*fr*.50 8° Belin, *Paris* [63] 85

Poetry.

PARIS, Gaston — La Poésie frç. au 15e. Siècle [*extr. fr.* Le Monde Poétique] 8° *Paris* 86

Jeanne d'Arc Poems.

HANEBUTH, Karl — Ueb. d. hauptsächl. Jeanne d'Arc Dichtungen d. 15-17 Jahrh. [diss.] 8° *Marburg* 93

Collections.

Anthologie Satyriaque: répert. d. meilleures poésies et chansons joyeuses parues en frç. depuis Clément Marot j.-à nos jours, 8 vols. [300 prin.] 12° Soc. d. Biblioph., *Luxemb.* 76

RAYNAUD, Gaston [ed.] — Rondeaux et autres Poésies du 15e. siècle — 8*fr*. 8° Soc. d. Anc. Textes (Didot), *Paris* 89

From MSS. in the Bibl. Nationale, Paris; by the Bibliothécaire Honor. du Dépt. des MSS.

Poetry.

DE BAÏF, Jean Ant. [1532-92] Oeuvres en Rime, ed. Chas. Marty Laveau, vols. i.-iv. [Pléiade Frç.] ea. 25*fr*. s 8° Lemerre, *Paris* 85-87

NAGEL, H. — Die metrischen Verse J. A. de Baïf [programme] 8° Fock, *Lps.* 78

BELLEAU, Rémy [1528-77].

BESSNER, Reinh. — Verhältn. v. Belleau z. d. früheren Steinbächern [diss.] 8° *Oppeln* 86

WAGNER, Herm. — Remy Belleau und seine Werke [dissert. inaug.] 8° Fock, *Lps.* 90

BUCHER, Germ.-Colin [16 cent.] Poésies, ed. Jos. Denais — 12*fr*.50 8° Techener, *Paris* 90

BUCHER was *secrétaire du grand-maître de Malte*; his poems are here pb. for 1st time, w. notes and glossary.

" " Supplémt. aux Poésies de Germ. Colin (Bucher), p. Em. Picot [*extr. fr.* Bull. d. Biblioph.] 1*fr*.50 8° Techener, *Paris* 90

Grant Garde Derrière [15 cent.]: ed. W. G. C. Bijvanck, *s.t.* Un Poète Inconnu d. l. Soc. de Villon; w. Introd. and gloss. 16° Champion, *Paris* 91

Appended is a hitherto inedited *ballade* of VILLON to his wife; fr. MS. in Bibl. Natl.

LE HOUX [1545 (-6)-1616] Vaux de Vire, w. tr. Jas. P. Muirhead; w. Introd., port., and pl. *o.p.* [*pb.* 21/-; *w.* 10/-] 8° Murray 75

Texts and trs. *en regard*. A colln. of drinking and convivial songs, formerly supposed to have been written by Olivier BASSELIN, and only collected and purified by Maître LE HOUX.

" " Vaux de Vire d'Olivier Basselin et Jean Le Houx, ed. P. L. Jacob — 2*fr*.50 12° Delahays, *Paris* 58

" " Olivier Basselin et le Vau de Vire, ed. Prf. Armand Gasté; w. Introd. & notes 5*fr*. 16° Lemerre, *Paris* 87

" " Les Noels Virois, ed. Arm. Gasté; w. Introd. and notes — 3*fr*.50 16° Clérisse, *Caen* 62

DE BEAUREPAIRE, Eug. — Etude sur Basselin, Jean le Houx et le Vaudevire Normand *o.p.* Tostain, *Avranches* 58

Extr. fr. vol. xxiii. of the *Mémoires de la Société des Antiquaires de Normandie* (1858).

DU BOIS, Louis — Vaux de Vire d'Olivier Basselin *o.p.* 8° *Caen* 21

GASTÉ, Prf. Armand — Olivier Basselin et les Compagnons du Vau-de-Vire; erreur histor. et littér.; facs. *o.p.* 8° " 66

" " Jean le Houx et le Vau de Vire à la fin de 16 Siècl. [*v. also* Intro. *to* Noels, *sup.*] 6*fr*. 8° " 74

MAROT, Clément [1497 (?)-1544].

GUY, Hy. — Les Sources du Poète Clément Marot [pp. 31] 8° Gadrat, *Foix* 90

DE RONSARD, Pierre [1524-85] Œuvres, ed. Ch. Marty Laveaux, vols. i.-v. [Pléide Frç.] ea. 25*fr*. 8° Lemerre, *Paris* 87-92

BIZOS, G. [ed.] — Ronsard [a coll. of facs. fr. the Bibl. Nat. and Musée de Versailles] 8° Lecène, *Paris* 91

FROGER, L. — Les premières Poésies de Ronsard [odes and sonnets] 8° Fleury, *Mamers* 92

LANGE, P. — Ueber Ronsards Franciade u. ihr. Verhältn. z. Vergils Aeneide [progr.] 1*m*.20 4° *Wurzen* (Fock, *Lps.*) 87

VILLON, Frç. [1431-*c.* 1456] Œuvres, ed. Aug. Longnon; w. glossary [good edn. fr. the MSS.] 10*fr*. s 8° Lemerre, *Paris* 92

" " " ed. Louis Moland; w. Introd, notes, and bibliogr. 18° Garnier, *Paris* 93

" " Petit Testament, ed. W. G. C. Bijvanck

" " --*a new ballade to his wife*, ed. W. G. C. Bijvanck—*in his ed. of* Grant Garde, *ut sup.*

REICHEL, Herm. — Syntaktische Studien zu Villon [dissert. inaug.] 8° *Leipzig* 91

" " Jargon et Jobelin, Le: ed. Pierre d'Alheim—*ut inf.* [5 hitherto ined. *ballades* fr. Stockh. MS.; of doubtful authenticity.]

D'ALHEIM, Pierre — Le Jargon jobelin de Maistre Frc. Villon 18° Savine, *Paris* 90

Text tr. and gloss., w. a short essay, condemning the *ballades* as a recent forgery, and VITU and the *Acad. Frçse.* as dupes.

SCHÖNE, Lucien [ed.] — Le Jargon et Jobelin d. Villon: suivi d. jargon au théâtre 20*fr*. s 8° Lemerre, *Paris* 88

Text, various readings, Mod.-Fch. tr., notes and glossaries.

SCHWOB, Marcel — Etude sur l'Argot français 1*fr*.50 8° Bouillon, *Paris* 89

Cf. also his paper *Le Jargon des Coquillards en* 1455 in vol. vii. of the *Mém. d. l. Soc. d. Linguistique d. Paris* (1890).

VITU, Aug. [ed.] — Le Jargon et Jobelin de Villon 12*fr*. 8° Ollendorff, *Paris* [83] 89

Crowned by the *Académie Française*. This 2nd edn. differs fr. the 1st only in its title-page and wrapper.

Fiction.

Cent Nouvelles Nouvelles: 2 vols.; w. Introd. and notes [Bibl. Elzévirienne] *o.p.* [*pb.* 10*fr*.] 18° Daffis, *Paris* 58

DE LA SALE (LA SALLE), Ant. [15 cent.] Quinze Joyes du Mariage [a satire]: ed. D. Jouaust, w. notes and gloss.; pref. L. Urbach 30*fr*. 16° Libr. d. Biblioph., *Paris* 87

An *édition de luxe*, with *eaux-fortes* by Ad. LALAUZE.

MARGUÉRITE D'ANGOULÊME [Qu. of Navarre; 1492-1549] Heptaméron—*vid* B.B. K § 278.

CAREL, G. — Das Heptaméron und seine Sprache, pt. i. [Einleitg., Laute, Wortformen] [progr.] 8° Fock, *Lps.* 96

RABELAIS, Frç. [1495-1553].
BRIERLEY, J. Rabelais—*ut* K § 35.
DUBOUCHET, A. Rabelais à Montpellier [1530-1538]; 1 facs. 20/*fr.* 4° Coulet, *Montpellier* 87
ERNST, Karl Syntaktische Studien zu Rabelais 1*m*.50 8° *Greifswald* (Fock, *Lpz.*) 90
HEULHARD, Arth. Rabelais: ses voyages en Italie, son exil à Metz; port., 9 pl., and 75 ill. 40/*fr.* 8° Allison, *Paris* 91
MILLET, René Rabelais; port. [Les Grands Ecriva. Frç.] 2/*fr.* 16° Hachette, *Paris* 92
PLATEN, E. Syntaktische Untersuchungen zu Rabelais 1*m*.50 8° Fock, *Lpz.* 91
SÄGCHE, Sam: Syntaktische Untersuchungen zu Rabelais [dissert. inaug.] 1*m*.80 8° *Halle* (Fock, *Lpz.*) 88
SCHÖNERMARK, W. Beiträge z. Gesch. d. frz. Sprache a. Rabelais Werken, 3 pts. [schl.-progrs.] 61; 66; 74
TÉNOT, F. Rabelais et sa Mission: étude en vieux français [pp. 88] 16° Péricat, *Tours* 93
TÖPEL, Carl Syntaktische Untersuchungen zu Rabelais [dissert. inaug.] 1*m*.50 8° *Oppeln* 87

Drama.

GARNIER, Robert [1545-*c.* 1601].
DHOM, Heinr. Welches ist d. Verhältniss v. Garniers Hippolyte z. s. Quellen? 1*m*.20 8° *Schweinfurt* 89
FROST, J. Robert Garnier und sein Theater [programme] 8° Fock, *Lpz.* 67
KÖRNER, P. Der Versbau Robert Garniers 2*m*.40 8° Vogt, *Berlin* 94
PROCOP Syntaktische Studien über Robert Garnier [dissert. inaug.] 8° *Erlangen* 86
RÄDER, H. Die Tropen u. Figuren Robert Garniers [dissert. inaug.] 8° *Kiel* 86
DE MAIRET, Jean [1604-1683].
DANNHEISSER, Ern. Studien zu Jean de Mairets Leben u. Wirken [dissert. inaug.] 1*m*.50 8° Fock, *Lpz.* 88
Mystère de l'Incarnation [repres. at Rouen 1474]: ed. P. Le Verdier, 3 vols. *Rouen* 83-85

Miscellaneous Prose.

BRANTOME, Pierre de Bourdeille, Sieur de [1540-1614].
Œuvres, ed. Prosp. Mérimée + Louis Lacour, vols. viii.-xi. [Bibl. Elzévir.] ea. 6*fr.* 12° Plon, *Paris* 91-94
DE COMMINES, Philippe [1447(?)-1511] Mémoires—*ut* B.B. K § 278.
CHANTELAUZE, Régis Philippe de Commines—*in his* Portraits Historiques 3/*fr*.50 12° Perrin, *Paris* [86] 87
TIMPE Philippe de Commines: sa vie et ses mémoires [schl.-progr.] 8° Fock, *Lpz.* 79
VOLMER Zur Beurtheilung Philippe Commynes [schl.-progr.] 8° „ „ 84
MARGUERITE DE VALOIS, Qu. of Navarre [1552-1615] Memoirs, tr. "Violet Fane" [= Mary M. Singleton]; w. Introd. and notes; ports. m 8° 21/- *nt.* Nimmo; $5 Scribner, *N.Y.* 92

A new tr. The 8 ill. are good reprods. fr. contemp. portraits mostly fr. the series executed by Thos. LE LEU. A handsome vol. Author was sister of HENRI III. and the 1st wife of HENRI IV. (the "Reine Margot" of DUMAS), and must not be confused w. the compiler of the *Heptameron* [*ut sup.*, *s.v.* Fiction], whose great-niece she was, nor w. MARGUERITE DE VALOIS who married the Dke. of SAVOY (all three bg. interesting 16-cent. princesses). These memoirs were 1st tr. into Engl. by Rob. CODRINGTON in 1641 [not 1648, as stated in Preface (he also tr. the *Heptam.* in 1654)]: the best Fch. edn. is that of GUESSARD (Soc. de l'Hist. de Frce.), a tr. of whose notes are incorpor. here. The *Bibl. Elzévir.* edn., w. notes by L. LALANNE [*o.p.* (*pb.* 5/*fr.*) 12° Daffis, *Paris* '58] is also a good one.

XXIX. Celtic Philology and Literature.

279. CELTIC PHILOLOGY (*a*): LINGUISTIC ETHNOLOGY. GENERAL PHILOLOGY.

Linguistic Ethnology.

ATKINS, T. de Courcy The Kelt or Gael: his ethnography, geography and philology 5/- 8° Unwin 93

Claims a good deal for Keltic, incl. maternity of Latin (wh. is "pure Keltic") and of Greek [a "Keltic dialect"], and impregnatn. of Basque and Etruscan among other things. Comparative vocabularies added.

BERTRAND, Alex. Nos Origines, 5 vols.; maps and ill. ea. 10/*fr.* 8° Leroux, *Paris* [76] 89-93 *in prg.*

Introduction: Archéol. Celtique et Gauloise .... [76] 89 | ii. *Les Celtes* 93
i. *La Gaule avant les Gaulois* .... [i.-iv. not prev. pb.] 91 | iii. *La Religion Gauloise*; iv. *La Gaule Romaine* .... *in prep.*

BOURKE, Can. Ulick J. The Aryan Origin of Gaelic Race and Language c 8° [75] 76
PRICHARD, J. Cowles The Eastern Origin of the Celtic Nations, ed. R. G. Lathan *o.p.* [*pb.* 16/-; *w.* 10/-] 8° Quaritch 57

A suppl. to his *Physical Hist. of Mankind* (*ut* B.B. E § 3). A comparison of Celtic dialects w. Sansc., Gk., Lat. and Teut. langs. Of no value now.

RHYS, Prf. Jno. The Early Ethnology of Brit. Isles [= six Rhind Lects. 1889] 8° Cymmrodorion Soc. 91

More especially the ethnology of Scotland, treated fr. pt.-of-view of Language. Regards the Picts as a non-Aryan race. Repr. fr. *Scottish Review*, 1890.

„ „ Celts and Pre-Celts *in prep.*

Will supplement his treatmt. of Pictish lang. Author is at present at wk. on Basque, expecting it to furnish a key to interpretn. of Pictish Oghams and other remains.

DE VALROGER, Lucien Les Celtes, la Gaule celtique: étude critique 7/*fr*.50 8° Didier, *Paris* 79
Dwarf Races —*v.* B § 5° (MACRITCHIE.)

General Philology.

DUPLAN, A. Prosp. Patois de Bigorre: lang. prim. d'ou tout. l. langs. celt. se sont form. 5/*fr.* 4° Larrieu, *Tarbes* 91

A comparative vocabulary of six languages.

Grammar.

SCHMIDT, Rich. Zur keltischen Grammatik [Leipzig dissert. inaug.] 8° Trübner, *Strassbg.* 91

280. CELTIC PHILOLOGY (*b*): CYMRIC BRANCH.

Generally.

Phonology.

LOTH, Jos. Les Mots Latins dans les Langues brittoniques : phonétique et commentaire 10*fr.* 8° Bouillon, *Paris* 92
Gallic, Armoric, Cornish; w. Introd. on the romanization of Britain.

Old Gallic, Breton, Cornish.

Etymology.

D'ARBOIS DE JUBAINVILLE, H. Noms Gaulois chez César et Hirtius *De Bello Gallico*, ser. i. 4*fr.* 8° Bouillon, *Paris* 91
The substance of 15 lects. del. at the Collège de Frce. in 1890–91, the notes on wh. they were founded being furnished by E. ERNAULT and G. DOTTIN, whose names are mentioned on title-p. as "*collaborateurs*." A v. suggestive bk. This 1st series deals w. *rix* [= Lat. *rex*], its etymol., use in pers., local and tribal names, and compounds as *-rix*.

LEROUX, Alcide Marche du Patois actuel dans l'anc. Pays d. La Mée [Hte. Bret.] 2*fr.*50 8° Lechevallier, *Paris* 86
SÉBILLOT, Paul Mémoires Originaux : La Lang. Brétonne, limite et statistique 8° *Paris* 86
THÉDENAT, Hy. Liste de Noms gaulois [fr. inscriptions; *extr. fr.* Revue Celtique] 8° Durand, *Chartres* 94
LAGADEUC, J. Le Catholicon, ed. R. F. Le Men *o.p.* 8° *Lorient* [1499] *n.d.* (67)
A Breton, Fch. and Latin dict., ed. fr. the edn. of AUFFRAT DE QUOTQUEUERAN, *Treguier* (Jehan Calvez) 1499. Of considerable (antiquarian) interest.

WILLIAMS, Chas. Alb. Die französischen Ortsnamen keltischer Abkunft—*ut* K § 270.

Dictionary.

DU RUSQUEC, H. Dictionnaire Français Breton 20*fr.* 8° *Morlaix* (Bouillon, *Paris*) 83–86

Chrestomathy.

*HOLDER, Prf. Alf. [ed.] Alt-Celtischer Sprachschatz, pts. i.–vi. r 8° ea. 8m. Teubner, *Lpz.* / ea. 10*fr.* Welter, *Paris* 91–94 *in prg.*
To be cpl. in 18 quarterly Pts. When finished, it will form a compl. colln. of materials for study of Old Celtic—fr. contemp. inscripp., monumental and numismatic, Gk. and Lat. writers, itineraries and glossaries. Words alphab. arrgd., illustrative quotns. chronologically, inscripp. locally. "Old Celtic" here designates Gaulish and the basis common to both Cymric and Gaelic.

LOTH, Jos. [ed.] Chrestomathie Cretonne (Armoricain, Gallois, Cornique), pt. i. [Bret.-Armor.] 10*fr.* 8° Bouillon, *Paris* 90

Dialect : Slang.

QUELLIEN, Narc. L'Argot des Nomades en Basse Bretagne 25*fr.*50 8° Maisonneuve, *Paris* 86

Welsh.

Linguistic Ethnology.

SOUTHALL, Jno. E. Wales and her Language; linguistic map 6/6 c 8° Southall, *Newpt., Mon.* 92
An interesting, but unsystematic, survey of Welsh hist., race, liter. and language : in form of a plea for preservn. of the last.

Grammar.

ROBERTS, Griffith A Welsh Grammar : and other tracts 15*fr.* 18° Bouillon, *Paris* 70–83
A page-for-page reprodn. of a celebrated *Welsh Grammar*, pub. at Milan in 1567.

Etymology : Dictionary.

*EVANS, Can. D. Silvan Geiriadur Cymraeg: dict. of Welsh lang., pt. iii. [letter C] 16/6 *nt.* r 8° Spurrell, Carmarthen (Simpkin) 93
Completes the first vol., 1264 pp. [A–C] 34/6 *nt.* An elaborate and researchful work.

281. CELTIC PHILOLOGY (*c*): IRISH-GAELIC BRANCH.

Irish.

Grammar.

HAYDEN, Rev. Wm. [S.-J.] Intro. to Study of the Irish Lang.: text, tr. and glossary [pp. 74] 2/6 8° Gill, *Dublin* (Nutt) 91
Based on the Preface to Rev. Andr. DONLEVY'S *Catechism* [1st ed., *sub tit. An Teagasg Criostuidhe* in catech. of Xtn. doctr. in Irish, w. Engl. tr. *en regard*), pub. *Paris* 1742; 2nd ed., ed. Rev. Jno. MCENCROE (text altered; preface modified), *Dublin* 1822; 3rd ed. (text restored; pref. omitted), *ib.* 1848.

Dictionary.

*ASCOLI, Prf. G. J. Glossarium Palæo-Hibernicum, in pts. [to end of S. by 1894] ?–94 *in prg.*

Inscriptions —*v. also* G § 14.

Christian Inscriptions in the Irish Language to Twelfth Century 10/- 4° Royal Soc. of Antiqs. of Irel. (Hodges, *Dubl.*) 86

Gaelic.

Etymology : Place-Names.

JOHNSTON, Rev. Jas. B. The Place-Names of Scotland 7/6 c 8° Douglas, *Edin.* 92
Conts. a General and Philolog. Introd., followed by a list of place-names coll. fr. the earliest documts., w. explans. of their meaning, and their old spellings (some dated). Represents much conscientious labour.

MACDONALD, Jas. Place-Names in Strathbogie, w. notes; map and plans 4/6 c 8° Wyllie, *Aberdeen* 91
Repr. fr. *Proceedings of Huntly Field Club* w. 4 indices: of places, persons, subjects, Gaelic words. Also *L.P.* (50 copies) w. 10/6.

MAXWELL, Sir Herb. Scottish Land-Names; their origin and meaning 6/- c 8° Blackwood 94
The Rhind Lects. 1893. Mainly a classif. list of place-names, chfly. in Galloway, w. Gaelic etymols. Not wholly trustworthy, but useful as a supplt. to JOHNSTON [*ut supra*], whose labours the author has freely used.

" " Studies in the Topography [= toponymy] of Galloway—*ut* B.B. K § 238.

282. CELTIC LITERATURE (a): CYMRIC BRANCH.

Generally.

History of Literature.

D'ARBOIS DE JUBAINVILLE + LOTH, Hy. Jos. [eds.] Cours de Littérature celtique, vols. iii.–iv. ea. 8/*fr.* 8° Thorin, *Paris* 89

iii.–iv. *Mabinogion*, trad. Jos. LOTH, 2 vols. [*ut* B.B. K § 282] 16/*fr.* '89.

SULLIVAN, Prf. W. K. —*article* Celtic Literature, *in* Encyclo. Britannica, 9th edn., *ut* B.B. K § 1.

Breton (incl. MODERN BRETON).

History of Literature. Bibliography.

KERVILER, René [ed.] Répertoire général de Bio-bibliogr. bretonne, pts. i.–ix. [*to* Don] 8° Plihon, *Rennes* 86-90 *in prg.*

LEROUX, Alcide La Poésie bretonne: discours [6 cent. to pres. day; pp. 31] 1/*fr.*50 8° Mellinet, *Nantes* 88

Collection.

TIERCELIN + ROPARTZ, Louis J. Guy [eds.] Le Parnasse Creton contemporain 6/*fr.* 8° Lemerre, *Paris* 89

Individual Texts.

"KERARDVEN, L." [= Louis DUFILHOL] Guionvac'h [1835]: Chronique bretonne; w. Introd. René Kerviler; ill. 10/*fr.* 4° Soc. d. Biblioph. Bret., *Nantes* 90

Mystère de Sainte Barbe: ed. Em. Ernault; w. Introd. and Fch. tr. [text of 1557] 12/*fr.* 4° ,, ,, ,, ,, 88

Good edn. of a Breton tragedy; w. etymol. dict. of Middle-Breton: crowned by the *Institut*. Forms vol. iii. of *Archives de Bretagne*.

Folklore —*v.* B § 15.

Welsh.

Manuscripts.

Historical MSS. Commissn.: Catalogue of Old Welsh Manuscripts *in prep.*

In 1894 the Chancellor of the Exchequer granted £400 for 2 yrs. towards the cost of examining and cataloguing old Welsh MSS., the wk. to be done under the direction of the Histor. MSS. Commission.

Literature. Modern Collections.

Hengwrt MSS. [15 cent.], Selection fr., preserved in Peniarth Libr., ed. & tr. Rev. Rob. Williams + Prf. G. Hartwell Jones, vols. i.–ii. [*c.* 1500 pp.] 50/– 8° Quaritch 74; 92

Parts: i.–iii. [= vol. i.] *Y Seint Greal* (an early Welsh versn.); w. glossary [WILLIAMS + JONES] *not sold sep.*, '74-'76; iv. *Campeu Charlymaen* Gests of Charlem.], 15/–, '78; v.–vi. [iv.–vi. = vol. ii.] *Purdan Padric* [*St. Patrick's Purgatory*] *Gospel of Nicodemus, etc.*, ea. 15/–, 88; 92.

LLOYD, J. W. V. [ed.] —*in his* History of the Princes, Lords Marcher, *etc.*, *ut* B.B. G § 22.

Conts. a number of ancient Welsh poems, several of considerable interest.

*Old Welsh Texts: ed. Prf. Jno. Rhys + J. Gwenogvryn Evans, vol. i.–iv. r 8° *priv. prin.*, *Oxford* 87–93 *in prg.*

i. *Red Bk. of Hergest*, i.: *Mabinogion* [*ut* B.B. K § 283] 21/– *nt.* 87
ii. *Black Bk. of Carmarthen*: *Facs. of* .... 33/– *nt.* 88
iii. *Red Bk. of Hergest*, ii.: *Y Llyvyr Coch o Hergest* [*ut infra*] 21/– *nt.* 89
iv. *Bk. of Llan Dâv* [*ut infra*] 93
v. *Bk. of Aneurin* [anc. Welsh poetry, 12-13 cent. .... *in prep.*

Ancient Collections and Individual Texts.

*Bruts: Y Llyvyr Coch o Hergest; yr ii Gyfrol; y Brutieu, ed. Prf. J. Evans + J. Gwenogvryn Evans [Old Welsh Texts] r 8° *priv. prin.*, *Oxford* 89

An excellent and accurate diplomatic reprodn. in a great variety of types to repres. differ. characters in the original (rendering it as useful to the student as the *Red Book* itself) of all the chronicles known as *Bruts* in the *Red Book of Hergest*. Incl. the romance of *Dares Phrygius*, the Welsh version of the *Hist. Regum Brit.* of GEOFFREY OF MONMOUTH, val. histor. documn., such as the *Brut y Tywysogion*, *Brut y Saeson*, *etc.*, and also the oldest extant list of the cantrefs and commotes of Wales (added to *Red Bk.*) of great value for Welsh topogr. Several facs. of early Welsh calligraphy.

Elucidarium, and other Tracts in Welsh, fr. Llyvyr Agkyr Llandewivrevi [A.D. 1346], ed. J. Morris Jones + Prf. Jno. Rhys. [Anecdota Oxon.] s 4° 21/– Clar. Press Macmillan, *N.Y.* 94

Edited from the MS. in Jesus Coll., Oxford.

*Llan Dâv., Bk. of [Liber Landavensis; 12 cent.]: ed. J. Gwenogvryn Evans + Prf. Jno. Rhys [Old Welsh Texts] r 8° *priv. prin.*, *Oxf'd.* 93

An extremely thorough diplomatic reprodn. of the orig. MS., letter for letter, the first time it has been reprod. in its entirety, the edn. of the old Welsh MSS. Soc. [1840] having been ed. fr. late transcripts. Various rgs., palæogr. notes and 40 pp. double-col. Index (incl. mod. equivalts. of anc. place-names) appended; also 14 autotype facs. (incl. four of the *Bk. of St. Chad.*, an 8 cent. MS. of the Gospels in Latin). The chief pt. of bk. consists of lives of the earlier bishops of Llandaff, tog. w. grants of land and other privileges conferred upon the See by the chieftains of the diocese (all in Latin).

Mabinogion:

OTHMER, K. Das Verhältniss v. Christian v. Troyes "Erec et Enide" z. d. Mabinogion—*ut* K § 277, *s.v.* Arthurian Romances.

Psalmau Dafydd o'r yn cyfieithiad a'r Beibl cyffredin; w. Introd. Prf. Thos. Powel; ill. s 4° C. J. Clark *in prep.*

A facs. reprodn. of the rare Welsh Psalter of 1588, of wh. only 4 copies are known.

283. CELTIC LITERATURE (b): IRISH-GAELIC BRANCH.

Irish.

History of Literature.

d'ARBOIS DE JUBAINVILLE, H. L'Epopée celtique en Irlande, vol. i. 8/*fr.* 8° *Paris* 91

SULLIVAN, Prf. W. K. —*article* Celtic Literature *in* Encyclo. Britannica, *ut* K § 282.

Modern Collections.

*O'GRADY, Standish H. [ed.] Silva Gadelica: i.–xxxi., 2 vols.; w. trs. and notes ea. 21/– r 8° Williams 92

A colln. of tales fr. *Bk. of Leinster*, *Bk. of Ballymote*, *Leabhar Breac*, *Bk. of Lismore* and other MSS., w. extra. ill. persons and places—of great importance for the folklorist, Celtic antiquary, and student of Church hist., and very interesting reading withal. Vol. i. conts. Text, ii. the (excellent) Tr., Notes and Index of Names and Places.

STOKES+WINDISCH, Dr. Whitley / Fr. E. [eds.] Irische Texte ; w. Germ. trs. and vocab. Ser. iii., pt. i. 8m. 8° Hirzel, *Lps.* 91

Series i. ed. by WINDISCH, alone, ser. ii. by WINDISCH+STOKES, ut B.B. K § 283, s. varr. Windisch, Windisch+Stokes.

Poetry.

CORNISH, C. M. [ed.] Celtic Irish Songs and Song-Writers : a seln. ; w. Introd. and memrs. 5/- c 8° Cornish 85

*HYDE, Dr. Dougl. [ed. and tr.] The Songs of the Connaught Bards, 3 vols. *in prep.*

* ,, ,, Abhráin Gradh Chuige Connacht : love-songs of Connacht ; w. trs. and notes 2/6 s 8° Unwin 93

With Engl. transcription. Forms the 4th chap. of former bk., pub. in advance, contg. 45 songs.

MONTGOMERY, H. R. [ed.] Specs. of the Early Native Poetry of Ireld. ; w. intro. & running comm. 6/- c 8° Hodges, *Dublin* [*v.y.*] 92

Tr. by various authors, Miss BURKE, J. ANSTER, *etc.*

SULLIVAN, T. D. [tr.] Blanaid : and other Irish historical and legendary poems fr. the Gaelic 3/6 f 8° Eason, *Dublin* 91

Folklore —*v. also* B § 15.

HYDE, Dr. Douglas [ed.] Leabhar Sgeulaighteachta ; w. notes [Irish folk-tales] 5/- c 8° Gill, *Dublin*

,, ,, [ed.] Covis na Teineadh [a further collection] 1/6 c 8° ,, ,, 92

LARMINIE, Wm. [ed. and tr.] West Irish Folk Tales and Romances—*ut* B § 15.

With specs. of the Gaelic originals in 3 dialects, phonetically spelt. Orally coll., w. name of each narrator. A good bk.

Individual Texts.

Aislinge Meic Conglinne ["Vision of Mac Conglinne"] ed. Dr. Kuno Meyer, w. Engl. tr. *en regard*, gloss., notes and index subscr. 7/6 raised to 10/- *nt.* c 8° Nutt 92

A 12 cent. Irish tale. With Introd. on Composition, date and origin of the tale by Prf. W. WOLLNER (*Lps.*).

Cath Ruis Na Rig for Boinn : ed. E. Hogan ; w. tr., preface and indices [Todd Lect. Ser.] 3/6 8° Roy. Irish Ac., *Dubl.* / Williams 92

Conts. also a treatise on Irish neuter substantives, and a Supplt. to the *Index Vocabulorum* of ZEUSS' *Gram. Celtica* [*ut* B.B. K § 279].

Cathreim Thoirdealbhaigh ["Triumphs of Turlough"] : ed. Standish H. O'Grady ; w. tr. and notes *in prep.*

A hist. of the wars betw. the Normans and the Irish in Thomond, written 1459 by Jno. MacRory MACCRAITH for Tadhg MACNAMARA, of Ranna.

Codex Palatino-Vaticanus, no. 830 : ed. B. MacCarthy ; w. trs. and indices [Todd Lect. Ser.] 7/6 8° Roy. Irish Ac., *Dubl.* / Williams 92

Dinnsenchas [*or* Dindsenchas] : ed. and tr. Dr. Whitley Stokes—*ut* B § 15.

Fate of the Children of Lir [Soc. f. Preservn. Irish Lang.] 1/6 12° Duffy, *Dublin* 88

,, of the Children of Tuireann—*v.* Oidhe Chloinne Tuireann, *infra.*

,, of the Children of Uisneach [Soc. f. Preservn. Irish Lang.] 12° Duffy, *Dublin*

KEATING, Geoff. The Three Shafts of Death, ed. Prf. Rob. Atkinson, v. ii., pt. 1 [Irish MS. Ser.] 3/6 8° Williams 90

O'CLERY, Lughaidh Life of Hugh Roe O'Donnell, Prince of Tyrconnell [1586–1602] ; ed. F'r. Denis Murphy ; w. histor. Introd., tr. and notes ; ill. and autogr. 7/6 *nt.* 4° Sealy, *Dublin* 92

From the MS. in Roy. Irish Acad. One of the bks. wh. the Four Masters used in compiln. of their *Annals* [*ut* B.B. F § 41]. The Introd. (pp. 168) gives detailed acc. of the Clan O'Donnell, narr. of events covered by the *Life*, full acc. of the long and disastrous struggle betw. O'DONNELL and O'NEILL agst. the power of ELIZABETH, *etc.* O'DONNELL was b. 1573.

Oidhe Chloinne Tuireann : fate of the children of Tuireann, ed. R. J. O'Duffy [Soc. for Preserv. Ir. Lang.] 2/- 12° Duffy, *Dublin* 88

Psalter : Hibernica Minora, fragmt. of Old-Ir. treat. on Psalter, ed. Dr. Kuno Meyer ; w. tr., notes and gloss. [Anecd. Oxon.] s 4° 7/6 Clar. Press / Macmillan, *N.Y.* 94

Pursuit of Diarmuid and Grainne : pt. i. 1/-, *cl.* 1/6 ; ii. 1/6, *cl.* 2/- [Soc. f. Preservn. Irish Lang., *Dubl.*] 12° Duffy, *Dublin* 8-

Vision of Mac Conglinne : Irish text, Engl. tr. Prf. Kuno Meyer, notes and glossary 10/6 c 8° Nutt 93

A Middle-Irish Wonder-book. The tr. (by no means faultless) is a revisn. of that by W. M. HENNESSY, wh. appeared in *Fraser's Mag.* twenty yrs. ago. Introd. by Prf. W. WOLLNER (*Lps.*).

Gaelic.

History of the Literature.

MACNEILL, Nigel Literature of the Highlanders [fr. earliest to pres. times] 5/- c 8° 62

Folklore —*v.* B § 15.

Manx.

FARGHER, J. C. [ed.] Manx Carols ; w. English tr. [in parallel cols.] [260 pp.] 2/- *nt.* 8° 91

The first collection of Manx carols ever brought together.

Prayer, Bk. of Common : tr. Bp. Jno. Phillips [17 cent.], ed. A. W. Moore ; w. Introd. Prf. Jno. Rhys *in prep.*

An edn. of the oldest Manx text in existence, tr. by PHILLIPS, Bp. of Sodor and Man in early 17 cent., and ed. by Edr. of *The Manx Note-Book.*

XXX. Slavonic Philology and Literature.

284. SLAVONIC PHILOLOGY: GENERALLY.

Generally.

Bibliography.

PASTRNEK, Fr. Bibliograph. Uebersicht üb. d. slav. Philologie: 1876-91—*in* Archiv. f. slav. Phil., Suppl. 15*m.* 8° Weidmann, *Berl.* 92

POPOV, A. J. Bibliografičeskie Materialy, izd. pod red. M. Speranskago [pp. 101] 8° *Moscow* 89

Linguistic Ethnology.

HEY, Gust. Die slavischen Siedelungen im Königr. Sachsen 6*m.* 8° Baensch, *Dresden* 93

Etymology : Place-Names.

KÜHNEL, P. Die slavischen Orts- u. Flurnamen d. Oberlausitz, pt. i. 1*m.*; ii. 2*m.*; iii. 1*m.*80 8° Koehler, *Lpz.* 91; 91; 94
MEYER, Gust. Die slav., alban. u. rumän. Lehnworte i. Neugriech. [Neugr. Stud. ii.]—*ut* K § 186.

Phonology.

LESKIEN, Aug. Untersuchungen üb. Quantität u. Betonung i. d. slav. Spr., Pt. I. 4*m.* 8° Hirzel, *Lpz.* 92–93
i. *Quantität im Serbischen, A, B, C,* 4*m.*, 92–'93. (Extr. fr. *Abhdgn. sächs. Gesellsch.*).
SOBOLEVSKIJ Old-slav. Phonol.; Old-slav. sounds [in Russn.; *extrs. fr.* Rusak. Fil. Vestn.] 8° 88; 88

History of Literature.

MIKLOSICH, Frz. Die Darstellung in slav. Volksepos [*extr. fr.* Denkschr. Wien. Akad.] 2*m.*60 4° Tempsky, *Vienna* 90
PYPINE + SPASOVIC, A. H. / W. D. Histoire des Littératures Slaves, trad. Prf. Ern. Denis [pp. 630] 16*fr.*; *red. to* 5*fr.* 8° Leroux, *Paris* 81
Bulgarian, Serbo-Croatian, Yougo-Russian. For orig. (and Germ. tr.) v. 𝔅.𝔅. K § 284.
VOLČEK, J. History of Slavonic Literature [in Russian] 6/- 8° *Kiew* 89

Albanian.

Etymology.

MEYER, Prf. Gust. Das latein. Element im Albanischen—*in* Gröber's Grundriss, *ut* K § 256.

Dictionary.

*MEYER, Prf. Gust. Etymologisches Wörterbuch d. albanes. Sprache [Samml. indog. W'bb.] 12*m.* 8° Trübner, *Strassb.* 90

Phonology.

MEYER, Prf. Gust. Alban. Stud., pt. iii. [Lautlehre d. indogerm. Bestandtheile d. Alban.] 2*m.* r 8° Tempsky, *Vienna* 92

Collected Essays.

v. HAHN, J. G. Albanesische Studien—*ut* 𝔅.𝔅. B § 19.
On the topography, archæol., history, manners and customs, folklore and language.

Basko-Slavonic.

TOPOLOVSEK, J. Die baskoslavische Spracheinheit, vol. I. 8*m.* r 8° Gerold, *Vienna* 94
This vol. deals w. Comparative Phonology, and conts. a General Introd. and an Appendix *Ire-Slavisches.*
UHLENBECK, C. C. Die lexicalische Urverwandtschaft d. Baltoslavischen u. Germanischen 2*m.* 8° Blankenberg, *Leyden* 90

Bohemian.

Grammar.

JONAS, Ch. [Am.] Bohemian Made Easy: pract. course for English-speaking people $1.75 c 8° Caspar, *Milwaukee* 91

Etymology : Dictionaries.

Dictionary of the Bohemian Language *Racine, Wisconsin* 79
Seems, from the great prominence given to trade and techn. terms, to have been primarily intended for the many Bohemian artisans in America. A good little book.
KUNZ, A. Böhmisch-deutsches u. deutsch-böhmisches Taschenwörterbuch 3*m.* 8° Neufeld, *Berlin* 93
v. STERZINGER, Jos. Deutsch-böhmisches Wörterbuch, ed. V. E. Mourek, pts. i.–ii. ea. 80*pf.* 8° Otto, *Prague* 94 *in prg.*

Literature —*for* Folklore *v.* B § 19, *for* Engl. trs. of Novels *v.* K § 56.

SAFARIK + PALACZKY, P. J. / F. [eds.] Die ältesten Denkmäler d. böhmischen Sprache; facss. 7*m.*50 4° Kronberger, *Prague* 40
Libuša's Gericht, Evangelium Johannis, Leitmeritzer Stiftungsbrief, Glossen d. Mater Verborum.
Seznam pover a zvyklosti pohanskych: ed. Dr. Cenek Zíbrt 94
On the popular superstns. of the Slavs, based on an 8 cent. MS. in Vatican; w. learned notes and bibliography.

Serial.

Athenæum: Listy pro Literaturu a Kritiku Vedeckou *Prague* 82 *sqq., in prg.*
Appears on 15th of every month, except August and September

Bulgarian: Old (Cyrillic, Palæoslavonic, Old-Slovenic).

BROZ, Ivan Oblici jezika staroga slovenskog s dodatkom [Old-Slov. accidence] 8° *Usagebru* 89
CHODZKO, Alex. Grammaire paléoslave; facss. [incl. some texts] 13*fr.* i 8° Impr. Nat. (Maisonneuve, *Paris*) 69
CIGALE [ed.] Deutsch-Slovenisches Wörterbuch 60 *sqq.*
The *Slovenisch-Deutsches* counterpart is now (1894) in preparation.
VONDRAK, W. Altslovenische Studien [*extr. fr.* Sitzber. Wien. Akad.] 1*m.*80 r 8° Tempsky, *Vienna* 90

Literature.

Carminum Christianorum Versio palæosloven.-rossica, ed. Dr. V. Jagic 20*m.* 4° *St. Petersb.* (Weidmann, *Berl.*) 86
JAGIČ, Dr. V. Der erste Cetinjer Kirchendruck v. 1494, 2 pts. [*extr. fr.* Sitzber. Wien. Akad.] 8*m.*40 r 8° Tempsky, *Vienna* 94; 94
i. Bibliographical and lexicographical, 4*m.*40; ii. Gk.-Slavonic glossary, w. Slav.-Gk. list of words, 4*m.*
" " Die Mendanersentenzen in d. altkirchenslav. Uebersetzung [*extr. fr.* Sitzber. Wien Akad.] 2*m.*20 r 8° Tempsky, *Vienna* 92
" " Das byzant. Lehrgedicht Spaneas i. d. Kirchenslav. Uebers. [*extr. fr.* Sitzber. Wien. Akad.] 1*m.* r 8° " " 92
" " [ed.] Slavische Beiträge z. d. bibl. Apocryphen, pt. i. [*extr. fr.* Abhgn. Wien. Akad.] 6*m.* 4° " " 93
" " + THALLÓCZY + WICKHOFF, L. / F. [eds.] Missale glagoliticum Hervoiae ducis Spalatensis; 41 ill. f° *Vienna* 91
MALTZEW, A. [ed. and tr.] Die Nachtwache d. orthodox.-kath. Kirche d. Morgenlandes 12*m.* 8° Siegesmund, *Berl.* 92
Slavonic text, w. German tr., of the evening and morning liturgy.
ZIVIER, Ezech. Studien über den Codex Suprasliensis [diss. inaug.] 8° *Breslau* 92

K §§ 284

Bulgarian : Modern.

CHODZKO, Alex. Etudes Bulgares 3*fr.* 8° Leroux, *Paris* 75

Article.

MILETIĆ, Lj. The Article in Bulgarian [in Bulgarian lang.] [pp. 54] 8° *Zagreb* 89

Literature. —*for* Folklore *v.* B § 19, *for* Engl. trs. of Novels *v.* K § 56.

Sbornik za Narodni Umotvorenia, Nauka i Knizhnina, vols. i.–x. 8° *Sofia* ?–94 *in prg.*

A Collection of National Scientific and Literary Works, now being issued by the Bulg. Minister of Education. It amounts to a pubn. at Govt. expense of all the literary and scientific essays and pamphlets, and is stimulating vigour in those departments.

MILLIEN, Achille [ed. and tr.] Ballades et Chansons pop. Tcheques et Bulgares Lemerre, *Paris* 94

Serial.

Bulgarski Pregled [crit. and liter. review; monthly] 8° *Sophia* 93 *in prg.*

Macedo-Slavonic Dialects.

Phonology.

MASING, Dr. Leonh. Zur Laut- und Akzentlehre d. macedo-slavonischen Dialekte 4*m.* 8° *St. Petersburg* 91

Specimens of Literature.

DRAGANOV, Prf. P. [ed.] Makedonsko-Slavianski Sbornik s'prilozheniem slovarya, pt. i.; w. notes *St. Petersburg* 94

A colln. of poems *etc.*, many dedic. to the natl. hero, Marko KRALJEVICH. A Dicty. is to be added.

VERKOVICH [ed.] —*has ed. a colln. of national songs of the country.*

" [ed.] Veda Slovena

Hungarian, Czech —*v.* K § 142.

Lithuanian. Lettish. Old Prussian.

Bibliography.

Bibliographie, Altpreussische—*pub. annually as a* Beilageheft *to the* Altpreuss. Monatsschr. *and repr.*: 1892 3*m.* r 8° Beyer, *Königsbg.* 94

STANKIEWICZ, Maur. Bibliografia litewska: 1547–1701 Studia Litewska, pt. ii] 2*m.* 8° Gebethner, *Cracow* 89

Serial.

Mittheilungen der Litauischen Litterarischen Gesellschaft, pts. i.–xv. ca. 1*m.*60 to 3*m.* 8° Winter, *Heidelbg.* 80–90 *in prg.*

Grammar.

AKIELEWICZ, Mik. Gramatyka jezyka litewskiego 3/6 8° Posnan, *Głąsownia* 90

Nouns.

LESKIEN, Aug. Die Bildung der Nomina im Litauischen 16*m.* 8° Hirzel, *Lpz.* 91

Syntax.

ALEKSANDROW, Alex. Nominalzusammensetzungen [Litauische Studien, i.; pp. 124] 8° *Dorpat* 88

Verb : *Preterite.*

WIEDEMANN, Osk. Das litauische Präteritum: Beitrag zur Verbalflexion 6*m.* 8° Trübner, *Strassb.* 91

Etymology.

Foreign Elements : *German.*

PRELLWITZ, W. Die deutschen Bestandteile in den lettischen Sprachen, pt. i. 2*m.*40 8° Vandenhöck, *Göttingen* 91

Specimens of Literature—*for* Folklore *v.* B § 19.

DONALITIUS Littauische Dichtungen, übers. u. erläut. Passarge *c.* 4*m.* Waisenhaus, *Halle* 94

Polish.

Etymology : *Dictionary.*

HORA, E. A. Polskoczeski slownik Kieszonkomy [Polish-Bohem. dict.] 8*m.* 16° *Prague* 90

Phonology.

HANUSZ, J. Lautlehre d. poln.-armen. Mundart v. Kuty [in Galicia] 5*m.* 8° Hölder, *Vienna* 87

Old Polish.

BAUDOIN, Prf. The Old Polish Language till the Fourteenth Century [in Russian] *Leipzig* 70

Pronoun and *Adjective.*

STEINER, Alois Flexion d. Pronomens u. d. Adjectivs in Altpoln. [bas. on Cod. Florianensis] [prog.] 8° *Brzezany* 89

History of Literature —*v. also* K § 40 (MORFILL); *for* Engl. trs. of Novels *v.* K § 56.

BRZEZA, Ad. Literatura Polska, pts. i.–iv. 8° Gebethner i Wolff, *Warsaw* 90–91

KALICZKOWSKI, A. Outlines of the History of Polish Literature [in Polish] 7*m.*50 8° *Lemberg* 89

Old Literature.

Bibl. Pisarzów Polskich [Lib. of Polish Writers], vs. i.–xxviii. [a coll. of reprts. of old and scarce Pol. pubns.] Acad. of Sciences, *Cracow*

Russian.

Grammar.

KÖRNER, Wilh. Ausführliches Lehrbuch der russischen Sprache 7m.80 m 8° Eupel, *Sondershausen* 92
MOTTI, Prf. Pietro. Russian Grammar for General Use, 5/-; Element. Russn. Gram. 2/6; Key 2/- 12° Nutt 90; 90
The larger Gram. is a fairly good bk., w. exx., dialogues, and commerc. corresp.; the smaller is a mere skeleton of the lang.

Etymology.

LEGER + BARDONNAUT, Prf. Louis / G. Les Racines de la Langue Russe 5fr. 8° Maisonneuve, *Paris* 94

Dictionary.

Academy, Russian: Russian Dictionary *in prg.*
BOOCH + FREY, Friedr. / Adam Hand-Wörterb. d. russisch. u. deut. Sprache, vol. i. [Deut.-Russ.] 6m.; ii. [R.-D.] 9m. 8° Haessel, *Lpz.* [71] 90; [71] 86
WERBLUNSKI, S. L. Neues ausführl. Handwb. d. russ. u. deut. Sprache, 2 vols. ea. 4m. r 16° Friedberg, *Berl.* 91; 91

Military Terms.

MANASSEWITSCH, B. Russisch-deutsches u. deutsch-russisches Militarisches Wb. 4m. 92

Pronunciation.

LUNDELL, J. A. Etudes sur la Prononciation russe, pt. i. [Bibliography] 5kr. 8° Akad. Bokh., *Upsala* 90

Chrestomathy.

ASBOTH, Osk. [ed.] Russische Chrestomathie [elementary; w. glossary] 2m.25 8° Brockhaus, *Lpz.* 90
MANDELKERN, S. [ed.] Historische Chrestomathie d. russischen Litteratur 6m. 8° 91

Literature.

History —*v. also* K § 40 (espec. POLEVOI).
LEGER, Louis La Littérature Russe [pp. xv., 561] 18° Colin, *Paris* 92
Notices of most of the princ. authors fr. earliest to pres. times; w. extracts fr. their writings.

Specimens —*for* Folklore *v.* B § 19, *for* Engl. trs. of Novels *v.* K § 56, of Poetry *v.* K § 77, of Drama *v.* K § 81.
Chronique dite de Nestor, trad. Prf. Louis Léger, sur texte slavo-russe; w. notes [Ecole Lang. Orient. Viv.] 15fr. 8° Bouillon, *Paris* 86
MILLIEN, Achille [ed. & tr.] Les Chants oraux du Peuple russe Lemerre, *Paris* 93

Servian and Croatian.

Syntax.

ZIVANOVIC, Prf. J. Servian Syntax [in Servian; for use of his pupils; pp. 96] 8° 89

Etymology: Dictionaries.

KARAGIC [KARAJICH], Vuk. Stef. Lexicon Serbico-germanico-Latinum [*ut* B.B. K § 285]: 3rd ed., pt. i. 5m.40 r 8° *Belgrade* (Gerold, *Vienna*) [52–77] 92
Univ. of Agram Serbo-Croatian Dictionary *in prg.*

Orthography.

MARETIC, T. History of Croatian Orthography in Latin Writings [pp. xiii., 406; in Servian] 8° *Usagrebu* 89

Literature —*for* Folklore *v.* B § 19.
NEDICH, Prf. Ljubomir Iz Novije Srpske Lirike 8° *Belgrade* 93
Critical studies on JAKSHICH, ZMAJ (JOVANOVICH), KACHANSKI, BOJISLAV, and other Servian lyrical poets.
Pjesme [colln. of Servian ballads] 8° *Belgrade* [c. 23] 93
STOJANOVIC, Ljubomir [ed.] Old Servian Golden Bulls, Acts, Biographies, Annals, *etc.* [in Servian] 4° 90

Slovenic: Old. —*v.* Bulgarian: Old, *supra.*

Wendic (Sorbic).

MUCKE, Karl Ern. Histor. u. vergleich. Laut- u. Formenlehre d. niedersorb. Spr. 20m. r 8° Hirzel, *Lpz.* 91
Crowned by the Jablonowski Society at Leipzig.

Magazine.

Casopis: *in prg.*
A journal of the Lusatian Wends, an interesting people inhabiting "a Slavonic island in the German Ocean"; often conts. papers of philol. interest.

Literature —*for* Folklore *v.* B § 19.

Butler & Tanner, The Selwood Printing Works, Frome, and London.

THE BEST BOOKS

A READER'S GUIDE

TO THE CHOICE OF THE BEST AVAILABLE BOOKS
(ABOUT 50,000)
IN EVERY DEPARTMENT OF SCIENCE ART AND LITERATURE
WITH THE DATES OF THE FIRST AND LAST EDITIONS
AND THE PRICE SIZE AND PUBLISHER'S NAME OF EACH BOOK

A Contribution towards Systematic Bibliography

BY

WILLIAM SWAN SONNENSCHEIN

WITH COMPLETE AUTHORS AND SUBJECTS INDEXES

LONDON
SWAN SONNENSCHEIN & CO.
NEW YORK: G. P. PUTNAM'S SONS
BOSTON: THE AMERICAN LIBRARY BUREAU
1896

First Edition: September, 1887.

Second Edition (Stereotyped): March, 1891; Reissued June, 1891; Reissued March, 1894; Reissued September, 1896.

The First Supplement, entitled "A Reader's Guide," bringing the work down to 1893-94, was published in 1895, uniform with this work.

A

READER'S GUIDE TO CONTEMPORARY LITERATURE

BEING THE FIRST SUPPLEMENT TO

The Best Books

A READER'S GUIDE TO THE CHOICE OF THE BEST AVAILABLE BOOKS (ABOUT 50,000) IN EVERY DEPARTMENT OF SCIENCE ART AND LITERATURE WITH THE DATES OF THE FIRST AND LAST EDITIONS AND THE PRICE SIZE AND PUBLISHER'S NAME OF EACH BOOK

BY

WILLIAM SWAN SONNENSCHEIN

With complete Authors and Subjects Index

Notitia librorum est dimidium studiorum et maxima eruditionis pars exactam librorum habere cognitionem.

London

SWAN SONNENSCHEIN & CO.

NEW YORK: G. P. PUTNAM'S SONS

1895

"If the sentence of a judge ever await anyone, to condemn him to hardships and punishments, let neither the penitentiary weary him with the manufacture of the raw material, nor let the ores dug from the mines hurt his hard hands; just let him compose a Lexicon. For why should I mention anything else? Surely, this single labour hath all the forms of torture."—SCALIGER.

"Nocturna versate manu, versate diurna."—HORACE.

"Go, little book, God send thee good passage,
And specially let this be thy prayer
Unto them all that thee will read or hear,
Where thou art wrong, after their help to call,
Thee to correct in any part or all."—CHAUCER.

www.ingramcontent.com/pod-product-compliance
Lightning Source LLC
Chambersburg PA
CBHW030348230426
43664CB00007BB/573

* 9 7 8 3 3 3 7 2 4 8 8 8 8 *